(ex·ploring)

S E R I E S

1. Investigating in a systematic way: examining. 2. Searching into or ranging over for the purpose of discovery.

Microsoft®

Office 365®

Access™ 2019

COMPREHENSIVE

Series Editor **Mary Anne Poatsy**

Williams | Rutledge

Vice President of Courseware Portfolio Management: Andrew Gilfillan
Executive Portfolio Manager: Samantha Lewis
Team Lead, Content Production: Laura Burgess
Content Producer: Alexandrina Wolf
Development Editor: Barbara Stover
Portfolio Management Assistant: Bridget Daly
Director of Product Marketing: Brad Parkins
Director of Field Marketing: Jonathan Cottrell
Product Marketing Manager: Heather Taylor
Field Marketing Manager: Bob Nisbet
Product Marketing Assistant: Liz Bennett
Field Marketing Assistant: Derrica Moser
Senior Operations Specialist: Maura Garcia
Senior Art Director: Mary Seiner
Interior and Cover Design: Pearson CSC
Cover Photo: Courtesy of Shutterstock® Images
Senior Product Model Manager: Eric Hakanson
Manager, Digital Studio: Heather Darby
Digital Content Producer, MyLab IT: Becca Golden
Course Producer, MyLab IT: Amanda Losonsky
Digital Studio Producer: Tanika Henderson
Full-Service Project Management: Pearson CSC (Amy Kopperude)
Composition: Pearson CSC

Credits and acknowledgments borrowed from other sources and reproduced, with permission, in this textbook appear on the appropriate page within text.

Microsoft and/or its respective suppliers make no representations about the suitability of the information contained in the documents and related graphics published as part of the services for any purpose. All such documents and related graphics are provided "as is" without warranty of any kind. Microsoft and/or its respective suppliers hereby disclaim all warranties and conditions with regard to this information, including all warranties and conditions of merchantability, whether express, implied or statutory, fitness for a particular purpose, title and non-infringement. In no event shall Microsoft and/or its respective suppliers be liable for any special, indirect or consequential damages or any damages whatsoever resulting from loss of use, data or profits, whether in an action of contract, negligence or other tortious action, arising out of or in connection with the use or performance of information available from the services.

The documents and related graphics contained herein could include technical inaccuracies or typographical errors. Changes are periodically added to the information herein. Microsoft and/or its respective suppliers may make improvements and/or changes in the product(s) and/or the program(s) described herein at any time. Partial screen shots may be viewed in full within the software version specified.

Microsoft® and Windows® are registered trademarks of the Microsoft Corporation in the U.S.A. and other countries. This book is not sponsored or endorsed by or affiliated with the Microsoft Corporation.

Cataloging-in-Publication Data is available on file at the Library of Congress.

ISBN 10:   0-13-543581-1
ISBN 13: 978-0-13-543581-6

Dedications

For my husband, Ted, who unselfishly continues to take on more than his share to support me throughout the process; and for my children, Laura, Carolyn, and Teddy, whose encouragement and love have been inspiring.

Mary Anne Poatsy

I offer thanks to my family and colleagues who have supported me on this journey. I would like to dedicate the work I have performed toward this undertaking to my little grandson, Yonason Meir (known for now as Mei-Mei), who as his name suggests, is the illumination in my life.

Jerri Williams

To Zac: thank you so much for your hard work and dedication on this project. The long (late) hours you spent did not go unnoticed. I have very much enjoyed working with you and hope there's more to come. To my husband Dan, whose encouragement, patience, and love helped make this endeavor possible. Thank you for taking on the many additional tasks at home so that I could focus on writing. To Emma and Jane, I love you. You inspire me to reach for my goals and never settle for less.

Amy Rutledge

About the Authors

Mary Anne Poatsy, Series Editor, Common Features Author

Mary Anne is a senior faculty member at Montgomery County Community College, teaching various computer application and concepts courses in face-to-face and online environments. She holds a B.A. in Psychology and Education from Mount Holyoke College and an M.B.A. in Finance from Northwestern University's Kellogg Graduate School of Management.

Mary Anne has more than 20 years of educational experience. She has taught at Gwynedd Mercy College, Bucks County Community College, and Muhlenberg College. She also engages in corporate training. Before teaching, she was Vice President at Shearson Lehman in the Municipal Bond Investment Banking Department.

Jerri Williams, Access Author

Jerri Williams is a Senior Instructor at Montgomery County Community College in Pennsylvania, and currently works as a technical editor and content developer in addition to her teaching responsibilities. Jerri worked as a live and virtual corporate trainer and developer in major pharmaceutical and other companies for many years prior to joining the Exploring Access 2013, 2016, and 2019 teams. She is interested in travel, history, cooking, theater, movies, and tending to her colonial farmhouse (a work in progress). Jerri is married to Gareth and is the mother of two daughters, Holly (an accountant/office manager, and mother of an adorable son, Meir) and Gwyneth (a corporate defense/employment attorney). Jerri and Gareth live outside of Philadelphia, and enjoy their home and garden, spending time with family and friends, watching the Philadelphia Eagles, and visiting the Jersey Shore any time of the year.

Amy Rutledge, Access Author

Amy Rutledge is a Special Instructor of Management Information Systems at Oakland University in Rochester, Michigan. She coordinates academic programs in Microsoft Office applications and introductory management information systems courses for the School of Business Administration. Before joining Oakland University as an instructor, Amy spent several years working for a music distribution company and automotive manufacturer in various corporate roles including IT project management. She holds a B.S. in Business Administration specializing in Management Information Systems, and a B.A. in French Modern Language and Literature. She holds an M.B.A from Oakland University. She resides in Michigan with her husband, Dan and daughters Emma and Jane.

Dr. Robert T. Grauer, Creator of the Exploring Series

Bob Grauer is an Associate Professor in the Department of Computer Information Systems at the University of Miami, where he is a multiple winner of the Outstanding Teaching Award in the School of Business, most recently in 2009. He has written numerous COBOL texts and is the vision behind the Exploring Office series, with more than three million books in print. His work has been translated into three foreign languages and is used in all aspects of higher education at both national and international levels. Bob Grauer has consulted for several major corporations including IBM and American Express. He received his Ph.D. in Operations Research in 1972 from the Polytechnic Institute of Brooklyn.

Brief Contents

Office   **Office 365 Common Features**   2

Access

CHAPTER 1	Introduction to Access	70
CHAPTER 2	Tables and Queries in Relational Databases	132
CHAPTER 3	Query Calculations and Expressions	202
CHAPTER 4	Basic Forms and Reports	248
CHAPTER 5	Data Validation and Data Analysis	302
CHAPTER 6	Action and Specialized Queries	344
CHAPTER 7	Advanced Forms and Reports	388
CHAPTER 8	Get Connected	438
CHAPTER 9	Fine-Tuning the Database	500
CHAPTER 10	Enhanced Database Techniques	552

Application Capstone Exercise

Access Application Capstone Exercise (Chs. 1–4)   600
Access Comprehensive Application Capstone Exercise (Chs. 5–10)   604

Microsoft Office 2019 Specialist Access   608

GLOSSARY   611
INDEX   616

Contents

Microsoft Office 2019

■ CHAPTER ONE Office 365 Common Features: Taking the First Step 2

CASE STUDY SPOTTED BEGONIA ART GALLERY   2
GET STARTED WITH OFFICE APPLICATIONS   4
  Starting an Office Application   5
  Working with Files   6
  Using Common Interface Components   9
  Getting Help   15
  Installing Add-ins   17
HANDS-ON EXERCISE 1   19
FORMAT DOCUMENT CONTENT   25
  Using Templates and Applying Themes   25
  Modifying Text   27
  Relocating Text   30
  Reviewing a Document   32
  Working with Pictures   34
HANDS-ON EXERCISE 2   37

MODIFY DOCUMENT LAYOUT AND PROPERTIES   45
  Changing Document Views   45
  Changing the Page Layout   46
  Creating a Header and a Footer   49
  Configuring Document Properties   50
  Previewing and Printing a File   51
HANDS-ON EXERCISE 3   53
CHAPTER OBJECTIVES REVIEW   58
KEY TERMS MATCHING   60
MULTIPLE CHOICE   61
PRACTICE EXERCISES   62
MID-LEVEL EXERCISES   65
RUNNING CASE   67
DISASTER RECOVERY   67
CAPSTONE EXERCISE   68

Microsoft Office Access 2019

■ CHAPTER ONE Introduction to Access: Navigating an Access Database 70

CASE STUDY MANAGING A BUSINESS IN THE GLOBAL
  ECONOMY   70
DATABASES ARE EVERYWHERE!   72
  Opening, Saving, and Enabling Content in a Database   72
  Recognizing Database Object Types   74
  Modifying, Adding, and Saving Data   85
  Using Database Utilities   88
HANDS-ON EXERCISE 1   91
FILTERS AND SORTS   98
  Working with Filters   98
  Performing Sorts   102
HANDS-ON EXERCISE 2   104

ACCESS DATABASE CREATION   109
  Creating a Database   109
HANDS-ON EXERCISE 3   115
CHAPTER OBJECTIVES REVIEW   119
KEY TERMS MATCHING   120
MULTIPLE CHOICE   121
PRACTICE EXERCISES   122
MID-LEVEL EXERCISES   127
RUNNING CASE   129
DISASTER RECOVERY   129
CAPSTONE EXERCISE   130

■ CHAPTER TWO Tables and Queries in Relational Databases: Designing Databases and Extracting Information   132

CASE STUDY BANK INTERNSHIP	132
TABLE DESIGN, CREATION, AND MODIFICATION	134
Designing a Table	134
Creating and Modifying Tables and Working with Data	138
HANDS-ON EXERCISE 1	145
MULTIPLE-TABLE DATABASES	149
Importing Data from External Sources	149
Establishing Table Relationships	152
HANDS-ON EXERCISE 2	157
SINGLE-TABLE QUERIES	164
Creating a Single-Table Query	164
Using the Query Wizard	167
Specifying Query Criteria	169
Specifying Query Sort Order and Running a Query	172
Copying and Modifying a Query	172

HANDS-ON EXERCISE 3	174
MULTITABLE QUERIES	177
Creating a Multitable Query	177
Modifying a Multitable Query	178
HANDS-ON EXERCISE 4	182
CHAPTER OBJECTIVES REVIEW	186
KEY TERMS MATCHING	188
MULTIPLE CHOICE	189
PRACTICE EXERCISES	190
MID-LEVEL EXERCISES	196
RUNNING CASE	198
DISASTER RECOVERY	199
CAPSTONE EXERCISE	200

■ CHAPTER THREE Query Calculations and Expressions: Performing Calculations and Summarizing Data Using Queries   202

CASE STUDY REAL ESTATE INVESTORS	202
CALCULATED FIELDS AND EXPRESSIONS	204
Creating a Query with a Calculated Field	204
Formatting Calculated Results	209
Recovering from Common Errors	210
Verifying Calculated Results	211
HANDS-ON EXERCISE 1	212
THE EXPRESSION BUILDER AND FUNCTIONS	217
Creating Expressions Using the Expression Builder	217
Using Built-In Functions	218
HANDS-ON EXERCISE 2	222

AGGREGATE FUNCTIONS	226
Adding Aggregate Functions to Datasheets	226
Creating Queries with Aggregate Functions	227
HANDS-ON EXERCISE 3	232
CHAPTER OBJECTIVES REVIEW	236
KEY TERMS MATCHING	237
MULTIPLE CHOICE	238
PRACTICE EXERCISES	239
MID-LEVEL EXERCISES	242
RUNNING CASE	244
DISASTER RECOVERY	245
CAPSTONE EXERCISE	246

■ CHAPTER FOUR Basic Forms and Reports: Simplifying Data Entry and Producing Information   248

CASE STUDY COFFEE SHOP STARTS NEW BUSINESS	248
CREATE BASIC FORMS TO SIMPLIFY DATA MANAGEMENT	250
Creating Forms Using Form Tools	250
Modifying Forms	258
Using the Form Layout Control	261
Sorting Records in a Form	263
HANDS-ON EXERCISE 1	264
CREATE BASIC REPORTS TO PRESENT INFORMATION	271
Creating Reports Using Report Tools	272
Using Report Views	277
Modifying a Report	278
Sorting and Grouping Records in a Report	281

HANDS-ON EXERCISE 2	283
CHAPTER OBJECTIVES REVIEW	288
KEY TERMS MATCHING	290
MULTIPLE CHOICE	291
PRACTICE EXERCISES	292
MID-LEVEL EXERCISES	296
RUNNING CASE	298
DISASTER RECOVERY	298
CAPSTONE EXERCISE	299

■ CHAPTER FIVE Data Validation and Data Analysis: Reducing Errors and Extracting Better Information · 302

CASE STUDY IMPLEMENTING A NEW DATABASE AT TOMMY'S SHELTER	302
RESTRICT TABLE DATA	304
Establishing Data Validation	304
Controlling the Format of Data Entry	307
Controlling Input with a Lookup Field	309
HANDS-ON EXERCISE 1	311
DATA ANALYSIS WITH ADVANCED QUERIES AND FUNCTIONS	317
Customizing Output Based on User Input	317
Using Advanced Functions	319

HANDS-ON EXERCISE 2	327
CHAPTER OBJECTIVES REVIEW	332
KEY TERMS MATCHING	333
MULTIPLE CHOICE	334
PRACTICE EXERCISES	335
MID-LEVEL EXERCISES	338
RUNNING CASE	340
DISASTER RECOVERY	341
CAPSTONE EXERCISE	342

■ CHAPTER SIX Action and Specialized Queries: Advancing Beyond the Select Query · 344

CASE STUDY VIRTUAL REGISTRY, INC.	344
ACTION QUERIES	346
Determining When to Use an Action Query	346
Updating Data with an Update Query	348
Adding Records to a Table with an Append Query	351
Creating a Table with a Make Table Query	353
Deleting Records with a Delete Query	355
HANDS-ON EXERCISE 1	357
SPECIALIZED QUERIES	364
Summarizing Data with a Crosstab Query	364
Finding Duplicate Records with a Query	369
Finding Unmatched Records with a Query	371

HANDS-ON EXERCISE 2	375
CHAPTER OBJECTIVES REVIEW	378
KEY TERMS MATCHING	379
MULTIPLE CHOICE	380
PRACTICE EXERCISES	381
MID-LEVEL EXERCISES	384
RUNNING CASE	385
DISASTER RECOVERY	386
CAPSTONE EXERCISE	387

■ CHAPTER SEVEN Advanced Forms and Reports: Moving Beyond the Basics · 388

CASE STUDY YELLOWSTONE COUNTY TECHNICAL SERVICES	388
ADVANCED FORMS	390
Restricting Edits in a Form	390
Understanding Combo Boxes	391
Setting the Tab Order	394
Understanding Subforms	396
HANDS-ON EXERCISE 1	399
CONTROLS AND SECTIONS	405
Understanding Controls	405
Understanding Sections	412

HANDS-ON EXERCISE 2	420
CHAPTER OBJECTIVES REVIEW	427
KEY TERMS MATCHING	428
MULTIPLE CHOICE	429
PRACTICE EXERCISES	430
MID-LEVEL EXERCISES	434
RUNNING CASE	435
DISASTER RECOVERY	436
CAPSTONE EXERCISE	437

■ CHAPTER EIGHT Get Connected: Exchanging Data Between Access and Other Applications   438

CASE STUDY PROPERTY MANAGEMENT DATA EXCHANGE	438	Linking to and Importing an Excel Spreadsheet	474
CONNECT ACCESS TO EXTERNAL FILES	440	Importing an Excel Spreadsheet	476
Creating a Hyperlink Field	440	Importing a Text File	477
Adding an Attachment Field	442	**HANDS-ON EXERCISE 3**	**480**
Adding Attachment Controls to Forms and Reports	445	CHAPTER OBJECTIVES REVIEW	489
HANDS-ON EXERCISE 1	**448**	KEY TERMS MATCHING	490
EXPORT DATA TO OFFICE AND OTHER APPLICATIONS	454	MULTIPLE CHOICE	491
Exporting Data to Excel	454	PRACTICE EXERCISES	492
Exporting Data to Word	457	MID-LEVEL EXERCISES	496
Exporting Data to a PDF or XPS Document	460	RUNNING CASE	497
Exporting Objects to Another Access Database	462	DISASTER RECOVERY	498
HANDS-ON EXERCISE 2	**464**	CAPSTONE EXERCISE	499
IMPORT AND LINK DATA IN ACCESS DATABASES	471		
Linking to an Access Table	471		

■ CHAPTER NINE Fine-Tuning the Database: Designing for Performance   500

CASE STUDY THE METROPOLITAN ZOO	500	DATABASE SECURITY	530
DATABASE NORMALIZATION	502	Controlling Navigation	530
Understanding First Normal Form	503	Encrypting and Password Protecting a Database	532
Understanding Second Normal Form	505	Creating an Executable Form of a Database	534
Understanding Third Normal Form	507	**HANDS-ON EXERCISE 3**	**536**
Finalizing the Design	509	CHAPTER OBJECTIVES REVIEW	540
HANDS-ON EXERCISE 1	**511**	KEY TERMS MATCHING	541
BUILT-IN ANALYSIS AND DESIGN TOOLS	515	MULTIPLE CHOICE	542
Using the Database Documenter Tool	516	PRACTICE EXERCISES	543
Using the Performance Analyzer Tool	518	MID-LEVEL EXERCISES	546
Using the Table Analyzer Tool	520	RUNNING CASE	548
Using the Database Splitter Tool	523	DISASTER RECOVERY	549
HANDS-ON EXERCISE 2	**525**	CAPSTONE EXERCISE	550

■ CHAPTER TEN Enhanced Database Techniques: Using Macros and SQL in Access   552

CASE STUDY RETIREMENT PLAN CONTRIBUTIONS	552	Interpreting an SQL SELECT Statement	579
MACRO DESIGN	554	Using an SQL SELECT Statement as a Record Source	581
Understanding the Purpose of a Macro	554	**HANDS-ON EXERCISE 3**	**584**
Creating a Standalone Macro	555	CHAPTER OBJECTIVES REVIEW	587
Attaching an Embedded Macro to an Event	557	KEY TERMS MATCHING	588
HANDS-ON EXERCISE 1	**561**	MULTIPLE CHOICE	589
DATA MACROS	568	PRACTICE EXERCISES	590
Identifying When to Use a Data Macro	568	MID-LEVEL EXERCISES	595
Creating an Event-Driven Data Macro	568	RUNNING CASE	597
Creating a Named Data Macro	569	DISASTER RECOVERY	597
HANDS-ON EXERCISE 2	**572**	CAPSTONE EXERCISE	598
STRUCTURED QUERY LANGUAGE	578		
Understanding the Fundamentals of SQL	578		

Application Capstone Exercises

Access Application Capstone Exercise (Chs. 1–4)   600

Access Comprehensive Application Capstone Exercise (Chs. 5–10)   604

Microsoft Office 2019 Specialist Access   608

GLOSSARY   611

INDEX   616

Acknowledgments

The Exploring team would like to acknowledge and thank all the reviewers who helped us throughout the years by providing us with their invaluable comments, suggestions, and constructive criticism.

A. D. Knight
Northwestern State University
Natchitoches–Louisiana

Aaron Montanino
Davenport University

Adriana Lumpkin
Midland College

Alan S. Abrahams
Virginia Tech

Alexandre C. Probst
Colorado Christian University

Ali Berrached
University of Houston–Downtown

Allen Alexander
Delaware Technical & Community College

Amy Rutledge
Oakland University

Andrea Marchese
Maritime College
State University of New York

Andrew Blitz
Broward College; Edison State College

Angel Norman
University of Tennessee–Knoxville

Angela Clark
University of South Alabama

Ann Rovetto
Horry–Georgetown Technical College

Astrid Todd
Guilford Technical Community College

Audrey Gillant
Maritime College, State University of
New York

Barbara Stover
Marion Technical College

Barbara Tollinger
Sinclair Community College

Ben Brahim Taha
Auburn University

Beverly Amer
Northern Arizona University

Beverly Fite
Amarillo College

Biswadip Ghosh
Metropolitan State University of Denver

Bonita Volker
Tidewater Community College

Bonnie Homan
San Francisco State University

Brad West
Sinclair Community College

Brian Kovar
Kansas State University

Brian Powell
West Virginia University

Carmen Morrison
North Central State College

Carol Buser
Owens Community College

Carol Roberts
University of Maine

Carol Wiggins
Blinn College

Carole Pfeiffer
Southeast Missouri State University

Carolyn Barren
Macomb Community College

Carolyn Borne
Louisiana State University

Cathy Poyner
Truman State University

Charles Hodgson
Delgado Community College

Chen Zhang
Bryant University

Cheri Higgins
Illinois State University

Cheryl Brown
Delgado Community College

Cheryl Hinds
Norfolk State University

Cheryl Sypniewski
Macomb Community College

Chris Robinson
Northwest State Community College

Cindy Herbert
Metropolitan Community College–Longview

Craig J. Peterson
American InterContinental University

Craig Watson
Bristol Community College

Dana Hooper
University of Alabama

Dana Johnson
North Dakota State University

Daniela Marghitu
Auburn University

David Noel
University of Central Oklahoma

David Pulis
Maritime College, State University of
New York

David Thornton
Jacksonville State University

Dawn Medlin
Appalachian State University

Debby Keen
University of Kentucky

Debra Chapman
University of South Alabama

Debra Hoffman
Southeast Missouri State University

Derrick Huang
Florida Atlantic University

Diana Baran
Henry Ford Community College

Diane Cassidy
The University of North Carolina at
Charlotte

Diane L. Smith
Henry Ford Community College

Dick Hewer
Ferris State College

Don Danner
San Francisco State University

Don Hoggan
Solano College

Don Riggs
SUNY Schenectady County Community
College

Doncho Petkov
Eastern Connecticut State University

Donna Ehrhart
Genesee Community College

Elaine Crable
Xavier University

Elizabeth Duett
Delgado Community College

Erhan Uskup
Houston Community College–Northwest

Eric Martin
University of Tennessee

Erika Nadas
Wilbur Wright College

Evelyn Schenk
Saginaw Valley State University

Floyd Winters
Manatee Community College

Frank Lucente
Westmoreland County Community College

G. Jan Wilms
Union University

Gail Cope
Sinclair Community College

Gary DeLorenzo
California University of Pennsylvania

Gary Garrison
Belmont University

Gary McFall
Purdue University

George Cassidy
Sussex County Community College

Gerald Braun
Xavier University

Gerald Burgess
Western New Mexico University

Gladys Swindler
Fort Hays State University

Gurinder Mehta
Sam Houston State University

Hector Frausto
California State University Los Angeles

Heith Hennel
Valencia Community College

Henry Rudzinski
Central Connecticut State University

Irene Joos
La Roche College

Iwona Rusin
Baker College; Davenport University

J. Roberto Guzman
San Diego Mesa College

Jacqueline D. Lawson
Henry Ford Community College

Jakie Brown, Jr.
Stevenson University

James Brown
Central Washington University

James Powers
University of Southern Indiana

Jane Stam
Onondaga Community College

Janet Bringhurst
Utah State University

Janice Potochney
Gateway Community College

Jean Luoma
Davenport University

Jean Welsh
Lansing Community College

Jeanette Dix
Ivy Tech Community College

Jennifer Day
Sinclair Community College

Jill Canine
Ivy Tech Community College

Jill Young
Southeast Missouri State University

Jim Chaffee
The University of Iowa Tippie College of
Business

Joanne Lazirko
University of Wisconsin–Milwaukee

Jodi Milliner
Kansas State University

John Hollenbeck
Blue Ridge Community College

John Meir
Midlands Technical College

John Nelson
Texas Christian University

John Seydel
Arkansas State University

Judith A. Scheeren
Westmoreland County Community College

Judith Brown
The University of Memphis

Juliana Cypert
Tarrant County College

Kamaljeet Sanghera
George Mason University

Karen Priestly
Northern Virginia Community College

Karen Ravan
Spartanburg Community College

Karen Tracey
Central Connecticut State University

Kathleen Brenan
Ashland University

Ken Busbee
Houston Community College

Kent Foster
Winthrop University

Kevin Anderson
Solano Community College

Kim Wright
The University of Alabama

Kirk Atkinson
Western Kentucky University

Kristen Hockman
University of Missouri–Columbia

Kristi Smith
Allegany College of Maryland

Laura Marcoulides
Fullerton College

Laura McManamon
University of Dayton

Laurence Boxer
Niagara University

Leanne Chun
Leeward Community College

Lee McClain
Western Washington University

Lewis Cappelli
Hudson Valley Community College

Linda D. Collins
Mesa Community College

Linda Johnsonius
Murray State University

Linda Lau
Longwood University

Linda Theus
Jackson State Community College

Linda Williams
Marion Technical College

Lisa Miller
University of Central Oklahoma

Lister Horn
Pensacola Junior College

Lixin Tao
Pace University

Loraine Miller
Cayuga Community College

Lori Kielty
Central Florida Community College

Lorna Wells
Salt Lake Community College

Lorraine Sauchin
Duquesne University

Lucy Parakhovnik
California State University–Northridge

Lynn Baldwin
Madison College

Lynn Keane
University of South Carolina

Lynn Mancini
Delaware Technical Community
College

Lynne Seal
Amarillo College

Mackinzee Escamilla
South Plains College

Marcia Welch
Highline Community College

Margaret McManus
Northwest Florida State College

Margaret Warrick
Allan Hancock College

Marilyn Hibbert
Salt Lake Community College

Mark Choman
Luzerne County Community College

Mary Beth Tarver
Northwestern State University

Mary Duncan
University of Missouri–St. Louis

Maryann Clark
University of New Hampshire

Melissa Nemeth
Indiana University–Purdue University
Indianapolis

Melody Alexander
Ball State University

Michael Douglas
University of Arkansas at Little Rock

Michael Dunklebarger
Alamance Community College

Michael G. Skaff
College of the Sequoias

Michele Budnovitch
Pennsylvania College of Technology

Mike Jochen
East Stroudsburg University

Mike Michaelson
Palomar College

Mike Scroggins
Missouri State University

Mimi Spain
Southern Maine Community College

Muhammed Badamas
Morgan State University

NaLisa Brown
University of the Ozarks

Nancy Grant
Community College of Allegheny
County–South Campus

Nanette Lareau
University of Arkansas Community
College–Morrilton

Nikia Robinson
Indian River State University

Pam Brune
Chattanooga State Community College

Pam Uhlenkamp
Iowa Central Community College

Patrick Smith
Marshall Community and Technical College

Paul Addison
Ivy Tech Community College

Paul Hamilton
New Mexico State University

Paula Ruby
Arkansas State University

Peggy Burrus
Red Rocks Community College

Peter Ross
SUNY Albany

Philip H. Nielson
Salt Lake Community College

Philip Valvalides
Guilford Technical Community College

Ralph Hooper
University of Alabama

Ranette Halverson
Midwestern State University

Richard Blamer
John Carroll University

Richard Cacace
Pensacola Junior College

Richard Hewer
Ferris State University

Richard Sellers
Hill College

Rob Murray
Ivy Tech Community College

Robert Banta
Macomb Community College

Robert Dušek
Northern Virginia Community College

Robert G. Phipps, Jr.
West Virginia University

Robert Sindt
Johnson County Community College

Robert Warren
Delgado Community College

Robyn Barrett
St. Louis Community College–Meramec

Rocky Belcher
Sinclair Community College

Roger Pick
University of Missouri at Kansas City

Ronnie Creel
Troy University

Rosalie Westerberg
Clover Park Technical College

Ruth Neal
Navarro College

Sandra Thomas
Troy University

Sheila Gionfriddo
Luzerne County Community College

Sherrie Geitgey
Northwest State Community College

Sherry Lenhart
Terra Community College

Shohreh Hashemi
University of Houston–Downtown

Sophia Wilberscheid
Indian River State College

Sophie Lee
California State University–Long Beach

Stacy Johnson
Iowa Central Community College

Stephanie Kramer
Northwest State Community College

Stephen Z. Jourdan
Auburn University at Montgomery

Steven Schwarz
Raritan Valley Community College

Sue A. McCrory
Missouri State University

Sumathy Chandrashekar
Salisbury University

Susan Fuschetto
Cerritos College

Susan Medlin
UNC Charlotte

Susan N. Dozier
Tidewater Community College

Suzan Spitzberg
Oakton Community College

Suzanne M. Jeska
County College of Morris

Sven Aelterman
Troy University

Sy Hirsch
Sacred Heart University

Sylvia Brown
Midland College

Tanya Patrick
Clackamas Community College

Terri Holly
Indian River State College

Terry Ray Rigsby
Hill College

Thomas Rienzo
Western Michigan University

Tina Johnson
Midwestern State University

Tommy Lu
Delaware Technical Community College

Troy S. Cash
Northwest Arkansas Community College

Vicki Robertson
Southwest Tennessee Community

Vickie Pickett
Midland College

Vivianne Moore
Davenport University

Weifeng Chen
California University of Pennsylvania

Wes Anthony
Houston Community College

William Ayen
University of Colorado at Colorado Springs

Wilma Andrews
Virginia Commonwealth University

Yvonne Galusha
University of Iowa

Special thanks to our content development and technical team:

Barbara Stover

Lisa Bucki

Lori Damanti

Sallie Dodson

Morgan Hetzler

Ken Mayer

Joyce Nielsen

Chris Parent

Sean Portnoy

Steven Rubin

LeeAnn Bates
MyLab IT content author

Becca Golden
Media Producer

Jennifer Hurley
MyLab IT content author

Kevin Marino
MyLab IT content author

Ralph Moore
MyLab IT content author

Jerri Williams
MyLab IT content author

Preface

The Exploring Series and You

Exploring is Pearson's Office Application series that requires students like you to think "beyond the point and click." In this edition, the *Exploring* experience has evolved to be even more in tune with the student of today. With an emphasis on Mac compatibility, critical thinking, and continual updates to stay in sync with the changing Microsoft Office 365, and by providing additional valuable assignments and resources, the *Exploring* series is able to offer you the most usable, current, and beneficial learning experience ever.

The goal of *Exploring* is, as it has always been, to go farther than teaching just the steps to accomplish a task—the series provides the theoretical foundation for you to understand when and why to apply a skill. As a result, you achieve a deeper understanding of each application and can apply this critical thinking beyond Office and the classroom.

New to This Edition

Continual eText Updates: This edition of *Exploring* is written to Microsoft® Office 365®, which is constantly updating. In order to stay current with the software, we are committed to twice annual updates of the eText and Content Updates document available as an instructor resource for text users.

Focus on Mac: Mac usage is growing, and even outstripping PC usage at some four-year institutions. In response, new features such as Mac Tips, On a Mac step boxes, Mac Troubleshooting, and Mac tips on Student Reference Cards help ensure Mac users have a flawless experience using *Exploring*.

Expanded Running Case: In this edition, the Running Case has been expanded to all applications, with one exercise per chapter focusing on the New Castle County Technical Services case, providing a continuous and real-world project for students to work on throughout the semester.

Pre-Built Learning Modules: Pre-built inside MyLab IT, these make course setup a snap. The modules are based on research and instructor best practices, and can be easily customized to meet your course requirements.

Critical Thinking Modules: Pre-built inside MyLab IT, these pair a Grader Project with a critical thinking quiz that requires students to first complete a hands-on project, then reflect on what they did and the data or information they interacted with, to answer a series of objective critical thinking questions. These are offered both at the chapter level for regular practice, as well as at the Application level where students can earn a Critical Thinking badge.

What's New for MyLab IT Graders

Graders with WHY: All Grader project instructions now incorporate the scenario and the WHY to help students critically think and understand why they're performing the steps in the project.

Hands-On Exercise Assessment Graders: A new Grader in each chapter that mirrors the Hands-On Exercise. Using an alternate scenario and data files, this new Grader is built to be more instructional and features Learning Aids such as Read (eText), Watch (video), and Practice (guided simulation) in the Grader report to help students learn, remediate, and resubmit.

Auto-Graded Critical Thinking Quizzes:

- Application Capstones that allow students to earn a Critical Thinking badge
- Chapter-level quizzes for each Mid-Level Exercise Grader project

Improved Mac Compatibility in Graders: All Graders are tested for Mac compatibility and any that can be made 100% Mac compatible are identified in the course. This excludes Access projects as well as any that use functionality not available in Mac Office.

Autograded Integrated Grader Projects: Based on the discipline-specific integrated projects, covering Word, Excel, PowerPoint, and Access in various combinations.

Final Solution Image: Included with Grader student downloads, final output images allows students to visualize what their solution should look like.

What's New for MyLab IT Simulations

Updated Office 365, 2019 Edition Simulations: Written by the *Exploring* author team, ensures one-to-one content to directly match the Hands-On Exercises (Simulation Training) and mirror them with an alternate scenario (Simulation Assessment).

Student Action Visualization: Provides a playback of student actions within the simulation for remediation by students and review by instructors when there is a question about why an action is marked as incorrect.

Series Hallmarks

The **How/Why Approach** helps students move beyond the point and click to a true understanding of how to apply Microsoft Office skills.

- **White Pages/Yellow Pages** clearly distinguish the theory (white pages) from the skills covered in the Hands-On Exercises (yellow pages) so students always know what they are supposed to be doing and why.

- **Case Study** presents a scenario for the chapter, creating a story that ties the Hands-On Exercises together and gives context to the skills being introduced.

- **Hands-On Exercise Videos** are tied to each Hands-On Exercise and walk students through the steps of the exercise while weaving in conceptual information related to the Case Study and the objectives as a whole.

An **Outcomes focus** allows students and instructors to know the higher-level learning goals and how those are achieved through discreet objectives and skills.

- **Outcomes** presented at the beginning of each chapter identify the learning goals for students and instructors.

- **Enhanced Objective Mapping** enables students to follow a directed path through each chapter, from the objectives list at the chapter opener through the exercises at the end of the chapter.
    - **Objectives List:** This provides a simple list of key objectives covered in the chapter. This includes page numbers so students can skip between objectives where they feel they need the most help.
    - **Step Icons:** These icons appear in the white pages and reference the step numbers in the Hands-On Exercises, providing a correlation between the two so students can easily find conceptual help when they are working hands-on and need a refresher.
    - **Quick Concepts Check:** A series of questions that appear briefly at the end of each white page section. These questions cover the most essential concepts in the white pages required for students to be successful in working the Hands-On Exercises. Page numbers are included for easy reference to help students locate the answers.
    - **Chapter Objectives Review:** Located near the end of the chapter and reviews all important concepts covered in the chapter. Designed in an easy-to-read bulleted format.

- **MOS Certification Guide** for instructors and students to direct anyone interested in prepping for the MOS exam to the specific locations to find all content required for the test.

End-of-Chapter Exercises offer instructors several options for assessment. Each chapter has approximately 11–12 exercises ranging from multiple choice questions to open-ended projects.

- **Multiple Choice, Key Terms Matching, Practice Exercises, Mid-Level Exercises, Running Case, Disaster Recovery, and Capstone Exercises** are at the end of all chapters.
    - **Enhanced Mid-Level Exercises** include a **Creative Case** (for PowerPoint and Word), which allows students some flexibility and creativity, not being bound by a definitive solution, and an **Analysis Case** (for Excel and Access), which requires students to interpret the data they are using to answer an analytic question.

- **Application Capstone** exercises are included in the book to allow instructors to test students on the contents of a single application.

The Exploring Series and MyLab IT

The *Exploring Series* has been a market leader for more than 20 years, with a hallmark focus on both the *how* and *why* behind what students do within the Microsoft Office software. In this edition, the pairing of the text with MyLab IT Simulations, Graders, Objective Quizzes, and Resources as a fully complementary program allows students and instructors to get the very most out of their use of the *Exploring Series*.

To maximize student results, we recommend pairing the text content with MyLab IT, which is the teaching and learning platform that empowers you to reach every student. By combining trusted author content with digital tools and a flexible platform, MyLab personalizes the learning experience and helps your students learn and retain key course concepts while developing skills that future employers are seeking in their candidates.

Solving Teaching and Learning Challenges

Pearson addresses these teaching and learning challenges with *Exploring* and MyLab IT 2019.

Reach Every Student

MyLab IT 2019 delivers trusted content and resources through easy-to-use, Prebuilt Learning Modules that promote student success. Through an authentic learning experience, students become sharp critical thinkers and proficient in Microsoft Office, developing essential skills employers seek.

Practice and Feedback: What do I do when I get stuck or need more practice?

MyLab IT features **Integrated Learning Aids** within the Simulations and now also within the Grader Reports, allowing students to choose to Read (via the eText), Watch (via an author-created hands-on video), or Practice (via a guided simulation) whenever they get stuck. These are conveniently accessible directly within the simulation training so that students do not have to leave the graded assignment to access these helpful resources. The **Student Action Visualization** captures all the work students do in the Simulation for both Training and Assessment and allows students and instructors to watch a detailed playback for the purpose of remediation or guidance when students get stuck. MyLab IT offers **Grader project reports** for coaching, remediation, and defensible grading. Score Card Detail allows you to easily see where students were scored correctly or incorrectly, pointing out how many points were deducted on each step. Live Comments Report allows you and the students to see the actual files the student submitted with mark-ups/comments on what they missed and now includes Learning Aids to provide immediate remediation for incorrect steps.

Application, Motivation, and Employability Skills: Why am I taking this course, and will this help me get a job?

Students want to know that what they are doing in this class is setting them up for their ultimate goal—to get a job. With an emphasis on **employability skills** like critical thinking and other soft skills, **digital badges** to prove student proficiency in Microsoft skills and critical thinking, and **MOS Certification practice materials** in MyLab IT, the *Exploring Series* is putting students on the path to differentiate themselves in the job market, so that they can find and land a job that values their schools once they leave school.

Application: How do I get students to apply what they've learned in a meaningful way?

The *Exploring Series* and MyLab IT offer instructors the ability to provide students with authentic formative and summative assessments. The realistic and hi-fidelity **simulations** help students feel like they are working in the real Microsoft applications and allow them to explore, use 96% of Microsoft methods, and do so without penalty. The **Grader projects** allow students to gain real-world context as they work live in the application, applying both an understanding of how and why to perform certain skills to complete a project. New **Critical Thinking quizzes** require students to demonstrate their understanding of why, by answering questions that force them to analyze and interpret the project they worked on to answer a series of objective questions. The new **Running Case** woven through all applications requires students to apply their knowledge in a realistic way to a long-running, semester-long project focused on the same company.

Ease of Use: I need a course solution that is easy to use for both me and my students

MyLab IT 2019 is the easiest and most accessible in its history. With new **Prebuilt Learning** and **Critical Thinking Modules** course set-up is simple! **LMS integration capabilities** allow users seamless access to MyLab IT with single sign-on, grade sync, and asset-level deep linking. Continuing a focus on accessibility, MyLab IT includes an **integrated Accessibility Toolbar** with translation feature for students with disabilities, as well as a **Virtual Keyboard** that allows students to complete keyboard actions entirely on screen. There is also an enhanced focus on Mac compatibility with even more Mac-compatible Grader projects,

Developing Employability Skills

High-Demand Office Skills are taught to help students gain these skills and prepare for the Microsoft Office Certification exams (MOS). The MOS objectives are covered throughout the content, and a MOS Objective Appendix provides clear mapping of where to find each objective. Practice exams in the form of Graders and Simulations are available in MyLab IT.

Badging Digital badges are available for students in Introductory and Advanced Microsoft Word, Excel, Access, and PowerPoint. This digital credential is issued to students upon successful completion (90%+ score) of an Application Capstone Badging Grader project. MyLab IT badges provide verified evidence that learners have demonstrated specific skills and competencies using Microsoft Office tools in a real project and help distinguish students within the job pool. Badges are issued through the Acclaim system and can be placed in a LinkedIn ePortfolio, posted on social media (Facebook, Twitter), and/or included in a résumé. Badges include tags with relevant information that allow students to be discoverable by potential employers, as well as search for jobs for which they are qualified.

> "The badge is a way for employers to actually verify that a potential employee is actually somewhat fluent with Excel."—Bunker Hill Community College Student

The new **Critical Thinking Badge** in MyLab IT for 2019 provides verified evidence that learners have demonstrated the ability to not only complete a real project, but also analyze and problem-solve using Microsoft Office applications. Students prove this by completing an objective quiz that requires them to critically think about the project, interpret data, and explain why they performed the actions they did in the project. Critical Thinking is a hot button issue at many institutions and is highly sought after in job candidates, allowing students with the Critical Thinking Badge to stand out and prove their skills.

Soft Skills Videos are included in MyLab IT for educators who want to emphasize key employability skills such as Accepting Criticism and Being Coachable, Customer Service, and Resume and Cover Letter Best Practices.

Resources

Instructor Teaching Resources	
Supplements Available to Instructors at www.pearsonhighered.com/ exploring	**Features of the Supplement**
Instructor's Manual	Available for each chapter and includes: • List of all Chapter Resources, File Names, and Where to Find • Chapter Overview • Class Run-Down • Key Terms • Discussion Questions • Practice Projects & Applications • Teaching Notes • Additional Web Resources • Projects and Exercises with File Names • Solutions to Multiple Choice, Key Terms Matching, and Quick Concepts Checks
Solutions Files, Annotated Solution Files, Scorecards	• Available for all exercises with definitive solutions • Annotated Solution Files in PDF feature callouts to enable easy grading • Scorecards to allow for easy scoring for hand-grading all exercises with definitive solutions, and scoring by step adding to 100 points.
Rubrics	For Mid-Level Exercises without a definitive solution. Available in Microsoft Word format, enabling instructors to customize the assignments for their classes
Test Bank	Approximately 75–100 total questions per chapter, made up of multiple-choice, true/false, and matching. Questions include these annotations: • Correct Answer • Difficulty Level • Learning Objective Alternative versions of the Test Bank are available for the following LMS: Blackboard CE/Vista, Blackboard, Desire2Learn, Moodle, Sakai, and Canvas
Computerized TestGen	TestGen allows instructors to: • Customize, save, and generate classroom tests • Edit, add, or delete questions from the Test Item Files • Analyze test results • Organize a database of tests and student results
PowerPoint Presentations	PowerPoints for each chapter cover key topics, feature key images from the text, and include detailed speaker notes in addition to the slide content. PowerPoints meet accessibility standards for students with disabilities. Features include, but are not limited to: • Keyboard and Screen Reader access • Alternative text for images • High color contrast between background and foreground colors

Scripted Lectures	• A lecture guide that provides the actions and language to help demonstrate skills from the chapter • Follows the activity similar to the Hands-On Exercises but with an alternative scenario and data files
Prepared Exams	• An optional Hands-On Exercise that can be used to assess students' ability to perform the skills from each chapter, or across all chapters in an application. • Each Prepared Exam folder includes the needed data files, instruction file, solution, annotated solution, and scorecard.
Outcome and Objective Maps	• Available for each chapter to help you determine what to assign • Includes every exercise and identifies which outcomes, objectives, and skills are included from the chapter
MOS Mapping, MOS Online Appendix	• Based on the Office 2019 MOS Objectives • Includes a full mapping of where each objective is covered in the materials • For any content not covered in the textbook, additional material is available in the Online Appendix document
Transition Guide	A detailed spreadsheet that provides a clear mapping of content from Exploring Microsoft Office 2016 to Exploring Microsoft Office 365, 2019 Edition
Content Updates Guide	A living document that features any changes in content based on Microsoft Office 365 changes as well as any errata
Assignment Sheets	Document with a grid of suggested student deliverables per chapter that can be passed out to students with columns for Due Date, Possible Points, and Actual Points
Sample Syllabus	Syllabus templates set up for 8-week, 12-week, and 16-week courses
Answer Keys for Multiple Choice, Key Terms Matching, and Quick Concepts Check	Answer keys for each objective, matching, or short-answer question type from each chapter

Student Resources

Supplements Available to Students at www.pearsonhighered.com/exploring	**Features of the Supplement**
Student Data Files	All data files needed for the following exercises, organized by chapter: • Hands-On Exercises • Practice Exercises • Mid-Level Exercises • Running Case • Disaster Recovery Case • Capstone Exercise
MOS Certification Material	• Based on the Office 2019 MOS Objectives • Includes a full mapping of where each objective is covered in the materials • For any content not covered in the textbook, additional material is available in the Online Appendix document

(ex·ploring)

SERIES

1. Investigating in a systematic way: examining. 2. Searching into or ranging over for the purpose of discovery.

Microsoft®

Office 365®

Access™ 2019

COMPREHENSIVE

Office 365 Common Features

LEARNING OUTCOME You will apply skills common across the Microsoft Office suite to create and format documents and edit content in Office 365 applications.

OBJECTIVES & SKILLS: After you read this chapter, you will be able to:

Get Started with Office Applications

OBJECTIVE 1: START AN OFFICE APPLICATION 5
Use Your Microsoft Account, Use OneDrive
OBJECTIVE 2: WORK WITH FILES 6
Create a New File, Save a File, Open a Saved File
OBJECTIVE 3: USE COMMON INTERFACE COMPONENTS 9
Use the Ribbon, Use a Dialog Box and Gallery,
Customize the Ribbon, Use the Quick Access Toolbar,
Customize the Quick Access Toolbar, Use a Shortcut
Menu, Use Keyboard Shortcuts
OBJECTIVE 4: GET HELP 15
Use the Tell Me Box, Use the Help Tab, Use Enhanced
ScreenTips
OBJECTIVE 5: INSTALL ADD-INS 17
Use an Add-in from the Store
HANDS-ON EXERCISE 1 19

Format Document Content

OBJECTIVE 6: USE TEMPLATES AND APPLY THEMES 25
Open a Template, Apply a Theme
OBJECTIVE 7: MODIFY TEXT 27
Select Text, Format Text, Use the Mini Toolbar

OBJECTIVE 8: RELOCATE TEXT 30
Cut, Copy, and Paste Text; Use the Office Clipboard
OBJECTIVE 9: REVIEW A DOCUMENT 32
Check Spelling and Grammar
OBJECTIVE 10: WORK WITH PICTURES 34
Insert a Picture, Modify a Picture
HANDS-ON EXERCISE 2 37

Modify Document Layout and Properties

OBJECTIVE 11: CHANGE DOCUMENT VIEWS 45
Change Document Views Using the Ribbon,
Change Document Views Using the Status Bar
OBJECTIVE 12: CHANGE THE PAGE LAYOUT 46
Change Margins, Change Page Orientation,
Use the Page Setup Dialog Box
OBJECTIVE 13: CREATE A HEADER AND FOOTER 49
Insert a Footer, Insert a Header
OBJECTIVE 14: CONFIGURE DOCUMENT PROPERTIES 50
View and Enter Document Properties
OBJECTIVE 15: PREVIEW AND PRINT A FILE 51
Preview a File, Change Print Settings, Print a File
HANDS-ON EXERCISE 3 53

CASE STUDY | Spotted Begonia Art Gallery

You are an administrative assistant for Spotted Begonia, a local art gallery. The gallery does a lot of community outreach to help local artists develop a network of clients and supporters. Local schools are invited to bring students to the gallery for enrichment programs.

As the administrative assistant for Spotted Begonia, you are responsible for overseeing the production of documents, spreadsheets, newspaper articles, and presentations that will be used to increase public awareness of the gallery. Other clerical assistants who are familiar with Microsoft Office will prepare the promotional materials, and you will proofread, make necessary corrections, adjust page layouts, save and print documents, and identify appropriate templates to simplify tasks. Your experience with Microsoft Office is limited, but you know that certain fundamental tasks that are common to Word, Excel, and PowerPoint will help you accomplish your oversight task. You are excited to get started with your work!

Dean Drobot/Shutterstock

Taking the First Step

CHAPTER 1

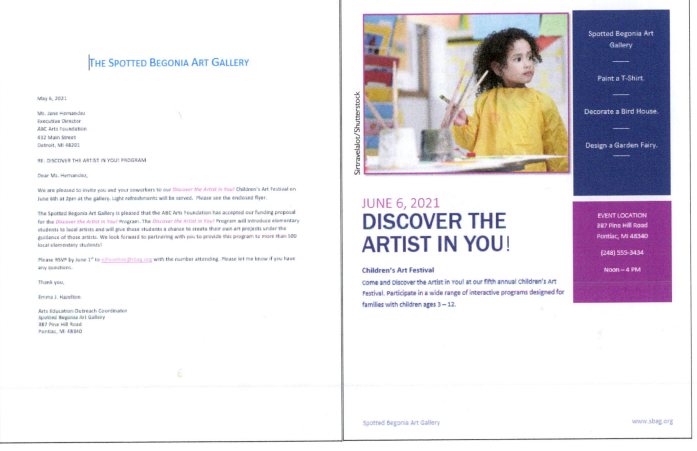

FIGURE 1.1 Spotted Begonia Art Gallery Documents

CASE STUDY | Spotted Begonia Art Gallery

Starting Files	Files to be Submitted
cf01h1Letter.docx	cf01h1Letter_LastFirst.docx
Seasonal Event Flyer Template	cf01h3Flyer_LastFirst.docx

MyLab IT Grader An alternate version of this project is available as a MyLab IT Grader Assessment

Get Started with Office Applications

Organizations around the world rely heavily on Microsoft Office software to produce documents, spreadsheets, presentations, and databases. **Microsoft Office** is a productivity software suite that includes a set of software applications, each one specializing in a specific type of output. There are different versions of Office. Office 365 is purchased as a monthly or annual subscription and is fully installed on your PC, tablet, and phone. With Office 365, you receive periodic updates of new features and security measures. Office 365 also includes access to OneDrive storage. Office 2019 is a one-time purchase and fully installed on your PC. Periodic upgrades are not available. Both Office 365 and Office 2019 have versions that run on a Mac.

All versions of Microsoft Office include Word, Excel, and PowerPoint, as well as some other applications. Some versions of Office also include Access. Office 365 for Mac and Office for Mac include Word, Excel, and PowerPoint, but not Access. **Microsoft Word** (Word) is a word processing application, used to produce all sorts of documents, including memos, newsletters, reports, and brochures. **Microsoft Excel** (Excel) is a financial spreadsheet program, used to organize records, financial transactions, and business information in the form of worksheets. **Microsoft PowerPoint** (PowerPoint) is presentation software, used to create dynamic presentations to inform and persuade audiences. Finally, **Microsoft Access** (Access) is a database program, used to record and link data, query databases, and create forms and reports. The choice of which software application to use really depends on what type of output you are producing. Table 1.1 describes the major tasks of the four primary applications in Microsoft Office.

TABLE 1.1	Microsoft Office Applications
Office Application	**Application Characteristics**
Word	Word processing software used with text and graphics to create, edit, and format documents.
Excel	Spreadsheet software used to store quantitative data and to perform accurate and rapid calculations, what-if analyses, and charting, with results ranging from simple budgets to sophisticated financial and statistical analyses.
PowerPoint	Presentation graphics software used to create slide shows for presentation by a speaker or delivered online, to be published as part of a website, or to run as a stand-alone application on a computer kiosk.
Access	Relational database software used to store data and convert it into information. Database software is used primarily for decision making by businesses that compile data from multiple records stored in tables to produce informative reports.

These programs are designed to work together, so you can integrate components created in one application into a file created by another application. For example, you could integrate a chart created in Excel into a Word document or a PowerPoint presentation, or you could export a table created in Access into Excel for further analysis. You can use two or more Office applications to produce your intended output.

In addition, Microsoft Office applications share common features. Such commonality gives a similar feel to each software application so that learning and working with each Office software application is easier. This chapter focuses on many common features that the Office applications share. Although Word is primarily used to illustrate many examples, you are encouraged to open and explore Excel and PowerPoint (and to some degree, Access) to examine the same features in those applications. As a note, most of the content in this chapter and book are for the Windows-based Office applications. Some basic information about Office for Mac is included in TIP boxes and in the Step boxes when there are significant differences to point out.

In this section, you will learn how to log in with your Microsoft account, open an application, and open and save a file. You will also learn to identify interface components common to Office software applications, such as the ribbon, Backstage view, and the Quick Access Toolbar. You will experience Live Preview. You will learn how to get help with an application. You will also learn about customizing the ribbon and using Office add-ins.

Starting an Office Application

Microsoft Office applications are launched from the Start menu. Select the Start icon ⊞ to display the Start menu and select the app tile for the application in which you want to work (see Figure 1.2). Note: The Start menu in Figure 1.2 may show different tiles and arrangement of tiles than what is on your Start menu. If the application tile you want is not on the Start menu, you can open the program from the list of all apps on the left side of the Start menu, or alternatively, you can use search on the taskbar. Just type the name of the program in the search box and press Enter. The program will open automatically.

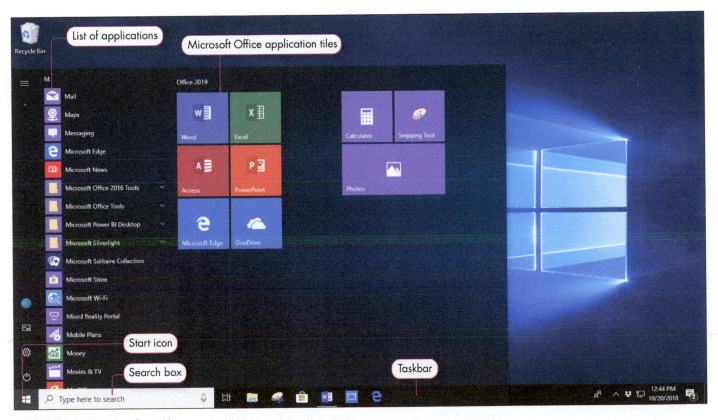

FIGURE 1.2 Windows Start Menu

Use Your Microsoft Account

When you have a Microsoft account, you can sign in to any Windows computer and you will be able to access the saved settings associated with your Microsoft account. That means any computer can have the same familiar look that you are used to seeing on your home or school computers and devices. Your Microsoft account will automatically sign in to all the apps and services that use a Microsoft account, such as OneDrive and Outlook. If you share your computer with another user, each user can have access to his or her own Microsoft account, and can easily switch between accounts by logging out of one Microsoft account and logging in to another Microsoft account. You can switch accounts within an application as well.

To switch between accounts in an application such as Word, complete the following steps:

1. Click the profile name at the top-right of the application.
2. Select Switch account.
3. Select an account from the list, if the account has already been added to the computer, or add a new account.

On a Mac, to switch between accounts in an application, complete the following steps:

1. Click the application menu (Word, Excel, etc.), click Sign Out, and then click Sign Out again.
2. Click File, click New From Template, and then click Sign in at top of the left pane.
3. Click Sign in again, type your user email, click Next, type password, and then click Sign in.

Use OneDrive

Having a Microsoft account also provides additional benefits, such as being connected to all of Microsoft's resources on the Internet. These resources include an Outlook email account and access to OneDrive cloud storage. *Cloud storage* is a technology used to store files and work with programs that are stored in a central location on the Internet. *OneDrive* is a Microsoft app used to store, access, and share files and folders on the Internet. OneDrive is the default storage location when saving Office files. Because OneDrive stores files on the Internet, when a document has been saved in OneDrive the most recent version of the document will be accessible when you log in from any computer connected to the Internet. Files and folders saved to OneDrive can be available offline and accessed through File Explorer—Windows' file management system. Moreover, changes made to any document saved to OneDrive will be automatically updated across all devices, so each device you access with your Windows account will all have the same version of the file.

OneDrive enables you to collaborate with others. You can share your documents with others or edit a document on which you are collaborating. You can even work with others simultaneously on the same document.

STEP 1 ▸ Working with Files

When working with an Office application, you can begin by opening an existing file that has already been saved to a storage medium or you can begin work on a new file or template. When you are finished with a file, you should save it, so you can retrieve it at another time.

Create a New File

After opening an Office application, you will be presented with template choices. Use the Blank document (workbook, presentation, database, etc.) template to start a new blank file. You can also create a new Office file from within an application by selecting New from the File tab.

The File tab is located at the far left of the ribbon. When you select the File tab, you see *Backstage view*. Backstage view is where you manage your files and the data about them—creating, saving, printing, sharing, inspecting for accessibility, compatibility, and other document issues, and accessing other setting options. The File tab and Backstage view is where you do things "to" a file, whereas the other tabs on the ribbon enable you to do things "in" a file.

Save a File

Saving a file enables you to open it for additional updates or reference later. Files are saved to a storage medium such as a hard drive, flash drive, or to OneDrive.

The first time you save a file, you indicate where the file will be saved and assign a file name. It is best to save the file in an appropriately named folder so you can find it easily later. Thereafter, you can continue to save the file with the same name and location using the Save command. If the file is saved in OneDrive, any changes to the file will be automatically saved. You do not have to actively save the document. If you want more control over when changes to your document are saved, you have the option to turn this feature off (or back on) with the AutoSave feature in the Quick Access Toolbar.

There are instances where you will want to rename the file or save it to a different location. For example, you might reuse a budget saved as an Excel worksheet, modifying it for another year, and want to keep a copy of both the old and revised budgets. In this instance, you would save the new workbook with a new name, and perhaps save it in a different folder. To do so, use the Save As command, and continue with the same procedure to save a new file: navigating to the new storage location and changing the file name. Figure 1.3 shows a typical Save As pane that enables you to select a location before saving the file. Notice that OneDrive is listed as well as This PC. To navigate to a specific location, use Browse.

FIGURE 1.3 Save As in Backstage View

To save a file with a different name and/or file location, complete the following steps:

1. Click the File tab.
2. Click Save As.
3. Select a location or click Browse to navigate to the file storage location.
4. Type the file name.
5. Click Save.

STEP 2 ## Open a Saved File

Often you will need to work on an existing file that has been saved to a storage location. This may be an email attachment that you have downloaded to a storage device, a file that has been shared with you in OneDrive, or a file you have previously created. To open an existing file, navigate in File Explorer to the folder or drive where the document is stored, and then double-click the file name to open the file. The application and the file will open. Alternatively, if the application is already open, from Backstage view, click Open, and then click Browse, This PC, or OneDrive to locate and open the file (see Figure 1.4).

> **MAC TIP:** To open an existing file, navigate in Finder to the folder or drive where the document is stored and double-click the file name to open the file.

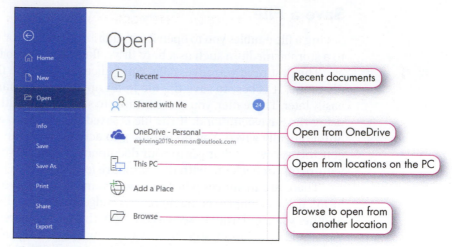

FIGURE 1.4 Open in Backstage View

Office simplifies the task of reopening files by providing a Recent documents list with links to your most recently used files, as shown in Figure 1.5. When opening the application, the Recent list displays in the center pane. The Recent list changes to reflect only the most recently opened files, so if it has been quite some time since you worked with a particular file, or if you have worked on several other files in between and you do not see your file listed, you can click More documents (or Workbooks, Presentations, etc).

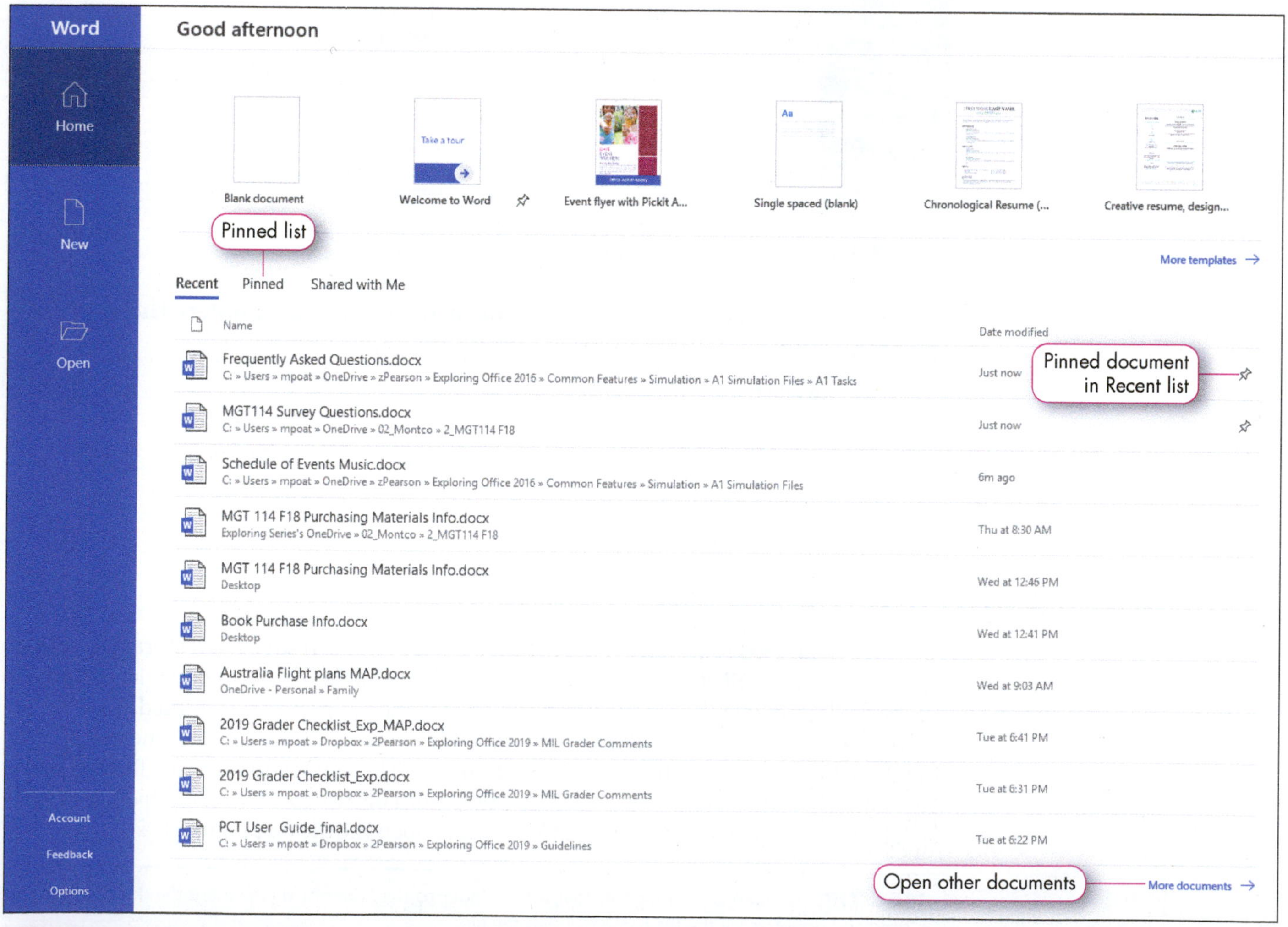

FIGURE 1.5 Recent Documents List

Using Common Interface Components

When you open any Office application, you will first notice the title bar and ribbon (see Figure 1.6) at the top of the document. These features enable you to identify the document, provide easy access to frequently used commands, and controls the window in which the document displays. The ***title bar*** identifies the current file name and the application in which you are working. It also includes control buttons that enable you to minimize, restore down, or close the application window. The Quick Access Toolbar, on the left side of the title bar, enables you to turn AutoSave on or off, save the file, undo or redo editing, and customize the Quick Access Toolbar. Located just below the title bar is the ribbon. The ***ribbon*** is the command center of Office applications containing tabs, groups, and commands. If you are working with a large project, you can maximize your workspace by temporarily hiding the ribbon. There are several methods that can be used to hide and then redisplay the ribbon:

- Double-click any tab name to collapse; click any tab name to expand
- Click the Collapse Ribbon arrow at the far-right side of the ribbon
- Use the Ribbon Display Option on the right side of the Title bar. These controls enable you to not only collapse or expand the ribbon, but also to choose whether you want to see the tabs or no tabs at all.

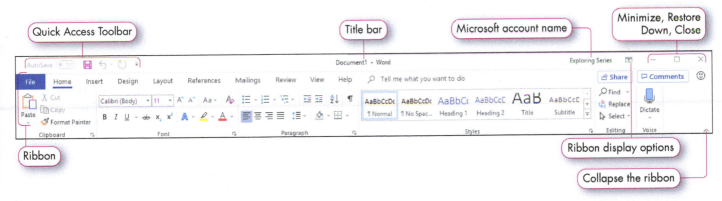

FIGURE 1.6 The Title Bar, Quick Access Toolbar, and Document Controls

Use the Ribbon

The main organizational grouping on the ribbon is tabs. The ***tab*** name indicates the type of commands located on the tab. On each tab, the ribbon displays several task-oriented groups. A ***group*** is a subset of a tab that organizes similar commands together. A ***command*** is a button or task within a group that you select to perform a task (see Figure 1.7). The ribbon with the tabs and groups of commands is designed to provide efficient functionality. For that reason, the Home tab displays when you first open a file in an Office software application and contains groups with the most commonly used commands for that application. For example, because you often want to change the way text is displayed, the Home tab in an Office application includes a Font group, with commands related to modifying text. Similarly, other tabs contain groups of related actions, or commands, many of which are unique to each Office application. The active tab in Figure 1.7 is the Home tab.

> **MAC TIP:** Office for Mac does not display group names in the ribbon by default. On a Mac, to display group names on the ribbon, click the application name menu (Word, Excel, PowerPoint) and select Preferences. Click View and click to select Show group titles in the Ribbon section of the View dialog box.

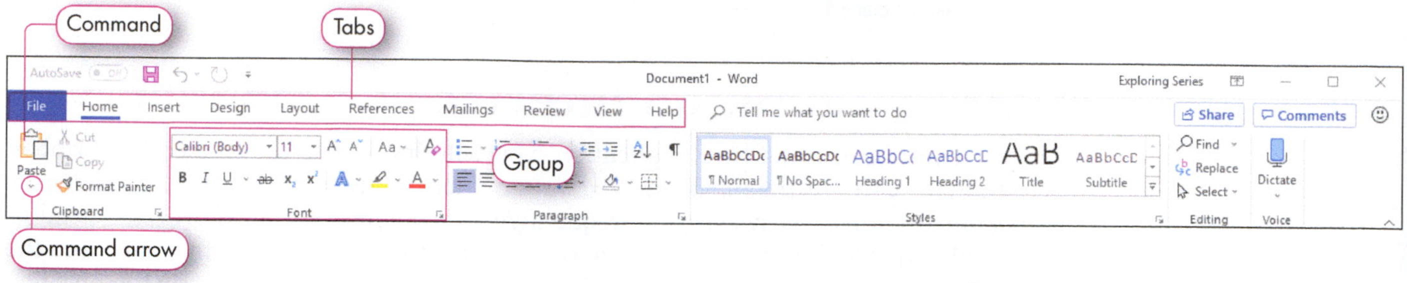

FIGURE 1.7 The Ribbon

As shown in Figure 1.7, some ribbon commands, such as Paste in the Clipboard group, contain two parts: the main command and an arrow. The arrow may be below or to the right of the main command, depending on the command, window size, or screen resolution. When selected, the arrow brings up additional commands or options associated with the main command. For example, selecting the Paste arrow enables you to access the Paste Options commands, and the Font color arrow displays a set of colors from which to choose. Instructions in the *Exploring* series use the command name to instruct you to click the main command to perform the default action, such as click Paste. Instructions include the word *arrow* when you need to select the arrow to access an additional option, such as click the Paste arrow.

Office applications enable you to work with objects such as images, shapes, charts, and tables. When you include such objects in a project, they are considered separate components that you can manage independently. To work with an object, you must first select it. When an object is selected, the ribbon is modified to include one or more ***contextual tabs*** that contain groups of commands related to the selected object. These tabs are designated as Tool tabs; for example, Picture Tools is the contextual tab that displays when a picture is selected. When the object is no longer selected, the contextual tab disappears.

Word, PowerPoint, Excel, and Access all share a similar ribbon structure. Although the specific tabs, groups, and commands vary among the Office programs, the way in which you use the ribbon and the descriptive nature of tab titles is the same, regardless of which program you are using. For example, if you want to insert a chart in Excel, a header in Word, or a shape in PowerPoint, those commands are found on the Insert tab in those programs. The first thing you should do as you begin to work with an Office application is to study the ribbon. Look at all tabs and their contents. That way, you will have a good idea of where to find specific commands, and how the ribbon with which you are currently working differs from one that you might have used in another application.

STEP 3 **Use a Dialog Box and Gallery**

Some commands and features do not display on the ribbon because they are not as commonly used. For example, you might want to apply a special effect such as Small caps or apply character spacing to some text. Because these effects are not found on the ribbon, they will most likely be found in a ***dialog box*** (in this case, the Font dialog box). When you open a dialog box, you gain access to more precise or less frequently used commands. Dialog boxes are accessed by clicking a ***Dialog Box Launcher*** ⌐, found in the lower right corner of some ribbon groups. Figure 1.8 shows the Font Group Dialog Box Launcher and the Font dialog box.

> **MAC TIP:** Dialog box launchers are not available in Office for Mac. Instead, click a menu option such as Format, Edit, or Insert for additional options.

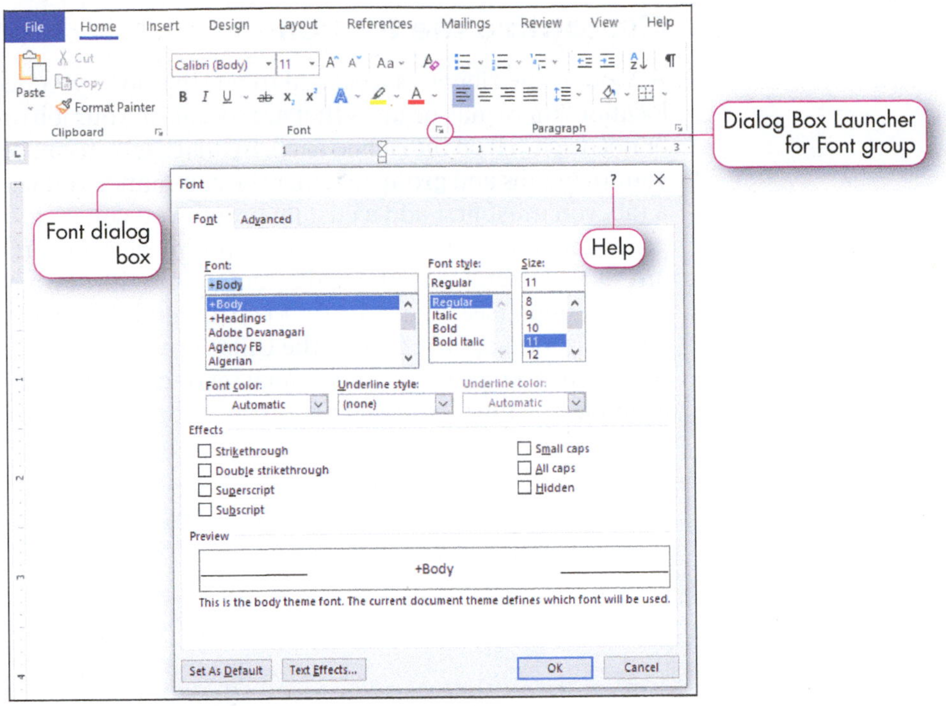

FIGURE 1.8 The Font Dialog Box in Word

> **TIP: GETTING HELP WITH DIALOG BOXES**
> You will find commands or options in a dialog box that you are not familiar with. Click the Help button that displays as a question mark in the top-right corner of the dialog box. The subsequent Help window offers suggestions or assistance in implementing the relevant feature.

Similarly, some formatting and design options are too numerous to include in the ribbon's limited space. For example, the Styles group displays on the Home tab of the Word ribbon. Because there are more styles than can easily display at once, the Styles group can be expanded to display a gallery of additional styles. A *gallery* is an Office feature that displays additional formatting and design options. Galleries in Excel and PowerPoint provide additional choices of chart styles and slide themes, respectively. Figure 1.9 shows an example of a PowerPoint Themes gallery. From the ribbon, you can display a gallery of additional choices by clicking More, which is located at the bottom right of the group's scroll bar found in some ribbon selections (see Figure 1.9).

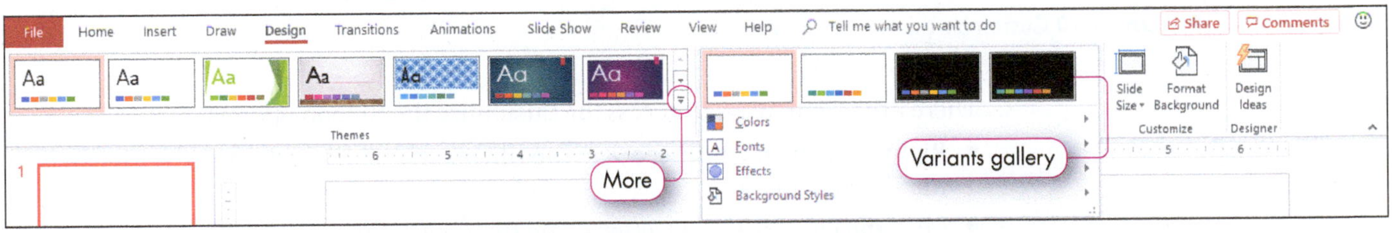

FIGURE 1.9 The Variants Gallery in PowerPoint

When editing a document, worksheet, or presentation, it is helpful to see the results of formatting changes before you make final selections. The feature that displays a preview of the results of a selection is called *Live Preview*. For example, you might be considering modifying the color of an image in a document or worksheet. As you place the pointer over a color selection in a ribbon gallery or group, the selected image will temporarily display the color to which you are pointing. Similarly, you can get a preview of how theme designs would display on PowerPoint slides by pointing to specific themes in the PowerPoint Themes group and noting the effect on a displayed slide. When you click the item, the selection is applied. Live Preview is available in various ribbon selections among the Office applications.

Customize the Ribbon

Although the ribbon is designed to put the tasks you need most in an easily accessible location, there may be tasks that are specific to your job or hobby that are on various tabs, or not displayed on the ribbon at all. In this case, you can personalize the ribbon by creating your own tabs and group together the commands you want to use. To add a command to a tab, you must first add a custom group. You can create as many new tabs and custom groups with as many commands as you need. You can also create a custom group on any of the default tabs and add commands to the new group or hide any commands you use less often (see Figure 1.10). Keep in mind that when you customize the ribbon, the customization applies only to the Office program in which you are working at the time. If you want a new tab with the same set of commands in both Word and PowerPoint, for example, the new tab would need to be created in each application.

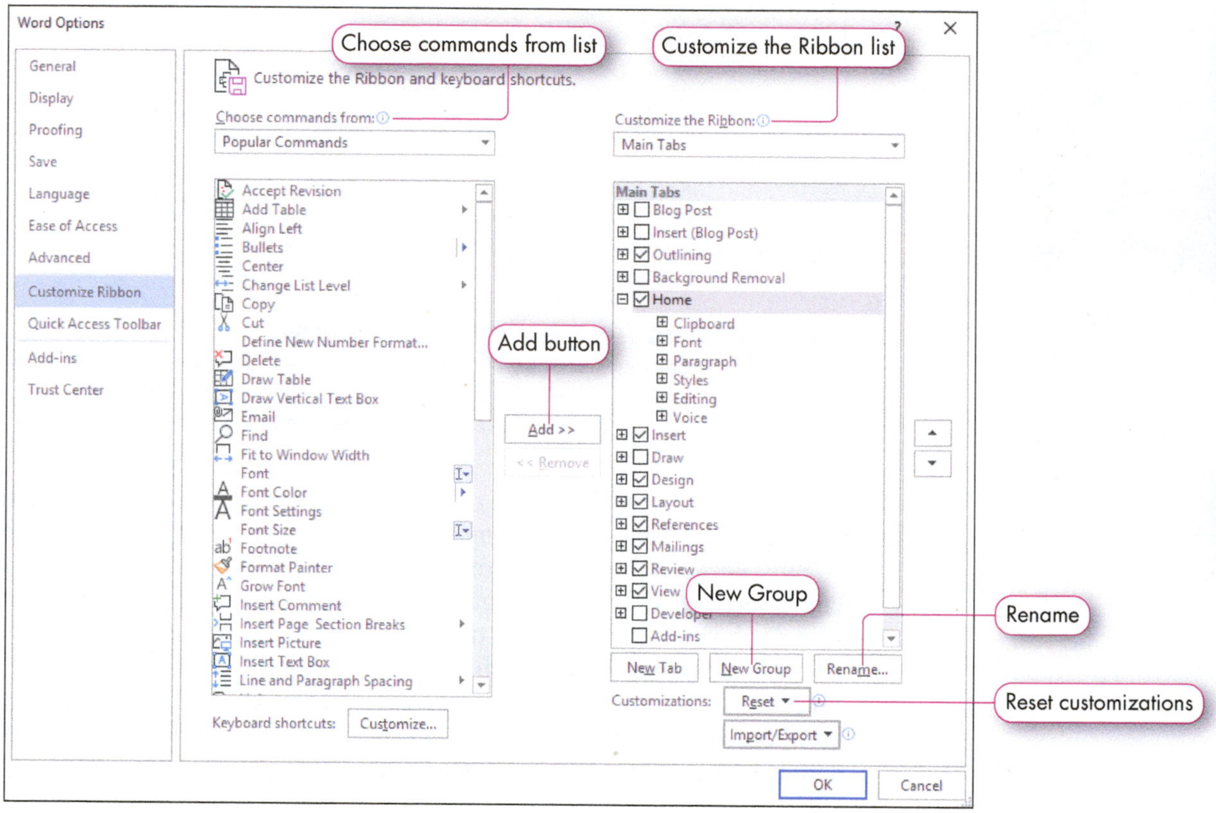

FIGURE 1.10 Customize the Ribbon in Word

There are several ways to access the Customize the Ribbon options:

- Right-click in an empty space in the ribbon and select Customize the Ribbon on the shortcut menu.
- Click the File tab, select Options, and then select Customize Ribbon.
- Click the Customize Quick Access Toolbar button, select More Commands, and then select Customize Ribbon.

The left side of the Customize the Ribbon window displays popular commands associated with the active application, but all available commands can be displayed by selecting All Commands in the *Choose commands from* list. On the right side of the Customize the Ribbon window is a list of the Main Tabs and Groups in the active application. You can also access the contextual Tool tabs by selecting the arrow in the Customize the Ribbon list and selecting Tool Tabs.

To customize the ribbon by adding a command to an existing tab, complete the following steps:

1. Click the File tab, click Options, and then select Customize Ribbon. (Alternatively, follow the other steps above to access the Customize the Ribbon window.)
2. Click the tab name that you want to add a group to under the Customize the Ribbon list. Ensure a blue background displays behind the tab name. Note that checking or unchecking the tab is not selecting the tab for this feature.
3. Click New Group. New Group (Custom) displays as a group on the selected tab.
4. Click Rename and give the new group a meaningful name.
5. Click the command to be added under the Choose commands from list.
6. Click Add.
7. Repeat as necessary, click OK when you have made all your selections.

On a Mac, to customize the ribbon, complete the following steps:

1. Click the Word menu (or whichever application you are working in) and select Preferences.
2. Click Ribbon & Toolbar in the Authoring and Proofing Tools (or in Excel, Authoring).
3. Click the plus sign at the bottom of the Main Tabs box and select New Group.
4. Click the Settings icon and click Rename. Give the new group a meaningful name. Click Save.
5. Continue using steps 5 and 6 in the PC step box above.

To revert all tabs or to reset select tabs to original settings, click Reset, and then click Reset all customizations or Reset only selected Ribbon tab (refer to Figure 1.10).

STEP 4 ## Use and Customize the Quick Access Toolbar

The **Quick Access Toolbar (QAT)**, located at the top-left corner of every Office application window (refer to Figure 1.6), provides one-click access to commonly executed tasks. By default, the QAT includes commands for saving a file and for undoing or redoing recent actions. You can recover from a mistake by clicking Undo on the QAT. If you click the Undo command arrow on the QAT, you can select from a list of previous actions in order of occurrence. The Undo list is not maintained when you close a file or exit the application, so you can only erase an action that took place during the current Office session. You can also Redo (or Replace) an action that you have just undone.

You can also customize the QAT to include commands you frequently use (see Figure 1.11). One command you may want to add is Quick Print. Rather than clicking

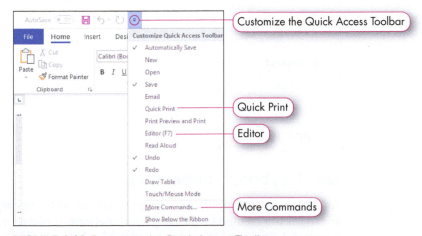

FIGURE 1.11 Customize the Quick Access Toolbar

the File tab, selecting Print, and then selecting various print options, you can add Quick Print to the QAT so that with one click you can print your document with the default Print settings. Other convenient commands can be added, such as Editor to run a spell check of the document.

You customize the QAT by selecting Customize Quick Access Toolbar arrow on the right side of the displayed QAT commands or by right-clicking an empty area on the QAT, and then selecting or deselecting the options from the displayed list of commands. Alternatively, you can right-click any command on the ribbon and select Add to Quick Access Toolbar from the shortcut menu.

To remove a command from the QAT, right-click the command and select Remove from Quick Access Toolbar. If you want to move the QAT to display under the ribbon, select Customize Quick Access Toolbar and click Show below the Ribbon.

STEP 5 ▸ Use a Shortcut Menu

In Office, you can usually accomplish the same task in several ways. Although the ribbon and QAT provide efficient access to commands, in some situations you might find it more convenient to access the same commands on a shortcut menu. A *shortcut menu* is a context-sensitive menu that displays commands and options relevant to the active object. Shortcut menus are accessed by selecting text or an object or by placing the insertion point in a document and pressing the right mouse button or pressing the right side of a trackpad. (On a Mac, press the Control key when you tap the mouse or use a two-finger tap on a trackpad). The shortcut menu will always include options to cut, copy, and paste. In addition, a shortcut menu features tasks that are specifically related to the document content where the insertion point is placed. For example, if your insertion point is on a selected word or group of words, the shortcut menu would include tasks such as to find a synonym or add a comment. If the active object is a picture, the shortcut menu includes options to group objects, provide a caption, or wrap text. As shown in Figure 1.12, when right-clicking a slide thumbnail in PowerPoint, the shortcut menu displays options to add a new slide, duplicate or delete slides, or to change slide layout.

FIGURE 1.12 A Shortcut Menu in PowerPoint

Use Keyboard Shortcuts

Another way to simplify initiating commands is to use *keyboard shortcuts*. Keyboard shortcuts are created by pressing combinations of two or more keys to initiate a software command. Keyboard shortcuts are viewed as being more efficient because you do not have to take your fingers off the keyboard. Some of the most common keyboard shortcuts in Office include Ctrl+C (Copy), Ctrl+X (Cut), Ctrl+V (Paste), and Ctrl+Z (Undo). Pressing Ctrl+Home moves the insertion point to the beginning of a Word document, to cell A1 in Excel, or to the first PowerPoint slide. To move to the end of those files, press Ctrl+End. There are many other keyboard shortcuts. To discover a keyboard shortcut for a command, point to a command icon on the ribbon to display the ScreenTip. If a keyboard shortcut exists, it will display in the ScreenTip. Many similar keyboard shortcuts exist for Office for Mac applications; however, press the Command key rather than the Ctrl key, such as Command+C for Copy.

> **TIP: USING KEYTIPS**
> Another way to use shortcuts, especially those that do not have a keyboard shortcut, is to press Alt to display KeyTips. You can use KeyTips to do tasks quickly without using the mouse by pressing a few keys—no matter where you are in an Office program. You can get to every command on the ribbon by using an access key—usually by pressing two to four keys sequentially. To stop displaying KeyTips, press Alt again.

Getting Help

No matter whether you are a skilled or a novice user of an Office application, there are times when you need help in either finding a certain ribbon command or need additional assistance or training for a task. Fortunately, there are features included in every Office application to offer you support.

STEP 6 ▸ ## Use the Tell Me Box

To the right of the last ribbon tab is a magnifying glass icon and the phrase "Tell me what you want to do." This is the **Tell me box** (see Figure 1.13). Use Tell me to enter words and phrases to search for help and information about a command or task you want to perform. Alternatively, use Tell me for a shortcut to a command or, in some instances (like Bold), to complete the action for you. Tell me can also help you research or define a term you entered. Perhaps you want to find an instance of a word in your document and replace it with another word but cannot locate the Find command on the ribbon. As shown in Figure 1.13, you can type *find* in the Tell me box and a list of commands related to the skill will display, including Find & Select and Replace. Find & Select gives options for the Find command. If you click Replace, the Find and Replace dialog box opens without you having to locate the command on the ribbon.

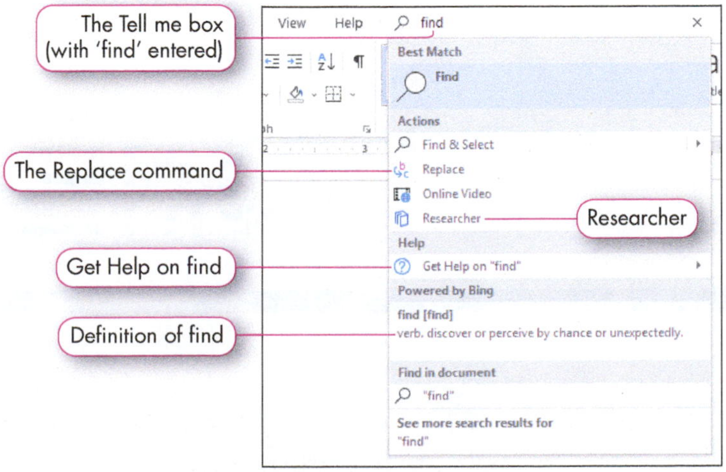

FIGURE 1.13 The Tell Me Box

Should you want to read about the feature instead of applying it, you can click *Get Help on "find,"* which will open Office Help for the feature. Another feature is Smart Lookup on the References tab. This feature opens the Smart Lookup pane that shows results from various online sources based on the search term. ***Smart Lookup*** provides information about tasks or commands in Office and can also be used to search for general information on a topic, such as *President George Washington*. Smart Lookup is also available on the shortcut menu when you right-click text as well as on the References tab in Word. Depending on your search, Researcher may display instead of, or in addition to, Smart Lookup. Researcher can be used to find quotes, citable sources, and images. Researcher is shown in Figure 1.13.

Use the Help Tab

If you are looking for additional help or training on certain features in any Microsoft Office application, you can access this support on the Help tab (see Figure 1.14). The Help command opens the Help pane with a list of tutorials on a variety of application-specific topics. Show Training displays application-specific training videos in the Help pane. Besides Help and Show Training, the Help tab also includes means to contact Microsoft support and to share your feedback. If you are using Office 365, you receive periodic updates with new features as they are released. To learn more about these features, or simply to discover what a new or previous update includes, use the What's New command. What's New brings you to a webpage that discusses all the newly added features organized by release date. You can also access What's New by clicking Account in Backstage view.

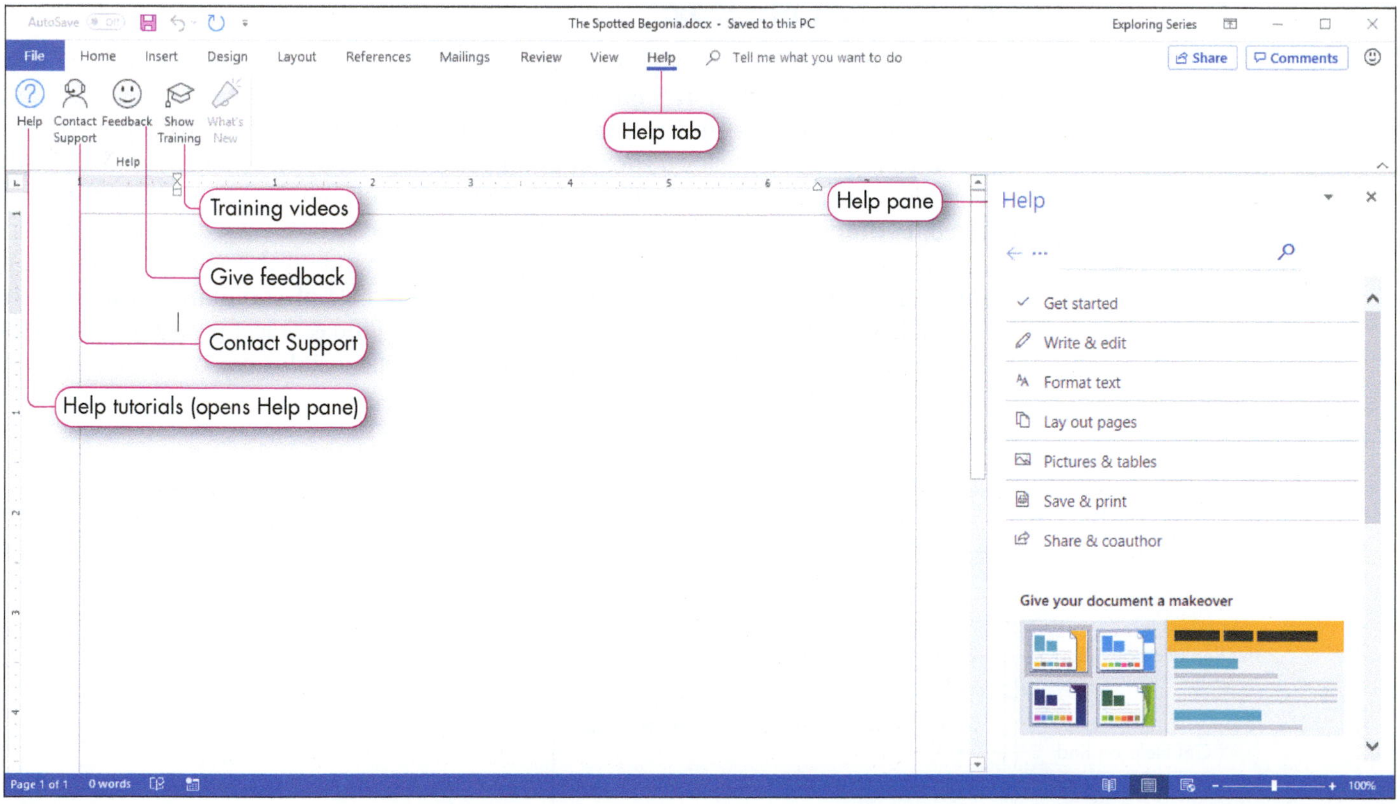

FIGURE 1.14 Help Tab

Use Enhanced ScreenTips

As you use the commands on the ribbon, there may be some that you would like to know more about its purpose, or would like assurance that you are selecting the correct command. For quick summary information on the name and purpose of a command button, point to the command until an **_Enhanced ScreenTip_** displays, with the name and a brief description of the command. If applicable, a keyboard shortcut is also included. Some ScreenTips include a _Tell me more_ option for additional help. The Enhanced ScreenTip, shown for **_Format Painter_** in Figure 1.15, provides a short description of the command in addition to the steps that discuss how to use Format Painter. Use Format Painter to copy all applied formatting from one set of text to another.

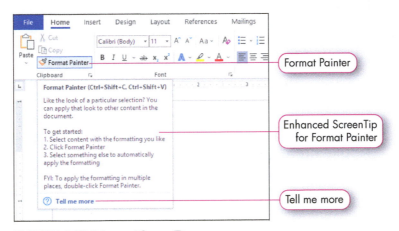

FIGURE 1.15 Enhanced ScreenTip

TIP: COPY FORMAT WITH FORMAT PAINTER
Use Format Painter to quickly apply the same formatting, such as color, font style, and size to other text. Format Painter can also be used to copy border styles to shapes. Format Painter is available in Word, Excel, and PowerPoint, and can be extremely useful when applying multiple formats to other text. Using Format Painter also ensures consistency in appearance between sets of text. To copy formatting to one location, single-click Format Painter, and then click where you want the format applied. To copy formatting to multiple locations, double-click Format Painter. Press Esc or click Format Painter again to turn off the command.

Installing Add-ins

As complete as the Office applications are, you still might want an additional feature that is not a part of the program. Fortunately, there are Microsoft and third-party programs called add-ins that you can add to the program. An **_add-in_** is a custom program that extends the functionality of a Microsoft Office application (see Figure 1.16). For example, in PowerPoint, you could add capability for creating diagrams, access free images, or obtain assistance with graphic design. In Excel, add-ins could provide additional functionality that can help with statistics and data mining. In Word, add-ins could provide survey or resume-creating capabilities. Some add-ins will be available for several applications. For example, the Pickit image app shown in Figure 1.16 is available for Word and PowerPoint. You can access add-ins through the My Add-ins or Get Add-ins commands on the Insert tab. Some templates may come with an add-in associated with it. Some add-ins are available for free, whereas others may have a cost.

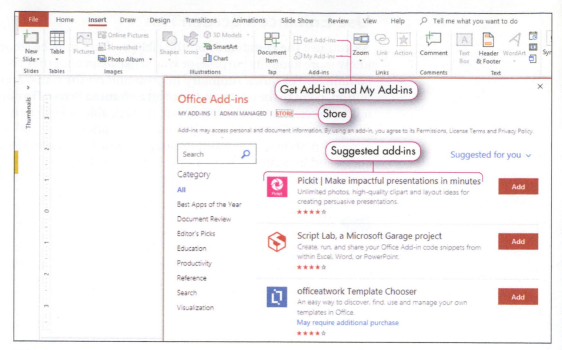

FIGURE 1.16 Add-ins for PowerPoint

Quick Concepts

1. Explain the benefits of logging in with your Microsoft account. *p. 5*

2. Describe when you would use Save and when you would use Save As when saving a document. *p. 7*

3. Explain how the ribbon is organized. *p. 9*

4. Describe the Office application features that are available to assist you in getting help with a task. *p. 15*

Hands-On Exercises

▶ Watch the Video for this Hands-On Exercise!

Skills covered: Open a Saved File • Save a File • Use a Shortcut Menu • Use the Tell me Box

1 Get Started with Office Applications

The Spotted Begonia Art Gallery just hired several new clerical assistants to help you develop materials for the various activities coming up throughout the year. A coworker sent you a letter and asked for your assistance in making a few minor formatting changes. The letter is an invitation to the *Discover the Artist in You!* program Children's Art Festival. To begin, you will open Word and open an existing document. You will use the Shortcut menu to make simple changes to the document. Finally, you will use the Tell me box to apply a style to the first line of text.

STEP 1 OPEN AND SAVE A FILE

You start Microsoft Word and open an event invitation letter that you will later modify. You rename the file to preserve the original and to save the changes you will make later. Refer to Figure 1.17 as you complete Step 1.

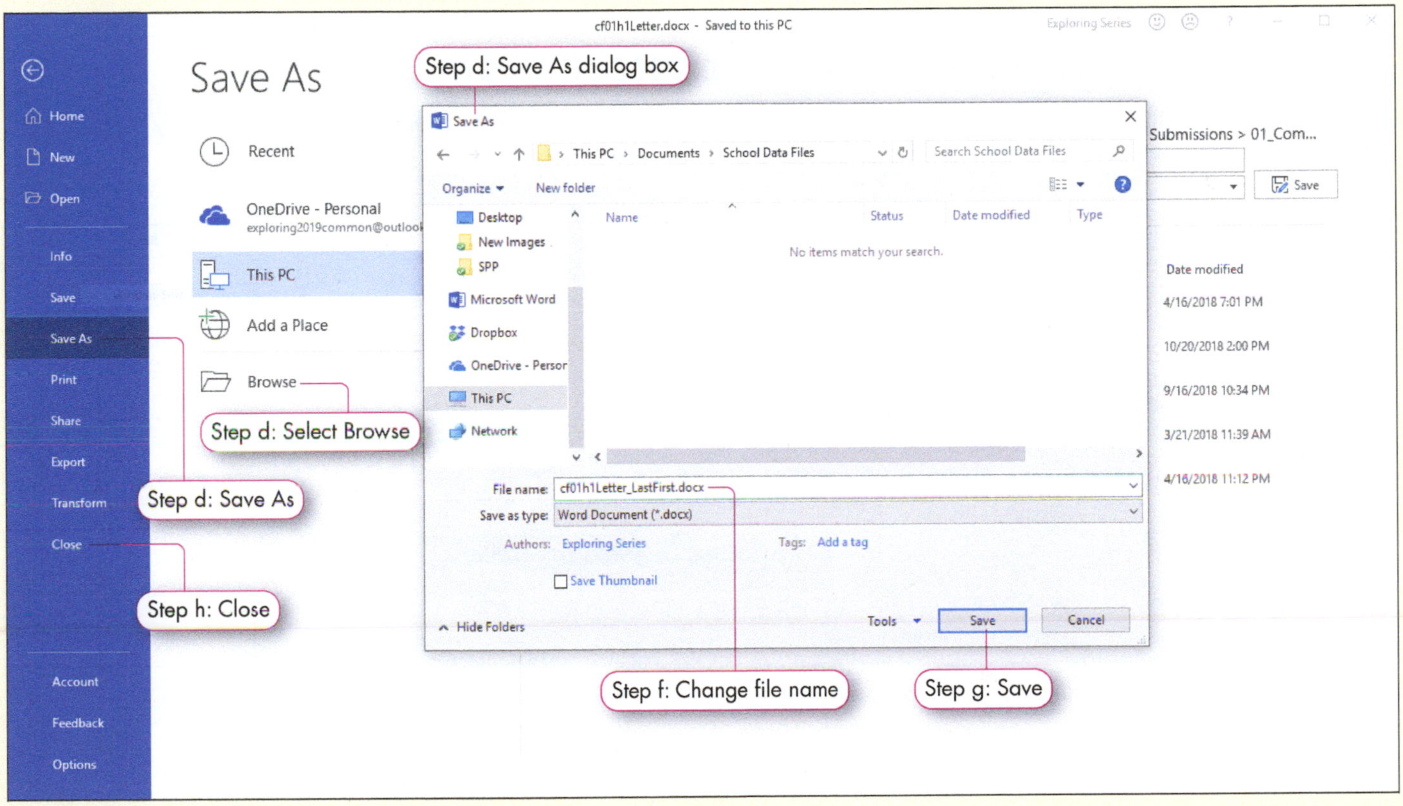

FIGURE 1.17 The Save As Dialog Box

a. Open the Word document *cf01h1Letter*.

The event invitation letter opens.

> **TROUBLESHOOTING:** When you open a file from the student files associated with this book, you may see an Enable Content warning in the Message Bar. This is a security measure to alert a user when there is potentially unsafe content in the file you want to open. You may be confident of the trustworthiness of the files for this book, and should click Enable Content to begin working on the file.

b. Click the **File tab**, click **Save As**, and then click **Browse** to display the Save As dialog box.

Because you will change the name of an existing file, you use the Save As command to give the file a new name. On a Mac, click the File menu and click Save As.

c. Navigate to the location where you are saving your files.

If you are saving the file in a different location than that of your data files, then you will also change the location of where the file is saved.

d. Click in the **File name box** (or the Save As box in Office for Mac) and type **cf01h1Letter_LastFirst**.

You save the document with a different name to preserve the original file.

When you save files, use your last and first names. For example, as the Common Features author, I would name my document "cf01h1Letter_PoatsyMaryAnne."

e. Click **Save**.

> **TROUBLESHOOTING:** If you make any major mistakes in this exercise, you can close the file, open *cf01h1Letter* again, and then start this exercise over.

The file is now saved as cf01h1Letter_LastFirst. Check the title bar of the document to confirm that the file has been saved with the correct name.

f. Click **File** and click **Close** to close the file. Keep Word open.

STEP 2 **OPEN A SAVED FILE AND USE THE RIBBON**

You now have time to modify the letter, so you open the saved file. You use ribbon commands to modify parts of the letter. Refer to Figure 1.18 as you complete Step 2.

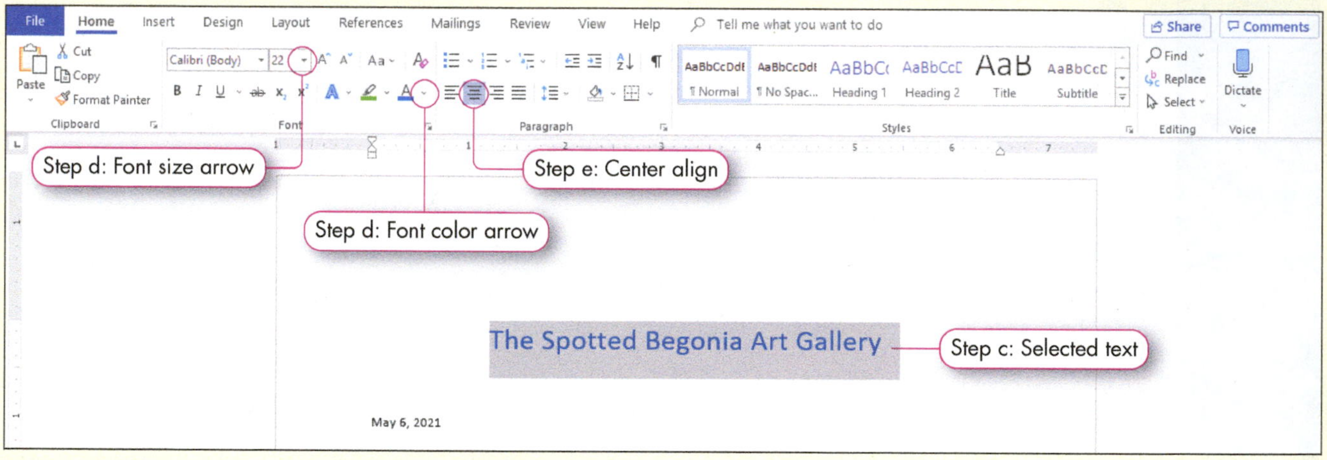

FIGURE 1.18 Use Ribbon Commands to Modify Text

a. Click the **File tab** and click **Open** from the left menu.

The Open window displays.

b. Click **cf01h1Letter_LastFirst** from the list of Recent documents on the right side of the Open window.

The letter you saved earlier opens and is ready to be modified.

c. Place the insertion point in the left margin just before the first line of text *The Spotted Begonia Art Gallery* so an angled right-pointing arrow displays and click.

This is an efficient way of selecting an entire line of text. Alternatively, you can drag the pointer across the text while holding down the left mouse button to select the text.

d. Click the **Font color arrow** in the Font group on the Home tab and select **Blue** in the Standard Colors section. With the text still selected, click the **Font Size arrow** in the Font group and select **22**.

You have changed the color and size of the Art Gallery's name.

e. Click **Center** in the Paragraph group.

f. Click **File** and click **Save**.

Because the file has already been saved, and the name and location are not changing, you use the Save command to save the changes.

USE A DIALOG BOX AND GALLERY

Some of the modifications you want to make to the letter require using tasks that are in dialog boxes and galleries. You will use a Dialog Box Launcher and More to expand the galleries to access the needed commands and features. Refer to Figure 1.19 as you complete Step 3.

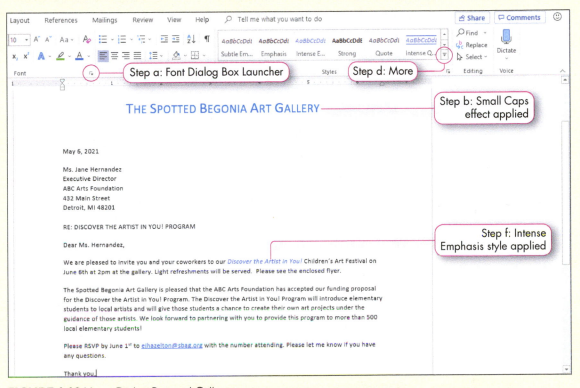

FIGURE 1.19 Use a Dialog Box and Gallery

a. Select the text **The Spotted Begonia Art Gallery**, if it is not already selected. Click the **Font Dialog Box Launcher** ⬜ in the Font group.

The Font dialog box displays.

> **MAC TROUBLESHOOTING:** Office for Mac does not have Dialog Box Launchers. Instead, open a menu and select an option. For example, to access Font options that display in the Font Dialog Box, click the Format menu, and then click Font.

b. Click the **Small caps check box** in the Effects section to select it and click **OK**.

The Small caps text effect is applied to the selected text.

c. Place the insertion point immediately to the left of the text *Discover the Artist in You!* in the first sentence of the paragraph beginning *We are pleased*. Hold the left mouse button down and drag the pointer to select the text up to and including the exclamation point.

> **TROUBLESHOOTING:** Be sure the file you are working on is displayed as a full window. Otherwise, use the vertical scroll bar to bring the paragraph into view.

d. Click **More** in the Styles group to display the Styles gallery. (On a Mac, click the right gallery arrow or click the down arrow to view more options.)

e. Point to Heading 1 style.

Notice how Live Preview shows how that effect will look on the selected text.

f. Click **Intense Emphasis**.

The Intense Emphasis style is applied to the program name.

g. Click **File** and click **Save**.

STEP 4 ## USE AND CUSTOMIZE THE QUICK ACCESS TOOLBAR

You make a change to the document and immediately change your mind. You use the Undo button on the QAT to revert to the original word. You also anticipate checking the spelling on the letter before sending it out. Because you use Spell Check often, you decide to add the command to the QAT. Finally, you realize that you could be saving the document more efficiently by using Save on the QAT. Refer to Figure 1.20 as you complete Step 4.

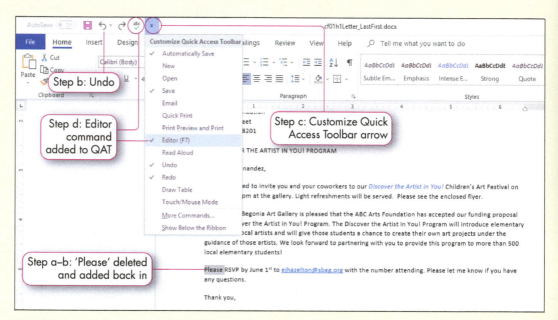

FIGURE 1.20 Customize the Quick Access Toolbar

a. Scroll down so the third paragraph beginning with *Please RSVP* is visible. Double-click **Please** and press **Delete** on the keyboard.

Please is deleted from the letter, but you decide to add it back in.

b. Click **Undo** on the QAT.

Please displays again.

c. Click the **Customize Quick Access Toolbar arrow** on the right side of the QAT.

A list of commands that can be added to the QAT displays.

d. Click **Editor**.

The Editor icon displays on the QAT so you can check for spelling, grammar, and writing issues.

e. Click **Save** on the QAT.

STEP 5 USE A SHORTCUT MENU

The letter inviting Ms. Hernandez also extends the invitation to her coworkers. Ms. Hazelton has asked that you use a different word for coworkers, so you use a shortcut menu to find a synonym. Refer to Figure 1.21 as you complete Step 5.

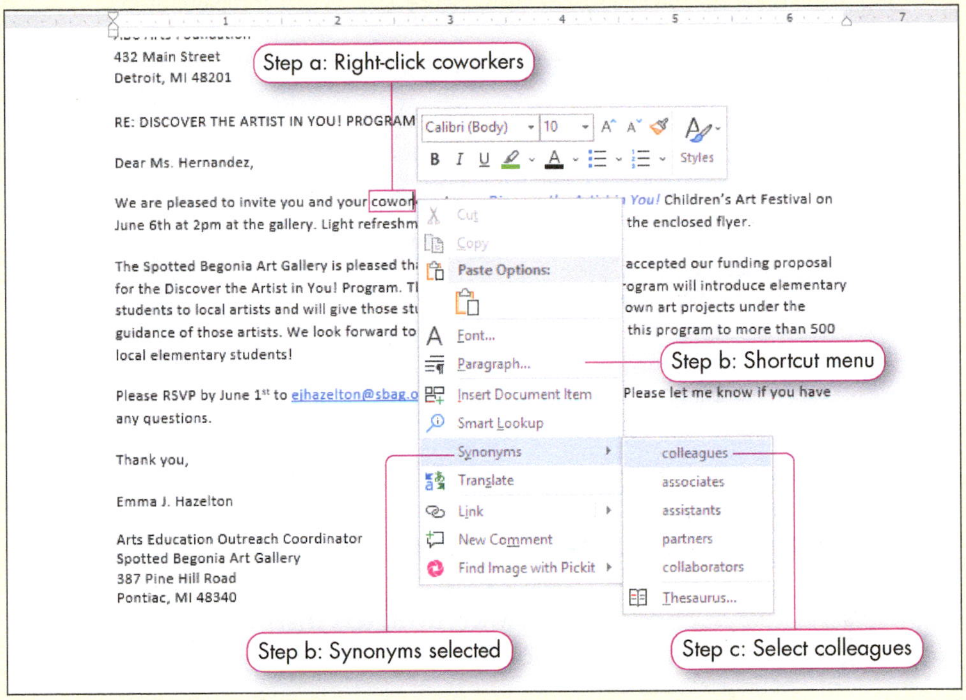

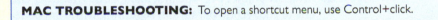

FIGURE 1.21 Use the Shortcut Menu to Find a Synonym

a. Point to and right-click the word **coworkers** in the first sentence of the letter that starts with *We are pleased*.

A shortcut menu displays.

MAC TROUBLESHOOTING: To open a shortcut menu, use Control+click.

b. Select **Synonyms** on the shortcut menu.

A list of alternate words for coworkers displays.

c. Select **colleagues** from the list.

The synonym *colleagues* replaces the word *coworkers*.

d. Click **Save** on the QAT.

You would like to apply the Intense Effect style you used to format *Discover the Artist in You!* to other instances of the program name in the second paragraph. You think there is a more efficient way of applying the same format to other text, but you do not know how to complete the task. Therefore, you use the Tell me box to search for the command and then you apply the change. Refer to Figure 1.22 as you complete Step 6.

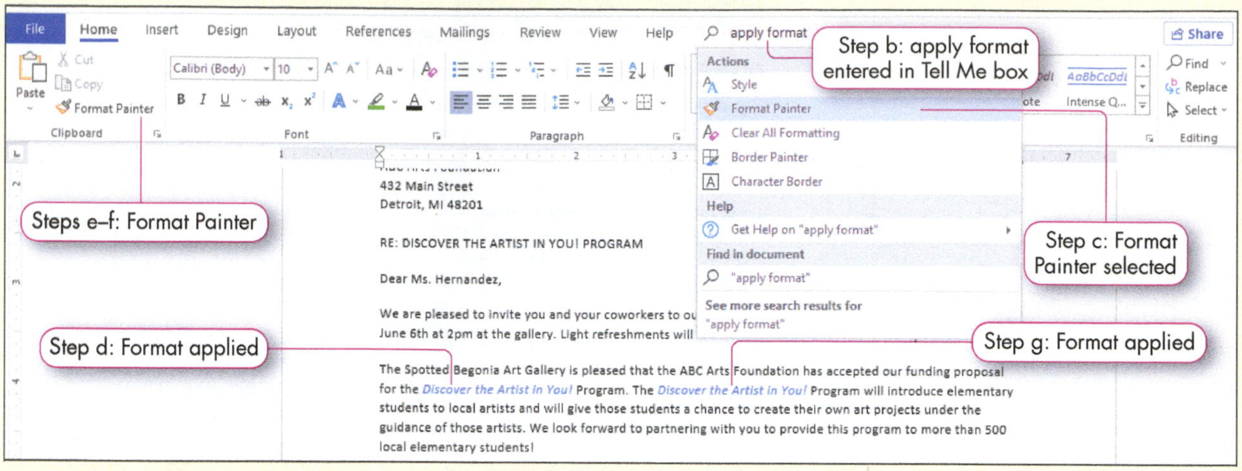

FIGURE 1.22 Use the Tell Me Box

a. Click anywhere in the text **Discover the Artist in You!** in the first sentence of the letter that starts with *We are pleased.*

b. Click the **Tell me box** and type **apply format**.

   The Tell me box displays a list of options related to apply format.

c. Select **Format Painter** from the list of options in the Tell Me results.

   Notice that the Format Painter command in the Clipboard group is selected and a paint-brush is added to the insertion point 🖌️I.

d. Drag the pointer over the first instance of **Discover the Artist in You!** in the second line of the second paragraph beginning with *The Spotted Begonia.*

   The Intense Emphasis style was applied to the selected text.

> **TROUBLESHOOTING:** If the format is not applied to the text, move to the next step, but double-click Format Painter and apply the format to both instances of Discover the Artist in You!

e. Point to **Format Painter** in the Clipboard group and read the Enhanced ScreenTip.

   You notice that to apply formatting to more than one selection, you must double-click Format Painter, but because you need to apply the format to only one more set of text, you will single-click the command.

f. Click **Format Painter** in the Clipboard group.

g. Drag the pointer over the second instance of **Discover the Artist in You!** in the second paragraph beginning with *The Spotted Begonia.*

   You used the Format Painter to copy the formatting applied to text to other text.

> **TROUBLESHOOTING:** Press Esc on the keyboard to turn off Format Painter if you had to double-click Format Painter in Step d above.

h. Save and close the document. You will submit this file to your instructor at the end of the last Hands-On Exercise.

Format Document Content

In the process of creating a document, worksheet, or presentation, you will most likely make some formatting changes. You might center a title, or format budget worksheet totals as currency. You can change the font so that typed characters are larger or in a different style. You might even want to bold text to add emphasis. Sometimes, it may be more efficient to start with a document that has formatting already applied or apply a group of coordinated fonts, font styles, and colors. You might also want to add, delete, or reposition text. Inserting and formatting images can add interest to a document or illustrate content. Finally, no document is finished until all spelling and grammar has been checked and all errors removed.

In this section, you will explore themes and templates. You will learn to use the Mini Toolbar to quickly make formatting changes. You will learn how to select and edit text, as well as check your grammar and spelling. You will learn how to move, copy, and paste text, and how to insert pictures. And, finally, you will learn how to resize and format pictures and graphics.

Using Templates and Applying Themes

You can enhance your documents by using a template or applying a theme. A ***template*** is a predesigned file that incorporates formatting elements and layouts and may include content that can be modified. A ***theme*** is a collection of design choices that includes colors, fonts, and special effects used to give a consistent look to a document, workbook, or presentation. Microsoft provides high-quality templates and themes, designed to make it faster and easier to create professional-looking documents.

STEP 1 ### Open a Template

When you launch any Office program and click New, the screen displays thumbnail images of a sampling of templates for that application (see Figure 1.23). Alternatively, if you are already working in an application, click the File tab and select New on the Backstage

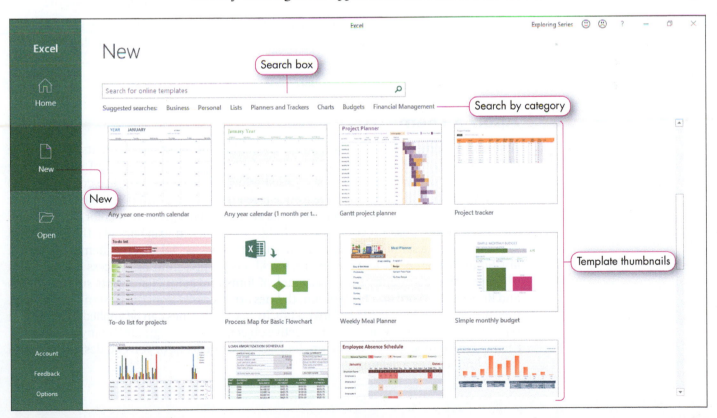

FIGURE 1.23 Templates in Excel

Navigation Pane. One benefit of starting with a template is if you know only a little bit about the software, with only a few simple changes you would have a well-formatted document that represents your specific needs. Even if you know a lot about the program, starting with a template can be much more efficient than if you designed it yourself from a blank file. Templates in Excel often use complex formulas and formatting to achieve a dynamic workbook that would automatically adjust with only a few inputs. Using a resume template in Word greatly simplifies potentially complex formatting, enabling you to concentrate on just inputting your personal experiences. PowerPoint templates can include single element slides (such as organization charts) but also include comprehensive presentations on topics such as Business Plans or a Quiz show game presentation similar to *Jeopardy!*

The Templates list is composed of template groups available within each Office application. The search box enables you to locate other templates that are available online. When you select a template, you can view more information about the template, including author information, a general overview about the template, and additional views (if applicable).

To search for and use a template, complete the following steps:

1. Open the Microsoft Office application with which you will be working. Or, if the application is already open, click File and click New.
2. Type a search term in the *Search for online templates box* or click one of the Suggested searches.
3. Scroll through the template options or after selecting a search term, use the list at the right to narrow your search further.
4. Select a template and review its information in the window that opens.
5. Click Create to open the template in the application.

On a Mac, to search for and use a template, complete the following steps:

1. Open the Microsoft Office application with which you will be working. Or, if the application is already open, click the File menu and click New from Template.
2. Continue with steps 2 through 5 in the PC steps above.

STEP 2 · **Apply a Theme**

Applying a theme enables you to visually coordinate various page elements. Themes are different for each of the Office applications. In Word, a theme is a set of coordinating fonts, colors, and special effects, such as shadowing or glows, that are combined into a package to provide a stylish appearance (see Figure 1.24). In PowerPoint, a theme is a file that includes the formatting elements such as a background, a color scheme, and slide layouts that position content placeholders. Themes in Excel are like those in Word in that they are a set of coordinating fonts, colors, and special effects. Themes also affect any SmartArt or charts in a document, workbook, or presentation. Access also has a set of themes that coordinate the appearance of fonts and colors for objects such as Forms and Reports. In Word and PowerPoint, themes are accessed from the Design tab. In Excel, they are accessed from the Page Layout tab. In Access, themes can be applied to forms and reports and are accessed from the respective object's Tools Design tab. In any application, themes can be modified with different fonts, colors, or effects, or you can design your own theme and set it as a default.

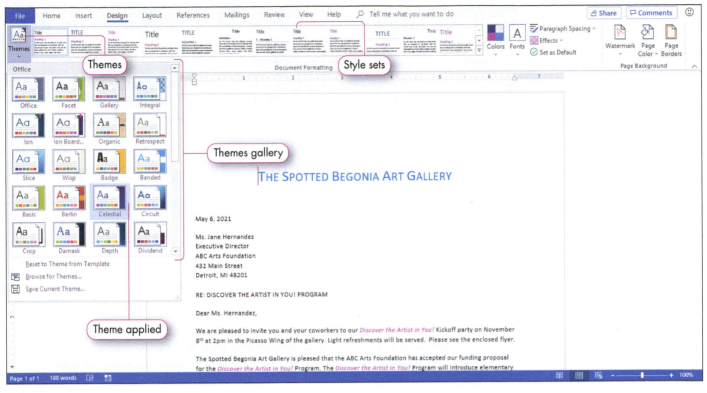

FIGURE 1.24 Themes in Word

Modifying Text

Formatting and modifying text in documents, worksheets, or presentations is an essential function when using Office applications. Centering a title, formatting cells, or changing the font color or size are tasks that occur frequently. In all Office applications, the Home tab provides tools for editing text.

Select Text

Before making any changes to existing text or numbers, you must first select the characters. A common way to select text or numbers is to place the pointer before the first character of the text you want to select, hold down the left mouse button, and then drag to highlight the intended selection. Note that in Word and PowerPoint when the pointer is used to select text in this manner, it takes on the shape of the letter *I*, called the *I-beam* $\boxed{\text{I}}$.

Sometimes it can be difficult to precisely select a small amount of text, such as a few letters or a punctuation mark. Other times, the task can be overwhelmingly large, such as when selecting an entire multi-page document. Or, you might need to select a single word, sentence, or paragraph. In these situations, you should use one of the shortcuts to selecting large or small blocks of text. The shortcuts shown in Table 1.2 are primarily applicable to text in Word and PowerPoint. When working with Excel, you will more often need to select multiple cells. To select multiple cells, drag the selection when the pointer displays as a large white plus sign $\boxed{+}$.

Once you have selected the text, besides applying formatting, you can delete or simply type over to replace the text.

TABLE 1.2	Shortcut Selection in Word and PowerPoint
Item Selected	**Action**
One word	Double-click the word.
One line of text	Place the pointer at the left of the line, in the margin area. When the pointer changes to an angled right-pointing arrow, click to select the line.
One sentence	Press and hold Ctrl and click in the sentence to select it.
One paragraph	Triple-click in the paragraph.
One character to the left of the insertion point	Press and hold Shift and press the left arrow on the keyboard.
One character to the right of the insertion point	Press and hold Shift and press the right arrow on the keyboard.
Entire document	Press and hold Ctrl and press A on the keyboard.

Format Text

At times, you will want to make the font size larger or smaller, change the font color, or apply other font attributes, for example, to emphasize key information such as titles, headers, dates, and times. Because formatting text is commonplace, Office places formatting commands in many convenient places within each Office application.

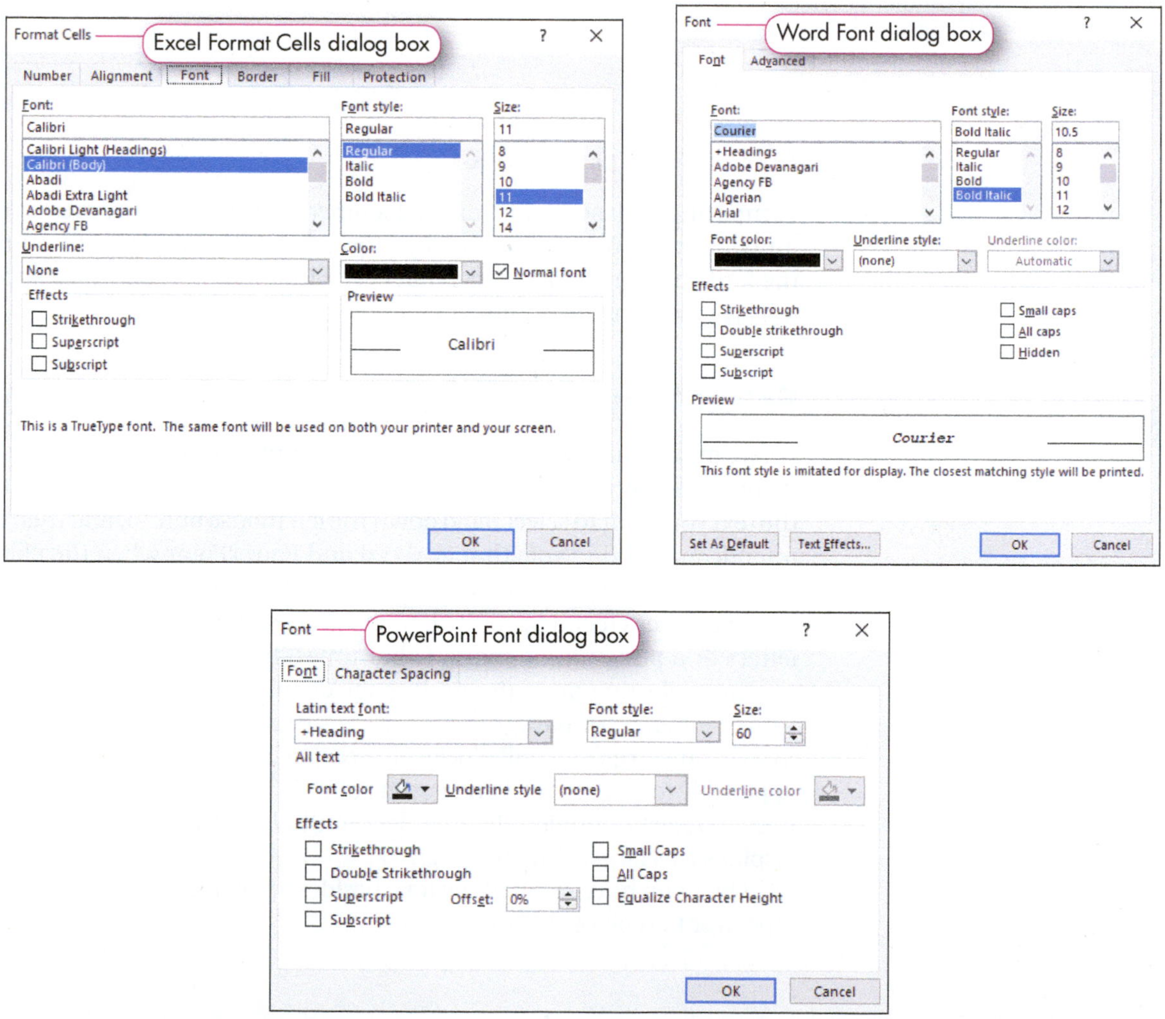

FIGURE 1.25 The Font Dialog Boxes

You can find the most common formatting commands in the Font group on the Home tab. As noted earlier, Word, Excel, and PowerPoint all share very similar Font groups that provide access to tasks related to changing the font, size, and color. Remember that you can place the pointer over any command icon to view a summary of the command's purpose, so although the icons might appear cryptic at first, you can use the pointer to quickly determine the purpose and applicability to your potential text change.

If the font change that you plan to make is not included as a choice on the Home tab, you may find what you are looking for in the Font dialog box. If you are making many formatting choices at once, using the Font dialog box may be more efficient. Depending on the application, the contents of the Font dialog box vary slightly, but the purpose is consistent—providing access to choices related to modifying characters (refer to Figure 1.25).

The way characters display onscreen or print in documents, including qualities such as size, spacing, and shape, is determined by the font. When you open a Blank document, you are opening the Normal template with an Office theme and the Normal style. The Office theme with Normal Style includes the following default settings: Calibri font, 11-point font size, and black font color. These settings remain in effect unless you change them. Some formatting commands, such as Bold and Italic, are called *toggle commands*. They act somewhat like a light switch that you can turn on and off. Once you have applied bold formatting to text, the Bold command is highlighted on the ribbon when that text is selected. To undo bold formatting, select the bold formatted text and click Bold again.

Use the Mini Toolbar

You have learned that you can always use commands on the Home tab of the ribbon to change selected text within a document, worksheet, or presentation. Although using the ribbon to select commands is simple enough, the **Mini Toolbar** provides another convenient way to accomplish some of the same formatting changes. When you select or right-click any amount of text within a worksheet, document, or presentation, the Mini Toolbar displays (see Figure 1.26) along with the shortcut menu. The Mini Toolbar provides access to the most common formatting selections, as well as access to styles and list options. Unlike the QAT, you cannot add or remove options from the Mini Toolbar. To temporarily remove the Mini Toolbar from view, press Esc. You can permanently disable the Mini Toolbar so that it does not display in any open file when text is selected by selecting Options on the File tab. Ensure the General tab is selected and deselect *Show Mini Toolbar on selection* in the User Interface options section.

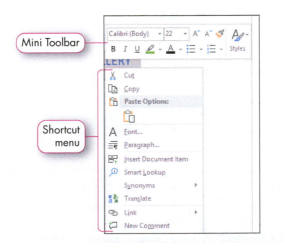

FIGURE 1.26 The Mini Toolbar and Shortcut Menu

Relocating Text

On occasion, you may want to relocate a section of text from one area of a Word document to another. Or suppose that you have included text on a PowerPoint slide that you believe would be more appropriate on a different slide. Or perhaps an Excel formula should be copied from one cell to another because both cells should show totals in a similar manner. In all these instances, you would use the cut, copy, and paste features found in the Clipboard group on the Home tab. The **Office Clipboard** is an area of memory reserved to temporarily hold selections that have been cut or copied and enables you to paste the selections to another location.

STEP 4 ## Cut, Copy, and Paste Text

To **cut** means to remove a selection from the original location and place it in the Office Clipboard. To **copy** means to duplicate a selection from the original location and place a copy in the Office Clipboard. To **paste** means to place a cut or copied selection into another location in a document. It is important to understand that cut or copied text remains in the Office Clipboard even after you paste it to another location. The Office Clipboard can hold up to 24 items at one time.

To cut or copy text, and paste to a new location, complete the following steps:

1. Select the text you want to cut or copy.
2. Click the appropriate command in the Clipboard group either to cut or copy the selection.
3. Click the location where you want the cut or copied text to be placed. The location can be in the current file or in another open file within most Office applications.
4. Click Paste in the Clipboard group on the Home tab.

You can paste the same item multiple times, because it will remain in the Office Clipboard until you power down your computer or until the Office Clipboard exceeds 24 items. It is best practice to complete the paste process as soon after you have cut or copied text.

In addition to using the commands in the Clipboard group, you can also cut, copy, and paste by using the Mini Toolbar, a shortcut menu (right-clicking), or by keyboard shortcuts. These methods are listed in Table 1.3.

TABLE 1.3	Cut, Copy, and Paste Options
Command	**Actions**
Cut	• Click Cut in Clipboard group. • Right-click selection and select Cut. • Press Ctrl+X.
Copy	• Click Copy in Clipboard group. • Right-click selection and select Copy. • Press Ctrl+C.
Paste	• Click in destination location and select Paste in Clipboard group. • Click in destination location and press Ctrl+V. • Right-click in destination location and select one of the choices under Paste Options in the shortcut menu. • Click Clipboard Dialog Box Launcher to open Clipboard pane. Click in destination location. With Clipboard pane open, click the arrow beside the intended selection and select Paste.

> ### TIP: USE PASTE OPTIONS
> When you paste text, you may not want to paste the text with all its formatting. In some instances, you may want to paste only the text, unformatted, so that special effects such as hyperlinks are not copied. In other instances, you might want to paste and match the formatting in the destination location or keep the current formatting in the new location. Paste Options commands are displayed when you click the Paste arrow or use the shortcut menu. Paste Options are different in each application, but in general, they include pasting contents without any formatting applied, pasting contents using the source formats, or pasting contents using the destination formats. In Excel, Paste Options also include pasting values to replace formulas, and transposing columns and rows to rows and columns. There are also options related to pasting pictures.

Use the Office Clipboard

When you cut or copy selections, they are placed in the Office Clipboard. Regardless of which Office application you are using, you can view the Office Clipboard by clicking the Clipboard Dialog Box Launcher, as shown in Figure 1.27.

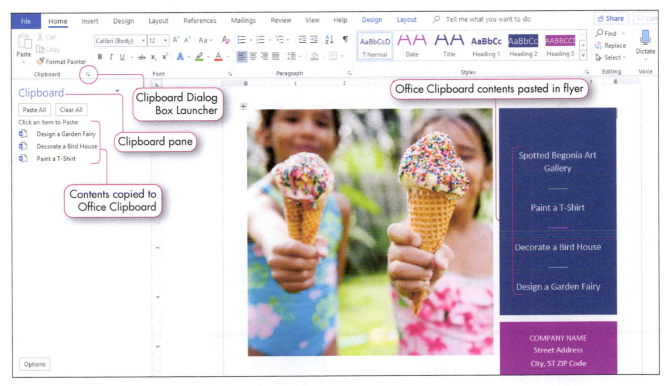

FIGURE 1.27 The Office Clipboard

Unless you specify otherwise when beginning a paste operation, the most recently added item to the Office Clipboard is pasted. If you know you will be cutting or copying and then pasting several items, rather than doing each individually, you can cut or copy all the items to the Office Clipboard, and then paste each or all Office Clipboard items to the new location. This is especially helpful if you are pasting the Office Clipboard items to a different Office file. Just open the new file, display the Clipboard pane, and select the item in the list to paste it into the document. The Office Clipboard also stores graphics that have been cut or copied. You can delete items from the Office Clipboard by clicking the arrow next to the selection in the Clipboard pane and selecting Delete. You can remove all items from the Office Clipboard by clicking Clear All. The Options button at the bottom of the Clipboard pane enables you to control when and where the Office Clipboard is displayed. Close the Clipboard pane by clicking the Close button in the top-right corner of the pane or by clicking the arrow in the title bar of the Clipboard pane and selecting Close.

Reviewing a Document

As you create or edit a file, and certainly as you finalize a file, you should make sure no spelling or grammatical errors exist. It is important that you carefully review your document for any spelling or punctuation errors, as well as any poor word choices before you send it along to someone else to read. Word, Excel, and PowerPoint all provide standard tools for proofreading, including a spelling and grammar checker and a thesaurus.

STEP 5 ### Check Spelling and Grammar

Word and PowerPoint automatically check your spelling and grammar as you type. If a word is unrecognized, it is flagged as misspelled or grammatically incorrect. Misspellings are identified with a red wavy underline, and grammatical or word-usage errors (such as using *bear* instead of *bare*) have a blue double underline. Excel does not check spelling as you type, so it is important to run the spelling checker in Excel. Excel's spelling checker will review charts, pivot tables, and textual data entered in cells.

Although spelling and grammar is checked along the way, you may find it more efficient to use the spelling and grammar feature when you are finished with the document. The Check Document command is found on the Review tab in the Proofing group in Word. In Excel and PowerPoint the Spelling command is on the Review tab in the Proofing group. When it is selected, the Editor pane will open on the right. For each error, you are offered one or more suggestions as a correction. You can select a suggestion and click Change, or if it is an error that is made more than one time throughout the document, you can select Change All (see Figure 1.28). If an appropriate suggestion is not made, you can always enter a correction manually.

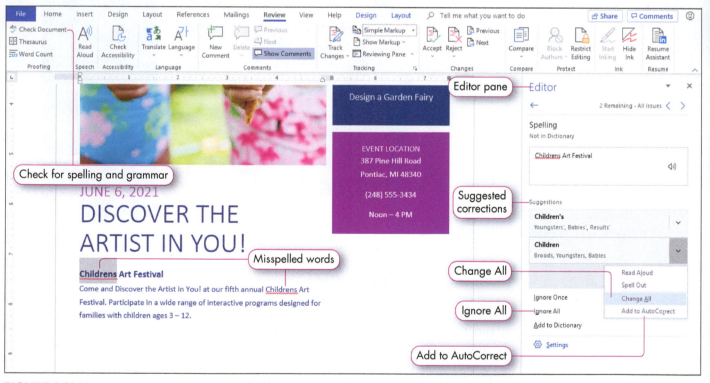

FIGURE 1.28 Using the Editor Pane to Correct Spelling

It is important to understand that the spelling and grammar check is not always correct, so you still need to proof a document thoroughly and review the errors carefully. For example, you might have a word that is truly misspelled in its context, but perhaps is still a valid word in the dictionary. Spell check might not pick it up as a misspelled word, but a careful read through would probably pick it up. There are times when the spelling and grammar check will indicate a word is misspelled and it really is not. This often happens with names or proper nouns or with new technical terms that may not be in the application's dictionary. In these instances, you can choose to Ignore, Ignore All, or Add. Choosing Ignore will skip the word without changing it. If you know there are multiple instances of that word throughout the document, you can choose Ignore All, and it will skip all instances of the word. Finally, if it is a word that is spelled correctly and that you use it often, you can choose to Add it to the dictionary, so it will not be flagged as an error in future spell checks.

If you right-click a word or phrase that is identified as a potential error, you will see a shortcut menu similar to that shown in Figure 1.29. The top of the shortcut menu will identify the type of error, whether it is spelling or grammar. A pane opens next to the shortcut menu with a list of options to correct the misspelling. These would be the same options that would display in the Editor pane if you ran the Spelling & Grammar command from the ribbon. Click on any option to insert it into the document. Similarly, you have the choices to Add to Dictionary or Ignore All. Each alternative also has options to Read Aloud or Add to AutoCorrect.

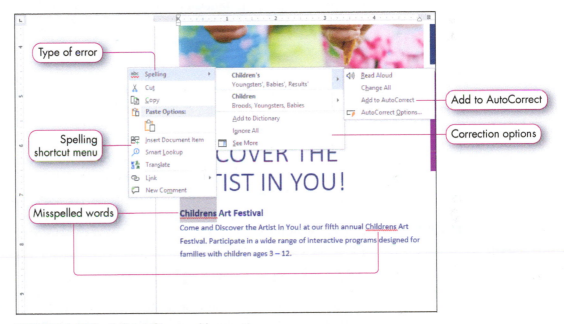

FIGURE 1.29 Spell Check Shortcut Menu options

You can use AutoCorrect to correct common typing errors, misspelled words, and capitalization errors, as well as to insert symbols (see Figure 1.30). There is a standard list of common errors and suggested replacements that is used in Excel, Word, and PowerPoint. So, if you type a word that is found in the Replace column, it will automatically be replaced with the replacement in the With column. For example, if you typed *accross* it would automatically correct to *across*. If you typed (tm) it would automatically change to the trademark symbol ™. You can add or delete terms and manage AutoCorrect by selecting Options from the File tab, and then in the Options dialog box, select Proofing and then click AutoCorrect Options.

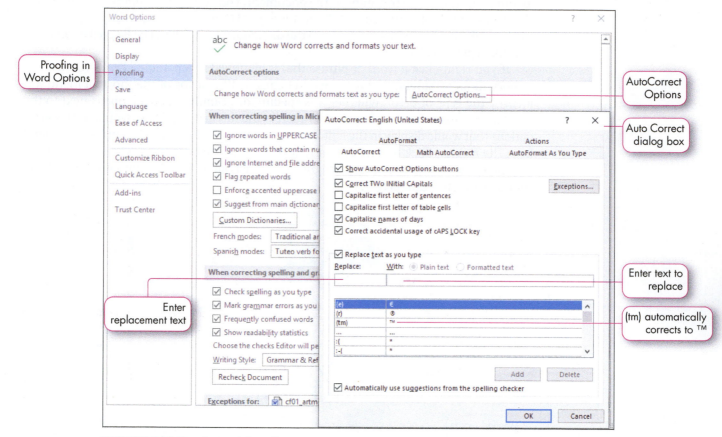

FIGURE 1.30 Proofing and AutoCorrect

Working with Pictures

Documents, worksheets, and presentations can include much more than just words and numbers. You can add energy and additional description to a project by including pictures and other graphic elements. A **picture** is just that—a digital photo. A picture can also be considered an illustration. Illustrations can also be shapes, icons, SmartArt, and Charts. While each of these types of illustrative objects have definitive differences, they are all handled basically the same when it comes to inserting and resizing. For the purposes of simplicity, the following discussion focuses on pictures, but the same information can be applied to any illustrative object you include in your document, worksheet, or presentation.

STEP 6 **Insert Pictures**

In Word, Excel, and PowerPoint, you can insert pictures from your own library of digital photos you have saved on your hard drive, OneDrive, or another storage medium. If you want a wider variety of pictures to choose from, you can search directly inside the Office program you are using for an online picture using Bing. Pictures and Online Pictures are found on the Insert tab.

To insert an online picture, complete the following steps:

1. Click in the file where you want the picture to be placed.
2. Click the Insert tab.
3. Click Online Pictures in the Illustrations group.
4. Type a search term in the Bing search box and press Enter.
5. Select an image and click Insert.

When the picture is inserted into a document, the Picture Tools Format tab displays. You can use these tools to modify the picture as needed.

> **TIP: CREATIVE COMMONS LICENSE**
> The Bing search filters are set to use the Creative Commons license system so the results display images that have been given a Creative Commons license. These are images and drawings that can be used more freely than images found directly on websites. Because there are different levels of Creative Commons licenses, you should read the Creative Commons license for each image you use to avoid copyright infringement.

STEP 7 ## Modify a Picture

Once you add a picture to your document, you may need to resize or adjust it. Before you make any changes to a picture, you must first select it. When the picture is selected, eight sizing handles display on the corners and in the middle of each edge (see Figure 1.31) and the Picture Tools tab displays on the ribbon. To adjust the size while maintaining the proportions, place your pointer on one of the corner sizing handles, and while holding the left mouse button down, drag the pointer on an angle upward or downward to increase or decrease the size, respectively. If you use one of the center edge sizing handles, you will

FIGURE 1.31 Formatting a Picture

stretch or shrink the picture out of proportion. In addition to sizing handles, a rotation handle displays at the top of the selected image. Use this to turn the image. For more precise controls, use the Size and Rotate commands on the Picture Tools Format tab. When a picture is selected, the Picture Tools Format tab includes options for modifying a picture. You can apply a picture style or effect, as well as add a picture border, from selections in the Picture Styles group. Click More to view a gallery of picture styles. As you point to a style, the style is shown in Live Preview, but the style is not applied until you select it. Options in the Adjust group simplify changing a color scheme, applying creative artistic effects, and even adjusting the brightness, contrast, and sharpness of an image (refer to Figure 1.31).

If a picture contains areas that are not necessary, you can crop it, which is the process of trimming edges that you do not want to display. The Crop tool is located on the Picture Tools Format tab (refer to Figure 1.31). Even though cropping enables you to adjust the amount of a picture that displays, it does not actually delete the portions that are cropped out. Therefore, you can later recover parts of the picture, if necessary. Cropping a picture does not reduce the file size of the picture or the document in which it displays. If you want to permanently remove the cropped portions of a figure and reduce the file size, you must compress the picture. Compress Pictures is found in the Adjust group on the Picture Tools Format tab (refer to Figure 1.31).

Quick Concepts

5. Discuss the differences between themes and templates. *p. 25*

6. Discuss several ways text can be modified. *p. 27*

7. Explain how the Office Clipboard is used when relocating text. *p. 31*

8. Explain how to review a document for spelling and grammar. *p. 32*

9. Explain why it is important to use the corner sizing handles of a picture when resizing. *p. 35*

Hands-On Exercises

▶ Watch the Video for this Hands-On Exercise!

Skills covered: Open a Template • Apply a Theme • Select Text • Format Text • Cut, Copy, and Paste Text • Check Spelling and Grammar • Insert a Picture • Modify a Picture

2 Format Document Content

As the administrative assistant for the Spotted Begonia Art Gallery, you want to create a flyer to announce the *Discover the Artist in You!* Children's Art Festival. You decide to use a template to help you get started more quickly and to take advantage of having a professionally formatted document without knowing much about Word. You will modify the flyer created with the template by adding and formatting your own content and changing out the photo.

STEP 1 ▶ OPEN A TEMPLATE

To facilitate making a nice-looking flyer, you review the templates that are available in Microsoft Word. You search for flyers and finally choose one that is appropriate for the event, knowing that you will be able to replace the photo with your own. Refer to Figure 1.32 as you complete Step 1.

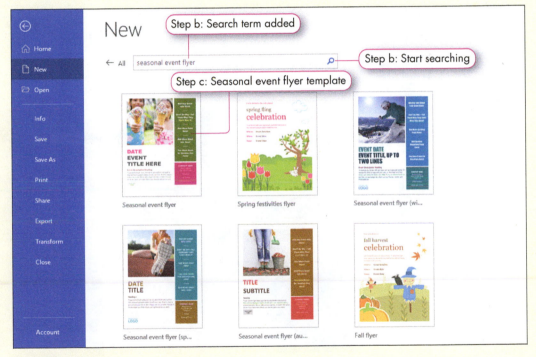

FIGURE 1.32 Search for a Template

a. Ensure Word is open. Click **File** and click **New**.

b. Type the search term **seasonal event flyer** in the *Search for online templates* box to search for event flyer templates. Click **Start searching**.

Your search results in a selection of event flyer templates.

c. Locate the Seasonal event flyer template as shown in Figure 1.32 and click to select it.

The template displays in a preview.

d. Click **Create** to open the flyer template.

The flyer template that you selected opens in Word.

e. Click **Save** on the QAT.

Because this is the first time you save the flyer file, clicking Save on the QAT opens the Save As window, in which you must indicate the location of the file and the file name.

f. Click **Browse** to navigate to where you save your files. Save the document as **cf01h2Flyer_LastFirst**.

STEP 2 ▷ APPLY A THEME

You want to change the theme of the template for a different font effect and theme color that matches more of the Spotted Begonia Art Gallery's other documents. Refer to Figure 1.33 as you complete Step 2.

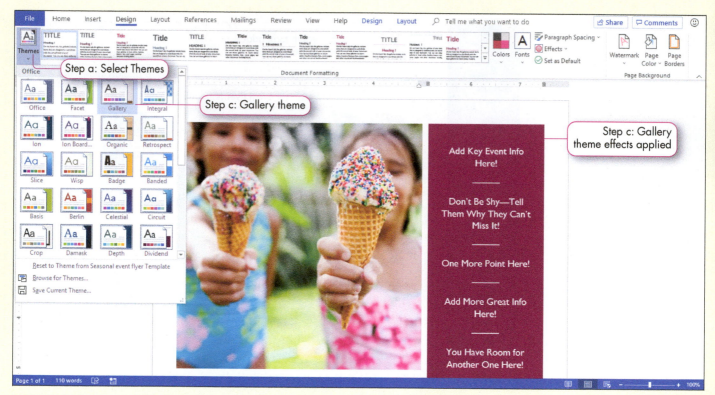

FIGURE 1.33 Select and Edit Text

a. Click the **Design tab** and click **Themes** in the Document Formatting group.

The Themes gallery displays.

b. Point to a few themes and notice how the template changes with each different theme.

c. Click **Gallery**.

The Gallery theme is applied, changing the color of the banners, and modifying the font and font size.

d. Save the document.

You will replace the template text to create the flyer, adding information such as a title, date, and description. After adding the text to the document, you will modify the formatting of the organization name in the flyer. Refer to Figure 1.34 as you complete Step 3.

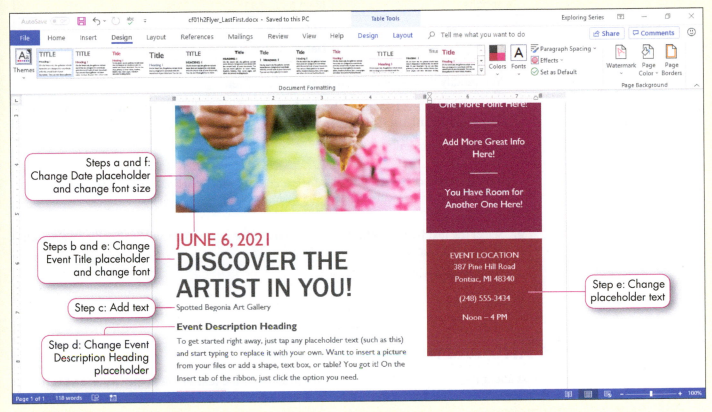

FIGURE 1.34 Edit Placeholder Text

a. Scroll to see the **Date placeholder** in the main body of the text, click, and then type **June 6, 2021** in the placeholder.

b. Click the **Event Title Here placeholder** and type **Discover the Artist in You!** in the placeholder.

c. Press **Enter** and continue typing **Spotted Begonia Art Gallery**.

d. Click the **Event Description Heading placeholder** and type **Childrens Art Festival**. (Ignore the misspelling for now.)

e. Select each text placeholder in the bottom box of the right table column and replace the content in each text placeholder with the content from the right column below.

Placeholder	Text Typed Entry
Company Name	**Event Location**
Street Address City ST Zip Code	**387 Pine Hill Road Pontiac, MI 48340**
Telephone	**(248) 555-3434**
Web Address	**Noon – 4 PM**
Dates and Times	**Delete the text**

You modify the placeholders to customize the flyer.

f. Select the title text **Discover the Artist in You!**. Click the **Font arrow** on the Mini Toolbar. Select **Franklin Gothic Medium**.

The font is changed.

> **TROUBLESHOOTING:** If the Mini Toolbar does not display after selecting the text, right-click the selected text and select the font Franklin Gothic Medium.

g. Select the text **June 6, 2021**. Click the **Font Size arrow** on the Mini Toolbar. Select **26** on the Font Size menu.

The font size is changed to 26 pt.

h. Click **Save** on the QAT to save the document.

STEP 4 CUT, COPY, AND PASTE TEXT

You add descriptive text about the event. You then decide to move some of the text to the banner panel on the right. You also copy the sponsor's name to the top of the banner. Finally, you delete some unwanted placeholders. Refer to Figure 1.35 as you complete Step 4.

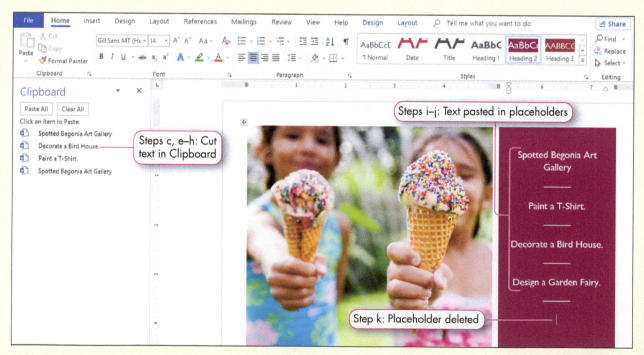

FIGURE 1.35 Use the Clipboard Commands

a. Select the **placeholder text** below Childrens Art Festival that begins with *To get started* and press **Delete**. Enter the following text and ignore any intentional misspellings. They will be corrected later.

Come and Discover the Artist in You! at our fifth annual Childrens Art Festival. Participate in a wide range of interactive programs designed for families with children ages 3–12. Paint a T-Shirt. Decorate a Bird House. Design a Garden Fairy.

b. Click the **YOUR LOGO HERE placeholder** and press **Delete**.

c. Select the text **Spotted Begonia Art Gallery**. Right-click the selected text and click **Cut** from the shortcut menu.

d. Scroll to the top of the flyer. Click the **Add Key Event Info Here! placeholder** in the right column. Click the **Home tab** and click **Paste** in the Clipboard group to paste the previously cut text.

The text is now moved to the banner.

e. Click the **Clipboard Dialog Box Launcher**.

The Office Clipboard displays. The cut text displays in the Clipboard pane.

> **MAC TROUBLESHOOTING:** For Step e, use Command+X. Select the Don't be Shy . . . placeholder text and press Command+V. Repeat for Steps f and g below, using Command+X to cut the indicated text, and Command+V to paste the text in the two placeholders below Paint a T-Shirt.

f. Scroll to the paragraph at the bottom of the flyer beginning with Come and Discover. Select the text **Paint a T-Shirt.** (include the period) and press **Ctrl+X**.

Notice that the cut text selection is in the Office Clipboard.

g. Select the text **Decorate a Bird House.** from the text you entered in Step a and press **Ctrl+X**.

h. Select the text **Design a Garden Fairy.** from the text you entered in Step a and press **Ctrl+X**.

The Office Clipboard displays the three cut selections of text.

i. Scroll to the top of the flyer. Select the **Don't Be Shy . . . placeholder text** and click **Paint a T-Shirt** from the Office Clipboard.

The text in the Office Clipboard is pasted in a new location.

j. Repeat Step i, replacing **One More Point Here! placeholder text** with **Decorate a Bird House** and **Add More Great Info Here placeholder text** with **Design a Garden Fairy**.

k. Select the last **placeholder text** in the banner and press **Delete**.

l. Click **Clear All** in the Clipboard pane and close the Office Clipboard. Save the document.

CHECK SPELLING AND GRAMMAR

Because this flyer will be seen by the public, it is important to check the spelling and grammar in your document. Refer to Figure 1.36 as you complete Step 5.

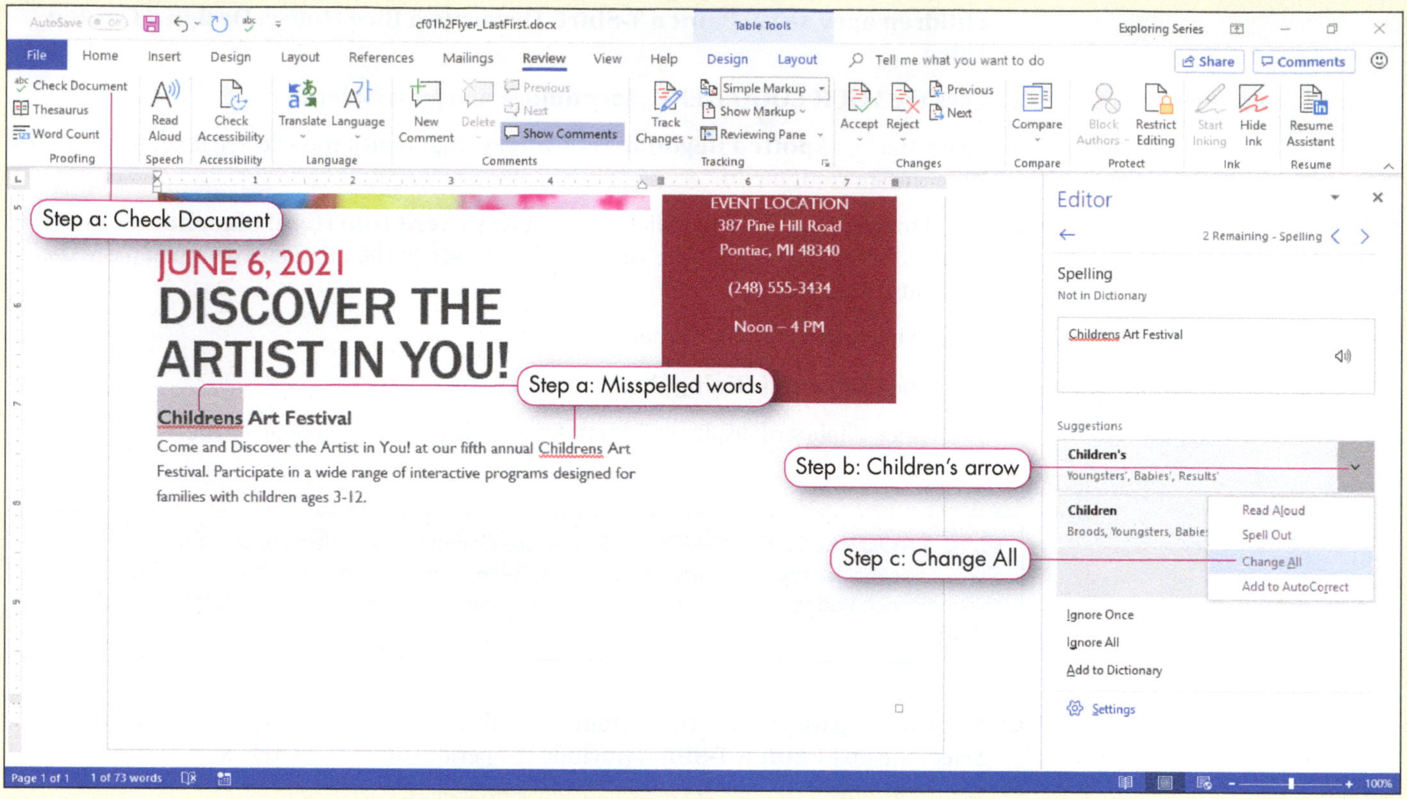

FIGURE 1.36 Check Spelling and Grammar

a. Press **Ctrl+Home**. Click the **Review tab** and click **Check Document** in the Proofing group.

The Editor pane opens and two spelling errors are identified.

b. Click Spelling in the Corrections box and click the **arrow** to the right of Children's in the Editor pane.

c. Select **Change All** to accept the suggested change to *Children's* in the Spelling pane for all instances. Make any other changes as needed. Click **OK** to close the dialog box.

The spelling and grammar check is complete.

d. Save the document.

You want to change the template image to an image that better reflects the children's event being held at the gallery. You use an image the Art Gallery director has provided you. Refer to Figure 1.37 as you complete Step 6.

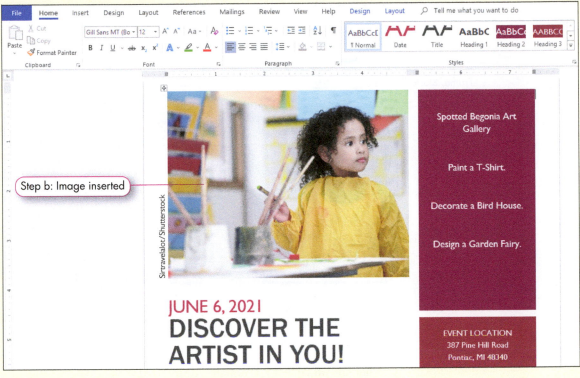

FIGURE 1.37 Insert Picture

a. Scroll to the top of the flyer. Click the **image** to select it and press **Delete**.

You have deleted the image you want to replace.

b. Click **Pictures** in the Illustrations group on the Home tab. Navigate to your Student Data files and select *cf01h2Art.jpg*. Click **Insert**.

The new image is placed in the document.

c. Save the document.

You want to make the picture stand out better, so you decide to add a border frame around the image. Refer to Figure 1.38 as you complete Step 7.

FIGURE 1.38 Modify a Picture

a. Click the **picture** if it is not already selected.

The Picture Tools Format tab displays on the ribbon and sizing handles display around the image. The Table Tools Design and Layout tabs also display. The flyer template uses a table to place the elements. Selecting the picture also selects the table.

b. Click the **Format tab** and click **More** in the Picture Styles group.

A gallery of Picture Styles displays.

c. Point to a few different Picture Styles to see the effects in Live Preview and select **Simple Frame, Black**. Keep the image selected.

A black border is applied around the image.

d. Click the **Picture Border arrow** and select **Pink, Accent 2, Darker 50%** under Theme Colors.

The border color is changed to coordinate with the colors on the flyer.

e. Save the document. Keep the document open if you plan to continue with the next Hands-On Exercise. If not, close the document and exit Word.

Modify Document Layout and Properties

When working with a document, before you send or print it, you will want to view the final product to make sure that your margins and page layout are as they should be. Moreover, you might want to add some details in a header or footer, or in document properties to help identify the author and contents of the document to help in later searches. Although you can always print a document using the default printer settings, you may want to change printer settings or page layout settings before printing.

In this section, you will explore how to view and edit document properties. You will learn about views and how to change a document view to suit your needs. In addition, you will learn how to modify the page layout, including page orientation and margins as well as how to add headers and footers. Finally, you will explore Print Preview and the various printing options available to you.

STEP 1 ## Changing Document Views

As you prepare or read a document, you may find that you want to change the way you view it. A section of your document may be easier to view when you can see it magnified, or you might want to display more of your document than what is showing onscreen. You can also select a different *view*, the way a file appears onscreen, to make working on your project easier.

Change Document Views Using the Ribbon

Views for Word, Excel, and PowerPoint are available on the View tab. Each application has views that are specific to that application. PowerPoint and Excel each have a Normal view, which is the typical view used to create and view presentation slides and workbooks. Word's Print Layout view is like Normal view in that it is the view used to create documents. Print Layout view is useful when you want to see both the document text and such features margins and page breaks. Table 1.4 outlines the other views in each application. Access does not have a View tab, but rather incorporates unique views that are visible when working with any Access object.

TABLE 1.4	Office Views	
Application	**View**	**Description**
	Print Layout	The default view used when creating documents.
	Read Mode	All editing commands are hidden. Arrows on the left and right sides of the screen are used to move through the pages of the document.
Word	Web Layout	All page breaks are removed. Use this view to see how a document will display as a webpage.
	Outline View	If Style Headings are used in a document, the document is organized by level. Otherwise, the document will display with each paragraph as a separate bullet.
	Draft View	A pared-down version of Print Layout view.
	Normal	The default view used when creating worksheets.
	Page Break Preview	Displays a worksheet with dashed lines that indicate automatic page breaks. Used to adjust page breaks manually.
Excel	Page Layout	Displays the worksheet headers and margins.
	Custom Views	Create custom views.
	Normal	The default view used when creating presentations.
	Outline View	Displays a presentation as an outline using titles and main text from each slide.
PowerPoint	Slide Sorter	Displays presentation slides in thumbnail form making it easier to sort and organize slide sequence.
	Notes Page	Makes the Notes pane, which is located under the Slide pane, visible. You can type notes that apply to the current slide. Notes do not display during a presentation.
	Reading View	Displays the presentation in full screen like Slide Show.

Change Document Views Using the Status Bar

The *status bar*, located at the bottom of the program window, displays information relevant to the application and document on which you are working, as well as some commands. On the left side of the status bar is application- and document-specific information. When you work with Word, the status bar informs you of the number of pages and words in an open document. Excel shows the status of the file and a Macro recording command. The PowerPoint status bar shows the slide number and total number of slides in the presentation. Word and PowerPoint also display a proofing icon that looks like an opened book. An x in the icon indicates there are proofing errors that need to be fixed ▣. Clicking the icon will start the spelling and grammar check.

Other pertinent document information for PowerPoint and Excel display on the right side of the status bar. The Excel status bar displays summary information, such as average and sum, of selected cells, and the PowerPoint status bar provides access to slide notes.

The right side of the status bar also includes means for changing the view and for changing the zoom size of onscreen file contents. The view buttons (see Figure 1.39) on the status bar of each application enable you to change the view of the open file. These views correspond to the most commonly used views in each application.

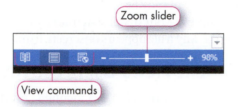

FIGURE 1.39 The Status Bar

The *Zoom slider* is a horizontal bar on the right side of the status bar that enables you to increase or decrease the size of the document onscreen. You can drag the tab along the slider in either direction to increase or decrease the magnification of the file (refer to Figure 1.39). Be aware, however, that changing the size of text onscreen does not change the font size when the file is printed or saved.

STEP 2 Changing the Page Layout

When you prepare a document or worksheet, you are concerned with the way the project appears onscreen and possibly in print. The Layout tab in Word and the Page Layout tab in Excel provide access to a full range of options such as margin settings and page orientation. PowerPoint does not have a Page Layout tab, because its primary purpose is displaying contents onscreen rather than in print.

Because a document or workbook is most often designed to be printed, you may need to adjust margins and change the page orientation, or to center a worksheet vertically or horizontally on a page for the best display. In addition, perhaps the document text should be aligned in columns. You will find these and other common page settings in the Page Setup group on the Layout (or Page Layout) tab. For less common settings, such as determining whether headers should print on odd or even pages, you use the Page Setup dialog box.

Change Margins

A **_margin_** is the area of blank space that displays to the left, right, top, and bottom of a document or worksheet. Margins display when you are in Print Layout or Page Layout view (see Figure 1.40), or in Backstage view previewing a document to print. There are Normal, Wide, and Narrow default margin settings for Word and Excel. Word also includes Moderate and Mirrored margins. If you want more customized margin settings, use the Custom Margins option at the bottom of the Margins gallery to display the Page Setup dialog box.

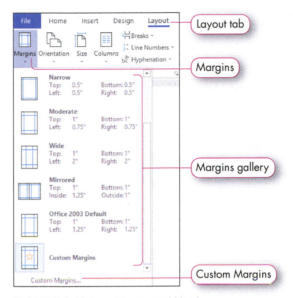

FIGURE 1.40 Page Margins in Word

To change margins in Word and Excel, complete the following steps:

1. Click the Layout (or Page Layout) tab.
2. Click Margins in the Page Setup group.
3. Do one of the following:
   - Select a preset margin option.
   - Click Custom Margins (refer to Figure 1.40) and set the custom margin settings. Click OK to accept the custom margin settings.

Change Page Orientation

Documents and worksheets can be displayed or printed in different page orientations. A page in **_portrait orientation_** is taller than it is wide. A page in **_landscape orientation_** is wider than it is tall. Word documents are usually displayed in portrait orientation, whereas Excel worksheets are often more suited to landscape orientation. In PowerPoint, you can change the orientation of slides as well as notes and handouts. Orientation is also an option in the Print page of Backstage view.

Use the Page Setup Dialog Box

Page Orientation settings for Word and Excel are found in the Layout (or Page Layout) tab in the Page Setup group. The Page Setup group contains Margins and Orientation settings as well as other commonly used page options for each Office application. Some are unique to Excel, and others are more applicable to Word. Other less common settings are available in the Page Setup dialog box only, displayed when you click the Page Setup Dialog Box Launcher. The Page Setup dialog box includes options for customizing margins, selecting page orientation, centering horizontally or vertically, printing gridlines, and creating headers and footers. Figure 1.41 shows both the Excel and Word Page Setup dialog boxes.

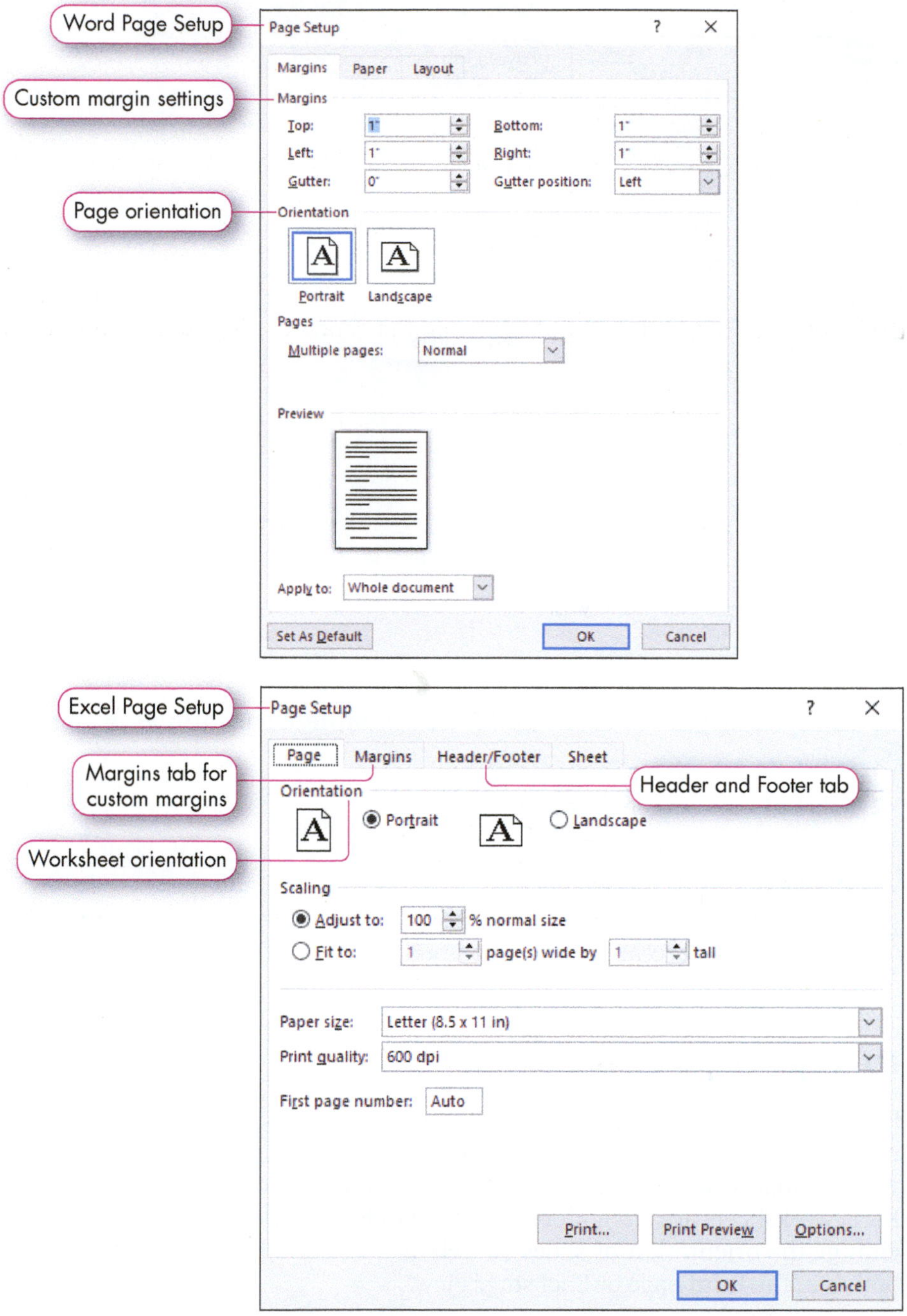

FIGURE 1.41 Page Setup Dialog Boxes in Word and Excel

Although PowerPoint slides are generally set to landscape orientation, you can change to portrait orientation by accessing the Slide Size controls on the Design tab and selecting Custom Slide Size. When choosing to print Notes Pages, Outline, or Handouts, the page orientation can be changed in Print Settings in Backstage view.

STEP 3 ▶ Creating a Header and a Footer

The purpose of including a header or footer is to better identify the document and give it a professional appearance. A **_header_** is a section in the top margin of a document. A **_footer_** is a section in the bottom margin of a document. Generally, page numbers, dates, author's name, or file name are included in Word documents or PowerPoint presentations. Excel worksheets might include the name of a worksheet tab, as well. Company logos are often displayed in a header or footer. Contents in a header or footer will appear on each page of the document, so you only have to specify the content once, after which it displays automatically on all pages. Although you can type the text yourself at the top or bottom of every page, it is time-consuming, and the possibility of making a mistake is great.

Header and footer commands are found on the Insert tab. In Word, you can choose from a predefined gallery of headers and footers as shown in Figure 1.42. To create your own unformatted header or footer, select Edit Header (or Edit Footer) at the bottom of the gallery. You can only add footers to PowerPoint slides (see Figure 1.42). You can apply footers to an individual slide or to all slides. To add date and time or a slide number, check each option to apply. Check the Footer option to add in your own content. In PowerPoint, the location of a footer will depend on the template or theme applied to the presentation. For some templates and themes, the footer will display on the side of the slide rather than at the bottom. Headers and footers are available for PowerPoint Notes and Handouts. Select the Notes and Handouts tab in the Header and Footer dialog box and enter in the content

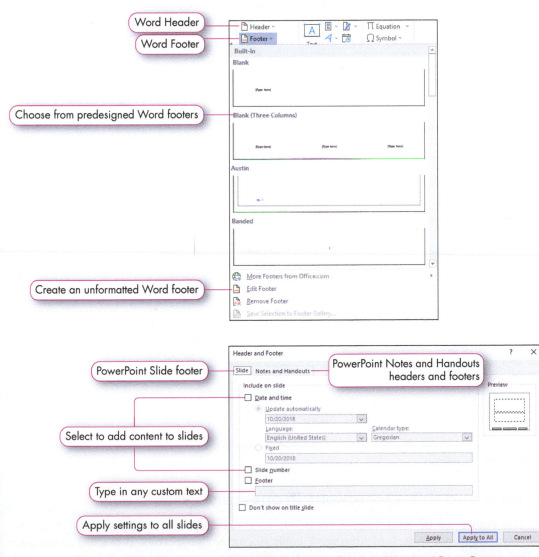

FIGURE 1.42 Insert Footer in Word and PowerPoint

similarly to how you would enter footer information on slides. In Excel, headers and footers are separated into left, center, and right sections. You can type your own contents or use a predefined header or footer element, such as date, file name, or sheet name.

After typing a header or a footer, it can be formatted like any other text. It can be formatted in any font or font size. In Word or Excel, when you want to leave the header and footer area and return to the document, click Close Header and Footer or double-click in the body of the document.

STEP 4 ▸ Configuring Document Properties

Recall that Backstage view is a component of Office that provides a collection of commands related to a file. Earlier in this chapter, you used Backstage view to open and save a file and template and to customize ribbon settings. Using Backstage view, you can also view or specify settings related to protection, permissions, versions, and properties of a file. A file's properties include the author, file size, permissions, and date modified. Backstage view also includes options for customizing program settings, signing in to your Office account, and exiting the application. In addition to creating a new document and opening and saving a document, you use Backstage view to print, share, export, and close files.

All the features of Backstage view are accessed by clicking the File tab and then selecting Info in the Backstage Navigation Pane (see Figure 1.43). The Info page will occupy the entire application window, hiding the file with which you are working. You can return to the file in a couple of ways. Either click the Back arrow in the top-left corner or press Esc on the keyboard.

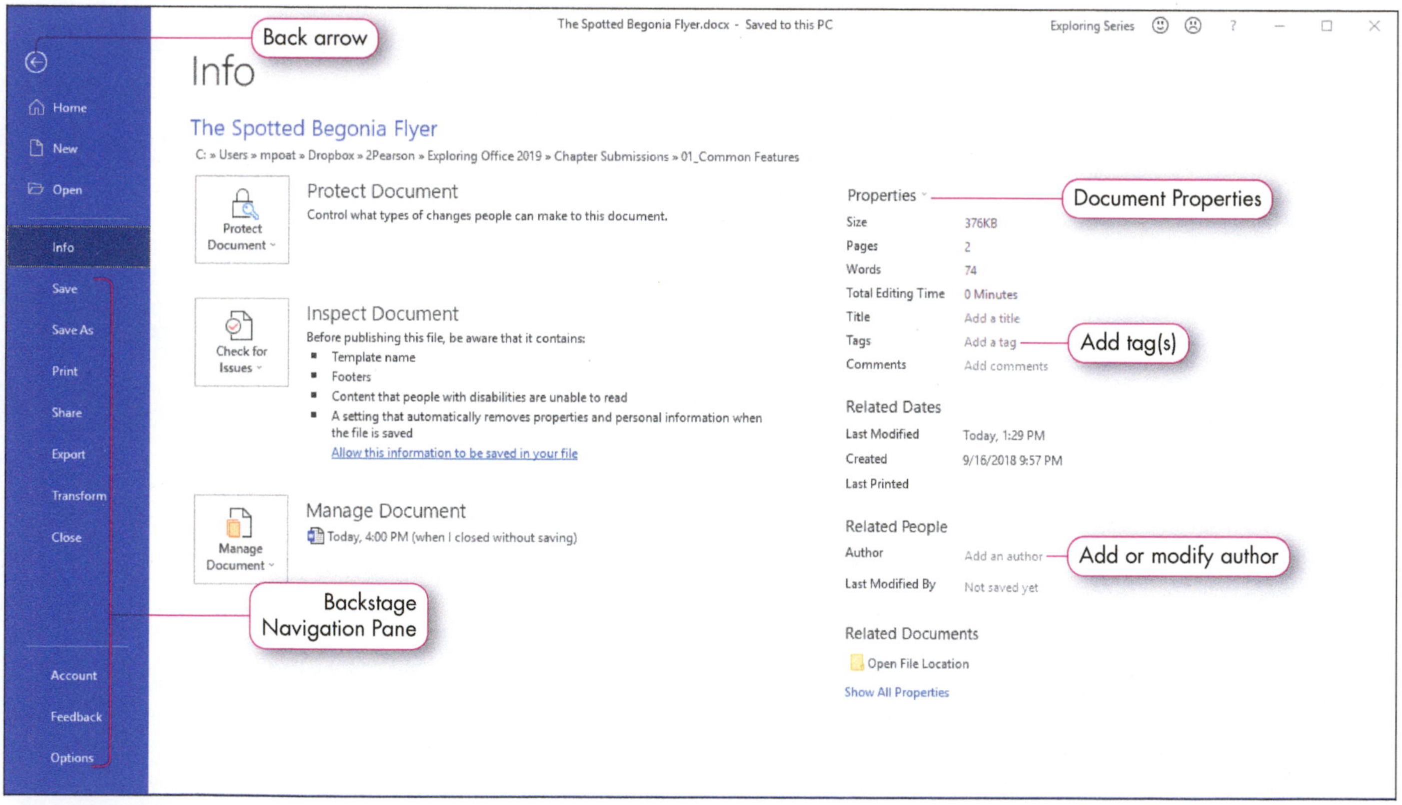

FIGURE 1.43 Backstage View and Document Properties

View and Edit Document Properties

The Info page of Backstage view is where you can protect, inspect, and manage your document as well as manage specific document properties. It is good to include information that identifies a document, such as the author and title. You can also add one or more tags (refer to Figure 1.43). A ***tag*** is a data element or metadata that is added as a document property. Like a keyword, you can search for a file based on tags you assign a document. For example, suppose you apply a tag of *Picasso* to all documents you create that are associated with that artist. Later, you can use that keyword as a search term, locating all associated documents. Statistical information related to the current document such as file size, number of pages, and total words are located on the Info page of Backstage view.

STEP 5 Previewing and Printing a File

When you want to print an Office file, you can select from various print options, including the number of copies and the specific pages to print. It is a good idea to look at how your document or worksheet will appear before you print it. When you select Print from Backstage view, the file previews on the right, with print settings located in the center of the Backstage view. Figure 1.44 shows a typical Backstage Print view. If you know that the page setup is correct and that there are no unique print settings to select, you can simply print without adjusting any print settings.

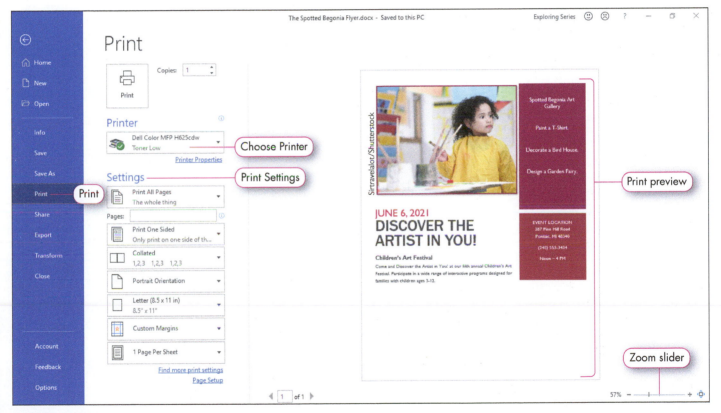

FIGURE 1.44 Backstage Print View in Word

> **TIP: CHANGING THE SIZE OF PRINT PREVIEW**
> Sometimes the preview image of your document shows only a part of the document page or shows a smaller image of the document page. You can change the size of the print preview by using the zoom slider in the bottom-right corner of the preview (refer to Figure 1.44).

Other options in the Backstage Print view vary depending on the application in which you are working. For example, PowerPoint's Backstage Print view includes options for printing slides and handouts in various configurations and colors, whereas Excel's focuses on worksheet selections and Word's includes document options. Regardless of the Office application, you will be able to access Settings options from Backstage view, including page orientation (landscape or portrait), margins, and paper size. To print a file, click the Print button (refer to Figure 1.44).

Quick Concepts

10. Discuss why you would need to change the view of a document. *p. 45*

11. Discuss the various ways you can change a page layout. *p. 46*

12. Explain what functions and features are included in Backstage view. *p. 50*

13. Discuss some document properties and explain why they are helpful. *p. 50*

Hands-On Exercises

Skills covered: Change Document Views Using the Ribbon • Change Document Views Using the Status Bar • Change Margins • Change Page Orientation • Insert a Footer • View and Enter Document Properties •Preview a File • Change Print Settings

3 Modify Document Layout and Properties

You continue to work on the flyer. You will review and add document properties, and prepare the document to print and distribute by changing the page setup. You will also add a footer with Spotted Begonia's information. As the administrative assistant for the Spotted Begonia Art Gallery, you must be able to search for and find documents previously created. You know that by adding tags to your flyer you will more easily be able to find it later. Finally, you will explore printing options.

STEP 1 CHANGE THE DOCUMENT VIEW

To get a better perspective on how your flyer would look if posted to the Gallery's website, you explore the Web Layout view available in Word. Refer to Figure 1.45 as you complete Step 1.

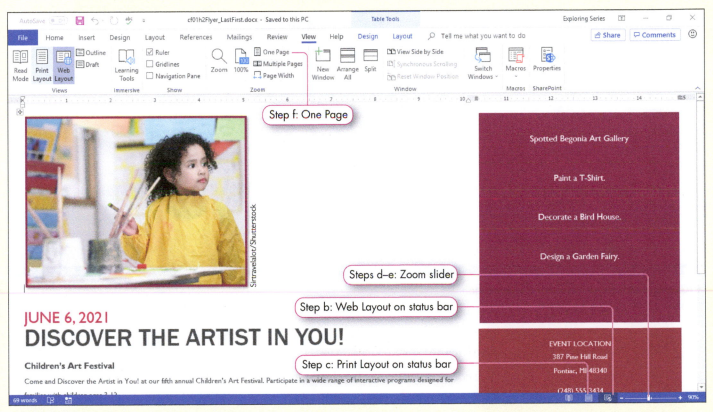

FIGURE 1.45 The Flyer in Web Layout View

a. Open *cf01h2Flyer_LastFirst* if you closed it at the end of Hands-On Exercise 2, and save it as **cf01h3Flyer_LastFirst**, changing h2 to h3.

b. Click **Web Layout** on the status bar. Observe the changes to the view.

The view is changed to Web Layout and simulates how the document would display on the Web.

c. Click **Print Layout** on the status bar. Observe the changes to the view.

The document has returned to Print Layout view.

d. Drag the **Zoom slider** to the left so you can see the full page of the flyer.

e. Drag the **Zoom slider** to the right to zoom in on the image.

f. Click the **View tab** and click **One Page** in the Zoom group.

The entire flyer is displayed.

CHANGE THE PAGE LAYOUT

You show the flyer to the Program Director. You both wonder whether changing the orientation and margin settings will make the flyer look better when it is printed. You change the orientation setting, but ultimately revert to Portrait orientation. You modify the margins in Portrait orientation to improve the spacing around the edges of the page. Refer to Figure 1.46 as you complete Step 2.

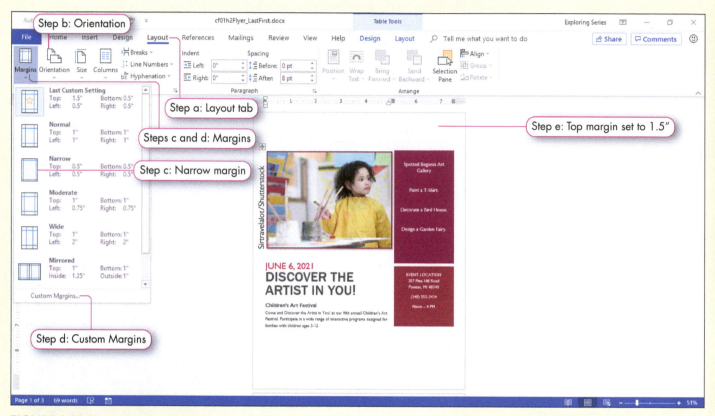

FIGURE 1.46 Change Margins and Orientation

a. Click the **Layout tab** and click **Orientation** in the Page Setup group. Select **Landscape.**

The document is now wider than it is tall.

b. Click **Orientation** and select **Portrait**.

The document returns to Portrait orientation.

c. Click **Margins** in the Page Setup group. Select **Narrow**.

The document margins were changed to Narrow. The Narrow margin allows for better spacing horizontally, but you would like the flyer to be centered better vertically on the page.

d. Click **Margins** and select **Custom Margins**.

The Page Setup dialog box opens.

e. Change the Top margin to **1.5"** Click OK.

f. Click the **View tab** and click **One Page** in the Zoom group.

The document looks well balanced on the page.

g. Save the document.

INSERT A HEADER AND A FOOTER

You decide to add the Gallery's name and website URL to the flyer as a footer so anyone who is looking for more information on the Spotted Begonia Art Gallery can access the website. Refer to Figure 1.47 as you complete Step 3.

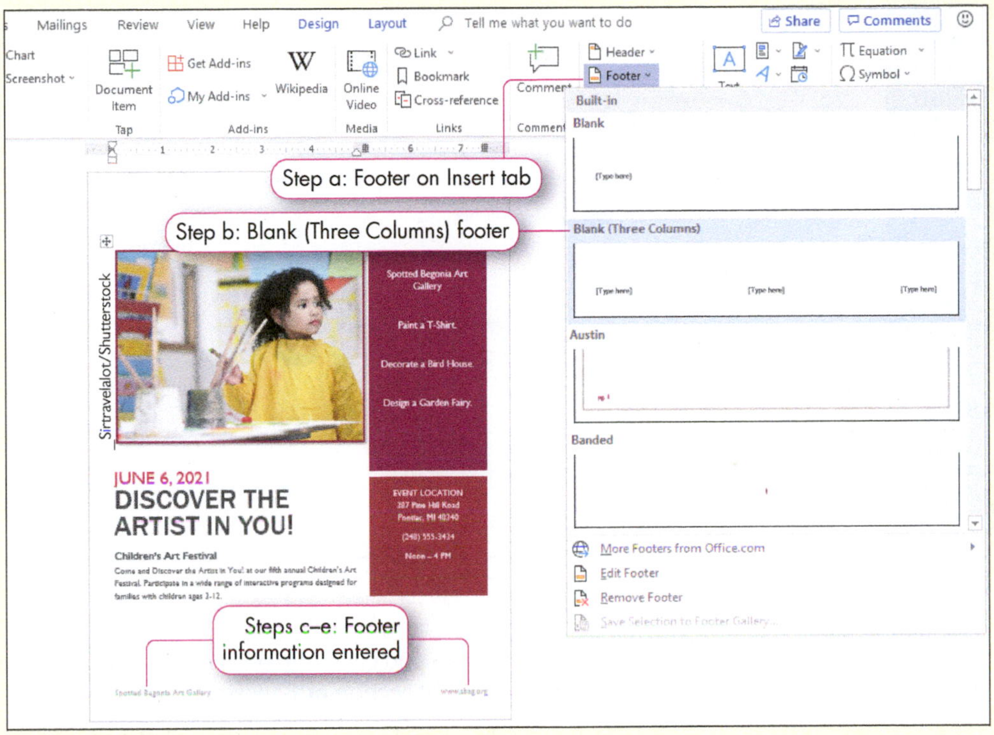

FIGURE 1.47 Insert a Footer

a. Click the **Insert tab** and click **Footer** in the Header & Footer group.

A footer gallery displays.

b. Click the **Blank (Three Columns) footer**.

You select a footer with three areas to add your own information.

c. Click **[Type here]** on the left side of the footer. Type **Spotted Begonia Art Gallery**.

d. Click **[Type here]** on the center of the footer. Press **Delete**.

e. Click **[Type here]** on the right side of the footer. Type **www.sbag.org**.

f. Click **Close Header and Footer** in the Close group.

The footer information is entered.

g. Save the document.

STEP 4 ENTER DOCUMENT PROPERTIES

You add document properties, which will help you locate the file in the future when performing a search of your files. Refer to Figure 1.48 as you complete Step 4.

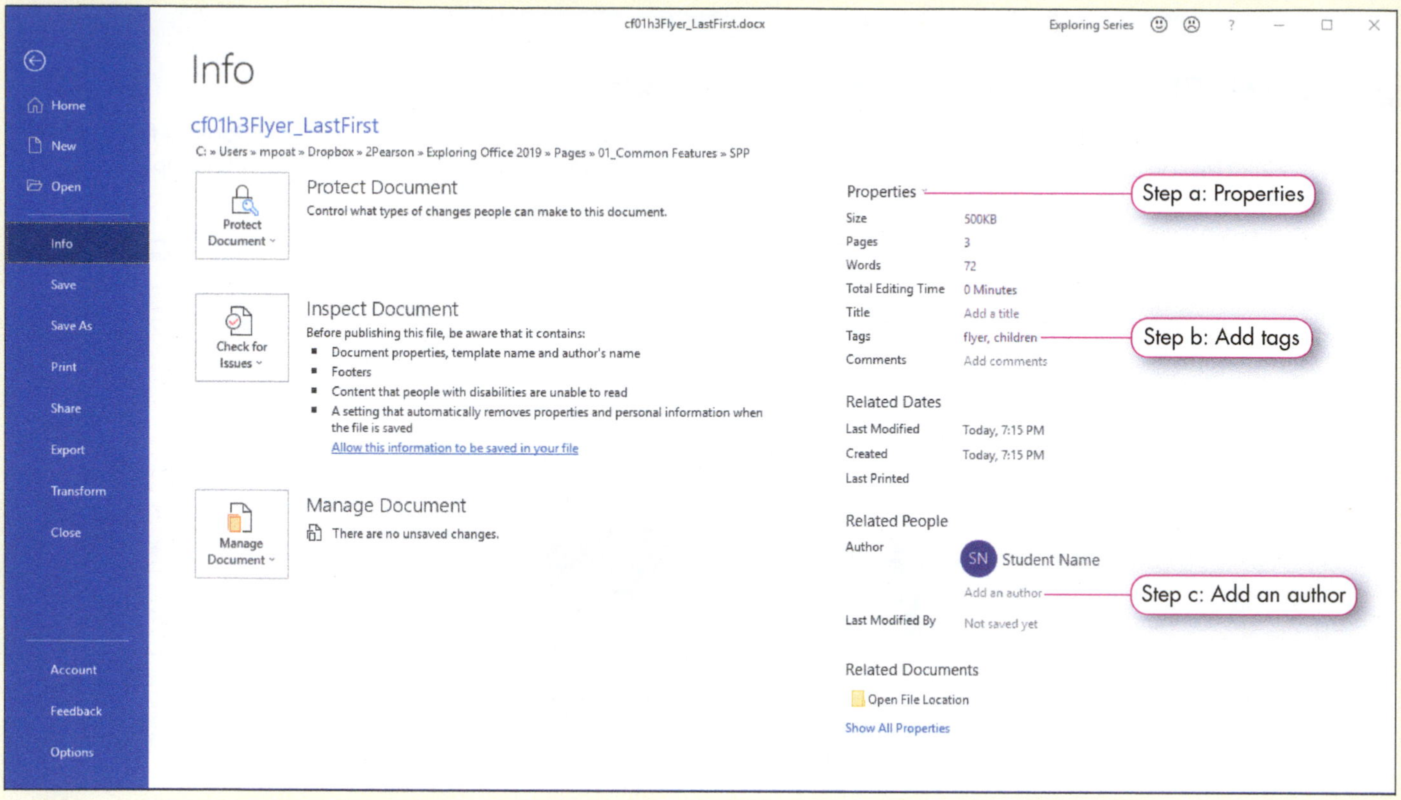

FIGURE 1.48 Enter Document Properties

a. Click the **File tab** and click Info on the Backstage Navigation Pane. Locate Properties at the top of the right section of Backstage view.

b. Click the **Add a tag box** and type **flyer, children**.

> **MAC TROUBLESHOOTING:** On a Mac, to add a tag click the File menu and select Properties. Click the Summary tab and enter text in the Keywords box.

You added tag properties to the flyer.

c. Click the **Add an Author box** and type your first and last name.

You added an Author property to the flyer.

d. Click **Save** in the Backstage Navigation Pane.

You have reviewed and almost finalized the flyer. You want to look at how it will appear when printed. You also want to look over Print Settings to ensure they are correct. Refer to Figure 1.49 as you complete Step 5.

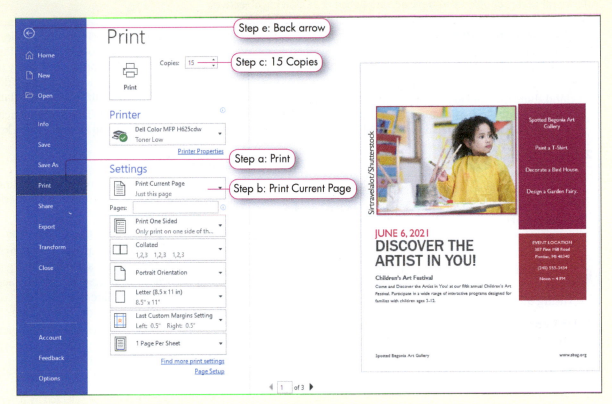

FIGURE 1.49 Backstage Print View

a. Click **Print** in the Backstage Navigation Pane.

   It is always a good idea before printing to use Print Preview to check how a file will look when printed.

b. Click **Print All Pages arrow** and select **Print Current Page**.

   You notice that the template created extra pages. You only want to print the current page.

c. Select the **1** in the Copies box and type **15**.

   The orientation and custom margins settings match what was done previously. Even though you will not print the document now, the print settings will be saved when you save the document.

d. Click the **Back arrow**.

e. Save and close the file. Based on your instructor's directions, submit the following:

   cfo1h1Letter_LastFirst
   cf01h3Flyer_LastFirst

Chapter Objectives Review

After reading this chapter, you have accomplished the following objectives:

1. Start an Office application.
- Use your Microsoft account: Your Microsoft account connects you to all of Microsoft's Internet-based resources.
- Use OneDrive: OneDrive is an app used to store, access, and share files and folders on the Internet. OneDrive is the default storage location for Microsoft Office files. OneDrive is incorporated directly in File Explorer.

2. Work with files.
- Create a new file: You can create a document as a blank document or from a template.
- Save a file: Saving a file enables you to open it later for additional updates or reference. Files are saved to a storage medium such as a hard drive, CD, flash drive, or to OneDrive.
- Open a saved file: You can open an existing file using the Open dialog box. Recently saved files can be accessed using the Recent documents list.

3. Use common interface components.
- Use the ribbon: The ribbon, the long bar located just beneath the title bar containing tabs, groups, and commands, is the command center of Office applications.
- Use a dialog box and gallery: Some commands are not on the ribbon. To access these commands, you need to open a dialog box with a Dialog Box Launcher. A gallery displays additional formatting and design options for a command. Galleries are accessed by clicking More at the bottom of a gallery scroll bar
- Customize the ribbon: You can personalize the ribbon by creating your own tabs and custom groups with commands you want to use. You can create a custom group and add to any of the default tabs.
- Use and Customize the Quick Access Toolbar: The Quick Access Toolbar, located at the top-left corner of any Office application window, provides one-click access to commonly executed tasks, such as saving a file or undoing recent actions.
- You can add additional commands to the QAT.
- Use a Shortcut menu: When you right-click selected text or objects, a context-sensitive menu displays with commands and options relating to the selected text or object.
- Use keyboard shortcuts: Keyboard shortcuts are keyboard equivalents for software commands. Universal keyboard shortcuts in Office include Ctrl+C (Copy), Ctrl+X (Cut), Ctrl+V (Paste), and Ctrl+Z (Undo). Not all commands have a keyboard shortcut. If one exists, it will display in the command ScreenTip.

4. Get help.
- Use the Tell me box: The Tell me box not only links to online resources and technical support but also provides quick access to commands.

- Use the Help tab: The Help tab includes resources for written and video tutorials and training, a means to contact Microsoft Support, and a way to share feedback. What's New displays a webpage that discusses all newly added features organized by release date.
- Use Enhanced ScreenTips: An Enhanced ScreenTip describes a command and provides a keyboard shortcut, if applicable.

5. Install add-ins.
- Add-ins are custom programs or additional commands that extend the functionality of a Microsoft Office program.

6. Use templates and apply themes.
- Open a template: Templates are a convenient way to save time when designing a document. A gallery of template options displays when you start any application. You can also access a template when you start a new document, worksheet, presentation, or database.
- Apply a theme: Themes are a collection of design choices that include colors, fonts, and special effects used to give a consistent look to a document, workbook, or presentation.

7. Modify text.
- Select text: Text can be selected by a variety of methods. You can drag to highlight text and select individual words or groups of text with shortcuts.
- Format text: You can change the font, font color, size, and many other attributes.
- Use the Mini Toolbar: The Mini Toolbar provides instant access to common formatting commands after text is selected.

8. Relocate text.
- Cut, copy, and paste text: To cut means to remove a selection from the original location and place it in the Office Clipboard. To copy means to duplicate a selection from the original location and place a copy in the Office Clipboard. To paste means to place a cut or copied selection into another location.
- Use the Office Clipboard: When you cut or copy selections, they are placed in the Office Clipboard. You can paste the same item multiple times; it will remain in the Office Clipboard until you exit all Office applications or until the Office Clipboard exceeds 24 items.

9. Review a document.
- Check spelling and grammar: As you type, Office applications check and mark spelling and grammar errors (Word only) for later correction. The Thesaurus enables you to search for synonyms. Use AutoCorrect to correct common typing errors and misspelled words and to insert symbols.

10. **Work with pictures.**
  - Insert a picture: You can insert pictures from your own library of digital photos saved on your hard drive, OneDrive, or another storage medium, or you can initiate a Bing search for online pictures directly inside the Office program you are using.
  - Modify a picture: To resize a picture, drag a corner-sizing handle; never resize a picture by dragging a center sizing handle. You can apply a picture style or effect, as well as add a picture border, from selections in the Picture Styles group.

11. **Change document views.**
  - Change document views using the ribbon: The View tab offers views specific to the individual application. A view is how a file will be seen onscreen.
  - Change document views using the status bar: In addition to information relative to the open file, the Status bar provides access to View and Zoom level options.

12. **Change the page layout.**
  - Change margins: A margin is the area of blank space that displays to the left, right, top, and bottom of a document or worksheet.

  - Change page orientation: Documents and worksheets can be displayed in different page orientations. Portrait orientation is taller than it is wide; landscape orientation is wider than it is tall.
  - Use the Page Setup dialog box: The Page Setup dialog box includes options for customizing margins, selecting page orientation, centering horizontally or vertically, printing gridlines, and creating headers and footers.

13. **Create a header and a footer.**
  - A header displays at the top of each page.
  - A footer displays at the bottom of each page.

14. **Configure Document Properties.**
  - View and edit document properties: Information that identifies a document, such as the author, title, or tags can be added to the document's properties. Those data elements are saved with the document as metadata, but do not appear in the document as it displays onscreen or is printed.

15. **Preview and print a file.**
  - It is important to preview your file before printing.
  - Print options can be set in Backstage view and include page orientation, the number of copies, and the specific pages to print.

Key Terms Matching

Match the key terms with their definitions. Write the key term letter by the appropriate numbered definition.

a. Add-in
b. Backstage view
c. Cloud storage
d. Footer
e. Format Painter
f. Group
g. Header
h. Margin
i. Microsoft Access
j. Microsoft Office

k. Mini Toolbar
l. Office Clipboard
m. OneDrive
n. Quick Access Toolbar
o. Ribbon
p. Status bar
q. Tag
r. Tell me box
s. Template
t. Theme

1. _____ A productivity software suite including a set of software applications, each one specializing in a type of output. **p. 4**

2. _____ The long bar located just beneath the title bar containing tabs, groups, and commands. **p. 9**

3. _____ A custom program or additional command that extends the functionality of a Microsoft Office program. **p. 17**

4. _____ A collection of design choices that includes colors, fonts, and special effects used to give a consistent look to a document, workbook, or presentation. **p. 25**

5. _____ A data element or metadata that is added as a document property. **p. 51**

6. _____ A component of Office that provides a concise collection of commands related to an open file and includes save and print options. **p. 6**

7. _____ A tool that displays near selected text that contains formatting commands. **p. 29**

8. _____ Relational database software used to store data and convert it into information. **p. 4**

9. _____ A feature in a document that consists of one or more lines at the bottom of each page. **p. 49**

10. _____ A predesigned file that incorporates formatting elements, such as a theme and layouts, and may include content that can be modified. **p. 25**

11. _____ A feature that enables you to search for help and information about a command or task you want to perform and will also present you with a shortcut directly to that command. **p. 15**

12. _____ A tool that copies all formatting from one area to another. **p. 17**

13. _____ Stores up to 24 cut or copied selections for use later in your computing session. **p. 30**

14. _____ A task-oriented section of a ribbon tab that contains related commands. **p. 9**

15. _____ An online app used to store, access, and share files and folders. **p. 6**

16. _____ Provides handy access to commonly executed tasks, such as saving a file and undoing recent actions. **p. 13**

17. _____ The long bar at the bottom of the screen that houses the Zoom slider and various View buttons. **p. 46**

18. _____ The area of blank space that displays to the left, right, top, and bottom of a document or worksheet **p. 47**

19. _____ A technology used to store files and to work with programs that are stored in a central location on the Internet. **p. 6**

20. _____ A feature in a document that consists of one or more lines at the top of each page. **p. 49**

Multiple Choice

1. In Word or PowerPoint, a quick way to select an entire paragraph is to:
   (a) place the pointer at the left of the line, in the margin area, and click.
   (b) triple-click inside the paragraph.
   (c) double-click at the beginning of the paragraph.
   (d) press Ctrl+C inside the paragraph.

2. When you want to copy the format of a selection but not the content, you should:
   (a) double-click Copy in the Clipboard group.
   (b) right-click the selection and click Copy.
   (c) click Copy Format in the Clipboard group.
   (d) click Format Painter in the Clipboard group.

3. Which of the following is *not* a benefit of using One Drive?
   (a) Save your folders and files to the cloud.
   (b) Share your files and folders with others.
   (c) Hold video conferences with others.
   (d) Simultaneously work on the same document with others.

4. What does a red wavy underline in a document or presentation mean?
   (a) A word is misspelled or not recognized by the Office dictionary.
   (b) A grammatical mistake exists.
   (c) An apparent formatting error was made.
   (d) A word has been replaced with a synonym.

5. Which of the following is *true* about headers and footers?
   (a) They can be inserted from the Layout tab.
   (b) Headers and footers only appear on the last page of a document.
   (c) Headers appear at the top of every page in a document.
   (d) Only page numbers can be included in a header or footer.

6. You can get help when working with an Office application in which one of the following areas?
   (a) The Tell me box
   (b) The Status bar
   (c) Backstage view
   (d) The Quick Access Toolbar

7. To access commands that are not on the ribbon, you need to open which of the following?
   (a) Gallery
   (b) Dialog box
   (c) Shortcut menu
   (d) Mini Toolbar

8. To create a document without knowing much about the software, you should use which of the following?
   (a) Theme
   (b) Live Preview
   (c) Template
   (d) Design Style

9. Which is the preferred method for resizing a picture so that it keeps its proportions?
   (a) Use the rotation handle
   (b) Use a corner-sizing handle
   (c) Use a side-sizing handle
   (d) Use the controls in the Adjust group

10. Which is *not* a description of a tag in a Word document?
   (a) A data element
   (b) Document metadata
   (c) Keyword
   (d) Document title

Practice Exercises

1 Designing Webpages

You have been asked to make a presentation at the next Montgomery County, PA Chamber of Commerce meeting. With the Chamber's continued emphasis on growing the local economy, many small businesses are interested in establishing a Web presence. The business owners would like to know more about how webpages are designed. In preparation for the presentation, you will proofread and edit your PowerPoint file. You decide to insert an image to enhance your presentation and use an add-in to include a map and contact information for the Chamber of Commerce. Refer to Figure 1.50 as you complete this exercise.

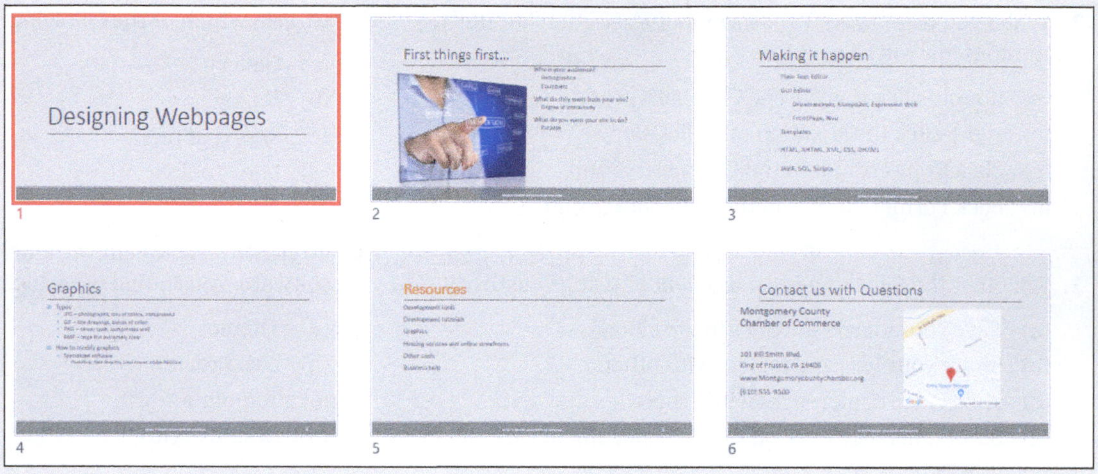

FIGURE 1.50 Designing Webpages Presentation

a. Open the PowerPoint presentation *cf01p1Design*.

b. Click the **File tab**, click **Save As**, and then save the file as **cf01p1Design_LastFirst**.

c. Click the **Design tab** and click **More** in the Themes group. Scroll through the themes to find and select **Retrospect theme**. Select the **third Variant** in the Variants group. Close the Design Ideas pane if it opens.

d. Click **Slide 2** in the Slides pane on the left. Double-click to select **Resources** on the slide title. Use the Mini Toolbar to click the **Font Color arrow**. Select **Orange, Accent 2** in the Theme Colors group. Click **Bold** on the Mini Toolbar.

e. Click **Slide 3** in the Slides pane. Click the **Pictures icon** in the left content placeholder. Browse to the student data files, locate and select *cf01p1Website.jpg*, and then click **Insert**. Close the Design Ideas pane if it opens.

f. Select the picture. Click the **Format tab** and click **More** in the Picture Styles group to open the Pictures Style Gallery. Click the **Reflected Perspective Right**. Click the **Height box** in the Size group and type **4**. Press **Enter**. Place the pointer over the image to display a 4-headed arrow and drag to position the image so it is centered vertically in the open space.

g. Click the **Home tab** and click the **Clipboard Dialog Box Launcher**. Click **Slide 7** and select all the placeholder content. Right-click the selected text and click **Cut** from the shortcut menu.

> **TROUBLESHOOTING:** If there is content in the Office Clipboard, click Clear All to remove all previously cut or copied items from the Office Clipboard.

> **MAC TROUBLESHOOTING:** On a Mac, select the text and press Control+X. Click Slide 4 and press Control+V. Repeat for Step h. Skip to Step j.

h. Click **Slide 5** and select all the placeholder content. Press **Ctrl+X**.

i. Click **Slide 4** and click the **content placeholder**. Click **Paste All** in the Office Clipboard. Close the Office Clipboard.

j. Click **Slide Sorter** on the status bar. Click **Slide 5** and press **Delete**. Click **Slide 6** and press **Delete**. Drag **Slide 2** to the right of **Slide 5**. Click the **View tab** and click **Normal**.

k. Click **Slide 6** in the Slides pane. Click the **Insert tab**, point to **My Add-ins** in the Add-ins group, and read the Enhanced Screen Tip to find out more about Add-ins. Click **My Add-ins**, click the **Store tab**, and then in the search box, type **map**. Press **Enter**.

l. Click **Add** to add OfficeMaps - Insert maps quick and easy!

m. Click Open OfficeMaps on the Insert tab. Click in the Enter a location box and type the address shown on Slide 6. Click Insert Map. Close the OfficeMaps pane.

n. Select the map, click the **Height box** in the Size group, and type **4**. Press **Enter**. Position the map attractively in the slide.

o. Click **Slide 1**. Click **Header & Footer** in the Text group on the Insert tab. Click the **Slide number check box** to select it. Click the **Footer box** to select it and type **Business Owners Association Presentation**. Click **Don't show on title slide check box** to select it. Click **Apply to All**.

p. Click the **Review tab** and click **Spelling** in the Proofing group. In the Spelling pane, click **Change** or **Ignore** to make changes as needed. The words *KompoZer* and *Nvu* are not misspelled, so you should ignore them when they are flagged. Click **OK** when you have finished checking spelling.

q. Click the **File tab.** Click the **Add a Tag box** and type **business, BOA, web design**.

r. Click **Print**. Click the **Full Page Slides arrow** and select **6 Slides Horizontal** to see a preview of all the slides as a handout.

> **MAC TROUBLESHOOTING:** Click the File menu, click Print, and then click Show Details. In the Print dialog box, click the Layout arrow and select Handouts (6 slides per page).

s. Click the **Portrait Orientation arrow** and select **Landscape Orientation**. Click the **Back arrow**.

t. Save and close the file. Based on your instructor's directions, submit cf01p1Design_LastFirst.

2 Upscale Bakery

You have always been interested in baking and have worked in the field for several years. You now have an opportunity to devote yourself full time to your career as the CEO of a company dedicated to baking cupcakes and pastries. One of the first steps in getting the business off the ground is developing a business plan so that you can request financial support. You will use Word to develop your business plan. Refer to Figure 1.51 as you complete this exercise.

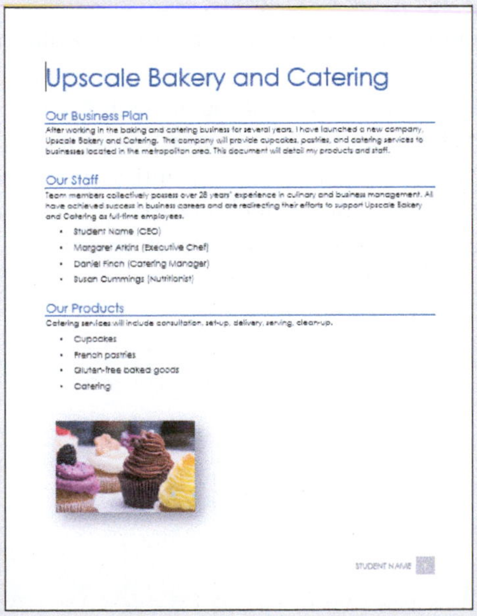
Upscale Bakery and Catering

Our Business Plan

After working in the baking and catering business for several years, I have launched a new company, Upscale Bakery and Catering. The company will provide cupcakes, pastries, and catering services to businesses located in the metropolitan area. This document will detail my products and staff.

Our Staff

Team members collectively possess over 28 years' experience in culinary and business management. All have achieved success in business careers and are redirecting their efforts to support Upscale Bakery and Catering as full-time employees.

- Student Name (CEO)
- Margaret Atkins (Executive Chef)
- Daniel Finch (Catering Manager)
- Susan Cummings (Nutritionist)

Our Products

Catering services will include consultation, set-up, delivery, serving, clean-up.

- Cupcakes
- French pastries
- Gluten-free baked goods
- Catering

STUDENT NAME

Sabuhi Novruzov/123RF

FIGURE 1.51 Upscale Bakery Business Plan

a. Open the Word document *cf01p2Business*. Click the **File tab**, click **Save As**, and save the file as **cf01p2Business_LastFirst**.

b. Click the **Design tab**, click **Themes**, and then select **Slice**.

c. Select the paragraphs beginning with *Our Staff* and ending with *(Nutritionist)*. Click the **Home tab** and click **Cut** in the Clipboard group. Click to the left of *Our Products* and click **Paste**.

d. Select the text **Your name** in the first bullet in the *Our Staff* section and replace it with your first and last names. Select the entire bullet list in the *Our Staff* section. On the Mini Toolbar, click the **Font Size arrow** and select **11**.

e. Click **Format Painter** in the Clipboard group. Drag the Format Painter pointer across all four *Our Products* bullets to change the bullets' font size to 11 pt.

f. Click the **Tell me box** and type **footer**. Click **Add a Footer**, scroll to locate the **Integral footer**, and click to add it to the page. Keep the footer open.

g. Right-click the **page number box** in the footer. Click the **Shading arrow** in the Paragraph group on the Home tab and select **White Background 1 Darker 50%**. Click **Close Header and Footer** on the Header & Footer Tools Design tab.

h. Triple-click to select the last line in the document, which says *Insert and position picture here*, and press **Ctrl+X**. Click the **Insert tab** and click **Online Pictures** in the Illustrations group.

i. Click in the **Bing Image search box**, type **Cupcakes**, and then press **Enter**.

j. Select any **cupcake image** and click **Insert**. Do not deselect the image.

k. Ensure the Picture Tools Format tab is active, and in the Picture Styles group, select the **Drop Shadow Rectangle**.

> **TROUBLESHOOTING:** If you are unable to find a cupcake image in Bing, you can use *cf01p2Cupcake* from the student data files.

l. Click the **Size Dialog Box Launcher** and ensure that Lock aspect ratio is selected. Click **OK**. Click the **Shape width box** in the Size group and change the width to **2.5**.

m. Click outside the picture.

n. Press **Ctrl+Home**. Click **Customize Quick Access Toolbar** and select **Spelling & Grammar** (ignore if present). Click **Spelling & Grammar** from the QAT. Correct the spelling error and click **OK**.

o. Click the **View tab** and select **Draft** in the Views group. Click **Print Layout** in the Views group and click **One Page** in the Zoom group.

p. Click the **Layout tab** and click **Margins** in the Page Setup group. Change to **Moderate Margins**.

q. Click the **File tab**. In the Properties section, click in Add a tag box and add the tag **business plan**. Click **Add an author** and add your first and last name to the Author property. Right-click the **current author** (should say Exploring Series) and click **Remove Person**.

r. Click **Print** in Backstage view. Notice the author name has changed in the footer. Change the number of copies to **2**. Click the **Back arrow**.

s. Save and close the file. Based on your instructor's directions, submit cf01p2Business_LastFirst.

Mid-Level Exercises

1 Reference Letter

MyLab IT Grader

You are an instructor at a local community college. A student asked you to provide her with a letter of reference for a job application. You have used Word to prepare the letter, but now you want to make a few changes before it is finalized.

a. Open the Word document *cf01m1RefLetter* and save it as **cf01m1RefLetter_LastFirst**.

b. Change the theme to **Gallery**. Point to Colors in the Document Formatting group and read the Enhanced ScreenTip. Click **Colors** and select **Red**.

c. Insert a **Blank footer**. Type **410 Wellington Parkway, Huntsville, AL 35611**. Center the footer. Close the footer.

d. Place the insertion point at the end of Professor Smith's name in the signature line. Press **Enter** twice. Insert a picture from your files using *cf01m1College.png*. Resize the image to **1"** tall. Click **Color** in the Adjust group and select **Dark Red, Accent color 1 Light**. Click **Center** in the Paragraph group on Home tab.

e. Press **Ctrl+Home**. Select the **date** and point to several font sizes on the Mini Toolbar. Use Live Preview to view them. Click **12**.

f. Right-click the word **talented** in the second paragraph starting with *Stacy is a* and click **Synonyms** from the shortcut menu. Replace *talented* with **gifted**.

g. Move the last paragraph—beginning with *In my opinion*—to position it before the second paragraph—beginning with *Stacy is a gifted*.

h. Press **Ctrl+Home**. Use Spelling & Grammar to correct all errors. Make any spelling and grammar changes that are suggested. Stacy's last name is spelled correctly.

i. Change the margins to **Narrow**.

j. Customize the QAT to add **Print Preview and Print**. Preview the document as it will appear when printed. Stay in Backstage view.

k. Click **Info** in Backstage view. Add the tag **reference** to the Properties for the file in Backstage view.

l. Save and close the file. Based on your instructor's directions, submit cf01m1RefLetter_LastFirst.

2 Medical Monitoring

MyLab IT Grader

You are enrolled in a Health Informatics study program in which you learn to manage databases related to health fields. For a class project, your instructor requires that you monitor your blood pressure, recording your findings in an Excel worksheet. You have recorded the week's data and will now make a few changes before printing the worksheet for submission.

a. Open the Excel workbook *cf01m2Tracker* and save it as **cf01m2Tracker_LastFirst**.

b. Change the theme to **Crop**.

c. Click in the cell to the right of *Name* and type your first and last names. Press **Enter**.

d. Select **cells H1, I1, J1, and K1**. Cut the selected cells and paste to **cell C2**. Click **cell A1**.

e. Press **Ctrl+A**. Use Live Preview to see how different fonts will look. Change the font of the worksheet to **Arial**.

f. Add the Spelling feature to the QAT and check the spelling for the worksheet to ensure that there are no errors.

g. Select **cells E22, F22, and G22**. You want to increase the decimal places for the values in cells so that each value shows one place to the right of the decimal. Use **Increase Decimal** as the search term in the Tell me box. Click **Insert Decimal** in the results to increase the decimal place to **1**.

h. Press **Ctrl+Home** and insert an **Online Picture** of your choice related to blood pressure. Resize and position the picture so that it displays in an attractive manner. Apply the **Drop Shadow Rectangle** picture style to the image.

i. Insert a footer. Use the Page Number header and footer element in the center section. Use the File Name header and footer element in the right section of the footer. Click in a cell on the worksheet. Return to Normal view.

j. Change the orientation to **Landscape**. Change the page margins so Left and Right are **1.5"** and Top and Bottom and **1"**. Center on page both vertically and horizontally. Close the dialog box.

k. Add **blood pressure** as a tag and adjust print settings to print two copies. You will not actually print two copies unless directed by your instructor.

l. Save and close the file. Based on your instructor's directions, submit cf01m2Tracker_LastFirst.

Running Case

New Castle County Technical Services

New Castle County Technical Services (NCCTS) provides technical support for companies in the greater New Castle County, Delaware, area. The company has been in operation since 2011 and has grown to become one of the leading technical service companies in the area. NCCTS has prided itself on providing great service at reasonable costs, but as you begin to review the budget for next year and the rates your competitors are charging, you are realizing that it may be time to increase some rates. You have prepared a worksheet with suggested rates and will include those rates in a memo to the CFO. You will format the worksheet, copy the data to the Office Clipboard, and use the Office Clipboard to paste the information into a memo. You will then modify the formatting of the memo, check the spelling, and ensure the document is ready for distribution before sending it on to the CFO.

a. Open the Excel workbook *cf01r1NCCTSRates* and save as **cf01r1NCCTSRates_LastFirst**.

b. Select **cells A4:C4**. Click **More** in the Styles group on the Home tab and select **Heading 2**.

c. Select **cells A5:C5**. Press **Ctrl** and select cells **A7:C7**. Change the font color to **Red** in Standard Colors.

d. Select **cells A5:C10** and increase the font size to **12**.

e. Select cells **A4:C10**. Open the **Office Clipboard**. Clear the Office clipboard if items display. Click **Copy** in the Clipboard group. Keep Excel open.

f. Open the Word document *cf01r1NCCTSMemo* and save it as **cf01r1NCCTSMemo_LastFirst**.

g. Change Your Name in the From: line to your own name.

h. Press **Ctrl+Home**. Insert image *cf01r1Logo.jpg*. Resize the height to **1"**.

i. Change the document theme to **Retrospect**.

j. Place insertion point in the blank line above the paragraph beginning with *Please*.

k. Open Office Clipboard and click the item in the Office Clipboard that was copied from the NCCTS Rates workbook. Clear then close the **Office Clipboard**.

l. Check the spelling. Correct all grammar and spelling mistakes.

m. Increase left and right margins to **1.5"**.

n. Insert a footer and click **Edit Footer**. Click **Document Info** in the Insert group on the Header and Footer Tools Design tab. Click **File Name**. Click **Close Header and Footer**.

o. Enter **2022**, **rates** as tags.

p. Save and close the files. Based on your instructor's directions, submit the following files:
cf01r1NCCTSMemo_LastFirst
cf01r1NCCTSRates_LastFirst

Disaster Recovery

Resume Enhancement

You are applying for a new position and you have asked a friend to look at your resume. She has a better eye for details than you do, so you want her to let you know about any content or formatting errors. She has left some instructions pointing out where you can improve the resume. Open the Word document *cf01d1Resume* and save it as **cf01d1Resume_LastFirst**. Add your name, address, phone and email in the placeholders at the top of the document. Change the theme of the resume to Office. Bold all the job titles and dates held. Italicize all company names and locations. Use Format Painter to copy the formatting of the bullets in the Software Intern description and apply them to the bullets in the other job description. Bold the name of the university and location. Apply italics to the degree and date. Change the margins to Narrow. Add resume as a tag. Check the spelling and grammar. Save and close the file. Based on your instructor's directions, submit cf01d1Resume_LastFirst.

Capstone Exercise

Social Media Privacy

You have been asked to create a presentation about protecting privacy on social media sites. You have given the first draft of your presentation to a colleague to review. She has come up with several suggestions that you need to incorporate before you present.

Open and Save Files

You will open, review, and save a PowerPoint presentation.

1. Open the PowerPoint presentation *cf01c1SocialMedia* and save it as **cf01c1SocialMedia_LastFirst**.

Apply a Theme and Change the View

You generally develop a presentation using a blank theme, and then when most of the content is on the slides, you add a different theme to provide some interest.

2. Apply the **Quotable theme** to the presentation and use the **Purple variant**.
3. Change to **Slide Sorter view**. Drag **Slide 2** to become **Slide 3** and drag **Slide 8** to become **Slide 6**.
4. Return to **Normal view**.

Select Text, Move Text, and Format Text

You make some changes to the order of text and change some word choices.

5. Click **Slide 5** and cut the second bullet. Paste it so it is the first bullet.
6. Right-click the second use of **regularly** in the first bullet to find a synonym. Change the word to **often**.
7. Double-click **location** in the fourth bullet. Drag it so it comes after *Disable* and add a space between the two words. Delete the word **of** so the bullet reads *Disable location sharing*.
8. Use the Mini Toolbar to format **Never** in the fifth bullet in italics.

Insert and Modify a Picture

You think Slide 2 has too much empty space and needs a picture. You insert a picture and add a style to give it a professional look.

9. Click **Slide 2** and insert the picture *cf01c1Sharing.jpg* from your data files.
10. Resize the picture height to **4.5"**.
11. Apply the **Rounded Diagonal Corner, White Picture Style**.

Use the Tell me Box

You also want to center the picture on Slide 2 vertically. You use the Tell Me box to help with this. You also need help to change a bulleted list on Slide 5 to SmartArt because many of your slides use SmartArt. You know that there is a way to convert text to SmartArt, but you cannot remember where it is. You use the Tell me box to help you with this function, too.

12. Ensure the picture on Slide 2 is still selected. Type **Align** in the Tell me box. Click **Align Objects** and select **Align Middle**.
13. Select the bulleted text on **Slide 5**. Use the Tell me box to search **SmartArt**.
14. Click the first instance of Convert text to SmartArt from your search and click **More SmartArt Graphics** to convert the text to a **Lined List**.

Insert Header and Footer

You want to give the audience printed handouts of your presentation, so you add a header and footer to the handouts, with page numbers and information to identify you and the topic.

15. Add **page numbers** to all Handouts.
16. Add **Social Media Privacy** as a Header in all Handouts.
17. Add **your name** as a Footer in all Handouts.

Customize the Quick Access Toolbar

You know to review the presentation for spelling errors. Because you run spell check regularly, you add a button on the QAT. You also add a button to preview and print your presentation for added convenience.

18. Add **Spelling** to the QAT.
19. Add **Print Preview and Print** to the QAT.

Check Spelling and Change View

Before you call the presentation complete, you will correct any spelling errors and view the presentation as a slide show.

20. Press **Ctrl+Home** and check the spelling.
21. View the slide show. Click after reviewing the last slide to return to the presentation.

Use Print Preview, Change Print Layout, and Adjust Document Properties

You want to print handouts of the presentation so that 3 slides will appear on one page.

22. Click the **Print Preview and Print command** on the QAT to preview the document as it will appear when printed.

23. Change Full Page Slides to **3 Slides**.

> **MAC TROUBLESHOOTING:** Click the File menu and click Print. Click Show Details. Click Layout and choose Handouts (3 slides per page).

24. Change the Page Orientation to **Landscape**.

25. Adjust the print settings to print **two** copies. You will not actually print two copies unless directed by your instructor.

26. Change document properties to add **social media** as a tag and change the author name to your own.

27. Save and close the file. Based on your instructor's directions, submit cf01c1SocialMedia_LastFirst.

Introduction to Access

You will demonstrate understanding of relational database concepts.

OBJECTIVES & SKILLS: After you read this chapter, you will be able to:

Databases Are Everywhere!

OBJECTIVE 1: OPEN, SAVE, AND ENABLE CONTENT IN A DATABASE   72
Open a Database, Enable Content in a Database, Save a Database with a New Name

OBJECTIVE 2: RECOGNIZE DATABASE OBJECT TYPES   74
Examine the Access Interface, Explore Table Datasheet View, Navigate Through Records, Explore Table Design View, Understand Relationships between Tables

OBJECTIVE 3: MODIFY, ADD, AND SAVE DATA   85
Modify Records in a Table, Add Records to a Table, Delete Records from a Table

OBJECTIVE 4: USE DATABASE UTILITIES   88
Back up a Database, Print Information

HANDS-ON EXERCISE 1   91

Filters and Sorts

OBJECTIVE 5: WORK WITH FILTERS   98
Use a Selection Filter to Find Exact Matches, Use a Selection Filter to Find Records Containing a Value, Use Filter By Form

OBJECTIVE 6: PERFORM SORTS   102
Sort Table Data

HANDS-ON EXERCISE 2   104

Access Database Creation

OBJECTIVE 7: CREATE A DATABASE   109
Create a Blank Database, Create a Database Using a Template, Explore and Customize a Database Template, Create a Table Using an Application Part

HANDS-ON EXERCISE 3   115

CASE STUDY | Managing a Business in the Global Economy

Northwind Traders is an international gourmet food distributor that imports and exports specialty foods from around the world. Keeping track of customers, vendors, orders, and inventory is a critical task. The owners of Northwind have just purchased an order-processing database created with Microsoft Access 2019 to help manage their customers, suppliers, products, and orders.

You have been hired to learn, use, and manage the database. Northwind's owners are willing to provide training about their business and Access. They expect the learning process to take about three months. After three months, your job will be to support the order-processing team as well as to provide detail and summary reports to the sales force as needed. Your new job at Northwind Traders will be a challenge, but it is also a good opportunity to make a great contribution to a global company. Are you up to the task?

Navigating an Access Database

Sfio Cracho/Shutterstock

CHAPTER

1

Customers

Customer I	Company Name	Contact Name	Contact Title	Address	City	Region
ANATR	Ana Trujillo Emparedados y helados	Ana Trujillo	Owner	Avda. de la Constitución 2222	México D.F.	
ANTON	Antonio Moreno Taquería	Antonio Moreno	Owner	Mataderos 2312	México D.F.	
BOLID	Bólido Comidas preparadas	Martín Sommer	Owner	C/ Araquil, 67	Madrid	
BONAP	Bon app'	Laurence Lebihan	Owner	12, rue des Bouchers	Marseille	
CHOPS	Chop-suey Chinese	Yang Wang	Owner	Hauptstr. 29	Bern	
DUMON	Du monde entier	Janine Labrune	Owner	67, rue des Cinquante Otages	Nantes	
FOLKO	Folk och fä HB	Maria Larsson	Owner	Åkergatan 24	Bräcke	
GROSR	GROSELLA-Restaurante	Manuel Pereira	Owner	5ª Ave. Los Palos Grandes	Caracas	DF
LETSS	Let's Stop N Shop	Jaime Yorres	Owner	87 Polk St.	San Francisco	CA
LINOD	LINO-Delicateses	Felipe Izquierdo	Owner	Ave. 5 de Mayo Porlamar	I. de Margarita	Nueva Espar
OTTIK	Ottilies Käseladen	Henriette Pfalzheim	Owner	Mehrheimerstr. 369	Köln	
PARIS	Paris spécialités	Marie Bertrand	Owner	265, boulevard Charonne	Paris	
SANTG	Santé Gourmet	Jo				
SIMOB	Simons bistro	Jy				
TORTU	Tortuga Restaurante	M				
WHITC	White Clover Markets	Ka				
WOLZA	Wolski Zajazd	Zb				

Contact Details ✕

Tanya Machuca

Go to [▼]   💾 Save and New   📧 E-mail   📇 Save As Outlook Contact   [Close]

General

First Name	Tanya	Business Phone	801-555-8108
Last Name	Machuca	Home Phone	
Company	Hobblecreek Mountain Dent ▼	Mobile Phone	801-555-8921
Job Title	D.D.S. ▼	Fax Number	
E-mail	HMDentistry@email.com		
Web Page			
Category	Business ▼		

Edit Picture

		Notes
	Click to Map	Available Tuesday - Friday 7 a.m. to 4 p.m.
Street	56 West 200 North	
City	Mapleton	
State/Province	UT	
Zip/Postal Code	84664	
Country/Region	USA	

FIGURE 1.1 Northwind Traders and Contact Management Databases

CASE STUDY | Managing a Business in the Global Economy

Starting File	Files to be Submitted
a01h1Traders	**a01h1Traders_LastFirst_*CurrentDate*** **a01h2Traders_LastFirst** **a01h3Contacts_LastFirst**

MyLab IT Grader An alternate version of this project is available as a MyLab IT Grader Assessment

Databases Are Everywhere!

A *database* is a collection of data organized as meaningful information that can be accessed, managed, stored, queried, sorted, and reported. You participate in data collection and are exposed to databases on a regular basis. Your college or university stores your personal and registration data. When you registered for this course, your data was entered into a database. If you have a bank account, a Social Security card, a medical history, or if you have ever booked a flight with an airline, your information is stored in a database.

You use databases online without realizing it, such as when you shop or check your bank statement. Even when you type a search phrase into Google and click Search, you are using Google's massive database with all of its stored webpage references and keywords. Look for something on Amazon, and you are searching Amazon's database to find a product that you want to buy.

A *database management system (DBMS)* is a software system that provides the tools needed to create, maintain, and use a database. Database management systems make it possible to access and control data and display the information in a variety of formats. *Microsoft Access* is the database management system included in professional editions of the Office 2019 suite. Access is a valuable decision-making tool used by many organizations. More advanced DBMS packages include Microsoft SQL Server, MySQL, and Oracle.

Organizations from all industries rely on data to conduct daily operations. Businesses maintain and analyze data about their customers, employees, orders, volunteers, activities, and facilities. Data and information are two terms that are often used interchangeably. However, when it comes to databases, the two terms mean different things. Data are what is entered into a database. Information is the finished product that is produced by the database. Data are converted to information by selecting, performing calculations, and sorting. Decisions in an organization are usually based on information produced by a database, rather than raw data. For example, the number 55 is just an item of data, because it could mean anything. Only when a label is attached to it (for example, as someone's age) does it take on meaning and become information.

In this section, you will learn the fundamentals of organizing data in a database, explore Access database objects and the purpose of each object, and examine the Access interface.

STEP 1 Opening, Saving, and Enabling Content in a Database

As you work through the material in this book, you will frequently be asked to open a database, save it with a new name, and enable content. You can also start by creating a new database if appropriate.

> **To open an existing Access database and enable content, complete the following steps:**
>
> 1. Start Access. Backstage view displays. (Note: If Access is already open, click the File tab to display Backstage view).
> 2. Click Open Other Files.
> 3. Click Browse to open the Open dialog box.
> 4. Locate and select the database and click Open.
> 5. Click Enable Content on the message bar (see Figure 1.2). Access will close and reopen the database, and the security warning disappears and will not display again for this database.

If you have been provided a database, open the file to get started. When you open any database for the first time, you will be presented with a warning that it might contain harmful code. By enabling the content, the database file will be trusted on the computer you are working on. All content from this publisher and associated with this book can be trusted.

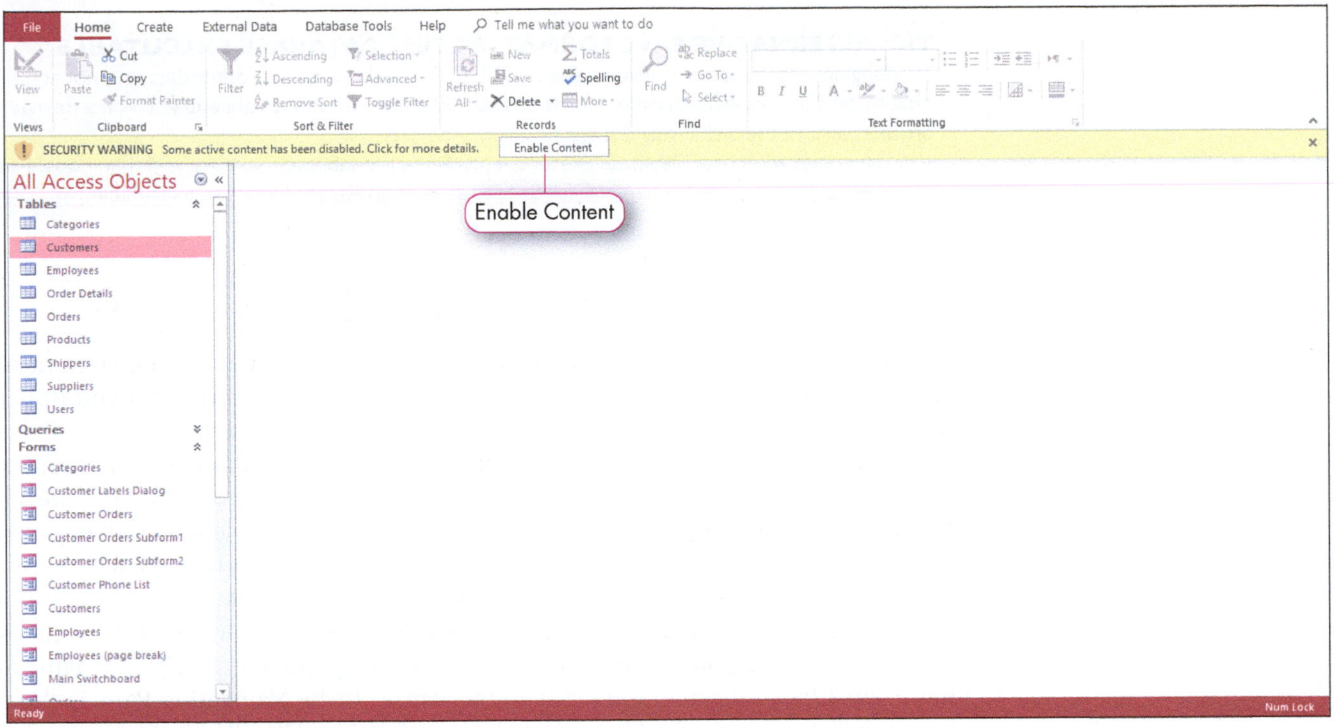

FIGURE 1.2 Access Security Warning

The File tab gives you access to the Save As command. Most assignments will have you save the starting database file with a new name. The name given to the file should help describe the purpose of the database. On the File tab, select Save As and ensure *Save Database As* is selected (see Figure 1.3). The saving process is similar to that of any other program except that in Access you have the option to save objects within the database. After you have named the file an appropriate name, click Save.

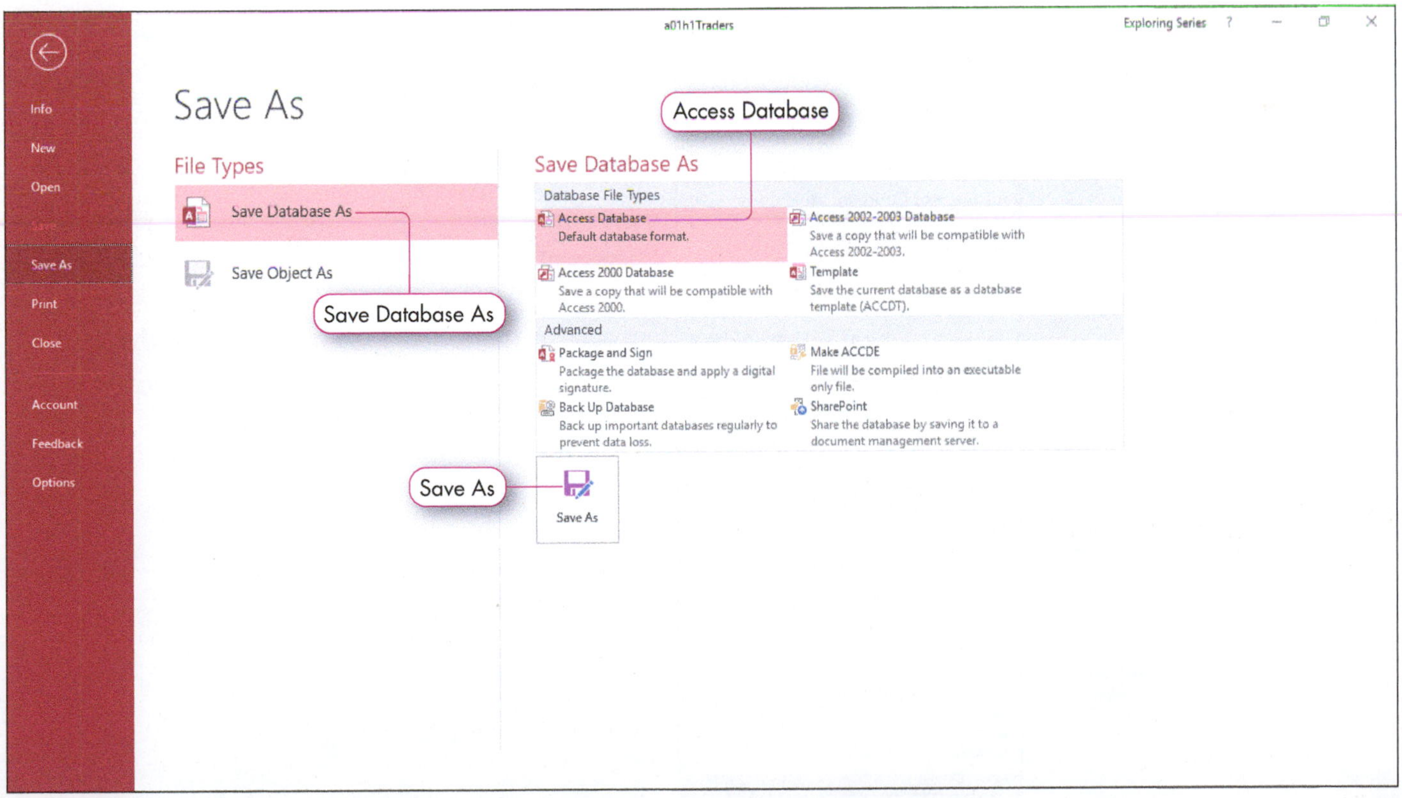

FIGURE 1.3 Access Save As Options

> **TIP: ALTERNATIVE SAVE FORMAT: ACCESS DATABASE EXECUTABLE**
> Creating an Access Database Executable (ACCDE) file enables users to enter data, but not add, modify, or delete objects. In other words, the only task they can do is data entry. This file format protects against users changing designs or deleting objects.
>
> To create an Access Database Executable, click the File tab, click Save As, and then double-click Make ACCDE. Enter the file name. Click Save to save as an Access Database Executable.

STEP 2 Recognizing Database Object Types

Databases must be carefully managed to keep information accurate. Data need to be changed, added, and deleted. Managing a database also requires that you understand when data are saved and when you need to use the Save commands.

In Access, each component created and used to make the database function is known as an *object*. Objects include tables, queries, forms, and reports, and can be found in the *Navigation Pane*. The Navigation Pane is an Access interface element that organizes and lists the objects in an Access database. The Navigation Pane is located on the left side of the screen and displays all objects. You can open any object by double-clicking the object's name in the list. You can toggle the display of the Navigation Pane by clicking the Shutter Bar Open/Close button at the top-right corner of the pane. The Navigation Pane Shutter Bar Open/Close button appears as a double arrow. If the Navigation Pane is shown, the button will display as a double arrow pointing left «, and it will hide the Navigation Pane when clicked. If the Navigation Pane is hidden, the button displays as a double arrow pointing right », and it will show the Navigation Pane when clicked. You can collapse the contents of an object group by clicking the group heading or the double arrows to the right of the group heading. To expand the contents of an object group that has been hidden, click the heading again or click the double arrows to the right of the group heading again. To change the way objects are grouped in the Navigation Pane, click the Object list arrow ⊙ on the Navigation Pane title bar and select your preferred configuration of the available options. See Figure 1.4 to see the features of the Navigation Pane.

FIGURE 1.4 Navigation Pane Features

Most databases contain multiple tables. By default, the objects display in groups by object type in the Navigation Pane. In other words, you will see a list of tables, followed by queries, followed by forms, followed by reports. The purpose of each of these objects is described below.

Tables are where all data are stored in your database and, thus, can be said to be the foundation of each database. Tables organize data into columns and rows. Each column represents a ***field***, a category of information we store in a table. For example, in the Northwind database, a table containing customer information would include fields such as Customer ID, Company Name, and City. Each row in a table contains a ***record***, a complete set of all the fields about one person, place, event, or concept. A customer record, for example, would contain all the fields about a single customer, including the Customer ID, the Company Name, Contact Name, Contact Title, Address, City, etc. Figure 1.5 shows both fields and records. The ***primary key*** is a field (or combination of fields) that uniquely identifies each record in a table. Common primary keys are driver's license number, government ID number (such as a Social Security number), passport number, and student ID. Many of these primary keys are generated by a database. Your college or university's database likely assigns a unique identifier to a student as soon as they apply, for example.

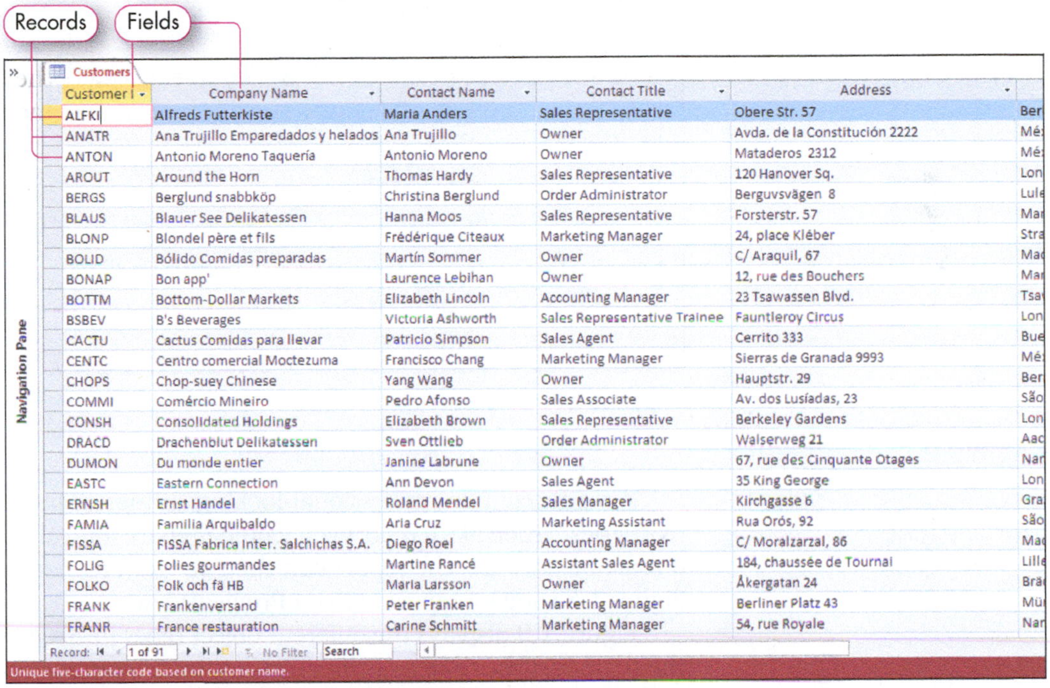

Customer I	Company Name	Contact Name	Contact Title	Address	
ALFKI	Alfreds Futterkiste	Maria Anders	Sales Representative	Obere Str. 57	Ber
ANATR	Ana Trujillo Emparedados y helados	Ana Trujillo	Owner	Avda. de la Constitución 2222	Mé
ANTON	Antonio Moreno Taquería	Antonio Moreno	Owner	Mataderos 2312	Mé
AROUT	Around the Horn	Thomas Hardy	Sales Representative	120 Hanover Sq.	Lon
BERGS	Berglund snabbköp	Christina Berglund	Order Administrator	Berguvsvägen 8	Lul
BLAUS	Blauer See Delikatessen	Hanna Moos	Sales Representative	Forsterstr. 57	Ma
BLONP	Blondel père et fils	Frédérique Citeaux	Marketing Manager	24, place Kléber	Stra
BOLID	Bólido Comidas preparadas	Martín Sommer	Owner	C/ Araquil, 67	Ma
BONAP	Bon app'	Laurence Lebihan	Owner	12, rue des Bouchers	Ma
BOTTM	Bottom-Dollar Markets	Elizabeth Lincoln	Accounting Manager	23 Tsawassen Blvd.	Tsa
BSBEV	B's Beverages	Victoria Ashworth	Sales Representative Trainee	Fauntleroy Circus	Lon
CACTU	Cactus Comidas para llevar	Patricio Simpson	Sales Agent	Cerrito 333	Bue
CENTC	Centro comercial Moctezuma	Francisco Chang	Marketing Manager	Sierras de Granada 9993	Mé
CHOPS	Chop-suey Chinese	Yang Wang	Owner	Hauptstr. 29	Ber
COMMI	Comércio Mineiro	Pedro Afonso	Sales Associate	Av. dos Lusíadas, 23	São
CONSH	Consolidated Holdings	Elizabeth Brown	Sales Representative	Berkeley Gardens	Lon
DRACD	Drachenblut Delikatessen	Sven Ottlieb	Order Administrator	Walserweg 21	Aac
DUMON	Du monde entier	Janine Labrune	Owner	67, rue des Cinquante Otages	Nar
EASTC	Eastern Connection	Ann Devon	Sales Agent	35 King George	Lon
ERNSH	Ernst Handel	Roland Mendel	Sales Manager	Kirchgasse 6	Gra
FAMIA	Familia Arquibaldo	Aria Cruz	Marketing Assistant	Rua Orós, 92	São
FISSA	FISSA Fabrica Inter. Salchichas S.A.	Diego Roel	Accounting Manager	C/ Moralzarzal, 86	Ma
FOLIG	Folies gourmandes	Martine Rancé	Assistant Sales Agent	184, chaussée de Tournai	Lill
FOLKO	Folk och fä HB	Maria Larsson	Owner	Åkergatan 24	Brä
FRANK	Frankenversand	Peter Franken	Marketing Manager	Berliner Platz 43	Mü
FRANR	France restauration	Carine Schmitt	Marketing Manager	54, rue Royale	Nar

FIGURE 1.5 An Access Table

A ***query*** (or queries, plural) is a question you ask about the data in your database. Notice the word query is similar to the word inquiry, which means "question." It produces a subset of data that provides information about the question you have asked. For example, a query may display a list of which customers live in a specific town or a list of children registered for a specific after-school program. You can double-click a query in the Navigation Pane and you will notice the interface is similar to that of a table, as shown in Figure 1.6.

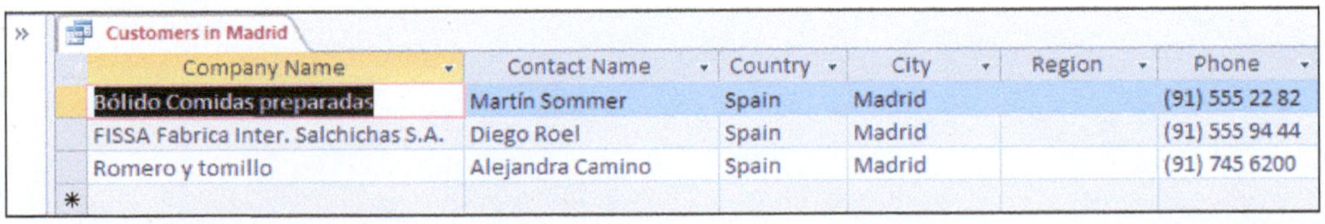

Company Name	Contact Name	Country	City	Region	Phone
Bólido Comidas preparadas	Martín Sommer	Spain	Madrid		(91) 555 22 82
FISSA Fabrica Inter. Salchichas S.A.	Diego Roel	Spain	Madrid		(91) 555 94 44
Romero y tomillo	Alejandra Camino	Spain	Madrid		(91) 745 6200

FIGURE 1.6 An Access Query

A *form* allows simplified entry and modification of data. Much like entering data on a paper form, a database form enables you to add, modify, and delete table data. Most forms display one record at a time, which helps prevent data entry errors. Forms are typically utilized by the users of the database, while the database designer creates and edits the form structure. Figure 1.7 shows a form. Notice a single record is displayed.

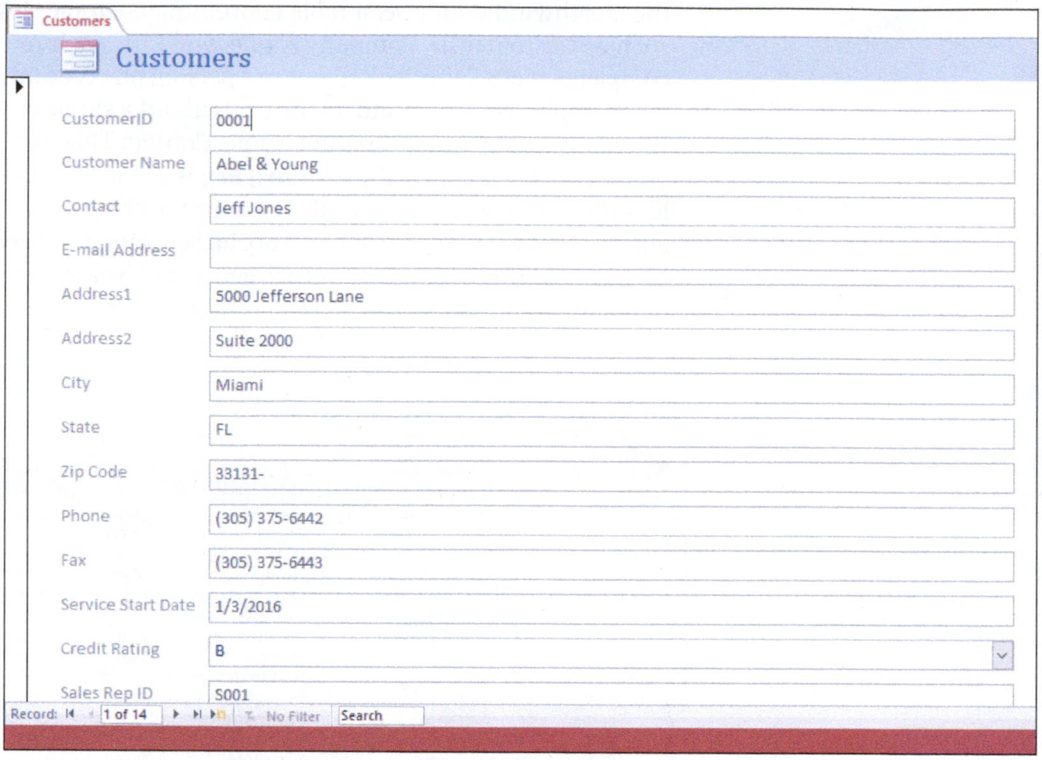

Customers	
Customers	
CustomerID	0001
Customer Name	Abel & Young
Contact	Jeff Jones
E-mail Address	
Address1	5000 Jefferson Lane
Address2	Suite 2000
City	Miami
State	FL
Zip Code	33131-
Phone	(305) 375-6442
Fax	(305) 375-6443
Service Start Date	1/3/2016
Credit Rating	B
Sales Rep ID	S001

Record: 1 of 14 · No Filter · Search

FIGURE 1.7 An Access Form

A *report* contains professional-looking, formatted information from underlying tables or queries. Much like a report you would prepare for a class, a report puts the results into a readable format. The report can then be viewed onscreen, saved to a file, or printed. Figure 1.8 shows a report in Print Preview view.

Figure 1.9 displays the different object types in Access with the foundation object—the table—in the center of the illustration. The purpose each object serves is explained underneath the object name. The flow of information between objects is indicated by single-arrowhead arrows if the flow is one direction only. Two-arrowhead arrows indicate that the flow goes both directions. For example, you can use forms to view, add, delete, or modify data from tables.

Customer Contacts

Contact Name	Company Name	Contact Title	Phone	City	Region	Country
Alejandra Camino	Romero y tomillo	Accounting Manager	(91) 745 6200	Madrid		Spain
Alexander Feuer	Morgenstern Gesundkost	Marketing Assistant	0342-023176	Leipzig		Germany
Ana Trujillo	Ana Trujillo Emparedados y helados	Owner	(5) 555-4729	México D.F.		Mexico
Anabela Domingues	Tradição Hipermercados	Sales Representative	(11) 555-2167	São Paulo	SP	Brazil
André Fonseca	Gourmet Lanchonetes	Sales Associate	(11) 555-9482	Campinas	SP	Brazil
Ann Devon	Eastern Connection	Sales Agent	(171) 555-0297	London		UK
Annette Roulet	La maison d'Asie	Sales Manager	61.77.61.10	Toulouse		France
Antonio Moreno	Antonio Moreno Taquería	Owner	(5) 555-3932	México D.F.		Mexico
Aria Cruz	Familia Arquibaldo	Marketing Assistant	(11) 555-9857	São Paulo	SP	Brazil
Art Braunschweiger	Split Rail Beer & Ale	Sales Manager	(307) 555-4680	Lander	WY	USA
Bernardo Batista	Que Delícia	Accounting Manager	(21) 555-4252	Rio de Janeiro	RJ	Brazil
Carine Schmitt	France restauration	Marketing Manager	40.32.21.21	Nantes		France
Carlos González	LILA-Supermercado	Accounting Manager	(9) 331-6954	Barquisimeto	Lara	Venezuela
Carlos Hernández	HILARIÓN-Abastos	Sales Representative	(5) 555-1340	San Cristóbal	Táchira	Venezuela
Catherine Dewey	Maison Dewey	Sales Agent	(02) 201 24 67	Bruxelles		Belgium
Christina Berglund	Berglund snabbköp	Order Administrator	0921-12 34 65	Luleå		Sweden
Daniel Tonini	La corne d'abondance	Sales Representative	30.59.84.10	Versailles		France

Page: 1 ▶ ▶I No Filter

FIGURE 1.8 An Access Report

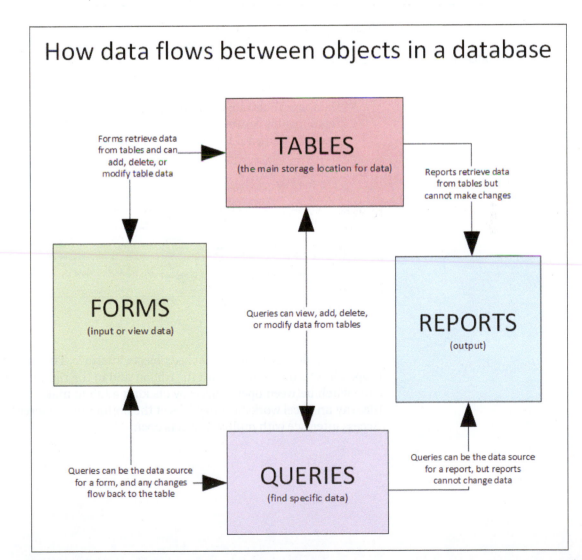

FIGURE 1.9 Flow of Information between Object Types

Two other object types, macros and modules, are rarely used by beginning Access users. A *macro* object is a stored series of commands that carry out an action. Macros are often used to automate tasks. A *module* is an advanced object written using the VBA (Visual Basic for Applications) programming language. Modules provide more functionality than macros but are not generally required for even intermediate users.

Examine the Access Interface

While Access includes the standard elements of the Microsoft Office applications interface such as the title bar, the ribbon, the Home tab, the File tab, and scroll bars, it also includes elements unique to Access.

The Access ribbon has six tabs that always display, as well as tabs that appear only when particular objects are open. The two tabs that are unique to Access are:

- External Data tab: Contains all the operations used to facilitate data import and export (see Figure 1.10).

FIGURE 1.10 External Data Tab

- Database Tools tab: Contains the feature that enables users to create relationships between tables and enables use of more advanced features of Access. Figure 1.11 shows the Database Tools tab.

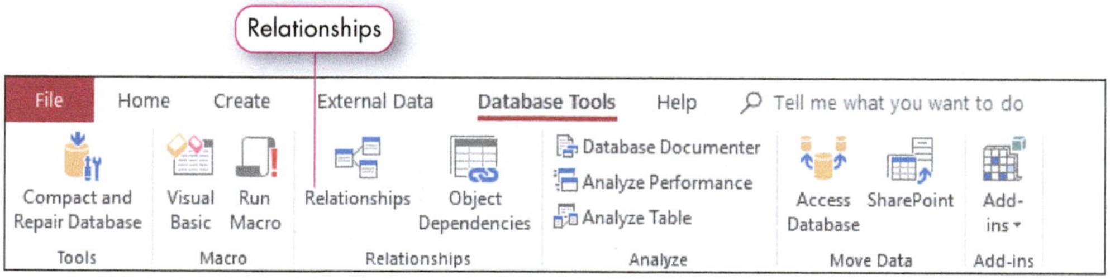

FIGURE 1.11 Database Tools Tab

By default, Access uses a tabbed objects interface. That means that each object that is open has its own tab beneath the ribbon and to the right of the Navigation Pane. You can switch between open objects by clicking a tab to make that object active, similar to the way an Excel worksheet has tabs at the bottom of the screen. Figure 1.12 shows the Access interface with multiple objects open.

Customers table open
Employees table open
Invoices query open

Employee ID	Last Name	First Name	Title	Title Of Courtesy	Birth Date	Hire Date	Address	City	Region	Posta
1	Davolio	Nancy	Sales Representative	Ms.	12/8/1983	5/1/2015	507 - 20th Ave. E.	Seattle	WA	98122
2	Fuller	Andrew	Vice President, Sales	Dr.	2/19/1957	8/14/2015	908 W. Capital Way	Tacoma	WA	98401
3	Leverling	Janet	Sales Representative	Ms.	8/30/1970	4/1/2012	722 Moss Bay Blvd.	Kirkland	WA	98033
4	Peacock	Margaret	Sales Representative	Mrs.	9/19/1986	5/3/2011	4110 Old Redmond Rd.	Redmond	WA	98052
5	Buchanan	Steven	Sales Manager	Mr.	3/4/1970	10/17/2008	14 Garrett Hill	London	EU	SW1 8
6	Suyama	Michael	Sales Representative	Mr.	7/2/1978	10/17/2009	Coventry House	London	EU	EC2 7
7	King	Robert	Sales Representative	Mr.	5/29/1985	1/2/2008	Edgeham Hollow	London	EU	RG1 9
8	Callahan	Laura	Inside Sales Coordinator	Ms.	1/9/1990	3/5/2014	4726 - 11th Ave. N.E.	Seattle	WA	98105
9	Dodsworth	Anne	Sales Representative	Ms.	1/27/1988	11/15/2013	7 Houndstooth Rd.	London	EU	WG2 1

All Access Objects
Tables
- Categories
- Customers
- Employees
- Order Details
- Orders
- Products
- Shippers
- Suppliers

FIGURE 1.12 Access Database with Multiple Objects Open

Explore Table Datasheet View

Access provides two different ways to view a table: Datasheet view and Design view. When you open a table, Datasheet view displays by default. **Datasheet view** is a grid containing fields (columns) and records (rows). You can view, add, edit, and delete records in Datasheet view. Figure 1.13 shows the Customers table in Datasheet view. Each row contains a record for a specific customer. The record selector, or row heading (when clicked), is used to select the entire record. Each column represents a field, or one attribute about a customer.

Field selector
Table Tools Fields tab
Table Tools Table tab

File	Home	Create	External Data	Database Tools	Help	Fields	Table

Record selector

Customer I	Company Name	Contact Name	Contact Title
ALFKI	Alfreds Futterkiste	Maria Anders	Sales Representative
ANATR	Ana Trujillo Emparedados y helados	Ana Trujillo	Owner
ANTON	Antonio Moreno Taquería	Antonio Moreno	Owner
AROUT	Around the Horn	Thomas Hardy	Sales Representative
BERGS	Berglund snabbköp	Christina Berglund	Order Administrator
BLAUS	Blauer See Delikatessen	Hanna Moos	Sales Representative
BLONP	Blondel père et fils	Frédérique Citeaux	Manager
BOLID	Bólido Comidas preparadas	Martín Sommer	Owner
BONAP	Bon app'	Laurence Lebihan	Owner
BOTTM	Bottom-Dollar Markets	Elizabeth Lincoln	Accounting Manager
BSBEV	B's Beverages	Victoria Ashworth	Sales Representative Trainee
CACTU	Cactus Comidas para llevar	Patricio Simpson	Sales Agent
CENTC	Centro comercial Moctezuma	Francisco Chang	Marketing Manager
CHOPS	Chop-suey Chinese	Yang Wang	Owner
COMMI	Comércio Mineiro	Pedro Afonso	Sales Associate
CONSH	Consolidated Holdings	Elizabeth Brown	Sales Representative
DRACD	Drachenblut Delikatessen	Sven Ottlieb	Order Administrator
DUMON	Du monde entier	Janine Labrune	Owner
EASTC	Eastern Connection	Ann Devon	Sales Agent
ERNSH	Ernst Handel	Roland Mendel	Sales Manager
FAMIA	Familia Arquibaldo	Aria Cruz	Marketing Assistant
FISSA	FISSA	Roel	Accounting Manager
FOLIG	Foli	ne Rancé	Assistant Sales Agent
FOLKO	Folk och fä HB	Maria Larsson	Owner
FRANK	Fran	Franken	Marketing Manager
FRANR	Fran	e Schmitt	Marketing Manager

Navigation Pane

Selected record number (18)

Number of total records (91)

Record: 18 of 91 No Filter Search

Unique five-character code based on customer name.

FIGURE 1.13 Datasheet View for Customers Table

Notice the Customers table shows records for 91 employees. The customer records contain multiple fields about each customer, including the Company Name, Contact Name, and so on. Occasionally a field does not contain a value for a particular record. For example, many customers do not have a Region assigned. Access shows a blank cell when data is missing.

Navigate and Locate Records

The Navigation bar at the bottom of Figure 1.14 shows that the Customers table has 91 records and that record number 18 is the current record. The navigation arrows enable you to go to the first record, the previous record, the next record, or the last record. Click the right arrow with a yellow asterisk to add a new (blank) record. Navigation works for more than just tables. Navigation arrows are also available in queries and forms.

FIGURE 1.14 Navigation Arrows in a Table

In addition to navigating, you also have access to the Find command. The Find command is located in the Find group on the Home tab and can be used to locate specific records. You can search for a single field or the entire record, match all or part of the selected field(s), move forward or back in a table, or specify a case-sensitive search. A Replace command is on the ribbon located next to the Find command. You can use this command to replace the found text with an updated value.

To find a record using the Find command, complete the following steps:

1. Open the table that contains the data you are searching for. Note that if you want to search a query, form, or report, you can follow the same steps, except open the appropriate object instead of the table.
2. Click any cell within the field you want to search. For example, if you want to search the City field in the Customers table, as shown in Figure 1.15, click any City value.
3. Ensure the Home tab is selected.
4. Click Find in the Find group.
5. Type the value you are searching for in the Find What box. Note that the entry is not case sensitive.
6. Click Find Next to find the next matching value.

The following table represents the Customers datasheet shown in the figure.

Customer ID	Company Name	Contact Name	Contact Title	Address	City	Region	Postal Code	Country	Phone
ALFKI	Alfreds Futterkiste	Maria Anders	Sales Representative	Obere Str. 57	Berlin		12209	Germany	030-007432 030
ANATR	Ana Trujillo Emparedados y helados	Ana Trujillo	Owner	Avda. de la Constitución 2222	México D.F.		05021	Mexico	(5) 555-472 (5)
ANTON	Antonio Moreno Taquería	Antonio Moreno	Owner	Mataderos 2312	México D.F.		05023	Mexico	(5) 555-393
AROUT	Around the Horn	Thomas Hardy	Sales Representative	120 Hanover Sq.	London		WA1 1DP	UK	(171) 555-7 (17
BERGS	Berglund snabbköp	Christina Berglund	Order Administrator	Berguvsvägen 8	Luleå		S-958 22	Sweden	0921-12 34 092
BLAUS	Blauer See Delikatessen	Hanna Moos	Sales Representative	Forsterstr. 57	Mannheim		68306	Germany	0621-08460 062
BLONP	Blondel père et fils	Frédérique Citeaux		24, place Kléber	Strasbourg		67000	France	88.60.15.31 88.6
BOLID	Bólido Comidas preparadas	Martín Sommer		C/ Araquil, 67	Madrid		28023	Spain	(91) 555 22 (91
BONAP	Bon app'	Laurence Lebihan	Owner	12, rue des Bouchers	Marseille		13008	France	91.24.45.40 91.2
BOTTM	Bottom-Dollar Markets	Eliza...		...ssen		BC	T2F 8M4	Canada	(604) 555-4 (60
BSBEV	B's Beverages	Victo...					EC2 5NT	UK	(171) 555-1
CACTU	Cactus Comidas para llevar	Patri...		...os Aires			1010	Argentina	(1) 135-555 (1)
CENTC	Centro comercial Moctezuma	Franc...		...o D.F.			05022	Mexico	(5) 555-339 (5)
CHOPS	Chop-suey Chinese	Yang...					3012	Switzerland	0452-07654
COMMI	Comércio Mineiro	Pedr...		...ulo	SP		05432-043	Brazil	(11) 555-76
CONSH	Consolidated Holdings	Eliza...					WX1 6LT	UK	(171) 555-2 (17
DRACD	Drachenblut Delikatessen	Sven...					52066	Germany	0241-03912 024
DUMON	Du monde entier	Janin...					44000	France	40.67.88.88 40.6
EASTC	Eastern Connection	Ann...					WX3 6FW	UK	(171) 555-0 (17
ERNSH	Ernst Handel	Rolan...					8010	Austria	7675-3425 767
FAMIA	Familia Arquibaldo	Aria Cruz	Marketing Assistant	Rua Orós, 92	São Paulo	SP	05442-030	Brazil	(11) 555-98
FISSA	FISSA Fabrica Inter. Salchichas S.A.	Diego Roel	Accounting Manager	C/ Moralzarzal, 86	Madrid		28034	Spain	(91) 555 94 (91
FOLIG	Folies gourmandes	Marti...	Sales A...		Lille		59000	France	20.16.10.16 20.1
FOLKO	Folk och fä HB	Maria...			Bräcke		S-844 67	Sweden	0695-34 67
FRANK	Frankenversand	Peter...	g Manag...		München		80805	Germany	089-087731 089
FRANR	France restauration	Carine Schmitt	Marketing Manager	54, rue Royale	Nantes		44000	France	40.32.21.21 40.3
FRANS	Franchi S.p.A.	Paolo Accorti	Sales Representative	Via Monte Bianco 34	Torino		10100	Italy	011-498826 011

Record: 1 of 91   No Filter   Search

Callouts: "Searching for Berlin", "Match: is set to Whole Field", "Look In: set to Current field (in this case, City)"

Find and Replace dialog box: Find | Replace tabs. Find What: Berlin. Look In: Current field. Match: Whole Field. Search: All. [ ] Match Case [✓] Search Fields As Formatted. Buttons: Find Next, Cancel.

FIGURE 1.15 The Find and Replace Dialog Box

Explore Table Design View

Design view gives you a detailed view of the table's structure and is used to create and modify a table's design by specifying the fields it will contain, the fields' data types, and their associated properties. Recall a table opens in Datasheet view by default. You switch between Datasheet and Design views by clicking View in the Views group on the Home tab (see Figure 1.16).

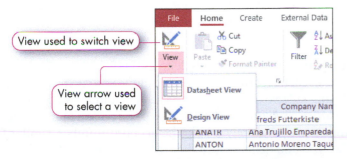

Callouts: "View used to switch view", "View arrow used to select a view"

FIGURE 1.16 View Button

View is a two-part command. Clicking the top part of the command toggles between Design and Datasheet view. Clicking the command arrow opens a menu from which you can select the view you want. Either way of performing this task is correct.

Figure 1.17 shows Design view for the Orders table. In the top portion, each row contains the field name, the data type, and an optional description for each field in the table. The fields listed in Design view correspond to the fields (or column headings) in Datasheet view. In the bottom portion, the Field Properties pane contains the properties (details) for a field.

Data types define the type of data that will be stored in a field, such as short text, numeric, currency, date/time, etc. Defining the type of data is important because Access will behave a specific way based on the type of data the field contains. Each field's data type determines the type of input accepted. For example, if you want to store the hire date of an employee, you would input a field name and select the Date/Time data type. Data types will be discussed further in a later chapter.

Next to the data type is Description, where a description of the field can be added. Some field names are obvious such as Student First Name. Other fields may require a bit more detail to better understand the values the field will capture.

Below the list of fields and data types are field properties. A *field property* defines the characteristics of a field in more detail. Field properties are displayed for the field selected and change as each field is selected. Figure 1.17 shows field properties for Order ID. For example, the field OrderDate has a Date/Time data type, then you can further choose the format for the date. A ShortDate format will display dates in the following format: mm/dd/yyyy or 4/19/2018. Furthermore, you can choose whether the field is required or not. Though some changes can be made to the field properties in Datasheet view, Design view gives you access to more properties.

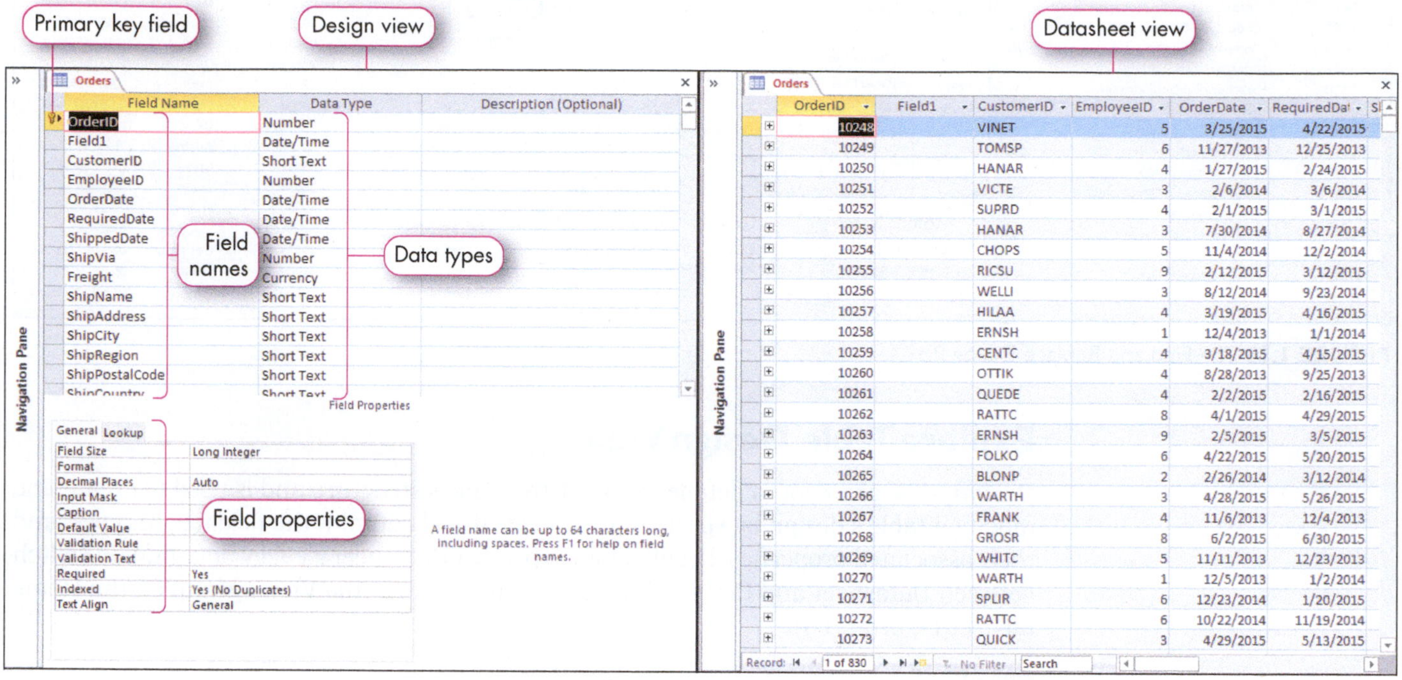

FIGURE 1.17 Orders Table Design and Datasheet View

Notice the key icon next to the OrderID field; this denotes this field is the primary key in the Orders table; it ensures that each record in the table is unique and can be distinguished from every other record. If you had two orders from the same customer, you could tell they are different because there are two separate OrderIDs. This is the reason many companies ask for your account number when you pay a bill. The account number, similar to an OrderID, uniquely identifies you and helps ensure that the payment is not applied to the wrong customer.

Rename and Describe Tables

To make a table easy to use, Access includes a few properties you can modify. Tables default to a name of Table 1 (or Table 2, etc.) if you do not specify otherwise. As you can imagine, this would make it very difficult to determine the contents of the table. Therefore, it is important to give a table a name that clearly defines the data it contains. It is simple to rename a table and give it a more descriptive name.

To rename a table, complete the following steps:

1. Verify that the table is closed. If it is not closed, right-click the table tab and select Close. A table cannot be renamed while it is open.
2. Right-click the table name in the Navigation Pane.
3. Select Rename from the shortcut menu.
4. Type the new name over the selected text and press Enter.

Tables also include a description, which provides documentation about the contents of a table. For example, most table names in the Northwind database are straightforward. However, the database comes with predefined descriptions for most tables to explain the purpose of each field. This can provide a user with additional clarification regarding the purpose of a table if they know where to look. By default, descriptions are not shown unless you right-click the table and select Table Properties. If you are working with a complex database, adding descriptions can be extremely helpful for new users. Figure 1.18 shows a table description.

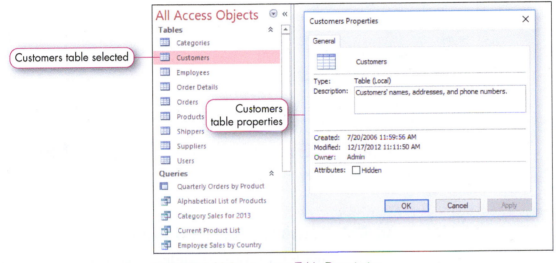

FIGURE 1.18 Previewing a Table Description

TIP: SHOWING OBJECT DETAILS

Most users will not need to see a description frequently. However, if necessary, you can change the Navigation Pane to display details by default. The details include the creation date, modification date, and description of the object. You may need to increase the size of the Navigation Pane to see the full description, so this works better on wider screens.

To show object details, right-click All Access Objects in the Navigation Pane and click View By. Select Details to display the full details. Resize the Navigation Pane so you can view the complete descriptions. Figure 1.19 shows a view of objects with descriptions.

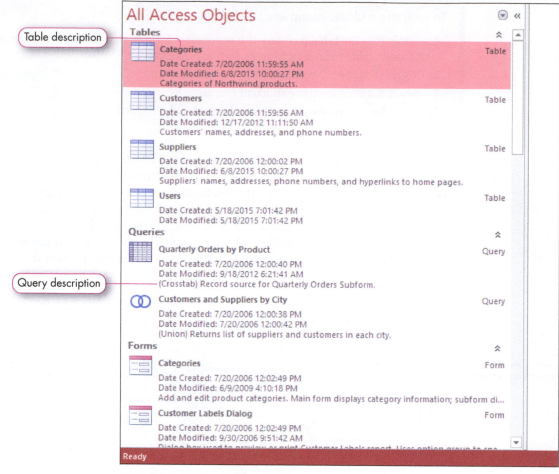

Table description

Query description

FIGURE 1.19 Detail View of Objects

Understand Relationships between Tables

A *relationship* is a connection between two tables using a common field. The benefit of a relationship is the ability to efficiently combine data from related tables to create queries, forms, and reports. If you are using an existing database, relationships are likely created already. The design of the Latte database, which contains multiple tables, is illustrated in Figure 1.20. The diagram shows the relationships that were created between tables using join lines. Join lines enable you to create a relationship between two tables using a common field. For example, the Customers table is joined to the Orders table using the common field CustomerID. These table connections enable you to query the database for information stored in multiple tables. This feature gives the manager the ability to ask questions like, "What orders are there for Katie's Casual Wear?" In this case, the name of the customer (Katie's Casual Wear) is stored in the Customers table, but the orders are stored in the Orders table. Notice in Figure 1.21, a plus sign ⊞ displays to the left of each Customer. If you click the plus sign, a subdatasheet will display with a list of related records from a related table. If there is not a plus sign, then a related record does not exist. Figure 1.21 is the Datasheet view of the Customers table. Because of the relationship with the Orders table, you can see what orders are associated with each customer by clicking the plus sign ⊞ next to each customer.

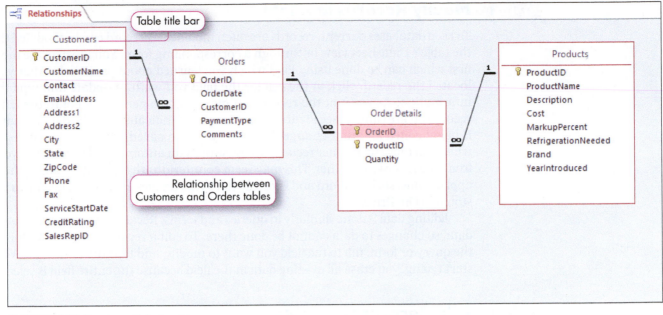

FIGURE 1.20 Database Relationships

CustomerID	Customer Name	Contact	E-mail Address	Address1	Address2	City	State	Zip Code
C0001	Abel & Young	Jeff Jones		5000 Jefferson Lane	Suite 2000	Miami	FL	33131-
C0002	Department of CIS	Eleanor Milgrom		1238 Walsh Drive	Suite 2202	Miami	FL	33131-
C0003	Advantage Sales	Neil Goodman	service@advantagesales.com	4215 South 81 Street		Miami	FL	33131-
C0004	Kinzer & Sons	Nicholas Colon		9020 N.W. 75 Street	Suite 302	Coral Springs	FL	33065-
C0005	Milgrom Associates	Ashley Geoghegan	ageoghegan@milgrom.net	7500 Center Lane		Coral Springs	FL	33070-
C0006	Lugo Computer Sales	Derek Anderson	service@lugocomputer.net	6000 Tigertail Avenue		Coconut Grove	FL	33133-
C0007	Bethune Appliance Sales	Michael Ware	bethune@bethune.com	276 Brickell Avenue	Suite 1403	Miami	FL	33131-
C0008	Baker Auto Supply	Robert Slane	rslane@bakerauto.com	4508 N.W. 7 Street		Miami	FL	33131-
C0009	Howard Animal Hospital	Luis Couto	lcouto@howardanimals.net	455 Bargello Avenue		Coral Gables	FL	33124-
C0010	Katie's Casual Wear	Jeffrey Muddell	katie@katiewear.com	9522 S.W. 142 Street		Miami	FL	33176-

Order ID	Order Date	Payment Type	Comments	Click to Add
O0013	1/12/2019	Check		
O0024	1/23/2019	Check		
O0029	1/25/2019	Cash		
(New)	9/18/2018			

CustomerID	Customer Name	Contact	E-mail Address	Address1	Address2	City	State	Zip Code
C0011	Little, Joiner, & Jones	Lauren Center	lcenter@ljj.com	7245 NW 8 Street		Miami	FL	33133-
C0012	Kline Bait & Tackle	Benjamin Lee	blee@klineb&t.com	1000 Call Street		Coconut Grove	FL	33133-
C0013	Computer Informations Sys	Eleanor Milgrom	emilgrom@cis.edu	1238 Walsh Drove	Suite 2202	Miami	FL	33186-
C0014	Coulter Office Supplies	Maryann Coulter	mcoulter@coulter.com	1000 Main Street		Coral Springs	FL	33071-
(New)								

FIGURE 1.21 Related Tables

Relationships will be discussed further in the next chapter. However, you can view the existing relationships in any database to familiarize yourself with the way tables work together. To view existing database relationships, click Relationships in the Relationships group on the Database Tools tab. Then, reposition tables by dragging the table's title bar (as shown in Figure 1.20) to a new location so all relationships are visible. This is not required but doing so may make the relationships easier to follow. Save and close the relationships window when you are finished.

Modifying, Adding, and Saving Data

Data in a database will be always changing. You should expect new records to be added or current records to be modified. If you are working with a Customer database, you would expect new customers to be added constantly. If you are dealing with a university database, new students will be added, some will graduate, and others will transfer from one program of study to another.

STEP 3 ## Modify Records in a Table

To keep databases current, records are often modified. A record can be modified through the table's Datasheet view or through a corresponding form. You must locate the record first which can be done using Find which you learned about previously. After you have located the record, click in the cell for the field you want to update and type the new information. As you edit the record you may notice a pencil symbol to the left of the record you are editing (see Figure 1.22). The pencil indicates that the data in that record is being edited and that changes have not yet been saved. The pencil icon disappears when you move to another record. Access saves data automatically as soon as you move from one record to another. This may seem counterintuitive at first because other Office applications, such as Word and Excel, do not save changes automatically unless they are stored in OneDrive.

Editing data is done similarly in queries and forms. Recall that reports cannot change data, so changes to data cannot be done there. To edit a record in a query or form, open the query or form, tab to the field you want to modify, and type the new data. When you start typing, you erase all existing data in the field because the entire field is selected.

STEP 4 ## Add Records to a Table

Often it is necessary to add new records to a table such as a new student record. New records can be added through the table's Datasheet view or through a corresponding form. Using a corresponding form displays records one at a time and can help to ensure that edits are being made to the correct record. You will learn more about using forms later in this chapter. However, often a quick change or edit can be done directly in the table in Datasheet view.

To add a new record to a table, complete the following steps:

1. Open the table in Datasheet view by double-clicking it in the Navigation Pane.
2. Click New in the Records group on the Home tab.
3. Begin typing.
4. Press Tab to move to the next field and enter data. Repeat this step until you have input all required data for this record.
5. Move to another record by clicking elsewhere or pressing Tab in the last field in a record. As soon as you move to another record, Access automatically saves the changes to the record you created or changed.

If you are unable to type in a field, then you have selected a field with a data type of AutoNumber, which Access assigns for you. If this is the case, click in a different field and begin typing. The asterisk record indicator changes to a pencil symbol to show that you are in editing mode (see Figure 1.22).

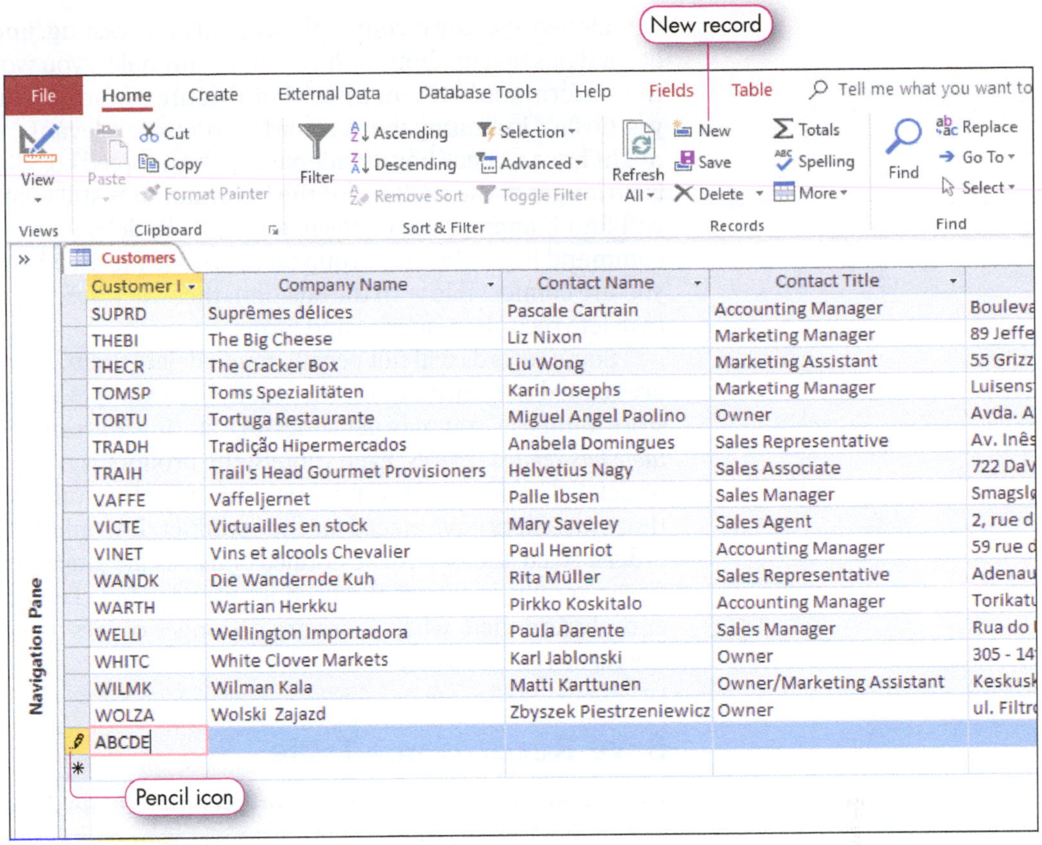

FIGURE 1.22 Adding a Record Using a Table

As with most of Microsoft Office applications, there are several ways to perform the same task. There are many ways to facilitate moving around a datasheet as you navigate from record to record. In addition to using commands on the ribbon, you can use keyboard shortcuts. See Table 1.1 for a list of some shortcuts you can use when performing data entry.

TABLE 1.1	Keyboard Shortcuts for Entering Data
Keystroke	**Result**
Up arrow (↑)	Moves insertion point up one row.
Down arrow (↓)	Moves insertion point down one row.
Left arrow (←)	Moves insertion point left one field in the same row.
Right arrow (→)	Moves insertion point right one field in the same row.
Tab or Enter	Moves insertion point right one field in the same row.
Shift+Tab	Moves insertion point left one field in the same row.
Home	Moves insertion point to the first field in the current row.
End	Moves insertion point to the last field in the current row.
Esc	Cancels any changes made in the current field while in Edit mode.
Ctrl+Z	Undo. Reverses the last unsaved edit.

STEP 5 ## Delete Records from a Table

Deciding to delete records is not a simple decision. Many times, deleting records is a bad idea. Say you are working in the database for an animal shelter. After an animal has been adopted, you may be tempted to delete the animal from the database. However, you would then lose any record of the animal ever existing, and if the owner calls asking if the animal has had its shots, or how old the animal is, you would no longer be able to provide that information. Often, instead of deleting information, it would be better to create a yes/no field indicating that a record is no longer relevant. For example, the shelter database might have a check box for adopted. If the adopted box displays a checkmark, the animal is no longer at the shelter, but the information is still available. That said, sometimes you will find it appropriate to delete a record. To delete a record from a table, use the Delete command in the Records group on the Home tab. Read any warning that might pop up. If you are comfortable with the deletion, then click Yes. Note that you can take similar steps to delete records in queries and forms.

Some records will not permit you to delete them, even if you wanted to, because they are related to records in another table. For example, if you try to delete a product from a store database, you may get a message stating *You cannot delete this record because another table has related records*. Even though the product is no longer available for sale, it cannot be deleted because related records exist in another table. In this case, there may be orders that customers have placed for that product. It would be best to know about outstanding orders, so customers can be notified of a possible alternative product rather than an order never arriving because the product was deleted. The order can be modified or deleted entirely and then, when there are no longer orders associated with the related product, the record can be deleted.

Save Records in a Table

When you make a change to a record's content in an Access table (for example, changing a customer's phone number), Access saves your changes as soon as you move to a different record. You will only be prompted to save if you make changes to the design of the table (such as changing the font or background color).

The Save function in Access works differently than in the other Office applications. Access works primarily from storage (i.e., the hard drive). As you enter and update the data in an Access database, the changes are automatically saved to the storage location you specified when you saved the database. If a power failure occurs, you will lose only the changes to the record that you are currently editing.

> **TIP: UNDO WORKS DIFFERENTLY**
> You can click Undo to reverse the most recent change (the phone number you just modified, for example) to a single record immediately after making changes to that record. However, unlike other Office programs that enable multiple Undo steps, you cannot use Undo to reverse multiple edits in Access. Undo (and Redo) are found on the Quick Access Toolbar.

STEP 6 ▶ Using Database Utilities

Database administrators spend a lot of time maintaining databases. Software utility programs make this process simpler. As Access is a database management utility, there are a few tools that can be used to protect, maintain, and improve the performance of a database.

Back Up a Database

Back Up Database is a utility that creates a duplicate copy of the entire database to protect data from loss or damage. Imagine what would happen to a firm that loses track of orders placed, a charity that loses the list of donor contributions, or a hospital that loses the digital records of its patients. Making backups is especially important when you have multiple users working with the database. Mistakes can be made, and records can unintentionally be deleted. When you use the Back Up Database utility, Access provides a file name for the backup that uses the same file name as the database you are backing up, an underscore, and the current date. This makes it easy for you to keep track of backups by the date they were created.

Keep in mind, backing up a database on the same storage device as the original database can leave you with no protection in the event of hardware failure. Backups are typically stored on a separate device, such as an external hard drive or network drive.

To back up a database, complete the following steps:

1. Click the File tab.
2. Click Save As.
3. Click Back Up Database under the Advanced group (see Figure 1.23).
4. Click Save As. Revise the location and file name if you want to change either and click Save.

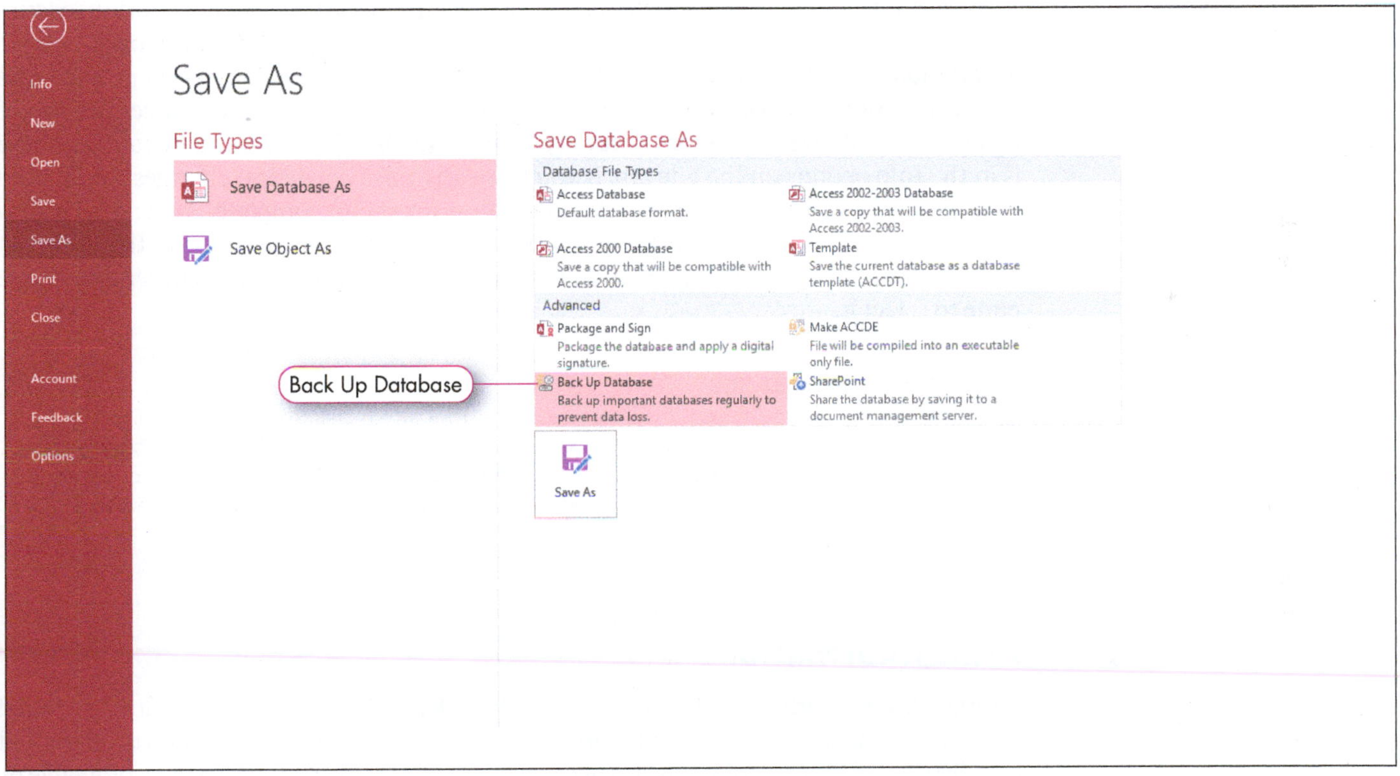

FIGURE 1.23 Back Up Database Option

TIP: RESTORE A DATABASE FROM A BACKUP
In the case of a total database failure, you can use a backup as the new database. If just particular information is missing, you can recover information to an existing database. To do so, open the database that has lost or corrupted information, delete the corrupted object from the current database and import the missing object from the backup.

To delete the corrupted object from the current database and import the missing object from the backup, complete the following steps:

1. Click the External Data tab, and click New Data Source in the Import & Link group. Select From Database and then click Access.
2. Click Browse, select the backup file, and click Open.
3. Ensure the option to Import tables, queries, forms, reports, macros, and modules into the current database is selected, and click OK.
4. Click the tab related to the object you want to restore (Tables, Queries, Forms, Reports, Macros, or Modules).
5. Click the object to select it and click OK.
6. Click Close to close the Get External Data – Access Database dialog box. The object is now restored to the current database.

Compact and Repair a Database

Occasionally Access databases experience corruption. Database corruption occurs when the data are stored improperly, resulting in the loss of data or database functionality. With everyday use, databases may become corrupt, so Access provides the *Compact and Repair Database* utility. Compact and Repair Database reduces the size of a database and fixes any errors that may exist in the file. Compact and Repair Database is in the Info options on the File tab. If you have any unsaved design changes, you will be prompted to save before the compact and repair process can complete. Alternatively, you can have Access perform a Compact and Repair automatically by clicking the Compact on Close check box under Application Options in the Options for the current database pane to select it.

> **TIP: SPLIT DATABASES**
>
> Another utility built into Access is the Database Splitter tool, which puts the tables in one file (the back-end database), and the queries, forms, and reports in a second file (the front-end). This way, each user can create their own queries, forms, and reports without potentially changing an object someone else needs. The Split Database option is found on the Database Tools tab. Click Access Database in the Move Data group.

Print Information

Though Access is primarily designed to store data electronically, you can produce a printed copy of your data. Reports are database objects that are specifically designed to be printed and distributed, but occasionally it is necessary to print out the Datasheet view of a table or query to check results. Each object in the database prints individually, so you would select the object you want to print from the Navigation Pane, and access the print commands from the File tab. It is good practice to preview your work before printing a document. This way, if you notice an error, you can fix it and not waste paper.

Quick Concepts

1. Describe each of the four main types of objects in an Access database. *pp. 75–76*
2. Discuss the difference between Datasheet view and Design view in a table. *pp. 79, 81*
3. Explain why it is important to define data types in Access. *p. 81*
4. Explain the purpose of using the compact and repair utility. *p. 90*

Skills covered: Open a Database • Save a Database with a New Name • Enable Content in a Database • Examine the Access Interface • Explore Table Datasheet View • Navigate Through Records • Explore Table Design View • Understand Relationships between Tables • Add Records in a Table • Modify Records in a Table • Delete Records from a Table • Back Up a Database • Print Information

1 Databases Are Everywhere!

Northwind purchases food items from suppliers around the world and sells them to restaurants and specialty food shops. Northwind depends on the data stored in its Access database to process orders and make daily decisions. You will open the Northwind database, examine the Access interface, review the existing objects in the database, and explore Access views. You will add, edit, and delete records using both tables and forms. Finally, you will back up the database.

STEP 1 OPEN, SAVE, AND ENABLE CONTENT IN A DATABASE

As you begin your job, you first will become familiar with the Northwind database. This database will help you learn the fundamentals of working with database files. Refer to Figure 1.24 as you complete Step 1.

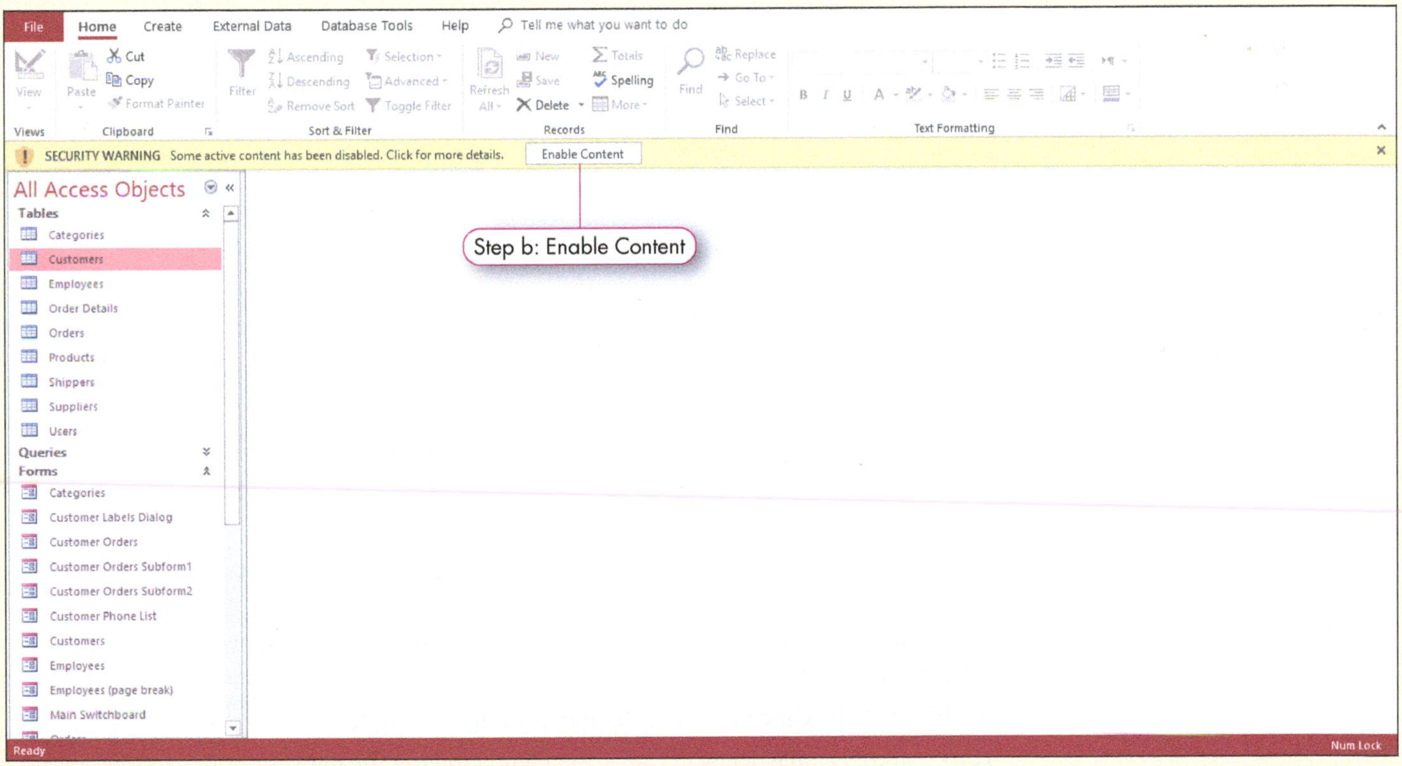

FIGURE 1.24 Northwind Database

a. Start your computer. Click **Start**, and click **Access** from the list of applications. Click **Open Other Files** and click **Browse**. Navigate to the location of your student files. Double-click *a01h1Traders*. Click the **File tab**, click **Save As**, and then click **Access Database**. Click **Save As** and save the file as **a01h1Traders_LastFirst**.

When you save files, use your last and first names. For example, as the Access author, I would save my database as "a01h1Traders_RutledgeAmy".

The Security Warning message bar displays below the ribbon, indicating that some database content is disabled.

TROUBLESHOOTING: If you make any major mistakes in this exercise, you can close the file, open *a01h1Traders* again, and then start this exercise over.

b. Click **Enable Content** on the Security Warning message bar.

When you open an Access file, you should enable the content.

STEP 2 RECOGNIZE DATABASE OBJECT TYPES

Now that you have opened the Northwind database, you should examine the Navigation Pane, objects, and views to become familiar with these fundamental Access features. Refer to Figure 1.25 as you complete Step 2.

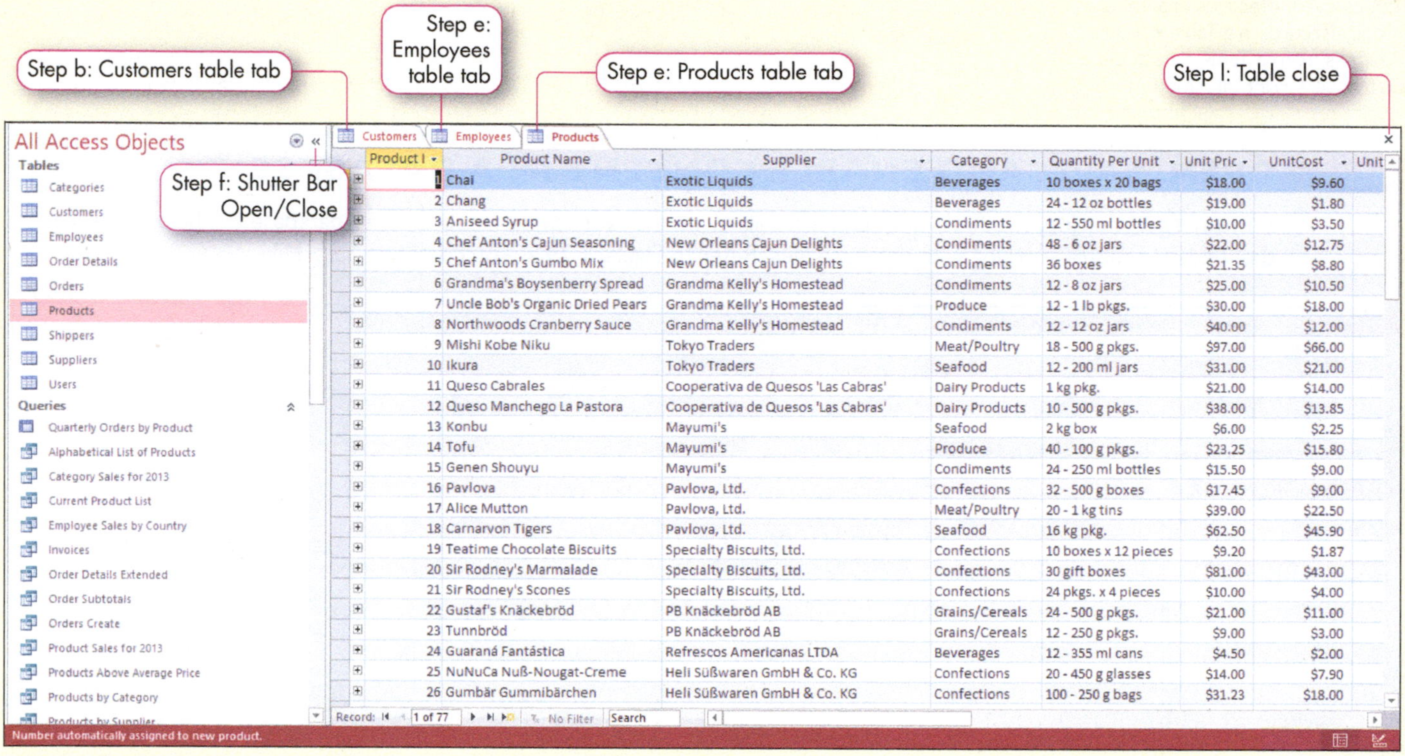

FIGURE 1.25 Northwind Objects

a. Scroll through the Navigation Pane and notice the Access objects listed under each expanded group.

The Tables group and the Forms group are expanded, displaying all the table and form objects.

b. Double-click the **Customers table** in the Navigation Pane.

The Customers table opens in Datasheet view, showing the data contained in the table. The Customers tab displays below the ribbon indicating the table object is open. Each customer's record displays on a table row. The columns of the table display the fields that comprise the records.

c. Click the **View arrow** and select **Design view**, in the Views group on the Home tab.

The view of the Customers table switches to Design view. The top portion of Design view displays and the field names match the field headings previously seen in Datasheet view. Additionally, the field's data type, and an optional description of what the field should contain can be seen. The bottom portion of Design view displays the field properties (details) for the selected field.

d. Click the **View arrow** and select **Datasheet view** in the Views group on the Home tab again.

Your view returns to Datasheet view, which shows the data stored in the table.

e. Double-click **Employees** in the Tables group of the Navigation Pane. Double-click **Products** from the same location.

The Employees and Products tables open. The tabs for three table objects display below the ribbon: Customers, Employees, and Products.

f. Click **Shutter Bar Open/Close** ⟪ on the title bar of the Navigation Pane to hide the Navigation Pane. Click ⟫ again to show the Navigation Pane.

The Navigation Pane collapses and expands to enable you to view more in the open object window, or to view your database objects.

g. Scroll down in the Navigation Pane and locate Reports.

The Reports group is expanded, and all report objects are displayed.

h. Scroll up until you see Forms. Click **Forms** in the Navigation Pane.

The Forms group collapses and individual form objects no longer display.

i. Click the **Database Tools tab** and click **Relationships** in the Relationships group.

j. Examine the join lines showing the relationships that connect the various tables. For example, the Orders table is connected to the Order Details table using the OrderID field as the common field.

k. Click **Relationship Report** in the Tools group. The report opens in a new tab. Right-click on the tab and select **Save** and click **OK**.

The report is now saved in the Reports section on the Navigation Pane.

l. Click **Close** ☒ the at the top right of the report to close the Relationships Report. Click **Close** ☒ the at the top right of the tab to close the Relationships window. Click **Close** ☒ the at the top right of the table to close the Products table.

<table>
<tr><td colspan="2">STEP 3</td><td colspan="11">**MODIFY RECORDS IN A TABLE**</td></tr>
</table>

You want to learn to edit the data in the Northwind database, because data can change. For example, employees will change their address when they move, and customers will change their order data from time to time. Refer to Figure 1.26 as you complete Step 3.

Step i: Table close

Step h: Record 1 remains unchanged

Step e: Your data replaces Margaret Peacock in record 4

Employee I ▾	Last Nam ▾	First Nam ▾	Title	Title Of Courte ▾	Birth Dat ▾	Hire Date ▾	Address	City	Region ▾	Postal (
1	Davolio	Nancy	Sales Representative	Ms.	12/8/1983	5/1/2015	507 - 20th Ave. E.	Seattle	WA	98122
2	Fuller	Andrew	Vice President, Sales	Dr.	2/19/1957	8/14/2015	908 W. Capital Way	Tacoma	WA	98401
3	Leverling	Janet	Sales Representative	Ms.	8/30/1970	4/1/2012	722 Moss Bay Blvd.	Kirkland	WA	98033
4	Peacock	Margaret	Sales Representative	Mrs.	9/19/1986	5/3/2011	4110 Old Redmond Rd.	Redmond	WA	98052
5	Buchanan	Steven	Sales Manager	Mr.	3/4/1970	10/17/2008	14 Garrett Hill	London	EU	SW1 8J
6	Suyama	Michael	Sales Representative	Mr.	7/2/1978	10/17/2009	Coventry House	London	EU	EC2 7JR
7	King	Robert	Sales Representative	Mr.	5/29/1985	1/2/2008	Edgeham Hollow	London	EU	RG1 9S
8	Callahan	Laura	Inside Sales Coordinato	Ms.	1/9/1990	3/5/2014	4726 - 11th Ave. N.E.	Seattle	WA	98105
9	Dodsworth	Anne	Sales Representative	Ms.	1/27/1988	11/15/2013	7 Houndstooth Rd.	London	EU	WG2 7L
(New)										

FIGURE 1.26 Northwind Employees Table

a. Click the **Employees tab** to view the Employees table.

b. Double-click **Peacock** (the value of the Last Name field in the fourth row); the entire name highlights. Type your last name to replace Peacock.

The pencil symbol in the record selector box indicates that the record is being edited but has not yet been saved.

c. Press **Tab** to move to the next field in the fourth row. Replace **Margaret** with your first name and press **Tab**.

You have made changes to two fields in the same record.

d. Click **Undo** on the Quick Access Toolbar.

Your first and last names revert to Margaret Peacock because you have not yet left the record.

e. Type your first and last names again to replace Margaret Peacock. Press **Tab**.

You should now be in the title field, and the title, Sales Representative, is selected. The record has not been saved, as indicated by the pencil symbol in the record selector box.

f. Click anywhere in the third row where Janet Leverling's data are stored.

The pencil symbol disappears, indicating that your changes have been saved.

g. Click the **Address field** in the first row, Nancy Davolio's record. Select the entire address and type **4004 East Morningside Dr.** Click anywhere on the second record, Andrew Fuller's record.

h. Click **Undo**.

Nancy Davolio's address reverts to 507 - 20th Ave. E. However, the Undo command is now faded. You can no longer undo the change that you made replacing Margaret Peacock's name with your own.

i. Click **Close** ☒ at the top right of the table to close the Employees table.

The Employees table closes. You are not prompted to save your changes; they have already been saved for you because Access works in storage, not memory. If you reopen the Employees table, you will see your name in place of Margaret Peacock's name.

STEP 4 ▶ ADD RECORDS TO A TABLE

You have been asked to add information about a new line of products to the Northwind database. You add records to the Products table through the Products Form. The two objects are directly connected. Refer to Figure 1.27 as you complete Step 4.

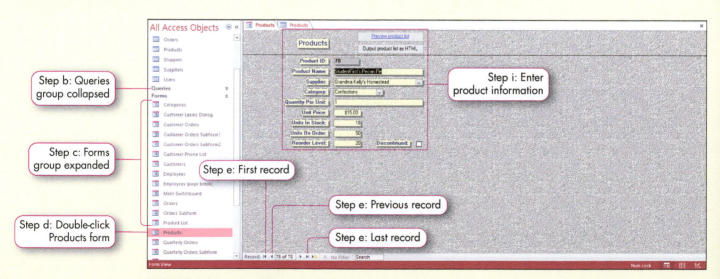

FIGURE 1.27 Adding Data Using Products Form

a. Right-click the **Customers tab** and click **Close All**.

b. Click the **Queries group** in the Navigation Pane to collapse it. Click the **Reports group** in the Navigation Pane to collapse it as well.

c. Click the **Forms group** in the Navigation Pane to expand the list of available forms.

d. Double-click the **Products form** to open it.

e. Click the Next record arrow in the Navigation bar at the bottom of the form window. Click **Last record**, click **Previous record**, and then click **First record**.

f. Click **Find** in the Find group on the Home tab, type **Grandma** in the Find What box, click the **Match arrow**, and then select **Any Part of Field**. Click **Find Next**.

You should see the data for Grandma's Boysenberry Spread. Selecting the Any Part of Field option will return a match even if it is contained as part of a word.

g. Click **Cancel** to close the Find dialog box.

h. Click **New** in the Records group on the Home tab.

i. Type the following information for a new product. Click, or press **Tab**, to move into the next cell. Notice as soon as you begin typing, Access will assign a ProductID to this product.

Field Name	Value to Type
Product Name	**Your name's Pecan Pie** (replacing Your name with your first name) For example, as the Access author, my Product name would be Amy's Pecan Pie.
Supplier	**Grandma Kelly's Homestead** (click the arrow to select from the list of Suppliers)
Category	**Confections** (click the arrow to select from the list of Categories)
Quantity Per Unit	I
Unit Price	**15.00**
Units In Stock	I8
Units On Order	50
Reorder Level	20
Discontinued	**No** (Ensure the checkbox is unchecked)

The Products form and Products table are linked so the new record was added to the Products table.

j. Click anywhere on the **Pecan Pie record** you just typed. Click the **File tab**, select **Print**, and then click **Print Preview**.

The first four records display in the Print Preview.

k. Click **Last Page** in the Navigation bar and click **Previous Page** to show the new record you entered.

The beginning of the Pecan Pie record is now visible. The record continues to the next page.

l. Click **Close Print Preview** in the Close Preview group.

m. Close the Products form.

To help you understand how Access stores data, you verify that the new product is in the Products table. You also attempt to delete a record. Refer to Figure 1.28 as you complete Step 5.

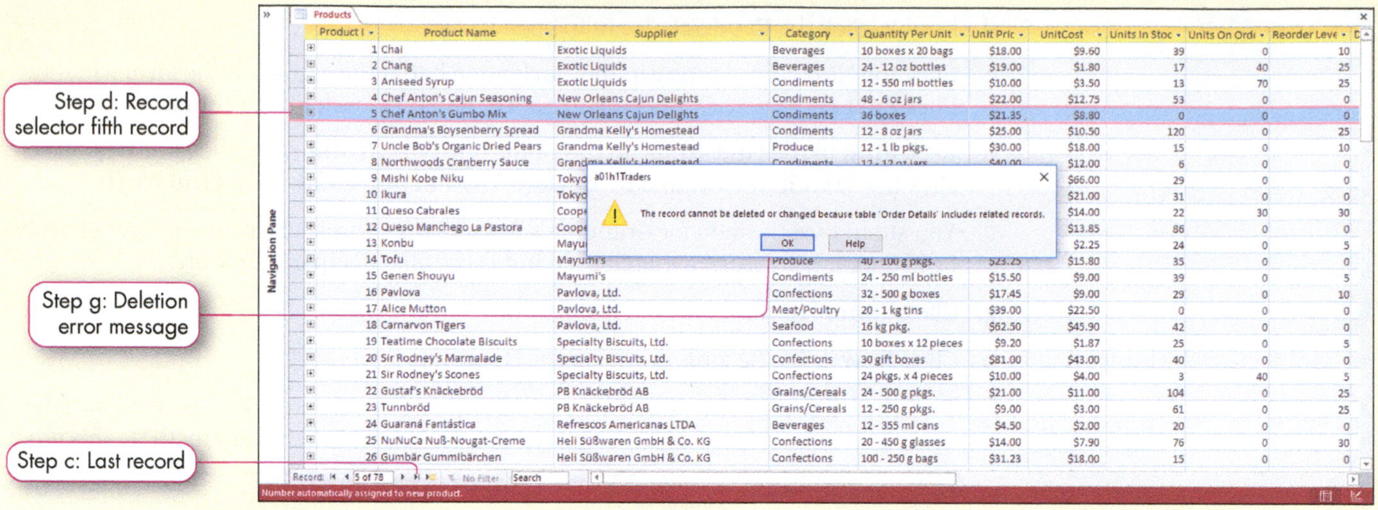

Step d: Record selector fifth record

Step g: Deletion error message

Step c: Last record

FIGURE 1.28 Deleting Data

a. Click the **Forms group** in the Navigation Pane to collapse it. Expand the **Tables group**.

b. Double-click the **Products table** to open it.

c. Click **Last record** in the Navigation bar.

The Pecan Pie record you entered in the Products form is listed as the last record in the Products table. The Products form was created from the Products table. Your newly created record, Pecan Pie, is stored in the Products table even though you added it using the form.

d. Navigate to the fifth record in the table and place the pointer in the record, Chef Anton's Gumbo Mix.

e. Scroll right using the horizontal scroll bar until you see the Discontinued field.

The check mark in the Discontinued check box tells you that this product has been discontinued.

f. Click the **record selector** to the left of the fifth record.

A border surrounds the record and the record is shaded, indicating it is selected.

g. Click **Delete** in the Records group and read the error message.

The error message tells you that you cannot delete this record because the table "Order Details" has related records. (Customers ordered this product in the past.) Even though the product is now discontinued and no stock remains, it cannot be deleted from the Products table because related records exist in the Order Details table.

h. Click **OK**.

i. Navigate to the last record and click the **record selector**.

The Pecan Pie record you added earlier is displayed.

j. Click **Delete** in the Records group. Read the warning.

The warning box tells you that this action cannot be undone. Although this product can be deleted because it was just entered and no orders were created for it, you do not want to delete the record.

k. Click **No**. You do not want to delete this record. Close the Products table.

> **TROUBLESHOOTING:** If you clicked Yes and deleted the record, return to Step 4d. Re-open the form and re-enter the information for this record. This will be important later in this lesson.

STEP 6 USE DATABASE UTILITIES

You will protect the Northwind database by using the Back Up Database utility. Refer to Figure 1.29 as you complete Step 6.

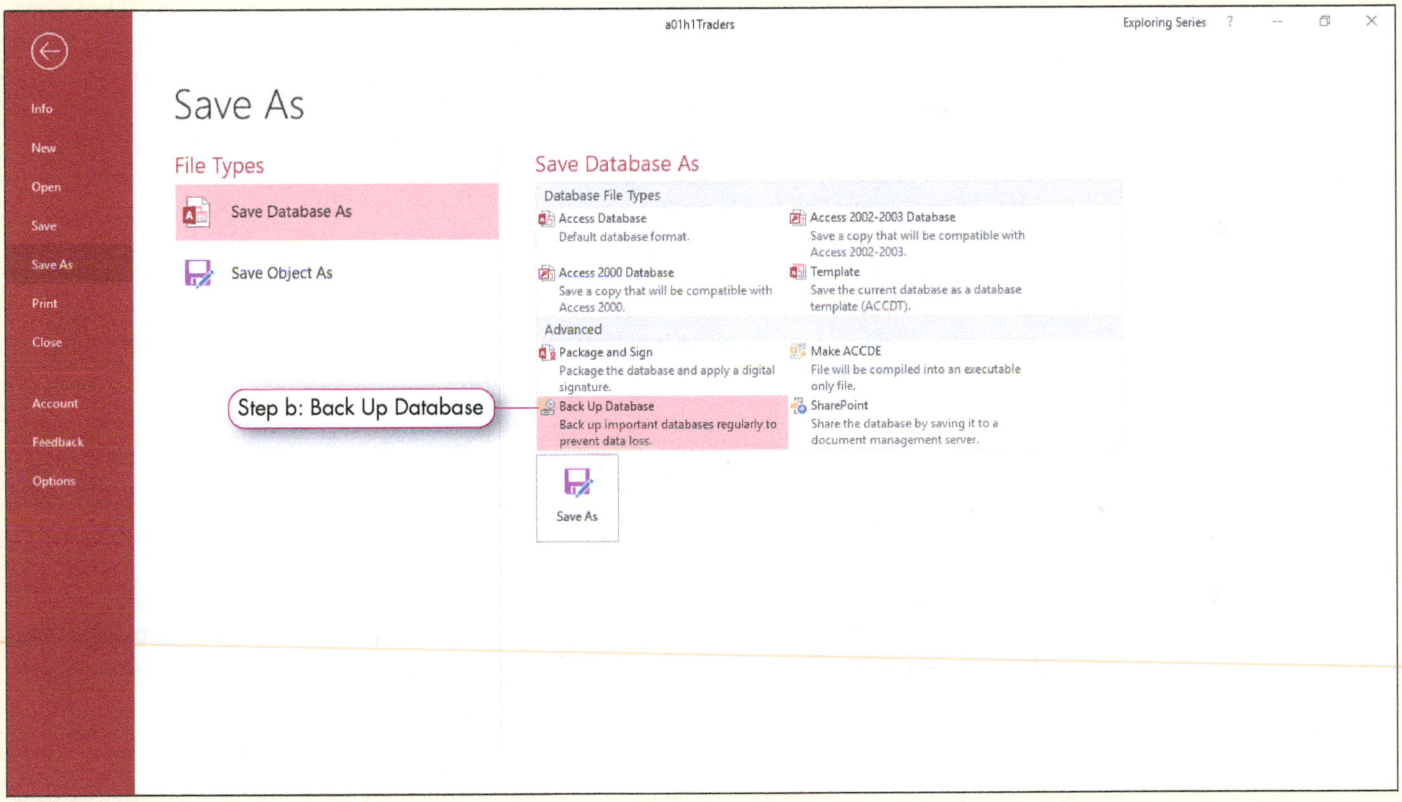

FIGURE 1.29 Backing Up a Database

a. Click the **File tab** and click **Save As**.

b. Double-click **Back Up Database** under the Advanced section to open the Save As dialog box.

The backup utility assigns the default name by adding a date to your file name.

c. Verify that the Save in folder displays the location where you want your file saved and click **Save**. You will submit this file to your instructor at the end of the last Hands-On Exercise.

You just created a backup of the database after completing Hands-On Exercise 1. The original database file remains onscreen.

d. Keep the database open if you plan to continue with the next Hands-On Exercise. If not, close the database and exit Access.

Filters and Sorts

Access provides many tools that you can use to change the order of information and to identify and extract only the data needed. You can find specific information, such as which suppliers are in Denton, TX, or which customers have placed orders in the last seven days. There may be other times you simply want to sort information rather than extract information.

In this section, you will learn how to use filters to create subsets of information that match one or more criteria. Next, you will learn how to organize data by sorting on single or multiple categories. Finally, you will learn how to locate records in a table based on criteria.

Working with Filters

Suppose you wanted to see a list of the products in the Confections category in the Northwind database. To obtain this list, you would open the Products table in Datasheet view and create a filter. A *filter* enables you to specify conditions that need to be met in order to display the desired records. These conditions are known as criteria (or criterion, singular) and are a number, a text phrase, or an expression (such as >50) used to select records from a table. Therefore, to view a list of all Confections, you would apply a filter to the Products table, displaying only records with a Category value of Confections. In this case, Category is the field, and Confections is the criterion that is applied to the field.

You can use filters to analyze data quickly. Applying a filter does not delete any records; filters only hide records that do not match the criteria. One or more filters can be applied to the same set of data. Filters narrow down the data so you can focus on specific data rather than view all of the data in a large set of records. Two types of filters are discussed in this section: Selection filter and Filter By Form.

STEP 1 ▶ Use a Selection Filter to Find Exact Matches

A *Selection filter* displays in Datasheet view only the records that exactly match a criterion you select. Access uses the current selection as the criterion. For example, if you filter a Job Title field and you select "equals Owner," you would only find customers who have a Job Title of Owner (but not any other variation such as Co-Owner). Selection filters are not case sensitive, so any variation of capitalization (OWNER, owner) would also display in the search results.

> **To use a Selection filter to find an exact match, complete the following steps:**
>
> 1. Click in any field in Datasheet view that contains the criterion on which you want to filter.
> 2. Click Selection in the Sort & Filter group on the Home tab.
> 3. Select Equals "criterion" from the list of options (*criterion* will be replaced by the value of the field).

Figure 1.30 displays a Customers table with 91 records. The records in the table are displayed in sequence according to the Job title. The Navigation bar at the bottom indicates that the active record is the second 34th row in the table. Owner in the Job Title field is selected.

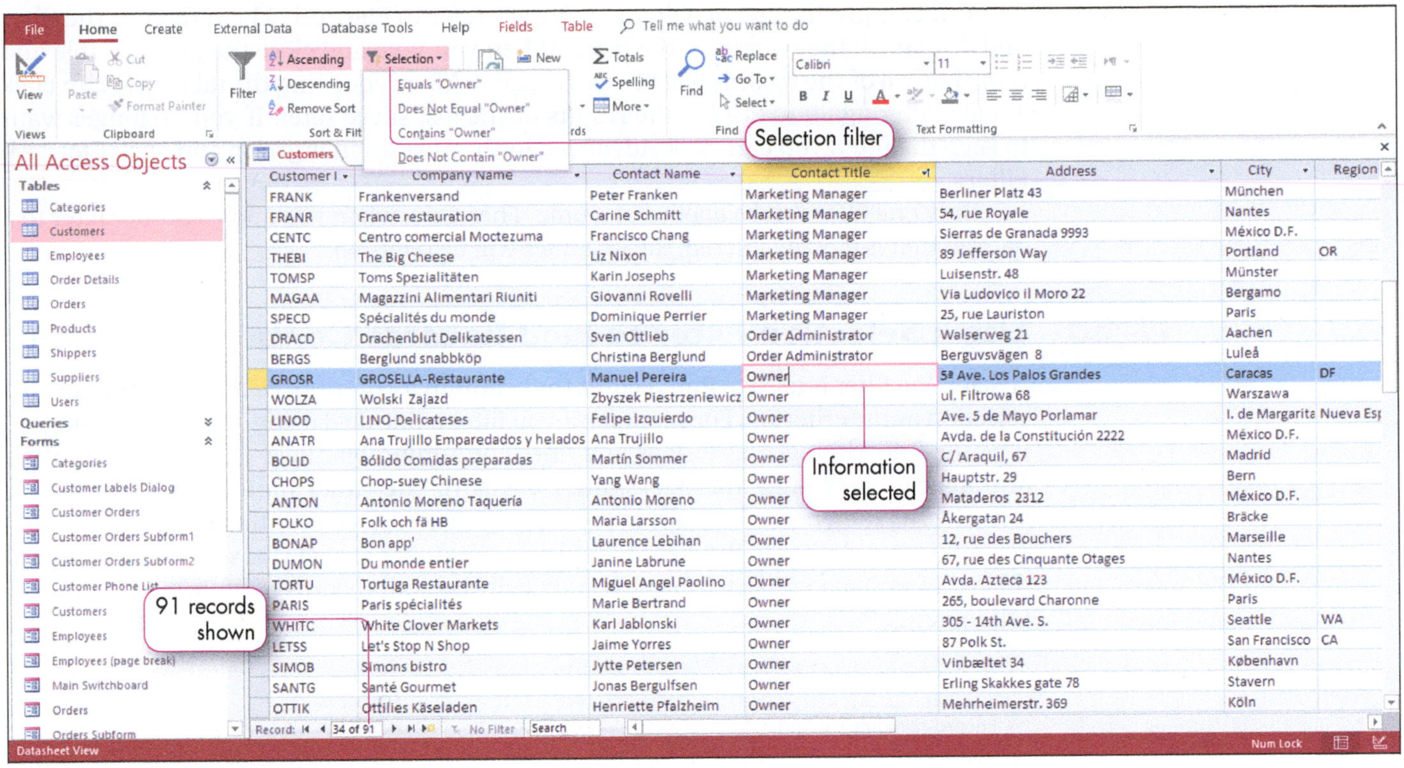

FIGURE 1.30 Unfiltered Customers Table

Figure 1.31 displays a filtered view of the Customers table, showing records with the job title Owner. The Navigation bar shows that this is a filtered list containing 17 records matching the criterion. The Customers table still contains the original 91 records, but only 17 records are visible with the filter applied.

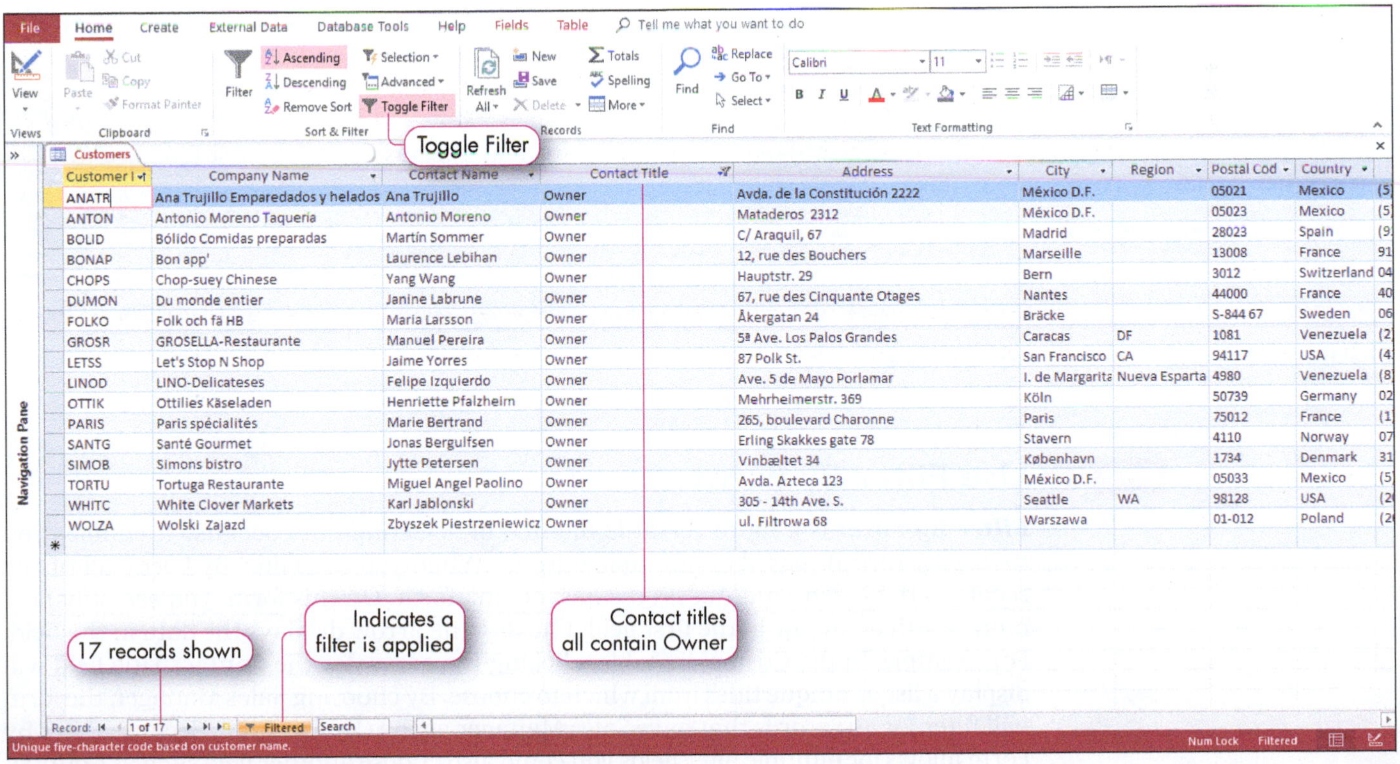

FIGURE 1.31 Filtered Customers Table

You can use the Toggle Filter command (refer to Figure 1.31) to remove the filter and display all the records in the table. When you save and close the filtered table and reopen it, all of the records will be visible again. After reopening the table, you can click Toggle Filter again to display the results of the last saved filter. If you no longer want to keep the filter, you can click Advanced in the Sort & Filter group and click Clear All Filters.

Only one filter can be applied at a time. Therefore, when you apply another filter to a dataset that is already filtered, the first filter will be removed.

STEP 2 ## Use a Selection Filter to Find Records Containing a Value

A Selection filter is used to find records that contain a criterion. Access uses the current selection as the criterion. For example, if you filter a title field using "contains Manager," it would find Manager, as well as any titles containing Manager (such as Accounting Managers, Marketing Managers, etc,). As with the exact match, this is not case sensitive, as shown in the results in Figure 1.32. The steps to locating values containing certain text is similar to the steps to find exact matches except you select *Contains* from the list of options presented. Your results will show all records containing a partial or full match.

Record contains Manager

Customer ID	Company Name	Contact Name	Contact Title	Address	City	Region	Postal Code	Country	P
BOTTM	Bottom-Dollar Markets	Elizabeth Lincoln	Accounting Manager	23 Tsawassen Blvd.	Tsawassen	BC	T2F 8M4	Canada	(604)
FISSA	FISSA Fabrica Inter. Salchichas S.A.	Diego Roel	Accounting Manager	C/ Moralzarzal, 86	Madrid		28034	Spain	(91) 5
HANAR	Hanari Carnes	Mario Pontes	Accounting Manager	Rua do Paço, 67	Rio de Janeiro	RJ	05454-876	Brazil	(21) 5
LILAS	LILA-Supermercado	Carlos González	Accounting Manager	Carrera 52 con Ave. Bolívar #65-98 Llano Largo	Barquisimeto	Lara	3508	Venezuela	(9) 33
QUEDE	Que Delícia	Bernardo Batista	Accounting Manager	Rua da Panificadora, 12	Rio de Janeiro	RJ	02389-673	Brazil	(21) 5
QUICK	QUICK-Stop	Horst Kloss	Accounting Manager	Taucherstraße 10	Cunewalde		01307	Germany	0372-
ROMEY	Romero y tomillo	Alejandra Camino	Accounting Manager	Gran Vía, 1	Madrid		28001	Spain	(91) 7
SUPRD	Suprêmes délices	Pascale Cartrain	Accounting Manager	Boulevard Tirou, 255	Charleroi		B-6000	Belgium	(071)
VINET	Vins et alcools Chevalier	Paul Henriot	Accounting Manager	59 rue de l'Abbaye	Reims		51100	France	26.47
WARTH	Wartian Herkku	Pirkko Koskitalo	Accounting Manager	Torikatu 38	Oulu		90110	Finland	981-4
BLONP	Blondel père et fils	Frédérique Citeaux	Manager	24, place Kléber	Strasbourg		67000	France	88.60
CENTC	Centro comercial Moctezuma	Francisco Chang	Marketing Manager	Sierras de Granada 9993	México D.F.		05022	Mexico	(5) 55
FRANK	Frankenversand	Peter Franken	Marketing Manager	Berliner Platz 43	München		80805	Germany	089-0
FRANR	France restauration	Carine Schmitt	Marketing Manager	54, rue Royale	Nantes		44000	France	40.32
GALED	Galería del gastrónomo	Eduardo Saavedra	Marketing Manager	Rambla de Cataluña, 23	Barcelona		08022	Spain	(93) 2
GREAL	Great Lakes Food Market	Howard Snyder	Marketing Manager	2732 Baker Blvd.	Eugene	OR	97403	USA	(503)
ISLAT	Island Trading	Helen Bennett	Marketing Manager	Garden House	Cowes	Isle of Wight	PO31 7PJ	UK	(198)
LAZYK	Lazy K Kountry Store	John Steel	Marketing Manager	12 Orchestra Terrace	Walla Walla	WA	99362	USA	(509)
MAGAA	Magazzini Alimentari Riuniti	Giovanni Rovelli	Marketing Manager	Via Ludovico il Moro 22	Bergamo		24100	Italy	035-6
SPECD	Spécialités du monde	Dominique Perrier	Marketing Manager	25, rue Lauriston	Paris		75016	France	(1) 47
THEBI	The Big Cheese	Liz Nixon	Marketing Manager	89 Jefferson Way	Portland	OR	97201	USA	(503)
TOMSP	Toms Spezialitäten	Karin Josephs	Marketing Manager	Luisenstr. 48	Münster		44087	Germany	0251-
ERNSH	Ernst Handel	Roland Mendel	Sales Manager	Kirchgasse 6	Graz		8010	Austria	7675-
FURIB	Furia Bacalhau e Frutos do Mar	Lino Rodriguez	Sales Manager	Jardim das rosas n. 32	Lisboa		1675	Portugal	(1) 35
GODOS	Godos Cocina Típica	José Pedro Freyre	Sales Manager	C/ Romero, 33	Sevilla		41101	Spain	(95) 5
LAMAI	La maison d'Asie	Annette Roulet	Sales Manager	1 rue Alsace-Lorraine	Toulouse		31000	France	61.77

Record: 9 of 33 ▶ ▶ Filtered Search

Datasheet View — Filtered

FIGURE 1.32 Finding Records Containing a Value

STEP 3 ## Use Filter By Form

Filter By Form is a more versatile method of selecting data because it enables you to display records based on multiple criteria. When you use Filter By Form, all of the records are hidden, and Access creates a blank form. On this form, you see only field names with an arrow in the first field. Clicking the arrow displays the data in the field. For example, in the Customers table, clicking the arrow for the Contact Title field will display a list of unique titles from which to choose. By choosing Sales Manager, the form will filter for all records that have Sales Manager as the Contact Title. Because Filter By Form allows for multiple filter fields you could also choose another field such as Country.

To apply the filter and view the results, click Toggle. Choosing Austria would result in two records that have Sales Manager as the Contact Title and where the person is also from Austria. Both criteria must be met in the same record for them to appear in the result. If a person has the title of Sales Manager but is not from the country of Austria, they will not be found in the filtered results. Figure 1.33 shows Filter By Form with these two criteria chosen.

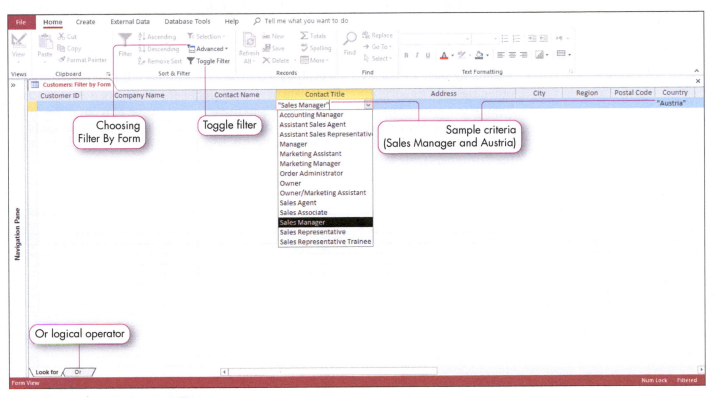

FIGURE 1.33 Filter By Form in a Table

An advantage of Filter By Form is that you can use a comparison operator such as equal (=), not equal (<>), greater than (>), less than (<), greater than or equal to (>=), and less than or equal to (<=). For example, you can locate employees with a Hire date after a specific date such as 2015. To add this criterion, you would click in the field and type the operator followed by the date, in this case you would type >1/1/2015 in the Hire date field.

Another advantage of using this filter method is that you can specify an OR logical operator. As previously discussed, using Filter By Form that displays a record in the results if ALL the criteria are true. However, if you use the OR operator, a record is included if at least one criterion is true. Figure 1.33 shows the location of the OR operator on the Filter by Form page.

To use Filter By Form, complete the following steps:

1. Open the table in Datasheet view and click Advanced in the Sort & Filter group on the Home tab.
2. Click Filter By Form.
3. Click in the field you want to use as a criterion. Click the arrow to select the criterion from existing data.
4. Add additional criterion and comparison operators as required.
5. Click Toggle Filter in the Sort & Filter group on the Home tab to apply the filter.

Performing Sorts

You can change the order of information by sorting one or more fields. A *sort* lists records in a specific sequence, such as alphabetically by last name or by ascending EmployeeID. Sorting adds organization to data and makes the records easier to visualize and understand. Records are not necessarily added in a specific order so sorting by Employee Last Name for example may be more beneficial than viewing the data sorted by an autonumber. Sorting does not change the order of the data in the database, only the way the data are viewed.

Sort Table Data

Ascending sorts a list of text data in alphabetical order or a numeric list in lowest to highest order. Descending sorts a list of text data in reverse alphabetical order or a numeric list in highest to lowest order. You can equate this to these terms outside of a database. When you are coming down from a high place (such as the top of a ladder), you are said to be descending, and when you are climbing a ladder, you are ascending. Figure 1.34 shows the Customers table sorted in ascending order by city name.

Customer I	Company Name	Contact Name	Contact Title	Address	City	Country	Region	Postal Cod
DRACD	Drachenblut Delikatessen	Sven Ottlieb	Order Administrator	Walserweg 21	Aachen	Germany		52066
RATTC	Rattlesnake Canyon Grocery	Paula Wilson	Assistant Sales Representative	2817 Milton Dr.	Albuquerque	USA	NM	87110
OLDWO	Old World Delicatessen	Rene Phillips	Sales Representative	2743 Bering St.	Anchorage	USA	AK	99508
VAFFE	Vaffeljernet	Palle Ibsen	Sales Manager	Smagsløget 45	Århus	Denmark		8200
GALED	Galería del gastrónomo	Eduardo Saavedra	Marketing Manager	Rambla de Cataluña, 23	Barcelona	Spain		08022
LILAS	LILA-Supermercado	Carlos González	Accounting Manager	Carrera 52 con Ave. Bolívar #65-98 Llano Largo	Barquisimeto	Venezuela	Lara	3508
MAGAA	Magazzini Alimentari Riuniti	Giovanni Rovelli	Marketing Manager	Via Ludovico il Moro 22	Bergamo	Italy		24100
ALFKI	Alfreds Futterkiste	Maria Anders	Sales Representative	Obere Str. 57	Berlin	Germany		12209
CHOPS	Chop-suey Chinese	Yang Wang	Owner	Hauptstr. 29	Bern	Switzerland		3012
SAVEA	Save-a-lot Markets	Jose Pavarotti	Sales Representative	187 Suffolk Ln.	Boise	USA	ID	83720
FOLKO	Folk och fä HB	Maria Larsson	Owner	Åkergatan 24	Bräcke	Sweden		S-844 67
KOENE	Königlich Essen	Philip Cramer	Sales Associate	Maubelstr. 90	Brandenburg	Germany		14776
MAISD	Maison Dewey	Catherine Dewey	Sales Agent	Rue Joseph-Bens 532	Bruxelles	Belgium		B-1180
CACTU	Cactus Comidas para llevar	Patricio Simpson	Sales Agent	Cerrito 333	Buenos Aires	Argentina		1010
OCEAN	Océano Atlántico Ltda.	Yvonne Moncada	Sales Agent	Ing. Gustavo Moncada 8585	Buenos Aires	Argentina		1010
RANCH	Rancho grande	Sergio Gutiérrez	Sales Representative	Av. del Libertador 900	Buenos Aires	Argentina		1010
THECR	The Cracker Box	Liu Wong	Marketing Assistant	55 Grizzly Peak Rd.	Butte	USA	MT	59801
GOURL	Gourmet Lanchonetes	André Fonseca	Sales Associate	Av. Brasil, 442	Campinas	Brazil	SP	04876-786
GROSR	GROSELLA-Restaurante	Manuel Pereira	Owner	5ª Ave. Los Palos Grandes	Caracas	Venezuela	DF	1081
SUPRD	Suprêmes délices	Pascale Cartrain	Accounting Manager	Boulevard Tirou, 255	Charleroi	Belgium		B-6000
HUNGO	Hungry Owl All-Night Grocers	Patricia McKenna	Sales Associate	8 Johnstown Road	Cork	Ireland	Co. Cork	
ISLAT	Island Trading	Helen Bennett	Marketing Manager	Garden House	Cowes	UK	Isle of Wight	PO31 7PJ
QUICK	QUICK-Stop	Horst Kloss	Accounting Manager	Taucherstraße 10	Cunewalde	Germany		01307
HUNGC	Hungry Coyote Import Store	Yoshi Latimer	Sales Representative	City Center Plaza	Elgin	USA	OR	97827
GREAL	Great Lakes Food Market	Howard Snyder	Marketing Manager	2732 Baker Blvd.	Eugene	USA	OR	97403
LEHMS	Lehmanns Marktstand	Renate Messner	Sales Representative	Magazinweg 7	Frankfurt a.M.	Germany		60528

Record: 1 of 91 • No Filter • Search

Unique five-character code based on customer name.

Records sorted by City value

FIGURE 1.34 Sorted Customers Table

To sort data in a table by one criterion, select the field that you want to use to sort the records. Then, select Ascending or Descending in the Sort & Filter group on the Home tab.

Access can sort records by more than one field, for example, sorting by City and State. When sorting by multiple criteria, Access first sorts in order of fields from left to right. It is important to understand that to sort by multiple fields, you must arrange your columns in the order you want them sorted by. So, for example, in most databases, State fields are usually added to the right (after) the City fields; however, if you want to first sort by State, and then by Cities listed in alphabetical order within each state, the order of the fields will need to change so the State field is to the left of the City field. In this case you would move the State field. To move a field, click the column heading and hold down the left mouse button. A thick line displays to the left of the column. Drag the field to the appropriate position and release the mouse button.

Once the column has been moved, you can perform a sort by selecting the field to the left, sorting, and then doing the same for the secondary sort column.

Quick Concepts

5. Explain the purpose of creating a filter. *p. 98*

6. Explain the difference between a Selection filter and a Filter By Form. *pp. 98, 100*

7. Discuss the benefits of sorting records in a table. *p. 102*

Hands-On Exercises

MyLab IT HOE2 Sim Training

Watch the Video for this Hands-On Exercise!

Skills covered: Use a Selection Filter to Find Exact Matches • Use a Selection Filter to Find Records Containing a Value • Use Filter By Form • Sort Table Data

2 Filters and Sorts

The sales manager at Northwind Traders wants quick answers to her questions about customer orders. You use the Access database to filter tables to answer these questions and sort the records based on the manager's requirements.

STEP 1 USE A SELECTION FILTER TO FIND EXACT MATCHES

The sales manager asks for a list of customers who live in London. You use a Selection filter with an equal condition to locate these customers. Refer to Figure 1.35 as you complete Step 1.

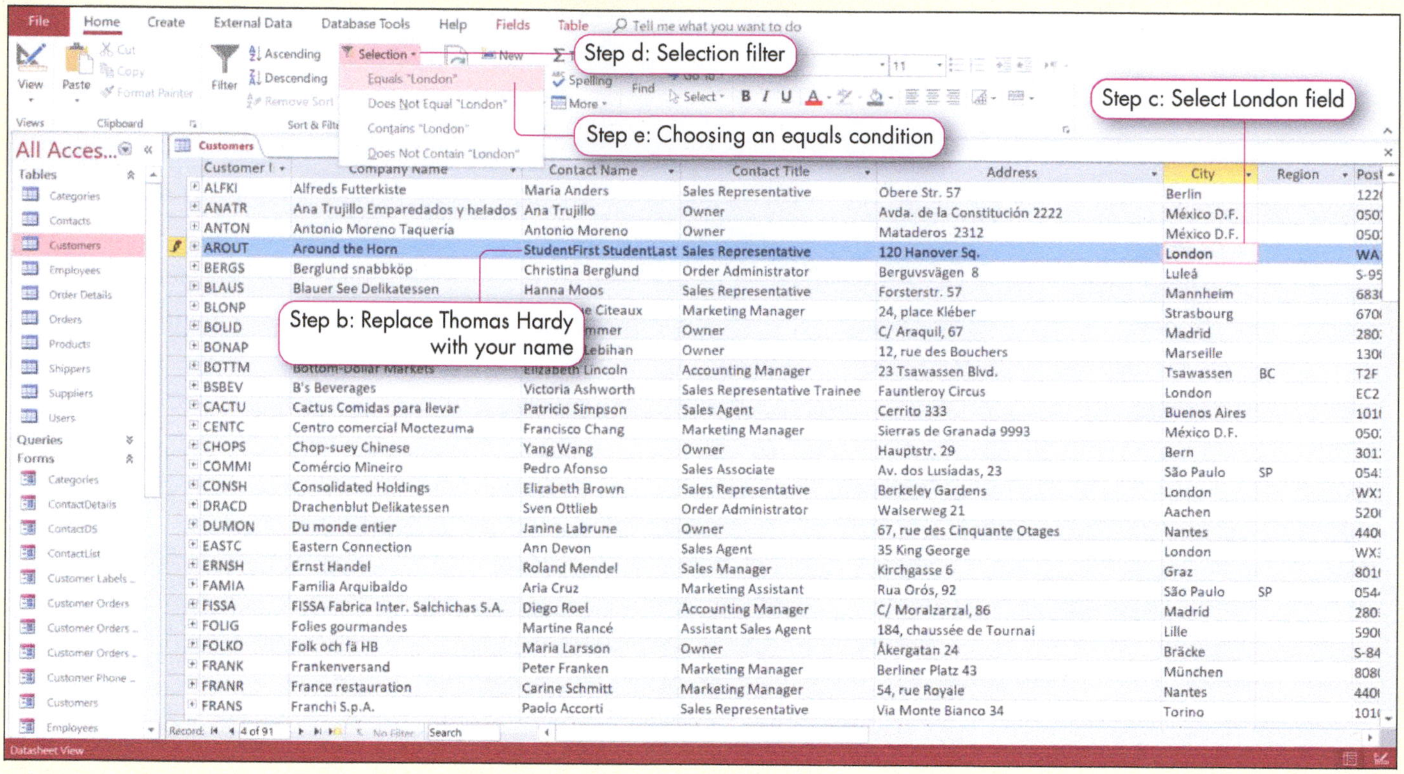

FIGURE 1.35 Filtering the Customers Table

a. Open the *a01h1Traders_LastFirst* database if you closed it at the end of Hands-On Exercise 1, and save it as **a01h2Traders_LastFirst**, changing h1 to h2. Click **Enable Content**.

b. Double-click the **Customers table** in the Navigation Pane, navigate to record **4**, and then replace **Thomas Hardy** with your name in the Contact Name field.

c. Scroll right until the City field is visible. The fourth record has a value of London in the City field. Click the **London field** to select it.

d. Click **Selection** in the Sort & Filter group on the Home tab.

e. Select **Equals "London"** from the menu. Six records are displayed.

> The Navigation bar display shows that six records that meet the London criterion are available. The other records in the Customers table are hidden. The Filtered icon also displays on the Navigation bar and column heading, indicating that the Customers table has been filtered.

f. Click **Toggle Filter** in the Sort & Filter group to remove the filter.

g. Click **Toggle Filter** again to reset the filter.

STEP 2 ## USE A SELECTION FILTER TO FIND RECORDS CONTAINING A VALUE

The sales manager asks you to narrow the list of London customers so that it displays only records that contain the title Sales Representatives. To accomplish this task, you add a second layer of filtering using a Selection filter. Refer to Figure 1.36 as you complete Step 2.

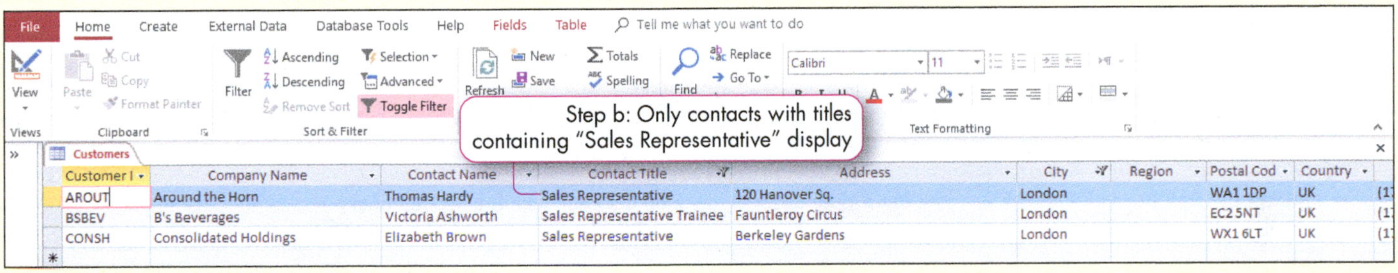

FIGURE 1.36 Filtered Customers

a. Click in any field value in the Contact Title field that contains the value **Sales Representative**.

b. Click **Selection** in the Sort & Filter group, select **Contains "Sales Representative,"** and then compare your results to those shown in Figure 1.36.

> Three records match the criteria you set. You have applied a second layer of filtering to the customers in London. The second layer further restricts the display to only those customers who have the words Sales Representative contained in their titles. Because you chose Contains as your filter, any representatives with the phrase Sales Representative appear. This includes Victoria Ashworth, who is a Sales Representative Trainee.

> **TROUBLESHOOTING:** If you do not see the record for Victoria Ashworth, you selected Equals "Sales Representative" instead of Contains "Sales Representative." Repeat Steps a and b, making sure you select Contains "Sales Representative."

c. Close the Customers table. Click **Yes** when prompted to save the design changes to the Customers table.

You are asked to provide a list of records that do not match just one set of criteria. You will provide a list of all extended prices less than $50 for a specific sales representative. Use Filter By Form to provide the information when two or more criteria are necessary. You also preview the results in Print Preview to see how the list would print. Refer to Figure 1.37 as you complete Step 3.

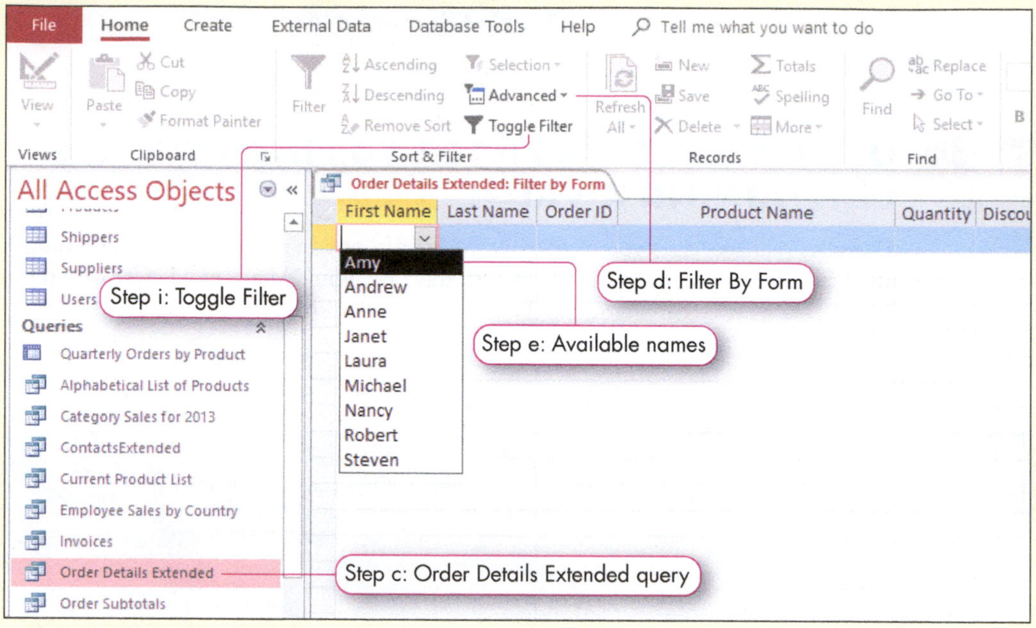

FIGURE 1.37 Using Filter By Form

a. Click the **Tables group** in the Navigation Pane to collapse the listed tables.

b. Click the **Queries group** in the Navigation Pane to expand the list of available queries.

c. Locate and double-click **Order Details Extended** to open it.

This query contains information about orders. It has fields containing information about the sales person, the Order ID, the product name, the unit price, quantity ordered, the discount given, and an extended price. The extended price is a field used to total order information.

d. Click **Advanced** in the Sort & Filter group and select **Filter By Form** from the list. The first field, First Name, is active by default.

All of the records are now hidden, and you see only field names and an arrow in the first field. Although you are applying Filter By Form to a query, you can use the same process as applying Filter By Form to a table. You are able to input more than one criterion using Filter By Form.

e. Click the **First Name arrow**.

A list of all available first names displays. Your name should be on the list. Figure 1.38 shows *Amy Rutledge*, which replaced Margaret Peacock in Hands-On Exercise 1.

> **TROUBLESHOOTING:** If you do not see your name and you do see Margaret on the list, you probably skipped steps in Hands-On Exercise 1. Close the query without saving changes, return to the first Hands-On Exercise, and then rework it, making sure not to omit any steps. Then you can return to this location and work the remainder of this Hands-On Exercise.

f. Select your first name from the list.

g. Click in the first row under the Last Name field to reveal the arrow. Locate and select your last name by clicking it.

h. Scroll right until you see the Extended Price field. Click in the first row under the Extended Price field and type **<50**.

This will select all of the items ordered where the total price was less than 50.

i. Click **Toggle Filter** in the Sort & Filter group.

You have specified which records to include and have executed the filtering by clicking Toggle Filter.

j. Click the **File tab**, click **Print**, and then click **Print Preview**.

You instructed Access to preview the filtered query results. The preview displays the query title as a heading. The current filter is applied, as well as page numbers.

k. Click **Close Print Preview** in the Close Preview group.

l. Close the Order Details Extended query. Click **Yes** when prompted to save your changes.

STEP 4 PERFORM SORTS

The Sales Manager is pleased with your work; however, she would like some of the information displayed in a different order. You will now sort the records in the Customers table using the manager's new criteria. Refer to Figure 1.38 as you complete Step 4.

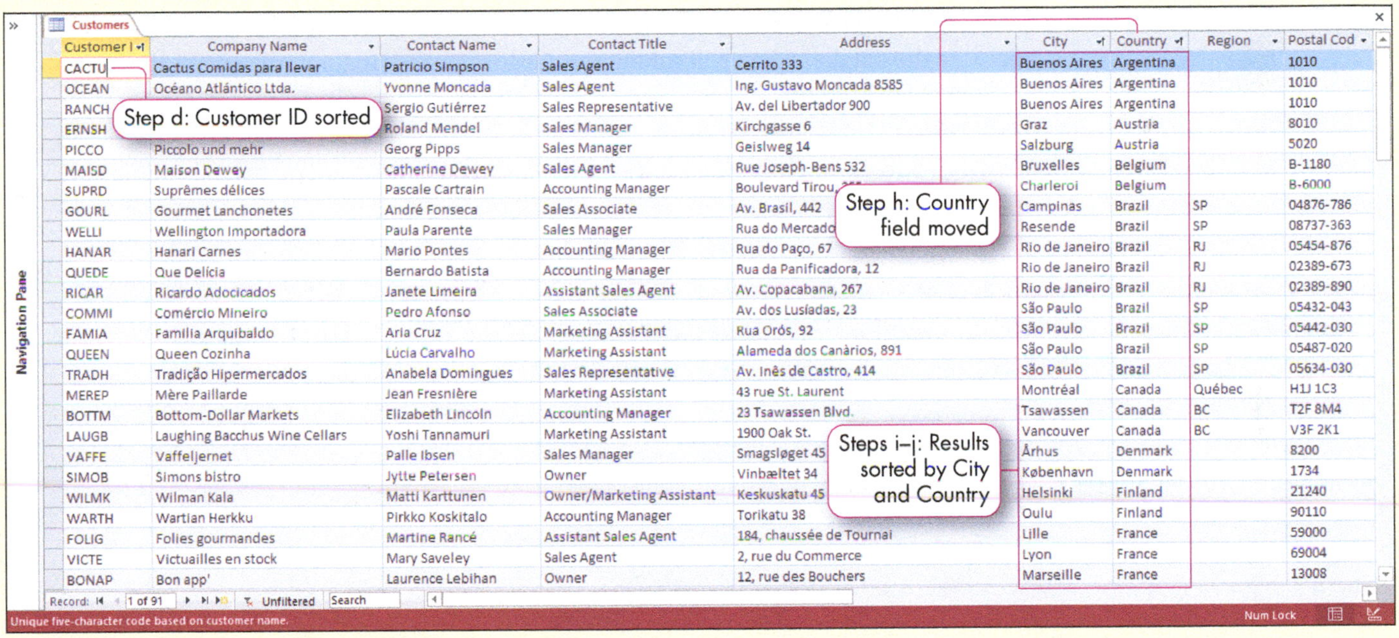

Customer I	Company Name	Contact Name	Contact Title	Address	City	Country	Region	Postal Cod
CACTU	Cactus Comidas para llevar	Patricio Simpson	Sales Agent	Cerrito 333	Buenos Aires	Argentina		1010
OCEAN	Océano Atlántico Ltda.	Yvonne Moncada	Sales Agent	Ing. Gustavo Moncada 8585	Buenos Aires	Argentina		1010
RANCH		Sergio Gutiérrez	Sales Representative	Av. del Libertador 900	Buenos Aires	Argentina		1010
ERNSH		Roland Mendel	Sales Manager	Kirchgasse 6	Graz	Austria		8010
PICCO	Piccolo und mehr	Georg Pipps	Sales Manager	Geislweg 14	Salzburg	Austria		5020
MAISD	Maison Dewey	Catherine Dewey	Sales Agent	Rue Joseph-Bens 532	Bruxelles	Belgium		B-1180
SUPRD	Suprêmes délices	Pascale Cartrain	Accounting Manager	Boulevard Tirou,	Charleroi	Belgium		B-6000
GOURL	Gourmet Lanchonetes	André Fonseca	Sales Associate	Av. Brasil, 442	Campinas	Brazil	SP	04876-786
WELLI	Wellington Importadora	Paula Parente	Sales Manager	Rua do Mercado	Resende	Brazil	SP	08737-363
HANAR	Hanari Carnes	Mario Pontes	Accounting Manager	Rua do Paço, 67	Rio de Janeiro	Brazil	RJ	05454-876
QUEDE	Que Delícia	Bernardo Batista	Accounting Manager	Rua da Panificadora, 12	Rio de Janeiro	Brazil	RJ	02389-673
RICAR	Ricardo Adocicados	Janete Limeira	Assistant Sales Agent	Av. Copacabana, 267	Rio de Janeiro	Brazil	RJ	02389-890
COMMI	Comércio Mineiro	Pedro Afonso	Sales Associate	Av. dos Lusíadas, 23	São Paulo	Brazil	SP	05432-043
FAMIA	Familia Arquibaldo	Aria Cruz	Marketing Assistant	Rua Orós, 92	São Paulo	Brazil	SP	05442-030
QUEEN	Queen Cozinha	Lúcia Carvalho	Marketing Assistant	Alameda dos Canàrios, 891	São Paulo	Brazil	SP	05487-020
TRADH	Tradição Hipermercados	Anabela Domingues	Sales Representative	Av. Inês de Castro, 414	São Paulo	Brazil	SP	05634-030
MEREP	Mère Paillarde	Jean Fresnière	Marketing Assistant	43 rue St. Laurent	Montréal	Canada	Québec	H1J 1C3
BOTTM	Bottom-Dollar Markets	Elizabeth Lincoln	Accounting Manager	23 Tsawassen Blvd.	Tsawassen	Canada	BC	T2F 8M4
LAUGB	Laughing Bacchus Wine Cellars	Yoshi Tannamuri	Marketing Assistant	1900 Oak St.	Vancouver	Canada	BC	V3F 2K1
VAFFE	Vaffeljernet	Palle Ibsen	Sales Manager	Smagsløget 45	Århus	Denmark		8200
SIMOB	Simons bistro	Jytte Petersen	Owner	Vinbæltet 34	København	Denmark		1734
WILMK	Wilman Kala	Matti Karttunen	Owner/Marketing Assistant	Keskuskatu 45	Helsinki	Finland		21240
WARTH	Wartian Herkku	Pirkko Koskitalo	Accounting Manager	Torikatu 38	Oulu	Finland		90110
FOLIG	Folies gourmandes	Martine Rancé	Assistant Sales Agent	184, chaussée de Tournai	Lille	France		59000
VICTE	Victuailles en stock	Mary Saveley	Sales Agent	2, rue du Commerce	Lyon	France		69004
BONAP	Bon app'	Laurence Lebihan	Owner	12, rue des Bouchers	Marseille	France		13008

FIGURE 1.38 Updated Customers Table

a. Click the **Queries group** in the Navigation Pane to collapse the listed queries.

b. Click the **Tables group** in the Navigation Pane to expand the list of available tables and double-click the **Customers table** to open it.

This table contains information about customers. The table is sorted in alphabetical order by CustomerID.

c. Click **Shutter Bar Open/Close** in the Navigation Pane to hide the Navigation Pane.

It will be easier to locate fields in the Customer table if the Navigation Pane is hidden.

d. Click any entry in the Customer ID field. Click **Descending** in the Sort & Filter group on the Home tab.

Sorting in descending order on a text field produces a reverse alphabetical order.

e. Scroll right until you can see both the Country and City fields.

f. Click the **Country column heading**.

The entire field is selected.

g. Click the **Country column heading** again and hold down the **left mouse button**.

A thick line displays on the left edge of the Country field.

h. Ensure that you see the thick line on the edge of the Country field. Drag the **Country field** to the left until the thick line moves between the City and Region fields. Release the mouse button and the Country field position moves to the right of the City field.

You moved the Country field next to the City field so that you can easily sort the table based on both fields.

i. Click any city name in the City field and click **Ascending** in the Sort & Filter group.

The City field displays the cities in alphabetical order.

j. Click any country name in the Country field and click **Ascending** in the Sort & Filter group.

The countries are sorted in alphabetical order. The cities within each country also are sorted alphabetically. For example, the customer in Graz, Austria, is listed before the customer in Salzburg, Austria.

k. Close the Customers table. Click **Yes** to save the changes to the design of the table.

l. Click **Shutter Bar Open/Close** in the Navigation Pane to show the Navigation Pane.

m. Close the database. You will submit this file to your instructor at the end of the last Hands-On Exercise.

Access Database Creation

Now that you have examined the fundamentals of an Access database and explored the power of databases, it is time to create one! A lot of careful thought should go into designing a database. Businesses may use a database only to keep track of customers, or they may use a database for much more, such as orders and inventory tracking. Databases can range from a simple table or two to complex business applications with many tables, forms, reports, etc. that become the core of the business operations. Depending on the purpose of the database, its size, and how many people will use it, one of two methods may be used to create a database.

In this section, you explore the benefits of creating a database from a blank database, which enables you to design it to your specific requirements. Additionally, you will learn how to create a database from a template to save time by having tables, forms, reports, etc. already available to modify to your specifications.

Creating a Database

When you first start Access, you can create a database using one of two methods:

- Create a blank database
- Create a database from a template (note: there will be many templates shown)

Creating a blank database enables you to create a database specific to your requirements. Rather than starting from scratch by creating a blank database, you can use a template to create a new database. An Access *template* is a predefined database that includes professionally designed tables, forms, reports, and other objects that you can use to jumpstart the creation of your database.

Figure 1.39 shows the options for creating a blank database and multiple templates from which you can select the method for which you want to create a database.

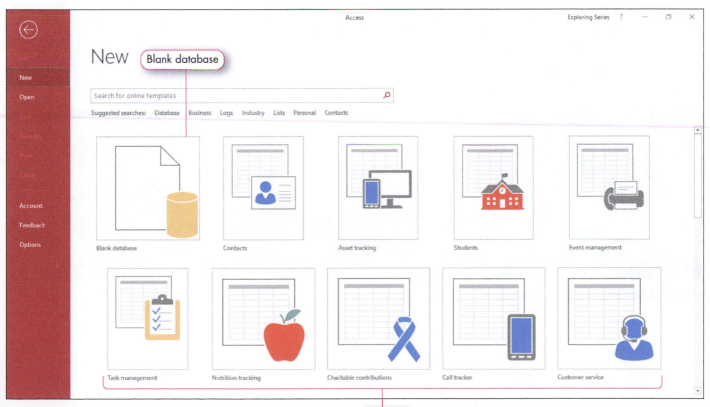

FIGURE 1.39 Options for Creating a New Database

Create a Blank Database

Often, if you are migrating data from Excel to Access, you would start by creating a blank database. At that point, you could import your existing structure and data into a new table. Another time you might use a blank database is when you are starting a project and want to design your own tables.

When you create a blank database, Access opens to a blank table in Datasheet view where you can add fields or data. You can also refine the table in Design view. You would then create additional tables and objects as necessary. Obviously, this task requires some level of Access knowledge, so unless you have requirements to follow, you may be better served using a template.

To create a blank database, complete the following steps:

1. Open Access. (If Access is already open, click the File tab and click New.)
2. Click Blank database.
3. Type the file name for the file in the text box, click Browse to navigate to the folder where you want to store the database file, and then click OK.
4. Click Create (see Figure 1.40).
5. Type data in the empty table that displays.

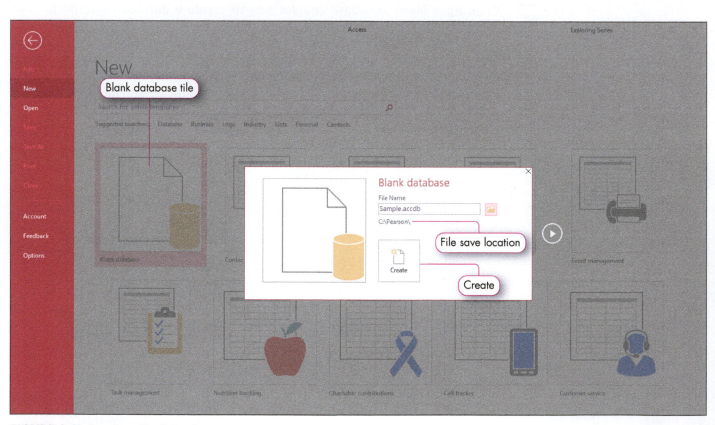

FIGURE 1.40 Creating a Blank Database

STEP 1 Create a Database Using a Template

Using a template to start a database saves you a great deal of creation time. Working with a database template can also help a new Access user become familiar with database design. Database templates are available from Backstage view, where you can select from a variety of templates or search online for more templates.

To create a database from a template, complete the following steps:

1. Open Access. (If Access is already open, click the File tab and click New.)
2. Click the desktop database template you want to use or use the search box at the top of the page to find templates for a specific purpose. Figure 1.41 shows some examples of templates.
3. Type the file name for the file in the text box, click Browse to navigate to the folder where you want to store the database file, and then click OK.
4. Click Create to download the template. The database will be created and will open.
5. Click Enable Content in the Security Warning message bar.

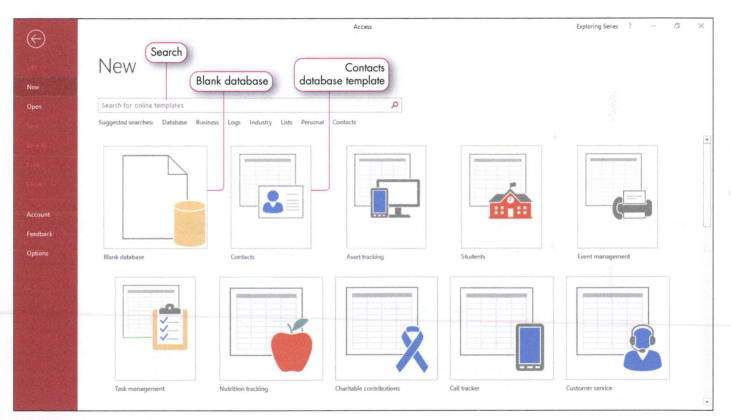

FIGURE 1.41 Database Templates

After the database opens, you may see a Welcome page that includes a video you can use to learn more about the database. When finished reviewing the learning materials, close the Welcome page to view the database. Figure 1.42 displays the Welcome page included with the Task management template. Because you downloaded a template, some objects will have already been created. You can work with these objects just as you did in the first two sections of this chapter. Edit any object to meet your requirements.

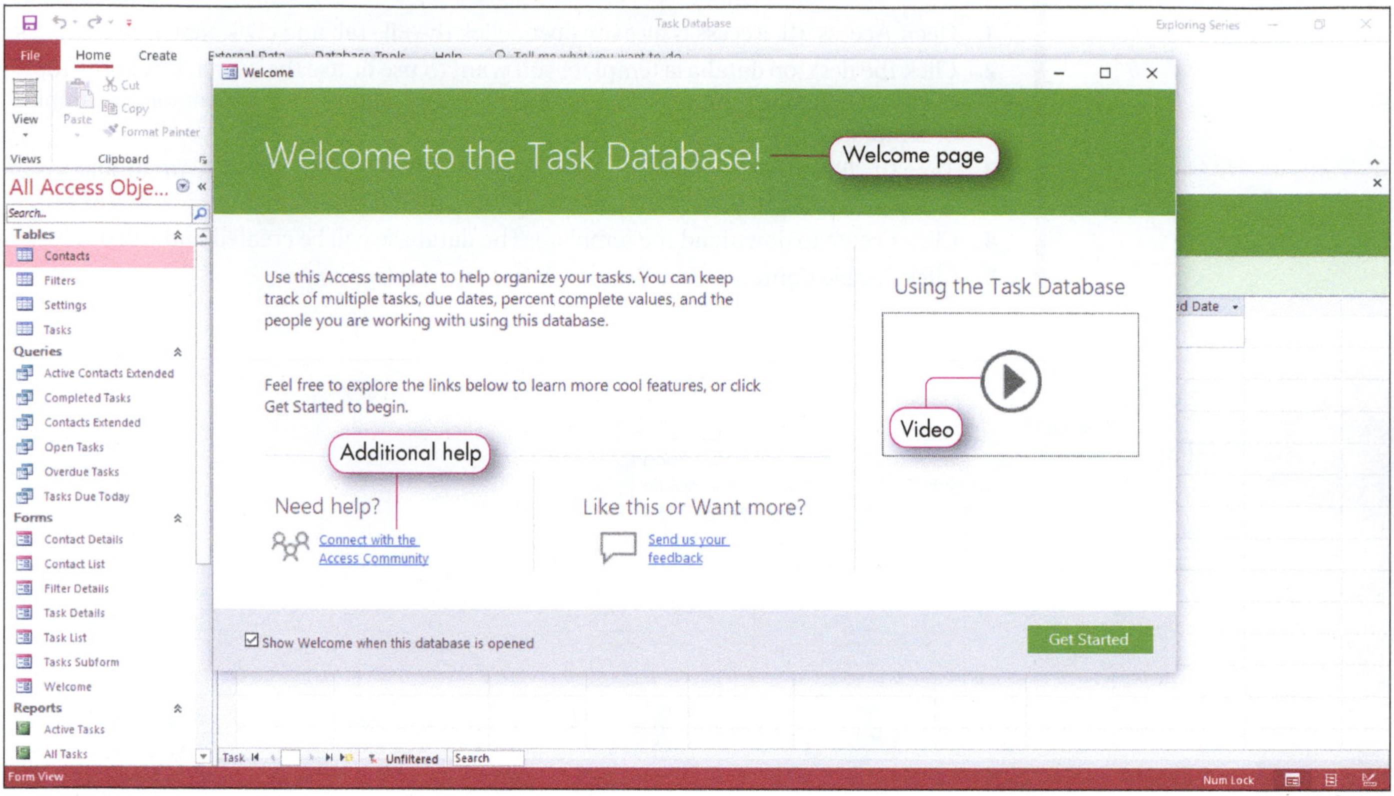

FIGURE 1.42 Getting Started Page for a Template

> **TIP: CREATE A TEMPLATE FROM A DATABASE**
> If you have a database you may want to reuse in the future, you can save it as a template. Doing so will enable you to create new databases with the same tables, queries, forms, and reports as the one you have created. You can also reuse just specific objects within the database such as a form or report. To create a template from an existing database, use the File tab option of Save As and select Template as the file type.

Explore and Customize a Database Template

Once a database template has been downloaded, you can use it as you would use any Access database. Figure 1.43 shows the Contact Details form from the Contact management database template.

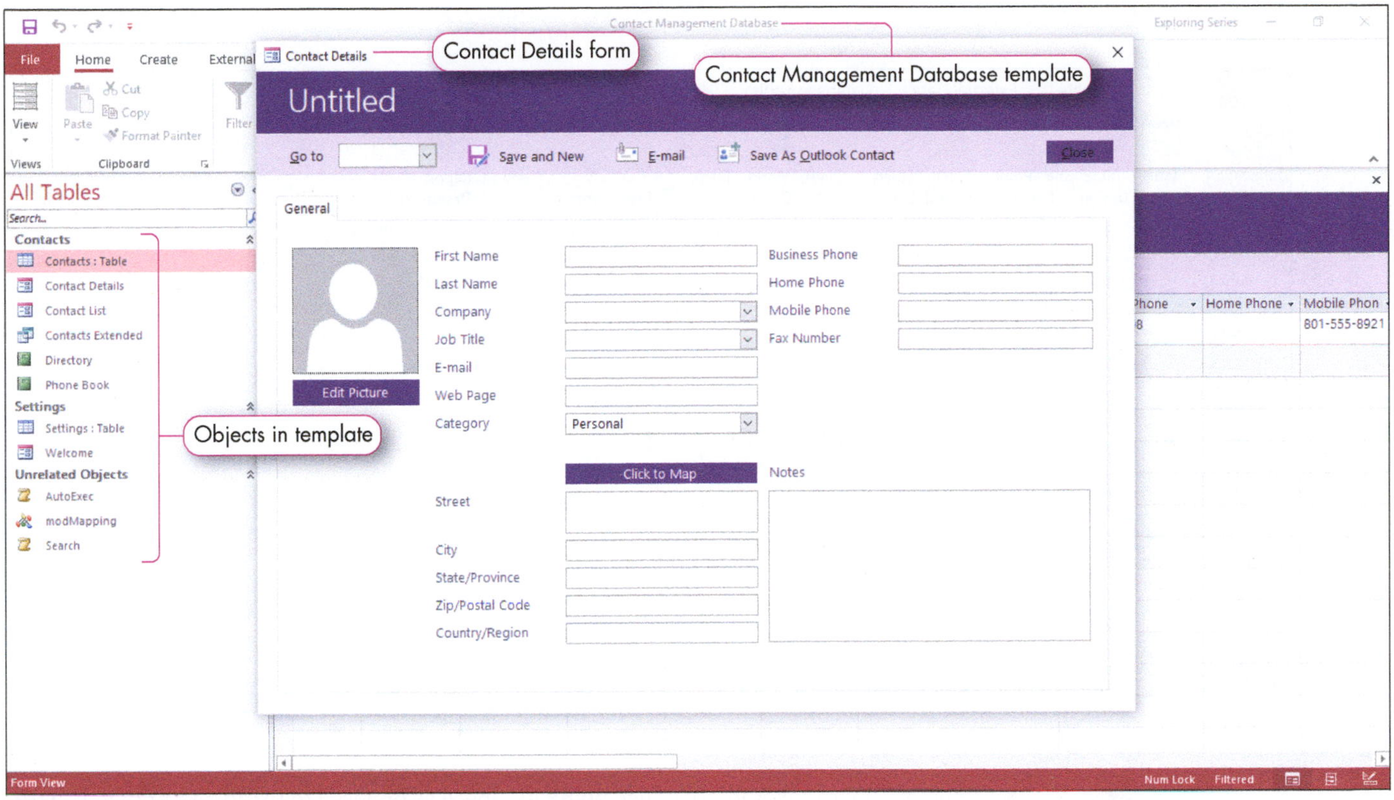

FIGURE 1.43 Contact Management Database

One of the reasons to use a template is so you do not have to create any of the objects. Therefore, you will notice each template comes with a varying number of predefined queries, forms, and reports. Familiarize yourself with the unique features of a template; because they are professionally designed, they are typically well thought out. Review the objects listed in the Navigation Pane. After you are familiar with the database design, you can enter your data using a table or form.

Create a Table Using an Application Part

An *application part* enables you to add a set of common Access components to an existing database, such as a table, a form, and a report for a related task. These are provided by Microsoft and offer components (for example, a Contacts table) you can add to an existing database, rather than creating an entirely new database, as shown in Figure 1.44. Using the pre-built application parts can save time and effort. A Contacts application part for example has a Contacts table with typical fields such as Last Name, First Name, Address, etc. Along with the table you will find there are also some queries, forms, and reports that would be useful for the Contacts table.

To add an application part to a database, click Application Parts in the Templates group on the Create tab. A list of options displays, with Quick Start options such as Contacts, Tasks, Issues, and Comments. Once you have made an option selection from the list, you will respond to the dialog boxes to complete the process of setting up the application part. After it is created, you will see the new components displayed in the Navigation Pane. You may be prompted to create a relationship between your tables. Setting up a relationship is not required but is recommended.

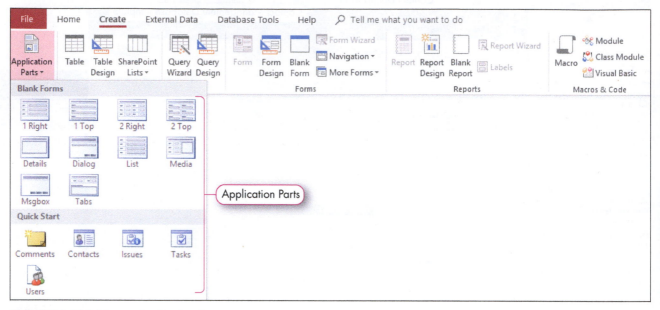

FIGURE 1.44 Adding an Application Part

Quick Concepts

8. Explain why you would use a new blank database as opposed to using a template. **p. 109**

9. Discuss two benefits of using a template to create a database. **pp. 111, 113**

10. Explain the purpose of using an application part. **p. 113**

Hands-On Exercises

MyLab IT HOE3 Sim Training

▶ Watch the Video for this Hands-On Exercise!

Skills covered: Create a Database Using a Template • Explore and Customize a Database Template

3 Access Database Creation

After working with the Northwind database on the job, you decide to use Access to create a personal contact database. Rather than start from a blank table, you use an Access Contacts template to make your database creation simpler. You explore the template objects and customize the database to suit your needs.

STEP 1 ▶ CREATE A DATABASE USING A TEMPLATE

You locate an Access template that you can use to create your personal contact database. This template not only enables you to store names, addresses, telephone numbers, and other information, but also helps you categorize your contacts, send email messages, and create maps of addresses. You download and save the template. Refer to Figure 1.45 as you complete Step 1.

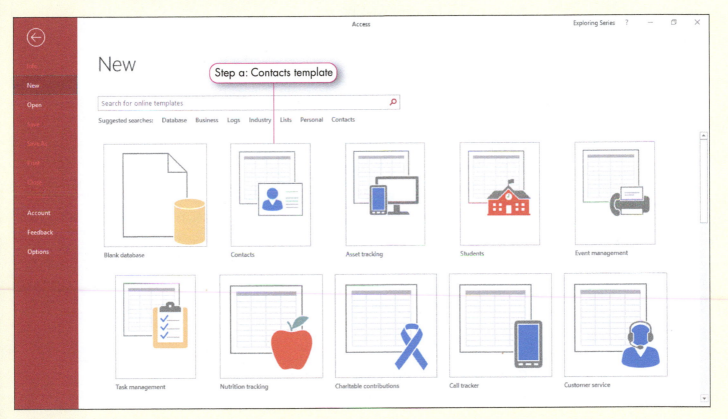

FIGURE 1.45 Contacts Template

a. Open Access. Click the **Contacts** template.

> **TROUBLESHOOTING:** If the Contacts template is not visible, type contacts in the search box at the top of the screen and click the magnifying glass. Note there may be slight differences to the name, so look for the template matching the icon above.

b. Click **Browse** to navigate to the folder where you are saving your files, type **a01h3Contacts_LastFirst** as the file name, and then click **OK**.

c. Click **Create** to download the template.

d. Click **Enable Content** on the Security Warning message bar.

e. Click the **Show Welcome when this database is opened check box** to deselect it. Close the Welcome to the Contacts Database page.

The database displays the Contact List form.

STEP 2 ## EXPLORE AND CUSTOMIZE A DATABASE TEMPLATE

Because the database opens in the Contact List form, you decide to begin by entering a contact in the form. You then explore the objects created by the template so that you understand the organization of the database. Refer to Figure 1.46 as you complete Step 2.

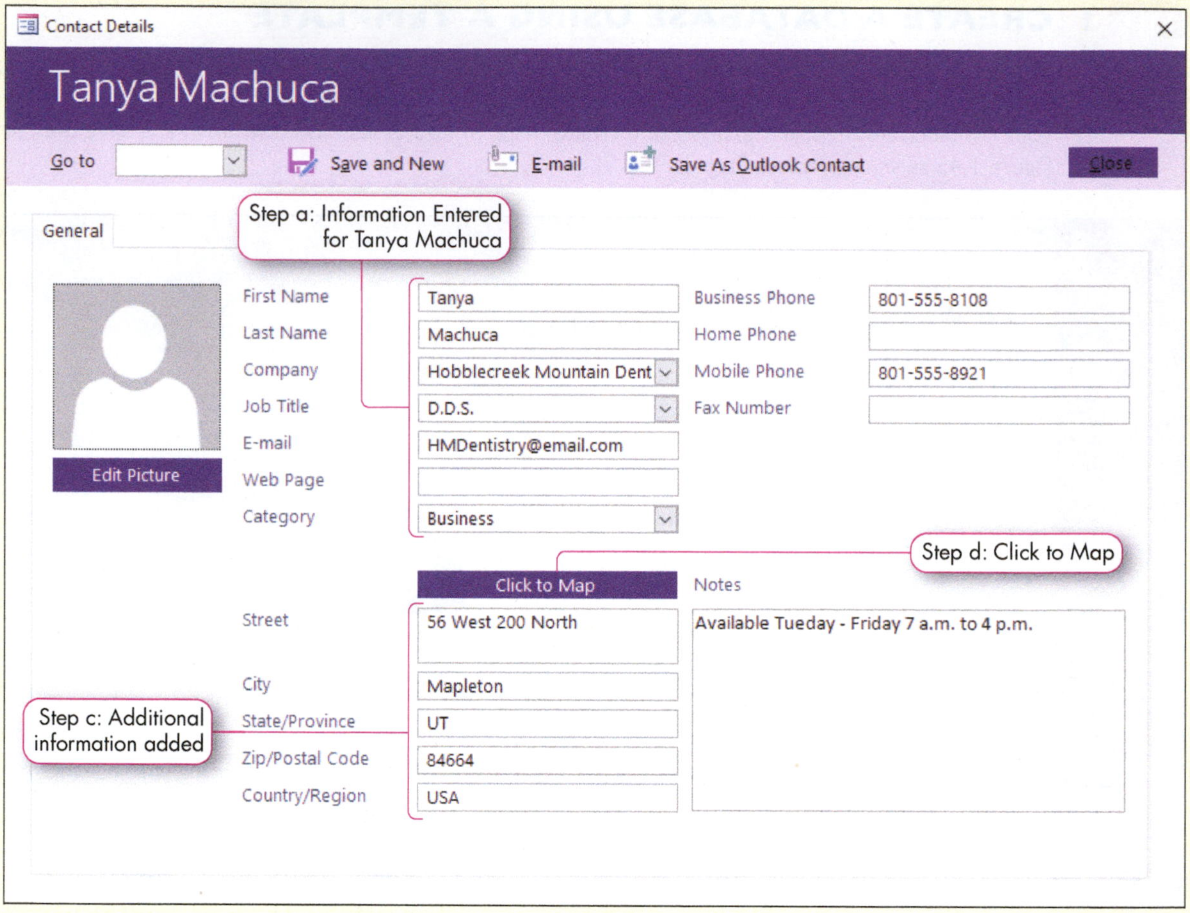

FIGURE 1.46 Contact Details for Tanya Machuca

a. Click in the **First Name field** of the first record. Type the following information, pressing **Tab** between each entry. Do not press Tab after entering the ZIP/Postal Code.

Field Name	Value to Type
First Name	**Tanya**
Last Name	**Machuca**
Company	**Hobblecreek Mountain Dentistry**
Job Title	**D.D.S.**
Category	**Business** (select from list)
Email	**HMDentistry@email.com**
Business Phone	**801-555-8108**
Home Phone	(leave blank)
Mobile Phone	**801-555-8921**
Zip/Postal Code	**84664**

b. Scroll back to the left if necessary to see the first field. Click **Open** in the first field of Dr. Machuca's record.

Open is a hyperlink to a different form in the database. The Contact Details form opens, displaying Dr. Machuca's information. More fields are available for you to use to store information. (Note that this form could also be opened from the Navigation Pane.)

c. Type the following additional information to the record:

Field Name	Value to Type
Street	**56 West 200 North**
City	**Mapleton**
State/Province	**UT**
Country/Region	**USA**
Notes	**Available Tuesday - Friday 7 a.m. to 4 p.m.**

d. Click the **Click to Map hyperlink** to view a map to Dr. Machuca's office.

Bing displays a map to the address in the record. You can get directions, locate nearby businesses, and use many other options.

TROUBLESHOOTING: You may be prompted to choose an application. Select any Web browser such as Microsoft Edge from the list.

e. Close the map. Click **Close** in the top right of the form to save and close the Contact Details form.

The record is saved.

f. Click **New Contact** beneath the Contact List title bar.

The Contact Details form opens to a blank record.

g. Type the following information for a new record, pressing **Tab** to move between fields. Some fields will be blank.

Field Name	Value to Type
First Name	**Rowan**
Last Name	**Westmoreland**
Company	**Phoenix Aesthetics**
Job Title	**Aesthetician**
Email	**Rowan55W5@email.com**
Category	**Personal**
Street	**425 North Main Street**
City	**Springville**
State/Province	**UT**
Zip/Postal Code	**84663**
Mobile Phone	**801-555-2221**
Notes	**Recommended by Michelle**

h. Click **Close**.

i. Double-click the **Contacts table** in the Navigation Pane.

The information you entered using the Contact List form and the Contact Details form displays in the Contacts table.

j. Double-click the **Phone Book report** in the Navigation Pane.

The Phone Book report opens displaying the contact name and phone information organized by category.

k. Double-click the **Directory report** in the Navigation Pane.

The Directory report opens, displaying a full alphabetical contact list. The Directory report was designed to display more fields than the Phone Book, but it is not organized by category.

l. Click **All Access Objects** on the Navigation Pane and select **Tables and Related Views**.

You can now see the objects that are based on the Contacts table.

m. Right-click the **Directory report tab** and select **Close All**.

n. Close the database and exit Access. Based on your instructor's directions, submit the following:

a01h1Traders_LastFirst_*CurrentDate*

a01h2Traders_LastFirst

a01h3Contacts_LastFirst

Chapter Objectives Review

After reading this chapter, you have accomplished the following objectives:

1. Open, save, and enable content in a database.
- A database is a collection of data organized as meaningful information that can be accessed, managed, stored, queried, sorted, and reported. A database management system (DBMS) is a software system that provides the tools to create, maintain, and use a database. Access is the database management system found in business versions of Microsoft Office. A database is opened from the File tab.
- When a database is first opened, Access displays a message bar with a security warning. Click Enable Content if you trust the database's source.

2. Recognize database object types.
- Examine the Access interface: The DBMS manages objects. Common object types are Tables, Queries, Forms, Reports. Objects are organized and listed in the Navigation Pane. Access also uses a Tabbed objects interface in which each object that is open has its own tab.
- Explore table Datasheet view: Datasheet view is a grid containing fields (columns) and records (rows).
- Navigate and locate records: Navigation arrows enable you to move through records, with arrows for the first, previous, next, and last records, as well as one to add a new record.
- Explore table Design view: Design view gives you a detailed view of the table's structure and is used to create and modify a table's design by specifying the fields it will contain, the fields' data types, and their associated properties.
- Rename and describe tables: Tables can be renamed as necessary and a description can be added. The description gives the user more information about what an object does.
- Understand relationships between tables: A relationship is a connection between two tables using a common field. The benefit of a relationship is the ability to efficiently combine data from related tables to create queries, forms, and reports.

3. Modify, add, and save data.
- Access works primarily from storage. Records can be added, modified, or deleted in the database, and as the information is entered, it is automatically saved. Undo cannot reverse edits made to multiple records.
- Modify records in a table: A pencil symbol displays in the record selector box to indicate when you are in editing mode. Moving to another record saves the changes.
- Add records in a table: New records can be added through the table's Datasheet view or through a corresponding form. To add a new record to a table, click New in the Records group on the Home tab and begin typing the values in the field for the new record. Press Tab to move to subsequent fields.
- Delete records from a table: To delete a record, click the record selector and click Delete in the Records group on the Home tab.
- Save records in a table: Access saves your changes as soon as you move to a different record.

4. Use database utilities.
- Back up a database: The Back Up Database utility creates a duplicate copy of the database. This may enable users to recover from failure.
- Compact and Repair a database: The Compact and Repair utility reduces the size of a database and fixes any errors that may exist in the file.
- Print information: Access can create a print copy of your data. Previewing before printing is a good practice to avoid wasting paper.

5. Work with filters.
- Filters enable the display of desired records that meet specific criteria.
- Use a selection filter to find exact matches: A selection filter can be used to find exact matches.
- Use a selection filter to find records containing a value: A selection filter can find partial matches, for example, find values containing a certain phrase.
- Use Filter By Form: Filter By Form displays records based on multiple criteria and enables the user to apply logical operators and use comparison operators.

6. Perform sorts.
- Sort table data: Sorting changes the order of information, and information may be sorted by one or more fields. Data can be sorted ascending (low to high) or descending (high to low).

7. Create a database.
- Create a blank database: Creating a blank database enables you to create a database specific to your requirements.
- Create a database using a template: A template is a predefined database that includes professionally designed tables, forms, reports, and other objects that you can use to jumpstart the creation of your database.
- Explore database objects and customize a database template: After you create a database using a template, explore it and become familiar with the contents.
- Create a table using an application part: If you require a certain type of table (such as Contacts) you can add them using an application part.

Key Terms Matching

Match the key terms with their definitions. Write the key term letter by the appropriate numbered definition.

a. Application part
b. Database
c. Database Management System (DBMS)
d. Datasheet view
e. Design view
f. Field
g. Filter
h. Filter By Form
i. Form
j. Navigation Pane

k. Object
l. Primary key
m. Query
n. Record
o. Relationship
p. Report
q. Selection filter
r. Sort
s. Table
t. Template

1. _____ A method which enables the user to specify conditions to display only those records that meet certain conditions. **p. 98**

2. _____ An Access object that simplifies entering, modifying, and deleting table data. **p. 76**

3. _____ An object used to store data, organizing data into columns and rows. **p. 75**

4. _____ A method of listing records in a specific sequence (such as alphabetically). **p. 102**

5. _____ A predefined database that includes professionally designed tables, forms, reports, and other objects. **p. 109**

6. _____ A question the user asks about the data in a database. **p. 75**

7. _____ An Access interface element that organizes and lists database objects in a database. **p. 74**

8. _____ A filtering method that displays records based on multiple criteria. **p. 100**

9. _____ A set of common Access components that can be added to an existing database. **p. 113**

10. _____ An object that contains professional-looking, formatted information from underlying tables or queries. **p. 76**

11. _____ A main component that is created and used to make a database function, such as a table or form. **p. 74**

12. _____ A complete set of all the fields about one person, place, event, or concept. **p. 75**

13. _____ The field (or combination of fields) that uniquely identifies each record in a table. **p. 75**

14. _____ A connection between two tables using a common field. **p. 84**

15. _____ A collection of data organized as meaningful information that can be accessed, managed, stored, queried, sorted, and reported. **p. 72**

16. _____ A view that enables the user to create and modify a table design. **p. 81**

17. _____ A grid that enables the user to add, edit, and delete the records of a table. **p. 79**

18. _____ A piece of information stored in a table, such as a company name or city. **p. 75**

19. _____ A software system that provides the tools needed to create, maintain, and use a database. **p. 72**

20. _____ A filtering method that displays only records that exactly match selected criteria. **p. 98**

Multiple Choice

1. All of the following are examples of an Access object *except*?

   (a) Table
   (b) Form
   (c) Record
   (d) Macro

2. Where are data stored in a database?

   (a) Form
   (b) Query
   (c) Report
   (d) Table

3. You edit several records in an Access table. When should you execute the Save command?

   (a) Immediately after you edit a record
   (b) Once at the end of the session
   (c) Records are saved automatically; the save command is not required
   (d) When you close the table

4. Which of the following is *not* true of an Access database?

   (a) Each field has a data type that establishes the kind of data that can be entered.
   (b) Every record in a table has the same fields as every other record.
   (c) Every table in a database contains the same number of records as every other table.
   (d) A primary key uniquely identifies a record.

5. Which of the following is true regarding table views?

   (a) You can add, edit, and delete records using Design view.
   (b) Datasheet view shows a detailed view of the table design.
   (c) Datasheet view provides access to more field properties than Design view.
   (d) Changes made in Datasheet view are automatically saved when you move the insertion point to a different record.

6. Which of the following utilities is used to recover in the event of loss or damage?

   (a) Back Up Database
   (b) Compact and Repair Database
   (c) Database Splitter
   (d) Encrypt Database

7. Which of the following would be matched if you use a Selection filter's exact match option for the title "Manager"?

   (a) Sales Manager
   (b) Manager (but not MANAGER)
   (c) Manager and MANAGER
   (d) Sales Manager and Manager (but not MANAGER)

8. Which of the following conditions is available through a Selection filter?

   (a) Equal condition
   (b) Delete condition
   (c) AND condition
   (d) OR condition

9. All of the following statements are true about creating a database *except*:

   (a) A single blank table is provided with a blank database.
   (b) When creating a blank database, Access opens to a blank table in Datasheet view.
   (c) Using a template to create a database saves time because it includes predefined objects.
   (d) The objects provided in a template cannot be modified.

10. To add a predefined table to an existing database, you should use which of the following?

    (a) Application part
    (b) Blank database
    (c) Custom web app
    (d) Database template

Practice Exercises

1 Replacement Parts

As a recent hire at Replacement Parts, you are tasked with performing updates to the customer database. You have been asked to open the company's database, save it with a new name, and then modify, add, and delete records. You will then back up the database, apply filters and sorts, and use an application part to add a new table that will be used to track customer shipping and receiving complaints. Refer to Figure 1.47 as you complete the exercise.

Issues											✕
ID ▾	Summary ▾	Status ▾	Priority ▾	Category ▾	Project ▾	Opened Date ▾	Due Date ▾	Keywords ▾	Resolution		
1	Multiple customers have repo	1 - New	1 - Critical	1 - Category	1 - Project	7/3/2018					
* (New)		1 - New	1 - Critical	1 - Category	1 - Project	9/18/2018					

FIGURE 1.47 Issues Table Added to Replacement Parts Database

a. Start your computer. Click **Start**, and click **Access** from the list of applications. Click **Open Other Files** and click **Browse**. Navigate to the location of your student files. Double-click to open the *a01p1Replace* file. Click the **File tab**, click **Save As**. Click **Access Database**, and click **Save As**. Save the database as **a01p1Replace_LastFirst**. Click **Enable Content** on the message bar.

b. Locate the Navigation Pane. Double-click the **Manufacturers table** to open the table in Datasheet view. Locate record 800552 (Haas). Click the **ManufacturerName field** for the record. Change the name from Haas to **Haas International**. For the same record, click the **CountryOfOrigin field** and change the CountryOfOrigin from Germany to **Austria**.

c. Locate the last (blank) record. Click the **MfgID field**. Type **801411** and press **Tab**. In the ManufacturerName field type **Bolshoy Fine China** and press **Tab**. In the CountryOfOrigin field type **Russia** and press **Tab**. In the EmployeeID field type **817080** and press **Tab**. Type the following new records:

MfgID	ManufacturerName	CountryofOrigin	EmplolyeeID
801422	Tejada and Sons	Dominican Republic	816680
801433	Lubitz UK	England	817580

d. Locate the sixth record, with MfgID **800661** (John Bradshaw). Right-click on the **row indicator** for the record and select **Delete Record**. Click **Yes** to delete the record.

e. Click **Close** ✕ the at the top right of the table to close the Manufacturers table.

f. Click the **File tab**, click **Save As**, and then double-click **Back Up Database**. Accept the default backup file name and click **Save**.

g. Double-click the **Customers table** in the Navigation Pane to open the table in Datasheet view.

h. Click the **State field** for the first record (Diego Martinez). Click **Selection** in the Sort & Filter group and select **Equals "OR"** to display the two customers in Oregon. Close the table. Click **Close** ✕ at the top right of the Customers table tab. Click **Yes** when prompted to save the changes to the table.

i. Double-click the **Employees table** to open the table in Datasheet view.

j. Click the **plus sign** next to Alfonso Torres. Notice he is assigned as the representative for the manufacturer Antarah. Click the **minus sign** next to Alfonso Torres to close the subdatasheet.

k. Click **Advanced** in the Sort & Filter group on the Home tab and select **Filter By Form.** Click in the **Salary field**. Type **>60000** and click **Toggle Filter** in the Sort & Filter group on the Home tab to apply the filter. Six employees are displayed. Click Close ✕ at the top right of the Employees table tab. Click **Yes** when prompted to save the changes to the table.

l. Double-click the **Manufacturers table** to open the table in Datasheet view.

m. Click any value in the **ManufacturerName** field. Click **Ascending** in the Sort & Filter group to sort the table by the name of the manufacturer. Click Close ⊠ at the top right of the Manufacturers table tab. Click **Yes** when prompted to save the changes to the table.

n. Click **Application Parts** in the Templates group on the Create tab. Select **Issues**. Select the option for "There is no relationship." Click **Create**.

o. Double-click the **Issues table** to open the table in Datasheet view.

p. Click in the Summary field and type **Multiple customers have reported damaged goods received in Denton, Texas.** (include the period). Leave all other fields as the default values. Click Close ⊠ at the top right of the Issues table tab. Click **Yes** when prompted to save the changes to the table.

q. Close the database and exit Access. Based on your instructor's directions, submit the following:

a01p1Replace_LastFirst

a01p1Replace_LastFirst_*CurrentDate*

2 Custom Coffee

The Custom Coffee Company provides coffee, tea, and snacks to offices in Miami. Custom Coffee also supplies and maintains the equipment for brewing the beverages. To improve customer service, the owner recently had an Access database created to keep track of customers, orders, and products. This database will replace the Excel spreadsheets currently maintained by the office manager. The company hired you to verify and input all the Excel data into the Access database. Refer to Figure 1.48 as you complete the exercise.

Product ID	ProductName	Description	Cost	MarkupPercent	RefrigerationNeeded	Brand	Click to Add
2	Coffee - Hazelnut	24/Case, Pre-Ground 1.75 Oz Bags	$23.00	1	No	Premium	
4	Coffee - Assorted Flavors	18/Case. Pre-Ground 1.75 Oz Bags	$23.00	0.5	No	House	
26	Robusto Chai Tea Latte K-Cups	40/Box	$26.00	0.75	No	Premium	
27	Robusto French Roast K-Cups	40/Box	$28.00	1	No	Premium	

FIGURE 1.48 Filtered Products Table

a. Start your computer. Click **Start** and click **Access** from the list of applications. Click **Open Other Files** and click **Browse**. Navigate to the location of your student files. Double-click to open the *a01p2Coffee* file. Click the **File tab**, click **Save As**. Click **Access Database**, and then click **Save As**. Save the database as **a01p2Coffee_LastFirst**. Click **Enable Content** on the message bar.

b. Click the **Database Tools tab** and click **Relationships** in the Relationships group. Review the table relationships. Notice the join line between the Customers and Orders tables. Click **Relationship Report** in the Tools group on the Relationship Tools Design tab. Right-click the **Relationships** for a01p2Coffee_LastFirst tab, and click **Save**. Click **OK** to save the report with the default name.

c. Click Close ⊠ at the top right of the Relationships Report tab. Click Close ⊠ at the top right of the Relationships tab. Click **No** if prompted to save the changes to the relationships.

d. Double-click the **Sales Reps table** in the Navigation Pane to open it in Datasheet view. For rep number 2, replace **YourFirstName** and **YourLastName** with your first and last names. Close the table by clicking **Close** on the right side of the Sales Reps window.

e. Double-click the **Customers table** to open it in Datasheet view. Click **New** in the Records group. Add a new record by typing the following information; press **Tab** after each field. The first field is an autonumber data type, therefore you will begin by adding data to the Customer Name field. Input masks will add the correct formatting to the Phone and Sales Rep ID fields.

Customer Name:	**Budrow Driving School**
Contact:	**Eric Cameron**
Address 1:	**1 Clausen Blvd**
Address 2:	**Floor 2**
City:	**Chesterton**
State:	**IN**
Zip Code:	**46304**
Phone:	**8575556661**
Credit Rating:	**A**
Sales Rep ID:	**2**

Notice the pencil symbol in the record selector for the new row. Press **Tab**. The pencil symbol disappears, and the new customer is automatically saved to the table.

f. Click the **City field** for the last record (Chesterton). Click **Selection** in the Sort & Filter group and select **Equals "Chesterton"** to display the three customers located in the town of Chesterton.

g. Save and close the table. Click **Yes** if prompted to save the changes to the table.

h. Double-click the **Products table** to open it in Datasheet view. Click **New** in the Records group. Add a new record by typing the following information:

Product ID:	**26**
ProductName:	**Robusto Chai Tea Latte K-Cups**
Description:	**40/Box**
Cost:	**26**
MarkupPercent:	**.75**
RefrigerationNeeded	**No**
Brand	**Premium**

i. Add a second product using the following information:

Product ID:	**27**
ProductName:	**Robusto French Roast K-Cups**
Description:	**40/Box**
Cost:	**28**
MarkupPercent:	**1**
RefrigerationNeeded	**No**
Brand	**Premium**

j. Click **Advanced** in the Sort & Filter group and select **Filter By Form**. Type **>=23** in the Cost field and click **Toggle Filter** in the Sort & Filter group.

k. Save and close the table.

l. Click the **File tab**, click **Save As**, and then double-click **Back Up Database**. Accept the default backup file name and click **Save**.

m. Click **Application Parts** in the Templates group on the Create tab. Select **Issues**. Click **Next** to accept the default relationship. Select "**CustomerName**" as the Field from "Customers," select **Sort Ascending** from Sort this field, and then type **Customer** as the name for the lookup column. Click **Create**.

n. Double-click the **Issues table** to open it in Datasheet view.

o. Click the **Customer field** for the first record. Click the **arrow** and select **Advantage Sales**. Click in the **Summary field** and type **Customer reports French roast coffee delivered instead of decaf.** Leave all other fields as the default values.

p. Close the table. Close the database and exit Access. Based on your instructor's directions, submit the following:

a01p2Coffee_LastFirst

a01p2Coffee_LastFirst_*CurrentDate*

3 Healthy Living

FROM SCRATCH

You and two friends from your gym have decided to use Access to help you reach your weight goals. You will use the Access Nutrition template to help you get organized. Refer to Figure 1.49 as you complete this exercise.

ID	TipDescription	TipCategory	Click to Add
150	Walk, jog, skate, or cycle.	Activity	
147	Replace a coffee break with a brisk 10-minute walk. Ask a friend to go with yc	Activity	
146	Get off the bus or subway one stop early and walk or skate the rest of the way	Activity	
141	Walk, skate, or cycle more, and drive less.	Activity	
139	Walk the dog—don't just watch the dog walk.	Activity	
138	Walk up and down the soccer or softball field sidelines while watching the kid	Activity	
135	Join a walking group in the neighborhood or at the local shopping mall. Recrui	Activity	
*	(New)		

FIGURE 1.49 Filtered Tips Table

a. Start your computer. Click **Start**, and click **Access** from the list of applications. Click the **Nutrition tracking template** in Backstage view.

> **TROUBLESHOOTING:** If the Nutrition tracking template is not visible, type nutrition in the search box at the top of the screen and click the magnifying glass. Note there may be slight differences to the name, so look for the template matching the image above.

b. Type **a01p3Nutrition_LastFirst** in the File name box. Click **Browse**. Navigate to the location where you are saving your files in the File New Database dialog box, click **OK** to close the dialog box, and then click **Create** to create the new database.

c. Click **Enable Content** on the message bar. A form titled *Today at a glance* is already open. Close the form.

d. Double-click the **My Profile table** in the Navigation Pane to open it in Datasheet view.

e. Click **record selector**, click **Delete** in the Records group. Click **Yes** to delete the existing record.

f. Click **New** in the Records group. Type the following information in as a new record, pressing **Tab** between each field:

Sex:	Male
Height:	64
Weight:	190
Age:	28
Lifestyle:	Lightly active
Goal:	Lose weight

g. Click **New** in the Records group. Type the following information, pressing **Tab** between each field:

Sex:	**Male**
Height:	**69**
Weight:	**140**
Age:	**20**
Lifestyle:	**Moderately active**
Goal:	**Gain weight**

h. Click **New** in the Records group. Type the following information, pressing **Tab** between each field:

Sex:	**Female**
Height:	**66**
Weight:	**140**
Age:	**23**
Lifestyle:	**Moderately active**
Goal:	**Maintain my weight**

i. Close the table by clicking **Close** on the right side of the My Profile window.

j. Double-click the **Foods table**. Click **Advanced** in the Sort and Filter group and select **Filter By Form**.

k. Click the **Calories field** for the first record. Type **<200** in the Calories field and **>=10** in the Fiber [grams] field. Click **Toggle Filter** in the Sort & Filter group.

l. Save and close the table by clicking **Close** on the right side of the Foods window and clicking **Yes** when asked if you want to save the changes.

m. Double-click the **Tips table** to open it in Datasheet view.

n. Click in the first **TipCategory**. Click **Ascending** in the Sort & Filter group to sort the tips in alphabetical order.

o. Place the pointer over the word **Walk** in the fifth record (ID #138) and drag to select it. Make sure you do not highlight the space after the word Walk when you select the text. Click **Selection** in the Sort & Filter group and select **Contains "Walk"**.

p. Save and close the table by clicking **Close** on the right side of the Tips window and clicking **Yes** when asked if you want to save the changes.

q. Click the **File tab**, click **Save As**, and then double-click **Back Up Database**. Use the default backup file name.

r. Close the database and exit Access. Based on your instructor's directions, submit the following:

a01p3Nutrition_LastFirst
a01p3Nutrition _LastFirst_*CurrentDate*

Mid-Level Exercises

1 Sunshine Mental Health Services

Sunshine Mental Health Services provides counseling and medication services. They have recently expanded their database to include patients in addition to the staff. You were hired to replace their former Information Technology support staff member. You will work to update the data in the database, familiarize yourself with the table relationships, filter and sort a table, and add a table to keep track of user accounts. Finally, you add an application part to track the users.

a. Open the *a01m1Sunshine* file and save the database as **a01m1Sunshine_LastFirst**. Click **Enable Content** on the Security Warning message bar.

b. Open the **Staff table** in Datasheet view.

c. Locate the record for Kovit Ang (StaffID 80073). Replace his Address with **11 Market Street**, replace his City with **Harrison**, and his ZIPCode with **04040**. Leave all other fields with their current values.

d. Add yourself as a new staff member. Type a StaffID of **99999** and type your name in the Full-Name field. Type **1 Clinton Terrace** for your Address, **Harrison** as your City, **ME** as your State, and **04040** as your ZIP. Type a JobCode of **300**, a Salary of **48500**, and a 401k contribution of **0.02**. Click the box in the Active field so a check mark appears in the box.

e. Delete record **80399** (Stan Marsh).

f. Sort the table by Salary in descending order. Save and close the table.

g. Click **Relationships** in the Relationships group on the Database Tools tab and notice the relationship between the Pos table and the Staff table, and the relationship between the Staff table and Patients table. Each position has staff associated with it, and staff members have patients associated with them. Close the Relationships window.

h. Rename the **Pos table** to **Position**. Add a description to the table stating **This table contains a list of all available job titles at the company**. Click **OK**.

i. Open the **Position table** in Datasheet view. Click the **plus sign** next to JobCode 100 (Social Worker). Notice seven social workers are employed by the company. Click the **plus sign** next to JobCode 300 (IT Support). Only your name should display. Close the table.

j. Open the **Patients table** in Datasheet view. Use a Selection filter to show all patients associated with **StaffID 80073**. Save and close the table.

k. Open the **Staff table** in Datasheet view. Use Filter By Form to display all staff members who earn a salary of more than **80000**. Toggle the filter to verify the results. Save and close the table.

l. Back up the database. Accept the default file name.

m. Add the **Users application part** to the database. Change the relationship so there is One "Staff" to many "Users" by clicking the arrow next to Patients and selecting **Staff**. Click **Next**. Select the **FullName** field from the Staff table, choose the **Sort Ascending** option, and then name the lookup column **User**. Click **Create**.

n. Open the **Users table** in Datasheet view.

o. Select **Adolfo Ortiz** in the User field. Type **aortiz@sunshinementalhealth.org** for Email and **aortiz** for Login. Leave the Full Name blank. Close the table.

p. Open the **Patient Data Entry** form in Form view. Delete the phone number for **PatientID 1** (Minoru Kobayashi). Close the form.

q. Close the database and exit Access. Based on your instructor's directions, submit the following:

a01m1Sunshine_LastFirst
a01m1Sunshine_LastFirst_*CurrentDate*

ANALYSIS CASE

The Association of Higher Education will host its National Conference on your campus next year. To facilitate the conference, the Information Technology department has replaced last year's Excel spreadsheets with an Access database containing information on the rooms, speakers, and sessions.

a. Open the *a01m2NatConf* file and save the database as **a01m2NatConf_LastFirst**. Click **Enable Content** on the Security Warning message bar.

b. Open **Relationships**.

c. Review the objects and relationships in the database. Notice that there is a relationship between Speakers and SessionSpeaker. Click **Relationship Report** in the Tools group on the Relationship Tools Design tab. Right-click the **Relationships** for the a01m2NatConf_LastFirst tab, and click **Save**. Click **OK** to save the report with the default name. Close the Relationship report tab. Close the relationships.

d. Open the **SessionSpeaker table**. Scroll to the first blank record at the bottom of the table and type a new record using SpeakerID **99** and SessionID **09**. (Note: Speaker 99 does not exist.) How does Access respond? Press **Escape** twice to cancel your change. Close the table.

e. Open the **Speakers table**. Replace *YourFirstName* with your first name and *YourLastName* with your last name. Close the Speakers table.

f. Open the **Sessions table** and use a Selection filter to identify the sessions that take place in room 101.

g. Sort the filtered results in ascending order by the **SessionTitle** field. Save and close the table.

h. Back up the database. Use the default backup file name.

i. Open the *a01m2Analysis.docx* document in Word and save the document as **a01m2Analysis_LastFirst .docx**. Use the database objects you created to answer the questions. Save and close the document.

j. Close the database and exit Access. Based on your instructor's directions, submit the following:

a01m2NatConf_LastFirst
a01m2NatConf_LastFirst_*CurrentDate*
a01m2Analysis_LastFirst.docx

Running Case

New Castle County Technical Services

New Castle County Technical Services (NCCTS) provides technical support for a number of companies in the greater New Castle County, Delaware, area. They are working to move their record keeping to an Access database. You will add, update, and delete some records, add filters, and create a backup.

a. Open the database *a01r1NCCTS* and save the database as **a01r1NCCTS_LastFirst**. Click **Enable Content** on the Security Warning message bar.

b. Open the **Call Types table** in Datasheet view. Type the following rates for the HourlyRate field and close the table:

Description	Hourly Rate
Hardware Support	30
Software Support	25
Network Troubleshooting	40
Network Installation	40
Training	50
Security Camera Maintenance	40
Virus Removal	25
Disaster Recovery	60
VoIP Service	45
Other	35

c. Open the **Reps table** in Datasheet view. Add a new record, filling in the value **8** for the RepID field, your last name as the rep's last name, and your first name as the rep's first name.

d. Sort the Reps table by **RepLast** in ascending order. Close the table.

e. Open the **Customers table** in Datasheet view. Locate the record for **Edwin VanCleef** (PC030). Delete the entire record.

f. Click in the **City field** for SVC Pharmacy. Use the Selection filter to only show customers who are located in the city of **Newark**. Save and close the table.

g. Open the **Calls table** in Datasheet view. Use **Filter By Form** to filter the HoursLogged field so only calls with 10 or more hours logged on the call (**>=10**) are displayed. Save and close the table.

h. Back up the database, using the default name.

i. Close the database and exit Access. Based on your instructor's directions, submit the following:

a01r1NCCTS_LastFirst
a01r1NCCTS_LastFirst_*CurrentDate*

Disaster Recovery

Lugo Web Hosting

Your Access database has become corrupted, and you are in the process of restoring it from a backup from two weeks ago. In the last two weeks, there have been only a few changes. All users who previously had a 900 GB quota have had their quotas increased to 1 TB. In addition, all users who were previously on the server named Aerelon have been moved to another server, Caprica. You have determined you can use filters to help fix the data in the Users table. Open the *a01d1Lugo_Backup* file and save the database as **a01d1Lugo_LastFirst**. Apply filters to show users who meet the conditions above and manually change the data for each user. Sort the table by the server in ascending order. Close the database and exit Access. Based on your instructor's directions, submit a01d1Lugo_LastFirst.

Capstone Exercise

Lending for Small Businesses

You are employed as a technical supervisor at a lending firm for small business loans. You will work with a form that is used to store loan officer information, add records, and sort tables.

Modify Data in a Table

You will open an original database file and save the database with a new name. You will then demonstrate modifying, adding, and deleting information by using tables and forms.

1. Open the *a01c1Loans* file and save the database as **a01c1Loans_LastFirst**.

2. Open the **Loan Officers table** in Datasheet view. Update the database with the information below and close the table.

First Name	Last Name	Email Address	Phone Ext	Title
John	Badman	john_badman@loanofficer.com	x1757	Loan Officer
Stan	Dupp	stan_dupp@loanofficer.com	x6720	Senior Loan Officer
Herb	Avore	herb_avore@loanofficer.com	x2487	Loan Officer
Polly	Esther	polly_esther@loanofficer.com	x8116	Senior Loan Officer
Strawberry	Fields	strawberry_fields@loanofficer.com	x3219	Loan Officer
Ann	Serdifone	ann_serdifone@loanofficer.com	x5962	Managing Loan Officer

3. Close the Loan Officers table.

4. Open the **Loans table** in Datasheet view. Add a new record with the following information:

OfficerID:	5
MemberID:	15
LoanAmount:	7000
Term:	36 months
InterestRate:	15.41%
Payment:	244.07
Grade:	D
IssueDate:	12/15/18
LoanStatus:	Late (31-120 days)

5. Open the **Maintain Members form**. In record 3 (for *Brynn Anderson*, MemberID 13), add a new loan to the subform:

OfficerID:	5
LoanAmount:	17000
Term:	36 months
InterestRate:	4.35%
Payment:	300.45
Grade:	B
IssueDate:	9/1/18
LoanStatus:	Fully Paid

6. Use the Navigation bar to search for MemberID **16**, and edit the subform so that the InterestRate is **0.1254** instead of 0.1899 for the LoanID *47*.

7. Close the Maintain Members form.

Sort a Table and Use Filter By Form

You will sort the Loan table and apply a filter to display only publishers located in New York.

8. Sort the records in the Loans table by the **IssueDate** field in descending order (newest to oldest).

9. Locate the loans that have a rate of less than **11%** (**<0.11**) and a term of **36 months**. Use the Filter By Form to apply the filters and preview the filtered table.

10. Close the table and save the changes.

Apply a Selection Filter and Sort a Query

You are interested in quickly filtering the data in the Loans, Officers, and Members query based on a specific loan officer. You then sort the filtered results to view the loans by loan status.

11. Open the **Loans, Officers, and Members query** in Datasheet view.

12. Use a Selection filter to show only the loans managed by the loan officer whose name is **John Badman**.

13. Sort the query by **LoanStatus** in alphabetical order. Save and close the query.

Back Up a Database and Add an Application Part

You will demonstrate adding an application part to the manager to show how tables are created. You will first back the database up to reinforce the importance of backing up the data.

14. Create a backup copy of your database, accepting the default file name.

15. Add a Comments application part, selecting the option **One 'Loans' to many 'Comments.'** Select the **LoanStatus field** for the Field from Loans and **Sort Ascending** for Sort this field. Name the lookup column **Status**.

16. Close the database and exit Access. Based on your instructor's directions, submit the following:

a01c1Loans_LastFirst
a01c1Loans_LastFirst_CurrentDate

Tables and Queries in Relational Databases

LEARNING OUTCOMES
You will create and modify tables for data input and organization.
You will develop queries to extract and present data.

OBJECTIVES & SKILLS: After you read this chapter, you will be able to:

Table Design, Creation, and Modification

OBJECTIVE 1: DESIGN A TABLE   134
Design a Table

OBJECTIVE 2: CREATE AND MODIFY TABLES AND WORK WITH DATA   138
Create a Table in Datasheet View, Delete a Field, Set a Table's Primary Key, Work with Field Properties, Create a New Field in Design View, Modify the Table in Datasheet View

HANDS-ON EXERCISE 1   145

Multiple-Table Databases

OBJECTIVE 3: IMPORT DATA FROM EXTERNAL SOURCES   149
Import Excel Data, Import Access Data, Modify an Imported Table's Design, Add Data to an Imported Table

OBJECTIVE 4: ESTABLISH TABLE RELATIONSHIPS   152
Establish Table Relationships, Enforce and Test Referential Integrity

HANDS-ON EXERCISE 2   157

Single-Table Queries

OBJECTIVE 5: CREATE A SINGLE-TABLE QUERY   164
Create a Single-Table Query

OBJECTIVE 6: USE THE QUERY WIZARD   167
Use the Simple Query Wizard

OBJECTIVE 7: SPECIFY QUERY CRITERIA   169
Use Query Design View, Specify Query Criteria

OBJECTIVE 8: SPECIFY QUERY SORT ORDER AND RUN A QUERY   172
Specify Query Sort Order, Run a Query

OBJECTIVE 9: COPY AND MODIFY A QUERY   172
Copy and Modify a Query, Change Query Data

HANDS-ON EXERCISE 3   174

Multitable Queries

OBJECTIVE 10: CREATE A MULTITABLE QUERY   177
Add Additional Tables and Fields to an Existing Query, Create a Multitable Query from Scratch

OBJECTIVE 11: MODIFY A MULTITABLE QUERY   178
Modify a Multitable Query, Add and Delete Fields in a Multitable Query, Use a Total Row to Summarize Data in a Query

HANDS-ON EXERCISE 4   182

CASE STUDY | Bank Internship

You have started an internship at Commonwealth Federal Bank in Wilmington, Delaware. The bank is considering converting its existing records into an Access application. To analyze whether that would be advantageous, the manager asks you to create a sample Access database made up of customers, accounts, and the bank's respective branches.

Designing Databases and Extracting Information

Sfio Cracho/Shutterstock

As you begin, you realize that some of the data are contained in external Excel and Access files that you will import directly into the new database. Importing from Excel and Access is fairly straightforward and will help to avoid common errors that are associated with data entry. Once the data have been imported, you will use queries to view the records in ways that are relevant to the bank's usage.

Once the new database is created and the data are entered, you will extract information about the customers, accounts, and branches by creating and running queries. The value of that information depends entirely on the quality of the underlying data—the tables. This chapter uses the bank database to present the basic principles of table and query design.

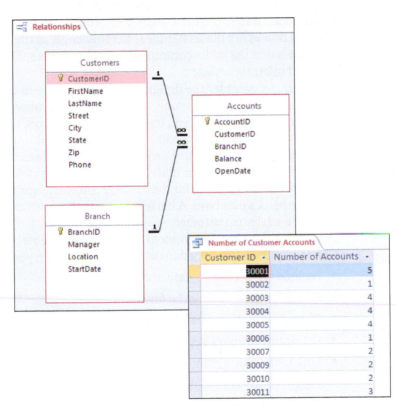

FIGURE 2.1 Bank Database

CASE STUDY | Bank Internship

Starting Files	File to be Submitted
Blank database **a02h2Accounts** **a02h2Customers.xlsx**	**a02h4Bank_LastFirst**

MyLab IT Grader An alternate version of this project is available as a MyLab IT Grader Assessment

Table Design, Creation, and Modification

A successful and usable database design begins with the tables. Because tables store all the data, they provide the basis for all the activities you perform in a database. If the tables are not designed properly, the database will not function as expected. Whether you are experienced in designing tables or are a new database designer, the process should not be done haphazardly. You should follow a systematic approach when creating tables for a database.

In this section, you will learn the essentials of good table design. After developing and analyzing the table design on paper, you will implement that design in Access. In addition, you will learn to create and refine tables by changing the properties of various fields.

Designing a Table

A table is a collection of records, with each record made up of a number of fields. During the table design process, consider the specific fields you will need in each table; list the proposed fields with their table names, and determine what type of data each field will store (numbers, dates, pictures, etc.). The order of the fields within the table and the specific field names are not as significant at this stage, as they can be modified later. What is important is that the tables contain all necessary fields so that the database can produce the required information later.

For example, consider the design process necessary to create a database for a bank. Typically, your bank has your name, address, phone number, and Social Security number. It also knows which accounts you have (checking, savings, money market), your account balances, and if you have a credit card with that bank. Additionally, your bank keeps information about its branches around the city or state. If you think about the data your bank maintains, you can make a list of the categories of data needed to store that information. These categories for the bank—customers, accounts, branches—become the tables in the bank's database. A bank's customer list is an example of a table; it contains a record for each bank customer.

After the tables have been identified, plan for the necessary fields using these six guidelines, which are discussed in detail in the following paragraphs:

- Include the necessary data.
- Design for now and for the future.
- Store data in their smallest parts.
- Determine primary keys.
- Link tables using common fields.
- Design to accommodate calculations.

Figure 2.2 shows a customer table and two other tables found in a sample bank database. It also lists fields that would be needed in each table.

Include Necessary Data

A good way to determine what data (inputs) are necessary in tables is to consider the output you will need from your database. You will probably need to create professional-looking reports for others, so begin by creating a rough draft of the reports you will need. Then design tables that contain the fields necessary to create those reports. In other words, ask yourself what information will be expected from the database (outputs) and determine the data required (inputs) to produce that information. Defining and organizing good data input will result in better output from your database. Consider, for example, the tables and fields in Figure 2.2. Is there required information that could not be generated from those tables?

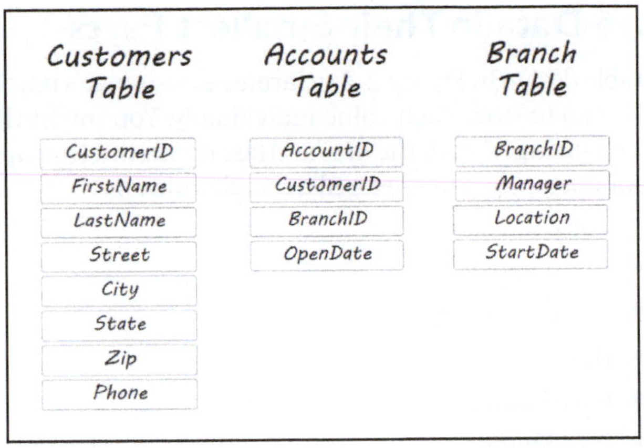

FIGURE 2.2 Rough Draft of Tables and Fields in a Sample Bank Database

- You will be able to determine how long a customer has banked with the branch because the date he or she opened the account is stored in the Accounts table, which will eventually connect to the Customers and Branch tables.

- You will be able to determine which branch a customer uses because the Accounts table includes both the CustomerID and the BranchID. The Accounts table will eventually connect to both the Customers and Branch tables, making it possible to gather this information.

- You will not be able to generate the monthly bank statement. To generate a customer bank statement (showing all deposits and withdrawals for the month), you would need to add an additional table—to track activity for each account.

- You will not be able to email a customer because the Customers table does not contain an email field at this time. If additional fields are required, such as a cell phone number, email address, or an emergency contact, you will want to include them in this stage of the design process. However, it is possible to add missing fields later.

Design for Now and for the Future

As the information requirements of an organization evolve over time, the database that stores and organizes the data must change as well. When designing a database, try to anticipate future needs and build in the flexibility to satisfy those demands. For example, you may also decide to create additional fields for future use (such as an email or customer photo field). However, additional fields will also require more storage space, which you will need to consider, especially when working with larger databases. Good database design must balance the data collection needs of the organization with the cost associated with collection and storage. Plans must also include the frequency and cost necessary to modify and update the database.

In the Customers table, for example, you would store each customer's name, address, and home phone number. You would also want to store additional phone numbers for many customers—a cell phone number, and perhaps a work number. As a database designer, you will design the tables to accommodate multiple entries for similar data.

Store Data in Their Smallest Parts

The table design in Figure 2.2 separates a customer's name into two fields (FirstName and LastName) to store each value individually. You might think it is simpler to use a single field consisting of both the first and last name, but that approach is too limiting. Consider a list of customer names stored as single values:

- Sue Grater
- Rick Grater
- Nancy Gallagher
- Harry Weigner
- Barb Shank
- Pete Shank

The first problem in this approach is the lack of flexibility: You could not easily create a salutation for a letter using the form *Dear Sue* or *Dear Ms. Gallagher* because the first and last names are not stored or retrievable individually.

A second difficulty is that the list of customers cannot be easily displayed in alphabetical order by last name because the last name begins in the middle of the value. The most common way to sort names is by the last name, which you can do more efficiently if the last name is stored as a separate field.

You may need to select customer records for a particular state or zip code, which will be easier if you store the data as separate fields. The customer's city, state, and zip code should always be stored as individual fields, along with any other values that you may want to sort by or retrieve separately.

Determine Primary Keys

When designing your database tables, it is important to determine the primary key. Recall that the primary key is the field whose values will uniquely identify each record in a table. For example, in Figure 2.2, the CustomerID field will uniquely identify each customer in the database. If you have two customers with the same first and last names, such as John Williams, how would you be able to distinguish one from the other when entering records? In a Customers table, the CustomerID values can be typed individually, or you could have a system that assigns these unique values automatically. Either way, each record should have its own unique primary key field value.

Plan for Common Fields Between Tables

As you create the tables and fields for the database, keep in mind that some tables will be joined in relationships using common fields. Creating relationships will enable you to extract data from more than one table when creating queries, forms, and reports. For example, you will be able to determine which customers have which accounts by joining the Customers and Accounts tables. CustomerID in the Customers table will join to the CustomerID field in the Accounts table. It may make sense to you to name the common fields the same way in each table, although that is not a firm requirement in Access. Draw a *join line* between common fields to indicate how the tables will be related, as shown in Figure 2.3. You will create join lines between tables when you learn to create table relationships later in the chapter.

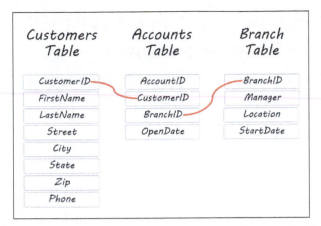

FIGURE 2.3 Determine Relationships Using Common Fields

Avoid *data redundancy*, which is the unnecessary storing of duplicate data in two or more tables. Having redundant or duplicate data in multiple tables can lead to serious errors. Suppose the customer address is stored in both the Customers and Accounts tables. If a customer moved to a new address, it is possible that the address would be updated in only one of the two tables. The result would be inconsistent and unreliable information. Depending on which table you would use to check an address, either the new or the old one might be given to someone requesting the information. Storing the address in only one table is more reliable; if it changes, it only needs to be updated one time (in the Customers table) and can be referenced again and again from that table. In the case of the bank database, each customer's address will only be stored one time. CustomerID in the Customers table will join to the CustomerID field in the Accounts table. Because of this relationship, the address will be retrievable when required by other objects created in the database.

> **TIP: COMMON FIELD NAMES AND DATA TYPES**
> Although it may make sense to name the common fields the same way between tables, it is not a requirement in Access. For example, you could use CustomerID in one table and CustomerNumber in another to identify your customers. However, the data types of the fields should match, so if you are using the Short Text data type in one table, use the same data type for the common field in the related table.

Design to Accommodate Calculations

A calculated field produces a value from an expression or function that references one or more existing fields. Calculated fields are frequently created in database objects with numeric data, such as a monthly interest field that multiplies the balance in a customer's account by 1% each month (Balance*.01). You can also create calculated fields using date/time data. For example, if you want to store the length of time a customer has had an account, you can create a calculated field that subtracts the opening date from today's date. The result will be the number of days each customer has been an account holder.

A person's age is another example of a calculated field using date arithmetic—the date of birth is subtracted from today's date and the result is divided by 365 (or 365.25 to account for leap years). It might seem easier to store a person's age as a number rather than the birth date to avoid using a calculated field, but that would be a mistake because age changes over time and the field would need to be updated each time it changes. You can use date arithmetic to subtract one date from another to find out the number of days, months, or years that have elapsed between them.

Access enables you to store calculated fields in a table using the calculated data type and to include those fields in queries, forms, and reports. However, many Access users prefer to create calculated fields in their query designs rather than in the tables themselves.

STEP 1 › Creating and Modifying Tables and Working with Data

Tables can be created in a new blank database or in an existing database by using any of the following methods:

- Enter field names and table data directly in Datasheet view.
- Type field names in rows in Design view and enter the data in Datasheet view.
- Import data from another database or application, such as Excel.
- Use a template.

Regardless of how a table is first created, you can always modify it later to include a new field or to change an existing field. Changes to existing fields should be handled with caution. Generally, we think about Datasheet view as the "front end" of the table, where data can be entered, edited, and viewed, although it is possible to create and modify a table using the datasheet. For more sophisticated options, you can switch to Design view of the table, which can be considered the "back end" of the table. More design changes can be made in Design view; however, you will need to return to Datasheet view to enter, edit, or view data. Figure 2.4 shows a table created by entering fields in Design view.

When you add a field to a table, the field must be given an appropriate name to identify the data it stores. The field name should be descriptive of the data and can be up to 64 characters in length, including letters, numbers, and spaces. Field names cannot begin with a leading blank space. Database developers sometimes use Pascal Case notation for field names. Instead of spaces in multiword field names, you can use uppercase letters to distinguish the first letter of each new word, for example, ProductCost or LastName (some developers use Camel Case, which is similar to Pascal Case, where the first letter of the first word is lowercase). It is sometimes preferable to avoid spaces in field names because spaces can cause naming conflicts with other applications that may use these fields, such as Microsoft Visual Basic for Applications. As mentioned previously, fields can be added, deleted, or renamed either in Design view or Datasheet view.

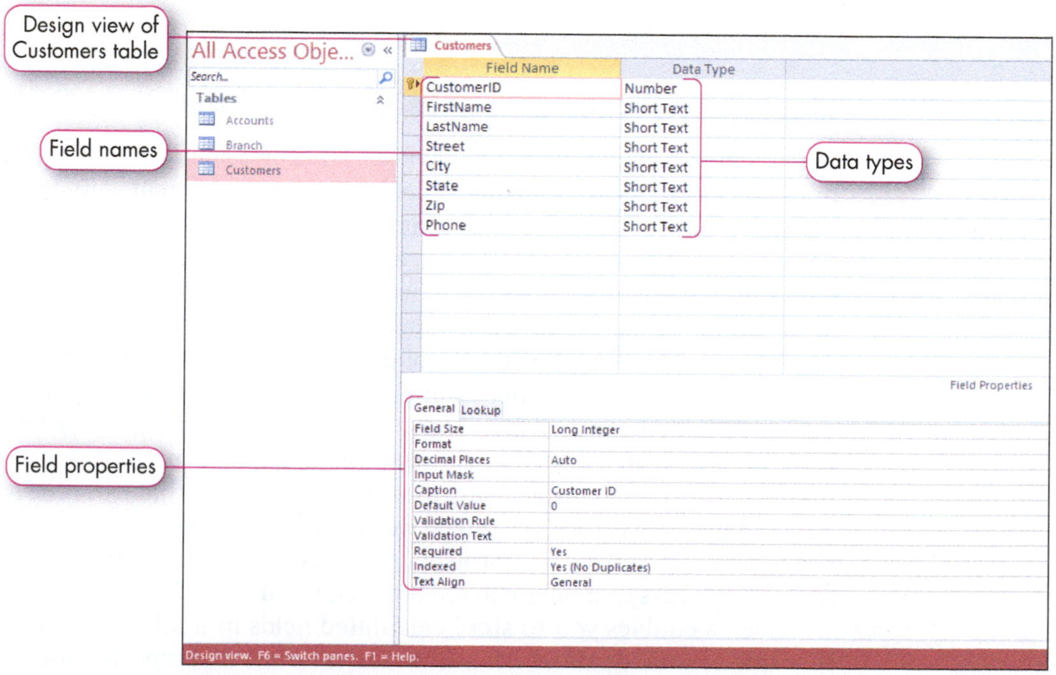

FIGURE 2.4 Customers Table Created in Design View

To rename a field, select the field name you want to change, type the new field name, press Enter, and then save the table. To delete a field from a table, use one of the following methods:

- In Datasheet view, select the field and press Delete. Click Yes in the message box.
- In Design view, click the record selector of the field you want to delete, and click Delete Rows in the tools group on the design tab. Click Yes in the message box that displays to confirm that you want to permanently delete the field and the data in it.

> **TIP: HIDE FIELDS IN AN ACCESS DATASHEET**
>
> At times, not all fields in a datasheet need to be displayed at once. You may only need to view or modify certain fields and not others. To hide a field in a datasheet, right-click the column selector that displays the field name and from the shortcut menu, select Hide Fields. To make the field visible again, right-click any column selector, select Unhide Fields, and then select the appropriate column's check box.

Determine Data Type

Every field in a table has an assigned ***data type*** that determines the type of data that can be entered and the operations that can be performed on that data. Table 2.1 lists the data types, their uses, and examples of each. Data types are important when creating and joining common fields in tables. The data types of the common fields must match (with a few minor exceptions). For example, if CustomerID is a Number field in one table, but a Short Text value in another, you will need to change the data type in one or the other to avoid a data type mismatch. You can change a data type after you have entered data into your table but do so with caution. In some cases, changing data types is inconsequential; for example, you may want to convert a number to a currency value. This type of change would only affect the formatting displayed with the values, not the underlying values themselves. Other types of changes could become more problematic. In any case, when designing tables, choose the initial data type carefully, and be sure to back up your database before changing data types.

> **TIP: KEYBOARD SHORTCUT FOR DATA TYPES**
>
> You also can type the first letter of the data type, such as d for Date/Time, s for Short Text, or n for Number. To use the keyboard shortcut, click in the field name and press Tab to advance to the Data Type column. Next, type the first letter of the data type.

TABLE 2.1 Data Types and Uses

Data Type	Description	Example
Short Text	Stores alphanumeric data, such as a customer's name or address. It can contain alphabetic characters, numbers, and/or special characters (e.g., an apostrophe in O'Malley). Social Security numbers, telephone numbers, and postal codes should be designated as text fields because they are not used in calculations and often contain special characters such as hyphens and parentheses. A short text field can hold up to 255 characters.	2184 Walnut Street
Long Text	Lengthy text or combinations of text and numbers, such as several sentences or paragraphs; used to hold descriptive data. Long text controls can display up to 64,000 characters.	A description of product packaging
Number	Contains a value that can be used in a calculation, such as the number of credits a course is worth. The contents are restricted to numbers, a decimal point, and a plus or minus sign.	12
Large Number	Used for storing very large numeric values in a database, allowing a greater range for calculations. Enabling this data type makes your database incompatible with versions of Access prior to 2016.	9,223,372,036,854,775,807
Date/Time	Stores dates or times that can be used in date or time arithmetic.	10/31/2018 1:30:00 AM
Currency	Used for fields that contain monetary values.	$1,200
AutoNumber	A special data type used to assign the next consecutive number each time you add a record. The value of an AutoNumber field is unique for each record in the table.	1, 2, 3
Yes/No	Only one of two values can be stored, such as Yes or No, True or False, or On or Off (also known as a Boolean). For example, is a student on the Dean's list: Yes or No.	Yes
OLE Object	Contains an object created by another application. OLE objects include pictures and sounds.	JPG image
Hyperlink	Stores a Web address (URL) or the path to a folder or file. Hyperlink fields can be clicked to retrieve a webpage or to launch a file stored locally.	http://www.irs.gov
Attachment	Used to store one or multiple images, spreadsheet files, documents, and other types of supported files in records.	An Excel workbook
Calculated	The results of an expression that references one or more existing fields.	[Price]*.05
Lookup Wizard	Creates a field that enables you to choose a value from another table or from a list of values by using a list box or a combo box.	Accounts table with a CustomerID field that looks up the customer from the records in the Customers table

STEP 2 Set a Table's Primary Key

The primary key is the field (or possibly a combination of fields) that uniquely identifies each record in a table. Access does not require that each table have a primary key. However, a good database design usually includes a primary key in each table. You should select unique and infrequently changing data for the primary key. For example, a credit card number may seem to be unique, but would not make a good primary key because it is subject to change when a new card is issued due to fraudulent activity.

You probably would not use a person's name as the primary key, because several people could have the same name. A value like CustomerID, as shown in the Customers table in Figure 2.5, is unique and is a better choice for the primary key. When no field seems to stand out as a primary key as a natural choice, you can create a primary key field with the AutoNumber data type. The **AutoNumber** data type is a number that automatically increments each time a record is added, starting with 1. The next added record would be 2, and so forth.

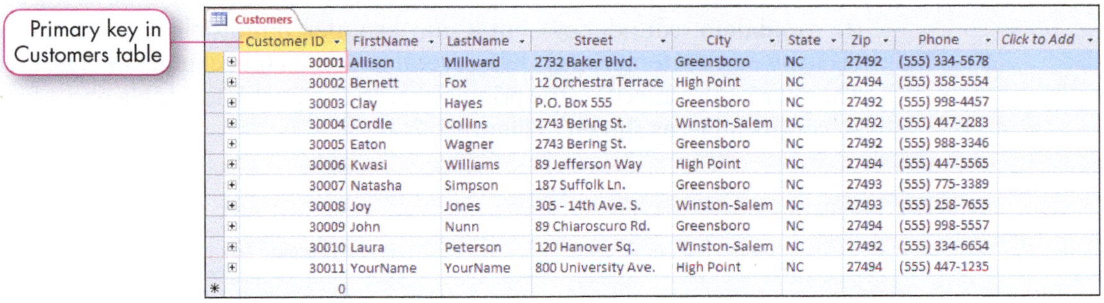

Primary key in Customers table

Customer ID	FirstName	LastName	Street	City	State	Zip	Phone	Click to Add
30001	Allison	Millward	2732 Baker Blvd.	Greensboro	NC	27492	(555) 334-5678	
30002	Bernett	Fox	12 Orchestra Terrace	High Point	NC	27494	(555) 358-5554	
30003	Clay	Hayes	P.O. Box 555	Greensboro	NC	27492	(555) 998-4457	
30004	Cordle	Collins	2743 Bering St.	Winston-Salem	NC	27492	(555) 447-2283	
30005	Eaton	Wagner	2743 Bering St.	Greensboro	NC	27492	(555) 988-3346	
30006	Kwasi	Williams	89 Jefferson Way	High Point	NC	27494	(555) 447-5565	
30007	Natasha	Simpson	187 Suffolk Ln.	Greensboro	NC	27493	(555) 775-3389	
30008	Joy	Jones	305 - 14th Ave. S.	Winston-Salem	NC	27493	(555) 258-7655	
30009	John	Nunn	89 Chiaroscuro Rd.	Greensboro	NC	27494	(555) 998-5557	
30010	Laura	Peterson	120 Hanover Sq.	Winston-Salem	NC	27492	(555) 334-6654	
30011	YourName	YourName	800 University Ave.	High Point	NC	27494	(555) 447-1235	
0								

FIGURE 2.5 Customers Table with a Natural Choice for the Primary Key

Figure 2.6 depicts a Speakers table, where no unique field can be identified from the data itself. In this case, you can identify the SpeakerID field with an AutoNumber data type. Access automatically numbers each speaker record sequentially with a unique ID as each record is added.

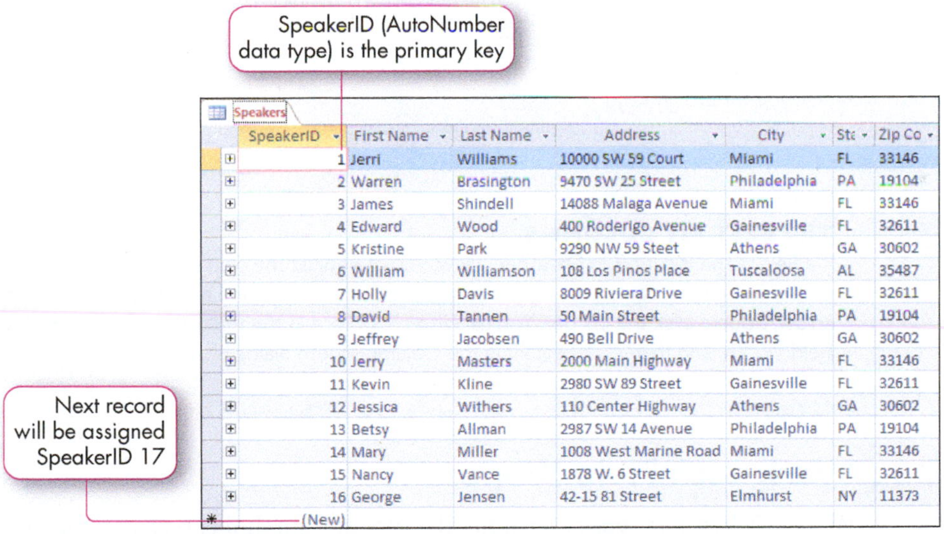

SpeakerID (AutoNumber data type) is the primary key

SpeakerID	First Name	Last Name	Address	City	State	Zip Code
1	Jerri	Williams	10000 SW 59 Court	Miami	FL	33146
2	Warren	Brasington	9470 SW 25 Street	Philadelphia	PA	19104
3	James	Shindell	14088 Malaga Avenue	Miami	FL	33146
4	Edward	Wood	400 Roderigo Avenue	Gainesville	FL	32611
5	Kristine	Park	9290 NW 59 Steet	Athens	GA	30602
6	William	Williamson	108 Los Pinos Place	Tuscaloosa	AL	35487
7	Holly	Davis	8009 Riviera Drive	Gainesville	FL	32611
8	David	Tannen	50 Main Street	Philadelphia	PA	19104
9	Jeffrey	Jacobsen	490 Bell Drive	Athens	GA	30602
10	Jerry	Masters	2000 Main Highway	Miami	FL	33146
11	Kevin	Kline	2980 SW 89 Street	Gainesville	FL	32611
12	Jessica	Withers	110 Center Highway	Athens	GA	30602
13	Betsy	Allman	2987 SW 14 Avenue	Philadelphia	PA	19104
14	Mary	Miller	1008 West Marine Road	Miami	FL	33146
15	Nancy	Vance	1878 W. 6 Street	Gainesville	FL	32611
16	George	Jensen	42-15 81 Street	Elmhurst	NY	11373
(New)						

Next record will be assigned SpeakerID 17

FIGURE 2.6 Speakers Table with an AutoNumber Primary Key

Explore a Foreign Key

Recall that part of good database planning is to plan for common fields between tables that will be joined in relationships. This is necessary so that data from different tables can be combined into meaningful queries and reports. One of the common fields will be the primary key in one table; the other common field in the related table is denoted as the *foreign key*. The CustomerID is the primary key (identified with a primary key icon) in the Customers table and uniquely identifies each customer in the database. CustomerID also displays as a foreign key in the related Accounts table to establish which customer owns the account(s). A CustomerID can be entered only one time in the Customers table (to avoid data redundancy), but it may be entered multiple times in the Accounts table because one customer may own several accounts (checking, savings, credit card, etc.). Therefore, CustomerID is the primary key in the Customers table and a foreign key in the Accounts table, as shown in Figure 2.7.

FIGURE 2.7 Two Tables Illustrating Primary and Foreign Keys

> **TIP: BEST FIT COLUMNS**
> If a field name is cut off in Datasheet view, you can adjust the column width by positioning the pointer on the vertical border on the right side of the column. When the pointer displays as a two-headed arrow, double-click the border. You can also click More in the Records group on the Home tab, select Field Width, and then click Best Fit in the Column Width dialog box.

STEP 3 ▶ Work with Field Properties

While a field's data type determines the type of data that can be entered and the operations that can be performed on that data, its *field properties* determine how the field is formatted and behaves. The field properties are set to default values according to the data type, but you can modify them as required. Field properties are commonly set in Design view, as shown in Figure 2.4; however, certain properties can be set in Datasheet view on the Table Tools Fields tab. Common properties are defined in Table 2.2.

TABLE 2.2	Common Access Table Properties and Descriptions
Property	**Description**
Field Size	Determines the maximum number of characters of a text field or the format of a number field. If you shorten a field size and save the change, a warning dialog box opens to indicate that "Some data may be lost" because the new field size is able to store less data.
Format	Changes the way a field is displayed or printed but does not affect the stored value.
Input Mask	Simplifies data entry by providing literal characters that are typed for every entry, such as hyphens in a Social Security number or slashes in a date. It also imposes data validation by ensuring that data entered conform to the mask.
Caption	Enables an alternate (or more readable) name to be displayed other than the field name; alternate name displays in datasheets, forms, and reports.
Default Value	Enters automatically a predetermined value for a field each time a new record is added to the table. For example, if most customers live in Los Angeles, the default value for the City field could be set to Los Angeles to save data entry time and promote accurate data entry.
Validation Rule	Requires data entered to conform to a specified rule.
Validation Text	Specifies the error message that is displayed when the validation rule is violated.
Required	Indicates that a value for this field must be entered. Primary key fields always require data entry.
Allow Zero Length	Allows entry of zero length text strings in a Hyperlink, or Short or Long Text fields.
Indexed	Increases the efficiency of a search on the designated field. When a primary key is set on a field, an index is automatically created by Access for that field. If you create a unique index on any field, Yes (No Duplicates), you cannot duplicate a value in that field.
Expression	Used for calculated fields only. Specifies the expression you want Access to evaluate and store.
Result Type	Used for calculated fields only. Specifies the format for the calculated field results.

Field Size is a commonly changed field property. The field size determines the amount of space a field uses in the database. A field with a Short Text data type can store up to 255 characters; however, you can limit the characters by reducing the field size property. For example, you might limit the State field to only two characters because state abbreviations are two letters. When setting field sizes, anticipate any future requirements of the database that might necessitate larger values to be stored. If you shorten a field size and save the change, a warning dialog box opens to indicate that "Some data may be lost" because the new field size is able to store less data. If your table contained State values that were longer than two characters earlier, this type of change could truncate the data in that field. Use caution when shortening field sizes and ensure that your data is backed up before making such changes.

You can set the ***Caption property*** to create a label that is more understandable than a field name. While Pascal Case is preferred for field names, adding a space between words is often more readable. When a caption is set, it displays at the top of a table or query column in Datasheet view (instead of the actual field name), and when the field is used in a report or form. For example, a field named CustomerID could have the caption *Customer Number*.

Set the ***Validation Rule*** property to restrict data entry in a field to ensure that correct data are entered. The validation rule checks the data entered when the user exits the field. If the value entered violates the validation rule, an error message displays and prevents the invalid data from being entered into the field. For example, if you set a rule on a date field that the date entered must be on or after today, and a date in the past is entered in the field, an error message will display. You can customize the error message (validation text) when you set the validation rule.

The ***Input Mask*** property simplifies data entry by providing literal characters that are typed for every entry, such as hyphens in a Social Security number or dashes in a phone number. Input masks ensure that data in fields such as these are consistently entered and formatted.

STEP 4 Create a New Field in Design View

At times, it may be necessary to add table fields that were not included in the original design process. While it is possible to add fields in Datasheet view (using the Click to Add arrow at the top of an empty column), Design view, as shown in Figure 2.4, offers more flexibility in setting field properties.

To add a new field in Design view, complete the following steps:

1. Click in the first empty field row in the top pane of the table's Design view.
2. Enter the Field Name, Data Type, and Description (optional), and set the Field Properties.
3. Click the row selector, and then click and drag the new field to place it in a different position in the table.
4. Click Save on the Quick Access Toolbar and switch to Datasheet view to enter or modify data.

STEP 5 Modify the Table in Datasheet View

Whereas Design view is commonly used to create and modify the table structure by enabling you to add and edit fields and set field properties, Datasheet view is used to add, edit, and delete records. In a Customers table, you might find that frequent data updates are common. New customers need to be added, and at times, customers may need to be deleted. If a customer changes his/her address, telephone number, or email address, the existing record will be edited. You may notice that when you call customer service representatives, they often ask you to update your personal information; up-to-date data produces the best possible information in a database.

Quick Concepts

1. Explain why it is important to "Plan for common fields" when designing database tables. *p. 136*
2. Consider why it is important to set a primary key in a table. *p. 136*
3. Discuss how the Validation Rule field property helps to control data entry and why that is important. *p. 143*

Hands-On Exercises

Skills covered: Design a Table • Create a Table in Datasheet View • Delete a Field • Set a Table's Primary Key • Work with Field Properties • Create a New Field in Design View • Modify the Table in Datasheet View

1 Table Design, Creation, and Modification

Creating a sample database as an intern for Commonwealth Federal Bank will be a great opportunity for you to showcase your database design and Access skills.

STEP 1 ▶ CREATE A TABLE IN DATASHEET VIEW

You create a new database and a table to store information about the bank's branches. You enter the data for the first record (BranchID, Manager, and Location). You examine the design of the table and realize that the BranchID field is a better unique identifier, making the ID field redundant. You delete the ID field. Refer to Figure 2.8 as you complete Step 1.

Step i: Save the table as Branch

Step h: Type the data directly into the datasheet

Steps d–g: Fields added to datasheet

BranchID	Manager	Location
B10	Cameron	Uptown
B20	Esposito	Eastern
B30	Amoako	Western
B40	Singh	Southern
B50	Student Name	Campus

FIGURE 2.8 Create the Branch Table in Datasheet View

a. Start Access and click **Blank database**.

b. Type **a02h1Bank_LastFirst** in the File Name box.

c. Click **Browse** to find the folder location where you will store the database and click **OK**. Click **Create** to create the new database.

Access will create the new database named a02h1Bank_LastFirst and a new table, Table1, will automatically open in Datasheet view. There is already an ID field in the table by default that uses the AutoNumber data type.

d. Click **Click to Add** and select **Short Text** as the Data type.

Click to Add changes to Field1. Field1 is selected to make it easier to change the field name.

e. Type **BranchID** and press **Tab**.

A list of data types for the third column opens so that you can select the data type for the third column.

f. Select **Short Text** in the Click to Add list, type **Manager**, and then press **Tab**.

g. Select **Short Text** in the Click to Add list and type **Location**.

h. Click in the **first column** (the ID field) next to the New Record asterisk, press **Tab**, and then type the data for the new table as shown in Figure 2.8, letting Access assign the ID field for each new record (using the AutoNumber data type). Replace *YourLastName* with your own last name.

i. Click **Save** on the Quick Access Toolbar. Type **Branch** in the Save As dialog box and click **OK**.

Entering field names, data types, and data directly in Datasheet view provides a simplified way to create the table initially.

j. Click **View** in the Views group on the Home tab to switch to Design view of the Branch table.

The field name for each of the four fields displays along with the data type.

k. Ensure that the ID field is selected, click **Delete Rows** in the Tools group on the Design tab. Click **Yes** to both warning messages.

Access responds with a warning that you are about to permanently delete a field and a second warning that the field is the primary key. You delete the field because you will set the BranchID field as the primary key.

STEP 2 SET A TABLE'S PRIMARY KEY

You determine that BranchID is a better choice as the table's primary key field. Rather than the sequential auto-numbering that Access uses by default for the key field, it is better to use the actual branch numbers. In this step, you will make the BranchID field the primary key field. Refer to Figure 2.9 as you complete Step 2.

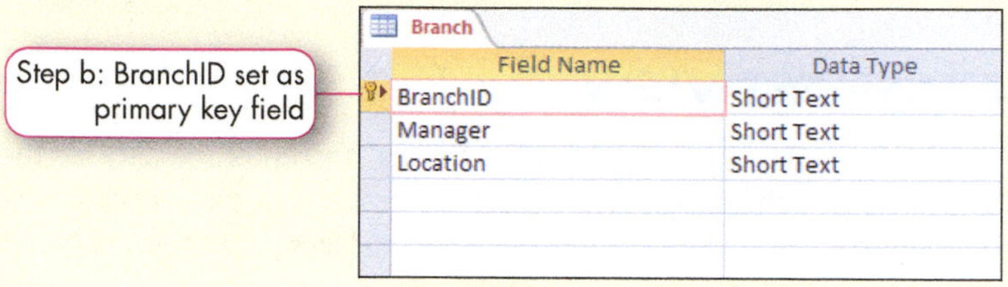

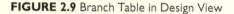

FIGURE 2.9 Branch Table in Design View

a. Ensure that the BranchID field is selected, as shown in Figure 2.9.

b. Click **Primary Key** in the Tools group on the Design tab.

You set BranchID as the primary key. The Indexed property in the Field Properties section at the bottom of the design window displays Yes (No Duplicates). When a primary key is set on a field, an index is automatically created by Access for that field to speed up searching through it.

c. Click **Save** on the Quick Access Toolbar to save the table.

STEP 3 WORK WITH FIELD PROPERTIES

You will modify the table design further to comply with the bank's specifications. Refer to Figure 2.10 as you complete Step 3.

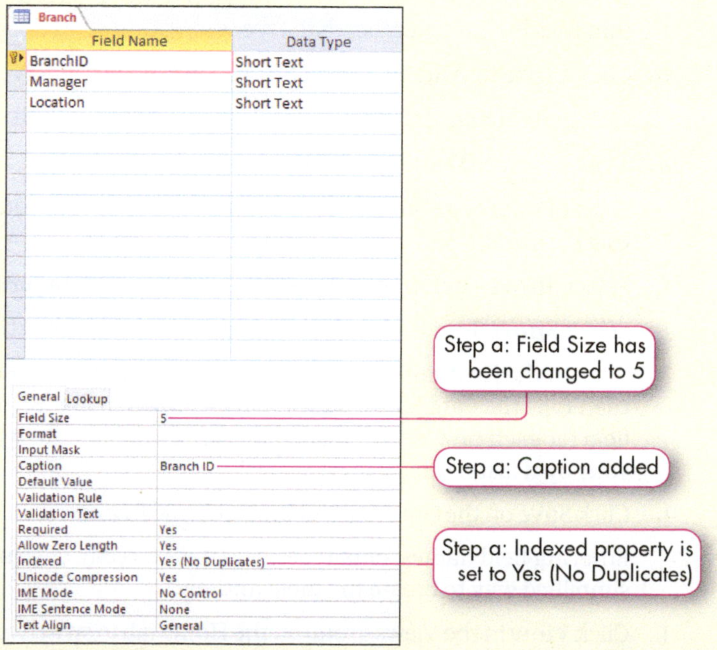

FIGURE 2.10 Changes to the Field Properties of the Branch Table in Design View

a. Click in the **BranchID field name**; modify the BranchID field properties by completing the following steps:

- Click in the **Field Size box** in the Field Properties pane and change 255 to **5**.
- Click in the **Caption box** and type **Branch ID**. Make sure Branch and ID have a space between them.
  A caption provides a more descriptive field name. It will display as the column heading in Datasheet view.
- Check the Indexed property; confirm it is Yes (No Duplicates).
- Check the Required property; confirm it is Yes. A primary key field always requires a value to be entered.

b. Click the **Manager field name**; modify the Manager field properties by completing the following steps:

- Click in the **Field Size box** in the Field Properties pane and change 255 to **30**.
- Click in the **Caption box** and type **Manager's Name**.

c. Click the **Location field name** and modify the following Location field properties by completing the following steps:

- Click in the **Field Size box** in the Field Properties pane and change 255 to **30**.
- Click in the **Caption box** and type **Branch Location**.

STEP 4 CREATE A NEW FIELD IN DESIGN VIEW

You notice that a date field is missing from your new table. Modify the table to add the new field. Refer to Figure 2.11 as you complete Step 4.

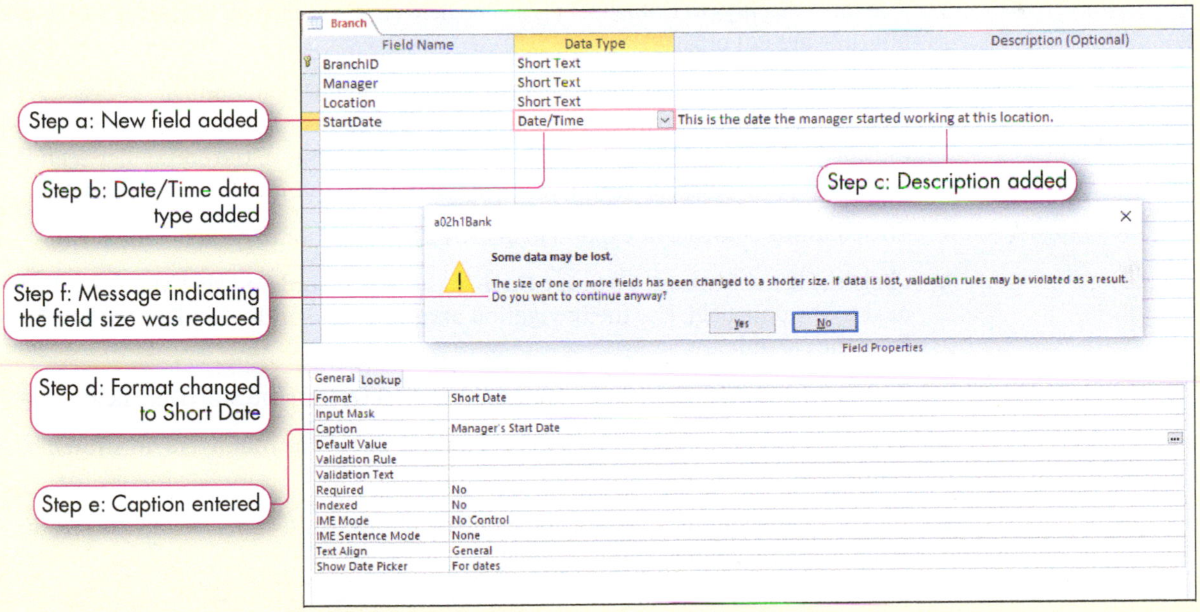

FIGURE 2.11 Adding a New Field to the Branch Table in Design View

a. Click in the **first blank field row** below the Location field name and type **StartDate**.

You added a new field to the table.

b. Press **Tab** to move to the Data Type column. Click the **Data Type arrow** and select **Date/Time**.

c. Press **Tab** to move to the Description column and type **This is the date the manager started working at this location.**

d. Click in the **Format box** in the Field Properties pane, click the **arrow**, and then select **Short Date** from the list of date formats.

e. Click in the **Caption box** and type **Manager's Start Date**.

f. Click **Save** on the Quick Access Toolbar.

A warning dialog box opens to indicate that "Some data may be lost" because the size of the BranchID, Manager, and Location field properties were shortened (in the previous step). It asks if you want to continue anyway. Always read the Access warning! In this case, you can click Yes to continue because you know that the existing and anticipated data values are no longer than the new field sizes.

g. Click **Yes** in the warning box.

STEP 5 MODIFY THE TABLE IN DATASHEET VIEW

As you work with the new sample, you will modify tables in the bank database by adding and modifying records. Refer to Figure 2.12 as you complete Step 5.

Step b: Expanded fields

Step c–d: Start dates

Branch ID	Manager's Name	Branch Location	Manager's Start Date	Click to Add
B10	Cameron	Uptown	12/5/2016	
B20	Esposito	Eastern	6/18/2015	
B30	Amoako	Western	3/13/2013	
B40	Singh	Southern	9/15/2016	
B50	Student Name	Campus	10/11/2018	

FIGURE 2.12 Start Dates Added to the Branch Table

a. Right-click the **Branch tab** and select **Datasheet View** from the shortcut menu.

The table displays in Datasheet view. The field captions display at the top of the columns, but they are cut off.

b. Position the pointer over the border between Branch ID and Manager's Name so that it becomes a double-headed arrow and double-click the border. Repeat the process for the border between Manager's Name and Branch Location, the border between Branch Location and Manager's Start Date, and the border after Manager's Start Date.

The columns contract or expand to display the best fit for each field name.

c. Click inside the **Manager's Start Date** in the first record and click the **Date Picker** 📅 next to the date field. Use the navigation arrows to find and select **December 5, 2016** from the calendar.

You can also enter the dates by typing them directly into the StartDate field.

d. Type the start date directly in each field for the rest of the managers, as shown in Figure 2.12.

e. Click the **Close** at the top-right corner of the Branch datasheet, below the ribbon. Click **Yes** to save the changes.

> **TROUBLESHOOTING:** If you accidentally click Close at the top of the ribbon, you will exit Access completely. To start again, launch Access and click the first file in the Recent list.

f. Double-click the **Branch table** in the Navigation Pane to open the table.

g. Click the **File tab**, click **Print**, and then click **Print Preview**.

Occasionally, users will print an Access table. However, database developers usually create reports to print table data.

h. Click **Close Print Preview** in the Close Preview group and close the Branch table.

i. Keep the database open if you plan to continue with the Hands-On Exercise. If not, close the database and exit Access.

Multiple-Table Databases

In Figure 2.2, the sample bank database contains three tables—Customers, Accounts, and Branch. You created one table, the Branch table, in the previous section using Datasheet view and modified the table fields in Design view. You will create the two remaining tables using different methods—by importing data from external sources.

In this section, you will learn how to import data from Excel and Access to populate the bank database. You will modify tables, create indexes, create relationships between tables, and enforce referential integrity.

Importing Data from External Sources

Often in organizations, files that can be used to create tables or add records to existing tables in databases are stored in external sources. Common sources are Excel spreadsheets, other Access databases, other file types (such as text files), and online sources. If data can be imported and are compatible with an existing database, it can save a great deal of data entry effort. Often, the data stored in external sources can be more efficiently managed in an Access database. Data can be imported as a new table in a database or added to an existing table (appended). Importing data copies records to your database and so will increase the file size, sometimes dramatically. It is also possible to link your database to an external source so that you can use the data that it contains without having to copy it into your own database file.

STEP 1 Import Excel Data

Access provides a wizard that guides you through the process of importing data from Excel. The process is relatively simple when the data are well-organized in the Excel worksheet, with column headings that will import as field names in the Access table.

To import an Excel spreadsheet to Access, complete the following steps:

1. Click the External Data tab.
2. Click New Data Source in the Import & Link group, point to From File, and then select Excel. The Get External Data – Excel Spreadsheet dialog box opens, as shown in Figure 2.13.
3. Click Browse to locate the Excel file you want to import, click the file to select it, and then click Open to specify this file as the source of the data.
4. Ensure the *Import the source data* option is selected and click OK. The Import Spreadsheet Wizard launches.
5. Select the worksheet from the list of worksheets shown at the top of the dialog box, as shown in Figure 2.14, and then click Next.
6. Ensure the *First Row Contains Column Headings* check box is selected and click Next, as shown in Figure 2.15. The column headings of the Excel spreadsheet will become the field names in the Access table.
7. Change the field options for the imported data, as shown in Figure 2.16, and click Next.
8. Click the *Choose my own primary key* option if the imported data have a field that is acceptable as a primary key, as shown in Figure 2.17, and click Next. Access will set the value in the first column of the spreadsheet (for example, AID) as the primary key field of the table. You can also allow Access to set the primary key if there is no value that is eligible to be a key field, or to set no primary key at all (not recommended).
9. Type the new table name in the Import to Table box, as shown in Figure 2.18, and click Finish.
10. Click Close when prompted to Save Import Steps.

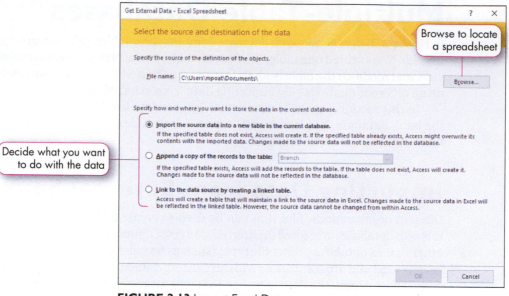

Browse to locate a spreadsheet

Decide what you want to do with the data

FIGURE 2.13 Import Excel Data

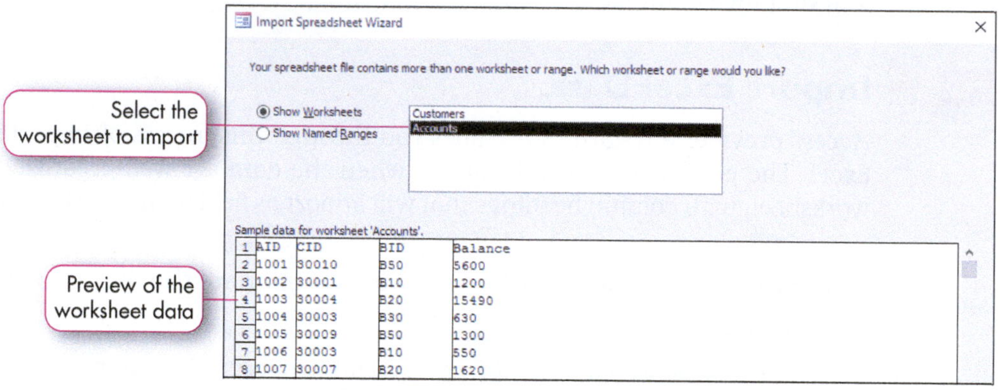

Select the worksheet to import

Preview of the worksheet data

FIGURE 2.14 Available Worksheets and Preview of Data

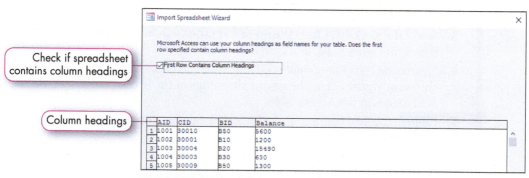

Check if spreadsheet contains column headings

Column headings

FIGURE 2.15 Excel Column Headings Become Access Field Names

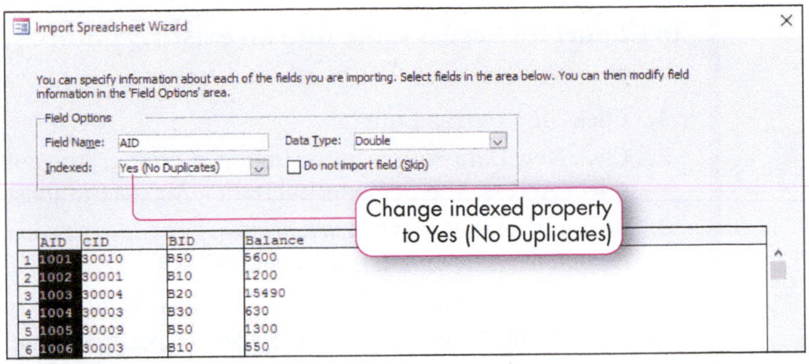

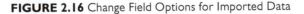

FIGURE 2.16 Change Field Options for Imported Data

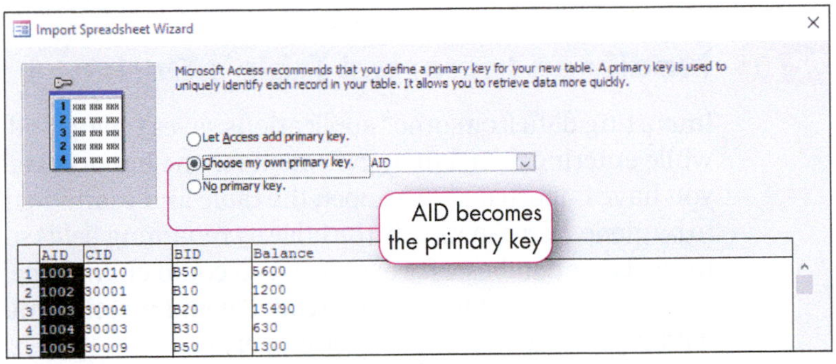

FIGURE 2.17 Set the Primary Key

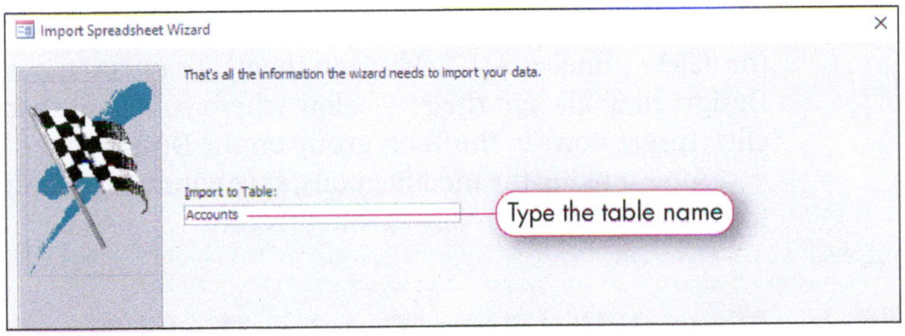

FIGURE 2.18 Enter a Table Name

TIP: LINKING TO EXTERNAL DATA

At times you might need to include a table in your database that already exists in another database. Instead of importing the data from this external source, you can create a link to it from within your database, and the table remains in the original database. You will be able to use the linked data as usual, but you will not be able to modify the original table's design. You can also link to existing spreadsheets from your database without having to copy a large amount of data into your file.

STEP 2 Import Access Data

A wizard can also guide you as you import data from Access databases. If there is an object in an external database (such as a table) that contains valuable data or suits another purpose in your application, there is no need to recreate it entirely. You can import an existing table's design only or a table with usable data. Likewise, if there is an existing form or report that will complement your data, you may not need to create it from scratch. You can import tables, queries, forms, reports, pages, macros, and modules from other databases. You can also modify the design of objects that are imported into your database to adapt them to your own application.

To import an Access table into an existing database, complete the following steps:

1. Click the External Data tab.
2. Click New Data Source in the Import & Link group, point to From Database, and then select Access. The Get External Data – Access Database dialog box opens.
3. Ensure that the *Import tables, queries, forms, reports, macros, and modules into the current database* option is selected.
4. Click Browse to locate the Access database from which you want to import.
5. Click the file to select it and click Open to specify this file as the source of the data.
6. Select the table you want to import and click OK. (Click Select All if the database contains multiple tables and you want to import all of them and click OK.)

STEP 3 ▶ Modify an Imported Table's Design

Importing data from other applications saves typing and prevents errors that may occur while entering data, but modifications to the imported tables will often be required. After you have imported a table, open the table and examine the design to see if changes need to be made. You can modify the table by renaming fields so that they are more meaningful. In the bank database, for example, you could change the name of the imported AID field to AccountID to make it more readable and meaningful. Use Design view to modify the data types, field sizes, and other properties.

STEP 4 ▶ Add Data to an Imported Table

After you have imported a table into your database, you can add new fields to the tables (or delete unnecessary fields from them). To create a new field between existing fields in Design view, click in the row below where you want the new field to be added, and then click Insert Rows in the Tools group on the Design tab.

After making the modifications, save your changes and switch back to Datasheet view to add new data or modify existing records.

STEP 5 ▶ Establishing Table Relationships

The benefit of a relationship is to efficiently combine data from related tables for creating queries, forms, and reports. In the example we are using, the customer data is stored in the Customers table. The Branch table stores data about the bank's branches, management, and locations. The Accounts table stores data about account ownership and balances. The common fields that were determined in the design phase of the tables can now be used to establish relationships between them.

To create the relationship between the common fields of two tables, complete the following steps:

1. Click the Database Tools tab.
2. Click Relationships in the Relationships group.
3. Drag the primary key field name from one table to the foreign key field name of the related table (for example, CustomerID in the Customers table to CustomerID in the Accounts table).
4. Set the options in the Edit Relationships dialog box and click Create. Figure 2.19 shows the bank database with relationships created by joining common fields.

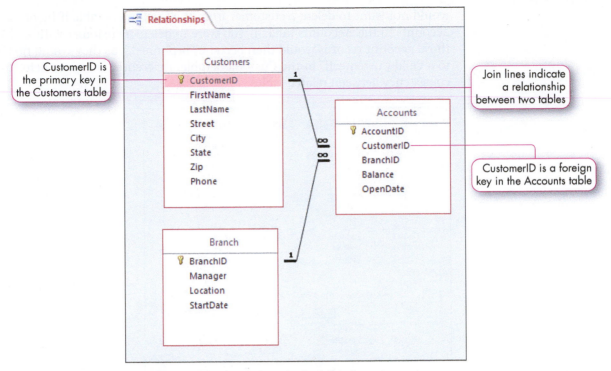

Customer ID is the primary key in the Customers table

Join lines indicate a relationship between two tables

CustomerID is a foreign key in the Accounts table

FIGURE 2.19 Relationships in the Bank Database

TIP: RETRIEVE DATA QUICKLY WITH INDEXING

When you set the primary key in Access, the Indexed property is automatically set to Yes (No Duplicates). The indexed property setting enables quick sorting in primary key order and quick retrieval based on the primary key. By default, Access tables are indexed and sorted by the primary key field. For non-primary key fields, it may sometimes be beneficial to set the Indexed property to Yes (Duplicates OK) so that data can be sorted and retrieved quickly on non-key fields.

Recall that in the bank database, CustomerID has been set as the primary key in the Customers table and is also a field in the Accounts table. The common fields share the same data type. Therefore, a relationship can be set between the Customers table and the Accounts table where CustomerID is the foreign key. Because there is a relationship between the two tables, when a customer is added to the Customers table, you will able to match him or her to their associated accounts; the same CustomerID is entered in both tables. Similarly, the Branch table can be joined to the Accounts table because BranchID has been set as the primary key in the Branch table, and BranchID is the foreign key in the Accounts table.

STEP 6 Enforce and Test Referential Integrity

When you begin to create a relationship in Access, the Edit Relationships dialog box displays. The first check box, Enforce Referential Integrity, should be checked in most cases. *Referential integrity* enforces rules in a database that are used to preserve relationships between tables when records are added, deleted, or changed.

When referential integrity is enforced, you cannot enter a foreign key value in a related table unless the value exists in the primary key field of the primary table. In the case of the bank database, the customer information is first entered in the Customers table before a customer's account information (which also includes CustomerID) can be entered into the Accounts table. If you attempt to enter an account for a new customer in the Accounts table prior to entering the new customer in the Customers table, an error will display, as shown in Figure 2.20. When referential integrity is enforced, usually you cannot delete a record in one table if it has related records in another table. For example, you probably would not want to delete a customer from the Customers table if he or she has active accounts in the Accounts table. If you were to delete a customer with active accounts, those account records would then become "orphaned," as they would no longer relate to a valid CustomerID in the Customers table. Referential integrity helps to guarantee consistency between related tables.

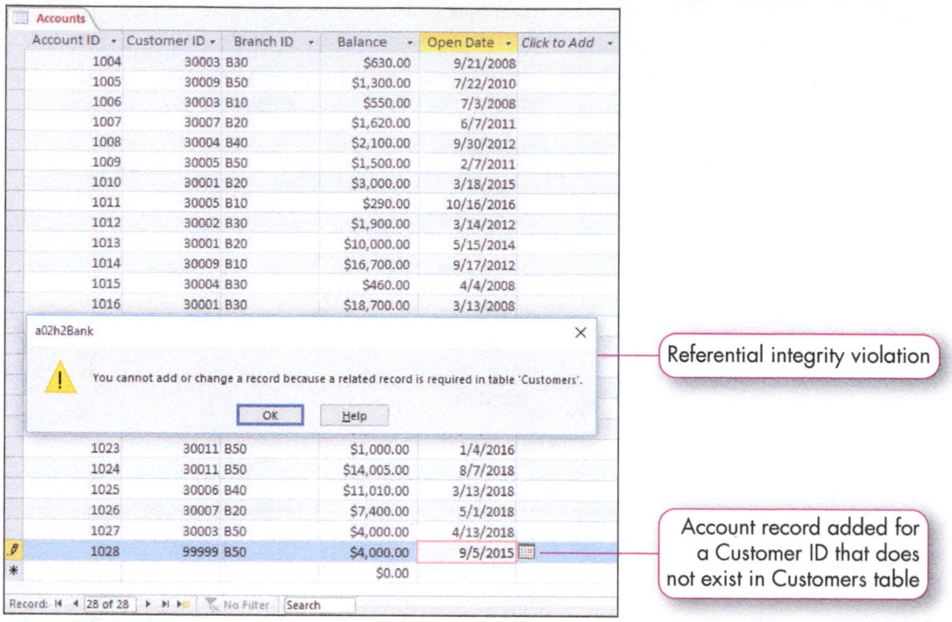

FIGURE 2.20 Error Message for Referential Integrity Violation

---

TIP: COMMON ERROR MESSAGES WHEN ENFORCING REFERENTIAL INEGRITY

When you set referential integrity between tables, common error messages can occur. For example, adding a value in a foreign key that does not exist as a primary key value produces an error, as shown in Figure 2.20. Common fields are not required to have the same names (although they often do), but they must have the same data type. If a CustomerID is a Number field in one table, but a Short Text value in another, you will need to change the data type in one or the other. Changing data types in tables can sometimes cause you to lose data, so setting data types carefully in the design process is a good strategy for avoiding this issue.

Set Cascade Options

When you create a relationship in Access and click the Enforce Referential Integrity check box, Access presents two additional options: Cascade Update Related Fields and Cascade Delete Related Records (see Figure 2.21). Select the *Cascade Update Related Fields* option so when the primary key value is modified in a primary table, Access will automatically update all foreign key values in a related table. If a CustomerID is updated for some reason, all of the matching CustomerID values in the Accounts table will update automatically. This option can save a great deal of data entry time and assures accuracy in the data updates.

Select the *Cascade Delete Related Records* option so when a record containing a primary key value is deleted in a primary table, Access will automatically delete all records in related tables that match the primary key. If one branch of a bank closes and its record is deleted from the Branch table, any account that is associated with this branch would then be deleted. Access will give a warning first to enable you to avoid the action of deleting records inadvertently.

Setting the Cascade Update and Cascade Delete options really depends on the business rules of an organization, and they should be set with caution. For example, if a branch of a bank closes, do you really want the accounts at that branch to be deleted? Another option might be to assign them to a different branch of the bank. Always ensure that your database is backed up; even though a warning message is displayed, it is still feasible to inadvertently delete valuable records from a database.

Establish a One-to-Many Relationship

Figure 2.21 also shows that the relationship that will be created is a one-to-many relationship. Access provides three different relationships for joining tables: one-to-one, one-to-many, and many-to-many. The most common type by far is the one-to-many relationship. A *one-to-many relationship* is established when the primary key value in the primary table can match many of the foreign key values in the related table.

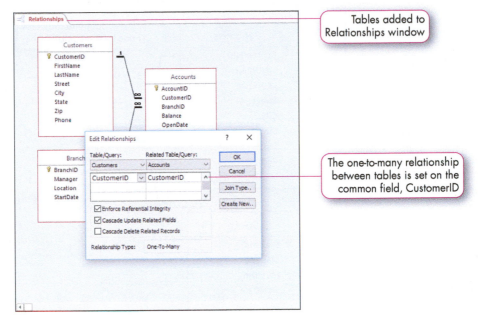

FIGURE 2.21 Cascade Update and Delete Options

For example, a bank customer will be added to the Customers table one time only. The primary key value, which is the CustomerID number, might be 1585. That same customer could set up a checking, a savings, and a credit card account. With each account, the CustomerID (1585) is required and, therefore, will occur three times in the Accounts table. The value is entered one time in the Customers table and three times in the Accounts table. The relationship between Customers and Accounts is described as one-to-many. Table 2.3 lists and describes all three types of relationships you can create between Access tables.

TABLE 2.3	Relationship Types
Relationship Type	**Description**
One-to-Many	The primary key table must have only one occurrence of each value. For example, each customer must have a unique identification number in the Customers table. The foreign key field in the related table may have repeating values. One customer can have many different account numbers.
One-to-One	Two different tables use the same primary key. Exactly one record exists in the second table for each record in the first table. Sometimes security issues require a single table to be split into two related tables. For example, in an organization's database anyone in the company might be able to access the Employee table and find the employee's office number, department assignment, or telephone extension. However, only a few people need to have access to the employee's network login password, salary, Social Security number, performance review, or marital status, which would be stored in a second table. Tables containing this information would use the same unique identifier to identify each employee.
Many-to-Many	This is an artificially constructed relationship allowing many matching records in each direction between tables. It requires construction of a third table called a junction table. For example, a database might have a table for employees and one for projects. Several employees might be assigned to one project, but one employee might also be assigned to many different projects. To create the junction table that connects the employees to their projects, a third table containing the primary key of each would be created.

Figure 2.22 displays the Relationships window for the bank database and all the relationships created using referential integrity. The join line between the CustomerID field in the Customers table and the CustomerID field in the Accounts table indicates that a one-to-many relationship has been set. The number 1 displays on the one side of the relationship and the infinity symbol displays the many side. You can rearrange the tables by dragging the tables by the title bar. You can switch the positions of the Branch and Accounts tables in the Relationships window without changing the relationship itself.

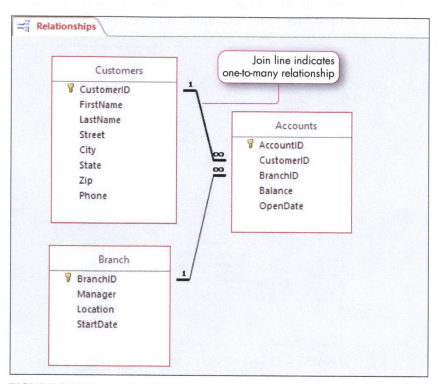

FIGURE 2.22 Relationships Window Displaying One-to-Many Relationships

---

TIP: NAVIGATING BETWEEN THE RELATIONSHIPS WINDOW AND A TABLE'S DESIGN

When you right-click a table's title bar in the Relationships window, the shortcut menu offers you the option to open the table in Design view. This is a convenient feature because if you want to link one table to another table, the joined fields must have the same data type. This shortcut enables you to check the fields and revise them if a table contains a field with the wrong data type. Change data types with caution, as data can be lost in the process.

Quick Concepts

4. Describe a scenario that may require you to import an Access table into your database. **p. 151**

5. Discuss the purpose of enforcing referential integrity between two tables. **p. 153**

6. Explain why you would you use the Cascade Update option when setting a relationship. **p. 154**

7. Describe two database tables that you might design that would contain a one-to-many relationship. **p. 155**

Hands-On Exercises

Skills covered: Import Excel Data • Import Access Data • Modify an Imported Table's Design • Add Data to an Imported Table • Establish Table Relationships • Enforce and Test Referential Integrity

2 Multiple-Table Databases

You created a new bank database and a new Branch table. Now you are ready to import additional tables—one from an Excel spreadsheet and one from an Access database. The data are formatted correctly and structured properly so that you can begin the import process.

STEP 1 IMPORT EXCEL DATA

You have discovered that one of Commonwealth's existing files contains reusable customer data. The data are related to the Branch table you created earlier, so you decide to import the data into your database. In this step, you import an Excel spreadsheet into the bank database. Refer to Figure 2.23 as you complete Step 1.

Steps c–j: Imported Customers table

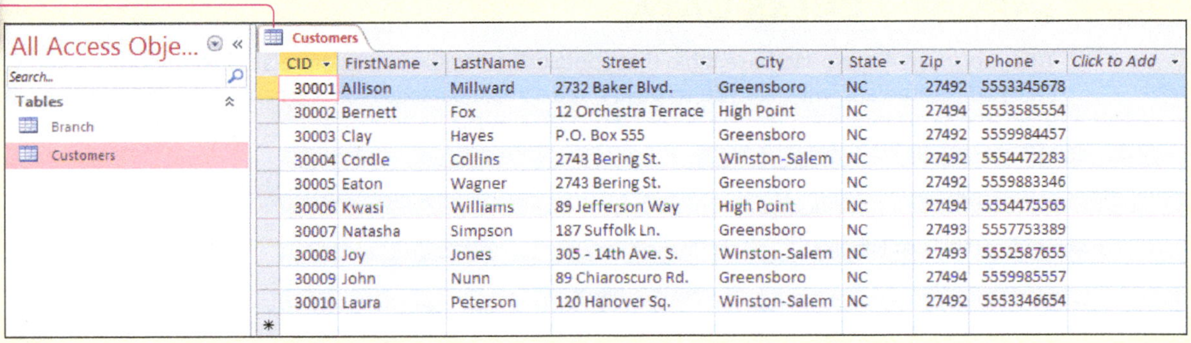

CID	FirstName	LastName	Street	City	State	Zip	Phone	Click to Add
30001	Allison	Millward	2732 Baker Blvd.	Greensboro	NC	27492	5553345678	
30002	Bernett	Fox	12 Orchestra Terrace	High Point	NC	27494	5553585554	
30003	Clay	Hayes	P.O. Box 555	Greensboro	NC	27492	5559984457	
30004	Cordle	Collins	2743 Bering St.	Winston-Salem	NC	27492	5554472283	
30005	Eaton	Wagner	2743 Bering St.	Greensboro	NC	27492	5559883346	
30006	Kwasi	Williams	89 Jefferson Way	High Point	NC	27494	5554475565	
30007	Natasha	Simpson	187 Suffolk Ln.	Greensboro	NC	27493	5557753389	
30008	Joy	Jones	305 - 14th Ave. S.	Winston-Salem	NC	27493	5552587655	
30009	John	Nunn	89 Chiaroscuro Rd.	Greensboro	NC	27494	5559985557	
30010	Laura	Peterson	120 Hanover Sq.	Winston-Salem	NC	27492	5553346654	

All Access Obje... — Tables: Branch, Customers

FIGURE 2.23 Imported Customers Table

a. Open *a02h1Bank_LastFirst* if you closed it at the end of Hands-On Exercise 1, and save it as **a02h2Bank_LastFirst**, changing h1 to h2.

b. Click **Enable Content** below the ribbon to indicate that you trust the contents of the database.

c. Click the **External Data tab**, click **New Data Source**, point to **From File** in the Import & Link group, and then select **Excel** to launch the Get External Data – Excel Spreadsheet dialog box. Ensure that the *Import the source data into a new table in the current database* option is selected.

> **TROUBLESHOOTING:** Ensure that you click Excel in the Import & Link group to import the spreadsheet and not the Excel command in the Export group.

d. Click **Browse** and navigate to your student data files. Select the *a02h2Customers.xlsx* workbook. Click **Open** and click **OK** to open the Import Spreadsheet Wizard.

e. Ensure that the *First Row Contains Column Headings* check box is selected to indicate to Access that column headings exist in the Excel file.

The field names CID, FirstName, LastName, Street, City, State, Zip, and Phone will import from Excel along with the data stored in the rows in the worksheet. You will modify the field names later in Access.

f. Click **Next**.

g. Ensure that CID is displayed in the Field Name box in Field Options. Click the **Indexed arrow** and select **Yes (No Duplicates)**. Click **Next**.

The CID (CustomerID) will become the primary key in this table. It needs to be a unique identifier, so you change the property to No Duplicates.

h. Click the **Choose my own primary key option**. Make sure that the CID field is selected. Click **Next**.

The final screen of the Import Spreadsheet Wizard prompts you to name your table. The name of the Excel worksheet is Customers, and Access defaults to the worksheet name.

i. Click **Finish** to accept Customers as the table name.

A dialog box opens prompting you to save the steps of this import to use again. If this is data that are to be collected in Excel and updated to the database on a regular basis, saving the import steps would save time. You do not need to save the import steps in this example.

j. Click **Close**.

The new table displays in the Navigation Pane of the bank database.

k. Open the imported Customers table in Datasheet view and double-click the **border** between each of the field names to adjust the columns to Best Fit. Compare your table to Figure 2.23.

l. Save and close the table.

STEP 2 IMPORT ACCESS DATA

You import an Access database table that contains account information related to the Branch and Customers tables that you created and will help you to build out a sample database for the bank that is a realistic example. You use the Import Wizard to import the database table. Refer to Figure 2.24 as you complete Step 2.

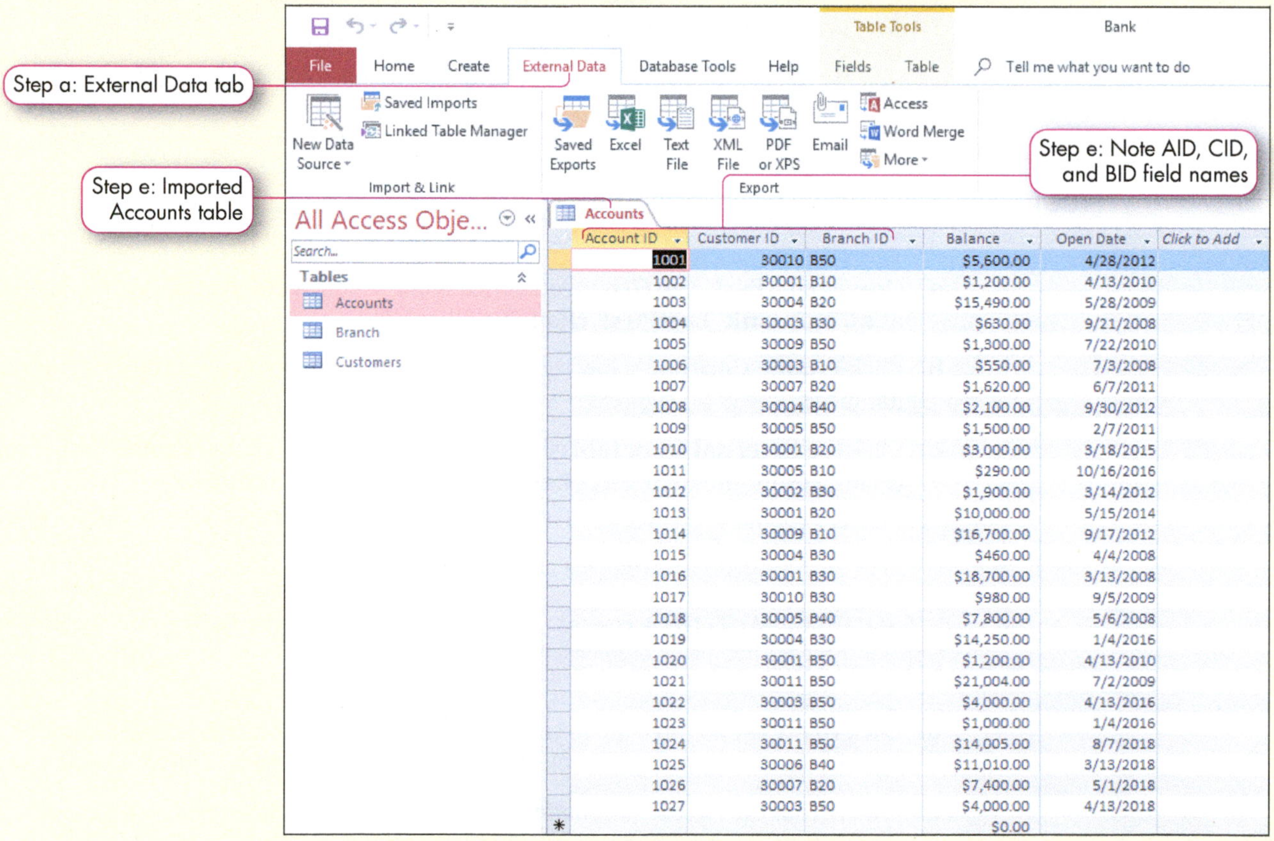

FIGURE 2.24 Imported Accounts Table

a. Click the **External Data tab**, click **New Data Source**, point to **From Database** in the Import & Link group, and then click **Access** to launch the Get External Data – Access Database dialog box. Ensure that the *Import tables, queries, forms, reports, macros, and modules into the current database* option is selected.

b. Click **Browse** and navigate to your student data files. Select the *a02h2Accounts* database. Click **Open** and click **OK** to open the Import Objects dialog box.

c. Click the **Accounts table** and click **OK**.

d. Click **Close** in the Save Import Steps dialog box.

The Navigation Pane now contains three tables: Accounts, Branch, and Customers.

e. Open the imported Accounts table in Datasheet view and compare it to Figure 2.24.

Notice that the imported table contains AID, CID, and BID fields. The fields need to be modified to be more readable, and to ensure that they work with the other tables in your database.

f. Close the table.

STEP 3 ## MODIFY AN IMPORTED TABLE'S DESIGN

When importing tables from either Excel or Access, the fields may have different data types and property settings than those required to create table relationships. You will modify the tables so that each field has the correct data type and field size. Refer to Figure 2.25 as you complete Step 3.

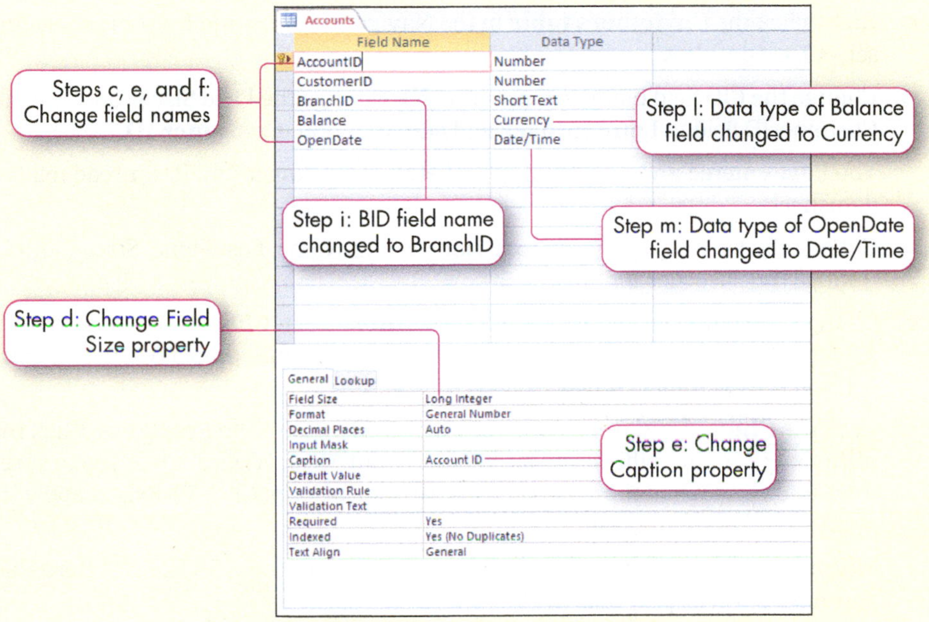

FIGURE 2.25 Modified Accounts Table Design

a. Right-click the **Accounts table** in the Navigation Pane.

b. Select **Design View** from the shortcut menu to open the table in Design view.

The Accounts table displays with the primary key AID selected.

c. Change the AID field name to **AccountID**.

d. Change the Field Size property to **Long Integer**.

Long Integer ensures that there will be enough numbers as the number of customers grows over time and may exceed 32,768 (the upper limit for Integer values).

e. Type **Account ID** in the Caption box for the AccountID field. The caption contains a space between Account and ID.

f. Click the **CID field**. Change the CID field name to **CustomerID**.

g. Change the Field Size property to **Long Integer**.

You can select the Field Size option using the arrow, or you can type the first letter of the option you want. For example, type l for Long Integer or s for Single. Make sure the current option is completely selected before you type the letter.

h. Type **Customer ID** in the Caption box for the CustomerID field. The caption contains a space between Customer and ID.

i. Click the **BID field**. Change the BID field name to **BranchID**.

j. Type **5** in the Field Size property box in the Field Properties.

k. Type **Branch ID** in the Caption property box for the Branch ID field.

l. Change the Data Type of the Balance field to **Currency**.

The Currency data type is used for fields that contain monetary values. In this case, changing the data type is not consequential; formatting the imported Balance field as Currency will not change the original data values.

m. Change the Data Type of the OpenDate field to **Date/Time** and set **Short Date** in the Format field property. Type **Open Date** in the Caption property box.

The OpenDate field stores the date that each account was opened.

n. Click **View** in the Views group to switch to Datasheet view. Read the messages and click **Yes** to each one.

In this case, it is acceptable to click Yes because the shortened fields will not cut off any data. Leave the table open.

o. Right-click the **Customers table** in the Navigation Pane and from the shortcut menu, select **Design View**.

p. Change the CID field name to **CustomerID**. Change the Field Size property of the CustomerID field to **Long Integer** and add a caption, **Customer ID**.

You have entered an intentional space between Customer and ID for readability in the datasheet.

q. Change the Field Size property to **20** for the FirstName, LastName, Street, and City fields. Change the Field Size for State to **2**.

r. Change the data type for Zip and Phone to **Short Text**. Change the Field Size property to **15** for both fields. Remove the @ symbol from the Format property where it exists for all fields in the Customers table.

s. Click the **Phone field name** and click **Input Mask** in Field Properties. Click the **ellipsis** ... on the right side to launch the Input Mask Wizard. Click **Yes** to save the table and click **Yes** to the *Some data may be lost* warning. Click **Finish** to apply the default phone number input mask.

The phone number input mask enables users to enter 6105551212 in the datasheet, and Access will display it as (610) 555-1212.

t. Click **Save** to save the design changes to the Customers table.

STEP 4 ADD DATA TO AN IMPORTED TABLE

Now that you have created the database tables, you discover that you need to add another customer and his account records. Refer to Figure 2.26 as you complete Step 4.

Customer ID	FirstName	LastName	Street	City	State	Zip	Phone	Click to Add
30001	Allison	Millward	2732 Baker Blvd.	Greensboro	NC	27492	(555) 334-5678	
30002	Bernett	Fox	12 Orchestra Terrace	High Point	NC	27494	(555) 358-5554	
30003	Clay	Hayes	P.O. Box 555	Greensboro	NC	27492	(555) 998-4457	
30004	Cordle	Collins	2743 Bering St.	Winston-Salem	NC	27492	(555) 447-2283	
30005	Eaton	Wagner	2743 Bering St.	Greensboro	NC	27492	(555) 988-3346	
30006	Kwasi	Williams	89 Jefferson Way	High Point	NC	27494	(555) 447-5565	
30007	Natasha	Simpson	187 Suffolk Ln.	Greensboro	NC	27493	(555) 775-3389	
30008	Joy	Jones	305 - 14th Ave. S.	Winston-Salem	NC	27493	(555) 258-7655	
30009	John	Nunn	89 Chiaroscuro Rd.	Greensboro	NC	27494	(555) 998-5557	
30010	Laura	Peterson	120 Hanover Sq.	Winston-Salem	NC	27492	(555) 334-6654	
30011	Student Name	Student Name	800 University Ave.	High Point	NC	27494	(555) 447-1235	

Step b: New record added to table

FIGURE 2.26 Customers Table Displaying the Added Customer ID 30011

a. Click **View** in the Views group to display the Customers table in Datasheet view.

The asterisk at the bottom of the table data in the row selector area is the indicator of a place to enter a new record.

b. Click next to the * in the **Customer ID field** in the new record row below 30010. Type **30011**. Fill in the rest of the data using your personal information as the customer. You may use a fictitious address and phone number.

Note the phone number format. The input mask you set formats the phone number as you type.

c. Close the Customers table. The Accounts table tab is open.

> **TROUBLESHOOTING:** If the Accounts table is not open, double-click Accounts in the Navigation Pane.

d. Click next to the * in the **Account ID field** in the new record row. Type **1024**. Type **30011** as the Customer ID and **B50** as the Branch ID. Type **14005** for the Balance field value. Type **8/7/2018** for the Open Date.

e. Add the following records to the Accounts table:

Account ID	Customer ID	Branch ID	Balance	Open Date
1025	30006	B40	11010	3/13/2018
1026	30007	B20	7400	5/1/2018

f. Close the Accounts table but keep the database open.

STEP 5 **ESTABLISH TABLE RELATIONSHIPS**

The tables for the sample bank database have been designed and populated. Now you will establish connections between the tables. Look at the primary and foreign keys as a guide. Refer to Figure 2.27 as you complete Step 5.

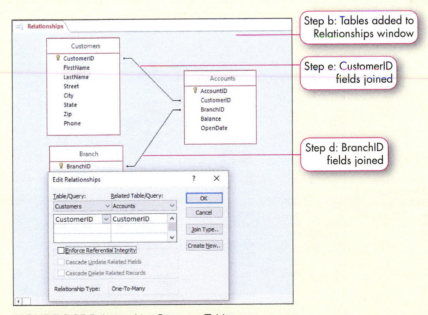

FIGURE 2.27 Relationships Between Tables

a. Click the **Database Tools tab** and click **Relationships** in the Relationships group.

The Relationships window opens, and the Show Table dialog box displays.

> **TROUBLESHOOTING:** If the Show Table dialog box does not open, click Show Table in the Relationships group on the Relationship Tools Design tab.

b. Double-click each of the three tables displayed in the Show Table dialog box to add them to the Relationships window. Click **Close** in the Show Table dialog box.

> **TROUBLESHOOTING:** If you have a duplicate table, click the title bar of the duplicated table and press Delete.

c. Click and drag the **border** of the Customers table field list to resize it so that all the fields are visible. Arrange the tables as shown in Figure 2.27.

d. Drag the **BranchID field** (the primary key) in the Branch table onto the BranchID field (the foreign key) in the Accounts table. The Edit Relationships dialog box opens. Click **Create**.

Access interprets a one-to-many relationship between the Branch and Accounts tables. Each single branch relates to many accounts. At this point, the tables are related by the BranchID field, but referential integrity is not yet enforced between them.

e. Drag the **CustomerID field** (the primary key) in the Customers table onto the CustomerID field (the foreign key) in the Accounts table. The Edit Relationships dialog box opens. Click **Create**.

Access interprets a one-to-many relationship between the Customers and Accounts tables. A customer will have only a single CustomerID number. The same customer may have many different accounts: Savings, Checking, Credit Card, and so forth. The tables are related by the CustomerID field, but referential integrity is not enforced between them.

f. Click **Save** on the Quick Access Toolbar to save the changes to the relationships.

STEP 6 ENFORCE AND TEST REFERENTIAL INTEGRITY

The design of the bank database must be 100% correct; otherwise, data entry may be compromised. Even though the table relationships are set, you need to enforce referential integrity. Next, you will test them by entering invalid data. If referential integrity is enforced, the invalid data will be rejected by Access. Refer to Figure 2.28 as you complete Step 6.

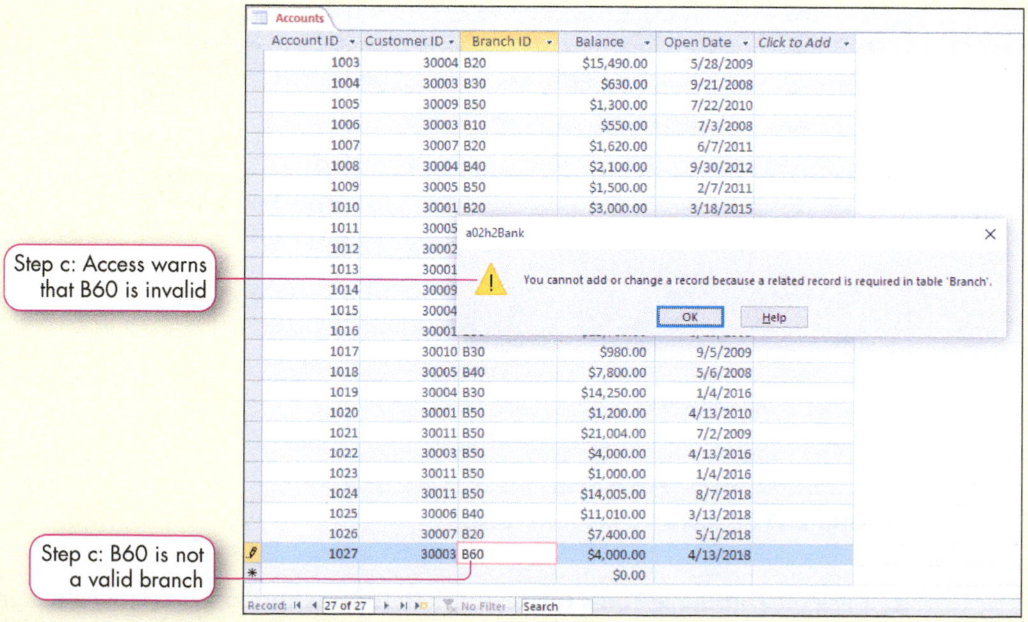

FIGURE 2.28 Referential Integrity Enforces Accurate Data Entry

a. Double-click the **join line** between the Branch and Accounts tables. The Edit Relationships dialog box opens. Click the **Enforce Referential Integrity** and **Cascade Update Related Fields check boxes** to select them. Click **OK**.

A black line displays, joining the two tables. It has a 1 at the end near the Branch table and an infinity symbol on the end next to the Accounts table. Referential integrity has been successfully enforced between the two tables; every BranchID in the Accounts table exists in the Branch table.

TROUBLESHOOTING: If you get an error message when you click OK, verify that the data types of the joined fields are the same. To check the data types from the Relationships window, right-click the title bar of a table and select Table Design from the shortcut menu. Modify the data type of the join fields, if necessary. Account ID should be Number, and Branch ID should be Short Text in both tables.

b. Double-click the **join line** between the Customers and Accounts tables. The Edit Relationships dialog box opens. Click the **Enforce Referential Integrity** and **Cascade Update Related Fields check boxes** to select them. Click **OK**. Close the Relationships window.

c. Double-click the **Accounts table** to open it in Datasheet view. Add a new record, pressing **Tab** after each field: Account ID: **1027**, Customer ID: **30003**, Branch: **B60**, Balance: **4000**, Open Date: **4/13/2018**. Press **Enter**.

You attempted to enter a nonexistent BranchID (B60) and were not allowed to make that error. A warning message is informing you that a related record in the Branch table is required because the Accounts table and the Branch table are connected by a relationship with Enforce Referential Integrity checked.

d. Click **OK**. Double-click the **Branch table** in the Navigation Pane and examine the data in the BranchID field. Notice the Branch table has no B60 record. Close the Branch table.

e. Replace B60 with **B50** in the new Accounts record and press **Tab** three times. As soon as the focus moves to the next record, the pencil symbol disappears, and your data are saved.

You successfully identified a BranchID that your Accounts table recognizes as a valid value. Because referential integrity between the Accounts and Branch tables has been enforced, Access looks at each data entry item in a foreign key and matches it to a corresponding value in the table where it is the primary key. In Step c, you attempted to enter a nonexistent BranchID and were not allowed to make that error. In Step e, you entered a valid BranchID. Access examined the BranchID field in the Branch table and found a corresponding value for B50.

f. Close the Accounts table. Close any open tables.

g. Keep the database open if you plan to continue with the next Hands-On Exercise. If not, close the database and exit Access.

Single-Table Queries

A *query* enables you to ask questions about the data stored in a database and provides the answers to the questions by creating subsets or summaries of data in a datasheet. If you wanted to see which customers have an account with a balance over $5,000, you could find the answer by creating an Access query. Unlike filters that you can apply to the table datasheets themselves, queries are saved as separate, named objects in your database. They can be copied for re-purposing, modified, and exported to other databases. Queries update dynamically as data changes in the underlying tables of a database and can be formed using one or more tables.

In this section, you will use the Simple Query Wizard and Query Design view to create queries from just one table. Multitable queries, queries that use two or more tables, will be covered in the next section.

Creating a Single-Table Query

Because data are stored in tables in a database, you always begin a query by determining which table (or tables) contain the data that you need. For the question about account balances over $5,000, you would use the Accounts table. You can create a single-table query in two ways—by using the Simple Query Wizard or the Query Design command in the Queries group on the Create tab. While the Simple Query Wizard offers a step-by-step guide to creating a query, the Query Design tool allows for more flexibility and customization and is often the preferred method for creating queries.

After you design a query, you run it to display the results in a datasheet. A query's datasheet looks like a table's datasheet, except that it is usually a subset of the fields and records found in the table on which it is based. The subset shows only the records that match the criteria that were added in the query design. The subset may contain different sorting of the records than the sorting in the underlying table. You can enter new records in a query, modify existing records, or delete records in Datasheet view. Any changes made in Datasheet view of a query are reflected in the underlying table on which the query is based. Likewise, changes made in tables are reflected in the queries that are built based on those tables.

Create a Single-Table Select Query

A Select query is a type of query that displays only the fields and records that match criteria entered in the query design process. Essentially, you are designing a query that selects specific values (a subset) from the original table data. The Select query is used to limit or filter output when you do not want to display all fields and records from your table(s).

To create a select query using the Query Design tool, complete the following steps:

1. Click the Create tab.
2. Click Query Design in the Queries group on the Create tab.
3. Select the table you want for your query from the Show Table dialog box.
4. Click Add to add the table to the top pane of the query design and close the Show Table dialog box.
5. Drag the fields needed from the table's field list to the query design grid (or alternatively, double-click the field names); then add criteria and sorting options.
6. Click Run in the Results group on the Design tab to show the results in Datasheet view.

Use Query Design View

Query Design view is divided into two sections: The top pane displays the table(s) from which the data will be retrieved, and the bottom pane (known as the query design grid) displays the fields and the criteria that you set. The query design grid (the bottom pane) contains columns and rows. Each field in the query design grid has its own column and contains multiple rows. The rows enable you to control the query results.

- The Field row displays the field name.
- The Table row displays the data source (in some cases, a field occurs in more than one table, for example, when it is a join field; therefore, it is often beneficial to display the table name in the query design grid).
- The Sort row enables you to sort in ascending or descending order (or neither).
- The Show row controls whether the field will be displayed or hidden in the query results. If the check box in this row is selected, the field will display.
- The **Criteria row** is used to set the rules that determine which records will be selected, such as customers with account balances greater than $ 5,000.

Figure 2.29 displays the query design grid with the Show Table dialog box open. The Show Table dialog box is used to define which table you will include in your query. The Accounts table is selected in the Show Table dialog box. After the Accounts table is added, the fields from that table are available for use in the query.

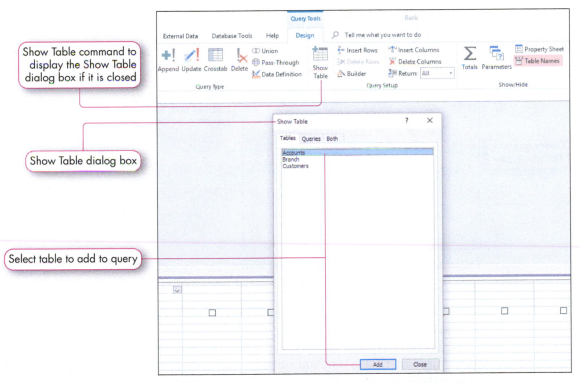

FIGURE 2.29 Query Design View with Show Table Dialog Box

Figure 2.30 shows the Design of a sample query with four fields, with a criterion set for one field. The results of the query display in Datasheet view, as shown in Figure 2.31.

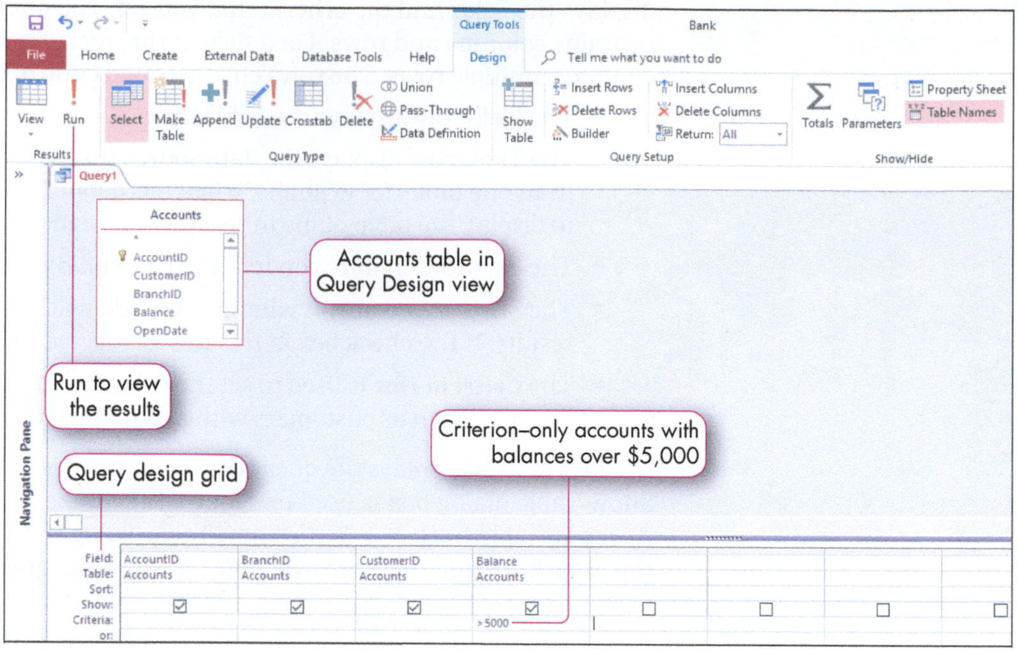

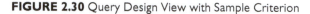

FIGURE 2.30 Query Design View with Sample Criterion

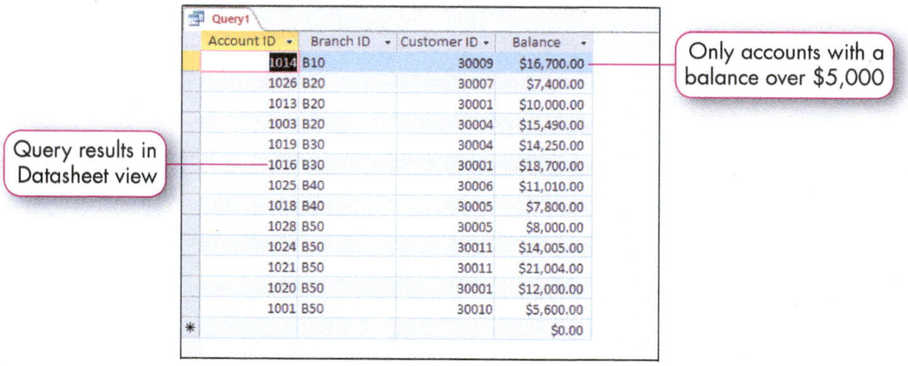

Account ID	Branch ID	Customer ID	Balance
1014	B10	30009	$16,700.00
1026	B20	30007	$7,400.00
1013	B20	30001	$10,000.00
1003	B20	30004	$15,490.00
1019	B30	30004	$14,250.00
1016	B30	30001	$18,700.00
1025	B40	30006	$11,010.00
1018	B40	30005	$7,800.00
1028	B50	30005	$8,000.00
1024	B50	30011	$14,005.00
1021	B50	30011	$21,004.00
1020	B50	30001	$12,000.00
1001	B50	30010	$5,600.00
*			$0.00

FIGURE 2.31 Query Results in Datasheet View

Should you need to fine-tune the query, switch back to Design view, make a change, and then run the query again to view the results. After you are satisfied with the results, you can save and name the query so it becomes a permanent part of the database and can be used later. Each time you run a query, the results will update based on the current data in the underlying table(s).

TIP: EXAMINE THE RECORDS

Be sure to examine the records returned in the query results. Verify that the records in the query results match the criteria that you specified in Design view. If the results are not what you anticipated, return to Design view, and check your criteria. If your criteria are inaccurate, your query may not return any results at all. Unexpected results can also occur from inaccurate data, so troubleshooting your queries is a skill that you will acquire as your experience progresses.

Using the Query Wizard

The **Simple Query Wizard** guides you through query design with a step-by-step process. The wizard is helpful for creating basic queries that do not require criteria. Any further modifications to the query after it has been created will be done in Design View. Launch the Query Wizard in the Queries group on the Create tab (see Figure 2.32). Select Simple Query Wizard in the New Query dialog box, as shown in Figure 2.33. In the first step of the Simple Query Wizard dialog box, you specify the tables or queries and fields required in your query. When you select a table from the Tables/Queries arrow (queries can also be based on other queries), a list of the table's fields displays in the Available Fields list box (see Figure 2.34).

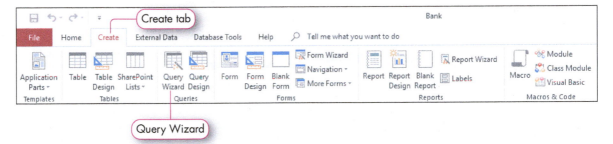

FIGURE 2.32 Launching the Query Wizard

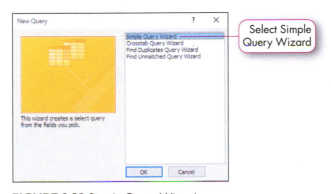

FIGURE 2.33 Simple Query Wizard

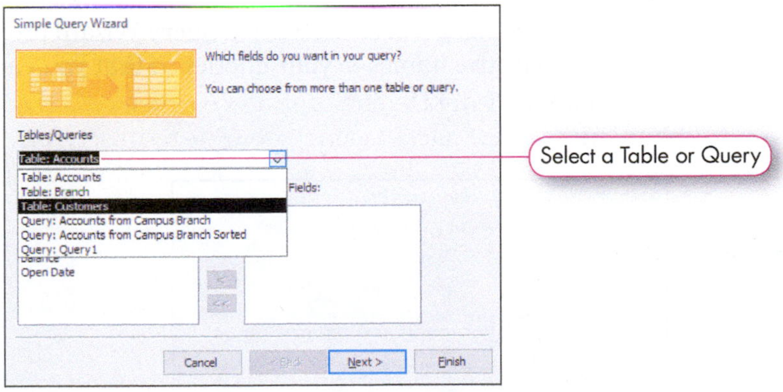

FIGURE 2.34 Specify Which Tables or Queries to Use

Select the necessary fields and add them to the Selected Fields list box using the directional arrows shown in Figure 2.35. In the next screen (shown in Figure 2.36), you choose between a detail and a summary query. The detail query shows every selected field of every record in the result. The summary query enables you to group data and view only summary records. For example, if you were interested in the total funds deposited at each of the bank branches, you would set the query to Summary, click Summary Options, and then click Sum on the Balance field. Access would then sum the balances of all selected accounts for each branch.

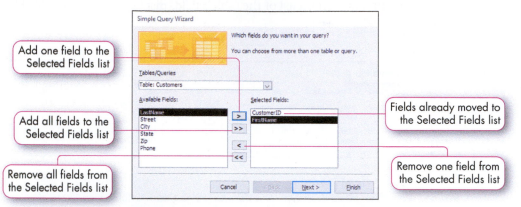

FIGURE 2.35 Specify the Fields for the Query

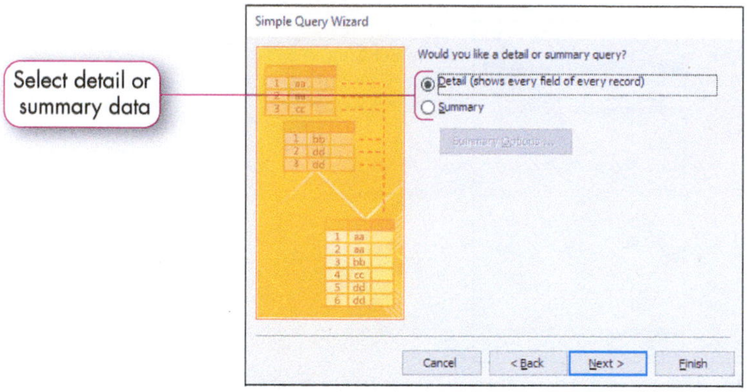

FIGURE 2.36 Choose Detail or Summary Data

The final dialog box of the Simple Query Wizard prompts for the name of the query. Assign descriptive names to your queries so that you can easily identify what each one does (see Figure 2.37).

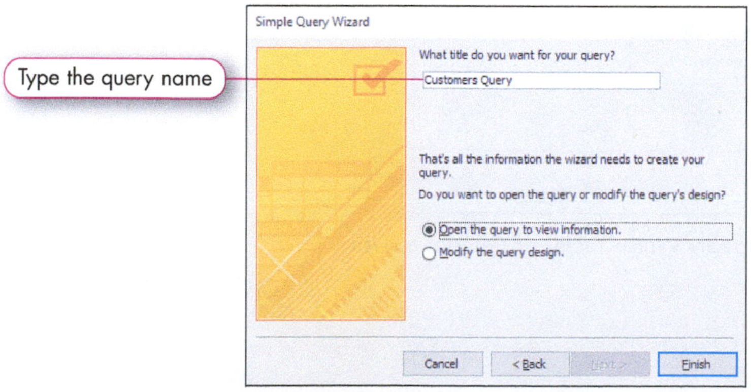

FIGURE 2.37 Name the Query

STEP 2 Specifying Query Criteria

Whether you started in Query Design View or with the Query Wizard, you can use criteria to further limit (or filter) the records to display only those that you require in the query results. Criteria are specified in the Criteria row by entering values that will extract records with matching values. For example, you might use the criterion "Campus" in the Branch field to display customers from the Campus branch in the bank database. Because criteria values are not case sensitive, typing "campus" is the same as typing "Campus" and both will return the same results.

When specifying a criterion for a query, Access may add delimiters—special characters that surround a criterion's value. The delimiter required is determined by the field's data type. Text fields require quotation marks before and after the text, for example, "Campus". When the criterion is in a date field, the criterion is enclosed in pound signs, such as #10/14/2019#. A date value can be entered using any allowed format, such as February 2, 2019, 2/2/2019, or 2-Feb-19. Use plain digits (no delimiter) for the criteria of a numeric field, currency, or AutoNumber. You can enter numeric criteria with or without a decimal point and with or without a minus sign. Commas and dollar signs are not allowed. You enter criteria for a Yes/No field as Yes or No. See Table 2.4 for query criteria and examples.

TABLE 2.4	Query Criteria	
Data Type	**Criteria**	**Example**
Text	"Harry"	For a FirstName field, displays only text that matches Harry specifically. The quotation marks can be typed, or Access will add them automatically.
Numeric	5000	For a Quantity field, displays only numbers that match 5000 exactly (do not specify commas, currency symbols, etc.).
Date	#2/2/2019#	For a ShippedDate field, shows orders shipped on February 2, 2019.
Yes/No	Yes	For a Discontinued field, returns records where the check box in the table is selected, denoting Yes.

> **TIP: COMMON ERRORS WHEN CREATING QUERIES**
>
> There are several common errors to be aware of when designing queries. A criterion that you enter in a query must match the data in the table. For example, if your table uses TH as a day of the week, and you use "Thursday" as your criterion, no matching records would display in the results. Ensure that you enter the correct criteria in the appropriate columns. The criteria enable you to filter for values in specific fields, and it is easy to type the right criteria in the wrong columns in the design grid. The correct spelling of the criteria is also essential to obtaining good results. Be alert to using the correct syntax for data types as well. For example, if you are querying a Number field but enter the value as text with surrounding quotation marks, a data type mismatch message will display.

Use Wildcards

Wildcards are special characters that can represent one or more characters in a text value. Suppose you want to use a criterion to select the last name of a customer, but you are not sure how to spell the name; however, you know that the name starts with the letters *Sm*. You can use a wildcard with a text value (such as Sm*) to search for the name.

You enter wildcard characters in text values in the Criteria row of a query. Therefore, if you want to search for names that start with the letters *Sm*, specify the criterion in the LastName field as *Sm**. All last names that begin with *Sm* would display in the results.

The wildcard characters stand in for the unknown characters. Wildcard characters can be placed in the beginning, middle, or end of a text string. There are several wildcards that you can use to produce different results. Table 2.5 shows more query criterion examples that use wildcards.

TABLE 2.5	Query Criteria Using Wildcards		
Character	Description	Example	Result
*	Matches any number of characters in the same position as the asterisk	Sm*	Small, Smiley, Smith, Smithson
?	Matches a single character in the same position as the question mark	H?ll	Hall, Hill, Hull
[ ]	Matches any single character within the brackets	F[ae]ll	Fall and Fell, but not Fill or Full
[!]	Matches any character not in the brackets	F[!ae]ll	Fill and Full, but not Fall or Fell

Use Comparison Operators in Queries

Comparison operators, such as equal (=), not equal (<>), greater than (>), less than (<), greater than or equal to (>=), and less than or equal to (<=), can be used in query criteria. Comparison operators enable you to limit the query results to only those records that meet the criteria. For example, if you only want to display accounts that have a balance greater than $5,000, you would type >5000 in the Criteria row of the Balance field. Table 2.6 shows more comparison operator examples. As an alternative to comparison operators, you can use the BETWEEN operator in criteria to specify inclusive values in a range. For example, to display accounts that have a balance of greater than or equal to (>=) 1000 and less than or equal to (<=) 5000, you can set the criteria as BETWEEN 1000 AND 5000.

TABLE 2.6	Comparison Operators in Queries
Expression	Example
=10	Equals 10
<>10	Not equal to 10
>10	Greater than 10
>=10	Greater than or equal to 10
<10	Less than 10
<=10	Less than or equal to 10

> **TIP: FINDING VALUES IN A DATE RANGE**
> To find the values contained within a date range, use the greater than (>) and less than (<) comparison operators. For example, to find the values of dates on or after January 1, 2019, and on or before December 31, 2019, use the criterion >=1/1/2019 and <=12/31/2019. You can also use the BETWEEN operator to find the same inclusive dates, for example, BETWEEN 1/1/2019 and 12/31/2019.

Work with Null

Sometimes finding missing (blank) values is an important part of making a decision. For example, if you need to know which orders have been completed but not shipped, you would create a query to find the orders with a missing (blank) ShipDate. The term that Access uses for a blank field is null (or not null for a populated field). Table 2.7 provides two examples of when to use the null criterion in a query.

TABLE 2.7 Establishing Null Criteria Expressions

Expression	Description	Example
Is Null	Used to find blank fields	For a SalesRepID field in the Customers table when the customer has not been assigned to a sales representative.
Is Not Null	Used to find fields with data	For a ShipDate field; a value has been entered to indicate that the order was shipped to the customer.

Establish AND, OR, and NOT Criteria

Recall the earlier question, "Which customers currently have an account with a balance over $5,000?" This question was answered by creating a query with a single criterion. At times, questions are more focused and require queries with more than one criterion. For example, you may need to know "Which customers from the Eastern branch currently have an account with a balance over $5,000?" To answer this question, you specify two criteria in different fields using the **AND condition**. This means that the query results will display only records that match *all* criteria. When the criteria are in the same row of the query design grid, Access interprets this as an AND condition. When you want to test two criteria in the same field, you can also use the AND logical operator as shown in Table 2.8.

When you have multiple criteria and you need to satisfy only one, not all the criteria, use the **OR condition**. The query results will display records that match any of the specified criteria. You can use the OR logical operator, and type the expression into the Criteria row, separating the criteria with the OR keyword. Table 2.8 shows an example of an OR condition created using this method. You can also type the first criterion in the Criteria row and type the next criterion in the Or row of the same field (to test for different values in the same field) or in a different field in the design grid (see Figure 2.38). The NOT logical operator returns all records except the specified criteria. For example, "Not Eastern" would return all accounts except those opened at the Eastern branch.

AND condition–criteria are in the same row

Field:	AccountID	CustomerID	BranchID	Balance
Table:	Accounts	Accounts	Accounts	Accounts
Sort:	Ascending			
Show:	☑	☑	☑	☑
Criteria:			"B50"	<5000
or:				

OR condition–criteria are in different rows

Field:	AccountID	CustomerID	BranchID	Balance
Table:	Accounts	Accounts	Accounts	Accounts
Sort:	Ascending			
Show:	☑	☑	☑	☑
Criteria:			"B50"	
or:				<5000

Use NOT to exclude specific records

Field:	AccountID	CustomerID	BranchID	Balance
Table:	Accounts	Accounts	Accounts	Accounts
Sort:		Ascending		Ascending
Show:	☑	☑	☑	☑
Criteria:			Not "B50"	<5000
or:				

FIGURE 2.38 Query Design Views Showing the AND, OR, and NOT Operators

TABLE 2.8	AND, OR, and NOT Queries	
Logical Operator	**Example**	**Result**
AND	>5000 AND <10000	For a Balance field, returns all accounts with a balance greater than $5,000 and less than $10,000.
OR	"Eastern" OR "Campus"	For a Location field, returns all accounts that are at the Eastern or the Campus branch.
NOT	Not "Campus"	For a Location field, returns all records except those in the Campus branch.

Specifying Query Sort Order and Running a Query

The query sort order determines the order of records in a query's Datasheet view. You can change the order of records by specifying the sort order in Design view. When you want to sort using more than one field, the sort order is determined from left to right. The order of columns should be considered when first creating the query. For example, a query sorted by LastName and then by FirstName must have those two fields in the correct order in the design grid. When modifying sort order, it is sometimes necessary to rearrange fields, or add and delete columns in the query design grid.

You can change the order, add, or delete fields in the query design grid, by completing one of the following steps:

- Change the order of a field: select the column you want to move by clicking the column selector. Click again and drag the selected field to its new location.
- Insert an additional column in the design grid: select a column and click Insert Columns in the Query Setup group on the Design tab. The additional column will insert to the left of the selected column.
- Delete a column: click the column selector to select the column and click Delete Columns in the Query Setup group, or press Delete on the keyboard.

Once your query is designed and saved, you run it to view the results. There are several ways to run a query. One method is from within Design view; click Run in the Results group on the Design tab. Another method is to locate the query in the Navigation Pane and double-click it (or select the query in the Navigation Pane and press Enter). The results will display in a datasheet as a tab in the main window.

STEP 3 ▶ Copying and Modifying a Query

After you create a query, you can create a copy of it to use as the basis for creating a similar query. Duplicating a query saves time when you need the same tables and fields but with slightly different criteria. For example, you need a list of accounts in each branch. In a case like this, you create a query for one branch, save a copy of the query, and then give it a new name. Finally, you would change the criteria to specify the next branch.

To create a query based on an existing query, complete the following steps:

1. Select, but do not open the query you want to copy in the Navigation Pane.
2. Right-click the query in the Navigation Pane and from the shortcut menu, select Copy.
3. Right-click in the empty space of the Navigation Pane and select Paste.
4. Type a name for the new query in the Paste As dialog box and click OK (see Figure 2.39).
5. Switch to Design view of the copied query and modify the query criteria.
6. Save and run the modified query.

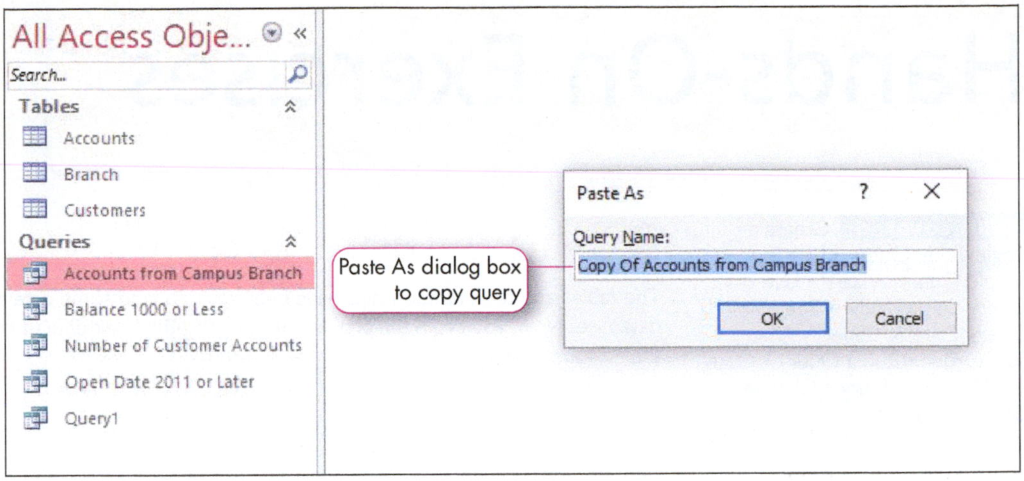

FIGURE 2.39 Using Copy Command and Paste As Dialog Box to Save a Copy of a Query

Change Query Data

Be aware that query results in the datasheet display the actual records that are stored in the underlying table(s). Being able to correct an error immediately while it is displayed in the query datasheet is an advantage. You can save time by not having to close the query, open the table, find the error, fix it, and then run the query again. However, use caution when editing records in query results because you will be changing the original table data.

Quick Concepts

8. Compare why you would create a single-table query as opposed to filtering a table. *p. 164*

9. Discuss an example of how to use a comparison operator to find certain records in a table. *p. 170*

10. Examine how you would use an AND condition in a query. *p. 171*

11. Discuss why you would want to copy an existing query. *p. 172*

Hands-On Exercises

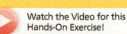

Skills covered: Create a Single-Table Query • Use the Simple Query Wizard • Use Query Design View • Specify Query Criteria • Specify Query Sort Order • Run a Query • Copy and Modify a Query • Change Query Data

3 Single-Table Queries

The tables and table relationships have been created, and some data have been entered in the bank database. Now, you begin the process of analyzing the bank data using queries. You decide to begin with the Accounts table.

STEP 1 USE THE QUERY WIZARD

You decide to start with the Query Wizard, knowing you can always alter the design of the query later in Design view. You will display the results in Datasheet view. Refer to Figure 2.40 as you complete Step 1.

Step h: Query named Accounts from Campus Branch

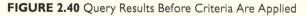

Account ID	Customer ID	Branch ID	Balance
1001	30010	B50	$5,600.00
1002	30001	B10	$1,200.00
1003	30004	B20	$15,490.00
1004	30003	B30	$630.00
1005	30009	B50	$1,300.00
1006	30003	B10	$550.00
1007	30007	B20	$1,620.00
1008	30004	B40	$2,100.00
1009	30005	B50	$1,500.00
1010	30001	B20	$3,000.00
1011	30005	B10	$290.00
1012	30002	B30	$1,900.00
1013	30001	B20	$10,000.00
1014	30009	B10	$16,700.00
1015	30004	B30	$460.00
1016	30001	B30	$18,700.00
1017	30010	B30	$980.00
1018	30005	B40	$7,800.00
1019	30004	B30	$14,250.00
1020	30001	B50	$1,200.00
1021	30011	B50	$21,004.00
1022	30003	B50	$4,000.00
1023	30011	B50	$1,000.00
1024	30011	B50	$14,005.00
1025	30006	B40	$11,010.00
1026	30007	B20	$7,400.00
1027	30003	B50	$4,000.00

Record: ◄ ◄ 1 of 27 ► ►I ►* No Filter Search

Step h: 27 records displayed

FIGURE 2.40 Query Results Before Criteria Are Applied

a. Open *a02h2Bank_LastFirst* if you closed it at the end of Hands-On Exercise 2, and save it as **a02h3Bank_LastFirst**, changing h2 to h3.

b. Click the **Create tab** and click **Query Wizard** in the Queries group.

   The New Query dialog box opens. Simple Query Wizard is selected by default.

c. Click **OK**.

d. Verify that Table: Accounts is selected in the Tables/Queries box.

e. Click **AccountID** in the Available Fields list and click **Add One Field** [>] to move it to the Selected Fields list. Repeat the process with **CustomerID**, **BranchID**, and **Balance**.

   The four fields should now display in the Selected Fields list box.

f. Click **Next**.

g. Confirm that Detail (shows every field of every record) is selected and click **Next**.

h. Name the query **Accounts from Campus Branch**. Click **Finish**.

This query name describes the data in the query results. Your query should have four fields: AccountID, CustomerID, BranchID, and Balance. The Navigation bar indicates that 27 records are present in the query results.

STEP 2 ▶ SPECIFY QUERY CRITERIA, SPECIFY SORT ORDER, AND RUN THE QUERY

You decide to modify your query to analyze accounts specifically for the Campus branch. Refer to Figure 2.41 as you complete Step 2.

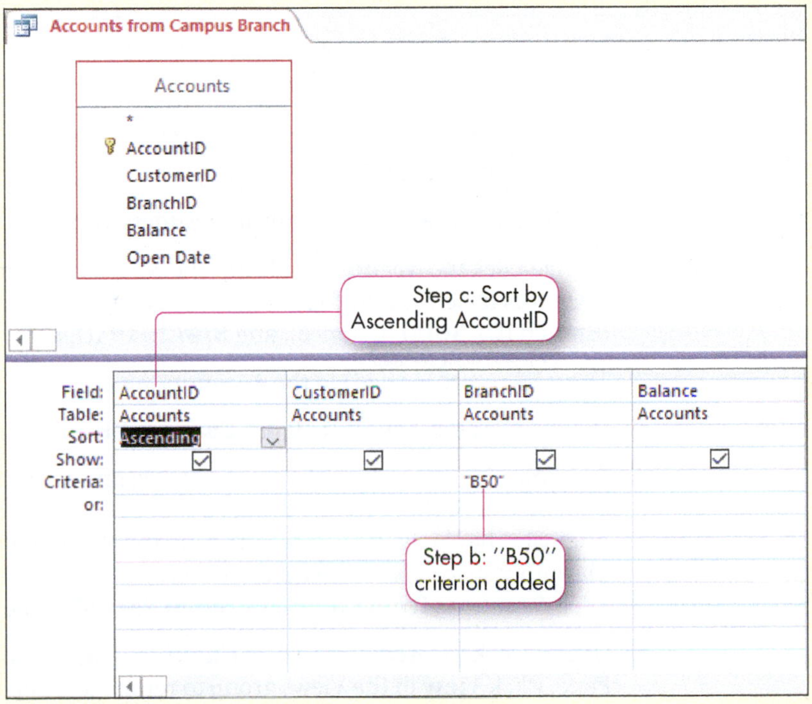

FIGURE 2.41 Enter Criteria and Add Sort Order

a. Click the **Home tab** and click **View** in the Views group.

The Accounts from Campus Branch query opens in Design view. You have created and named this query to view only those accounts at the Campus branch. However, other branches' accounts also display. You need to limit the query results to only the records for the branch of interest.

b. Click in the **Criteria row** (fifth row) in the BranchID column of the query design grid, type **B50**, and then press **Enter**.

B50 is the BranchID for the Campus branch. Access criteria are not case sensitive; therefore, b50 and B50 will produce the same results. Access adds quotation marks around text criteria after you press Enter, or you can type them yourself.

c. Click in the **Sort row** (third row) in the AccountID column and select **Ascending**.

d. Click **Run** in the Results group.

You decide to modify a value directly in the query datasheet and add a new record using the Accounts table. To create a second query that sorts the records in a different way, you copy and modify the existing query. Refer to Figure 2.42 as you complete Step 3.

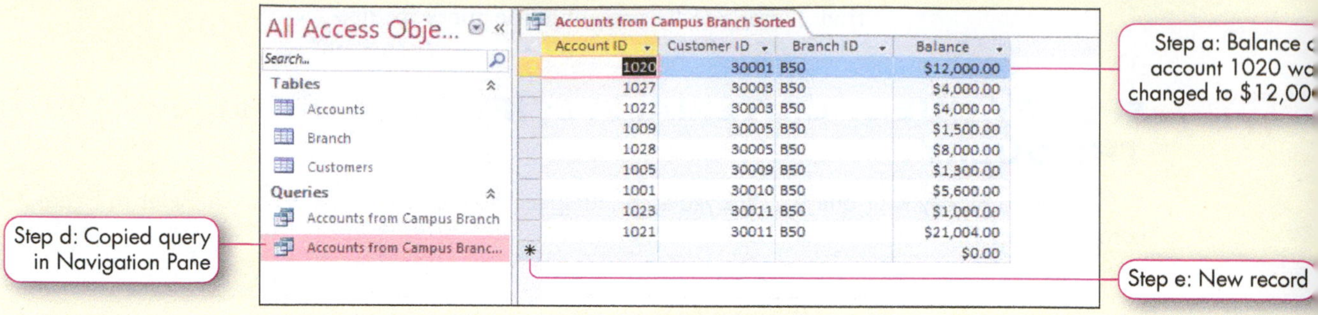

FIGURE 2.42 Modified Query with Updated Records

a. Click in the **Balance field** in the record for account 1020. Change $1,200 to **$12,000**. Press **Enter**. Save and close the query.

   You modified the record directly in the query results.

b. Double-click the **Accounts table** in the Navigation Pane. Add a new record to the Accounts table with the following data: **1028** (Account ID), **30005** (Customer ID), **B50** (Branch ID), **8000** (Balance), and **8/4/2019** (Open Date). Press **Tab**.

   The new record is added to the Accounts table.

c. Double-click the **Accounts from Campus Branch query** in the Navigation Pane.

d. Customer 30005 now shows two accounts: one with a balance of $1,500 and one with a balance of $8,000. Close the query. Right-click the **Accounts from Campus Branch query** in the Navigation Pane, and from the shortcut menu, select **Copy**. Right-click in the empty space in the **Navigation Pane**, and from the shortcut menu, select **Paste**. Type **Accounts from Campus Branch Sorted** as the query name. Click **OK**.

e. Double-click the **Accounts from Campus Branch Sorted** query in the Navigation Pane. Click **View** in the Views group to return to Design view of the duplicate query.

f. Click in the **Sort row** of the AccountID field, click the **arrow**, and then select **(not sorted)**. Click in the **Sort row** of the CustomerID field and select **Ascending**. Click in the **Sort row** of the Balance field and select **Ascending**.

g. Click **Run** in the Results group.

   Customer 30005 now shows two accounts with the two balances sorted in ascending order. The record for Account ID 1028 was added in the underlying Accounts table, and the query updates automatically to display it with the others. All other customers with more than one Campus branch account are listed in ascending order by balance.

h. Save the query. Close the Accounts from Campus Branch Sorted query and close the Accounts table.

i. Keep the database open if you plan to continue with the next Hands-On Exercise. If not, close the database and exit Access.

Multitable Queries

Multitable queries contain two or more tables and enable you to take advantage of the relationships that have been established in your database. When you extract information from a database with a query, often you will need to pull data from multiple tables. One table may contain the core information that you want, while another table may contain the related data that make the query provide the complete results. The query will then combine data from both tables into one datasheet.

For example, the sample bank database contains three tables: Customers, Accounts, and Branch. You connected the tables through relationships in order to store data efficiently and to enforce consistent data entry between them. The Customers table provides the information for the owners of the accounts. However, the Accounts table includes the balances of each account—the key financial information. Recall that these two tables were joined by the CustomerID field. Because the Accounts table only contains a CustomerID but no personal data, if you want to include information such as the customer's name in your query results, both the Customers and Accounts tables are needed to provide the information that you want.

In this section, you will learn different ways to create and modify multitable queries. As you acquire these new skills, you will realize the power of using related tables in your database.

Creating a Multitable Query

There are several ways to create multitable queries. One method is to add tables to an existing query; another way is to copy an existing query and add to it. You can also create a multitable query from scratch either using the Query Wizard or the Query Design tool.

STEP 1 ▸ Add Additional Tables and Fields to an Existing Query

One way to create a multitable query is to add additional tables and fields to an existing query. For example, you may want to add branch or customer data to a query that already includes account information.

To add tables to an existing query, complete the following steps:

1. Open the existing query in Design view.
2. Drag additional tables from the Navigation Pane directly into the top pane of the query design window.
3. Add fields, criteria, and sorting options in the query design grid.
4. Run and save the query.

The Branch and Customers tables were added to the Accounts from Campus Branch query, as shown in Figure 2.43. The join lines between tables indicate that relationships were previously set in the Relationships window. With the additional tables and fields available, you can now add the customer's name (from Customers) and the branch location name (from Branch) rather than using CustomerID and BranchID in your results. The datasheet will contain more readily identifiable information than ID numbers for customers and locations.

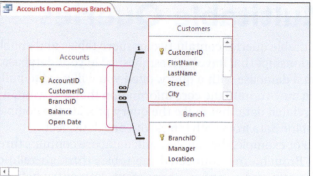

Join lines indicate Customers and Branch tables are related to the Accounts table

FIGURE 2.43 Two Additional Tables Added to a Query

STEP 2 Create a Multitable Query from Scratch

Creating a multitable query from scratch is similar to creating a single-table query except that you are adding two or more tables to the query design grid. However, choosing the right tables and managing the relationships in the query might require some additional skills. First, you should only use related tables in a multitable query. Related tables are tables that are joined in a relationship using a common field. Once tables are joined by a common field, you can pull related data from each to create complete and usable information in queries. Using Figure 2.43 as a guide, creating a query with the Accounts and Branch tables would be acceptable, as would using Accounts and Customers tables, or Accounts, Branch, and Customers tables. All three scenarios include related tables. However, creating a query with only the Branch and Customers tables would not be acceptable because these tables are not directly related to one another (in other words, they do not have a common field).

To create a multitable query, complete the following steps:

1. Click the Create tab.
2. Click Query Design in the Queries group.
3. Add the tables you want in your query from the Show Table dialog box. Close the Show Table dialog box.
4. Drag the fields you want to display from the tables to the query design grid (or alternatively, double-click the field names); then add criteria and sorting options.
5. Click Run in the Results group on the Design tab to display the results in Datasheet view.

TIP: PRINT THE RELATIONSHIP REPORT TO HELP CREATE A MULTITABLE QUERY

When you create a multitable query, you only include related tables. As a guide, when the Relationships window is open, you can print the Relationship Report. Click the Database Tools tab and click Relationship Report in the Tools group on the Relationship Tools Design tab. This report will provide a diagram that displays the tables, fields, and relationships in your database. A Relationship Report is also very useful when you need to understand a database that is unfamiliar to you. The report is exportable to other formats such as Word if you want to share it with colleagues.

STEP 3 Modifying a Multitable Query

After creating a multitable query, you may find that you did not include all the fields you needed or that you included fields that are unnecessary to the results. To modify multitable queries, use the same techniques you learned for single-table queries.

- To add tables, use the Show Table dialog box in the Query Setup group on the Query Tools Design tab (or drag the tables into the top pane of the query design from the Navigation Pane).
- To remove tables, select the unwanted tables and press Delete.

- To add fields, double-click the fields you want to include.
- To remove fields, click the column selector of each field and press Delete.

Join lines between related tables should display automatically in a query if the relationships were previously established, as shown in Figure 2.43.

> **TIP: MULTITABLE QUERIES INHERIT RELATIONSHIPS**
> When you add two or more related tables to a query, join lines display automatically. Each time you create a query with the same tables, the relationships between them will be inherited from the database.

Add and Delete Fields in a Multitable Query

In Figure 2.44, the design grid and fields from all three tables display. Figure 2.44 shows that Location (from the Branch table) replaced BranchID and LastName (from the Customers table) replaced CustomerID to make the results more useful. BranchID was deleted from the query; therefore, the "B50" criterion was removed as well. "Campus" was added to the Location field's Criteria row to extract the names of the branches rather than their BranchID numbers. The results of the revised query are shown in Figure 2.45.

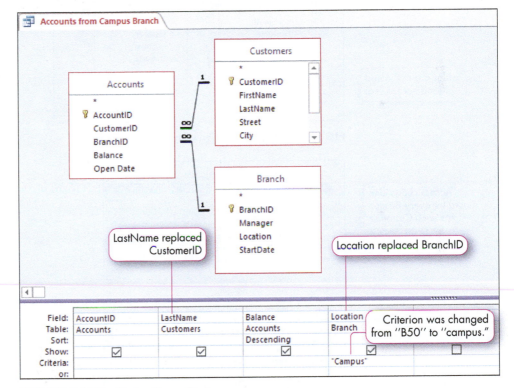

FIGURE 2.44 Modify the Query Design

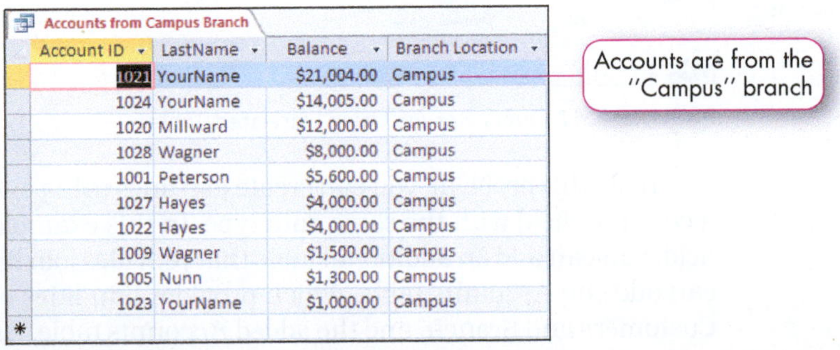

FIGURE 2.45 Datasheet View of a Multitable Query

Add Join Lines in a Multitable Query

Over time, your databases may grow, and additional tables might be added. Occasionally, new tables are added to the database but not to the Relationships window. When queries are created with the newly added tables, join lines will not be established. When this happens, you can create temporary join lines in the query design window. These join lines will provide a temporary relationship between tables (for that query only) and enable Access to interpret the query properly. It may be that you are not planning to save the query in your database or even make the additional table a permanent object. However, if you plan to extract data from related tables repeatedly, it is preferable to create a permanent relationship between the tables in the Relationships window.

In Figure 2.46, two tables are added to a new query's design, but no join line connects them. The results of the query will be unpredictable and will display more records than expected. The Customers table contains 11 records, and the Branch table contains 5 records. Because Access does not know how to interpret the unrelated tables, the results will show 55 records—every possible combination of customer and branch (11 × 5). See Figure 2.47.

FIGURE 2.46 Query Design with Unrelated Tables

LastName	Branch ID	Branch Location	Manager's Start Date
Millward	B10	Uptown	12/3/2014
Millward	B20	Eastern	6/18/2013
Millward	B30	Western	3/13/2011
Millward	B40	Southern	9/15/2014
Millward	B50	Campus	10/11/2016
Fox	B10	Uptown	12/3/2014
Fox	B20	Eastern	6/18/2013
Fox	B30	Western	3/13/2011
Fox	B40	Southern	9/15/2014
Fox	B50	Campus	10/11/2016
Hayes	B10	Uptown	12/3/2014
Hayes	B20	Eastern	6/18/2013
Hayes	B30	Western	3/13/2011
Hayes	B40	Southern	9/15/2014
Hayes	B50	Campus	10/11/2016
Collins	B10	Uptown	12/3/2014
Collins	B20	Eastern	6/18/2013
Collins	B30	Western	3/13/2011
Collins	B40	Southern	9/15/2014
Collins	B50	Campus	10/11/2016
Wagner	B10	Uptown	12/3/2014
Wagner	B20	Eastern	6/18/2013
Wagner	B30	Western	3/13/2011
Wagner	B40	Southern	9/15/2014
Wagner	B50	Campus	10/11/2016
Williams	B10	Uptown	12/3/2014
Williams	B20	Eastern	6/18/2013

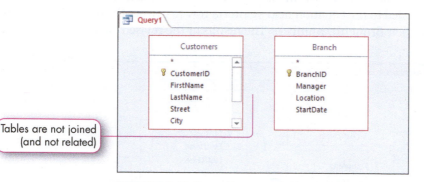

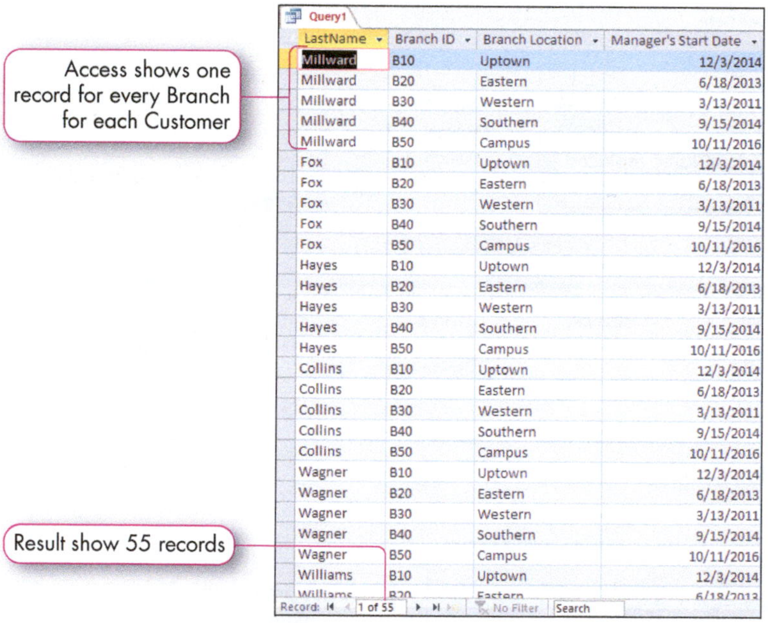

FIGURE 2.47 Query Results Using Unrelated Tables

To fix this problem, you can create join lines using existing tables if the tables contain a common field with the same data type. In this example, in which there is no common field, you can add an additional table that provides join lines between all three tables. You can add the Accounts table, which provides join lines between the two existing tables, Customers and Branch, and the added Accounts table. As soon as the third table is added to the query design, the join lines display automatically.

Use a Total Row to Summarize Data in a Query

You can get valuable information from your database using a multitable query. For example, if you want to know how many accounts each customer has, you would create a new query and add both the Customers and Accounts tables to Design view. After you verify that the join lines are correct, you add the CustomerID field from the Customers table and the AccountID field from the Accounts table to the query design grid. When you initially run the query, the results show duplicates in the CustomerID column because some customers have multiple accounts. Suppose that you want to display a single row for each Customer ID in the query, with a count of how many accounts each customer has. To summarize information this way, you can add a Total row to the query, create one group (or effectively one record) for each customer and use a function to count the number of accounts each customer has.

To summarize this information (how many accounts each customer has), in Design view, select Totals in the Show/Hide group on the Query Tools Design tab. The Total row displays. Both fields show the Group By option in the Total row. The Total row enables you to summarize records by using functions such as Sum, Average, Count, etc. Before selecting a function that will summarize the values for each group, you must determine which field will represent your groupings. In this case, you will group the records by the Customer ID field and use the Count function to count the number of accounts per group.

With Group By selected in the Customer ID field, click in the Total row of the AccountID field, select Count from the list of functions, and then run the query again. This time the results show one row for each customer and the number of accounts for each customer, as shown in Figure 2.48. There are additional ways of aggregating data in queries, which will be covered in a later chapter.

Customer ID	CountOfAccountID
30001	5
30002	1
30003	4
30004	4
30005	4
30006	1
30007	2
30009	2
30010	2
30011	3

FIGURE 2.48 Datasheet Results with the Count of Accounts per Customer

Quick Concepts

12. Discuss the advantage of creating a multitable query. *p. 177*

13. Explain a situation where you would use a Total row in a query. *p. 181*

14. Consider what happens when you create a query with tables that have no common field. *p. 180*

Hands-On Exercises

MyLab IT HOE4 Sim Training

Watch the Video for this
Hands-On Exercise!

Skills covered: Add Additional Tables and Fields to an Existing Query • Create a Multitable Query from Scratch • Modify a Multitable Query • Add and Delete Fields in a Multitable Query • Use a Total Row to Summarize Data in a Query

4 Multitable Queries

In order to evaluate the sample set of data further, you will create queries that are based on multiple tables rather than on a single table. To create a multitable query, you decide to open an existing query, add additional tables and fields to it, and then save the query.

STEP 1 ADD ADDITIONAL TABLES AND FIELDS TO A QUERY

The previous query was based on the Accounts table, but now you want to add information to the query from the Branch and Customers tables. You will add the Branch and Customers tables along with some additional fields from these tables to the query. Refer to Figure 2.49 as you complete Step 1.

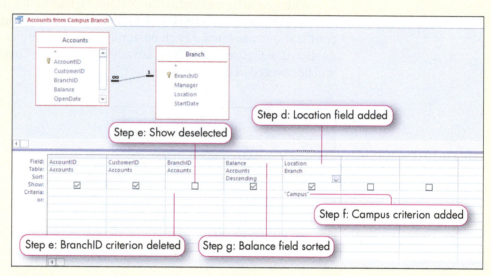

FIGURE 2.49 Add Tables to an Existing Query

a. Open *a02h3Bank_LastFirst* if you closed it at the end of Hands-On Exercise 3, and save it as **a02h4Bank_LastFirst**, changing h3 to h4.

b. Right-click the **Accounts from Campus Branch query** in the Navigation Pane and select **Design View** from the shortcut menu.

c. Drag the **Branch table** from the Navigation Pane to the top pane of the query design window to the right of the Accounts table.

   A join line connects the Branch table to the Accounts table. The tables in the query inherit the relationship created earlier in the Relationships window.

d. Drag the **Location field** from the Branch table to the first empty column in the design grid.

   The Location field should be positioned to the right of the Balance field.

e. Click the **Show check box** below the BranchID field to deselect it and hide this field from the results.

   The BranchID field is no longer needed in the results because the Location field provides the branch name instead. Because you deselected the BranchID Show check box, the BranchID field will not display the next time the query is run.

f. Delete the B50 criterion in the BranchID column.

g. Type **Campus** as a criterion in the Location field and press **Enter**.

Access adds quotation marks around Campus for you because Campus is a text criterion. You are substituting the Location criterion (Campus) in place of the BranchID criterion (B50).

h. Click in the AccountID field **Sort row**, click the **arrow**, and then select **not sorted**. Click in the **Sort row** of the Balance field. Click the **arrow** and select **Descending**.

i. Click **Run** in the Results group.

The BranchID field does not display in Datasheet view because you hid the field in Step e. Only Campus accounts display in the datasheet (10 records). Next, you will add the Customers LastName field to, and delete the CustomerID field from, the query.

j. Save the changes to the query design.

k. Click **View** in the Views group to return to Design view. Point to the column selector at the top of the BranchID field, and when an arrow displays, click to select it. Press **Delete**.

The BranchID field has been removed from the query design grid.

l. Drag the **Customers table** from the Navigation Pane to the top pane of the query design window and reposition the tables so that the join lines are not blocked (see Figure 2.49).

The join lines automatically connect the Customers table to the Accounts table (similar to Step c above).

m. Drag the **LastName field** in the Customers table to the second column in the design grid.

The LastName field should be positioned to the right of the AccountID field.

n. Click the **column selector** in the CustomerID field to select it. Press **Delete**.

The CustomerID field is no longer needed in the results because you added the LastName field instead.

o. Click **Run** in the Results group.

The last names of the customers now display in the results.

p. Save and close the query.

STEP 2 **CREATE A MULTITABLE QUERY FROM SCRATCH**

You realize that another query is needed to show those customers with account balances of $1,000 or less. You create the query and view the results in Datasheet view. Refer to Figure 2.50 as you complete Step 2.

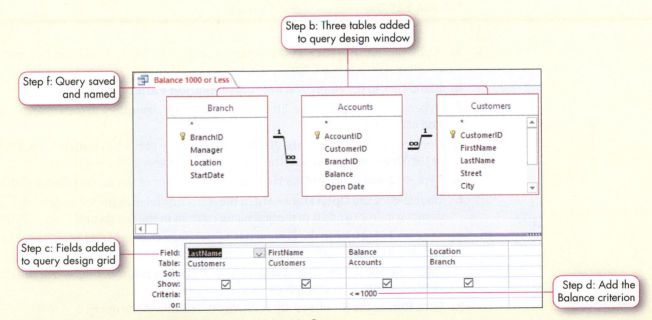

FIGURE 2.50 Create a Multitable Query

a. Click the **Create tab** and click **Query Design** in the Queries group.

b. Double-click the **Branch table name** in the Show Table dialog box. Double-click **Accounts** and **Customers** so that all three are added to Design view. Click **Close** in the Show Table dialog box.

Three tables are added to the query. The join lines were set earlier in the Relationships window.

c. Double-click the following fields to add them to the query design grid: **LastName**, **FirstName**, **Balance**, and **Location**.

d. Type **<=1000** in the Criteria row of the Balance column.

e. Click **Run** in the Results group to see the query results.

Six records that have a balance of $1,000 or less display.

f. Click **Save** on the Quick Access Toolbar and type **Balance 1000 or Less** as the Query Name in the Save As dialog box. Click **OK**.

g. Close the query.

STEP 3 ▶ MODIFY A MULTITABLE QUERY

You decide to make additional changes to the Balance 1000 or Less query you just created. You will create a copy of the existing query and modify the criteria to display the accounts that were opened on or after January 1, 2011, with balances of $2,000 or less. Refer to Figure 2.51 as you complete Step 3.

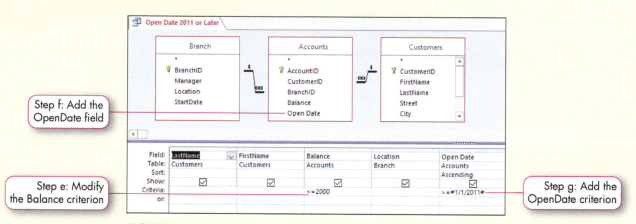

FIGURE 2.51 Query Using the And Condition

a. Right-click the **Balance 1000 or Less query** in the Navigation Pane, and from the shortcut menu, select **Copy**.

b. Right-click in the empty space of the **Navigation Pane** and select **Paste**.

c. Type the name **Open Date 2011 or Later** for the new query in the Paste As dialog box and click **OK**.

d. Double-click the **Open Date 2011 or Later** query in the Navigation Pane. Click **View** in the Views group to switch the query to Design view.

e. Type **<=2000** in place of <=1000 in the Criteria row of the Balance field and press **Enter**.

f. Double-click the **Open Date field** in the Accounts table in the top pane of the query design window to add it to the first blank column in the design grid.

g. Type **>=1/1/2011** in the Criteria row of the Open Date field and press **Enter** to extract only accounts that have been opened since January 1, 2011.

After you type the expression and move to a different column, Access will add the # symbols around the date automatically.

h. Click **Run** in the Results group to display the results of the query.

Five records display in the query results.

i. Click **View** in the Views group to return to Design view of the duplicate query.

j. Click in the **Sort row** of the Open Date field and select **Ascending**.

k. Click **Run** in the Results group.

> The records are sorted from the earliest open date on or after January 1, 2011, to the most recent open date.

l. Save and close the query.

STEP 4 ▶ USE A TOTAL ROW TO SUMMARIZE DATA IN A QUERY

You will to create a query that displays the number of accounts each customer has opened. You create a query using a Total row to summarize the number of accounts per customer. Refer to Figure 2.52 as you complete Step 4.

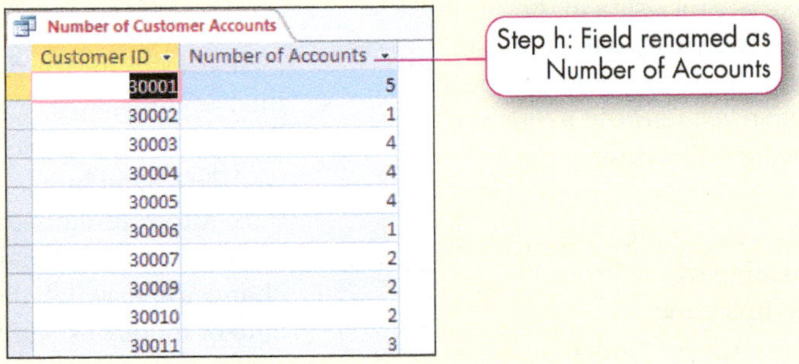

Number of Customer Accounts	
Customer ID ▾	Number of Accounts ▾
30001	5
30002	1
30003	4
30004	4
30005	4
30006	1
30007	2
30009	2
30010	2
30011	3

Step h: Field renamed as Number of Accounts

FIGURE 2.52 Number of Accounts per Customer

a. Click the **Create tab** and click **Query Design** in the Queries group.

b. Add the **Accounts table** and the **Customers table** to the top pane of the query design window. Click **Close** in the Show Table dialog box.

c. Double-click the **CustomerID** in the Customers table in the top pane of the query design window to add it to the first blank column in the design grid and double-click the **AccountID** in the Accounts table to add it to the second column.

d. Click **Run** in the Results group.

> The results show there are 28 records. Every account for every customer is displayed in its own record. You want only the total number of accounts a customer has, so you modify the query to group the records by the CustomerID and summarize the AccountIDs using a function.

e. Click **View** in the Views group to return to Design view of the query.

f. Click **Totals** in the Show/Hide group.

> Both columns show the Group By option in the Total row.

g. Click **Group By** in the Total row of the AccountID field and select **Count**.

> The Count function will count the number of Account IDs per customer. You will give the AccountID field a more identifiable description to display in the results.

h. Modify the AccountID field to read **Number of Accounts: AccountID**.

> You typed a descriptive name followed by a colon that will display Number of Accounts in the datasheet when you run the query.

i. Click **Run** in the Results group. Resize the columns of the datasheet to fully display the results.

> The results show one row for each customer and the number of accounts each customer has opened since the database was created.

j. Click **Save** on the Quick Access Toolbar and type **Number of Customer Accounts** as the query name. Click **OK**. Close the query.

k. Close the database and exit Access. Based on your instructor's directions, submit a02h4Bank_LastFirst.

Chapter Objectives Review

After reading this chapter, you have accomplished the following objectives:

1. Design a table.

- Include necessary data: Consider the output requirements when creating your table design. Determine the data (input) required to produce the expected information (output) later.
- Design for now and for the future: When designing a database, anticipate the future needs of the system and build in the flexibility to satisfy those demands.
- Store data in their smallest parts: Store data in their smallest parts for more flexibility. Storing a full name in a Name field is more limiting than storing a first name in a separate FirstName field and a last name in a separate LastName field. Separating values allows for easier sorting/filtering of records.
- Determine primary keys: When designing your database tables, it is important to determine which field will uniquely identify each record in a table.
- Plan for common fields between tables: Tables are joined in relationships using common fields. You are not required to name the common fields with the same name, but make sure they have the same data type.
- Design to accommodate calculations: Calculated fields are frequently created with numeric data. You can use date arithmetic to subtract one date from another to find the number of days, months, or years that have elapsed between them.

2. Create and modify tables and work with data.

- You can create tables in Datasheet view or Design view. Alternatively, you can import data from another database or an application such as Excel to create tables in an Access database.
- Determine data type: Data type assignments determine the type of data that can be entered and the operations that can be performed on that data. Access recognizes 13 data types.
- Set a table's primary key: The primary key is the field that uniquely identifies each record in a table.
- Explore a foreign key: A foreign key is a field in one table that is also the primary key of another table. A CustomerID might be the primary key field in a Customers table and the foreign key field in a related Accounts table.
- Work with field properties: Field properties determine how the field looks and behaves. Examples of field properties are the Field Size property and the Caption property.
- Create a new field in Design view: It may be necessary to add table fields that were not included in the original design process. While it is possible to add fields in Datasheet view, Design view offers more flexibility.
- Modify the table in Datasheet view: Datasheet view is used to add, edit, and delete records. Design view is used

to create and modify the table structure by enabling you to add and edit fields and set field properties. You cannot work with records in Design view.

3. Import data from external sources.

- Import Excel data: You can import data from other applications such as an Excel spreadsheet.
- Import Access data: You can import data from another database by using the Import Wizard.
- Modify an imported table's design: After importing a table, examine the design and make necessary modifications. Use Design view to modify the field names, data types, field sizes, and other properties.
- Add data to an imported table: After you have imported a table into your database, you may want to add new fields to the tables. After making the modifications, save your changes and switch back to Datasheet view to add new data or modify existing records.

4. Establish table relationships.

- Relationships enable you to extract records from more than one table and help to avoid data redundancy. Use the Show Table dialog box to add tables to the Relationships window. Drag a field name from one table to the corresponding field name in another table to join the tables.
- Enforce and test referential integrity: Referential integrity enforces rules in a database that are used to preserve relationships between tables when records are changed.
- Set cascade options: The Cascade Update Related Fields option ensures that when the primary key is modified in a primary table, Access will automatically update all foreign key values in a related table. The Cascade Delete Related Records option ensures that when the primary key is deleted in a primary table, Access will automatically delete all records in related tables that reference the primary key.
- Establish a one-to-many relationship: A one-to-many relationship is established when the primary key value in the primary table can match many of the foreign key values in the related table. One-to-one and many-to-many are also relationship possibilities, but one-to-many relationships are the most common.

5. Create a single-table query.

- Create a single-table select query: A single-table select query uses fields from one table to display only those records that match certain criteria.
- Use Query Design view: Use Query Design view to create and modify a query. The top pane of the query design window contains tables with their respective field names and displays the join lines between tables. The bottom pane, known as the query design grid, contains columns and rows that you use to build and control the query results.

6. Use the Query Wizard.
- The Simple Query Wizard is an alternative method for creating queries. It enables you to follow a series of prompts to select tables and fields from lists. The last step of the wizard prompts you to save and name the query.

7. Specify query criteria.
- Different data types require different syntax. Date fields are enclosed in pound signs and text fields in quotations. Numeric and currency fields require no delimiters.
- Use wildcards: Wildcards are special characters that can represent one or more characters in a text value. A question mark is a wildcard that stands for a single character in the same position as the question mark, while an asterisk is a wildcard that stands for any number of characters in the same position as the asterisk.
- Use comparison operators in queries: Comparison operators such as equal, not equal, greater than, less than, greater than or equal to, and less than or equal to can be used in the criteria of a query to limit the query results to only those records that meet the criteria.
- Work with null: Access uses the term null for a blank field. Null criteria can be used to find missing information.
- Establish AND, OR, and NOT criteria: The AND, OR, and NOT conditions are used when queries require logical criteria. The AND condition returns only records that meet all criteria. The OR condition returns records meeting any of the specified criteria. The NOT logical operator returns all records except the specified criteria.

8. Specify query sort order and run a query.
- The query sort order determines the order of records in a query's Datasheet view. You can change the order of records by specifying the sort order in Design view.
- The sort order is determined from the order of the fields from left to right. Move the field columns to position them in left to right sort order.

- To obtain the results for a query, run the query. To run the query, click Run in the Results group in Design view. Another method is to locate the query in the Navigation Pane and double-click it. A similar method is to select the query and press Enter.

9. Copy and modify a query.
- To save time, after specifying tables, fields, and conditions for one query, copy the query, rename it, and then modify the fields and criteria in the copied query.
- Change query data: You can correct an error immediately while data are displayed in the query datasheet. Use caution when editing records in query results because you will be changing the original table data.

10. Create a multitable query.
- Add additional tables and fields to an existing query: Open the Navigation Pane and drag the tables from the Navigation Pane directly into the top pane of the query design window.
- Create a multitable query from scratch: Multitable queries contain two or more tables enabling you to take advantage of the relationships that have been set in your database.

11. Modify a multitable query.
- Add and delete fields in a multitable query: Multitable queries may need to be modified. Add fields by double-clicking the field name in the table you want; remove fields by clicking the column selector and pressing Delete.
- Add join lines in a multitable query: If the tables have a common field, create join lines by dragging the field name of one common field onto the field name of the other table. Or you can add an additional table that will provide a join between all three tables. Multitable queries inherit the relationships that have been set in the Relationships window.
- Use a Total row to summarize data in a query: Use the Total Row options of a field such as Group By and Count to aggregate and summarize values in queries.

Key Terms Matching

Match the key terms with their definitions. Write the key term letter by the appropriate numbered definition.

a. AND condition   **k.** Foreign key

b. AutoNumber   **l.** Input mask

c. Caption property   **m.** Join line

d. Cascade Delete Related Records   **n.** One-to-many relationship

e. Cascade Update Related Fields   **o.** OR condition

f. Comparison operator   **p.** Query

g. Criteria row   **q.** Referential integrity

h. Data redundancy   **r.** Simple Query Wizard

i. Data type   **s.** Validation rule

j. Field property   **t.** Wildcard

1. _____ Connects two tables together by their common field in the Relationships window. **p. 137**

2. _____ The unnecessary storing of duplicate data in two or more tables. **p. 137**

3. _____ Determines the type of data that can be entered and the operations that can be performed on that data. **p. 139**

4. _____ A number that automatically increments each time a record is added. **p. 140**

5. _____ A field in one table that is also the primary key of another table. **p. 141**

6. _____ Characteristic of a field that determines how it looks and behaves. **p. 142**

7. _____ Used to create a more understandable label than a field name label that displays in the top row in Datasheet view and in forms and reports. **p. 143**

8. _____ Checks the data for allowable value when the user exits the field. **p. 143**

9. _____ Simplifies data entry by providing literal characters that are typed for every entry. **p. 143**

10. _____ Rules in a database that are used to preserve relationships between tables when records are added, deleted, or changed. **p. 153**

11. _____ An option that directs Access to automatically update all foreign key values in a related table when the primary key value is modified in a primary table. **p. 154**

12. _____ When the primary key value is deleted in a primary table, Access will automatically delete all foreign key values in a related table. **p. 154**

13. _____ When the primary key value in the primary table can match many of the foreign key values in the related table. **p. 155**

14. _____ Enables you to ask questions about the data stored in a database and provides answers to the questions in a datasheet. **p. 164**

15. _____ A row in the Query Design grid that determines which records will be selected. **p. 165**

16. _____ Provides a step-by-step guide to help you through the query design process. **p. 167**

17. _____ Special character that can represent one or more characters in the criterion of a query. **p. 169**

18. _____ Uses greater than (>), less than (<), greater than or equal to (>=), and less than or equal to (<=), etc. to limit query results that meet these criteria. **p. 170**

19. _____ Returns only records that meet all criteria. **p. 171**

20. _____ Returns records meeting any of the specified criteria. **p. 171**

Multiple Choice

1. All of the following are suggested guidelines for table design *except*:
   (a) include all necessary data.
   (b) store data in their smallest parts.
   (c) avoid date arithmetic.
   (d) link tables using common fields.

2. Which of the following determines the amount of space a field uses in the database?
   (a) Field size
   (b) Data type
   (c) Caption property
   (d) Normalization

3. When entering, deleting, or editing data:
   (a) the table must be in Design view.
   (b) the table must be in Datasheet view.
   (c) the table can be in either Datasheet or Design view.
   (d) data can only be entered in a form.

4. With respect to importing data into Access, which of the following statements is *true*?
   (a) The Import Wizard works only for Excel files.
   (b) The Import Wizard is found on the Create tab.
   (c) You can assign a primary key while you are importing Excel data.
   (d) Imported table designs cannot be modified in Access.

5. The main reason to set a validation rule in Access is to:
   (a) limit the entry of incorrect values in a table.
   (b) make it possible to delete records.
   (c) keep your database safe from unauthorized users.
   (d) keep redundant data from being entered in a table.

6. An illustration of a one-to-many relationship would be:
   (a) an employee listed in the Employees table earns a raise, so the Salaries table must be updated.
   (b) a customer may have more than one account in an accounts table.
   (c) each employee in an Employees table has a matching entry in the Salaries table.
   (d) an employee leaves the company so that when he is deleted from the Employees table, his salary data will be deleted from the Salaries table.

7. A query's specifications as to which records to include must be entered on the:
   (a) table row of the query design grid.
   (b) show row of the query design grid.
   (c) sort row of the query design grid.
   (d) Criteria row of the query design grid.

8. When adding date criteria to the Query Design view, the dates you enter will be delimited by:
   (a) parentheses.
   (b) pound signs.
   (c) quotes.
   (d) at signs.

9. It is more efficient to make a copy of an existing query rather than to create a new query when which of the following is *true*?
   (a) The existing query contains only one table.
   (b) The existing query and the new query use the same tables and fields.
   (c) The existing query and the new query have the exact same criteria.
   (d) The original query is no longer being used.

10. Which of the following is *true* for the Query Wizard?
   (a) No criteria can be added as you step through the Wizard.
   (b) You can only select related tables as a source.
   (c) Fields with different data types are not allowed.
   (d) You are required to summarize the data.

Practice Exercises

1 Philadelphia Bookstore

FROM SCRATCH Tom and Erin Mullaney own and operate a bookstore in Philadelphia, Pennsylvania. Erin asked you to help her create an Access database to store the publishers and the books that they sell. The data for the publishers and books are currently stored in Excel worksheets that you decide to import into a new database. You determine that a third table—for authors—is also required. Your task is to create and populate the three tables, set the table relationships, and enforce referential integrity. You will then create queries to extract information from the tables. Refer to Figure 2.53 as you complete this exercise.

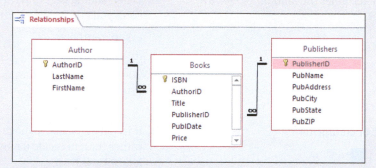

FIGURE 2.53 Books Relationships Window

a. Open Access and click **Blank database**. Type **a02p1Books_LastFirst** in the File Name box. Click **Browse** to navigate to the location where you are saving your files in the File New Database dialog box, click **OK** to close the dialog box, and then click **Create** to create the new database.

b. Type **11** in the Click to Add column in the new Table1 and click **Click to Add**. The field name becomes Field1 and *Click to Add* now displays as the third column. In the third column, type **Beschloss** and press **Tab**. Repeat the process for the fourth column; type **Michael R.** and press **Tab** two times. The insertion point returns to the first column where (New) is selected.

c. Press **Tab**. Access will automatically increment the ID field. Type the rest of the data using the following table. These data will become the records of the Author table.

ID	Field1	Field2	Field3
1	11	Beschloss	Michael R.
(New)	12	Turow	Scott
	13	Rice	Anne
	14	King	Stephen
	15	Connelly	Michael
	16	Rice	Luanne
	17	*your last name*	*your first name*

d. Click **Save** on the Quick Access Toolbar. Type **Author** in the Save As dialog box and click **OK**.

e. Click **View** in the Views group to switch to Design view of the Author table.

f. Select **Field1**—in the second row—in the top portion of the table design and type **AuthorID** to rename the field. In the Field Properties section in the lower pane of the table design, type **Author ID** in the Caption box and verify that Long Integer displays for the Field Size property.

g. Select **Field2** and type **LastName** to rename the field. In the Field Properties section in the bottom portion of Design view, type **Author's Last Name** in the Caption box and type **20** as the field size.

h. Select **Field3** and type **FirstName** to rename the field. In the Field Properties section in the bottom portion of the table design, type **Author's First Name** as the caption and type **15** as the field size.

i. Click the **ID field row selector** (which displays the primary key) to select the row and click **Delete Rows** in the Tools group. Click **Yes** two times to confirm both messages.

j. Click the **AuthorID row selector** and select **Primary Key** in the Tools group to set the primary key.

k. Click **Save** on the Quick Access Toolbar to save the design changes. Click **Yes** to the *Some data may be lost* message. You will not lose any data because of the field size changes you made. Close the table.

l. Click the **External Data tab**, click **New Data Source**, point to **From File** in the Import & Link group, and then select **Excel** to launch the Get External Data – Excel Spreadsheet dialog box. Verify that the *Import the source data into a new table in the current database* option is selected, click **Browse**, and then navigate to your student data folder. Select the *a02p1Books.xlsx* workbook, click **Open**, and then click **OK**. This workbook contains two worksheets. Follow the steps below:

- Select the **Publishers worksheet** and click **Next**.
- Click the **First Row Contains Column Headings check box** to select it and click **Next**.
- Ensure that the PubID field is selected, click the **Indexed arrow**, select **Yes (No Duplicates)**, and then click **Next**.
- Click the **Choose my own primary key arrow**, ensure that PubID is selected, and then click **Next**.
- Accept the name Publishers for the table name, click **Finish**, and then click **Close** without saving the import steps.

m. Use the Import Wizard again to import the Books worksheet from the *a02p1Books.xlsx* workbook into the Access database. Follow the steps below:

- Ensure that the Books worksheet is selected and click **Next**.
- Ensure that the **First Row Contains Column Headings check box** is selected and click **Next**.
- Click the **ISBN column**, click the **Indexed arrow**, set the Indexed property box to **Yes (No Duplicates)**, and then click **Next**.
- Click the **Choose my own primary key arrow**, select **ISBN** as the primary key field, and then click **Next**.
- Accept the name Books as the table name. Click **Finish** and click **Close** without saving the import steps.

n. Right-click the **Books table** in the Navigation Pane and select **Design View**. Make the following changes:

- Click the **PubID field** and change the name to **PublisherID**.
- Set the caption property to **Publisher ID**.
- Change the PublisherID Field Size property to **2**.
- Click the **ISBN field** and change the Field Size property to **13**.
- Change the AuthorCode field name to **AuthorID**.
- Change the AuthorID Field Size property to **Long Integer**.
- Click the **ISBN field row selector** (which displays the primary key) to select the row. Click and drag to move the row up to the first position in the table design. You want the primary key field to display in the first column of the table.
- Click **Save** on the Quick Access Toolbar to save the design changes to the Books table. Click **Yes** to the *Some data may be lost* warning. You will not lose any data because of the field size changes you made.
- Close the table.

o. Right-click the **Publishers table** in the Navigation Pane and select **Design View**. Make the following changes:

- Click the **PubID field** and change the name to **PublisherID**.
- Change the PublisherID Field Size property to **2**.
- Change the Caption property to **Publisher's ID**.
- Change the Field Size property to **50** for the PubName and PubAddress fields.
- Change the Pub Address field name to **PubAddress** (remove the space).
- Change the PubCity Field Size property to **30**.

- Change the PubState Field Size property to **2**.
- Change the Pub ZIP field name to **PubZIP** (remove the space).
- Click **Save** on the Quick Access Toolbar to save the design changes to the Publishers table.
- Click **Yes** to the *Some data may be lost* warning. You will not lose any data because of the field size changes you made. Close the Publishers table.

p. Click the **Database Tools tab** and click **Relationships** in the Relationships group. Click **Show Table**, if the Show Table dialog box does not open automatically. Follow the steps below:
- Double-click each **table name** in the Show Table dialog box to add it to the Relationships window and close the Show Table dialog box.
- Drag the **AuthorID field** from the Author table onto the AuthorID field in the Books table.
- Click the **Enforce Referential Integrity** and **Cascade Update Related Fields check boxes** in the Edit Relationships dialog box to select them. Click **Create** to create a one-to-many relationship between the Author and Books tables.
- Drag the **PublisherID field** from the Publishers table onto the PublisherID field in the Books table.
- Click the **Enforce Referential Integrity** and **Cascade Update Related Fields check boxes** in the Edit Relationships dialog box to select them. Click **Create** to create a one-to-many relationship between the Publishers and Books tables.
- Click **Save** on the Quick Access Toolbar to save the changes to the Relationships window, then in the Relationships group, click **Close**.

q. Click **Query Wizard** in the Queries group on the Create tab. With Simple Query Wizard selected, click **OK**. Follow the steps below:
- Ensure that the **Publishers table** is selected and double-click to add **PubName**, **PubCity**, and **PubState** to the Selected Fields list. Click **Next** and click **Finish**. In Datasheet view, double-click the **border** to the right of each column to set the column widths to Best Fit to view the results. Click **Save** on the Quick Access Toolbar. Close the query.

r. Right-click the **Publishers Query** in the Navigation Pane, and from the shortcut menu, select **Copy**. Right-click in the **Navigation Pane**, and from the shortcut menu, select **Paste**. Type **New York Publishers Query** as the query name. Click **OK**. Follow the steps below:
- Open the New York Publishers Query. Click **View** in the Views group on the Home tab to switch to Design view of the query. Click and drag the **Books table** from the Navigation Pane into the top pane of the query design window.
- Select the **Books table**, double-click **Title** and **PublDate** to add the fields to the query design grid.
- Click in the **Criteria row** of the PubState field and type **NY**. Click the **Sort cell** of the PublDate field, click the arrow, and then select **Descending**.
- Click **Run** in the Results group (12 records display in the Datasheet sorted by PublDate in descending order). Double-click the border to the right of each column to set the column widths to Best Fit to view the results.
- Save and close the query.

s. Right-click the **New York Publishers Query** in the Navigation Pane, and from the shortcut menu, select **Copy**. Right-click in the **Navigation Pane**, and from the shortcut menu, select **Paste**. Type **Summary by Publisher** as the query name. Click **OK**.

t. Open the query. Click **View** in the Views group on the Home tab to switch to Design view of the query.

u. Click in the **Criteria row** of the PubState field and delete "**NY**". Click the **Sort cell** of the PubName field, click the **arrow**, and then select **Ascending**.

v. Click the gray **column selector** at the top of the PubCity field and press **Delete**. Delete the **PubState** and **PublDate** fields from the query. There are now two fields remaining in the query, PubName and Title.

w. Click **Totals** in the Show/Hide group on the Query Tools Design tab. Click in the **Total row** of the Title field, click the **arrow**, and then select **Count**. The records will be grouped by the publisher's name and the titles for each publisher will be summarized.

x. Modify the field name of the Title column as **Title Count: Title** to make the field name more identifiable.

y. Click **Run** in the Results group (8 records display in the Datasheet). The results display the title count for each publisher.

z. Save and close the query.

aa. Close the database and exit Access. Based on your instructor's directions, submit a02p1Books_LastFirst.

2 Employee Salary Analysis

The Morgan Insurance Company offers a full range of insurance services. They store the firm's employee data in an Access database. This file contains each employee's name and address, job performance, salary, and title, but the data need to be imported into a different existing database. A database file containing two of the tables (Location and Titles) already exists; your job is to import the employee data from Access to create the third table. Once imported, you will modify field properties and set new relationships. The owner of the company, Victor Reed, is concerned that some of the Atlanta and Boston salaries may be below the guidelines published by the national office. He asks that you investigate the salaries of the two offices and create a separate query for each city. Refer to Figure 2.54 as you complete this exercise.

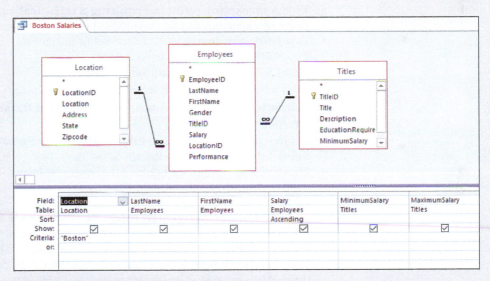

FIGURE 2.54 Boston Salaries Query Design

a. Open *a02p2Insurance* and save it as **a02p2Insurance_LastFirst**. Double-click the **Location table** and review the data to become familiar with the field names and the type of information stored in the table. Review the Titles table. Double-click the **border** to the right of the TitleID column to set the column width to Best Fit. Save the table. Close both tables.

b. Click the **External Data tab**, click **New Data Source**, point to **From Database**, and then select **Access** in the Import & Link group. Complete the following steps:

- Click **Browse** and navigate to the *a02p2Employees* database in your student data folder. Select the file, click **Open**.
- Click **OK** in the Get External Data – Access Database dialog box.
- Select the **Employees table** in the Import Objects dialog box and click **OK**.
- Click **Close** without saving the import steps.

c. Double-click the **Employees table** in the Navigation Pane, then click **View** in the Views group on the Home tab to switch to Design view of the Employees table. Make the following changes:

- Ensure that the EmployeeID field is selected and click **Primary Key** in the Tools group on the Table Tools Design tab.
- Click the **LastName field** and change the Field Size property to **20**.
- Change the Caption property to **Last Name**.
- Click the **FirstName field** and change the Field Size property to **20**.
- Change the Caption property to **First Name**.
- Click the **LocationID field** and change the Field Size property to **3**.
- Change the Caption property to **Location ID**.
- Click the **TitleID field** and change the Field Size property to **3**.
- Change the Caption property to **Title ID**.
- Change the Salary field data type to **Currency**.
- Save the design changes. Click **Yes** to the *Some data may be lost* warning.

d. Click **View** in the Views group to view the Employees table in Datasheet view and examine the data. Click any record in the Title ID column and click **Ascending** in the Sort & Filter group on the Home tab.

e. Double-click the **Titles table** in the Navigation Pane to open it in Datasheet view. Notice that the T04 title is not in the list.

f. Add a new record in the first blank record at the bottom of the Titles table. Use the following data:
- Type **T04** in the TitleID field.
- Type **Senior Account Rep** in the Title field.
- Type **A marketing position requiring a technical background and at least three years of experience** in the Description field.
- Type **Four year degree** in the Education Requirements field.
- Type **45000** in the Minimum Salary field.
- Type **85000** in the Maximum Salary field.

g. Close all tables. Click **Yes** if you are prompted to save changes to the Employees table.

h. Click **Relationships** in the Relationships group on the **Database Tools tab** and Click **Show Table**. Follow the steps below:
- Double-click each of the three **table names** in the Show Table dialog box to add it to the Relationships window and close the Show Table dialog box.
- Click and drag to adjust the height of the Employees table so that all fields display in each one.
- Drag the **LocationID field** in the Location table onto the LocationID field in the Employees table.
- Click the **Enforce Referential Integrity** and **Cascade Update Related Fields check boxes** in the Edit Relationships dialog box to select them. Click **Create** to create a one-to-many relationship between the Location and Employees tables.
- Drag the **TitleID field** in the Titles table onto the TitleID field in the Employees table (move the field lists by clicking and dragging their title bars as needed so that they do not overlap).
- Click the **Enforce Referential Integrity** and **Cascade Update Related Fields check boxes** in the Edit Relationships dialog box to select them. Click **Create** to create a one-to-many relationship between the Titles and Employees tables.
- Click **Save** on the Quick Access Toolbar to save the changes to the Relationships window and close the Relationships window.

i. Click the **Create tab** and click the **Query Wizard** in the Queries group. Follow the steps below:
- Select **Simple Query Wizard** and click **OK**.
- Select **Table: Employees** in the Tables/Queries box.
- Double-click **LastName** in the Available Fields list to move it to the Selected Fields list.
- Double-click **FirstName** in the Available Fields list to move it to the Selected Fields list.
- Double-click **LocationID** in the Available Fields list to move it to the Selected Fields list.
- Click **Next**.
- Type **Employees Location** as the query title and click **Finish**.

- Click **View** in the Views group on the Home tab to switch to Design view of the query. Click and drag the **Titles table** from the Navigation Pane into the top pane of the query design window.
- Double-click **Title** in the Titles table to add the field to the query design grid.
- Click the **Sort cell** of the LocationID field, click the **arrow**, and then click **Ascending**.
- Click **Run** in the Results group (311 records display in the Datasheet sorted by LocationID in ascending order). Double-click the **border** to the right of each column to set the column widths to Best Fit.
- Click **View** in the Views group on the Home tab to switch to Design view of the query.
- Click the gray **column selector** at the top of the **LastName field** and press **Delete**. Delete the **FirstName field** from the query. There are now two fields remaining in the query, LocationID and Title.
- Click **Totals** in the Show/Hide group on the Query Tools Design tab. Click in the **Total row** of the Title field, click the **arrow**, and then select **Count**. The records will be grouped by the location and the titles for each location will be summarized.
- Modify the field name of the Title column as **Count by Title: Title** to make the field name more identifiable.
- Click **Run** in the Results group (11 records display in the Datasheet). The results display the title count for each active location.
- Save and close the query.

j. Click **Query Design** in the Queries group on the Create tab. Follow the steps below:
  - Add **Location**, **Employees**, and **Titles tables** to the top pane of the query window.
  - Double-click **Location** in the Location table to move it to the first field in the query design grid.
  - Double-click **LastName**, **FirstName**, and **Salary** in the Employees table to add the next three fields.
  - Double-click **MinimumSalary** and **MaximumSalary** in the Titles table to add the next two fields.
  - Save the query as **Atlanta Salaries** and run the query.

k. Click **View** in the Views group on the Home tab to switch to Design view of the Atlanta Salaries query. Follow the steps below:
  - Click in the **Criteria row** of the Location field, and type **Atlanta**. Click the **Sort cell** of the Salary field, click the **arrow**, and then select **Ascending**.
  - Click **Run** in the Results group. Review the data to determine if any of the Atlanta employees have a salary less than the minimum or greater than the maximum when compared to the published salary range. You notice that several salaries fall below the minimum value specified by the company. These salaries will be investigated and updated later.
  - Save and close the query.

l. Right-click the **Atlanta Salaries query** in the Navigation Pane and from the shortcut menu, select **Copy**. Right-click a blank area in the **Navigation Pane** and select **Paste**. In the Paste As dialog box, type **Boston Salaries** for the query name. Click **OK**.

m. Right-click the **Boston Salaries query** in the Navigation Pane and select **Design View**. In the Criteria row of the Location field, replace Atlanta with **Boston**. Follow the steps below:
  - Click **Run** in the Results group. Review the data to determine if any of the Boston employees have a salary less than the minimum or greater than the maximum when compared to the published salary range. You notice that several salaries fall below the minimum value specified by the company.
  - Modify some data that were incorrectly entered in the data that you imported. In the query results, for the first employee, Frank Cusack, change the salary to **$48,700.00**; for Brian Beamer, **$45,900.00**; for Lorna Weber, **$45,700.00**; for Penny Pfleger, **$45,800.00**.
  - Save and close the query.

n. Close the database and exit Access. Based on your instructor's directions, submit a02p2Insurance_LastFirst.

Mid-Level Exercises

1 My Game Collection

ANALYSIS CASE

You have cataloged your vintage video games in an Access database. In this project, you add two tables to a database you have started—one to identify the game system that runs your game and the other to identify the category or genre of the game. Then you will join each table in a relationship so that you can query the database.

a. Open *a02m1Games* and save the database as **a02m1Games_LastFirst**. Open the Games table and review the fields containing the game information. Close the table.

b. Create a new table in Design view. Add the field name **SystemID** and select **AutoNumber** as the Data Type. Add the caption **System ID**. Set the SystemID field as the primary key for the table.

c. Add a second field named **SystemName** with the **Short Text Data Type**. Change the SystemName field size property to **15**. Add the caption **System Name**. Save the table as **System**.

d. Switch to Datasheet view and enter the following system names, letting Access assign the System ID:

System Name

XBOX 360

PS3

Wii

NES

PC Game

Nintendo 3DS

Double-click the **border** to the right of the System Name column to set the column width to Best Fit. Save and close the table.

e. Create a new table in Design view. Add the field name **CategoryID** and select **AutoNumber** as the Data Type. Add the caption **Category ID**. Set the **CategoryID field** as the Primary Key for the table.

f. Add a second field named **CategoryDescription** and accept **Short Text** as the Data Type. Change the field size property to **25**. Add the caption **Category Description**. Save the table as **Category**.

g. Switch to Datasheet view, and enter the following Category Description names, letting Access assign the Category ID:

Category Description

Action

Adventure

Arcade

Racing

Rhythm

Role-playing

Simulation

Sports

Close the table.

h. Establish relationships in the database by adding the **Category** and **System tables** to the Relationships window. Close the Show Table dialog box. Create a one-to-many relationship between the **SystemID field** in the System table and the **SystemID field** in the Games table, enforcing Referential Integrity. Select the option to cascade update the related fields.

i. Create a one-to-many relationship between the **CategoryID field** in the Category table and the **CategoryID field** in the Games table, enforcing Referential Integrity. Select the option to cascade update the related fields. Save and close the Relationships window.

j. Create a simple query using the Query Wizard. From the Games table, add the **GameName** and **Rating** fields (in that order). Save the query using the title **Ratings**.

k. Switch to Design view. Sort the Rating field in ascending order. Click the **gray column selector** at the top of the Rating field, then click and drag the **column** to move it to the first position of the query design grid. Add a Total row, click in the **Total row** of the GameName column, click the **arrow**, and then select **Count**. The records will be grouped by rating, and the number of games will be counted for each group. Run, close, and save the query.

l. Create a new query in Design view. Add the Category, Games, and System tables to the query design window. Add the following fields to the query (in this order):

- **GameName**
- **CategoryDescription**
- **Rating**
- **SystemName**
- **DateAcquired**

m. Sort the query in ascending order by GameName and run the query. Save the query as **Game List** and close the query.

n. Copy the **Game List query** in the Navigation Pane and paste it with the name **PS3 Games**. Modify the query in Design view by using **PS3** as the criteria for SystemName. Remove the sort by GameName and sort in ascending order by CategoryDescription. Save and run the query. Close the query.

o. Create a query named **Thanksgiving Games** that shows the name of the game, its rating, the category description of the game, and the system name for each. You only want to display **Wii** games with a rating of **Everyone** or **Teen**. Because the system name is the same for the games you plan to pack and share, hide this value from the results. Run the query. Save and close the query.

p. Close the database and exit Access. Based on your instructor's directions, submit a02m1Games_LastFirst.

2   The Prestige Hotel   MyLab IT Grader

The Prestige Hotel chain caters to upscale business travelers and provides state-of-the-art conference, meeting, and reception facilities. It prides itself on its international, four-star cuisine. Last year, it began a member reward club to help the marketing department track the purchasing patterns of its most loyal customers. All of the hotel transactions are stored in a database. Your task is to help the managers of the Prestige Hotels in Denver and Chicago identify their customers who stayed in a room last year and who had three persons in their party.

a. Open *a02m2Hotel* and save the file as **a02m2Hotel_LastFirst**. Review the data contained in the three tables. Specifically, study the tables and fields containing the data you need to analyze: dates of stays in Denver and Chicago rooms, the members' names, and the numbers in the parties.

b. Import the location data from the Excel file *a02m2Location.xlsx* as a new table in the current database. Using the wizard, specify that the first row contains column headings, set the LocationID field to be indexed with no duplicates, and set the LocationID field as the primary key. Import the table with the default name Location and do not save the import steps.

c. View the Location table in Design view and change the field size for the LocationID field to **Long Integer**. Save the table. Click **Yes** in the dialog box indicating that some data may be lost. Close the table.

d. Add the **Location**, **Orders**, **Members**, and **Service tables** to the Relationships window to begin establishing relationships in the database. Close the Show Table dialog box. Create a one-to-many relationship between the Location table and the Orders table using the LocationID field. Enforce Referential Integrity. Select the option to cascade update the related fields.

e. Create a relationship between the Members and Orders tables using the MemNumber field, ensuring that you enforce referential integrity and cascade update related fields.

f. Create a relationship between the Service and Orders tables using the ServiceID field, ensuring that you enforce referential integrity and cascade update related fields. Save and close the Relationships window.

g. Create a new query in Design view using **Location**, **Members**, **Orders**, and **Service tables**. Add the following fields to the query (in this order): **ServiceDate** from the Orders table; **City** from the Location table, **NoInParty** from Orders table; **ServiceName** from the Service table; and **FirstName** and **LastName** from the Members table. Set the criteria in city field to limit the output to **Denver**.

h. Display only service dates from 7/1/2017 to 6/30/2018 (Hint: Use the Between operator).

i. Set the NoInParty criterion to **2**. Sort the results in ascending order by the ServiceDate. Run and save the query with the name **Denver Rooms 2 Guests**.

j. Use Design view to change the order of the query fields so that they display as FirstName, LastName, ServiceDate, City, NoInParty, and ServiceName. Run, save the changes to the query, and close the query.

k. Copy the **Denver Rooms 2 Guests query** and paste it in the **Navigation Pane**, renaming the new query **Chicago Rooms 2 Guests**.

l. Open the Chicago Rooms 2 Guests query in Design view and change the City criterion from Denver to **Chicago**. Run the query and save the changes. Close the query.

m. Close the database and exit Access. Based on your instructor's directions, submit a02m2Hotel_LastFirst.

Running Case

New Castle County Technical Services

New Castle County Technical Services (NCCTS) provides technical support for several companies in the greater New Castle County, Delaware area. Once you have completed the changes to the database tables and set the appropriate relationships, you will be ready to extract information by creating queries.

a. Open the database *a02r1NCCTS* and save it as **a02r1NCCTS_LastFirst**.

b. Open the Call Types table in Design view. Before you create your queries, you want to modify some of the table properties:
  • Set the caption of the HourlyRate field to **Hourly Rate**.
  • View the table in Datasheet view and save the changes when prompted.

c. Close the table.

d. Make the following additional changes to the tables:
  • Open the Calls table in Design view. Set the caption of the HoursLogged field to **Hours Logged**.
  • Set the caption of the OpenedDate field to **Opened Date**.
  • Set the caption of the ClosedDate field to **Closed Date**.
  • Set the caption of the CustomerSatisfaction field to **Customer Satisfaction**.
  • View the table in Datasheet view and save the changes when prompted. You will not lose any data by making this change, so click **Yes** in the message box when prompted. Close the table.
  • Open the Customers table in Design view. Set the field size of CompanyName to **50** and the caption to **Company Name**. View the table in Datasheet view and save the changes when prompted. You will not lose any data by making this change, so click **Yes** in the message box when prompted. Close the table.

- Open the Reps table in Design view. Set the caption of the RepFirst field to **Rep First Name**. Set the caption of the RepLast field to **Rep Last Name**. View the table in Datasheet view and save the changes when prompted. Close the table.

e. Open the Relationships window. Create a join line between the Call Types and Calls tables, ensuring that you enforce referential integrity and cascade update related fields. Set a relationship between Reps and Calls and between Customers and Calls using the same options. Save and close the Relationships window.

f. Create a multitable query, following the steps below:
- Add the following fields (in this order): **CallID** (from Calls), **Description** (from Call Types), **CompanyName** (from Customers), and **RepFirst** and **RepLast** (from Reps).
- Run the query, and then modify it to add **HoursLogged** (from Calls).
- Sort the query by HoursLogged in ascending order. Set the criteria of the HoursLogged field to **Is Not Null** and run the query again.
- Modify the criteria of the HoursLogged field to **>=5** and **<=10**, the Description to **Disaster Recovery**, and the RepFirst to **Barbara** (do not enter RepLast criterion).
- Save the query as **Complex Disaster Recovery Calls_Barbara**. Run and close the query.

g. Create a copy of the **Complex Disaster Recovery Calls_Barbara query** and modify it following the steps below:
- Save the copy of the query as **Complex Network Installation Calls_Barbara**.
- Modify the query so that the description displays Barbara's network installation calls that logged between 5 and 10 hours.
- Save, run, and then close the query.

h. Close the database and exit Access. Based on your instructor's directions, submit a02r1NCCTS_LastFirst.

Disaster Recovery

May Beverage Sales

If criteria in a query are inaccurate, the query may not return any results at all. Unexpected results can also occur from inaccurate data, so troubleshooting queries is a skill that you can put to work in your organization. A coworker explained that he was having difficulty with queries that were not returning correct results and asked you to help diagnose the problem. Open *a02d1Traders* and save it as **a02d1Traders_LastFirst**. It contains two queries, *May 2019 Orders of Beverages and Confections* and *2019 Beverage Sales by Ship Country*. He also asked for your help in adding the CompanyName from the Customers table to the last column of the *2019 Beverage Sales by Ship Country* query. You will correct the errors in the criteria of both queries and add the extra field to one of them.

The May 2019 Orders of Beverages and Confections query is supposed to contain only information for orders shipped in May 2019. You find other shipped dates included in the results. Change the criteria to exclude the other dates. Run and save the query. Close the query.

The 2019 Beverage Sales by Ship Country query returns no results. Check the criteria in all fields and modify so that the correct results are returned. Add the **CompanyName** from the Customers table to the last column of the *2019 Beverage Sales by Ship Country* query. Run and save the query. Close the query.

Close the database and exit Access. Based on your instructor's directions, submit a02d1Traders_LastFirst.

International Foodies

International Foodies is an importer of exotic foods from all over the world. You landed a summer internship with the company and discovered that their product lists and the suppliers they buy from are stored in Excel workbooks. You offer to help by using your newly gained knowledge of Access to create a relational database for them. You will begin by importing the workbooks from Excel into a new Access database. Your manager mentions that she also wants a table that specifies food categories so that you can relate the products you sell to specific categories in the database. You will create a table from scratch to track categories, create relationships between the tables, and create some baseline queries.

Create a New Database

You will examine the data in the Excel worksheets to determine which fields will become the primary keys in each table and which fields will become the foreign keys so that you can join them in the database.

1. Open the *a02c1Suppliers.xlsx* Excel workbook, examine the data, and then close the workbook.

2. Open the *a02c1Products.xlsx* Excel workbook, examine the data, and then close the workbook.

3. Create a new, blank database named **a02c1Foodies_LastFirst**. Close the new blank table created automatically by Access without saving it.

Import Data from Excel

You will import two Excel workbooks that contain supplier and product information into the database.

4. Click the **External Data tab**, click **New Data Source**, point to **From File** in the Import & Link group, and then select **Excel**.

5. Navigate to and select the *a02c1Suppliers.xlsx* workbook to be imported as a new table in the current database.

6. Select **First Row Contains Column Headings option**.

7. Set the SupplierID field Indexed option to **Yes (No Duplicates)**.

8. Select **SupplierID** as the primary key when prompted and accept the table name Suppliers. Do not save the import steps.

9. Import the *a02c1Products.xlsx* workbook, set the ProductID Indexed option to **Yes (No Duplicates)**, and then select **ProductID** as the primary key.

10. Accept the table name Products.

11. Change the Field Size of the QuantityPerUnit field to **25** in Design view of the Products table. Set the Field Size of ProductID and CategoryID to **Long Integer**. Save the changes and open the table in Datasheet view.

12. Open the Suppliers table in Datasheet view to examine the data. Close the tables.

Create a New Table

You will create a new table that will enable International Foodies to associate each product with a food category in the database.

13. Create a new table in Design view and save the table as **Categories**.

14. Add the following fields in Design view and set the properties as specified:

   - Add the primary key field as **CategoryID** with the **Number Data Type** and **Number assigned to a new category.** (type the period) as the Description. Set the Caption property to **Category ID**.

   - Add **CategoryName** with the **Short Text Data Type** and **Name of food category.** (type the period) as the Description. Change the field size to **15**. Set the Caption property to **Category Name** and the Required property to **Yes**.

   - Add **CategoryDescription** with the **Long Text Data Type**. Set the Caption property to **Category Description**.

15. Switch to Datasheet view and save the table when prompted. You will enter Category data into the table in a later step. Close the table.

Create Relationships

You will create the relationships between the tables using the Relationships window.

16. Add all three tables to the Relationships window. Identify the primary key fields in the Categories table and the Suppliers table and join them with their foreign key counterparts in the related Products table. Select the **Enforce Referential Integrity** and **Cascade Update Related Fields check boxes**. Save and close the Relationships window.

Add Data to the Categories Table

You will add 8 records to the Categories table so that you have some sample data to test in the database.

17. Add the following records to the Categories table:

Category ID	Category Name	Category Description
1	Beverages	Soft drinks, coffees, teas
2	Condiments	Sauces, relishes, seasonings
3	Confections	Desserts, candies, sweet breads
4	Dairy Products	Cheeses
5	Grains/Cereals	Breads, pasta, cereal
6	Meat/Poultry	Prepared meats
7	Produce	Dried fruit, bean curd
8	Seafood	Seaweed and fish

18. Close the table.

Use the Query Wizard

You will use the Simple Query Wizard to create a query of all products that you import in the seafood category.

19. Add the **ProductName**, **SupplierID**, and **CategoryID** fields from Products (in that order).

20. Save the query as **Seafood Products**.

21. Add a criterion in Design view, to include only products with **8** as the CategoryID. Sort the query results in ascending order by ProductName.

22. Run, save, and close the query.

Copy and Modify a Query in Design View

You want to create a query that displays actual category names rather than the CategoryIDs. You are interested to know which meat and poultry products are imported. You will copy the Seafood Products query and modify it to delete a field, then add an additional table and field.

23. Copy the Seafood Products query and paste it using **Seafood Or Meat/Poultry** as the query name.

24. Open the **Seafood Or Meat/Poultry query** in Design view and delete the **CategoryID column**.

25. Add the **Categories table** to the top pane of the query design window. Add the **CategoryName field** to the last column of the design grid and set the criterion as "**Seafood**" Or "**Meat/Poultry**".

26. Run, save, and close the query.

Create a Multitable Query

You will create a query that identifies suppliers and their associated products. Because there is a relationship between the two tables, you can now pull data from each of them together as usable information.

27. Create a query in Design view that includes the **Suppliers** and **Products** tables. The query should list the company name, contact name, phone number (in that order), then the product name and the product cost (in that order).

28. Sort the query by company name in ascending order, then by product cost in descending order.

29. Run, close, and save the query as **Company by Product List**.

Use a Total Row to Summarize Data in a Query

You determine that the data in the Company by Product List query could be summarized with a Total row. You will group the records by company name and count the number of products you buy from each of them.

30. Copy the **Company by Product List query** and paste it using **Summary of Company by Product** as the query name.

31. Open the **Summary of Company by Product query** in Design view and delete the **ContactName**, **Phone**, and **ProductCost columns**.

32. Click **Totals** in the Show/Hide group on the Query Tools Design tab. Click in the **Total row** of the ProductName field, click the **arrow**, and then select **Count**. The records will be grouped by the company's name and the products for each company will be summarized.

33. Modify the field name of the Title column as **Product Count: ProductName** to make the field name more identifiable.

34. Click **Run** in the Results group (20 records display in the Datasheet). The results display the product count for each company that supplies your organization.

35. Save and close the query.

36. Close the database and exit Access. Based on your instructor's directions, submit a02c1Foodies_LastFirst.

Query Calculations and Expressions

LEARNING OUTCOME You will create queries to perform calculations and summarize data.

OBJECTIVES & SKILLS: After you read this chapter, you will be able to:

Calculated Fields and Expressions

OBJECTIVE 1: CREATE A QUERY WITH A CALCULATED FIELD 204
Build Expressions, Understand the Order of Operations

OBJECTIVE 2: FORMAT CALCULATED RESULTS 209
Format Fields

OBJECTIVE 3: RECOVER FROM COMMON ERRORS 210
Recognize and Correct Common Errors

OBJECTIVE 4: VERIFY CALCULATED RESULTS 211
Evaluate Results

HANDS-ON EXERCISE 1 212

The Expression Builder and Functions

OBJECTIVE 5: CREATE EXPRESSIONS USING THE EXPRESSION BUILDER 217
Use the Expression Builder

OBJECTIVE 6: USE BUILT-IN FUNCTIONS 218
Calculate a Loan Payment with the Pmt Function

HANDS-ON EXERCISE 2 222

Aggregate Functions

OBJECTIVE 7: ADD AGGREGATE FUNCTIONS TO DATASHEETS 226
Display a Total Row for a Query

OBJECTIVE 8: CREATE QUERIES WITH AGGREGATE FUNCTIONS 227
Create a Totals Query, Add Grouping to a Totals Query, Add Conditions to a Totals Query, Add a Calculated Field to a Totals Query

HANDS-ON EXERCISE 3 232

CASE STUDY | Real Estate Investors

After completing their degrees in Business at Passaic County Community College (PCCC) and a weekend seminar in real estate investing, Donald Carter and Matthew Nevoso were ready to test their skills in the marketplace. Don and Matt had a simple strategy—buy distressed properties at a significant discount, then resell the properties for a profit. Based on their seminar, they knew to gather key information such as the asking price, the number of bedrooms, square feet, and days on the market. Because they are just starting out, they decided to consider less expensive houses.

Based on a tip from the real estate seminar, they decided to create a database using Access, using data from a variety of home listing services. They approached you to help them find houses that meet their criteria. This new database approach should hopefully help them acquire their first investment property.

CHAPTER 3

Performing Calculations and Summarizing Data Using Queries

Sfio Cracho/Shutterstock

First Name	Last Name	List Price	Square Feet	Listing	Sold	Price Per Sq Ft	Payment
Philip	DeFranco	$109,140.00	1133	10004	No	$96.33	$416.84
Chardae	Myles	$129,780.00	1132	10028	No	$114.65	$495.67
Makarem	Abdeljawad	$136,680.00	1375	10008	No	$99.40	$522.02
Meera	Shah	$138,990.00	1276	10016	No	$108.93	$530.85
StudentFirst	StudentLast	$140,693.00	1490	10069	No	$94.42	$537.35
Makarem	Abdeljawad	$140,904.00	1301	10061	No	$108.30	$538.16
Makarem	Abdeljawad	$142,380.00	1373	11028	No	$103.70	$543.80
Chardae	Myles	$163,737.00	1476	10910	No	$110.93	$625.36
Jaynish	Mody	$164,436.00	1850	10117	No	$88.88	$628.03
Jaynish	Mody	$166,320.00	1437	10082	No	$115.74	$635.23
Chardae	Myles	$166,552.00	1623	10851	No	$102.62	$636.12
Chardae	Myles	$166,800.00	1598	10014	No	$104.38	$637.06
Philip	DeFranco	$168,000.00	1680	10002	No	$100.00	$641.65
Chardae	Myles	$168,354.00	1651	10885	No	$101.97	$643.00
Philip	DeFranco	$174,230.00	1771	10104	No	$98.38	$665.44
StudentFirst	StudentLast	$174,720.00	1610	10921	No	$108.52	$667.31
Meera	Shah	$174,720.00	1694	11035	No	$103.14	$667.31
Chardae	Myles	$175,336.00	1855	10868	No	$94.52	$669.66
StudentFirst	StudentLast	$175,560.00	1562	11036	No	$112.39	$670.52
Meera	Shah	$176,176.00	1761	10025	No	$100.04	$672.87
Jaynish	Mody	$177,984.00	1707	10066	No	$104.27	$679.78
Chardae	Myles	$179,088.00	1837	10010	No	$97.49	$683.99
Chardae	Myles	$179,100.00	1946	11079	No	$92.03	$684.04
Chardae	Myles	$179,712.00	1854	10102	No	$96.93	$686.38
Chardae	Myles	$180,180.00	1896	10019	No	$95.03	$688.17
Makarem	Abdeljawad	$180,810.00	1667	10044	No	$108.46	$690.57
Total		**$167,100.47**		**32**		**$102.10**	

Record: 1 of 32 — No Filter — Search

NameOfList	AvgOfSalePrice	Number Sold	DaysOnMarket
Algernon Listings	$324,697.22	18	24
FastHouse	$288,314.50	6	22
Houses 4 Sale	$218,039.00	2	24
Local Listings	$341,085.67	9	24
Major Houses	$235,757.88	8	25
Trullo	$236,885.21	19	26
Wholesaler	$276,654.92	26	26
Total		**88**	

FIGURE 3.1 Real Estate Investors Property Database

CASE STUDY | Real Estate Investors

Starting File	File to be Submitted
a03h1Property	**a03h3Property_LastFirst**

MyLab IT Grader An alternate version of this project is available as a MyLab IT Grader Assessment

Calculated Fields and Expressions

As you are manipulating data in an Access database, you will often want to perform calculations using the existing fields in your tables. By inserting a calculated field, you could, for example, create a field that calculates gross pay for an employee, by multiplying values stored in the number of hours worked field by values stored in the hourly pay rate field. Unfortunately, calculations may not always be that simple. If you have received a paycheck, you realize your gross pay is not the same as the amount of your paycheck. Your net pay will be lower, due to common deductions such as Social Security, Medicare, federal and state income taxes, unemployment insurance, and union dues. Some deductions may be a flat rate, and others are calculated based on the paycheck amount, so even what appears to be a simple calculation can be complex. A database that is used for payroll will need to calculate monthly pay taking into account all of these deductions. This can be accomplished through a calculation. Access includes many built-in calculations. Calculations are added commonly to queries, but can also be added to tables, forms, and reports.

In this section, you will learn how to use expressions to create a calculated field. You will also format the calculations to enhance readability and finally learn about how to avoid or recover from common errors.

Creating a Query with a Calculated Field

Rather than performing a calculation outside the database and inputting the result into your database, you should instead store the components of the calculation as fields and conduct the calculation using a calculated field in the database. A *calculated field* is a field that displays the result of a calculation that is based on an existing field or fields in the database. Calculating values rather than inputting values reduces errors and inconsistencies.

While calculated fields can be placed in both tables and queries, it is recommended to create calculated fields in a query. First, when a calculated field is placed in a table, the calculation cannot utilize the fields from other tables or queries. Second, using a calculated field in a table requires storing values (the results of a calculation) that depend on other fields. This eventually can cause confusion and irregularities and often breaks the rules of normalization. Because the very nature of queries is dependent on data from tables, queries are the better alternative for calculated fields.

For example, you would store a person's date of birth instead of their age because their age will change over time. Moreover, you can calculate a person's age with a calculated field, subtracting the date of birth from today's date. If you stored the person's current age, then next year it would be incorrect, and you would be constantly updating your tables. On the other hand, if you create a calculated field to determine a person's age, when you run the query you will have the person's current and correct age.

As another example, a table contains the times when employees clock in and out of work. You create a calculation in a query to determine how many hours each employee worked in a day by using a calculated field that subtracts data stored in the Clock In and Clock Out fields.

STEP 1 ▶ Build Expressions

An *expression* is a formula used in a calculated field that contains several different elements such as values and operations. Expressions can be typed manually or inserted into a calculated field using Access tools.

While some expressions are simple to create such as "sales price * sales tax", others are more complicated. Consider the following scenario. A company plans on allowing customers to pay off their purchase balance, interest free, in 12 monthly payments. The balance for each customer is stored in an Access database in a field named Balance. To calculate the monthly payment, you would use a calculated field with an expression that divides Balance by 12. You are left with a monthly payment of $100. See Figure 3.2 for an example of the calculated field, Balance, added to a query.

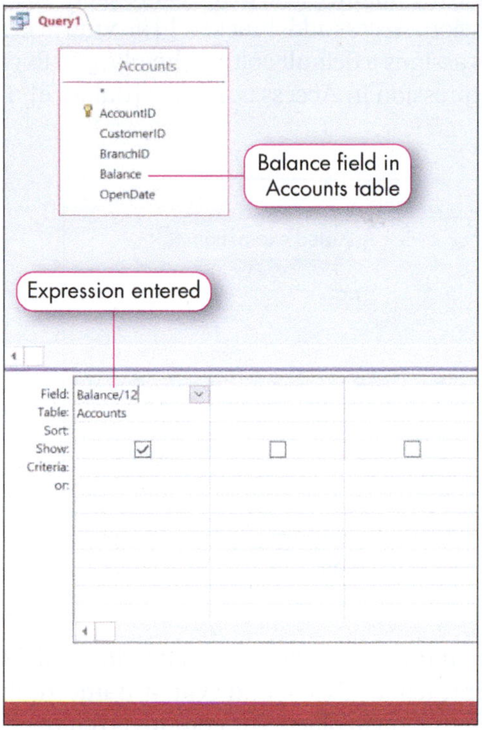

FIGURE 3.2 Balance Field in a Query

However, many companies will apply some sort of surcharge or add interest when customers pay balances off in installments, making the calculation more complex. The company may decide to add a surcharge of 20% (or 0.20) of the balance. In this case, you include a multiplication step in the above calculation. You multiply the results by 1.2. Then, divide that by 12 to get the monthly payment of $120 (see Figure 3.3). Note that there are multiple ways to implement this calculation, so this is not the only solution.

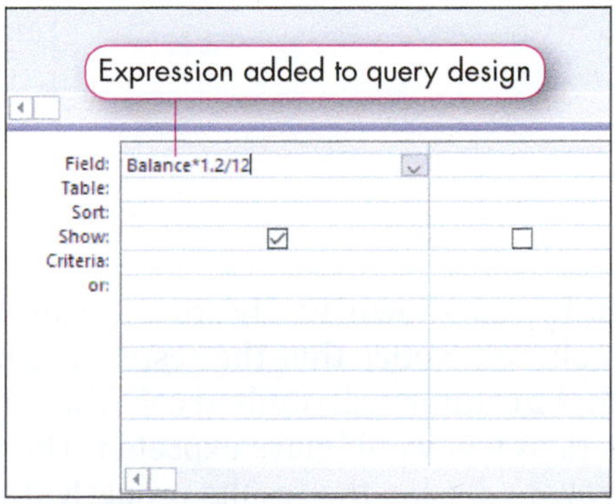

FIGURE 3.3 Sample Expression in a Query

To calculate the monthly installment with a 20% surcharge you would enter as an expression the following formula: Balance*1.2/12. You cannot exactly type that formula as it appears in the preceding sentence – a few modifications will need to be made. To input an expression in a way Access can understand, first add a new calculated field by clicking the field row. Then, to begin entering the expression, double-click the Balance field in the table above, to add the Balance field to the expression. You might notice that as you type the rest of the expression, Access adds brackets [ ] around field names as shown in Figure 3.4. In addition, Access assigns a default column heading of Expr1: to the start of the expression. The resulting expression in Access is: Expr1: [Balance]*1.2/12.

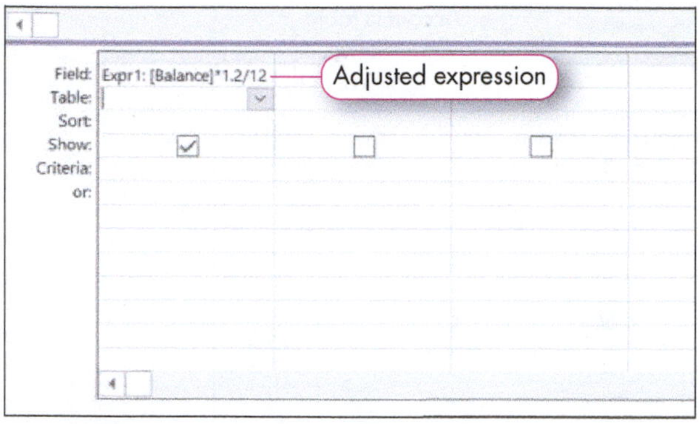

FIGURE 3.4 Modified Expression

When you run the query, the column heading will be *Expr1*. To rename this column MonthlyPayment, delete *Expr1* and type a name such as MonthlyPayment, making certain to leave the colon in place. The column is renamed MonthlyPayment in Figure 3.5. Alternatively, you can include the field name when you start to build the expression, followed by a colon, and then enter the expression.

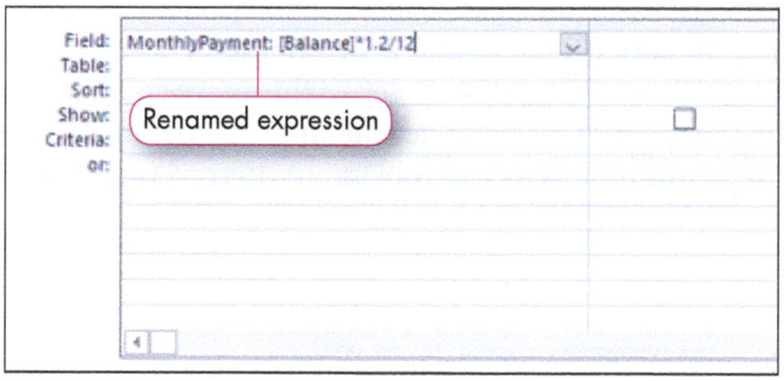

FIGURE 3.5 Expression Renamed

The query results, as shown in Figure 3.6, display a decimal number in the MonthlyPayment column. Notice that the results are not easy to read and should be formatted. Sometimes a column will result in cells that are filled with pound signs #### rather than numbers as you would have expected. The pound signs represent that the column is too narrow to display the results properly. To fix this issue, double-click the outer edge of the column to widen it and view the numbers. You will learn more about formatting the results in the next section.

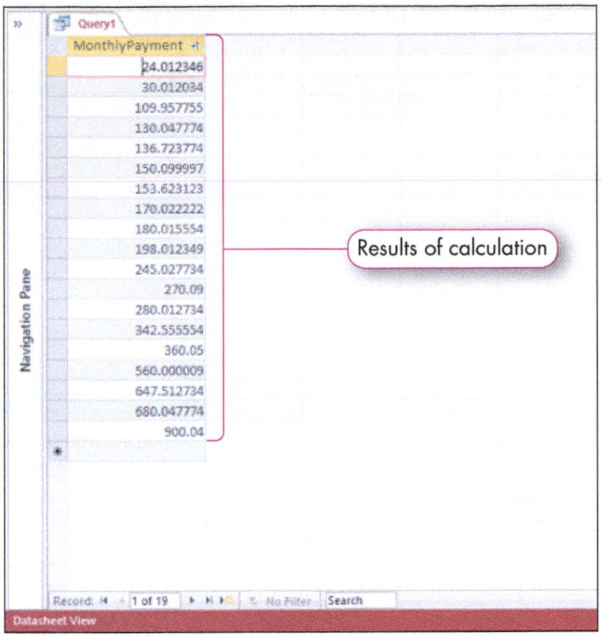

FIGURE 3.6 Unformatted Results

As you create expressions in a calculated field, you may find one or more of the following elements in the calculated field:

- Arithmetic operator (for example: *, /, +, or −)
- **Constant**, a value that does not change (such as a person's birthdate)
- Function (built-in calculations like Pmt)
- Identifier (the names of fields – such as *Balance* from the example above, controls, or properties)

To see the entire calculated field expression in Design view, right-click the Field row and select Zoom. A dialog box (the Zoom box) will open to enable you to easily see and edit the entire contents of the cell, as shown in Figure 3.7. Once you have finished modifying a field, click Close in the top-right corner of the Zoom box.

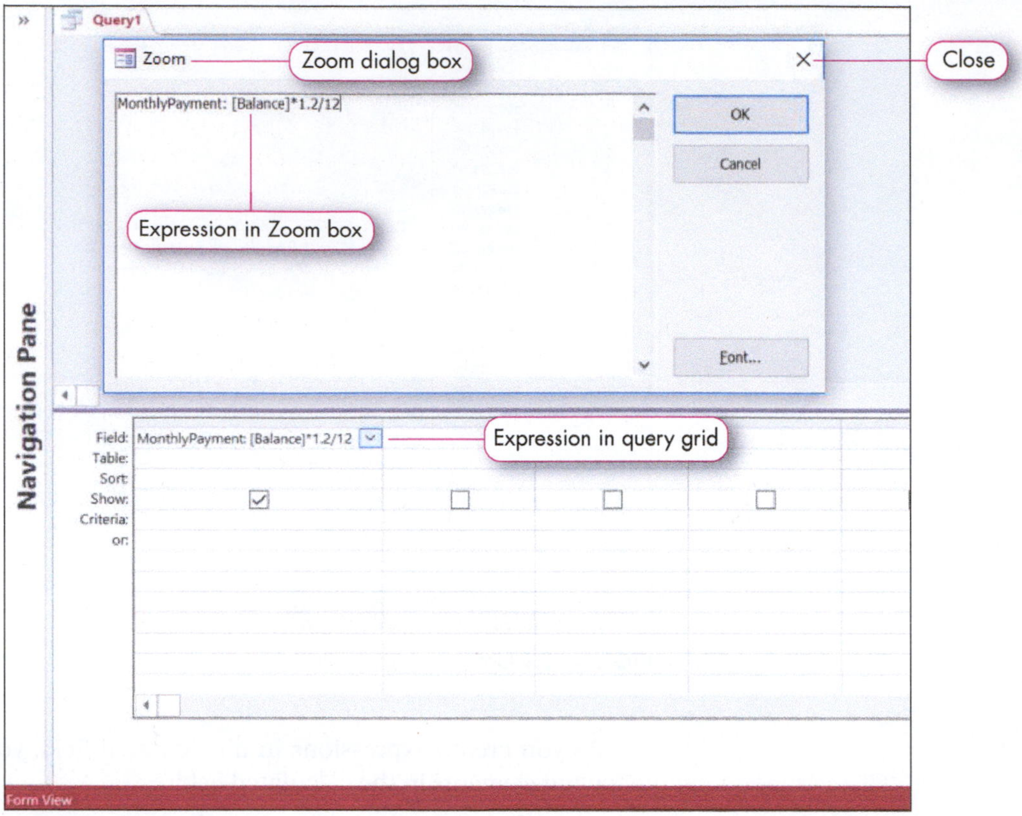

FIGURE 3.7 Zoom box

Understand the Order of Operations

The *order of operations* determines the sequence by which operations are calculated in a mathematical expression. Access performs mathematical calculations left to right in this order: **P**arentheses, **E**xponentiation, **M**ultiplication or **D**ivision, and finally **A**ddition or **S**ubtraction. Some people remember the order of operations with the phrase Please Excuse My Dear Aunt Sally or PEMDAS. Use parentheses to ensure a lower-order operation occurs first. Table 3.1 shows some examples of the order of operations. Access uses the following symbols:

• Parentheses	( )
• Exponentiation	^
• Multiplication	*
• Division	/
• Addition	+
• Subtraction	–

TABLE 3.1	Examples of Order of Operations	
Expression	**Order to Perform Calculations**	**Output**
=2+3*3	Multiply first and then add.	11
=(2+3)*3	Add the values inside the parentheses first and then multiply.	15
=2+2^3	Evaluate the exponent first, $2^3=2*2*2$ (or 8). Then add.	10
=10/2+3	Divide first and then add.	8
=10/(2+3)	Add first to simplify the parenthetical expression and then divide.	2
=10*2–3*2	Multiply first and then subtract.	14

STEP 2 Formatting Calculated Results

When using calculated fields in queries, you will format the results to make your query results more readable. For example, if you are calculating net pay, you do not need to display more than two decimal places. Even though you are formatting to display only two decimal places to conform to normal conventions, the database still stores the full decimal places and uses the entire number when that value is used in other calculations. Similarly, a decimal value can be formatted as a percentage (0.02 to 2%) but Access will store the full number.

To format a field in a query, use the **Property Sheet**. The Property Sheet enables you to change the way a field displays. For example, a numeric field has settings such as *number format* and *number of decimal places*, while other data types will have settings specific to that type. The Property Sheet is in many ways similar to the Field Properties in a table.

To format a calculated field using the Property Sheet in a query, complete the following steps:

1. Open the query in Design view.
2. Click the Field row of the field you want to format.
3. Click Property Sheet in the Show/Hide group on the Design tab.
4. Click the appropriate option and choose the setting. You can change the format by clicking the Format property arrow and selecting a format (such as Currency for numeric fields). For numeric fields, the Decimal Places property enables you to choose the number of decimal places that display. To change the caption (which displays as the name of the column), click the text box next to the Caption property and type the column heading. Figure 3.8 shows the Property Sheet options related to a numeric field.
5. Close the Property Sheet, by clicking Close as shown in Figure 3.8. After using the Property Sheet, it will be displayed when the query is opened in Design view, unless you close it. However, as most of your users will not be viewing the query in Design view, it should not matter either way if the Property Sheet is closed or not.

FIGURE 3.8 Property Sheet Options

Recovering from Common Errors

When creating calculated fields, a number of common errors can occur. Learning how to recognize errors and recover from issues is important. Some common types of errors:

Syntax Error: Forgetting the Colon

A correct formula looks like this: MonthlyPayment: [Balance]*1.2/12

If you forget the colon, you will get an invalid syntax error, indicating something is wrong with the way the formula is written, as shown in Figure 3.9.

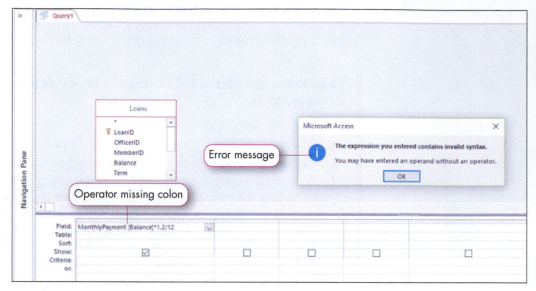

FIGURE 3.9 Syntax Error Warning

Syntax Error: Spelling Error

If you mistype the field name as *Baalance*, you will get an error when you run the query that prompts you to give a value for *Baalance* as shown in Figure 3.10.

Access cannot complete the calculation because the database does not recognize a field named *Baalance*. Correct the misspelling, and the calculation is made.

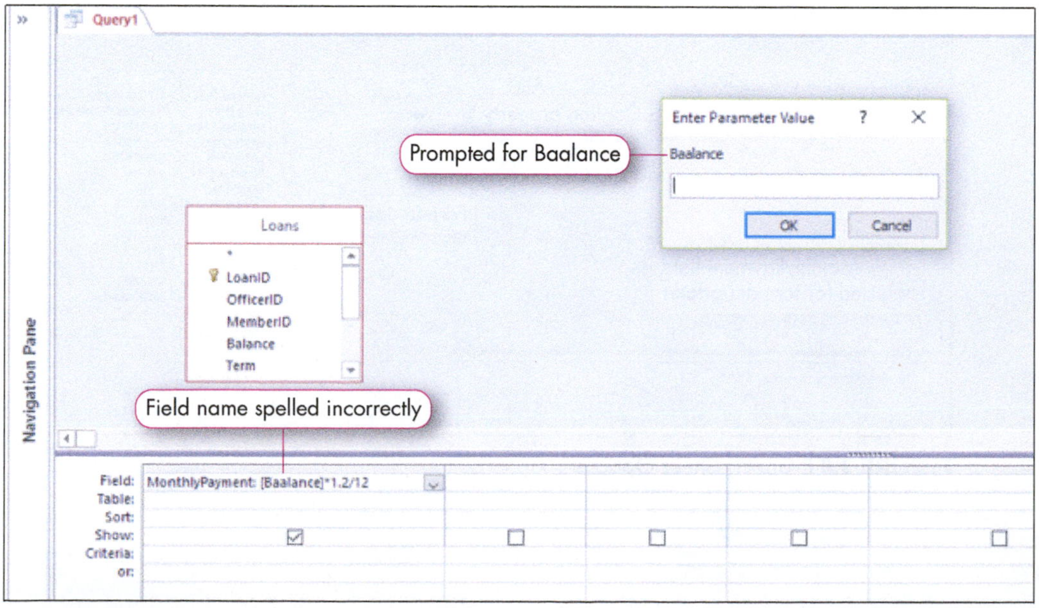

FIGURE 3.10 Result of Spelling Error in Field Name

Syntax Error: Order of Operations Error

If you do not check your formulas, you may get incorrect results. For example, the following would not produce the expected output:

NewMonthlyBalance: [Balance] + 100/12

If you want addition to be done before division, you must remember the parentheses:

NewMonthlyBalance: ([Balance] + 100)/12

Verifying Calculated Results

After the query runs, review the field values and calculated values in Datasheet view to make sure the results make sense. As noted above, you might have forgotten to add in parentheses causing the wrong order of operations to be conducted. In a real-world scenario, you will not be given step-by-step directions and instead will apply critical thinking skills to your work. Access will calculate exactly what you tell it to calculate, even if you make logical errors in the calculation.

Assume you are calculating a car payment for a $10,000 car, with monthly payments for 5 years. If your results indicated that the monthly payment is $1,000, you should ask yourself, "Does it make sense for me to pay $1,000 every month for five years to finance a $10,000 car?"

You can verify results with a calculator. Alternatively, you could check the results in Excel by copying and pasting the data into a worksheet, conducting the calculations in Excel, and then comparing the answers to the query results in Access. The Access calculated field, the calculator, and the Excel calculations should all return identical results.

Quick Concepts

1. Discuss the four types of elements that can appear as part of an expression in Access. **p. 207**

2. Briefly describe the order of operations. Give an example of how the order of operations makes a difference in a calculation. **p. 208**

3. Explain how Access responds when you spell a field name incorrectly in a query. **p. 210**

Hands-On Exercises

Skills covered: Build Expressions • Format Fields • Recognize and Correct Common Errors • Evaluate Results

1 Calculated Fields and Expressions

Using the data from the homes for sale lists that Don and Matt acquired, you can help them target properties that meet their criteria. As you examine the data, you discover other ways to analyze the properties. You create several queries and present your results to the two investors for their comments.

STEP 1 ▶ BUILD EXPRESSIONS

You begin your analysis by creating a query using the Properties and Agents tables from the Property database. The Properties table contains all the properties the investors will evaluate; the Agents table contains a list of real estate agents who represent the properties' sellers. In this exercise, you will add requested fields and only show properties that have not been sold. You will then build an expression to calculate the price per square foot for each property. Refer to Figure 3.11 as you complete Step 1.

Step e: First Name and Last Name fields added to query

Step f: ListPrice, SqFeet, and Sold fields added to query

Step i: ListPrice sorted in ascending order

Step l: New calculated field added

Step h: Sold criterion

Step m: Calculated field results

First Name	Last Name	List Price	Square Feet	Sold	PricePerSqFt
Philip	DeFranco	$109,140.00	1133	No	96.3283318623124
Chardae	Myles	$129,780.00	1132	No	114.646643109541
Makarem	Abdeljawad	$136,680.00	1375	No	99.4036363636364
Meera	Shah	$138,990.00	1276	No	108.926332288401
Student Name	Student Name	$140,693.00	1490	No	94.4248322147651
Makarem	Abdeljawad	$140,904.00	1356	No	108.304381245196
Makarem	Abdeljawad	$142,380.00	1373	No	103.699927166788
Chardae	Myles	$163,737.00	1476	No	110.932926829268
Jaynish	Mody	$164,436.00	1850	No	88.8843243243243
Jaynish	Mody	$166,320.00	1437	No	115.741127348643
Chardae	Myles	$166,552.00	1623	No	102.619839802834
Chardae	Myles	$166,800.00	1598	No	104.380475594493
Philip	DeFranco	$168,000.00	1680	No	100
Chardae	Myles	$168,354.00	1651	No	101.970926711084
Philip	DeFranco	$174,230.00	1771	No	98.3794466403162
Meera	Shah	$174,720.00	1694	No	103.140495867769
Student Name	Student Name	$174,720.00	1610	No	108.521739130435
Chardae	Myles	$175,336.00	1855	No	94.5207547169811
Student Name	Student Name	$175,560.00	1562	No	112.394366197183
Meera	Shah	$176,176.00	1761	No	100.04315729699
Jaynish	Mody	$177,984.00	1707	No	104.267135325132
Chardae	Myles	$179,088.00	1837	No	97.4893848666304
Chardae	Myles	$179,100.00	1946	No	92.0349434737924
Chardae	Myles	$179,712.00	1854	No	96.9320388349515
Chardae	Myles	$180,180.00	1896	No	95.0316455696203
Makarem	Abdeljawad	$180,810.00	1667	No	108.464307138572

Record: 1 of 215

Step j: 215 results

FIGURE 3.11 Modified Expression

---

a. Open *a03h1Property*. Save the database as **a03h1Property_LastFirst**.

> **TROUBLESHOOTING:** If you make any major mistakes in this exercise, you can close the file, open *a03h1Property* again, and then start this exercise over.

b. Open the Agents table and replace the name *Student Name* with your name. Close the table.

c. Click the **Create tab** and click **Query Design** in the Queries group to create a new query.

The Show Table dialog box opens so you can specify the table(s) and/or queries to include in the query design.

d. Select the **Agents table** and click **Add**. Select the **Properties table** and click **Add**. Click **Close** to close the Show Table dialog box.

e. Double-click the **FirstName** and **LastName fields** in the Agents table to add them to the query.

f. Double-click the **ListPrice**, **SqFeet**, and **Sold fields** in the Properties table to add them to the query.

g. Click **Run** in the Results group to display the results in Datasheet view.

A total of 303 properties display in the results.

h. Switch to Design view. Type **No** in the Criteria row of the Sold field.

> **TROUBLESHOOTING:** As you begin typing *No* the designer will popup a suggestion of "Now()." Press Esc to close the dialog box.

i. Click the **Sort row** in the ListPrice field. Click the **arrow** and select **Ascending**.

j. Click **Run** in the Results group to display the results.

The 215 unsold properties display in the datasheet, with the least expensive houses displayed first.

k. Click **Save** on the Quick Access Toolbar and type **Price Per Square Foot** as the Query Name in the Save As dialog box. Click **OK**.

l. Switch to Design view. Click the **Field row** of the first blank column of the query design grid. Right-click and select **Zoom** to show the Zoom box. Type **PricePerSqFt: ListPrice/SqFeet** and click **OK**.

Access inserts square brackets around the fields for you. The new field divides the values in the ListPrice field by the values in the SqFeet field.

m. Click **Run** in the Results group to view the results. Adjust column widths as necessary.

The new calculated field, PricePerSqFt, is displayed. Compare your results to those shown in Figure 3.11.

> **TROUBLESHOOTING:** If you see pound signs (#####) in an Access column, double-click the vertical line between column headings to increase the width.

> **TROUBLESHOOTING:** If, when you run the query, you are prompted for a parameter value, cancel and return to Design view. Ensure that you have entered the correct spelling for the field name from Step l in the first row of a blank column.

n. Save the changes to the query.

STEP 2 FORMAT CALCULATED RESULTS

Don and Matt want the calculated field formatted with two decimal places. You will change the format to Currency and add a caption to the calculated field. Refer to Figure 3.12 as you complete Step 2.

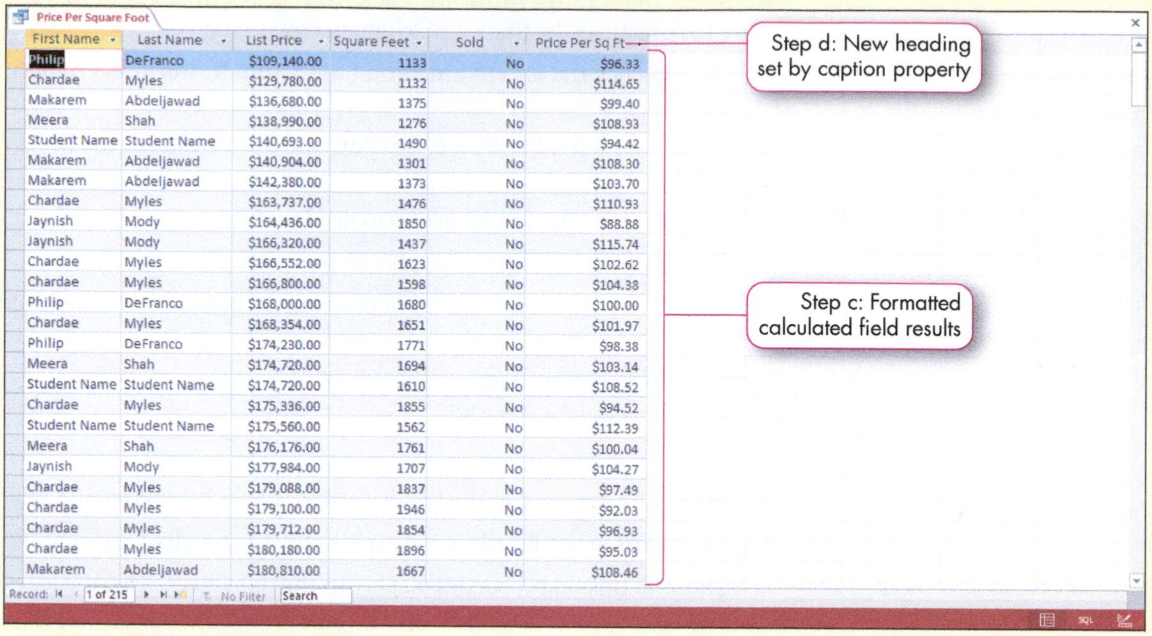

First Name	Last Name	List Price	Square Feet	Sold	Price Per Sq Ft
Philip	DeFranco	$109,140.00	1133	No	$96.33
Chardae	Myles	$129,780.00	1132	No	$114.65
Makarem	Abdeljawad	$136,680.00	1375	No	$99.40
Meera	Shah	$138,990.00	1276	No	$108.93
Student Name	Student Name	$140,693.00	1490	No	$94.42
Makarem	Abdeljawad	$140,904.00	1301	No	$108.30
Makarem	Abdeljawad	$142,380.00	1373	No	$103.70
Chardae	Myles	$163,737.00	1476	No	$110.93
Jaynish	Mody	$164,436.00	1850	No	$88.88
Jaynish	Mody	$166,320.00	1437	No	$115.74
Chardae	Myles	$166,552.00	1623	No	$102.62
Chardae	Myles	$166,800.00	1598	No	$104.38
Philip	DeFranco	$168,000.00	1680	No	$100.00
Chardae	Myles	$168,354.00	1651	No	$101.97
Philip	DeFranco	$174,230.00	1771	No	$98.38
Meera	Shah	$174,720.00	1694	No	$103.14
Student Name	Student Name	$174,720.00	1610	No	$108.52
Chardae	Myles	$175,336.00	1855	No	$94.52
Student Name	Student Name	$175,560.00	1562	No	$112.39
Meera	Shah	$176,176.00	1761	No	$100.04
Jaynish	Mody	$177,984.00	1707	No	$104.27
Chardae	Myles	$179,088.00	1837	No	$97.49
Chardae	Myles	$179,100.00	1946	No	$92.03
Chardae	Myles	$179,712.00	1854	No	$96.93
Chardae	Myles	$180,180.00	1896	No	$95.03
Makarem	Abdeljawad	$180,810.00	1667	No	$108.46

FIGURE 3.12 Formatted Field

a. Ensure the Price Per Square Foot query is open in Design view.

b. Click the **PricePerSqFt calculated field cell**. Click **Property Sheet** in the Show/Hide group on the Design tab.

   The Property Sheet displays.

c. Click the **Format property**. Click the **Format property arrow** and select **Currency**.

d. Click the **Caption property** and type **Price Per Sq Ft**. (Do not include the period.) Press **Enter**. Close the Property Sheet.

e. Click **Run** to view your changes.

   The calculated field values are formatted as Currency, and the column heading displays Price Per Sq Ft instead of PricePerSqFt.

f. Compare your result to Figure 3.12. Save the changes to the query.

STEP 3 RECOVER FROM COMMON ERRORS AND VERIFY RESULTS

A few errors arise as you test a new calculated field. You check the spelling of the field names in the calculated fields because that is a common mistake. You decide to verify your data prior to showing it to the investors. You use the estimation method to check your calculations. Refer to Figure 3.13 as you complete Step 3.

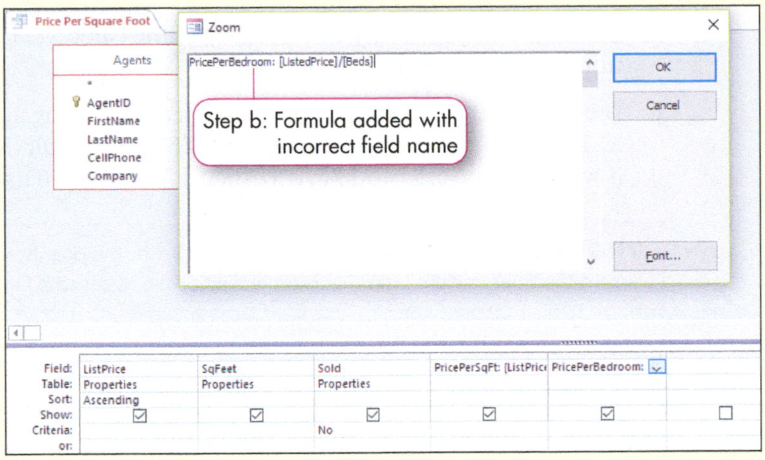

FIGURE 3.13 Incorrect Expression

a. Switch to Design view of the Price Per Square Foot query. Scroll to the first blank column of the query design grid and click the **Field row**.

b. Right-click and select **Zoom** to display the Zoom box. Type **PricePerBedroom: [ListedPrice]/[Beds]**. Your formula should match Figure 3.13. Click **OK** in the Zoom dialog box.

You are intentionally misspelling the field name for the ListPrice (as ListedPrice which does not exist as a field in the database) to see how Access will respond.

c. Click **Property Sheet** in the Show/Hide group of the Design tab. Click the **Format property**. From the menu, select **Currency**. Click the **Caption box** and type **Price Per Bedroom**. Press **Enter**. Close the Property Sheet.

d. Click **Run** in the Results group.

You should see the Enter Parameter Value dialog box. Access does not recognize ListedPrice in the tables defined for this query in the first record. When Access does not recognize a field name, it will ask you to supply a value.

e. Type **100000** in the first parameter box. Press **Enter**.

The query has the necessary information to run and returns the results in Datasheet view.

f. Examine the results of the calculation for Price Per Bedroom.

All the records display 50000 because you entered the value 100000 into the parameter box. Because Access could not recognize the field name and use individual values for the field, to run the query, you supplied the constant value 100000, which Access used for the calculation in each record. The value was treated as a constant and gave the same results for all records.

g. Return to Design view. Display the Zoom box. Change the formula to **PricePerBedroom: [ListPrice]/[Beds]**. Click **OK**.

You corrected the error in the field name, ListPrice.

h. Run and save the query.

The calculated values in the last two columns should not give you an error message. Correct any issues by reexamining the previous steps and formulas to ensure correct spelling and proper formatting of the formula.

i. Examine the PricePerSqFt field.

One of the ways to verify the accuracy of the calculated data is to ask yourself if the numbers make sense.

j. Locate the 20th record with Meera Shah as the listing agent, an asking price of $176,176.00, and square footage of 1761. The result ($100.04) makes sense, because if we round the price to 176,100, then 176,100/1761 = 100.

> **TROUBLESHOOTING:** If the 20th record is not the one listed above, ensure that you have sorted the query by the List Price in ascending order, as specified in Step 1i.

k. Save and close the query.

l. Keep the database open if you plan to continue with the next Hands-On Exercise. If not, close the database and exit Access.

The Expression Builder and Functions

In the last Hands-On Exercise, you calculated the price per square foot for real estate properties to help evaluate properties on the investment list. You typed the names of two fields to create the expression: ListPrice/SqFeet. Manually typing field names can lead to errors. Instead, use the Expression Builder. The **Expression Builder** is a tool that enables you to build expressions more quickly and accurately. The Expression Builder uses objects, operators, and functions to help build simple to complex calculations. The Expression Builder's size enables you to easily see complex formulas and functions in their entirety.

In this section, you will learn how to create expressions with the Expression Builder. You also will learn how to use Built-In Functions.

STEP 1 Creating Expressions Using the Expression Builder

The Expression Builder enables you to create expressions by supplying you with access to fields, operators, and functions. Another advantage is that when you insert a function, placeholders for the function's arguments tell you which values belong where. Experienced users may have functions memorized, but new users have the Expression Builder to provide support.

When in Query Design view, you will find the Builder on the Query Tools Design tab in the Query Setup Group. Its icon resembles a magic wand. Once you open the Expression Builder, the Expression Builder dialog box displays. The top portion is an empty rectangular box known as the expression box. The left column of the Expression Builder dialog box contains Expression Elements (see Figure 3.14), which include the Built-In Functions, objects from the current database (including tables), and common expressions.

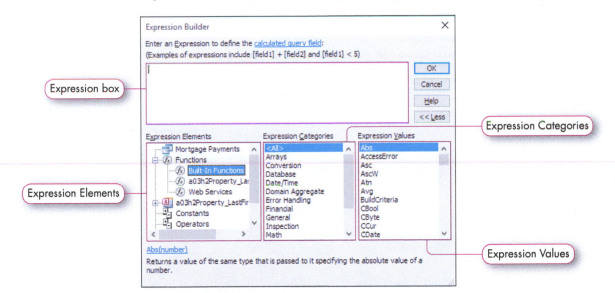

FIGURE 3.14 Expression Builder

The middle column displays the Expression Categories based on the item selected in the Expression Elements box (refer to Figure 3.14). For example, when the Built-In Functions item is selected in the Expression Elements box, the available Built-In Function categories, such as the Math category, are displayed in the Expression Categories box.

The right column displays the Expression Values, if any, for the categories that you selected in the Expression Categories box (refer to Figure 3.14). For example, if you click Built-In Functions in the Expression Elements box and click Date/Time in the Expression Categories box, the Expression Values box lists the Built-In Functions in the Date/Time category. When using dates in an expression, it is important to understand how Access stores the date. Microsoft stores a date as a number, more specifically, the number of days since January 1, 1900. A date with a time is stored as a fraction of that day. For example, January 1, 2019 would be stored as 43831.00. If the time were noon on that same day (1/1/2019 12:00 PM), the number stored would be 43831.50—for half the day. Storing dates as numbers enables you to perform mathematical calculations on those dates. For example, we can determine someone's age today or the number of days a property has been for sale by subtracting one date from another.

> **To create a calculated field with the Expression Builder, complete the following steps:**
>
> 1. Open a query in Design view (or create a new query).
> 2. Click the Field row of a blank column.
> 3. Click Builder in the Query Setup group of the Design tab to launch the Expression Builder.
> 4. Type the calculated field name and type a colon to name the column. Although this is not required, as mentioned earlier in this chapter, this will change the title of the column in Datasheet view.
> 5. Click the source table or query listed in the Expression Elements section and double-click the field you want. This will insert a field in a format resembling [Properties]![Beds] as shown in Figure 3.15. In this example, the table name Properties displays in brackets, followed by an exclamation point, followed by the field name Beds in brackets. As long as you do not have multiple fields with the same name, you can safely delete the table name and exclamation point (leaving you with [Beds] in this example). If you want to use operators (such as +) you can type those manually.
> 6. Repeat the previous step for each field you want to add to the calculation, remembering to take the order of operations into account. See Figure 3.15 as an example formula created in the Expression Builder.
> 7. Click OK to close the Expression Builder window.
> 8. Click Run in the Results group to view the results in Datasheet view.

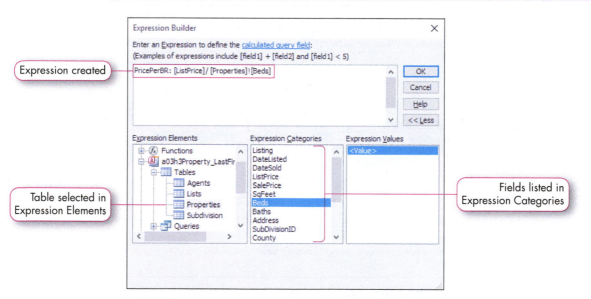

FIGURE 3.15 Expression Created in Expression Builder

Using Built-In Functions

A *function* is a predefined computation that performs a complex calculation. Each function has a specific name that describes the purpose of the function. It also has *arguments*, which are specific inputs used to complete the calculation. The order and type of argument is particular to each function. Additionally, some functions have optional arguments, which are not required but may be necessary for your task. Each function has a specific *syntax* that determines the layout and order of the function and its arguments.

Figuring out the payment of a loan or isolating the year portion of a date is made easier with the use of Built-In Functions. There are around 150 functions built into Access. Many of the functions in Access are similar to those in Excel. Once you identify what you need to calculate, you can review the Built-In Functions in the Expression Builder to see if the function exists. The functions are organized into Expression Categories or as an alphabetical list. See Figure 3.16 for an example function inserted using the Expression Builder. When you select a function, a description of the function's purpose is displayed at the bottom of the dialog box. When clicked, the blue hyperlink, located at the bottom of the dialog box, will open further help documentation to discuss the function in more detail.

All functions have one or more placeholder fields, called arguments, that are identified by <<>> symbols. Function arguments provide the values used to perform calculations. The layout and order of a function is referred to as syntax, and in general is written as: Function name(<<argument>>, <<argument>>,<<argument>>, . . .). Notice an example of placeholder text in Figure 3.16. Functions work the same in Access, Excel, and programming languages (such as C#, Java, or Python).

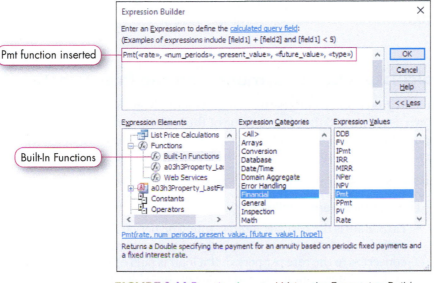

FIGURE 3.16 Function Inserted Using the Expression Builder

To create an expression using a function with the Expression Builder, complete the following steps:

1. Open a query in Design view (or create a new query).
2. Click the Field row of a blank column.
3. Click Builder in the Query Setup group of the Design tab to launch the Expression Builder.
4. Type the calculated field name and type a colon if you want to name the column.
5. Click Functions in the Expression Elements section of the window (see Figure 3.16). Click Built-In Functions to display a list of available functions.
6. Locate and click the function category in the Expression Categories section, as shown in Figure 3.17. If you are unsure of the category, you can use Help or search through the category labeled.
7. Ensure the function is selected, double-click the function name in the Expression Values section to add it.
8. Click a placeholder text element to select it, unless your function does not have placeholder text.
9. Replace each argument with a number, a field name, or calculation. (For example, in Figure 3.17, the first argument placeholder text was replaced by 0.05/12.)
10. Click OK to close the Expression Builder window.
11. Click Run in the Results group to view the results in Datasheet view.

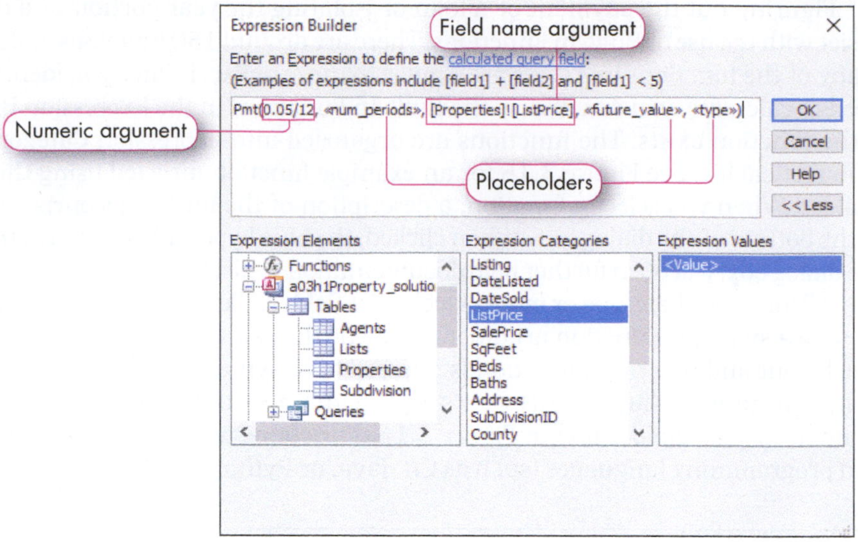

FIGURE 3.17 Expression with Some Arguments Filled In

Calculate a Loan Payment with the Pmt Function

The **Pmt function** calculates the loan payment given the rate, number of periods (also known as term), and the present value of the loan (the principal). If necessary, two other arguments (future value and type) can be used, but they are not necessary for many calculations. The Pmt function uses the following syntax:

Pmt(<<rate>>, <<num_periods>>, <<present_value>>, <<future_value>>, <<type>>)

The arguments are as follows:

- **rate**: Rate is the periodic interest rate. The period must match the payment period. Interest rates are usually stated as yearly rates, so the annual rate must be converted to the rate per period. If a loan is paid monthly, divide the annual rate by 12. If interest rate is a field in one of the tables, then the rate argument would display as [InterestRate]/12, where [InterestRate] is the field from the table and 12 is the number of payments. Otherwise, when entered manually, this is entered as a decimal followed by the division (for example, 0.05/12).

- **num_periods**: Num_periods is the total number of payments. Typically, you will multiply the number of years of the loan by the number of payments per year. The total number of payments for a monthly payment would be calculated as the number of years multiplied by 12.

- **present_value**: The present_value is the total amount of the loan. By default, the Pmt function will return a negative value, as a loan payment is considered a debit. If you want to display this as a positive number, place a negative sign in front of the loan amount. In a mortgage there is typically a down payment required. The present value in that situation would be the price of the home minus the down payment.

- **future_value** and **type**: The last two arguments—future value and type—are both optional, so they are usually left blank or filled in with zero. Future_value is the amount that a loan is future value or cash balance you want after you've made the final payment. For a mortgage or car loan, you will be required to pay the loan amount until there is a zero balance. Type is the time frame when the payments are due. For a mortgage or car loan, the payments will typically be due at the end of the period.

The following example shows how to use the Pmt function to calculate the payment for a loan with a 5% interest rate, paid 12 times a year. This loan will be paid for four years and has a present value of $12,500. Figure 3.18 shows how it displays in the Expression Builder. Observe that a negative sign has been placed in front of the present_value argument, which is 12500 in this expression. This ensures that the function will return a positive value.

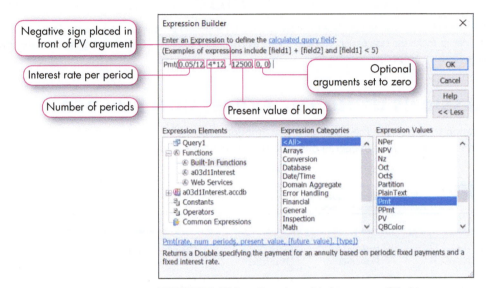

FIGURE 3.18 Pmt Function with Arguments Filled In

4. Discuss two benefits of using the Expression Builder to create expressions. *p. 217*

5. Explain the purpose of one of the arguments in the Pmt function. *p. 220*

6. Given the following function: describe what argument each component represents. Pmt(0.05/12, 5*12, −50000, 0, 0). *p. 220*

Hands-On Exercises

MyLab IT HOE2 Sim Training

Watch the Video for this Hands-On Exercise!

Skills covered: Use the Expression Builder • Calculate a Loan Payment with the Pmt Function

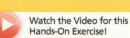

2 The Expression Builder and Functions

Don and Matt ask you to calculate the down payment for unsold properties; you use the Expression Builder to make the task easier. You also create an additional calculated field showing the estimated mortgage for each property.

STEP 1 CREATE EXPRESSIONS USING THE EXPRESSION BUILDER

You will create one calculation to determine the down payment amount given a 20% down payment. The calculation you will create is shown in Figure 3.19. Your expected output is shown in Figure 3.20.

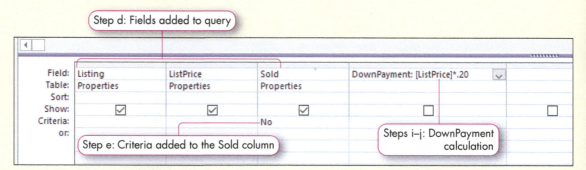

FIGURE 3.19 Calculation in Expression Builder

Listing	List Price	Sold	DownPayment
10001	$202,342.00	No	$40,468.40
10002	$168,000.00	No	$33,600.00
10003	$232,960.00	No	$46,592.00
10004	$109,140.00	No	$21,828.00
10005	$224,770.00	No	$44,954.00
10006	$269,696.00	No	$53,939.20
10007	$212,592.00	No	$42,518.40
10008	$136,680.00	No	$27,336.00
10010	$179,088.00	No	$35,817.60
10012	$198,144.00	No	$39,628.80
10014	$166,800.00	No	$33,360.00
10016	$138,990.00	No	$27,798.00
10017	$249,872.00	No	$49,974.40
10018	$205,524.00	No	$41,104.80
10019	$180,180.00	No	$36,036.00
10020	$228,984.00	No	$45,796.80
10022	$226,590.00	No	$45,318.00
10023	$275,616.00	No	$55,123.20
10024	$183,312.00	No	$36,662.40
10025	$176,176.00	No	$35,235.20
10026	$225,720.00	No	$45,144.00
10028	$129,780.00	No	$25,956.00
10031	$219,996.00	No	$43,999.20
10035	$345,708.00	No	$69,141.60
10039	$234,036.00	No	$46,807.20
10040	$192,864.00	No	$38,572.80

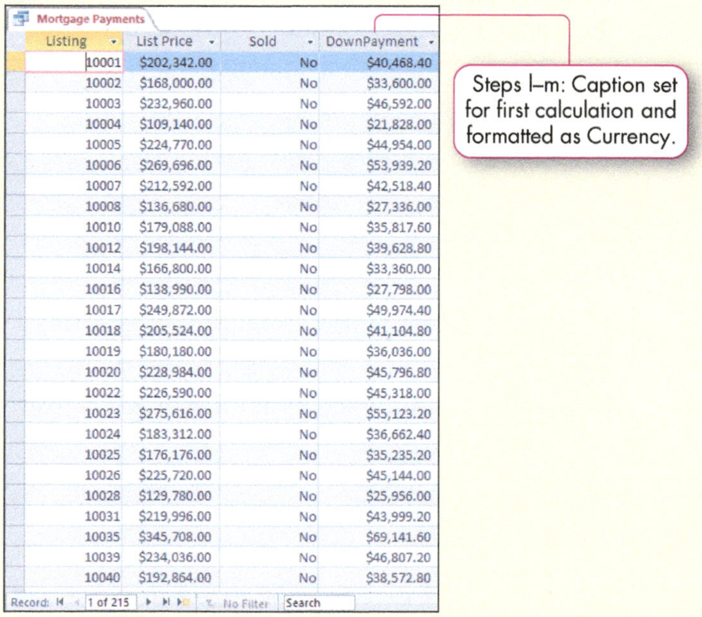

FIGURE 3.20 Down Payment Calculation

a. Open *a03h1Property_LastFirst* if you closed it at the end of Hands-On Exercise 1, and save it as **a03h2Property_LastFirst**, changing h1 to h2.

b. Click the **Create tab** and click **Query Design** in the Queries group.

c. Select the **Properties table**, click **Add**, and then click **Close** to close the Show Table dialog box.

d. Double-click the **Listing**, **ListPrice,** and **Sold fields** to add them to the query.

e. Type **No** in the criteria box in the Sold column.

Typing No for the Sold field will ensure that only available properties will display.

> **TROUBLESHOOTING:** As you begin typing *No* the designer will popup a suggestion of "Now()." Press Esc to close the dialog box.

f. Click the **Field row** in the first blank column of the query design grid and click **Builder** in the Query Setup group.

The Expression Builder dialog box opens.

g. Click the **plus sign** next to the a03h2Property_LastFirst database in the Expression Elements box to expand the list. Click the **plus sign** next to Tables and select the **Properties table**.

The fields from the Properties table are now listed in the middle column (Expression Categories).

h. Double-click the **ListPrice field** to add it to the expression box.

i. Highlight the **[Properties]! prefix** in front of ListPrice and press **Delete**.

The expression now reads [ListPrice]. As the ListPrice field name is unique within the query, the table name is not necessary. Removing this makes the query easier to read. If a field named ListPrice was in more than one table in our query, removing the table name would cause problems.

j. Type ***** and **0.2** after [ListPrice] in the Expression Builder dialog box.

You want to see the potential down payment for each of the properties. A down payment of 20% of the purchase price must be made to secure a mortgage for these properties. Therefore, you multiply the ListPrice field by 0.20. The expression now reads [ListPrice]*0.2.

k. Click **OK** and click **Run** in the Results group to view the query results.

Observe that the column heading reads Expr1. Also notice that the column's contents are not formatted.

l. Switch to Design view and ensure that the Expr1 field is selected. Change the Expr1 to **DownPayment**. Ensure that the colon remains in the expression.

The DownPayment column now has an appropriate name.

m. Ensure that the DownPayment field is still selected. Click **Property Sheet** in the Show/Hide group. Click the **Format box** and select **Currency**. Close the Property Sheet.

The field is now formatted as currency.

n. Run the query and examine the changes. Adjust column widths as necessary. Compare your results to Figure 3.20.

o. Click **Save** on the Quick Access Toolbar and save the query as **Mortgage Payments**.

Don and Matt are close to making an offer on a house. They want to restrict the query to houses that cost $190,000 or less. They also want to calculate the estimated mortgage payment for each house. You create this calculation using the Pmt function. You make the following assumptions: 80% of the sale price to be financed, a 30-year term, monthly payments, and a fixed 6.0% annual interest rate. Refer to Figures 3.21 and 3.22 as you complete Step 2.

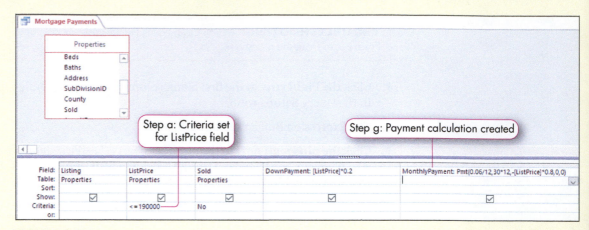

FIGURE 3.21 Mortgage Payments Design View

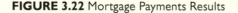

FIGURE 3.22 Mortgage Payments Results

a. Ensure the Mortgage Payments query is open in Design view, type **<=190000** in the Criteria row of the ListPrice column. (Do not add a comma or dollar signs when typing the amount.) Press **Enter**.

The query, when it is run, will show only the houses that cost $190,000 or less.

b. Click the **Field row** of the first blank column. Click **Builder** in the Query Setup group to open the Expression Builder dialog box.

c. Double-click **Functions** in the Expression Elements box and select **Built-In Functions**.

d. Select **Financial** in the Expression Categories box.

e. Double-click **Pmt** in the Expression Values box.

f. Position the insertion point before the Pmt function. Type **MonthlyPayment:** to the left of the Pmt function, with a space after the colon.

g. Click each argument to select it and substitute the appropriate information as shown in the following table. Make sure there is a comma between each argument.

Argument	Replacement Value
«rate»	0.06/12
«num_periods»	30*12
«present_value»	[ListPrice]*0.8
«future_value»	0
«type»	0

Note that the loan is a 30-year loan with 12 payments per year, hence the calculation for the number of payments. Also note, Don and Matt plan on financing 80% of the cost. Therefore, you will multiply the list price by 0.8 (80%).

h. Click **OK**.

The expression should read:

MonthlyPayment: Pmt(0.06/12,30*12,[ListPrice]*0.8,0,0)

i. Open the Property Sheet for the MonthlyPayment field and change the format to **Currency**. Close the Property Sheet. Run the query.

Notice that the payment amounts are negative numbers (displayed in parentheses). You will edit the formula to change the negative payment values to positive.

j. Switch to Design View. Select the MonthlyPayment column and click **Builder**. Add a **minus sign (−)** to the left of [ListPrice] and click **OK**.

By adding the negative sign in front of Pmt, you ensure that the value is displayed as a positive number.

k. Run the query and examine the results. Adjust column widths as necessary.

The query displays a column containing the calculated monthly mortgage payment, formatted as currency, as shown in Figure 3.22.

l. Save and close the query. Keep the database open if you plan to continue with the next Hands-On Exercise. If not, close the database and exit Access.

Aggregate Functions

So far, you have learned to create calculations and build expressions for single value calculations. Many times, you want to know the total of a column or the average of a set of values. In these cases, you would use an aggregate function. An *aggregate function* performs a calculation on an entire column of data and returns a single value. One example of an aggregate function is Sum. If you wanted to add up or find the sum of an entire column of numbers, you would be creating aggregate data. Aggregate data enables you to see the data as a whole. Access refers to aggregate functions as Totals. Totals can be added to Datasheet view of a query, or they can be added to a query's Design view. Access provides two methods of adding aggregate function:

- The *Total row* enables you to use an aggregate function in one or more columns of a data table or a query result without having to change the design of your query.
- A *totals query* calculates subtotals for groups of records, whereas a Total row calculates grand totals for one or more columns (fields) of data.

For example, if you wanted to find the grand total of all sales, you use a Total row. However, if you wanted to subtotal sales by department or by sales rep, you use a totals query to group your records by the category and then sum the sales figures.

Based on the data type, different aggregate functions will be available for both the totals query and Total row. Only number and currency data types are eligible for use with the Sum aggregate function. Numeric fields are eligible for all of the functions, whereas Short Text fields would be eligible for the count function. A list of common aggregate functions is shown in Table 3.2.

TABLE 3.2 Common Aggregate Functions	
Function	**Description**
Avg (Average)	Calculates the average value for a column.
Count	Counts the number of values in a column.
Max (Maximum)	Returns the item with the highest value.
Min (Minimum)	Returns the item with the lowest value.
Sum	Totals the items in a column.

In the Property database, the average home price per county could be presented in a query or a report. This would give prospective buyers a good idea of home prices in their target counties. Almost every company or organization that uses a database will aggregate data.

In this section, you will learn how to create and work with aggregate functions. Specifically, you will learn how to use the Total row and create a totals query.

STEP 1 Adding Aggregate Functions to Datasheets

Aggregate data enables users to evaluate values in a single record to the aggregate of all the records. If you are considering buying a property in Story County, Iowa, for $150,000, and the average price of a property in that county is $450,000, you know you are getting a good deal (or buying a bad property).

Adding a Total row to a query is simple and has the advantage of displaying the totals along with displaying the individual records. Figure 3.23 shows the Total row added to Datasheet view of a query. In this image, the average of the List Price is displayed. The available aggregate functions are shown in the Price Per Sq Ft column.

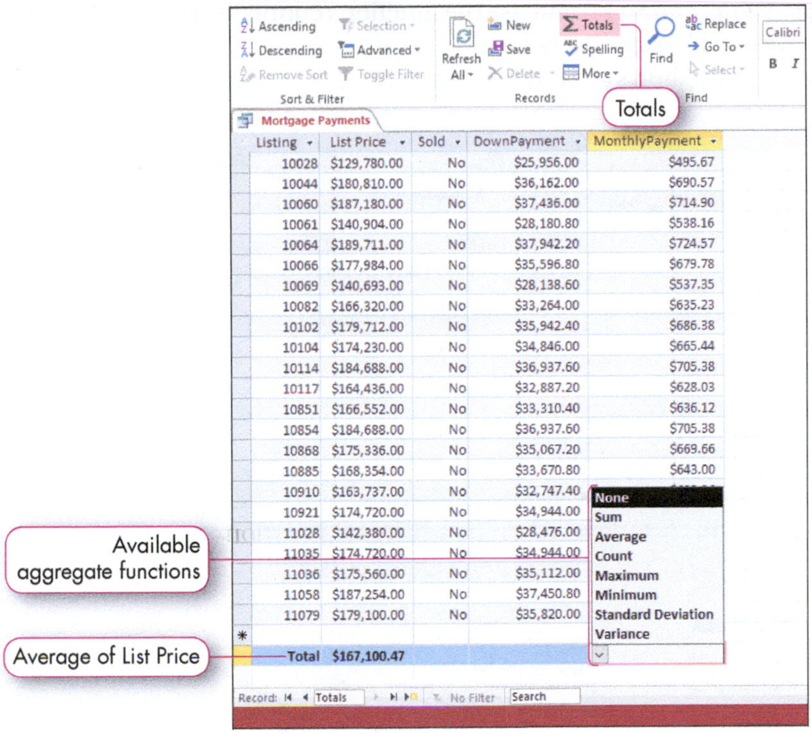

FIGURE 3.23 Total Row in Datasheet View

To add a Total row to the Datasheet view of a query or table, complete the following steps:

1. View the query or table in Datasheet view.
2. Click Totals in the Records group on the Home tab. The Total row is added at the bottom of the datasheet, below the new record row.
3. Select one of the aggregate functions (such as Average, Count, or Sum) in the new Total row by clicking in the cell and clicking the arrow.

Creating Queries with Aggregate Functions

Many times, you may require in-depth statistics that using a Total row does not provide. For example, instead of wanting to see the average sale price for houses, you may want to see the average sale price by city. Instead of seeing the average price for every item your store sells, you may want to see the average price for each category. Using the Total row, this is not feasible. Another limitation of the Total row is that it cannot provide aggregate data such as the average sale price, minimum sale price, or maximum sale price at the same time.

STEP 2 ## Create a Totals Query

Another way to display aggregate functions is by using a totals query. A totals query is created in Query Design and displays aggregate data when the query is run. This provides two distinct advantages over the Total row. The first enables you to show only the results of the aggregate functions (and not the detail), and the second to see statistics by category.

A totals query is particularly advantageous when a table or query has hundreds of records. Instead of showing detail that a Total row provides, a totals query displays the summary statistics for the entire table or query. For example, if you want to see the total number of listings, the average sale price, and the average home size in square feet for all properties in the table, you can use a totals query. The query will only include the fields Listings, Value, and Sq Ft, and use the functions count, average, and average in the Total row of each field, respectively.

Figure 3.24 shows a totals query in Design view, and Figure 3.25 shows the results.

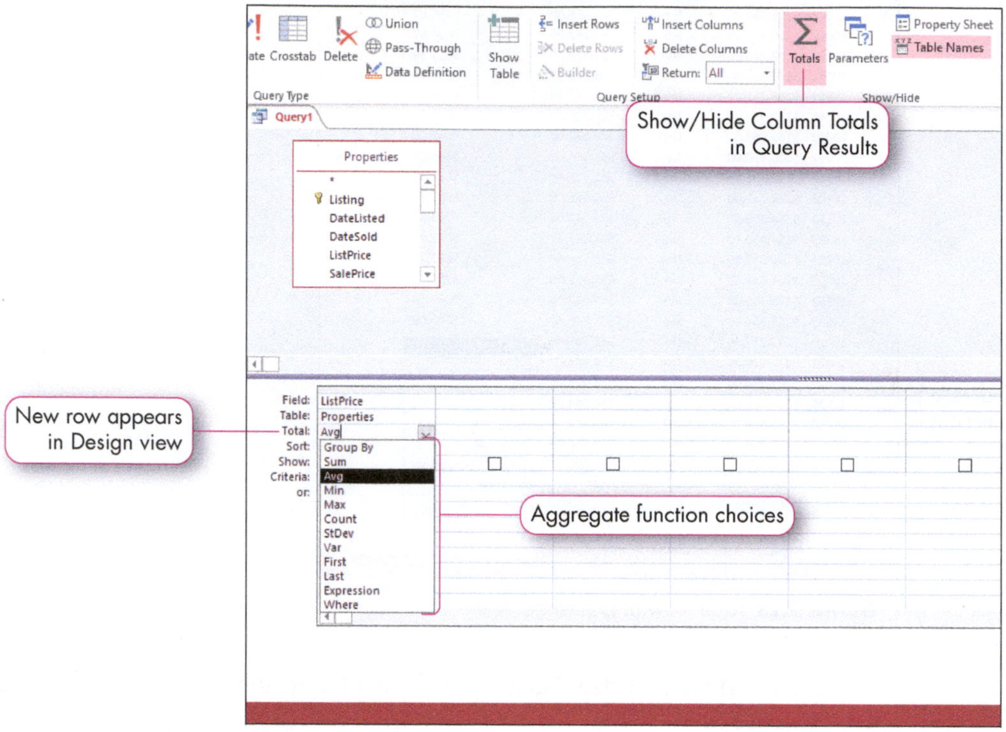

FIGURE 3.24 Totals Query Design View

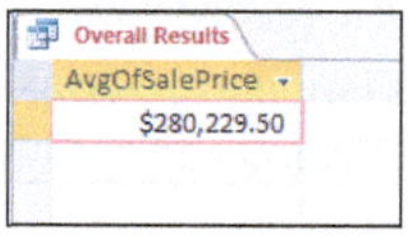

FIGURE 3.25 Totals Query Results

To create a totals query, complete the following steps:

1. Create a query in Design view using the fields for which you want to get statistics.
2. Click Totals in the Show/Hide group on the Design tab. A new Total row displays in the query design grid between the Table and Sort rows. Notice that it defaults to Group By.
3. Click Group By and select the aggregate function you want applied for each field.
4. Click the Field row of the field, click Property Sheet in the Show/Hide group on the Design tab, and adjust settings for each of the fields to meet your requirements.
5. Click Run in the Results group.

> **TIP: USE MULTIPLE AGGREGATE FUNCTIONS FOR THE SAME FIELD IN A QUERY**
>
> If you want to see the results of multiple aggregate functions for a single field, you can add the same field multiple times to a query. Display the Total row in Query design and select a different aggregate function for each column. When you run the query, you will see the results of each aggregate function in separate columns.

Add Grouping to a Totals Query

Grouping a query enables you to summarize the data by the values of a field. For example, instead of seeing overall averages, you may want to see the results for each county. In this case, add the County field as a grouping level to see statistics by County. To group an existing totals query, you will add the field you want to group by to the query in Design view. For readability, the field should be the first field in the query. Then, verify that the Total row displays Group By for the added field (see Figure 3.26), and run the query.

Figure 3.26 shows Design view of a totals query with five columns, the first of which is the grouping field. Figure 3.27 shows the results of this query. Notice that the resulting query shows one row for each county.

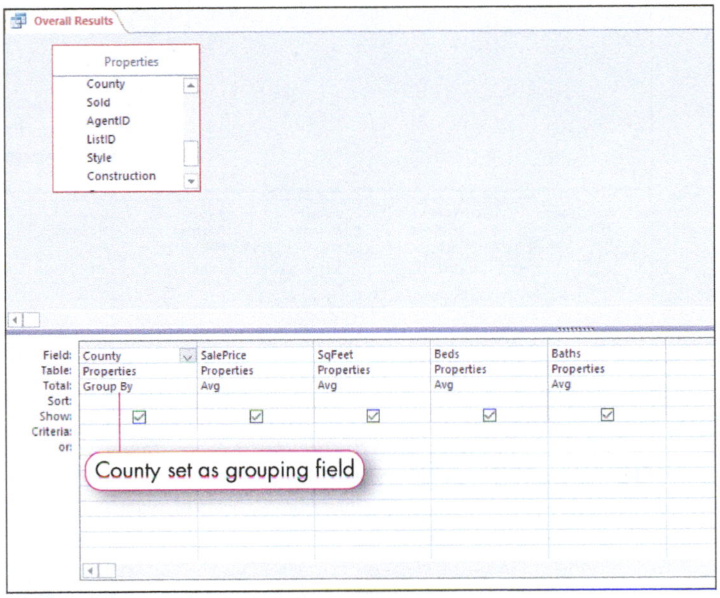

FIGURE 3.26 Grouped Totals Query Design View

County	AvgOfSalePrice	AvgOfSqFeet	AvgOfBeds	AvgOfBaths
Bergen	$220,431.12	2218.08163265306	3.12244897959184	1.63265306122449
Essex	$284,091.38	2844.50574712644	3.90804597701149	1.86206896551724
Hudson	$243,285.50	2645.23529411765	3.41176470588235	1.64705882352941
Mercer	$341,085.67	3242.675	4.45	2
Morris	$322,404.05	3105.6875	4.140625	1.890625
Passaic	$219,325.20	2049.03846153846	2.80769230769231	1.75
Sussex	$269,411.17	2968	4.5	2.1

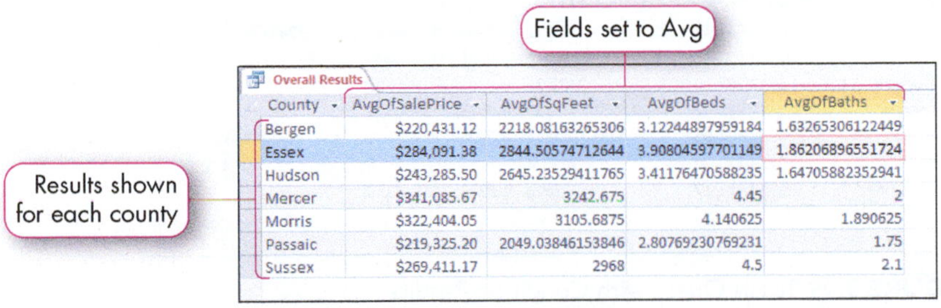

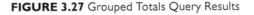

FIGURE 3.27 Grouped Totals Query Results

Add Conditions to a Totals Query

Totals queries can provide additional information when you add criteria. Criterion permits you to drill down to more specific information. For example, if you wanted to see the number of houses, average price, and average square feet for only the sold properties, grouped by county, you can add the Sold field to the query. Set the Sold field criteria to *Yes* to include in the query results only properties that have been sold.

To add conditions to an existing totals query, complete the following steps:

1. Double-click the field you want to limit by to add it to the design grid. The location of this field is not important, as it will not be displayed.
2. Select Where from the menu in the Total row.
3. Enter the condition.
4. Run the query.

Figure 3.28 shows a query with a condition added, and Figure 3.29 shows the results. In Figure 3.28, the Yes condition was added to the Sold field to so only Properties that were sold are added to the Aggregate query. Compare this to Figure 3.27 to see the change in results.

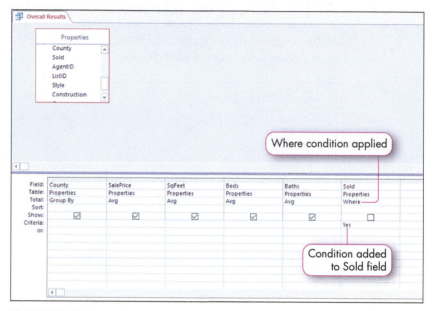

FIGURE 3.28 Totals Query with Condition Design View

FIGURE 3.29 Totals Query with Condition Results

> **TIP: MULTIPLE GROUPING LEVELS**
> At times, you may want to add multiple grouping fields. For example, instead of grouping by state, you might want to group by city. However, if you group by city, customers with the same city name in different states would be grouped together. For example, all 50 states have a location named Greenville. If you grouped by city, all customers with a city of Greenville, regardless of state, would appear as a group. This is probably not your intent. Instead, you probably would want to see results by city and state and, thus would want to add both fields to a query and select Group By.

Add a Calculated Field to a Totals Query

Calculated fields can also have aggregate functions applied to them. For example, you may want to calculate mortgage payments and see the average of your calculation (see Figure 3.30). The results of the query will resemble Figure 3.31. Note that you can also use any of the other methods shown earlier, so you can add grouping (as shown in the figures below) and format the field as required.

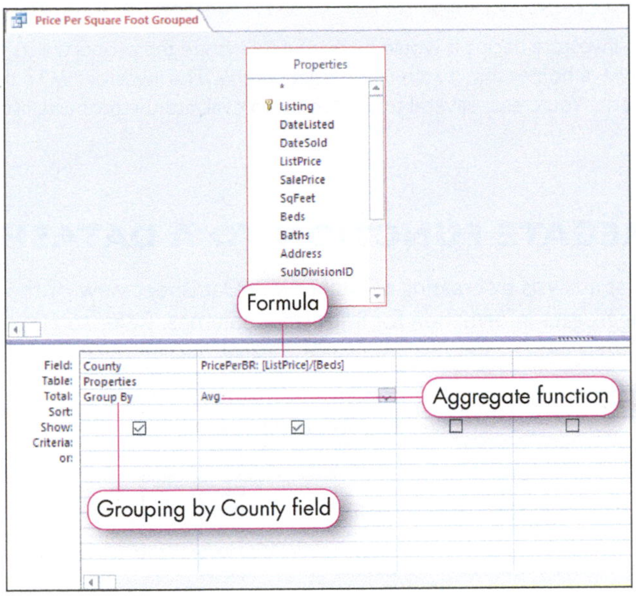

FIGURE 3.30 Adding Calculated Field to Totals Query

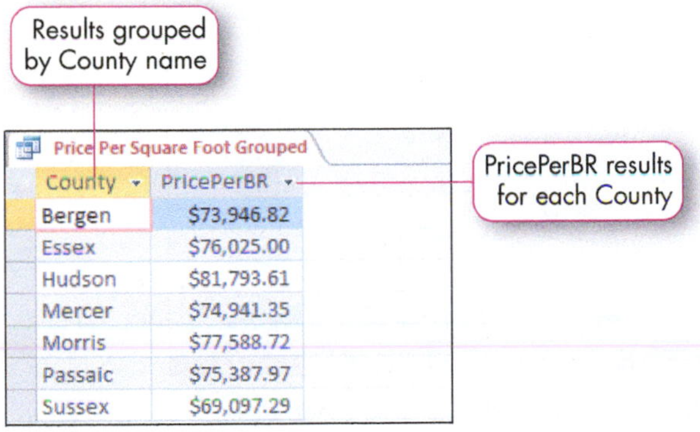

FIGURE 3.31 Calculated Field Results

Quick Concepts

7. Discuss the purpose of using aggregate functions. *p. 226*

8. Explain when you would use a Total row and when you would use a totals query. *p. 226*

9. Explain what is meant by a query that is "grouped by" state. *p. 229*

Hands-On Exercises

Skills covered: Display a
Total Row for a Query • Create
a Totals Query • Add Grouping to
a Totals Query • Add Conditions
to a Totals Query • Add a Calculated Field to a Totals Query

3 Aggregate Functions

The investors decide it would be helpful to analyze the property lists they purchased. Some of the lists do
not have homes that match their target criteria. The investors will either purchase new lists or alter their
criteria. You create several totals queries to evaluate the property lists.

STEP 1 ADD AN AGGREGATE FUNCTION TO A DATASHEET

You begin your property list analysis by creating a Total row in Datasheet view of the Mortgage Payments query. This
will give you a variety of aggregate information for important columns. Refer to Figure 3.32 as you complete Step 1.

Step b: Mortgage
Payments query opened

Step e: Average List Price

Step f: Count of Listing

Listing	List Price	DownPayment	MonthlyPayment
10016	$138,990.00	$27,798.00	$666.65
10025	$176,176.00	$35,235.20	$845.01
10064	$189,711.00	$37,942.20	$909.93
11035	$174,720.00	$34,944.00	$838.03
10002	$168,000.00	$33,600.00	$805.80
10004	$109,140.00	$21,828.00	$523.48
10024	$183,312.00	$36,662.40	$879.24
10104	$174,230.00	$34,846.00	$835.68
10066	$177,984.00	$35,596.80	$853.68
10082	$166,320.00	$33,264.00	$797.74
10114	$184,688.00	$36,937.60	$885.84
10117	$164,436.00	$32,887.20	$788.70
10008	$136,680.00	$27,336.00	$655.57
10044	$180,810.00	$36,162.00	$867.24
10061	$140,904.00	$28,180.80	$675.83
11028	$142,380.00	$28,476.00	$682.91
10069	$140,693.00	$28,138.60	$674.82
10854	$184,688.00	$36,937.60	$885.84
10921	$174,720.00	$34,944.00	$838.03
11036	$175,560.00	$35,112.00	$842.06
10010	$179,088.00	$35,817.60	$858.98
10014	$166,800.00	$33,360.00	$800.04
10019	$180,180.00	$36,036.00	$864.22
10028	$129,780.00	$25,956.00	$622.48
10060	$187,180.00	$37,436.00	$897.79
32	$167,100.47		

FIGURE 3.32 Totals Added to Datasheet View

a. Open *a03h2Property_LastFirst* if you closed it at the end of Hands-On Exercise 2 and
save it as **a03h3Property_LastFirst**, changing h2 to h3.

b. Open the **Mortgage Payments query** in Datasheet view.

c. Click **Totals** in the Records group on the Home tab.

d. Click the **cell** that intersects the Total row and the List Price column.

e. Click the **arrow** and select **Average** to display the average value of all the properties that
have not sold. Adjust column widths as necessary to ensure that all values are displayed.

The average list price of all properties is $167,100.47.

f. Click the **arrow** in the Total row in the Listing column and select **Count** from the list.

The count of properties in this datasheet is 32.

g. Compare your results to Figure 3.32. Save and close the query.

STEP 2 CREATE A TOTALS QUERY AND ADD GROUPING AND CONDITIONS

You create a totals query to help Don and Matt evaluate the properties in groups by the Name of the List. Refer to Figure 3.33 and Figure 3.34 as you complete Step 2.

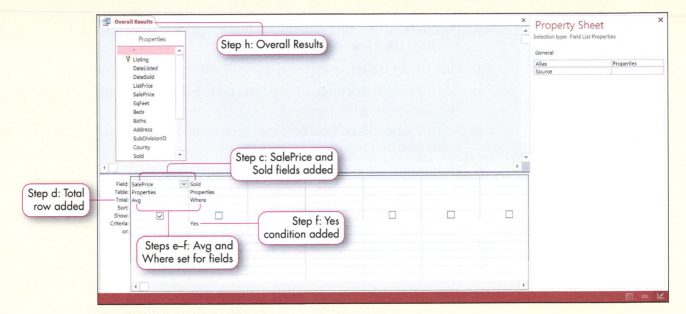

FIGURE 3.33 Overall Results Query

NameOfList	AvgOfSalePrice	Number Sold
Algernon Listings	$324,697.22	18
FastHouse	$288,314.50	6
Houses 4 Sale	$218,039.00	2
Local Listings	$341,085.67	9
Major Houses	$235,757.88	8
Trullo	$236,885.21	19
Wholesaler	$276,654.92	26

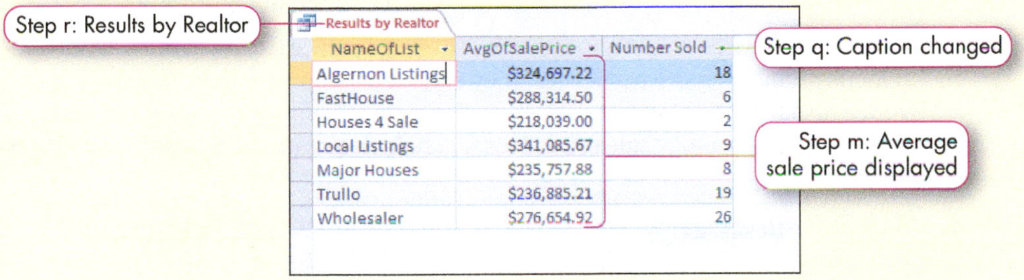

FIGURE 3.34 Results by Realtor Query Output

a. Click **Query Design** in the Queries group of the Create tab.

You create a new query in Query Design; the Show Table dialog box opens.

b. Click the **Properties table** in the Show Table dialog box and click **Add**. Close the Show Table dialog box.

c. Double-click the **SalePrice** and **Sold fields** to add them to the query.

d. Click **Totals** in the Show/Hide group of the Design tab to show the Total row.

A new row labeled Total displays in the query design grid, between the Table and Sort rows. Each field has Group By listed in the new row by default.

e. Click the **Group By arrow** in the SalePrice column Total row and select **Avg**.

f. Click the **Group By arrow** in the Sold column Total row and select **Where**. Type **Yes** in the Criteria row.

This criterion will limit the results to sold houses only.

g. Click the **SalePrice field** and click **Property Sheet** in the Show/Hide group. Change the SalePrice format to **Currency**. Close the Property Sheet. Run the query. Ensure each column width displays the full values for the column. Compare your results to Figure 3.34.

The results show an overall average of $280,229.50 for the sold properties in the database.

h. Click **Save** on the Quick Access Toolbar and type **Overall Results** in the Save As dialog box. Click **OK**. Close the query.

i. Click **Query Design** in the Query group of the Create tab to create a new query.

j. Add the **Properties table** and the **Lists table** from the Show Table dialog box. Close the Show Table dialog box.

k. Add the **NameOfList field** from the Lists table and the **SalePrice**, **Listing**, and **Sold fields** from the Properties table to the query.

l. Click **Totals** in the Show/Hide group to show the Total row.

A new row labeled Total displays between the Table and Sort rows.

m. Change the Total row for SalePrice to **Avg**.

n. Change the Total row for Listing to **Count**.

o. Change the Total row for Sold to **Where**. Type **Yes** in the Criteria row.

This criterion will limit the results to sold houses only.

p. Click the **SalePrice field** and click **Property Sheet** in the Show/Hide group. Change the SalePrice format to **Currency**.

q. Click the **Listing field** and change the caption to **Number Sold**. Close the Property Sheet. Run the query and widen the columns as shown in Figure 3.34.

Notice that Houses 4 Sale has the lowest average sale price. As Don and Matt are hoping to focus on inexpensive properties, they can focus on properties offered by this source. Notice also that the query results show the number of properties sold in each source, in addition to the average sale price. This will help determine which sources have been more effective.

r. Click **Save** on the Quick Access Toolbar and type **Results by Realtor** in the Save As dialog box. Click **OK**. Keep the query open for the next step.

STEP 3 ▸ ADD A CALCULATED FIELD TO A TOTALS QUERY

The previous query shows the average value of the properties by realtor. However, Don and Matt learned at the seminar they attended that the longer a property has been on the market, the better your chances of negotiating a better price. You will revise the query to show, on average, how long each realtor takes to sell a house. Refer to Figure 3.35 as you complete Step 3.

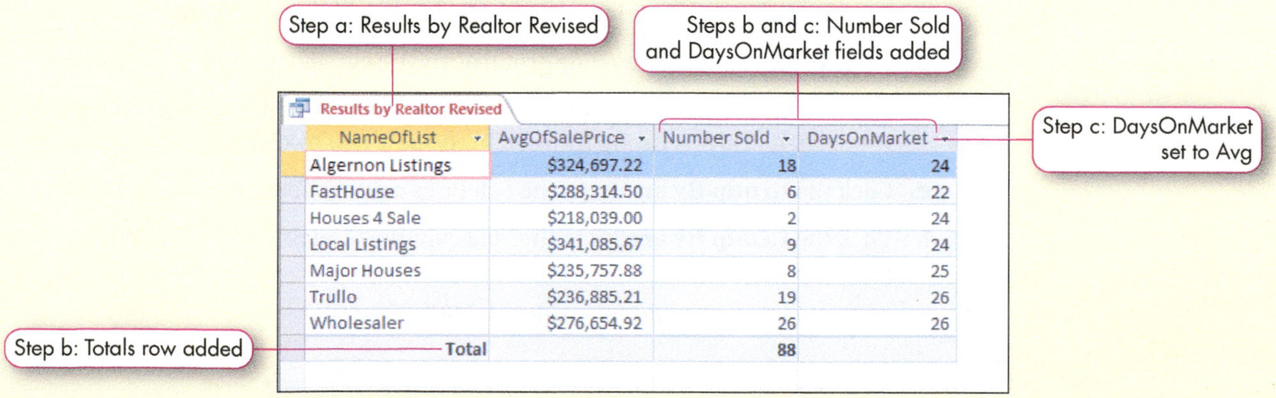

Step a: Results by Realtor Revised

Steps b and c: Number Sold and DaysOnMarket fields added

Step c: DaysOnMarket set to Avg

Results by Realtor Revised

NameOfList	AvgOfSalePrice	Number Sold	DaysOnMarket
Algernon Listings	$324,697.22	18	24
FastHouse	$288,314.50	6	22
Houses 4 Sale	$218,039.00	2	24
Local Listings	$341,085.67	9	24
Major Houses	$235,757.88	8	25
Trullo	$236,885.21	19	26
Wholesaler	$276,654.92	26	26
Total		88	

Step b: Totals row added

FIGURE 3.35 Results by Realtor Revised Query Output

a. Click the **File tab**, select **Save As**, and click **Save Object As**. Click **Save As** and type **Results By Realtor Revised**. Click **OK**.

You are making a copy of the previous query.

b. Click **Totals** in the Records group of the Home tab. Click in the Total row for the **Number Sold** column, click the **arrow**, and then select **Sum**.

The total number of houses sold (88) now displays at the bottom of the Number Sold column.

c. Switch to Design view. In the field row of the first blank column, type **DaysOnMarket: [DateSold]-[DateListed]** to create a new calculated field. Change the Total row from Group By to **Avg**.

The DaysOnMarket field will show the average number of days on the market for each sold listing.

d. Display the Property Sheet for the DaysOnMarket field and change the Format property to **Fixed**. Change the Decimal Places property to **0**. Close the Property Sheet.

e. Run the query and examine the DaysOnMarket field. Widen the columns and compare your results to Figure 3.35.

Houses 4 Sale listings have an average of 24 days on the market. Because this is in-line with their competitors, it lets you know they are neither fast nor slow with sales.

f. Save and close the query.

g. Close the database and exit Access. Based on your instructor's directions, submit a03h3Property_LastFirst.

Chapter Objectives Review

After reading this chapter, you have accomplished the following objectives:

1. Create a query with a calculated field.

- Expressions can contain a combination of arithmetic operators, constants, functions, and identifiers.
- Build expressions: Expressions must be written following Access rules. Correct syntax is very important.
- Understand the order of operations: Calculated fields follow the same order of operations as mathematical equations—parentheses, then exponentiation, then multiplication and division, and finally addition and subtraction.

2. Format calculated results.

- Calculated results may not have the format you want; change the properties of a calculated field using the Property Sheet.

3. Recover from common errors.

- Common errors include forgetting the colon in the appropriate location, spelling errors, and misuse of the order of operations.

4. Verify calculated results.

- Always check the results of your equation; Access will check for errors in the way something is written, but not logic errors.

5. Create expressions using the Expression Builder.

- The Expression Builder will enable you to create complex expressions by choosing fields and Built-In Functions. Click the Builder icon to open the tool.

6. Use Built-In Functions.

- Access includes 150 Built-In Functions, or predefined computations that perform complex calculations.

- Some functions require arguments, which are inputs (often fields or constants) given to a function.
- Calculate a loan payment with the Pmt function: The Pmt function accepts the rate, number of payments, and loan amount and calculates a loan payment. Two other arguments, future value and type, are typically left as zero.

7. Add aggregate functions to datasheets.

- Aggregate functions, including functions such as Sum, Avg, and Count, perform calculations on an entire column of data and return a single value. The Total row displays at the bottom of a query or table; it can perform any aggregate function on each column.

8. Create queries with aggregate functions.

- Create a totals query: Create a query as usual and click the Totals command in Design view.
- Add grouping to a totals query: Grouping enables you to summarize your data by the values of a field. For example, instead of showing overall averages, add County as a grouping field and see averages for each county.
- Add conditions to a totals query: Totals queries can provide additional information when you add criteria.
- Add a calculated field to a totals query: Similar to other queries, conditions can be added to totals queries, such as only showing listings with the Sold field equal to No.

Key Terms Matching

Match the key terms with their definitions. Write the key term letter by the appropriate numbered definition.

a. Aggregate function

b. Argument

c. Calculated field

d. Constant

e. Expression

f. Expression Builder

g. Function

h. Grouping

i. Order of operations

j. Pmt function

k. Property Sheet

l. Total row

m. Totals query

1. _____ A combination of elements that produce a value. **p. 204**

2. _____ A field that displays the result of an expression rather than data stored in a field. **p. 204**

3. _____ A way to display aggregate data when a query is run. **p. 226**

4. _____ A value that does not change. **p. 207**

5. _____ A method of summarizing data by the values of a field. **p. 229**

6. _____ A predefined computation that performs a complex calculation. **p. 218**

7. _____ An Access tool that enables you to create more complicated expressions. **p. 217**

8. _____ A function that calculates the loan payment given the rate, number of periods (also known as term), and the present value of the loan (the principal). **p. 220**

9. _____ The sequence by which operations are performed in a mathematical expression. **p. 208**

10. _____ A method to display aggregate function results as the last row in Datasheet view of a table or query. **p. 226**

11. _____ The input used to produce output for a function. **p. 218**

12. _____ The location where you change settings such as number format and number of decimal places. **p. 209**

13. _____ A calculation performed on an entire column of data that returns a single value. Includes functions such as Sum, Avg, and Count. **p. 226**

Multiple Choice

1. Which of the following *cannot* be used in a calculated field?

   (a) The number 12
   (b) An asterisk (*)
   (c) [HoursWorked] (a field in the current database)
   (d) The % symbol

2. When creating a calculation, which of the following would be identified as an error by Access?

   (a) A field name spelled wrong in a calculation
   (b) An incorrect formula (for example, adding two numbers instead of subtracting)
   (c) An order of operations error (for example, [HourlyPay]+2*[HoursWorked])
   (d) A missing colon in the expression (for example: TotalHours [OTHours]+[RegHours])

3. What is the result of the following expression?
$2 * 7 + 8 - 6/2$

   (a) 19
   (b) 8
   (c) 20
   (d) 12

4. Which of the following *cannot* be adjusted in the Property Sheet?

   (a) Caption
   (b) Mathematical expression
   (c) Number format (for example, displaying numbers as Currency)
   (d) Number of decimal places

5. Which of the following could *not* be done using an aggregate function?

   (a) Averaging a series of numbers
   (b) Calculating the payment amount of a loan
   (c) Counting the number of values that exist
   (d) Finding the smallest value

6. Which of the following *cannot* be added to a totals query?

   (a) Conditions
   (b) Grouping fields
   (c) Aggregate functions
   (d) All of these can be added to a totals query.

7. Which statement about a totals query is *true*?

   (a) A totals query is created in Datasheet view.
   (b) A totals query may contain several grouping fields but only one aggregate field.
   (c) A totals query is limited to only two fields, one grouping field, and one aggregate field.
   (d) A totals query may contain several grouping fields and several aggregate fields.

8. Which of the following statements is *true*?

   (a) A total order cost is an example of a common field to group by.
   (b) A last name is an example of a common field to group by.
   (c) For best results, add as many "group by" fields as possible.
   (d) None of these statements is true.

9. Which of the following about the Total row in Query design is *false*?

   (a) The Total row enables you to apply aggregate functions to the fields.
   (b) The Total row is hidden by default in all new queries.
   (c) The Total row is located between the Table and Sort rows.
   (d) The Total row applies only to non-numeric fields.

10. If you want to calculate aggregate statistics about graduation rates for students in a college database, which of the following would provide the *least* useful information if you were to group by it?

   (a) High School
   (b) Gender
   (c) Race
   (d) Driver's License Number

Practice Exercises

Conforto Insurance

The Conforto Insurance Agency is a mid-sized company with offices located across the country. Each employee receives an annual performance review. The review determines employee eligibility for salary increases and the annual performance bonus. The employee data is stored in an Access database, which is used to monitor and maintain employee records. Your task is to calculate the salary increase for each employee; you will also calculate the average salary for each position. Refer to Figure 3.36 as you complete this exercise.

Average Salary By Location	
Location	AvgOfSalary
Atlanta	$48,470.41
Boston	$45,597.50
Chicago	$47,113.68
Kansas City	$48,426.79
Los Angeles	$46,272.37
Miami	$45,839.00
New York	$47,116.71
Orlando	$42,537.89
Phoenix	$44,844.25
Pittsburgh	$50,579.36
San Francisco	$48,705.00

FIGURE 3.36 Average Salary by Location Results

a. Open *a03p1Insurance*. Save the database as **a03p1Insurance_LastFirst**.

b. Click the **Create tab** and click **Query Design** in the Queries group to create a new query. Select the **Employees table** and click **Add**. Select the **Titles table** and click **Add**. Click **Close** to close the Show Table dialog box.

c. Double-click the **LastName**, **FirstName**, **Performance**, and **Salary fields** from the Employees table to add them to the query. Double-click the **Increase field** from the Titles table to add it to the query.

d. Click the **Field row** of the first blank column in the query design grid and type **NewSalary: [Salary]+[Salary]*[Increase]** to create a calculated field that adds the existing salary to the increase.

e. Click **Run** in the Results group to run the query.

f. Switch to Design view. Ensure the NewSalary calculated field is selected. Click **Property Sheet** in the Show/Hide group to display the Property Sheet. Click the **Format property** in the Property Sheet. Click the **Format property arrow** and select **Currency**. Type **New Salary** in the Caption box.

g. Click **Run** in the Results group to view the results. Adjust column widths as necessary. Save the query as **Updated Salaries**. Close the query.

h. Click the **Create tab** and click **Query Design** in the Queries group to create a new query. Select the **Employees table** and click **Add**. Select the **Location table** and click **Add**. Click **Close** to close the Show Table dialog box.

i. Double-click the **Location field** from the Location table. Double-click the **Salary field** from the Employees table.

j. Click **Totals** in the Show/Hide group to display the Total row. Change the Total row for Salary to **Avg**. Leave the Location field set to Group By.

k. Click the **Salary field**. Click the **Format property** in the Property Sheet. Click the **Format property arrow** and select **Currency**.

l. Click **Run** in the Results group to view the results. Adjust column widths to display all the data. Save the query as **Average Salary By Location** and compare your results to Figure 3.36. Close the query.

m. Close the database and exit Access. Based on your instructor's directions, submit a03p1Insurance_LastFirst.

2 South Bend Yachts

South Bend Luxury Motor Yachts, a local boat seller, hired a new Chief Financial Officer (CFO). The new CFO, Rosta Marinova, asked the financing department to provide her with some summaries. She would like to determine how much financing the company is currently offering, offer financing with interest to customers, and see aggregate purchase statistics for local cities. Refer to Figure 3.37 as you complete this exercise.

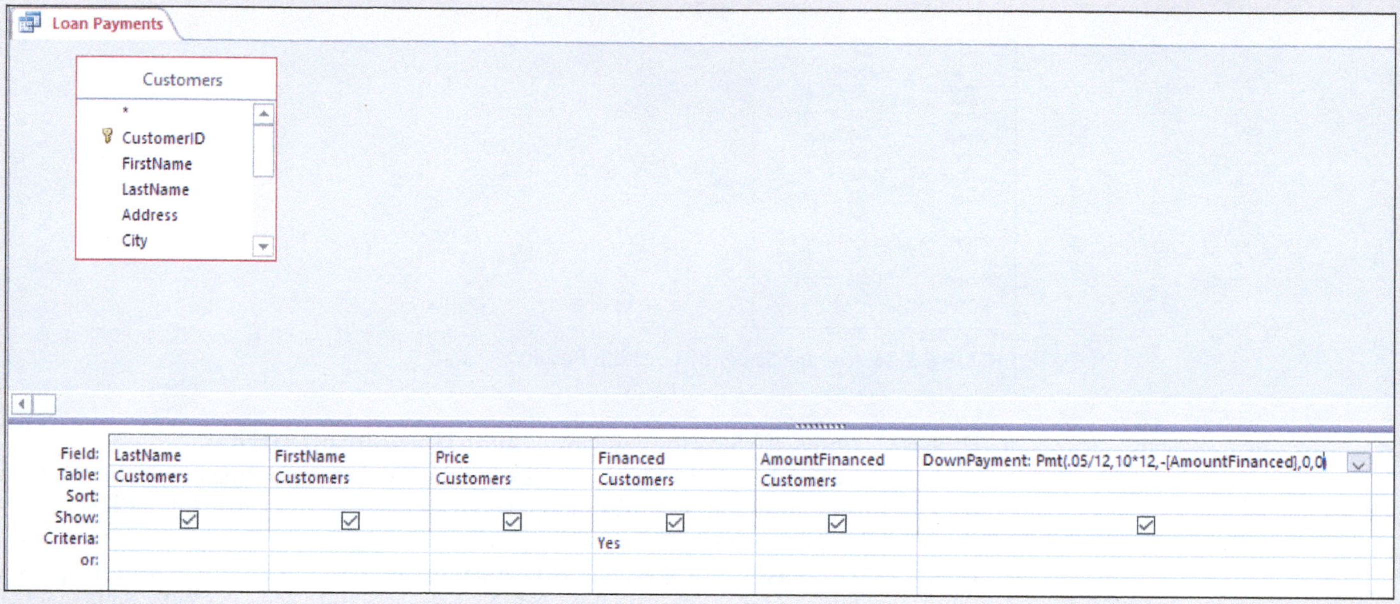

FIGURE 3.37 Loan Payments Design

a. Open *a03p2Yachts* and save the database as **a03p2Yachts_LastFirst**.

b. Click the **Create tab** and click **Query Design** in the Queries group to create a new query. Select the **Customers table** and click **Add**. Click **Close** to close the Show Table dialog box.

c. Double-click the **LastName**, **FirstName**, **Price**, **Financed**, and **AmountFinanced fields**.

d. Click the **Field row** of the first blank column and type
DownPayment: [Price]-[AmountFinanced].

e. Click **Run** in the Results group to run the query. Examine the results. Adjust column widths to display all data.

f. Click **Save** on the Quick Access Toolbar and type **Down Payment Amounts** as the Query Name in the Save As dialog box. Click **OK**.

g. Switch to Design view. Click the **Criteria row** for the Financed field and type **Yes**.

This will limit the results to financed boats. Boats that were not financed were paid for in full when purchased.

h. Click the **check box** on the Show row of the Financed field to deselect it, so it does not display when the query is run.

i. Sort the query by DownPayment in descending order by clicking the **Sort row** for the DownPayment field and selecting **Descending**.

j. Click **Property Sheet** in the Show/Hide group. In the Caption box, type **Down Payment**.

k. Click **Run** in the Results group to view the results. Adjust column widths to display all data. Notice that the column heading for the DownPayment field appears with a space in the name.

l. Save and close the query.

m. Click the **Create tab** and click **Query Design** in the Queries group to create a new query. Select the **Customers table** and click **Add**. Click **Close** to close the Show Table dialog box.

n. Double-click the fields **LastName**, **FirstName**, **Price**, **Financed**, and **AmountFinanced** to add them to the query.

o. Click the **Field row** of the first blank column. Click **Builder** in the Query Setup group to open the Expression Builder. Double-click **Functions** and select **Built-In Functions**. Select **Financial** and double-click **Pmt** in the Expression Values box.

p. Position the insertion point before the Pmt function. Type **MonthlyPayment:** to the left of the function (including the colon).

q. Click each argument to select it, and substitute the appropriate information below. Once you have entered the information, click **OK**.

- Type **0.06/12** for rate (6% interest, paid monthly).
- Type **10*12** for num_periods (10 year loan, 12 payments per year).
- Use **[AmountFinanced]** for the present_value.
- Use **0** in place of future_value and type.

r. Click **Property Sheet** in the Show/Hide group. In the Caption box, type **Monthly Payment**. Select **Currency** as the format.

s. Click the **Criteria row** for the Financed field and type **Yes.** Click the **Show check box** to deselect it.

t. Click **Run** in the Results group to examine the results.

u. Click **Totals** in the Show/Hide group on the Design tab. Click **Group By** in the Monthly Payment column, click the arrow, and then select **Avg**.

v. Switch to Design view. Add a **minus sign** in front of [AmountFinanced] in the DownPayment calculation to display the results as positive numbers. Compare your design to Figure 3.37.

w. Click **Run** in the Results group to examine the results. Adjust column widths to display all data. Save the query as **Loan Payments** and close the query.

x. Close the database and exit Access. Based on your instructor's directions, submit a03p2Yachts_LastFirst.

Mid-Level Exercises

1 Small Business Loans

ANALYSIS CASE

You are the manager of a regional business loan department for the U.S. Small Business Administration office. You have decided to evaluate whether Access could be used in place of the Excel worksheet you are currently using. You will create a blank desktop database, add a table, add some sample customers, and then import some recent data from an Excel spreadsheet. You will calculate the payments for the loans that are currently on the books by creating a query using the Pmt function. You will also summarize loans by the type of loan (M = Mortgage, C = Car, and O = Other).

a. Open Access and create a new blank desktop database named **a03m1Loans_LastFirst**.

b. Switch to Design view. Type **Customers** in the Save As dialog box and click **OK**.

c. Change the first Field Name to **CustomerID** and accept AutoNumber as the Data Type. Type **Company** in the second row and press **Tab**. Accept Short Text as the Data Type. Type **FirstName** in the third row and press **Tab**. Accept Short Text as the Data Type.

d. Add LastName, City, State, and Zip as fields selecting Short Text as the data type for each field.

e. Verify that the CustomerID field is set as the primary key.

f. Switch to Datasheet view. Click **Yes** to save the table. Add the records as shown in the following table. Note that Access will assign an ID. Once you have typed the records, close the Customers table.

Company	FirstName	LastName	City	State	Zip
Jones and Co	Robert	Paterson	Greensboro	NC	27401
Elements, Inc.	Merve	Kana	Paterson	NJ	07505
Godshall Meats, LLC	Francisco	De La Cruz	Beverly Hills	CA	90210

g. Click the **External Data tab** and click **New Data Source** in the Import & Link group. Point to **From File** and click **Excel**. Click **Browse** to locate the *a03m1Loans.xlsx* spreadsheet. Select the workbook and click **Open** at the bottom of the dialog box.

h. Ensure that *Import the source data into a new table in the current database* is selected and click **OK**. Click **Next** three times, accepting the defaults, until you are asked to add a primary key. Click the **Choose my own Primary Key option** and ensure **LoanID** is selected. Click **Next** once more and click **Finish**, accepting Loans as the table name. Click **Close** in the Get External Data dialog box.

i. Open the Loans table in Design view. Select the **InterestRate field** and change the format to **Percent**. Change the field size for the CustomerID field to **Long Integer**. Save and close the table, selecting **Yes** when prompted that some data may be lost.

j. Click the **Database Tools tab** and click **Relationships** in the Relationships group. Add both tables to the Relationships window and close the Show Table dialog box.

k. Drag the **CustomerID field** from the Customers table and drop it onto the **CustomerID field** in the Loans table. Check the **Enforce Referential Integrity check box** in the Edit Relationships dialog box to select it and click **Create**. Save and close the Relationships window.

l. Create a query in Design view using the two tables. Add the **Company field** from the Customers table and the **LoanID, Amount, InterestRate, Term**, and **LoanClass fields** from the Loans table. Sort the query by LoanID in ascending order. Save the query as **Loan Payments**.

m. Add a calculated field named **Payment** in the first blank column to calculate the loan payment for each loan, using the Expression Builder. Use the Pmt function. Insert the appropriate field names in place of the placeholder arguments. Assume that the loans have monthly payments (12 payments per year). Ensure that the payment displays as a positive number. Run the query. The first loan should have a value of 472.25725417464 . . . (the extra decimal places will be removed shortly).

> **TROUBLESHOOTING:** If you cannot see the fields from your current query, ensure that you have saved the query. Try closing and reopening the query.

n. Switch to Design view and change the format for the Payment field to **Currency**. Run the query again to verify your change.

o. Click **Totals** in the Records group on the Home tab. Change the value for the Total row for the Amount column to **Sum** and the values for the InterestRate and Term to **Average**. Adjust column widths as necessary. Save and close the query.

p. Create a copy of Loan Payments. Save the new query as **Loan Payments Summary**.

q. Open the Loan Payments Summary query in Design view and rearrange the columns as follows: LoanClass, LoanID, Amount, and InterestRate. Delete columns Company, Term, and Payment. Click **Totals** in the Show/Hide group. Change the Total row for LoanID field to **Count**, for the Amount field to **Sum**, and for the InterestRate field to **Avg**. Run the query.

r. Switch to Design view and display the Property Sheet. For the LoanID field, change the caption to **Loans**. For the Amount field, change the caption to **Total Amount** and change the format to **Currency**. For the InterestRate field, change the caption to **Avg Interest Rate** and change the format to **Percent**. Run the query. Adjust column widths to display all data. Save and close the query.

s. Close the database and exit Access. Based on your instructor's directions, submit a03m1Loans_LastFirst.

2 Investment Properties

MyLab IT Grader

You oversee Dysan Investment's database, which contains all of the information on the properties your firm has listed and sold. Your task is to determine the length of time each property was on the market before it sold. You also have been tasked with calculating the sales commission from each property sold. Two agents will receive commission on each transaction: the listing agent and the selling agent. You also will summarize the sales data by employee and calculate the average number of days each employee's sales were on the market prior to selling and the total commission earned by the employees.

a. Open *a03m2Homes*. Save the database as **a03m2Homes_LastFirst**.

b. Create a new query, add the Agents, Properties, and SubDivision tables, and then add the following fields: from the Agents table, add the LastName field; from the Properties table, the DateListed, DateSold, SalePrice, SellingAgent, and ListingAgent fields; and from the SubDivision table, the Subdivision field.

c. Add criteria to the table to ensure that the DateSold field is not empty (in other words, properties that have not been sold). You will need to use a condition involving Null to accomplish this. Format the SalePrice field as **Currency**. Save the query as **Sales Report**.

d. Create a calculated field using the Expression Builder named **DaysOnMarket** by subtracting DateListed from DateSold. This will calculate the number of days each sold property was on the market when it sold. Add a caption of **Days on Market**.

e. Calculate the commissions for the selling and listing agents using two calculated fields. The listing commission rate is 3.5% of the sale price and the selling commission rate is 2.5% of the sale price. You can type these in directly or use the Expression Builder. Name the newly created fields **ListComm** and **SellComm**. Add captions of **Listing Commission** and **Selling Commission** and format the fields as **Currency**.

f. Run the query. Adjust column widths to display all data. Display the Total row. Calculate the average number of days on the market, and the sum for the SalePrice and the two commission fields. Adjust column widths so all values are visible, and save and close the query.

g. Create a copy of the Sales Report query named **Sales Summary by Last Name**. Remove the DateListed, SellingAgent, ListingAgent, and Subdivision fields.

h. Display the Total row. Group by LastName and change the DateSold field Total row to **Where**, so the condition carries over. Show the sum of SalePrice, the average of DaysOnMarket, and the sum for both ListComm and SellComm. Change the caption for the SalePrice field to **Total Sales** and format the DaysOnMarket field as **Fixed**. Run the query. Adjust column widths to display all data.

i. Adjust the Total row in Datasheet view so it shows the sum of TotalSales. Adjust column widths to display all data. Save and close the query.

j. Create a copy of the Sales Summary by Last Name query named **Sales Summary by Subdivision** and open the query in Design view. Remove the LastName field. Add the Subdivision field to the query and ensure the Total row is set to Group By. Sort the query results on the DaysOnMarket field in Ascending order. Limit the results to only return the top five values. (Hint: look in the Query Setup group of the Design tab).

k. Run the query and ensure only the top 5 values display. Save and close the query.

l. Close the database and exit Access. Based on your instructor's directions, submit a03m2Homes_LastFirst.

Running Case

New Castle County Technical Services

New Castle County Technical Services (NCCTS) provides technical support for a number of local companies. Part of their customer service evaluation involves logging how calls are closed and a quick, one-question survey given to customers at the end of a call, asking them to rate their experience from 1 (poor) to 5 (excellent). Since the last time you worked with the database, additional call data has been logged. You are now being asked to create queries to help evaluate the effectiveness of their performance.

a. Open *a03r1NCCTS* and save the database as **a03r1NCCTS_LastFirst**.

b. Open the Reps table in Datasheet view. Locate record 8, fill in your last name as the rep's last name, and your first name as the rep's first name. Close the Reps table.

c. Create a new query in Design view. Add the Reps table and the Calls table to the query. Select the rep first and last names from the Reps table, and the CallID and CustomerSatisfaction fields from the Calls table.

d. Group by the RepFirst and RepLast fields. Display the count of the CallID field and average for the CustomerSatisfaction field.

e. Change the caption for the CallID field to **Num Calls**.

f. Format the CustomerSatisfaction average in Standard format and change the caption to **Avg Rating**.

g. Add a new calculated field named **AvgResponse**. Subtract the OpenedDate from the Closed-Date. Format the field as **Fixed**. Display the average for this field.

h. Run the query. Adjust column widths to ensure all data are displayed. Save the query as **Tech Ratings** and close the query.

i. Create a new query in Design view. Add the CallTypes, CallID, and Calls tables. Select the Description field from the Call Types table, and the CallID and CustomerSatisfaction field from the Calls table.

j. Group by the Description field. Display the count of the CallID field and average for the CustomerSatisfaction field.

k. Change the caption for the CallID field to **Num Calls**.

l. Format the CustomerSatisfaction average in Standard format and change the caption to **Avg Rating**.

m. Run the query. Adjust column widths to display all data. Save the query as **Call Type Effectiveness** and close the query.

n. Create a new query in Design view. Add the Customers, CallID, and Calls tables. Select the CompanyName field from the Customers table, and the CallID and CustomerSatisfaction field from the Calls table.

o. Group by the CompanyName field. Display the count of the CallID field and average for the CustomerSatisfaction field.

p. Format the CustomerSatisfaction average in Standard format and change the caption to **Avg Rating**.

q. Change the caption for the CallID field to **Num Calls**.

r. Run the query. Display the Total row. Show the sum of the Num Calls column. Adjust column widths to display all data.

s. Save the query as **Customer Happiness** and close the query.

t. Close the database and exit Access. Based on your instructor's directions, submit a03r1NCCTS_LastFirst.

Disaster Recovery

Too Many Digits

This chapter introduced you to calculated fields and totals queries. Open the database *a03d1Interest* and save the database as **a03d1Interest_LastFirst**. Your colleague, Jenny Yun, is having issues with her queries and has asked you for help fixing the issues. Open the Average Balance by Location query in Datasheet view. Notice the Locations are repeated several times in the query result. Group the query by the Location field to fix the query so that an average for the Balance is displayed for each location.

Next, open the Five Year Anniversary Query in Design view. Observe the Parameter Query message for OpeningDate. Resolve the issue with the expression in the DaysOpen calculated field. The expression should calculate the number of days the account has been open from January 1, 2020, which is the company's anniversary. The criteria for that field has been set so they will be able to recognize any clients who have been account holders for 5 years or more.

Finally, open the Monthly Interest Payments query in Datasheet view. Notice the multiple digits to the right of the decimal in the MonthlyInterest column; there should only be two digits. Search the Internet or Access Help to find further information about the round function, a function that will resolve this rounding problem. You only want to display two digits to the right of the decimal. Display the Total row in Datasheet view and display the total of the MonthlyInterest field. Adjust column widths as necessary. Save and close the query. Close the database and exit Access. Based on your instructor's directions, submit a03d1Interest_LastFirst.

Capstone Exercise

Brilton Madley Games

Brilton Madley, a board game manufacturer, hired a new CEO. She asked for your assistance in providing summaries of data that took place before she started with the company. To help her with her strategic planning, you will create queries to perform data analysis. Based on your meeting, you plan on creating four queries. One query will find orders with minor delays. Another query will summarize company revenue and cost by country. A third query will be used to help evaluate payments made by customers on their orders. The final query will calculate the total sales by sales representative title.

Database File Setup

You will open the Brilton Madley games database, use Save As to make a copy of the database, and then use the new database to complete this capstone exercise. You will add yourself as a Sales Representative to the employee table.

1. Open *a03c1Games* and save the database as **a03c1Games_LastFirst**.
2. Open the Sales Reps table. Add yourself as a sales rep. Fill in all information, including the RepID field. Set your Title to **Managing Partner**, salary to $105,144, and the country field to **United States**.
3. Close the Sales Reps table.

Shipping Efficiency Query

You will create a query to calculate the number of days between the date an order was placed and the date the order was shipped for each order. The result of your work will be a list of orders that took more than 30 days to ship. The salespeople will be required to review the records and report the source of the delay for each order. The CEO feels there may be issues with one of the products and would like data to back that up.

4. Create a query using Query Design. Add the Customers and Orders tables. From the Customers table, include the fields FirstName, LastName, and Phone (in that order). From the Orders table, include the fields OrderID, OrderDate, and ShippedDate (in that order).
5. Run the query and examine the records. Save the query as **Shipping Efficiency**.
6. Add a calculated field named **DaysToShip** to calculate the number of days taken to fill each order. (Hint: the expression will include the OrderDate and ShippedDate fields; the results will not contain negative numbers.)
7. Run the query and examine the results. Does the data in the DaysToShip field look accurate? Save the query.
8. Add criteria to limit the query results to include only orders that took more than 30 days to ship.
9. Add the Quantity field from the Orders table and the ProductName field from the Products table to the query (in that order). Sort the query by ascending LastName.
10. Add the caption **Days to Ship** to the DaysToShip field. Switch to Datasheet view to view the results. Adjust column widths to display all data.
11. Save and close the query.

Revenue and Cost by Country Query

The CEO is considering the financial impact of shipping to other countries. She asked for a query showing the total revenue and total cost for each country to which orders were shipped. She hopes to understand the distribution of revenue across the world.

12. Create a query using Query Design and add the Customers, Orders, and Products tables. Add the Country field from the Customers table. Set the field's Total row to **Group By**. Save the query as **Revenue and Cost by Country**.
13. Add a calculated field in the second column. Name the field **TotalRevenue**. This field should multiply the quantity ordered (from the Orders table) by the unit price for that item (from the Products table). Format the calculated field as Currency and change the caption to **Total Revenue**. Change the Total row for the TotalRevenue field to **Sum**.
14. Add a calculated field in the third column. Name the field **TotalCost**. The field should multiply the quantity ordered (from the Orders table) by the unit cost for that item (from the Products table). Format the calculated field as Currency and add a caption of **Total Cost**. Change the Total row to **Sum**.
15. Run the query. Examine the results. Save the query. Return to Design view.
16. Add the OrderDate field and criteria to that field so that only orders made between 7/1/2018 and 12/31/2018 are displayed. Change the Total row to **Where**. This expression will display only orders that were completed during the second half of 2018.
17. Run the query and view the results. Adjust column widths to display all data. Save and close the query.

Customer Payments Query

The CEO wants the salespeople to discuss financing with customers. In order to do so, she asked you to create a query showing the impact on price for prior orders. This way, the reps can give customers a comparison with an order they have already placed. For the moment, she is considering a 5% interest rate, paid over 12 months. She wants you to leave the results as negative numbers.

18. Create a copy of the Revenue and Cost by Country query named **Customer Payments**.

19. Switch to Design view of the new query and remove the Country, TotalCost, and OrderDate fields. Add the FirstName and LastName fields. Move the TotalRevenue field to the end. Rename the TotalRevenue field to OrderTotal. Change the caption to **Order Total**.

20. Add a new field using the Expression Builder named **SamplePayment**. Insert the Pmt function with the following parameters:
    - Use **0.05/12** for the rate argument (5% interest, paid monthly).
    - Use the number **12** for the num_periods argument (12 months).
    - Use the calculated field **[OrderTotal]** for the present_value.
    - Use the value **0** for both future_value and type.

21. Change the Total row to **Expression** for the SamplePayment field.

22. Change the Format for the SamplePayment field to **Currency**.

23. Run the query and examine the results. Adjust column widths to display all data. The results appear as negative numbers, as requested. Save and close the query.

Revenue by Sales Rep Query

The company is planning on evaluating the success of each tier of sales representative. The previous CEO had been considering raises at each level, but he was working from older data. You will provide a list of total revenue earned by each sales rep tier for the year before the current CEO started to best inform her decision making.

24. Create a copy of the Revenue and Cost by Country query named **Revenue by Sales Rep**.

25. Switch to Design view of the new query and remove the entire Customers table, the TotalCost, and Order-Date fields. Add the Sales Rep table. Add the Title field from the Sales Rep table and move it to the front of the TotalRevenue field.

26. Run the query and examine the summary records; there should be four sales rep titles listed.

27. Switch to Design view and change the sort order so that the title with the highest TotalRevenue is first and the title with the lowest TotalRevenue is last.

28. Run the query and verify the results.

29. Save and close the query.

30. Close the database and exit Access. Based on your instructor's directions, submit a03c1Games_LastFirst.

Basic Forms and Reports

LEARNING OUTCOMES
You will develop and modify forms to input and manage data.
You will create and modify reports to present information.

OBJECTIVES & SKILLS: After you read this chapter, you will be able to:

Create Basic Forms to Simplify Data Management

OBJECTIVE 1: CREATE FORMS USING FORM TOOLS   250
Identify a Record Source, Use the Form Tool, Work with a Subform, Create a Split Form, Create a Multiple Items Form, Create a Navigation Form

OBJECTIVE 2: MODIFY FORMS   258
Edit Data in Form View, Use Layout View to Modify a Form Design, Adjust Column Widths in a Form, Delete a Form Field, Add a Form Field, Modify Form Controls

OBJECTIVE 3: USE THE FORM LAYOUT CONTROL   261
Modify a Form Layout

OBJECTIVE 4: SORT RECORDS IN A FORM   263
Sort Records in a Form

HANDS-ON EXERCISE 1   264

Create Basic Reports to Present Information

OBJECTIVE 5: CREATE REPORTS USING REPORT TOOLS   272
Use the Report Tool, Use the Report Wizard

OBJECTIVE 6: USE REPORT VIEWS   277
Use Print Preview, Export a Report

OBJECTIVE 7: MODIFY A REPORT   278
Add a Field to a Report, Remove a Field from a Report, Adjust Column Widths in a Report, Change Orientation, Apply a Theme

OBJECTIVE 8: SORT AND GROUP RECORDS IN A REPORT   281
Sort and Group Records in a Report

HANDS-ON EXERCISE 2   283

CASE STUDY | Coffee Shop Starts New Business

Coffee shop owner Ryung Park decided to use her knowledge of the coffee and retail industries to sell her specialty products to businesses around the country. She created an Access database to help track her customer, product, and order information.

Ryung created a database with tables to store data for customers, products, sales reps, and orders. She is currently using these tables to enter data and retrieve information. However, Ryung realizes that forms have an advantage over tables because they can be designed to display one record at a time—this can reduce potential data-entry errors. It is simpler to add or edit a single record on screen rather than to try to manage records in a very large table containing hundreds or thousands of records. Forms also offer special functionality in some cases that tables do not. Ryung wants to create several forms and reports to facilitate data management and to review important business information. Ryung asked you to help create the new forms and reports that she needs.

CHAPTER 4

Simplifying Data Entry and Producing Information

Sfio Cracho/Shutterstock

FIGURE 4.1 Coffee Shop Enhanced Database with Forms and Reports

CASE STUDY | Coffee Shop Starts New Business

Starting File	Files to be Submitted
a04h1Coffee	**a04h2Coffee_LastFirst** **a04h2Products_LastFirst.pdf**

MyLab IT Grader An alternate version of this project is available as a MyLab IT Grader Assessment

Create Basic Forms to Simplify Data Management

Most Access database applications use forms rather than tables for data entry and for viewing information. A *form* is a database object used to view, add, or edit data in a table. Three main reasons exist for using forms rather than tables for working with data:

- You are less likely to edit the wrong record by mistake, which is easy to do in a large table containing many records.
- You can create a form that displays data from more than one table simultaneously.
- You can create customized Access forms to resemble the paper (or other types of) forms that users employ in their data entry processes.

When you are adding or editing data using a table with many records, you may select and edit the wrong record accidentally. A form is less likely to allow this type of error because many form types restrict entry to one record at a time. This enables you to focus on working with a single record rather than viewing many records at the same time.

Some forms require more than one table as their basis. For example, you may want to view a customer's details (name, address, email, phone, etc.) as well as all the orders the customer placed at the same time. This would require using data from both the Customers and the Orders tables (when there is a relationship set between them) in one form. Such a form enables a user to view two sources at the same time and make changes—additions, edits, or deletions—to one or both sources of data. When a change is made in the form, the data in the underlying table (or tables) are affected. A form is really a mirror image of the data in the tables and simply presents a user-friendly interface for users of the database.

Access forms can be designed to emulate the paper documents already used by an organization. When paper forms are currently used to collect data, it is a good idea to customize the electronic forms to resemble the paper forms. This will make the data entry process more efficient and ease the transition from paper to electronic form.

In this section, you will learn the basics of form design. You will discover multiple methods to create and modify Access forms.

STEP 1 Creating Forms Using Form Tools

Access provides a variety of options for creating forms. You will eventually develop a preference for one or two types of form layouts, but keep in mind that you have a good variety of options, if needed. You will want your forms to balance ease of use with the power to be effective.

Access provides 14 different tools for creating forms. You can find these options in the Forms group on the Create tab. The Forms group contains four of the most common form tools (Form, Form Design, Blank Form, and Form Wizard), a list of Navigation forms, and More Forms. The Navigation list provides six templates to create a user interface for a database; the More Forms list provides four additional form tools (Multiple Items, Datasheet, Split Form, and Modal Dialog).

A list of many of the Form tools available in Access is found in Table 4.1. Some tools will not be covered in detail, because they are not commonly used or because they are beyond the scope of this chapter (for example, Form Design, Blank Form, and Modal Dialog Form). Use Microsoft Access Help to find more information about Form tools that are not covered in this chapter.

TABLE 4.1	Form Tools in Access
Form Tool	**Use**
Form	Creates a form with a stacked layout that displays all the fields in the record source.
Form Design	Creates a new blank form in Design view.
Blank Form	Creates a new blank form in Layout view.
Form Wizard	Creates a custom form based on your answers to a series of step-by-step questions.
Navigation	Creates handy user-interface forms that enable users to switch between various forms and reports in a database. Six different Navigation form layouts are available from the list.
Split Form	Creates a two-part form with a stacked layout in one section and a tabular layout in the other.
Multiple Items	Creates a tabular layout form that includes all the fields from the record source.
Datasheet	Creates a form that resembles the datasheet of a table or query.
Modal Dialog	Creates a custom dialog box that requires user input that is needed for a database object.

> **TIP: USABILITY TESTING**
> After a database object (such as a form) is finalized, it should be tested by both the database designer and the end users. The designer should be certain that the form meets any requirements the users have given him or her. The designer should also browse through the records to make sure the values in all records (and not just the first record) display correctly. After testing is completed by both the designer and end users, the form should be modified and tested again before it is deployed with the database.

Ideally, a form should simplify data entry and editing. Creating a form is a collaborative process between the database designer and the end users. This process continues throughout the life of the form because the data management needs of an organization may change over time. Forms designed long ago to collect data for a new customer account may not include an email or a website field; both the customer table and its associated form would have to be modified to include these fields. The designer needs to strike a balance between collecting the data required for use by the database and cluttering the form with extraneous fields. The database users generally offer good opinions about which fields should be on a form and how the form should behave. If you listen to their suggestions, your forms will function more effectively, the users' work will be easier, and the data will contain fewer data-entry errors.

Similar to designing a table, you can make a sketch in advance to determine which fields are required in a form and what the order of the fields should be. Your form design should be approved by the client or users for whom you are building it before actual development begins.

Identify a Record Source

Before you create a form, you must identify the record source. A *record source* (or data source) is the table or query that supplies the records for a form or report. Use a table if you want to include all the records from a single table. Create a query first and use it as the record source if you want to filter the records in the source table, combine records from two or more related tables, or if you do not want to display all fields from the table(s) on your form. For example, if you want to create a form that displays customers from a single state only, you should base the form on a query.

TIP: MODIFY DATA SOURCES

To modify a data (record) source for a form that has already been created, from Layout view or Design view, open the form's Property sheet, click the Data tab, and then click in the Record Source property box. Click the arrow, and from the list, select an object as the new data source.

Use the Form Tool

The most common tool for creating forms, the *Form tool*, is used to create data entry forms for customers, employees, products, and other types of tables. A usable form can be created easily: select a table or query in the Navigation Pane and click Form in the Forms group on the Create tab.

Based on the table or query selected, Access automatically creates a new form in a stacked layout. A *stacked layout* displays fields in a vertical column for one record at a time, as shown in Figure 4.2. The other type of layout you can use is a *tabular layout*, which displays data horizontally across the page.

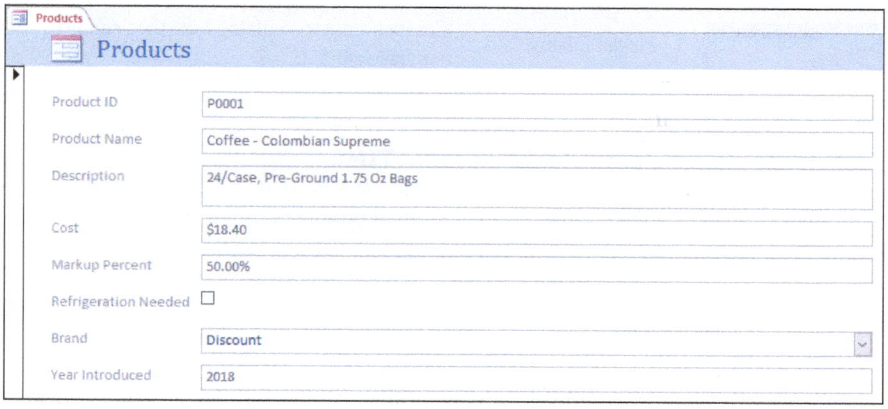

FIGURE 4.2 Form with a Stacked Layout

Understand Controls

Controls are the text boxes, buttons, labels, and other tools you use to add, edit, and display the data in a form or report. Notice in Figure 4.3 that each field has a label on the left and a text box on the right, both of which are referred to as controls. The form controls that display values are generally text box controls, and the boxes describing those values are label controls. In Figure 4.3, Product ID, Product Name, Description, etc. are label controls. The boxes containing the values for each field (P0001, Coffee–Colombian Supreme, etc.) are text box controls.

A *layout control* provides guides to help keep controls aligned horizontally and vertically and give your form a neat appearance, as shown in Figure 4.3. There may be times when you will select controls to format, delete, or move them during your design process. To select an individual control, click the text box or the label as needed.

You can select multiple controls to work with simultaneously, by completing one of the following methods:

- Click the first control, press and hold Ctrl, and then click the additional controls you want to include in the selection.

- Press Ctrl+A to select all the controls on a form at one time.

- If a layout control is displayed, click the Layout selector (+) in the upper left corner of the control.

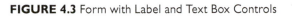

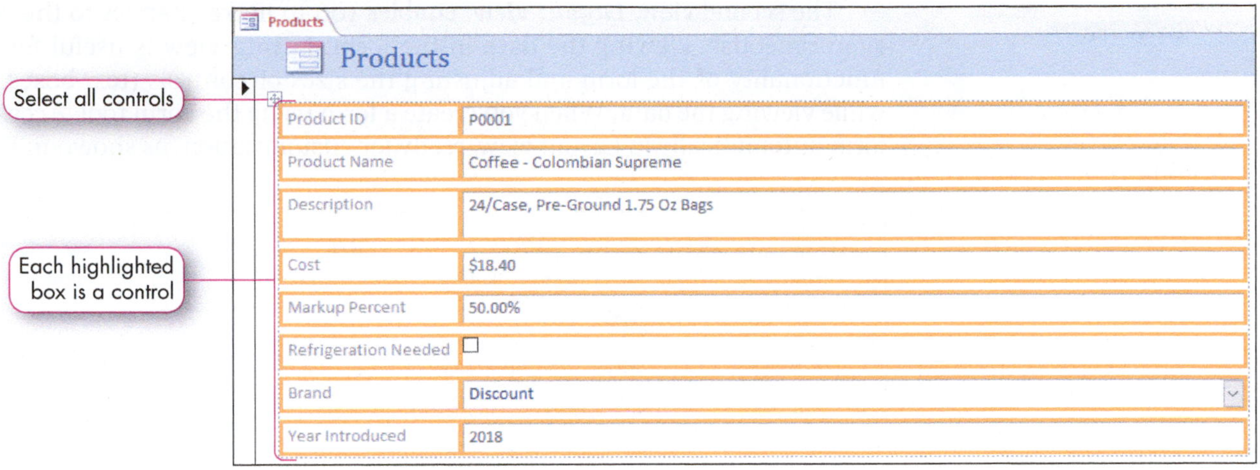
Select all controls
Each highlighted box is a control
Products
Products
Product ID
P0001
Product Name
Coffee - Colombian Supreme
Description
24/Case, Pre-Ground 1.75 Oz Bags
Cost
$18.40
Markup Percent
50.00%
Refrigeration Needed
Brand
Discount
Year Introduced
2018

FIGURE 4.3 Form with Label and Text Box Controls

Work with Form Views

There are three different views of a form available. The first, ***Form view***, is the user interface primarily used for data entry and data changes. You cannot make modifications to the form layout or design in Form view. Figure 4.4 shows a form in Form view. Notice that forms can be designed to include time-saving features such as lists and check boxes.

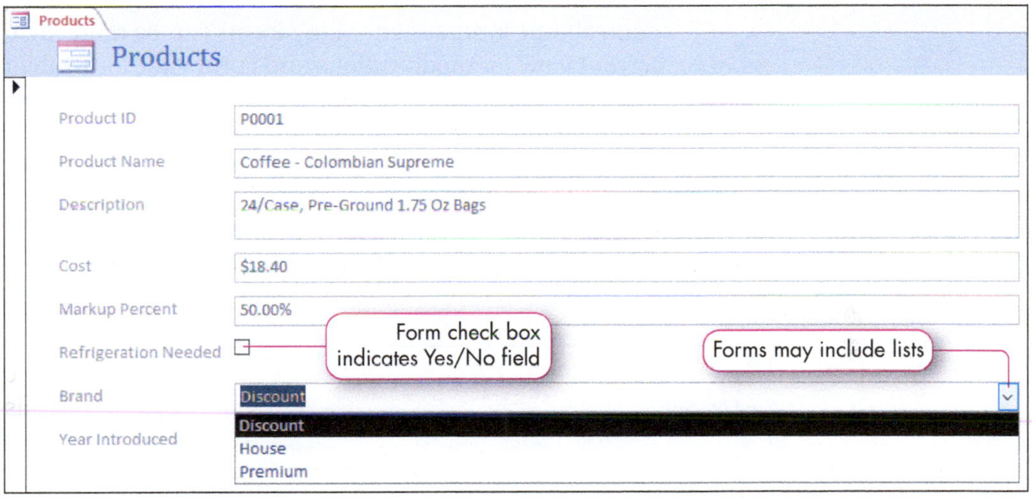
Products
Products
Product ID
P0001
Product Name
Coffee - Colombian Supreme
Description
24/Case, Pre-Ground 1.75 Oz Bags
Cost
$18.40
Markup Percent
50.00%
Refrigeration Needed
Form check box indicates Yes/No field
Forms may include lists
Brand
Discount
Year Introduced
Discount
House
Premium

FIGURE 4.4 Form in Form View

The second view, *Layout view*, enables you to make changes to the layout while simultaneously viewing the data in the form. Layout view is useful for testing the functionality of the form and adjusting the sizes of controls (text boxes and labels) while viewing the data. When you create a form using the Form tool, Access opens the form automatically in Layout view, ready for customization, as shown in Figure 4.5.

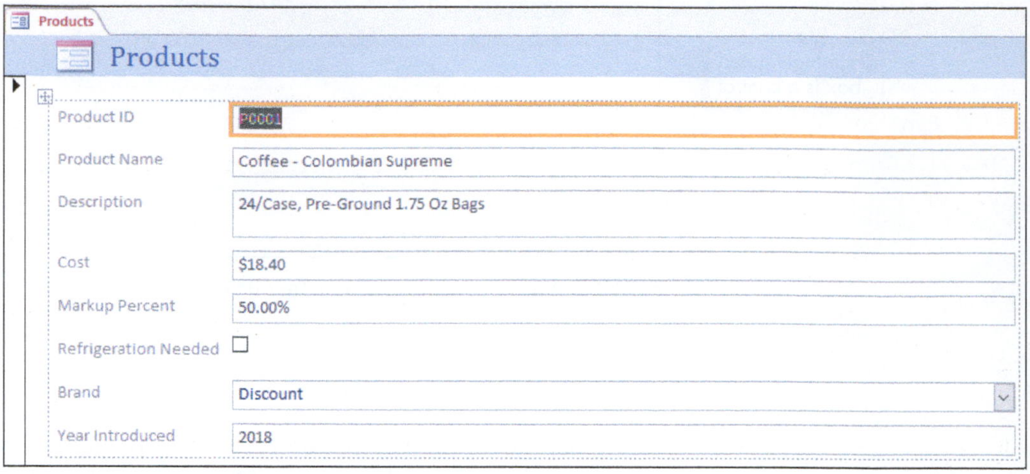

FIGURE 4.5 Form in Layout View

The third view, *Design view*, enables you to change advanced design settings that are not available in Layout view, such as removing a layout control, and gives you even more control over form design. Many forms can be made by toggling back and forth between Layout view for modifications and Form view for usability testing; however, Design view offers possibilities for more advanced adjustments. Figure 4.6 shows a form in Design view. Form views will be described in more detail later in this chapter.

Use the View arrow in the Views group on the Home tab to select either Form View, Layout View, or Design View. Alternatively, click the View buttons on the status bar at the bottom of the Access window, as shown in Figure 4.6, or right-click the form's window tab and select an option from the shortcut menu.

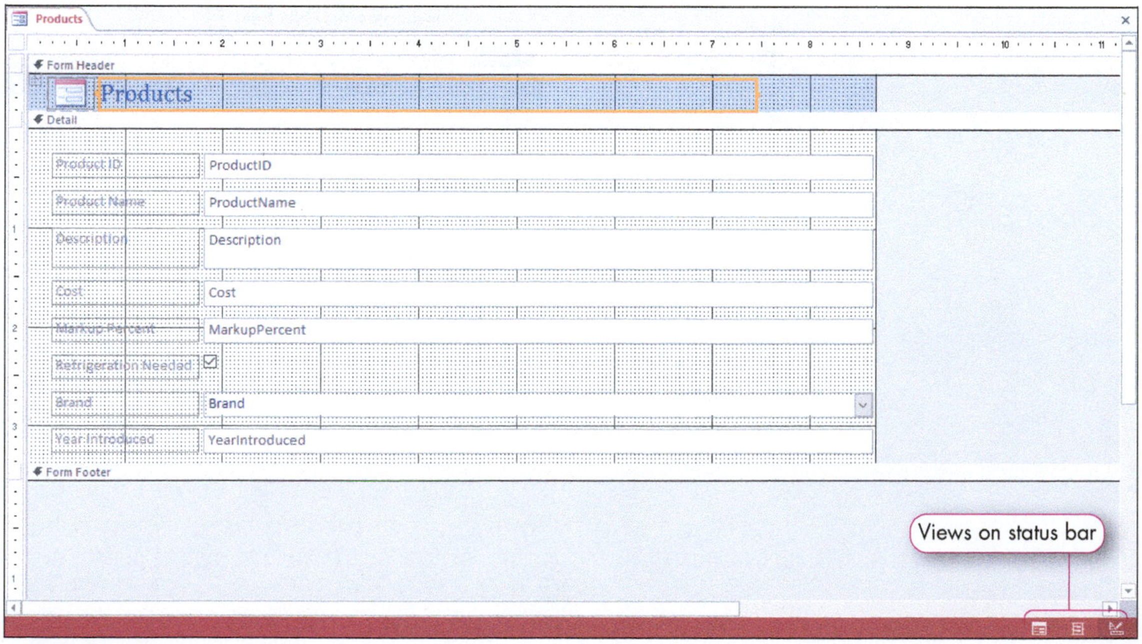

FIGURE 4.6 Form in Design View

Work with a Subform

When you use the Form tool to create a form, Access analyzes the table relationships in the database. If the table that the form is based upon is related to another table, Access automatically adds a subform to the main form. The subform displays records in the related table, generally laid out in a datasheet format. For example, assume you have sales representatives stored in a Sales Reps table and related customer information stored in a Customers table. In this example, if you create a new form based on the Sales Reps table using the Form tool, Access will add a Customers subform to the bottom of the main form, displaying all customers assigned to each sales representative (see Figure 4.7). At times, you may want the subform as part of your form; at other times, you may want to remove it if it is not relevant to the requirements of the form design. In Design view, click anywhere in the subform control, delete the subform, and then save the form.

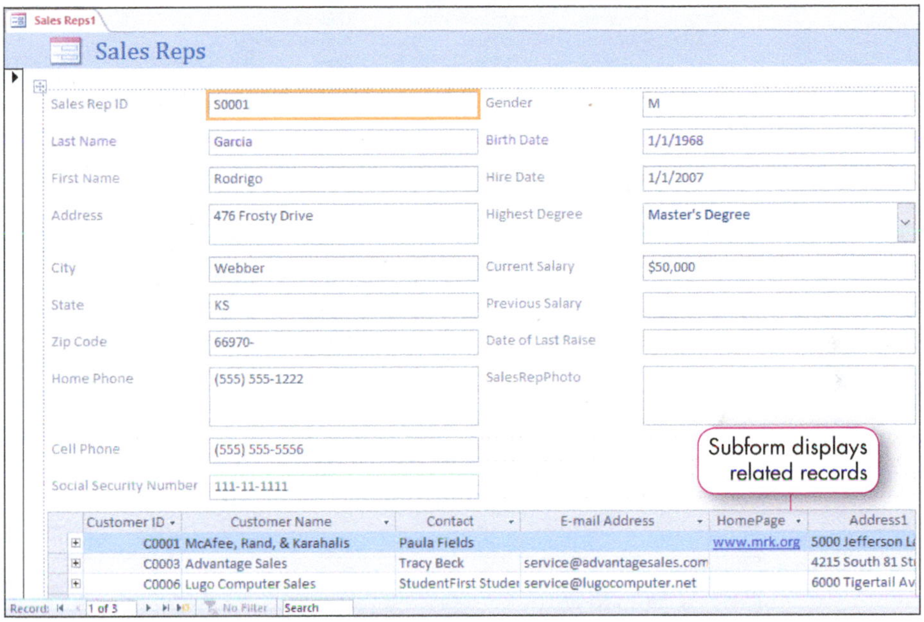

FIGURE 4.7 Sales Reps Form with Related Customers Subform

TIP: ADD A SUBFORM TO AN EXISTING FORM

It is possible to add a subform to an existing form by using the SubForm Wizard. In Design view of the form, click the Subform/Subreport tool in the Controls group on the Form Design Tools Design tab [icon], and then click in the form where you want the subform to display. The wizard will prompt you for the record source and through the steps for creating the subform.

Create a Split Form

A *split form* combines two views of the same record source—by default, the top section is displayed in a stacked layout (Form view), and the bottom section is displayed in a tabular layout (Datasheet view). If you select a record in the top section of the form, the same record will be selected in the bottom section of the form and vice versa. For example, if you create a split form based on an Orders table, you can select an Order in the bottom (datasheet) section and enter or edit the order's information in the top (Form view) section (see Figure 4.8). This gives you the option to navigate between orders more quickly in the bottom section, and when you locate the one you need, you can move to the top section to work with the record in Form view; however, you can add, edit, or delete records in either section. The splitter bar divides the form into two panes. You can adjust the splitter bar up or down (unless this option is disabled). To create a split form, select a table or query in the Navigation Pane, click More Forms, and then select Split Form in the Forms group on the Create tab.

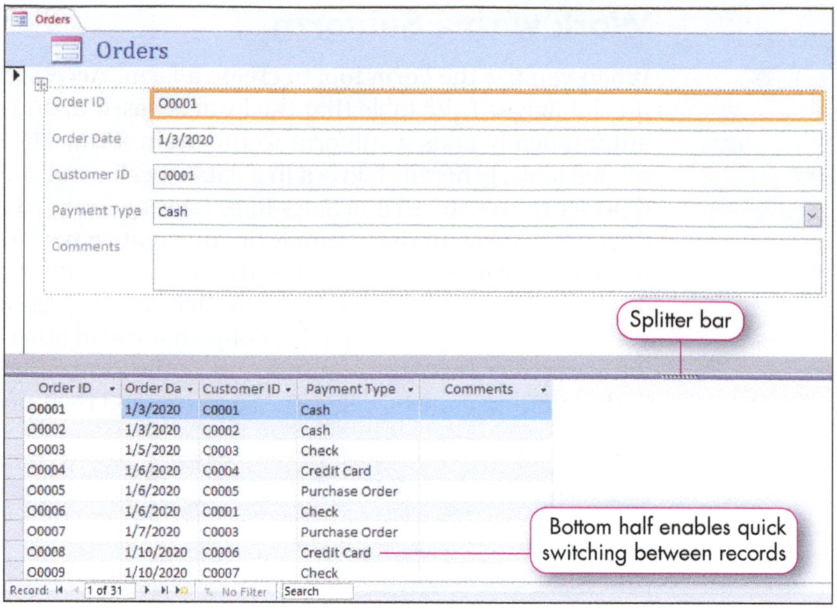

FIGURE 4.8 Split Form

Create a Multiple Items Form

A *multiple items form* displays multiple records in a tabular layout similar to a table's Datasheet view. However, a multiple items form provides you with more customization options than a datasheet, such as the ability to add graphical elements, buttons, and other controls. Figure 4.9 shows a multiple items form created from the Sales Rep table. Select a table or query in the Navigation Pane, click More forms, and then click Multiple Items in the Forms group on the Create tab.

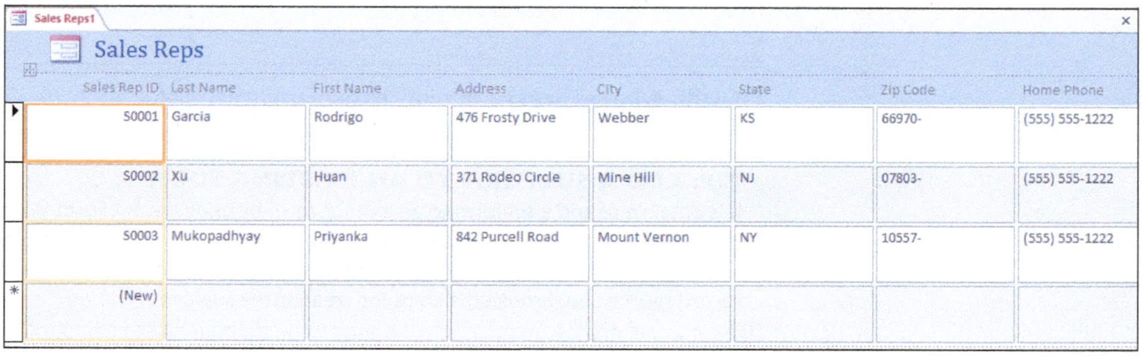

FIGURE 4.9 Multiple Items Form

Create a Navigation Form

The *Navigation form* options in the Forms group enable you to create user interfaces that have the look and feel of Web-based forms and enable users to quickly navigate between the objects of a database. For example, you can create a form where users click buttons for the various forms, reports, and other objects in the database that you want them to view. This is an excellent way to simplify the database navigation for data-entry personnel who may not be that familiar with finding their way around in Access. It is possible to set an option so that the Navigation form is the first one users see when they launch a database (see Figure 4.10). Click Navigation in the Forms group on the Create tab and select a layout to create a Navigation form.

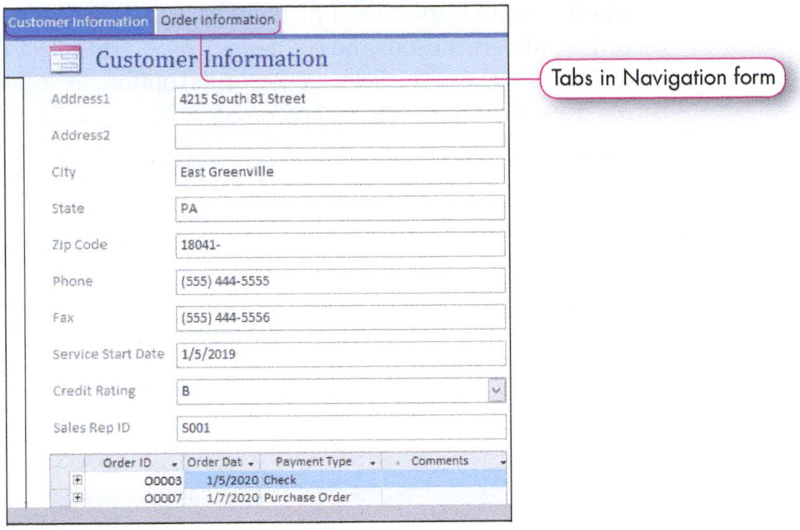

FIGURE 4.10 Horizontal Tabs Navigation Form

> **TIP: THE FORM WIZARD**
>
> The Form Wizard creates a customizable form based on your answers to a series of questions. The record source for the form can be a table or a query. As you proceed through the wizard, there are grouping and layout options and the possibility of creating a main form with a subform when the form is based on related tables. You can customize a form made with the wizard in Layout view or Design view anytime, so even though you create a form with the Form Wizard, you are never completely locked into its design and function. To get started, click Form Wizard, in the Forms group on the Create tab.

Create Forms Using the Other Form Tools

A Datasheet form is a replica of a table or query's Datasheet view except that it allows form properties to be set to control the behavior of the form. For example, you can create a datasheet form to display data in a table-like format but change the form's property so as not to allow a record to be deleted. This protects the data from accidental deletions while still providing users with the familiar Datasheet view.

> **TIP: FORM PROPERTIES**
>
> A form's Property Sheet enables you to control the behavior and formatting of controls in your forms. Display the Property Sheet in Layout view or Design view, by clicking Property Sheet in the Tools group on the Design tab. At the top of the Property Sheet, use the list arrow to select a control; you will see multiple tabs containing many individual attributes of the selected control that you can change. For example, the Format tab contains options for changing the styling of a control. Each tab of the Property Sheet contains a long list of attributes, so if you are looking for a specific one to modify, click the Sort properties in ascending order button in the top right corner of the pane.

The Form Design tool and the Blank Form tools can be used to create forms manually from scratch in Design view or Layout view, respectively. Use these form types if you want to have complete control over your form's design. In either case, after opening a completely blank form, click Add Existing Fields in the Tools group on the Design tab, and then add the required fields by dragging and dropping them onto the blank form from the Field List pane.

The Modal Dialog Form tool can be used to create a dialog box. This feature is useful when you need to gather information from the user or provide information to the user, such as a message. Dialog boxes are common in all Microsoft Office applications.

Print Selected Records in a Form

You can print a form by clicking the Print option on the File tab. However, printing from a form should be handled with caution. Forms are not generally designed for printing, so you may end up with hundreds of pages of printouts. A form with a stacked layout and 1,000 records could print thousands of pages unless you select the Selected Record(s) option in the Print dialog box. The Selected Record(s) option, as shown in Figure 4.11, will only print the current record (or selected records).

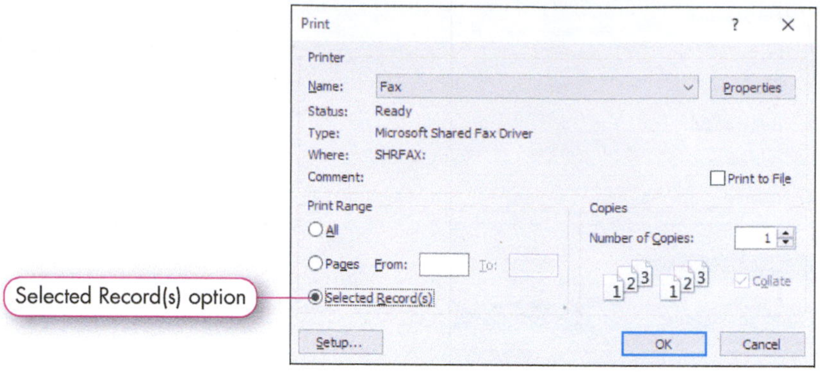

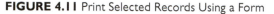

FIGURE 4.11 Print Selected Records Using a Form

> **TIP: POSITION A FORM WHEN PRINTING**
> If it becomes necessary to print a form, you can set the page margins to position the form on the printed sheet. To set the page margins, click the File tab, click Print, and then click Print Preview. Click Margins in the Page Size group of the Print Preview tab, and then select one of the predefined margin settings.

Modifying Forms

As previously mentioned, Access provides different views for a form; most forms display Layout, Form, and Design views. As you work with the form tools to create and modify forms, you will need to switch between the three form views in Access. Much of your design work can be done in Layout view; sometimes, you will need to switch to Design view to use a more advanced feature, such as changing the order of the fields as you press Tab to move from one to the next, or to use an option that is otherwise unavailable. Users of the form will typically only work in Form view; there is little reason for a user to switch to Layout or Design view, and these views can be disabled by the database designer to protect the integrity of the form. Modifications to the form should ideally be done only by a designated designer.

STEP 2 ## Edit Data in Form View

Use Form view to add, edit, and delete data in a form; the layout and design of the form cannot be changed in this view. The Navigation bar at the bottom of the form displays buttons to move between records, and you can click the New (blank) record button to add a new record. You can move from one field to another field by pressing Tab or clicking a field. Form view provides tools like those in Datasheet view of a table for finding, sorting, and filtering records. Using the Find command is a convenient way of locating a specific record when the record needs to be viewed, modified, or deleted.

STEP 3 ## Use Layout View to Modify Form Design

Use Layout view to modify the form design while viewing the data. The data are not editable in this view. You use Layout view to add or delete fields in a form, change the order of fields, modify field or form properties (such as which views are available), change the widths of controls, and enhance a form by adding a theme or styling. Reviewing the data in Layout view makes it easier to move and size controls and to ensure that all data are visible in Form view. You can move controls in Layout view by dragging and dropping them into a new location. It is good practice to toggle back and forth between Layout view and Form view when making changes to the form's design.

Forms have a good number of options that you can use in your design process. In Layout view, under the Form Layout Tools tab, you have access to three contextual tabs on the ribbon that provide a number of tools for modifying forms as follows:

- Design tab: To make changes to the design of the form, such as applying themes, inserting headers and footers, and additional controls.
- Arrange tab: To change the layout of a form, to move fields up or down, or to control margins.
- Format tab: To work with different fonts, font sizes, and colors; to add or remove bolding, italics, or underlining; to adjust text alignment; or to add a background image.

Similarly, in Design view, the Form Design Tools tabs are available (Design, Arrange, and Format) with many of the same options you will find in Layout view.

Adjust Column Widths in a Form

When column widths are adjusted in a form with a stacked layout, all field sizes will increase and decrease in size together. Therefore, it is best to make sure that the columns are wide enough to accommodate the widest value in each field. For example, if a form contains information such as a customer's first name, last name, address, city, state, ZIP, phone, and email address, you will need to make sure the longest address and the longest email address are completely visible (because those fields are likely to contain the longest data values). To increase or decrease column widths in a form with a stacked layout, display the form in (Stacked) Layout view and click the text box control of the first field to select it. Point to the right border of the control until the pointer turns into a double-headed arrow. Drag the right edge of the control to the left or right until you arrive at the required width.

You will notice that all field sizes change as you change the width of the first field. All fields that are included in the layout will have a standard width. If you want to resize one specific field, remove that field from the layout control. Select the field and the label to be removed, right-click, click Layout, and then select Remove Layout. If you remove a field from the layout control, it stays on the form but can be moved and resized more freely.

It is also possible to resize form fields by setting a specific width or height using the Property sheet. In Layout view or Design view of the form, select Property Sheet in the Tools group on the Design tab. Use the Width and Height boxes to set specific values by typing them.

Add and Delete Form Fields

There will be instances when you will want to add or delete form fields. At times, new fields may be added to tables and then incorporated into forms. At other times, you may decide that while a field is present in a table, it is not necessary to display it to users in a form.

To add a field to a form, complete the following steps:

1. Display the form in (Stacked) Layout view and click Add Existing Fields in the Tools group on the Design tab. In the Field List pane, you will see a list of fields from the table (record source), as shown in Figure 4.12. For a multiple-table form, click the plus sign (+) to the left of the appropriate table to expand it and locate the desired field(s).
2. Click and drag the desired field to the precise location on the form, using the shaded line as a guide for positioning the new field. Alternatively, double-click a field to add it to the form; the field will be added below the selected field. The other fields will automatically adjust to make room for the new field.

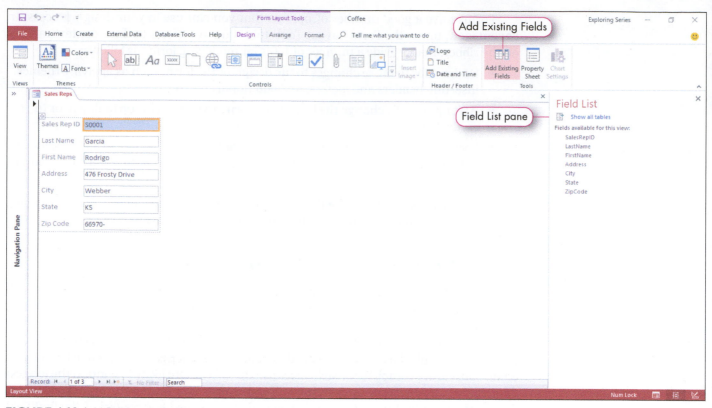

FIGURE 4.12 Add Fields to a Form

> **To delete a field from a form, complete the following steps:**
>
> 1. Display the form in (Stacked) Layout view and click the text box control of the field to be deleted (note the shaded border around the control).
> 2. Click Select Row in the Rows & Columns group on the Arrange tab to select the text box and its associated label. Alternatively, click the text box control, press and hold Ctrl, and then click the associated label control to select them both.
> 3. Press Delete. The other fields will automatically adjust to close the gap around the deleted field.

Modify Form Controls

When you view a form in Layout view, the Form Layout Tools tab displays the Design, Arrange, and Format tabs. The Format tab contains a series of commands that enable you to change the font, display, and alignment of the controls on a form. At times, you may want to change the formatting of one or more controls. For example, if you have a form that shows the information about the sale of vehicles, you might want to emphasize the net profit of each transaction by changing the font or background color of the control.

Modifying the font sizes, changing the font colors, and adding background colors to controls can enhance a form and make it more user-friendly. Select familiar fonts, such as Arial or Calibri, for both the form label and text box controls. Apply bold to the labels to help the user distinguish labels from the text boxes. Consider aligning the labels and the text box controls. You may also want to separate the primary key field from the rest of the form fields by providing a visual boundary, as illustrated in Figure 4.13. One note of caution: using too many fonts, font sizes, colors, and other effects can detract from your design and make your form confusing to users.

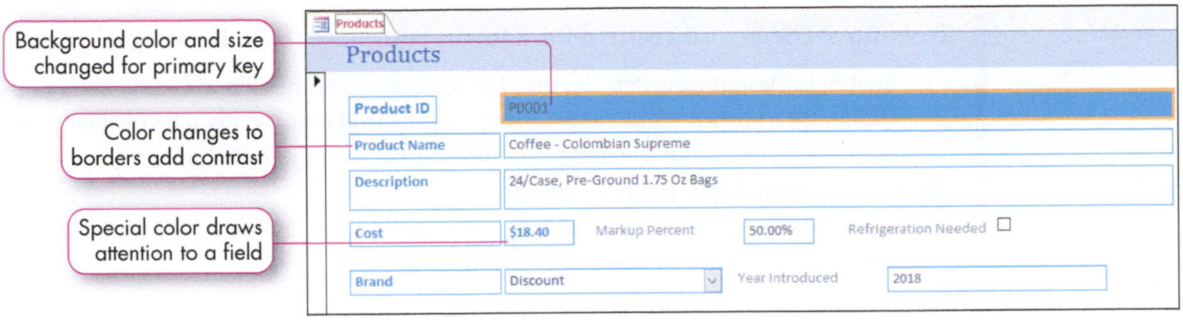

Background color and size changed for primary key

Color changes to borders add contrast

Special color draws attention to a field

Products

Products

Product ID	PI0001
Product Name	Coffee - Colombian Supreme
Description	24/Case, Pre-Ground 1.75 Oz Bags
Cost	$18.40	Markup Percent	50.00%	Refrigeration Needed ☐
Brand	Discount	Year Introduced	2018

FIGURE 4.13 A Well-Designed Form with Styling

From the Form Layout Tools Format tab, you can change a number of control attributes. Table 4.2 illustrates some of the commands you can use.

TABLE 4.2	Common Attributes for Form Controls
Format	**Method to apply format**
Font size	Click the Font Size arrow in the Font group.
Font emphasis	Click Bold, Italic, or Underline in the Font group.
Alignment	Click Align Left, Center, or Align Right in the Font group.
Background color	Click the Background Color arrow in the Font group.
Font color	Click the Font Color arrow in the Font group.
Number format	Use the tools in the Number group to select number formats such as Currency, Percent, Comma formatting, or to increase or decrease decimal places.

STEP 4 Using the Form Layout Control

When you use one of the form tools to create a new form, Access adds a layout control to keep controls aligned and to give your form a neat appearance. The layout control provides structure for the fields but is also somewhat restrictive. You can remove a single control from the layout to move it independently of the other fields. Select the field and label to be removed, right-click, and from the shortcut menu point to Layout, and then select Remove Layout. You can then drag and drop the control(s) to a different location on the form. If you want to have more control over the location of your fields, you can remove the layout control completely and position the controls manually on the form. You can also modify the layout of the form to determine whether the fields are arranged vertically or horizontally.

You can use the tools on the Arrange tab to change the layout of a form, to move fields up and down, and to control margins. The Arrange tab displays in both Layout view and Design view. The Table group of the Arrange tab contains commands that enable you to add gridlines to a form's layout, change the layout from stacked to tabular (and vice versa), or remove the layout (the Remove Layout command is available only in Design view).

To apply a layout or change the layout of a form, complete the following steps:

1. Open the form in Layout or Design view.
2. Select multiple controls by clicking the first control, pressing and holding Ctrl, and then clicking the additional controls you want to include in the layout. To select all the controls on a form, press Ctrl+A. If the controls already have a layout applied, click any control that is part of the layout, and click Select Layout in the Rows & Columns group on the Arrange tab.
3. Click Tabular or Stacked in the Table group on the Arrange tab.

To remove the layout control for a form, complete the following steps:

1. Switch to Design view (the Remove Layout option on the ribbon is only available in Design view) and click any one of the controls that is currently part of the layout.
2. Click Select Layout in the Rows & Columns group on the Arrange tab.
3. Click Remove Layout in the Table group.
4. Switch to Layout view. Drag and drop the control(s) to a different location on the form.

The Rows & Columns group also contains commands that enable you to insert rows and columns in a form's layout. In a form with a stacked layout, you may want to separate some controls from the rest of the fields or create some empty space so that fields can be added or repositioned. For example, you can select a control and click Insert Below. This will create an empty row (or space) below the selected control. This group also contains the Select Layout, Select Column, and Select Row commands, which you can use to select the entire layout or a single column or row in a layout. In Figure 4.14, three empty rows have been inserted above the Cost field.

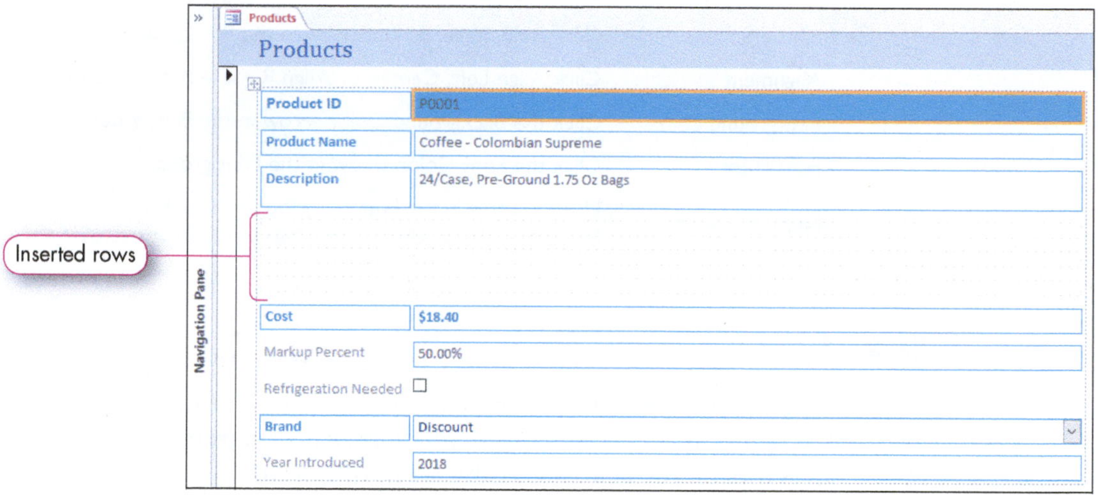

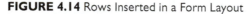

FIGURE 4.14 Rows Inserted in a Form Layout

TIP: APPLY A BACKGROUND IMAGE TO A FORM

To apply a background image to a form, open the form in Layout or Design view, and then click Background Image in the Background group on the Format tab. Next, click Browse to locate the image you want to apply to the form. Once the image has been applied to the form, you can change the properties of the image so that the image displays correctly. You can use the same technique to add a background image to a report.

Sorting Records in a Form

When a form is created using a Form tool, the sort order of the records in the form is initially dependent on the sort order of the record source—the underlying table or query. Tables are usually sorted by the primary key, whereas queries can be sorted in a variety of ways. No matter how the records are initially sorted, you can modify the sort order in a form so that it is different from the sort order of the underlying table or query. The sort options for a form are shown in Figure 4.15.

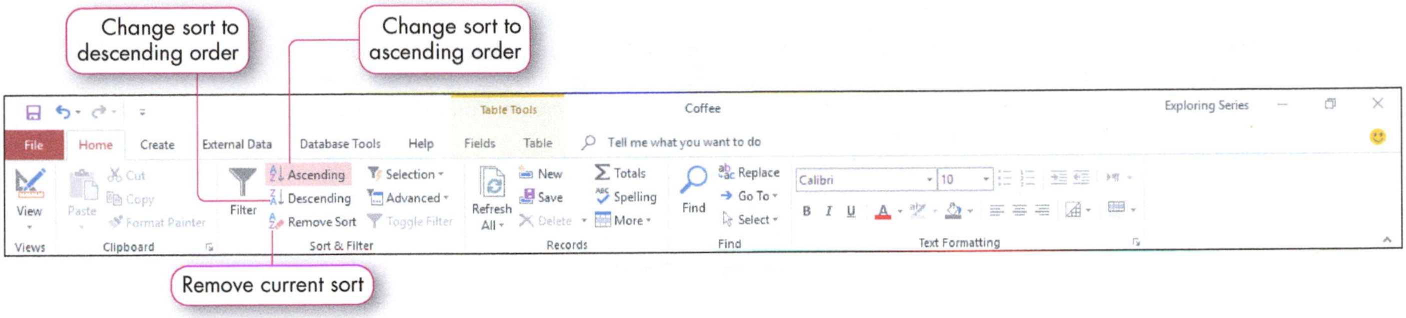

FIGURE 4.15 Adding and Removing Sort Order

You can easily sort on a single field, in ascending or descending order. Open the form in Form view and select the field by which you want to sort. Click Ascending or Descending in the Sort & Filter group on the Home tab.

If you want to sort on multiple fields, you would create a query with a more advanced sort order, and base the form on the query. For example, you might want to sort your records first by a state name, and within each group of state records, sort them by city. Open the query in Design view, add the sort settings you want, save the query, and then use the query as the record source of the form. To remove the sort order in a form, open the form in Form view, and then click Remove Sort in the Sort & Filter group on the Home tab.

Quick Concepts

1. Explain how a form simplifies data entry (when compared to entering data into a table). *p. 250*

2. Discuss the benefit of creating a Navigation form for users of a database. *p. 256*

3. Consider how to determine the record source of a form. *p. 251*

4. Explain the advantage of creating a form with a subform. *p. 255*

5. Discuss the best strategy for creating a form that sorts by more than one field. *p. 263*

Hands-On Exercises

MyLab IT HOE1 Sim Training

▶ Watch the Video for this Hands-On Exercise!

Skills covered: Identify a Record Source • Use the Form Tool • Create a Split Form • Create a Multiple Items Form • Work with a Subform • Create a Navigation Form • Edit Data in Form View • Delete a Form Field • Add a Form Field • Adjust Column Widths in a Form • Modify Form Controls • Modify a Form Layout • Sort Records in a Form

1 Create Basic Forms to Simplify Data Management

After talking with Ryung about her data entry needs, you decide to create several sample forms using different formats. You will use the Form tool and others to determine which options provide the best solutions and modify the design of the forms you create. You will show each form to Ryung to get feedback and see if she has any preferences.

STEP 1 CREATE FORMS USING FORM TOOLS

You will create several forms using different layouts. Refer to Figure 4.16 as you complete Step 1.

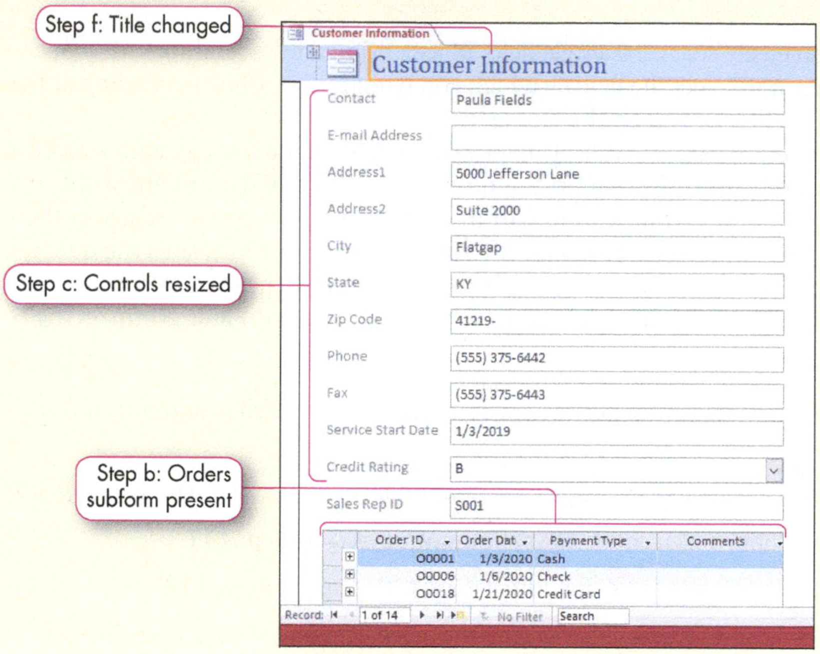

Step f: Title changed

Step c: Controls resized

Step b: Orders subform present

FIGURE 4.16 Customer Information Form

a. Open *a04h1Coffee* and save it as **a04h1Coffee_LastFirst**.

> **TROUBLESHOOTING:** If you make any major mistakes in this exercise, you can close the file, open *a04h1Coffee* again, and then start this exercise over.

b. Click the **Customers table** in the Navigation Pane to select the table but not open it. Click the **Create tab** and click **Form** in the Forms group.

Access creates a new form with two record sources—Customers (with stacked layout, on top) and Orders (with datasheet layout, below). Access detected a one-to-many relationship between the Customers and Orders tables, and so it created a main form with its associated subform below it. The form opens in Layout view.

c. Ensure that the top text box containing *C0001* is selected. The text box is outlined with a shaded border. Move the pointer to the right edge of the shaded border until the pointer changes to a double-headed arrow. Drag the right edge to the left until the text box is approximately half of its original size.

All of the text boxes and the subform at the bottom adjust in size when you adjust the top text box. This is a characteristic of Layout view—enabling you to modify all controls at once.

> **TROUBLESHOOTING:** You may need to maximize the Access window or close the Navigation Pane if the right edge of the text box is not visible.

d. Ensure that the labels to the left of the text boxes display without being cut off. If they are cut off, adjust the size of the labels as you did in Step c.

e. Click **Save** on the Quick Access Toolbar and type **Customer Information** as the form name in the **Save As dialog box**. Click **OK**.

f. Click the **Customers title** at the top of the form to select it, click the title again, and then change the title to **Customer Information**. Press **Enter** to accept the change. Your form should now look like Figure 4.16. Save and close the form.

> **TROUBLESHOOTING:** If you make a mistake that you cannot easily recover from, consider deleting the form and creating it again. With the form closed, right-click the form name in the Navigation Pane, and from the shortcut menu, select Delete. If you named the form incorrectly, right-click the form in the Navigation Pane, and from the shortcut menu, select Rename.

g. Ensure that the Customers table is selected in the Navigation Pane. Click the **Create tab**, click **More Forms** in the Forms group, and then select **Split Form**.

Access creates a new form with a split view, one view in stacked layout and one view organized like a datasheet.

h. Scroll down and click anywhere in the *Coulter Office Supplies* customer record in the bottom pane (datasheet) of the form (record 14).

The top pane shows all the information for this customer in a stacked layout view.

i. Click the **Customers title** at the top of the form to select it, click **Customers** again, and then change the title to **Customers - Split View**. Press **Enter** to accept the change.

j. Click **Save** on the Quick Access Toolbar and type **Customers - Split View** in the Form Name box. Click **OK**. Close the form.

k. Click the **Products table** in the Navigation Pane. Click the **Create tab**, click **More Forms** in the Forms group, and then select **Multiple Items**.

Access creates a new multiple-items form based on the Products table. The form resembles a table's Datasheet view.

l. Click the **Products title** at the top of the form to select it, click **Products** again, and then change the title to **Products - Multiple Items**. Press **Enter** to accept the change.

m. Save the form as **Products - Multiple Items** and close the form.

n. Click the **Orders table** in the Navigation Pane. Click **Form** in the Forms group on the Create tab.

A main form with a subform is created. The main form is based on the Orders table, and the subform is based on the related Order Details table, displaying a record for each product associated with the order selected in the main form.

o. Click **Next record** on the Navigation bar at the bottom of the Orders (main) form. The next order displays the Order Details associated with Order ID O0002.

p. Click the **Home tab**. Click the **View arrow** in the Views group and select **Design View**. Click anywhere inside the Table.Order Details subform control and press **Delete**.

The subform control that displayed the associated order details is removed.

q. Switch to Form view to observe the change. Save the form as **Order Information**.

r. Click the **Create tab**, click **Navigation** in the Forms group, and then select **Horizontal tabs**.

s. Drag the **Customer Information form icon** from the Navigation Pane onto the **[Add New] tab** at the top of the form.

t. Drag the **Order Information form icon** from the Navigation Pane onto the **[Add New] tab** at the top of the form. Click the **Customer Information tab** and click the **Order Information tab**.

The Navigation form enables you to view and switch between objects readily.

u. Save the Navigation form with the default name and close all open objects.

USE FORM VIEW TO EDIT DATA

Now that you have created several forms, you will test the forms for usability. Refer to Figure 4.17 as you complete Step 2.

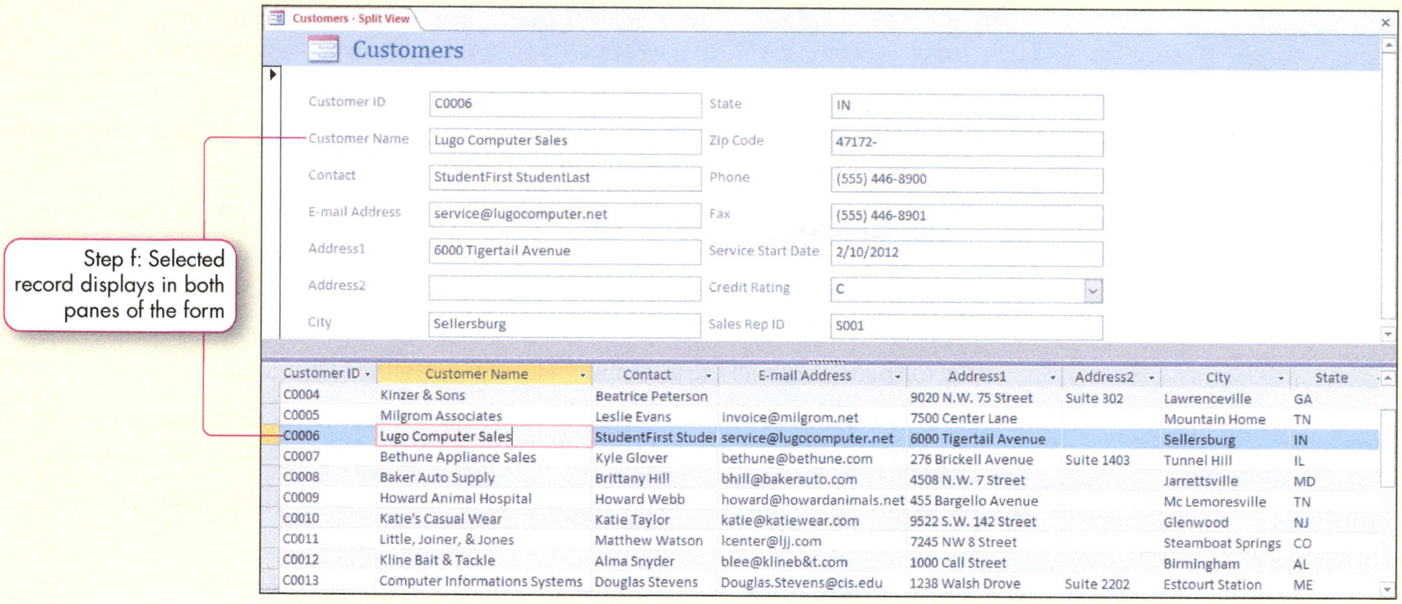

Step f: Selected record displays in both panes of the form

FIGURE 4.17 Customers – Split View form

a. Right-click the **Customer Information form** in the Navigation Pane, and from the shortcut menu, select **Open**. Select **Next record** on the Navigation bar at the bottom of the form to advance to the sixth customer, *Lugo Computer Sales*.

> **TROUBLESHOOTING:** Two Navigation bars exist, the inside one for the subform and the bottom-most one for the main form. Make sure you use the bottom-most one that displays the record count of 14.

b. Double-click the **Customers table** in the Navigation Pane.

Two tabs now display in the main window. You will compare the table data and the form data while you make changes to both.

c. Verify that the sixth record of the Customers table is *Lugo Computer Sales*, which corresponds to the sixth record in the Customer Information form. Click the tabs to switch between the table and the form.

d. Click the **Customer Information tab** (the form tab) and replace *Adam Sanchez*, the contact for Lugo Computer Sales, with **your name**. Advance to the next record to automatically save the changes. Click the **Customers tab** (the table tab) to see that the contact name changed in the table as well.

Changes to the Contact field and the other fields in the Customer Information form automatically change the data in the underlying table. Likewise, if you change data in the table, they will update automatically in the form.

> **TROUBLESHOOTING:** If the change from *Adam Sanchez* to your name does not display in the Customers table, check the Customer Information form to see if the pencil [🖉] displays in the left margin of the record. If it does, save the record by advancing to the next customer in the form and recheck to see if the name has changed in the underlying table.

e. Close the Customer Information form and the Customers table.

f. Open the Customers – Split View form. In the bottom pane of the split form, click **Lugo Computer Sales**, the sixth record. Notice that the top pane now displays the information for Lugo Computer Sales in a stacked layout. Notice also that there is an error in the email address—*service* is misspelled. In the top pane of the form, change the email address to **service@lugocomputer.net**.

g. Click another record in the bottom pane and click back on **Lugo Computer Sales,** as shown in Figure 4.17.

The pencil disappears from the record selector box in the form and the changes are saved to the underlying table.

STEP 3 USE LAYOUT VIEW TO MODIFY A FORM DESIGN

You will make some design changes to the forms based on feedback that Ryung gave you after some additional testing. You will also add a missing field to the main table and add it to the form. Refer to Figure 4.18 as you complete Step 3.

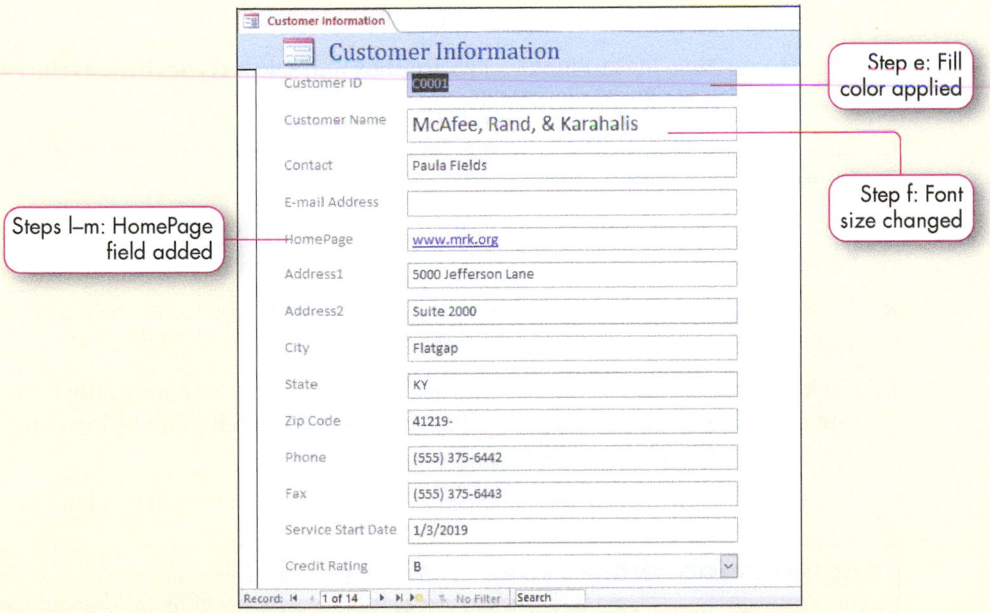

FIGURE 4.18 Completed Customer Information Form

a. Ensure that the Customers – Split View form is open and switch to Layout view. Point to the **splitter bar**, the border between the top and bottom panes of the window. When the pointer shape changes to a double-headed arrow, drag the **splitter bar** until it almost touches the Sales Rep ID field. Save and close the form.

b. Open the Products – Multiple Items form in Layout view. Point to the bottom edge of **Product ID P0001** until the pointer shape changes to a double-headed arrow. Drag the bottom edge up to reduce the height of the rows so they are as tall as they need to be to accommodate the information.

Changing the height of one row affects the height of all the rows in the form.

c. Click anywhere in the **Cost column** and click **Select Column** in the Rows & Columns group on the Arrange tab. Press **Delete** to remove the column (alternatively, right-click in the column, and from the shortcut menu, select Delete Column). Delete the **MarkupPercent column**.

d. Click the **Refrigeration Needed label** to select it. Change the label to the abbreviation **Refrig?** Resize the column so it is wide enough to display the label text. Save and close the form.

e. Open the Customer Information form in Layout view. Ensure that the CustomerID field is selected and click the **Format tab**. Click **Shape Fill** in the Control Formatting group. Select **Blue, Accent 1, Lighter 60%** under Theme Colors.

The background color of the CustomerID field changes to light blue.

> **TROUBLESHOOTING:** If the entire form background changes to blue, click Undo and ensure that only the Customer ID text box containing *C0001* is selected when you apply the color.

f. Select the **Customer Name field** (*McAfee, Rand, & Karahalis*). Change the font size to **16**. Save and close the form.

The customer name displays in a larger font, setting it apart from the other fields.

g. Right-click the **Customers table** in the Navigation Pane and select **Design View**.

You will add the HomePage hyperlink field to the Customers table.

h. Click the **Address1 field** and click **Insert Rows** in the Tools group on the Design tab.

A new row is inserted above the Address1 field.

i. Type **HomePage** in the blank Field Name box and select **Hyperlink** as the Data Type. Save and close the Customers table.

j. Right-click the **Customer Information form** in the Navigation Pane and select **Layout View**.

You will add the HomePage field from the Customers table to the Customer Information form.

k. Click **Add Existing Fields** in the Tools group on the Design tab to display the Field List pane.

l. Click the **HomePage field**. Drag the field from the Field List pane to the form below the E-mail Address field, until a shaded line displays between E-mail Address and Address1 and then drop it. Close the Field List pane.

Access displays a shaded line to help you place the field in the correct location.

> **TROUBLESHOOTING:** If the placement of the field is incorrect, you can click Undo and try again. Alternatively, select the label and text box controls and use the Move Up or Move Down commands in the Arrange group.

m. Switch to Form view. Press **Tab** until you reach the HomePage field, type **www.mrk.org**, and press **Tab**.

Because HomePage is a hyperlink field, Access formats it automatically in the form.

n. Save and close the Customer Information form.

STEP 4 ## USE THE FORM LAYOUT CONTROL AND SORT RECORDS IN A FORM

You will create a new form to view revenue data, but because the form is not organized the way you want, you will remove the form's layout control and move some fields to a new location. Ryung has an old Sales Reps form that she hopes you can make easier to read but keep in the vertical (stacked) format. She also tested the Customer Information form and likes the way it is working; however, she asks you to change the sort order to make it easier to find customers alphabetically by their names. Refer to Figure 4.19 as you complete Step 4.

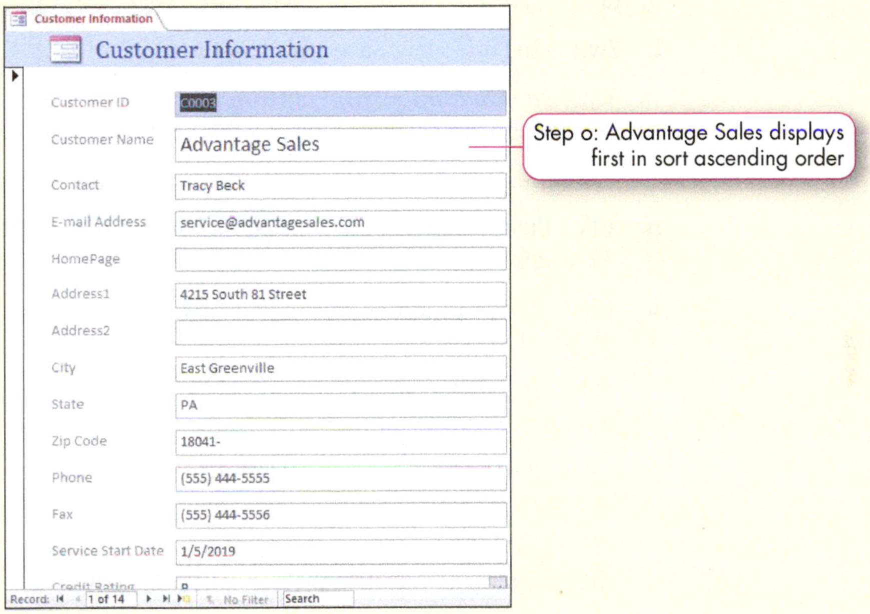

FIGURE 4.19 Customer Information Form Sorted

a. Click the **Revenue query** in the Navigation Pane. Click **Form** in the Forms group on the Create tab to create a new form based on this query.

The Revenue query is the record source for the form.

b. Switch to Design view. Click the first label, **Last Name**, press and hold **Ctrl**, and then click each of the other controls.

You have selected all label and text box field controls (from Last Name down to Revenue).

c. Click **Remove Layout** in the Table group on the Arrange tab. Switch back to Layout view.

> **TROUBLESHOOTING:** Recall that the Remove Layout option only displays on the ribbon in Design view, so if you do not see the command, ensure that you are in Design view.

d. Press Ctrl and click to select the text box controls. Resize the text box controls so they are approximately half of their original widths.

e. Click the **Price control**. Press and hold **Ctrl**, and click the **Revenue control**, the **Price label**, and the **Revenue label**. Drag the fields so that Price is positioned to the right of Cost and Revenue is to the right of Markup Percent. Switch to Form view.

Because the form's layout was removed, you can resize and move the controls independently.

f. Save the form as **Revenue by Order Item**. Close the form.

g. Open the **Sales Reps form** in Layout view. Notice that the form is not attractively organized.

h. Click **Select All** in the Selection group on the Format tab (alternatively press Ctrl+A).

All 14 controls are selected in the form.

i. Click **Tabular** in the Table group on the Arrange tab.

The controls are lined up horizontally across the top of the form.

j. Click **Stacked** in the Table group on the Arrange tab.

The controls are lined up vertically and the form is much easier to read.

k. Click the first **Sales Rep ID text box** and click the **Format tab**. Click **Shape Fill** in the Control Formatting group. Select **Blue, Accent 1, Lighter 60%** under Theme Colors.

l. Switch to Form view. Save and close the form.

m. Open the **Customer Information form** in Form view. Click **Next record** in the Navigation bar at the bottom several times to advance through the records.

Note that the customers are in Customer ID order.

n. Click **First record** in the Navigation bar to return to the customer *McAfee, Rand, & Karahalis*.

o. Click in the **Customer Name text box** and click **Ascending** in the Sort & Filter group on the Home tab.

Advantage Sales displays (Customer ID C0003) because it is the first customer name in alphabetical order, as shown in Figure 4.19.

p. Click **Next record** in the Navigation bar at the bottom of the form to advance through the records.

The records are now in Customer Name order, whereas in the original Customers table, they are sorted by the primary key field, CustomerID.

q. Save and close the Customer Information form.

r. Keep the database open if you plan to continue with the next Hands-On Exercise. If not, close the database, and exit Access.

Create Basic Reports to Present Information

By now, you know how to plan a database, create tables, establish relationships between tables, enter data into tables, and extract data using queries. In the previous section of this chapter, you learned how to create and modify several types of data-entry forms. Next, you will learn how to create professional reports using the report-generating tools in Access.

A *report* is a document that displays meaningful information from a database to its users. Access reports can be printed, viewed onscreen, or even saved as files, such as Word documents. A report is designed for output of information only based on data from tables or queries in your database (record sources); you cannot use reports to change data in your database.

The following are all examples of reports that might be created in Access:

- A contacts list sorted by last name and then by first name
- A customer report grouped by orders for each customer
- An employee list grouped by department
- A monthly statement from a bank
- A transcript of a student and his/her grades
- A set of mailing labels

Reports are used to help the reader understand and analyze information. For example, in a report you can group the customers together for each sales rep and highlight the customers who have not placed an order in six months. This is an example of using a list of customers from the Customers table together with sales rep data in the database as an effective business analysis tool. To increase business, the sales reps could contact their customers who have not ordered in the past six months and review the findings with the sales manager. A sales report could be run each month to see if the strategy has helped to produce any new business.

Before you create a report in Access, you should consider the following questions:

- What is the purpose of the report?
- Who will use the report?
- Which tables, queries, and fields are needed for the report?
- How will the report be distributed? Will users view the report directly from the Access database, or will they receive it through email, fax, or the Internet?
- Will the results be converted to Word, Excel, HTML, or another format?

In the Forms section of this chapter, you learned that it is helpful to talk to users and design a form before you begin to create it in Access. The same applies to creating an Access report. Users can give you solid input and creating a design in advance of working in Access will help you determine which report tool to use to create the report. Interview end users of a report (employer, customer, organization for whom you are creating the report) to determine which records and fields need to be included as well as any formatting or readability concerns they may have. Once you agree on the basic format of the report, you can begin to consider how to handle the execution of it in Access.

The next step in planning your report is to create or identify an optimal record source. You may use one or more tables, queries, or a combination of tables and queries as the report's record source. Sometimes, a single table contains all the records you need for the report. Other times, you will incorporate several tables. When data from multiple related tables are needed to create a report, you can first create a single query (with criteria, if necessary) and then base the report on that query. Multiple tables used in a query must be related, as indicated with join lines. Make sure that whatever record source you decide to use, you will be able to access all the data required for the report.

Reports can contain text and numeric data as well as formatting, calculated fields, graphics, and so forth. For example, you can add a company logo to the report header. Be sure that you have appropriate permission to use any company logo, graphic, or photo in your reports to avoid inappropriate or illegal use of an asset.

In this section, you will create reports in Access by first identifying a record source, then designing the report, and finally choosing a Report tool. You will learn how to modify a report by adding and deleting fields, resizing columns, and sorting records. You will also learn about the report sections, the report views, and controls on reports.

STEP 1 # Creating Reports Using Report Tools

Access provides five different report tools for creating reports. The report tools are located on the Create tab in the Reports group, as shown in Figure 4.20. The most common of the tools, the Report tool, is used to instantly create a tabular report based on a selected table or query. Table 4.3 provides a summary of the five report tools and their usages. Once you create a report using one of the report tools, you can perform modifications in either Layout view or Design view.

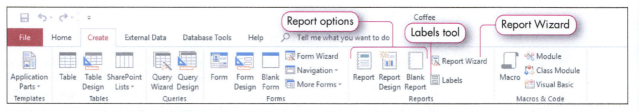

FIGURE 4.20 Reports Group on the Create Tab

TABLE 4.3	Report Tools and Their Usages
Report Tool	**Usage**
Report	Create a tabular report that displays all the fields in the selected record source (table or query).
Report Design	Create a new blank report in Design view. Add fields and controls manually. This tool is used by advanced users who want to create a report from scratch with no help from Access.
Blank Report	Create a new blank report in Layout view. Drag and drop to add fields and controls manually.
Report Wizard	Answer a series of step-by-step questions, and Access will design a custom report for you.
Labels	Select a preformatted label template and create printable labels.

Use the Report Tool

The easiest way to create a report is with the Report tool. The **Report tool** is used to create a tabular report based on the selected table or query. Select a table or query in the Navigation Pane and click Report in the Reports group on the Create tab.

Access creates a tabular layout report instantly. Notice that this type of report displays data horizontally in columns across the page, as shown in Figure 4.21.

Sales Reps													

Sales Reps					Sunday, April 1, 2018 2:42:12 PM								
Sales Rep ID	Last Name	First Name	Address	City	State	Zip Code	Home Phone	Cell Phone	Social Security Number	Gender	Birth Date	Hire Date	Highest Degree
S0001	Garcia	Rodrigo	476 Frosty Drive	Webber	KS	66970-	(555) 555-1222	(555) 555-5556	111-11-1111	M	1/1/1968	1/1/2007	Master's Degree
S0002	Xu	Huan	371 Rodeo Circle	Mine Hill	NJ	07803-	(555) 555-1222	(555) 555-5556	111-22-3333	F	11/23/1981	3/15/2014	Bachelor's Degree
S0003	Mukopadhyay	Priyanka	842 Purcell Road	Mount Vernon	NY	10557-	(555) 555-1222	(555) 555-5556	111-33-5555	F	1/1/1961	1/1/2009	Master's Degree

FIGURE 4.21 Tabular Report Created with the Report Tool

If you prefer, you can display a report using a stacked layout, which displays fields in a vertical column. This type of report is less common because it would result in longer printouts. The number of pages depends on the number of records in the record source.

Use the Report Wizard

The **Report Wizard** prompts you for input in a series of steps to generate a customized report. The wizard enables you to make certain customizations quickly and easily without having to be an expert in report design.

Select the report's record source (table or query) in the Navigation Pane and click Report Wizard in the Reports group on the Create tab. The wizard opens with the selected table or query (the record source) displayed in the first dialog box. Click the Tables/Queries list arrow to display a list of available tables or queries, if you want to choose a different record source. Select the fields you want to include in the report. You can select an available field and click $>$ to add a single field to the Selected Fields list, $>>$ to select all fields, $<$ to remove a field, and $<<$ to remove all fields from the report (see Figure 4.22). Set the fields, then advance to the next screen.

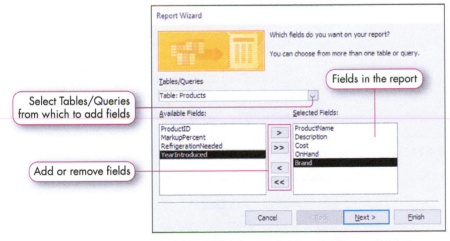

FIGURE 4.22 Selecting Fields in the Report Wizard

Apply the grouping levels, as shown in Figure 4.23. Grouping enables you to organize and summarize the data in a report, based on values in a field. For example, you can group products by their brand name and average the cost of products in each group. To group records in a report, select the field you want to group by and click Add One Field $>$ to add the new group. If you need a second or third grouping level, add those field names in order. The order in which you select the groups determines the order of display in the report. In Figure 4.23, the products are grouped by the Brand field. Once you have selected the appropriate options, advance to the next step. For a basic report, you would not select any grouping fields and instead just skip this screen.

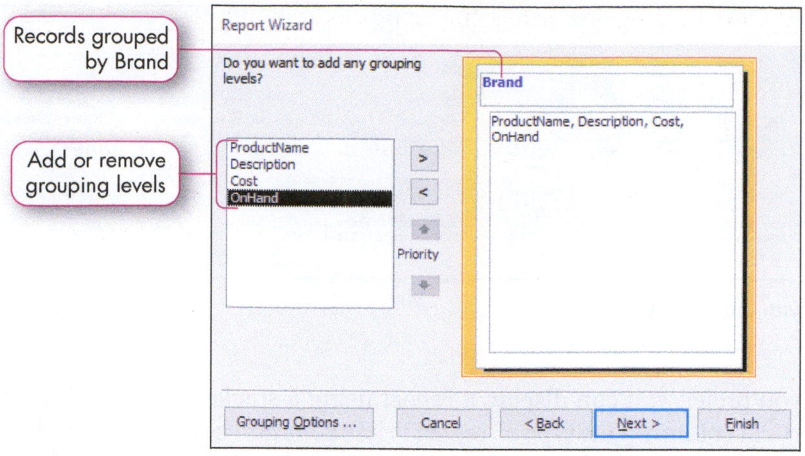

Records grouped by Brand

Add or remove grouping levels

FIGURE 4.23 Grouping Options in the Report Wizard

Apply the sorting and summary options in the next dialog box. Figure 4.24 displays the sort options for a grouped report. You can click Summary Options if you want to apply aggregating functions (e.g., Sum, Average, Minimum, and Maximum) and to specify whether you want to see detailed records on the report or only the aggregated results (see Figure 4.25). You can also choose to calculate values as percentages of totals in your report results. If no grouping is specified in your report, the summary options are not available. In Figure 4.25, no summary options are selected. Click OK to return to the Report Wizard.

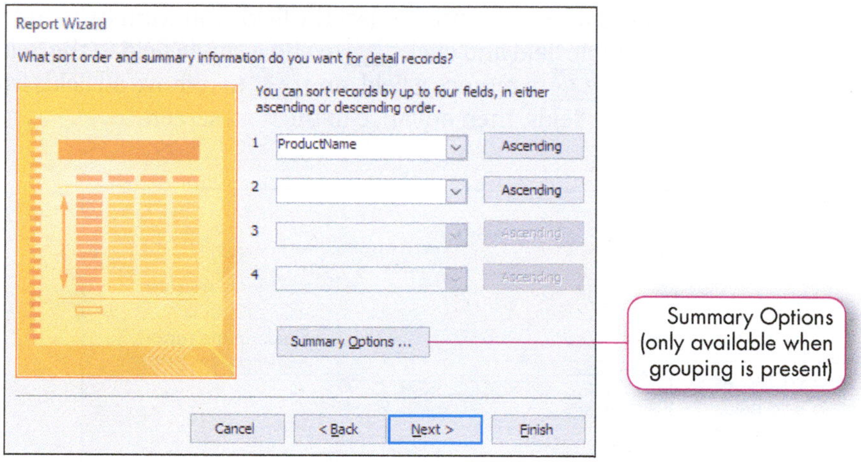

Summary Options (only available when grouping is present)

FIGURE 4.24 Sort and Summarize Grouped Data in the Report Wizard

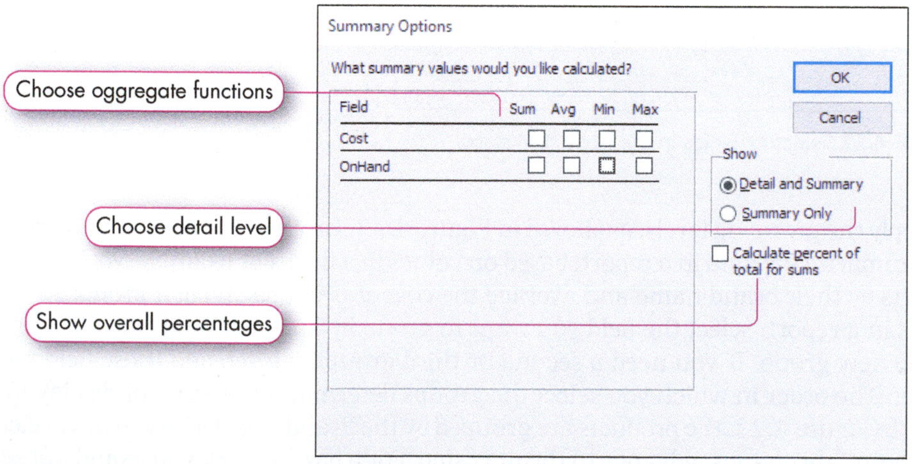

Choose oggregate functions

Choose detail level

Show overall percentages

FIGURE 4.25 Summary Options Dialog Box

In the next dialog box, select the layout as shown in Figure 4.26, to determine the report's appearance. In a grouped report, you will be prompted to select the layout from three options:

- Stepped Layout will display column headings at the top of the page and keep the grouping field(s) in their own row.
- Block Layout will include the grouping field(s) in line with the data, saving some space when printing. It has one set of column headings at the top of each page.
- Outline Layout will display the grouping field(s) on their own separate rows and has column headings inside each group. This leads to a longer report when printing but may help make the report easier to read.

Clicking any of these layouts will give you a general preview in the preview area. In a report without grouping, the layouts are Columnar, Tabular, and Justified. You can determine how the data fit on a page by selecting Portrait or Landscape.

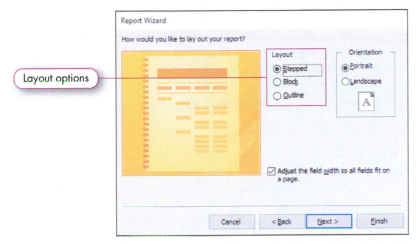

FIGURE 4.26 Layout Options for Grouped Data in the Report Wizard

Finish the wizard by giving the report a name. Your grouped report will resemble Figure 4.27.

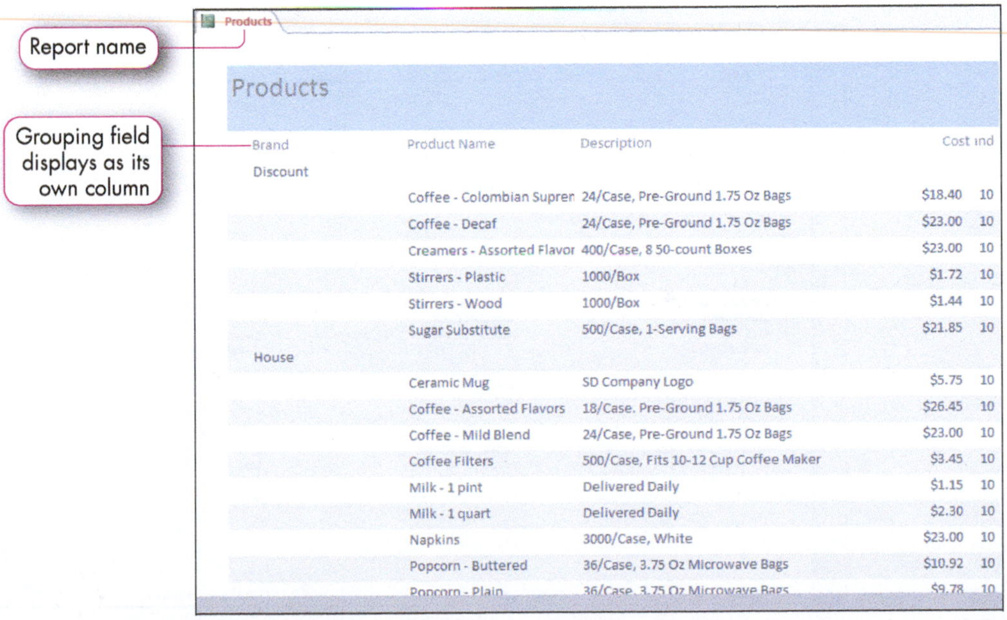

FIGURE 4.27 Grouped Report

Use the Label Wizard

The *Label Wizard* enables you to easily create mailing labels, name tags, and other specialized tags. A mailing label report is a specialized report that you can create and print with name-brand labels, such as Avery and many others. If you purchase a store brand label from an office supply store, it will generally state the comparable manufacturer and product number; the wizard provides a long list of both manufacturers and label sizes.

To use the Label Wizard, complete the following steps:

1. Select the table or query that you will use as the record source for the report.
2. Click Labels in the Reports group on the Create tab.
3. Select the manufacturer, product number, unit of measure, label type, and then click Next.
4. Select the font and color options and click Next.
5. Add the fields to the prototype label, as shown in Figure 4.28. You add the fields exactly as you would like them to display, including adding commas, spacing, and pressing Enter to move to the next line, where applicable.
6. Add sort fields, for example, you may want to sort by state or zip code, and then click Next.
7. Name the report and click Finish to generate your label report. The results using the Customers table are shown in Figure 4.29.

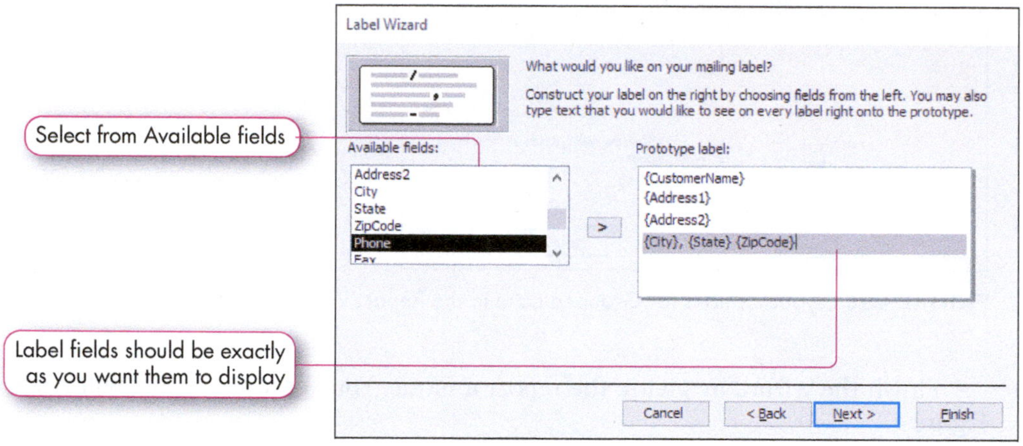

FIGURE 4.28 Create a Customers Prototype Label

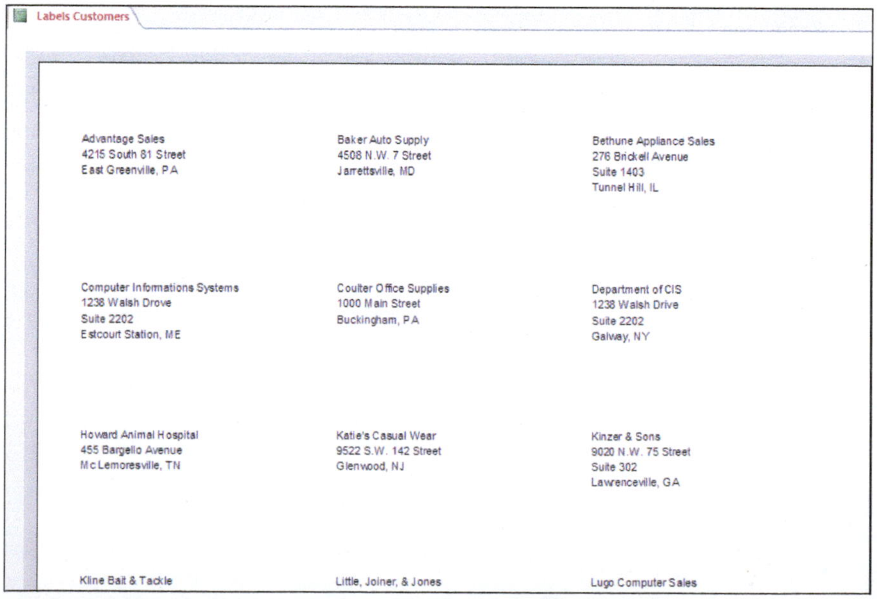

FIGURE 4.29 Customer Mailing Labels Created by Label Wizard

Using Report Views

As you work with the report tools to create and modify reports, you might need to switch between the four report views in Access—Report, Layout, Design, and Print Preview. Report view and Print Preview are generally used only for viewing or printing the report. To make modifications to a report, use Layout view and Design view. Most of the design work can be done in Layout view, but sometimes Design view is necessary to apply a more advanced feature, such as setting the tab order of the controls. Click the View arrow in the Views group and select the view to switch between the four views (alternatively, right-click the report tab and select the desired view from the shortcut menu).

View a Report in Report View

Report view enables you to view a report onscreen in a continuous page layout. However, because the data cannot be changed in Report view, it is simply a way of viewing the information without having to worry about accidentally moving a control. You can also use Report view to filter data if you only want to view a selected group of records.

STEP 2 Use Print Preview and Export a Report

Print Preview enables you to see exactly what the report will look like when it is printed. You cannot modify the design of the report or the data in Print Preview. By default, Print Preview will display all the pages in the report. Figure 4.29 displays the mailing labels report in Print Preview.

From Print Preview, you have the option to export and save the report to a different file type, such as Word. This is a useful option if you plan to share a report electronically but do not want to distribute the entire database. Alternatively, you can share a report with an individual or group who does not have Access installed on their computer or is not conversant with Access. In the Data group, on the Print Preview tab, you will find several eligible file types, as shown in Figure 4.30. Select the option in the Data group and follow the onscreen prompts to export your report. Commonly used formats include Excel, Word, and Portable Document Format (PDF).

Portable Document Format (PDF) is a file type that was created for exchanging documents independently of software applications and operating system environments. In other words, you can email a report in PDF format to users running various operating systems, and they can open it even if they do not have Microsoft Access installed. PDF files open in Adobe Reader, a free downloadable program; recent versions of Windows have a Reader program that displays PDF files as well. The Reader app can be downloaded from the Microsoft store for free if it is not installed on your system.

Because databases contain a great deal of information, Access reports can become very long, requiring many pages to print. At times, reports can be formatted incorrectly, or blank pages might print in between each page of information. Be sure to troubleshoot your reports before sending them to the printer, or to recipients via email.

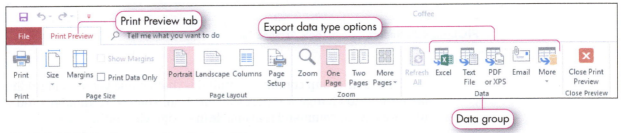

FIGURE 4.30 Data Group on Print Preview Tab

Use Layout View to Modify a Report

Use Layout view to modify the report's design while still viewing the data. You should use Layout view to add or delete fields in the report, modify field properties, change the column widths, group, sort, and summarize data. The Page Setup tab presents options for setting the page size, orientation, and margins. Although you will be able to view your modifications along with the data in Layout view, you will still need to check the report in Print Preview to evaluate all the changes before printing it.

STEP 3 Modifying a Report

After you create a report by using one of the report tools, you may want to modify it. Some of the common changes you make in reports are adding and deleting controls, changing the arrangement, widths, and formatting of controls, and modifying the title. From either Layout or Design view, there are four tabs available for report modification:

- Design: Use this tab to make changes to the design of the report, such as adding fields, grouping and sorting records, changing themes, and inserting additional controls.

- Arrange: Use this tab to change the layout of a report, to move fields up and down, and to control margins and spacing.

- Format: Use this tab to work with fonts, font sizes, and colors; add or remove bolding, italics, or underlining; adjust text alignment; or add a background image or color.

- Page Setup: Use this tab to change paper size, margins, or page orientation or to format reports into multiple columns.

Change the Report Layout

When you use one of the report tools to create a new report, Access will add a layout control to help align the fields. Layout controls in reports work similarly to layout controls in forms. The layout control provides guides to help keep controls aligned horizontally and vertically and give your report a neat appearance. The Arrange tab displays in both Layout view and Design view and contains commands for working with the layout of a report. Some key commands on the Arrange tab from Layout view are highlighted in Figure 4.31.

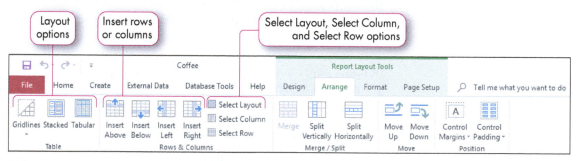

FIGURE 4.31 Report Layout Tools Arrange Tab

The Table group contains commands that enable you to add gridlines to a report's layout and to change a report's layout from stacked to tabular (and vice versa). The Remove Layout command is available in Design view only.

To change a report's layout from tabular to stacked, complete the following steps:

1. Open the report in Layout view and click the Arrange tab.
2. Click any text box in the Detail section of the report.
3. Click Select Layout in the Rows & Columns group.
4. Click Stacked in the Table group.

The Rows & Columns group contains commands that enable you to insert rows and columns inside a report's layout. In a report with a stacked layout, you may want to separate some controls from the rest of the fields or create some empty space so that fields can be added or repositioned. For example, you can select a control and click Insert Below. This will create an empty row (or space) below the selected control. This group also contains the Select Layout, Select Column, and Select Row commands, which you can use to select the entire layout, or a single column or row in a layout.

The Merge/Split group contains commands that enable you to merge and split the controls on a report. There are times when you might want to deviate from the basic row and column formats that the report tools create. For example, you can make a label such as *Product Name* display in two controls (Product and Name), with one positioned below the other rather than in one single control.

The Move group contains commands to move a field up or down in a stacked layout. Moving controls up or down in a report may cause unexpected results; you can always click Undo if you need to reverse your changes.

The Position group contains commands to control the margins and the padding (the spacing between controls) in a report. The preset margin settings are convenient to use; make sure that if you change the margins, you preview the report to view the result.

Remove a Report Layout Control

If you want to have more control over the location of the fields, you can remove the layout control and position the controls manually on the report.

To remove the layout control from a report, complete the following steps:

1. Open the report in Design view (the option is not available on the ribbon in Layout view) and click anywhere in the layout control you want to remove.
2. Click Select Layout in the Rows & Columns group on the Arrange tab.
3. Click Remove Layout in the Table group. All of the controls are still available in the report but can now be managed individually.

You can add a layout control to a report by first selecting all the controls you want to include in the layout. To select multiple controls, click the first control, press and hold Ctrl, and then click the additional controls you want to include. Press Ctrl+A to select all the controls on a form. Click Tabular or Stacked in the Table group.

Modify Report Controls

The Format tab contains a series of commands that enable you to change the font, display, and alignment of the controls on a report, as shown in Figure 4.32. The formatting tools in Access are like those in other Microsoft Office applications. To format report controls, open the report in Layout view (or Design view) and select the control(s) you want to format. Click the Format tab and click the formatting tools as desired.

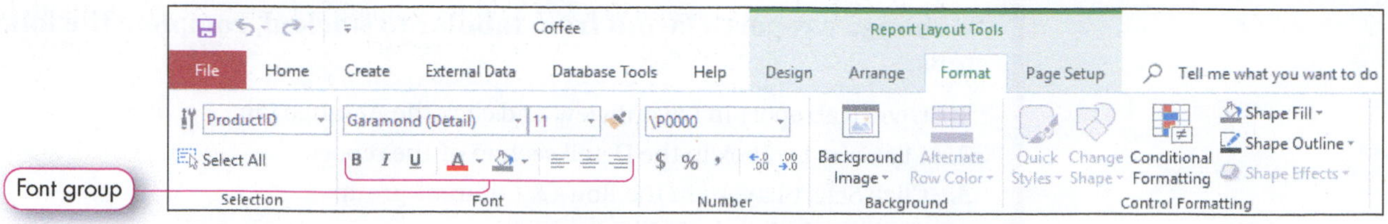

FIGURE 4.32 Report Layout Tools Format Tab

> **TIP: INSERT A LOGO IN A REPORT**
> To insert a logo in a report, open the report in Layout (or Design) view, and then click Logo in the Header/Footer group on the Design tab. In the Insert Picture dialog box, locate the image, click the file, and then click Open. The picture will display in the Report Header section; use the Property Sheet to modify the size and other attributes.

Add a Field to a Report

At times, new fields may be added to tables and then need to be incorporated into reports. Alternatively, you might be creating a customized report and want to add fields individually. Adding a field to a report with a stacked or tabular layout is similar to adding a field to a form.

To add a field to a report, complete the following steps:

1. Open the report in Layout view and click Add Existing Fields in the Tools group on the Design tab. The Field List pane displays at the right of the report. For a single-table report, a list of fields from the table (record source) is displayed. For a multiple-table report, click the + (plus sign) to the left of the appropriate table to expand it, and locate the field(s) you want to add.
2. Click and drag the field to the precise location on the report, using the shaded line as a guide for positioning the new field. Alternatively, you can double-click a field to add it to the report; the field will be added below the selected field. The other fields will automatically adjust to make room for the new field.

Remove a Field from a Report

You may decide that even though a field was available in a table or in a query that was used as the record source, it is not necessary to display it to users in a report. Not all fields in a database are necessarily relevant to reports that you create.

To remove a field from the Detail section of a report, complete the following steps:

1. Open the report in Layout view and click the text box control of the field to be deleted (note the shaded border around the control).
2. Click Select Row in the Rows & Columns group on the Arrange tab to select the text box and its associated label. Alternatively, click the text box control, press and hold Ctrl, and then click the associated label control to select them both.
3. Press Delete. The other fields will automatically adjust to close the gap around the deleted field.

Adjust Column Widths in a Report

You can adjust the width of each column in a tabular report individually so that each column is wide enough to accommodate the widest value in the field. For example, if a report contains first name, last name, address and city, and email address, you will need to make sure the longest value in each field is completely visible. Scroll through the records to ensure that all values can be viewed by report users. To modify a column width in a tabular report, open the report in Layout view, and then click the text box control of the field you want to resize. Point to the right border of the control until the pointer turns into a double-headed arrow. Drag the right edge of the control to the left or right until you arrive at the desired width.

Change Margins and Orientation

At times, you will want to print a report in Landscape orientation as opposed to Portrait, which is the default setting; that decision will depend upon how many columns you want to display across the page, the widths of the fields, and other formatting considerations. The Page Setup tab contains options like those you may have used in Word. In the Page Size group, you can change the margins, and in the Page Layout group, you can work with Page Setup options, including setting the orientation of your report, as shown in Figure 4.33.

FIGURE 4.33 Report Layout Tools Page Setup Tab

Apply a Theme

You can enhance the report's appearance by applying one of the built-in Access themes. A theme ensures a consistent use of fonts and a color scheme that uses complimentary colors. Open the report in Layout or Design view and select Themes in the Themes group on the Design tab. Point to a theme to see its name in the ScreenTip and a Live Preview of the theme in the report, then click to select it. By default, the theme will be applied to all objects in your database. Right-click a theme in the gallery to apply it to the current report only, or to all the reports in your database that share a common theme. Be sure to preview your report after applying a theme to ensure that applied font changes do not prevent your data from displaying correctly.

STEP 4 Sorting and Grouping Records in a Report

When a report is created using the Report tool, the sort order of the records in the report is initially dependent on the sort order of the record source—similar to the way records are sorted in a form. The primary key of the record source often controls the sort order. For example, if the report is sorted in primary key order, such as by CustomerID, sorting by a field like LastName might be a better choice. Users can locate the records in alphabetical order by the customer's last name, or by a different sort order that they find more useful. An Access report has an additional feature for sorting records, as well as grouping them by a common value, such as a customer's name. While in Layout view or Design view, click Group & Sort in the Grouping & Totals group on the Design tab. The Group, Sort, and Total pane displays at the bottom of the report. This pane enables you to group records together and to override the sort order in the report's record source. Note that if you do not use the Report Wizard, this is generally how you would add grouping and totals to a report.

To change the sorting in a report, complete the following steps:

1. Open the report in Layout or Design view and click Group & Sort in the Grouping & Totals group on the Design tab.
2. Click *Add a sort* and select the field by which you want to sort. The default sort order is ascending.
3. Add another sort by clicking *Add a sort* again. For example, you could sort first by Brand and then by ProductName, as shown in Figure 4.34.

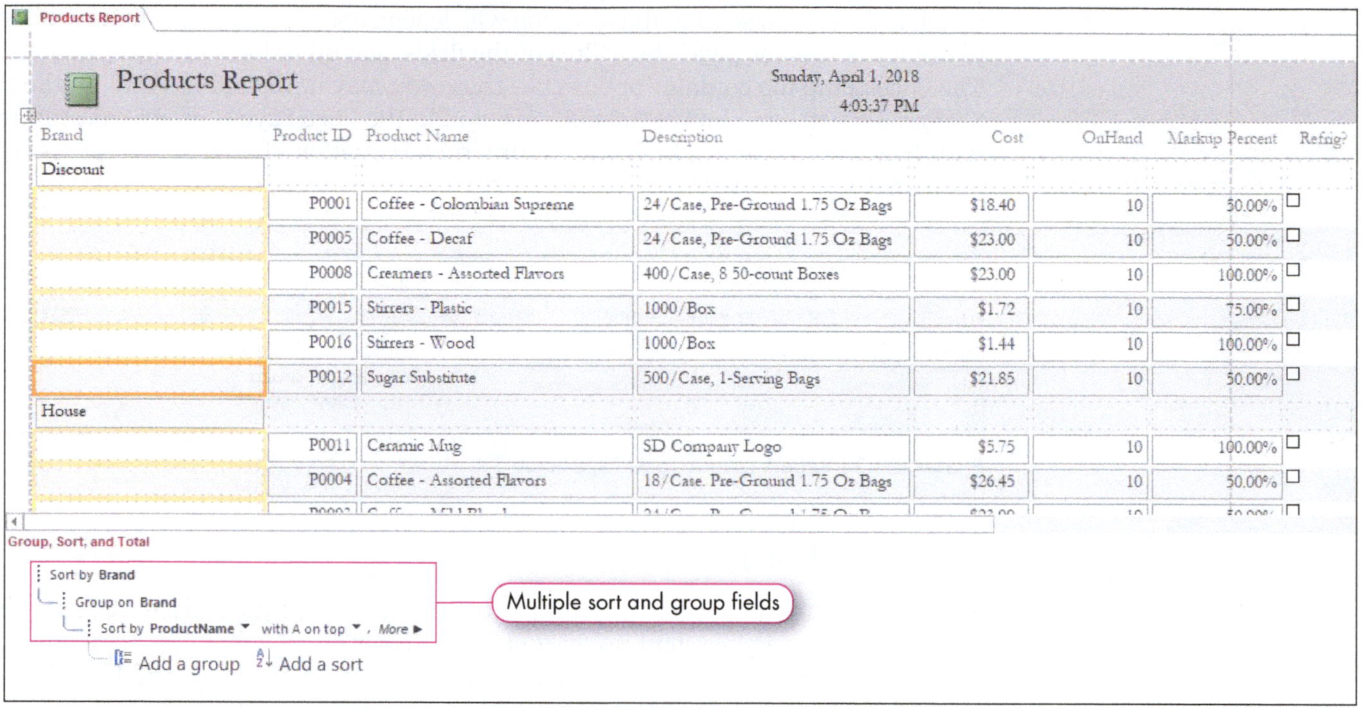

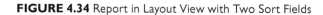

Brand	Product ID	Product Name	Description	Cost	OnHand	Markup Percent	Refrig?
Discount							
	P0001	Coffee - Colombian Supreme	24/Case, Pre-Ground 1.75 Oz Bags	$18.40	10	50.00%	☐
	P0005	Coffee - Decaf	24/Case, Pre-Ground 1.75 Oz Bags	$23.00	10	50.00%	☐
	P0008	Creamers - Assorted Flavors	400/Case, 8 50-count Boxes	$23.00	10	100.00%	☐
	P0015	Stirrers - Plastic	1000/Box	$1.72	10	75.00%	☐
	P0016	Stirrers - Wood	1000/Box	$1.44	10	100.00%	☐
	P0012	Sugar Substitute	500/Case, 1-Serving Bags	$21.85	10	50.00%	☐
House							
	P0011	Ceramic Mug	SD Company Logo	$5.75	10	100.00%	☐
	P0004	Coffee - Assorted Flavors	18/Case. Pre-Ground 1.75 Oz Bags	$26.45	10	50.00%	☐

Group, Sort, and Total

Sort by **Brand**
└ Group on **Brand**
   └ Sort by **ProductName** ▾ with A on top ▾ , More ▶ ← Multiple sort and group fields

Add a group   Add a sort

FIGURE 4.34 Report in Layout View with Two Sort Fields

Quick Concepts

6. Discuss the difference between Report view and Print Preview. **p. 277**
7. Explain why it is beneficial to save a report in the PDF format. **p. 277**
8. Consider the advantage of viewing your reports in Layout view. **p. 278**
9. Discuss an example for which you would remove a report layout control while modifying a report. **p. 278**
10. Describe how sorting records in a report can be helpful. **p. 281**

Hands-On Exercises

2 Create Basic Reports to Present Information

You create a products report using the Access Report tool to help Ryung stay on top of the key information for her business. You will modify the column widths so that they all fit across one page. You will also use the Report Wizard to create additional reports that Ryung requires.

STEP 1 ▸ **CREATING REPORTS USING REPORT TOOLS**

You use the Report tool to create an Access report to help Ryung manage her product information. This report is especially useful for determining which products she needs to order to fill upcoming orders. You also use the Report Wizard to determine sales by city. Refer to Figure 4.35 as you complete Step 1.

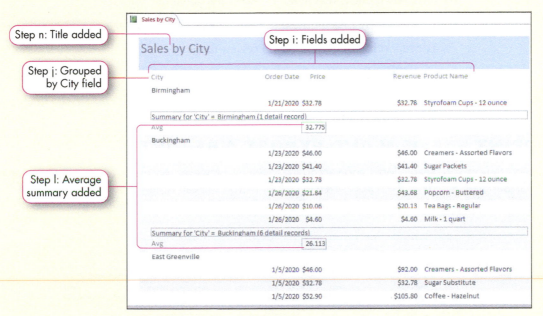

FIGURE 4.35 Sales by City Report

a. Open *a04h1Coffee_LastFirst* if you closed it at the end of Hands-On Exercise 1 and save it as **a04h2Coffee_LastFirst**, changing h1 to h2.

b. Select the **Products table** in the Navigation Pane. Click the **Create tab** and click **Report** in the Reports group.

   Access creates a new tabular layout report based on the Products table. The report opens in Layout view, ready for editing.

c. Click the **Products title** at the top of the report to select it, click again on **Products**, and then change the title to **Products Report**. Press **Enter** to accept the change.

d. Right-click the **Products report tab** and select **Print Preview**.

   The report is too wide for the page; you will close Print Preview and change the orientation to Landscape.

e. Click **Close Print Preview** in the Close Preview group to return to Layout view.

f. Click the **Page Setup tab** and click **Landscape** in the Page Layout group.

The report changes to Landscape orientation. Most of the columns now fit across one page. You will make further revisions to the report later so that it fits on one page.

g. Save the report as **Products Report**. Close the report.

h. Select the **Revenue query** in the Navigation Pane. Click the **Create tab** and click **Report Wizard** in the Reports group.

The Report Wizard launches.

i. Click the **City field** and click **Add One Field** > to add the City field to the report. Repeat the same process for the **OrderDate**, **Price**, **Revenue**, and **ProductName** **fields**. Click **Next**.

j. Ensure that City is selected, click **Add One Field** > to add grouping by city. Click **Next**.

k. Click the **arrow** in the first sort box and select **OrderDate**. Accept the default sort order as Ascending. Click **Summary Options**.

l. Click the **Avg check box** in the Price row to summarize the Price field. Click **OK**.

m. Click **Next**. Click **Next** again to accept the default layout.

n. Type **Sales by City** for the title of the report. Click **Finish**.

The report is displayed in Print Preview mode.

o. Click **Close Print Preview**.

p. Save and close the report.

USE PRINT PREVIEW AND EXPORT A REPORT

The Products Report you created looks good according to Ryung. However, Access does not run on her smart device, and she wants to have a copy of the report saved in PDF format so she can review it outside of the office. You will export a copy of the report to PDF format for her. Refer to Figure 4.36 as you complete Step 2.

Step a: Report in PDF format

Products Report					Monday, March 26, 2018 7:34:50 PM		
Product ID	Product Name	Description	Cost	Markup Percent	Refrigeration Needed		Brand
P0001	Coffee - Colombian Supreme	24/Case, Pre-Ground 1.75 Oz Bags	$18.40	50.00%	☐		Discount
P0002	Coffee - Hazelnut	24/Case, Pre-Ground 1.75 Oz Bags	$26.45	100.00%	☐		Premium
P0003	Coffee - Mild Blend	24/Case, Pre-Ground 1.75 Oz Bags	$23.00	50.00%	☐		House
P0004	Coffee - Assorted Flavors	18/Case, Pre-Ground 1.75 Oz Bags	$26.45	50.00%	☐		House
P0005	Coffee - Decaf	24/Case, Pre-Ground 1.75 Oz Bags	$23.00	50.00%	☐		Discount
P0006	Tea Bags - Regular	75/Box, Individual Tea Bags	$5.75	75.00%	☐		House
P0007	Tea Bags - Decaf	75/Box, Individual Tea Bags	$8.05	75.00%	☐		House
P0008	Creamers - Assorted Flavors	400/Case, 8 50-count Boxes	$23.00	100.00%	☐		Discount
P0009	Creamers - Liquid	200/Case, Individual Creamers	$17.25	100.00%	☑		Premium
P0010	Sugar Packets	2000/Case	$20.70	100.00%	☐		House
P0011	Ceramic Mug	SD Company Logo	$5.75	100.00%	☐		House
P0012	Sugar Substitute	500/Case, 1-Serving Bags	$21.85	50.00%	☐		Discount
P0013	Coffee Filters	500/Case, Fits 10-12 Cup Coffee Maker	$3.45	50.00%	☐		House
P0014	Napkins	3000/Case, White	$23.00	100.00%	☐		House
P0015	Stirrers - Plastic	1000/Box	$1.72	75.00%	☐		Discount
P0016	Stirrers - Wood	1000/Box	$1.44	100.00%	☐		Discount
P0017	Spoons	500/Box, White Plastic	$17.25	100.00%	☐		House
P0018	Popcorn - Plain	36/Case, 3.75 Oz Microwave Bags	$9.78	100.00%	☐		House
P0019	Popcorn - Buttered	36/Case, 3.75 Oz Microwave Bags	$10.92	100.00%	☐		House
P0020	Soup - Chicken	50 Envelopes	$11.50	100.00%	☐		Premium
P0021	Soup - Variety Pak	50 Envelopes	$13.80	100.00%	☐		Premium
P0022	Styrofoam Cups - 10 ounce	1000/Case	$19.55	50.00%	☐		House

Page 1 of 2

FIGURE 4.36 Products Report Saved in PDF Format

a. Open the Products Report, click the **File tab**, click **Print**, and then select **Print Preview**. Click **PDF or XPS** in the Data group on the Print Preview tab. Navigate to where you are saving your files, type the file name **a04h2Products_LastFirst**, ensure that *Open file after publishing* is selected, and then click **Publish**.

Windows will open the report in your system's default PDF viewer, which may be Adobe Reader or the Windows Reader app. Close the reader window.

b. Ensure that you return to the Access window, and in the Export – PDF dialog box, click **Close** when prompted to save the export steps.

c. Click **Close Print Preview** and close the report.

MODIFYING A REPORT

Ryung realized the Products table is missing a field that she requires for her reports. She asked you to add the field to the table and update the report to include the new field. She also wants to make sure the report fits nicely across one landscape page. She also asked you to show her some sample color schemes. Refer to Figure 4.37 as you complete Step 3.

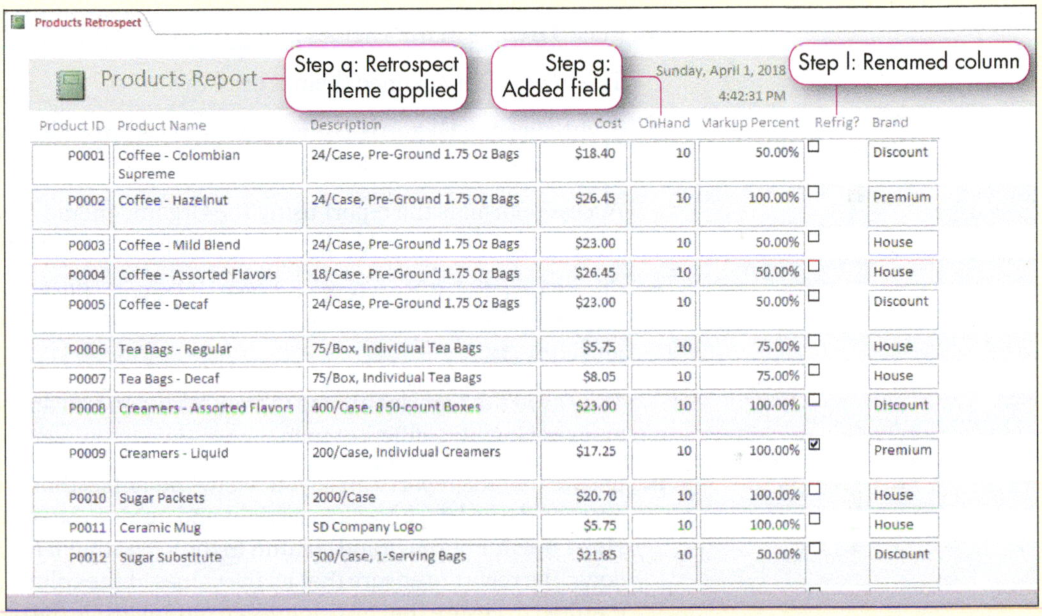

FIGURE 4.37 Products Retrospect Report

a. Right-click the **Products table** and select **Design View**.

You need to add the OnHand field to the Products table.

b. Click in the **MarkupPercent field** and click **Insert Rows** in the Tools group on the Design tab.

A new blank row displays above the MarkupPercent field.

c. Type **OnHand** in the Field Name box and select **Number** as the Data Type.

d. Save the table. Click **View** in the Views group to switch to Datasheet view.

The new OnHand column contains no data. Next, you will add some sample data to the new field for testing purposes only.

e. Type the number **10** for each item's OnHand value. Close the Products table.

f. Right-click **Products Report** in the Navigation Pane and select **Layout View**. Click **Add Existing Fields** in the Tools group on the Design tab to open the Field List pane, if necessary.

g. Drag the **OnHand field** from the Field List pane between the Cost and MarkupPercent fields. Close the Field List pane.

Because of the tabular layout control, Access adjusts all the columns to make room for the new OnHand field.

h. Display the report in Print Preview.

The report is still too wide for a single page.

i. Click **Close Print Preview**. Ensure that you are in Layout view.

j. Scroll to and click anywhere in the **Year Introduced column**. Click the **Arrange tab** and click **Select Column** in the Rows & Columns group. Press **Delete** to remove the column.

The Year Introduced column is removed from the report.

k. Scroll to and click the **ProductID column heading** and drag the right border to the left until the Product ID heading still fits, but any extra white space is removed.

l. Scroll to and click the **Refrigeration Needed column heading** and rename the column **Refrig?**. Adjust the width of the *Refrig?* column heading so that any extra white space is removed.

m. Click **Themes** in the Themes group on the Design tab.

The available predefined themes display.

n. Right-click the **Organic theme** and select **Apply Theme to This Object Only**. Display the report in Print Preview.

Access reformats the report using the Organic theme. The report is still too wide for a single page. You will make further adjustments in the next steps.

o. Click **Close Print Preview** and save the report. Click the **File tab**, select **Save As**, select **Save Object As**, and then click **Save As**. Type **Products Organic** as the report name and click **OK**.

You saved the report with one theme. Now, you will apply a second theme to the report and save it with a different name.

p. Ensure that the report is in Layout view. You notice that the Brand column is extending over the dashed page break to its right and needs to be resized to fit on the page. Drag the **right border** of the Brand column to the left so that it fits inside the page break. Scroll down the report to ensure that all the values in the column are visible. Narrow columns as required to ensure that all columns are fitting inside the dashed page break. Save the report.

q. Click **Themes** in the Themes group to apply a different theme. Right-click the **Retrospect theme** and select **Apply Theme to This Object Only**. Display the report in Print Preview.

If you do not apply the theme to this object only, all database objects will adopt the Retrospect theme.

r. Click **Close Print Preview**. Click the **File tab**, select **Save As**, select **Save Object As**, and then click **Save As**. Type **Products Retrospect** as the report name and click **OK**. Close the report.

You will be able to show Ryung two product reports with different themes applied.

STEP 4 SORTING AND GROUPING RECORDS IN A REPORT

Ryung wants the Products Report records to be sorted and grouped by Brand. You will change the sort order, group the records, and preview the report to see the results. Refer to Figure 4.38 as you complete Step 4.

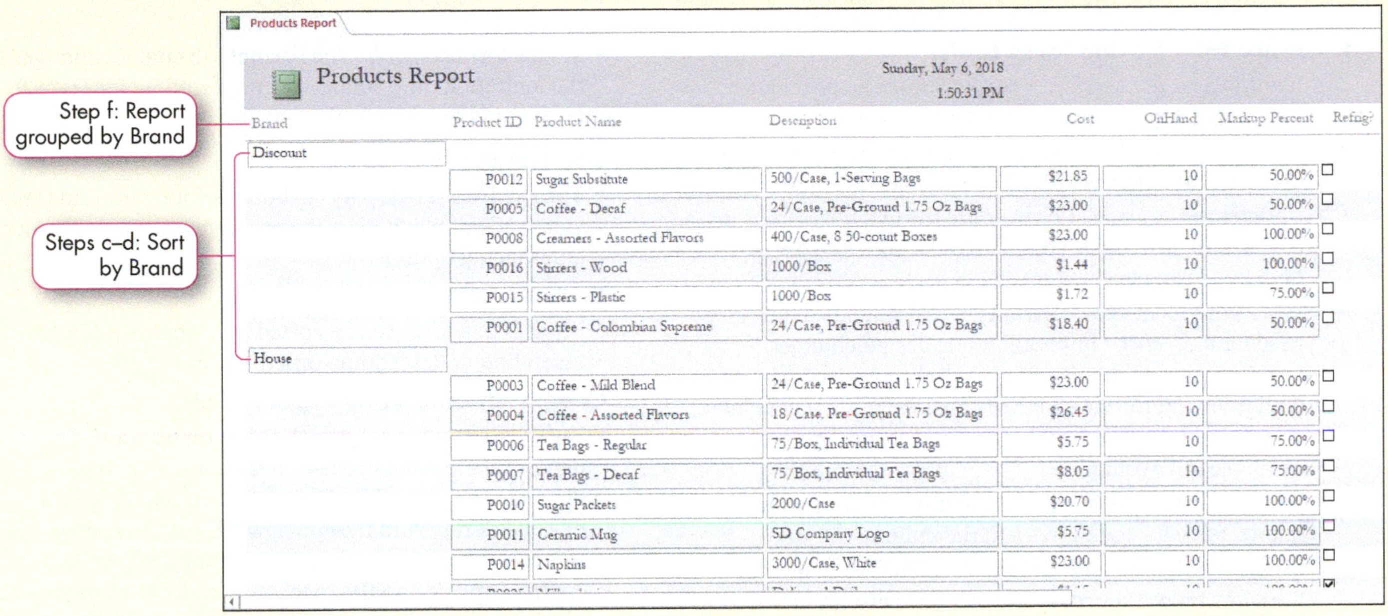

FIGURE 4.38 Products Report Grouped by Brand

a. Open **Products Report** in Layout view.

b. Click **Group & Sort** in the Grouping & Totals group on the Design tab.

The *Add a group* and *Add a sort* options display at the bottom of the report in the Group, Sort, and Total pane.

> **TROUBLESHOOTING:** If the options do not display, the Group, Sort, and Total pane may have been open. If the pane is closed after selecting the command, try clicking Group & Sort again.

c. Click **Add a sort**.

A new Sort bar displays at the bottom of the report.

d. Select **Brand** from the list.

The report is now sorted by Brand in ascending order (with the Discount brand at the top).

e. Click **Add a group**.

f. Select **Brand** from the list.

The report is now grouped by Brand.

g. View the report in Report view. Save and close the report.

h. Close the database and exit Access. Based on your instructor's directions, submit the following:

a04h2Coffee_LastFirst

a04h2Products_LastFirst.pdf

Chapter Objectives Review

After reading this chapter, you have accomplished the following objectives:

1. Create forms using form tools.

- Identify a record source: A record source is the table or query that supplies the records for the form.
- Use the Form tool: The Form tool creates a basic form that opens in Layout view.
- Understand controls: Controls are the text boxes, buttons, labels, and other tools you use to add, edit, and display data in a form or report.
- Work with form views: Form view is a simplified interface used for data entry, but it allows no design changes. Layout view enables users to make changes to the layout while viewing the data in the form. Design view enables you to change advanced design settings that are not available in Layout view.
- Work with a subform: A subform displays data from a related table for each record in the main table.
- Create a split form: A split form combines two views of the same record source—one section is displayed in a stacked layout, and the other section is displayed in a tabular layout.
- Create a multiple items form: This form displays multiple records in a tabular layout like a table's Datasheet view, with more customization options.
- Create a Navigation form: A Navigation form enables you to create user interfaces that have the look and feel of Web-based forms and allows users to open and close the objects of a database.
- Create forms using the other form tools: A datasheet form is a replica of a table or query's Datasheet view except that it still retains form properties. The Form Design tool and the Blank Form tools can be used to create a form manually. The Modal Dialog Form tool can be used to create a dialog box.
- Print selected records in a form: Use the Selected Record(s) option in the Print dialog box to print one or more selected records.

2. Modify forms.

- Edit data in Form view: Most users will work in Form view. This enables changes to data but not to design elements.
- Use Layout view to modify form design: Layout view enables you to change the design of a form while viewing data.
- Adjust column widths in a form: Column widths often need to be adjusted. Size the columns to accommodate the widest entry in a field.
- Add and delete form fields: Fields can be added to an existing form using the Field List. Fields can be removed by selecting the text box and the label control and pressing Delete.

- Modify form controls: The Format tab enables changes to the font, including bold, italic, underlining, font size, font color, font background, and alignment.

3. Use the form layout control.

- The Arrange tab displays in both Layout view and Design view and enables you to change form layout, field order, and spacing options.

4. Sort records in a form.

- Records in a form can be sorted by a single field in either ascending or descending order.

5. Create reports using report tools.

- Use the Report tool: Access has five report tools. The Report tool instantly creates a tabular report based on a table or query. The Report Design tool creates a new blank report in Design view. The Blank Report tool creates a new blank report so that you can insert controls and design the report manually in Layout view. The Report Wizard tool steps you through the process to create a report. The Labels tool creates a page of mailing labels using a template.
- Use the Report Wizard: The Report Wizard will guide you step by step through creating a report, prompting you for input and generating output. The wizard enables you to group records of a common type and summarize data in your reports.
- Use the Label Wizard: The Label Wizard can produce printable labels. Access includes predefined standard formats for common labels.

6. Use report views.

- View a report in Report view: Report view is ideal for viewing data onscreen. Neither data nor the design can be changed in this view.
- Use Print Preview and export a report: Print Preview shows how the report will display when printed. It also enables you to export the report as a file in several formats, such as Word and PDF.
- Use Layout view to modify a report: Layout view enables you to change the design of a report while viewing data.

7. Modify a report.

- Change the report layout: The Arrange tab displays in both Layout view and Design view. The tools on the Arrange tab enable you to work with the layout of a report to give it a more uniform appearance.
- Remove a report layout control: To have more control over the location of your fields, you can remove the layout control and position the controls manually on the report.
- Modify report controls: The Format tab enables changes to the font, including bold, italic, underlining, font size, font color, font background, and alignment.

- Add a field to a report: Fields can be added to an existing report using the Field List pane.
- Remove a field from a report: Fields can be deleted either in Layout or Design view.
- Adjust column widths in a report: Column widths often need to be adjusted. Be sure to make the column wide enough to display the widest value in a field.
- Change margins and orientation: You can display the report in portrait or landscape mode and increase or decrease margin sizes.

- Apply a theme: Themes can be applied to a single report or to all objects in the database.

8. Sort and group records in a report.
- Access reports can be sorted differently from their underlying record sources, as well as grouped by a common value, such as a customer's name. Use the Group, Sort, and Total pane to add a sort or grouping level to a report.

Key Terms Matching

Match the key terms with their definitions. Write the key term letter by the appropriate numbered definition.

a. Control
b. Design view
c. Form
d. Form tool
e. Form view
f. Label Wizard
g. Layout control
h. Layout view
i. Multiple Items form
j. Navigation form

k. Portable Document Format (PDF)
l. Print Preview
m. Record source
n. Report
o. Report tool
p. Report view
q. Report Wizard
r. Split form
s. Stacked layout
t. Tabular layout

1. _____ A database object that is used to add data into, or edit data in, an underlying table. **p. 250**

2. _____ Used to create data entry forms for customers, employees, products, and other tables. **p. 252**

3. _____ The table or query that supplies the records for a form or report. **p. 251**

4. _____ Arrangement that displays fields in a vertical column. **p. 252**

5. _____ Arrangement that displays fields horizontally across the screen or page. **p. 252**

6. _____ A text box, button, label, or other tool you use to add, edit, and display the data in a form or report. **p. 252**

7. _____ Provides guides to help keep controls aligned horizontally and vertically and give your form or report a uniform appearance. **p. 252**

8. _____ A simplified user interface primarily used for data entry; does not allow you to make changes to the layout. **p. 253**

9. _____ Enables users to make changes to a layout while viewing the data in the form or report. **p. 254**

10. _____ Enables you to change advanced design settings you cannot see in Layout view, such as removing a layout control. **p. 254**

11. _____ Combines two views of the same record source—one section is displayed in a stacked layout and the other section is displayed in a tabular layout. **p. 255**

12. _____ Displays multiple records in a tabular layout like a table's Datasheet view, with more customization options. **p. 256**

13. _____ User interface that allows users to switch between various forms and reports in a database. **p. 256**

14. _____ A database document that outputs meaningful information to its readers. **p. 271**

15. _____ Used to instantly create a tabular report based on the table or query currently selected. **p. 272**

16. _____ Prompts you for input and then uses your answers to generate a customized report. **p. 273**

17. _____ Enables you to easily create mailing labels, name tags, and other specialized tags. **p. 276**

18. _____ Enables you to determine what a printed report will look like in a continuous page layout. **p. 277**

19. _____ Enables you to see exactly what the report will look like when it is printed. **p. 277**

20. _____ A file type that was created for exchanging documents independent of software applications and operating system environment. **p. 277**

Multiple Choice

1. A form or report can be made from one or more tables or a query. The object(s) that is the underlying basis for a form or a report is the:
   - (a) control source.
   - (b) record source.
   - (c) grouped object.
   - (d) Multiple Items form.

2. Which of the following statements is *false*?
   - (a) Both forms and reports can use tabular and stacked layouts.
   - (b) A stacked layout displays data in a vertical column.
   - (c) A tabular layout displays data horizontally.
   - (d) Stacked layouts are more common for reports because they use less paper when printed.

3. To summarize data in a report and override the sort order of the record source you would use:
   - (a) a text box.
   - (b) a button on a report.
   - (c) the Group, Sort, and Total pane.
   - (d) a label on a report.

4. The view you can use to export a report to a different format is:
   - (a) Layout view.
   - (b) Form view.
   - (c) Design view.
   - (d) Print Preview.

5. Which of the following views provides you with the option to view data while making design and layout changes?
   - (a) Design view
   - (b) Layout view
   - (c) Form view/Report view
   - (d) Print Preview

6. Which of the following statements about reports is *false*?
   - (a) Reports can be saved to a file (such as a Word document) on your computer.
   - (b) Reports are primarily used to modify data.
   - (c) Reports can produce output in several ways, including mailing labels.
   - (d) Reports can be created simply by using the Report tool.

7. Create a _____ form as a user interface that enables you to switch between forms and reports in a database.
   - (a) Stacked
   - (b) Multiple items
   - (c) Split
   - (d) Navigation

8. If you need to send a report to a user who does not have Microsoft Office available, which of the following file formats would be the best choice to ensure it can be opened?
   - (a) Word
   - (b) Excel
   - (c) Reader
   - (d) Portable Document Format (PDF)

9. Which of the following statements is *false*?
   - (a) Reports are generally used for printing, emailing, or viewing data on the screen.
   - (b) Themes are the predefined sets of colors, fonts, and graphics.
   - (c) Forms are used for viewing but not inputting data.
   - (d) Forms and reports both include controls, such as text boxes, that can be resized.

10. Which of the following statements is *true*?
    - (a) You can add grouping and sorting to records in a report that vary from the underlying record source.
    - (b) You can sort records in reports but not in forms.
    - (c) The default sort order for a field is descending.
    - (d) You can either group or sort records (but not both).

Practice Exercises

The Human Resources department of the Comfort Insurance Agency has initiated its annual employee performance reviews. You will create forms for them to perform data entry using the Form tool, a split form, and a multiple items form. You will create a report to display locations, and a report displaying employee salary increases grouped by location. Additionally, you will export the salary increases report as a PDF file. Refer to Figure 4.39 as you complete this exercise.

Location YearHired	LastName	FirstName	Salary	2020Increase	2020Raise
Employee Compensation					
L01					
2019	Abrams	Wendy	$47,500.00	3.00%	$1,425.00
2015	Anderson	Vicki	$47,900.00	4.00%	$1,916.00
2019	Bichette	Susan	$61,500.00	4.00%	$2,460.00
2017	Block	Leonard	$26,200.00	3.00%	$786.00
2018	Brown	Patricia	$25,000.00	5.00%	$1,250.00
2016	Brumbaugh	Paige	$49,300.00	3.00%	$1,479.00
2018	Daniels	Phil	$42,600.00	3.00%	$1,278.00
2017	Davis	Martha	$51,900.00	4.00%	$2,076.00
2016	Drubin	Lolly	$37,000.00	3.00%	$1,110.00
2015	Gander	John	$38,400.00	3.00%	$1,152.00
2017	Grippando	Joan	$26,100.00	3.00%	$783.00
2019	Harrison	Jenifer	$44,800.00	3.00%	$1,344.00
2018	Imber	Elise	$63,700.00	4.00%	$2,548.00
2019	Johnshon	Billy	$22,800.00	5.00%	$1,140.00
2019	Johnson	Debbie	$39,700.00	3.00%	$1,191.00
2019	McCammon	Johnny	$43,100.00	4.00%	$1,724.00
2015	Mills	Jack	$44,600.00	3.00%	$1,338.00

FIGURE 4.39 Employee Compensation Report

a. Open *a04p1Insurance*. Save the database as **a04p1Insurance_LastFirst**.

b. Click the **Locations table** in the Navigation Pane. Click **Form** in the Forms group on the Create tab.

c. Click the **View arrow** in the Views group on the Home tab and select **Design View**. Click anywhere in the **Table.Employees subform control** and press **Delete**. Switch to Layout view.

d. Ensure that the LocationID text box containing *L01* in Record 1 is selected. Drag the **right border** to the left to resize the column to approximately half of its original width (to about 3.4"). The other text boxes will resize as well.

e. Change the font size of the Location text box control (containing *Atlanta*) to **14** and change the Background Color to **Blue, Accent 1, Lighter 60%**.

f. Click **Select Row** in the Rows & Columns group on the Arrange tab. Click **Move Up** in the Move group until Location displays above LocationID.

g. Save the form as **Locations Data Entry**.

h. Delete the **LocationID field**. Delete the **Office Phone label**. Move the **Office Phone field** to the row immediately below the Location field.

i. Click **Add Existing Fields** in the Tools group on the Form Layout Tools Design tab. Click and drag to add **LocationID** back to the form from the Field List pane, immediately below the Address field. Close the Field List pane.

j. Switch to Form view, and then save and close the form.

k. Click the **Titles table** in the Navigation Pane. Click **More Forms** in the Forms group on the Create tab to create a Multiple Items form based on the Titles table. Resize the width of the Title field to approximately **1"** and the EducationRequired field to approximately **1.5"** so that all fields are visible onscreen without scrolling.

l. Click the **File tab**, click **Print**, and then select **Print Preview**. Click **Landscape** in the Page Layout group. Click **Close Print Preview** in the Close Preview group.

m. Save the form as **Job Titles Multiple Items**. Close the form.

n. Click the **Employees table** in the Navigation Pane. Click **More Forms** in the Forms group on the Create tab to create a Split Form based on the Employees table. Switch to Form view.

o. Select the bottom pane of the form, scroll down and click in the record for **EmployeeID 22** (Denise Smith). In the top pane of the form, select the existing Performance value (*Average*), and replace it with **Good**. Press Tab two times to save the record.

p. Save the form as **Employees Split Form**. Close the form.

q. Click the **Locations table** in the Navigation Pane. Click **Report** in the Reports group on the Create tab.

r. Click and drag the **right border** of each label to the left to reduce the column widths until there are no controls on the right side of the vertical dashed line (page break). Drag the control containing the page number to the left so that it is inside the page break.

s. Display the report in Report view. Verify that the report is only one page wide in Report view. Save the report as **Locations** and close the report.

t. Click the **Employees Query** in the Navigation Pane. Click **Report Wizard** in the Reports group on the Create tab. Respond to the prompts as follows:

- Add all the fields to the Selected Fields list. Click **HireDate** and remove the field from the Selected Fields. Remove **YearHired** from the Selected Fields. Click **Next**.
- Accept grouping by Location. Click **Next**.
- Select **LastName** for the first sort order, and **FirstName** for the second (ascending order for both). Click **Summary Options**.
- Click **Sum** for Salary, and **Avg** for 2020Increase. Click **OK**. Click **Next**.
- Accept the Stepped layout. Change Orientation to **Landscape**. Click **Next**.
- Type **Employee Compensation** for the title of the report. Click **Finish**.

u. Click **Close Print Preview**. Switch to Layout view.

v. Adjust the widths of the controls so that all the data values are visible and the columns all fit within the vertical dashed border (page break). Some of the text boxes and labels will need to be relocated; select the control to be moved and click and drag it to a new location but keep them in the same order.

w. Click **Themes** in the Themes group on the Design tab. Right-click the **Slice theme** and select **Apply Theme to This Object Only**. Adjust the label widths and report title so that they are fully visible. Scroll to the bottom of the report and move any text boxes, such as the page number control, so that they are inside the page break. Resize all text boxes and labels so that their values are fully visible.

x. Click and drag **YearHired** from the Field List into the report layout. Drag and drop the column into the space immediately to the right of the Location column. Close the Field List. Display the report in Print Preview. Compare your report to Figure 4.39. Make adjustments as required.

y. Export the report as a PDF file named **a04p1Employee_Compensation_LastFirst**. Close the reader window. Do not save the export steps.

z. Save and close the Employee Compensation report.

aa. Click the **Create tab**, click **Navigation** in the Forms group, and then select **Horizontal Tabs**.

ab. Drag the **Job Titles Multiple Items form icon** from the Navigation Pane onto the **[Add New] tab** at the top of the form.

ac. Drag the **Employee Compensation report icon** from the Navigation Pane onto the **[Add New] tab** at the top of the form. Click the **Job Titles Multiple Items tab** and click the **Employee Compensation tab**.

ad. Save the Navigation form with the default name and close all open objects.

ae. Close the database and exit Access. Based on your instructor's directions, submit the following:

a04p1Insurance_LastFirst

a04p1Employee Compensation_LastFirst.pdf

2 Financial Management Prospects

You are working as a customer service representative for a financial management firm. Your task is to contact a list of prospective customers and introduce yourself and the services of your company. You will create a form to view, add, and update data for one customer at a time. After creating the form, you will customize it and add sorting. You will also create a report to display all the information on one screen, for viewing purposes. Refer to Figure 4.40 as you complete this exercise.

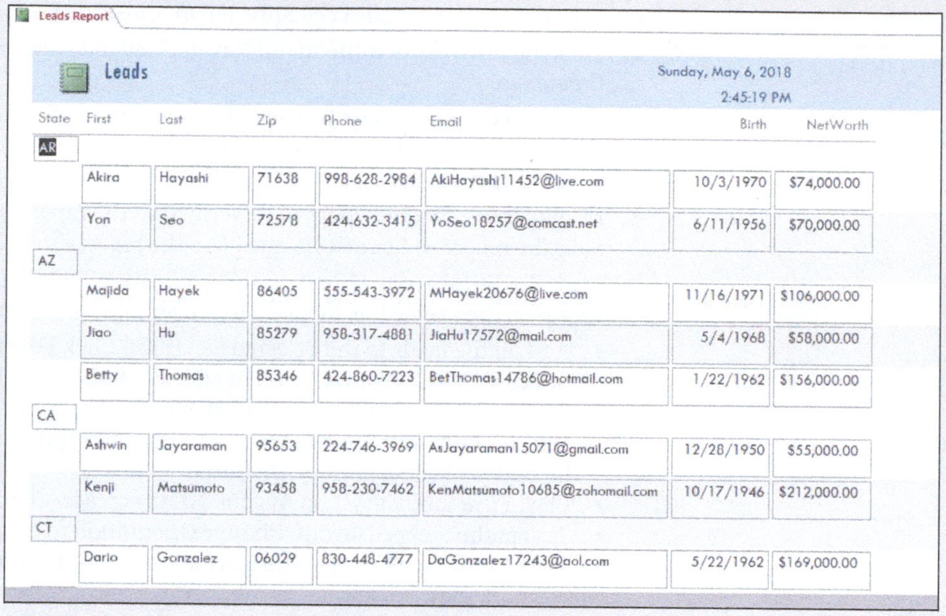
Leads Report

Leads

Sunday, May 6, 2018
2:45:19 PM

State	First	Last	Zip	Phone	Email	Birth	NetWorth
AR							
	Akira	Hayashi	71638	998-628-2984	AkiHayashi11452@live.com	10/3/1970	$74,000.00
	Yon	Seo	72578	424-632-3415	YoSeo18257@comcast.net	6/11/1956	$70,000.00
AZ							
	Majida	Hayek	86405	555-543-3972	MHayek20676@live.com	11/16/1971	$106,000.00
	Jiao	Hu	85279	958-317-4881	JiaHu17572@mail.com	5/4/1968	$58,000.00
	Betty	Thomas	85346	424-860-7223	BetThomas14786@hotmail.com	1/22/1962	$156,000.00
CA							
	Ashwin	Jayaraman	95653	224-746-3969	AsJayaraman15071@gmail.com	12/28/1950	$55,000.00
	Kenji	Matsumoto	93458	958-230-7462	KenMatsumoto10685@zohomail.com	10/17/1946	$212,000.00
CT							
	Dario	Gonzalez	06029	830-448-4777	DaGonzalez17243@aol.com	5/22/1962	$169,000.00

FIGURE 4.40 Grouped and Sorted Leads Report

a. Open *a04p2Prospects*. Save the database as **a04p2Prospects_LastFirst**.

b. Click the **Leads table** in the Navigation Pane. Click **Form** in the Forms group on the Create tab.

c. Select the **LeadID text box** of Record 1 and drag the right border to the left to resize the column to approximately half of its original width (to about 3.4"). The other text boxes will resize as well.

d. Change the title of the form to **New Leads**.

e. Change the font size of the NetWorth text box control to **14** and change the Background Color to **Blue, Accent 5, Lighter 60%**.

f. Click **Select Row** in the Rows & Columns group on the Arrange tab. Click **Move Up** in the Move group until NetWorth displays above First.

> **TROUBLESHOOTING:** If the text box and the label do not move together, click Undo, ensure that both controls are selected, and then follow the instructions in Step f.

g. Save the form as **Leads Form**. Switch to Form view.

h. Navigate to Record 63. Enter **your name** in both the first and last fields. Leave the Email field blank.

i. Click in the **Last field** and click **Ascending** in the Sort & Filter group on the Home tab. Farrah Aaron should be the first record displayed unless your last name appears before hers alphabetically.

j. Save and close the form.

k. Click the **Leads table** in the Navigation Pane. Click **More Forms** in the Forms group on the Create tab and select **Split Form**.

l. Modify the form title to read **Leads-Split Form**. Save the form as **Leads-Split Form** and close the form.

m. Click the **Leads table**. Click **Report** in the Reports group on the Create tab.

A new report is created based on the Leads table.

n. Make the fields as narrow as possible to remove any extra white space in them. Change the report's orientation to **Landscape**.

o. Delete the **LeadID**, **Address**, and **City** columns from the report.

p. Click Group & Sort in the Grouping & Totals group on the Design tab. Group the records by **State** and sort them by **LastName** in ascending order. Close the Group, Sort, and Total pane.

q. Click **Themes** in the Themes group on the Design tab. Right-click the **Integral theme** and select **Apply Theme to This Object Only**. At the bottom of the report, change the font size of the control that displays the total to **10**. Move any text boxes, such as the page number control, so that they are inside the page break.

r. Export the report as a PDF file named **a04p2LeadsReport_LastFirst**. Close the reader window. Do not save the export steps.

s. Save the report as **Leads Report**. Close the report.

t. Click the **Create tab**, click **Navigation** in the Forms group, and then select **Vertical Tabs, Left**.

u. Drag the **Leads Form form icon** from the Navigation Pane onto the **[Add New] tab** at the left of the form.

v. Drag the **Leads Report report icon** from the Navigation Pane onto the second **[Add New] tab** at the left of the form. Click the **Leads Form tab** and click the **Leads Report tab**.

w. Save the Navigation form with the default name and close all open objects.

x. Close the database and exit Access. Based on your instructor's directions, submit the following:

a04p2LeadsReport_LastFirst

a04p2Prospects_LastFirst.pdf

Mid-Level Exercises

1 Hotel Chain

ANALYSIS CASE

You are the general manager of a large hotel chain. You track revenue by categories, such as conference room rentals and weddings. You want to create a report that shows which locations are earning the most revenue in each category. You will also create a report to show you details of your three newest areas: St. Paul, St. Louis, and Seattle.

a. Open *a04m1Rewards*. Save the database as **a04m1Rewards_LastFirst**.

b. Select the **Members table** and create a Multiple Items form. Save the form as **Maintain Members**.

c. Change the MemNumber label to **MemID** and use the Property Sheet to reduce the MemNumber column width to **0.6"**.

d. Change the widths of the LastName, FirstName, City, and Phone fields to **1.25"**; change the width of the State and Zip fields to **0.75"**; and change the width of the Address field to **1.75"**. Delete the form icon (the picture next to the title of the form) in the Form Header.

e. Change the sorting on the MemberSince control so that the members who joined most recently are displayed first.

f. Click the **LastName field**. Change the Control Padding to **Wide**. (Hint: Search **Control Padding** in the *Tell me* box.)

g. Save and close the form.

h. Select the **Revenue query** and create a report using the Report Wizard. Include all fields in the report and add grouping first by **City** and then by **ServiceName**. Add a **Sum** to the Revenue field and click the **Summary Only option**. Select **Outline Layout** and name the report **Revenue by City and Service**.

i. Scroll through all the pages to check the layout of the report while in Print Preview mode. Close Print Preview. Switch to Layout view and delete the **NumInParty** and **PerPersonCharge** controls.

j. Select the result of the aggregate sum function for the city's revenue. Change the font size to **12**, change the font color to **Dark Blue, Text 2**, and change the background color of the control to **Yellow**.

k. Change the sort on the report, so that it sorts by city in descending order—that is, so that the last city alphabetically (St. Paul) is displayed first.

l. Examine the data in the report to determine which city (of these three: St. Paul, St. Louis, or Seattle) has the highest Sum of event revenue. You will use this information to modify a query. Save and close the report. Modify the Totals by Service query so the criteria for the City field is the city you determined had the highest sum of event revenue (St. Paul, St. Louis, or Seattle). Run, save, and close the query.

m. Create a report using the Report tool based on the Totals by Service query. Name the report **Targeted City**. Close the report.

n. Close the database and exit Access. Based on your instructor's directions, submit a04m1Rewards_LastFirst.

2 Benefit Auction

FROM SCRATCH

You are helping to organize a benefit auction to raise money for families who lost their homes in a natural disaster. The information for the auction is currently stored in an Excel spreadsheet, but you have volunteered to import it into Access. You will create a database that will store the data from Excel in Access. You will create a form to manage the data-entry process. You also create two reports: one that lists the items collected in each category and one for labels so you can send the donors a thank-you letter after the auction.

a. Open Access and create a new database named **a04m2Auction_LastFirst**.

b. Switch to Design view. Type **Items** in the Save As dialog box and click **OK**.

c. Change the ID Field Name to **ItemID**. Add a second field named **Description**. Accept **Short Text** as the data type for the Description field and change the field size to **50**.

d. Enter the remaining field names in the table (in this order): **DateOfDonation**, **Category**, **Price**, **DonorName**, **DonorAddress1**, and **DonorAddress2**. Change the data type of the DateOfDonation field to **Date/Time** and the Price field to **Currency**. Accept **Short Text** as the data type for the remaining fields.

e. Open Excel and open the file *a04m2Items.xlsx*. Examine the length of the Category, DonorAddress1, and DonorAddress2 columns. Return to Access. Change the field size for the Category to **15**, DonorAddress1 to **25**, and DonorAddress2 to **30**. Save the table, and switch to Datasheet view.

f. Copy and paste the 26 rows from the Excel spreadsheet into the Items table. To paste the rows, locate the * to the left of the first blank row, click the **Record Selector**, right-click the **Record Selector**, and then from the shortcut menu, select **Paste**. AutoFit all the column widths so all data are visible. Save and close the table. Close the workbook and exit Excel.

> **TROUBLESHOOTING:** Once you have pasted the data, ensure that your chosen field sizes did not cause you to lose data. If so, update the field sizes, delete the records you pasted to the table, and then repeat Step f.

g. Verify that the Items table is selected in the Navigation Pane. Create a new form using the Form tool.

h. Select all of the fields and labels in the Detail section of the form. Change the layout of the form to a **Tabular Layout**. With all of the fields selected, switch to Design view and use the Property Sheet to set their widths to **1.3"**. Then change the width of the ItemID, Category, and Price columns to **0.75"**.

i. Add conditional formatting so that each Price that is **greater than 90** has a font color of **Green** (in the first row, under Standard Colors). (Hint: Search **Conditional Formatting** in the *Tell me* box.)

j. Save the form as **Auction Items Form**.

k. Switch to Form view and create a new record. Enter **iPad** as the Description; **12/31/2018** as the DateOfDonation; **House** as the Category; **$400** as the Price; **Staples** as the DonorName; **500 Market St** as the DonorAddress1; and **Brick, NJ 08723** as the DonorAddress2.

l. Add a sort to the form, so that the lowest priced items display first. Save and close the form.

m. Select the **Items table** in the Navigation Pane, and create a report using the Report Wizard. Include all fields except the two donor address fields, group by Category, include the Sum of Price as a Summary Option, accept the default layout, and then save the report as **Auction Items by Category**.

n. Switch to Layout view. Resize the **DateOfDonation control** so that the left edge of the control aligns with the left edge of the column label. Select the **Price** and **Sum of Price controls** and increase the width to **0.75"**. Select any value in the **DonorName column** and drag the left edge of the controls to the right to decrease the width of the column. Resize the **Grand Total control** so that its value displays. Preview the report to verify the column widths are correct.

o. Switch to Layout view and sort the report so the least expensive item is displayed first in each group. Save and close the report.

p. Select the **Items table** in the Navigation Pane. Create mailing labels based on the Avery 5660 template. (Hint: Search **Labels** in the *Tell me* box and click the **Labels** tool in the results.) Place **DonorName** on the first line, **DonorAddress1** on the second line, and **DonorAddress2** on the third line. Sort the labels by **DonorName**. Name the report **Donor Labels**. After you create the labels, display them in Print Preview mode to verify that all values will fit onto the label template. Close the label report.

q. Close the database and exit Access. Based on your instructor's directions, submit a04m2Auction_LastFirst.

Running Case

New Castle County Technical Services (NCCTS) provides technical support for a number of companies in the greater New Castle County, Delaware, area. Now that you have completed the database tables, set the appropriate relationships, and created queries, you are ready to create a form and a report.

a. Open the database *a04r1NCCTS* and save it as **a04r1NCCTS_LastFirst**.

b. Create a split form based on the Calls table.

c. Add the **Description field** by dragging and dropping it immediately below the CallTypeID. (Hint: Click Show all tables in the Field List pane and locate the field by expanding the Call Types table.) Close the Field List pane. Switch to Form view and ensure that the records are sorted by CallID in ascending order.

d. Save the form as **Calls Data Entry** and close the form.

e. Use the Report tool to create a basic report based on the Customer Happiness query.

f. Sort the records by the **Avg Rating field** in ascending order.

g. Apply the **Integral theme** to this report only.

h. Change the title of the report to **Customer Satisfaction Ratings** and format the background color of the control to **Medium Gray** (under Standard Colors).

i. Set the font color of the title control to **Blue, Accent 2**, the font size to **20**, and the alignment to **Center**. Click the default logo in the report header and press **Delete**.

j. Switch to Report view. Save the report as **Customer Satisfaction Survey** and close the report.

k. Close the database and exit Access. Based on your instructor's directions, submit a04r1NCCTS_LastFirst.

Disaster Recovery

A co-worker is having difficulty with an Access report and asked for your assistance. He was trying to fix the report and seems to have made things worse. Open the *a04d1Sales* database and save the file as **a04d1Sales_LastFirst**. Open the Properties Report in Report view. The report columns do not fit across one page. In addition, there is a big gap between two fields, and he moved the Beds and Baths fields so they are basically on top of one another. Add all the fields to a tabular layout. Group the records first by City in ascending order, and then by Beds in descending order. Within each group, sort the report by ListPrice in ascending order. Change the report to Landscape orientation and adjust the column widths so they all fit across one page (inside the dashed vertical page break). Apply the Organic theme to this report only, and switch to Report view. Save the new report as **Properties by City**, close the report, and then delete the original **Properties Report** from the database (right-click the report in the Navigation Pane, and from the shortcut menu, select **Delete**). Close the database and exit Access. Based on your instructor's directions, submit a04d1Sales_LastFirst.

Capstone Exercise

Foodies Forms and Reports

You will create a form so that users of the database can enter and edit suppliers of products to your business easily. You create an attractive report that groups the products that you purchase by their suppliers and export it to PDF format for easy distribution. Finally, you create a Navigation form so that database users can switch between major objects in the database readily.

Create and Customize a Form

You will create a form to manage the data in the Suppliers table. Use the Form tool to create the form and modify the form as required. You will also remove the layout control from the form so that the controls can be repositioned freely.

1. Open the *a04c1Foodies* database and save it as **a04c1Foodies_LastFirst**.

2. Select the **Suppliers table** as the record source for a form. Use the Form tool to create a new form with a stacked layout.

3. Change the form's title to **Enter/Edit Suppliers**.

4. Reduce the width of the text box controls to approximately half of their original size (about 3.4").

5. Delete the **Products subform** control from the form.

6. View the form and the data in Form view. Sort the records by **CompanyName** in ascending order.

7. Set the background color of the CompanyName text box to **Blue, Accent 1, Lighter 80%** and set the font size to **14**.

8. Save the form as **Edit Suppliers**.

9. Open the Edit Suppliers form in Design view. Select all controls in the form and remove the layout.

10. View the form in Layout view. Delete the **Contact Title label** from the form and move the text box up and to the right of ContactName so that their top edges are aligned.

11. Delete the **Country label** from the form and move the text box up and to the right of PostalCode so that their top edges are aligned. Move the **Phone** and **Fax labels** and text boxes up to below PostalCode so that they close in the white space, keeping the spacing close to that of the rest of the controls.

12. View the form in Print Preview and set the orientation to **Landscape**.

13. Switch to Form view, and then save and close the form.

Create a Report

You will create a report based on the Company by Product List query. You decide to use the Report Wizard to accomplish this task. You are planning to email a copy of the report to your business partner, who is not conversant in Access, so you will export the report as a PDF file prior to sending it.

14. Select the **Company by Product List query** in the Navigation Pane as the record source for the report.

15. Activate the Report Wizard and use the following options as you proceed through the wizard steps:
    - Select all the available fields for the report.
    - View the data by Suppliers.
    - Accept the default grouping levels and click **Next**.
    - Use **ProductName** as the primary sort field in ascending order.
    - Accept the Stepped and Portrait options.
    - Save the report as **Products by Suppliers**.
    - Switch to Layout view and apply the **Organic theme** to this report only.
    - Set the width of the **ProductCost label** to approximately 0.8" so that the entire text of the label is visible.

16. Switch to Report view to determine whether all the columns fit across the page. Switch to Layout view and drag the left edge of the **ProductName text box** to the left so that the column width is wide enough to display the values in the field (approximately 2.5").

17. Delete the **ContactName label** and **text box** from the report. Drag the right edge of the **CompanyName text box** to the right so that the column width is wide enough to display the values in the field (approximately 2.6"). Save the report.

18. Switch to Print Preview and export the report as a PDF file named **a04c1ProductsbySuppliers_LastFirstpdf**.

19. Close the reader program that displays the PDF report and return to Access. Close Print Preview. Save and close the report.

Add an Additional Field to the Query and the Report

You realize that the Country field was not included in the query that is the record source for your report. You add the field to the query and modify the report in Layout view to include the missing field.

20. Open the **Company by Product List query** in Design view.

21. Add the **Country field** from the Suppliers table to the query design grid, after the ProductCost field. Run, save, and close the query.

22. Open the Products by Suppliers report in Layout view. Add the **Country field** from the Field List pane by dragging it into the report layout. Click the selection handle at the top of the Country column and move

the column immediately to the left of the Phone field. Resize the Country text box so that the column width is wide enough to display the values in the field (approximately .75"). Switch to Print Preview, and then save and close the report.

Create a Navigation Form

You will create a Navigation form so that users can switch between objects in the database readily.

23. Create a **Vertical Tabs, Left** Navigation form.

24. Drag the **Edit Suppliers form icon** from the Navigation Pane onto the **[Add New] tab** at the left of the form.

25. Drag the **Products by Suppliers report icon** from the Navigation Pane onto the second **[Add New] tab** at the left of the form. Save the Navigation form with the default name and close all open objects.

26. Close the database and exit Access. Based on your instructor's directions, submit the following:

    a04c1Foodies_LastFirst

    a04c1ProductsbySuppliers_LastFirst.pdf

Data Validation and Data Analysis

LEARNING OUTCOMES

You will use data validation features to improve data entry.
You will perform data analysis using advanced queries.

OBJECTIVES & SKILLS: After you read this chapter, you will be able to:

Restrict Table Data

OBJECTIVE 1: ESTABLISH DATA VALIDATION   304
Require a Field, Add a Default Field Value, Add a
Validation Rule with Validation Text
OBJECTIVE 2: CONTROL THE FORMAT OF DATA ENTRY   307
Create an Input Mask
OBJECTIVE 3: CONTROL INPUT WITH A LOOKUP FIELD   309
Create a Lookup Field, Modify a Lookup Field

HANDS-ON EXERCISE 1   311

Data Analysis with Advanced Queries and Functions

OBJECTIVE 4: CUSTOMIZE OUTPUT BASED ON USER INPUT   317
Create a Parameter Query, Create a Parameter Report
OBJECTIVE 5: USE ADVANCED FUNCTIONS   319
Use the Date Function, Use the Round Function,
Use the IIf Function, Use the IsNull Function,
Use the DatePart Function

HANDS-ON EXERCISE 2   327

CASE STUDY | Implementing a New Database at Tommy's Shelter

Tommy Mariano operates a small animal shelter. He has been keeping records by hand, but due to a large turnover in volunteers, recordkeeping can be a challenge. He has decided to move to a database solution, and his hope is that this will help reduce errors. Although volunteers may still make mistakes, he believes that a well-designed database will prevent some common errors. As a volunteer, you have offered to create a database to assist him in this process. You have created the tables and done some data entry, and you will now work to make sure data validation takes place.

In addition to the problem of data entry, Tommy has been examining a lot of the data from his shelter by hand. As someone with some database experience, you know that advanced queries are the answer here. You will use advanced queries to help streamline his data gathering and reporting so Tommy can focus on what is important—finding homes for the animals in his shelter.

Reducing Errors and Extracting Better Information

Sfio Cracho/Shutterstock

FIGURE 5.1 Tommy's Shelter Database

CASE STUDY | Implementing a New Database at Tommy's Shelter

Starting File	File to be Submitted
a05h1Tommys	**a05h2Tommys_LastFirst**

MyLab IT Grader An alternate version of this project is available as a MyLab IT Grader Assessment

Restrict Table Data

When filling out forms online, you may notice certain pieces of information are required. If you are attempting to purchase something, you will not be able to complete the purchase if you leave the credit card number blank. You may also notice that information you enter is checked for validity. On many sites, you cannot enter an email address without the @ sign. Some fields appear as drop-down menus. Instead of typing a state name, a menu offering only valid responses will be displayed. Picking from a list helps narrow the possible answers as well as eliminates spelling and interpretation errors. Access contains validation features similar to those found in Web forms. Many of these features are found in the table settings; some are available in forms as well.

In this section, you will explore setting validation of data in tables to create more reliable data in your database. By setting up data validation, you reduce user errors, which is a key reason to use a database.

Establishing Data Validation

Data validation is a set of constraints or rules that help control data entered into a field. Access provides some data validation automatically. For example, you cannot enter text into a field with a number data type or add two records with identical primary key values. Access provides several additional data validation methods to help minimize data entry errors. These can be found in the Field Properties pane in a table's Design view.

> **TIP: GOOD DATA VERSUS INCLUSION**
>
> Database administrators need to balance good data and inclusion to avoid controversy because users do not see an option for their gender, religion, or something else. Sometimes it is best to look to large companies for help. For example, Google provides three options for Gender: Female, Male, or Other. Microsoft offers Female, Male, or Not Specified. Giving users a third option for Gender avoids excluding users who do not identify as female or male, while still protecting the integrity of your data. If you are unsure of how to proceed, you can always discuss this with your company's Human Resources Department.

STEP 1 ▸ Require a Field

When a field is required, it simply means a field cannot be left without a value. Although this does not prevent incorrect data from being entered, it does at least prevent the user from skipping the item. Recall that when you add a primary key field to a table the Required property is set to "Yes" by default, requiring that a value be entered. You can control whether other fields in a table require an entry by setting the Required field property to Yes. To ensure the integrity of the records in a table, you should set the Required property to "Yes" for critical fields. To change a field's Required property, open the table in Design view, select the field for which you want a required value, select *Required* in the Field Properties pane, and then change the value to "Yes" (see Figure 5.2). When you save the table, you may be prompted about data integrity rules; click No for that message.

FIGURE 5.2 Setting a Field to Required

For all new records, Access requires you to enter data into the required field. If you leave a required field blank during data entry, an error message displays, as shown in Figure 5.3.

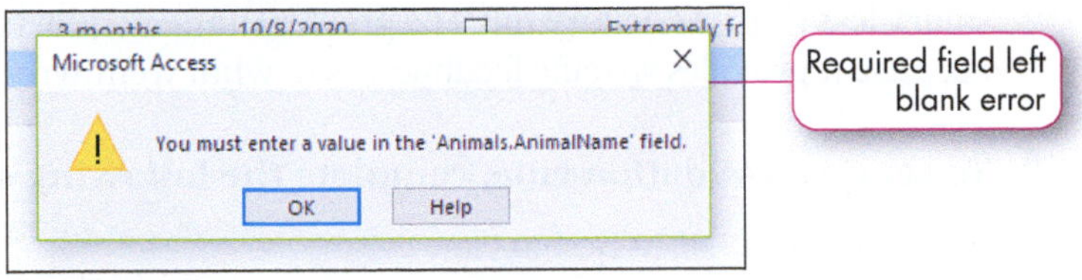

FIGURE 5.3 Results of a Required Field Being Left Blank

> **TIP: CHECK FOR EXISTING BLANK FIELDS BEFORE SETTING REQUIRED FIELDS**
> If you set the Required property to Yes after data has already been entered in a table, you will see the message, "Data integrity rules have been changed; existing data may not be valid for the new rules. This process may take a long time. Do you want the existing data to be tested with the new rules?" If an error message displays, you must manually fix the data. Use a filter to check for blank fields in the Datasheet view and resolve any inconsistencies before setting the Required property to Yes.

Add a Default Field Value

A *default value* specifies a value that is automatically entered into a field when a new record is added to a table. When a majority of new records contain a common value, set a default value for that field to reduce data entry time. For example, suppose many of the animals the shelter handles are cats. If you type Cat in the Default Value property, all new records entered in Datasheet view will display Cat, as shown in Figure 5.4. You can overwrite this default value if you have a different type of animal.

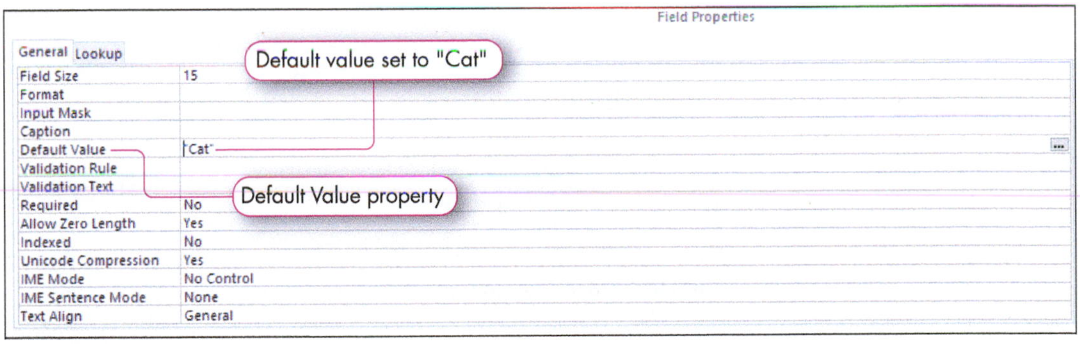

FIGURE 5.4 Default Field Value of Cat

STEP 2 Add a Validation Rule with Validation Text

A *validation rule* limits the data values a user can enter in a field. At the most basic level, all the comparison operators are available in creating a validation rule. An appropriate validation rule for an hourly wage field might be $>=12$ to make sure a person's hourly wage is greater than or equal to the state minimum wage of 12 dollars. As with queries, you can use comparison operators, including greater than ($>$), greater than or equal to ($>=$), less than ($<$), less than or equal to ($<=$), equal to ($=$), not equal to ($<>$), Between, In, and Like. If a validation rule is violated, Access does not enable the user to continue until an appropriate value is entered, or the record is discarded.

You can help improve the user experience by providing **validation text**, which displays a custom error message to the user when incorrect data are entered. Ideally, the validation text will explain which value is rejected and why. If you have entered a validation rule to require salary to be greater than or equal to 12 and the user enters an incorrect value such as 9, the validation text displays. A meaningful error message such as "You entered a salary less than 12. Salary must be greater than or equal to 12." would be helpful for users because it provides specific feedback as to what went wrong.

To set up a validation rule, complete the following steps:

1. Open the table in Design view.
2. Click the field for which you want to add a validation rule.
3. Click Validation Rule in the Field Properties pane.
4. Enter the validation rule, as shown in Figure 5.5. For example, *>0* or *Between 50 and 300*.
5. Enter a meaningful error message in the Validation Text property in the Field Properties pane, as shown in Figure 5.5 (optional, but recommended). This text will display when an incorrect value is entered, as shown in Figure 5.6.

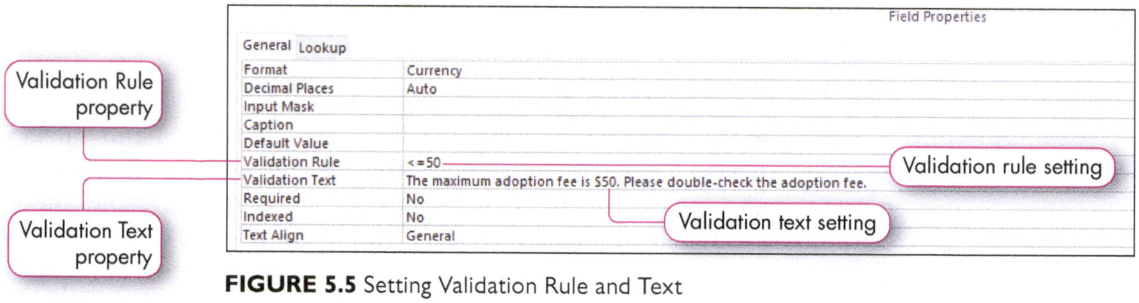

FIGURE 5.5 Setting Validation Rule and Text

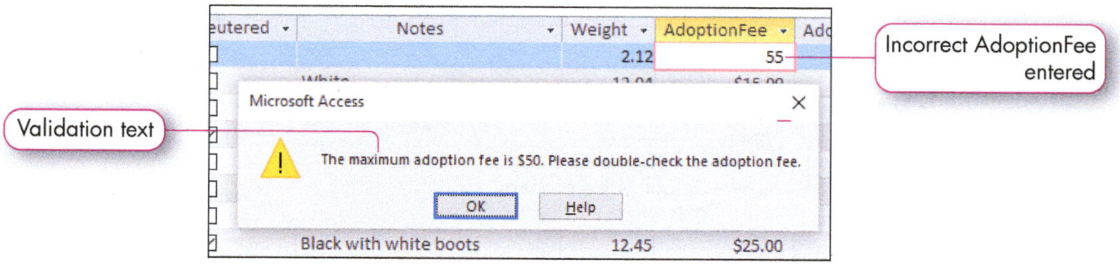

FIGURE 5.6 Validation Rule Violation

Validation rules only check values entered for a field. They do not prevent users from skipping the field. Unless you set the Required property to Yes, having a validation rule does not force data entry for the field. Therefore, if you add a validation rule to a field, you should also consider setting the Required property to Yes. Validation rules cannot be applied to some data types such as AutoNumber, OLE Object, and Attachment.

> **TIP: EXISTING DATA VIOLATE NEW VALIDATION RULE**
> If you add a validation rule to a table with existing records, some data in those records may violate the rule. For example, you might add validation to the hourly wage field, indicating it must be greater than or equal to 12 dollars. However, if there are employees who have wages less than 12 dollars, Access warns that existing data may violate the new validation rule. You can click Yes to test the data. If adding a validation rule uncovers an underlying problem in the data, you can switch to Datasheet view and apply a filter to find the records in violation and update the records accordingly.

Controlling the Format of Data Entry

In addition to controlling what users enter into a data table, database designers can also control the format of the data entry. For example, a phone number might be stored in a Short Text field with a size of 14. The database designer might expect users to enter a number in a format such as (959) 555-6000. However, users could enter 959.555.6000, 9595556000, 959-555-6000, or even 99999999999999 if there are no restrictions. Although this might not seem like a problem because each entry reflects the same phone number, the inconsistent way the number is formatted will lead to problems with sorting, filtering, and querying data.

An *input mask* restricts the data being input into a field by specifying the exact format of the data entry. Phone number and Social Security number are two common text fields that often use input masks because the consistency for their format is important. Figure 5.7 shows a field with a phone number input mask applied.

When adding an input mask, it is necessary to consider the data that users will add to the field. It may not be appropriate to use a mask. For example, when local and international data may be entered in the same field, the Zip Code input mask will not allow for foreign zip codes because they follow a different format.

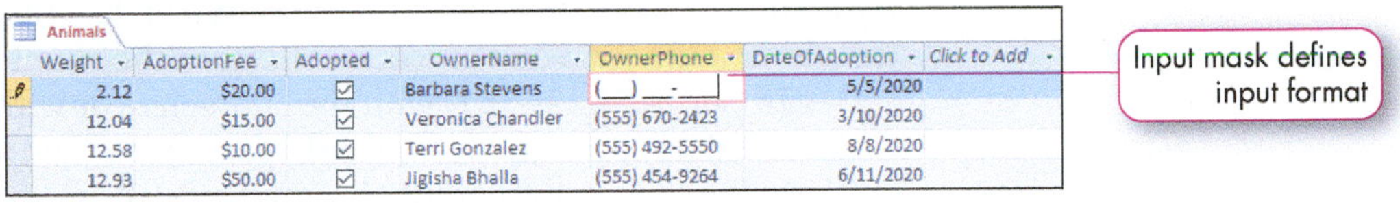

FIGURE 5.7 Phone Number Input Mask

STEP 3 ▶ Create an Input Mask

The *Input Mask Wizard* is a tool used to quickly assist with applying an input mask to a field (as shown in Figure 5.8). Although you can type an input mask manually, the code for these can be complicated to understand. Access includes some common input masks automatically, including phone number, Social Security number, ZIP code, and more. Table 5.1 shows examples of common input masks, examples, and the code format Access applies to the property field for that mask.

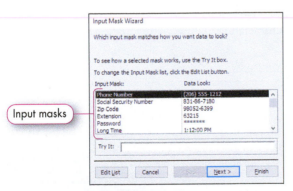

FIGURE 5.8 Built-in Input Masks

TABLE 5.1 Examples of Common Input Masks

Field	Example Data with Mask Applied	Input Mask Property Field Code
Social Security Number	555-55-5555	000\-00\-0000;0;;
Phone Number	(555) 555-1234	!\(999") "000\-0000;;_
Zip Code	00000-9999	00000\-9999;0;_
Password	******	Password
Date (various date types available; short date shown in example)	__/__/____	99/99/0000;0;

To add an input mask to a field using the Input Mask Wizard, select the field where you want to add an input mask, and then click the Build button (ellipsis) to start the wizard. After choosing the type of input mask you want, you can use the Try It feature to see how the mask will display. You can apply the mask format as you see it without making any changes, or you can edit the mask to fit your data. You can choose your own placeholder characters as shown in Figure 5.9. If you want to keep the mask, your next decision is if you want to store the characters. For example, when users enter data for a phone number, they will typically see (___) ____- _____, which lets them know the expected format of the phone number. You can choose to store the number for example, as either (555) 123-4567 or 5551234567, with the characters or without. Although storing with the characters does require additional disk space, it is a good idea to store the characters. After finishing the steps in the wizard, the input mask displays in the Input Mask property box. For example, a phone number field is !\(999") "000\-0000;;_ as shown in Figure 5.10.

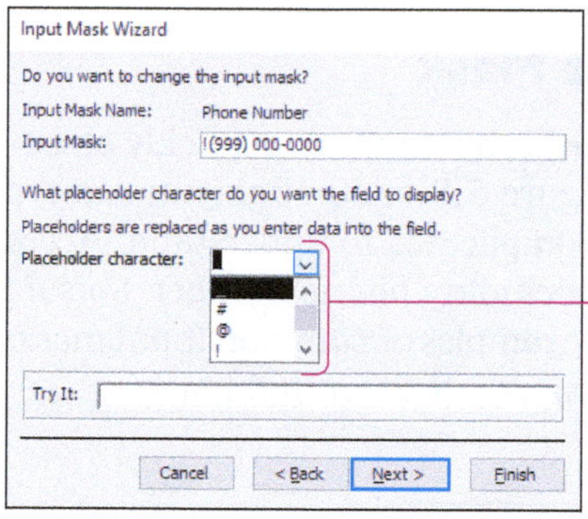

FIGURE 5.9 Placeholder Characters

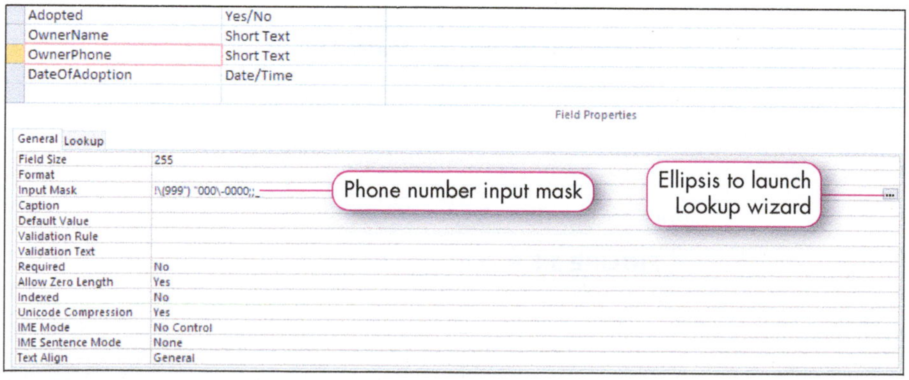

FIGURE 5.10 Input Mask for a Phone Number in Design View

> **TIP: CUSTOM INPUT MASKS**
> You can create custom input masks. For example you can create a mask PC-LL0000 where PC is required, LL indicates two required letters, and 0000 are required numbers. Use Microsoft Help or search the Internet for other options.

Controlling Input with a Lookup Field

Input masks provide good format for data entry, but they do not necessarily validate that correct information has been entered. If only a specific range of entries are appropriate for a field, a state field for example, then it is better to use a ***lookup field***, which provides the user with a predefined list of values to choose from in a menu. It is safer to protect your data and help guide your users by displaying acceptable options. If you let users enter a value for a State field, they may not all enter the data the same way. For example, you might have Mich, Michigan, MI, or some misspelled variations for that state. When gathering data from users, your priority is often protecting data so that it can be more easily filtered, sorted, and queried. In addition to the added accuracy, data entry is faster if the options for this field are limited to the values in a drop-down list format. Changing the data type to a lookup field will display only those options and ensure uniformity and consistency of the data.

> **TIP: STATE AS A LOOKUP FIELD**
> If you use a lookup field for State, do not forget to include DC as an abbreviation for Washington D.C. You might also want to include abbreviations for US territories and countries with free associations with the US such as PR (Puerto Rico) and VI (Virgin Islands).

To add a lookup field, you must first choose whether to store the field options list in a separate table or by entering the values directly into the wizard. The latter is best for options that are limited to a small list that may not change often. The options for a lookup field are often put in a separate table, which has been created ahead of time. Generally, a separate simple table is created as the source for the list. Storing the options in a separate table makes it easier to update the list. This table does not need to a have a relationship with any other table. For example, if an AnimalType field includes options such as cat, dog, and bird, you could create a separate table to store those values. The table would include a record for each animal, one for each option. The AnimalType field would be the primary key, but a primary key is not necessary. Additional list options would be added to the table directly as needed. Figure 5.11 shows an example of a lookup field in Datasheet view.

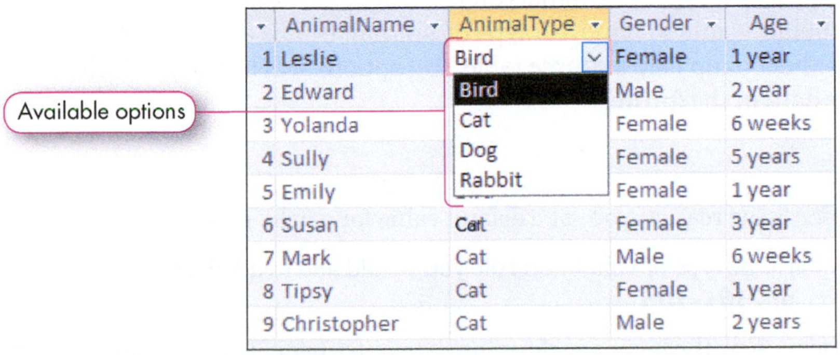
Available options
AnimalName
AnimalType
Gender
Age
1 Leslie
Bird
Female
1 year
2 Edward
Male
2 year
3 Yolanda
Female
6 weeks
4 Sully
Female
5 years
5 Emily
Female
1 year
6 Susan
Cat
Female
3 year
7 Mark
Cat
Male
6 weeks
8 Tipsy
Cat
Female
1 year
9 Christopher
Cat
Male
2 years
Bird
Cat
Dog
Rabbit

FIGURE 5.11 Lookup Field

Access provides a Lookup Wizard to help you create a lookup field. The **Lookup Wizard** creates the menu of predefined values (lookup fields) by asking you questions and using your answers to create the options list.

STEP 4 > Create a Lookup Field

The first step in creating a lookup field is often to create a new table that will hold the options. As mentioned, it is usually best to look up the values in a table because the list can be more easily updated. Lookup fields can be created in either Datasheet view or Design view.

> **To create a lookup field that references an existing table using the Lookup Wizard, complete the following steps:**
>
> 1. Open the table in Design view.
> 2. Click the field you want to change to a lookup list and select Lookup Wizard as the Data Type.
> 3. Click Next to accept the default *I want the lookup field to get the values from another table or query.*
> 4. Choose the table that contains the lookup values. Click Next.
> 5. Select the field (or fields) from the table for the lookup field list and click the Add One Field `>` icon. Click Next.
> 6. Specify a sort order for the lookup list. Click Next.
> 7. Adjust the column width for the lookup column. Columns should be wide enough to display the longest value. You may choose to *Hide key column*, although this is not necessary in cases where you only have a single field table. Click Next.
> 8. Name the lookup field. You can also choose to check the Enable Data Integrity check box, so users can only enter values found on the lookup list. Click Finish.
> 9. Click Yes if prompted that the table must be saved before the relationships can be created.

To add a Lookup in Datasheet view, click the arrow for the new field, to the right of *Click to Add*, and then follow steps 3–9 above. For the AnimalType field in the Animals table, shown previously in Figure 5.11, the table Types of Animals contains four records.

STEP 5 > Modify a Lookup Field

You can add, delete, or edit values in the lookup field to accommodate changing data needs. For example, if the shelter expands the types of animals it cares for to include rabbits, open the Types of Animals table and add the new record to the bottom of the table. If the shelter wants to remove a type of animal, that is done in the same way. When you change the lookup field's source table, the options will be updated when the user tries to change data in the future.

Quick Concepts

1. Discuss the reasons you set a default value for a field. **p. 305**
2. Explain the type of validation rule you would add to a Salary field with a Number data type. **pp. 305-306**
3. Discuss how the person performing data entry benefits if you add an input mask to a field. **pp. 307-308**
4. Explain whether or not a LastName field would be a good candidate for a lookup field. **pp. 309-310**

Hands-On Exercises

MyLab IT HOE1 Sim Training

Watch the Video for this Hands-On Exercise!

Skills covered: Require a Field • Add a Default Field Value • Add a Validation Rule with Validation Text • Create an Input Mask • Create a Lookup Field • Modify a Lookup Field

1 Restrict Table Data

You want to modify the shelter database to reduce data entry errors, so you will add some data validation rules to the tables. You will set default field values, set validation rules, create input masks, and establish a lookup field.

STEP 1 REQUIRE A FIELD AND ADD A DEFAULT FIELD VALUE

You decide to review the Animals table and require the AnimalName field because you do not want animals added to the database without names. You will also set the default value for the AnimalType field to Cat because cats are the most common animal in the shelter. Refer to Figure 5.12 as you complete Step 1.

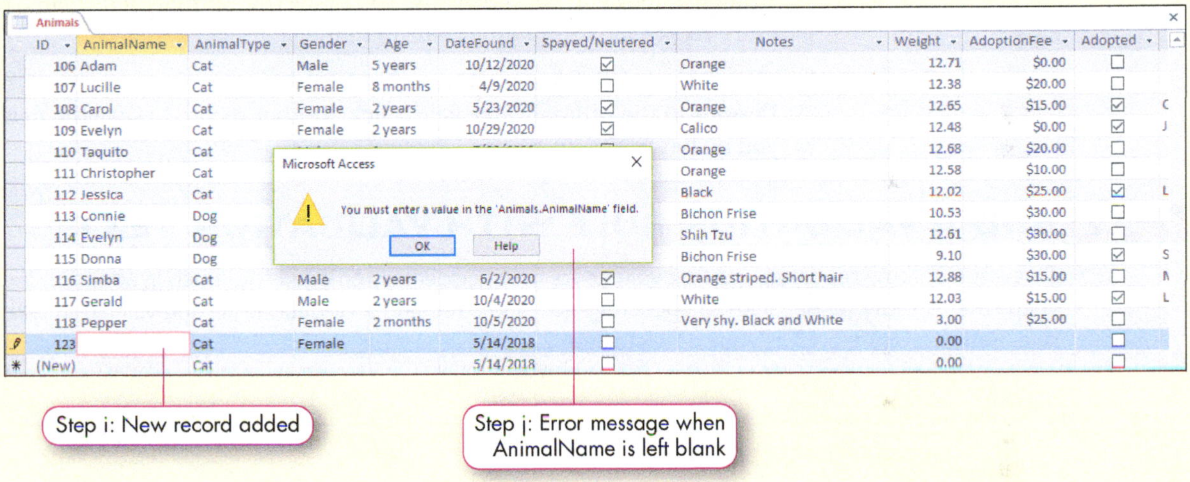

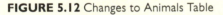

FIGURE 5.12 Changes to Animals Table

Step i: New record added

Step j: Error message when AnimalName is left blank

---

a. Open *a05h1Tommys*. Save the file as **a05h1Tommys_LastFirst**.

> **TROUBLESHOOTING:** If you make any major mistakes in this exercise, you can close the file, open *a05h1Tommys* again, and then start this exercise over.

b. Open the Animals table in Design view.

c. Click the **AnimalName field** in the design grid.

d. Click **Required** in the Field Properties pane. Click the **Required property box arrow** and select **Yes** from the list.

An entry in the AnimalName field is now required for each animal.

e. Click the **AnimalType field**.

f. Click **Default Value** in the Field Properties pane and type **Cat**.

Because most of the animals in the shelter are cats, you set the default value to Cat. You now will test the changes you made to the table design.

g. Click **Save** on the Quick Access Toolbar. Click **Yes** in response to the warning about testing the data integrity rules.

h. Switch to the Datasheet view of the Animals table. Click **New** in the Records group of the Home tab to add a new record. Ensure the AnimalType is displayed as Cat by default (see Figure 5.12).

i. Click the **Gender field** of the new record and type **Female**. Type **2 months** in the Age field and type **10/5/2020** in the DateFound field. Type **Very shy. Black and White** in the Notes field. Type **3** in the Weight field and type **25** in the AdoptionFee field. The AnimalName, Spayed/Neutered, Adopted, OwnerName, OwnerPhone, and DateOfAdoption fields are left blank.

To test data validation rules, you have left a required field blank.

j. Press **Tab** until an error message displays.

The error message, as shown in Figure 5.12, indicates that you must enter a value in the AnimalName field. This is because you made the AnimalName field a required field, so every record must contain a value in that field.

k. Click **OK**, click the **AnimalName field** for the new record you just typed, and then type **Pepper** in the AnimalName field. Click another record to save the new record. Notice you no longer see an error.

STEP 2 ▶ **ADD A VALIDATION RULE WITH VALIDATION TEXT**

One issue Tommy reported was that volunteers have accidentally charged too much in adoption fees. The shelter keeps the fees low (under $50) to encourage adoption. You add a validation rule and validation text to enforce this rule. Refer to Figure 5.13 as you complete Step 2.

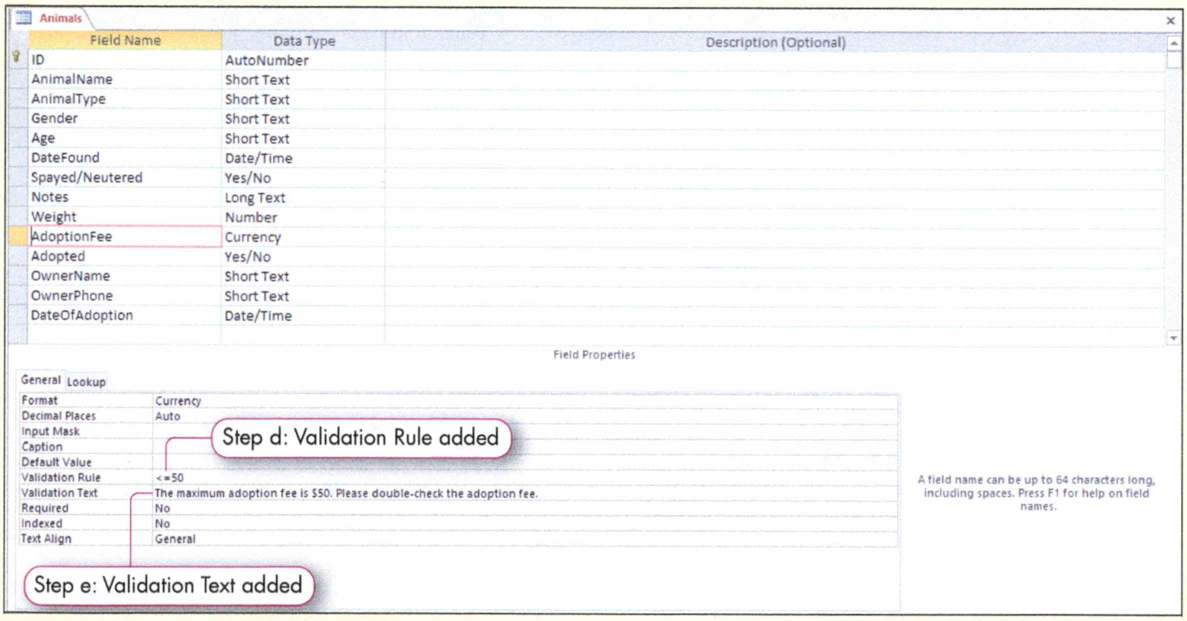

FIGURE 5.13 Validation Added to AdoptionFee field

a. Switch to Design view of the Animals table.

b. Click the **AdoptionFee field**.

c. Click **Validation Rule** in the Field Properties pane.

d. Type **<=50** in the Validation Rule property box.

The maximum adoption fee is $50. You have added a rule that notifies the user when a value that is not less than or equal to $50 (that is, greater than $50) is entered in the AdoptionFee field.

e. Click the **Validation Text property** and type **The maximum adoption fee is $50. Please double-check the adoption fee.**

When a user enters an adoption fee that is too high, a message displays telling the user to modify the entry.

f. Switch to the Datasheet view of the Animals table.

g. Click **Yes** in response to the message about changed data integrity rules.

You can respond Yes because the data will not be affected by the new rule.

h. Click the **AdoptionFee field** of the first record. Replace the current value with **51** and press **Tab**.

The validation text you entered earlier appears.

i. Click **OK** in the error message box. Change the first record value to **20** for the AdoptionFee field. Press **Tab**.

Because $20 is an acceptable value, you do not receive an error message.

STEP 3 ▶ CREATE AN INPUT MASK

You decide to add an input mask to the owner's phone number field so that all users follow a consistent data entry format. Refer to Figure 5.14 as you complete Step 3.

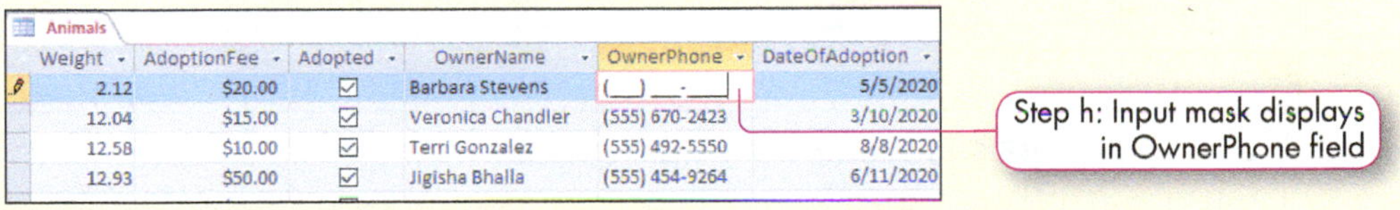

FIGURE 5.14 Input Mask for OwnerPhone Field

a. Switch to Design view of the Animals table.

b. Click the **OwnerPhone field** in the Field Name column.

c. Click **Input Mask** in the Field Properties pane. Click the **ellipsis** on the right side of the Input Mask property box to open the Input Mask Wizard.

The Phone Number input mask is already selected.

d. Click the **Try It box** in the Input Mask Wizard dialog box. (__) __-__ displays. Press **Home** to position the insertion point at the first character and type **5556667777** to verify that the mask displays the phone numbers correctly.

e. Click **Next** twice.

You accept the mask with the default placeholder character.

f. Click the **With the symbols in the mask, like this option**. Click **Next** and click **Finish**.

The data will be stored in the Animals table with the symbols (the parentheses and the dash). This is important to note if you plan on querying the data later.

g. Save the table. Switch to the Datasheet view of the Animals table and scroll to the OwnerPhone field.

The phone numbers display in the preset format with parentheses and hyphens.

h. Type your phone number into the first record, replacing the existing phone number, to test the input mask. Press **Esc** to return the record to its original state.

CREATE A LOOKUP FIELD

Rather than having volunteers enter a type of animal and risk the possibility of a misspelled or invalid animal type, you decide to create a lookup field that enables the volunteers to choose from a list. Refer to Figure 5.15 as you complete Step 4.

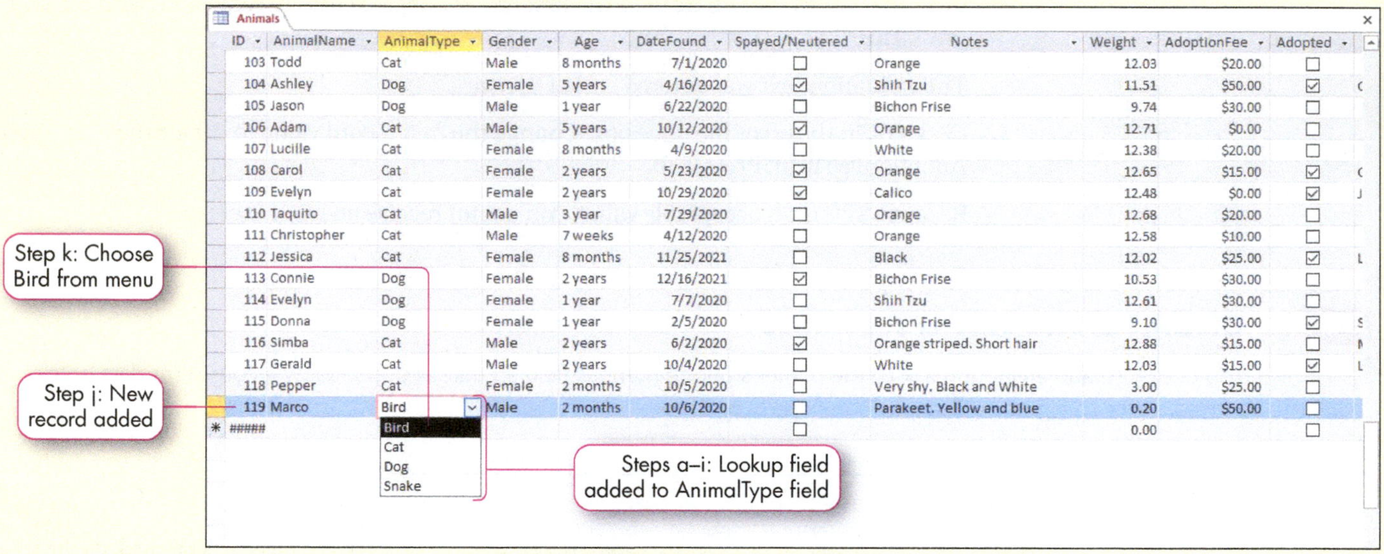

FIGURE 5.15 Lookup for AnimalType Field

a. Switch to Design view of the Animals table.

b. Click the blank cell to the right of the **AnimalType field**.

c. Click the **Data Type arrow** and choose **Lookup Wizard** from the list.

The Lookup Wizard launches.

d. Verify that the following option is selected: **I want the lookup field to get the values from another table or query**. Click **Next**.

e. Click **Table: Types of Animals** and click **Next**.

This table was prefilled with animal types.

f. Click **AnimalType** and click the **Add One Field** > icon to move it to the Selected Fields box. Click **Next**.

g. Click the arrow in the first sort box and select **AnimalType**. Click **Next**.

h. Click **Next** to accept the default column width.

You may adjust the column width to your preference.

i. Click **Finish**. Click **Yes** to save the table and click **Yes** when prompted that some data may be lost.

The Lookup Field has now been established.

j. Switch to the Datasheet view of the Animals table. Click **New** in the Records group of the Home tab to add a new animal using the following data, pressing **Tab** between each entry. Note that once you enter an AnimalName, a primary key, named ID, is automatically assigned:

AnimalName	Marco
AnimalType	Bird
Gender	Male
Age	2 months
DateFound	10/6/2020
Spayed/Neutered	Unchecked
Notes	Parakeet. Yellow and blue
Weight	0.2
AdoptionFee	50

The Adopted, OwnerName, OwnerPhone, and DateOfAdoption fields are left blank. The lookup field displays a menu of animal types, as shown in Figure 5.15. The default is Cat from Step 1.

k. Close the Animals table.

STEP 5 MODIFY A LOOKUP FIELD

After a few days of testing, you decide to modify the table containing the lookup values for the lookup field. Volunteers have pointed out that the shelter does not have the facilities to care for snakes, but they can care for rabbits, which is not listed as an option. Refer to Figure 5.16 as you complete Step 5.

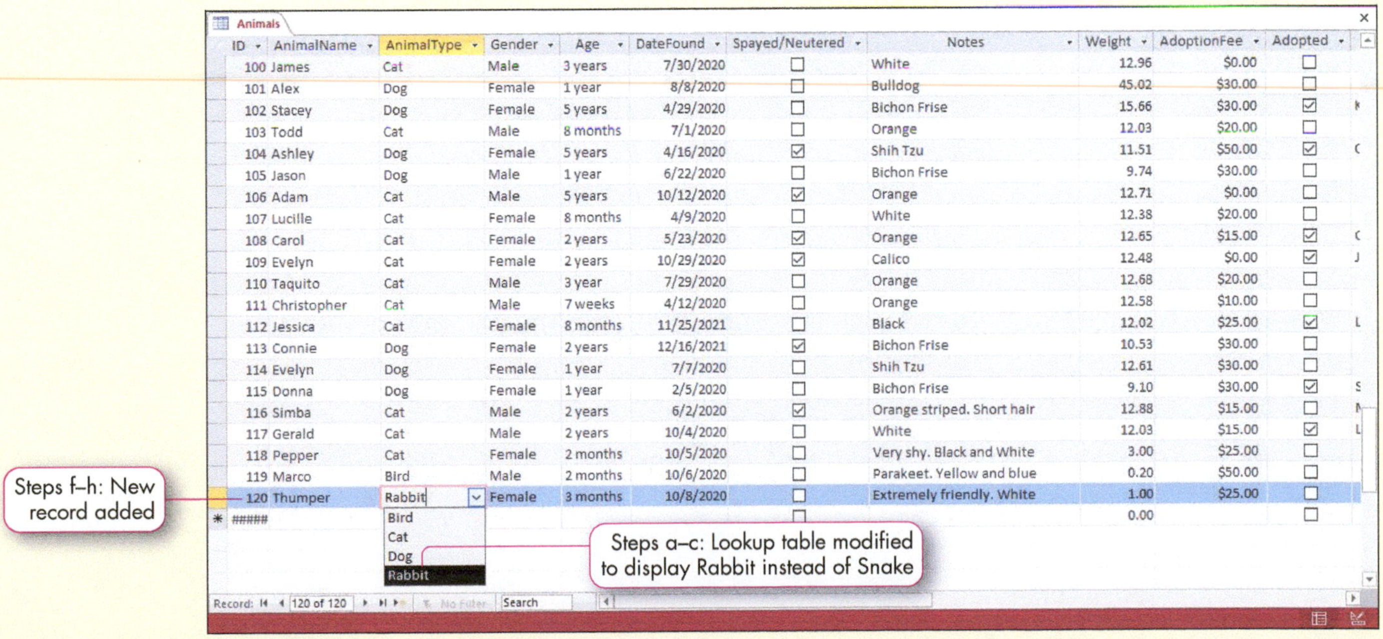

FIGURE 5.16 New Record Added to Animals Table

a. Open the Types of Animals table in Datasheet view.

b. Click the **Snake record**. Click **Delete** in the Records group of the Home tab. Click **Yes** when prompted that you will not be able to undo this Delete operation.

c. Add a new row with **Rabbit** as the AnimalType.

d. Close the Types of Animals table.

e. Open the Animals table in Datasheet view.

f. Click **New** in the Records group on the Home tab to add a new record to the table. Accept the default ID and type **Thumper** as the value for the AnimalName field.

g. Click the arrow to select the menu for AnimalType. Notice that Snake is no longer an option, but Rabbit is. Select **Rabbit** for the AnimalType.

> **TROUBLESHOOTING:** If you see #DELETED instead of Rabbit, then go back to Step d and close the Types of Animals table.

h. Type the rest of the data below, leaving any fields not mentioned blank:

Gender	**Female**
Age	**3 months**
DateFound	**10/8/2020**
Spayed/Neutered	**Unchecked**
Notes	**Extremely friendly. White**
Weight	**1**
AdoptionFee	**25**

i. Close the Animals table.

j. Keep the database open if you plan to continue with the next Hands-On Exercise. If not, close the database and exit Access.

Data Analysis with Advanced Queries and Functions

Extracting and manipulating data are the center of the database experience. Creating multiple queries to extract similar information can result in wasted effort. For example, if you have one query to extract all information about dogs and one to extract all information about cats, you will be maintaining two similar queries and doubling your maintenance time. You can apply special conditions that enable you to make a query more versatile, so when a user runs a query, he or she is prompted for the criteria.

In addition to selecting information, Access includes a number of functions through the Expression Builder (as discussed in a previous chapter). There are many built-in functions you can use to perform a variety of different tasks. You might be surprised at how many things can be done using a query.

In this section, you will create special queries to prompt the user for criteria when run. You will also use advanced functions in the Expression Builder to analyze data.

Customizing Output Based on User Input

Access provides a variety of query types to help make decisions. To determine how many pets of a certain animal type were adopted at Tommy's this year, you could construct a query with the relevant fields, and then enter Cat into the Criteria row of the AnimalType field to restrict the results to display only cats for adoption. You could then save the query as Cat Adoptions. If you wanted to see the same information for dogs, you could copy the first query, rename the copy as Dog Adoptions, and then enter Dog into the Criteria row of the AnimalType field. However, you might ask yourself if there is a better way to handle this situation. The answer is yes—using a parameter query.

A **_parameter query_** is a query that prompts the user for criterion (the parameter) at run time. It enables you to create a generic query and generate results based on the parameter provided. A parameter query reduces development time because the query can be used repeatedly without modifying the design because only the criterion changes.

STEP 1 ### Create a Parameter Query

A parameter query is not different from the queries you have used before—it is still a select query. The process to create it is very similar to the way you have created queries. However, instead of putting a specific value as a criterion, such as Cat or Dog, you would put a phrase in brackets, for example [Enter animal type]. When the query is run, a dialog box displays with the prompt you entered "Enter animal type." After the user enters a type of animal, Access will complete the query as if the user's response was entered as criterion initially (Figure 5.17). Then, Access will display any values that match the user's data entry exactly.

Creating a parameter query is similar to creating most other queries; the major difference is in the criteria. If you want to be a little more flexible, you can combine a comparison operator with the parameter. For example, you may ask a user to enter a value that will serve as a minimum age. In this case, you would type >=[Enter Minimum Age]. Access will process this by displaying all values greater than or equal to the user's data entry. You can use any of the comparison operators you may have used in the past, including greater than (>), greater than or equal to (>=), less than (<), less than or equal to (<=), equal to (=), not equal to (<>), Between, In, or Like. If you do not specify a comparison operator, Access will default to equal to as the operator.

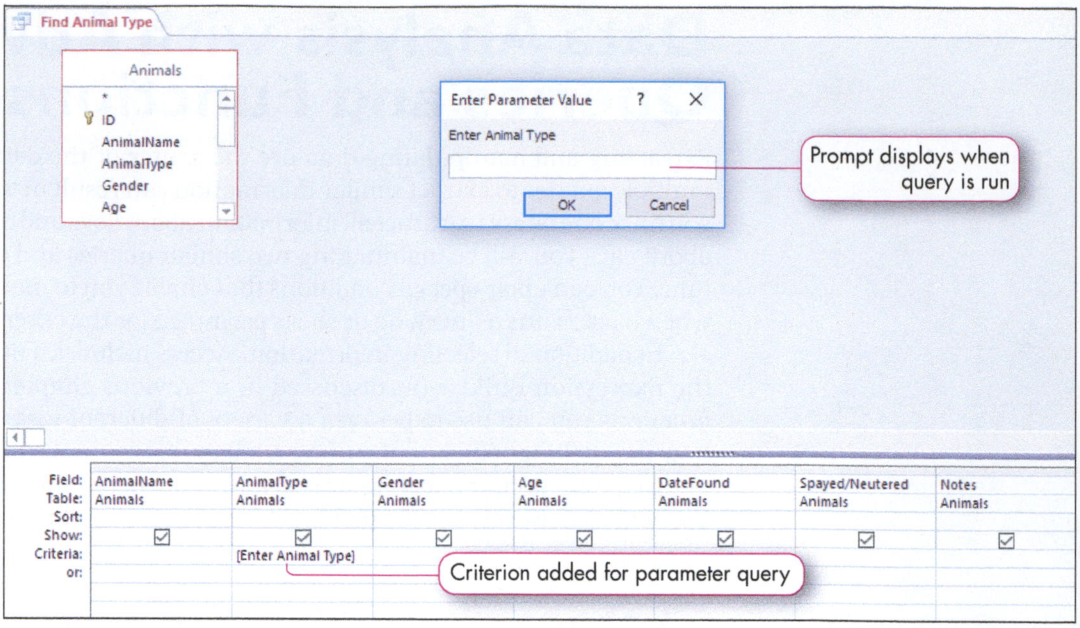

FIGURE 5.17 Parameter Query Prompt

Recall from previous query discussions you could use the Between operator to create a range of acceptable data. You can do the same with a parameter query by entering *Between [Enter Start Date] And [Enter End Date]* into the criteria of the EventDate column. This expression generates two Enter Parameter Value dialog boxes, one for the starting date and one for the ending date. After the user supplies the dates, Access then evaluates those dates as the query criteria. For example, if you enter 6/1/2021 when prompted for the starting date and 6/30/2021 as the ending date, Access interprets that as Between #6/1/2021# And #6/30/2021#. Recall that Access encloses date fields with the # character.

You can also use the Like operator to create a parameter query. Instead of searching for an exact match, you can use the Like operator to locate records that match the pattern you specify. For example, if you were to set the parameter to [Enter City] for a City field, you could revise the criterion to enable users to enter the partial name of a city. The new criterion would be Like [Enter Partial City] & '*' (use single quotation marks around the *). This new expression enables you to enter P at the prompt, and Access finds all cities that begin with P. The results might include cities named Paterson, Pompton Lakes, and Passaic, but not cities named West Paterson.

You can also use multiple parameters within a single query. For example, you could prompt for a maximum adoption fee and then prompt for gender. In this case, you would add one parameter to the AdoptionFee field and one parameter to the Gender field.

TIP: RESTRICT PARAMETER INPUT WITH THE PARAMETERS WINDOW

If your users run queries and end up with no results, it may be because their input is not in the form the query expects. Access provides a Parameters tool to restrict data types that will be accepted. This gives an additional level of control for parameter queries. For example, you may have a field named BirthDate and set the criterion to [Enter Start Date] for that field. The user would be prompted to enter a date. However, any value could be accepted. To add a layer of protection from errors, you can restrict the data that will be accepted. For example: >1/1/1900 for a birth date.

To display the Query Parameters window, open the query in Design view, click Parameters on the Show/Hide group of the Design tab, and then add the criteria. You can choose a data type for each parameter.

Create a Parameter Report

The effectiveness of parameter queries can be extended to reports. By creating a report based on a parameter query, you automatically receive the benefits of a parameter query—adding flexibility that enables a user to control the content of the report. The creation of a parameter report is simple once the parameter query has been created.

To create a parameter report from an existing parameter query, complete the following steps:

1. Select a parameter query in the Navigation Pane. Click Report in the Reports group of the Create tab.
2. Create a new report and the Enter Parameter Value dialog box displays, asking you to enter the criterion.
3. Enter a value and click OK. If you only have one parameter, the report opens in Layout view. Otherwise, you will be prompted for the other parameters.
4. Save the report. Note each time the report is opened, you are prompted for new criteria.

Any other type of report can be created as well using the same process that you used in previous chapters. This can work well with labels reports, for example, if you want to generate labels for customers who live in a certain state or ZIP code.

Using Advanced Functions

Effective functions can make a huge difference in the power of a database. Recall from an earlier chapter that there are several built-in functions in Access, each of which serve to perform some sort of calculation. Functions can include arguments; some arguments are required to perform the calculation, and others are optional. Some functions are relatively straightforward. For example, Sqr(NumberField) displays the square root of a field named Number.

However, for more complex tasks, you may end up with some sort of long expression that might take some time and understanding to develop. For example, the following function is created to isolate only the last name of a person by locating a space in the field FullName and displaying the values that appear after the space: Mid([FullName],InStr.(1,[FullName]," ")+1,Len([FullName])).

In a database, functions are often used to manipulate text, perform a calculation, or extract part of a date to calculate time. A few common functions, Date, Round, IIf, IsNull, and DatePart have been presented in this chapter. Functions can be added to database field properties, queries, forms, and more.

Recall when adding a function to a query, if you know the function and its arguments, you can type them directly into the first blank column of a query in Design view. However, it may be easier to use the Expression Builder to locate your function and add it to your query. The first few steps to add a function using the Builder are the same, no matter the function. Use these steps as your reference as you use the functions discussed in the remainder of this chapter.

To insert a function in a query using the Expression Builder, complete the following steps:

1. Open a query in Design view (or create a new query).
2. Click the Field row of a blank column.
3. Click Builder in the Query Setup group of the Design tab to launch the Expression Builder.
4. Double-click Functions in the Expression Elements section of the Expression Builder window.
5. Click Built-In Functions.
6. Locate and click the function category in the Expression Category section. If you are unsure of the category, you can use Help or search through the category labeled *All*.
7. Double-click the function name in the Expression Values section. The function and its argument placeholders are added to the Expression Builder window.
8. Type the number, field name, or calculation you want to replace the placeholder.
9. Click OK to close the Expression Builder window.
10. Replace Expr1 with a field name.

TIP: PLANNING FOR A FUNCTION

Many times, creating customized solutions for your users requires planning and research as well as combining multiple functions. These will not always be functions with which you are familiar. Once you identify what functionality is required, you can check the Built-In Functions in the Expression Builder to see if the function exists, add the function to the expression box, and replace «placeholder text» with the argument values. If a function is not available in the Expression Builder, use search engines or Microsoft Help.

STEP 2 ▶ **Use the Date Function**

The **Date function** is a function that returns the current date and can be found in the Date/Time category in Expression Builder. Access updates the value each time the system date changes. The Date function takes no arguments and can be entered directly in a field row of an existing query: =Date() as shown in Figure 5.18. Recall that in an earlier chapter, you performed simple date arithmetic with a fixed date to calculate the number of days a property was listed on the market before it was sold. In that instance, the difference between the DateSold and the DateListed fields was calculated. Creating a function with only fixed dates is not always realistic. You may want to run the same query over and over based on the current date, which will change every time you open the database. For example, you could calculate the number of days an animal was in the shelter by using the Date function in an expression. You could form your expression as: DaysInShelter: Date()-[DateFound].

=DATE()

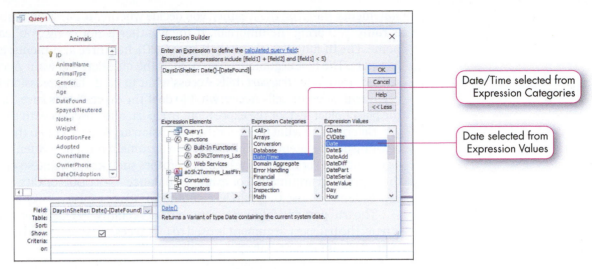

FIGURE 5.18 Date Function

> **TIP: DEFAULT A DATE FIELD TO TODAY**
> You can type Date() in the Default Value property in Table Design view to insert the current date when a new record is added. This type of default value is useful for many date fields where the person is inputting data for the current date, such as a hire date or an order date. In the future, the field will display the current date when data entry is performed.

Use the Round Function

The **Round function** returns a number rounded to a specified number of decimal places and is found in the Math Expression category. The Round function has two arguments: number and precision. The first argument, *number*, is the value to be rounded. The second argument, *precision*, is the number of decimal places to which you will round the number. If you leave the precision parameter blank, Access defaults to the nearest whole number.

For example, you may want to round animal weights to the nearest tenth of a pound. This can be accomplished using a query. See Figure 5.19. Notice the main function is written as Round([Weight],1). In this case, the first argument is the value to be rounded (the Weight field), and the second is to what decimal place (1, or the tenths). An animal weighing 25.05 pounds would be listed as 25.1 pounds, whereas an animal weighing 25.21 pounds would be listed as 25.2 pounds.

=ROUND(<<number>>, <<precision>>)

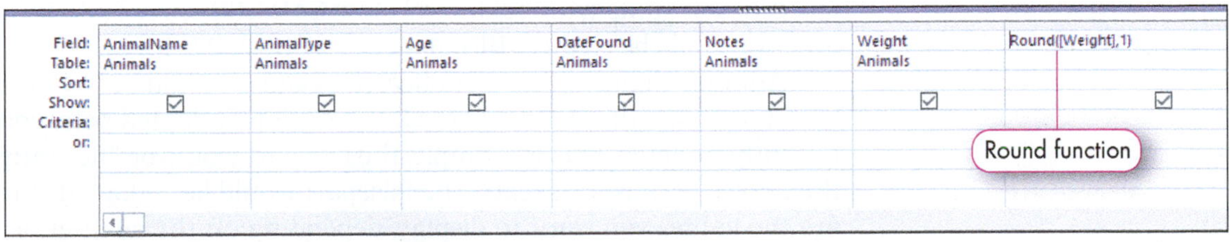

Field:	AnimalName	AnimalType	Age	DateFound	Notes	Weight	Round([Weight],1)
Table:	Animals	Animals	Animals	Animals	Animals	Animals	
Sort:							
Show:	☑	☑	☑	☑	☑	☑	☑
Criteria:							
or:							

Round function

FIGURE 5.19 Round Function in Design View

STEP 3 ▶ Use the IIf Function

Another commonly used Access function is the **IIf function**, which evaluates an expression and displays one value when the expression is true and another value when the expression is false. The IIf function is available in the Expression Builder in the Built-In Functions, in the Program Flow category. In your day-to-day life, you are constantly performing IIf statements. Based on the weather, you decide whether to carry an umbrella. If the weather is rainy, you bring the umbrella. If the weather is not rainy, you leave the umbrella at home. The IIf function (shown in Figure 5.20), has three arguments: expression, truepart, falsepart. The first argument, *expression*, is the question you want Access to evaluate. The second argument, *truepart*, tells Access what to do if the expression is true, and the last argument, *falsepart*, tells Access what to do if the expression is false. Once inserted, replace the placeholder text for the expression, truepart, and falsepart with the values you want.

Determining what to use for the expression argument is often the most difficult part of creating an IIf statement. The expression argument must be written so that it can evaluate as yes (or true) or no (or false) only. Operators such as >, <, and so on, are used as part of the expression argument. For example, Balance >= 10000 or City = "Sarasota" are valid expressions because they can be evaluated as true or false.

The truepart and falsepart arguments are relatively straightforward. If the expression is true, the truepart argument is used to tell Access what it should do. Alternatively, if the expression is false, the falsepart argument tells Access what it should do. You can output text, a numeric value, or even embed another function or calculation. When using text and dates as the true or false results, you need to remember to include quotation marks (") around a text value, and pound signs (#) around a date value.

=IIF(<<expression>>, <<truepart>>, <<falsepart>>)

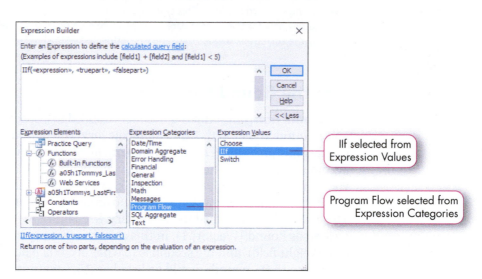

FIGURE 5.20 IIf Function

For example, if accounts with balances of $10,000 or more earn 3.5% interest, whereas accounts with balances below $10,000 earn 1.5% interest, the following IIf function could be created: IIf(Balance>=10000, 0.035, 0.015).

Another slightly more complicated example would be if you categorize adopted pets based on when they were adopted. For recently adopted pets, you may want to display Recently Adopted. In this example, the truepart would be "Recently Adopted" (remember the quotes because it is text). The falsepart would be "Adopted" (again, in quotes). These are the values you want to display, depending on the evaluation of the expression. To create an expression that determines if the date of adoption is within (less than or equal to) 30 days of the current date, you will include the Date function and the DateOfAdoption field to create an expression: Date() – DateOfAdoption <=30. Putting it all together, the IIf function would be: IIf(Date() – DateOfAdoption <=30, "Recently Adopted", "Adopted"). The expression is shown in the Expression Builder in Figure 5.21.

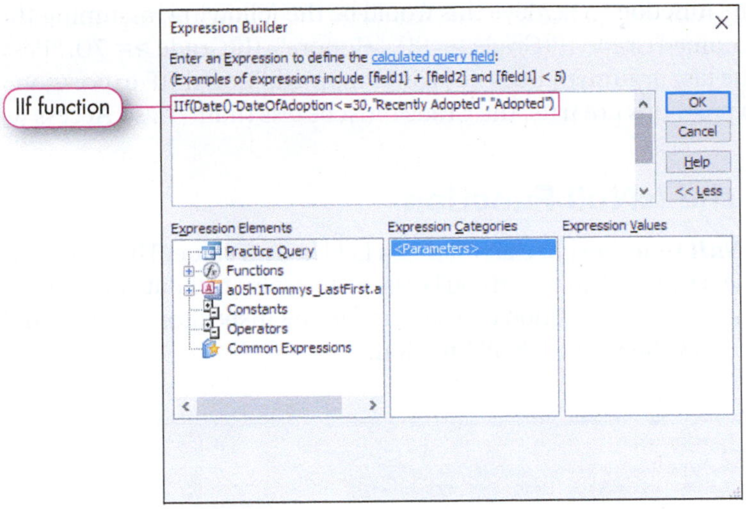

FIGURE 5.21 IIf Function to Evaluate DateOfAdoption

The results of the function are shown in Figure 5.22. For that example, the date it is run—that is, Date()—is 12/20/2021. You can see Rachel, who was adopted on 12/20/2021, is listed as recently adopted because her adoption date was within 30 days of the current date.

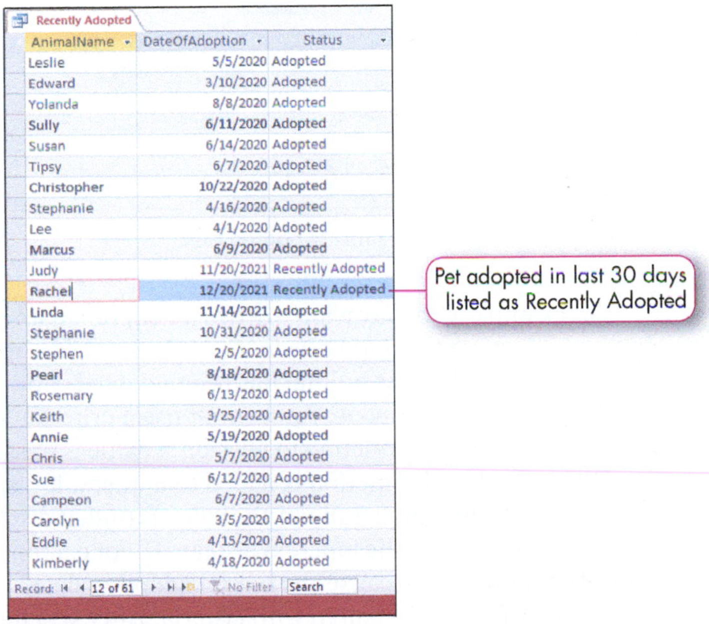

FIGURE 5.22 IIf Function Results

Sometimes it is necessary to use IIf functions within an IIf function. This happens when two conditions are not sufficient to evaluate an expression. When a function is used within another function, it is referred to as a nested function. Suppose you have three choices you need to evaluate for a grade field (as illustrated in Table 5.2):

TABLE 5.2	Grading IIF Function Example
Grade	**Result**
Grade > = 90	Honors
Grade > = 70	Pass
Grade < 70	Fail

The function to achieve this would be the following, assuming the Grade is stored in a field named Grade:IIf(Grade >=90, "Honors", IIf(Grade >= 70, "Pass", "Fail")). Observe that the last argument does not contain an additional IIF expression. If neither of those first expressions are true, the Grade must be less than 70, so Access will display Fail.

Use the IsNull Function

The *IsNull function* checks whether a field has no value. The word *null* means an absence of value. The IsNull function can be useful to evaluate if data are missing. In the Expression Builder, the IsNull function can be found in the Inspection category of Built-In Functions. Figure 5.23 shows the IsNull function.

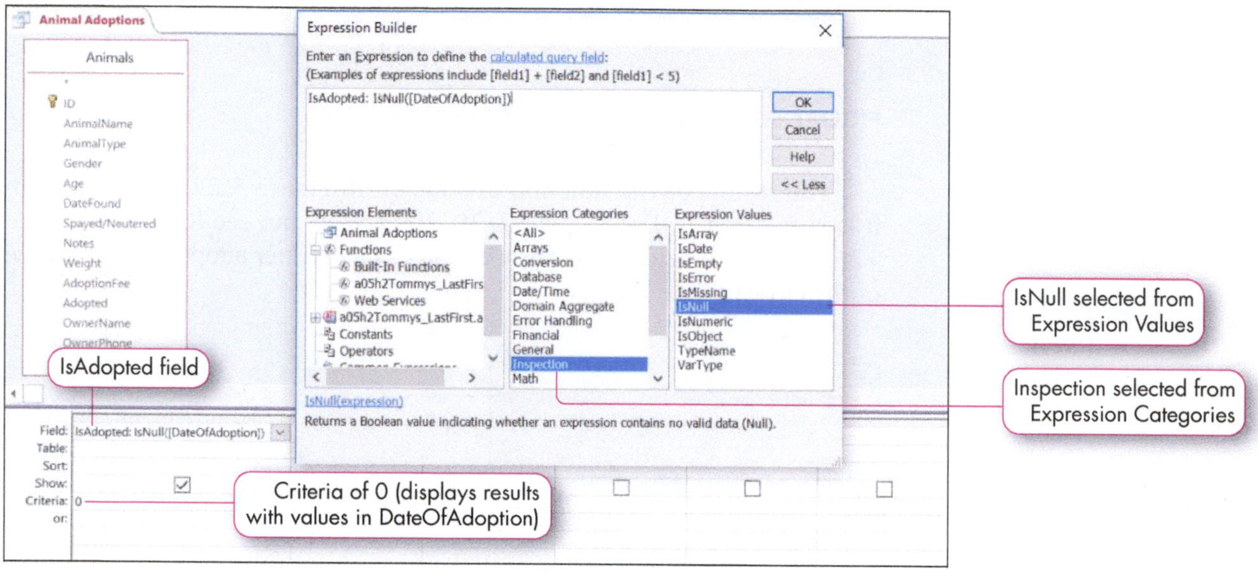

FIGURE 5.23 IsNull Function and Setting Criteria for IsAdopted Field

For example, you may want to extract adoption date information about the pets in the database. Assume the database does not have a field named Adopted that stores as a Yes or No value whether the animal has been adopted. How would you extract only the pets that have not been adopted? You cannot use a criterion of AdoptedDate = 0. You would need to use the IsNull function to check if a value is missing.

When the IsNull function is added to a query, it displays one of two values. Access determines "Is this value null?" If the value is null, it displays -1. If the value is not null—that is, it has a value—the function displays 0. For example, the results of IsNull for Leslie's DateOfAdoption is 0 because she has an adoption date.

IsNull is frequently paired with criteria. After you have created a calculated column using the IsNull function, you could evaluate the results and display only certain values. You could display non-null values by setting the Criteria row to 0, or display null values by setting the Criteria row to -1. Figure 5.23 shows setting the criteria for the calculated IsAdopted field to 0, so it will only show pets with valid adoption dates.

=ISNULL(<<expression>>)

STEP 4 Use the DatePart Function

Date manipulation is a task most database administrators will perform frequently. Users will typically seek out information with dates attached, whether it is finding orders placed in the last few days or seeking out information about past transactions. The *DatePart function* examines a date and displays a portion of the date. You can find this function through the Expression Builder in the Date/Time category of Built-In Functions.

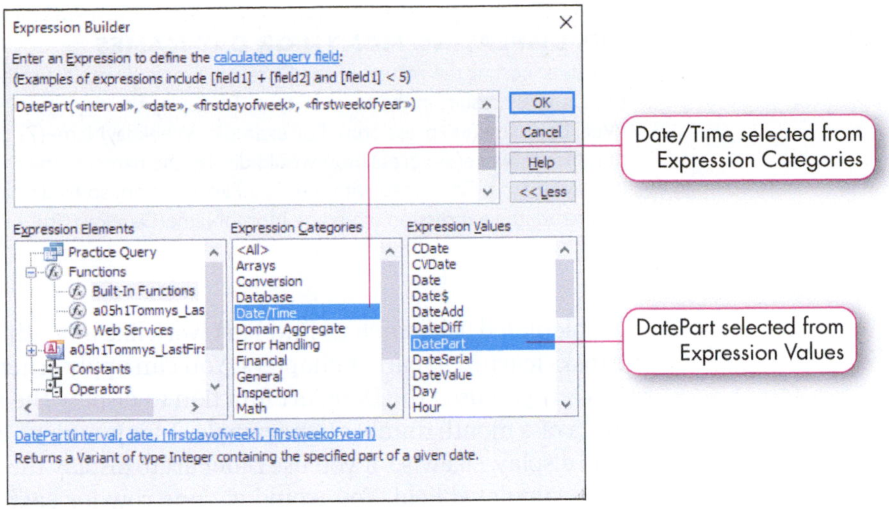

Date/Time selected from Expression Categories

DatePart selected from Expression Values

FIGURE 5.24 DatePart Function

DatePart (see Figure 5.24) is used to extract the year, month, or day, and a few other intervals as well. You could use this function, for example, to find all pets adopted in the current month (for example, January) and send the owner a birthday card for the pet. The AdoptedDate field in the shelter database has a Short Date format and stores the date as 1/10/2020. If you want to know only the month, you must extract that from the date in the field using the DatePart function. The first argument, the interval, describes the portion of the date that you want to display. The second argument, the date, tells Access where to find the Date/Time information. Table 5.3 shows some common values for the interval argument.

The result of the DatePart function displays a numeric value, so if you extract the month, you get a number from 1 (representing January) through 12 (representing December). If you extract the weekday, you get a number from 1 (representing Sunday) through 7 (representing Saturday).

DatePart(«interval», «date», «firstdayofweek», «firstweekofyear»)

TABLE 5.3   DatePart Interval Values

Common Values for Interval Argument, and Explanation

Interval Argument	Explanation
"yyyy"	Year
"m"	Month (displays a number 1 through 12, 1 represents January)
"d"	Day (displays a number, 1 through 366, representing the day of the year)
"w"	Day of the Week (displays a number 1 through 7, 1 represents Sunday)
"h"	Hour
"n"	Minute

Table 5.4 shows a few examples of the DatePart function being used on a Date/Time field named HireDate. For these examples, assume HireDate is 8/31/2020.

TABLE 5.4   Evaluating the DatePart Function

Function Portion	Resulting Value	Explanation
DatePart("yyyy",HireDate)	2020	August 31, 2020, has a year of 2020
DatePart("m",HireDate)	8	August is the eighth month of the year
DatePart("w",HireDate)	2	August 31, 2020, is a Monday (the second day of the week).

Calculated fields such as DatePart work like any other field when it comes to some of the tasks learned in earlier chapters. You can apply criteria (including using a parameter query). If you used the DatePart function to display the month number, you could add a criteria of a month number (for example, 1 for January), and only results from that month would display. Likewise, if you use DatePart to display the month number, you could group by the calculated field. You would get one row for each month. Figure 5.25 shows the results of the animals grouped by the month each animal was found. The Month column was created using the DatePart function, as shown in Figure 5.26.

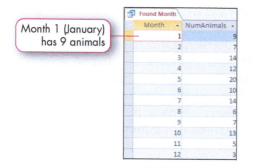

Month 1 (January) has 9 animals

FIGURE 5.25 Query Showing Animals by Month

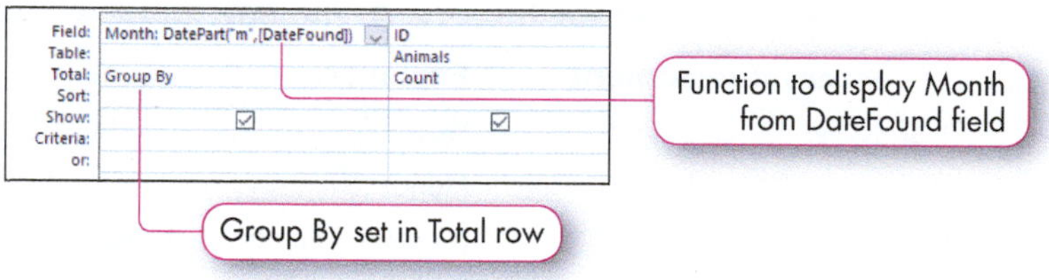

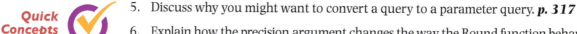

Function to display Month from DateFound field

Group By set in Total row

FIGURE 5.26 Grouping by DatePart Function Results

Quick Concepts

5. Discuss why you might want to convert a query to a parameter query. *p. 317*

6. Explain how the precision argument changes the way the Round function behaves. *p. 321*

7. You want to use the IIf function to display Yes for all applicants with a value of 700 or more in their CreditScore field and No for all other applicants. Provide and explain the values of the *expression*, *truepart*, and *falsepart* arguments for this function. *pp. 321–323*

8. Explain the purpose of the IsNull function. *p. 324*

9. Demonstrate, using an expression, how you would direct the DatePart function to display only the month of a field named BirthDate. *pp. 324–326*

Hands-On Exercises

Skills covered: Create a
Parameter Query • Create a
Parameter Report • Use the Date
Function • Use the Round Function •
Use the IIf Function • Use the
IsNull Function • Use the DatePart
Function

2 Data Analysis with Advanced Queries and Functions

After applying data validation rules to the tables, you will perform some advanced queries against the database. You will create a parameter query, use advanced Expression Builder functions, and use date arithmetic to manipulate the data.

STEP 1 CREATE A PARAMETER QUERY AND REPORT

Tommy wants you to create a query that will enable the volunteers to input the animal type and display all animals matching the type. He also wants to create a report based on that query to be viewed on the computer. In addition, he wants you to create a query to display all animals dropped off at the shelter in a certain date range. Refer to Figure 5.27 as you complete Step 1.

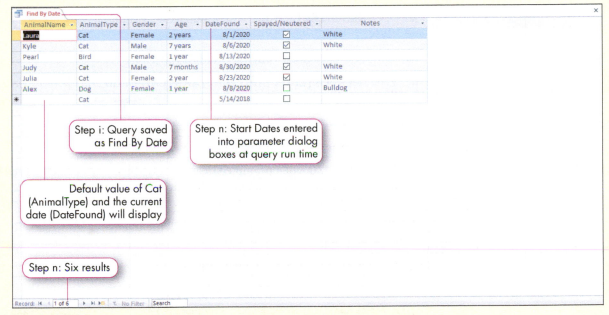

FIGURE 5.27 Find By Date Results for August 2020

a. Open *a05h1Tommys_LastFirst* if you closed it at the end of Hands-On Exercise 1, and save it as **a05h2Tommys_LastFirst**, changing h1 to h2.

b. Click the **Create tab**. Click **Query Design** in the Queries group to create a new query. Double-click the **Animals table** to add it to the query. Click **Close**.

c. Double-click each of the following fields to add them to the query: **AnimalName**, **AnimalType**, **Gender**, **Age**, **DateFound**, **Spayed/Neutered**, and **Notes**.

d. Type **[Enter Animal Type]** in the Criteria row for the AnimalType field.

e. Save the query as **Find Animal Type**. Run the query.

You are prompted to enter an animal type in a box labeled Enter Animal Type.

> **TROUBLESHOOTING:** If you are not prompted to Enter Animal Type, ensure your criterion for the AnimalType field is enclosed in brackets exactly as shown in Step d.

f. Type **Bird** in the Enter Animal Type box and click **OK**.

All nine birds in the database are displayed, including Marco, who was entered in Hands-on Exercise 1.

> **TROUBLESHOOTING:** If you get no results, ensure you typed [Enter Animal Type] in the correct field's criteria.

g. Close the Find Animal Type query.

h. Double-click the **Find Animal Type query** in the Navigation Pane to run the query again. Enter **Cat** when prompted and click **OK**. Verify 86 records are displayed. Close the query.

i. Right-click the **Find Animal Type query** and select **Copy**. Right-click a blank area of the Navigation Pane and select **Paste**. Name the query **Find By Date** and click **OK**.

j. Open the Find By Date query in Design view by right-clicking and selecting **Design view**.

k. Remove the criterion from the AnimalType field.

l. Type **Between [Enter Start Date] and [Enter End Date]** on the Criteria row for the DateFound field.

m. Save the query. Run the query.

You will be prompted for one date and then for a second date.

n. Type **8/1/2020** when prompted to Enter Start Date and click **OK**. Type **8/31/2020** when prompted to Enter End Date and click **OK**. Verify six animals are displayed, as shown in Figure 5.27. Close the query.

o. Click the **Find Animal Type query**. Click the **Create tab** and click **Report** in the Reports group.

You are prompted to Enter Animal Type.

> **TROUBLESHOOTING:** If you are prompted to enter a Start Date, cancel and ensure you have clicked the Find Animal Type query first.

p. Type **Bird** when prompted and click **OK**.

The same nine records displayed earlier appear in report form. Because this is designed to be viewed on screen and not printed, you will not worry about resizing the fields.

q. Save the report as **Animal Report** and close the report.

Tommy requested some modifications to the database that you can achieve using advanced functions. You will assist him by setting a default date and rounding animal weights. Refer to Figure 5.28 as you complete Step 2.

AnimalName	AnimalType	Age	DateFound	Notes	Weight	Rounded
Leslie	Bird	1 year	4/25/2020		2.12	2
Edward	Cat	2 year	3/7/2020	White	12.04	12
Yolanda	Cat	6 weeks	7/20/2020	Black	12.58	13
Sully	Dog	5 years	5/15/2020	Bichon Frise	12.93	13
Emily	Bird	1 year	3/24/2020		2.13	2
Susan	Cat	3 year	5/21/2020	Black	12.47	12
Mark	Cat	6 weeks	1/4/2020	Orange	12.01	12
Tipsy	Cat	1 year	5/18/2020	Black with white boots	12.45	12
Christopher	Cat	2 years	9/24/2020	Black	12.46	12
Laura	Cat	2 years	8/1/2020	White	12.88	13
Leo	Cat	5 months	6/3/2020	Calico	7.44	7
Stephanie	Cat	5 years	4/5/2020	White	12.32	12
Lee	Bird	1 year	3/4/2020		2.11	2
Sylvia	Cat	2 years	11/7/2021	Calico	12.72	13
Marcus	Bird	1 year	5/27/2020		2.20	2
Judy	Cat	5 years	11/11/2021	White	12.60	13
Rodney	Bird	1 year	10/9/2020		2.13	2
Rachel	Cat	2 years	12/16/2021	Black	12.61	13
Lawrence	Cat	9 months	9/9/2020	Black	12.94	13
Kyle	Cat	7 years	8/6/2020	White	12.63	13
Linda	Cat	6 months	11/6/2021	Orange	7.92	8
Stephanie	Cat	2 year	10/6/2020	Black	12.67	13
Elaine	Cat	3 year	3/6/2020	Calico	12.44	12
Jet	Bird	1 year	5/18/2020	Parakeet	2.09	2
Jill	Cat	5 weeks	3/22/2020	Calico	12.69	13

Record: 1 of 120   No Filter   Search

> Steps h–k: Rounded field rounds Weight field to nearest whole number

FIGURE 5.28 Rounded Weights Query Results

a. Open the Animals table in Design view. Click the **DateFound field**.

b. Click **Default Value** in the Field Properties. Type **Date()** as the default value.

The default value for all new records is the current date.

c. Switch to Datasheet view. Save the changes when prompted. Scroll to the new record at the bottom of the table.

The first blank record has a default value of the current date. Note if you are working on this before 2020, your default date may be before some of the other dates.

d. Close the Animals table.

e. Click the **Create tab**. Click **Query Design** in the Queries group to create a new query. Double-click the **Animals table** in the Show Table dialog box. Click **Close**.

f. Double-click the **AnimalName**, **AnimalType**, **Age**, **DateFound**, **Notes**, and **Weight fields** to add them to the query.

g. Click the top row of the first column after the Weight field.

You will create a new column to round the Weight field.

h. Click **Builder** in the Query Setup group. Double-click **Functions** in the Expression Elements section of the window. Click **Built-In Functions**. Click **Math** in the Expression Categories section of the Expression Builder.

i. Double-click **Round** in the Expression Values section.

Round(«number», «precision») displays in the Expression Builder.

j. Remove «number», «precision» from the expression and replace them with **Weight**.

Round(Weight) displays in the Expression Builder.

k. Click **OK**. Replace Expr1 in your new column with **Rounded**. Run the query. Check the Rounded column against the Weight column to make sure the animal weights are rounded to the nearest whole number (see Figure 5.28).

l. Save the query as **Rounded Weights** and close the query.

STEP 3 USE IIF AND ISNULL FUNCTIONS

Tommy wants to find data entry errors in his database. Due to the sheer number of volunteers, he has noticed mistakes in the database, and he wants a query to find any pets that are listed as adopted but do not have an owner name. You will help him to accomplish this by using an IsNull function inside an IIf function. Refer to Figure 5.29 as you complete Step 3.

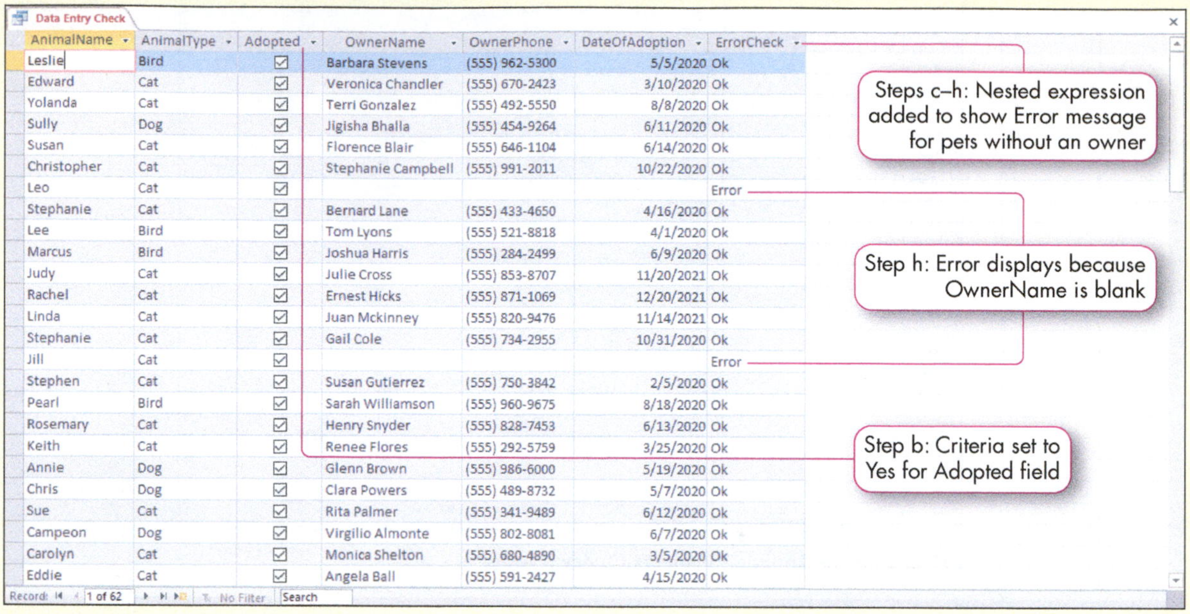
Data Entry Check

AnimalName	AnimalType	Adopted	OwnerName	OwnerPhone	DateOfAdoption	ErrorCheck
Leslie	Bird	☑	Barbara Stevens	(555) 962-5300	5/5/2020	Ok
Edward	Cat	☑	Veronica Chandler	(555) 670-2423	3/10/2020	Ok
Yolanda	Cat	☑	Terri Gonzalez	(555) 492-5550	8/8/2020	Ok
Sully	Dog	☑	Jigisha Bhalla	(555) 454-9264	6/11/2020	Ok
Susan	Cat	☑	Florence Blair	(555) 646-1104	6/14/2020	Ok
Christopher	Cat	☑	Stephanie Campbell	(555) 991-2011	10/22/2020	Ok
Leo	Cat	☑				Error
Stephanie	Cat	☑	Bernard Lane	(555) 433-4650	4/16/2020	Ok
Lee	Bird	☑	Tom Lyons	(555) 521-8818	4/1/2020	Ok
Marcus	Bird	☑	Joshua Harris	(555) 284-2499	6/9/2020	Ok
Judy	Cat	☑	Julie Cross	(555) 853-8707	11/20/2021	Ok
Rachel	Cat	☑	Ernest Hicks	(555) 871-1069	12/20/2021	Ok
Linda	Cat	☑	Juan Mckinney	(555) 820-9476	11/14/2021	Ok
Stephanie	Cat	☑	Gail Cole	(555) 734-2955	10/31/2020	Ok
Jill	Cat	☑				Error
Stephen	Cat	☑	Susan Gutierrez	(555) 750-3842	2/5/2020	Ok
Pearl	Bird	☑	Sarah Williamson	(555) 960-9675	8/18/2020	Ok
Rosemary	Cat	☑	Henry Snyder	(555) 828-7453	6/13/2020	Ok
Keith	Cat	☑	Renee Flores	(555) 292-5759	3/25/2020	Ok
Annie	Dog	☑	Glenn Brown	(555) 986-6000	5/19/2020	Ok
Chris	Dog	☑	Clara Powers	(555) 489-8732	5/7/2020	Ok
Sue	Cat	☑	Rita Palmer	(555) 341-9489	6/12/2020	Ok
Campeon	Dog	☑	Virgilio Almonte	(555) 802-8081	6/7/2020	Ok
Carolyn	Cat	☑	Monica Shelton	(555) 680-4890	3/5/2020	Ok
Eddie	Cat	☑	Angela Ball	(555) 591-2427	4/15/2020	Ok

Record: 1 of 62 No Filter Search

FIGURE 5.29 Data Entry Check Query Results

a. Click the **Create tab**. Click **Query Design** in the Queries group to create a new query. Double-click the **Animals table**. Click **Close**. Double-click the **AnimalName**, **AnimalType**, **Adopted**, **OwnerName**, **OwnerPhone**, and **DateOfAdoption fields** to add them to the query.

You will use a combination of an IIf and IsNull function to find animals that are listed as adopted but do not have owners listed.

b. Type **Yes** in the Criteria row of the Adopted field.

You will limit your query results to animals that are listed as adopted.

c. Click the top row of the first blank column following the DateOfAdoption column. Click **Builder** in the Query Setup group.

d. Double-click **Functions** in the Expression Elements section of the window. Click **Built-In Functions**. Click **Program Flow** in the Expression Categories section of the Expression Builder. Double-click **IIf** in the Expression Values section of the window.

IIf(«expression», «truepart», «falsepart») displays in the Expression Builder.

e. Click **«expression»**. Press **Delete**. Click **Inspection** in the Expression Categories section of the Expression Builder. Double-click **IsNull**.

IIf(IsNull(«expression»), «truepart», «falsepart») displays in the Expression Builder.

f. Click **«expression»**. Type **OwnerName**.

IIf(IsNull(OwnerName), «truepart», «falsepart») displays in the Expression Builder.

g. Click **«truepart»**. Type "**Error**". Click **«falsepart»**. Type "**Ok**".

IIf(IsNull(OwnerName), "Error", "Ok") displays in the Expression Builder.

h. Click **OK**. Replace Expr1 with **ErrorCheck**. Run the query and compare the results with Figure 5.29.

An error message will appear for any pet record that has been listed as adopted but has no owner. Tommy can now review his records and fix the errors.

i. Save the query as **Data Entry Check**. Close the query.

STEP **4** # USE THE DATEPART FUNCTION

Tommy was asked by a local animal control agency to provide a list of all animals that have been found in the month of January in any year. The agency is hoping to use this information to determine whether to add more part-time workers for January. You will help him get a list of all animals the shelter has collected during any January. Refer to Figure 5.30 as you complete Step 4.

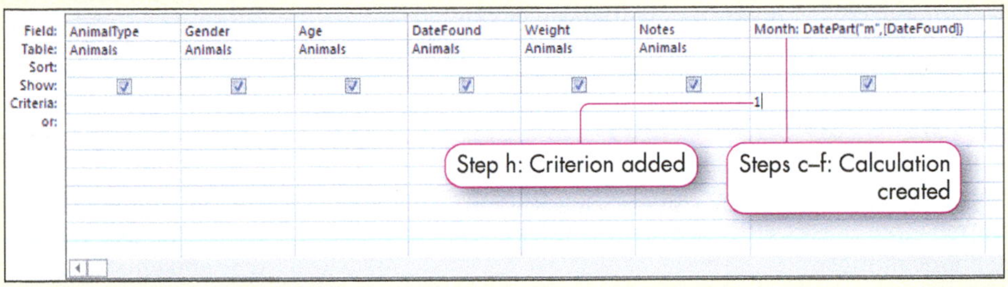

FIGURE 5.30 January Animals Design

a. Click the **Create tab**. Click **Query Design** in the Queries group to create a new query. Double-click the **Animals table**. Click **Close**. Double-click the **AnimalType**, **Gender**, **Age**, **DateFound**, **Weight**, and **Notes fields** to add them to the query.

b. Click the top row of the first blank column after the Notes field. Click **Builder** in the Query Setup group.

c. Double-click **Functions** in the Expression Elements section of the window. Click **Built-In Functions** and click **Date/Time** in the Expression Categories section of the Expression Builder. Double-click **DatePart** in the Expression Values section of the window.

DatePart(«interval», «date», «firstdayofweek», «firstweekofyear») displays in the Expression Builder.

d. Click **«firstdayofweek»** and press **Delete**. Repeat the process for **«firstweekofyear»** and the extra spaces and commas.

DatePart(«interval», «date») displays in the Expression Builder.

e. Click **«interval»**. Type "**m**". Click **«date»**. Type **DateFound**.

DatePart("m", DateFound) now displays in the Expression Builder.

f. Click **OK**. Replace Expr1 with **Month**.

g. Run the query. Examine the new column.

The new column now contains a number corresponding to the number of the month of the year (for example, 1 for January and 12 for December).

h. Switch to Design view. Type **1** in the Criteria row for the newly created column and compare your design with Figure 5.30. Run the query.

The nine animals found in the month of January appear.

i. Save the query as **January Animals**. Close the query.

j. Close the database and exit Access. Based on your instructor's directions, submit a05h2Tommys_LastFirst.

Chapter Objectives Review

After reading this chapter, you have accomplished the following objectives:

1. Establish data validation.

- Require a field: Required fields cannot be left without a value, and existing records do not have to be updated if you set this property.
- Add a default field value: A default field value automatically enters a value in a field, which is useful if a majority of new records have the same value.
- Add a validation rule with validation text: Validation rules limit the type or range of data that can be entered, and validation text provides more information when the user violates a validation rule.

2. Control the format of data entry.

- Create an input mask: Input masks specify the exact format of the data entry. You can use the wizard to create common input masks, such as Social Security number and phone number.

3. Control input with a lookup field.

- Create a lookup field: A field with several repeated values may be better suited as a lookup field, which provides the user with a finite list of values to choose from in a menu.
- Modify a lookup field: Lookup field options are usually in a separate table, so changes can be performed in that table.

4. Customize output based on user input.

- Create a parameter query: A parameter query is a select query for which the user provides the criterion at run time. It enables you to create a query for one situation and then expand it into a query for unlimited situations.
- Create a parameter report: Base a report on a query with parameters, and the same option to enter parameters at run time is available. This extends the effectiveness of the parameter query to a report.

5. Use advanced functions.

- Use the Date function: The Date function returns the current date. There are no parameters.
- Use the Round function: The Round function displays a number rounded to a specific number of decimal places. The number of decimal places is specified by changing the precision parameter.
- Use the IIf function: The IIf function evaluates an expression and returns one value when the expression is true and another value when the expression is false. The expression involves a comparison that can be evaluated as yes or no.
- Use the IsNull function: The IsNull function checks whether a field has no value.
- Use the DatePart function: DatePart enables you to isolate part of a date (day of the week, week number, month, year, etc.). A calculated field using DatePart can have criteria applied for it. Grouping also works with the DatePart function.

Key Terms Matching

Match the key terms with their definitions. Write the key term letter by the appropriate numbered definition.

a. Data validation

b. Date function

c. DatePart function

d. Default value

e. IIf function

f. Input mask

g. Input Mask Wizard

h. IsNull function

i. Lookup field

j. Lookup Wizard

k. Parameter query

l. Round function

m. Validation rule

n. Validation text

1. _____ A function that examines a date and displays a portion of the date. **p. 324**

2. _____ A function that checks whether a field has no value. **p. 324**

3. _____ A function that evaluates an expression and displays one value when the expression is true and another value when the expression is false. **p. 321**

4. _____ A function that calculates the current date. **p. 320**

5. _____ A query for which the user provides the criterion at run time. **p. 317**

6. _____ A way to provide the user with a predefined list of values from which to choose in a menu. **p. 309**

7. _____ A tool that helps you create a menu of predefined values by asking you questions and using your answers to create the options list. **p. 310**

8. _____ A setting that limits the data values a user can enter into a field. **p. 305**

9. _____ A tool used to generate data restrictions for a field. **p. 307**

10. _____ A set of constraints or rules that help control data entered into a field. **p. 304**

11. _____ A setting that restricts the data being input into a field by specifying the exact format of the data entry. **p. 307**

12. _____ A function that returns a number rounded to a specific number of decimal places. **p. 321**

13. _____ A way to specify what value is automatically entered into a field when a new record is added to a table. **p. 305**

14. _____ A setting that provides a custom error message to the user when incorrect data are entered. **p. 306**

Multiple Choice

1. Which of the following is *not* a data validation technique?

   (a) Round function
   (b) Lookup fields
   (c) Default values
   (d) Input masks

2. Which of the following fields is *most likely* to be set to required?

   (a) An account number in a credit union database
   (b) A student's major in a college's database
   (c) The middle name of a student in a high school swimming database
   (d) The vehicle color in a motor vehicles office database

3. Which of the following tool enables users to assign commonly used formats to ease data entry?

   (a) Report Wizard
   (b) Lookup Wizard
   (c) Input Mask Wizard
   (d) Query Design Wizard

4. The string of characters !\(999") "000\-0000;0;_ represents which of the following?

   (a) Lookup field
   (b) Validation text
   (c) Input mask
   (d) Parameter

5. A parameter query enables you to:

   (a) specify criteria for a field when you run the query.
   (b) find and display specific parts of a date, for example the month.
   (c) restrict the data a user enters into a field, such as requiring the data to appear as a Social Security number.
   (d) perform mathematical operations, such as rounding.

6. When would you use the Date function?

   (a) To display the current date
   (b) To display only the year from a date field
   (c) When doing math involving two date fields
   (d) To convert a value from a number into a date

7. Which of the following statements about the Round function is *false*?

   (a) The Round function has two parameters: the value you want to round and the precision.
   (b) A Round function with a precision of 1 rounds to the nearest integer.
   (c) A Round function without a precision parameter displays an integer.
   (d) Round(210.61,0) would display 211.

8. Which of the following statements is *false*?

   (a) The IsNull function works on date fields.
   (b) IsNull can be used to determine if a field has no value.
   (c) A null value means that the value is 0 for any type of field.
   (d) A null value means that the value is -1 for any type of field.

9. Which of the following is *not* a valid condition for an IIf function?

   (a) Credits >= 60
   (b) State IN ("CA","WA","OR")
   (c) City <> "Nashua"
   (d) Between 10 and 22

10. Which of the following *cannot* be extracted by the DatePart function?

    (a) Weekday
    (b) Month
    (c) Year
    (d) Leap Year

Practice Exercises

Willow Insurance Agency

The Willow Insurance Agency recently migrated to an Access database. Based on a recommendation from a colleague, the agency has hired you to consult on its database design. You will help to improve the quality of the data by implementing data validation and also create a query to help extract information. Refer to Figure 5.31 as you complete this exercise.

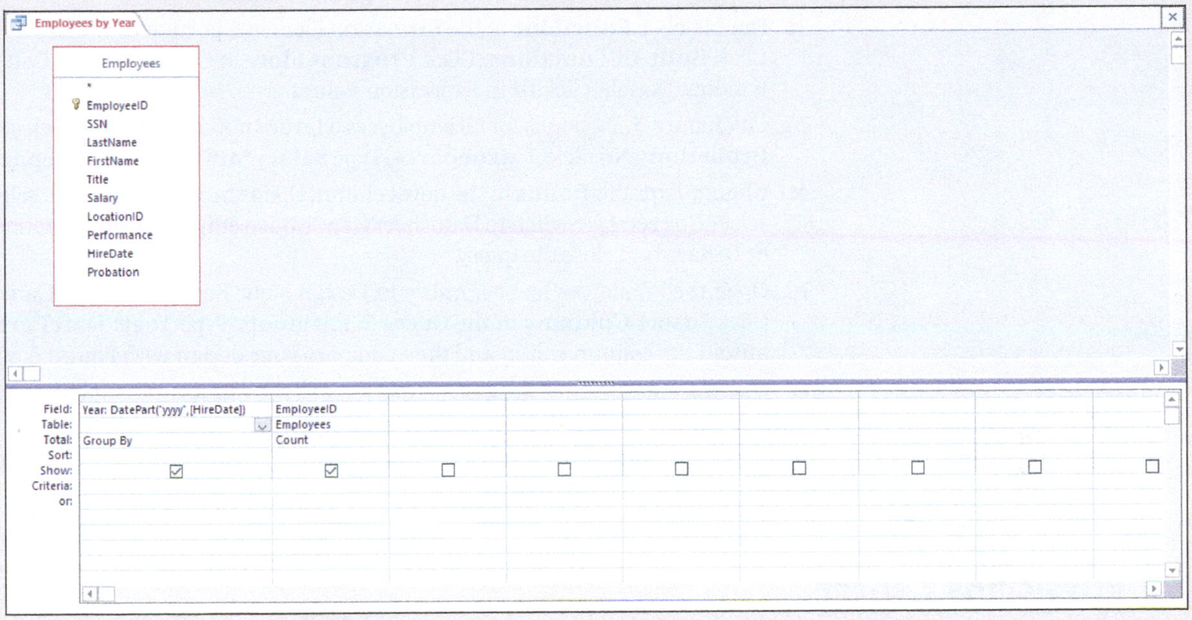

FIGURE 5.31 Employees by Year Design

a. Open *a05p1Willow*. Save the database as **a05p1Willow_LastFirst**.

b. Open the Employees table in Design view. Click the **Salary field**.

c. Click **Required** in the Field Properties pane. Click the arrow at the right of the row and select **Yes**.a

d. Click **Validation Rule** in the Field Properties pane. Type **>=18000**.

e. Click **Validation Text** in the Field Properties pane. Type **Minimum salary is $18,000**.

f. Click the **Title field**. Click **Default Value** in the Field Properties pane. Type **T03**. As most employees start as trainees, this is a good choice for default value.

g. Click the **SSN field**. Click **Input Mask** in the Field Properties pane. Click the **ellipsis** . Click **Yes** when prompted to save the table, and click **No** if asked if you want the existing data to be tested. Select **Social Security Number** and click **Next** twice. When asked how you want to store the data, select the option for **With the symbols in the mask**. Click **Finish**.

h. Click the **LocationID field**. Click **Data Type** and select **Lookup Wizard** from the list. Click **Next** to accept the default of getting values from another table or query. Click **Table: Location** and click **Next**. Click **Location** and click **Add One Field** to add it to the Selected Fields. Click **Next**. Select **Location** for the sort order and click **Next**. Click **Finish**. Click **Yes** in response to the prompt about saving the table.

i. Switch to Datasheet view. Click **New** in the Records group on the Home tab. Type an EmployeeID of **312**. Type a SSN of **999999999** (without the dashes) and notice Access fills dashes in automatically. Enter **Tarquinio** for the last name and **Jennifer** for the first name. Accept the default value of T03 for the Title field. Leave Salary blank.

j. Select **Miami** for LocationID. Type **Excellent** for Performance and **1/1/2020** for HireDate. Leave Probation deselected.

k. Click **EmployeeID 311**. Respond to the error message that indicates you must enter a value in the salary field and click **OK**.

l. Enter a value of **4000** for Jennifer Tarquinio's salary. Click **Employee 311** again. Click **OK** for the prompt, *Minimum salary is $18,000*. Type a salary of **40000** and click **Employee 311**. Close the table.

m. Open the Bonus Amounts query in Design view. Click the **Field row** of the first blank column and click **Builder** in the Query Setup group.

n. Double-click **Functions** in the Expression Elements portion of the Expression Builder window. Click **Built-In Functions**. Click **Program Flow** in the Expression Categories portion of the window. Double-click **IIf** in Expression Values.

o. Calculate a 5.5% bonus for all employees who are not on probation. Select **«expression»**. Type **Probation=No**. Select **«truepart»**. Type **Salary*.055**. Select **«falsepart»**. Type **0**. Click **OK**.

p. Change Expr1 to **Bonus** in the new column. Open the Property Sheet, select **Format**, and then select **Currency**. Switch to Datasheet view. Notice employees on probation will receive a bonus of 0. Save and close the query.

q. Open the Employees by Year query in Design view. Remove the HireDate field from the query. Click **Insert Columns** in the Query Setup group. Type **Year: DatePart("yyyy",HireDate)**, autofit the column width, and then compare your design with Figure 5.31.

r. Run the query. Notice the query now displays the number of employees hired in each calendar year. Save and close the query.

s. Close the database and exit Access. Based on your instructor's directions, submit a05p1Willow_LastFirst.

2 Physicians Center

The Paterson Physicians Center asked you to improve its data entry process. Management wants to create a lookup field to enroll new physicians. Because the data entry personnel sometimes misspell the members' specializations, you decide to create a lookup table. If all the specialty areas are entered uniformly, a query of the data will produce accurate results. Before you create the form, you decide to apply some of the data validation techniques you learned. You will also create a parameter query to assist a doctor in finding potential new volunteers for studies. Refer to Figure 5.32 as you complete this exercise.

First Name	Last Name	Phone Number	BirthDate	Cholesterol	StudyID	BirthYear
Jian	Zhou	(822) 828-8020	12/1/1971	236	S08	1971
Ashlyn	Harris	(555) 848-2655	9/8/1970	226	S01	1970
Yong	Hwang	(351) 476-8559	2/14/1971	241	S05	1971
Alondra	Ramirez	(327) 234-9297	7/13/1971	212	S02	1971
James	Allen	(958) 384-8646	9/26/1972	206	S08	1972
Ana	Cruz	(555) 906-3693	5/28/1972	203	S05	1972
Adolfo	Rivera	(424) 736-3836	5/8/1971	205	S01	1971
Ju	Huang	(236) 900-9510	10/10/1971	241	S04	1971
				0	S00	

FIGURE 5.32 High Cholesterol Query Results

a. Open *a05p2Physicians*. Save the database as **a05p2Physicians_LastFirst**.

b. Open the Physicians table in Design view.

c. Click the **FirstName field** and change the Required property to **Yes** in the Field Properties pane. Do the same for the **LastName**, **State**, and **PhoneNumber fields**.

d. Click the **State field**. Click **Default Value**, and type **NJ**.

e. Click the **Specialization field**. Select **Lookup Wizard** in the Data Type box.

f. Respond to the wizard as follows:

- Select **I want the lookup field to get the values from another table or query**. Click **Next**.
- Select **Table: Specialization** as the lookup table. Click **Next**.
- Click **Add One Field** to move Specialization to the Selected Fields box. Click **Next**.
- Click the arrow of the first sort box and select **Specialization**. Click **Next**.
- Widen the Specialization column by dragging the right border to the right. Click **Next**.
- Click **Finish** to accept the default field name.
- Click **Yes** to save the table and click **Yes** in response to the dialog boxes that display.

g. Close the table. Open the Specialization **table** in Datasheet view.

h. Click **New** in the Records group of the Home tab. Type **Pulmonary Disease** as the name of the specialization. Close the table.

i. Open the **Physicians table** in Datasheet view. Select a record, click the **Specialization field**, and then click the arrow to verify the new lookup field is working. For each physician, click the **Specialization arrow** and select the correct specialization as listed below. Once you have completed that, close the table.

First Name	Last Name	Specialization
Qiturah	Hamade	**Hematology**
Takeo	Yamada	**Obstetrics**
Kazuo	Yamaguchi	**Pulmonary Disease**

j. Open the High Cholesterol query in Design view. Click **Criteria** for the BirthDate field. Type **Between [Start Date] and [End Date]** so the user can enter a start and end date.

k. Click the **Field row** of the first blank column. Type **BirthYear: DatePart("yyyy",BirthDate)**.

l. Run the query. Type **1/1/1970** as the Start Date and **1/1/1973** as the End Date. You should see eight results, as shown in Figure 5.32. Notice the year of birth is displayed as the final column. Save and close the query.

m. Click the **High Cholesterol query** in the Navigation Pane. Click **Report** in the Reports group of the Create tab. Type **1/1/1968** as the Start Date and **1/1/1971** as the End Date.

n. Click the **Page Setup tab**. In the Page Layout group, click **Landscape**. Save the report as **High Cholesterol Report** and close the report.

o. Close the database and exit Access. Based on your instructor's directions, submit a05p2Physicians_LastFirst.

Mid-Level Exercises

1 Hotel Chain

MyLab IT Grader

You are the general manager of a large hotel chain. Your establishment provides a variety of guest services ranging from rooms and conferences to weddings. The data entry accuracy of your staff could bear some improvement, so you have decided to move to Microsoft Access and implement several data validation techniques. You also will take advantage of Access's Expression Builder to help analyze data.

a. Open *a05m1Hotel*. Save the database as **a05m1Hotel_LastFirst**.

b. Open the Members table in Design view. Add a phone number input mask to the Phone field. Save with the symbols and close the table.

c. Open the Location table in Design view. Change the Required property for the City and Address fields to **Yes**.

d. Convert the LastRenovation field to a Lookup Wizard. Look the values up in the Renovation table. Save and close the Location table.

e. Open the Orders table in Design view. Add a validation rule that requires the value of the NumInParty field to be less than or equal to 80. Type the validation text **Party sizes cannot exceed 80.** Save and close the Orders table.

f. Create a copy of the Average By Day query. Name the new query **Average By Month**.

g. Ensure the Average By Month query is displayed. Delete the ServiceDate field. Add a new column and then use the Expression Builder to create a formula that will result in the month name of the ServiceDate field. To do so, use the DatePart function to extract the month number from the ServiceDate field and use the MonthName function (nest the DatePart function inside of the MonthName function) to change the results of the DatePart function from the month number to the month name. Name the column **Month** and move the Month field to the left of the NumInParty field.

h. Run the query. Save and close the query.

i. Create a copy of the Average By Month query. Name the new query **Average By Month and Year**.

j. Ensure the Average By Month and Year query is displayed. Add a second grouping field between the Month and NumInParty fields. The field should display the four-digit year in the ServiceDate field. Run the query. Verify your results show both an April 2019 average as well as an April 2020 average. Name the new field **Year**. Sort by Year in ascending order. Save and close the query.

k. Close the database and exit Access. Based on your instructor's directions, submit a05m1Hotel_LastFirst.

2 Northwind Traders

ANALYSIS CASE

You are the office manager of the Northwind Traders specialty food wholesaler. You will modify the company's Access database to help produce more reliable information. You create a lookup field in which data cannot be modified by users. You also create queries and reports to validate data.

a. Open *a05m2Traders*. Save the database as **a05m2Traders_LastFirst**.

b. Open the Employees table in Design view. Add a phone number input mask to the HomePhone field using the Input Mask Wizard. Do not store the symbols.

c. Change the TitleOfCourtesy field to be a lookup field. Find values in the TitleOfCourtesy table. Sort by the TitleOfCourtesy field. Accept the default name. Save and close the table, ignoring the warning that data may be lost.

d. Open the TitleOfCourtesy table in Datasheet view. Add the titles **Sr.**, **Sra.**, and **Srta.** on separate lines because the company has hired a Spanish-speaking representative and may hire more. Save and close the table.

e. Open the Employees table in Datasheet view. Scroll to record 10 for Claudia Mendiola. Change her TitleOfCourtesy to **Srta.** by selecting it from the menu. Close the table.

f. Open the Customers table in Design view. Add an input mask to the CustomerID field so the user must enter five nonnumeric characters and ensure the characters are converted to uppercase. In the input mask list, click Edit List and add a new field to the list. Type **CustomerID** in the Description box, type **>LLLLL** in the Input Mask box (to represent uppercase letters), leave the Placeholder box blank, and then type **ABCDE** in the Sample Data box. Click **Close**. Click **Next**. Choose _ (the underscore symbol) from the Placeholder character list. Click **Next**. Select **Without the symbols in the mask, like this:** and click **Finish**.

g. Switch to Datasheet view. Locate the record for the company with the name Around the Horn. Change the name of the company to **London Specialties**. Attempt to change the CustomerID to **99999**. If your input mask is working correctly, you will not be able to type it.

h. Change the CustomerID for London Specialties to **LONSP**. Close the table.

i. Create a copy of the Shipments By Vendor query. Name the query **Shipments By Year and Vendor**. Open the query in Design view.

j. Add a new field before Company Name. Extract the four-digit year from the ShippedDate field using a function and ensure the Total row is set to Group By. Name the column **Year**.

k. Add a parameter to the Year column so the user can type a year at run time and see one year's results at a time. The user should be prompted with the text **Enter Year**. Save and close the query.

l. Open the Revenue query in Design view. Create a new field named **Net** that calculates the difference between Revenue and TotalCost. Round the Net field to the nearest dollar.

m. Add a new field to the Revenue query that displays **Profit** when the value of the Net field is greater than zero and **Loss** when it is less than or equal to zero. Name the field **ProfitOrLoss**. Run the query and ensure orders with negative Net fields display Loss.

n. Save and close the query.

o. Open the *a05m2Traders.docx* document from your data files. Save the document as **a05m2Traders_LastFirst**. Use the queries you created and modified to answer the questions in the Word document. Save and close the document.

p. Save and close the database. Exit Access. Based on your instructor's directions, submit the following:

a05m2Traders_LastFirst

a05m2Traders_LastFirst.docx

Running Case

New Castle County Technical Services

New Castle County Technical Services (NCCTS) provides technical services to clients in the greater New Castle County, Delaware area. Your manager, Dora Marquez, requested your assistance in creating a parameter query, a query that summarizes the calls by day of the week, and a query that rounds the hours a technician worked on a call.

a. Open the database *a05r1NCCTS* and save the database as **a05r1NCCTS_LastFirst**.

b. Open the Calls table in Design view and click the **OpenedDate field**. Change the default value to display the current date (using the Date function). Change the field so it is required. Save the table. Click **No** when prompted to test the existing data with the new rules.

c. Switch to Datasheet view. Click the **Last record button** at the bottom of the datasheet to verify the new record (marked with an *) shows your current date as the default value. Close the table.

d. Open the **Calls By Type query** in Design view. Click the **Criteria row** of the CallTypeID field.

e. Add a parameter that displays **Enter Call Type Number** to the user. Run the query. Enter **1** when prompted. Verify 29 records are displayed. Save and close the query.

f. Create a new query in Query Design. Include the Calls table. Open Builder.

g. Insert the **DatePart function**. Display the day of the week for the OpenedDate field. Delete the remaining parameters, leaving them blank.

h. Rename the field **Weekday**.

i. Add the **CallID field** to the query after the Weekday field.

j. Display the Totals row and change the **Total row** for CallID to Count. Run the query. Verify Saturday (weekday 6) has the lowest volume of calls. Save the query as **Calls By Day** and close the query.

k. Open the **Customer Billing query** in Design view. Click the field row in the first empty column (following the HoursLogged column) and launch the Expression Builder. Round the **HoursLogged field** to a precision of **0**. Rename the column **Rounded**. Run the query and verify the new column lists only whole numbers. Save and close the query.

l. Open the **Call Status query** in Design view. Click the first empty column and launch Builder. Insert the **IIf function**. The expression should check if the ClosedDate field is null, the result when true should display **Open** and the result when false should read **Closed**.

m. Rename the field **OpenOrClosed**. Run the query. Notice the cases with a ClosedDate are listed as Closed in the OpenOrClosed column, while the cases with no ClosedDate are listed as Open. You can use a filter to verify. Save and close the query

n. Close the database and exit Access. Based on your instructor's directions, submit a05r1NCCTS_LastFirst.

Disaster Recovery

FROM SCRATCH

Amy Lee, owner of Moody Training, has an issue with her database. Her computer crashed, and she did not have a backup. She wants you to help her recover her database, but all she has is a recent spreadsheet of job applicants. This will be a start in recovering from failure and helping rebuild the database. Start Access and create a new, blank desktop database named **a05d1 Applicants_LastFirst**. Import the Excel spreadsheet *a05d1Applicants.xlsx* contents into a new table, ensuring the first row contains column headings. Accept default data types. Select the SSN field as the primary key and save the table as **Applicants**. To help her recover, you will perform the following tasks:

- Apply the appropriate input mask to the SSN field.
- Require the LastName and FirstName fields.
- Provide a default value of the current date for the DateOfApplication field.
- Create a table named **DegreeTypes** containing the seven degree types found in the database (B.A., B.F.A., B.S., M.A., M.B.A., M.F.A., M.S.). This table should have one field (HighestDegreeType). Set the HighestDegreeType as the primary key.
- Change the HighestDegreeType field in the Applicants table to be a lookup field, getting values from the DegreeTypes table.
- Create a query named **Missing Degrees** to display the first name, last name, and email for all applicants with missing (null) highest degree names so they can be contacted via email for clarification. You will need to add a new, calculated field and set appropriate criteria so only the applicants with a null degree name appear. Name the calculated field MissingDegree and do not display it in the query results.

Close the database and exit Access. Based on your instructor's directions, submit a05d1Applicants_LastFirst.

Capstone Exercise

Varmel Studio Toys

You work as the database manager at Varmel Studio Toys, located in Lansing, Michigan. Varmel Studio Toys has the world's largest selection of collectible superhero posters and action figures. Your task is to add validation rules, create a lookup field that data entry associates can use to add new items to the inventory, and create a new table to classify items as a poster or action figure. You will also use queries to analyze existing data.

Database File Setup and Add New Table

You will save the database file with a new name and create a new table that will be the source for a lookup.

1. Open *a05c1Toys* and save it as **a05c1Toys_LastFirst**.
2. Use Design view to create a new table. Add **ItemTypeID** as the first field name, with data type AutoNumber; add **ItemTypeDescription** as the second field name, with data type Short Text and field size 15. Set ItemTypeID is set as the primary key. Save the table and name it **Item Types**. Add two records: **Action Figure** and **Poster**. Close the table.

Establish Data Validation

You will edit the Inventory table design to validate data. You will make two fields required and add a validation rule to a field. You will also test the validation to make sure the rules work as intended.

3. Open the Inventory table in Design view.
4. Set the InventoryQty and ItemTypeID fields to **Required**.
5. Establish a validation rule for the InventoryQty field that requires the value to be greater than or equal to zero.
6. Create validation text for the InventoryQty: **The value of this field must be 0 or greater.**
7. Save the table. Switch to Datasheet view and test the data with the new rules.
8. Change the InventoryQty in the first record to **−2** and click another record. Review the validation text that displays.
9. Press **Esc** to restore the original InventoryQty value. Close the Inventory table.

Control the Format of Data Entry

To help keep data input consistent, you will add input masks to the Phone fields in the Employees and Customer tables.

10. Open the Employees table in Design view.

11. Add a phone number input mask for the Phone field using the Input Mask Wizard.
12. Save and close the table.

Control Input with a Lookup Field

You will convert the ItemTypeID field in the Inventory table to a lookup field, using the new table you created previously as the source for the values in the lookup field.

13. Open the Inventory table in Design view.
14. Change the Data Type of the ItemTypeID field to **Lookup Wizard**. Use the Item Types table for the values in the lookup field, select both fields in the table, leave the sort blank, hide the key field from the user, and then accept the default name ItemTypeID.
15. Save the table, ignoring the warning about field size changes. Switch to Datasheet view.
16. Change the item type to **Poster** in the first record and click the second record. Change the first record back to **Action Figure**.
17. Close the table.

Customize Output Based on User Input

You will modify an existing query to add a parameter so employees doing data entry can quickly get a list of inventories below a certain level.

18. Open the Find Low Inventory query in Design view.
19. Add criteria for the InventoryQty field. The user should be prompted to Enter Threshold. The query should display all results between 1 and the parameter.
20. Run the query. Enter **2** when prompted to Enter Threshold. You should have two results.
21. Save and close the query.

Use Advanced Functions

You will modify the Rounded Item Prices query to round retail values for items in the inventory. You will also create a query to display employees who are in line for a performance review.

22. Open the Rounded Item Prices query in Design view.
23. Create a new column to round the Retail price of each item to the nearest dollar. Name the field **RoundedRetail**.
24. Create a new column to display **Premium** for all items that have a RoundedRetail value of 35 or more and **Standard** for items that are less than 35. Name the field **Class**.

25. Run the query. Ensure the correct values appear.

26. Save and close the query.

27. Open the Overdue Employee Reviews query in Design view.

28. Add a new column to determine if an employee's performance review is overdue. If the employee's DateOfLastReview is null, it should display **Overdue**. If not, it should display nothing. Name the column **ReviewStatus**.

29. Add criteria of **Overdue** to the column you just created, so only the employees who are Overdue display.

30. Run the query. Ensure only employees with null DateOfLastReview display.

31. Save and close the query.

Perform Date Arithmetic

You will modify an existing query displaying daily totals to instead display monthly totals.

32. Open the Order Totals By Month query in Design view.

33. Change the first column to group by Month rather than OrderDate. Use the DatePart function to extract the month from the date. Name the column **MonthNumber**.

34. Run the query. The first line should read 5 (as the month, representing May) with a total of $658.72.

35. Save and close the query.

36. Close the database and exit Access. Based on your instructor's directions, submit a05c1Toys_LastFirst.

Action and Specialized Queries

LEARNING OUTCOME | You will use action queries to update, add, and delete data and create queries for specialized purposes.

OBJECTIVES & SKILLS: After you read this chapter, you will be able to:

Action Queries

OBJECTIVE 1: DETERMINE WHEN TO USE AN ACTION QUERY   346
Back Up a Database when Testing an Action Query

OBJECTIVE 2: UPDATE DATA WITH AN UPDATE QUERY   348
Create a Select Query Before Running an Update Query, Convert a Select Query to an Update Query, Test an Update Query, Verify an Update Query

OBJECTIVE 3: ADD RECORDS TO A TABLE WITH AN APPEND QUERY   351
Create an Append Query, Preview and Run an Append Query

OBJECTIVE 4: CREATE A TABLE WITH A MAKE TABLE QUERY   353
Create a Make Table Query, Preview and Run a Make Table Query

OBJECTIVE 5: DELETE RECORDS WITH A DELETE QUERY   355
Create a Delete Query

HANDS-ON EXERCISE 1   357

Specialized Queries

OBJECTIVE 6: SUMMARIZE DATA WITH A CROSSTAB QUERY   364
Use the Crosstab Query Wizard, Modify a Crosstab Query

OBJECTIVE 7: FIND DUPLICATE RECORDS WITH A QUERY   369
Create a Find Duplicate Records Query Using the Wizard

OBJECTIVE 8: FIND UNMATCHED RECORDS WITH A QUERY   371
Create a Find Unmatched Query Using the Wizard

HANDS-ON EXERCISE 2   375

CASE STUDY | Virtual Registry, Inc.

Virtual Registry, Inc. is a web-based firm that sells china, crystal, and flatware to customers who use their online registry service. As the new database administrator for Virtual Registry, Inc., you will perform several important database operations. The most urgent is the need to increase retail prices for a key manufacturer, Spode China, by 5 percent because they have recently announced a price hike to their wholesale customers. You will use an update query to make this price increase; you will create other action queries that make changes to the firm's database: adding records to and deleting records from existing tables and making a new table from data in current tables.

Before you run the action queries, you decide to make a backup copy of the database. If a problem occurs with any of the queries, you will be able to recover data by reverting to the backup copy. In addition to backing up

CHAPTER 6

Advancing Beyond the Select Query

Sfio Cracho/Shutterstock

the database as a precaution, you will verify that the action queries identify the correct records before you run them, ensuring that the records will be processed as required.

You will create another special type of query known as the crosstab query; a crosstab query will summarize data in the Virtual Registry, Inc. database and help the managers evaluate the sales and other company statistics. Finally, you will create two queries that will identify related tables that contain mismatched data and tables with duplicate data.

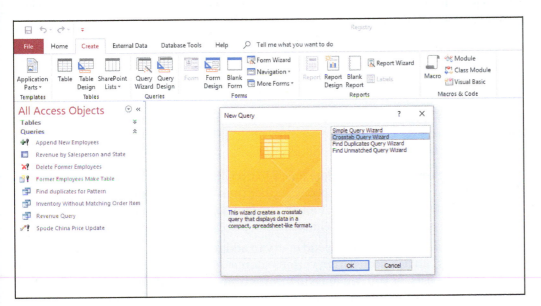

FIGURE 6.1 Virtual Registry, Inc. Queries

CASE STUDY | Virtual Registry, Inc.

Starting File	File to be Submitted
a06h1Registry	**a06h2Registry_LastFirst**

MyLab IT Grader An alternate version of this project is available as a MyLab IT Grader Assessment

Action Queries

When you create a new query, by default you are creating a select query. You begin your query design process by selecting the necessary tables and selecting the required fields to add to the query design grid. The select query is used to limit or filter output when you do not want to display all fields and records from your table(s). A select query provides a subset of the original data that answers questions that users ask about the data in their databases. A select query is also flexible; you can update the underlying table data via the query if you notice an error in your data or discover a missing field value. Another advantage of a select query is that you can create a query for one condition—for example, banquet sales in Boston hotels—and then copy the query, rename the copy, and change the criteria to extract data for a second city, for example, Miami.

Access provides four additional query types—update, append, make table, and delete—that you can use to edit records, add records, make a new table, or delete records, respectively, based on criteria that you specify. The four queries are collectively referred to as *action queries*. Because action queries make changes to data in the underlying tables that cannot be undone, Access displays a warning when you attempt to run them. Access warns you that you are about to change data in a specified number of records and enables you to cancel the proposed changes to avoid any unintended changes to the data.

In this section, you will learn about action queries and how they are used to maintain databases. Specifically, you will create the following types of action queries: update, append, make table, and delete.

Determining When to Use an Action Query

Action queries change the data in your database, so it is important to understand how each action query functions before you implement it in your database. Four main action queries can be used to maintain a database:

- **Update query.** Use an update query to update or change data automatically based on criteria that you specify. Rather than modifying data manually or by using the Find and Replace tool, the update query is automatic and accurate. You can use an update query to implement a price change to products in a table.

- **Append query.** Use an append query to add records to an existing table. Records can be selected from various sources, such as external databases and spreadsheets, or you can append records from one table to another in an existing database. Rather than entering data manually or performing multiple copy-and-paste operations to a table, the append query is an automated process. An append query can be created to add new customers from an alternate source or from one table to another existing table.

- **Make table query.** A make table query automatically creates a new table from data that already exists in a database. You can create the new table in the current or another database. For example, a make table query can make a new table from a subset of existing records, such as customers in a specific state.

- **Delete query.** A delete query automatically removes records from a table based on criteria that you specify. After a make table query is run to create records in another table, you can remove those same records from the current table. For example, after older sales records are copied into a separate table, they can be deleted from your active working table.

One situation that requires an action query is that in which an end user is required to enter the same information in many records. For example, at Virtual Registry, Inc., if your objective is to locate customer orders with missing dates, you can replace every null date with a value manually by creating a select query to list them and then typing in a correct date. Alternatively, you can convert the select query to an update query and enter a date for all missing (null) order dates automatically. In a table that contains many records, an update query is a great time saver with respect to data entry and reduces the possibility of introducing errors by entering data updates manually.

Another situation in which an Access designer would create action queries is in a college's student database. When students enroll in a school or program, they are classified as current students and are entered in an active students table. After graduation, the school moves the student records from the student table to an alumni table. An append query is a convenient way to copy records from one table to another. Use a delete query to remove the graduated students from the active students table to avoid storing the same data in two separate tables.

A make table query is useful when a subset of your original data needs to be its own separate table, for example, a table that displays customers from a specific state with their total orders summarized for a given period.

Prior to changing data in a table, you will first want to locate the records that need to be modified. For example, at Virtual Registry, Inc. you discover that one or more orders contain a missing order date—key information required to process the order. To find orders with missing order dates, you can first create a select query and use criteria to locate the records with null date values. You already learned how to create select queries in previous chapters. In this example, you would add the table that contains the order data to the query design window, add the relevant fields to the query design grid, and then add any necessary criteria. As shown in Figure 6.2, Is Null is added as the criterion of the OrderDate field. Run the query to see how many orders are missing an order date, as shown in Figure 6.3. You can create a new select query or use one that already exists in your database, if it specifies the tables and field names that you need for the action query. You can also copy and modify an existing select query as the basis to create an action query.

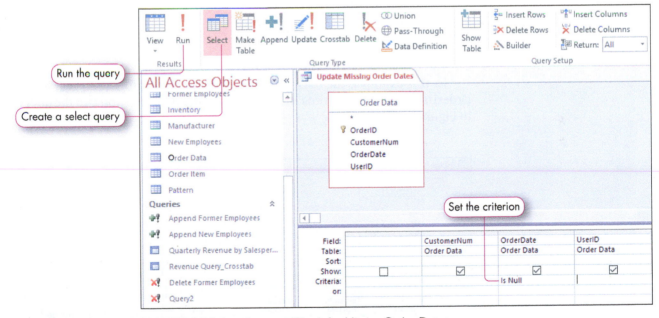

FIGURE 6.2 Select Query to Check for Missing Order Dates

FIGURE 6.3 Query Results Display Records with Missing Order Dates

STEP 1 **Back Up a Database When Testing an Action Query**

Action queries locate and change data that meet specific criteria. You cannot undo updates or deletions performed with an action query. Before running an action query, it is best to back up the entire database. This provides you with some insurance in case you need to recover from a mistake. Once you run an action query, you are committing yourself to an irreversible change.

STEP 2 # Updating Data with an Update Query

An *update query* changes the data values in one or more fields for all records that meet specific criteria. For example, the phone company announces that all of its customers in a specific area code will now have a different area code. You can construct an update query to identify records of all customers who currently have that specific area code and then change their existing area code to the new area code.

Convert a Select Query to an Update Query

Your goal is to update records with missing order dates. Once the records with missing order dates are located by a select query, you convert it to an update query and add a date to any records with a null order date so that the orders can be processed.

To create the update query, complete the following steps:

1. Create a select query or modify an existing query using the necessary fields and criteria as shown in Figures 6.2 and 6.3.
2. View the select query in Design view.
3. Click Update in the Query Type group.
4. Enter the new value into the Update To row.

In this example, the current date (using the Date() function) will be added to the OrderDate field for all records with a missing order date after you run the query, as shown in Figure 6.4.

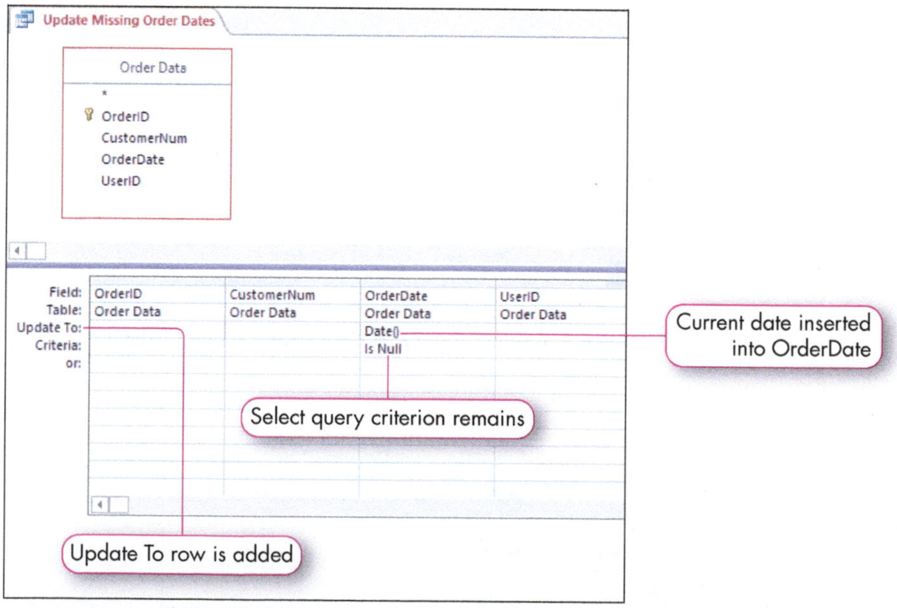

FIGURE 6.4 Update Query Created from a Select Query

You can test an update query before running it to verify that the correct number of records will be updated by switching to Datasheet view first. You can preview the records that will update before the changes are implemented. Once you run an update query, you cannot undo the modifications to your records, so it is important to preview the records that will change beforehand.

> **To test an update query before running it, complete the following steps:**
>
> 1. Click View in the Results group on the Design tab and select Datasheet view.
> 2. Examine the records in the datasheet carefully to ensure that the correct values will update when you run the query. Only the columns with a value in the Update To row display.
> 3. Click View in the Views group of the Home tab and select Design view to verify the criteria, if necessary.
> 4. Select Run in the Results group to run the query.

Datasheet view will look different than usual—most of the columns that displayed in Datasheet view of the select query are no longer shown in Datasheet view of the update query (see Figure 6.5). Only the field name and records that conform to the Update To criteria display. You can use this information to evaluate the number of records that will be updated when you run the update query. Look at the number of records shown in the Navigation bar at the bottom of the Datasheet view. If the number of records is what you expect, then it is safe to run the update query. If the number of records that display seems unreasonable, return to Design view and verify your criteria. In the example shown in Figure 6.5, the datasheet is indicating that five order dates are missing. When the update query is run, a warning message is displayed. Because you have previewed the results and are assured they are accurate, respond Yes to the warning message *Are you sure you want to update these records?*

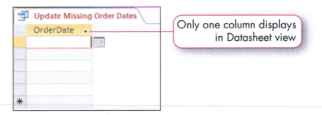

Only one column displays in Datasheet view

FIGURE 6.5 Datasheet View of an Update Query

The update query executes and adds the date to the order date field. The five records will have the current date in the order date field after you click Yes to the Access message, as shown in Figure 6.6.

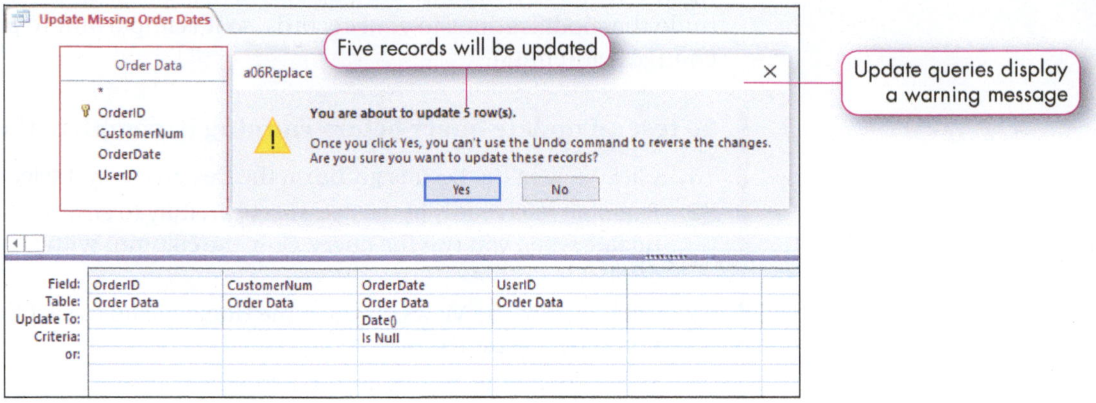

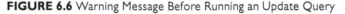

FIGURE 6.6 Warning Message Before Running an Update Query

Verify an Update Query

Running an update query from Design view does not display the results in a datasheet like a select query does; Access simply returns you to the query design window. One method of verification is to locate records that have changed in the updated table and to check that those records no longer exist in their original state. In this example, you can revert the update query back to a select query and attempt to locate records where the order dates are null. In Design view of the Update Missing Order Dates query, click Select in the Query Type group. With Is Null as the criterion in the order date field, run the select query. The query results show that there are no longer records with missing (null) order dates (see Figure 6.7).

FIGURE 6.7 Verify the Data After Running the Update Query

> **TIP: DO NOT RERUN UPDATE QUERIES**
> After you run an action query, it might appear that nothing has happened except that the warning box disappears. You might be tempted to click Run again—but you should not; you may find that data are updated again unnecessarily. For example, if you create an update query to lower the sale price of all products by 15 percent, entering [Sale Price]* .85 into the Update To row for the sale price field would work correctly. However, running the query a second time would lower the price an additional 15 percent. In this case, the total reduction would be a 27.75 percent discount (lower than the intended 15 percent). If you run an update query inadvertently, you can restore your data from the backup copy of your database.

Adding Records to a Table with an Append Query

An ***append query*** copies records from one or more tables—the source(s)—and adds them to an existing table—the destination. The appended records display in the destination table in primary key order, or they are added to the bottom of the table if no primary key exists. If any appended record violates the primary key rule or another rule created for the destination table, the record is rejected. You can use an append query to copy employee records in the Virtual Registry, Inc. database. Suppose the company hires new employees each month. The company may place new hires into a Candidates table until their background checks are complete. Once the checks are completed, the candidates can be appended to the Employees table and then deleted from the Candidates table. Append queries are frequently used in conjunction with delete queries to move records from one table to another. If you use an append query to copy a record from one table to another, the original record still exists in the source table. The same data are now stored in two different places—a practice that should be avoided in a well-designed database. After the records meeting your criteria are copied into the destination table, you can use a delete query to remove them from the source table.

Often, organizations store current records in one table and append them to a more permanent table after they are completed. The tables involved with an append query—the source and destination—usually contain the same field names. The rules for appending data from one table to another are as follows:

- Data types of the fields in both tables must match in most cases; however, some minor exceptions to this rule exist.

- All the normal rules for adding a new record to the destination table apply. For example, a record is not appended if a value is missing in the source table when the field in the destination table is a required field.

- The destination table should usually not contain an AutoNumber field. An AutoNumber in the source table should append to a Number field in the destination table.

- If a field in the source table does not exist in the destination table, Access leaves a blank in the Append To row, and you will need to manually specify the destination field name (or just delete the unneeded source field from the query design grid). If the destination table has nonrequired fields that are not in the source table, the record appends, and the missing field values are blank.

Similar to an update query, the first step in creating an append query is to create a select query or modify an existing select query. You can use one or multiple tables for the data source. Next, select the fields you want to append from the table(s) to the query design grid. Enter the criteria to filter only the records you want to append. For example, if Virtual Registry, Inc. wants to move employees who have left the company from the Employees table to the Former Employees table, you can create a select query, and add criteria to find employees where the termination date is not null. The results of this select query are shown in Datasheet view in Figure 6.8. Review the data to ensure that the records to be appended are the correct records prior to running the query.

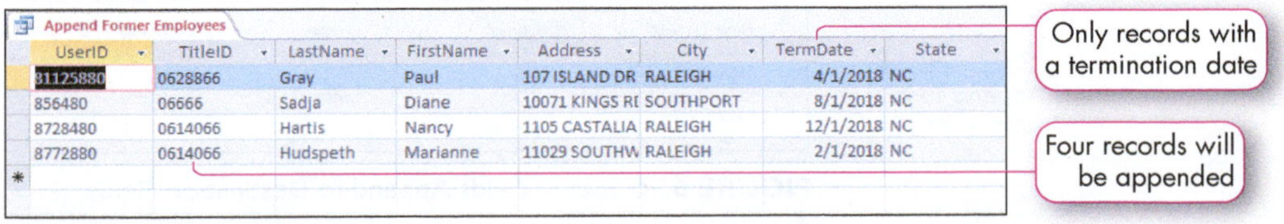

FIGURE 6.8 Verify the Data Before Running the Append Query

Create an Append Query

After you verify that the correct records are selected, switch to Design view, and then change the select query to an append query. When you convert the select query to an append query, you will be prompted to select the destination table, as shown in Figure 6.9. When you convert a select query to an append query, the Show row in the query design grid is removed and the Append To row is added in its place. If the fields in the source and destination tables are the same, Access automatically inserts the correct field names into the Append To row, as shown in Figure 6.10.

To create the append query, complete the following steps:

1. Create a select query or modify an existing query using the necessary fields and criteria.
2. View the select query in Design view.
3. Click Append in the Query Type group.
4. Click the Table Name arrow, select the destination table, and then click OK, as shown in Figure 6.9.

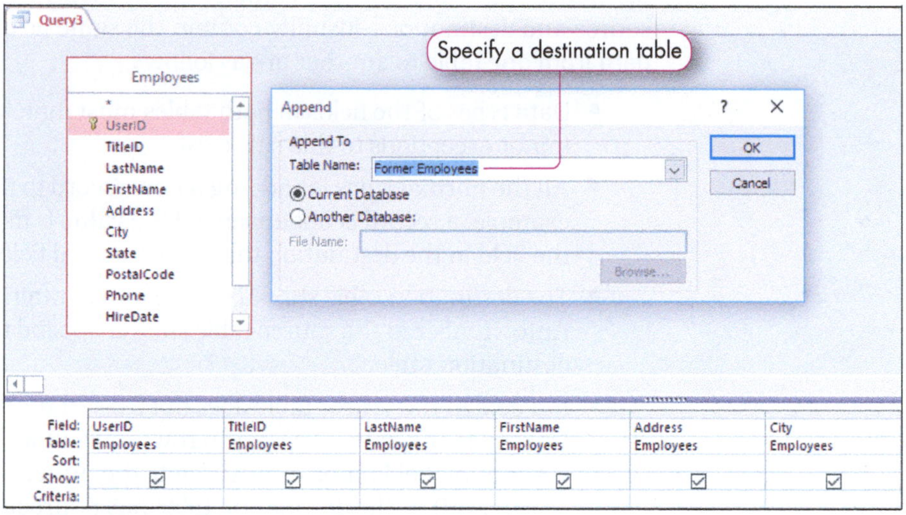

FIGURE 6.9 Create an Append Query

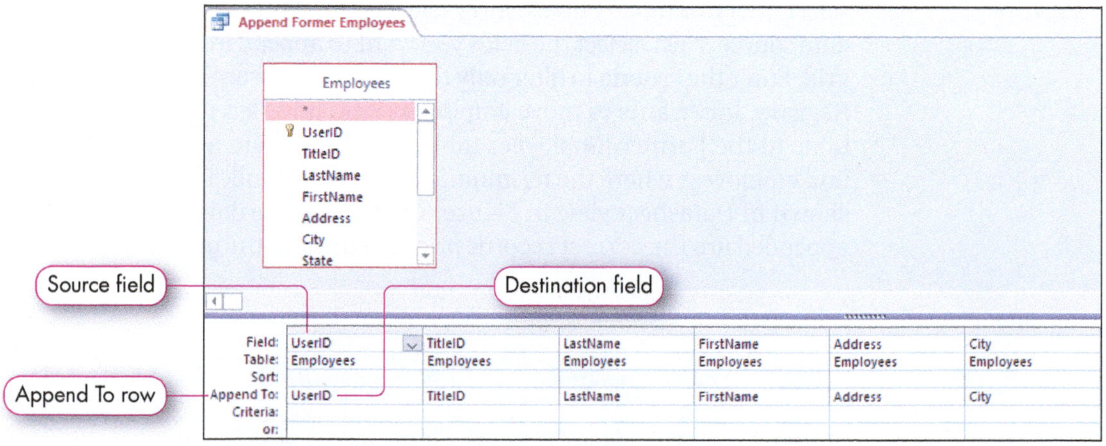

FIGURE 6.10 Source Fields Append to Destination Fields

Preview and Run an Append Query

You can preview the records to be appended before you actually run the query. Review the data to ensure that the records to be appended are the same ones you intended to select for this action. To preview the records to be appended, click View in the Results group to double-check in Datasheet view. After verifying the records, switch back to Design view.

To run an append query, complete the following steps:

1. Click Run in the Results group in Design view. You will receive a message informing you that you are about to append the number of records selected, as shown in Figure 6.11.

2. Click Yes to continue. As with all the action queries, you cannot undo the action after it is run.

3. Save and close the append query if you intend to use it again. Otherwise, close it without saving.

4. Open the destination table and verify that the appended records are in the table.

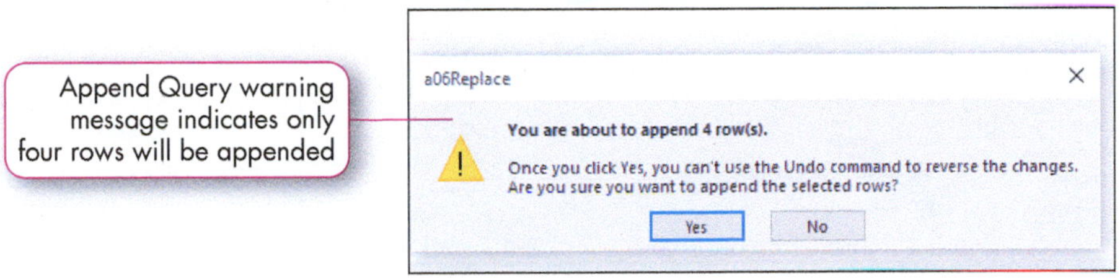

Append Query warning message indicates only four rows will be appended

FIGURE 6.11 Informational Message Displays When Append Query Runs

---

TIP: WHEN AN APPEND QUERY DOES NOT APPEND

If Access cannot append the records to the destination table, a message displays explaining the reasons why the append query failed. If the primary key value of a record you are attempting to append already exists in the destination table, you will not be able to add the record that is causing the key violation. When this failure occurs, close the message box and examine the source and destination tables. Locate the records that have duplicate primary key values and determine the best way to handle necessary changes.

STEP 5 # Creating a Table with a Make Table Query

The third type of action query is the make table query. A *make table query* selects records from one or more tables and uses them to create a new table. A make table query is useful when you want a subset of your data to be its own separate table. For example, a table that displays customers from a specific state with their total orders summarized for a given period could be used in a different context, copied into another database, or converted to another format, such as an Excel spreadsheet.

At Virtual Registry, Inc., the sales manager wants to know the total year-to-date order values for each customer. You can create a make table query that would gather this information from one or more existing tables in a new table—Customer Order Totals, for example.

Create a Make Table Query

The process of creating a make table query is very similar to other action queries in that a select query is needed as the basis for a make table query. The difference is that a make table query creates the structure of a new table and then adds the records to that table. By comparison, an append query requires a destination table to exist first; otherwise, it cannot append additional records. You can use the make table query to copy some or all records from a source table to a newly named destination table. Once the new table is created, if you run the make table query again, Access prompts you before it overwrites the table and creates it again with new data as specified by the make table query. Ensure that you determine in advance that you want to create an entirely new table with the records that meet your criteria rather than appending those records to the existing table, which would be handled with an append query. Figure 6.12 displays the design for a make table query that will copy summarized order data to a new table.

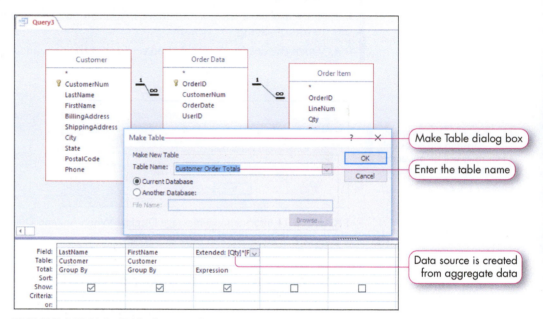

FIGURE 6.12 Make Table Query in Design View

To create a make table query, complete the following steps:

1. Create a select query; specify the tables and field names that you want to add to the new table in the query design window.
2. Specify the criteria that will result in selecting the correct records for your new table.
3. Click Make Table in the Query Type group of the Design view.
4. Specify the table name that you want to create in the Table Name box.
5. Click OK.

Preview and Run a Make Table Query

As with the other action queries, you should preview the datasheet prior to running the query to verify that the records are those that you intend to insert into a new table. Running the make table query will create a new table in your database. Recall that if you run the same make table query at a later date, the first table will be replaced with a new, up-to-date table.

To preview and run a make table query, complete the following steps:

1. Click View in the Results group to view the records in Datasheet view.
2. Verify that the previewed records are correct and click View again to return to Design view.
3. Click Run in the Results group and Access displays a message warning you that you are about to append records to a new table.
4. Click Yes, and the new table is created.
5. Open the new table and verify the records are correct.
6. Save and close the query if you intend to use it again. Otherwise, close it without saving.

> **TIP: SAVING AND REUSING ACTION QUERIES**
> At times, you will use an action query one time for a specific task, such as a price change, and then you will close the query without saving it. However, there are times when you will want to reuse queries to append and delete records at certain intervals or to make new tables as the requirements of your database change. If you think you will use an action query on a regular basis, save it with an identifiable name in your database. Remember to preview records in Datasheet view before you run action queries.

STEP 6 Deleting Records with a Delete Query

The final type of action query is the delete query. A **delete query** selects and removes records from a table. Sometimes it is necessary to identify and delete data from tables in a database. For example, if you copy the Virtual Registry, Inc. inactive customers from the Customers table to the Inactive Customers table using an append query, you will want to delete those records from the original Customers table. As with other action queries, you should always take precautions prior to running a delete query; you cannot undo the results of a delete query. If you create a backup copy of the database prior to running a delete query, you can always recover from an error.

Create a Delete Query

The delete query begins the same way as all of the other action queries, with a select query. You can create a new select query or use one that already exists in your database, if it specifies the tables and field names that you need for the delete query.

At Virtual Registry, Inc. there may be times when they want to remove orders that were incorrectly entered on a specific date. Figure 6.13 displays the criterion to delete the orders that were placed on 6/10/2019. If you fail to specify a criterion, Access will attempt to delete all of the records in the orders table. Access displays a warning message and enables you to avoid running the delete query.

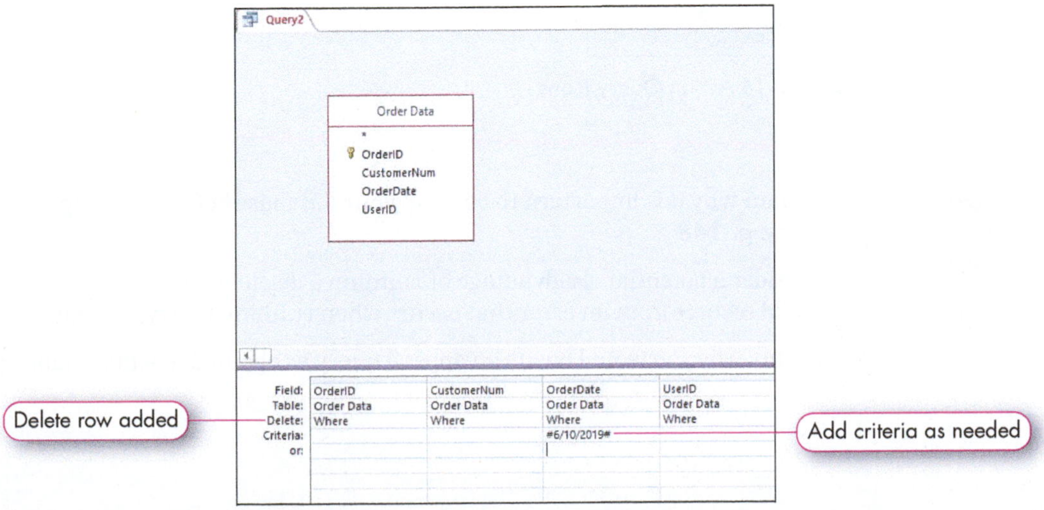

FIGURE 6.13 Delete Query in Design View

To create a delete query, complete the following steps:

1. Create or select an existing select query; specify the tables and field names that you want to remove from the table in the query design window.
2. Specify the criteria in the fields that will result in deleting the correct records from your table.
3. Click Delete in the Query Type group of Design view.

Preview and Run a Delete Query

As with the other action queries, always preview the records to be deleted in Datasheet view prior to running the delete query. At this point, no records have been deleted. You are simply specifying which records will be selected for deletion. You have changed the query type from a select to a delete query, but you will need to run the query before the actual deletions occur. After you verify the number of records in the datasheet, run the query.

To preview and run the delete query, complete the following steps:

1. Click View in the Results group to view the records in Datasheet view.
2. Verify that the previewed records are correct and click View again to return to Design view.
3. Click Run in the Results group to run the query and delete the records.
4. Click Yes when the warning message displays. Verify the results of the delete query by opening the table to confirm that the records were deleted.
5. Save and close the query if you intend to use it again. Otherwise, close it without saving.

TIP: ACTION QUERY ICONS

Access denotes the action queries differently from select queries by displaying a specific icon for each action query type in the Navigation Pane (see Figure 6.14). This may prevent users from accidentally running an action query and getting unexpected results. For example, if an update query is created to increase prices by 10 percent, running the query a second time would increase those prices again. Exercise caution when running action queries.

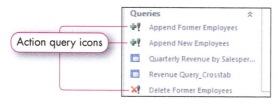

FIGURE 6.14 Action Query Icons

Quick Concepts

1. Explain why it is important to back up your database before running an action query. **p. 348**

2. Consider a potential disadvantage of running a delete query and describe how you would recover from an error that occurs when running this type of query. **p. 356**

3. Discuss why you would create an append query as opposed to a make table query. **p. 354**

Hands-On Exercises

MyLab IT HOE1 Sim Training

Watch the Video for this Hands-On Exercise!

Skills covered: Back Up a Database When Testing an Action Query • Create a Select Query Before Running an Update Query • Convert a Select Query to an Update Query • Test an Update Query • Verify an Update Query • Create an Append Query • Preview and Run an Append Query • Create a Make Table Query • Preview and Run a Make Table Query • Create a Delete Query

1 Action Queries

Several maintenance tasks are required at Virtual Registry, Inc. Before you begin to change data, you back up the database to make it easy to recover from a mistake. Each task requires an action query. After you create and run each query, you verify the changes by checking the records in the modified table.

STEP 1 BACK UP A DATABASE WHEN TESTING AN ACTION QUERY

You will create a backup copy of the Virtual Registry, Inc. database before you create any action queries. If you make a mistake along the way, revert to the original file and start again. Refer to Figure 6.15 as you complete Step 1.

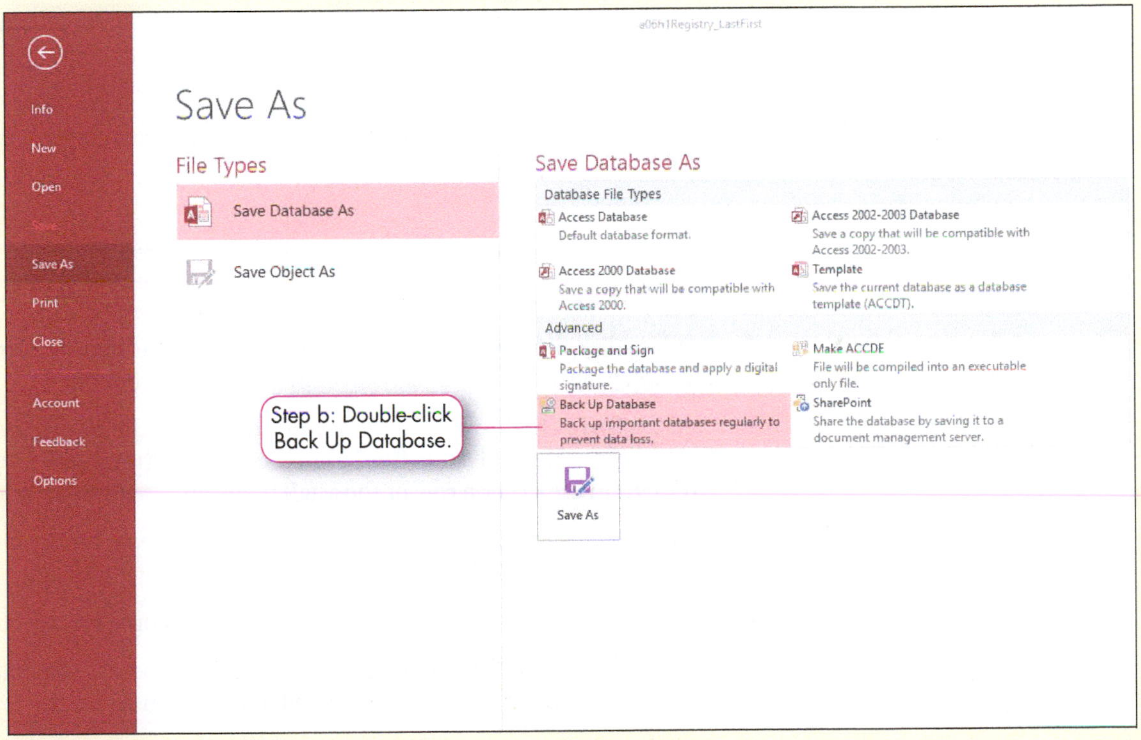

FIGURE 6.15 Create a Backup Copy of the Database

a. Open *a06h1Registry* and save it as **a06h1Registry_LastFirst**.

> **TROUBLESHOOTING:** If you make any major mistakes in this exercise, you can close the file, open *a06h1Registry* and then start this exercise over.

b. Click the **File tab**, click **Save As**, and then double-click **Back Up Database**.

Before you execute an action query, you should make a backup copy of the entire database. If data are changed or deleted inadvertently, you can use the backup copy to recover it.

c. Click **Save** to accept the default file name for the backup copy of the a06h1Registry_LastFirst_*CurrentDate* database.

A backup copy of the database now exists in the folder where you store your exercise files.

d. Verify the backup file exists in your folder where you stored it.

One of your suppliers, Spode China, has increased its prices for the upcoming year. At Virtual Registry, Inc., you decide to increase your retail prices by the same amount for items supplied by Spode China. You create an update query to increase the retail price by 5 percent for those items only. Refer to Figure 6.16 as you complete Step 2.

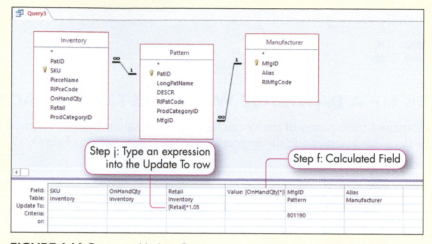

FIGURE 6.16 Create an Update Query

a. Click **Query Design** in the Queries group on the Create tab.

The Show Table dialog box opens.

b. Double-click the **Inventory**, **Pattern**, and **Manufacturer tables** to add these tables to the query design space. Close the Show Table dialog box.

c. Add the **SKU, OnHandQty**, and **Retail fields** from the Inventory table; **MfgID field** from the Pattern table; and **Alias field** from the Manufacturer table to the design grid. Type **801190** in the Criteria row of the MfgID column.

You added the criteria to select only Spode China pieces for the price updates. The MfgID for Spode China is 801190.

d. Switch to Datasheet view and verify the correct records are selected.

The results include four Spode China records. No updates are made at this time; you are simply previewing the records to be updated in the next steps.

e. Switch to Design view. Click the **MfgID column** and click **Insert Columns** in the Query Setup group.

A new blank column displays between Retail and MfgID.

f. Type **Value:[OnHandQty]*[Retail]** in the top (Field) row of the new blank column and press **Enter**. Click in the Value column and click **Property Sheet** in the Show/Hide group. Select **Currency** from the list in the Format box and close the Property Sheet.

You created a calculated field so that you can check the total value of the inventory before and after the update.

g. Switch to Datasheet view. Click **Totals** in the Records group.

h. Click in the **Total row** of the Value column, click the arrow, and then select **Sum**.

The total of the Value column is $16,637.64. The value after you update the prices by 5 percent will be $17,469.52 ($16,637.64 × 1.05).

i. Click **View** to return to Design view. Click **Update** in the Query Type group.

You changed the query type from a select to an update query. The Sort and Show rows of the select query are replaced by the Update To row in the query design grid.

j. Click the **Update To row** under the Retail field in the query design grid. Type **[Retail]*1.05** and press **Enter**. Click in the **Retail column** and click **Property Sheet** in the Show/Hide group. Select **Currency** from the list in the Format box and close the Property Sheet.

The expression will be used to update the current retail value of these products with a value that is 5 percent higher.

k. Compare your screen with Figure 6.16.

You created an update query to increase the retail price of Spode China products by 5 percent, but you want to verify the values before you run the query. Once you update the prices, you will not be able to undo the changes. Refer to Figure 6.17 as you complete Step 3.

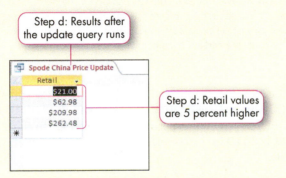

FIGURE 6.17 Query Results After Update

a. Switch to Datasheet view and examine the records before running the query.

You should see a list of retail prices ($20.00, $59.98, $199.98, $249.98) but no other columns. Access only displays the columns that have a value in the Update To row. These are the current prices that will be updated when you run the query.

b. Click **View** to return to Design view.

c. Click **Run** in the Results group to update the prices. Click **Yes** in response to the *You are about to update 4 row(s)* warning.

Although it may seem as though nothing happened, the prices have changed.

d. View the results in Datasheet view.

The four retail prices are now $21.00, $62.98, $209.98, and $262.48, as shown in Figure 6.17. These prices are 5 percent higher than the original retail prices you observed in Step a above.

e. Return to Design view. Click **Select** in the Query Type group.

f. Switch to Datasheet view.

The prices in the Retail column reflect the updated prices, and the bottom of the Retail column is now $17,469.52, which verifies that the update query worked correctly. This value is 5% more than the total of the original total observed before the update in a previous step.

g. Return to Design view.

h. Click **Update** in the Query Type group to change it back to an update query. Save the query as **Spode China Price Update**. Close the query.

The query icon in the Navigation Pane indicates the query is an update query.

CREATE AN APPEND QUERY

Virtual Registry, Inc. hired several new employees who were placed into the New Employees table for a 30-day probation period. The probation period is over, and now you want to add them to the Employees table. Refer to Figure 6.18 as you complete Step 4.

Step i: Append query will add four records

UserID	TitleID	LastName	FirstName	Address	City	State	PostalCode	Phone	HireDate
8965985	0626266	Thomasson	Aaron	5437 PRINCE CHARLES DR	GIBSONVILLE	NC	27215	3365551364	9/3/19
8965990	063566	DePaul	Mason	376C GATE DR.	BURLINGTON	NC	27217	3365555307	11/9/19
8965995	0648266	Scott	Angie	101 BOSTON ST.	SALISBURY	NC	28146-8856	7045559158	9/10/19
8966000	0626266	Student Name	Student Name	340 DEKALB PIKE	BLUEBELL	NC	27217	3368472393	9/11/19

FIGURE 6.18 Records to be Appended to the Employees Table

> **TROUBLESHOOTING:** You could make a backup copy of the database to revert back to the original data in the event of an error. You backed up the database at the beginning of this exercise, but you may want another backup in case the append query causes a problem. If you complete this step on the same day as you completed the last step, Access adds (1) to the end of the backup file name to distinguish it from the earlier file name.

a. Open the **New Employees table** in Datasheet view and add a new record. Type **8966000** in the **UserID field**; **0626266** in the **TitleID field**; your last name, first name, address, city, state, postal code, and phone number in the respective name fields; and **9/11/2019** in the **HireDate field**. Note that there are now four new employees in the table.

b. Close the New Employees table.

c. Open the **Employees table** and note the total records in the Navigation bar at the bottom of the window.

The Navigation bar displays 115 current employees.

d. Close the Employees table.

e. Click **Query Design** in the Queries group on the Create tab. Double-click the **New Employees table**. Close the Show Table dialog box.

You have begun to create a select query.

f. Click **Append** in the Query Type group.

You changed the query design to an append query to add the four newly hired employees to the Employees table. The Append dialog box opens, prompting you to supply the destination table name.

g. Click the **Table Name arrow** and select **Employees**. Verify the Current Database option is selected and click **OK**.

The Append To row displays on the query design grid, ready for you to add fields. You need all of the fields in the New Employees table added to the Employees table.

h. Double-click the **title bar** of the New Employees table in the top pane of the Design view window. Double-clicking the title bar of the field list is a shortcut to ensure that all the fields are selected. Drag the selected fields to the first field cell in the query design grid.

i. Click **View** in the Results group and preview the data you are about to append.

You should see 4 rows and 10 fields, as shown in Figure 6.18.

j. Click **View** in the Views group to return to Design view.

k. Click **Run** in the Results group to run the query. Click **Yes** in response to the *You are about to append 4 row(s)* warning.

Nothing obvious happens after the query runs; you will open the appended table to confirm that the four records were added to it.

l. Open the Employees table. Sort the table in descending order (Newest to Oldest) by the HireDate field and make sure the four newest records were added.

The Employees table should now contain a total of 119 employees. Your own name should be one of the top four records.

m. Click the **Query1 tab** and click **Save** on the Quick Access Toolbar. Save the query as **Append New Employees**. Close the open objects. Save the design of the Employees table.

The query icon in the Navigation Pane indicates the query is an append query.

CREATE A MAKE TABLE QUERY

Virtual Registry, Inc. wants you to create a Former Employees table for all employees who are no longer with the company. The records of these former employees are currently stored in the Employees table. You will copy them to a Former Employees table. Refer to Figure 6.19 as you complete Step 5.

Step j: Nine records added to the Former Employees table

UserID	TitleID	LastName	FirstName	Address	City	State	PostalCode	Phone	HireDate	TermDate	TermReason
81013580	0628866	Woodham	Trevor	10729 TRAPPERS	RALEIGH	NC	27615-5313	9198463129	6/1/2004	1/2/2009	Ret
81040480	0626266	Fangmeier	Angie	108 LOCHBERRY I	RALEIGH	NC	27615-2815	3362991750	1/31/2009	2/3/2010	Vol
81094880	0649066	Cox	Tim	1012 TRADERS TF	SAN FRANCISCO	CA	94116-3039	9195671893	1/31/2009	3/4/2010	Term
81095180	0648266	Bowman	Jeanette	1018 WENTWOR	SALISBURY	NC	28146-8856	9198512318	4/16/2006	4/5/2007	Vol
81100280	063566	Seeber	Carol	104 LITTLE RIVER	ROCKY MOUNT	NC	27801-3052	9198512318	7/21/2009	5/6/2012	Ret
81102780	0660466	Gregory	Joni	1010 MEADOWG	SCOTIA	NY	12302	9198469158	1/20/2005	6/7/2009	Vol
81105380	0626266	Mesimer	John	1102 KINDLEY CT	RALEIGH	NC	27609-2800	9197839369	12/25/2011	2/2/2012	Term
81105880	069266	Rhynes	Judy	100 CIRCLEVIEW	STEAMBOAT SPRI	CO	80488-1895	9103926711	12/12/2004	8/9/2005	Ret
81110980	0626266	Aaron	Bev	1102 BRITTLEY W	RALEIGH	NC	27609-3625	9198472095	12/12/2004	9/10/2006	Vol

FIGURE 6.19 Former Employees Table Created by Make Table Query

a. Click **Query Design** in the Queries group on the Create tab.

b. Double-click the **Employees table** to add it to the query. Close the Show Table dialog box.

Some of the employees listed in the Employees table no longer work for Virtual Registry, Inc. You need to retain this information but do not want these records included in the Employees table; the records will be stored in an archive table named Former Employees and later deleted from the current table.

c. Double-click the **title bar** of the Employees table in the top pane of the query design window to select all the fields. Drag the selected fields to the first field box in the design grid.

d. Type **Is Not Null** in the Criteria row of the TermDate field, and press **Enter**.

This criterion will select only those employees with a value in the termination date field.

e. Display the results in Datasheet view.

You should find that nine employees are no longer with the company. These are the employees you want to copy to a new table using a make table query.

f. Click **View** to switch back to Design view.

g. Click **Make Table** in the Query Type group.

The Make Table dialog box opens and prompts you for the name and storage location information for the new table. You will archive the out-of-date data, but the new table can reside in the same database.

h. Type **Former Employees** in the Table Name box. Make sure the Current Database option is selected. Click **OK**.

i. Click **Run** in the Results group to run the query. Click **Yes** in response to the *You are about to paste 9 row(s) into a new table* warning.

j. Open the **Former Employees table** to verify the nine former employees are present, as shown in Figure 6.19. Close the table.

> **TROUBLESHOOTING:** If the table did not display properly, delete the query and the newly created table. You can try this query again by beginning from Step 5a. Be sure to check that the correct criterion is entered to locate employees with termination dates.

k. Save Query1 as **Former Employees Make Table**.

The query icon in the Navigation Pane indicates the query is a make table query.

l. Close the query.

STEP 6 CREATE A DELETE QUERY

You copied the former employees from the Employees table to the Former Employees table in the Virtual Registry, Inc. database. Now you will delete the former employees from the Employees table. It is not good database design practice to have the same records stored in two different tables. Refer to Figure 6.20 as you complete Step 6.

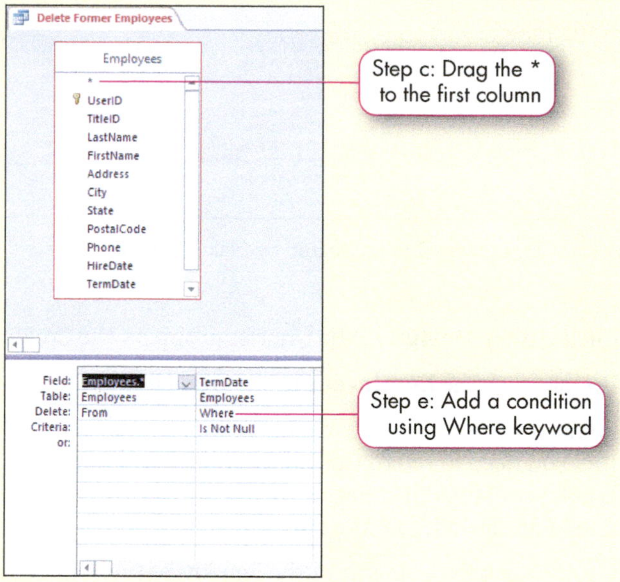

FIGURE 6.20 Delete Query to Remove Former Employees

a. Click **Query Design** in the Queries group on the Create tab.

b. Double-click the **Employees table** in the Show Table dialog box to add it to the query. Close the Show Table dialog box.

c. Drag the ***** from the Employees table field list to the first column of the query design grid.

The * field only takes up one column in the design grid. The * field represents all the fields in the Employees table. This is another shortcut for adding all of the fields to the query design grid in one step rather than one by one.

d. Drag the **TermDate field** from the Employees table to the second column of the query design grid.

When you use the * to add all the fields to the query design grid simultaneously, you need to add the TermDate field separately to use it to set the criteria for the select query. The outcome of the query is no different than adding the fields to the query design grid in the conventional way.

e. Type **Is Not Null** in the Criteria row for the TermDate field. Click **View** to switch to Datasheet view.

You created a select query to make sure you have correctly identified the nine records for deletion prior to changing it to a delete query. Nine records are displayed in Datasheet view. The TermDate field that you added separately to set the criteria is named Field0 by default in the datasheet. The query results will not be affected by the temporary name.

f. Switch to Design view. Click **Delete** in the Query Type group.

The Delete row now contains *From* in the Employees.* column and *Where* in the TermDate column. This delete query will delete all records in the Employees table that have a termination date.

g. Click **Run** in the Results group. Click **Yes** in response to the *You are about to delete 9 row(s) from the specified table* warning.

You deleted the nine former employees from the Employees table.

h. Save the query as **Delete Former Employees**. Close the query.

i. Open the Employees table and verify that the number of total employees has been reduced from 119 to 110. Close the table.

j. Keep the database open if you plan to continue with the next Hands-On Exercise. If not, close the database and exit Access.

Specialized Queries

Specialized queries help you to analyze and improve the integrity of the data in a database. Three specialized queries enable you to group and summarize data, find mismatched records, and locate duplicate records.

- A crosstab query calculates data using a sum, average, or other function, and groups values, with at least one value displayed along the left side of the datasheet, and one across the top. For example, you can sum the revenues earned by each salesperson by month, quarter, or year.

- A find unmatched query enables you to identify mismatched records. An unmatched record is a record in one table without a matching record in a related table. For example, you might want to locate customers who have no orders, or items for sale that have not been purchased.

- A find duplicates query identifies duplicate records. A duplicate record is one in which the same information is entered extraneously in a table, sometimes by data entry error, such as two customers with the same name or address. A find duplicates query will help you to locate those records so that you can make necessary corrections.

In this section, you will learn about three types of queries that are used for special conditions. You will create three specialized queries: a crosstab query to group and summarize data, a find unmatched query to find mismatched records, and a find duplicates query to locate duplicate records.

Summarizing Data with a Crosstab Query

You can group and summarize data with a crosstab query. A *crosstab query* summarizes a data source (which can be a table or a query) into a grid of rows and columns (a datasheet). A crosstab query is often created to show trends in values (e.g., sales) over time. For example, to evaluate the sales force at Virtual Registry, Inc., you can create a crosstab query to examine the revenue generated by each salesperson over a specific time period.

The grouping in a crosstab query comes from the definitions of row and column headings. A field selected as a *row heading* displays values from that field along the left side of a crosstab query datasheet. A *column heading* displays values from a selected field name along the top of a crosstab query. The summarizing or aggregating data in a crosstab query is displayed at the intersection of the rows and columns. The values that are displayed depend on which aggregate function you choose when you create the crosstab query—sum, average, and count are common examples. If you want to display the quarterly revenue for each salesperson for the current year, use the salespersons' names as the row headings, order dates as the column headings, and the total quarterly sales in dollars as the intersecting values. When you assign a date field to the column heading, Access gives you an option for summarizing by year, quarter, month, or date; in this case, you will summarize the Virtual Registry, Inc. data by quarter. You can also create additional levels of grouping by adding extra rows to the crosstab query.

STEP 1 ## Use the Crosstab Query Wizard

You will generally use the Crosstab Query Wizard to build a crosstab query, although you can build one from scratch using the query design grid. As with any query wizard, you first identify the source of the data that will be the basis of the crosstab query. Unlike other queries, you can only reference one object (table or query) as the data source in a crosstab query. Therefore, if you want to use fields stored in different tables, you must first combine the required data into a query. Once the data are combined in a single source, you can create the crosstab query.

To create a crosstab query, complete the following steps:

1. Click Query Wizard in the Queries group on the Create tab.
2. Click Crosstab Query Wizard in the New Query dialog box.
3. Click OK, as shown in Figure 6.21.
4. Identify the data source and click Next. You can display tables, queries, or both tables and queries by selecting the appropriate view option button (see Figure 6.22).
5. Identify up to three row heading fields in the next step of the wizard, as shown in Figure 6.23. To make a selection, double-click the field name, or click the field name, and click Add One Field $\boxed{>}$. Click Next. Access limits the number of row heading fields to three.
6. Select the field for the column headings, as shown in Figure 6.24. You can specify one field for column headings.
7. Click Next. If the field contains date data, this step will prompt you for the date interval (see Figure 6.25). Click Next. In this example, the sales data for each salesperson will be summarized by quarter.
8. Select the field to use in a calculation at the intersection of each row and column; then select which aggregate function to apply, such as Avg, Count, or Sum. You can have as many aggregate fields as you want, but more than two or three makes the crosstab query difficult to read. Click Next. Figure 6.26 shows the result of selecting the Revenue field and the Sum function.
9. Name the query and click an option to determine how you want to view the new query (see Figure 6.27).

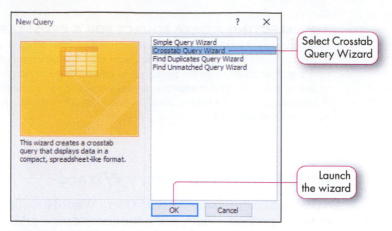

FIGURE 6.21 Open the Crosstab Query Wizard

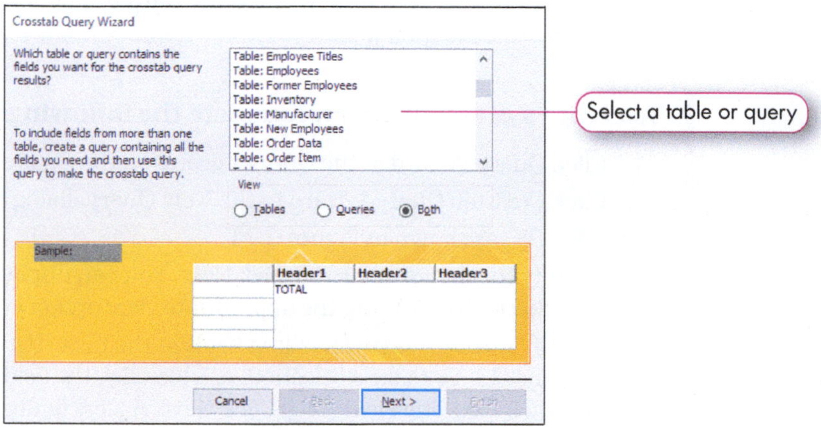

FIGURE 6.22 Select the Data Source

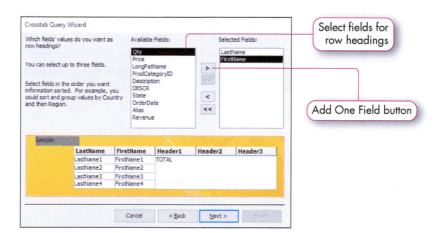

FIGURE 6.23 Select the Row Headings

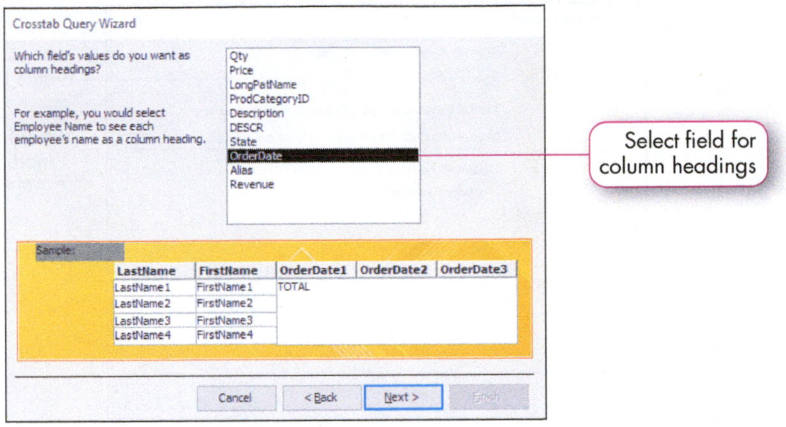

FIGURE 6.24 Select the Column Headings

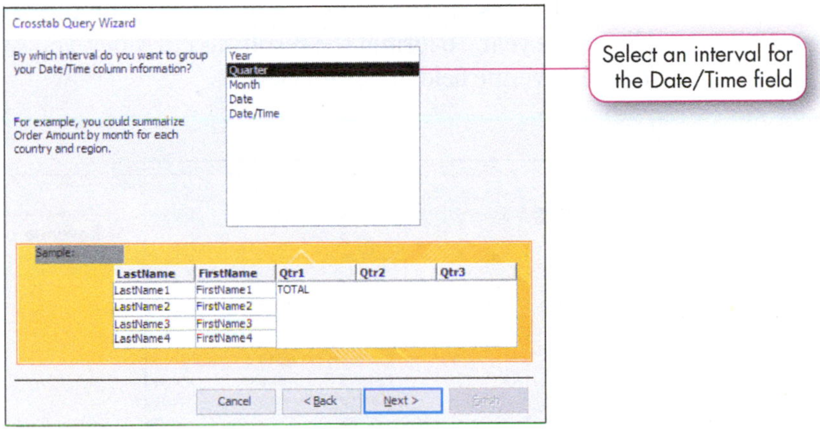

FIGURE 6.25 Specify the Date/Time Interval

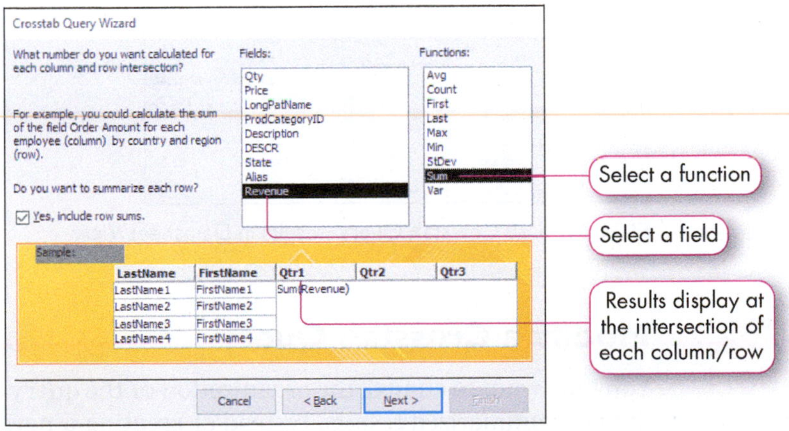

FIGURE 6.26 Select the Value to be Summarized

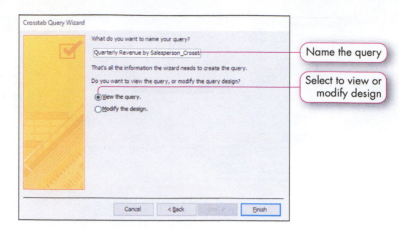

FIGURE 6.27 Name the Crosstab Query

Figure 6.28 shows the results of a crosstab query with the total quarterly sales for each salesperson. The Total of Revenue column displays totals for each salesperson for the entire year. To format the results as currency, you would modify the Format property of the Revenue field in Design view.

LastName	FirstName	Total Of Rev	Qtr 2	Qtr 3
Abdel-Hameed	W ROBERT	19.995	19.995	
Adams	Suzanne	244.9	244.9	
Adams	Teresa	56.47		56.47
Albee	Sue	148.95	90.98	57.97
Allen	Sandra	398.855	351.865	46.99
Alphin	Rich	391.68	309.72	81.96
Alphin	Rick	339.415	311.92	27.495
Austin	JOY	1397.435	1397.435	
Austin	Judy	1299.215	844.35	454.865
Bailey	Jeanette	383.05	174.925	208.125
Bantel	Dick	26.995		26.995
Behnke	Zack	787.21	384.53	402.68
Behrend	Wynn	256.32	256.32	
Bolick	Violet	908.36	547.535	360.825
Bourbeau	Trevor	0	0	
Bremer	Tim	174.75	174.75	
Chesson	Susan	2956.375	2498.02	458.355
Chut Jr.	Susan	2104.9	451.185	1653.715
Cowan	Sherol	62.735		62.735
Dietz	Sally	37.975	37.975	
Dunn	Rudy	76.48	76.48	
Eichler	Ron	1337.635	225.17	1112.465
Eklund	Ron	589.535	392.67	196.865
Faggart	Robert	43.22	43.22	
Fairbanks	Rob	26.995	26.995	
Ferguson	Richard	207.34	150.275	57.065
Frantz	Rev. Charlie	117.43	108.44	8.99

Record: 1 of 93 — No Filter — Search

Callouts: Employee last names • Revenue produced each quarter • Total revenue produced for the entire year

FIGURE 6.28 Crosstab Query Results in Datasheet View

STEP 2 Modify a Crosstab Query

You may want to change the organization of the query to display different categories of data or summarized results. Instead of creating a new crosstab query, you can switch to Design view to modify the crosstab query design by changing row and column heading fields, modifying the aggregate function, or altering the field selection for the aggregate calculation. You also can include additional row heading (grouping) fields in the crosstab query. Modify properties, fields, and field order for a crosstab as you would in any select query.

Figure 6.29 shows the Design view of a crosstab query. The crosstab query has been modified to show the product category IDs instead of the salesperson's names as the first row headings. Figure 6.30 shows the Datasheet view of the crosstab query after it has been modified, and all calculations have been formatted as currency.

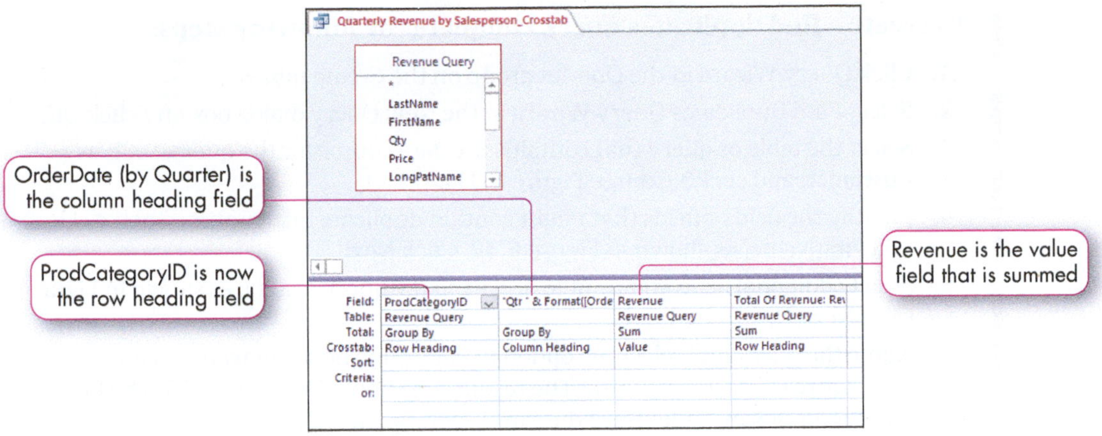

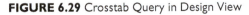

OrderDate (by Quarter) is the column heading field

ProdCategoryID is now the row heading field

Revenue is the value field that is summed

FIGURE 6.29 Crosstab Query in Design View

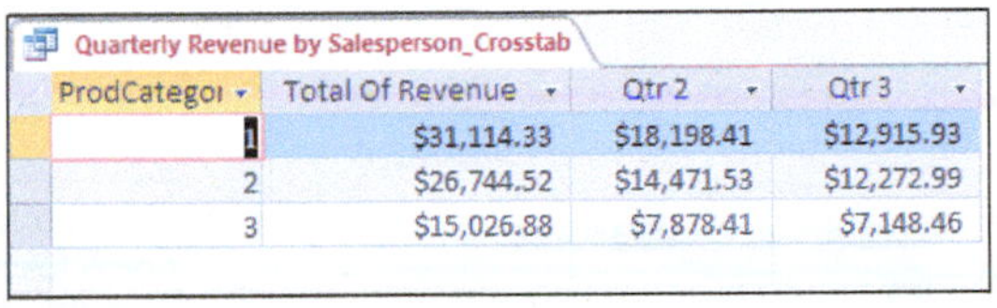

FIGURE 6.30 Modified Crosstab Query Results in Datasheet View

STEP 3 Finding Duplicate Records with a Query

If two records with the same name and address exist in a table, it may indicate a duplicate entry. You might expect a well-designed database to restrict a user from entering more than one record into a table with the same name and address; however, because most tables use unique (primary key) values to identify each record separately, as long as each ID (or primary key value) is different, a user might be able to enter one, two, three, or more records with the same name and address (for example, two or more entries for the same customer). Access can create a query to display records that are potential duplicates, such as duplicated customer or order information that can occur as the result of data entry error.

Sometimes data are entered more than one time by mistake. However, not all duplicated data in a database are the result of errors. For example, if the CustomerID field is the unique identifier (primary key) in a Customer table, no two customers can have the same ID number. However, the same CustomerID field also exists as a foreign key field in the related Orders table. Because of the one-to-many relationship between the Customer table and the Orders table, the CustomerID can repeat in the Orders table; thus one customer can place many orders. Repeating data values in a foreign key on the many side of a one-to-many relationship is typical and expected.

Additionally, some data values repeat by necessity in a table. The city field will contain many records with duplicating values. The LastName field may contain records with the same name, such as Smith, Lee, or Rodriguez. Duplicated values such as these are not errors, so they should not be removed; however, there may be occasions when you will need to locate, manage, or delete unwanted duplicates.

You can use a ***find duplicates query*** to help identify duplicate values in a table. For example, if you inherit a poorly designed table (or import a spreadsheet into your database), with duplicate values in the field you propose to use as the primary key field, you might not be able to set a primary key. After you identify the problem records, you can modify or delete them, and then set the primary key. After the primary key is assigned, you can create appropriate relationships in the database and enforce referential integrity between tables. Finding duplicate values and knowing what to do with them is one of the challenges of good database design.

To create a find duplicates query, complete the following steps:

1. Click Query Wizard in the Queries group on the Create tab.
2. Select Find Duplicates Query Wizard in the New Query dialog box and click OK.
3. Select the table or query that contains the data source for the query, such as Customer, and click Next (see Figure 6.31).
4. Identify the field or fields that might contain duplicate information, such as LastName and FirstName, as shown in Figure 6.32. Click Next.
5. Select additional fields you want to display in the query results, as shown in Figure 6.33. Click Next.
6. Name the query and select the option to determine how you want to view it initially (see Figure 6.34). Click Finish. The results are shown in Figure 6.35. The first two records for Susan Agner have the same address; therefore, one of them should probably be removed.

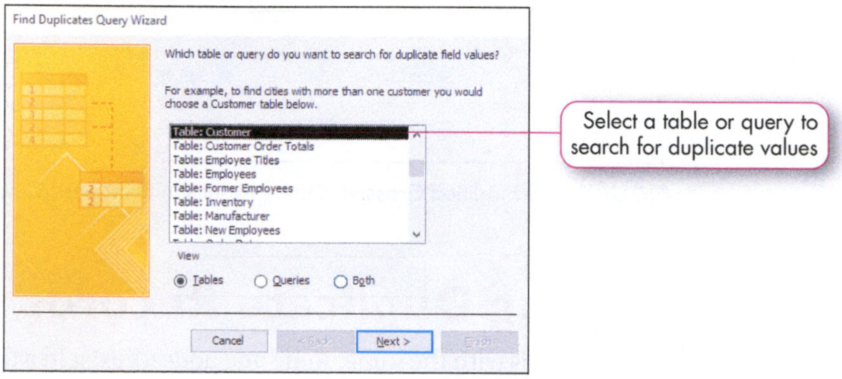

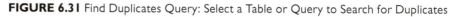

FIGURE 6.31 Find Duplicates Query: Select a Table or Query to Search for Duplicates

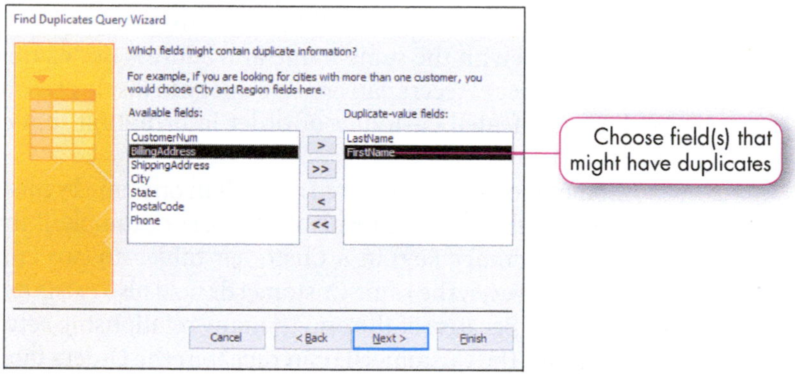

FIGURE 6.32 Find Duplicates Query: Select Fields to Display

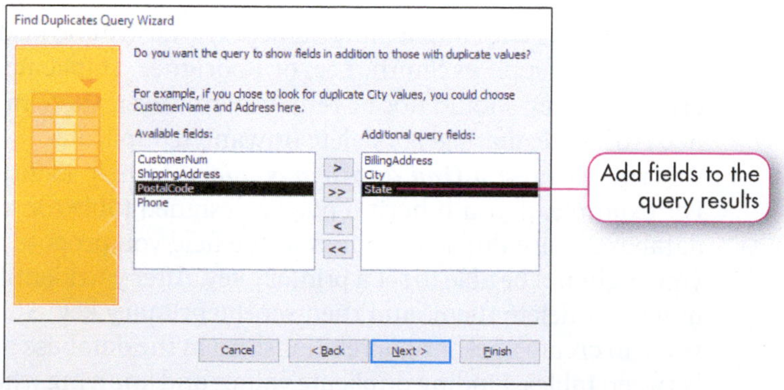

FIGURE 6.33 Find Duplicates Query: Select Additional Fields to Display

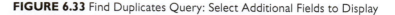

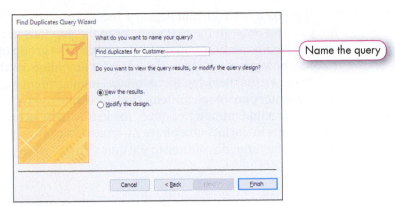

FIGURE 6.34 Name the Find Duplicates Query

LastName	FirstName	CustomerNu	BillingAddre	City	State
Agner	Susan	0517750	6503 BARWICK	CORNELIUS	NC
Agner	Susan	0518850	6503 BARWICK	CORNELIUS	NC
Beaver	Beth	0525850	1227 GENEVA A	WILMINGTON	NC
Beaver	Beth	0582050	4209 FROST CT	HARRISBURG	NC
Blade	Wanda	510986	776 LEWISVILLE	CHARLOTTE	NC
Blade	Wanda	0520250	PO BOX 391	AUSTIN	TX
Bolick	Vicki	0526750	6020-103 WINT	FAYETTEVILLE	NC
Bolick	Vicki	0522050	6026 BELLOW S	FAYETTEVILLE	NC
Bowman	Tommy	511029	5916 PRESCOTT	FAYETTEVILLE	NC
Bowman	Tommy	511012	5947 DIXON DR	FAYETTEVILLE	NC
Boyer	Tom	566655	7220 RABBIT RU	CHARLOTTE	NC
Boyer	Tom	0529850	4603 WHITBY P	GREENSBORO	NC
Carlson	Sylvia	557051	5312 NEWHALL	GRAHAM	NC
Carlson	Sylvia	557653	609 ELLYNN DR	ELON	NC
Cates	Susan	0537050	3513 LAYTON R	KINGS MOUNT	NC
Cates	Susan	520993	3507 CHIPPEND	KINGS MOUNT	NC
Cline	Sue	0567050	136 WESTVIEW	WASHINGTON	NC
Cline	Sue	0569950	5205 HUNTERS	GREENSBORO	NC
Cogan	Steve	0537950	4731 JAMESFOI	GREENSBORO	NC
Cogan	Steve	510899	929 LYNNVIEW	BURNSVILLE	MN
Coleman	Steve	510868	PO BOX 915	ALAMANCE	NC
Coleman	Steve	610991	3687 WILLOW L	KANNAPOLIS	NC
Cook	Shirley	0582150	514 BARTLING I	GREENSBORO	NC
Cook	Shirley	586754	514 I AVENUE	GREENSBORO	NC
Cormier	Sherry	610987	105 CANTERFIE	WILMINGTON	NC

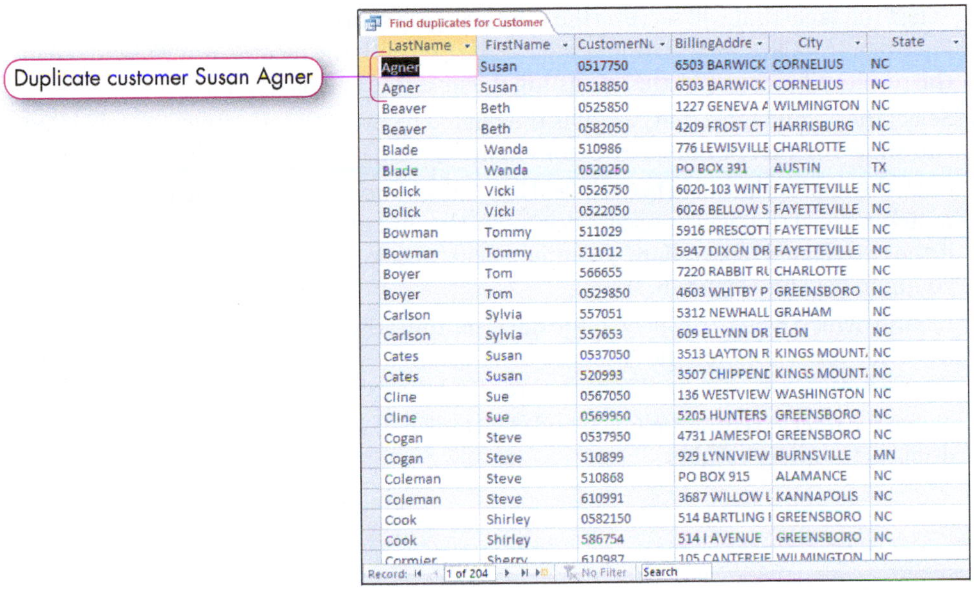

FIGURE 6.35 Duplicated Customers in the Find Duplicates Query Results

TIP: DELETING DUPLICATE RECORDS

Double-check yourself when deleting duplicate records. For example, if two customers in a table have the same exact details but unique ID (primary key) values, records (such as orders) may be stored using each of the two customer IDs. This could be the result of errant data entry. Ensure that when you delete the duplicated customer record, you do not delete associated orders in a related table. Associate the orders with the customer ID that you are keeping.

STEP 4 Finding Unmatched Records with a Query

A ***find unmatched query*** compares records in two related tables and displays the records found in one table but not the other. In a student database, an instructor might want to find students with missing assignment grades. The find unmatched query would require two tables (Students and Grades) with a common field (StudentID) where one of the tables is missing information (Grades). The find unmatched query could become the source for a Missing Assignments Report.

It is possible for Virtual Registry, Inc. to run reports that show which customers did not place an order in the past week, or in the previous month, or in the past 12 months, or ever. No matter how you decide to handle this group of customers, it could be useful to know how many who have signed up for an online catalog have never placed an order.

In the Virtual Registry, Inc. database, management may want to know which items in their inventory are obsolete: items that the company stocks that have never been sold. You can create a find unmatched query to identify these obsolete items. The results will show which items in the inventory have no related sales entries. These items can be returned to the manufacturer, discounted to sell quickly, or used as a write-off.

To create an unmatched query, complete the following steps:

1. Click Query Wizard in the Queries group on the Create tab.
2. Select the Find Unmatched Query Wizard in the New Query dialog box and click OK.
3. Select the table that will serve as the primary table source for this query (see Figure 6.36). Click Next. The first table is the one with the records you want to see in the results—for example, the one listing the inventory items that have never sold.
4. Select the second table that contains the related records—for example, the table that can show whether or not an inventory item was sold (see Figure 6.37). Click Next.
5. Click the appropriate field in each field list. Click Matching Fields to determine the matching field that will be used. Click Next. The find unmatched query only works if the two related tables share a common field. Access automatically recognizes the common field (see Figure 6.38).
6. Identify which fields to display in the query output. Use Add One Field > to move the fields you want from the Available fields box to the Selected fields list, as shown in Figure 6.39. Click Next. In this case, three fields have been selected for the query.
7. Name the query (see Figure 6.40) and click Finish to view the results. Figure 6.41 displays the query results.

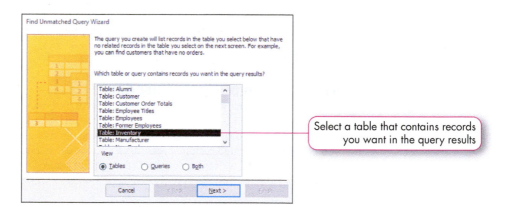

FIGURE 6.36 Find Unmatched Query: Select a Primary Table

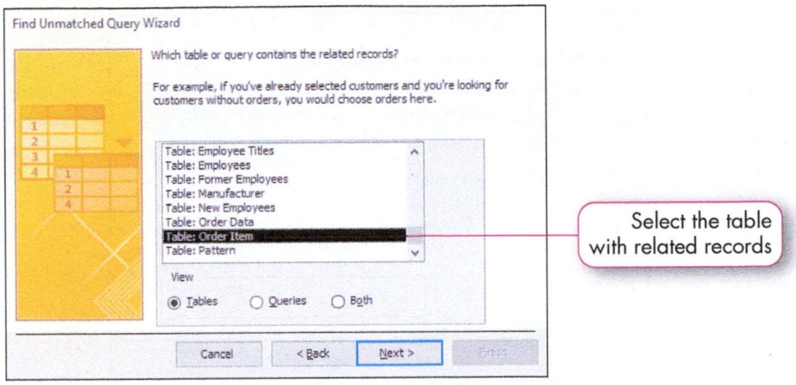

FIGURE 6.37 Find Unmatched Query: Select a Related Table

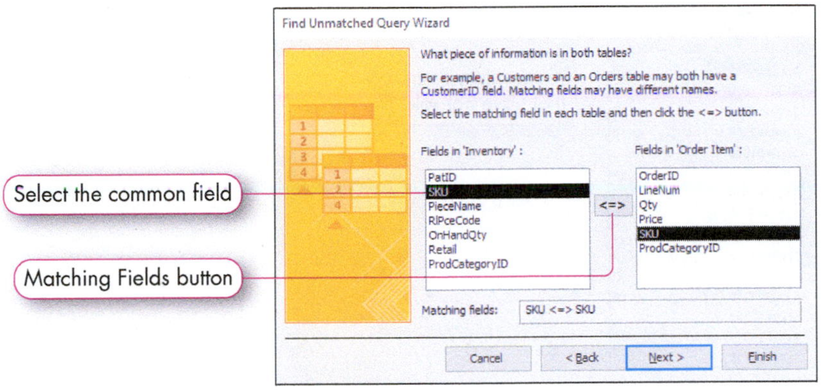

FIGURE 6.38 Find Unmatched Query: Identify the Common Field

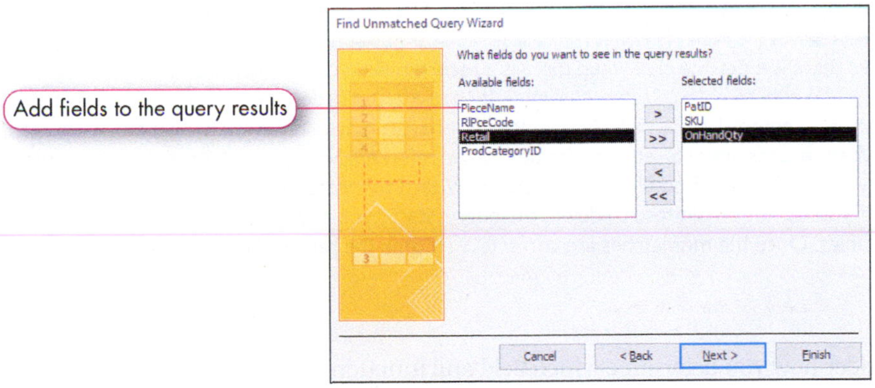

FIGURE 6.39 Find Unmatched Query: Select the Output Fields

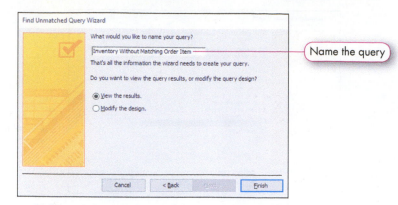

FIGURE 6.40 Find Unmatched Query: Name the Query

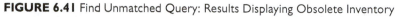

FIGURE 6.41 Find Unmatched Query: Results Displaying Obsolete Inventory

---

TIP: LOCATE UNMATCHED RECORDS TO HELP ENFORCE REFERENTIAL INTEGRITY

Sometimes there is a definite clue when there is a record mismatch between tables. For example, you may not be able to enforce referential integrity between an orders table and a customers table if a customer ID entered in the orders table does not have a match in the customers table. This can happen when records are entered in tables before the referential integrity rules are set or because of data entry errors. Run the Find Unmatched Query Wizard to locate the mismatches and correct the records. If you do not obtain results, delete the query, start over, and then try reversing the order of the two tables. Once the mismatches are corrected, enforce the referential integrity rules.

Quick Concepts

4. Consider how you determine which field and function is good to use for aggregating the data in a crosstab query. ***p. 364***

5. Discuss a situation in which it is important to delete duplicate data in a database. ***p. 374***

6. Determine a strategy for how you would correct records after running a find unmatched query. ***p. 372***

Hands-On Exercises

Skills covered: Use the Crosstab Query Wizard • Modify a Crosstab Query • Create a Find Duplicate Records Query Using the Wizard • Create a Find Unmatched Query Using the Wizard

2 Specialized Queries

Virtual Registry, Inc. management asked you to review their database and make a few improvements. You create a crosstab query that summarizes their revenue by state to help them analyze sales history. You also check tables for unmatched data and duplicate data using the built-in query tools.

STEP 1 USE THE CROSSTAB QUERY WIZARD

You want to analyze the revenue generated by each salesperson at Virtual Registry, Inc. You decide to group and analyze the results by salesperson and by state. This type of summary can be accomplished using a crosstab query. Refer to Figure 6.42 as you complete Step 1.

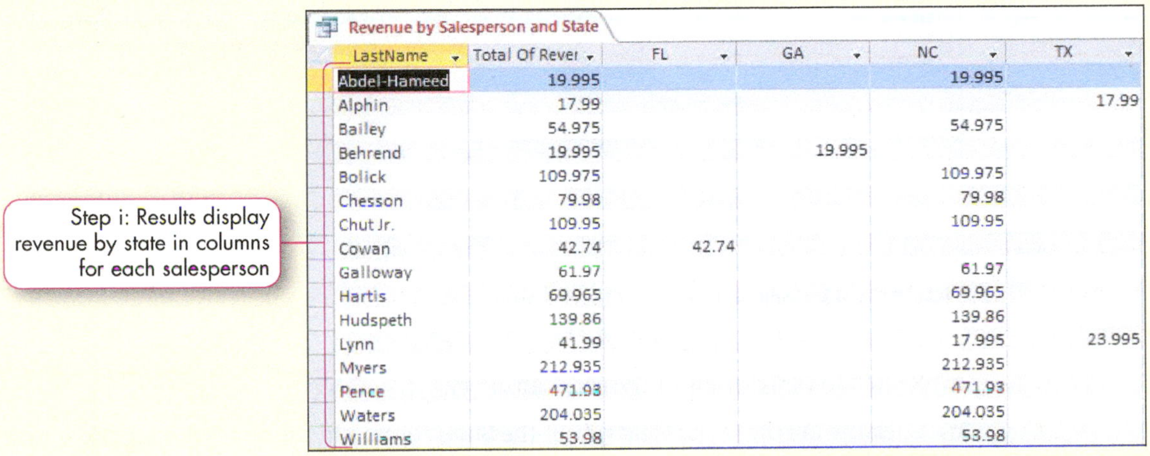

Step i: Results display revenue by state in columns for each salesperson

FIGURE 6.42 Crosstab Query Results

a. Open *a06h1Registry_LastFirst* if you closed it at the end of Hands-On Exercise 1, and save it as **a06h2Registry_LastFirst**, changing h1 to h2.

b. Click **Query Wizard** in the Queries group on the Create tab.

c. Click **Crosstab Query Wizard**. Click **OK**.

The Crosstab Query Wizard opens.

d. Click **Queries** in the View section of the Crosstab Query Wizard dialog box. Select *Query: Revenue Query* and click **Next**.

You selected the Revenue query as the data source that contains order data by salesperson and state. However, the data are not summarized the way you want it, so you will organize it using the crosstab query.

e. Double-click the **LastName field** in the Available Fields box to move it to the Selected Fields list. Click **Next**.

You selected the LastName field as the row headings. The crosstab query will summarize the data for each salesperson by last name.

f. Click the **State field** to select it as the column headings. Click **Next**.

The states will be listed across the top of the datasheet as column headings in the results.

g. Click the **Revenue field** in the list to select it as the summarizing field. Click **Sum** in the Functions list to specify which aggregate function to perform. Click **Next**.

   The crosstab query will display the sum of revenue for each salesperson by state.

h. Change the query name to **Revenue by Salesperson and State**. Ensure that the *View the query.* option is selected. Click **Finish**.

i. Examine the results.

   The datasheet displays the sum of revenue for each salesperson in each state. However, you discover that the results are not organized exactly the way that the sales reps want to view them. You will modify the crosstab query in the next step.

STEP 2 MODIFY A CROSSTAB QUERY

The sales reps at Virtual Registry, Inc. asked you to change the column heading field from State to ProdCategoryID. This will help the sales reps identify the sales for each product category. Refer to Figure 6.43 as you complete Step 2.

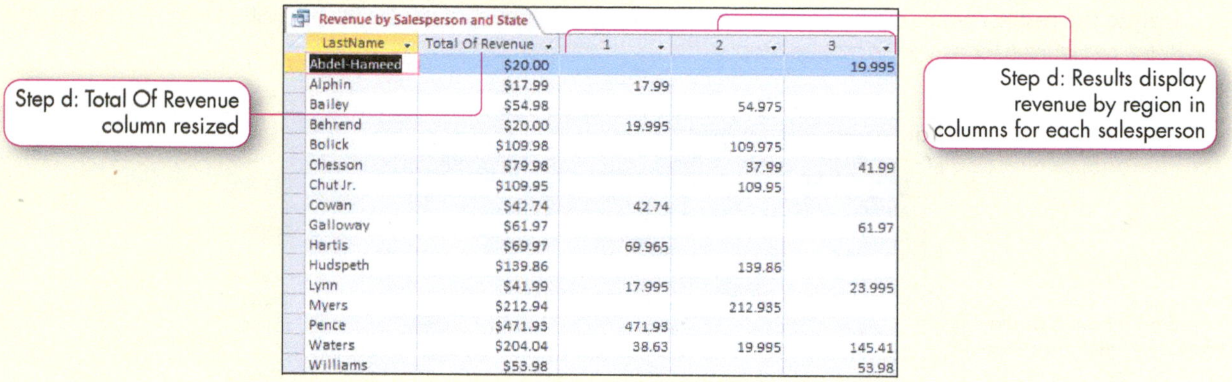

LastName	Total Of Revenue	1	2	3
Abdel-Hameed	$20.00			19.995
Alphin	$17.99	17.99		
Bailey	$54.98		54.975	
Behrend	$20.00	19.995		
Bolick	$109.98		109.975	
Chesson	$79.98		37.99	41.99
Chut Jr.	$109.95		109.95	
Cowan	$42.74	42.74		
Galloway	$61.97			61.97
Hartis	$69.97	69.965		
Hudspeth	$139.86		139.86	
Lynn	$41.99	17.995		23.995
Myers	$212.94		212.935	
Pence	$471.93	471.93		
Waters	$204.04	38.63	19.995	145.41
Williams	$53.98			53.98

FIGURE 6.43 Modified Crosstab Query Results

a. Switch to Design view of the crosstab query.

b. Click the **arrow** in the Field row of the State column in the query design grid and select **ProdCategoryID**. Click **Run** in the Results group.

   The column headings in the datasheet now display the product category IDs rather than the state names.

c. Switch to Design view, click in the **Total Of Revenue field**, open the Property Sheet, and then change the Format field property to **Currency**. Close the Property Sheet.

d. Click **Run** in the Results group to see the new results. Double-click the **right border** of the Total of Revenue column so the entire column displays.

e. Save the changes and close the query.

STEP 3 CREATE A FIND DUPLICATES QUERY USING THE WIZARD

One of the data entry employees believes that duplicate entries may exist in the Pattern table. You create a query to find duplicates in the LongPatName field in the Pattern table. If duplicates do exist, the company will need to move all existing orders to one pattern and then delete the other pattern. Refer to Figure 6.44 as you complete Step 3.

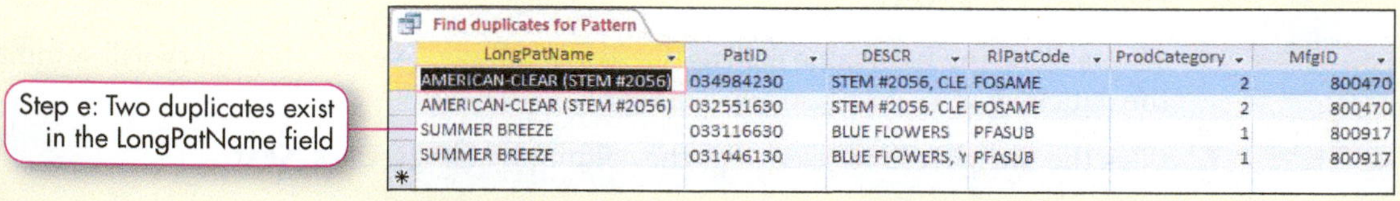

LongPatName	PatID	DESCR	RIPatCode	ProdCategory	MfgID
AMERICAN-CLEAR (STEM #2056)	034984230	STEM #2056, CLE	FOSAME	2	800470
AMERICAN-CLEAR (STEM #2056)	032551630	STEM #2056, CLE	FOSAME	2	800470
SUMMER BREEZE	033116630	BLUE FLOWERS	PFASUB	1	800917
SUMMER BREEZE	031446130	BLUE FLOWERS, Y	PFASUB	1	800917

FIGURE 6.44 Results of the Find Duplicate Records Query

a. Click **Query Wizard** in the Queries group on the Create tab and select **Find Duplicates Query Wizard**. Click **OK**.

b. Scroll down and click **Table: Pattern**. Click **Next**.

c. Double-click **LongPatName** in the Available fields list to move it to the Duplicate-value fields box. Click **Next**.

d. Click **Add All Fields** [>>] to move the rest of the fields in the table from the Available fields box to the Additional query fields box. Click **Next**.

e. Click **Finish** to accept the default name, *Find duplicates for Pattern*, and the option to view the results. Double-click the **right border** of the LongPatName column so the entire column displays.

   The datasheet displays four records showing two duplicate LongPatName fields. Although the patterns have unique ID (PatID) values in the Pattern table, two pattern names have been repeated. Going forward, the company will need to make some changes to the database to correct this issue.

f. Save the query. Close the query.

STEP 4 CREATE A FIND UNMATCHED QUERY USING THE WIZARD

The marketing manager at Virtual Registry, Inc. asked you to identify the items in inventory that have no orders associated with them. You create a find unmatched query to find the SKU numbers that have no records in the Order Data table. With this information, the marketing department will determine whether to continue to carry these items. Refer to Figure 6.45 as you complete Step 4.

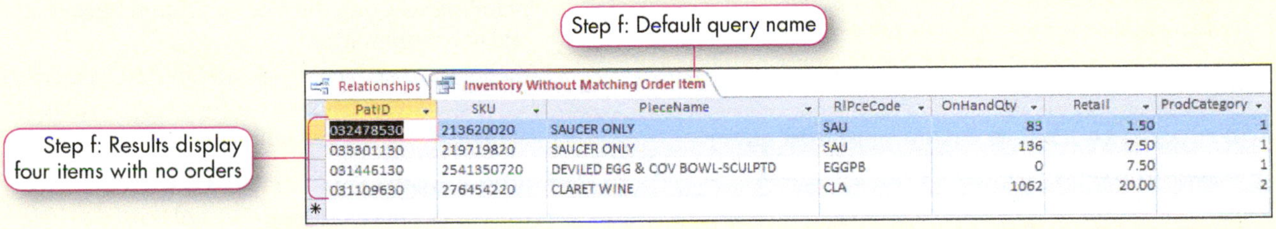

PatID	SKU	PieceName	RIPceCode	OnHandQty	Retail	ProdCategory
032478530	213620020	SAUCER ONLY	SAU	83	1.50	1
033301130	219719820	SAUCER ONLY	SAU	136	7.50	1
031446130	2541350720	DEVILED EGG & COV BOWL-SCULPTD	EGGPB	0	7.50	1
031109630	276454220	CLARET WINE	CLA	1062	20.00	2

FIGURE 6.45 Inventory Without Matching Orders

a. Click **Query Wizard** in the Queries group on the Create tab. Click **Find Unmatched Query Wizard** in the New Query dialog box and click **OK**.

   Your goal in creating a find unmatched query is to find the items for which there are no orders.

b. Select **Table: Inventory** and click **Next**.

   You selected the Inventory table as the first table, as you are trying to find items that customers have not ordered.

c. Click **Table: Order Item** and click **Next**.

   You selected the Order Item table as the second table, so you can find items that have no order data listed in this table. The Find Unmatched Query Wizard identifies SKU as the common field between the two tables that you selected.

d. Click **Next**.

e. Click **Add All Fields** [>>] to add all the fields to the query results. Click **Next**.

f. Click **Finish** to accept the default name and the option to view the results.

   Four items in the Inventory table have no orders placed for them at this time. This is a good opportunity to determine whether these items should be discontinued; alternatively, whether the inventory for these items should be reduced.

g. Save the query. Close the query.

h. Close the database and exit Access. Based on your instructor's directions, submit a06h2Registry_LastFirst.

Chapter Objectives Review

After reading this chapter, you have accomplished the following objectives:

1. Determine when to use an action query.

- Action queries edit, add, or delete data in a database. These four queries—update, append, make table, and delete—are used for updating records that meet certain criteria, for appending records to a table, for making a new table, and for deleting specific records from a table.
- Back up a database when testing an action query: Action queries change data in your database, so it is important to back up your database in case it needs to be restored.

2. Update data with an update query.

- Use a select query to define the fields and criteria to be used in your update query.
- Convert a select query to an update query: An update query changes the data values in one or more fields for all records that meet specific criteria. The update query defines precisely how field values will be updated.
- Test an update query: View the update query in Datasheet view to determine which records will be affected before you run it.
- Verify an update query: Open the table to determine the results of the updates. Verifying update query results is a good database practice.

3. Add records to a table with an append query.

- Create an append query: An append query selects records from one or more tables and adds them to another table. The append query defines precisely which fields and records will be appended.
- Preview and run an append query: If you want to verify the records to be appended, you can preview them in Datasheet view before you run the query. Open the appended table after running the append query to ensure that the records have been added appropriately.

4. Create a table with a make table query.

- Create a make table query: A make table query selects records from one or more tables and uses them to create a new table.
- Preview and run a make table query: View the make table query in Datasheet view to determine which records

will be added to the new table before you run it. Open the new table after running the make table query to ensure that the records have been added appropriately.

5. Delete records with a delete query.

- Create a delete query: A delete query selects records from a table and removes them from the table.
- Preview and run a delete query: View the delete query in Datasheet view to determine which records will be deleted from the table before you run it. Open the table after running the delete query to ensure that the records have been deleted as expected.

6. Summarize data with a crosstab query.

- A crosstab query summarizes a data source into a grid of rows and columns (a datasheet); the intersection of each row and column displays valuable aggregate (summarized) data.
- Use the Crosstab Query Wizard: The wizard guides you through the steps of creating the crosstab query, including selecting the row and column headings and the field to be summarized.
- Modify a crosstab query: In Design view, you can modify the row/column headings of the query, format fields, and summarize the data in different ways.

7. Find duplicate records with a query.

- The Find Duplicates Query Wizard is used to help identify duplicated values in a table. The wizard guides you through the steps of creating the query, including identifying which fields to search for duplicated data.

8. Find unmatched records with a query.

- The Find Unmatched Query Wizard creates a query that compares records in two related tables and returns the records found in one table but not the other. The wizard guides you through the steps of creating the query, including identifying which fields to search for unmatched data.

Key Terms Matching

Match the key terms with their definitions. Write the key term letter by the appropriate numbered definition.

a. Action query
b. Append query
c. Column heading
d. Crosstab query
e. Delete query

f. Find duplicates query
g. Find unmatched query
h. Make table query
i. Row heading
j. Update query

I. _____ A query that compares records in two related tables, and then displays the records found in one table but not the other. **p. 379**

2. _____ A query that selects records from one or more tables (the source) and adds them to an existing table (the destination). **p. 351**

3. _____ A query that selects records from one or more tables and uses them to create a new table. **p. 353**

4. _____ A query that summarizes a data source into a few key rows and columns; the intersection of each row and column displays aggregate data. **p. 364**

5. _____ A query that selects records from a table and then removes them from the table. **p. 355**

6. _____ The field name used to display values along the left side of a crosstab query. **p. 364**

7. _____ The field name used to display values at the top of a crosstab query. **p. 364**

8. _____ A query that adds, updates, or deletes data in a database. **p. 346**

9. _____ A query that helps you identify repeated values in a table. **p. 369**

10. _____ A query that changes the data values in one or more fields for all records that meet specific criteria. **p. 349**

Multiple Choice

1. Which one of the following tasks *cannot* be completed with an action query?

    (a) Deleting records from a table

    (b) Updating records in a table

    (c) Finding unmatched values between tables

    (d) Creating a new table based on a group of selected records

2. Which statement is *true* about update queries?

    (a) Only database administrators can run update queries.

    (b) If you run an update query more than once, you will receive an error message.

    (c) You can only use an update query to change text values in a table.

    (d) Update queries should be executed with caution because you cannot undo their changes.

3. Which type of query would you run to preview the results before running one of the other three?

    (a) Select query

    (b) Update query

    (c) Delete query

    (d) Append query

4. In a large products table that you have acquired from an external source, you find that there are repeating product IDs. You need to set ProductID as the primary key field in this table. What is the best way to resolve this problem?

    (a) Delete the duplicate product IDs manually.

    (b) Create a delete query to delete the repeating values.

    (c) Leave the table as is because there are already orders related to the duplicate product IDs.

    (d) Use a find duplicates query to locate duplicate product IDs. Delete the duplicates and associate all orders for that product to the remaining product ID.

5. Why is it a good idea to delete an update query after it runs?

    (a) Update queries are capable of changing values (such as prices) more than one time.

    (b) Update queries can be used to delete records from your tables.

    (c) It is not important; you can always undo the results of an update query.

    (d) An update query can erase your table and create a new one in its place.

6. When is it generally useful to run a delete query?

    (a) A delete query is usually run after an update query.

    (b) A delete query is usually run before an update query.

    (c) A delete query is usually run after an append or make table query.

    (d) A delete query should only be run when you need to delete data permanently from a database.

7. Why would you use an append query?

    (a) Because users need to be able to select records based on varied selection criteria

    (b) To determine which records may need to be deleted from the database

    (c) To summarize the data in a firm's database to help managers evaluate their financial position

    (d) To copy records from one table to another based on criteria that you specify

8. What is the purpose of a row heading in a crosstab query?

    (a) To determine which values you want to update

    (b) To display values from a selected field along the top of a crosstab query

    (c) To use a function to summarize data in the intersecting cells

    (d) To display values from a selected field along the left side of the datasheet in the results

9. What would you do if you ran an update query inadvertently?

    (a) Use the Undo command to reverse the changes to the records.

    (b) Manually modify all of the changes that were updated in the table.

    (c) Restore the original records from your backed-up copy of the database.

    (d) Run a delete query to delete the modified records.

10. What is the best way to find students who have not handed in a certain assignment?

    (a) Create a select query for assignments and compare the results with the student roster.

    (b) Create a select query for assignments and examine the results for missing dates.

    (c) Create a select query of assignments for the students in the class and examine the results for missing student names for each assignment.

    (d) Create a find unmatched query using the student and assignment tables.

Practice Exercises

1 National Bank

You are the DBA for a national bank, working on a project to restructure the loans program. The bank has decided to increase mortgage loan rates by a half percent. You will use an update query to modify the mortgage rates. In addition, you will move all mortgage loans from the original loans table to a new mortgages table and delete the mortgages from the loans table. You will also create a query to determine which customers have multiple car or personal loans with the bank. Finally, you decide to summarize the payments made so that you can analyze the payments for car and personal loans by quarter. Refer to Figures 6.46 and 6.47 as you complete this exercise.

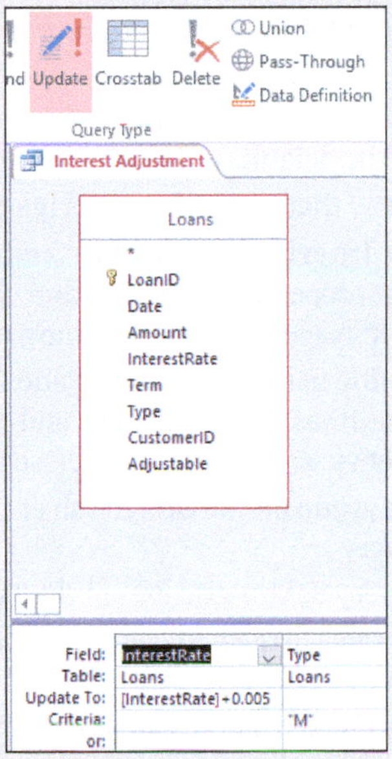

FIGURE 6.46 Update Query to Increase Mortgage Rates by 0.50 Percent

FIGURE 6.47 Delete Query to Delete Mortgages from Loans Table

a. Open *a06p1Bank* and save it as **a06p1Bank_LastFirst**. Click **Save As** on the File tab and double-click **Back Up Database**. Click **Save** to accept the default file name for the backup copy of the a06p1Bank_LastFirst_*CurrentDate* database.

b. Click **Query Design** in the Queries group on the Create tab. Double-click the **Loans table** in the Show Table dialog box to add it to the query. Close the Show Table dialog box.

c. Double-click the **LoanID**, **InterestRate**, and **Type fields**. Click **Run** in the Results group. Save the query as **Interest Adjustment**.

d. Switch to Design view. Type **"M"** in the Criteria row of the Type column.

   Entering *"M"* in the Criteria row of the Type column will filter out only those loans that are mortgages.

e. Click in the **Field row** of the fourth column and type **NewRate: [InterestRate] + 0.0050**. Press **Enter**.

   You have created a new calculated field to determine the new proposed interest rate, which will increase by 0.50 percent.

f. Ensure the calculated field column is selected and click **Property Sheet** in the Show/Hide group. Change the Format property to **Percent**. Close the Property Sheet.

g. Click **Run** in the Results group and examine the results of the NewRate calculated field.

h. Switch to Design view. Click **Update** in the Query Type group. Click in the **Update To row** of the InterestRate field and type **[InterestRate] + 0.0050**.

   The update query will change the existing interest rates to the higher interest rates that you calculated in the NewRate field. Compare your query design with Figure 6.46.

i. Click **View** in the Results group to verify that 12 records will be updated. Switch back to Design view.

j. Click **Run** in the Results group. Click **Yes** in response to the Warning message box. Save and close the query.

k. Open the Loans table and verify the Mortgage loan interest rates are 0.50 percent higher than in the original records. Close the table.

l. Click **Query Design** in the Queries group on the Create tab. Double-click the **Loans table** in the Show Table dialog box. Close the Show Table dialog box.

m. Double-click the **title bar** of the Loans table to select all the fields and drag them to the first column in the query design grid.

n. Click **Run** in the Results group to run the query.

o. Switch back to Design view. Type **"M"** in the Criteria row of the Type column. Click **Run** in the Results group.

p. Switch back to Design view. Click **Make Table** in the Query Type group and type **Mortgages** as the new table name. Accept the default setting of *Current Database* and click **OK**.

q. Switch to Datasheet view to verify that only the 12 mortgage loans will be affected.

r. Switch to Design view. Select the **InterestRate column** and click **Property Sheet** in the Show/Hide group. Change the Format property to **Percent** and close the Property Sheet. Click **Run** in the Results group. Click **Yes** in response to the Warning message box.

s. Double-click the **Mortgages table** in the Navigation Pane. Verify that the 12 mortgages are in the table. In Design view, set LoanID as the primary key and change the InterestRate field format to **Percent**. Switch to Datasheet view, save, and then close the table.

t. Click **Delete** in the Query Type group on the Design tab of the make table query to change the make table query to a delete query.

u. Delete all the columns in the query design grid except the Type column.

v. Drag the *** field** from the Loans table to the first column in the query design grid. Compare your query design with Figure 6.47.

w. Click **Run** in the Results group. Click **Yes** in response to the Warning message box.

x. Save the query as **Delete Mortgages Query**. Close the query.

y. Open the Loans table to verify that there are no mortgages (Type *M*) in the table. Close the table.

z. Click **Query Wizard** in the Queries group on the **Create tab**. Click **Find Duplicates Query Wizard** and click **OK**.

aa. Click **Table: Loans** and click **Next**. Add **CustomerID** and **Type** as the duplicate-value fields and click **Next**. Add all remaining fields as the additional query fields and click **Next**.

Note that even though there are duplicate CustomerID and Type values listed in the results, each LoanID is unique. Therefore, displaying four results in the datasheet is accurate.

ab. Accept the default name and finish the query.

ac. Close the query.

ad. Click **Query Wizard** in the Queries group on the Create tab. Click **Crosstab Query Wizard** and click **OK**.

ae. Click the **Queries option button** in the View area and click **Query: Loan Payments by Type**. Click **Next**.

af. Add the **LoanName field** for the row headings and click **Next**. Select the **PaymentDate field** for the column headings, **Quarter** as the date interval, and the **AmountReceived field** for the column and row intersection. Sum the **AmountReceived field**. Click **Next**.

ag. Accept the default name, *Loan Payments by Type_Crosstab*, and finish the query.

The crosstab query displays the amounts received for car and personal loans by quarter.

ah. Close the query.

ai. Close the database and exit Access. Based on your instructor's directions, submit a06p1Bank_LastFirst.

Car Dealership

You have been asked to modify a car dealership database that tracks employee data, sales records, and vehicle information. You will identify the sold vehicles in the database and move them to a separate table. You will also summarize data in the database and locate unmatched records. Refer to Figure 6.48 as you complete this exercise.

VehicleID	VehicleYear	VehicleMake	VehicleModel	VehicleColor	VehicleCost	VehicleSalePrice	VehicleAquisitionDate	VehicleSoldDate
1000	2015	Honda	Accord	Gray	$25,000.00	$26,999.00	5/1/2020	
1002	2015	Honda	Accord	Red	$23,500.00	$27,500.00	5/5/2020	
1003	2014	Honda	Accord EX	Black	$24,900.00	$28,950.00	3/1/2020	
1004	2013	Honda	Civic	White	$11,300.00	$14,500.00	5/11/2020	
1007	2014	BMW	325i	White	$25,000.00	$32,000.00	4/26/2020	
1008	2015	BMW	528i	Black	$28,000.00	$35,900.00	5/20/2020	
1009	2012	BMW	M3	Red	$25,900.00	$31,500.00	5/29/2020	
*	(New)							

FIGURE 6.48 Vehicles Without Matching Sales Agreements

a. Open *a06p2Car* and save it as **a06p2Car_LastFirst**.

b. Click **Query Design** in the Queries group on the Create tab. Double-click the **Vehicles table** in the Show Table dialog box to add it to the query. Close the Show Table dialog box. Create a select query based on all of the fields from the Vehicles table. Add criteria to show only vehicles where the sold date **"Is Not Null"**. Run the query.

c. Convert the select query to a make table query. Name the new table **Vehicles Sold**. Run the query and save it as **Make Table Query_Sold**. Close the query. Open the **Vehicles Sold table** to verify the results.

d. Set the VehicleSoldDate of VehicleID 1001 (*Honda Accord Dark Blue*) in the Vehicles table to **4/30/2020**. Save the record and close the table.

e. Make a copy of the **Make Table Query_Sold** in the Navigation Pane and name the copy **Append Query_Sold**. Right-click the new append query, and from the shortcut menu, select **Design View**.

f. Change the query type to **Append**. Append records to the Vehicles Sold table. Modify the criteria to select VehicleID **1001** and delete the existing criterion. Run the query. Save and close the query.

g. Open the **Vehicles Sold table** in Design view. Change the Data Type of the **VehicleID field** to **Number** and set this field as the primary key. Save and close the table.

h. Make a copy of the **Append Query_Sold** in the Navigation Pane and name the copy **Delete Query_Sold**. Right-click the new delete query, and from the shortcut menu, select **Design View**.

i. Change the query type to **Delete**. Modify the criteria to delete only vehicles where the sold date **"Is Not Null"** and delete the existing criterion. Run the query. Save and close the query. Open the **Vehicles table** and note that the sold cars are now deleted. Close the table.

j. Create a crosstab query based on the **Available Inventory query**. Use the **VehicleMake field** for the row headings, the **VehicleYear field** for the column headings, and the **VehicleSalePrice field** for the column and row intersection. Average the **VehicleSalePrice field**. Save the query as *Available Inventory_Crosstab*, the default name assigned by Access.

k. Set the caption of the Total Of VehicleSalePrice: [VehicleSalePrice] field to **Average Sale Price**. Save and close the query.

l. Click **Query Wizard** in the Queries group on the Create tab. Click **Find Unmatched Query Wizard**, and click **OK**.

m. Create an unmatched query to display vehicles that have no sales agreement and include all of the fields from the Vehicles table.

n. Select records in which the VehicleID field in the Vehicles table does not have a match in the AgreementVehicleID field in the SalesAgreement table. Accept the default query name. Finish and close the query.

o. Close the database and exit Access. Based on your instructor's directions, submit a06p2Car_LastFirst.

Mid-Level Exercises

1 Northwind Traders

Northwind Traders is a small international specialty foods distribution firm. Management has decided to close the North and South American operations and concentrate on European markets. They asked you to update certain customer records and to move all deactivated customers to another table. Once you move the records, you will delete them from the original table.

a. Open *a06m1Exporters* and save it as **a06m1Exporters_LastFirst**.

b. Create a select query based on all of the fields from the **Customers table**. Add criteria to show only customers in the **USA**. Run the query.

c. Change the query to an update query that replaces all instances of *USA* with **United States**. Run the query and save it as **Update US Customers**. Close the query.

d. Create a make table query that is based on all of the fields in the **Customers table**. Name the new table **Deactivated Customers**. Add criteria to select only **United States** customers. Run the query and save it as **Make Table Query**. Close the query.

e. Make a copy of the **Make Table Query** in the Navigation Pane and name the copy **Append Query**. Right-click the new **Append Query**, and from the shortcut menu, select **Design View**.

f. Change the query type to **Append**. Append records to the Deactivated Customers table. Change the criteria of the Country field to **Venezuela**. Run the query. Save and close the query.

g. Make a copy of the **Append Query** in the Navigation Pane and name the copy **Delete Query**. Right-click the new **Delete Query**, and from the shortcut menu, select **Design View**.

h. Change the query type to **Delete**. Change the Country criteria to **United States Or Venezuela**. Delete all the columns in the query design grid except the Country column. Run the query and click **Yes** in the message box. Save and close the query. Open the Deactivated Customers table to view the records added by the make table and append queries. Close the table.

i. Close the database and exit Access. Based on your instructor's directions, submit a06m1Exporters_LastFirst.

2 Hotel Analysis

ANALYSIS CASE

You are assisting the general manager of a large hotel chain. You will create several queries in the company's database, including calculating total revenues by quarter for each service and then by city for the Raleigh and St. Louis properties. You will also create queries to find unmatched records and to find duplicate names in the members table.

a. Open *a06m2Hotels* and save it as **a06m2Hotels_LastFirst**.

b. Create a crosstab query based on the **Revenue query**. Use the **ServiceName field** for the row headings, the **Service Date field** for the column headings grouped by **Quarter** intervals, and the **Revenue field** for the row and column intersection. Sum the Revenue field. Save the query as *Revenue_Crosstab*, the default name assigned by Access.

c. Format the Revenue and Total of Revenue crosstab values as **Currency**. Run the query. Save and close the Revenue_Crosstab query.

d. Create a copy of the Revenue_Crosstab query and save it as **Revenue_Crosstab2**.

e. Open the **Revenue_Crosstab2 query** in Design view. Modify the query so that the City field is used for the row headings. Run the query, save the query, and then close it.

f. Create a find unmatched query that displays repeat members from Raleigh who have no matching orders. Records from the **Repeat Members Club table** should display in the results. Include all fields from the table. Run the query and save it as **Raleigh Members Without Matching Orders**.

g. Create a copy of the Raleigh Members Without Matching Orders query and save it as **Charlotte Members Without Matching Orders**.

h. Modify the query so that **Charlotte** members who have no matching orders are displayed in the results. Run, save, and then close the query.

i. Create a find duplicates query that displays any repeat members who have the same address and city (add fields in that order). Display the **MemNumber**, **LastName**, and **FirstNames fields** (in that order) as additional fields in the query. Run the query and save it as **Find Duplicate Members**. Examine the results to ensure that each member is uniquely identified in the database by checking the MemNumber, LastName, and FirstName of each record.

j. Close the database and exit Access. Based on your instructor's directions, submit a06m2Hotels_LastFirst.

Running Case

New Castle County Technical Services

New Castle County Technical Services (NCCTS) provides technical support for a number of companies in the greater New Castle County, Delaware area. Now that you have created a parameter query and used functions, you are ready to create action and specialized queries. You will create action queries to move closed call records to an archive table and a crosstab query to summarize call data.

a. Open the database *a06r1NCCTS* and save it as **a06r1NCCTS_LastFirst**.

b. Create a select query based on all the fields from the Calls table. Add criteria to display only closed dates between 1/1/2020 and 1/31/2020. Run the query.

c. Convert the select query to a make table query. Name the new table **Archived Calls**. Run the query and save it as **Make Table_Archive**. Close the query. Open the **Archived Calls table** to verify the results (15 records display). Close the table.

d. Make a copy of the **Make Table_Archive query** in the Navigation Pane and name the copy **Append Table_Archive**. Right-click the new append query, and from the shortcut menu, select **Design View**.

e. Change the query type to **Append**. Append records to the Archived Calls table. Modify the existing criterion to append records with closed dates between 2/1/2020 and 2/28/2020. Run the query.

f. Save and close the query. Open the **Archived Calls table** to verify the results (39 records display). Close the table.

g. Make a copy of the **Append Table_Archive query** in the Navigation Pane and name the copy **Delete Calls Query**. Right-click the new delete query, and from the shortcut menu, select **Design View**.

h. Change the query type to **Delete**. Modify the criteria to delete records with closed dates between 1/1/2020 and 2/28/2020. Run the query. Save and close the query. Open the Calls table and note that the calls closed in January and February of 2020 are deleted. Close the table.

i. Create a crosstab query based on the Calls table. Use the **CallTypeID field** for the row headings, the **CustomerSatisfaction field** for the column headings, and the **HoursLogged field** for the row and column intersection. Average the HoursLogged field. Accept the default name and finish the query.

j. Format the [HoursLogged] and Total Of HoursLogged: [HoursLogged] fields as **Fixed** with two decimal places. Set the criteria of the CustomerSatisfaction field to **Is Not Null**. Run the query again. Widen the Total Of HoursLogged field to give it the best fit. Save and close the query.

k. Close the database and exit Access. Based on your instructor's directions, submit a06r1NCCTS_LastFirst.

Disaster Recovery

Prohibit Duplicate Append

Northwind Traders is an international specialty foods distributor that relies on an Access database to track customers and process its orders. A make table query moved all the owners from the Customers table to a new Customer Owners table. A colleague converted a copy of the make table query to an append query and ran it again (expecting it would not add another set of records). Unfortunately, it did add the same set of owners to the table, and now every owner is duplicated. Consider the best way to fix this problem. You need the append query so that you can run it when new owners are added to the database. However, running the append query should not add duplicate records to the Customer Owners table. Open *a06d1Food* and save it as **a06d1Food_LastFirst**. Correct the problem in the table that is allowing this type of error. Run the append query to ensure that duplicate records are no longer getting added to Customer Owners. Ensure that no duplicate records remain in the Customer Owners table. Close the database and exit Access. Based on your instructor's directions, submit a06d1Food_LastFirst.

Northwind Traders Sales Analysis

Northwind Traders is a small international gourmet foods wholesaler. You will update the company's database by increasing the price of all of the meat and poultry products. You will make a table for archiving older order information. You will also summarize quantities sold by category and identify customers who have no orders.

Database File Setup

You will prepare the database for changes by opening the original database file and saving a copy to use to complete this capstone exercise.

1. Open *a06c1Prices* and save it as **a06c1Prices_LastFirst**.

Identify and Update Selected Category Prices

Using a select query, you will identify all of the products with a category of meat or poultry, and then use an update query to increase the prices of the products.

2. Create a select query that includes the CategoryID and CategoryName from the Categories table and the UnitPrice and ProductName fields from the Products table. Run the query and note the CategoryID for Meat/Poultry.

3. Add the appropriate CategoryID criterion to limit the query output to only Meat/Poultry.

4. Convert the query to an update query. Update the UnitPrice for Meat/Poultry only by increasing it by 6 percent. View the query in Datasheet view prior to running it to make sure you are updating the correct (four) records. Return to Design view and run the query.

5. Save the query as **Update Meat/Poultry Prices**. Close the query.

Create a New Table and Delete Archived Records

You will identify orders shipped during the first half of the year and create a new table in which to store them. You will then delete the orders from the current orders table.

6. Create a select query that identifies all of the orders shipped **Between 1/1/2020 and 3/31/2020**. Include all fields from the Orders table.

7. Convert the select query to a make table query.

8. Name the new table **Orders Archive**. Run the query.

9. Save the query as **Make Orders Archive Table**. Close the query.

10. Make a copy of the **Make Orders Archive Table query** and save it as **Append Orders Archive Table**. Open the **Append Orders Archive Table query** in Design view. Convert the make table query to an append query. The query will append to the Orders Archive table.

11. Modify the criteria to append orders shipped **Between 4/1/2020 and 6/30/2020**. Run the query, save it, and then close it.

12. Open the **Orders Archive table** in Design view and set **OrderID** as the primary key field. Switch to Datasheet view, save, and then close the table.

13. Make a copy of the **Append Orders Archive Table query** and save it as **Delete Archived Orders**. Open the **Delete Archived Orders query** in Design view. Convert the append query to a delete query.

14. Modify the criteria to delete all archived orders (six records). Run, save, and then close the query.

Calculate Summary Statistics

You want to determine how sales are performing with respect to each product category. You will create a crosstab query that displays quantities by category and salesperson.

15. Open the Profit query in Design view and add the **LastName field** from the Employees table to the last column of the query design grid. Run, save, and then close the query.

16. Use the query wizard to create a crosstab query based on the Profit query that sums the total **Quantity** by **Ship Country** (row heading) and **Category-Name** (column heading). Accept the query name as *Profit_Crosstab*.

17. Modify the query to display **CategoryName** as a row heading field and **LastName** as a column heading field. Run, save, and then close the query.

Create a Find Unmatched Query

You will create a query to determine which customers have no matching orders. The customers will be contacted to determine if they would like to place an order.

18. Create a query to find out if any of the customers have no current order details. Add all of the fields from the Customers table to the results.

19. Save the query as **Customers With No Orders**. Run the query and close it.

20. Close the database and exit Access. Based on your instructor's directions, submit a06c1Prices_LastFirst.

Advanced Forms and Reports

LEARNING OUTCOME | You will use advanced form and report features to create customized solutions.

OBJECTIVES & SKILLS: After you read this chapter, you will be able to:

Advanced Forms

OBJECTIVE 1: RESTRICT EDITS IN A FORM 390
Convert a Form to Read-Only

OBJECTIVE 2: UNDERSTAND COMBO BOXES 391
Convert a Text Box to a Combo Box, Customize a
Combo Box

OBJECTIVE 3: SET THE TAB ORDER 394
Set Tab Order Using Auto Order, Set Tab Order
Manually, Remove a Tab Stop

OBJECTIVE 4: UNDERSTAND SUBFORMS 396
Create a Subform

HANDS-ON EXERCISE 1 399

Controls and Sections

OBJECTIVE 5: UNDERSTAND CONTROLS 405
Add a Calculated Control, Add a Label Control,
Add a Chart Control, Add Emphasis to a Form or
Report Using Line and Rectangle Controls, Add
Text and Images to a Form or Report, Add a Page
Break Control

OBJECTIVE 6: UNDERSTAND SECTIONS 412
Show, Hide, and Resize Sections; Add a
Group Header/Footer to Reports; Add Totals
to a Footer

HANDS-ON EXERCISE 2 420

CASE STUDY | Yellowstone County Technical Services

Yellowstone County Technical Services is a small company that provides technical support for several businesses in Yellowstone County, Montana. You have been tasked with updating the customer tracking database to expand the input and output capabilities of the system. In your experience with the company, you have seen some of the common errors users make when performing data entry and have also seen what is effective and what is not effective in forms. In addition, you have seen which reports users utilize and have heard suggestions about changes they would like made.

You realize everyone benefits when you are proactive and help users prevent errors. In addition, finding ways to extract more information from the same amount of data is important as well. Being able to interpret and present the information in a database so management can use it can be what makes or breaks your career as a database administrator.

In your role as supervisor, you also want to lead your technicians by example, and implementing improvements in your database is a good start. After implementing the changes, you can use the database as a case study to train your technicians in effective database design.

CHAPTER 7

Moving Beyond the Basics

Sfio Cracho/Shutterstock

FIGURE 7.1 Yellowstone County Technical Services

CASE STUDY | Yellowstone County Technical Services

Starting Files	File to be Submitted
a07h1Yellowstone a07h2Logo. jpg	a07h2Yellowstone_LastFirst

MyLab IT Grader An alternate version of this project is available as a MyLab IT Grader Assessment

Advanced Forms

For basic database solutions, a simple form created with the Form tool suffices. However, at times, you might want to go beyond the basics. There are several changes you can make to customize a form. Part of your goal when administering a database is to make the database easy to use, and well-designed forms provide that functionality. For example, you can create a form that enables users to look up information but not change it, so a user cannot accidentally change data. You can convert a field from a text box to a menu. You can choose to adjust the sequence in which the fields are ordered as you press Tab. Access enables you to create and manipulate subforms, which show related records from other tables.

In this section, you will restrict edits in forms to ensure data cannot be changed. You will create combo boxes and set the tab order on a form. You will create subforms to display additional records.

STEP 1 Restricting Edits in a Form

One method of protecting data in a database is to restrict casual users from editing the data. Those using a database to retrieve information, such as a person's address or phone number, or to review the details of an order are examples of casual users. However, the people who want to look up information most likely are not the people you want adding, editing, or deleting records. When many users make changes to the data, the data can become unreliable and difficult to maintain.

Most databases have forms to easily and efficiently enter data into the database. They can be used to add new products, customers, and so on. Moreover, forms can also be used to look up information to make an edit or simply to confirm the information is correct. For example, a customer service employee speaking with a customer may need to ensure that the company has the correct contact information for the customer. Sometimes, it is best to allow an employee to look up the customer information without giving the employee permission to make changes to the data. You can limit the employee to only looking up an address or phone number. When users want to look up information without making changes, it is best to restrict editing on a form. A form that enables users to view but not change data is a ***read-only form***.

Before you change a form to read-only, you should consider whether this form will be used to edit data. In addition, do you want users to add new records? Also, should they be able to delete records? All these properties can be adjusted once you have created a form or converted it to read-only.

> **To convert an existing form to a read-only form, complete the following steps:**
>
> 1. Open the form in Layout view.
> 2. Click Property Sheet in the Tools group on the Design tab.
> 3. Select Form in the Selection type box at the top of the Property Sheet, as shown in Figure 7.2.
> 4. Click Allow Edits on the Data tab and change the Allow Edits property to No.
> 5. Change Allow Additions and Allow Deletions to No, if you want to restrict these types of changes.
> 6. Switch to Form view and test the form by attempting to change data.
> 7. Save the form.

If you change the Allow Deletions property to No, you can see the results of this change when you attempt to click Delete in the Records group on the Home tab—Delete is no longer available. Likewise, if you set the Allow Additions property to No, you cannot click New in the Records group on the Home tab. There are no obvious cues that a form cannot be used to edit data. It is suggested that you change the form title and name to indicate it is read-only. Otherwise, you can frustrate users who might open the form and wonder why they cannot change data.

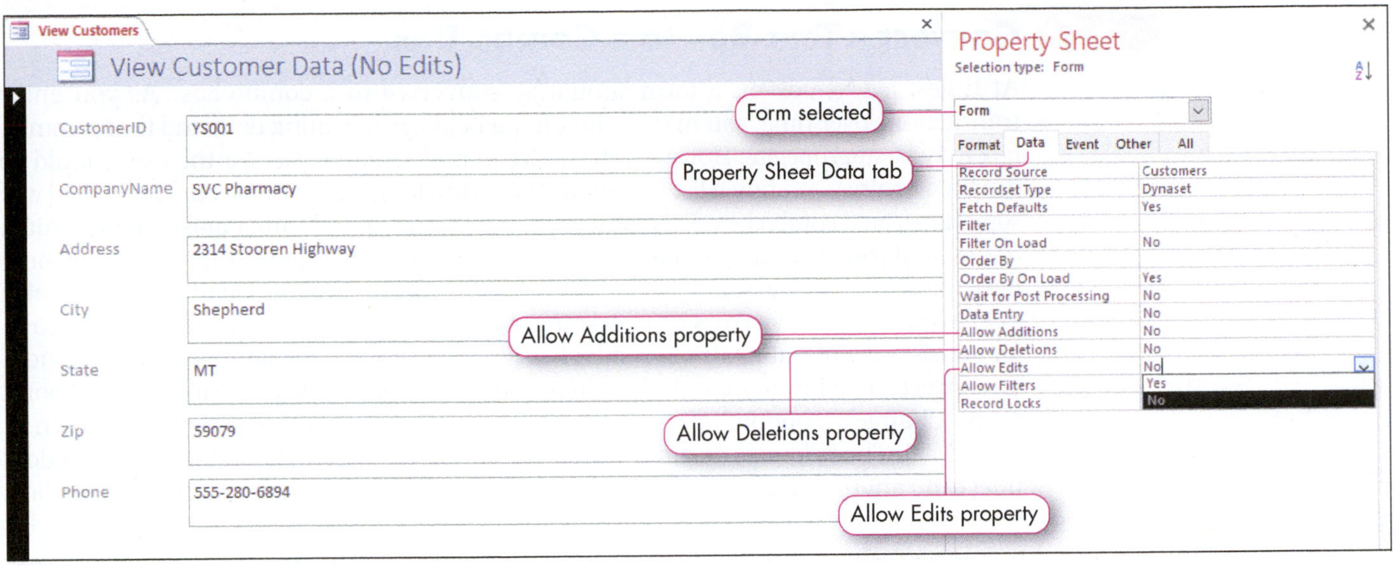

FIGURE 7.2 Changing a Form to Read-Only

Understanding Combo Boxes

If you create a form based on a table with a lookup field, the lookup field becomes a Combo Box control on the new form. A **Combo Box control**, as shown in Figure 7.3, displays a menu of options from which the user can select a single value. Combo boxes make data entry faster and easier. Text boxes that exist in a form can be converted to combo boxes to facilitate this ease of use.

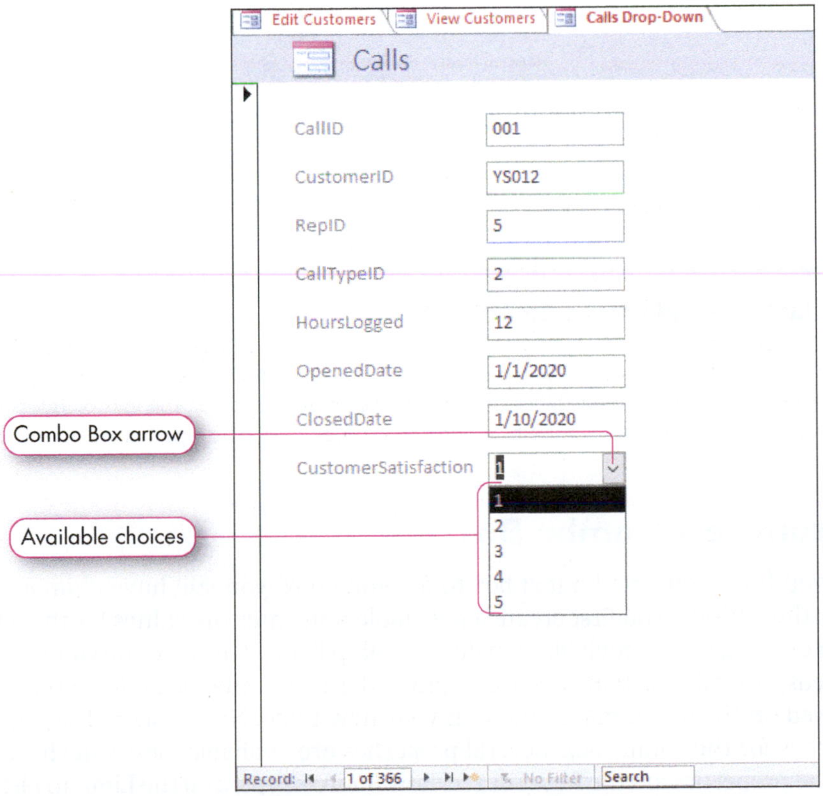

FIGURE 7.3 Combo Box in Form View

Convert a Text Box to a Combo Box

At times, a text box on a form should be converted to a combo box. As you enter transactions over time, you may realize that a field has repeating data and that a combo box may be appropriate. However, the desire to make input easier for the user should be weighed against creating a list of options that is too long. For example, the State field will sometimes be a combo box. Fifty states and the District of Columbia make up the United States, and you may prefer not to have a menu containing 51 items. However, if you only need to reference a few states, a combo box would be a good option. Combo boxes can also help avoid data entry errors by restricting the entries to those in the list, in which case, for consistency of data entry, a combo box listing all 51 states might be a better option. To convert a text box to a combo box, in Layout view, right-click on the text box and point to the Change To option, and select Combo Box from the shortcut menu, as shown in Figure 7.4. The field now displays with an arrow on the right side of the text box. It does not yet do anything, however. To enable the menu, you need to customize the combo box.

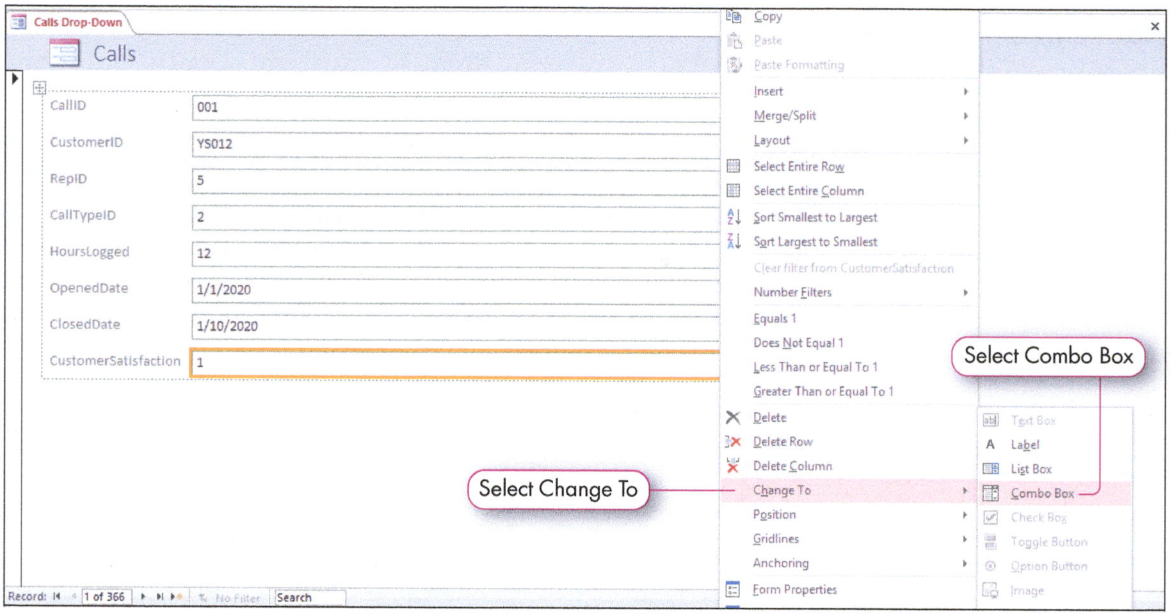

FIGURE 7.4 Changing a Field to a Combo Box

TIP: LIST BOX VERSUS COMBO BOX

When converting a text box, another option is to choose a list box. A list box control is similar to a combo box control but has a couple of differences. A list box displays several rows of the list at all times, whereas the combo box hides the list until the arrow is clicked. The list box is less compact than a combo box. Unlike a combo box, additional values cannot be typed in the list box by the user.

Customize a Combo Box

Once you have converted a text box to a combo box, you still have changes to make to enable the options. You first create a new table and enter the values for the option list, or use an existing table, much like you do for lookup fields. This way, the values can be found in an easy-to-edit location. Then, the source for the combo box can be set so the values displayed on the menu match those in your new table. Next, you will set any necessary properties for the combo box. Several properties are available for combo boxes, but three essential properties are the Row Source, Row Source Type, and the Limit to List properties. Figure 7.5 shows Data properties you can set to customize a combo box. The Row Source property designates the source for the combo box list. This property works in conjunction with the Row Source Type, which designates the list source: table/query, value list, or a field list. For a table/query Row Source Type, the Row Source will be a SQL statement. The value list Row Source Type is a fixed list of values that you type yourself. Individual values are separated by semicolons (;). The field list Row Source Type shows a list of values from a selected table or query. The table or query used for the field list is typically designed for use in the combo box. The values for the option list can contain one or more fields from the table, for example customer number followed by the customer name.

To set a source for a combo box, complete the following steps:

1. Switch to Design view of the form.
2. Click the field you want to customize.
3. Click the Property Sheet in the Tools group on the Design tab.
4. Select a Row Source Type on the Data tab.
5. Select the Row Source on the Data tab.
6. Select from the list (field list), type the SQL statement (table/query), or type the list options separated by semicolons (value list), depending on the Row Source Type chosen.
7. Switch to Form view to test the combo box.

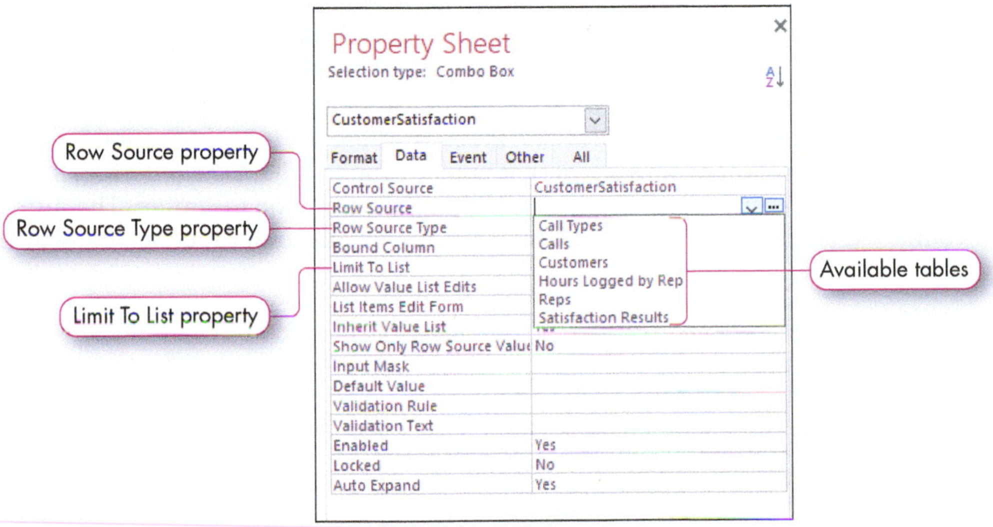

FIGURE 7.5 Combo Box Properties

You may also want to ensure your users only enter values that exist in the menu. The Limit to List property ensures they enter a value you have set as allowable.

To limit the values to the contents of the source table, complete the following steps:

1. Switch to Design view of the form.
2. Click the Property Sheet in the Tools group on the Design tab.
3. Change the Limit To List property to Yes on the Data tab.
4. Switch to Form view to test the combo box.

If you have set the Limit To List option and the user types a value not on the list, Access generates an error that reads, *The text you entered isn't an item in the list.* Similar to lookup fields, storing values in a separate table makes it very easy to change the values accepted in a combo box if the values ever change. For example, you may have initially dealt with customers in Idaho, Montana, and Wyoming. If you want to add Oregon and Washington to the combo box, you can add new rows to the table storing the state names.

Setting the Tab Order

When entering data into a table, users often press Tab to advance from one field to the next in a logical order, such as top to bottom or left to right. The **tab order** in a form is the sequential advancing from one field or control to the next when you press Tab. Each time Tab is pressed, the insertion point moves to a location known as the **tab stop**. When working with forms, the designer must remember to check the tab order before delivering the form to the end users; when a form is created, the initial tab order is not necessarily the order that is most useful to the user. Furthermore, if a control is moved on the form, the control retains is original tab order, which, with the move, may now be out of order.

STEP 3 ## Set Tab Order Using Auto Order

As a designer, you want to enable users to be as efficient and forms to be as logical as possible. Setting the tab order helps prevent errors and simplifies data entry. For example, there is usually a common order to a form requiring a person's address. The person's street address, city, state, zip code is typically presented in that order. As you insert controls into a form Access will set the tab order. At times, it will be set to an order that is not logical for the user. Access provides a tool that enables you to adjust the ordering, if the form has a Stacked layout and you want set the tab order from top to bottom. The Auto Order command (see Figure 7.6) can attempt to automatically order the tabbing, which may fix the problem.

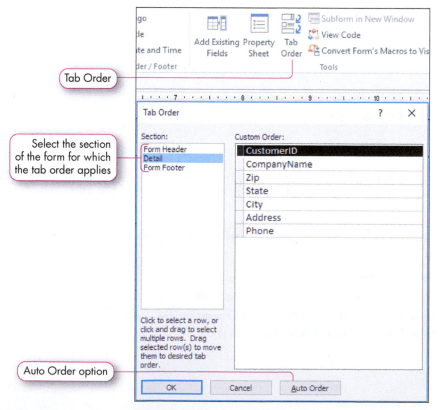

FIGURE 7.6 Tab Order for Form

> **To automatically set the tab order in a form, complete the following steps:**
>
> 1. Switch to Design view.
> 2. Click Tab Order in the Tools group on the Design tab. The Tab Order dialog box displays all the controls in each section of the form.
> 3. Ensure Detail is selected in the Section box to display the tab order for the fields.
> 4. Click Auto Order.
> 5. Click OK to accept the changes.

STEP 4 ## Set Tab Order Manually

The order in which the fields display in the Tab Order dialog box list, from top to bottom, (as shown in Figure 7.6) will be the order in which the tab stops flow.

If you create a custom form without a wizard or layout, the tab order generated might not flow in a logical order. Access does its best to set the tab order properly; however, if Access cannot fix the tabbing using Auto Order, you can also set it manually. For example, Auto Order does not work well if you have a form with multiple columns. In this case, you will need to manually rearrange the tab order.

> **To customize the tab order, complete the following steps:**
>
> 1. Switch to Design view.
> 2. Click Tab Order in the Tools group on the Design tab.
> 3. Ensure Detail is selected to display the tab order for the fields.
> 4. Click the record selector to the left of a field name and drag the field into position in the tab order. For example, if two fields are next to each other but in the wrong order, click the second field and drag the second field on top of the first one.
> 5. Click OK to accept the changes.
> 6. Switch to Form view and test the order by pressing Tab to advance through the fields on the form.

Remove a Tab Stop

At times, you want the tab order to skip a field completely. For example, if you add a calculated field to the form, you would not want to stop at this field. Calculated fields do not require data entry. Another example occurs when you have an AutoNumber field as the primary key. Your user does not add data to that field, so it should not have a tab stop. The Tab Stop property for a field can be changed to No to indicate that the field does not have a tab stop.

> **To remove the Tab Stop property for a field, complete the following steps:**
>
> 1. Switch to Layout view (or Design view).
> 2. Click the field for which you want to remove the tab stop.
> 3. Click Property Sheet in the Tools group on the Design tab.
> 4. Click the Other tab in the Property Sheet.
> 5. Click the Tab Stop property and change the property setting to No, as shown in Figure 7.7.
> 6. Switch to Form view and test the change by pressing Tab to advance through the fields on the form. The field you modified should be skipped when you press Tab.

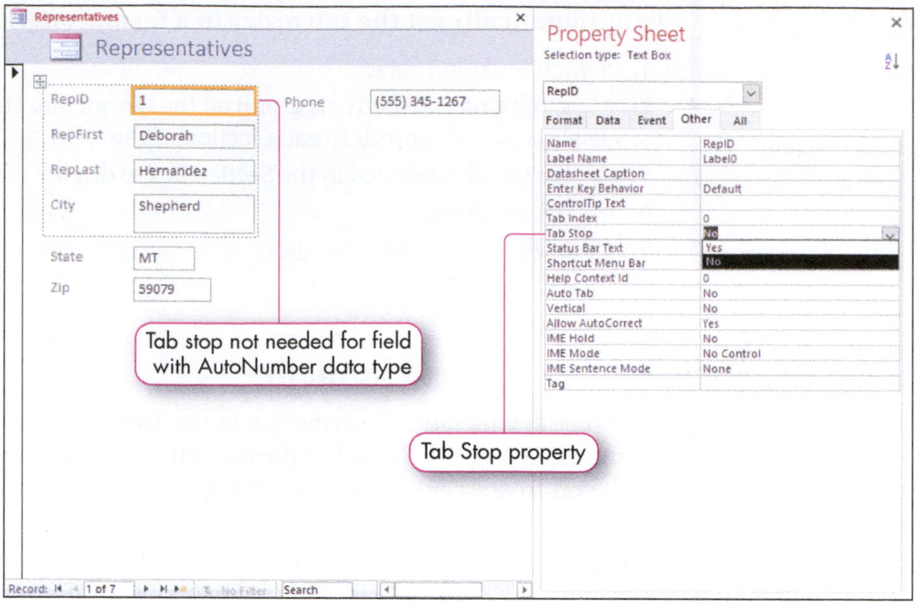

FIGURE 7.7 Removing a Tab Stop

STEP 5 ▶ Understanding Subforms

Relationships between tables usually exist in Access databases, which can lead to more complicated forms. In order to properly display information from multiple tables, a form will often have a **subform**, which is a form inserted into another form that displays records that are related to the records in a main form. Subforms are generally laid out in a tabular fashion, as shown in Figure 7.8.

When you create a form using the Form Wizard, if the table you are basing the form on has a relationship with another table, then Access will create a form with a subform automatically. The subform is based on the related table. In some instances, you may want to add a subform manually. You can add a subform to an existing form using the Subform/Subreport tool.

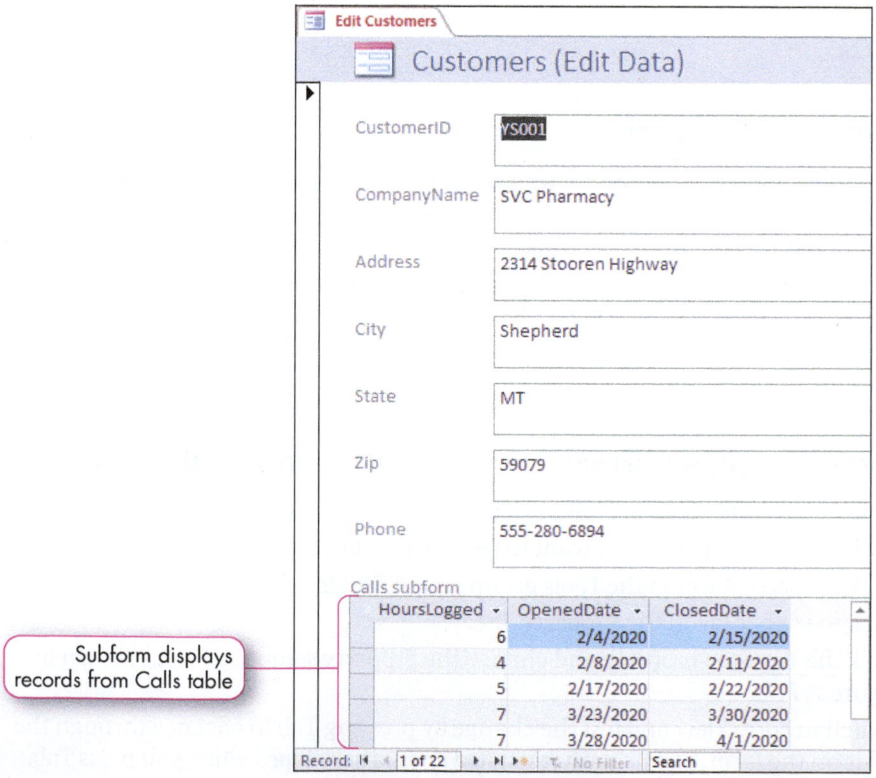

FIGURE 7.8 Form with a Subform

To manually add a subform using the Subform/Subreport tool, complete the following steps:

1. Open the form in Design view.
2. Click the Subform/Subreport control ▦ in the Controls group on the Design tab. If it is not visible, click More at the lower right of the Controls box.
3. Draw the subform. It can be resized later as. The SubForm Wizard Launches.
4. Choose the source for the subform, as shown in Figure 7.9. You can use an existing form or view data in a table or query.
5. Choose the appropriate fields from the table (or query) source, as shown in Figure 7.10. Click Next.
6. Choose the relationship you want to use, as shown in Figure 7.11. This step may not display if there is only one relationship. Click Next.
7. Accept the default name or create your own name for the subform. Click Finish.
8. Switch to Form view to see the results.

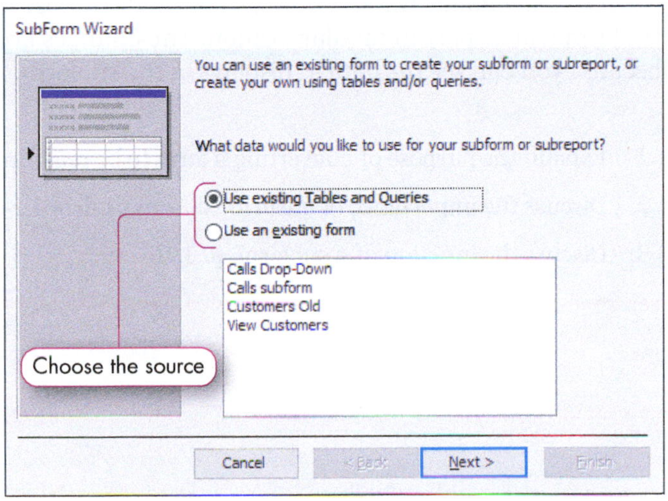

FIGURE 7.9 Selecting Source in SubForm Wizard

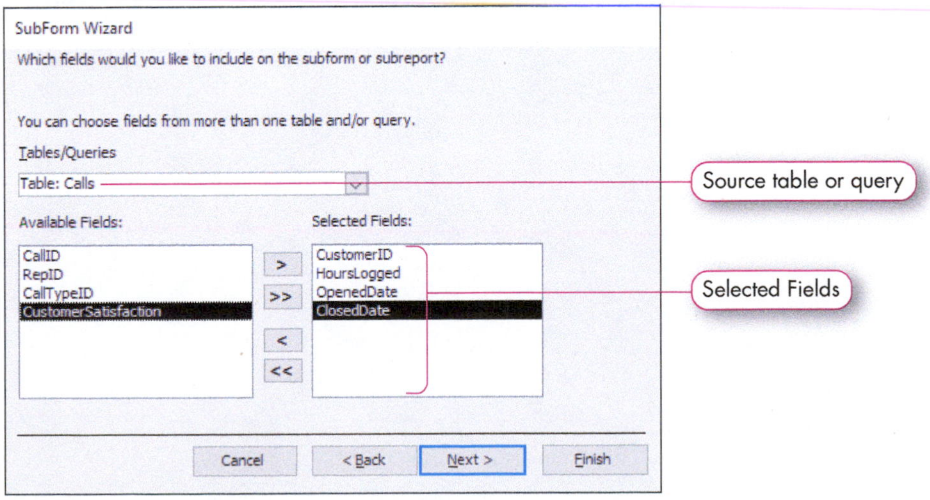

FIGURE 7.10 Selecting Fields in SubForm Wizard

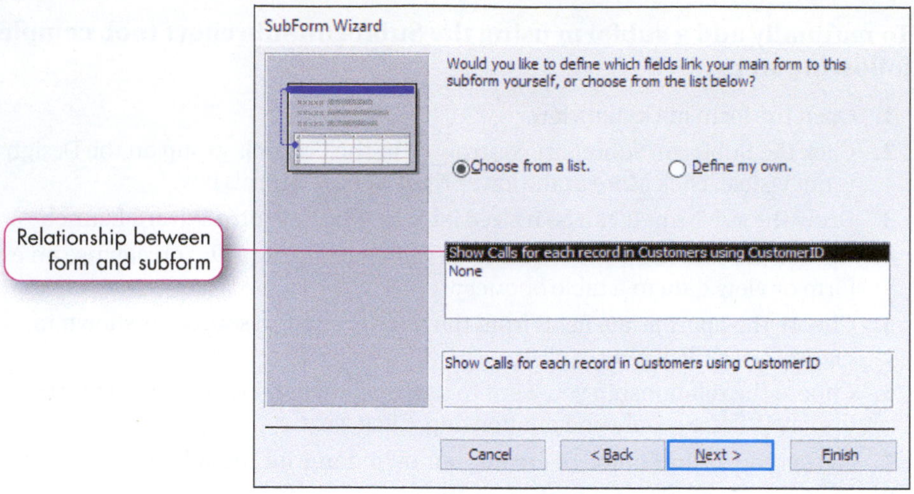

Relationship between form and subform

FIGURE 7.11 Selecting a Relationship in SubForm Wizard

You can change the size of the subform or the size of the fields in the subform. The subform will display in tabular fashion. The changes are easier to make in Layout view because you can see the data as displays in the subform.

Quick Concepts

1. Explain the purpose of converting a form to be read-only. **p. 390**

2. Discuss the importance of ensuring a form's tab order is logical. **p. 394**

3. Discuss the function of a subform. **p. 396**

Hands-On Exercises

MyLab IT HOE1 Sim Training

Watch the Video for this Hands-On Exercise!

Skills covered: Convert a Form to Read-Only • Convert a Text Box to a Combo Box • Customize a Combo Box • Set Tab Order Using Auto Order • Set Tab Order Manually • Remove a Tab Stop • Create a Subform

1 Advanced Forms

You have decided to create a read-only form for customer data. You will also create a form with a drop-down menu to enable users to record customer call satisfaction. You will repair an existing form that has problems with tab ordering. You will also create a form with a subform.

STEP 1 CONVERT A FORM TO READ-ONLY

You will use the Form tool to create a Customers form to enable users to look up customer information. You will make the form read-only so users do not accidentally alter data when looking up information. Refer to Figure 7.12 as you complete Step 1.

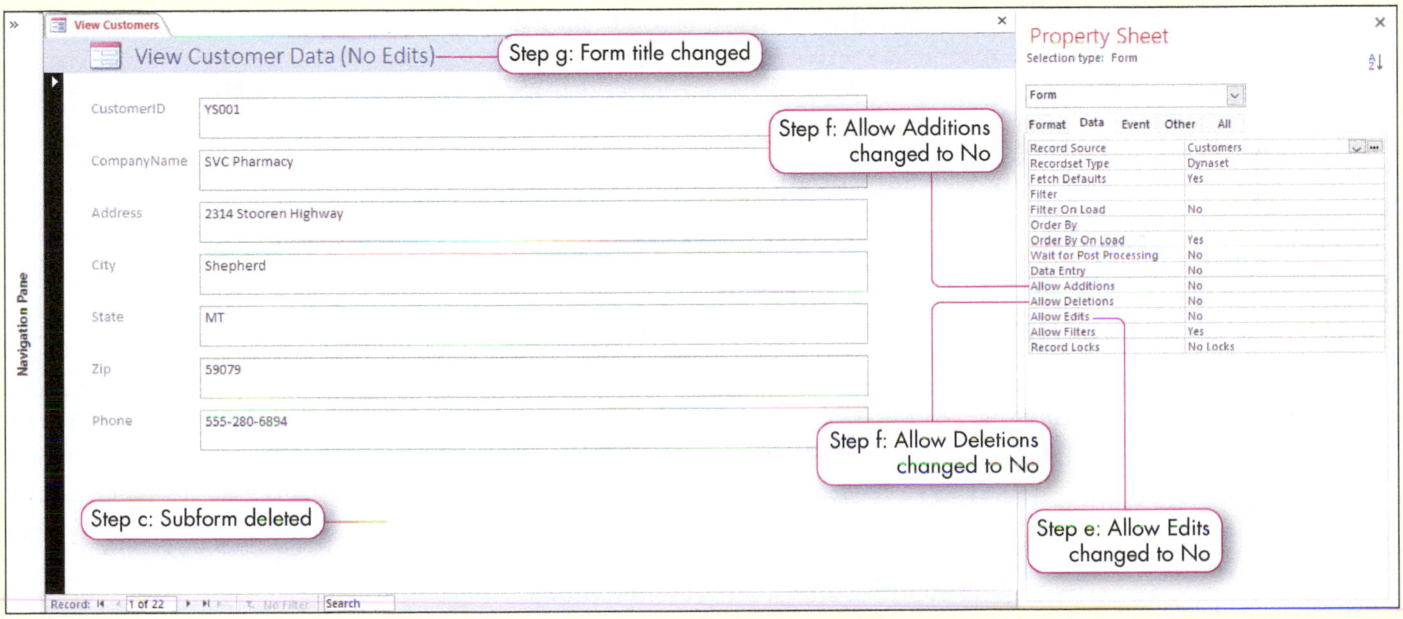

FIGURE 7.12 View Customers Form

a. Open *a07h1Yellowstone* and save it as **a07h1Yellowstone_LastFirst**.

> **TROUBLESHOOTING:** If you make any major mistakes in this exercise, you can close the file, open *a07h1Yellowstone* again, and then start this exercise over.

b. Select the **Customers table** in the Navigation Pane. Click the **Create tab** and click **Form** in the Forms group.

Access creates a new form based on the Customers table. The form opens in Layout view, ready to edit.

c. Click anywhere in the subform at the bottom of the window, click the border of the subform, and then press **Delete** to delete the subform.

The subform is removed.

> **TROUBLESHOOTING:** If you are prompted to confirm deleting of records, click No and ensure you have clicked the border before pressing Delete.

d. Click **Property Sheet** on the Design tab in the Tools group if it is not already displayed.

The Property Sheet displays on the right side of your screen.

e. Click the **Data tab** in the Property Sheet pane. Click the **Allow Edits box**, which currently displays *Yes*, and click the arrow at the right. Select **No**.

f. Repeat Step e to change the **Allow Additions** and **Allow Deletions property values** to **No**. Close the Property Sheet.

g. Click the **form title**. Change the title of the form to **View Customer Data (No Edits)**. Compare your results with Figure 7.12.

h. Switch to Form view.

i. Attempt to type in the CompanyName box.

You should not be able to change the field value.

> **TROUBLESHOOTING:** If you are able to type in the CompanyName box, switch to Layout view and check that you completed Step e.

j. Attempt to click **New** and **Delete** in the Records group on the Home tab.

You should not be able to add or delete a record.

> **TROUBLESHOOTING:** If you are able to click New or Delete, switch to Layout view and check that you completed Step f.

k. Click **Save** in the Quick Access Toolbar and save the form as **View Customers**. Close the form.

STEP 2 **CONVERT A TEXT BOX TO A COMBO BOX AND CUSTOMIZE A COMBO BOX**

You will use the Form tool to create an Access form to help manage customer call data. This form will enable you to record customer satisfaction data using a combo box rather than a manually typed entry. Therefore, you will convert the customer satisfaction text box to a combo box. Refer to Figure 7.13 as you complete Step 2.

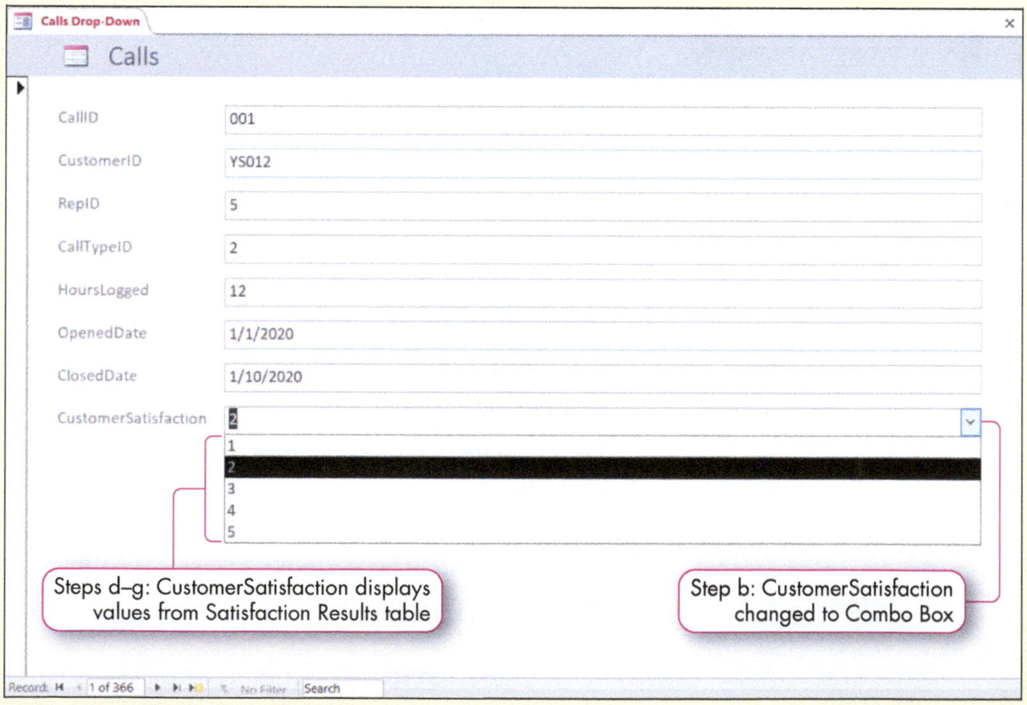

FIGURE 7.13 Calls Drop-Down Form

a. Select the **Calls table** in the Navigation Pane. Click the **Create tab** and click **Form** in the Forms group.

b. Right-click the **CustomerSatisfaction text box**, point to the **Change To option**, and then select **Combo Box** from the shortcut menu.

The CustomerSatisfaction text box changes to a combo box with an arrow on the right side of the box.

c. Click **Property Sheet** in the Tools group on the Design tab if it is not already displayed.

d. Click the **Row Source property** on the Data tab of the Property Sheet, click the arrow at the right of the Row Source box, and then select **Satisfaction Results**.

e. Click the **Limit To List property** and change the value to **Yes**.

You are limiting the list so manual entries will no longer be permitted.

f. Switch to Form view.

g. Click the **CustomerSatisfaction field**. Notice an arrow now displays on the right of the box. Click the arrow and notice values of 1, 2, 3, 4, and 5 as shown in Figure 7.13.

h. Type the value **6** for the CustomerSatisfaction field and press **Tab**.

Access will display an error message that the text you entered is not an item in the list.

> **TROUBLESHOOTING:** If Access does permit the value to be entered, ensure you set the Limit To List property to Yes in Step e.

i. Click **OK**. Change the value for the first record's CustomerSatisfaction field to **2** and press **Tab**.

You will not receive an error message because the value is in range.

j. Save the form as **Calls Drop-Down**, and close the form.

STEP 3 SET TAB ORDER USING AUTO ORDER

The users of the current Edit Customers form have reported problems with the tab order. You will fix the tab order using Auto Order. Refer to Figure 7.14 as you complete Step 3.

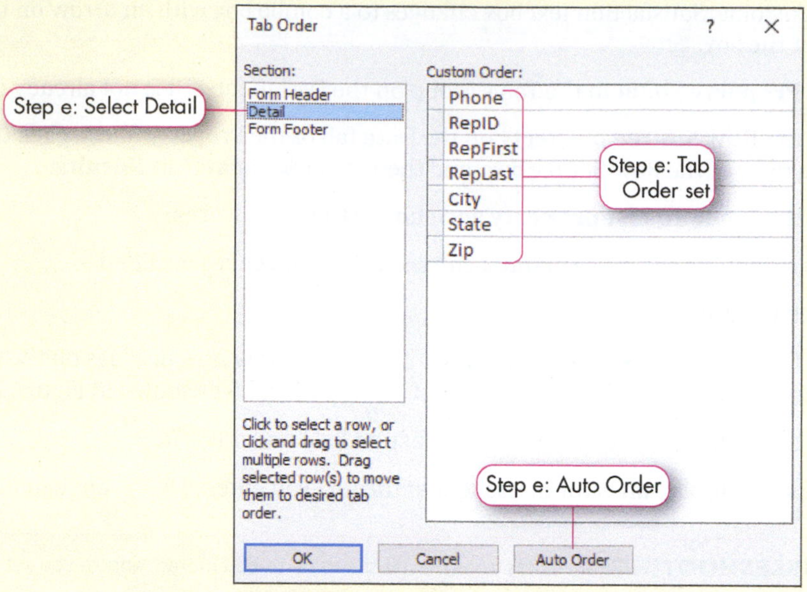

FIGURE 7.14 Tab Order for Edit Customers Form

a. Open the **Edit Customers form** in Form view.

b. Press **Tab**.

When you press Tab, the State field becomes active, rather than the CompanyName.

c. Press **Tab** five more times noticing the order in which the fields display.

The fields are not tabbed in a logical order.

d. Switch to Design view and click **Tab Order** in the Tools group on the Design tab.

e. Ensure Detail is selected in the section box and click **Auto Order**.

Notice State is no longer the second field on the list. The order now reflects the order of the fields, top to bottom. Because this is a Stacked Layout form, Access changes the tab order so it moves down one field at a time.

f. Click **OK**. Switch to Form view. Press **Tab** six times and verify that the tab order progresses in a logical order. Save and close the form.

STEP 4 SET TAB ORDER MANUALLY AND REMOVE A TAB STOP

You will also fix an old form so that the tabs appear in the correct order and remove a tab stop to prevent the user from stopping at a field they cannot update. Refer to Figure 7.15 as you complete Step 4.

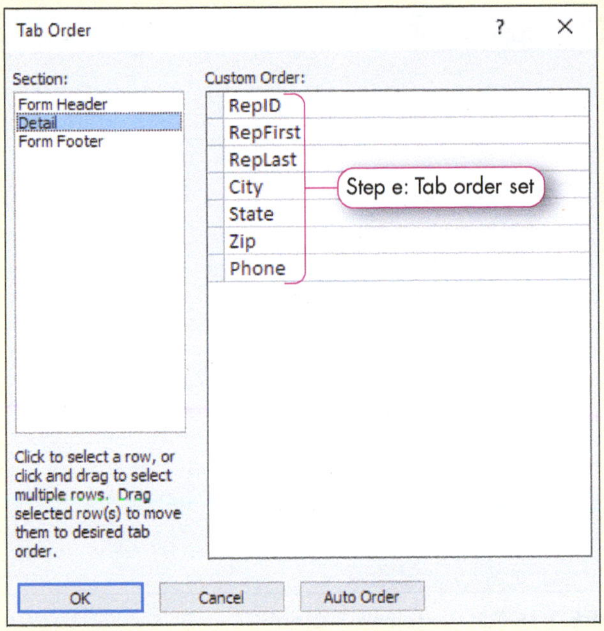

FIGURE 7.15 Tab Order for Representatives Form

a. Open the **Representatives form** in Form view. Press **Tab**.

The Phone field becomes active. You will change the tab order so Phone is the last field to become active.

b. Switch to Design view. Click **Tab Order** in the Tools group on the Design tab. Ensure **Detail** is selected and click **Auto Order**.

Notice *Phone* is displayed at the top of the list, which would make it the first field displayed. This is not the logical order.

c. Click the record selector to the left of the Phone field. Drag the **Phone field** beneath the Zip field. The tab order should match Figure 7.15. Click **OK**.

d. Click the **RepID field**. Display the Property Sheet, if it is not already displayed.

e. Click the **Other tab** in the Property Sheet. Click the Tab Stop property and change the property setting to **No**.

Pressing Tab is no longer necessary as the RepID field value is set by the AutoNumber.

f. Switch to Form view. Tab through the fields.

The default field is now the RepFirst and pressing Tab will bring you through RepLast City, State, Zip, and Phone, in that order. Note pressing Tab does not bring you to the RepID field.

g. Save and close the form.

The Edit Customers form does not display the related call information for each customer. You will modify the Edit Customers form so the subform containing the call information displays. Refer to Figure 7.16 as you complete Step 5.

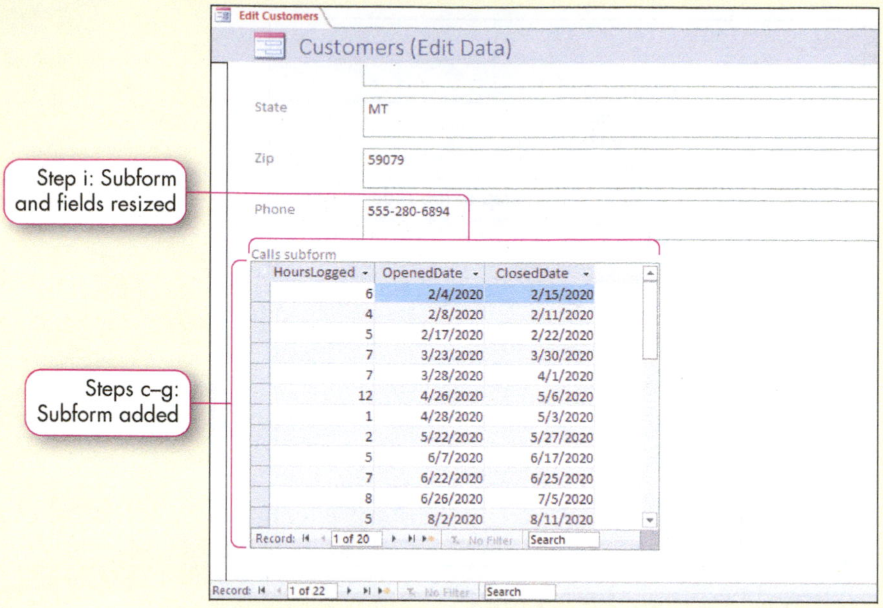

FIGURE 7.16 Edit Customers Subform

a. Open the **Edit Customers form** in Design view.

b. Click **More** and click the **Subform/Subreport control** in the Controls group on the Design tab.

> **TROUBLESHOOTING:** If the Subform/Subreport control is not visible, click More at the lower right of the Controls box.

c. Draw a box below the Phone field in the location shown in Figure 7.16. The size does not matter because it will be resized later.

   The Subform Wizard dialog box displays.

d. Click **Next** to accept the default *Use existing Tables and Queries* option.

e. Click the **Tables/Queries arrow**, and select **Table: Calls**. Double-click the **HoursLogged**, **OpenedDate**, and **ClosedDate fields**. Click **Next**.

f. Click **Next** to accept the default relationship.

g. Accept the default Calls subform name, and click **Finish**.

h. Switch to Layout view.

   Notice the Calls subform appears at the bottom of the screen.

i. Resize the subform and the fields to be approximately the size shown in Figure 7.16.

> **TROUBLESHOOTING:** If it is difficult to resize the bottom of the subform, first drag the Form Footer section bar which will expand the Detail section and allow you to resize more easily.

j. Save and close the form.

k. Keep the database open if you plan to continue with the next Hands-On Exercise. If not, close the database and exit Access.

Controls and Sections

Within each form or report, you find at least one *control*, which is an object on a form or report. Controls can display data, perform calculations, and add visual effects (such as boxes or lines). Text boxes, labels, combo boxes, and subforms are all examples of controls.

As you work with tools to create and modify forms and reports, you will often switch between the three views in Access—Form or Report view, Layout view, and Design view. You use Layout view to perform most changes, but Design view gives you, as a designer, a higher level of control. Forms and reports have similar functionality in Design view, so the skills you use in forms can generally be applied to reports and vice versa.

In this section, you will learn about unbound controls such as label controls, which insert a label to display a field name or other text, and calculated controls, which display the result of expressions or functions. You will also learn about bound controls, which are bound to a source of data. Additionally, you will learn about page break controls as well as sections in forms and reports.

Understanding Controls

When you use the form and report wizards to create basic objects, the resulting forms and reports contain controls that were added automatically, such as a title, field values, and field names. The most common control is the text box, but others include labels, calculations, and images. At the most basic level, all controls are parts on a form or report that are used to enter or display data. Controls fall into one of three categories: bound, unbound, or calculated. A *bound control* is any control whose source of data is a field in a table or query. Bound controls are dynamic in that the values update every time data is changed. An *unbound control* is any control not tied to a specific field and, thus, is generally unchanging. A *calculated control* is an unbound control that displays the result of an expression in a form or report. Calculated controls include simple math functions created using the Expression Builder.

Figure 7.17 shows one label and one value for each field in this record. The label CustomerID is an unbound label control and will always display CustomerID. The bound field value control for CustomerID, in this case YS001, is a bound control and will change depending on what record is being displayed.

FIGURE 7.17 Bound and Unbound Controls in a Form

Controls are located in the Controls group on the Form Layout Tools Design tab. Table 7.1 shows some of the common controls.

TABLE 7.1 Common Control Icons

Control Icon	Control Name	Description
abl	Text Box control	Inserts a text box to display data from a record source or data that are the result of a calculation
Aa	Label control	Inserts a label to display a field name or other text
	Combo box control	Inserts a menu displaying a list of options
	Rectangle control	Inserts a rectangle shape
	Subform/Subreport control	Inserts a subform or subreport
	Insert Page Break control	Inserts a page break
	Image control	Inserts an image
	Chart control	Inserts a chart based on table or query data
	Line control	Inserts a line

STEP 1 ## Add a Text Box Control

The Text Box control is used to display the data found in a record source (often, a table). Although the term *text box* may imply that it only displays Short Text values, it can display numeric data, currency, and dates, depending on the field's data type. Because it is tied to a field and is dynamic, a text box is considered a bound control. This is how forms and reports display the most current information; they use controls that are bound to fields.

> **TIP: USE THE ARRANGE TAB TO ORGANIZE TEXT BOX CONTROLS**
> When you add a new Text Box control to a report, you may find it puts the label in the same row as the data. In other words, the label, instead of appearing in a header, may appear in the data section. If this happens, click Tabular in the Table group on the Arrange tab while both the Label and Text Box controls are selected. The label will then move to a more appropriate location.

STEP 2 ## Add a Calculated Control

Forms and reports based on queries that contain calculated fields will display calculated fields like any other field. However, some forms and reports are based on a table rather than a query. In this case, you can add a calculated field that does not already exist to a form or report by using a text box and a calculated control. Calculated controls include simple math, aggregate functions such as Average, Count, and Sum, and functions created using the Expression Builder and are typically inserted into a Text Box control.

The expression for the calculated control can be typed directly into the text box, as shown in Figure 7.18.

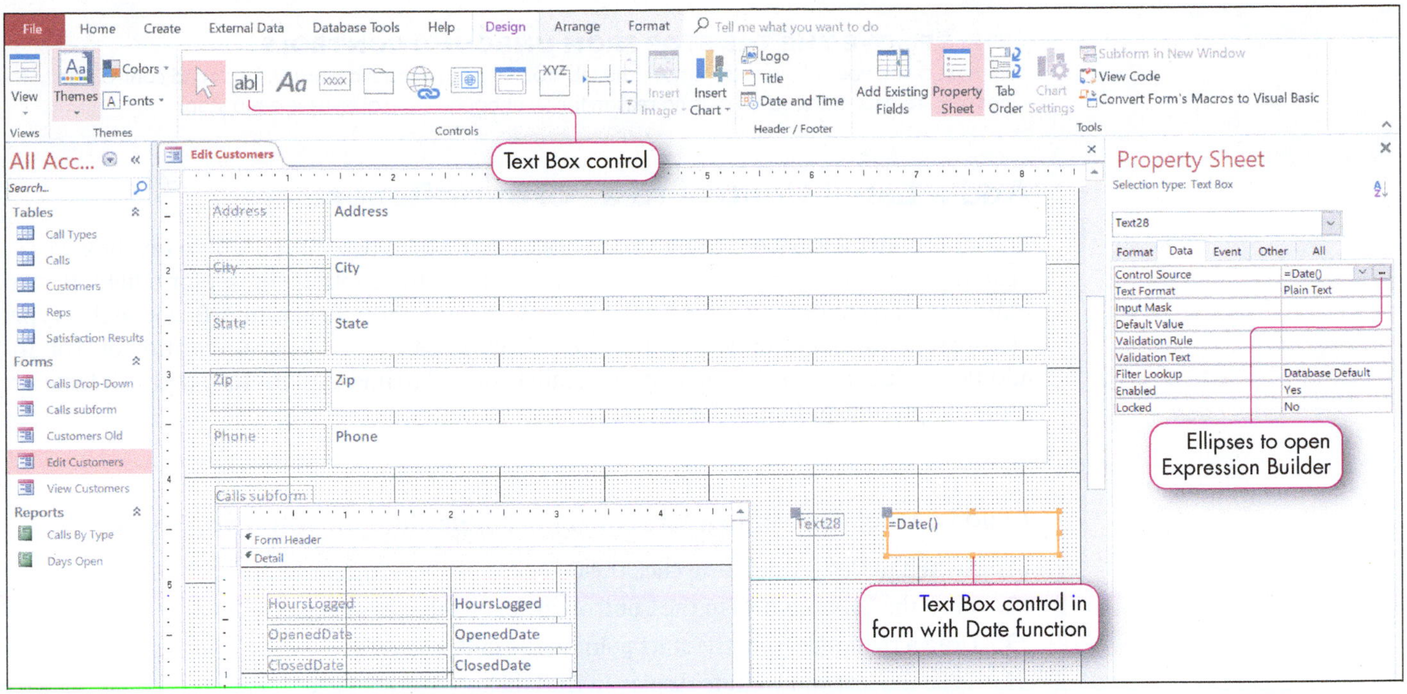

FIGURE 7.18 Calculated Control

To add a calculated control to a form or report using the Expression Builder, complete the following steps:

1. Switch to Design view and ensure the Design tab is selected.
2. Click the Text Box control in the Controls group, as shown in Figure 7.18.
3. Drag a rectangle from the start point to the end point. The word *Unbound* displays in the text box. Access also displays a label by default, often to the left of the text box. You can choose to delete or modify the label.
4. Display the Property Sheet if it is not displayed at the right side of your screen.
5. Click the Data tab on the Property Sheet and click the ellipses found next to the Control Source property to open the Expression Builder.
6. Create the expression.
7. Click OK.

If you are comfortable with formulas and functions, you do not have to use the Expression Builder. You could simply type the formula into the text box, preceded by an equal sign. For example, you could type =Date() to show the current date.

To format the results of a calculated control, complete the following steps:

1. Switch to Design view.
2. Click the text box you want to format.
3. Click Property Sheet in the Tools group on the Design tab, if it is not already visible.
4. Click the Format property on the Format tab of the Property Sheet to change the format. You will also find other options regarding formatting as well, such as a property for number of decimal places for a numeric field.

TIP: REMOVE THE TAB STOP FROM UNBOUND CONTROLS

In most cases, you will want to remove the tab stop from an unbound control. Unbound controls do not require data entry, so there is no reason for an unbound control to have a tab stop.

Add a Label Control to a Form or Report

The label control is a word or phrase to describe the data associated with a text box. For a field in a form or report, the label control defaults to the caption you set for a field. If you have not set a caption for a field, the label will default to the field name. Because this type of control does not change as you switch between records, it is an unbound control. In addition to label controls, you can use a label control to add explanatory text to a form or report to provide guidance for users.

To add a label control to a form or report, complete the following steps:

1. Switch to Design view and click the Design tab.
2. Click the Label control in the Controls group, as shown in Figure 7.19.
3. Drag a rectangle from the start point to the end point.
4. Type the text you want to display in the label.

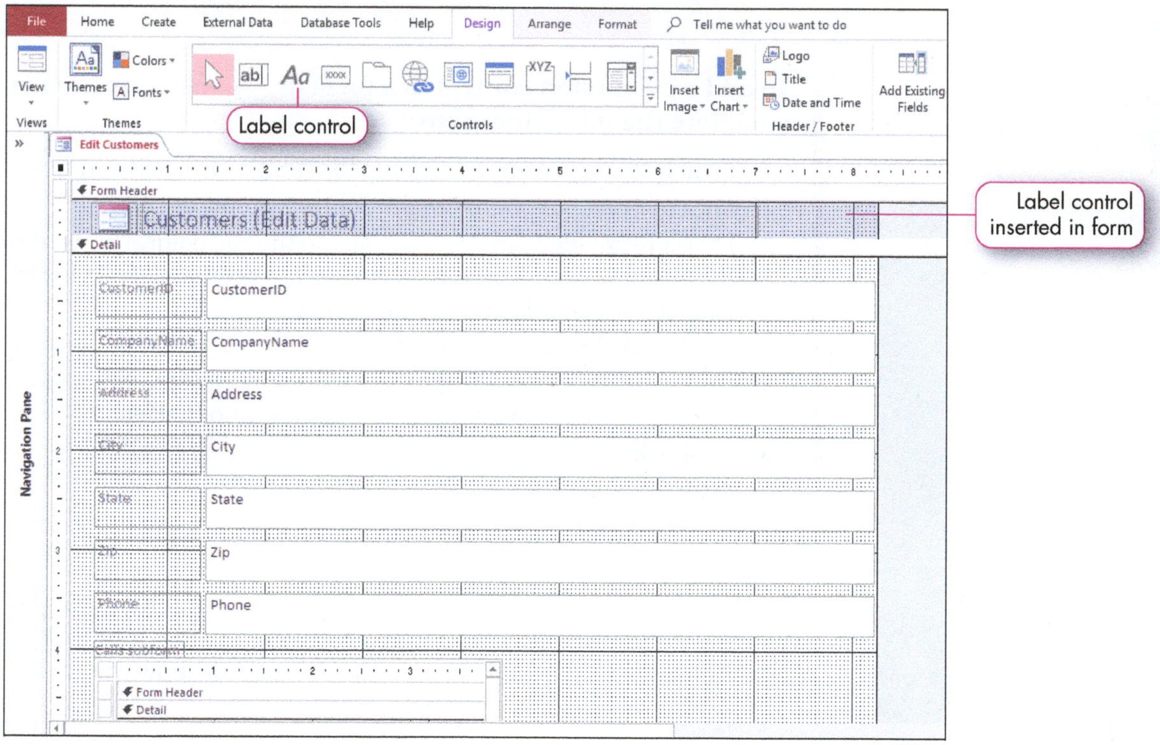

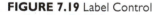

FIGURE 7.19 Label Control

STEP 3 Add a Chart Control to a Form or Report

The chart control enables you to display numeric data graphically. A chart can be added to a form or report and can be based on table or query data. In Access, you can create column, line, bar, pie, and combo charts. When you create a chart in an Access form or report, you need to specify the data source, the Axis (Category or X axis) and the Values Axis (Y axis). A legend is automatically created when two or more value fields are selected.

- Data Source: The data source for an Access chart can be either a table or query. If the data source is a table with many fields, it may be easier to first create a query that uses only the fields you want displayed in the chart, and then create the chart based on the query.
- Axis (Category or X Axis): This axis displays text labels for the chart. Two or more fields can be selected for the axis.
- Values (Y Axis): This axis displays the numeric scale corresponding to a data series. Two or more fields can be selected for the axis.

To add a chart control to a form or report, complete the following steps:

1. Switch to Design view and click the Design tab.
2. Click Insert Chart in the Controls group on the Design tab and select a chart type.
3. Drag a rectangle from the start point to the end point. The Chart Settings pane displays.
4. Select the data source for the chart on the Data tab in the Chart Settings pane and select the fields for each axis by clicking the checkbox next to the field name. The default aggregation is a sum and will be shown next to the field name. Click the arrow next to the selected field to change the aggregation.
5. Click the Format tab on the Chart Settings task pane and modify the options as necessary.

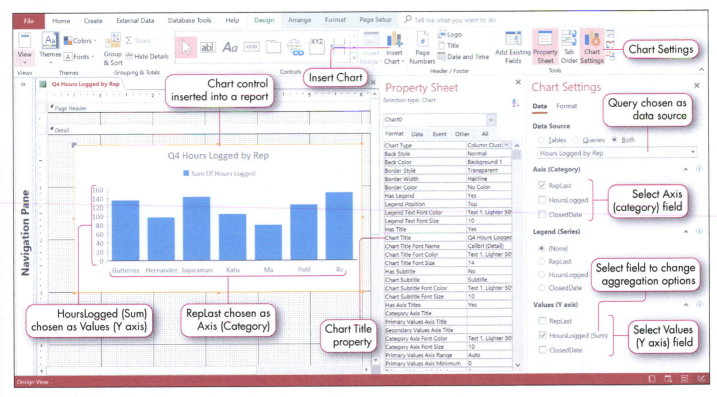

FIGURE 7.20 Chart Control

If the data source contains nonaggregated data, by default, Access will aggregate the data in the chart using functions such as Sum, Average, and Count. However, if your data are already aggregated, you can remove the default aggregate calculations in the chart creation process by clicking the selected field in the Values list and then selecting None in the list.

Similar to charts in Excel, the chart can be customized with a title, axis labels, legends, colors, and more. Customization of the chart is done through the Chart Settings task pane. When creating the chart, it may be easier to base the chart on a query rather than a table. You can create a dynamic chart that uses a value in a parameter query as a filter of the chart data. For example, you could create a query to view data only between specific dates set by the parameter value. When the form or report containing the chart is run, a dialog box prompts for the two date values, and the chart will show only the data between those two dates.

Add Emphasis to a Form or Report Using Line and Rectangle Controls

If you want to break up your form or report into sections, the line control and rectangle control are two options. As the names imply, the line control enables you to insert a line into your form or report, and the Rectangle control enables you to add a rectangle. After inserting these into an object, you can modify the shape to have a different line color, line thickness, and line type (such as dashed or dotted), and in the case of rectangles, the fill color. You will only find these options in Design view; they are not available in Layout view. To add a line or rectangle control to a form or report, click the line or rectangle control and drag a rectangle from the start point to the end point to display the control.

To format a line or rectangle control, use the options in the Control Formatting group on the Format tab, as shown in Figure 7.21. Choose the Shape Outline menu to change the color, thickness, and line type for a rectangle or line. Choose Shape Fill to add a fill color to a rectangle.

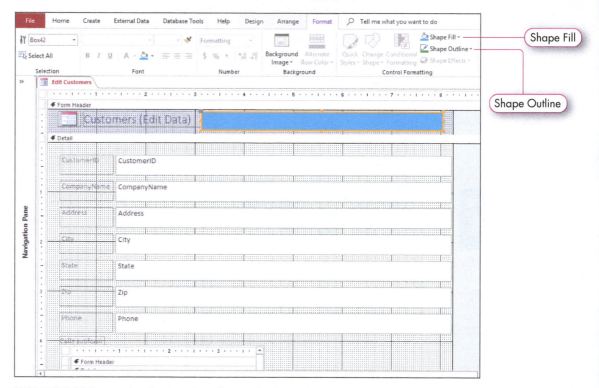

FIGURE 7.21 Formatting Options for a Rectangle Control

Add a Page Break Control

Pagination can be important for forms and especially reports. For example, you may want to print a report that keeps all of the orders for a particular product together. Doing so will make the report easier to read. You can add a page break to control where the break occurs as opposed to an automatic page break, which does not give you that control.

To add a page break to a form or report, complete the following steps:

1. Open the form or report in Design view.
2. Click the Insert Page Break control on the Design tab in the Controls group, as shown in Figure 7.22.
3. Click the section of the form or report where you want the page break. When you click the Insert Page Break control, the pointer changes to a crosshair with a small report icon (even in forms).
4. View the object in Print Preview to test the page break.

After you insert a page break on the form or report, a series of six dots appears on the left margin (see Figure 7.22). To remove the page break, click the six dots and press Delete.

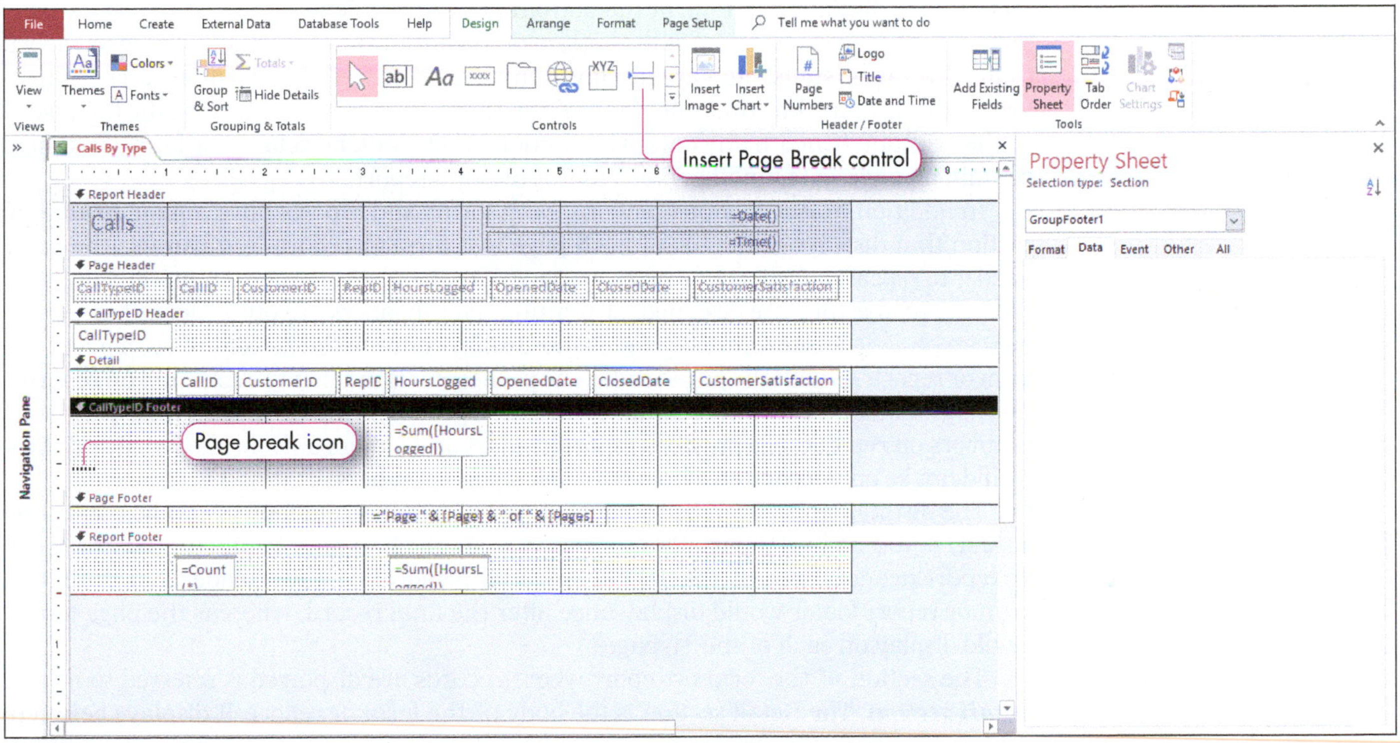

FIGURE 7.22 Page Break in Report

TIP: CHANGING DEFAULT BEHAVIOR OF CONTROLS

If you find you have to change properties to the same thing often, you can change the default behavior. For example, when inserting a text box, a label always appears by default. You can change default properties for any control by viewing any form or report in Design view, clicking the appropriate control in the Controls group on the Design tab, and clicking Property Sheet in the Tools group. The Property Sheet will list Default plus the name of the control, such as Default Tab Control or Default Text Box. Common changes include the default size of the control; border appearance, thickness, and color; and text and background color.

Understanding Sections

In Access, the design of a report or form is divided into sections. Each section has a specific use. A **section** is a part of a form or report that can be manipulated separately from other parts of a form or report. Sections are visible in Design view. Each section can be collapsed or expanded. Forms and reports both have some common sections, as well as sections that differ only by the name of the object. In order to create useful forms or reports you should understand how each section works.

The **form header** is a section that displays one time at the top of the form. Likewise, the **report header** is a section that displays one time at the top of a report. Often information such as the author name, report title, or date is inserted into a report header. If viewed on screen, both headers display one time above the data in the object. If the form or report is printed, each of these headers will print one time on the first page of the printout. Column headings (labels) display in report headers and in some form headers.

Similarly, there are sections at the bottom of a form or report. The **form footer** is a section that displays one time at the bottom of a form. Likewise, the **report footer** is a section that displays one time at the bottom of a report. Often information such as report totals (averages, sums, etc.) are displayed in a report footer. If viewed on screen, these footers display one time underneath the data. If printed, they print only on the final page of the printout, beneath any data. This section is left blank by default for forms and may contain an aggregate function (such as Count) for a report.

In addition to the previous sections, both forms and reports have a **page header**, a section that displays at the top of each page in a form or report. You can use the page header to repeat the report title on every page. Page headers are more commonly used for reports because they are designed for printing. Page headers are off by default for forms but can be added. Likewise, the **page footer** displays once at the bottom of each page in a form or report. As with the page header, the page footer is much more common on reports. The page footer is also off by default for forms. Page footers are often used to display page numbers on reports. The previous report headers and footers only display once and thus would not be an appropriate choice to display page numbers.

The distinction between the different types of headers and footers can be confusing at first. If you had a 10-page form or report, only the first page would display the form or report header. Each of the 10 pages would display the page header. Likewise, the form or report footer would display once after the final record, whereas the page footer would display on each of the 10 pages.

The section of the form or report where records are displayed is referred to as the **Detail section**. The Detail section is the body of the form or report. It displays between the header and footer sections in both forms and reports. Figure 7.23 shows the various form sections in Design view, and Figure 7.24 shows the form in Form view.

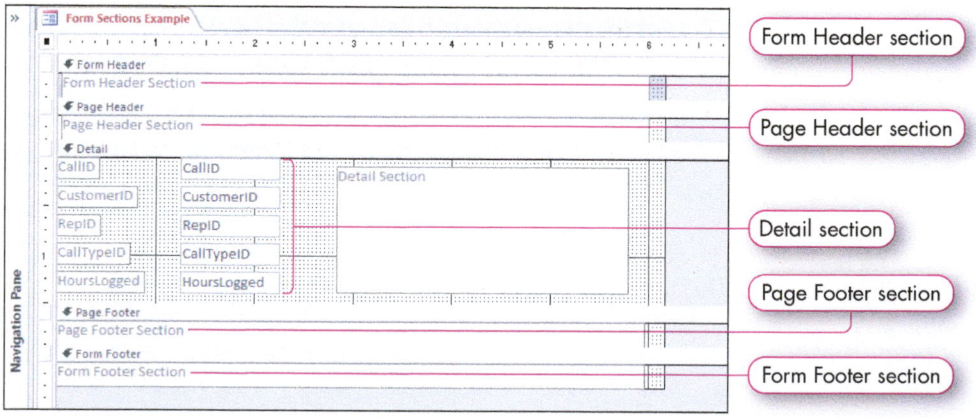

FIGURE 7.23 Form Sections in Design View

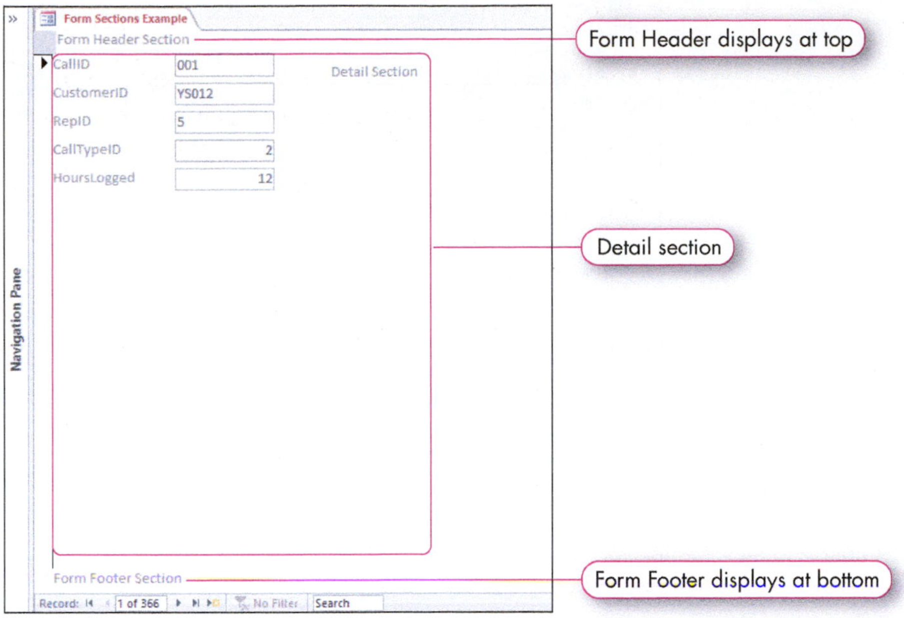

FIGURE 7.24 Form Sections in Form View

Reports are very similar to forms. Figure 7.25 shows the report sections in Design view, and Figure 7.26 shows the sections in Report view.

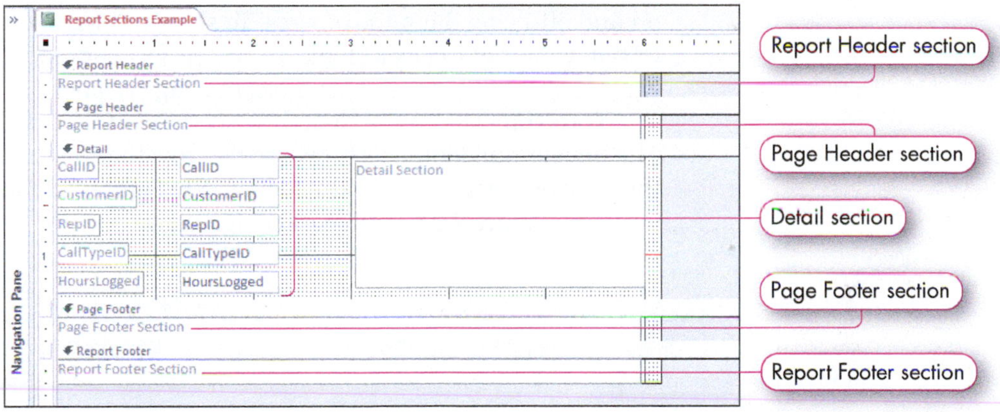

FIGURE 7.25 Report Sections in Design View

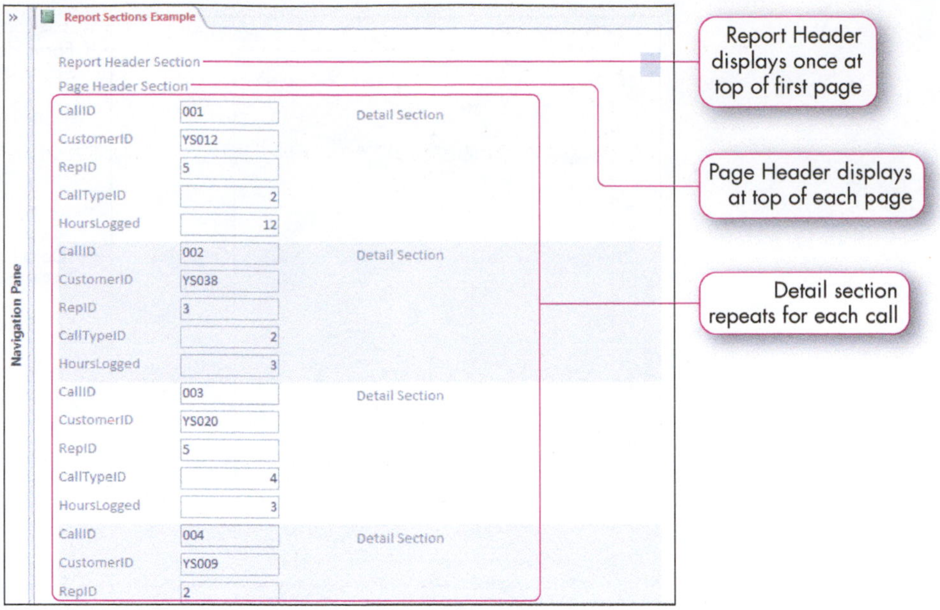

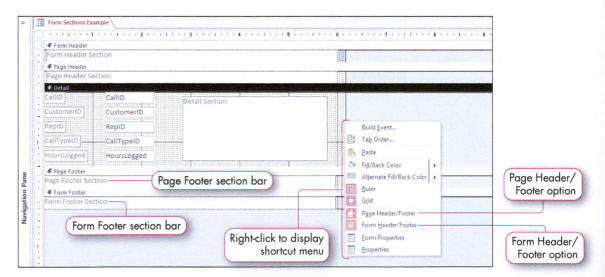

FIGURE 7.26 Report Sections in Report View

Show, Hide, and Resize Sections

Forms and reports display the Detail and Form/Report Header and Footer sections by default. Reports also include the page header/footer by default. All sections can be switched on and off using the same process. To show or hide a section, open the form or report in Design view, right-click a blank area of the form or report, and then select the section you want to show or hide—for example, the Page Header.

Note that when you switch a section off, it deletes all controls in the section. The header and footer sections are tied together; if you hide the form or report header, the form or report footer is also hidden. See Figure 7.27 for an illustration in Form Design view and Figure 7.28 for Report Design view.

FIGURE 7.27 Displaying Sections in Forms

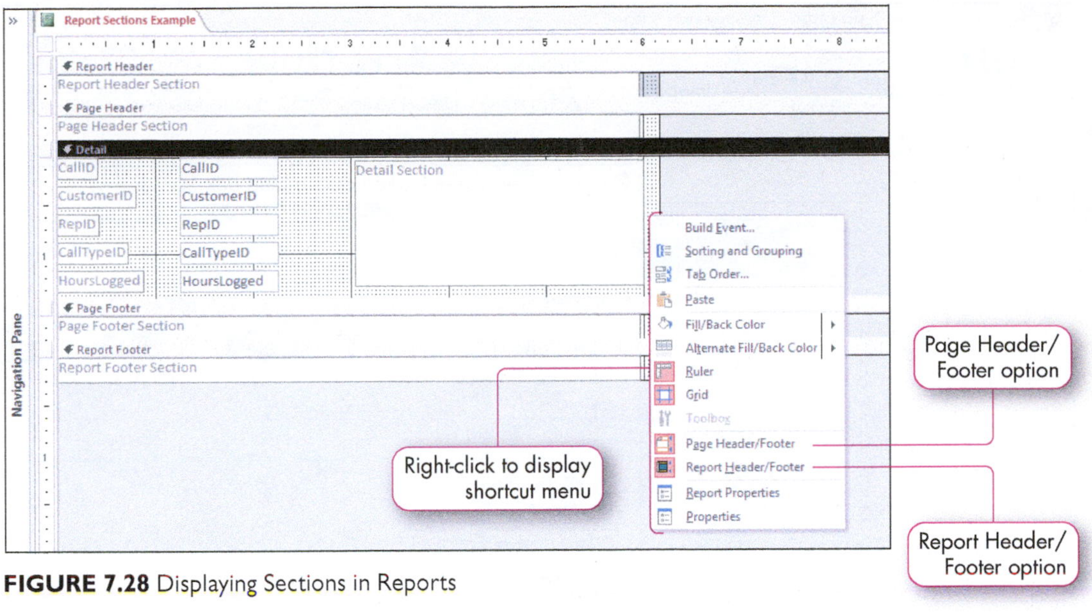

FIGURE 7.28 Displaying Sections in Reports

Within a form or report, you may want to change the height or width of portions of a section. The width is a global property. You cannot change the width of one section without changing it for the entire object. However, you can change the height of each section independently. In Figures 7.27 and 7.28, a **section bar** marks the top boundary of a section. You can expand or collapse the space between sections by moving the pointer over the section bar and dragging to the desired location. The top bar denotes the top boundary of the header. The bottom bar displays the top boundary of the footer. The grid-like area under the bars shows the space allotted to that section. If you decide that the allotted space for a particular section is not necessary, you can collapse that section fully so that the section bars are touching. The section remains in the report's design but will not take up any room on the Print Preview or the printed page.

Add Images to Form or Report Headers

Images can be useful especially when dealing with corporate forms and reports. Companies commonly use the same logo and colors on official publications. When creating a form or report, you can insert an image file containing the company logo or any other image. Often, the image is inserted in the header, so it displays on each page when printed or viewed on the screen.

To add an image to a form or report, complete the following steps:

1. Switch to Design view, and click the Design tab.
2. Click the Image control in the Controls group, as shown in Figure 7.29. If it is not visible, click More at the lower right of the Controls box.
3. Drag from the start point to the end point. The Insert Picture dialog box displays.
4. Browse to the location containing the image.
5. Click the image you want to insert and click Open.
6. Resize the image control as necessary.

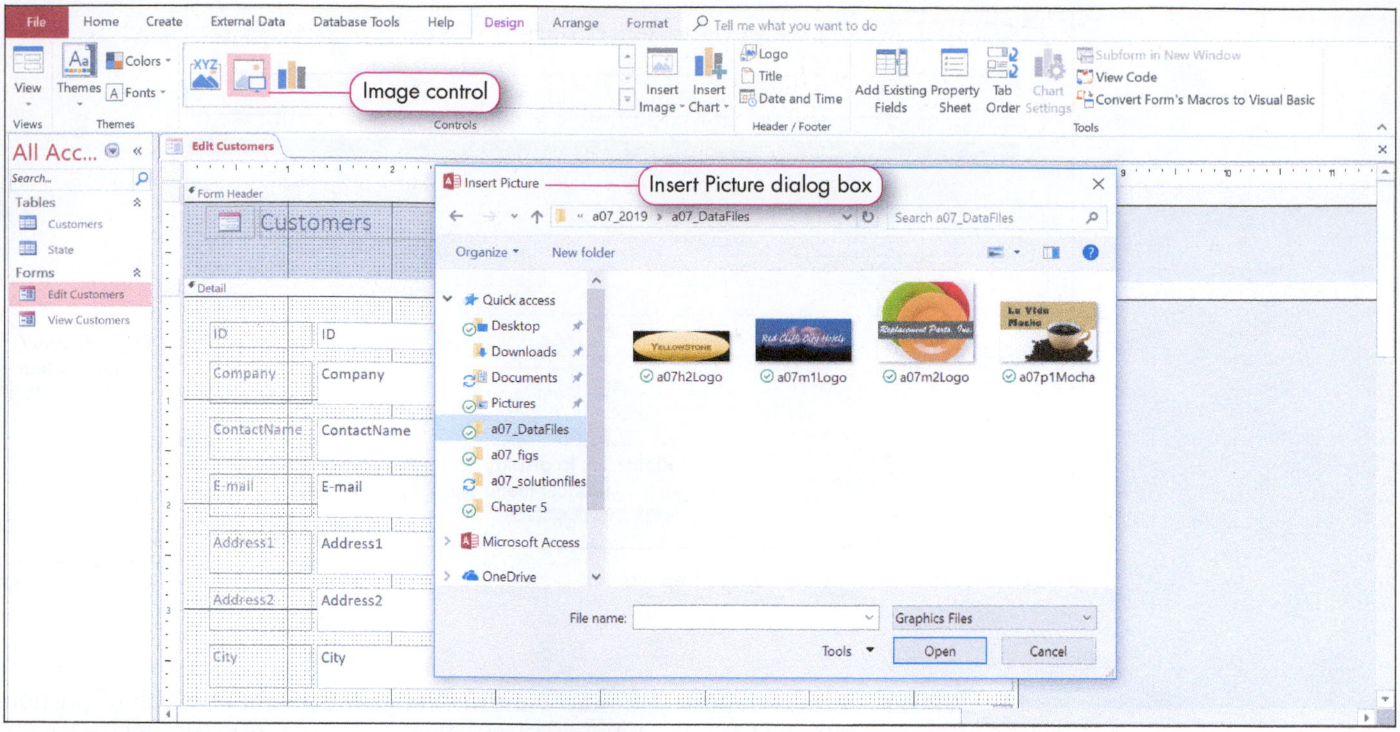

FIGURE 7.29 Image Control and Insert Picture Dialog Box

STEP 5 **Add a Group Header to Reports**

When grouping is added to a report, a group header and group footer are added to display the information. Note group headers and footers cannot be added to a form because forms do not support grouping. The *group header* is a section in a report that displays just above the Detail section in Design view along with the name of the field by which you are grouping. The group header displays once each time the grouping field value changes. For example, if you group by a State field, there can be up to 51 separate groups (including Washington, DC), and therefore, the group header could appear 51 times. Unlike the previous report, form, or page headers, the group header will not be identified by the name. Instead, it is identified by the field name followed by the word Header, so in the previous example, you would find a State Header section.

If you use the Report Wizard to create a report, you may have specified grouping and thus would find a group header in the report when you open in Design view. However, you can add a group header without the Report Wizard tool.

To add a group header to an existing report, complete the following steps:

1. Switch to Design view.
2. Click Group & Sort in the Grouping & Totals group on the Design tab (if the Group, Sort, and Total pane is not displayed at the bottom of the screen, as shown in Figure 7.30).
3. Click Add a group in the Group, Sort, and Total pane at the bottom of the screen.
4. Select the field to group by.

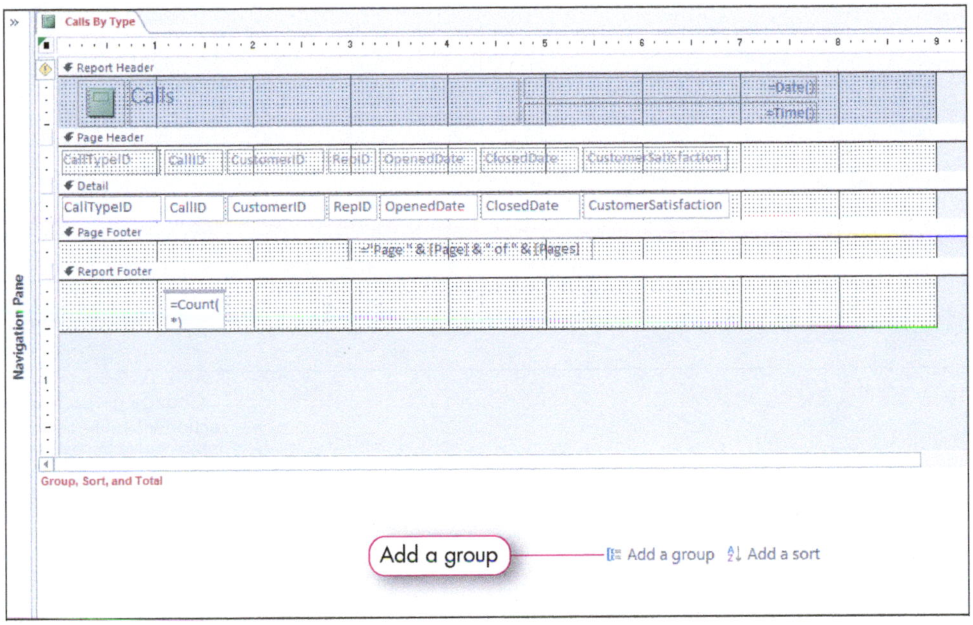

FIGURE 7.30 Group Header in a Report

Add a Group Footer to Reports

Likewise, the ***group footer*** is a section in a report that displays one time for each unique value in the grouping, below the group detail section. The Group footer displays aggregate data (count, sum, average, etc.) for the group. For example, it could show an average of customer satisfaction for each of the states.

The Group Footer section does not show by default. It displays below the Detail section in Design view, but only when you select this option in the Group, Sort, and Total pane. The group footer is useful for totalling the data at the end of each group. If you want to display the total number of calls for each technician, this could be displayed in the group footer.

Often, reports require totals at the group level and/or at the grand total level. For example, a report might contain a count of the number of calls each technician has handled and also display an overall total of the number of calls at the end of the report.

To add totals to a report that is grouped, complete the following steps:

1. Open the report in Design view.
2. Click More on the Group, Sort, and Total pane.
3. Click the option to the right of *without a footer section* and select *with a footer section*, as shown in Figure 7.31.
4. Select the *with no totals* option, and select the field, the function, and the options, as shown in Figure 7.32.

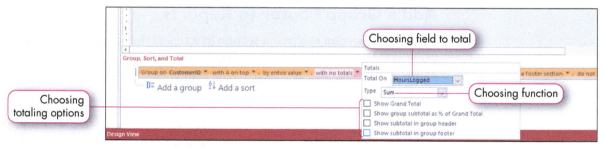

FIGURE 7.31 Group Footer in a Report

FIGURE 7.32 Adding Sum for HoursLogged Field

Figure 7.33 shows the sum for the HoursLogged field in Report view. Notice the total displays after Customer YS007 and the next set of records for customer YS009 begin.

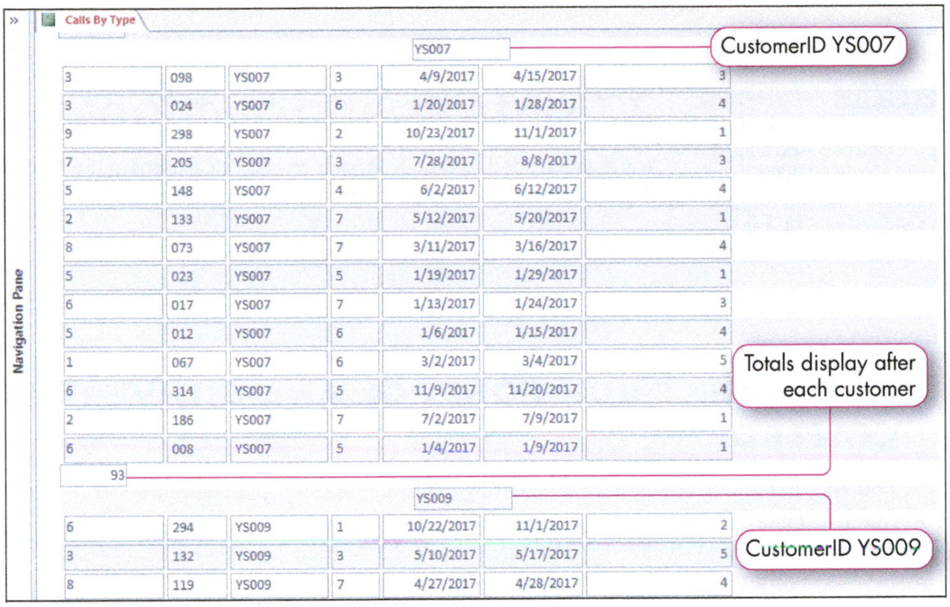

			YS007				CustomerID YS007
3	098	YS007	3	4/9/2017	4/15/2017	3	
3	024	YS007	6	1/20/2017	1/28/2017	4	
9	298	YS007	2	10/23/2017	11/1/2017	1	
7	205	YS007	3	7/28/2017	8/8/2017	3	
5	148	YS007	4	6/2/2017	6/12/2017	4	
2	133	YS007	7	5/12/2017	5/20/2017	1	
8	073	YS007	7	3/11/2017	3/16/2017	4	
5	023	YS007	5	1/19/2017	1/29/2017	1	
6	017	YS007	7	1/13/2017	1/24/2017	3	
5	012	YS007	6	1/6/2017	1/15/2017	4	
1	067	YS007	6	3/2/2017	3/4/2017	5	Totals display after each customer
6	314	YS007	5	11/9/2017	11/20/2017	4	
2	186	YS007	7	7/2/2017	7/9/2017	1	
6	008	YS007	5	1/4/2017	1/9/2017	1	
	93						
			YS009				
6	294	YS009	1	10/22/2017	11/1/2017	2	
3	132	YS009	3	5/10/2017	5/17/2017	5	CustomerID YS009
8	119	YS009	7	4/27/2017	4/28/2017	4	

FIGURE 7.33 Report with Totals

TIP: ADD A PAGE BREAK TO A GROUP FOOTER
A page break is commonly used in a group footer. Doing so causes each group to print on a separate page. For example, if you had a report grouped by customer, the report would print each customer's data on a separate page (rather than continuing with the next customer on the same page). This type of report is useful when the information is distributed to each customer. In the case that a customer's information takes up more than one page, the page break is inserted after each customer's information.

Quick Concepts

4. Explain the difference between a bound control and an unbound control. *p. 405*

5. List and briefly describe two controls found in the Controls group on the Design tab. *p. 406*

6. Discuss the purpose of a calculated control. *p. 405*

7. List and briefly describe the five default sections of a report. *p. 412*

8. Explain the purpose of a group header and footer. *p. 412*

Hands-On Exercises

MyLab IT HOE2 Sim Training

 Watch the Video for this Hands-On Exercise!

Skills covered: Add Text and Images to a Form or Report • Add a Calculated Control • Add a Page Break Control • Add a Chart Control • Show, Hide, and Resize Sections • Add a Group Header/Footer to Reports • Add Totals to a Footer

2 Controls and Sections

You have decided to modify reports to add calculations and to modify the different header and footer sections of forms and reports to improve the print and on-screen readability.

STEP 1 ADD A TEXT BOX CONTROL AND CONVERT TO A CALCULATED CONTROL

You will be making changes to an existing form and adding a calculated control to determine if a call is Open or Closed. Refer to Figure 7.34 as you complete Step 1.

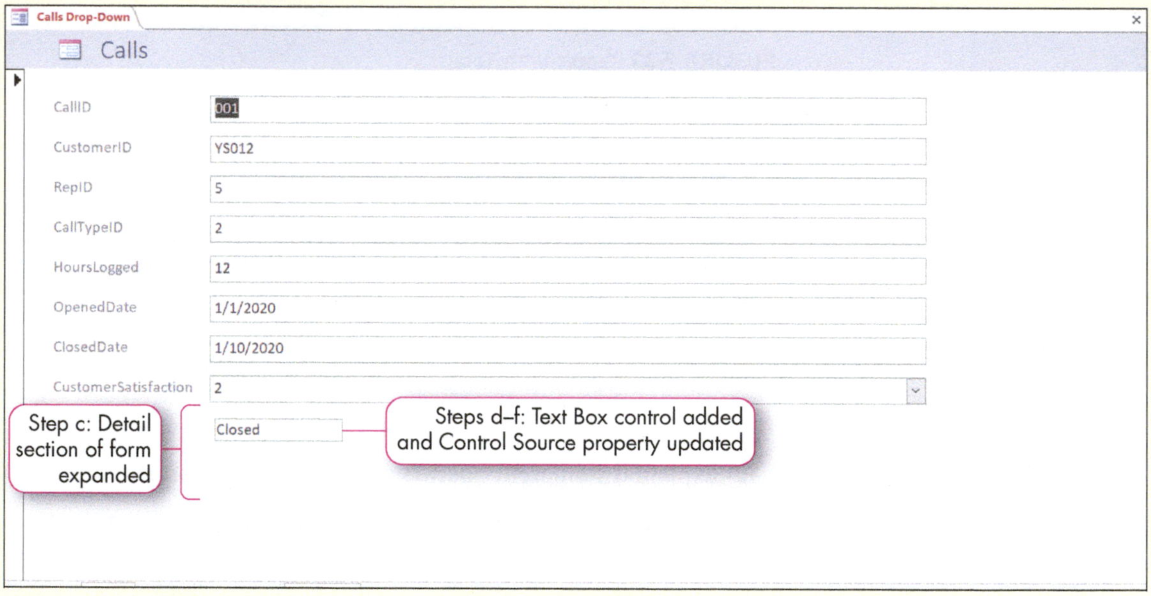

FIGURE 7.34 Calls Drop-Down Form

> Step c: Detail section of form expanded

> Steps d–f: Text Box control added and Control Source property updated

a. Open *a07h1Yellowstone_LastFirst* if you closed it at the end of Hands-On Exercise 1. Save the database as **a07h2Yellowstone_LastFirst**, changing h1 to h2.

b. Open the Calls Drop-Down form in Design view.

c. Click on the horizontal line above Form Footer, and drag the end of the Detail section (displayed right above the form footer) to about **4"** on the vertical ruler.

The Detail section of the form is expanded to accommodate the Text Box control to be added.

d. Click **Text Box** in the Controls group on the Design tab. Click beneath the last control in the form (CustomerSatisfaction) to insert the control. It should be placed approximately where it is shown in Figure 7.34.

e. Ensure the Property Sheet is displayed. Click the **Data tab** on the Property Sheet, click the **Control Source box**, and then click the **ellipses** next to the Control Source property to display the Expression Builder.

f. Type **IIf(IsNull([ClosedDate]), "Open","Closed")** and click **OK**.

This expression will display *Open* when the ClosedDate is null (in other words, when no value exists in the ClosedDate field) and *Closed* otherwise.

g. Click the label for the new control (the word *Text* followed by a number) and press **Delete**.

h. Switch to Form view. Ensure the first few records display *Closed*. Click the **Last record Navigation button**, and ensure the last record in the table has a value of *Open*.

As the open calls are going to be the most recent, most older calls will be closed, whereas most new calls will be open.

i. Save and close the form.

STEP 2 ## ADD A CALCULATED CONTROL TO A REPORT

You will make changes to an existing report to display the number of days each call has been open. Refer to Figure 7.35 as you complete Step 2.

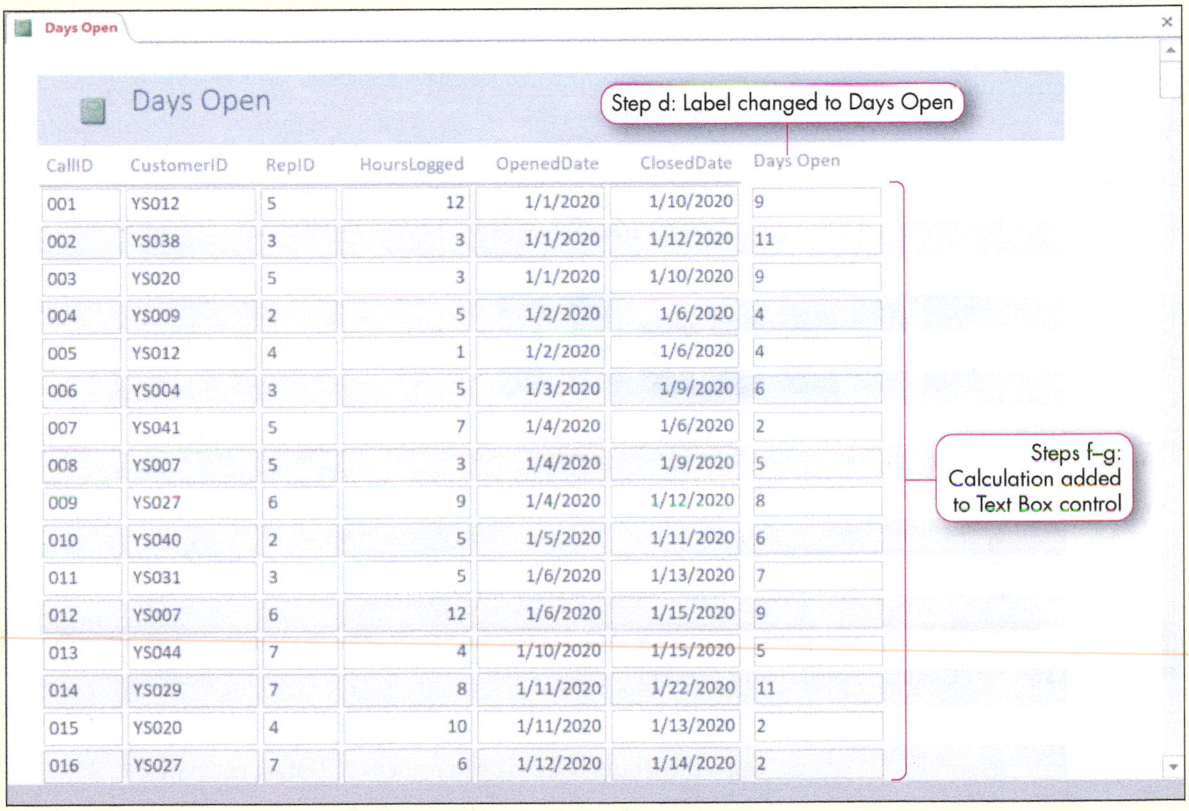

CallID	CustomerID	RepID	HoursLogged	OpenedDate	ClosedDate	Days Open
001	YS012	5	12	1/1/2020	1/10/2020	9
002	YS038	3	3	1/1/2020	1/12/2020	11
003	YS020	5	3	1/1/2020	1/10/2020	9
004	YS009	2	5	1/2/2020	1/6/2020	4
005	YS012	4	1	1/2/2020	1/6/2020	4
006	YS004	3	5	1/3/2020	1/9/2020	6
007	YS041	5	7	1/4/2020	1/6/2020	2
008	YS007	5	3	1/4/2020	1/9/2020	5
009	YS027	6	9	1/4/2020	1/12/2020	8
010	YS040	2	5	1/5/2020	1/11/2020	6
011	YS031	3	5	1/6/2020	1/13/2020	7
012	YS007	6	12	1/6/2020	1/15/2020	9
013	YS044	7	4	1/10/2020	1/15/2020	5
014	YS029	7	8	1/11/2020	1/22/2020	11
015	YS020	4	10	1/11/2020	1/13/2020	2
016	YS027	7	6	1/12/2020	1/14/2020	2

Step d: Label changed to Days Open

Steps f–g: Calculation added to Text Box control

FIGURE 7.35 Days Open Report with Calculation

a. Open the Days Open report in Design view.

b. Click the **Text Box control** in the Controls group on the Design tab. Click to the right of the ClosedDate text box in the Detail section of the report to add a new field.

c. Click the **Arrange tab**, and click **Tabular** in the Table group.

The new field lines up after the final column in the report.

d. Click the **Label control** for the new column in the Page Header section. Select the existing text and press **Delete**. Type **Days Open**.

e. Click the **Text Box control** for the new column (which currently displays the word *Unbound*). Display the Property Sheet, if it is not displayed.

f. Click the **Data tab** on the Property Sheet and click **Control Source**. Click the **ellipses** to launch the Expression Builder.

g. Type **=[ClosedDate]-[OpenedDate]** in the Expression box. Click **OK**.

h. Switch to Report view. Verify the calculation correctly displays the number of days each call was open, as shown in Figure 7.35.

i. Save and close the report.

STEP 3 ADD A CHART CONTROL TO A REPORT

You will create a new report to display a chart showing call data by the representative's last name. A query based on this data has already been created, and you will base the report on this query. Refer to Figure 7.36 as you complete Step 3.

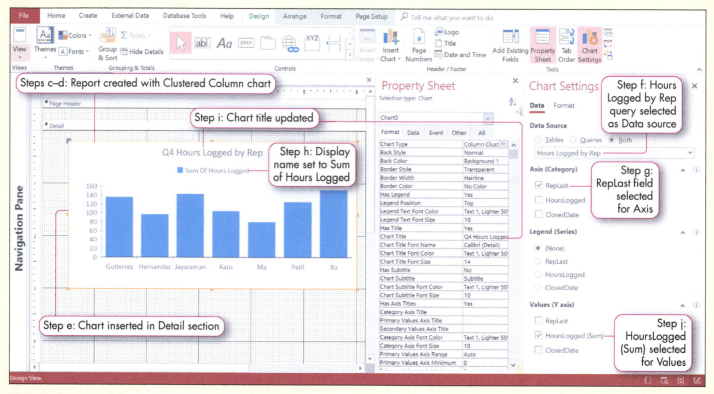

FIGURE 7.36 Chart Control Inserted into a Report

a. Open the Hours Logged by Rep query in Datasheet view.

The records for the query display the Representative last name, hours logged, and the date the call was closed. The query contains criteria to show only hours logged for the fourth quarter of 2020, between 9/1/2020 and 12/31/2020.

b. Close the query.

c. Click the **Create tab** and click **Report Design** in the Reports group.

A new blank report opens in Design view.

d. Click **Insert chart** on the Design tab, select **Column**, and then click **Clustered Column**.

e. Point to approximately **0.5"** on the horizontal ruler, drag the pointer to approximately **6.0"** on the horizontal ruler and approximately **3.0"** on the vertical ruler.

The chart control displaying sample data has been placed on the design grid. The Chart Settings task pane displays.

f. Click **Queries** on the Data tab in the Chart Settings task pane and select **Hours Logged by Rep** from the menu.

The chart is now bound to the Hours Logged by Rep query.

g. Select the **RepLast** field in the Axis section of the Chart Settings task pane and select the **HoursLogged (Sum)** field in the Values section of the Chart Settings task pane.

The chart now displays the total hours logged on the category axis and the representative last names along the bottom of the chart, the value axis. Observe that (Sum) has been placed next to the HoursLogged field on task pane. This is the default aggregate setting for the chart control. It can be changed by clicking the field name and changing the aggregation.

h. Click **Format tab** on the Chart Settings task pane and click the box next to Display name. Change the text to read: **Sum Of Hours Logged**. (Do not include the period.)

The chart legend now displays the text with the additional spaces.

i. Double-click the **Chart Title** to open the Chart Property sheet. Locate the Chart Title property on the Format tab and enter **Q4 Hours Logged by Rep** as the title. Close the Property Sheet.

The chart title is updated. Note the other chart settings that can be changed through the property sheet.

j. Click **Layout view** and review the report. Save the report as **Q4 Hours Logged by Rep** and close the report.

STEP 4 ## USE SECTIONS AND ADD AN IMAGE

You will adjust an existing form by adding a logo to the form header and adding a page header. Refer to Figure 7.37 as you complete Step 4.

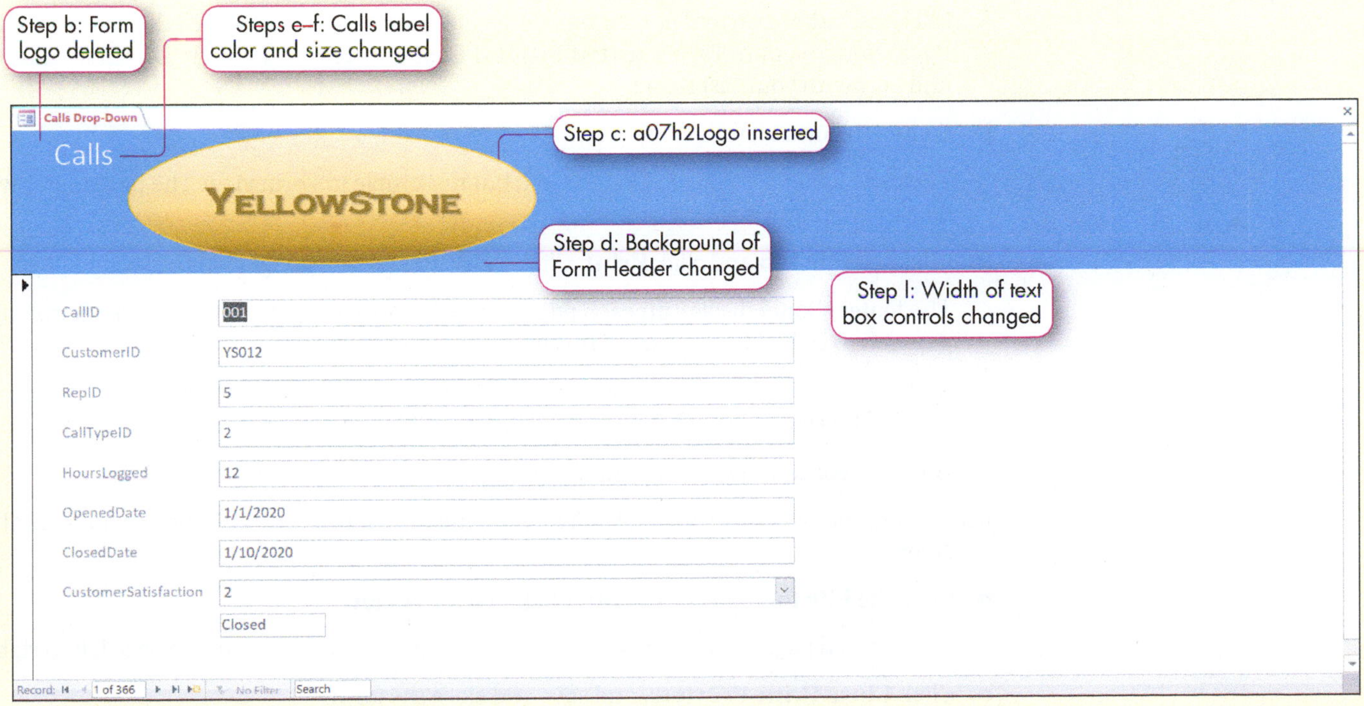

FIGURE 7.37 Updated Logo and Header

a. Open the Calls Drop-Down form in Design view.

b. Click the **form logo** (to the left of the word Calls) in the Form Header section and press **Delete**.

The form logo is removed from the form.

c. Click the **Image control** in the Controls group on the Design tab. Click to the right of the word *Calls* in the form header. Browse to the location of your data files and select *a07h2Logo.jpg*. Click **OK**.

> **TROUBLESHOOTING:** If you are unable to see the Image control in the Controls group on the Design tab, click More in the Controls group, and then click the Image control.

A logo for Yellowstone displays in the form header.

d. Click the **gray background** of the Form Header section. Click the **Format tab** and click the **Shape Fill arrow** in the Control Formatting group. Select **Blue, Accent 1** (first row, fifth column). Recall you can see the names for each color by pointing to a color and waiting for the ScreenTip to display.

e. Click the **Calls label** in the Form Header section. Click the **Font Color arrow** in the Font group on the Format tab. Select **White, Background 1** (first row, first column).

f. Click the **Font Size arrow** in the Font group on the Format tab. Change the size to **22**.

g. Switch to Form view and compare your form with Figure 7.37.

h. Switch to Design view. Right-click the grey background area in the Detail section and select **Page Header/Footer** from the shortcut menu.

A Page Header section displays above the Detail section and a Page Footer section displays below the Detail section.

i. Click the **Label control** in the Controls group on the Design tab. Click the left side of the Page Footer section. Type **Created by First Last**, replacing First with your first name and Last with your last name.

j. Switch to Form view.

The page footer is visible in Design view, but not visible in Form view. The page footer will display when printed.

k. Click the **File tab** and click **Print**. Click **Print Preview**. Navigate to the second page.

The footer should display on each page. You will notice the form is too wide to fit on one page left to right. When printed, this might lead to extra pages.

l. Right-click the **Calls Drop-Down tab** and select **Design View**. Scroll right and click the **CallID text box**, and change the width to **5.5"** on the horizontal ruler.

All other controls adjust as well.

m. Point to the right edge of the Detail section and drag it to about **7.5"** on the horizontal ruler.

n. Click the **File tab** and click **Print**. Click **Print Preview**.

As a printed page in Portrait is 8.5" wide, this report will now fit on one page left to right.

o. Click **Close Print Preview**, and save and close the form.

ADD A GROUP HEADER TO A REPORT

You will create a new report based on the Calls table and use the group headers and footers to summarize the data. Refer to Figure 7.38 as you complete Step 5.

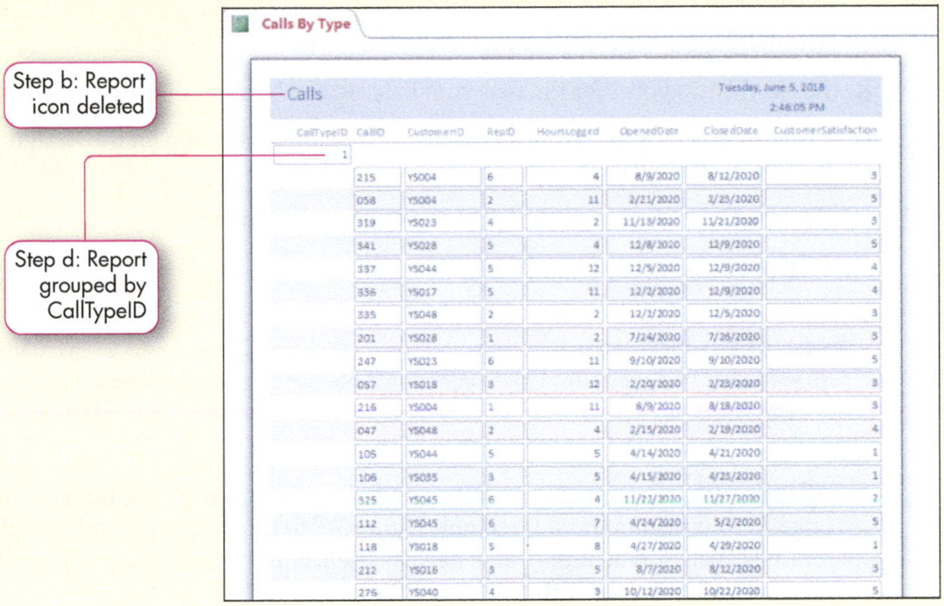

Step b: Report icon deleted

Step d: Report grouped by CallTypeID

FIGURE 7.38 Final Calls by Type Report

a. Click the **Calls table** in the Navigation Pane. Click **Report** in the Reports group on the Create tab.

b. Click the report icon (which displays to the left of the word *Calls*) from the report header and press **Delete**.

The report icon is deleted.

c. Click **Group & Sort** in the Grouping & Totals group on the Design tab, if it is not already shown.

The Group, Sort, and Total pane displays at the bottom of the report.

d. Click **Add a group** in the Group, Sort, and Total pane, and select **CallTypeID**.

The report will be grouped by the type of call.

e. Resize the RepID field so it fits on one page, left to right.

f. Switch to Design view.

Notice a CallTypeID Header section displays between the Page Header and Detail sections.

g. Click **More** in the Group, Sort, and Total pane. Click the **without a footer section arrow** and select **with a footer section**.

A CallTypeID footer section displays between the Detail and Page Footer sections.

h. Click the **HoursLogged text box**. Click **Totals** in the Grouping & Totals group on the Design tab and select **Sum**.

A Sum function appears in both the CallTypeID Footer and the report footer. A Count function displays in the CallID report footer section.

i. Right-click the **CallTypeID Footer section bar** and click **Properties**. Click the **All tab** on the Property Sheet. Change the height to **0.5"**.

The height of the CallTypeID Footer section is 0.5" tall.

j. Click the **Report Footer section bar**. On the Property Sheet for the Report Footer section bar, change the height to **0.5"**.

The height of the Report Footer section is 0.5" tall.

k. Resize the text boxes for the new sum fields to be about double the current height.

l. Click the **Insert Page Break control** in the Controls group on the Design tab. Click the bottom of the CallTypeID footer.

Six small dots display on the left of the CallTypeID footer.

m. Display the report in Print Preview.

> **TROUBLESHOOTING:** If an error message displays stating *The section width is greater than the page width, and there are no items in the additional space, so some pages may be blank*, try making the rows slightly less tall.

All calls with a CallTypeID display on page 1, with a total of 188 hours shown on page 2. Your results should resemble Figure 7.38. Due to the number of calls, the totals for CallTypeID 1 will display on a page by itself. Scroll forward and notice a total of 208 hours for all calls with a CallTypeID of 2.

n. Save the report as **Calls By Type** and close the report.

o. Close the database and exit Access. Based on your instructor's directions, submit a07h2Yellowstone_LastFirst.

Chapter Objectives Review

After reading this chapter, you have accomplished the following objectives:

1. Restrict edits in a form.
- Read-only forms enable users to view but not change data to help prevent erroneous data entry. Forms can be set to restrict changes, additions, and/or deletions.

2. Understand combo boxes.
- Convert a text box to a combo box: A Combo Box control displays a menu of options from which the user can choose a single value.
- Customize a combo box: Information can be looked up in a table or, less commonly, added manually to a combo box. You can restrict data entry to only the provided values.

3. Set the tab order.
- The tab order is the sequential advancing in a form from one field or control to the next when you press Tab. The tab order can be set automatically or manually.
- Set the tab order using Auto Order: The Auto Order command will attempt to order tabs in a logical order.
- Set tab order manually: If the Auto Order command does not fix the tab order, the order can be set manually. This is often the case with multiple columns.
- Remove a tab stop: Tab stops can be removed from any field. Often, they are removed from fields that do not require data entry, such as an Autonumber.

4. Understand subforms.
- A form can display records from a related table using a subform.
- Subforms are generally laid out as a table and are used when a relationship exists between two tables.
- Subforms can be manually added to any form using the Subform/Subreport tool. Assuming a relationship exists between two tables, it is a straightforward process.

5. Understand controls.
- Controls fall into one of three categories—bound, unbound, or calculated.
- A bound control is a category of control that is connected to a field in a table or query.
- An unbound control is a category of control not tied to a specific field, often decorative elements, such as titles, lines, pictures, and logos.
- Add a text box control: The Text Box control is used to display the data found in a record source (often, a table).
- Add a calculated control: A calculated control is placed inside a text box. It contains an expression that generates a calculated result. The Expression Builder enables you to create complex calculated controls.
- Add a label control to a form or report: The label control is a word or phrase to describe the data associated with a text box. For a field in a form or report, the label control defaults to the caption you set for a field.
- Add a chart control to a form or report: The chart control is a new feature for Office 2019 and enables you to display numeric data from a table or query.
- Add emphasis to a form or report using line and rectangle controls: The Line and Rectangle controls are among the options to add emphasis. Formatting can be adjusted.
- Add a Page Break control: You can specify exactly where to add a page break using the Page Break control.

6. Understand sections.
- A section is a part of a form or report that can be manipulated separately from other parts of the form or report. They are viewable in Design view.
- The Form Header section and the Report Header section are headers that display one time at the top of each form or report. The Form Footer and Report Footer sections are footers that display one time at the bottom of the form or report.
- The page header is a section that displays once at the top of each page in a form or report. The page footer is a section that displays once at the bottom of each page in a form or report.
- The Detail section displays the records in the data source.
- Show, hide, and resize sections: You can show or hide any missing section in Design view by right-clicking and selecting the section. Section boundaries are marked by a section bar that can be dragged up or down to resize a section.
- Add images to form or report headers: Images such as company logos can be added to forms and reports.
- Add a group header to reports: The group header is a section in a report that displays just above the Detail section in Design view along with the name of the field by which you are grouping. The group header displays once each time the grouping field value changes.
- Add a group footer to reports: The group footer is a section in a report that displays one time for each unique value in the grouping, below the group detail section.

Key Terms Matching

Match the key terms with their definitions. Write the key term letter by the appropriate numbered definition.

a. Bound control

b. Calculated control

c. Combo Box control

d. Control

e. Detail section

f. Form footer

g. Form header

h. Group footer

i. Group header

j. Page footer

k. Page header

l. Read-only form

m. Report footer

n. Report header

o. Section

p. Section bar

q. Subform

r. Tab order

s. Tab stop

t. Unbound control

1. _____ A form that enables users to view but not change data. **p. 390**

2. _____ A part of a form or report that can be manipulated separately from other parts of a form or report. **p. 412**

3. _____ A section that displays one time for each unique value in the grouping, above the group. **p. 416**

4. _____ A section that displays one time for each unique value in the grouping, below the group. **p. 417**

5. _____ A section that displays one time at the bottom of a form. **p. 412**

6. _____ A section that displays one time at the bottom of a report. **p. 412**

7. _____ A section that displays one time at the top of the report. **p. 412**

8. _____ An object on a form or report. **p. 405**

9. _____ A section that displays at the bottom of each page in a form or report. **p. 412**

10. _____ A section that displays at the top of each page in a form or report. **p. 412**

11. _____ A section that displays one time at the top of the form. **p. 412**

12. _____ A control not tied to a specific field. **p. 405**

13. _____ A control that is connected to a field in a table or query. **p. 405**

14. _____ A control that displays the result of an expression in a form or report. **p. 405**

15. _____ A form contained within another form. **p. 396**

16. _____ A control that provides a menu displaying a list of options from which the user can choose a single value. **p. 391**

17. _____ The section of the form or report where data is displayed. **p. 412**

18. _____ A marking that designates the top boundary of a section. **p. 415**

19. _____ The sequential advancing in a form from one field or control to the next when you press Tab. **p. 394**

20. _____ The location to which the insertion point moves each time Tab is pressed. **p. 394**

Multiple Choice

1. A form that is fully read-only permits you to:
   - (a) delete records.
   - (b) change data.
   - (c) view records.
   - (d) add records.

2. A menu can be created with a:
   - (a) calculated control.
   - (b) combo box.
   - (c) line control.
   - (d) section bar.

3. Which of the following statements about tab order is *true*?
   - (a) You *must* manually assign tab order if you wish to enable it.
   - (b) Fields cannot have their tab stop removed.
   - (c) Auto Order works well with two or more columns.
   - (d) Tab order can be automatically assigned by Access.

4. Which of the following would most likely be a subform?
   - (a) A list of primary care doctors for each patient
   - (b) A list of employees for a location
   - (c) A list of model names for a specific vehicle
   - (d) A list of birth mothers for a child

5. A control displaying the value of a field from a table or query is a(n):
   - (a) bound control.
   - (b) calculated control.
   - (c) rectangle control.
   - (d) unbound control.

6. A control containing =Date() is most likely to be a:
   - (a) bound control.
   - (b) calculated control.
   - (c) rectangle control.
   - (d) page break control.

7. Which of the following prints on every page of a form?
   - (a) Form header
   - (b) Group header
   - (c) Page header
   - (d) Report header

8. Which of the following statements is *false*?
   - (a) The Detail section displays the values of records.
   - (b) A Label control is used for text, such as titles.
   - (c) A calculated field is created with a Text Box control.
   - (d) Forms cannot display calculated controls.

9. Which of the following prints once per report?
   - (a) Form header
   - (b) Group header
   - (c) Page header
   - (d) Report header

10. Which of the following is available in a report but not in a form?
    - (a) Detail section
    - (b) Group Header section
    - (c) Form Header/Report Header section
    - (d) Page Footer section

Practice Exercises

1 La Vida Mocha

FROM SCRATCH

You are helping La Vida Mocha, a small coffee supply store, migrate to Access. You will add data basic validation and create two forms, one for data entry and one for viewing data. Refer to Figure 7.39 as you complete this exercise.

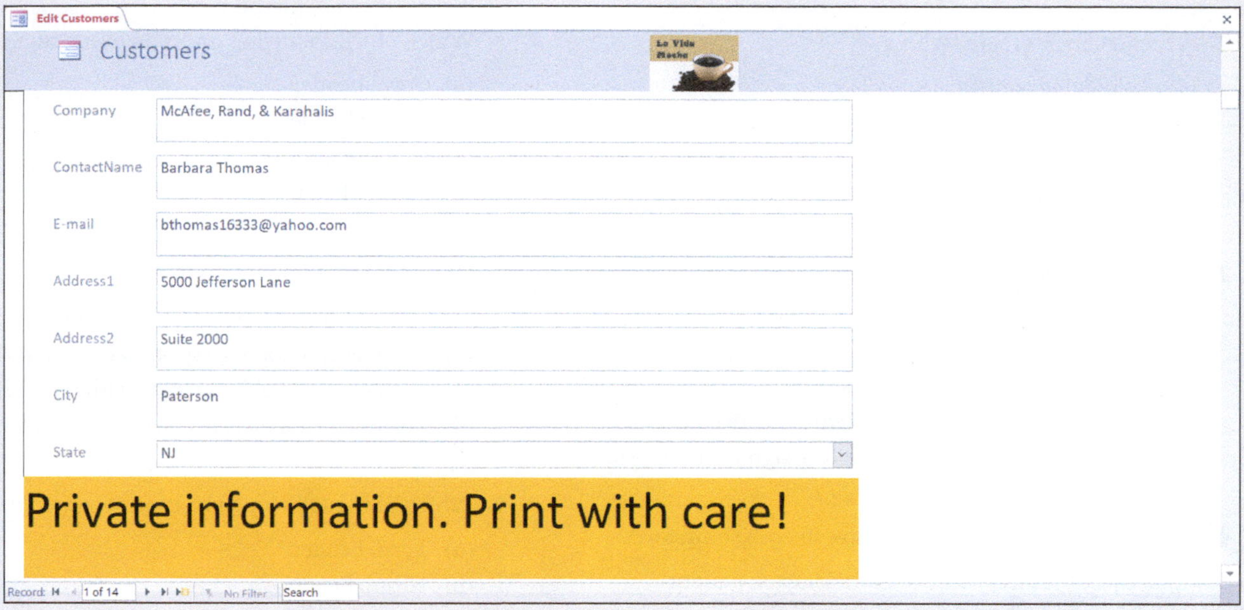

Big Pants Production/Shutterstock

FIGURE 7.39 Edit Customers Form

a. Open Access and create a new blank database named **a07p1Coffee_LastFirst**.

b. Close **Table1**. Click the **External Data tab** and click **New Data Source** in the Import & Link group. Select From File and click **Text File**. Ensure that the *Import the source data into a new table in the current database* is selected. Click **Browse** and navigate to your student data files. Select the file *a07p1States.txt*. Step through the wizard, naming the field **StateName**, changing the StateName field Indexed option to *Yes (No Duplicates)*, and choosing the StateName field as the primary key. Accept all other default properties. In the last step of the wizard, save the table as **State**.

c. Click the **External Data tab** and click **New Data Source** in the Import & Link group. Select From File and click **Text File**. Ensure that the *Import the source data into a new table in the current database* is selected. Click **Browse** and navigate to your student data files. Select the file *a07p1Customers.txt*. Step through the wizard, ensuring you check the **First Row Contains Field Names option** to select it. Accept default field names. For the ID field, change Indexed to *Yes (No Duplicates)*. Choose **ID** when asked to select a primary key. In the last step of the wizard, name the table **Customers**.

d. Click the **Customers table** in the Navigation Pane. Click **Form** in the Forms group on the Create tab. Save the form as **Edit Customers**.

e. Right-click the **State text box**, point to **Change To**, and then select **Combo Box** from the shortcut menu. If the Property Sheet is not displayed at the right of the screen, click **Property Sheet** in the Tools group on the Design tab to display it.

f. Change the Row Source property on the Data tab to **State**. Change the Limit To List property to **Yes**. Switch to Form view.

g. Change the State for the first customer to **NJ**, press **Tab**, type **Paterson** in the City, press **Tab**, and then type **07505** for Zip. You will notice the tab order is not logical (State, then City, then Zip).

h. Switch to Design view. Click **Tab Order** in the Tools group on the Design tab. Click **Detail** in the Section box of the Tab Order dialog box. Click the **record selector** to the left of the State field and drag it below the City field. Click **OK**.

i. Click the **Image control** in the Controls group. If it is not visible, click **More** at the lower right of the Controls box to display all controls first. Click at about **6"** on the horizontal ruler in the Form Header section and draw a box from the 6" on the horizontal ruler to the 7" on the horizontal rule and down to the bottom of the Header section, approximately 1". Browse to the location of your data files and select *a07p1Mocha.jpg*. Click **OK**.

j. Select the **Logo control** next to the Customers title and press **Delete**. Drag the **section bar** below the Form Footer section down to approximately **1"** on the vertical ruler.

k. Click the **Label control** in the Controls group on the Design tab. Click the **upper-left corner** of the Form Footer section (which is currently gray with dots in the background). Type the text **Private information. Print with care!** in the label. Click anywhere else in the Form Footer section to deselect the label.

l. Click the **border** of the label you created in the previous step to select the entire control. Click **Font Size arrow** in the Font group on the Format tab. Change the font size for the Label control to **36**. Resize the control so it is about 8" wide and 1" tall. Ensure the text is visible.

m. Click **Font Color arrow** in the Font group on the Format tab. Select the **Black, Text 1 color** in the first row.

n. Click **Background Color arrow** in the Font group on the Format tab. Select the **Gold, Accent 4 color** in the first row.

o. Click the **Design tab**. Click **Insert Page Break control** in the Controls group. If it is not visible, click More at the lower right of the Controls box to display all controls first. Click along the left margin underneath the SalesRepID field in the Details section to add a page break after each customer.

p. Drag the **right border** of the Detail section to be about **8"** wide. Switch to Form view and compare your form with Figure 7.39.

q. Click the **File tab** and click **Print**. Click **Print Preview**. Notice only one customer displays on the first page. Click **Next Page** three times to notice how each page contains a single customer.

r. Save and close the form. Create a copy of the form and name it **View Customers**. Open View Customers form in Design view.

s. Change the title at the top of the form to **Customers (View Only)**.

t. Display the Property Sheet. Ensure the menu at the top of the Property Sheet displays *Form*. Ensure the Data tab is displayed and change the options **Allow Additions**, **Allow Deletions**, and **Allow Edits** to **No** to create a read-only form. Switch to Form view and ensure you cannot add, change, or delete records.

u. Save and close the form.

v. Close the database and exit Access. Based on your instructor's directions, submit a07p1Coffee_LastFirst.

2 International Importers

You are a technical supervisor at International Importers. The technician who handles most Access tasks just went on paternity leave, and he was unable to address user change requests before going on leave. You will create a form and report based on user requests. Refer to Figure 7.40 as you complete this exercise.

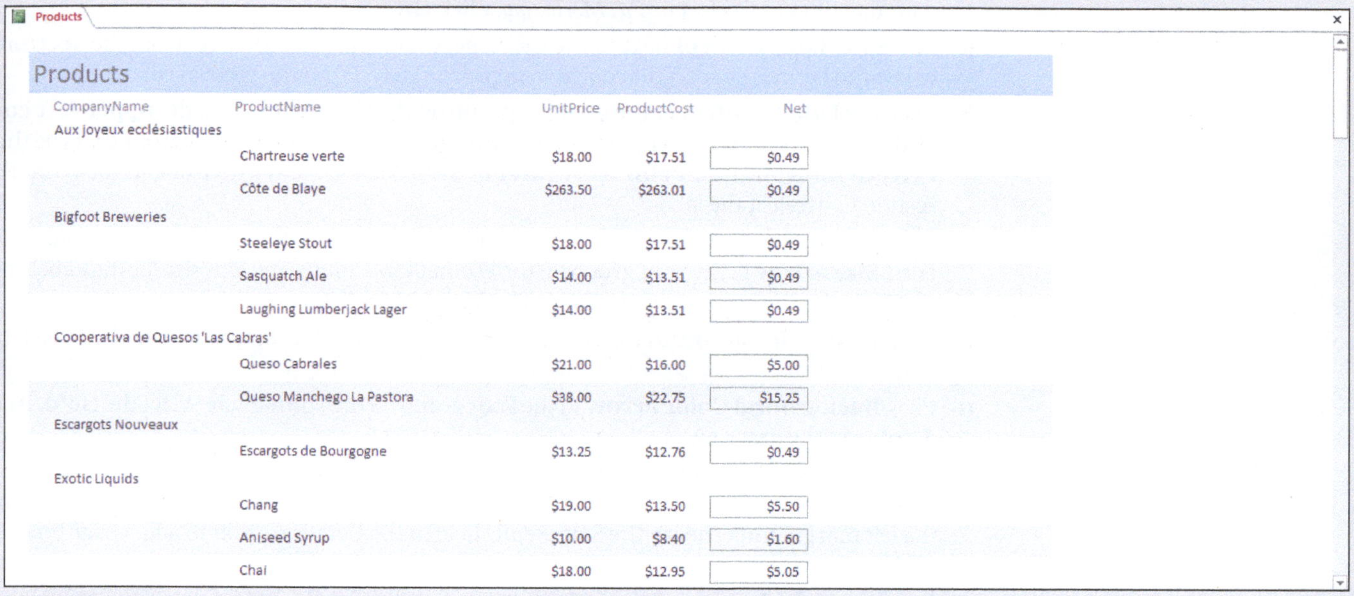
Products

CompanyName	ProductName	UnitPrice	ProductCost	Net
Aux joyeux ecclésiastiques				
	Chartreuse verte	$18.00	$17.51	$0.49
	Côte de Blaye	$263.50	$263.01	$0.49
Bigfoot Breweries				
	Steeleye Stout	$18.00	$17.51	$0.49
	Sasquatch Ale	$14.00	$13.51	$0.49
	Laughing Lumberjack Lager	$14.00	$13.51	$0.49
Cooperativa de Quesos 'Las Cabras'				
	Queso Cabrales	$21.00	$16.00	$5.00
	Queso Manchego La Pastora	$38.00	$22.75	$15.25
Escargots Nouveaux				
	Escargots de Bourgogne	$13.25	$12.76	$0.49
Exotic Liquids				
	Chang	$19.00	$13.50	$5.50
	Aniseed Syrup	$10.00	$8.40	$1.60
	Chai	$18.00	$12.95	$5.05

FIGURE 7.40 Products Report

a. Open *a07p2Importers*. Save the database as **a07p2Importers_LastFirst**.

b. Open the Orders form in Design view.

c. Click **Subform/Subreport** in the Controls group on the Design tab. If it is not visible, click More at the lower right of the Controls box to display all controls first. Click below the Freight label along the left margin.

d. Answer the Subform Wizard as follows:
- Accept the default Use Existing Tables and Queries and click **Next**.
- Select **Table: Orders** from the Tables/Queries list. Double-click **ProductID Quantity**, and **Discount**. Click **Next**.
- Accept the default relationship (Show Order Details for each record in Orders using OrderID). Click **Next**.
- Accept the default name of Order Details subform. Click **Finish**.

e. Switch to Layout view. Select the Order Details subform label and press **Delete**. Adjust the column widths in the subform so all fields are displayed.

f. Right-click the **ShipVia text box**. Point to **Change To** and select **Combo Box** from the shortcut menu.

g. Click **Property Sheet** in the Tools group, if it is not displayed on the right side of the screen. Click the Row Source Property on the Data tab. Click in the box and click the arrow to the right of the box. Select **Shippers** from the menu. Click the **ellipsis** to the right of the Row Source Property. In the query window, double-click the **ShipperID** and the **CompanyName** fields (in that order) to add them to the query. Save and close the query window.

h. Click the **Limit To List property** and change the value to **Yes** so users can only input values found in the list.

i. Switch to Form view. Notice the arrow at the right side of the ShipVia field, indicating you can now choose the Shipper from a menu. Close the form, saving all changes.

j. Open the Products report in Layout view. Click **Add a group** in the Group, Sort, and Total pane at the bottom of the screen. Select **CompanyName**. Notice the CompanyName field is not wide enough to display all values.

k. Switch to Design view. Drag the right margin of the CompanyName field (displayed in the CompanyName Header) to **4"** on the horizontal ruler. Widen the ProductCost in the Detail section to ensure the field name is completely visible.

l. Click the **Text Box control** in the Controls group on the Design tab. Click to the right of the ProductCost box in the Detail section.

m. Click **Tabular** in the Table group on the Arrange tab to move the label to the Page Header section.

n. Click the **label** for the control (which currently displays the word *Text* followed by a number) to select the label. Double-click the **label** to select the text in the label. Change the text in the label from the existing text to **Net**.

o. Double-click the **text box** for the new field (which currently displays *Unbound*) and type **=[UnitPrice]-[ProductCost]** in the box.

p. Click the **Format tab** on the Property Sheet. Change the format property to **Currency** and change the Decimal Places property to **2**. Close the Property Sheet.

q. Click the **Rectangle control** in the Controls group on the Design tab. If it is not visible, click **More** at the lower right of the Controls box to display all controls first. Draw a rectangle around the text box you just created (which currently displays =[UnitPrice]-[ProductCost]).

r. Click the **Format tab**. Click the **Shape Fill arrow** in the Control Formatting group. Select **Transparent**.

s. Switch to Report view. Compare your report with Figure 7.40.

t. Save and close the report.

u. Close the database and exit Access. Based on your instructor's directions, submit a07p2Importers_LastFirst.

Mid-Level Exercises

1 Red Cliffs City Hotels

ANALYSIS CASE

You are the general manager of a large hotel chain. You track revenue by categories: hotel rooms, conference rooms, and weddings. You will create a form that includes a menu for the state and the company logo in the header, uses the company colors, and has a correct tab order. You also plan on modifying a report so it displays the number of years that each customer has been a member.

a. Open *a07m1Rewards*. Save the database as **a07m1Rewards_LastFirst**.

b. Select the **Members table** and create a form using the Form tool. Save the form as **Maintain Members**.

c. Switch to Design view. Change the State text box to a combo box.

d. Change the Row Source to **States**.

e. Delete the form logo and the Label control (containing the word *Members*) from the Form Header section.

f. Insert an Image control in the upper-left corner of the Form Header section about 5" wide and 2" tall. Insert the *a07m1Logo.jpg* file.

g. Change the background color of the Detail section to the orange color found in the first row (**Orange, Accent 6**). Use the Property Sheet to make this change.

h. Select all the labels in the Detail section by drawing a box around them. Using the Property Sheet, change the font color of the labels to **Black, Text 1**. Change the border width of the labels to **2 pt** and the border color to **Blue, Accent 1**.

i. Switch to Form view. Verify the tab order does not work as expected by pressing **Tab** to visit each field (State comes before City). Correct the tab order so it proceeds in a logical order from top to bottom. Save and close the form.

j. Open the Members By State report in Design view.

k. Add a formula in the **Time as Member box** in the Details section (which currently displays *Unbound*) to determine the number of years they have been a member. Use **#12/31/2020#** as the current date (recall dates must be surrounded by # signs), subtract the **MemberSince** field, and divide the result by **365**.

l. Change the format of the formula from the previous step using the Property Sheet, to display as **Standard format** with **1** decimal place. Select the MemberSince field label and change the Gridline Style Bottom property to **Solid**. Align the field label as necessary.

m. Add grouping by the State field ensuring *with a header section* is selected. Add a sort (after the State grouping) to the MemberSince field. Sort oldest to newest.

n. Switch to Report view. Ensure the values displayed make sense. For example, assuming a current date of 12/31/2020, member Melissa Remaklus has been a member since 11/8/2006, so she has been a member for slightly more than 14 years. Also notice after the members from Alaska (AK), there is a break before the members from Alabama (AL) due to the grouping you added.

o. Save and close the report.

p. Open the *a07m1Analysis.docx* document in Word and save as **a07m1Analysis_LastFirst**. Use the database objects you created to answer the questions. Save and close the document.

q. Close the database. Exit Access. Based on your instructor's directions, submit the following files:

a07m1Rewards_LastFirst

a07m1Analysis_LastFirst.docx

2 Replacement Parts

You are working as a stockperson in the warehouse for Replacement Parts. You have received an internship in the Information Technology Department. You have been tasked with making modifications to the company database. Because you hope to move from being a stockperson to being a member of the technology staff, you want to impress and go above and beyond what has been asked of you.

a. Open *a07m2Replace*. Save the database as **a07m2Replace_LastFirst**.

b. Create a new form based on the Employees table using the Form tool. Save the form as **Employees Lookup**.

c. Delete the subform. Change the form to be read-only, ensuring users cannot add, delete, or edit records.

d. Change the title in the form header to **Employees (Lookup Only)**. Save and close the form.

e. Open the Customer Orders report in Design view.

f. Insert the *a07m2Logo.jpg* image using an Image control in the report header to the right of the Customer Orders text. Resize the image so that it is approximately 2" wide by 1" tall. Ensure the report header is approximately 1" tall.

g. Change the option in the Group, Sort, and Total pane so the grouping on OrderID displays with a footer section. Change the option from *with no totals* to total on the **Qty field** and to show the subtotal in the group footer. Add a Label control at about **5"** (to the left of the sum of the Qty field) in the OrderID footer that displays **Total Qty Ordered**.

h. Add a new Text Box control after the Price field in the Detail section. Click **Tabular** in the Table group on the Arrange tab.

i. Change the label for the new control to **Line Total**. Add a formula in the text box to multiply the Qty field by the Price field.

j. Change the format of the Line Total text box to **Currency**.

k. Use the Line control to add a horizontal line at the bottom of the OrderID footer that covers half of the width of the report. Press and hold **Shift** as you draw the line to help keep it straight.

l. Switch to Report view and ensure the Total Qty Ordered values display correctly. Switch to Design view.

m. Save and close the report.

n. Close the database and exit Access. Based on your instructor's directions, submit a07m2Replace_LastFirst.

Running Case

New Castle County Technical Services

New Castle County Technical Services (NCCTS) provides technical support for a number of local companies. You will be creating a new form to enable call information to be added and deleted (but not modified). To ease data entry, you will convert the call type to a combo box. You will also modify an existing form to fix problems with the tabbing, add a subform, and make the form more attractive. You will then modify an existing report to add grouping by customer, display average satisfaction for each customer, and set the form so at the most one customer displays on a page.

a. Open *a07r1NCCTS* and save the database as **a07r1NCCTS_LastFirst**.

b. Create a new form based on the Calls table using the Form tool. Change the form properties for Allow Edits, Allow Deletions, and Allow Additions to **No**.

c. Change the CallTypeID field to a Combo Box and set the row source to the Call Types table. Set the Limit to List property to **Yes**.

d. Save the form as **Call Logs** and close the form.

e. Open the Customer Information form in Form view. Press **Tab** six times and notice the inconsistent ordering of the fields. Switch to Design view.

f. Change the tab order so the fields display in the following order: CustomerID, CompanyName, Address, City, State, Zip, Phone.

g. Change the Tab Stop property for the CustomerID field to **No**.

h. Switch to Design view. Create a new subform using the **Subform/Subreport control** beneath the Phone field label. You should include all fields from the Calls table, use the default relationship, and accept the default name for the subform.

i. Switch to Layout view and resize the subform to be as wide as necessary to display all the data.

j. Switch to Design view. Add a vertical **Line Control**, starting to the right of the CustomerID field in the Detail section and continuing down to the bottom of the page.

k. Add a Label control to the Form Header section at the **5"** mark. Type **New Castle County Technical Services** in the control and change the font color to **Black, Text 1**.

l. Save and close the form.

m. Open the Calls by Customer report in Layout view.

n. Change the option so the CompanyName grouping displays with a footer section.

o. Display the average of the CustomerSatisfaction field, choosing the **Show subtotal in group footer** option.

p. Format the average of the CustomerSatisfaction field as **Standard** with **2** decimal places.

q. Switch to Design view and add a Page Break control to the bottom of the CompanyName footer.

r. Click in the Report Header section. Add a Hyperlink control. You plan on creating a link to the NCCTS website, but the website is not yet published, so you will create a link and modify it later. For the moment, the hyperlink should link to the address **http://www.google.com**, and the text to display should be **Google**. Move the hyperlink to the **4"** mark.

s. Switch to Report view and click the **Google link** to test it. The link should open in your default browser. Close the browser and return to Access.

t. Switch to Print Preview. Ensure the average of the CustomerSatisfaction field is displayed for each customer and each customer starts on a new page. Save and close the report.

u. Close the database and exit Access. Based on your instructor's directions, submit a07r1NCCTS_LastFirst.

Disaster Recovery

Ramos Medical Care

As a recent graduate of a Medical Informatics program, you are working in the healthcare field at Ramos Medical Care. A database recently crashed, and you were able to restore the database from a backup. The data are correct, but your supervisor identified some form and report issues. Open *a07d1Ramos* and save it as **a07d1Ramos_LastFirst**. Address the following problems:

- The Patient Lookup form used to be read-only, and users could not change, add, or delete information from the form. In addition, there used to be a single rectangular box with a black border surrounding all the fields in the Detail section. Add the rectangular box back to the form.
- The Intake form's tab order no longer works correctly. In addition, the State field used to be a menu, displaying the values found in the State Abbreviations table. The list should limit input to only the values on the list.
- The Medications by Room report used to be grouped by the patient's SSN and was sorted by MedicationName.
- The Illness Statistics report prompts for "Date" every time it is opened and no longer displays the current date in the page footer.

After updating the database, close the database and exit Access. Based on your instructor's directions, submit a07d1Ramos_LastFirst.

International Specialties Inc.

International Specialties Inc. asked you to assist them in updating the database they are using. The company requires a form that can be used to find customer information but not change that information. In addition, you will enhance the new form and generate a report showing which employees report to each supervisor.

Database File Setup

You will save a copy of the original database to complete this capstone exercise.

1. Open *a07c1Specialties*.
2. Save the database as **a07c1Specialties_LastFirst**.

Create a Read-Only Form

You will create a form to view customer information. Use the Form tool to create the form, and then switch the form to be read-only.

3. Select the **Customers table** and use the Form tool to create a new form.
4. Change the title to **View Customers**.
5. Delete the **Orders subform**.
6. Change the Allow Edits, Allow Additions, and Allow Deletions settings to **No**.
7. View the form in Form view and ensure you cannot edit, add, or delete records.
8. Save the form as **View Customers**.

Convert a Text Box to a Combo Box and Customize Tabbing

You will modify the newly created form to implement a menu and modify the tab order.

9. Create a new table named **Countries** using data imported from the file *a07c1Specialties.xlsx*. There should be one field named Country. Ensure a data type of **Short Text**. There should not be a primary key.
10. Ensure the View Customers form is open in Design view and change the Country field to a combo box.
11. Fix the tab order so the Postal Code field comes before the Country field. Test the form. Save the form.

Add Controls to Forms and Reports and Use Sections

You were asked to add some privacy information to the bottom of the View Customers form and make some design changes. You were also asked to create a report for managers that shows the name of all employees who work for them and calculates the number of years the employees have been employed at the company.

12. Open the **View Customers form** in Design view. Increase the size of the Form Footer section and add a new Label control on the left side of the form footer that displays the text **Customer information is considered private. All employees must adhere to GDPR guidelines.**
13. Change the font color to **Black, Text 1** and bold the text.
14. Save and close the form.
15. Create a new report in Design view.
16. Insert a Pie chart in the Details section starting at 0.5" on the vertical ruler and 0.5" on the horizontal ruler. The right side of the chart should align with the 6" mark on the horizontal ruler and the 3" mark on the vertical ruler.
17. Use the **Freight Costs query** as the data source, the **ShipCountry** as the Category Axis and the **Freight** as the Value Axis. Add a chart title, **Freight Costs by Country** and display data labels for the chart.
18. Save the report as **Freight Costs**. Close the report.
19. Create a new report using the Report Wizard. From the Employees table, select the **ReportsTo**, **FirstName**, **LastName**, **HireDate**, and **HomePhone fields** in that order. Accept all other default options.
20. Switch to Layout view. Add grouping by the **ReportsTo** field.
21. Switch to Design view. Switch the option to **with a footer section** in the Group, Sort, and Total pane. Use the pane to also display the count of the First Name field in the Group Footer section.
22. Add an **Insert Page Break control** at the bottom of the ReportsTo footer section.
23. Resize the Home Phone field so the right side lines up with the 8" on the horizontal ruler.
24. Add a new **Text Box control** to the right of the Home Phone box. Use **Tabular** in the Table group on the Arrange tab to place it correctly.
25. Change the label for the field to **Yrs Employed** and resize the Years Employed field so the right side lines up with the 9" on the horizontal ruler.
26. Add a formula in the text box to calculate the number of years since the employee's hire date, assuming the current date is #12/31/2020#. Format the field as **Standard** with **1** decimal place.
27. Adjust the height of the Detail section, using the Properties Sheet, to 0.375". Change the report orientation to **Landscape**.
28. Close and save the report. Close the database and exit Access. Based on your instructor's directions, submit a07c1Specialties_LastFirst.

LEARNING OUTCOME   You will exchange data between Access and other applications or websites.

OBJECTIVES & SKILLS: After you read this chapter, you will be able to:

Connect Access to External Files

OBJECTIVE 1: CREATE A HYPERLINK FIELD   440
Add a Hyperlink Field in Design View, Enter Hyperlinks in Datasheet View, Edit a Hyperlink Value

OBJECTIVE 2: ADD AN ATTACHMENT FIELD   442
Create an Attachment Field in Design View, Add Attachments in Datasheet View, Remove an Attachment in Datasheet View

OBJECTIVE 3: ADD ATTACHMENT CONTROLS TO FORMS AND REPORTS   445
Add an Attachment Control to a Report

HANDS-ON EXERCISE 1   448

Export Data to Office and Other Applications

OBJECTIVE 4: EXPORT DATA TO EXCEL   454
Export a Query to Excel, Export a Report to Excel

OBJECTIVE 5: EXPORT DATA TO WORD   457
Export a Query to Word, Modify an RTF File in Word

OBJECTIVE 6: EXPORT DATA TO A PDF OR XPS DOCUMENT   460
Export to a PDF or XPS Document

OBJECTIVE 7: EXPORT OBJECTS TO ANOTHER ACCESS DATABASE   462
Export a Table to Another Database, Export a Form to Another Database

HANDS-ON EXERCISE 2   464

Import and Link Data in Access Databases

OBJECTIVE 8: LINK TO AN ACCESS TABLE   471
Examine the Tables in the Source Database, Link to an Access Table, Append Linked Data to an Existing Table

OBJECTIVE 9: LINK TO AND IMPORT AN EXCEL SPREADSHEET   474
Examine the Format of an Excel Spreadsheet, Link to an Excel Spreadsheet, Create a Table from a Linked Spreadsheet

OBJECTIVE 10: IMPORT AN EXCEL SPREADSHEET   476
Import a Spreadsheet into Access

OBJECTIVE 11: IMPORT A TEXT FILE   477
Examine the Text File Before Importing, Import a Text File into Access, Append Imported Data to an Existing Table

HANDS-ON EXERCISE 3   480

CASE STUDY | Property Management Data Exchange

The Blackwood Maintenance Service (BMS) is a property management company located in Pineville, North Carolina. The owners want to attract new customers by expanding the services they offer. Many of the properties that are maintained by BMS belong to residents' associations.

Your task is to contact the board members of each association and ask them if you can send information about the new services. You will also ask permission to send the homeowners a flyer by regular mail.

After contacting each association, you send the association manager a list of the new services that BMS can offer the homeowners. In addition, you create a list of homeowners whom BMS will contact by mail. Each association has its own preferred format, so you prepare the information in a variety of ways. Information is also received by BMS in a variety of formats that you incorporate as new data into the database.

CHAPTER 8

Exchanging Data Between Access and Other Applications

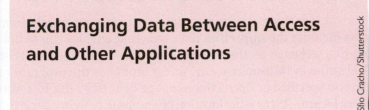

Sfio Cracho/Shutterstock

All Access Obj... «

Tables ≫
- Agents
- Customers
- Inspection Properties
- New Properties CSV
- New SubDivisions Homes
- Properties
- SubDivision
- Staffing Agents
- New SubDivisions

Queries ≫
- Append Davidson Propert...
- Append Staffing Agents
- Properties Built on or Bef...
- Service Request
- The Woodlands Owners

Forms ≫
- Agents
- Properties

Reports ≫
- Service Request Report

Service Request Report

Service Request Report

Listing	Subdivision	Contact Person	Homeowner	Address	City	Photo
10033	The Woodlands	Louise Davis	Lucy Ericson	864 Balsamwood	Woodlyn	
10068	The Woodlands	Louise Davis	Lucy Ericson	3510 Pinewood	Woodlyn	

Page 1 of 1

top: Artazum/Shutterstock; bottom: Artazum/Shutterstock

FIGURE 8.1 Property Management Data Exchange Database

CASE STUDY | Property Management Data Exchange

Starting Files	Files to be Submitted
a08h1Property	**a08h2Woodlands_LastFirst.xlsx**
a08h1Photos folder	**a08h2Service_LastFirst.xlsx**
a08h2Propexport	**a08h2Sub_LastFirst.docx**
a08h3Propstaff	**a08h2Service_LastFirst.pdf**
a08h3Propsub.xlsx	**a08h2Propexport_LastFirst**
a08h3Propinspect.xlsx	**a08h3Property_LastFirst**
a08h3Propnew.csv	

MyLab IT Grader An alternate version of this project is available as a MyLab IT Grader Assessment

Connect Access to External Files

At times, it is advantageous to connect to data that exist separately from an Access database. Access includes the *hyperlink* data type that enables you to link to a file on your computer, to a webpage on the Internet, or to an email address. When you click a hyperlink field value in Datasheet view, Access launches the program required and displays the file you specified or opens the webpage defined by the URL you entered. A *uniform resource locator (URL)* is the location of a website or webpage on the Internet. If the hyperlink is an email address, Access launches a new email window and automatically enters the email address in the To field.

Access also offers you the option of attaching files to records in a database through an attachment field. An attachment field enables you to attach multiple files of different types. Rather than links that direct you outside of your database, attachments are stored within the database file itself. For example, in a customers table, you can attach a photo of a key contact with whom you work. You can also attach other file types, such as Word documents, Excel spreadsheets, or documents in PDF format.

In this section, you will learn to create a hyperlink field to store website addresses. In addition, you will learn how to attach files to records. Finally, you will learn how to use an attachment control in forms and reports.

STEP 1 Creating a Hyperlink Field

You can add a hyperlink field in Design view (or Datasheet view) of a table to store website locations (URLs), email addresses, or links to files on your system. In addition to adding a hyperlink field in Design view of a table, you can also add it in Datasheet view by selecting *Click to Add* in the column header. You can access information about customers or organizations you are working with—the addresses, phone numbers, or contact information—from within an Access table by adding hyperlinks to their websites or other relevant documents stored outside the database. For example, if you have a database that contains a customers table, you can add a hyperlink field to store the website address of each customer.

After creating the new field with the Hyperlink data type assigned, you would then add the URLs, email addresses, or links to files in the datasheet, as shown in Figure 8.2, or in a form. Clicking a hyperlink value launches the appropriate program, such as a Web browser, Word, or Excel; if the hyperlink opens a file, you can make changes and save them within the host application. For example, if you launch an Excel workbook from Access, you can make and save changes to it in Excel. Additionally, if other collaborators can access and make changes to the same workbook, the next time you launch the file from the hyperlink, the updated version displays.

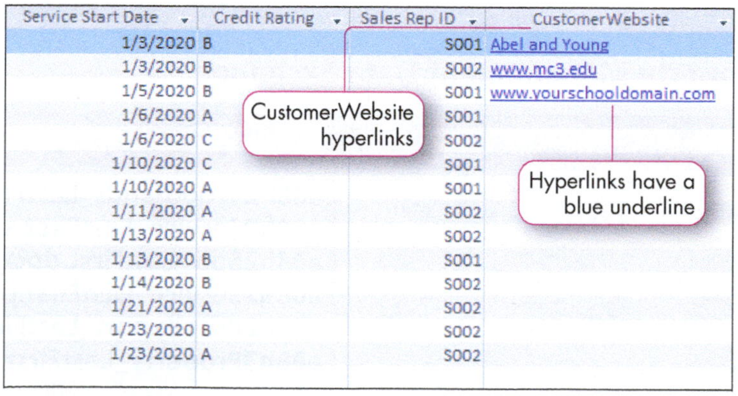

FIGURE 8.2 Hyperlink Fields

Edit a Hyperlink Value

At times, you will want to modify a hyperlink field. Several options exist in the Edit Hyperlink dialog box, such as the Text to display box, the ScreenTip button, and the Address box, as shown in Figure 8.3. If the URL, email address, or file name or location that the hyperlink points to changes, you can enter its new value in the Address box. You can modify the text that displays in the datasheet (or form) to a shortened or more descriptive value than what is specified by a URL or lengthier address. A ScreenTip is used to display pop-up text when you point to the hyperlink. ScreenTips are often used to explain a hyperlink's function, for example "Click here to send email." When you attempt to edit a hyperlink by clicking it, you will launch the software application; therefore, you need to use a different process to edit the hyperlink.

To edit a hyperlink field, complete the following steps:

1. Right-click the hyperlink field value, point to Hyperlink, and from the shortcut menu, select Edit Hyperlink.
2. Change the Text to display value to modify what the user sees when he or she views the field.
3. Select the Address box and modify the value that Access uses to locate a file and open it with the appropriate software.
4. Click ScreenTip to create pop-up text that will display when you point over the hyperlink text.
5. Click OK.

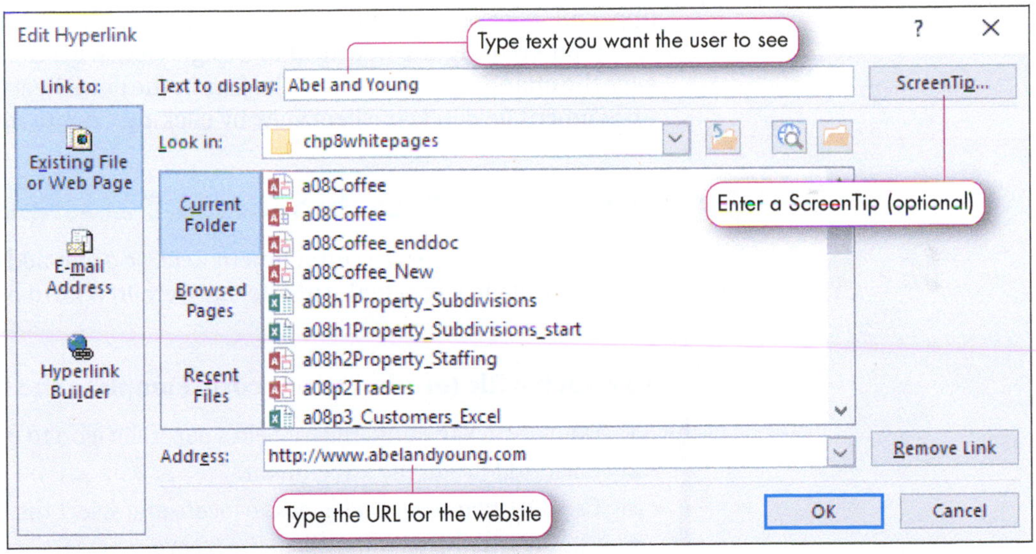

FIGURE 8.3 Edit Hyperlink Dialog Box

TIP: PRESS F2 TO EDIT HYPERLINK VALUES IN THE DATASHEET

As a shortcut to edit the text of a hyperlink value in a datasheet without opening the Edit Hyperlink dialog box, press Tab or the arrow keys to navigate to the value in the field you want to edit. With the value selected, press F2, and when the blinking insertion point displays, edit the value," and then press Enter or Tab.

It is possible to accidentally click and launch a website or a program when you only want to edit the hyperlink. For this reason, some database designers define hyperlink fields as text fields. Users can still store the URLs, email addresses, and file name paths as field values, but the references will not automatically launch any software when clicked. Users must copy and paste the text value into an appropriate application, such as a Web browser.

> **TIP: REMOVE A HYPERLINK FROM A FIELD**
> To remove a hyperlink from the datasheet, right-click the hyperlink field, point to Hyperlink, and select Remove Hyperlink. Access will remove the current hyperlink without asking for confirmation.

Adding an Attachment Field

Recall that an Access database is primarily used to store and analyze data, and to retrieve information. Data are usually typed directly into the tables or entered using an Access form. Sometimes you may want to store a reference to one or more external files—an image or photo, a scanned document, an Excel spreadsheet, a PDF document—and then open that file or files from within Access. These situations can be handled by adding an attachment field to a table.

STEP 3 ▸ ## Create an Attachment Field

An *attachment field* is similar to an email attachment; you can use an attachment field to attach multiple files of different types, and then launch those files using their native applications from within Access. The attached files are copied into the database itself. However, to work with a file, you need to open it from Access and use the source application associated with it.

After creating the new field in Design view with the Attachment data type assigned, save the changes, and then add the files in the datasheet or in a form. You can also add an attachment field in Datasheet view by clicking *Click to Add* in the column header.

STEP 4 ▸ ## Add or Edit Attachments in Datasheet View

Once you have created the attachment field, you can add one or more files to the new field in Datasheet view of a table (or alternatively, in a form based on a table) (see Figure 8.4).

To attach a file (or files) to a record, complete the following steps:

1. Double-click the attachment field's paperclip icon to open the Attachments dialog box.
2. Click Add to add the attachment.
3. Use the Choose File dialog box to locate and select the file to attach.
4. Click Open to attach the file to the record.
5. Click Add again to add the next file and each additional file.
6. Click OK to close the Attachments dialog box. The paperclip icon indicates how many files are attached to the current record.
7. Click the record below the current record to save the attached files.

Attachments   ✕

Attachments (Double-click to open)

📎 C0002.jpg | Add... |
                                                     | Remove |
                    Attach files | Open |
                                                     | Save As... |
                                                     | Save All... |

                                  | OK | | Cancel |

FIGURE 8.4 Attachments Dialog Box

When the new field with the attachment data type is created, a paperclip icon displays in every record with a (0) that indicates no attachments have been assigned to the records yet. After you add attachments to a record, the paperclip icon changes to indicate the number of files attached. In Figure 8.5, record 6 shows that two attachments were added. You can easily work with attached files by double-clicking the attachment field of the record. A dialog box displays with options to add, remove, open, or save a file. You can edit existing attachments later as the requirements of the database change. For example, you may need to remove a photo of a customer or employee and replace it with another or update a document, such as a contract that was previously attached to a record.

| 📋 Customers |
CustomerID ▾	Customer Name ▾	Customer Web site ▾	📎	Click to Add ▾
⊞	C0001	Abel & Young	Abel and Young	📎(0)	
⊞	C0002	Department of CIS	www.mc3.edu	📎(0)	
⊞	C0003	Advantage Sales	www.yourschooldomain.cor	📎(0)	Paperclip icon
⊞	C0004	Kinzer & Sons		📎(0)	indicates an
⊞	C0005	Milgrom Associates		📎(0)	Attachment field
⊞	C0006	Lugo Computer Sales		📎(2)	
⊞	C0007	Bethune Appliance Sales		📎(0)	
⊞	C0008	Baker Auto Supply		📎(0)	Number of attachments is
⊞	C0009	Howard Animal Hospital		📎(0)	indicated in parentheses (2)
⊞	C0010	Katie's Casual Wear		📎(0)	
⊞	C0011	Little, Joiner, & Jones		📎(0)	
⊞	C0012	Kline Bait & Tackle		📎(0)	
⊞	C0013	Computer Informations Sys		📎(0)	
⊞	C0014	Coulter Office Supplies		📎(0)	
＊	(New)			📎(0)	

FIGURE 8.5 Datasheet View Showing Attachments

Viewing an attachment from a datasheet or form launches the application that was used to create the file, such as Word, if you are viewing a Word document. As with linked files, you will make edits in the native application, and not in Access itself. If the application needed to open the file is not available on your system, you will be prompted to select another application that you can use to view it. Any changes that you make to attached files are saved in a temporary file on your hard drive; you can save the updated attachment to the database permanently when you are prompted in the Save Attachment dialog box (see Figure 8.6).

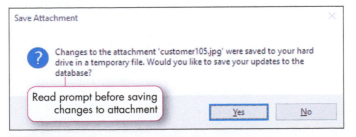

FIGURE 8.6 Save Attachment Message

To view or edit attached files, complete the following steps:

1. Double-click the attachment field's paperclip icon to open the Attachments dialog box.
2. Select the file to view or modify.
3. Click Open. Use the program associated with the file to make necessary changes.
4. Save and close the file once the change has been made.
5. Click OK in the Attachments dialog box.
6. Click Yes in the Save Attachment dialog box to save your changes.
7. Click the record below the current record to save the changes.

Table 8.1 summarizes the available options in the Attachments dialog box.

TABLE 8.1	Using the Attachments Dialog Box
Option	**Description**
Add	Add one or more files to a record.
Remove	Remove previously attached files.
Open	Launch the appropriate application and open the file in its associated program.
Save As	Save a copy of an attached file to your local storage device or network. If you open and modify the file in its associated application, remember to save the changes and add the modified file back into the database.
Save All	Save all attachments in a record to a local, temporary folder.

STEP 5 Remove Attachments in Datasheet View

Attachments can increase the file size of a database substantially. It is important to remove unnecessary or incorrect attachments to avoid excessive bloating of the database. Double-click the attachment field's paperclip icon to open the Attachments dialog box. Select the file to remove, click Remove, and click OK. Save the record.

If the database grows too large, you can remove some attachments, resize the files, and reattach the files in a smaller format if you want to keep them in the database. Remember to compact the database after you remove attachments.

To monitor the file size of a database, complete the following steps:

1. Compact the database.
2. Check the size of the database file:
   • Click the File tab, and from the Info page, click View and edit database properties.
   • Note the file size on the General tab of the Properties dialog box.
3. Add or remove the file attachment(s).
4. Compact the database and check the size of the database file again.

Adding Attachment Controls to Forms and Reports

In a form or report, you can work with attachments using an attachment control. It is more likely that database users will work with forms and reports rather than the tables themselves. An **attachment control** is a control that enables you to manage attached files in forms and reports. The attachment field must be defined in a table before you can include the attachment control in a form or report. If the attachment is a photo, the control displays the photos as you navigate through the records. If the attachment is a document, you will only see an icon representing the application (such as Word) that you click to launch the file. In Form view and Report view, you can navigate through multiple attachments in a form or report when there are several associated with a record, such as a photo and a performance review in an employee table. If an attachment field was not included in the original form or report design, you can add it later. If you add an attachment field to an existing table or include it in a query, and then decide to include that field in a form or report that is based on the underlying database object, you would then need to add the attachment control to the form or report in Layout view.

Add an Attachment Control to a Form

When you add an attachment control to a form, you can work with attachments such as photos and files that are associated with the individual records. You attach a control using the Field List pane, which you learned about in an earlier chapter when adding fields from tables to forms. An attachment field also displays in the Field List pane (when it has been added to a table) as a parent field with three child fields (see Figure 8.7). The expand symbol (+) enables you to expand, and the collapse symbol (−) enables you to collapse the child fields. Ensure that you use the parent field (that displays the field name itself) when adding the attachment to the form.

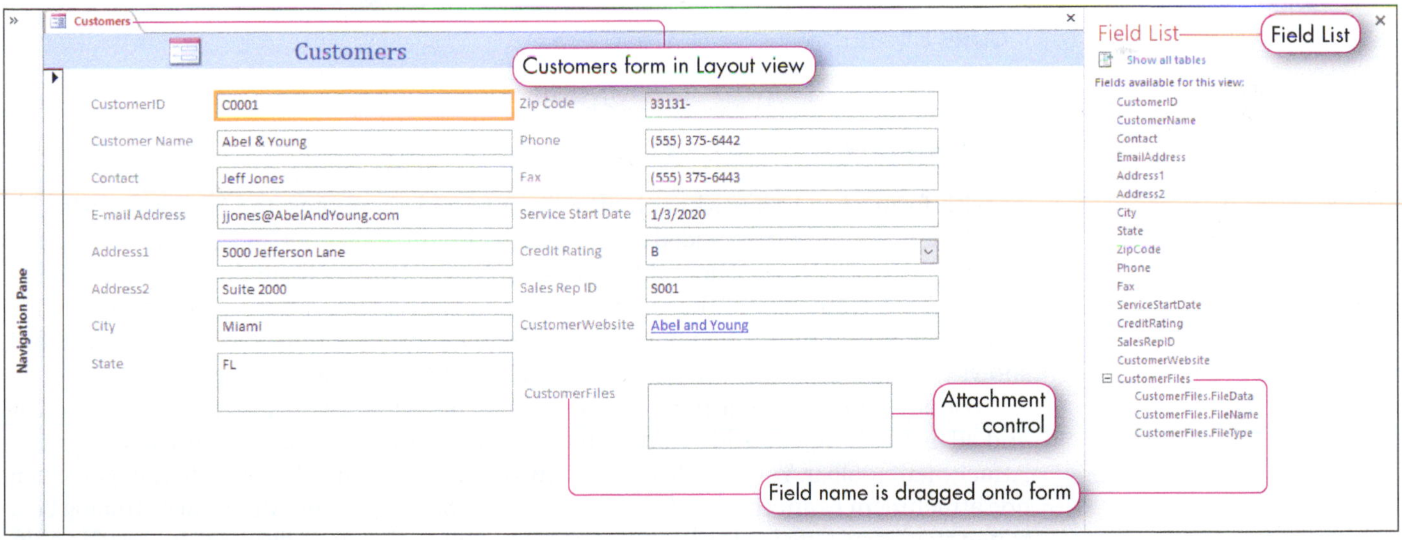

FIGURE 8.7 Add an Attachment Control to a Form

> **To add an attachment control to a form, complete the following steps:**
>
> 1. Open the form in Layout view.
> 2. Click Add Existing Fields in the Tools group on the Design tab.
> 3. Drag the field name from the Field List pane to the form and drop it in the location on the form. Access adds the bound attachment control and the associated label to the form.
> 4. Resize the bound control to ensure that the images display correctly.
> 5. Save the changes and then switch to Form view.

When the attachment control is in place, in Form view, click the control to view the Attachment toolbar (see Figure 8.8). The Attachment toolbar displays arrows that enable you to advance through multiple attachments. The Attachment toolbar also displays a paperclip icon that you can click to open the Attachments dialog box. This dialog box is the same one that opens when you click an attachment field in a table. Return to Layout view to make additional modifications to the form.

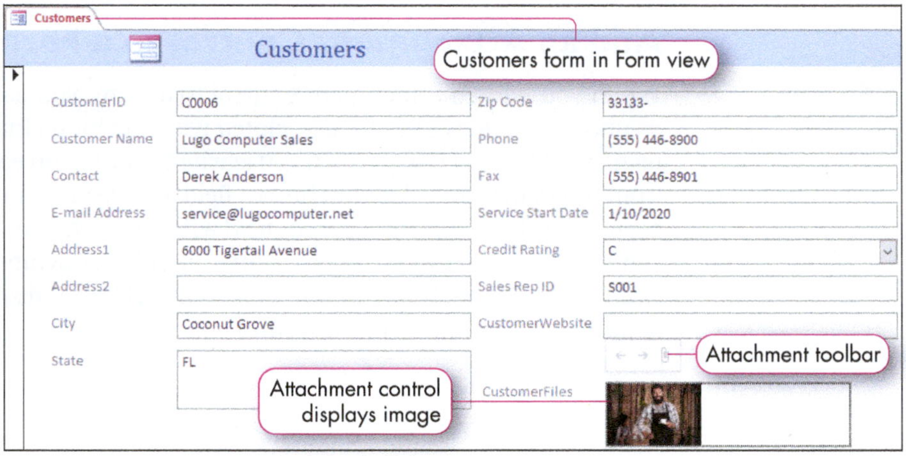

FIGURE 8.8 Attachment Control in Form View

STEP 6 ## Add an Attachment Control to a Report

As with forms, you can work with attachments such as photos and files in reports. An attachment control can be added to an existing report if it was not included in the original report design. The process for adding an attachment control is similar to adding one to the form: in Layout view of the report, select Add Existing Fields in the Tools group on the Design tab and drag the field name from the Field List pane onto the report. Figure 8.9 shows the CustomerFiles field added in Layout view of the Customers report.

Usually, attachments are viewed by users in Report view. To use the Attachment toolbar and advance through multiple attachments in Report view, click the control to view the Attachment toolbar. You can click the arrows on the Attachment toolbar to navigate from one attachment to another or click the paperclip icon to open the Attachments dialog box. When the report is viewed in Print Preview, the attachment field displays the first file only. The Attachment toolbar does not display in Print Preview.

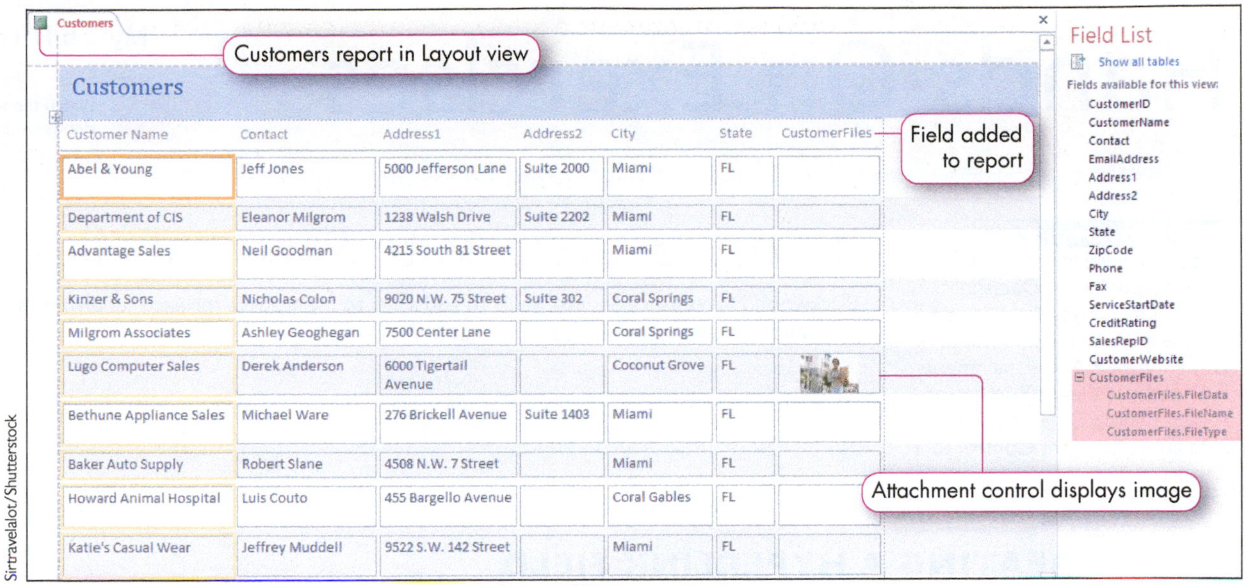

FIGURE 8.9 Attachment Control Added to a Report in Layout View

Quick Concepts

1. Describe when you would use a linked file as opposed to an attachment **p. 440**

2. Consider a potential disadvantage of storing attachments in your databases. **p. 444**

3. Discuss examples of hyperlinks that you could add to a database that you are designing. **p. 440**

Hands-On Exercises

MyLab IT HOE1 Sim Training

Watch the Video for this Hands-On Exercise!

Skills covered: Add a Hyperlink Field in Design View • Enter Hyperlinks in Datasheet View • Edit a Hyperlink Value • Create an Attachment Field in Design View • Add Attachments in Datasheet View • Remove an Attachment in Datasheet View • Add an Attachment Control to a Report

1 Connect Access to External Files

Blackwood Maintenance Service wants to add a link to the website for each subdivision's school district. You will also add photos of properties that BMS now serves.

STEP 1 CREATING A HYPERLINK FIELD

You will create a new field that will link to the school district's website for each subdivision served by Blackwood. Refer to Figure 8.10 as you complete Step 1.

Steps f–h: Type School District URLs in Datasheet view

SubDivision

SubDI	Subdivision	ContactPerson	Pool	RecreationCer	BikeTrail	School District
1	Fair Brook	Irma Stark	Yes	No	No	http://abss.k12.nc.us
2	King's Forests	Red Donner	No	Yes	Yes	http://www.gcncs.com
3	Dale	Al Sicas	Yes	Yes	Yes	http://www.gcncs.com
4	Eagle Valley	Tony Salvatores	No	No	No	http://www.orange.k12.nc.us
5	Running Brook	Jerry Kudash	Yes	Yes	No	http://www.orange.k12.nc.us
6	North Point	Reggie Elder	No	Yes	Yes	http://abss.k12.nc.us
7	Red Canyon	Kevin Kellie	Yes	No	No	http://abss.k12.nc.us
8	Seeley Lake	Glen Hughes	Yes	Yes	Yes	http://www.gcncs.com
9	The Links	Hugh Hyatt	Yes	No	Yes	http://abss.k12.nc.us
10	The Estates	Deb Dahl	No	No	No	http://www.orange.k12.nc.us
11	The Orchards	John Erthal	Yes	Yes	Yes	http://www.gcncs.com
12	The Pines	Ralph Borden	Yes	Yes	No	http://abss.k12.nc.us
13	Water Valley	Jansen Kunkelman	No	Yes	Yes	http://www.orange.k12.nc.us
14	The Woodlands	Louise Davis	No	No	No	http://www.orange.k12.nc.us

FIGURE 8.10 Enter Hyperlinks in Datasheet View

a. Open *a08h1Property* and save it as **a08h1Property_LastFirst**.

TROUBLESHOOTING: If you make any major mistakes in this exercise, you can close the file, open *a08h1Property* again, and then start this exercise over.

b. Open the Agents table and expand the Subdatasheet to view the properties managed by each agent. Close the Agents table.

c. Open the SubDivision table in Design view. In the blank field row below the BikeTrail field name, type **SchoolDistrict**. Click the **Data Type arrow** and select **Hyperlink**.

d. Type **School District** in the Caption property box in the Field Properties pane of the Table Design view.

e. Save the changes to the table. Switch to Datasheet view.

You are ready to add the school districts' website addresses to the new hyperlink field.

f. Type **http://abss.k12.nc.us** into the School District field for records 1, 6, 7, 9, and 12.

Fair Brook, North Point, Red Canyon, The Links, and The Pines are all located in the Alamance-Burlington School System.

g. Type **http://www.gcncs.com** into the School District field for records 2, 3, 8, and 11.

King's Forest, Dale, Seeley Lake, and The Orchards are in the Guilford District.

h. Type **http://www.orange.k12.nc.us** into the School District field for the remaining records (records 4, 5, 10, 13, and 14).

The remaining subdivisions are in the Orange County School District.

> **TROUBLESHOOTING:** If you make a mistake, do not click in the School District field to correct it. Instead, click in the BikeTrail column and press Tab to select the field that contains an error. Retype the information.

i. Click the **School District hyperlink** in record 1. The browser opens and the school district's website opens. Close the browser window.

j. Widen the School District field so that all data are displayed, and compare your screen with Figure 8.10.

STEP 2 EDIT A HYPERLINK VALUE

You realized that you entered an incorrect URL for the Guilford school district. You will fix the links in this step so that the URL links to schools in North Carolina. Refer to Figure 8.11 as you complete Step 2.

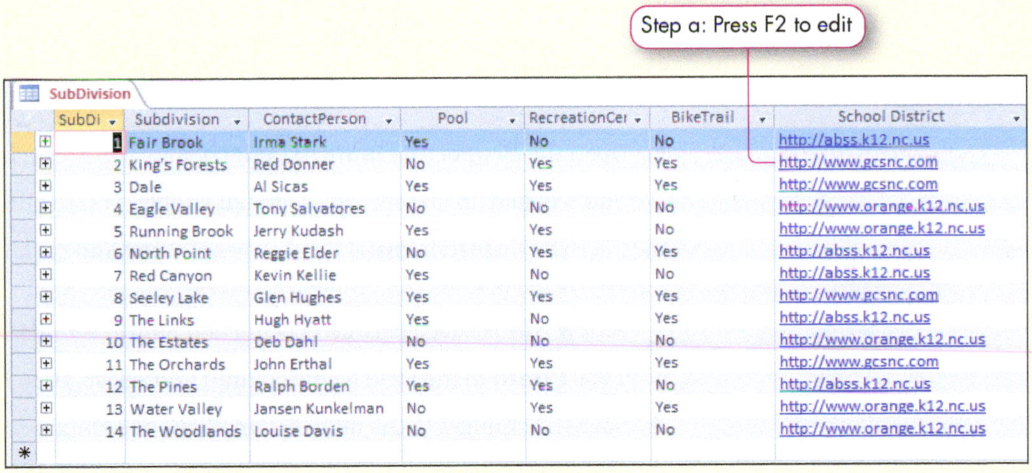

Step a: Press F2 to edit

SubDi	Subdivision	ContactPerson	Pool	RecreationCer	BikeTrail	School District
1	Fair Brook	Irma Stark	Yes	No	No	http://abss.k12.nc.us
2	King's Forests	Red Donner	No	Yes	Yes	http://www.gcsnc.com
3	Dale	Al Sicas	Yes	Yes	Yes	http://www.gcsnc.com
4	Eagle Valley	Tony Salvatores	No	No	No	http://www.orange.k12.nc.us
5	Running Brook	Jerry Kudash	Yes	Yes	No	http://www.orange.k12.nc.us
6	North Point	Reggie Elder	No	Yes	Yes	http://abss.k12.nc.us
7	Red Canyon	Kevin Kellie	Yes	No	No	http://abss.k12.nc.us
8	Seeley Lake	Glen Hughes	Yes	Yes	Yes	http://www.gcsnc.com
9	The Links	Hugh Hyatt	Yes	No	Yes	http://abss.k12.nc.us
10	The Estates	Deb Dahl	No	No	No	http://www.orange.k12.nc.us
11	The Orchards	John Erthal	Yes	Yes	Yes	http://www.gcsnc.com
12	The Pines	Ralph Borden	Yes	Yes	No	http://abss.k12.nc.us
13	Water Valley	Jansen Kunkelman	No	Yes	Yes	http://www.orange.k12.nc.us
14	The Woodlands	Louise Davis	No	No	No	http://www.orange.k12.nc.us

FIGURE 8.11 Edit a Hyperlink Field in Datasheet View

a. Click in the **BikeTrail column** of record 2 and press **Tab** until the School District field is selected. Press **F2** and edit the link so it reads **http://www.gcsnc.com**.

The *gcnsc* segment of the hyperlink was changed to *gcsnc,* with the *s* and *n* moved. The hyperlink is enclosed with pound signs (#), which Access uses to activate the link when clicked.

b. Click in the **BikeTrail column** of record 3 to save the changes.

You will use another method to edit the remaining Guilford URLs.

c. Right-click the hyperlink in record 3, point to **Hyperlink**, and then select **Edit Hyperlink** from the shortcut menu.

The Edit Hyperlink dialog box opens.

d. Change the *gcncs* segment of the hyperlink to **gcsnc** in the Address field at the bottom of the dialog box. Click **OK** to accept your changes and press ↓ to save your changes.

The Text to display changes.

e. Edit the remaining Guilford URLs (change *gcncs* to **gcsnc**) using the Edit Hyperlink dialog box. Compare your results with Figure 8.11.

f. Close and save the SubDivision table.

STEP 3 ## CREATE AN ATTACHMENT FIELD

BMS has collected photos of its properties for the past several years. The photos are stored in a folder where employees can access them as needed. The owners have asked you to create an attachment field so you can attach each photo to its corresponding property. Refer to Figure 8.12 as you complete Step 3.

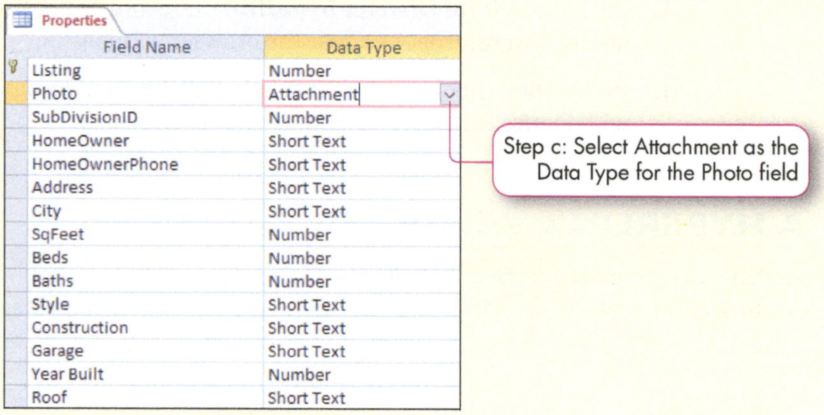

Field Name	Data Type
Listing	Number
Photo	Attachment
SubDivisionID	Number
HomeOwner	Short Text
HomeOwnerPhone	Short Text
Address	Short Text
City	Short Text
SqFeet	Number
Beds	Number
Baths	Number
Style	Short Text
Construction	Short Text
Garage	Short Text
Year Built	Number
Roof	Short Text

Step c: Select Attachment as the Data Type for the Photo field

FIGURE 8.12 Create an Attachment Field in Design View

a. Open the **Properties table** in Design view.

You will add an attachment field that enables you to attach the photos of the properties.

b. Click the **SubDivisionID field row selector** and click **Insert Rows** in the Tools group on the Design tab.

A new row is added between Listing and SubDivisionID.

c. Type **Photo** in the Field Name column and select **Attachment** as the data type.

d. Save the changes to the table design. Switch to Datasheet view.

The new attachment field displays a paperclip symbol with a (0), indicating no attachments are in any of the property records.

ADD OR EDIT ATTACHMENTS IN DATASHEET VIEW

You will attach four photos to their corresponding properties. Having these photos attached to the properties enables the agents to access them when working with the property owners. Refer to Figure 8.13 as you complete Step 4.

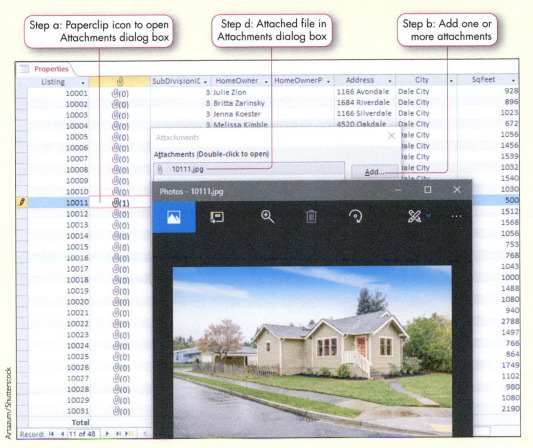

FIGURE 8.13 Add Attachments in Datasheet View

a. Double-click the **paperclip icon** in the Photo field in the record for listing 10011 to open the Attachments dialog box.

b. Click **Add**. Locate the *10011.jpg* photo in the a08h1PhotosFolder. Double-click the file to add it to the Attachments dialog box.

   The file displays in the Attachments dialog box.

c. Click **OK** to close the Attachments dialog box. Click the record for listing 10012 to save the record.

d. Double-click the **paperclip** in record 11 to open the Attachments dialog box again. Double-click the **10011.jpg photo** to open your computer's default photo software.

   Compare your screen with Figure 8.13.

e. Close the photo software and click **OK** in the Attachments dialog box.

f. Double-click the **paperclip** in listing 10033.

g. Click **Add** in the Attachments dialog box, and then locate and attach photo *10033.jpg* to the record. Click **OK**.

h. Double-click the **paperclip** in listing 10068 and attach photo *10068.jpg* to the record.

i. Select the record for listing 10025. Double-click the **paperclip** to open the Attachments dialog box. Click **Add** and add photo *10025.jpg* to the Attachments dialog box. Click **OK**. Click the record for listing 10026 to save the record.

STEP 5 REMOVE AN ATTACHMENT IN DATASHEET VIEW

One of the properties was sold, and the new owners are not going to use BMS to manage their property. You decide to remove the photo from this property's record. Refer to Figure 8.14 as you complete Step 5.

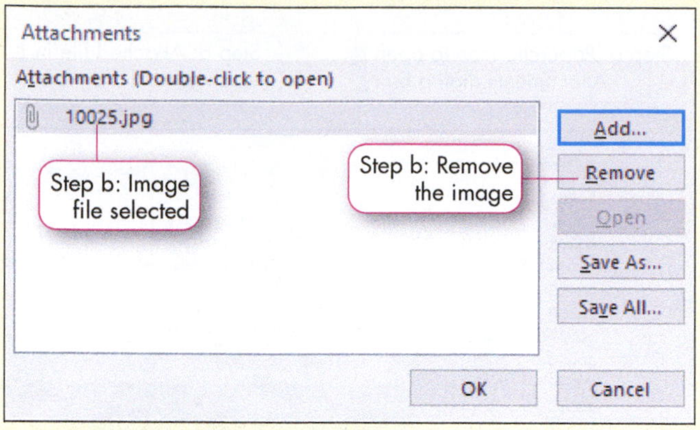

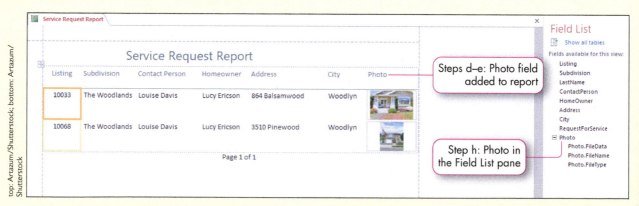

FIGURE 8.14 Remove an Attachment in Datasheet View

a. Double-click the **paperclip** in listing 10025 to open the Attachments dialog box.

b. Click **10025.jpg** and click **Remove**.

The photo has been removed from the Attachments dialog box.

c. Click **OK** to close the Attachments dialog box and click the record below to save the record.

d. Close the Properties table.

e. Click the **File tab** and click **Compact & Repair Database**.

You decide to compact the database because adding and removing attachments can increase the size of the database.

STEP 6 ADD AN ATTACHMENT CONTROL TO A REPORT

BMS asks you to create a report showing the properties with an outstanding service request. You decide to include a photo of each property, but only a thumbnail will display in the report. Refer to Figure 8.15 as you complete Step 6.

top: Artazum/Shutterstock; bottom: Artazum/Shutterstock

FIGURE 8.15 Attachment Field in a Report

a. Open the Service Request query in Design view. Type the name **"Lucy Ericson"** in the Criteria row of the HomeOwner field and press **Enter**.

b. Switch to Datasheet view and examine the query results.

Two properties display with *Lucy Ericson* as the homeowner. The Photo field is missing; you will return to Design view to add it to the query design.

c. Switch to Design view.

d. Drag the **Photo field** from the Properties table and drop it into the first blank field cell in the query design grid.

> **TROUBLESHOOTING:** If you drag one of the three child fields, delete the column and try again. Make sure you add the parent photo field, the field with a (+) or (–) symbol to its left.

e. Switch to Datasheet view and notice the Photo (attachment) field in the query results. Save and close the query.

f. Double-click **Service Request Report** in the Navigation Pane and switch to Layout view.

g. Click **Add Existing Fields** in the Tools group on the Design tab.

h. Click **Woodlyn** to select the City column. Double-click **Photo** in the Field List pane to add the field to the right side of the report.

> **TROUBLESHOOTING:** If you double-click one of the three child fields, click Undo and try again. Make sure you double-click the parent photo field, the field with a (+) or (–) symbol to its left.

The Photo field is added as the last column on the right of the report. The photos are positioned on the outside of the right margin. You will resize the other columns to reduce the layout width to one page.

i. Close the Field List pane. Reduce the width of the Listing column by dragging the right border of the Listing column heading to the left.

j. Reduce the width of the City column until no photos are positioned on the second page (ensure that they are inside the dashed page break).

k. View the report in Print Preview.

All the fields now fit onto one page.

l. Click **Close Print Preview** in the Close Preview group. Save and close the report.

m. Keep the database open if you plan to continue with the next Hands-On Exercise. If not, close the database and exit Access.

Export Data to Office and Other Applications

Using Access to collect and store data and to extract and analyze information is useful for any organization. But what happens when information must be shared with other departments, or with other companies that might not have the software or whose employees might not be familiar with Access? One way to deliver information is via hard copies. However, this does not work if the recipients want to manipulate the data themselves or to analyze it further from a different angle. A common way to distribute data stored in an Access database is to export them to another application.

In this section, you will learn how to export Access data to Excel and Word. Because these two applications are also part of the Microsoft Office suite, exporting from Access is straightforward. In addition to exporting to Excel and Word, you will also learn how to create a PDF or XPS document and how to export objects from one Access database to another Access database.

Exporting Data to Excel

Access users export data to Excel for several reasons. One is to take advantage of Excel's charting and data analysis functions. You can manipulate data to test different scenarios and analyze the results; manipulating and testing data in Excel is preferable to changing data in a database. You want the raw data in Access to stay the same! Another reason for exporting to Excel is to be able to distribute the Access data to users who do not have Access or who do not know how to use Access. Exporting data from Access to Excel is generally uncomplicated because the data in Access are usually structured in a manner that Excel understands, in a row and column format.

If the record source you want to export to Excel is a table, such as the Customers table shown in Figure 8.16, then the export-to-Excel process is straightforward. When you export a table to Excel, the field names become the column headings and the table records become the rows in the Excel spreadsheet. You can export an entire Access table to Excel or only selected records; records can be selected individually in a table, or the table can be filtered to display a subset of the records before the export is initiated.

When you export a table from Access, all columns and designated records in the table are exported, even if the table is open and not all the data are visible. In Figure 8.16, some field names such as Zip Code are not visible. If no records are selected or filtered in advance, all records are exported. In this example, the result is a new Excel worksheet containing all the columns and all of the records in the Customers table, as shown in Figure 8.17.

CustomerID	Customer Name	Contact	E-mail Address	Address1	Address2	City	State	Custo
C0001	Abel & Young	Jeff Jones	jjones@AbelAndYoung.com	5000 Jefferson Lane	Suite 2000	Miami	FL	Abel and
C0002	Department of CIS	Eleanor Milgrom		1238 Walsh Drive	Suite 2202	Miami	FL	www.m
C0003	Advantage Sales	Neil Goodman	service@advantagesales.com	4215 South 81 Street		Miami	FL	www.yo
C0004	Kinzer & Sons	Nicholas Colon		9020 N.W. 75 Street	Suite 302	Coral Springs	FL	
C0005	Milgrom Associates	Ashley Geoghegan	ageoghegan@milgrom.com	7500 Center Lane		Coral Springs	FL	
C0006	Lugo Computer Sales	Derek Anderson	service@lugocomputer.net	6000 Tigertail Avenue		Coconut Grove	FL	
C0007	Bethune Appliance Sales	Michael Ware	bethune@bethune.com	276 Brickell Avenue	Suite 1403	Miami	FL	
C0008	Baker Auto Supply	Robert Slane	rslane@bakerauto.com	4508 N.W. 7 Street		Miami	FL	
C0009	Howard Animal Hospital	Luis Couto	lcouto@howardanimals.net	455 Bargello Avenue		Coral Gables	FL	
C0010	Katie's Casual Wear	Jeffrey Muddell	katie@katiewear.com	9522 S.W. 142 Street		Miami	FL	
C0011	Little, Joiner, & Jones	Lauren Center	lcenter@ljj.com	7245 NW 8 Street		Miami	FL	
C0012	Kline Bait & Tackle	Benjamin Lee	blee@klineb&t.com	1000 Call Street		Coconut Grove	FL	
C0013	Computer Informations Sys	Eleanor Milgrom	emilgrom@cis.edu	1238 Walsh Drove	Suite 2202	Miami	FL	
C0014	Coulter Office Supplies	Maryann Coulter	mcoulter@coulter.com	1000 Main Street		Coral Springs	FL	
(New)								

FIGURE 8.16 Customers Table in Access Before Exporting to Excel

	A	B	C	D	E	F	G	H	I	J	K
1	CustomerID	Customer Name	Contact	E-mail Address	Address1	Address2	City	State	Zip Code	Phone	Fax
2	C0001	Abel & Young	Jeff Jones	jjones@AbelAndYoung.com	5000 Jefferson Lane	Suite 2000	Miami	FL	33131-	(555) 375-6442	(555) 375-644
3	C0002	Department of CIS	Eleanor Milgrom		1238 Walsh Drive	Suite 2202	Miami	FL	33131-	(555) 385-4431	(555) 385-443
4	C0003	Advantage Sales	Neil Goodman	service@advantagesales.com	4215 South 81 Street		Miami	FL	33131-	(555) 444-5555	(555) 444-555
5	C0004	Kinzer & Sons	Nicholas Colon		9020 N.W. 75 Street	Suite 302	Coral Springs	FL	33065-	(555) 753-9887	(555) 753-988
6	C0005	Milgrom Associates	Ashley Geoghegan	ageoghegan@milgrom.net	7500 Center Lane		Coral Springs	FL	33070-	(555) 753-7830	(555) 753-783
7	C0006	Lugo Computer Sales	Derek Anderson	service@lugocomputer.net	6000 Tigertail Avenue		Coconut Grove	FL	33133-	(555) 446-8900	(555) 446-890
8	C0007	Bethune Appliance Sales	Michael Ware	bethune@bethune.com	276 Brickell Avenue	Suite 1403	Miami	FL	33131-	(555) 444-3980	(555) 444-398
9	C0008	Baker Auto Supply	Robert Slane	rslane@bakerauto.com	4508 N.W. 7 Street		Miami	FL	33131-	(555) 635-3454	(555) 635-345
10	C0009	Howard Animal Hospital	Luis Couto	lcouto@howardanimals.net	455 Bargello Avenue		Coral Gables	FL	33124-	(555) 666-4801	(555) 666-480
11	C0010	Katie's Casual Wear	Jeffrey Muddell	katie@katiewear.com	9522 S.W. 142 Street		Miami	FL	33176-	(555) 253-3908	(555) 253-390
12	C0011	Little, Joiner, & Jones	Lauren Center	lcenter@ljj.com	7245 NW 8 Street		Miami	FL	33133-	(555) 974-1234	(555) 974-123
13	C0012	Kline Bait & Tackle	Benjamin Lee	blee@klineb&t.com	1000 Call Street		Coconut Grove	FL	33133-	(555) 327-4124	(555) 327-412
14	C0013	Computer Informations Systems	Eleanor Milgrom	emilgrom@cis.edu	1238 Walsh Drove	Suite 2202	Miami	FL	33186-	(555) 385-4431	(555) 385-443
15	C0014	Coulter Office Supplies	Maryann Coulter	mcoulter@coulter.com	1000 Main Street		Coral Springs	FL	33071-	(555) 123-9876	
16											

FIGURE 8.17 Customers Table Exported to Excel

STEP 1 ## Export a Query to Excel

If you want to export only a subset of a table, you can filter a table or select specific records before exporting. Alternatively, you can create a query to then export to Excel. For example, if you only need the address fields for customers in a certain zip code, you can create a query, and then export the query records to Excel.

To export a table or query to Excel, complete the following steps:

1. Select or open the object in the Navigation Pane.
2. Click Excel in the Export group on the External Data tab. Access opens the Export – Excel Spreadsheet dialog box (shown in Figure 8.18) to guide you through the export process.
3. Specify the file name and destination and the format for the exported file.
4. Specify whether to export the data with formatting and layout.
5. Specify if you want to open the destination file after the export operation is complete.
6. Specify if you want to export only the selected records (if you have selected one or more records in the datasheet).
7. Click OK.

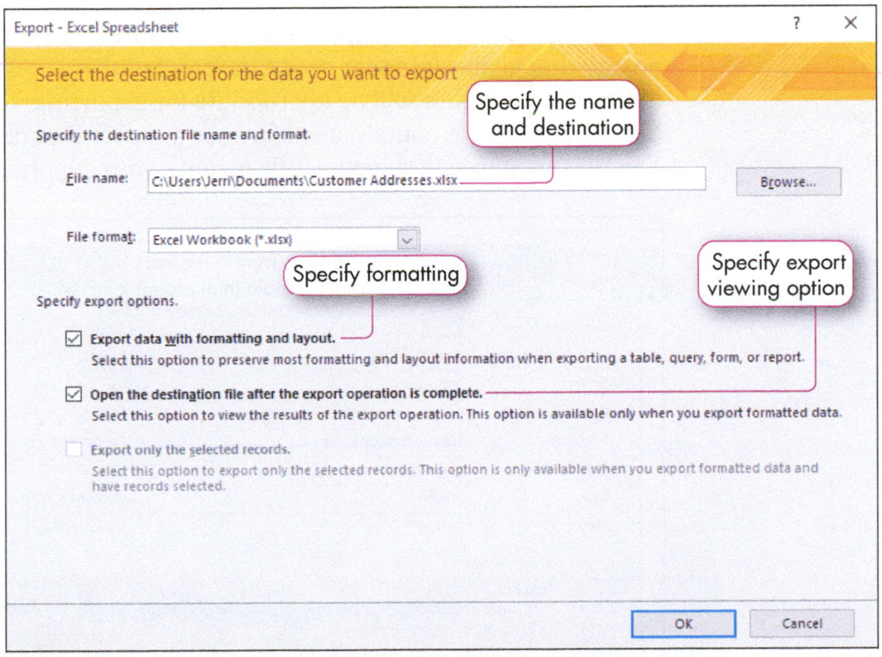

FIGURE 8.18 Export – Excel Spreadsheet Dialog Box

The Excel spreadsheet will display (see Figure 8.19). Once you are finished reviewing the exported Excel spreadsheet, and then return to the Access window, one final screen requires a response. Access asks you, *Do you want to save these export steps?* Click to select the *Save export steps* check box if you want to repeat the same export process later. Saving export steps is useful if you need to repeatedly export the same database object. The saved steps are stored under Saved Exports in the Export group.

FIGURE 8.19 Customer Addresses Query Exported to Excel

STEP 2

Export Forms and Reports to Excel

Exporting tables and queries to Excel usually yields predictable and consistent results. The main reason is the similarity between an Access datasheet and an Excel worksheet. Both have column headings, and both have multiple rows of data below the column headings. Most of the cells have data in them (blank cells are the exception). However, when you export forms and reports from Access to Excel, the results can be unpredictable. For example, if you export a form that contains customers' data and a subform showing the orders for each customer, the customers' data exports but the related orders (in the subform) do not. Figure 8.20 shows an Access form based on a Customers table and the related Orders for each customer. Figure 8.21 shows the same form after it is exported to Excel. The records from the related (Orders) table do not display. Furthermore, if you attempt to export a grouped report in Access, the grouping in Excel may not match the grouping in the Access report. Always be sure to open the exported object in Excel to ensure that all the data that need to be portrayed are present; otherwise, create or modify a record source that will be appropriate for exporting. For example, you could create a form that does not contain a subform or a report that does not contain grouping levels. You will want to experiment a little to make your exported data display suitably in Excel.

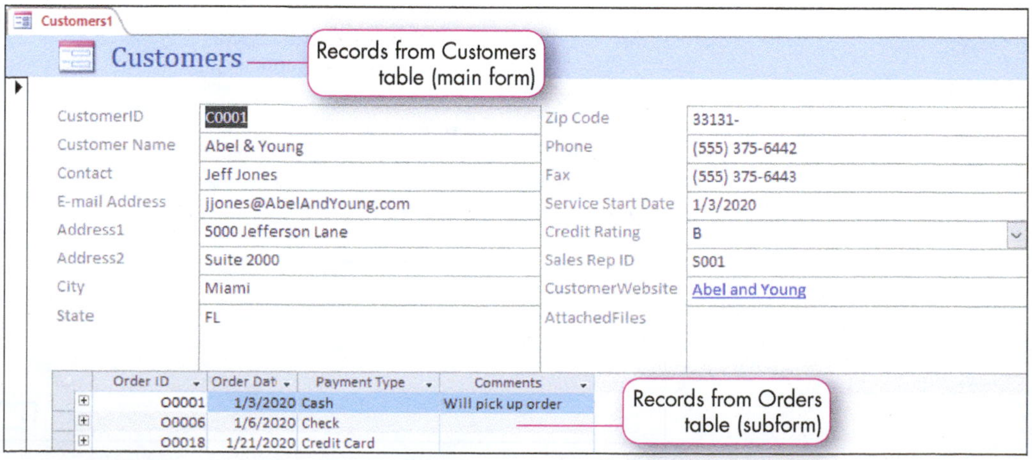

FIGURE 8.20 Customers with Orders Form in Access

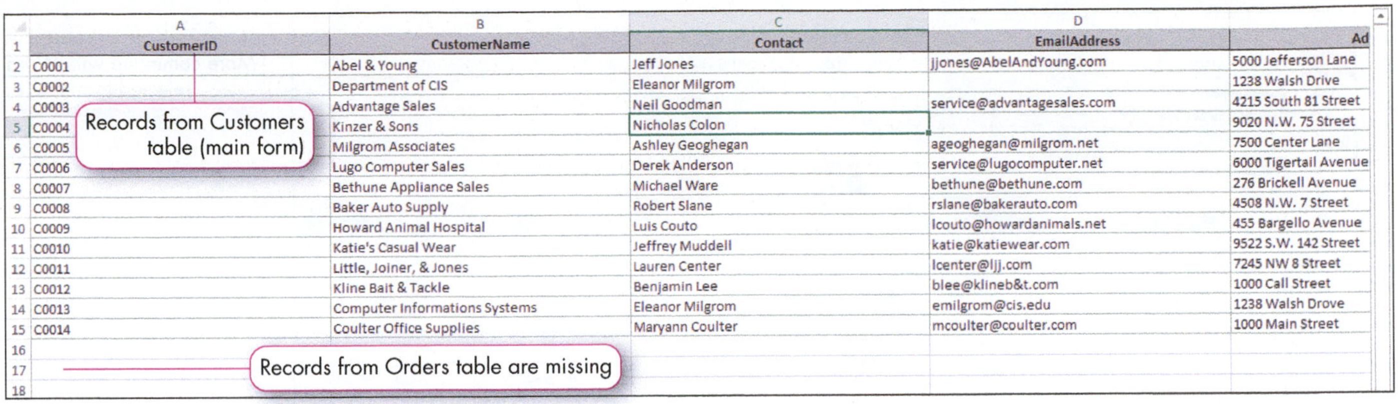

	A	B	C	D	Ad
1	CustomerID	CustomerName	Contact	EmailAddress	
2	C0001	Abel & Young	Jeff Jones	jjones@AbelAndYoung.com	5000 Jefferson Lane
3	C0002	Department of CIS	Eleanor Milgrom		1238 Walsh Drive
4	C0003	Advantage Sales	Neil Goodman	service@advantagesales.com	4215 South 81 Street
5	C0004	Kinzer & Sons	Nicholas Colon		9020 N.W. 75 Street
6	C0005	Milgrom Associates	Ashley Geoghegan	ageoghegan@milgrom.net	7500 Center Lane
7	C0006	Lugo Computer Sales	Derek Anderson	service@lugocomputer.net	6000 Tigertail Avenue
8	C0007	Bethune Appliance Sales	Michael Ware	bethune@bethune.com	276 Brickell Avenue
9	C0008	Baker Auto Supply	Robert Slane	rslane@bakerauto.com	4508 N.W. 7 Street
10	C0009	Howard Animal Hospital	Luis Couto	lcouto@howardanimals.net	455 Bargello Avenue
11	C0010	Katie's Casual Wear	Jeffrey Muddell	katie@katiewear.com	9522 S.W. 142 Street
12	C0011	Little, Joiner, & Jones	Lauren Center	lcenter@ljj.com	7245 NW 8 Street
13	C0012	Kline Bait & Tackle	Benjamin Lee	blee@klineb&t.com	1000 Call Street
14	C0013	Computer Informations Systems	Eleanor Milgrom	emilgrom@cis.edu	1238 Walsh Drove
15	C0014	Coulter Office Supplies	Maryann Coulter	mcoulter@coulter.com	1000 Main Street
16					
17					
18					

Records from Customers table (main form)

Records from Orders table are missing

FIGURE 8.21 Customers with Orders Form Exported to Excel

STEP 3

Exporting Data to Word

When you export data to Word, it will most likely be used for reporting purposes rather than for analysis. Although you can modify data exported into a Word table, those changes do not update the totals or other calculated fields (as they do in Excel). Generally, the exported data will not be manipulated but instead formatted as a report for distribution outside of its original Access database.

The process for exporting data from Access to Word is similar to that for exporting data to Excel. When you export an object from Access to Word, Access creates a file in the Rich Text Format. *Rich Text Format (RTF)* is a format that enables text-based documents to be opened in a variety of word-processing applications.

> **TIP: WHAT IS RTF (RICH TEXT FORMAT)?**
> RTF is a useful format for basic formatted text documents, such as instruction manuals, résumés, letters, and other documents. These documents support special text formatting, such as bold, italic, and underline. RTF documents also support left-, center-, and right-justified text. Furthermore, font specifications and document margins are supported in RTF documents. The RTF format uses the .rtf file extension; Word is the default software application for opening files with the .rtf extension. Once the RTF file is opened in Word, you can convert it to the Word Document format by using the Save As command on the File tab. From that point forward, the document retains the Word format.

The objects you select to export from Access to Word should have a tabular layout, such as tables, queries, and tabular reports. For example, if you want to export a products table from an Access database into a Word document, as shown in Figure 8.22, the export-to-Word process is uncomplicated. For the Products table, the field names become the column headings, and the records become the table rows in the RTF file.

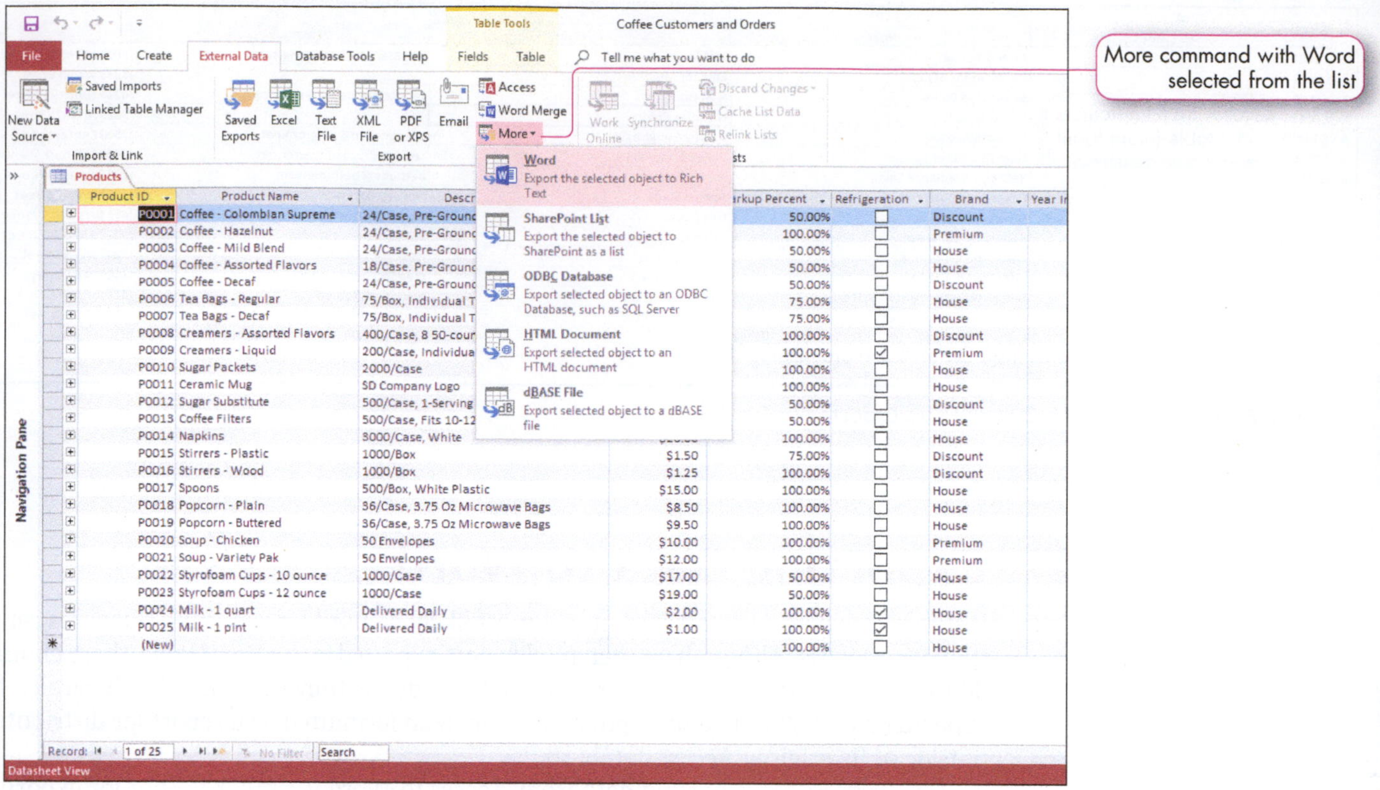

FIGURE 8.22 Product Data in Access

When you export tabular reports to Word, Access preserves the report's grouping aggregate functions, although some of the formatting may be lost. While other object types such as columnar forms and reports do export to Word, the results are unpredictable and poorly formatted. You should test the export of these objects to see if they produce usable data.

To export a table or query to Word, complete the following steps:

1. Select the table or query in the Navigation Pane (or open the table or query first) and click the External Data tab.

2. Click More in the Export group.

3. Select Word. Access opens the Export – RTF File dialog box (shown in Figure 8.23) to guide you through the export process.

4. Specify the file name, destination, and format for the exported file.

5. Specify if you want to open the destination file after the export operation is complete.

6. Specify if you want to export only the selected records (if you have selected one or more records in the datasheet).

7. Click OK.

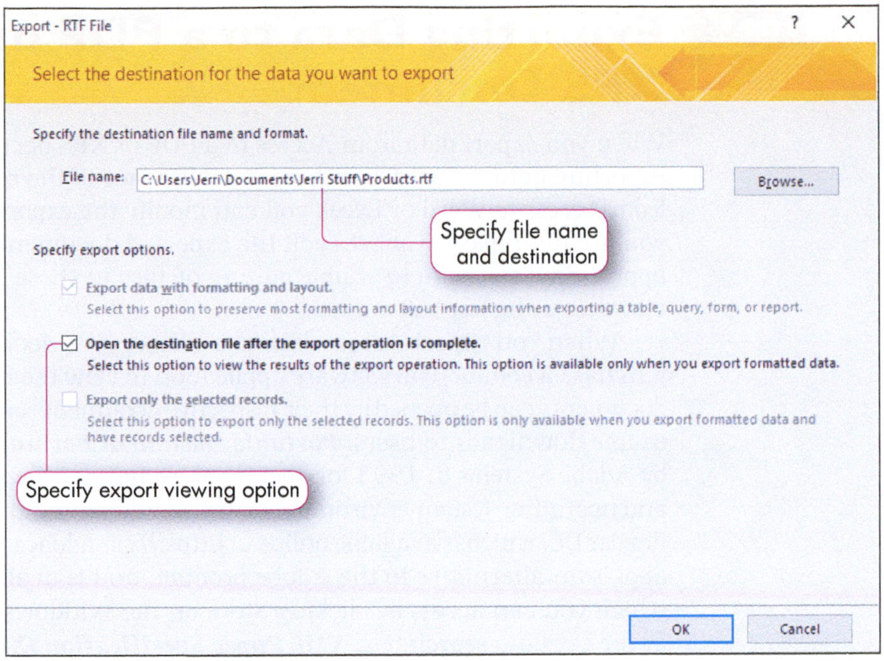

FIGURE 8.23 Export – RTF File Dialog Box

Modify an RTF File in Word

After you export an Access table to an RTF file, such as a products table, you can edit the file in Word and add additional text to the content. For example, if you want to send the exported products table to a few vendors to check current prices, you can add additional lines above the table to change the document to a memo format, as shown in Figure 8.24.

With an RTF file open, you can change the file type to Word Document so that you can take full advantage of Word's features and formatting tools.

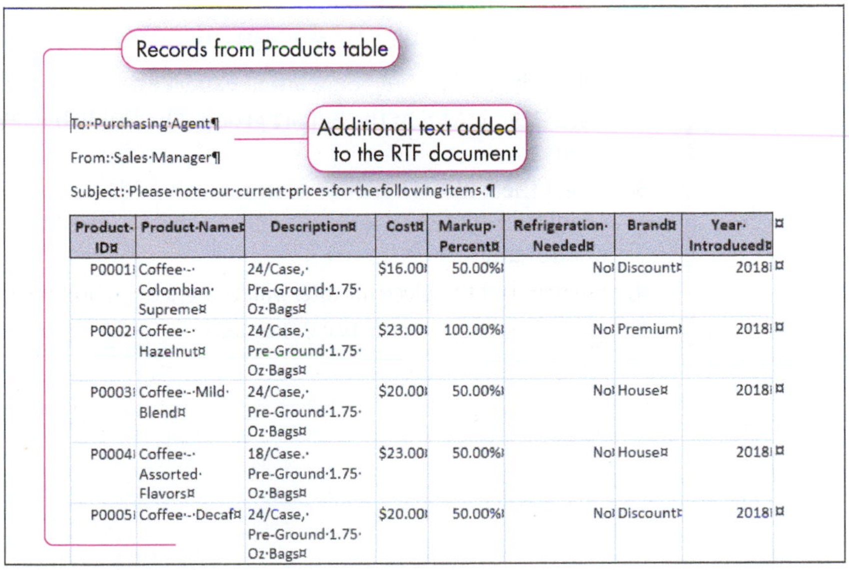

Product ID	Product Name	Description	Cost	Markup Percent	Refrigeration Needed	Brand	Year Introduced
P0001	Coffee - Colombian Supreme	24/Case, Pre-Ground 1.75 Oz Bags	$16.00	50.00%	No	Discount	2018
P0002	Coffee - Hazelnut	24/Case, Pre-Ground 1.75 Oz Bags	$23.00	100.00%	No	Premium	2018
P0003	Coffee - Mild Blend	24/Case, Pre-Ground 1.75 Oz Bags	$20.00	50.00%	No	House	2018
P0004	Coffee - Assorted Flavors	18/Case. Pre-Ground 1.75 Oz Bags	$23.00	50.00%	No	House	2018
P0005	Coffee - Decaf	24/Case, Pre-Ground 1.75 Oz Bags	$20.00	50.00%	No	Discount	2018

FIGURE 8.24 Product Data Exported to RTF Document

Exporting Data to a PDF or XPS Document

When you export data from Access to a PDF or XPS document, the process is similar to exporting data to Word, but there is a difference in the resulting files. When you export from Access to Word or Excel, you can modify the exported files. In PDF or XPS format you are not typically able to edit the exported documents. Most end users do not have appropriate software to enable editing of files in these formats; however, the files are viewable using free software.

When you export Access data to a PDF or XPS document, you are not required to purchase a commercial software application to view the information. Both PDF and XPS documents can be opened by their respective document readers. Both readers are available as free downloads to users. ***Portable Document Format (PDF)*** is a file format created by Adobe Systems in 1993 for document exchange independent of software application and operating system environment. PDF documents can be viewed with Adobe Acrobat Reader DC, which is available online at https://get.adobe.com/reader/. Reader, a Windows app, is an alternative to the Adobe product, and is available from the Microsoft Store, which you can access by clicking Store on the Windows 10 taskbar or by typing Store in the Cortana search box. ***XML Paper Specification (XPS)*** is a file format designed by Microsoft to display a printed page on screen identically on any computer platform. The XPS format is considered an alternative to PDF. An XPS document can be viewed with an XPS Viewer, which may be preinstalled with your operating system; otherwise, various free XPS viewers are available online.

Tables, queries, forms, and reports can be exported to a PDF or XPS document. If you attempt to export a single record from a form, you will be surprised to find the results contain all the records in the record source; you cannot selectively export form records. Be sure to check the number of pages after the objects are exported. Reports tend to be better choices for creating PDF and XPS documents, particularly if they do not need modification or data analysis. Documents in PDF or XPS format are generally intended for reviewing and printing. If your exported data do not display as intended, consider modifying an existing record source or creating a new one that will deliver better results.

To export to a PDF or XPS document, complete the following steps:

1. Select the object that you want to export and click the External Data tab.
2. Click PDF or XPS in the Export group. The Publish as PDF or XPS dialog box opens.
3. Select the folder where the document should be saved, type the name of the exported document, and then select the document type, either PDF or XPS Document.
4. Ensure that the *Open file after publishing* check box is selected.
5. Click Publish to create the document.

A document opens using the reader associated with the document type (PDF or XPS). The document contains multiple pages if the source has multiple pages. If the source document is too wide, then two pages may be required to display one page of data in the reader program. See Figure 8.25 as an example of a PDF document and Figure 8.26 as an example of an XPS document. XPS documents can be viewed with your browser (e.g., Microsoft Edge) or Reader if an XPS Viewer has not been installed. XPS documents are not as widely used and distributed as PDF documents. For that reason, PDF documents are the preferred format when exporting this type of document from Access.

Customers

Customer Name	Contact	Address1	Address2	City	State	CustomerFiles
Abel & Young	Jeff Jones	5000 Jefferson Lane	Suite 2000	Miami	FL	
Department of CIS	Eleanor Milgrom	1238 Walsh Drive	Suite 2202	Miami	FL	
Advantage Sales	Neil Goodman	4215 South 81 Street		Miami	FL	
Kinzer & Sons	Nicholas Colon	9020 N.W. 75 Street	Suite 302	Coral Springs	FL	
Milgrom Associates	Ashley Geoghegan	7500 Center Lane		Coral Springs	FL	
Lugo Computer Sales	Derek Anderson	6000 Tigertail Avenue		Coconut Grove	FL	
Bethune Appliance Sales	Michael Ware	276 Brickell Avenue	Suite 1403	Miami	FL	
Baker Auto Supply	Robert Slane	4508 N.W. 7 Street		Miami	FL	
Howard Animal Hospital	Luis Couto	455 Bargello Avenue		Coral Gables	FL	
Katie's Casual Wear	Jeffrey Muddell	9522 S.W. 142 Street		Miami	FL	
Little, Joiner, & Jones	Lauren Center	7245 NW 8 Street		Miami	FL	
Kline Bait & Tackle	Benjamin Lee	1000 Call Street		Coconut Grove	FL	
Computer Informations Systems	Eleanor Milgrom	1238 Walsh Drove	Suite 2202	Miami	FL	
Coulter Office Supplies	Maryann Coulter	1000 Main Street		Coral Springs	FL	

14

FIGURE 8.25 PDF Document Created from an Access Report

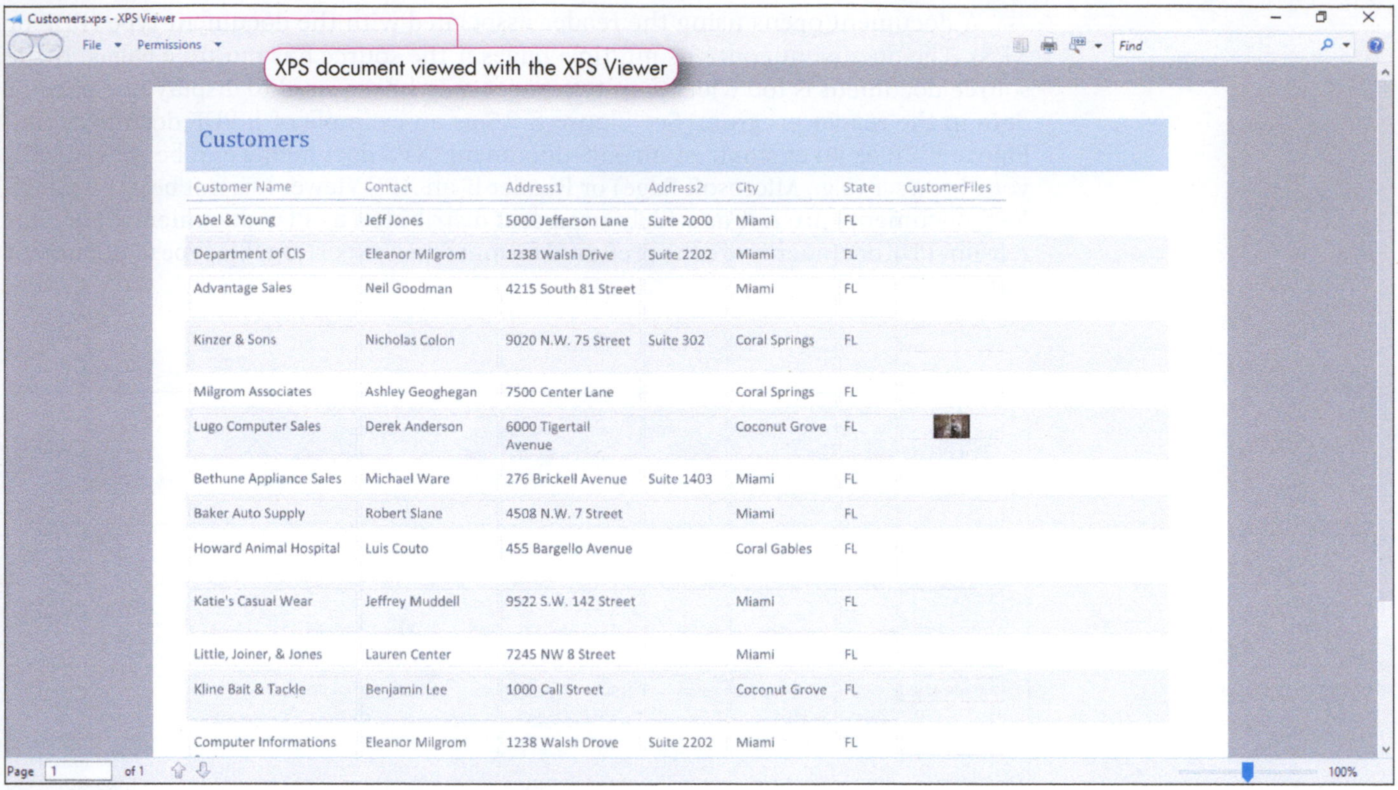

FIGURE 8.26 XPS Document Created from an Access Report

Exporting Objects to Another Access Database

After you create a database for one purpose, you may be able to use the structure of certain objects in a different database. For example, if you are designing databases for businesses, you will notice that many business databases require an employees table, a customers table, and an orders table. Companies often need a data entry form for each of those three tables. There may be common reports that can also be exported from one database to another—for example, an employee list report or a customer list report. However, you might have to modify the imported objects slightly to match the requirements of the new database. Exporting objects from one Access database to another saves time because you do not have to create the objects (tables, forms, reports) from scratch.

STEP 5 ### Export a Table to Another Database

When you export a table to another database, the Export dialog box prompts you to determine if you want to export the data along with the definition (e.g., the field names, data types) as shown in Figure 8.27. Sometimes, you will not want the data exported to the new database, depending on circumstances. If you are creating a new database for a different organization, the existing data would not be useful. However, the exported data could be extremely useful to a different department within the same company. After the table is successfully exported, you can delete unwanted fields and add new fields to create the table structure you need for the new purpose. Before you can export a table to another database, you must first create the new database if one does not already exist.

To export a table from one database to another, complete the following steps:

1. Select the table to be exported in the Navigation Pane.
2. Click the External Data tab.
3. Click Access in the Export group. The Export – Access Database dialog box displays.
4. Click Browse to locate the destination file, click the file to select it, and then click Save.
5. Click OK to proceed to the Export dialog box. Enter the name of the table (or accept the default name) and whether to export the Definition and Data or Definition Only.
6. Click OK in the Export dialog box; the table is then exported to the destination database.
7. Return to the Access window. Close the Save Export Steps window.

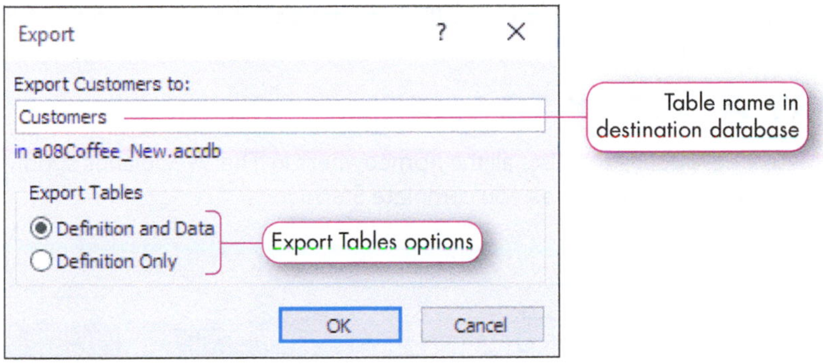

FIGURE 8.27 Export to Access Dialog Box

It is always a good idea to verify that the exported table was successfully exported to the destination database. Open the destination database and the exported table. After you verify that the table fields and records (if exporting data) are correct, close the table, and then close the database.

STEP 6 ▶ **Export Other Objects to Another Database**

In addition to tables, you may find that you can share queries, forms, and reports that you have designed with other databases by using the same process as that of exporting a table.

Verify that the exported object is available in the destination database by opening the database, then in the Navigation Pane, locate the exported object. After you verify the object was exported correctly, return to the original database.

Quick Concepts

4. Discuss a specific advantage of exporting an Access table to Excel. *p. 462*

5. Determine a scenario in which it would be useful to export an Access report to PDF format. *p. 460*

6. Consider a situation in which you would export the definition of a table to a different database, but not the data. *p. 462*

Hands-On Exercises

MyLab IT HOE2 Sim Training

▶ Watch the Video for this Hands-On Exercise!

Skills covered: Export a Query to Excel • Export a Report to Excel • Export a Query to Word • Modify an RTF File in Word • Export to a PDF or XPS Document • Export a Table to Another Database • Export a Form to Another Database

2 Export Data to Office and Other Applications

Blackwood Maintenance Service wants to contact the homeowners from the subdivisions they serve to tell them about their new services. You will export data to several different formats, depending on the preference of each subdivision's contact person. Some prefer an Excel spreadsheet, some prefer a Word document, one prefers PDF, and one prefers data in an Access table.

STEP 1 EXPORT A QUERY TO EXCEL

You will create a new query that lists all the homeowners in The Woodlands subdivision and export it to an Excel spreadsheet. Refer to Figure 8.28 as you complete Step 1.

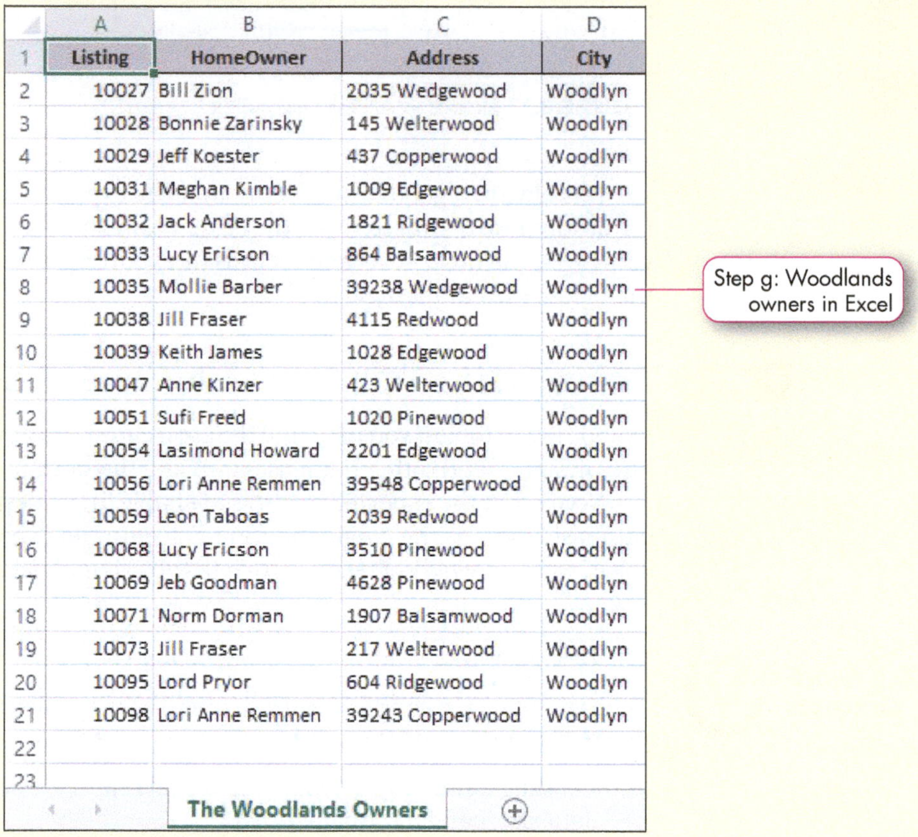

	A	B	C	D
1	**Listing**	**HomeOwner**	**Address**	**City**
2	10027	Bill Zion	2035 Wedgewood	Woodlyn
3	10028	Bonnie Zarinsky	145 Welterwood	Woodlyn
4	10029	Jeff Koester	437 Copperwood	Woodlyn
5	10031	Meghan Kimble	1009 Edgewood	Woodlyn
6	10032	Jack Anderson	1821 Ridgewood	Woodlyn
7	10033	Lucy Ericson	864 Balsamwood	Woodlyn
8	10035	Mollie Barber	39238 Wedgewood	Woodlyn
9	10038	Jill Fraser	4115 Redwood	Woodlyn
10	10039	Keith James	1028 Edgewood	Woodlyn
11	10047	Anne Kinzer	423 Welterwood	Woodlyn
12	10051	Sufi Freed	1020 Pinewood	Woodlyn
13	10054	Lasimond Howard	2201 Edgewood	Woodlyn
14	10056	Lori Anne Remmen	39548 Copperwood	Woodlyn
15	10059	Leon Taboas	2039 Redwood	Woodlyn
16	10068	Lucy Ericson	3510 Pinewood	Woodlyn
17	10069	Jeb Goodman	4628 Pinewood	Woodlyn
18	10071	Norm Dorman	1907 Balsamwood	Woodlyn
19	10073	Jill Fraser	217 Welterwood	Woodlyn
20	10095	Lord Pryor	604 Ridgewood	Woodlyn
21	10098	Lori Anne Remmen	39243 Copperwood	Woodlyn
22				
23				

Step g: Woodlands owners in Excel

The Woodlands Owners ⊕

FIGURE 8.28 Woodlands Query Exported to Excel

a. Open *a08h1Property_LastFirst* if you closed it at the end of Hands-On Exercise 1, and save it as **a08h2Property_LastFirst**, changing the h1 to h2.

b. Click **Query Design** in the Queries group on the Create tab. Add the **Properties table** to the query design window and close the Show Table dialog box.

c. Double-click the **SubDivisonID**, **Listing**, **HomeOwner**, **Address**, and **City fields** to add them to the query design grid.

d. Type **14** into the Criteria row of the SubDivisionID field. Click the **Show check box** to deselect it. Save the query as **The Woodlands Owners**.

You entered 14 in the Criteria row, which represents The Woodlands subdivision.

e. Run the query and widen the columns of the query so that all the data values are visible.

When you export to Excel, the Excel spreadsheet columns will be the same width as the Access columns, so it is important that all the data displays before exporting.

f. Click **Excel** in the Export group on the External Data tab. Click **Browse** to navigate to where you save your files. Type **a08h2Woodlands_LastFirst** in the File name box. Click **Save**.

> **TROUBLESHOOTING:** If you inadvertently click Excel in the Import & Link group, cancel the dialog box and click Excel in the Export group.

g. Click the **Export data with formatting and layout check box** and click the **Open the destination file after the export operation is complete check box** to select them in the Export – Excel Spreadsheet dialog box. Click **OK**.

A new Excel spreadsheet window opens showing The Woodlands owners' data.

> **TROUBLESHOOTING:** If you attempt to create an Excel file that already exists, Access displays the message, *Do you want to replace the existing one?* If you attempt to create an Excel file that is already open, Access displays a warning, *Microsoft Office Access can't save the output data.* Close the open Excel file and try again.

h. Return to the Access window. Click **Close** to close the Save Export Steps window without saving the export steps.

i. Save and close the query.

j. Review the workbook to ensure that all records have been exported as expected. Close the workbook and exit Excel. You will submit this file at the end of the last Hands-On Exercise.

STEP 2 **EXPORT A REPORT TO EXCEL**

You want to send the Service Request Report to one of the BMS subcontractors. You will export the report to Excel. Refer to Figure 8.29 as you complete Step 2.

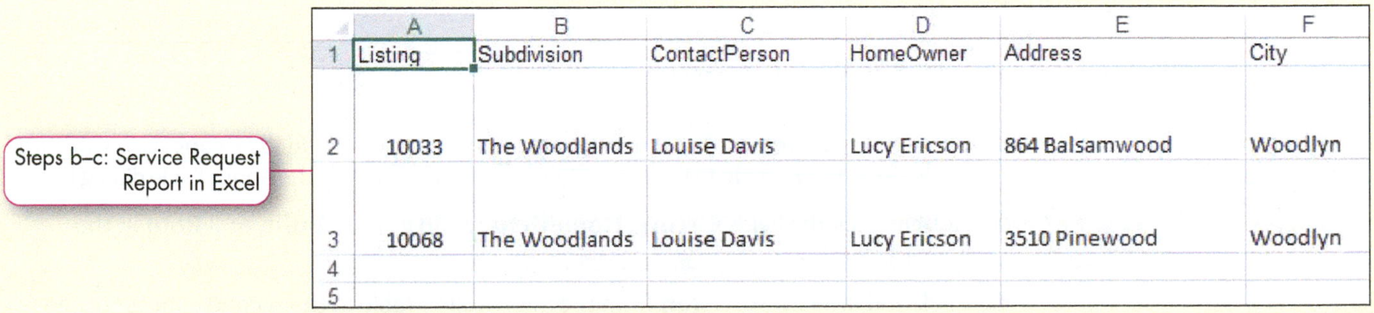

	A	B	C	D	E	F
1	Listing	Subdivision	ContactPerson	HomeOwner	Address	City
2	10033	The Woodlands	Louise Davis	Lucy Ericson	864 Balsamwood	Woodlyn
3	10068	The Woodlands	Louise Davis	Lucy Ericson	3510 Pinewood	Woodlyn
4						
5						

Steps b–c: Service Request Report in Excel

FIGURE 8.29 Report Exported to Excel

a. Double-click the **Service Request Report** in the Navigation Pane to open it.

You will export this report to Excel.

b. Click **Excel** in the Export group on the External Data tab.

c. Click **Browse** and navigate to where you save your files. Change the file name to **a08h2Service_LastFirst**. Click **Save**. Click the **Export data with formatting and layout check box** and click the **Open the destination file after the export operation is complete check box** to select them. Click **OK**.

A new Excel spreadsheet window opens, showing the Service Request Report data. The photos are missing and the report title was deleted.

d. Return to the Access window. Click **Close** to close the Save Export Steps window without saving the export steps.

e. Close the Access report.

f. Close the workbook and exit Excel. You will submit this file at the end of the last Hands-On Exercise.

STEP 3 EXPORT A QUERY TO WORD AND MODIFY AN RTF FILE IN WORD

You will create a query showing all homes with a tile roof built in or before 1997; these roofs may need to be repaired or replaced. Export the query results to Word. You will modify the exported document to include the typical memo elements. Refer to Figure 8.30 as you complete Step 3.

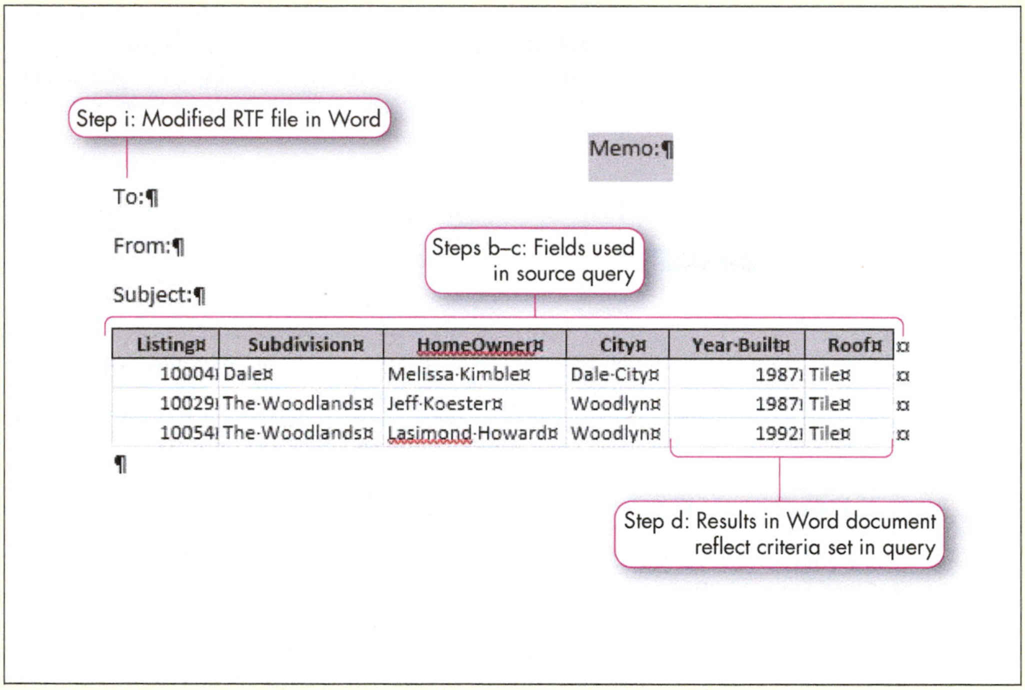

FIGURE 8.30 Query Data Exported to Word

a. Click **Query Design** in the Queries group on the Create tab. Add the **Properties table** and the **SubDivision table** to the query design window and close the Show Table dialog box.

b. Double-click the fields **Listing**, **HomeOwner**, **City**, **Year Built**, and **Roof** in the Properties table.

c. Click and drag **Subdivision** from the SubDivision table to the second column in the query design grid.

The other fields shift to the right to make room for the Subdivision field.

d. Type **<=1997** in the Criteria row of the YearBuilt column, and type **Tile** in the Criteria row of the Roof column.

You only want to see properties with a tile roof that were built on or before 1997.

e. Save the query as **Properties Built on or Before 1997**.

f. Run the query. Widen the columns of the query so that all the data values are visible.

When you export to Word, the columns show all the data if the column widths are wide enough in Access and the total width of the exported table does not exceed the Word document width.

g. Click the **External Data tab**, click **More** in the Export group, and then select **Word** from the displayed list.

You will use the list of properties to create a memo to send to the roofer, so he can inspect the roofs for damage.

h. Click **Browse** and navigate to where you save your files. Type **a08h2Sub_LastFirst** in the File name box. Click **Save**. Click the **Open the destination file after the export operation is complete check box** in the Export – RTF File dialog box to select it. Click **OK**.

Although you are exporting to Word, the file is saved in an RTF format. A new Word window opens, showing the Properties Built on or Before 1997 data.

> **TROUBLESHOOTING:** If you attempt to create a Word file that already exists, Access displays the message, *Do you want to replace the existing one?* If you attempt to create a Word file that is already open, Access displays a warning, *Microsoft Office Access can't save the output data.* Close the open Word file and try again.

i. Ensure that the insertion point is at the top of the document—the insertion point will be in the column heading of the first column. Press **Enter** one time and type **Memo:** Press **Enter** and type **To:**. Press **Enter**, type **From:**, press **Enter**, type **Subject:**, and then center-align the word *Memo*, as shown in Figure 8.30.

j. Click the **File tab** and click **Save As** to save the new Word document as **a08h2Sub_LastFirst**. Change the *Save as type* to **Word Document**. Click **Save**. Click **OK** in the warning dialog box if it displays. Close the document and exit Word.

k. Return to the Access window. Click **Close** to close the Save Export Steps window without saving.

l. Save and close the query. You will submit this file at the end of the last Hands-On Exercise.

STEP 4 ## EXPORT TO A PDF OR XPS DOCUMENT

You want to send the Service Request Report to one of the BMS contractors. The contractor asks that you send him the report in PDF format file because he does not have Microsoft Office on his device. Refer to Figure 8.31 as you complete Step 4.

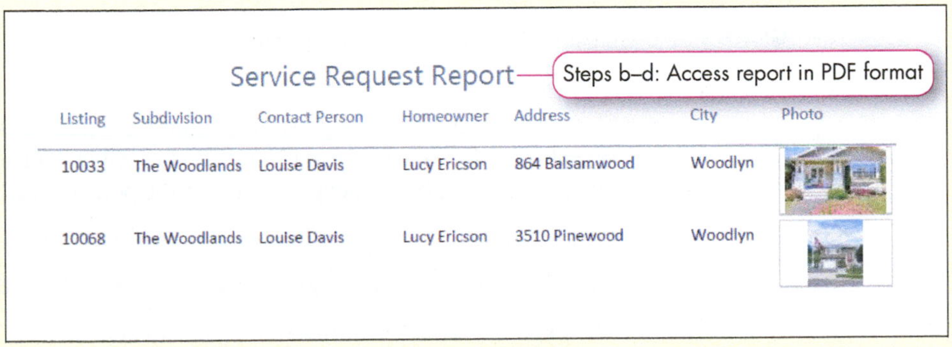

FIGURE 8.31 Service Request Report Exported to PDF

a. Select the **Service Request Report** in the Navigation Pane.

You will use this report to create a PDF document.

b. Click **PDF or XPS** in the Export group on the External Data tab.

c. Navigate to where you save your files.

d. Change the file name to **a08h2Service_LastFirst** and ensure that PDF is selected for the *Save as type*. Click **Publish**.

A new PDF document is created in the folder where you save your files and opens in the reader window. The images display in the PDF document, whereas they did not display in the Excel file.

> **TROUBLESHOOTING:** You might notice another file by the same name already in the file list, as it was used to export Excel data in a previous step.

e. Close the reader window.

f. Click **Close** to close the Save Export Steps window without saving. You will submit this file at the end of the last Hands-On Exercise.

STEP 5 EXPORT A TABLE TO ANOTHER DATABASE

Blackwood's landscaping contractor asked you for a list of all properties for which BMS provides landscaping services. Because his office manager knows Access, he asks you to send him the information in an Access database. Refer to Figure 8.32 as you complete Step 5.

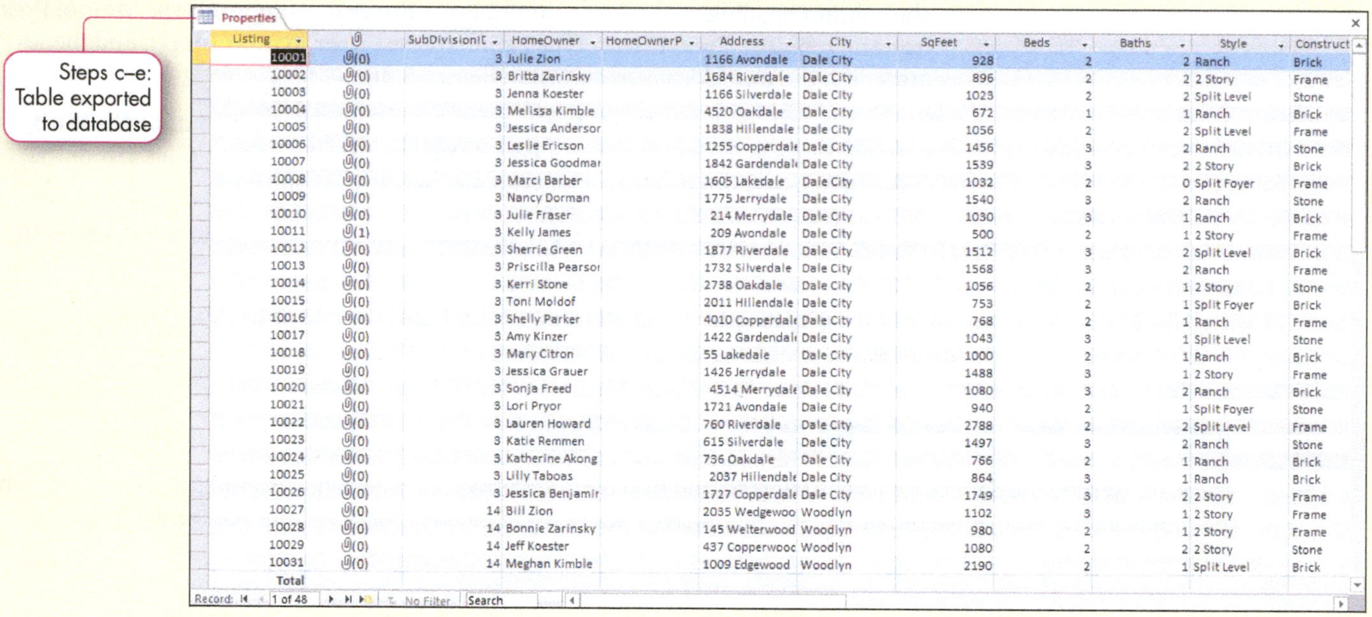

Steps c–e: Table exported to database

FIGURE 8.32 Destination Database with the Properties Table

a. Close the a08h2Property_LastFirst database. Open the *a08h2Propexport* database and save it as **a08h2Propexport_LastFirst**. Verify that this database does not contain any tables. Close a08h2Propexport_LastFirst. Open *a08h2Property_LastFirst*.

b. Select, but do not open, the **Properties table** in the Navigation Pane.

c. Click **Access** in the Export group on the External Data tab.

The Export – Access Database dialog box displays.

d. Click **Browse** and navigate to where you saved the a08h2Propexport_LastFirst database. Select the **a08h2Propexport_LastFirst database** and click **Save**. When you return to the Export – Access Database dialog box, click **OK**.

The Export dialog box displays, prompting for additional information about the table you are exporting.

e. Confirm that *Properties* is in the Export Properties to box. Accept the Definition and Data option. Click **OK**.

You are sending the properties data to the landscaping contractor.

f. Click **Close** to close the Save Export Steps window without saving.

Next, you want to verify that the table is in the destination database.

g. Close a08h2Property_LastFirst. Locate *a08h2Propexport_LastFirst* and open the database. Open the Properties table.

h. Close the a08h2Propexport_LastFirst database.

STEP 6 ## EXPORT A FORM TO ANOTHER DATABASE

The landscaping contractor wants you to send him a form to make it easier to work with the properties data. You will use the Form tool to quickly make a form with stacked layout. You will export the form to the same destination database as in Step 5. Refer to Figure 8.33 as you complete Step 6.

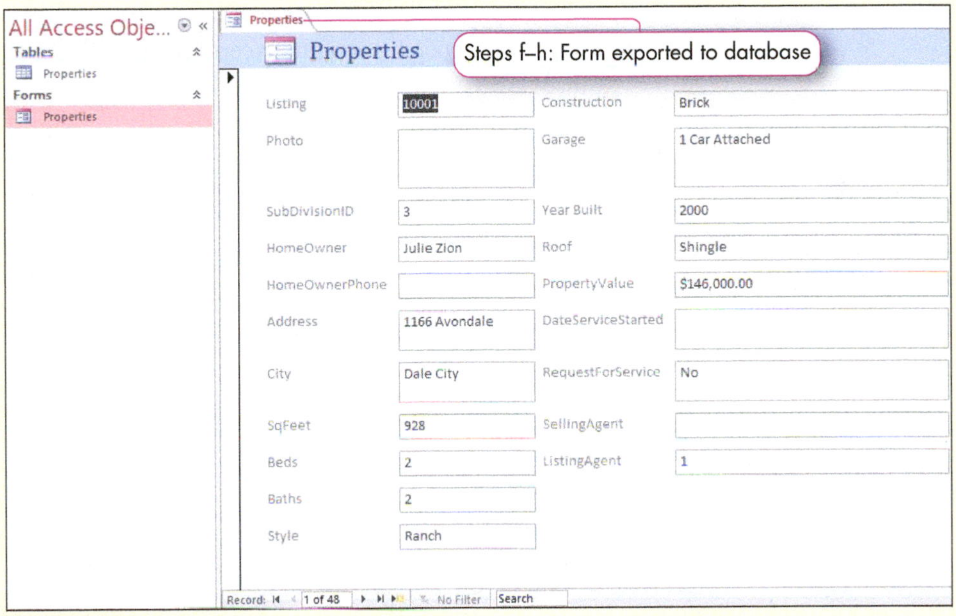

FIGURE 8.33 Destination Database with the Properties Form

a. Open the *a08h2Property_LastFirst* database. Ensure that the **Properties table** is selected in the Navigation Pane.

b. Click **Form** in the Forms group on the Create tab.

Access creates a new stacked layout form based on the Properties table.

c. Reduce the width of the Listing control by clicking on the right border and dragging it to the left. Reduce the width by approximately half. All the fields in the column will be resized.

d. Save the form as **Properties**. Close the form. Select **Properties form** in the Navigation Pane.

e. Click **Access** in the Export group on the External Data tab.

The Export – Access Database dialog box displays.

f. Click **Browse** and navigate to where you saved the a08h2Propexport_LastFirst database. Select the **a08h2Propexport_LastFirst database** and click **Save**. When you return to the Export – Access Database dialog box, click **OK**.

The Export dialog box displays, prompting you to type the name of the form you are exporting.

g. Confirm that *Properties* is in the Export Properties Form to box. Click **OK**.

You accept the default name of Properties.

h. Click **Close** to close the Save Export Steps window without saving.

Next you want to verify that the form is in the destination database.

i. Close the a08h2Property_LastFirst database. Locate *a08h2Propexport_LastFirst* and open the database. Verify the Properties form is in the database.

j. Open the form to view the data. Compare your screen with Figure 8.33.

k. Close the form.

l. Close the a08h2Propexport_LastFirst database. You will submit this file at the end of the last Hands-On Exercise.

m. Keep Access open if you plan to continue with the next Hands-On Exercise. If not, exit Access.

Import and Link Data in Access Databases

In the previous section, you learned about the benefits of exporting information from Access to Excel, Word, PDF, or XPS, and from one Access database to another. Sometimes you want to perform the opposite process—**importing** data into Access, which enables you to copy external data directly into a database. A variety of data file formats can be imported into Access. Alternatively, you can create links to use data from Access databases, Excel worksheets, and other applications without importing it into a database.

When you work with Access, much of the data entry is achieved by typing directly into tables or forms. However, you may want to import Access database objects from another database into your database. Importing tables from external databases is a convenient way to reuse data from other sources; you can modify an imported table or its records or append the table data to an existing table. You can also import and use other database objects, such as queries, forms, and reports from existing databases.

You might obtain data in Excel spreadsheets that can be imported directly into your Access database. Once the Excel data are imported into Access, you can add them to an existing table and save a lot of data entry time. Alternatively, you can use the imported Excel spreadsheet as a stand-alone table in Access.

You can also import text files into your Access databases rather than typing the data that originates from this type of source file. If you receive data in text format from systems that use text files, you can manage this type of data in Access if they are organized properly.

In this section, you will learn how to link a table from one Access database to another. You will also learn to use Excel data in a database by creating a link to and importing an Excel worksheet. Finally, you will learn how to import data into Access using a text file.

Linking to an Access Table

When a table in another database is relevant to your database, two options are available to use that data in your database. One is to import the table from the external database into your database; the other is to create a link to a table in another Access database. Importing a table from an external database provides direct access to the data, but also increases the size of your database. If the table you are importing is very large, you might want to consider linking it to your database. **Linking** enables you to connect to a table without having to import the table data into your database. You can only link to tables in another Access database; you cannot link to queries, forms, reports, macros, or modules.

When you link to a table in another Access database, Access creates a linked table that maintains a connection to the source table. You cannot change the structure of a linked table in the destination database (e.g., you cannot add or delete a field in a linked table, and you cannot modify the data type of a field). You can make changes to the data in a linked table in either instance of the database, and any changes you make are reflected in the table in both the source and destination database.

The ability to link to Access tables is important because databases are sometimes intentionally split so that non-table objects (queries, forms, and reports) reside in one database, and tables reside in another. To join the two databases, links are created from the database *without* tables to the database *with* tables. Users can add, delete, and edit data (in the linked objects) as if the tables reside in the first database (when they actually reside in the second).

Examine the Tables in the Source Database

Before you link to tables in another Access database, it is best to examine the tables in the source database first. Open the table that contains the information you need. Make sure the contents, field names, and other elements are correct prior to linking to the table.

STEP 2 **Link to an Access Table**

After you examine the data in the source table—the data you want to link to Access—you are ready to create a link from within the Access database. To add the new data into an existing table, you can append all or only a subset of the new table records to the table. You accomplish this by creating an append query based on the linked Access table. An append query is an action query that adds records to an existing table. Similar to the process of exporting data that was covered earlier in this chapter, linking to an Access table in another database uses a wizard (see Figure 8.34).

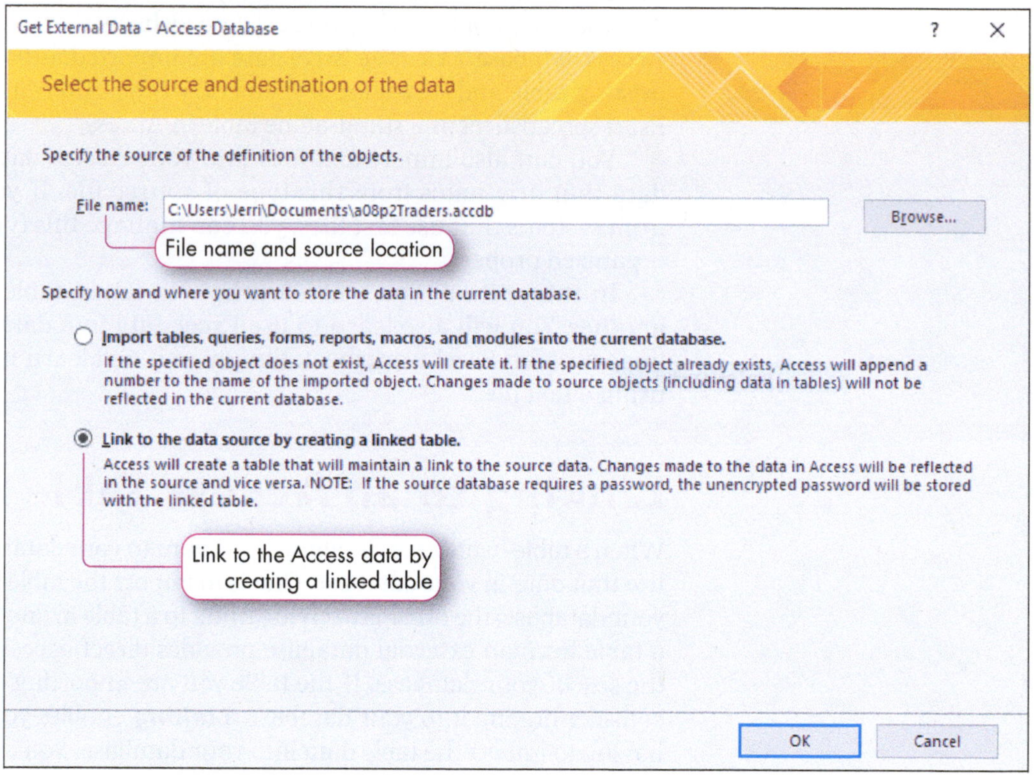

Get External Data - Access Database

Select the source and destination of the data

Specify the source of the definition of the objects.

File name: C:\Users\Jerri\Documents\a08p2Traders.accdb   Browse...

File name and source location

Specify how and where you want to store the data in the current database.

○ Import tables, queries, forms, reports, macros, and modules into the current database.
If the specified object does not exist, Access will create it. If the specified object already exists, Access will append a number to the name of the imported object. Changes made to source objects (including data in tables) will not be reflected in the current database.

◉ Link to the data source by creating a linked table.
Access will create a table that will maintain a link to the source data. Changes made to the data in Access will be reflected in the source and vice versa. NOTE: If the source database requires a password, the unencrypted password will be stored with the linked table.

Link to the Access data by creating a linked table

OK   Cancel

FIGURE 8.34 Get External Data – Access Database Dialog Box

To link to an Access table in another database, complete the following steps:

1. Click the External Data tab, then in the Import & Link group, click New Data Source, point to From Database, and then select Access. The Get External Data – Access Database dialog box opens.
2. Click *Link to the data source by creating a linked table.*
3. Click Browse to locate the Access database you want to link to.
4. Click the file to select it and click Open to specify this file as the source of the data.
5. Ensure that the *Link to the data source by creating a linked table* option is selected and click OK. The Link Tables dialog box displays, as shown in Figure 8.35.
6. Select the table you want to link to and click OK. Click Select All if the database contains multiple tables and you want to link to all of them.

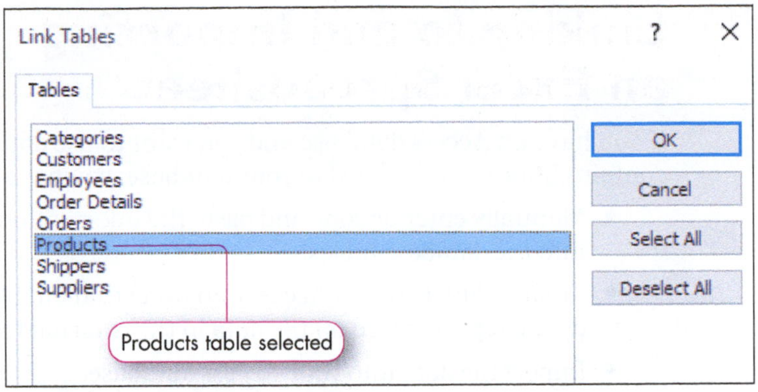

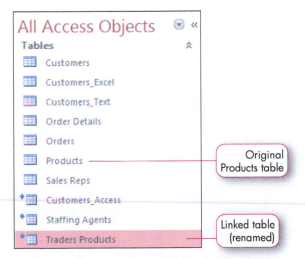

FIGURE 8.35 Link Tables Dialog Box

Once the link is created, you will see a special arrow icon next to the table name in the Navigation Pane that indicates the table is linked to an Access table. If the name of the linked table is the same as a table that already exists in the destination database, Access will add the number 1 to the end of the table name. For example, Access renames the linked table Products1 if a Products table already exists. If you link to another table with the same name, Products, Access renames the third table Products2. To further distinguish the linked Products table from the existing Products table, the Products1 table could be renamed (as Traders Products, for example), as shown in Figure 8.36.

FIGURE 8.36 Link to Access Table – Renamed

Linking to and Importing an Excel Spreadsheet

If you have an Access database and you want to use data from an Excel spreadsheet that contains information related to your database, you have three options:

- Manually enter or copy and paste the information contained in the spreadsheet into the database tables.
- Create a link between Access and Excel that enables you to update tables or create reports based on the data in the external Excel spreadsheet.
- Import the data into your Access database.

Linking and importing may appear to produce the same results; however, some differences do exist with respect to the resulting size of the database and the ability to modify data. Linking enables you to view the Excel data without increasing the size of the Access database. Linking does not enable you to update data from within Access; if errors exist in the worksheet, you must correct the errors in Excel and redisplay the linked table in Access. Importing an Excel worksheet enables you to modify the data in the imported table, which is a separate and distinct copy of the Excel worksheet.

STEP 3

Examine the Format of an Excel Spreadsheet

Before linking to the spreadsheet, you want to be sure the data are organized so that the import will be successful. First open the spreadsheet in Excel and examine the data, as shown in Figure 8.37. The data should be in continuous rows and columns with no blank rows, columns, or extraneous explanatory text. Ideally, the column headings and data formats should be an exact match to those in your database and in the same order, particularly if you are planning to merge the linked spreadsheet into an existing table. For example, the data in the Excel spreadsheet contains titles in cells A1 and A2 and a blank row in row 3. These first three rows will not import or link properly and should be deleted prior to importing or linking the data. It is a good idea to create a backup copy of the original spreadsheet before altering the spreadsheet to prepare it for linking or importing. This enables you to retrieve the original data in case this information is needed at another time.

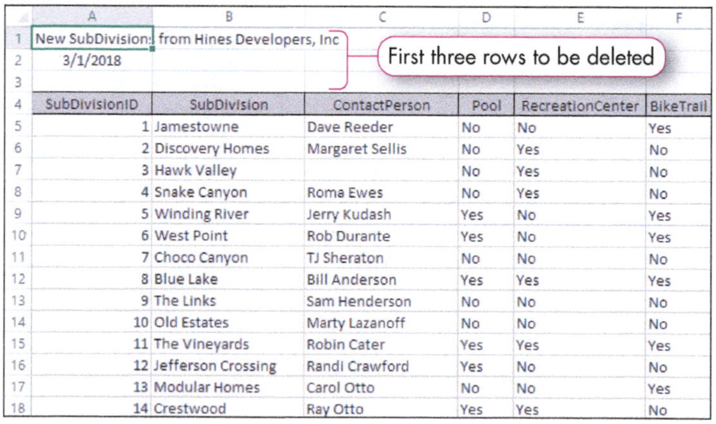

	A	B	C	D	E	F
1	New SubDivisions	from Hines Developers, Inc				
2	3/1/2018					
3						
4	SubDivisionID	SubDivision	ContactPerson	Pool	RecreationCenter	BikeTrail
5	1	Jamestowne	Dave Reeder	No	No	Yes
6	2	Discovery Homes	Margaret Sellis	No	Yes	No
7	3	Hawk Valley		No	Yes	No
8	4	Snake Canyon	Roma Ewes	No	Yes	No
9	5	Winding River	Jerry Kudash	Yes	No	Yes
10	6	West Point	Rob Durante	Yes	No	Yes
11	7	Choco Canyon	TJ Sheraton	No	No	No
12	8	Blue Lake	Bill Anderson	Yes	Yes	Yes
13	9	The Links	Sam Henderson	No	No	No
14	10	Old Estates	Marty Lazanoff	No	No	No
15	11	The Vineyards	Robin Cater	Yes	Yes	Yes
16	12	Jefferson Crossing	Randi Crawford	Yes	No	No
17	13	Modular Homes	Carol Otto	No	No	Yes
18	14	Crestwood	Ray Otto	Yes	Yes	No

First three rows to be deleted

FIGURE 8.37 Property SubDivisions Spreadsheet to Import into Access

Link to an Excel Spreadsheet

After you modify the Excel spreadsheet so the data will properly link to Access, you are ready to create a link to it from within Access. Similar to linking to an Access table in another database, linking to an Excel spreadsheet uses a wizard.

To link the Excel spreadsheet to Access, complete the following steps:

1. Click the External Data tab, then in the Import & Link group, click New Data Source, point to From File, and then select Excel. The Get External Data – Excel Spreadsheet dialog box launches.

2. Click Browse to locate the Excel file you want to link to, click the file to select it, and then click Open to specify this file as the source of the data.

3. Click the *Link to the data source* option and click OK. The Link Spreadsheet Wizard launches, as shown in Figure 8.38.

4. Select the worksheet from the list of worksheets if there is more than one sheet shown at the top of the dialog box and click Next.

5. Ensure that *First Row Contains Column Headings* check box is selected and click Next. The column headings of the Excel spreadsheet become the field names in the Access table.

6. Enter the new table name in the Linked Table Name box and click Finish.

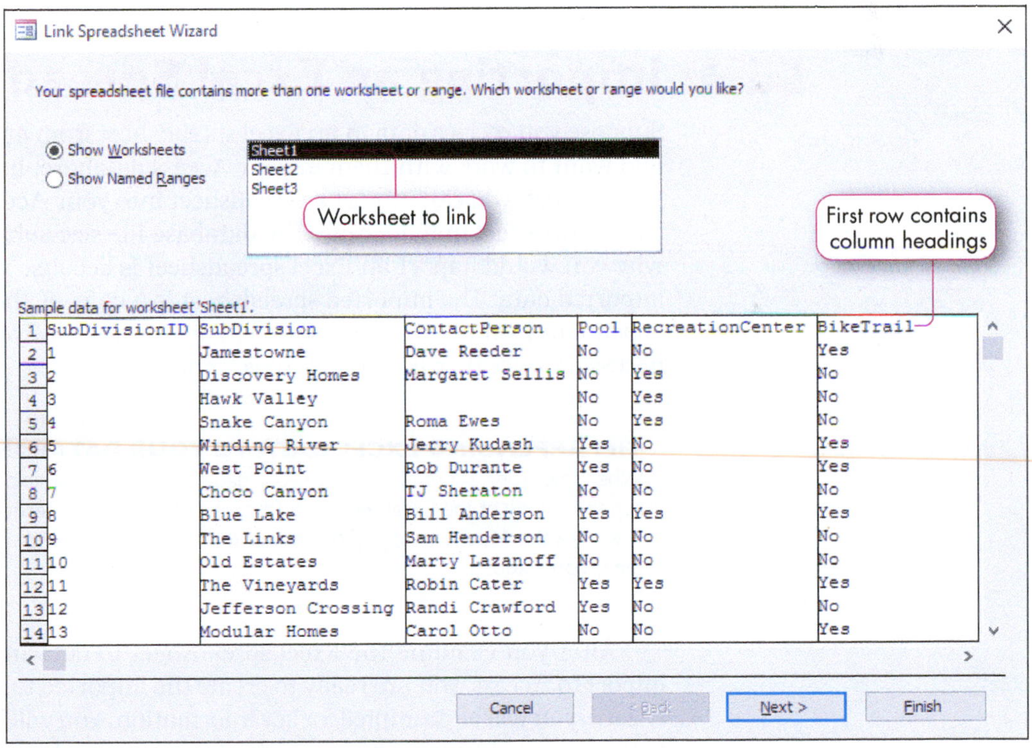

FIGURE 8.38 Link Spreadsheet Wizard

Because Access can only link to one sheet at a time, you might have to create multiple links, one for each worksheet. Make sure you label the links with descriptive names.

Once the link is created, you will see a special arrow icon next to the table name in the Navigation Pane that indicates the table is linked to the Excel file (see Figure 8.39). Double-click the table name and the table opens. The data look similar to data in the other tables, even though the data reside in an external Excel file. Although you have the linked table open in Access, you can still open the file in Excel (and vice versa).

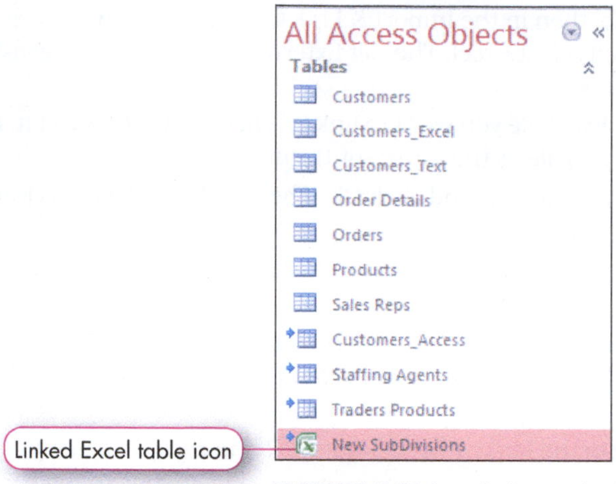

FIGURE 8.39 Icon Indicates Linked Excel Table

STEP 5 ▶ Importing an Excel Spreadsheet

Suppose you receive data in an Excel spreadsheet from another branch of your company and want to work with them in your Access database. In addition to linking to an Excel spreadsheet, you can import a spreadsheet into your Access database. Importing a large Excel worksheet may increase the database file size substantially; however, one reason why you would import an Excel spreadsheet is because you have more control over the imported data. The imported spreadsheet is a copy of the original spreadsheet, with no dependency on the external source. For that reason, you can manipulate the data as necessary once they is available in your database.

TIP: APPENDING EXCEL DATA TO YOUR DATABASE

When importing a spreadsheet into your database, if a comparable table exists, you can choose to append a copy of the Excel records to the table. In the Get External Data – Excel Spreadsheet dialog box, click the *Append a copy of the records to the table* option and select the table to which you want the records added.

After you examine the Excel spreadsheet to determine that the data will properly import to Access, you are ready to create the imported table. As you proceed through the wizard, you will be prompted for key information. You will be asked to assign a primary key to the imported table. If the spreadsheet contains a column that is eligible as a primary key, you can designate it as the key field in the Access table. Otherwise, you can allow Access to assign a generic primary key field using an AutoNumber data type. Alternatively, you can choose not to assign a primary key at all.

When you finish the import process, you will be asked to enter a name for the imported table. Ensure the name you assign is not one already used by an existing table and avoid the issue of having a duplicated table name in the database.

To import the Excel spreadsheet to Access, complete the following steps:

1. Click the External Data tab, then in the Import & Link group, click New Data Source, point to From File, and then select Excel. The Get External Data – Excel Spreadsheet dialog box launches.
2. Click Browse to locate the Excel file you want to import, click the file to select it, and then click Open to specify this file as the source of the data.
3. Ensure that the *Import the source data* option is selected and click OK. The Import Spreadsheet Wizard launches.
4. Select the worksheet from the list of worksheets if there is more than one sheet shown at the top of the dialog box and click Next.
5. Click the First Row Contains Column Headings check box and click Next two times.
6. Click the *Choose my own primary key* option if the imported data have a field that is acceptable as a primary key (as shown in Figure 8.40) and click Next.
7. Enter the new table name in the Import to Table box and click Finish.
8. Click Close when prompted to Save Import Steps.

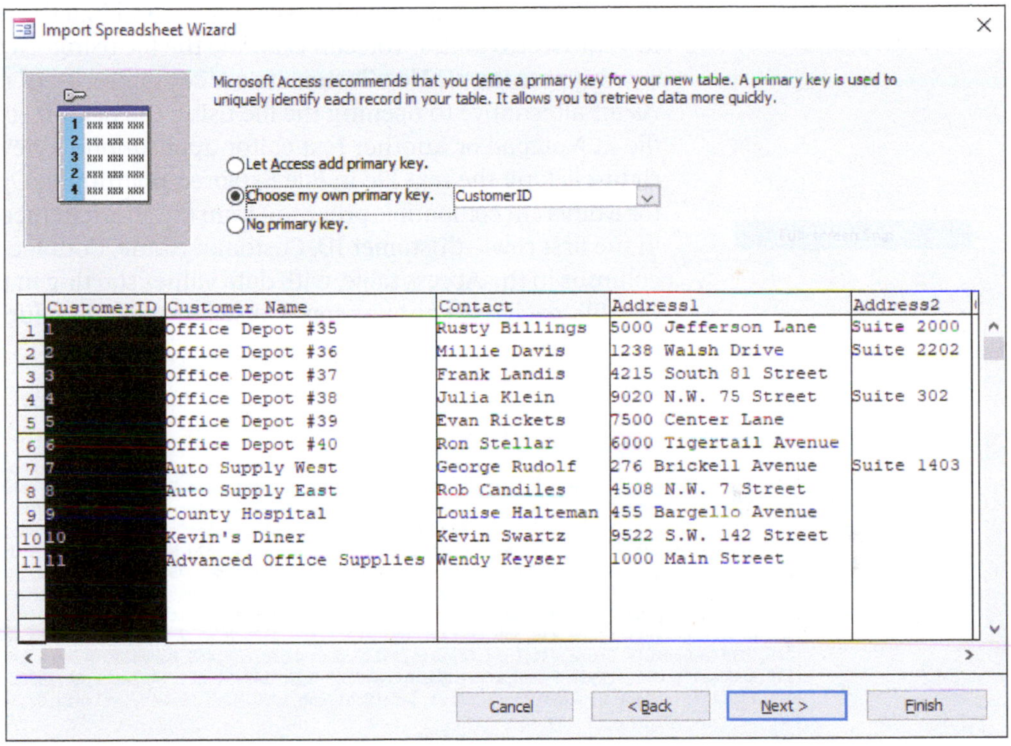

FIGURE 8.40 Choose My Own Primary Key Option

The imported table will display in the Navigation Pane, but it will not have an icon like a linked table would; it will look like any other table in the database.

Importing a Text File

In the preceding examples, you learned how to link to a table in another Access database and to link to and import an Excel spreadsheet. In addition, text files can be imported directly into an existing Access database. *Text files* store data without formatting and are commonly used for exchanging information between two computer systems.

Importing text files does not typically involve what we often consider to be text-based documents, such as Word or RTF files. The two most common text file types used for import are comma-separated values (CSV) and fixed-length files. **CSV text files** use a comma to separate one column from the next column, enabling the receiving software to distinguish one set of field values from the next. A text file of the CSV type has a .csv extension. Excel is the the default software application associated with CSV files and will launch when you open a file of this type. **Fixed-length text files** allocate a certain number of characters for each field. A fixed-length file containing company data might contain the fields Company Name with 25 characters allocated, Address with 20 characters, City with 20 characters, Region with 2 characters, and Postal Code with 10 characters. Any values with fewer than the allocated characters have spaces added to the end of the value, and any value that is longer than its allocated characters is cut off at the position where the characters exceed the maximum allowed.

STEP 6 ▶ ## Examine the Text File Before Importing

If you want to import a text file into Access, you should examine the file before performing the import. Confirm that the contents of the text file are relevant to your database. Also, verify that the format of the file is consistent and that the fields and data values correspond to your Access tables. You can examine the file using Excel.

Suppose the file NewCustomers.csv contains a list of new prospects for your company. As an alternative to opening the file using the default software, Excel, you can open the file in Notepad or another text editor application to view the comma-separated text by right-clicking the text file in File Explorer, pointing to *Open with*, and selecting Notepad (or a different compatible program) from the shortcut menu. The data contain field names in the first row—Customer ID, Customer Name, Contact, etc., each of which will become columns in the Access table, with data values starting in the second row. Because this is a CSV file, each row contains commas separating one value from the next (see Figure 8.41).

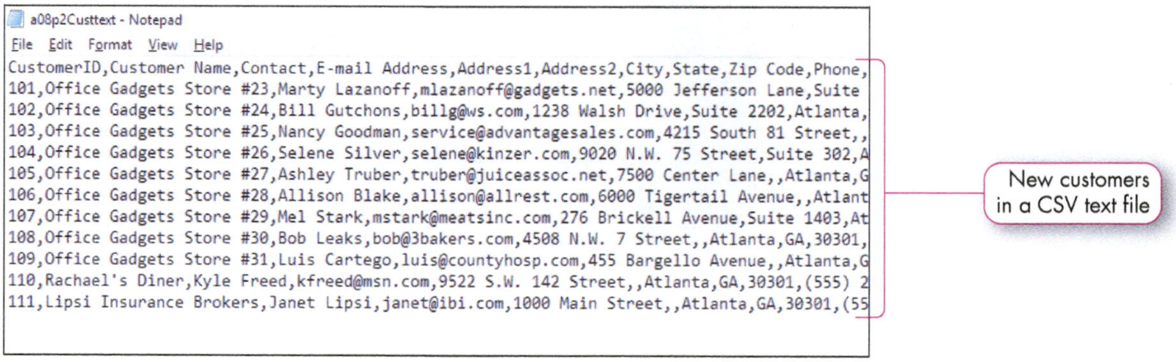

FIGURE 8.41 CSV File Opened with Notepad

STEP 7 ▶ ## Import a Text File into Access

After you examine the data in the CSV file, you are ready to import the data into an Access database.

To import a text file into an Access database, complete the following steps:

1. Click the External Data tab, then in the Import & Link group, click New Data Source, point to From File, and then select Text File. The Get External Data – Text File dialog box launches.

2. Click Browse to locate the CSV file you want to import (e.g., NewCustomers.csv), click the file to select it, and then click Open to specify this file as the source of the data.

3. Ensure that the *Import the source data into a new table* option is selected and click OK. The Import Text Wizard dialog box displays, as shown in Figure 8.42.

4. Click Next to proceed through the questions in the wizard.

5. Click the *First Row Contains Field Names* check box to select it and click Next two times.

6. Click the *Choose my own primary key* option and click Next. Access sets the value in the first field name of the text file as the primary key field of the table by default. Otherwise, you can specify a different value. You can also allow Access to set the primary key if no value that is eligible to be a key field exists, or to set no primary key at all.

7. Enter the new table name in the *Import to Table* box and click Finish.

8. Click Close at the Save Import Steps prompt. The new table displays in the Navigation Pane.

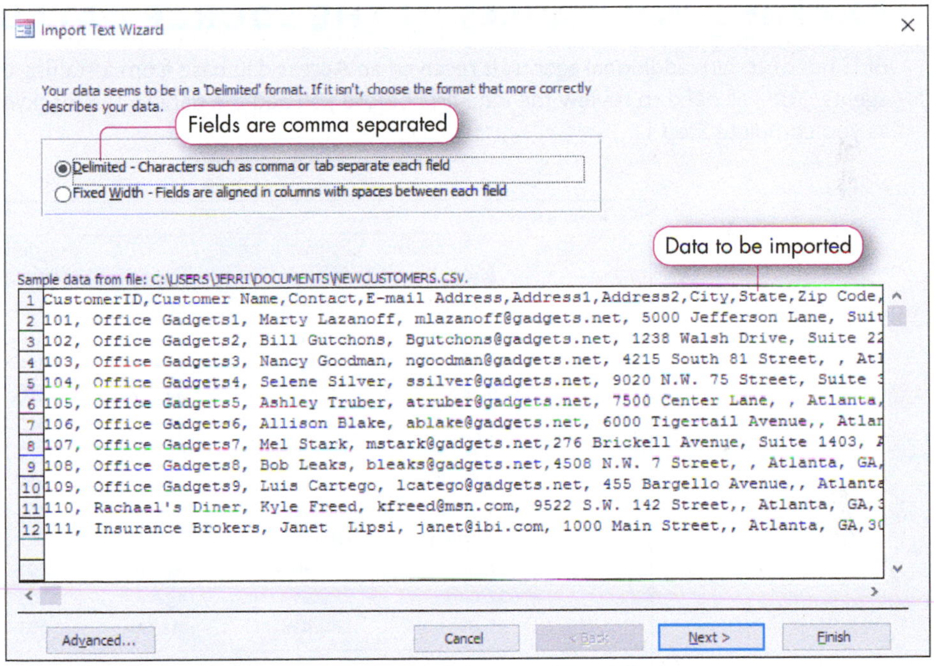

FIGURE 8.42 Import Text Wizard

The imported table will display in the Navigation Pane, with no special icon; it will look like any other table in the database.

Quick Concepts

7. Discuss a benefit and a disadvantage of linking a table to your database rather than importing it. *p. 474*

8. Consider what types of changes you would need to make to a spreadsheet before importing it into Access. *p. 474*

9. Examine how data are organized in a CSV file and discuss how Access imports them into a database table. *p. 478*

Hands-On Exercises

MyLab IT HOE3 Sim Training

Watch the Video for this Hands-On Exercise!

Skills covered: Examine the Tables in the Source Database • Link to an Access Table • Append Linked Data to an Existing Table • Examine the Format of an Excel Spreadsheet • Link to an Excel Spreadsheet • Create a Table from a Linked Spreadsheet • Import a Spreadsheet into Access • Examine the Text File Before Importing • Import a Text File into Access • Append Imported Data to an Existing Table

3 Import and Link Data in Access Databases

Blackwood Maintenance Service is adding additional subdivisions to its portfolio. It will need several new employees to manage the new subdivisions—you will review the list of agents provided in an external Access database and link it to the BMS database. BMS has obtained some subdivision information in an Excel spreadsheet, which you will link and import to the database. Another spreadsheet containing potential properties to be inspected also needs to be imported. Finally, BMS purchased a list of properties that might need its services. You will import the text file into the current database.

STEP 1 EXAMINE THE TABLES IN THE SOURCE DATABASE

BMS needs to hire additional agents. It received an Access database from a staffing company with a list of possible agents. You will need to review the data first before you add the data to the Blackwood database. Refer to Figure 8.43 as you complete Step 1.

Staffing Agents

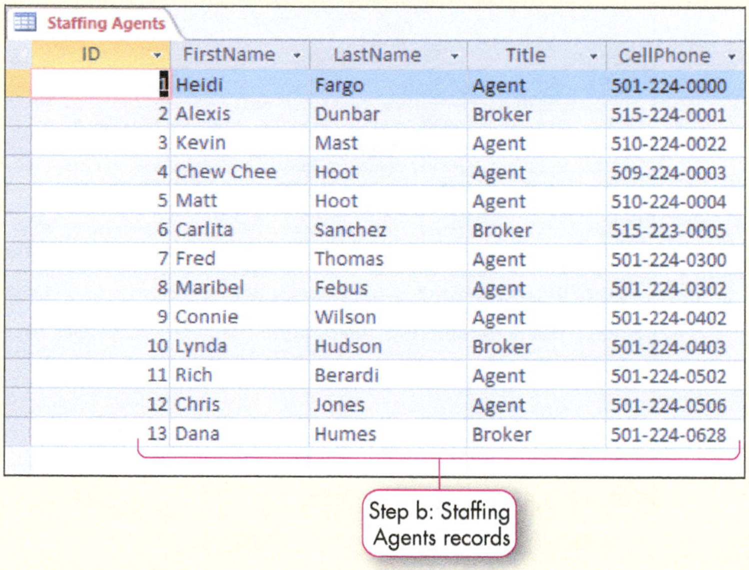

ID	FirstName	LastName	Title	CellPhone
1	Heidi	Fargo	Agent	501-224-0000
2	Alexis	Dunbar	Broker	515-224-0001
3	Kevin	Mast	Agent	510-224-0022
4	Chew Chee	Hoot	Agent	509-224-0003
5	Matt	Hoot	Agent	510-224-0004
6	Carlita	Sanchez	Broker	515-223-0005
7	Fred	Thomas	Agent	501-224-0300
8	Maribel	Febus	Agent	501-224-0302
9	Connie	Wilson	Agent	501-224-0402
10	Lynda	Hudson	Broker	501-224-0403
11	Rich	Berardi	Agent	501-224-0502
12	Chris	Jones	Agent	501-224-0506
13	Dana	Humes	Broker	501-224-0628

Step b: Staffing Agents records

FIGURE 8.43 Open the Source Database and Table

a. Open the *a08h3Propstaff* database file.

Access opens a08h3Propstaff database, and the Staffing Agents table displays in the Navigation Pane.

b. Open the Staffing Agents table in Datasheet view.

Thirteen agents are in the table.

c. Close the Staffing Agents table. Save the database as **a08h3Propstaff_LastFirst**. Close the database.

After examining the data from the staffing company, BMS management wants to link the data to its database. You will create a link to the table in the staffing database; you will then append the data to the Agents table in the Blackwood database. Refer to Figure 8.44 as you complete Step 2.

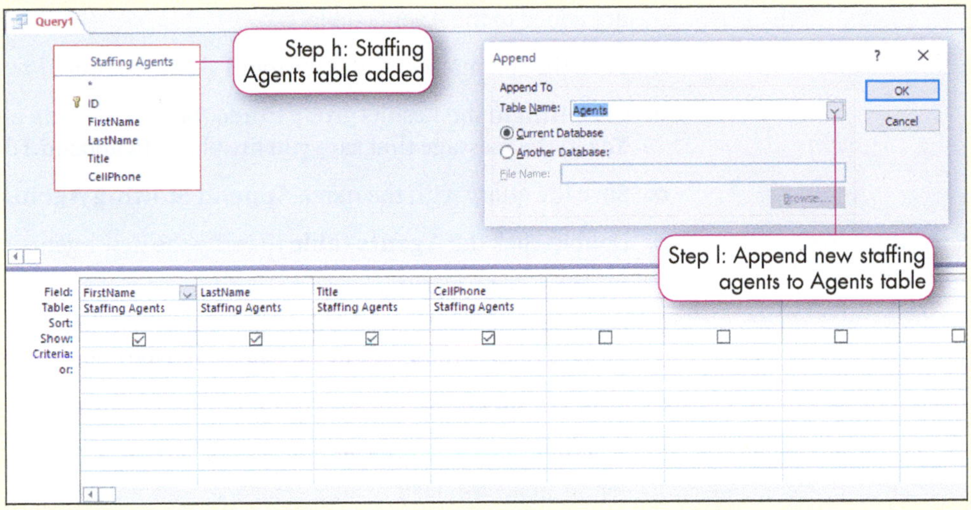

FIGURE 8.44 Append Staffing Agents to Agents Table

a. Open *a08h2Property_LastFirst* and save it as **a08h3Property_LastFirst**, changing h2 to h3.

b. Click the **External Data tab**. In the Import & Link group, click **New Data Source**, point to **From Database**, and then select **Access**.

c. Click **Browse** to locate the *a08h3Propstaff_LastFirst* database. Click the file to select it and click **Open**.

d. Select the **Link to the data source by creating a linked table option** and click **OK**.

e. Select the **Staffing Agents table** in the Link Tables dialog box and click **OK**.

You created a link to the Staffing Agents table in the staffing database. Note the arrow next to the table icon that indicates that the table is linked.

f. Double-click the **Staffing Agents table** in the Navigation Pane.

The table contains the same 13 records that are in the staffing database. You are now prepared to add the new agents to the Agents table so that all the agents can be merged into one table.

g. Close the Staffing Agents table.

h. Click **Query Design** in the Queries group on the Create tab. Add the **Staffing Agents table** to the query design and close the Show Table dialog box.

You began to create a select query, which you will convert to an append query.

i. Double-click the **title bar** of the Staffing Agents table to select all the fields. Drag the fields to the first field cell of the query design grid.

j. Switch to Datasheet view.

The new staffing agents are listed as expected, and you are now ready to append the records to the existing Agents table.

k. Switch back to Design view.

l. Click **Append** in the Query Type group and select **Agents** using the Table Name arrow. Click **OK**.

The *Append to* row displays in the query design grid with the corresponding field names listed. Some of the new IDs are the same as the existing IDs. You decide to remove the ID field from the append query. The new records will be automatically numbered when they are added to the Agents table.

m. Click the column selector at the top of the ID column. Press **Delete** to remove the column.

n. Click **Run** in the Results group to add the new staffing agents to the Agents table. Click **Yes** in the message that says you are about to append 13 rows to the Agents table.

o. Save the query with the name **Append Staffing Agents**. Close the query.

p. Double-click the **Agents table** to verify the new agents are in the table.

The ID numbers of the appended agents are automatically assigned by the Agents table because the ID field has the data type AutoNumber. Note that some of the missing data, such as home phone numbers, will need to be added later.

q. Close the table.

STEP 3 EXAMINE THE FORMAT OF AN EXCEL SPREADSHEET

You will open the list of new subdivisions that BMS received in an Excel spreadsheet format and decide whether you want to add the information to your existing subdivision table. Refer to Figure 8.45 as you complete Step 3.

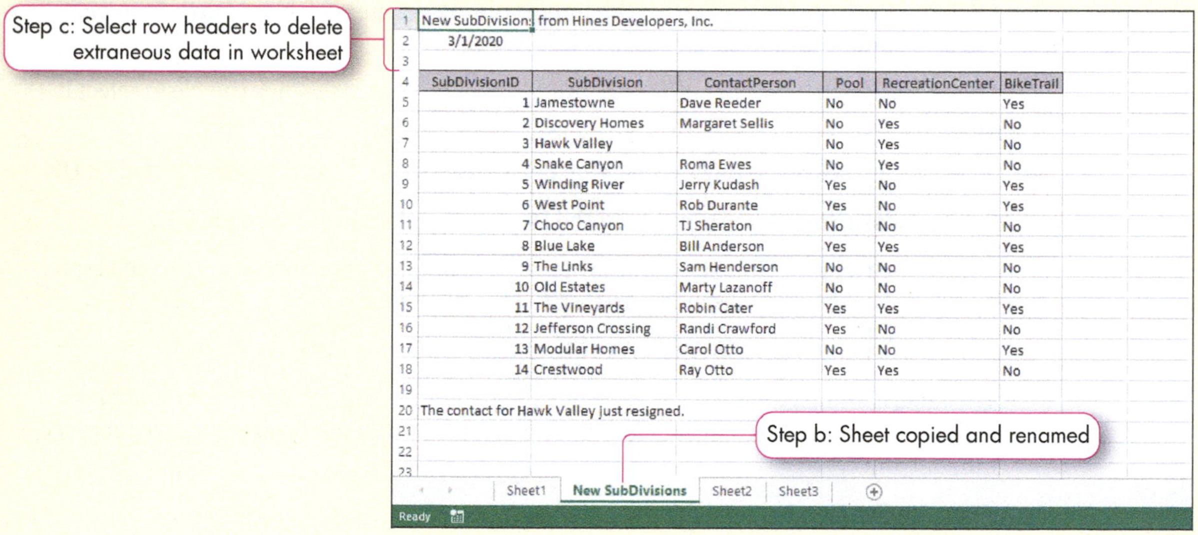

SubDivisionID	SubDivision	ContactPerson	Pool	RecreationCenter	BikeTrail
1	Jamestowne	Dave Reeder	No	No	Yes
2	Discovery Homes	Margaret Sellis	No	Yes	No
3	Hawk Valley		No	Yes	No
4	Snake Canyon	Roma Ewes	No	Yes	No
5	Winding River	Jerry Kudash	Yes	No	Yes
6	West Point	Rob Durante	Yes	No	Yes
7	Choco Canyon	TJ Sheraton	No	No	No
8	Blue Lake	Bill Anderson	Yes	Yes	Yes
9	The Links	Sam Henderson	No	No	No
10	Old Estates	Marty Lazanoff	No	No	No
11	The Vineyards	Robin Cater	Yes	Yes	Yes
12	Jefferson Crossing	Randi Crawford	Yes	No	No
13	Modular Homes	Carol Otto	No	No	Yes
14	Crestwood	Ray Otto	Yes	Yes	No

FIGURE 8.45 Copied Excel Worksheet to Be Modified

a. Open the Excel workbook *a08h3Propsub.xlsx* and save it as **a08h3Propsub_LastFirst**.

You will decide if the data will fit into the existing subdivision table and whether the data are formatted properly and do not contain extraneous rows.

b. Click **Enable Editing** in the Excel window if it displays. Right-click the **Sheet1 tab**. Select **Move or Copy**. Select **Sheet2** in the *Before sheet:* box and click to select the **Create a copy check box**. Click **OK**. Double-click the **copied sheet tab**, rename the worksheet **New SubDivisions**, and then press **Enter**.

The new worksheet is the second worksheet.

c. Click and drag the **row headers** to select the first three rows of the worksheet, as shown in Figure 8.45. Click **Delete** in the Cells group on the Home tab.

The first row of a spreadsheet that is being linked or imported must contain column headings that can be recognized as field names by Access.

d. Click **cell A17**, which contains *The contact for Hawk Valley just resigned*. Press **Delete**.

There should not be any data after the last row of formatted data.

e. Save and close the workbook and exit Excel.

The revised Excel spreadsheet can now be linked to the Access database.

STEP 4 ▶ **LINK TO AN EXCEL SPREADSHEET**

You will create a link to the new subdivisions worksheet and use the linked worksheet to create a new table in the database. Refer to Figure 8.46 as you complete Step 4.

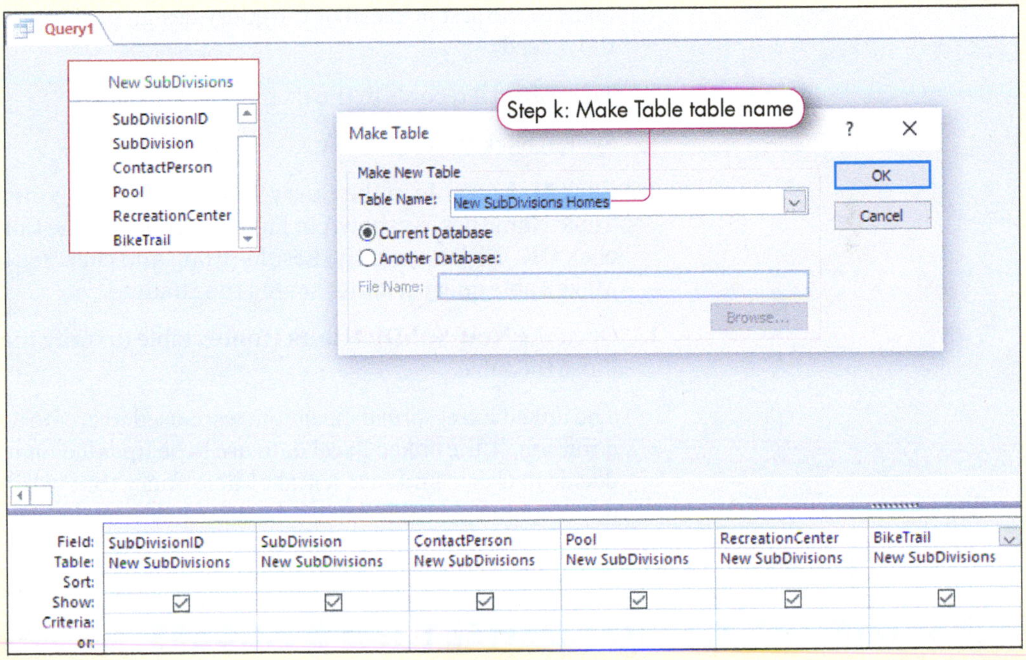

FIGURE 8.46 Use a Make Table Query to Create a New Table

a. Click Access on the taskbar to return to the Access window and click the **External Data tab**.

b. Click **New Data Source** in the Import & Link group, point to **From File**, and then select **Excel**.

The Get External Data – Excel Spreadsheet dialog box launches.

c. Click **Browse** to locate the spreadsheet *a08h3Propsub_LastFirst.xlsx*. Click **Open**.

d. Select the **Link to the data source by creating a linked table option** and click **OK**.

e. Select **New SubDivisions** in the Show Worksheets box of the Link Spreadsheet Wizard. Click **Next**.

You selected the revised worksheet for the link.

f. Click the **First Row Contains Column Headings check box** to select it. Click **Next**.

g. Accept the name *New SubDivisions* for the Access linked table name. Click **Finish**. Click **OK** in the message box that displays.

The Excel linked icon displays next to the New SubDivisions table.

h. Click **Query Design** in the Queries group on the Create tab. Add the **New SubDivisions table** to the query design and close the Show Table dialog box.

You decide to create a new table from the linked spreadsheet using a Make Table query.

i. Double-click the **title bar** of the New SubDivisions table to select all the fields. Drag the fields to the first field cell of the query design grid. Switch to Datasheet view to examine the records.

There are 14 records in the query results.

j. Switch back to Design view.

k. Click **Make Table** in the Query Type group. Type **New SubDivisions Homes** in the Table Name box, as shown in Figure 8.46. With the Current Database option selected, click **OK**. Click **Run** in the Results group and click **Yes** to the warning message. Close the Make Table query without saving the changes.

l. Open the **New SubDivisions Homes** table to verify that 14 records display in the table. Close the table.

The linked Excel spreadsheet data were used to create a new Access table in the database. If the linked Excel data are to be updated on a continuous basis, you could decide to create and save a Make Table query that will overwrite the table with the new data regularly.

STEP 5 IMPORT A SPREADSHEET INTO ACCESS

BMS received an Excel spreadsheet containing a list of potential new properties to be inspected. You need to examine the data prior to adding them to BMS's database; for now, the imported data will be used as a stand-alone table. Refer to Figures 8.47 and 8.48 as you complete Step 5.

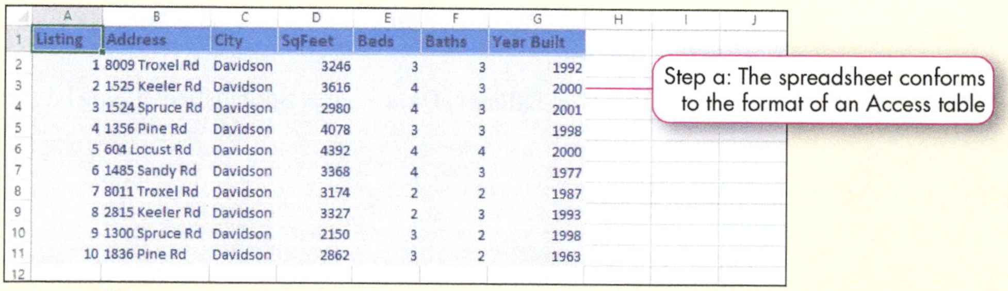

Listing	Address	City	SqFeet	Beds	Baths	Year Built
1	8009 Troxel Rd	Davidson	3246	3	3	1992
2	1525 Keeler Rd	Davidson	3616	4	3	2000
3	1524 Spruce Rd	Davidson	2980	4	3	2001
4	1356 Pine Rd	Davidson	4078	3	3	1998
5	604 Locust Rd	Davidson	4392	4	4	2000
6	1485 Sandy Rd	Davidson	3368	4	3	1977
7	8011 Troxel Rd	Davidson	3174	2	2	1987
8	2815 Keeler Rd	Davidson	3327	2	3	1993
9	1300 Spruce Rd	Davidson	2150	3	2	1998
10	1836 Pine Rd	Davidson	2862	3	2	1963

FIGURE 8.47 Spreadsheet to be Imported into Access

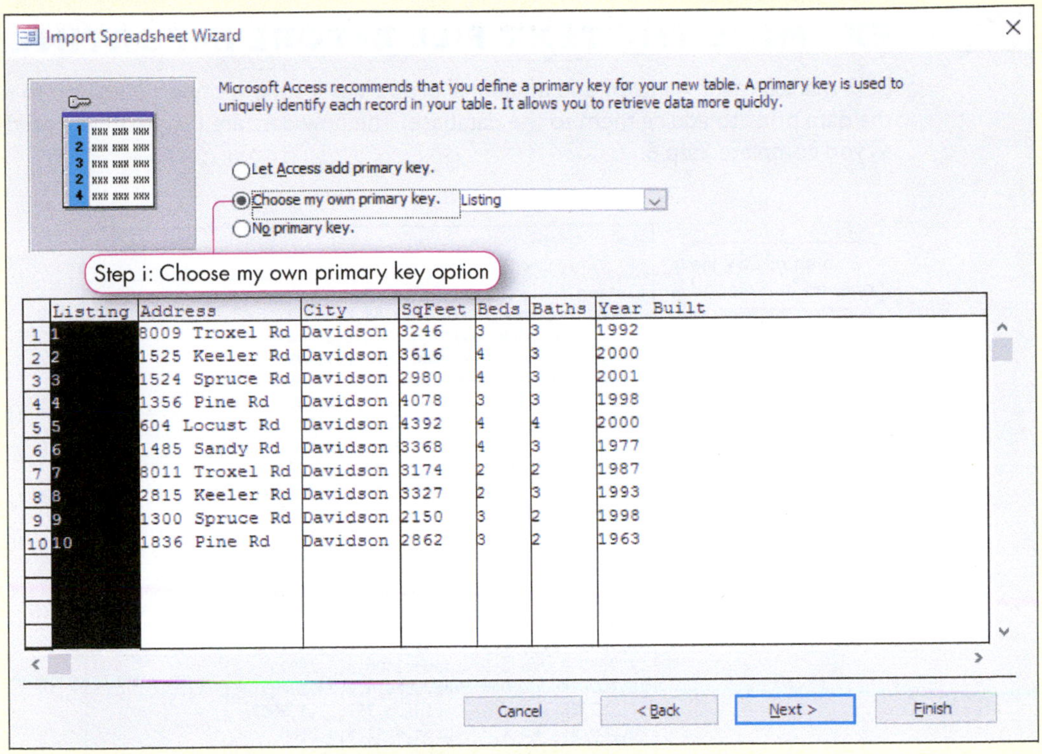

FIGURE 8.48 Importing a Spreadsheet to Access

a. Open the *a08h3Propinspect.xlsx* workbook.

The spreadsheet conforms to the format of an Access table, so you do not need to make any changes to it.

b. Close the workbook and exit Excel without making any changes to the file.

c. Click **Access** on the taskbar to return to the Access window and click the **External Data tab**.

d. Click **New Data Source** in the Import & Link group, point to **From File**, and then select **Excel**. The Get External Data – Excel Spreadsheet dialog box launches.

e. Click **Browse** to locate the spreadsheet *a08h3Propinspect.xlsx*. Click **Open**.

f. Ensure that the *Import the source data into a new table in the current database* option is selected and click **OK**.

g. Ensure that *First Row Contains Column Headings* is checked and click **Next** in the Import Spreadsheet Wizard.

The first row of the spreadsheet contains column headings that will be used as the field names for the Access table.

h. Click **Next**.

i. Click the **Choose my own primary key option**, verify that Listing displays as the primary key, and then click **Next**.

Access sets the value in the first column of the spreadsheet, Listing, as the primary key field of the table.

j. Enter the new table name, **Inspection Properties**, in the Import to Table box, and click **Finish**.

k. Click **Close** in the Save Import Steps dialog box.

The imported table displays in the Navigation Pane.

l. Open the **Inspection Properties table** to verify that 10 records display in the table. Close the table.

BMS management wants to add additional properties from the city of Davidson to its database. You want to examine the data prior to adding them to the database. The new data are in a text file with the CSV format. Refer to Figure 8.49 as you complete Step 6.

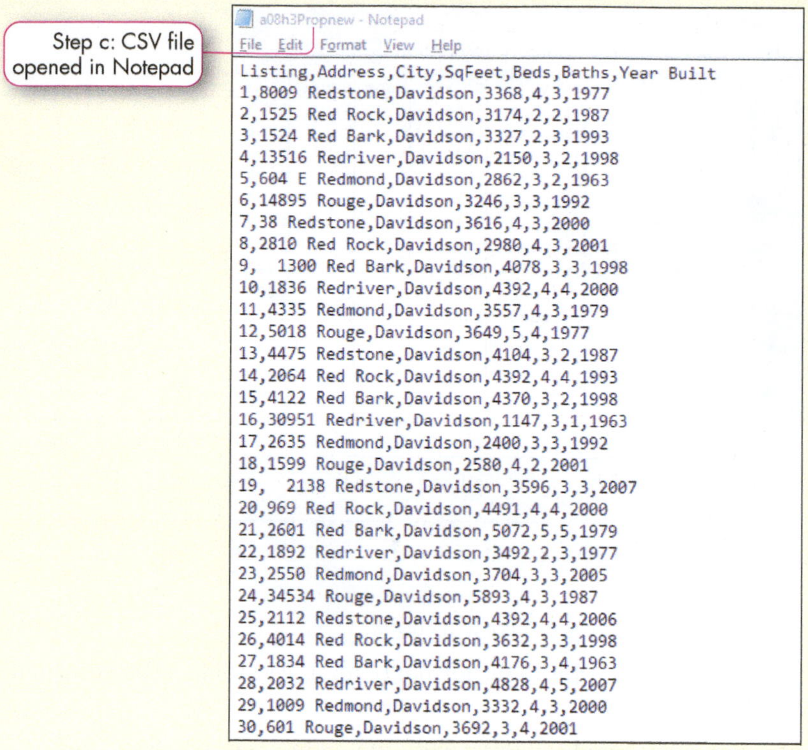

Step c: CSV file opened in Notepad

```
a08h3Propnew - Notepad
File  Edit  Format  View  Help
Listing,Address,City,SqFeet,Beds,Baths,Year Built
1,8009 Redstone,Davidson,3368,4,3,1977
2,1525 Red Rock,Davidson,3174,2,2,1987
3,1524 Red Bark,Davidson,3327,2,3,1993
4,13516 Redriver,Davidson,2150,3,2,1998
5,604 E Redmond,Davidson,2862,3,2,1963
6,14895 Rouge,Davidson,3246,3,3,1992
7,38 Redstone,Davidson,3616,4,3,2000
8,2810 Red Rock,Davidson,2980,4,3,2001
9,  1300 Red Bark,Davidson,4078,3,3,1998
10,1836 Redriver,Davidson,4392,4,4,2000
11,4335 Redmond,Davidson,3557,4,3,1979
12,5018 Rouge,Davidson,3649,5,4,1977
13,4475 Redstone,Davidson,4104,3,2,1987
14,2064 Red Rock,Davidson,4392,4,4,1993
15,4122 Red Bark,Davidson,4370,3,2,1998
16,30951 Redriver,Davidson,1147,3,1,1963
17,2635 Redmond,Davidson,2400,3,3,1992
18,1599 Rouge,Davidson,2580,4,2,2001
19,  2138 Redstone,Davidson,3596,3,3,2007
20,969 Red Rock,Davidson,4491,4,4,2000
21,2601 Red Bark,Davidson,5072,5,5,1979
22,1892 Redriver,Davidson,3492,2,3,1977
23,2550 Redmond,Davidson,3704,3,3,2005
24,34534 Rouge,Davidson,5893,4,3,1987
25,2112 Redstone,Davidson,4392,4,4,2006
26,4014 Red Rock,Davidson,3632,3,3,1998
27,1834 Red Bark,Davidson,4176,3,4,1963
28,2032 Redriver,Davidson,4828,4,5,2007
29,1009 Redmond,Davidson,3332,4,3,2000
30,601 Rouge,Davidson,3692,3,4,2001
```

FIGURE 8.49 CSV File Opened in Notepad

a. Open *a08h3Propnew.csv* using File Explorer.

Note that the file has consistent formatting for importing into Access.

b. Exit Excel without making any changes to the file.

c. Right-click the *a08h3Propnew.csv* file in File Explorer, point to **Open with**, and then select **Notepad** from the shortcut menu.

You use Notepad to examine the file in its native format.

d. Close Notepad.

The BMS owners want to import and append the Davidson properties to the Properties table in the Blackwood database. The Listing values will have to be modified when the data are appended so that they are higher than the existing values in the table. Refer to Figure 8.50 as you complete Step 7.

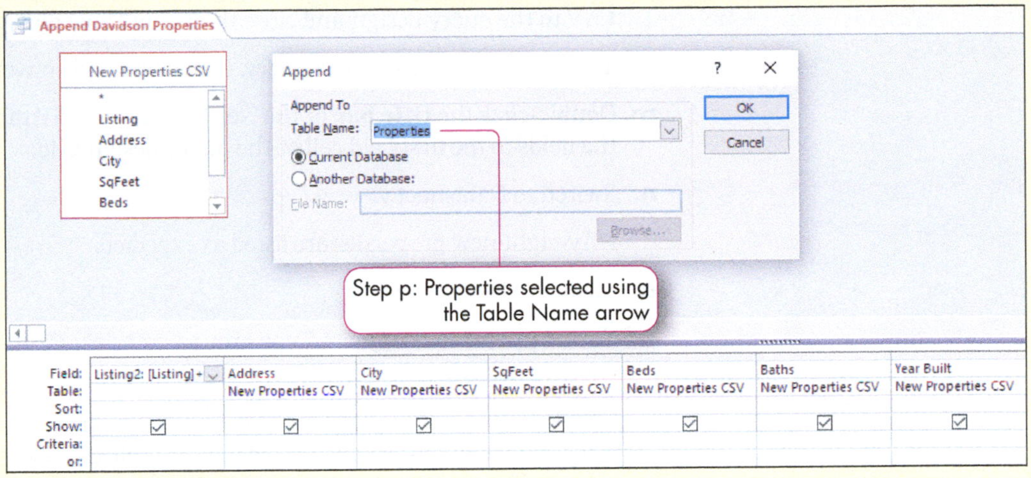

FIGURE 8.50 Append CSV Records to an Access Table

a. Click Access on the taskbar to return to Access. Click the **External Data tab**.

b. Click **New Data Source** in the Import & Link group, point to **From File**, and then select **Text File**.

The Get External Data – Text File dialog box launches.

c. Click **Browse** to locate the *a08h3Propnew.csv* file. Click **Open**.

> **TROUBLESHOOTING:** An error message might display if the file you are trying to import is open. Ensure that the text file is closed and return to the import process.

d. Ensure that *Import the source data into a new table in the current database* option is selected and click **OK**.

The Import Text Wizard starts. Delimited should be selected by default.

e. Click **Next** to accept the default options in this dialog box.

f. Click the **First Row Contains Field Names check box** to select it. Click **Next**.

g. Click **Next** to accept the default field options in this dialog box.

h. Click the **No primary key option**. Click **Next**.

When the records are appended to an existing table in the database, a unique value will be assigned to each of the imported records.

i. Type the new table name, **New Properties CSV**, in the Import to Table box, and click **Finish**.

j. Click **Close** in the Save Import Steps dialog box.

The imported table displays in the Navigation Pane.

k. Open the **Properties table**. Scroll down through the table and note that the existing Listing numbers consist of five digits. Close the table.

When the imported records are appended to an existing table in the database, similar values will be assigned to each of the records.

l. Click **Query Design** in the Queries group on the **Create tab**. Add **New Properties CSV** to the query design and close the Show Table dialog box.

You began to create a select query, which you will convert to an append query.

m. Double-click the **title bar** of the New Properties CSV table to select all the fields. Drag the fields to the first field cell of the query design grid.

n. Switch to Datasheet view.

Fifty-eight new properties are listed as expected.

o. Switch to Design view.

p. Click **Append** in the Query Type group and select **Properties** using the Table Name arrow. Click **OK**.

The *Append to* row displays in the query design grid with the corresponding field names listed. The new listing values need to be modified so they conform to the format of the existing listings. You decide to add 10300 to each new listing number using a calculated field.

q. Select the **Listing field name** in the first column. Type the calculated field:

Listing2:[Listing]+10300.

r. Switch to Datasheet view to see the results of the calculated field.

All the listing values are now higher than the listing numbers of the existing properties.

s. Switch to Design view.

t. Click **Run** in the Results group to add the new (Davidson) properties to the Properties table.

u. Click **Yes** in response to the *You are about to append 58 row(s)* message.

v. Save the query with the name **Append Davidson Properties**. Close the query.

w. Close the database and exit Access. Based on your instructor's directions, submit:

a08h2Woodlands_LastFirst.xlsx

a08h2Service_LastFirst.xlsx

a08h2Sub_LastFirst.docx

a08h2Service _LastFirst.pdf

a08h2Propexport_LastFirst

a08h3Property_LastFirst

Chapter Objectives Review

After reading this chapter, you have accomplished the following objectives:

1. Create a hyperlink field.
- A hyperlink in a table or form launches the appropriate software and enables you to interact with the file.
- Enter hyperlinks in Datasheet view to access information about customers or organizations you are working with from within an Access table.
- Edit a hyperlink value: Edit a hyperlink value if it navigates to an incorrect webpage, file, or location.

2. Add an attachment field.
- Create an attachment field: An attachment field stores file or files in a database, and you can open files from within Access.
- Add or edit attachments in Datasheet view: Manage your attachments from the datasheet using the Attachments dialog box.
- Remove attachments in Datasheet view: Attachments can be removed using the Attachments dialog box.

3. Add attachment controls to forms and reports.
- Add an attachment control to a form: An attachment control enables you to manage attached files in forms.
- Add an attachment control to a report: You can also manage attached files in reports. In a report, only the first file displays in Print Preview; to use the Attachment toolbar and advance through multiple attachments in a report, switch to Report view.

4. Export data to Excel.
- Tables, queries, forms, and reports can all be exported to Excel if their formats are compatible with spreadsheets.
- Export a query to Excel: Tables and queries tend to export well to Excel because their datasheet formats are compatible with spreadsheets.
- Export forms and reports to Excel: Subforms or grouped data may not export or display correctly.

5. Export data to Word.
- Data that have been exported to Word cannot always be manipulated or analyzed, so select record sources to be exported carefully.
- Export objects that have a tabular layout (e.g., tables and queries).
- Modify an RTF file in Word: When an object is exported to Word, Access creates a file in Rich Text Format that opens in Word by default. You can save the file in the Word document format.

6. Export data to a PDF or XPS document.
- PDF and XPS documents can be opened by their respective readers and do not require Microsoft Office to be installed on your system.

7. Export objects to another Access database.
- Export a table to another database: After you create a table for one database, you may be able to use it again (definition or both definition and data) for another database.
- Export other objects to another database: There may be common queries, forms, or reports that could also be exported from one database to another.

8. Link to an Access table.
- Examine the tables in the source database: Ensure that the data and format are relevant to your database.
- Link to an Access table: Linking enables you to connect to a table without having to import the table data into your database.
- Create an append query to add linked (or imported) data to an existing table in a database.

9. Link to and import an Excel spreadsheet.
- Examine the format of an Excel spreadsheet: Ensure that the data will display properly in Access; delete extraneous or blank rows.
- Link to an Excel spreadsheet: Create a link from Access to Excel that enables you to view Excel data in Access.
- Create a table from a linked spreadsheet by creating a make table query using the linked data.

10. Import an Excel spreadsheet.
- Examine the spreadsheet before importing to ensure that the data will display properly in Access. Import the data into your Access database; use the table as a stand-alone object or evaluate it before attempting to append it to an existing table.

11. Import a text file.
- Examine the text file before importing: Ensure that the data are eligible to be separated into columns and are consistent from row to row.
- Import a text file into Access: You can manipulate the data after they are imported into Access without changing the original text file.
- Append imported data to an existing table by using an append query.

Key Terms Matching

Match the key terms with their definitions. Write the key term letter by the appropriate numbered definition.

a. Attachment control
b. Attachment field
c. CSV text file
d. Fixed-length text file
e. Hyperlink
f. Importing

g. Linking
h. Portable Document Format (PDF)
i. Rich Text Format (RTF)
j. Text file
k. Uniform resource locator (URL)
l. XML Paper Specification (XPS)

1. _____ A file format developed by Microsoft and designed to display a printed page on screen identically on any computer platform. **p. 460**

2. _____ A file format that uses a comma to separate one column from the next column, enabling the receiving software to distinguish one set of field values from the next. **p. 478**

3. _____ A data type that enables you to quickly link to a file on your computer or to a webpage on the Internet. **p. 440**

4. _____ A file that stores data without formatting and is commonly used for exchanging information between two computer systems. **p. 471**

5. _____ The location of a website or webpage on the Internet. **p. 440**

6. _____ A process that enables you to connect to a table or spreadsheet without having to import the data into your database. **p. 477**

7. _____ A format that enables text-based documents to be opened in a variety of word-processing applications. **p. 471**

8. _____ A process that may result in increasing the size of the Access database substantially. **p. 457**

9. _____ A file format created by Adobe Systems for document exchange independent of software application and operating system environment. **p. 460**

10. _____ A field used to store multiple files of various formats and then launch those files from within Access. **p. 442**

11. _____ A file type that allocates a certain number of characters for each field. **p. 478**

12. _____ A control that enables you to manage attached files in forms and reports. **p. 445**

Multiple Choice

1. Which statement is *true* about hyperlink fields?

   (a) Hyperlinks cannot be used to launch webpages.

   (b) Hyperlinks cannot launch Excel spreadsheets or Word documents.

   (c) You can edit a hyperlink value in Datasheet view.

   (d) You can edit a hyperlink value in Design view.

2. Which statement is *true* about attachments?

   (a) You can attach only one file per record in a table.

   (b) You cannot use attachment files in forms and reports.

   (c) Attached photos display as thumbnails in queries.

   (d) Attachment files increase the size of an Access database.

3. You want to attach each employee's photo to his or her record in the Employees table. What is the correct process for adding the photos?

   (a) In the Employees table, add a hyperlink field, and then create a link to each photo file in Datasheet view of the table.

   (b) In the Employees table, add an attachment field, and then attach the photo to each employee's record in Design view of the table.

   (c) In the Employees table, add an attachment field, and then attach the photo to each employee's record in Datasheet view of the table.

   (d) Import the table that contains all of the photos of the employees into your database.

4. What is the primary difference between an imported table and a linked table?

   (a) Data in an imported table can be modified from Access; data in a linked table cannot be modified.

   (b) A linked table increases the size of the database, but an imported table does not.

   (c) Users cannot create queries with a linked table.

   (d) The data in imported tables resides inside the database; the data in linked tables resides outside the database.

5. You have exported an Access table to an Excel spreadsheet because:

   (a) you cannot create reports in Access.

   (b) the data can be manipulated by a user who does not know Access or does not own the software but is conversant with Excel.

   (c) data cannot be formatted in Access.

   (d) the Access database has grown too large.

6. What is the default format when you export data to Word?

   (a) PDF

   (b) RTF

   (c) XPS

   (d) DOCX

7. What is a major reason for exporting an Access report to a PDF document?

   (a) PDF does not require reader software to open the document.

   (b) PDF documents can be opened outside of Access with a reader program or Internet browser, irrespective of operating system used.

   (c) It is more convenient to modify data in a PDF document as opposed to an Access file.

   (d) Reports opened in Access cannot be formatted.

8. You have linked an Excel spreadsheet named *Inventory* to your database. It displays in the Navigation Pane as:

   (a) the Inventory table with a special icon to its left.

   (b) the Inventory form.

   (c) the Inventory report.

   (d) the Inventory query.

9. Which type of object(s) can be exported from one database to another?

   (a) Tables only

   (b) Tables and queries

   (c) All objects

   (d) Reports only

10. Importing a text file requires the data to be:

    (a) in table format, with a primary key assigned.

    (b) stored in a Word table.

    (c) separated, for example, by delimiters, such as commas.

    (d) in RTF file format.

Practice Exercises

As database administrator for Houston Bank, your manager wants you to attach photos of the customers to the records in the Customers table. You create an attachment field in the Customers table and begin to attach photos to the datasheet. You create an email hyperlink field for the customers and add an email address to the table. You add the photo attachment control to a form and export a report and a query to various file formats. Finally, you edit a hyperlink in a datasheet. Refer to Figures 8.51 and 8.52 as you complete this exercise.

top: Sirtravelalot/Shutterstock; bottom: Wavebreakmedia/shutterstock

Customers and Pictures

Customers

Sunday, November 18, 2018
12:42:54 PM

CustomerID	First Name	Last Name	Phone Number	AccountType	Email	Photo
C0001	Eileen	Faulkner	(555) 894-1511	Gold		
C0002	Scott	Wit	(555) 753-0345	Silver		
C0003	Benjamin	Grauer	(555) 444-5555	Platinum		
C0004	Wendy	Solomon	(555) 427-3104	Platinum		
C0005	Alex	Rey	(555) 555-6666	Silver		
C0006	Ted	Myerson	(555) 942-7654	Gold		
C0007	Lori	Sangastiano	(555) 542-3411	Gold		
C0008	Student Name	Student Name	(555) 374-5660	Gold	Student@pearson.edu	

FIGURE 8.51 Hyperlink and Attachment Control in a Report

To: Management Team¶

From: Loan Department¶

Subject: Receivables Qtr 1 and 2¶

LoanName¤	Total Of AmountReceived¤	Qtr 1¤	Qtr 2¤	¤
Car¤	$11,125.33¡	$1,996.62¡	$9,128.71¡¤	
Mortgage¤	$78,231.08¡	$15,577.55¡	$62,653.53¡¤	
Personal¤	$7,641.98¡	$1,367.12¡	$6,274.86¡¤	

¶

FIGURE 8.52 Loan Payments by Type_Crosstab Query Exported to Word

a. Open *a08p1Bank* and save it as **a08p1Bank_LastFirst**. Open the Customers table in Datasheet view and replace *Your_Name* with your own name. Switch to Design view.

b. Type **Email** in the first blank row of the Field Name column. Select **Hyperlink** as the Data Type.

c. Add another field, **Photo**, under Email, and then select **Attachment** as the Data Type. Save the table. Switch to Datasheet view.

d. Type your email address into the Email column of the eighth record.

e. Double-click the **paperclip** in the first record. Click **Add** in the Attachments dialog box. Locate and double-click the photo file *C0001.jpg* to attach it to the record and click **OK** in the Attachments dialog box.

f. Double-click the **paperclip** in the second record. Click **Add**. Double-click the photo file *C0002.jpg* to attach it to the record and click **OK**.

g. Click the **Create tab** and click **Report** in the Reports group to create a new report based on the Customers table.

h. Modify the report in Layout view. Delete the **Address**, **City**, **State**, and **Zip Code** columns by clicking each column heading, pressing **Shift**, clicking the first text box below it, and then pressing **Delete**. Delete the empty columns by clicking the column heading of each one and pressing **Delete**.

i. Resize the remaining columns so that all the fields will fit on one page. Display the report in Print Preview to verify that all columns fit on one page. If the report does not fit on one page, switch to Design view, and drag the page numbers text box to the left. Reduce the width of the report grid until the report fits on one page.

j. Save the report as **Customers and Pictures**. Close the report. Close the Customers table.

k. Double-click the **Customers and Loans form** in the Navigation Pane and switch to Layout view.

l. Click **Add Existing Fields** in the Tools group on the Design tab. Double-click **Photo** in the Field List pane to add the field to the form. Click and drag the control to move it so that it is aligned with the top and immediately to the right of the CustomerID field.

m. Close the Field List pane.

n. Switch to Form view. In Record 1, click the **photo**, and when the Attachment toolbar displays, click the **paperclip** (Manage Attachments). In the Attachments dialog box, click **Open** to view the image in your default photo viewer. Close the photo viewer window and then click **OK** in the Attachments dialog box. Save and close the form.

o. Select the **Customers and Pictures report** in the Navigation Pane. Click **PDF or XPS** in the Export group on the External Data tab. Navigate to the folder where you save your files.

p. Change the file name to **a08p1Bank_LastFirst** and ensure that **PDF** is selected as the *Save as type*. Click **Publish**. Close the reader. Click **Close** in the Save Export Steps window in Access.

q. Select the **Loan Payments by Type_Crosstab query** in the Navigation Pane. Click the **External Data tab** and click **Excel** in the Export group. Click **Browse** to navigate to the location where you save your files. Type **a08p1Bank_LastFirst** in the File name box. Click **Save**.

r. Click the **Export data with formatting and layout check box** and click the **Open the destination file after the export operation is complete check box** in the Export – Excel Spreadsheet dialog box. Click **OK**. Exit Excel. Click **Close** in the Save Export Steps window in Access.

s. Select the **Loan Payments by Type report** in the Navigation Pane. Click the **External Data tab** and click **Excel** in the Export group. Click **Browse** to navigate to the location where you save your files. Type **a08p1BankReport_LastFirst** in the File name box. Click **Save**.

t. Click the **Open the destination file after the export operation is complete check box** in the Export – Excel Spreadsheet dialog box. Click **OK**. Exit Excel. Click **Close** in the Save Export Steps window in Access.

u. Select the **Loan Payments by Type_Crosstab** query in the Navigation Pane. Click the **External Data tab**, click **More** in the Export group, and then select **Word** from the list. Click **Browse** to navigate to the location where you save your files. Type **a08p1Bank_LastFirst** as the file name. Ensure that the *Save as type* is Rich Text Format. Click **Save** to return to the Export – RTF File dialog box. Click the **Open the destination file after the export operation is complete check box** to select it. Click **OK**.

v. Verify that the data exported correctly to Word, press **Enter**, and then type the **To**, **From**, and **Subject** lines, as shown in Figure 8.52.

w. Save **a08p1Bank_LastFirst** as a Word document. Click **OK** in the compatibility message box if it displays. Close the document and exit Word. Click **Close** in the Save Export Steps window in Access.

x. Open the Customers table. In Record 8, CustomerID C0008, right-click the email address, point to **Hyperlink**, and then select **Edit Hyperlink** from the shortcut menu. Change the email address and the text to display to **student@pearson.edu**. Click **OK**. Press the down arrow to move to the next record. Close the table.

y. Close the database and exit Access. Based on your instructor's directions, submit:

a08p1Bank_LastFirst

a08p1Bank_LastFirst.pdf

a08p1Bank_LastFirst.xlsx

a08p1BankReport_LastFirst.xls

a08p1Bank_LastFirst.docx

2 Break Room Suppliers, Inc.

Break Room Suppliers, Inc., provides coffee, tea, beverages, and snacks to businesses in its area. To expand their business, the owners have obtained several customer-prospect lists. You will link and import the prospect lists into Access so the owners can determine how best to use them in their database. You will also import an Excel spreadsheet containing newly developed sales rep information. Finally, you will export a products table and form to an external database. Refer to Figure 8.53 as you complete this exercise.

CustomerID	Customer Name	Contact	E-mail Address	Address1	Address2	City	State	Zip Code
1	Drinks On Us	Jeff Jones	jeff@drinksonus.net	5000 Jefferson Lane	Suite 2000	Miami	FL	33131-
2	Water Department	Ed Milgrom		1238 Walsh Drive	Suite 2202	Miami	FL	33131-
3	Advantage Foods	Nancy Goodman	service@advantagesales.com	4215 South 81 Street		Miami	FL	33131-
4	Kinzer Snackfood	Selene Silver	selene@kinzer.com	9020 N.W. 75 Street	Suite 302	Coral Springs	FL	33065-
5	Juice & Associates	Ashley Truber	truber@juiceassoc.net	7500 Center Lane		Coral Springs	FL	33070-
6	Allisons Restaurant	Allison Blake	allison@allrest.com	6000 Tigertail Avenue		Coconut Grove	FL	33133-
7	Meats & Sauces	Mel Stark	mstark@meatsinc.com	276 Brickell Avenue	Suite 1403	Miami	FL	33131-
8	Three Bakers	Bob Leaks	bob@3bakers.com	4508 N.W. 7 Street		Miami	FL	33131-
9	County Hospital	Luis Cartego	luis@countyhosp.com	455 Bargello Avenue		Coral Gables	FL	33124-
10	Katie's Diner	Katie Mast	katie@msn.com	9522 S.W. 142 Street		Miami	FL	33176-
11	Advanced Office Supplies	Maryanne Ross	maryanne@advanced.com	1000 Main Street		Coral Springs	FL	33071-

FIGURE 8.53 Customers Imported from Another Access Database

a. Open *a08p2Coffee* and save it as **a08p2Coffee_LastFirst**.

b. Open *a08p2Custexcel.xlsx* and verify that the content and formatting of the worksheet is compatible with an Access table. Exit Excel. You will link the worksheet to your database.

c. Click the **External Data tab**, then in the Import & Link group, click **New Data Source**, point to **From File**, and then select **Excel**.

d. Click **Browse** in the Get External Data – Excel Spreadsheet dialog box and locate and select the file *a08p2Custexcel.xlsx*. Click **Open** to return to the Get External Data dialog box.

e. Click the **Link to the data source by creating a linked table option**. Click **OK**.

f. Click the **First Row Contains Column Headings check box** to select it. Click **Next**.

g. Confirm Customers_Excel is the Linked Table Name. Click **Finish**. Click **OK** in the message box.

h. Double-click the **Customers_Excel table** in the Navigation Pane to view the customer records. Close the table.

i. Open *a08p2Repsexcel.xlsx* and verify that the content and formatting of the worksheet is compatible with an Access table. Exit Excel. You will import the worksheet to your database.

j. Click the **External Data tab**, then in the Import & Link group, click **New Data Source**, point to **From File**, and then select **Excel**.

k. Click **Browse** in the Get External Data – Excel Spreadsheet dialog box and locate and select the file *a08p2Repsexcel.xlsx*. Click **Open** to return to the Get External Data dialog box.

l. Ensure that the **Import the source data into a new table in the current database option** is selected and click **OK**.

m. Click the **First Row Contains Column Headings check box** to select it. Click **Next** two times.

n. Click the **Choose my own primary key option** and verify that Sales Rep ID is selected. Click **Next**.

o. Confirm Sales Reps is the Import to Table name. Click **Finish**. Click **Close** in the Save Import Steps dialog box.

p. Double-click the **Sales Reps table** in the Navigation Pane to view the records. Close the table.

q. Open the database *a08p2Custaccess*. Open the Customers_Access table and examine the contents. You will link your database to this table. Close the table and close the database.

r. Return to the *a08p2Coffee_LastFirst* database. Click the **External Data tab**, then in the Import & Link group, click **New Data Source**, point to **From Database**, and then select **Access**.

s. Click **Browse** in the Get External Data – Access Database dialog box and locate and select the file *a08p2Custaccess*. Click **Open** to return to the Get External Data dialog box.

t. Click the **Link to the data source by creating a linked table option** to select it. Click **OK**.

u. Click **Customers_Access** in the Link Tables dialog box. Click **OK**.

v. Double-click the **Customers_Access table** in the Navigation Pane to view the customer records. Close the table.

w. Open File Explorer, right-click *a08p2Custtext.csv*, point to **Open with**, and then select **Notepad**. Examine the content of the .csv file. Close Notepad and return to the a08p2Coffee_LastFirst database.

x. Click the **External Data tab**, then in the Import & Link group, click **New Data Source**, point to **From File**, and then select **Text File**. Click **Browse** in the Get External Data – Text File dialog box and locate and select the file *a08p2Custtext.csv*. Click **Open** to return to the Get External Data dialog box. Verify that the *Import the source data into a new table in the current database* option is selected. Click **OK**.

y. Click **Next** when the Import Text Wizard displays. Click the **First Row Contains Field Names check box** to select it. Click **Next**. Click **Next** to confirm the field options. Click the **No primary key option** in the next dialog box. Click **Next**.

z. Change the Import to Table name to **Customers_Text**. Click **Finish**. Click **Close** in the Save Import Steps dialog box. Close the window.

aa. Open the **Customers_Text table** in the Navigation Pane to view the customer records. Close the table and close the database.

ab. Open *a08p2Custaccess* and save it as **a08p2Custaccess_LastFirst**. Close a08p2Custaccess_LastFirst. Open *a08p2Coffee_LastFirst*. Select, but do not open, the **Products table** in the Navigation Pane.

ac. Click **Access** in the Export group on the **External Data tab**. Click **Browse** to locate the destination database file. Select the *a08p2Custaccess_LastFirst* database and click **Save**. When you return to the Export – Access Database dialog box, click **OK**.

ad. Confirm that Products is in the *Export Products to* box. Accept the **Definition and Data option**. Click **OK**. Click **Close** to close the Save Export Steps window without saving.

ae. Select, but do not open, the **Products form** in the Navigation Pane. Click **Access** in the Export group on the **External Data tab**. Click **Browse** to locate the destination database file. Select the *a08p2Custaccess_LastFirst* database and click **Save**. When you return to the Export – Access Database dialog box, click **OK**.

af. Confirm that Products is in the *Export Products to* box. Click **OK**. Click **Close** to close the Save Export Steps window without saving.

ag. Close the database and exit Access. Based on your instructor's directions, submit:

a08p2Coffee_LastFirst

a08p2Custaccess_LastFirst

Mid-Level Exercises

1 | Morrison Arboretum

The Morrison Arboretum at NC University wants to add a few new features to its database. They want to add photos of the plants to the Plant Descriptions table and a hyperlink field that points to a website that describes each plant. You also want to create a report showing the plant names, the corresponding hyperlinks, and the plant photos. You export this report to Word and notice that the photos do not display in the Word document; instead, you publish the report as a PDF document to distribute via email to members. Finally, you export a query to Excel to be used as a mailing list.

a. Open *a08m1Arbor* and save it as **a08m1Arbor_LastFirst**.

b. Create a new hyperlink field named **PlantLink** in the Plant Descriptions table below the PlantName field.

c. Create a new attachment field named **Picture** in the Plant Descriptions table below the PlantLink field.

d. Open **Wikipedia.org** in a browser and search for **viburnum**. Copy the URL and paste it into the correct PlantLink field in Datasheet view.

e. Use the Attachments dialog box to add the appropriate photo for each plant. The photos are stored in the *a08m1PlantPhotos* folder. Close the table.

f. Create a basic report based on the Plant Descriptions table. Set the title of the report as **Plants with Links and Pictures**.

g. Center the report title text in the control and delete the logo to the left of the title control. Switch to Design view, drag the right edge of the report to the 8.25-inch mark, and then change the page layout to **Landscape**. Save the report as **Plants with Photos**. Switch to Print Preview, then close the report.

h. Export the Plants with Photos report to Word, in RTF format and save the document in Word format as **a08m1Plants_LastFirst.docx**. Note that no pictures were exported to the report. Close the document and exit Word. Close the Save Export Steps window without saving the export steps.

i. Publish the report in PDF format and save the document as **a08m1Plants_LastFirst.pdf**. View the PDF report in your reader program, note that the pictures were exported, and then close the reader. Close the Save Export Steps window without saving the export steps.

j. Export the **ENewsletter Members query** to Excel to use as a mailing list. Select **Export data with formatting and layout** and **Open the destination file after the export operation is complete**. Save the workbook as **a08m1Email_LastFirst.xlsx**. Review the exported data, and close Excel. Close the Save Export Steps window without saving the export steps.

k. Import the Excel spreadsheet back into the database as a linked table named **ENewsletter List**, using the first row headings as field names.

l. Open the linked ENewsletter List table and close the table.

m. Close the database and exit Access. Based on your instructor's directions, submit:

a08m1Arbor_LastFirst

a08m1Plants_LastFirst.pdf

a08m1Email_LastFirst.xlsx

a08m1Plants_LastFirst.docx

2 | Hotel Services

ANALYSIS CASE

As the database manager of a hotel chain, you monitor the services ordered using a summary query. The hotel chain's manager asks you to send him a summary of the Raleigh location orders as an Excel spreadsheet. He also asks you to export the Repeat Members Club table to a different database. Several hotels in Los Angeles are for sale, and you decide to import their order data to determine their activity levels.

a. Open *a08m2Hotel* and save it as **a08m2Hotel_LastFirst**. Open *a08m2Hotelexport* and save it as **a08m2Hotelexport_LastFirst**. Close a08m2Hotelexport_LastFirst and return to the a08m2Hotel_LastFirst database.

b. Export the Repeat Members Club table to a08m2Hotelexport_LastFirst. Verify that the table was exported correctly and return to the a08m2Hotel_LastFirst database. Do not save the export steps.

c. Modify the Summary by ServiceID query so that it displays only orders from location 3 (which is Raleigh). Save, run, and then close the query. Export the query to Excel and save the workbook as **a08m2Raleighorders_LastFirst.xlsx**.

d. Review the exported data, and close Excel. Do not save the export steps. Import the *a08m2Raleighorders_LastFirst.xlsx* Excel spreadsheet back into the a08m2Hotel_LastFirst database as a linked table named **Raleigh Property Updates**, with the first row headings as field names. Open the Raleigh Property Updates table and close the table. Do not save the import steps.

e. Open *a08m2Ordersexcel.xslx* and review the data in the spreadsheet. Exit Excel and return to a08m2Hotel_LastFirst. Import *a08m2Ordersexcel.xslx* as a table named **Orders_Excel** with the first row as column headings and OrderID as the primary key field. Do not save the import steps.

f. Open *a08m2Ordersaccess* and review the data in the Orders_Access table. Close a08m2Ordersaccess and return to a08m2Hotel_LastFirst. Create a link to the **Orders_Access** table in the a08m2Ordersaccess database. Do not save the import steps.

g. Open *a08m2Orderstext.csv* and review the data. Exit Excel and return to a08m2Hotel_LastFirst. Import the data from the *a08m2Orderstext.csv* text file using the first row headings as field names and **OrderID** as the primary key field into the database, saving the table as **Orders_Text**. Do not save the import steps.

h. Save a copy of *a08m2Orderstext.csv* as **a08m2Orderstext_LastFirst.txt** with the text file format (.txt). Edit the file using the Notepad program to delete the first data record, *OrderID 4001*, and reimport the modified text file into your database as **Orders_Text**. Overwrite the original table when prompted.

i. Close the database and exit Access. Based on your instructor's directions, submit:
    a08m2Hotel_LastFirst
    a08h2Hotelexport_LastFirst

Running Case

New Castle County Technical Services

New Castle County Technical Services (NCCTS) provides technical support for a number of companies in the greater New Castle County, Delaware area. Now that you have completed the form and report design, you are ready to share data between Access and other applications.

a. Open the database *a08r1NCCTS* and save it as **a08r1NCCTS_LastFirst**.

b. Create a Hyperlink field named **EmailAddress** in the last position of the Customers table. Save the table.

c. Type the email address **ITDept@SVCPharm.com** in the first record of the Customers table datasheet and close the table.

d. Create an Attachment field named **RepPhoto** in the last position of the Reps table. Save the table.

e. Add the photo named *a08r1Barbara.jpg* to the first record of the Reps table datasheet and close the table.

f. Export the Calls by Customer report to Excel as **a08r1ServiceCallsGrouped_LastFirst.xls**. Open the destination file after the export operation is complete. When the file opens in Excel, press **Ctrl+A** to select the entire worksheet, and set the font color to Automatic.

g. Save the Excel workbook and close it. Click **Access** on the taskbar to return to the Access window, and do not save the export steps.

h. Export the Calls_Crosstab query to Word in RTF format as **a08r1CallsCrosstab_LastFirst.rtf**. Open the destination file after the export operation is complete. When the file opens in Word, save a copy as a Word document using the same file name.

i. Click the **Layout tab**, click the **Orientation arrow** in the Page Setup group, and then select **Landscape**. Ensure that the insertion point is at the top of the document, press Enter, and then type **Average Hours Logged by Call Type and Customer Satisfaction Rating**. Center and bold the heading.

j. Save and close the Word document. Return to the Access window, and do not save the export steps.

k. Import the Excel workbook *a08r1CallGroups.xlsx* into a new table in the database. Select CallTypeID as the primary key, and save the table using the name **Call Groups**.

l. Close the database and exit Access. Based on your instructor's directions, submit:

a08r1NCCTS_LastFirst

a08r1ServiceCallsGrouped_LastFirst.xls

a08r1CallsCrosstab_LastFirst.docx

Disaster Recovery

Workplace Sensitivity Training

You have discovered that some of the new employees in the *a08d1Sensitivity* database require an in-service on workplace sensitivity. Open the database and save it as **a08d1Sensitivity_LastFirst**. You realize that there is a similar query in the *a08d1Etiquette* database that you can import and modify to be used for your requirement. Import the query named Require Etiquette Inservice into the a08d1Sensitivity_LastFirst database and rename it as **Require Sensitivity Inservice**. Modify the Require Sensitivity Inservice query so that the fourth field refers to the correct field name in the destination database, and only employees who have *not* had sensitivity training display in the results. You want to export the query results as a PDF file so that your report can be opened by recipients who do not have Access installed on their PCs. Export the query results to PDF format. Save the PDF file as **a08d1SensitivityInservice_LastFirst.pdf**. Close the PDF reader. Do not save the export steps. Close the database and exit Access. Based on your instructor's directions, submit the PDF file a08d1SensitivityInservice_LastFirst.pdf.

Capstone Exercise

Virtual Registry, Inc.

You work as a database manager at Virtual Registry, Inc. This firm specializes in supplying china, crystal, silver, and collectible gifts online. You will add a hyperlink field that will store a URL for each manufacturer's website. The HR Department manager wants to store a photo and the most recent performance review for each employee. You will also export data from the database to three different formats. Finally, you import information from Excel, Access, and text files.

Create Attachment and Hyperlink Fields

You will add a hyperlink field to the Manufacturer table to store each company's website address. You will also add an attachment field to the Employees table to store the employee's performance reviews and photos.

1. Open *a08c1Registry* and save it as **a08c1Registry_LastFirst**.

2. Create a new field in the Manufacturer table after RlMfgCode named **Website** with the Hyperlink data type. Save the table.

3. Switch to Datasheet view, add the website **https://www.spode.co.uk/** to the Spode China record (11), and then add **https://www.wedgwood.com** to the Wedgwood China record (15). Click each link to make sure it launches a browser and locates the appropriate website. Close the table.

4. Create a new field in the Employees table after HireDate named **EmployeeFiles** with the Attachment data type. Save the table.

5. Switch to Datasheet view and locate the record for UserID 81094880 (Tim Cox). Add the Word document named *81094880.docx* and the picture file named *81094880.jpg* to the EmployeeFiles field. Additional attachments will be added in the future.

6. Create a basic form based on the Employees table; the form will be open in Layout view. For UserID *81094880*, (record 1), click the **Word icon** and click the **Forward arrow** on the Attachment toolbar to view the picture file.

7. Save the form as Employees. Close the form and the table.

Export Filtered Records to Excel, Word, and PDF

You want to determine current sales for a specific product line. You will filter the Revenue Query to locate records and export the records to Excel and Word. You will also export inventory records to create a report in PDF format.

8. Open the Revenue Query. Use Filter by Selection to display records in the Alias column where the value equals *Waterford Crystal*.

9. Export the filtered records to an Excel file. Save the file as **a08c1Crystal_LastFirst**. Do not save the export steps.

10. Hide the **ProdCategoryID**, **DESCR,** and **Alias** fields from the results in the Revenue Query. Export the same filtered records to a Word file. Open the destination file after the export operation is complete. On the Layout tab, change the orientation of the document to Landscape. Press **Enter** one time and add the title **Waterford Crystal Orders** to the Word file. Format the title as bold and center aligned. Save the file as a Word document with the name **a08c1Crystal_LastFirst**. Close the document and exit Word. Do not save the export steps. Save and close the filtered Revenue Query.

11. Use Filter by Selection to display records in the Inventory table where the OnHandQty value equals *0* (five records will display). Export the filtered records to a PDF document. Save the file as **a08c1Inventory_LastFirst**. Close the PDF reader program. Do not save the export steps. Save and close the filtered Inventory table.

Import and Link Data from Excel, Access, and a Text File

You will import new customer records from Excel. You will also import customer records from an Access database and a text file.

12. Open the *a08c1Customers.xlsx* workbook, examine the Customers1 worksheet, and then close the workbook. Create a linked table in the database by importing the workbook named *a08c1Customers.xlsx*. Use the first row of the Customers1 worksheet as row headings and accept all other default options.

13. Open the *a08c1Customers* database, examine the Customers2 table, and then close the database. Create a linked table in the database by importing the Customers2 table from the database named *a08c1Customers*.

14. Open the *a08c1Textcust.csv* text file, examine the content, and then close the file. Create a table in the database by importing the text file named *a08c1Textcust.csv*. Use the first row of the file as field names, CustomerNum as the primary key, and name the table **Customers Text**. Accept all other default options.

15. Append the linked customer records to the original Customer table in the database. Append the 32 records from Customers1 and the 36 records from Customers2. Open the Customer table to view the appended records. Close the Customer table.

16. Close the database and exit Access. Based on your instructor's directions, submit:

    a08c1Registry_LastFirst
    a08c1Crystal_LastFirst.xlsx
    a08c1Crystal_LastFirst.docx
    a08c1 Inventory_LastFirst.pdf

Fine-Tuning the Database

LEARNING OUTCOMES

You will demonstrate a basic understanding of database normalization.
You will protect and optimize your database using advanced Access database tools.

OBJECTIVES & SKILLS: After you read this chapter, you will be able to:

Database Normalization

OBJECTIVE 1: UNDERSTAND FIRST NORMAL FORM 503
Implement First Normal Form

OBJECTIVE 2: UNDERSTAND SECOND NORMAL FORM 505
Implement Second Normal Form

OBJECTIVE 3: UNDERSTAND THIRD NORMAL FORM 507
Implement Third Normal Form

OBJECTIVE 4: FINALIZE THE DESIGN 509
Create Relationships

HANDS-ON EXERCISE 1 511

Built-In Analysis and Design Tools

OBJECTIVE 5: USE THE DATABASE DOCUMENTER TOOL 516
Run the Database Documenter

OBJECTIVE 6: USE THE PERFORMANCE ANALYZER TOOL 518
Run the Performance Analyzer, Add an Index

OBJECTIVE 7: USE THE TABLE ANALYZER TOOL 520
Run the Table Analyzer

OBJECTIVE 8: USE THE DATABASE SPLITTER TOOL 523
Run the Database Splitter, Work with a Front-End Database

HANDS-ON EXERCISE 2 525

Database Security

OBJECTIVE 9: CONTROL NAVIGATION 530
Create a Navigation Form, Start a Navigation Form Automatically, Hide the Navigation Pane

OBJECTIVE 10: ENCRYPT AND PASSWORD PROTECT A DATABASE 532
Add a Password to a Database

OBJECTIVE 11: CREATE AN EXECUTABLE FORM OF A DATABASE 534
Create an Access Database Executable

HANDS-ON EXERCISE 3 536

CASE STUDY | The Metropolitan Zoo

You have been working at the Metropolitan Zoo for the past two months, performing data entry and creating forms and reports for the Access database. Now that you are familiar with the functions of the database, you have suggested to your supervisor, Selene Platt, that you can improve the design and performance of the database.

Given your expertise in Access, you will run some diagnostic utilities to check the performance of your database. You know that when the tables are designed poorly the database can become unnecessarily large, causing it to perform more slowly. Furthermore, poorly designed tables are prone to data redundancy, which can cause data inconsistencies in the database. You will also plan to improve security on the database.

CHAPTER 9

Designing for Performance

Sfio Cracho/Shutterstock

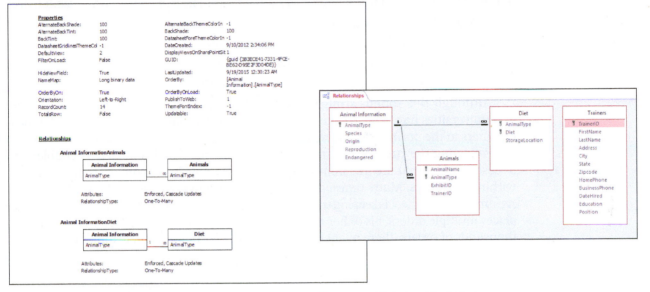

FIGURE 9.1 The Metropolitan Zoo Database—Documenter Report and Relationships Window

CASE STUDY | The Metropolitan Zoo

Starting Files	Files to be Submitted
a09h1Zoo	a09h1Zoo_LastFirst
a09h2ZooAnalyzer	a09h2ZooDocumenter_LastFirst.pdf
	a09h2ZooAnalyzer_LastFirst
	a09h2ZooSplit_LastFirst_be
	a09h3ZooExecutable_LastFirst

MyLab IT Grader An alternate version of this project is available as a MyLab IT Grader Assessment

Database Normalization

To this point, you have used common sense to determine which fields to include in each table. The process changes when you deal with a more complex system. Database designers generally start by performing customer interviews, reviewing existing documents, examining existing files, and anticipating needed inputs and outputs. They then divide the fields into tables and identify potential primary keys. Finally, they go through a process to refine the tables and remove issues. ***Normalization*** is the process of efficiently organizing data so that the same data are not stored in more than one table and that related data are stored together. Experienced database designers may instinctively create tables that follow the rules of normalization. Less-experienced designers generally use the process of normalization to guide them when creating tables. The benefits of normalization are:

- Minimization of data redundancy
- Improvement of referential integrity enforcement
- Ease of maintaining data (add, update, delete)
- Accommodation of future growth of a database

Although this sounds straightforward, it can present challenges. Many colleges and universities have multiple graduate-level database classes to train future database designers in the normalization process.

Following the rules of normalization while creating tables in Access enables you to design tables that are free from anomalies. An ***anomaly*** is an error or inconsistency within a database. Many times, these errors occur when you add, edit, or delete data. Assume a spreadsheet is keeping track of company orders, one order per row. If a customer places multiple orders, his or her name and location would be repeated. Mixed in among thousands of orders, there might be the following information for customer Laura Jones:

Order Date	Customer Name	Customer Address	City	Product #	Qty	Price
9/1/2021	Laura Jones	3312 West Rd	Washington, MI	#456789	3	$12.50
9/10/2021	Laura Jones	3312 West Rd	Washington, MI	#894561	1	$2.95
9/25/2021	Laura Jones	3312 West Rd	Washington, MI	#981156	1	$.95

Laura Jones may call in and change her address, which introduces an update anomaly. How does the database administrator know which record to update—the first, the second, the third, or all three? A user might try to update the records manually, but this would produce an anomaly as well if only one or two of the three records are changed. What if the town's name has changed from Washington to Washington Township, should it change for all other customers? Furthermore, do we know if this is the same person? There could be two or more people in the database with the same name.

The rules to optimize and fix potential repetition issues (data redundancy) in a database are known as ***normal forms*** and indicate the current state of a table. Before a table has been analyzed, it can be said to be unnormalized. You may also see the term 0NF, or zero normal form to refer to an unnormalized table. As you work to normalize a table, you will work with first normal form (1NF), second normal form (2NF), and third normal form (3NF). By definition, a table cannot be in 2NF unless it is already in 1NF, and it cannot be in 3NF unless it is in 2NF.

A table that meets 1NF criteria will have fewer problems than a table that does not. Similarly, a table that meets 2NF criteria will have fewer problems than a table that is in 1NF, and a table that meets 3NF criteria will have fewer problems than a table that is in 2NF. The majority of database designs only require the first three normal forms. Additional normal forms exist, but only 1NF, 2NF, and 3NF will be discussed in this chapter.

In this section, you will learn the first three rules of normalization to reduce data redundancy and data integrity issues. You will apply those rules to a database to create a more efficient database.

Understanding First Normal Form

First normal form is the first rule to apply. A table is defined as being in **first normal form (1NF)** if it contains no repeating groups or repeating columns. A table that does not conform to 1NF can be demonstrated by using an Excel spreadsheet that contains information about authors, books, and publishers (see Figure 9.2). In the spreadsheet, Dan Brown is listed as an Author in columns C and D; the titles of the books that Brown authored are listed in row 5 in column D. The remaining fields contain additional information related to the books. This example would not pass the 1NF test because column E—including the books that Brown authored—has multiple values in a single cell. Brown, the author, is listed once, and the books he wrote are listed in one cell. Moreover, column A has multiple values in a single cell—the ISBNs for those two books listed in column E. The same goes for other authors such as Dave Barry. Even though the individual titles are formatted to be on their own line, there are still multiple values in a single cell. If this Excel spreadsheet were imported into Access, the corresponding Access table with repeating groups would be as shown in Figure 9.3. This table shows the same condition with multiple values in the Title, ISBN, Publisher, and Pub Year fields. Repeating groups are not allowed in a normalized table.

	A	B	C	D	E	F	G
1	ISBN	AuthorID	AuthorFirst	AuthorLast	Title	Publisher	PubYear
2	9781401208417	ALMO01	Alan	Moore	V for Vendetta	DC Comics	2005
3	9780767931557	BEME01	Ben	Mezrich	The Accidental Billionaires	Anchor Books	2009
4	0805029648 / 9780399154379	DABA01	Dave	Barry	Bad Habits / History of the Millenium (So Far)	Henry Holt & Co. / G. P. Putman's Sons	1987 / 2007
5	0312995423 / 9780593054277	DABR01	Dan	Brown	Digital Fortress / The Lost Symbol	St. Martin / Doubleday	1998 / 2009
6	0809400774	DABR02	Dale	Brown	American Cooking: The Northwest	Time Life	1970
7	9780307405807	DOSA01	Douglas	Sarine	The Ninja Handbook	Three Rivers Press	2008
8	9781572439597	JAST01	Jayson	Stark	The Stark Truth	Triumph Books	2007
9	0380788624	NEST01	Neal	Stephenson	Cryptonomicon	Perennial	1999
10	9780345517951	ROJA01	Ron	Jaworski	The Games that Changed the Game	ESPN Books	2010

> Multiple values in the ISBN, Title, Publisher, and PubYear columns

FIGURE 9.2 Poorly Designed Excel Spreadsheet

ISBN	AuthorID	AuthorFirst	AuthorLast	Title	Publisher	PubYear
9781401208417	ALMO01	Alan	Moore	V for Vendetta	DC Comics	2005
9780767931557	BEME01	Ben	Mezrich	The Accidental Billionaires	Anchor Books	2009
080502964897 / 80399154379	DABA01	Dave	Barry	Bad Habits / History of the Millenium (So Far)	Henry Holt & Co. / G. P. Putman's Sons	1987 / 2007
031299542397 / 80593054277	DABR01	Dan	Brown	Digital Fortress / The Lost Symbol	St. Martin / Doubleday	1998 / 2009
0809400774	DABR02	Dale	Brown	American Cooking: The Northwest	Time Life	1970
9780307405807	DOSA01	Douglas	Sarine	The Ninja Handbook	Three Rivers Press	2008
9781572439597	JAST01	Jayson	Stark	The Stark Truth	Triumph Books	2007
0380788624	NEST01	Neal	Stephenson	Cryptonomicon	Perennial	1999
9780345517951	ROJA01	Ron	Jaworski	The Games that Changed the Game	ESPN Books	2010

> Mutliple values in the ISBN, Title, Publisher, and PubYear fields

FIGURE 9.3 Poorly Designed Access Database

In the book example, the Title column containing multiple values might be replaced with Title1, Title2, and Title3. This might appear to correct the problem because each cell contains one piece of information; however, this type of design still violates 1NF because it presents a repeating groups problem. With that "correction," it would still be difficult to find data efficiently.

Violations of the 1NF rule come in many forms. Each of the following situations violates the 1NF rule that there cannot be multiple values in the same field:

- An Author field listing multiple authors separated by commas like *Poatsy, Rutledge, Williams*
- An Address2 field listing the city, state, and ZIP together such as *Paterson, NJ 07501*
- An Instructor field that contains the following values for the same class on two lines:

  Poatsy

  Rutledge

Likewise, you cannot have multiple columns in the same record that store the same sort of data. A table with an Author1 field set to *Poatsy*, Author2 field set to *Rutledge*, and Author3 field set to *Williams* is a violation of 1NF.

When the 1NF rule is violated, it makes it difficult to find specific pieces of information, and that is the essence of the repeating groups problem. Tables containing repeating groups make it more difficult to add new entries, update existing entries, and properly extract information when running queries. For example, if you were to try to locate a specific book that Dan Brown wrote, and the database were set up with multiple title fields such as Title1, Title2, etc., which title field would you need to search to find a specific title? You would have to do multiple searches in each title field, which is not efficient. As a matter of fact, when you attempt to filter the data (as shown in Figure 9.4), two book names are listed as one piece of data. Similar problems would exist with queries searching for a specific book. In other words, there is no easy way to only show the information for a single book such as *Digital Fortress*. This occurs because all the books by one author are contained in the same record.

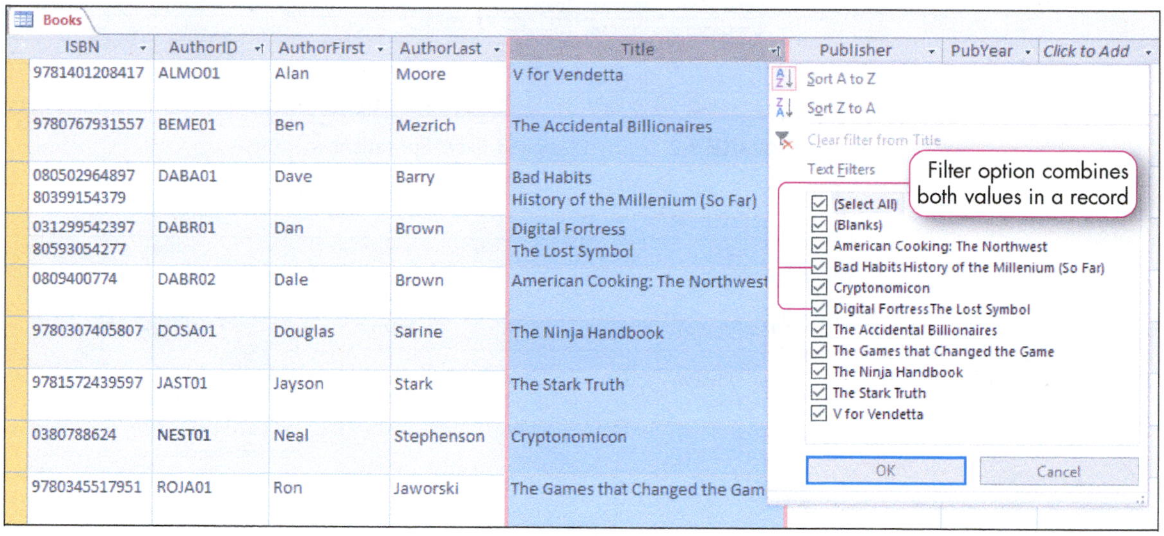

FIGURE 9.4 Filter Issues with Repeating Groups

STEP 1 ▶ Implement First Normal Form

To fix a table that has repeating groups, change the table so each unique piece of information is stored on a separate record in the same field. You can do this in Excel before importing to Access, or alternately add rows in Access and separate the repeating data into individual rows.

Figure 9.5 shows the Books table in Access after it has been put into first normal form; the single Brown row has been split into two rows with each book by Dan Brown as its own record.

At this point, although the table is in 1NF, it still has redundancy issues. Observe in Figure 9.5 that the author's names are repeated in the Books table, which introduces redundancy into the table. However, because normalization is a process, further normalization will remove the redundancies.

ISBN	AuthorID	AuthorFirst	AuthorLast	Title	Publisher	PubYear
9781401208417	ALMO01	Alan	Moore	V for Vendetta	DC Comics	2005
9780767931557	BEME01	Ben	Mezrich	The Accidental Billionaires	Anchor Books	2009
0805029648	DABA01	Dave	Barry	Bad Habits	Henry Holt & Co.	1987
9780399154379	DABA01	Dave	Barry	History of the Millenium (So Far)	G. P. Putman's Sons	2007
0312995423	DABR01	Dan	Brown	Digital Fortress	St. Martin	1998
9780593054277	DABR01	Dan	Brown	The Lost Symbol	Doubleday	2009
0809400774	DABR02	Dale	Brown	American Cooking: The Northwest	Time Life	1970
9780307405807	DOSA01	Douglas	Sarine	The Ninja Handbook	Three Rivers Press	2008
9781572439597	JAST01	Jayson	Stark	The Stark Truth	Triumph Books	2007
0380788624	NEST01	Neal	Stephenson	Cryptonomicon	Perennial	1999
9780345517951	ROJA01	Ron	Jaworski	The Games that Changed the Game	ESPN Books	2010

FIGURE 9.5 Books Table in First Normal Form (1NF)

Each book is a record

Understanding Second Normal Form

A table is in **second normal form (2NF)** if it meets 1NF criteria and all non-key fields are functionally dependent on the entire primary key. A **non-key field** is defined as any field that is not part of the primary key. **Functional dependency** occurs when the value of one field is determined by the value of another. For example, in a government database, given a Social Security number, you can determine a person's first and last name, but the opposite is not true. Given a first and last name, you cannot determine the Social Security number because many people can share the same name. In this case, the first and last names are functionally dependent upon the Social Security number.

STEP 2 Implement Second Normal Form

Second normal form tells you that when fields are not functionally dependent upon the primary key, you must remove those fields from the table. Most of the time, this results in new tables, although it may be possible to move fields into another existing table.

Most bookstore databases contain information about location and quantity in stock. For the purposes of this example, assume the bookstore has two locations, one in the town of Paterson and another one in the town of Wanaque. Therefore, the Books table from the earlier example has been expanded to include three extra fields, as shown in Figure 9.6. Because the location has been added, a problem has now been introduced. Notice in Figure 9.6 that the ISBN cannot be the primary key for this table because the same book (with the same ISBN) can be available in both locations. This situation violates 2NF.

ISBN	AuthorID	AuthorFirst	AuthorLast	Title	Publisher	PubYear	Location	OnHand	Aisle
9781401208417	ALMO01	Alan	Moore	V for Vendetta	DC Comics	2005	Paterson	2	5
9780767931557	BEME01	Ben	Mezrich	The Accidental Billionaires	Anchor Books	2009	Paterson	11	5
9780767931557	BEME01	Ben	Mezrich	The Accidental Billionaires	Anchor Books	2009	Wanaque	6	5
0805029648	DABA01	Dave	Barry	Bad Habits	Henry Holt & Co.	1987	Wanaque	1	4
9780399154379	DABA01	Dave	Barry	History of the Millenium (So Far)	G. P. Putman's Sons	2007	Wanaque	1	2
0312995423	DABR01	Dan	Brown	Digital Fortress	St. Martin	1998	Wanaque	3	1
0312995423	DABR01	Dan	Brown	Digital Fortress	St. Martin	1998	Paterson	2	5
9780593054277	DABR01	Dan	Brown	The Lost Symbol	Doubleday	2009	Paterson	11	3
9780593054277	DABR01	Dan	Brown	The Lost Symbol	Doubleday	2009	Wanaque	5	4
0809400774	DABR02	Dale	Brown	American Cooking: The Northwest	Time Life	1970	Paterson	1	8
9780307405807	DOSA01	Douglas	Sarine	The Ninja Handbook	Three Rivers Press	2008	Paterson	1	3
9781572439597	JAST01	Jayson	Stark	The Stark Truth	Triumph Books	2007	Wanaque	1	6
0380788624	NEST01	Neal	Stephenson	Cryptonomicon	Perennial	1999	Paterson	1	1
9780345517951	ROJA01	Ron	Jaworski	The Games that Changed the Game	ESPN Books	2010	Paterson	2	1

FIGURE 9.6 Expanded Books Table

Repeated information for a book found in two locations

In Figure 9.6 all the information related to the book *Digital Fortress* is repeated—the ISBN, AuthorFirst, AuthorLast, Title, Publisher, and PubYear. To resolve the anomaly, two tables are created: Books and Stock. The Books table contains fields that relate to the books, such as ISBN, AuthorID, AuthorFirst, AuthorLast, Title, Publisher, and PubYear. The primary key of this table is ISBN (see Figure 9.7). All non-key fields are now functionally dependent on the ISBN. The Stock table contains the fields ISBN, Location, OnHand, and Aisle, as shown in Figure 9.8. The primary key for this table is a **composite key**, a primary key that is made of two or more fields. In the new Stock table, the primary key (or composite key) is the combination of ISBN and Location. In the Stock table, all non-key fields are functionally dependent on both components of the primary key. In addition, notice that the data, once divided into two tables, have less repetition of book information.

Books

ISBN	AuthorID	AuthorFirst	AuthorLast	Title	Publisher	PubYear
9781401208417	ALMO01	Alan	Moore	V for Vendetta	DC Comics	2005
9780767931557	BEME01	Ben	Mezrich	The Accidental Billionaires	Anchor Books	2009
0805029648	DABA01	Dave	Barry	Bad Habits	Henry Holt & Co.	1987
9780399154379	DABA01	Dave	Barry	History of the Millenium (So Far)	G. P. Putman's Sons	2007
0809400774	DABA02	Dale	Brown	American Cooking: The Northwest	Time Life	1970
0312995423	DABR01	Dan	Brown	Digital Fortress	St. Martin	1998
9780593054277	DABR01	Dan	Brown	The Lost Symbol	Doubleday	2009
9780307405807	DOSA01	Douglas	Sarine	The Ninja Handbook	Three Rivers Press	2008
9781572439597	JAST01	Jayson	Stark	The Stark Truth	Triumph Books	2007
0380788624	NEST01	Neal	Stephenson	Cryptonomicon	Perennial	1999
9780345517951	ROJA01	Ron	Jaworski	The Games that Changed the Game	ESPN Books	2010

Each book displays in one record only

FIGURE 9.7 Books Table in Second Normal Form (2NF)

Stock

ISBN	Location	OnHand	Aisle
0312995423	Paterson	2	5
0312995423	Wanaque	3	1
0380788624	Paterson	1	1
0805029648	Wanaque	1	4
0809400774	Paterson	1	8
9780307405807	Paterson	1	3
9780345517951	Paterson	2	1
9780399154379	Wanaque	1	2
9780593054277	Paterson	11	3
9780593054277	Wanaque	5	4
9780767931557	Paterson	11	5
9780767931557	Wanaque	6	5
9781401208417	Paterson	2	5
9781572439597	Wanaque	1	6

ISBN and Location fields are composite key for the Stock table

FIGURE 9.8 Stock Table Created from Books Information

Tables with a composite key may require some additional changes. You must ensure that all other non-key fields are functionally dependent on the entire primary key. Some fields are functionally dependent on both the ISBN and Location fields. For example, to determine the number of books on hand for any specific title, both the ISBN and the Location fields are required. Similarly, to determine the aisle in which a book is stored, both the ISBN and the Location fields are required. However, some fields, such as Title, are only dependent on the ISBN component. Regardless of whether a book is in Paterson or Wanaque, a book with an ISBN of 0312995423 is always *Digital Fortress*. The same goes for the rest of the non-key fields shown in the Books table (Figure 9.7). Therefore, having the Title field in the Stock table would violate 2NF and the Title field would need to be moved to the Books table.

In Figure 9.8, adding an AutoNumber field labeled as the primary key would not solve the issue. It is, therefore, the combination of the ISBN and Location fields that would determine the other information in the table.

Understanding Third Normal Form

A table is in *third normal form (3NF)* if it meets 2NF criteria and no transitive dependencies exist. A *transitive dependency* occurs when the value of one non-key field is functionally dependent on the value of another non-key field. AuthorFirst and AuthorLast are dependent on AuthorID and, therefore, are an example of a transitive dependency. Whenever you know the AuthorID, the AuthorFirst and AuthorLast are automatically known. This can lead to repetition within a database, and, therefore, should be fixed.

STEP 3 ## Implement Third Normal Form

To conform to 3NF, AuthorFirst and AuthorLast must be moved to another table, as shown in Figure 9.9. The new Authors table contains three fields: AuthorID, AuthorFirst, and AuthorLast. The Books table can now reference the author using the AuthorID field, as shown in Figure 9.10. The Books table is in 3NF because the transitive dependency was removed. In effect, moving to 3NF requires some work because a new table is created and data are moved. For a large database, this may require creation of a Make Table query(see the Action Queries section of this textbook for more information). In the worst case, this could require large amounts of tedious data entry. However, the trade-off is less repeated data and less data inconsistency, which leads to fewer anomalies. For example, if you had a typographical error for an author's name (say, Steven King instead of Stephen King), you would only change the spelling in one place to correct it.

Each author name and AuthorID displays only once

Authors		
AuthorID	AuthorFirst	AuthorLast
ALMO01	Alan	Moore
BEME01	Ben	Mezrich
DABA01	Dave	Barry
DABR01	Dan	Brown
DABR02	Dale	Brown
DOSA01	Douglas	Sarine
JAST01	Jayson	Stark
NEST01	Neal	Stephenson
ROJA01	Ron	Jaworski

FIGURE 9.9 Authors Table Created from Books Information

Author first and last names are no longer repeated for each book

Books				
ISBN	AuthorID	Title	Publisher	PubYear
9781401208417	ALMO01	V for Vendetta	DC Comics	2005
9780767931557	BEME01	The Accidental Billionaires	Anchor Books	2009
0805029648	DABA01	Bad Habits	Henry Holt & Co.	1987
9780399154379	DABA01	History of the Millenium (So Far)	G. P. Putman's Sons	2007
0312995423	DABR01	Digital Fortress	St. Martin	1998
9780593054277	DABR01	The Lost Symbol	Doubleday	2009
9780307405807	DOSA01	The Ninja Handbook	Three Rivers Press	2008
9781572439597	JAST01	The Stark Truth	Triumph Books	2007
0809400774	NEST01	American Cooking: The Northwest	Time Life	1970
0380788624	NEST01	Cryptonomicon	Perennial	1999
9780345517951	ROJA01	The Games that Changed the Game	ESPN Books	2010

FIGURE 9.10 Books Table in Third Normal Form (3NF)

Another way to handle a conversion to 3NF is to delete fields that may not be necessary. In this specific case, the AuthorID field is important because it is the first and last names of the author. In other cases, ask yourself if there is an extra field that can be eliminated. For example, would you need to store the Publisher's City, or could you remove that information from the database all together?

To summarize, the normalization process for the Bookstore database first started with one table ONF (Fig 9.3), then, applying the rules of 1NF, the table was corrected so that each entry was a separate record. Next, the rules of 2NF were applied to the database. A Stock table was added to accommodate stock information for the two store locations. The ISBN field was made the primary key of the Books table, and any non-key fields that were not functionally dependent on the ISBN were moved to the Stock table. The ISBN and Location fields were combined for a composite primary key. All non-key fields in the new Stock table are functionally dependent on both ISBN and Location. Finally, the rules of 3NF were applied to the database. The authors' first and last names were moved into a new Author table. The AuthorID field remained in the Books table.

Table 9.1 presents a summary of the three normal forms covered in this chapter.

TABLE 9.1 Normalization Summary		
Form	**What It Does**	**Notes**
First Normal Form	Removes repeating groups	Introduces redundancy, which is fixed by later normal forms.
Second Normal Form	Removes dependencies on part of a composite primary key	Commonly an issue when a table has a composite key. If the primary key is a single field, a table is often in 2NF. Changes usually result in added tables.
Third Normal Form	Removes dependencies on any field that is not a primary key	Changes usually result in new tables.

> **TIP: CITY, STATE, ZIP, 3NF?**
> For most locations in the United States, if you have the ZIP code, you can look up the city and state. This might lead you to believe that this is a transitive dependency. However, on some rare occasions, this is not true. For example, the ZIP code 42223 covers parts of Christian County, Kentucky and Montgomery County, Tennessee. In this case, the same ZIP code not only crosses county borders, it also crosses state lines! Note that in this case, this oddity has to do with an army base that crosses state borders. Due to issues such as these, it is safe to consider a database with the city, state, and ZIP in the same table to be in 3NF.
>
> On the other hand, if you have two customers who live in North Brunswick, New Jersey, one person doing data entry might type it into the database as North Brunswick and the other may abbreviate it as N Brunswick. If you created a filter or query to locate all towns listed as North Brunswick, only one of those two customers would display in the results. The argument for putting ZIP in a separate table is to avoid issues such as that.

Finalizing the Design

Once you have created new tables, you will need to create relationships between the tables. This should be done after completion of the normalization process. The tables should be connected, and the Enforce Referential Integrity option should be checked. Remember, the purpose of normalization is to remove repetition, but you still have to be able to retrieve data. Relationships make that possible in a multiple-table database.

STEP 4 ## Create Relationships

Figure 9.11 shows the relationships in the Books database after normalization. Observe that the Stock and Author tables created during the normalization process now are related to the Books table through their primary keys. When you add a new table to a database, a relationship is not automatically created. You will need to create the relationships using the same procedure you have used in previous chapters. After the relationships have been set up, the flow of information becomes more obvious. Notice in Figure 9.12, the Authors table, in Datasheet view, now has a plus symbol to the left of each record to indicate that the records are connected to another table—in this case, the Books table. When clicked, the related records from the books table display for each author record.

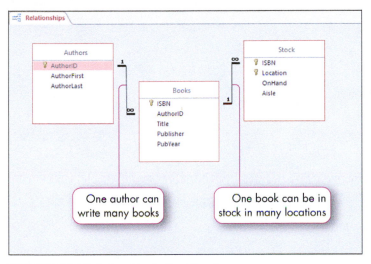

FIGURE 9.11 Relationships in Final Database

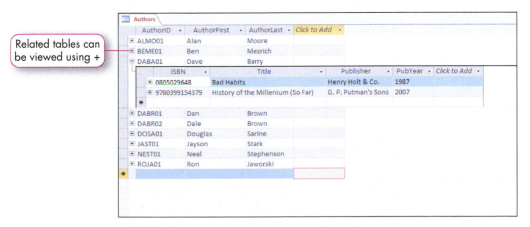

FIGURE 9.12 Related Records Using a Subdatasheet

Creating relationships can be a way to test for normalization. Normalization should not result in data loss, so if you cannot create a relationship between the tables with the Enforce Referential Integrity set, there is likely an issue with the way you have normalized. It may be frustrating to see an error saying a relationship cannot be created, but this is Access's way of letting you know there is a problem. To fix the problem, determine which records in one table do not match the records in another table. For example, you might have a book assigned to an author who does not exist, and you can fix that by assigning the book to a valid author.

Quick Concepts

1. Discuss the purpose of normalizing a database. *p. 502*

2. Explain the problems that the first normal form fixes. *p. 503*

3. Discuss the problems that the second normal form fixes. *p. 505*

4. Explain the problems that the third normal form fixes. *p. 507*

Hands-On Exercises

Skills covered: Implement First Normal Form • Implement Second Normal Form • Implement Third Normal Form • Create Relationships

1 Database Normalization

Your job at the Metropolitan Zoo has been fun and challenging. You have been making daily updates to the zoo's database with the help of your boss, Selene Platt. Based on your understanding of the rules of normalization, you decide to recommend some design changes to the database.

STEP 1 IMPLEMENT FIRST NORMAL FORM

Selene has asked you to review the table structure to see if any changes should be made. You decide to apply the rules of normalization to the Animals table. Refer to Figure 9.13 as you complete Step 1.

Step c: Diet field deleted

Step b: Multiple values in one field

AnimalName	AnimalType	Diet	Origin	Endangered	ExhibitID	TrainerID	TrainerName
Anny	Mockingbird	Insects	North America		1	1	Asha
Archie	Zebra	Plants	South Africa		2	3	Elizabeth
Bronstein	Komodo Dragon	Deer, Boar	Indonesia	✓	1	3	Elizabeth
Cara	Manatee	Plants	Central America		1	1	Asha
Cassandra	Emerald Tree Boa	Mice, Birds	South America		3	1	Asha
Cassandra	Ostrich	Alfalfa	Africa		2	2	Keisha
Dietre	Clouded Leopard	Small animals	Southeast Asia		1	2	Keisha
Farunn	White Rhinoceros	Plants	Africa	✓	2	2	Keisha
Khamen	Cuban Crocodile	Fish, Small animals	Cuba	✓	3	3	Elizabeth
Palom	Black Rhinoceros	Plants	Africa	✓	2	2	Keisha
Perenolde	Komodo Dragon	Deer, Boar	Indonesia	✓	1	1	Asha
Pocho	Cuban Crocodile	Fish, Small animals	Cuba	✓	3	4	Ruben
Rakshiri	Bengal Tiger	Animals, Fish	India	✓	1	4	Ruben
Sindall	Bengal Tiger	Animals, Fish	India	✓	1	4	Ruben
Sophie	Giraffe	Leaves, Stems	West Africa	✓	2	2	Keisha
Stampy	Elephant	Plant parts, Grass	Africa		2	3	Elizabeth
Uhkloc	Gorilla	Leaves, Fruit	Central Africa		2	4	Ruben
Zhevra	Zebra	Plants	South Africa		2	4	Ruben

FIGURE 9.13 Animals Table in First Normal Form (1NF)

a. Open *a09h1Zoo*. Save the database as **a09h1Zoo_LastFirst**.

> **TROUBLESHOOTING:** If you make any major mistakes in this exercise, you can close the file, open *a09h1Zoo* again, and then start this exercise over.

b. Open the Animals table in Datasheet view. Look for repeating groups in the Animals table.

The Diet field has multiple values separated by commas. This qualifies as a repeating group, and therefore, this information will be added to a new table and removed from this table to conform to 1NF.

c. Switch to Design view. Click the **row selector** for the Diet field and click **Delete rows** on the Table Tools Design tab in the Tools group. Click **Yes** when asked for confirmation and switch to Datasheet view. Click **Yes** when prompted to save.

The Animals table now meets 1NF criteria. Diet data were moved to a new table and the multiple values were removed from the Animals table.

d. Open the Diet table in Datasheet view.

For the purposes of this exercise, the diet information for each animal type was already added to the Diet table. This table has been provided to expedite the normalization process. You will relate the Diet and Animals tables in a future step.

e. Close the Diet table.

With the Diet data now in a separate table, you will examine the Animals table and convert to second normal form. Refer to Figure 9.14 as you complete Step 2.

Step d: Origin and Endangered fields deleted

Step a: Duplicate animal names

AnimalName	AnimalType	ExhibitID	TrainerID	TrainerName
Anny	Mockingbird	1	1	Asha
Archie	Zebra	2	3	Elizabeth
Bronstein	Komodo Dragon	1	3	Elizabeth
Cara	Manatee	1	1	Asha
Cassandra	Emerald Tree Boa	3	1	Asha
Cassandra	Ostrich	2	2	Keisha
Dietre	Clouded Leopard	1	2	Keisha
Farunn	White Rhinoceros	2	2	Keisha
Khamen	Cuban Crocodile	3	3	Elizabeth
Palom	Black Rhinoceros	2	2	Keisha
Perenolde	Komodo Dragon	1	1	Asha
Pocho	Cuban Crocodile	3	4	Ruben
Rakshiri	Bengal Tiger	1	4	Ruben
Sindall	Bengal Tiger	1	4	Ruben
Sophie	Giraffe	2	2	Keisha
Stampy	Elephant	2	3	Elizabeth
Uhkloc	Gorilla	2	4	Ruben
Zhevra	Zebra	2	4	Ruben

FIGURE 9.14 Animals Table in Second Normal Form (2NF)

a. Examine the Animals table and notice there are two animals named *Cassandra*.

   You check to make sure the table is in 2NF. Origin and Endangered are all determined by AnimalType and are attributes of a type of animal, not a specific animal. ExhibitID, TrainerID, and TrainerName are attributes of a specific animal. Fields will need to be removed to satisfy 2NF.

b. Open the Animal Information table in Datasheet view. Observe this table includes the Origin and Endangered fields as well as other fields regarding animals.

   These fields will be moved to the Animal Information table, which has been provided so you do not have to perform data entry.

c. Close the Animal Information table.

d. Open the Animals table in Design View. Observe that the table has a composite key (the combination of AnimalName and AnimalType). This table is not in 2NF because some fields are dependent on part of the primary key. Click the **row selector** for the Origin field and click **Delete Rows** in the Tools group on the Table Tools Design tab, clicking **Yes** in response to the warning. Click the **row selector** for the Endangered field and click **Delete Rows** in the Tools group on the Table Tools Design tab, clicking **Yes** in response to the warning.

   You deleted these two fields because they are not functionally dependent on the entire primary key. The Origin and Endangered data were already added to the Animal Information table.

e. Save the Animals table. Switch to Datasheet view.

   Your table should match Figure 9.14. All the remaining fields are functionally dependent on the entire primary key. Therefore, the table now meets 2NF criteria.

The final step to improve the zoo's Animals table is to convert to third normal form: The value of a non-key field cannot be functionally dependent on the value of another non-key field. Refer to Figure 9.15 as you complete Step 3.

AnimalName ▾	AnimalType ▾	ExhibitID ▾	TrainerID ▾
Anny	Mockingbird	1	1
Archie	Zebra	2	3
Bronstein	Komodo Dragon	1	3
Cara	Manatee	1	1
Cassandra	Emerald Tree Boa	3	1
Cassandra	Ostrich	2	2
Dietre	Clouded Leopard	1	2
Farunn	White Rhinoceros	2	2
Khamen	Cuban Crocodile	3	3
Palom	Black Rhinoceros	2	2
Perenolde	Komodo Dragon	1	1
Pocho	Cuban Crocodile	3	4
Rakshiri	Bengal Tiger	1	4
Sindall	Bengal Tiger	1	4
Sophie	Giraffe	2	2
Stampy	Elephant	2	3
Uhkloc	Gorilla	2	4
Zhevra	Zebra	2	4

Step d: TrainerName field deleted

FIGURE 9.15 Animals Table in Third Normal Form (3NF)

a. Look for any non-key field values in the Animals table that are functionally dependent on another non-key field value.

TrainerName (non-key) is functionally dependent on TrainerID (non-key). If you know the TrainerID, you can determine the TrainerName. For example, if you enter value 1 for the TrainerID, then the trainer's name will always be Asha. A Trainers table was established to include the contact information for each trainer. There is no need to repeat the trainer name in the Animals table. Just the TrainerID is needed. Any other information is available by establishing a relationship between the Trainers table and the Animals table.

b. Open the Trainers table in Datasheet view. Observe the non-key data have been moved from the Animals table to the Trainers table. Close the Trainers table.

c. Switch to Design view in the Animals table.

d. Delete the TrainerName field, clicking **Yes** in response to the warning.

You delete the TrainerName field because it is functionally dependent on the TrainerID field and, therefore, is not allowed in the Animals table for 3NF. Because the same information is already included in an existing table, you can delete the field. Otherwise, a new table would need to be established prior to deleting the data in the Animals table.

e. Switch to Datasheet view, saving the table. Compare your results with Figure 9.15.

The table now meets 3NF criteria.

f. Close the Animals table.

Now that all tables conform through 3NF, relationships can be established to ensure the database functions properly. Refer to Figure 9.16 as you complete Step 4.

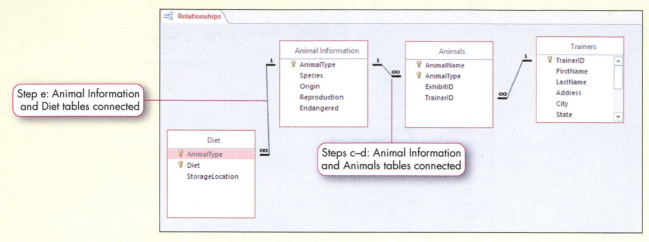

FIGURE 9.16 Zoo Relationships

a. Click the **Database Tools tab** and click **Relationships** in the Relationships group to show the Relationships window.

> **TROUBLESHOOTING:** If all the tables are not closed, you will get a warning about tables being locked. If you receive this warning, exit the Relationships window, close all open tables, and repeat Step a.

b. Click **Show Table** in the Relationships group. Double-click each **table** to add it to the Relationships window. Once you have added all four tables, click **Close** to close the Show Table dialog box.

c. Drag the **AnimalType field** from the Animal Information table to the AnimalType field in the Animals table.

The Animals and Animal Information tables are related by the common AnimalType field.

d. Select the **Enforce Referential Integrity** and **Cascade Update Related Fields checkboxes** in the Edit Relationships dialog box. Click **Create**.

e. Repeat Steps c and d to connect the AnimalType field in the Animal Information table to the AnimalType field in the Diet table. Compare your results with Figure 9.16.

You may also notice the Animals and Trainers tables are not yet linked. You are leaving these tables unlinked intentionally because you want to discuss the contents with your supervisor. This will be linked in Hands-On Exercise 2.

> **TROUBLESHOOTING:** There are three tables with an AnimalType field. If you cannot create the relationship, make sure you are connecting the AnimalType in the Animals, Diet, and Animal Information tables.

f. Save the relationships and close the Relationships window.

g. Keep the a09h1Zoo_LastFirst database open if you plan to continue with the next Hands-On Exercise. If not, save and close the database, and exit Access.

Built-In Analysis and Design Tools

As new tables, queries, forms, and reports are added to a database, the performance of the database may decline. This slower performance may be because Access databases are often created by users who lack formal training in database design. For example, a user who creates a database with 10 tables might not understand how to join the tables to produce efficient results and thus end up with repetition of data, poor performance, and data entry errors. Even if a database is well designed, deficiencies causing poor performance may exist. Some IT administrators may try to compensate for a poorly designed database by migrating to an enterprise-level database management system (DBMS), such as Microsoft SQL Server, MySQL, or Oracle. Enterprise-level DBMS database programs can manage larger amounts of data than Microsoft Access can. Unlike Access, these programs were designed to handle hundreds or thousands of users simultaneously. Large corporations such as Walmart, with *billions* of rows of transactional data use Oracle or other database servers to run their businesses.

Moving to an enterprise-level DBMS may have a positive net effect on the speed of processing; however, the design problems that existed in Access will still exist. It is best to resolve the design issues first in Access and then evaluate whether Access can handle the processing demands of the database. If it can, other reasons to use Access rather than move to an enterprise-level DBMS may exist. These reasons include wizards to help create tables, forms, and reports and a graphical user interface (GUI) that is intuitive to Access users. Also, Access can run on a desktop computer and does not require its own dedicated server as enterprise-level DBMS programs do. Another reason is cost. Microsoft SQL Server and Oracle are much more expensive than Access. MySQL, though free, still requires more expertise than an Access database. If you recommend migrating to one of those solutions, it is best to be sure it is worth the investment.

Sometimes, you can fix problems using the built-in Access tools. For example, you can split an Access database into two database files. If many users are accessing the same database, splitting the database may improve performance. One file would contain all the tables and reside on a server, while the other would reside with each user. Each user could create his or her own queries, forms, and reports on local machines but still access the same tables everyone else is using.

Access provides useful tools that database administrators can use to analyze and improve database performance—the Database Documenter tool, the Performance Analyzer tool, the Table Analyzer tool, and the Database Splitter. Figure 9.17 shows the tools available on the Database Tools tab.

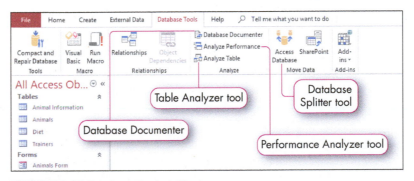

FIGURE 9.17 Database Analysis Tools

In this section, you will learn how to use the tools to analyze performance and tables, and document the database. You will also learn how to split an Access database into two databases using the Database Splitter tool.

Using the Database Documenter Tool

The **Database Documenter** creates a report that contains detailed information for each selected object in a database. The Database Documenter report shows the field names, data types, properties, indexes, and permissions for each of the selected objects. This can be helpful in many ways. New database administrators can become familiar with the structure of the database if you provide them a report. If someone will be working on a database, having this sort of documentation handy as he or she becomes familiar with a database is invaluable. You can also use this report to view details that are not necessarily apparent by looking at an object. The report can provide information about when an object was last modified or even when a field in a table was last modified. This can fix issues related to unintentional (or even intentional) changes introduced by a user. You may not need this level of information for a database with two tables, but this is more important the larger your database grows.

STEP 1 ## Run the Database Documenter

If you run the Database Documenter tool for small databases similar to the zoo database discussed in this chapter, the report generated can be nearly 100 pages if every option is selected. Important information can be missed due to the sheer amount of data. Before running the Documenter, you should narrow the options so only the pertinent information is displayed. Each tab in the Documenter dialog box represents a database object that can be documented (see Figure 9.18). Additionally, there is a Current Database tab and an All Object Types tab. For the Current Database tab, you can choose to analyze the database Properties or Relationships. For the other tabs in the Documenter window, a number of options are available, including choosing which objects to analyze and what level of detail to show found under Options (shown in Figure 9.19). A brief explanation of each of these options is listed in Table 9.2. You will most commonly run the Documenter to gather information about tables.

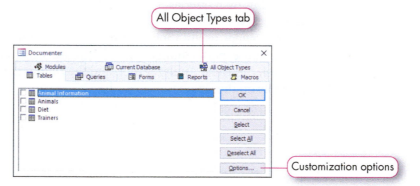

FIGURE 9.18 Database Documenter Dialog Box

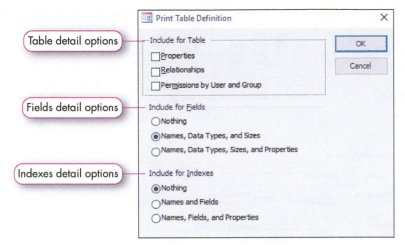

Table detail options

Fields detail options

Indexes detail options

FIGURE 9.19 Print Table Definition Dialog Box

TABLE 9.2	Database Documenter Options Found in Print Table Definition Dialog Box
Option	**Function**
Include for Table: Properties	Documents table properties, including number of records, date of last update, and formatting.
Include for Table: Relationships	Documents table relationships, including which fields are common between tables and type of relationship, such as one to many.
Include for Table: Permissions by User and Group	Shows permissions for the tables based on users and/or groups. If the database does not have user-based permissions, deselect this option.
Include for Fields: Nothing	Includes no detail about the fields in the selected tables.
Include for Fields: Names, Data Types, and Sizes	Includes field names, data types, and field sizes for each field in the selected tables.
Include for Fields: Names, Data Types, Sizes, and Properties	Includes field names, data type, and field size for each field in the selected tables and options such as whether a zero-length value (or null value) is allowed, column width, and text alignment. This makes the report much longer.
Include for Indexes: Nothing	Includes no detail about the indexes in the selected tables.
Include for Indexes: Names and Fields	Includes the names of all indexes and the fields with which they are associated.
Include for Indexes: Names, Fields, and Properties	Includes the names of all indexes, the fields with which they are associated, and the index properties, including the number of distinct index values and whether the index is required and must be unique. This makes the report much longer.

To run the Database Documenter, complete the following steps:

1. Click Database Documenter in the Analyze group on the Database Tools tab.
2. Select the specific objects or click the All Object Types tab, and Select All to analyze everything in the database.
3. Click Options to display the Print Table Definition dialog box and select the appropriate options.
4. Click OK to generate the report.

The Documenter creates a report that contains detailed information about the tables and other selected objects in your database; the report opens in Print Preview mode, as shown in Figure 9.20. Only the first page summary displays here. You can save the report in several formats. To open the full report, you can save the file as a PDF. The PDF format is especially useful when sharing the results with someone else electronically.

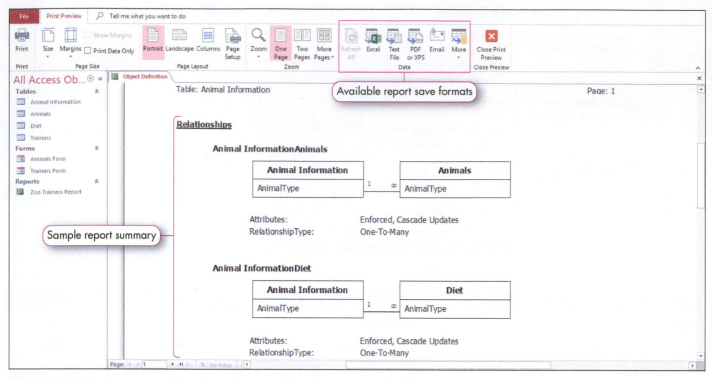

FIGURE 9.20 Database Documenter Report in Print Preview

Using the Performance Analyzer Tool

The Database Documenter is useful for listing the properties of each object in a database. However, the Documenter does not identify flaws in the design of the database. The ***Performance Analyzer*** evaluates each object in a database and makes recommendations for optimizing the database. Figure 9.21 shows the Performance Analyzer dialog box, where you can select objects to analyze. Similar to the Documenter, there is an All Object Types tab and a Current Database tab. You can analyze only one type of object at a time or all objects at the same time. You can easily deselect certain objects such as VBA projects.

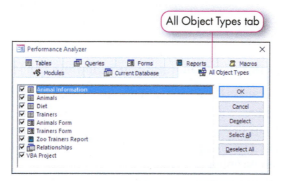

FIGURE 9.21 Performance Analyzer Options

STEP 2 ## Run the Performance Analyzer

Analyze Performance is located on the Database Tools tab in the Analyze group. Once the Analyze Performance dialog box is open, you will select the appropriate objects to analyze. The Tables tab is selected by default, as they are the most likely cause of slowdowns. When you click an item in the Analysis Results list, information about the proposed optimization is displayed in the Analysis Notes box, as shown in Figure 9.22. After the analysis is run, the Performance Analyzer lists results in a dialog box as recommendations, suggestions, or ideas.

- Recommendation—a recommendation will be marked with an exclamation point and is a change that will improve your database with little risk. Recommendations can be fixed automatically with the Performance Analyzer.

- Suggestion—a suggestion is marked by a question mark and potential compromises may have to be made when carrying out a suggested change. Suggestions can be fixed automatically with the Performance Analyzer.

- Idea—an idea is labeled with a lightbulb and must be performed manually by the database administrator.

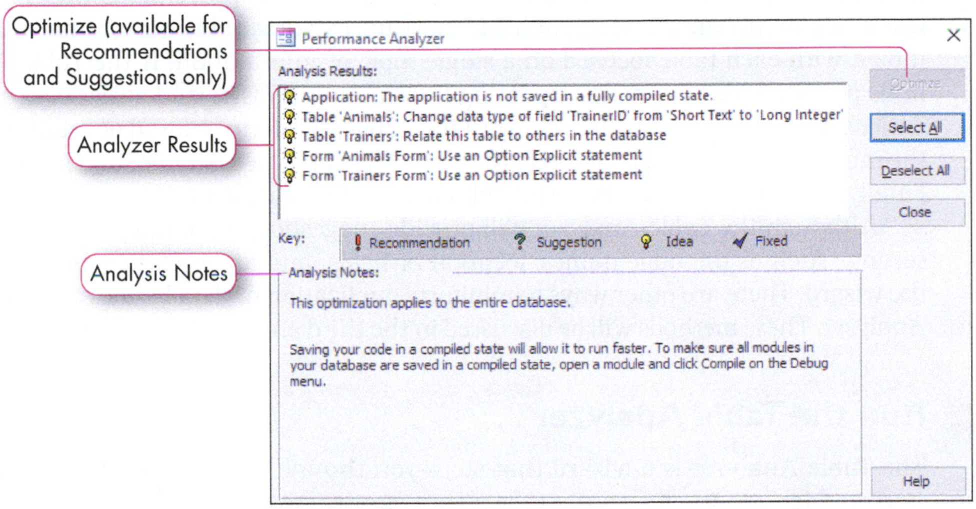

FIGURE 9.22 Performance Analyzer Results

Before implementing any changes, you should read the information provided in the Analysis Notes box and, if you are unsure, spend a little time doing research online first. The Performance Analyzer does not catch all possible database problems. Although a useful tool, the Performance Analyzer may miss some issues, so think of this tool as a supplement to your own analysis, not a replacement for it.

> **TIP: BACK UP DATABASE BEFORE OPTIMIZING**
> Before optimizing your database by making the changes suggested by the Performance Analyzer, it is best to back up your database. That way, you can revert back to the copy if the optimization yields unexpected results.

Add an Index

Some commonplace ideas you may see in the Performance Analyzer report include changing data types, relating a table to other tables in the database, and saving the database as an MDE file. One common suggestion made by the Performance Analyzer is to add an index. This is a simple change to a field (or fields) in a table that could improve performance when implemented. An **index** is a setting for a field that reduces the time it takes to run queries and reports. It is similar to the index in the back of a textbook in that it provides a convenient way to find information quickly. If you wanted to find where a topic is introduced in this book, you could flip through page by page, but you would probably instead turn to the index and find out what pages reference the topic. An index works similarly for the database.

Generally, you should add an index to any field that will be searched or sorted often. For example, in a college database, a student's name would likely be indexed, but not a phone number. However, in a cell phone service provider's database, a phone number would probably be indexed because customer service representatives would use it to find a customer. Adding an index saves time searching but will increase the time it takes to add information to the database. A database the size of the zoo database may not require an index, but in a larger project, this is a common suggestion of the Performance Analyzer tool.

Using the Table Analyzer Tool

The **Table Analyzer** evaluates the tables in a database and makes suggestions to minimize duplication of data. This primarily involves improvements that implement the rules of normalization, such as splitting existing tables into smaller, related tables, with each table focused on a single topic of information. If the Table Analyzer finds potential improvements, updating information is faster and easier because fewer data changes are required. Second, with the duplicated data removed or minimized, only the minimum information is stored; therefore, the database is smaller and more efficient. Finally, the database stores more reliable data because data are not repeated.

Although the Table Analyzer will provide suggestions for changes, you can adjust settings such as the table names, location of fields, and table relationships as you use the wizard. There are other ways to minimize duplication of data besides using the Table Analyzer. These methods will be discussed in the third section of this chapter.

STEP 3 ▶ Run the Table Analyzer

The Table Analyzer is a wizard that steps you though the analysis process. The first step enables you to choose the tables you want to analyze (see Figure 9.23). If it is recommended that new tables be created, the next steps will give you the opportunity to name the tables and designate the primary key. As you walk through the steps in the Table Analyzer Wizard (see Figure 9.23), you can decide which fields should be included in new tables, or you can let the wizard create the fields in the new tables. The wizard will offer suggestions, but it is best to think about whether they make sense in your database. Some of the suggestions made by the analyzer may be too extreme. For example, you may be advised to split a table into four new tables; however, for your purposes only two tables would make sense. The analyzer will also find data inconsistencies such as the same patient with two different social security numbers. The wizard creates a list of data you can change or accept. Perhaps it was just a typo with the numbers, and the data can be updated, or perhaps the name can be updated because it was a different person. The wizard will also create a query so existing forms and reports will still function. Furthermore, it creates a back-up of the original table data. This way if you do not like the outcome of the wizard's design you can revert back to the original table and try a different design.

To use the Table Analyzer Wizard, complete the following steps:

1. Click the Database Tools tab and select Analyze Table.
2. Click Next twice to advance past the introductory pages.
3. Select a table (see Figure 9.23) and click Next.
4. Click Next to let the wizard propose changes to the table. If no changes are recommended, Access will inform you and enable you to exit the wizard.
5. Rename tables by clicking the Rename Table, as shown in Figure 9.24, to clearly define the table content. You can also drag fields from one table to another if what Access suggests does not match what you have in mind. Click Next.
6. Confirm the primary keys in each proposed table, as shown in Figure 9.25. If you want to mark a field as a primary key, select it, and click Set Unique Identifier. To have Access create a primary key field for you, click in the table, and click Add Generated Key. Click Next.
7. Correct any inconsistent data, if prompted. If there are no problems with inconsistent data, this step does not display. However, if there are errors (such as the same animal having two different origins declared in two different records), this will be indicated, as shown in Figure 9.26.
8. Choose whether or not to create a query that simulates the original table. If you create the query, Access will manipulate the database so the existing queries, forms, and reports do not need to be rebuilt. In a database without any of these objects, you should select not to create the query.
9. Close the help window that displays.

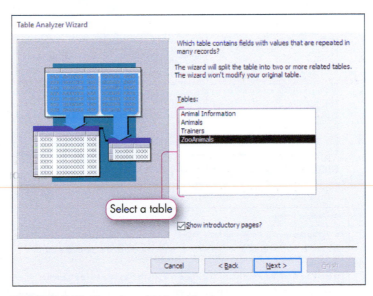

FIGURE 9.23 Choosing a Table to Analyze

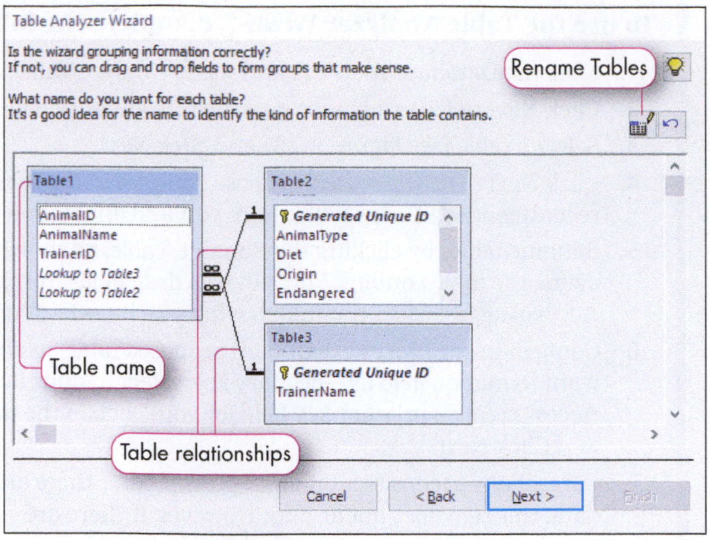

FIGURE 9.24 Renaming Tables

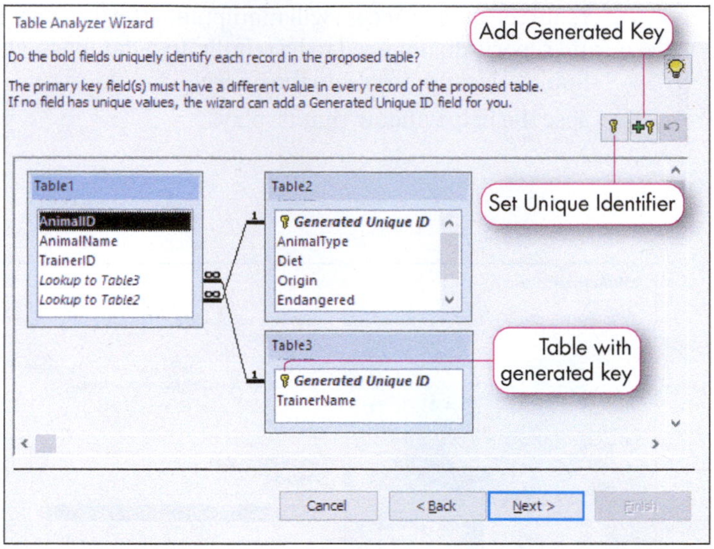

FIGURE 9.25 Identifying Primary Keys

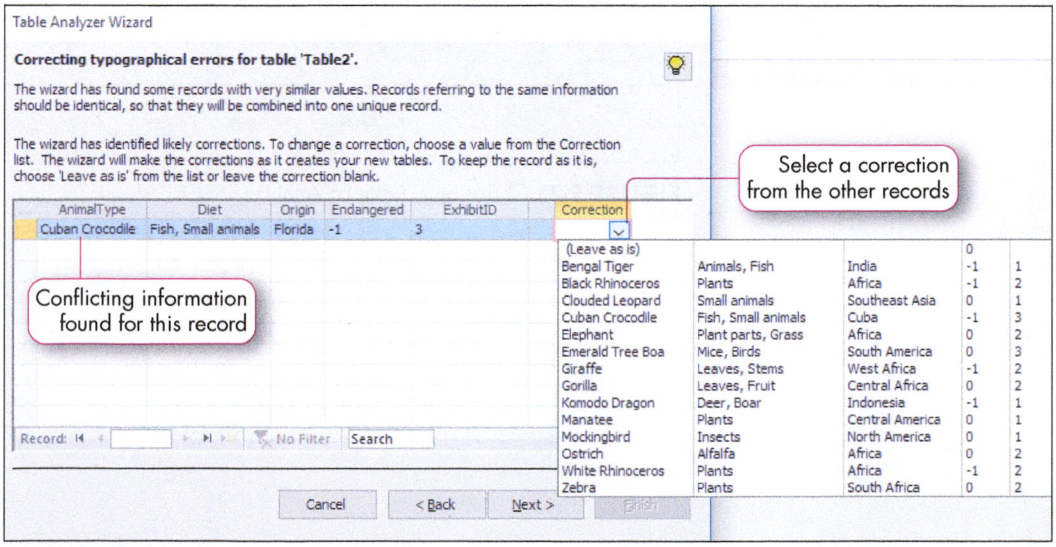

FIGURE 9.26 Identifying Data Entry Errors

After the Table Analyzer Wizard is finished, you should examine the new table structure. Click the Database Tools tab and click Relationships in the Relationships group. From there, because new tables will be added, relationships will need to be created. You could also use the Database Documenter tool to generate a new set of documentation for reference.

Using the Database Splitter Tool

A single-file Access database may work fine for a small office with a handful of users. However, when the number of users grows beyond that, you can use the *Database Splitter* tool, which enables you to split a database into two files: a back-end and a front-end database. A *back-end database* contains the tables of the database. A *front-end database* contains the queries, forms, and reports of the database. You could even have multiple front-end databases for different users or applications, all of whom are using the same back-end database.

The main advantages of splitting an Access database are improved reliability, security, and flexibility. By storing the back-end database on a server, the tables of the database will be backed up with the server, thus improving reliability. In addition, if the front-end database becomes corrupted, it would not affect the back-end database because they are two separate files. Security is improved because the security on the server is often better than that of a client machine. Finally, enabling each user to modify his or her own front-end database adds flexibility. Instead of trying to satisfy all users, the database administrator can enable each user to manage and customize his or her own front-end database, without affecting other users.

STEP 4 ## Run the Database Splitter

Once you have made the decision to split a database, the important decision is to choose where to store the back-end database. As discussed, storing the back-end database on a server would enable multiple users to use the tables.

To start the Database Splitter, complete the following steps:

1. Click Access Database in the Move Data group of the Database Tools tab.
2. Click Split Database.
3. Choose the folder and name for the new back-end database. Be aware Access will often default to your Documents folder, so make sure the correct folder is selected. The default name will be the original name plus "_be" for "back-end."
4. Click Split.
5. Click OK.

Work with a Front-End Database

After Access creates the back end, the front-end database remains open. The tables that existed in the original database are linked tables with the same table names. Linked tables have an arrow icon to indicate they are linked to another Access database (see Figure 9.27). When you point to a table name, a ScreenTip shows the path to the physical table to which the front-end database is linked. As users add data to the linked tables using the front-end database, the data become available to other users of the back-end tables. The linked tables cannot be redesigned by the end users. All users who will work with the front-end of the database must have Access installed on their local computer.

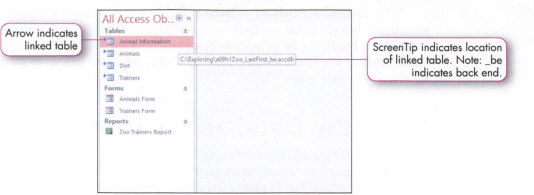

FIGURE 9.27 Linked Tables

TIP: ERRORS OPENING FRONT-END DATABASES

Note that if you use the front-end database on a different machine, or if you move the files into a different folder, you may get an error stating network access has been interrupted or the file path is not valid. If the database linking fails, you can right-click any linked table and select Linked Table Manager. Click Select All and click OK to update the location of the back-end database.

TIP: COMPARE DATABASES

Business editions of Microsoft Office 2019 include a tool called Database Compare, which was introduced in Office 2013. This tool is not part of Access; instead, it is a tool you can launch from your Start screen or Start menu. As the name implies, you can compare two database files to see the difference. Refer to online help for more assistance with the tool.

Quick Concepts

5. Explain three reasons that you would use the Database Documenter tool. *p. 516*

6. Discuss the three possible result types the Performance Analyzer tool might propose. *p. 519*

7. Explain how the Table Analyzer tool makes you more productive. *p. 520*

8. Discuss why a database administrator would decide to split a database. *p. 523*

Hands-On Exercises

MyLab IT HOE2 Sim Training

Watch the Video for this Hands-On Exercise!

Skills covered: Run the Database Documenter • Run the Performance Analyzer • Run the Table Analyzer • Run the Database Splitter • Work with a Front-End Database

2 Built-In Analysis and Design Tools

The Metropolitan Zoo database has been working well, but you decide to examine the database to see if further improvements can be made. Before you begin, you will create a report of the database relationships for your reference. You will use some built-in tools to analyze the database; you also decide to split the database into two files to enable different users to create their own queries, forms, and reports.

STEP 1 RUN THE DATABASE DOCUMENTER

You will create a report with the Database Documenter to show information on relationships in the zoo database. You will save this report as a PDF file for your reference. Refer to Figure 9.28 and Figure 9.29 as you complete Step 1.

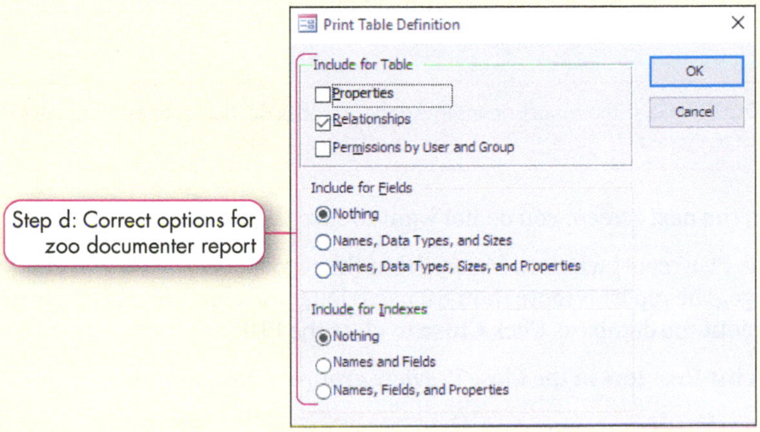

FIGURE 9.28 Database Documenter Options

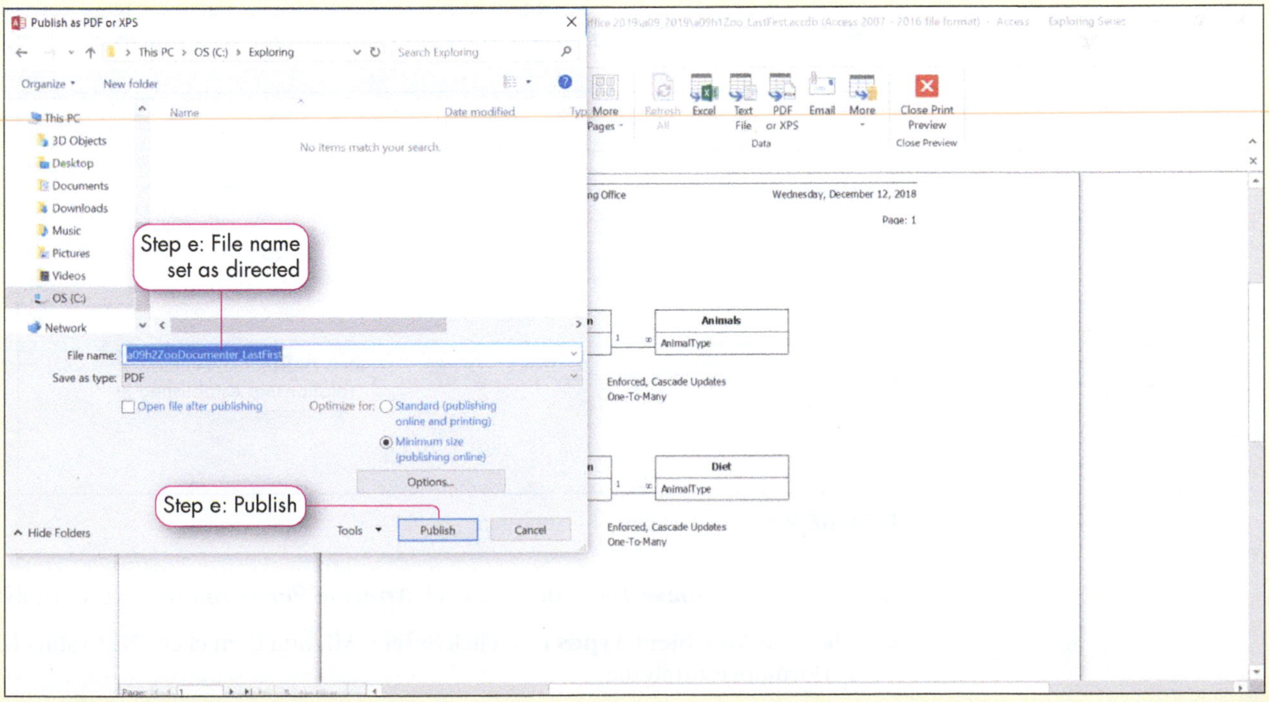

FIGURE 9.29 Publish Options for Documenter Report

a. Open *a09h1Zoo_LastFirst* if you closed it at the end of Hands-On Exercise 1 and save the database as **a09h2Zoo_LastFirst** changing h1 to h2.

b. Click **Database Documenter** in the Analyze group on the Database Tools tab. Click the **All Object Types tab**.

The complete set of objects in the database, including the forms, reports, properties, and relationships, are available to select.

c. Click **Select All** on the All Object Types tab and click **Options**.

d. Ensure the Relationships box in the *Include for Table* section is selected. Click the **Properties** and **Permission by User and Group check boxes** to deselect them. Click **Nothing** in the *Include for Fields* section and click **Nothing** in the *Include for Indexes* section. Your dialog box should resemble Figure 9.28. Click **OK**. Click **OK** to run the report.

You have changed the options so only the required information is present in the report.

e. Select **PDF or XPS** in the Data group on the Print Preview tab. Type **a09h2ZooDocumenter_LastFirst** for the file name. Click the **Open file after publishing check box** to deselect it, and click **Publish** to save the file, as shown in Figure 9.29. You will submit this file to your instructor at the end of the last Hands-On Exercise.

> **TROUBLESHOOTING:** If the report opens in Adobe Acrobat Reader or another tool, close the program and return to Access.

f. Click **Close** on the next screen, you do not want to save the steps.

g. Navigate to the PDF report window. Observe that the report documents the relationships on the first page. The report is more than 80 pages long and contains extremely detailed information about the database. Click **Close** to close the PDF.

h. Click **Close Print Preview** in the Close Preview group to close the report.

STEP 2 ▶ RUN THE PERFORMANCE ANALYZER

To evaluate the performance of the zoo database, you decide to run the Performance Analyzer tool. You will review the recommendations, suggestions, and ideas, and decide which to implement. Refer to Figure 9.30 as you complete Step 2.

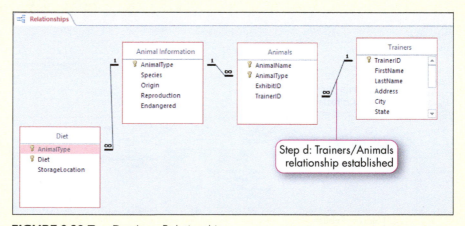

FIGURE 9.30 Zoo Database Relationships

a. Click the **Database Tools tab** and click **Analyze Performance** in the Analyze group.

b. Click the **All Object Types tab**, click **Select All**, and then click **OK** to start the Performance Analyzer.

The results window displays ideas to improve the zoo database.

c. Review the results of the Performance Analyzer and click the idea *Table Trainers; Relate this table to others in the database*. Read the idea suggested at the bottom of the dialog box, which further explains the idea text. This relationship should be established. Click **Close** to close the Performance Analyzer dialog box.

You consult with your supervisor and decide to establish a relationship between the Trainers and Animals tables as your supervisor suggests.

d. Click **Relationships** in the Relationships group on the Database Tools tab and create a relationship between the Trainers and Animals tables, using the common field TrainerID. Click to select the **Enforce Referential Integrity** and **Cascade Update Related Fields check boxes** and click **Create**.

The relationships should now match Figure 9.30. The tables may appear in a different order or of a different height in your database.

e. Save and close the Relationships window.

f. Repeat the procedure in Steps a and b above to run the Performance Analyzer again and see if the results are different this time.

The idea to relate the previous tables is no longer displayed. The suggestion to relate the Diet and Animals remains.

g. Close the Performance Analyzer dialog box and close the database.

STEP 3 **RUN THE TABLE ANALYZER**

You are curious what suggestions the Table Analyzer would have suggested with the original one table database you previously normalized. To do this, you will open an older version of the database, run the Table Analyzer, and then compare the results with the current database. Refer to Figure 9.31 as you complete Step 3.

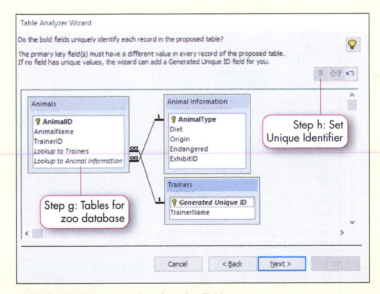

FIGURE 9.31 Unique Identifiers for Tables

a. Open *a09h2ZooAnalyzer*. Save the database as **a09h2ZooAnalyzer_LastFirst**.

b. Double-click the **ZooAnimals table** to open it in Datasheet view.

Observe that the table does not have any rules of normalization applied.

c. Close the ZooAnimals table.

d. Click the **Database Tools tab** and click **Analyze Table** in the Analyze group.

The Table Analyzer Wizard starts.

e. Click **Next** twice to skip the information steps.

Access displays a screen asking you to select tables.

f. Click **Next** twice ensuring "*Yes, let the wizard decide.*" is selected.

The ZooAnimals table was selected by default, and the wizard has suggested it be split into three tables.

g. Click the **Rename Table icon**, type **Animals** as the name of Table1, and then click **OK**. Select **Table2** and use the same process to rename Table2 as **Animal Information**. Select **Table3** and rename it **Trainers**. Click **Next**.

h. Click the **AnimalID field** in the Animals table and click **Set Unique Identifier** to set the primary key. Click the **AnimalType field** in the Animal Information table and use the same process to set the primary key. Compare your screen with Figure 9.31, and click **Next**.

Note that Access correctly identified the primary key for the Trainers table.

i. Select the **No, don't create the query option**, and click **Finish**. Click **OK** in response to the warning message.

There are still some repetition issues in the Diet field, but the Table Analyzer did reduce repetition of data.

j. Close the database. You will submit this file to your instructor at the end of the last Hands-On Exercise.

STEP 4 ## RUN THE DATABASE SPLITTER AND WORK WITH A FRONT-END DATABASE

You decide to split the zoo database to see if the performance of the database improves. You use the Database Splitter to divide the database into a front-end and a back-end file. Refer to Figure 9.32 as you complete Step 4.

FIGURE 9.32 Split Database

a. Open *a09h2Zoo_LastFirst*. Save the database as **a09h2ZooSplit_LastFirst**.

A database back up should be performed prior to splitting a database. The new database is displayed.

b. Click the **Database Tools tab** and click **Access Database** in the Move Data group.

The Database Splitter Wizard starts.

c. Click **Split Database**. Accept **a09h2ZooSplit_LastFirst_be** as the file name and click **Split**.

The Database Splitter splits the database into two files. You will submit the back-end file to your instructor at the end of the last Hands-On Exercise.

d. Click **OK**.

The database is split successfully. Notice arrows now appear to the left of each table, indicating they are stored in the back-end database.

e. Open the tables and the other objects to verify the database is working properly. Ensure the tables have arrows to the left of them, as shown in Figure 9.32.

f. Close the a09h2ZooSplit_LastFirst and a09h2ZooSplit_LastFirst_be databases.

g. Keep Access open if you plan to continue with the next Hands-On Exercise. If not, exit Access.

Database Security

Computer security can be defined as the protection of data from unauthorized access, modification, or destruction and can be divided into two general categories: physical security and logical security. Physical security involves protecting assets you can touch, such as computers, storage devices, and backup devices. Logical security protects the information that resides on the physical devices, including databases and other computer software. Security measures should be taken to protect your assets against both physical and logical threats.

In this section, you will learn several techniques available in Access to keep your database application safe. You will learn about controlling navigation, encrypting and password protecting the database, and prohibiting users from making other changes to the database that would affect other users' access to objects.

Controlling Navigation

To simplify data entry, a database designer can create a menu for users, highlighting commonly used objects. This can be accomplished using a **Navigation form**. Not to be confused with the Navigation Pane at the left side of the screen, the Navigation form is a tabbed menu system created by the database developer that ties the objects in the database together so that the database is easy to use. This can also help secure the database, as objects can be hidden from user view. The interface displays a menu enabling a nontechnical person to open various objects within the database and to move easily from one object to another. When adding a Navigation form, it is best to also hide the Navigation Pane from the user.

STEP 1 Create a Navigation Form

When you create a Navigation form, you drag and drop forms and reports onto tabs. An important point to note here is that a Navigation form is designed for forms and reports only. Tables and queries cannot be accessed through the Navigation form.

An added benefit of a Navigation form is that it can be easily converted to a Web form if the Access database is deployed on a company intranet or on the Internet. Navigation forms have the look and feel of forms you might find on a website such as Amazon or a mobile application. The Navigation tool in the Forms group on the Create tab enables you to select one of several form layouts. To add items to the Navigation form, drag the forms and/or reports from the Navigation Pane onto *Add New*, as shown in Figure 9.33. After creating a Navigation form, switch to Form view, cycling through each tab to view and test each form or report.

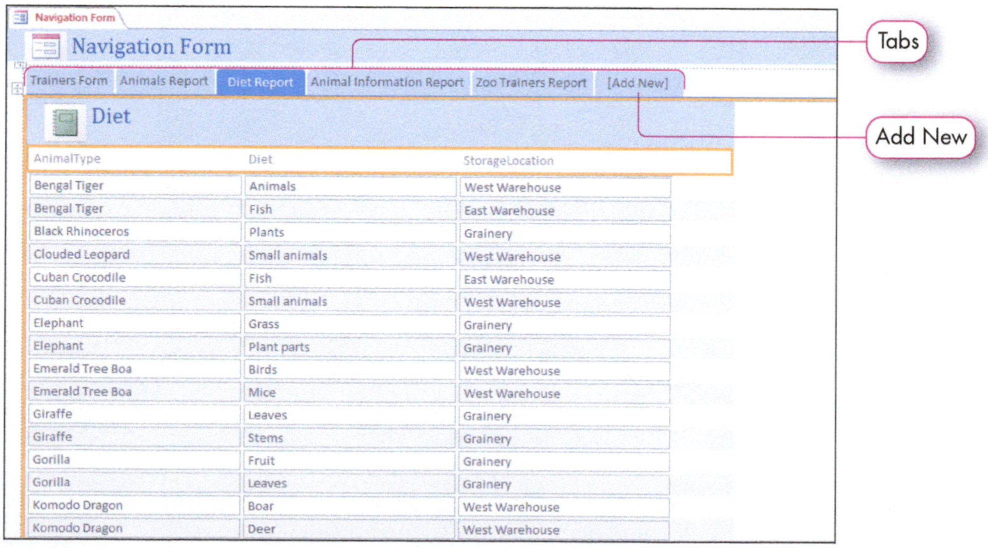

FIGURE 9.33 Navigation Form in Layout View

By default, Access will use the name of each form or report to identify the tab. In other words, if you drag a report named Animals to the Navigation form, the new tab is named Animals. To modify the tab name, double-click the name and replace the text.

Start a Navigation Form Automatically

To benefit users, the Navigation Pane should display automatically when the database is opened. To integrate a Navigation form as seamlessly as possible, you can set an option so the Navigation form opens automatically when the database is opened. Note this can be done with any form, not just a Navigation form. To start a form automatically, in the Options section on the File tab, choose Current Database, and select the name of the Navigation form you created from the Display Form menu as shown in Figure 9.34.

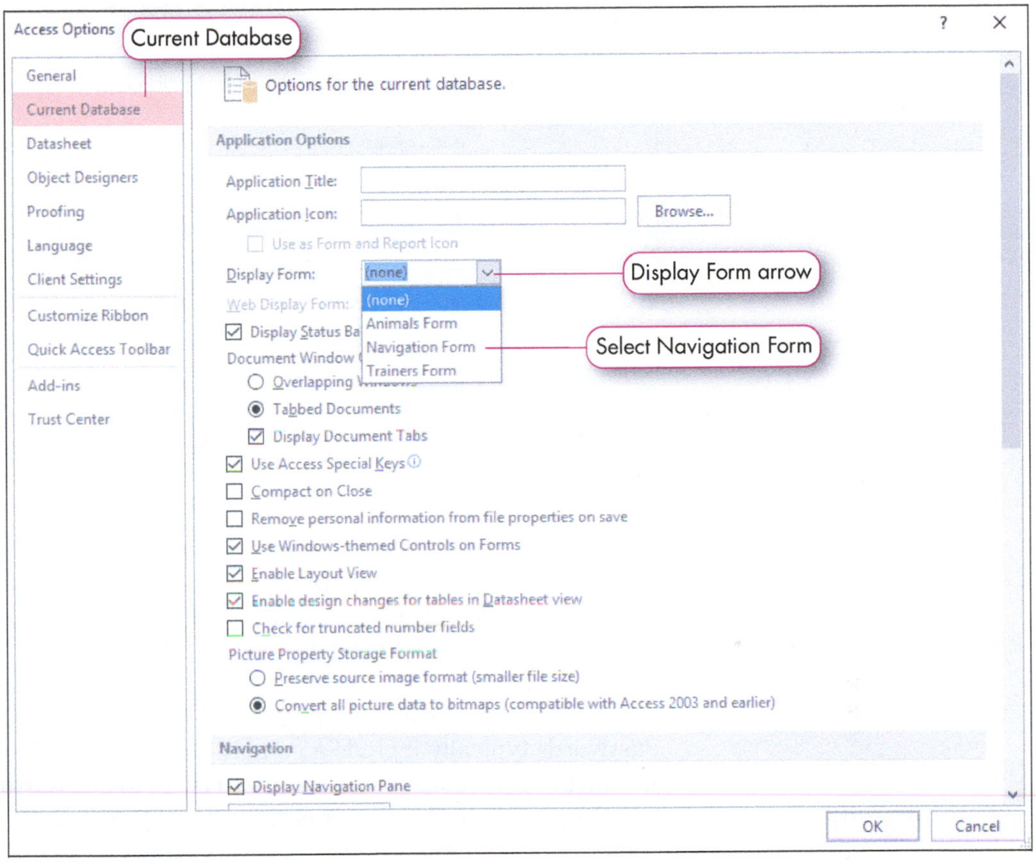

FIGURE 9.34 Starting a Form Automatically

Hide the Navigation Pane

The Navigation Pane, which is located at the left of the Access window, provides access to objects in the database. If you are using a Navigation form, you may decide to hide the Navigation Pane altogether from users. Hiding the Navigation Pane can be accomplished using a macro or by turning off the check box in the Access Options dialog box on the File, Options menu as shown in Figure 9.35. Alternatively, with or without a Navigation form, you can customize the Navigation Pane to prevent access to some objects. Giving users access to *all* database objects may not only confuse users but may undermine the database if inadvertent changes to objects were made. In customizing the Navigation Pane, groups of objects can be completely hidden, and macros can be added to control what actions users can perform, such as moving objects in the pane, deleting objects, or adding objects. The Navigation Options section below the checkmark enables you to give users access to some of the objects as needed.

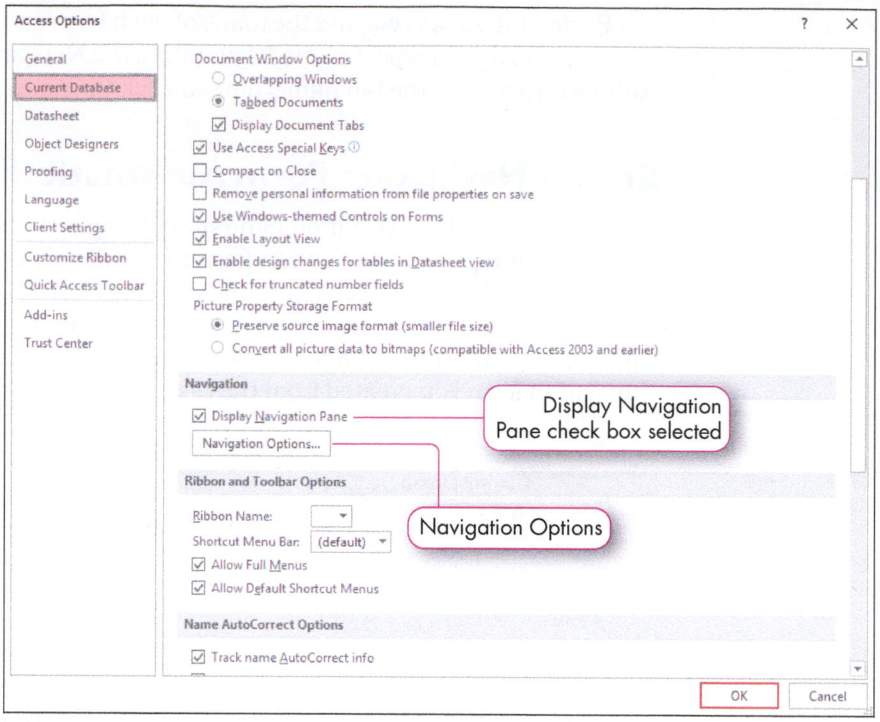

FIGURE 9.35 Navigation Pane Option

Encrypting and Password Protecting a Database

Access incorporates encryption methods to help keep your databases secure. *Encryption* makes the data unreadable to anyone except those who possess the password. Because the point of encryption is to protect your data, choose a strong password when setting up encryption. Encrypting a database is especially useful if you intend to distribute your database via email or store your database on removable media such as a USB flash drive.

Adding a password to an Access database prevents unauthorized access to the file. Passwords typically include a combination of letters and numbers. A strong password should be impossible for unauthorized users to guess. An example of a weak password is the word *password*. A stronger password is *eXploring!2019*. Notice the password includes a capital letter, a number, and a special character, which make the password harder to guess. Including capital letters, numbers, and special characters helps to make the password more secure. You can also improve security by using longer passwords and avoiding words found in a dictionary—such as *exploring*. Consider switching out a letter with a number or character, for example: *eXpl0ring* which uses zero instead of the letter o.

> **TIP: PASSWORD SECURITY**
> It is not advisable to use the same password for different accounts. If one account password is compromised, then all of them are compromised. This can be difficult to remember the countless number of passwords for all your accounts. You can consider using a prefix and that password. The prefix would vary for each account. For example, if you had an account for ABC company you could use abc + yourpassword, such as *abceXploring!2019*. With all the passwords to remember, you may feel compelled to write it down. However, writing down the password on a sticky note and leaving it on your monitor is not a good choice for protecting a truly secure password. If you must write down your passwords, store them in a secure location such as a locked file cabinet or a safe.
>
> The easiest way to solve both issues is to download or purchase an application to manage your passwords or use a secure online password manager. Of course, those tools require a password, so make sure you do not forget the password that protects your passwords.

STEP 2 ## Add a Password to a Database

Adding a password and encryption to a database requires the database to be opened in exclusive mode. Opening the database in exclusive mode guarantees that you are the only one currently using the database. Open Access, and from the File tab, open the database you want to open in exclusive mode, then select Open Exclusive from the list of options displayed by the Open arrow at the bottom dialog box (see Figure 9.36). You can then assign a password to a database by clicking Encrypt with Password as shown in Figure 9.37. Encrypt with Password enables you to type and verify a password for the open database.

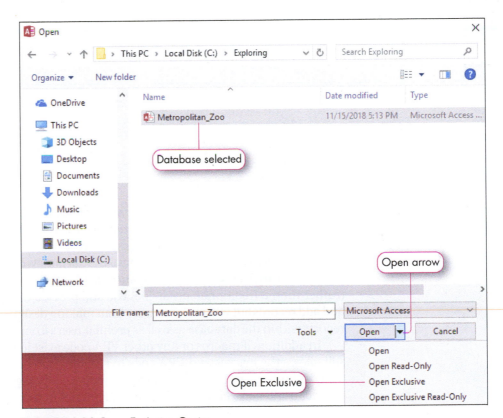

FIGURE 9.36 Open Exclusive Option

The next time you open this database, it will prompt for a password. Keep the password safe and secure to protect your database. To remove a password, you must open the database using the Open Exclusive option. On the File tab, choose Decrypt Database, and in the Unset Database Password dialog box, type the password, and click OK to remove the password.

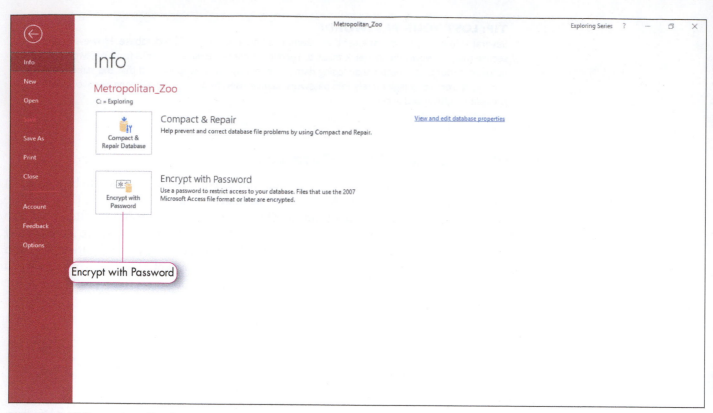

FIGURE 9.37 Encrypting a Database

Creating an Executable Form of a Database

After a database has been created, there are times where the database administrator will have to help correct mistakes. Users may accidentally change, delete, or rename objects and find the database no longer works. To avoid these unnecessary types of problems, if you have created an Access database that others will be using, you can convert the database to an ***Access Database Executable (ACCDE)***. A database saved as an .accde file (rather than a traditional .accdb file) will still provide the necessary functions to modify and add records but will prohibit users from making design and name changes to forms or reports within the database as well as prohibit users from creating new forms and reports.

In addition, if macros or any other VBA code exist in the database, an ACCDE format still allows the macros and VBA code to run but protects the code from being viewed or edited. This is especially useful if proprietary code is being used in the database. Note that users can still make changes to tables and queries in this case.

STEP 3 ### Create an Access Database Executable

Creating an Access Database Executable is a straightforward process. The existing database is saved with the new file extension, making a copy of the last saved version of the database.

> **To create an ACCDE file, complete the following steps:**
> 1. Click the File tab.
> 2. Click Save As and select Make ACCDE (see Figure 9.38).
> 3. Click Save As.
> 4. Provide a name and location and click Save.

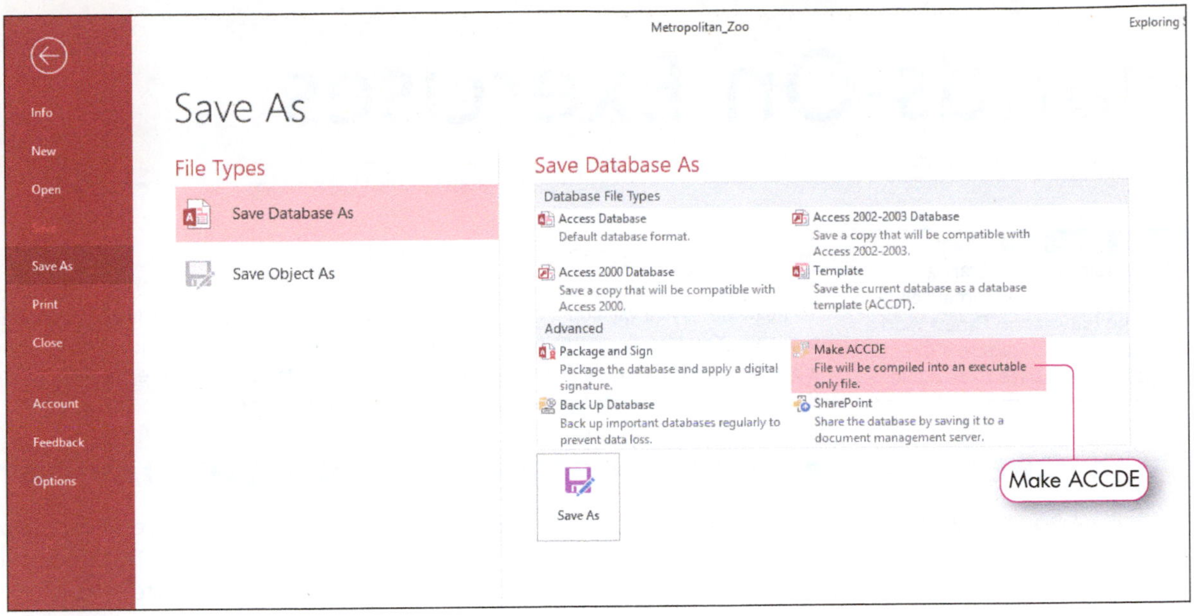

Save As

File Types

Save Database As

📇 Save Database As

💾 Save Object As

Save Database As

Database File Types

📇 Access Database
Default database format.

📇 Access 2002-2003 Database
Save a copy that will be compatible with Access 2002-2003.

📇 Access 2000 Database
Save a copy that will be compatible with Access 2000.

📇 Template
Save the current database as a database template (ACCDT).

Advanced

📇 Package and Sign
Package the database and apply a digital signature.

📇 Make ACCDE
File will be compiled into an executable only file.

📇 Back Up Database
Back up important databases regularly to prevent data loss.

📇 SharePoint
Share the database by saving it to a document management server.

💾 Save As

Make ACCDE

FIGURE 9.38 Creating an Access Database Executable

Similar to a database saved as .accdb, you cannot create an Access Database Executable file unless you have clicked Enable Content. Because these files can cause potentially dangerous code to be executed, you first should ensure that the file is trustworthy. When the database has been converted to an Access Database Executable, it cannot be converted back to its source format (.accdb). Therefore, keep your original database in a safe place. Without your original database, you would not be able to make changes to forms or reports.

> **TIP: DIGITAL SIGNATURES**
> Digital signatures confirm who created the file, that the file is valid, and that no changes have been made to the file after its authentication. As only the publisher can digitally sign the software, the signature enables users to trust the software. You can either create a signature yourself, use one created by your organization, or purchase one from a company such as VeriSign that issues and validates identities using digital signatures. If your company requires this level of security, it has likely purchased one and set it up to be available through your company's network. If you do not have a security certificate from a commercial vendor, you can create one by using the SelfCert tool (included with business editions of Microsoft Office). Find this by searching for Digital Certificate for VBA Projects on your computer or find help through the Microsoft website.

Quick Concepts

9. Describe the guidelines for creating a secure password. *p. 532*

10. Explain two advantages of a Navigation form. *p. 530*

11. Describe the advantage of an Access Database Executable file. *p. 534*

Hands-On Exercises

Skills covered: Create a Navigation Form • Start a Navigation Form Automatically • Hide the Navigation Pane • Add a Password to a Database • Create an Access Database Executable

3 Database Security

To help users, you will add a Navigation form so the important objects in the zoo database are readily available. You also decide to put several safety and security measures into action, including the addition of a password to protect against unauthorized use of the database and the creation of an executable form of the database to protect against accidental changes to the objects.

STEP 1 ▸ CREATE A NAVIGATION FORM AND HIDE THE NAVIGATION PANE

You decide to create a Navigation form to make it easier to open the daily forms and reports. You performed an informal survey of the employees to determine which objects they use the most and will add them to the Navigation form. You decide to use the Horizontal Tabs style. Refer to Figure 9.39 as you complete Step 1.

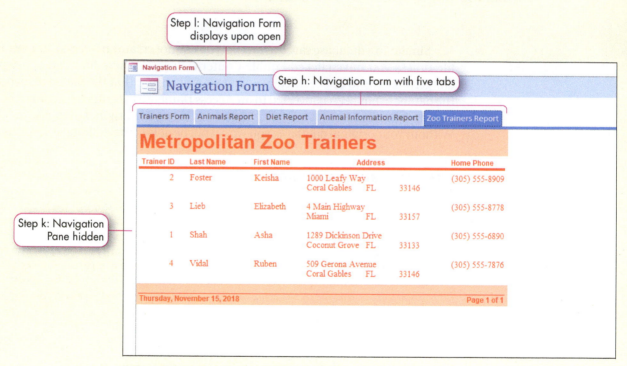

FIGURE 9.39 Zoo Database Navigation Form

a. Open *a09h2Zoo_LastFirst* if you closed it at the end of Hands-On Exercise 2, and save it as **a09h3Zoo_LastFirst**, changing h2 to h3.

b. Select the **Animals table** click the **Create tab**, and then click **Report** to create a basic report using the Report tool. Save the report as **Animals Report**. Close the report.

c. Repeat Step b to create a report based on the Diet table. Save the report as **Diet Report**. Close the report.

d. Repeat Step b to create a report based on the Animal Information table. Save the report as **Animal Information Report**. Close the report.

e. Click the **Create tab** and click **Navigation** in the Forms group. Select the **Horizontal Tabs option**.

A new Horizontal Tabs Navigation form displays.

f. Drag the **Trainers Form** from the Navigation Pane to **Add New** on the Navigation form.

g. Repeat Step f to add **Animals Report**, **Diet Report**, **Animal Information Report**, and **Zoo Trainers Report**, in that order.

h. Switch to **Form view** and click each **tab** to test the form. The form should match Figure 9.39.

i. Save the Navigation form with the default name and close the form.

j. Click the **File tab**, click **Options**, and in the Access Options dialog box, click **Current Database**.

k. Scroll to the Navigation section of the dialog box and deselect Display Navigation Pane.

The Navigation Pane will now be hidden from view.

l. Scroll to the Application Options section and click the **Display Form arrow**. Select **Navigation Form**. Click **OK** to close the dialog box. Click **OK**. Click **OK** to close the warning message that appears.

The Navigation form will now display upon opening the database.

m. Save and close the database. Re-open the database to test the changes.

The Navigation form displays when you open the database and the Navigation Pane should not be visible.

STEP 2 ▶ ADD A PASSWORD TO A DATABASE

To protect the database, you will add a password, in case the laptop it is stored on is lost or stolen. You discuss the password with Selene and decide to use a combination of letters, numbers, and symbols. Refer to Figure 9.40 as you complete Step 2.

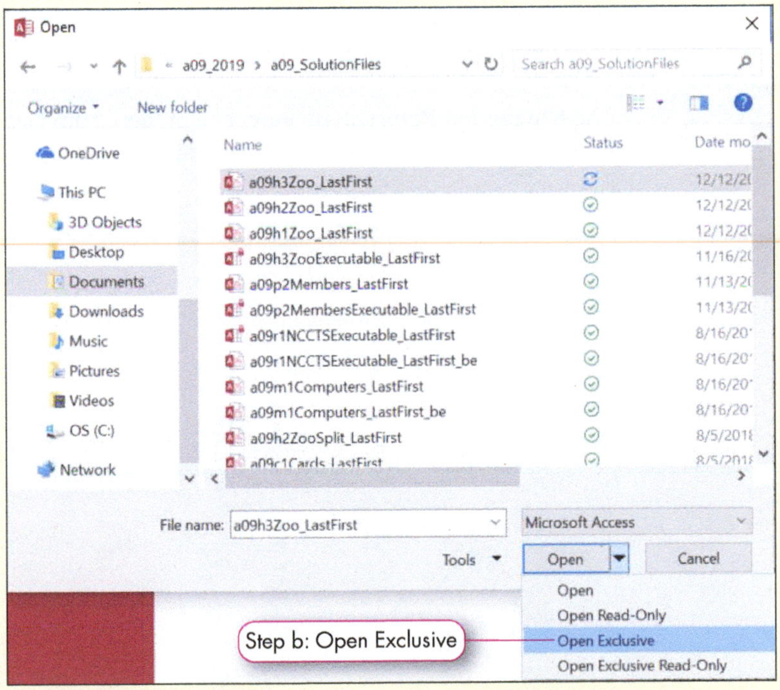

FIGURE 9.40 Opening Zoo Database in Exclusive Mode

a. Click the **File tab** and click **Encrypt with Password**.

A message displays telling you that you must have the database open for exclusive use.

b. Click **OK**. Click the **File tab** and click **Close**. Click the **File tab** and click **Open**. Click **Browse**. Locate and click the **a09h3Zoo_LastFirst database**, click the **Open arrow** at the bottom of the dialog box, and then select **Open Exclusive** from the list. Refer to Figure 9.40.

c. Click the **File tab** and click **Encrypt with Password**.

This time the warning message should not display.

d. Type the password **eXploring!2019** in the Password box and type the same password in the Verify box. Click **OK** to set the password and encrypt the database. Click **OK** in response to the warning message.

You will test the password to be sure that it works.

e. Close the database and open it again.

The Password Required dialog box opens, prompting you to type the password to open the database.

f. Type **eXploring!2019** in the *Enter database password* box and click **OK**. Close the database.

The database opens as expected.

g. Click the **File tab** and click **Open**. Click **Browse**. Locate and click the **a09h3Zoo_LastFirst database**, click the **Open arrow** at the bottom of the dialog box, and then select **Open Exclusive** from the list. Click **Info** on the File tab and click **Decrypt Database**. Type **eXploring!2019** in the *Enter database password* box and click **OK**.

You open the database in exclusive mode and remove the password so that you can more easily make changes to the database prior to distribution.

h. Click the **File tab**, click **Options**, and then in the Access Options dialog box, click **Current Database**.

i. Scroll to the Navigation section of the dialog box and select **Display Navigation Pane**.

The Navigation Pane will no longer be hidden from view so additional work may resume on the database. The Navigation form still displays.

STEP 3 CREATE AN ACCESS DATABASE EXECUTABLE

You decide to make the database more secure by creating an Access Database Executable. This will prevent zoo employees from making changes to forms and reports. Refer to Figure 9.41 as you complete Step 3.

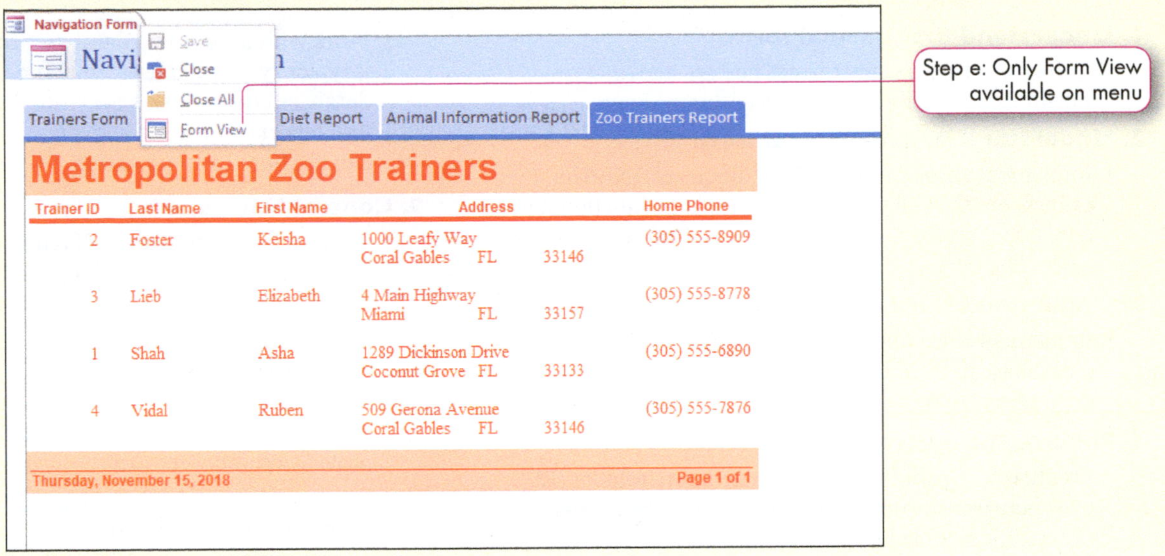

FIGURE 9.41 Executable Form of Zoo Database

a. Click the **File tab**, click **Save As**, and then double-click **Make ACCDE** in the Advanced section.

The Save As dialog box opens. The default Save as type is ACCDE File (*.accde), and the suggested file name is a09h3Zoo_LastFirst.

b. Type **a09h3ZooExecutable_LastFirst** as the file name and click **Save** to create the database.

c. Click the **File tab** and click **Close**.

d. Click the **File tab** and click **Open**. Click **Browse** to display the Open dialog box. Locate the **a09h2ZooExecutable file** you created, click the **Open arrow** at the bottom of the dialog box, and then select **Open Exclusive** from the list.

The database is opened in Exclusive mode, which guarantees that you are the only one currently using the database.

e. Right-click the **Trainers Form tab** and observe that Design View and Layout View are grayed out and unavailable, as shown in Figure 9.41. Because changes cannot be made, you have verified this database is in Access Database Executable form.

f. Close the form.

g. Close the database and exit Access. Based on your instructor's directions, submit the following:

a09h2ZooDocumenter_LastFirst.pdf

a09h2ZooAnalyzer_LastFirst

a09h2ZooSplit_LastFirst_be

a09h3Zoo_LastFirst

a09h3ZooExecutable_LastFirst

Chapter Objectives Review

After reading this chapter, you have accomplished the following objectives:

1. Understand first normal form.
- Implement first normal form: The first step to normalizing a table removes repeating groups.

2. Understand second normal form.
- Implement second normal form: Requires 1NF. The criteria are that all non-key fields must be functionally dependent on the entire primary key. If no composite key exists, the table is often in 2NF.

3. Understand third normal form.
- Implement third normal form: Requires 2NF. Converting a database to third normal form removes transitive dependencies, or dependencies on non-key fields.

4. Finalize the design.
- Create relationships: After normalization, relationships exist between the tables. If a table cannot be connected to others, there is likely a problem with normalization.

5. Use the Database Documenter tool.
- Run the Database Documenter: Database Documenter creates a report containing detailed information for each selected object. Database Documenter can be run on specific objects (for example, only tables, or only forms and reports). Users can select varying levels of detail.

6. Use the Performance Analyzer tool.
- Run the Performance Analyzer: Performance Analyzer evaluates a database and makes optimization recommendations.
- Add an index: Performance Analyzer may recommend adding an index, which will speed up searches such as queries or filters.

7. Use the Table Analyzer tool.
- Run the Table Analyzer: The Table Analyzer helps minimize the duplication of information. The Table Analyzer includes a wizard that enables you to split tables, rename newly created tables, rearrange fields in the new tables, and create relationships.

8. Use the Database Splitter tool.
- Run the Database Splitter: The Database Splitter tool is useful when the number of database users grows beyond a few. The tool splits a database into two files—a front-end database containing queries, forms, and reports, and a back-end database containing tables. Splitting a database may improve the speed of data processing. The back-end database is generally on a server.

- Work with a front-end database: The front-end database is typically on each user's machine. The front-end database enables users to create their own queries, forms, and reports. The front-end links to back-end tables, which can be shared among users.

9. Control Navigation.
- Create a Navigation form: Navigation forms help users open important forms and reports quickly. Choose one of six prebuilt layouts. Drag and drop forms and reports directly on tabs. A Navigation form can be easily converted to a Web form.
- Start a Navigation form automatically: Navigation forms can start automatically when a database opens to help provide guidance to users.
- Hide the Navigation Pane: If you are using a Navigation form, you may decide to hide the Navigation Pane altogether from users. Hiding the Navigation Pane can be accomplished using a macro or by turning off the check box in the Access Options dialog box on the File, Options menu.

10. Encrypt and password protect a database.
- Add a password to a database: Encryption alters digital information using an algorithm, making it unreadable without the password. Encrypted databases are very difficult to break into. Encryption is suggested especially if a database is sent via email or put on removable storage such as a USB drive.

11. Create an executable form of a database.
- Create an Access Database Executable: An Access Database Executable, or ACCDE, file is an executable form of the database—objects such as forms, reports, and VBA code cannot be changed. Saving as an ACCDE file adds an extra layer of protection.

Key Terms Matching

Match the key terms with their definitions. Write the key term letter by the appropriate numbered definition.

a. Access Database Executable (ACCDE)
b. Anomaly
c. Back-end database
d. Composite key
e. Database Documenter
f. Database Splitter
g. Encryption
h. First normal form (1NF)
i. Front-end database
j. Functional dependency

k. Index
l. Navigation form
m. Non-key field
n. Normal form
o. Normalization
p. Performance Analyzer
q. Second normal form (2NF)
r. Table Analyzer
s. Third normal form (3NF)
t. Transitive dependency

1. _____ A type of database file that prohibits users from making design and name changes to forms or reports within the database and prohibits users from creating new forms and reports. **p. 534**

2. _____ A primary key that is made up of two or more fields. **p. 506**

3. _____ A tool that enables you to convert a database into two files, a back-end database and a front-end database. **p. 523**

4. _____ A tool that creates a report containing detailed information for each selected object. **p. 516**

5. _____ An error or inconsistency that occurs when you add, edit, and delete data. **p. 502**

6. _____ A tabbed menu that ties the objects in the database together so that the database is easy to use. **p. 530**

7. _____ A tool that evaluates the tables in a database and normalizes them. **p. 520**

8. _____ Any field that is not part of the primary key. **p. 505**

9. _____ A criterion satisfied when a table that meets 1NF criteria and all non-key fields are functionally dependent on the entire primary key. **p. 505**

10. _____ A database that contains the queries, forms, and reports of the database. **p. 523**

11. _____ The process of efficiently organizing data so that the same data is not stored in more than one table, and that related data is stored together. **p. 502**

12. _____ The process of altering digital information using an algorithm to make it unreadable to anyone except those who possess the password. **p. 532**

13. _____ A database that contains the tables of the database. **p. 523**

14. _____ A tool that evaluates a database and then makes recommendations for optimizing the database. **p. 518**

15. _____ A condition that occurs when the value of one non-key field is functionally dependent on the value of another non-key field. **p. 505**

16. _____ A criterion satisfied when a table contains no repeating groups or repeating columns. **p. 503**

17. _____ A criterion satisfied when a table meets 2NF criteria and no transitive dependencies exist. **p. 507**

18. _____ A condition that occurs when the value of one field is determined by the value of another. **p. 507**

19. _____ The rules to optimize and fix potential repetition issues (data redundancy) in a database. **p. 502**

20. _____ A setting for a field that reduces the time it takes to run queries and reports. **p. 520**

Multiple Choice

1. The Database Documenter:

   (a) lists the properties of selected objects in the database.

   (b) suggests ways the database can be optimized.

   (c) searches for rows of repeating data and suggests design changes to improve performance.

   (d) is a wizard that provides step-by-step instructions on the creation of tables and forms.

2. Which tool makes recommendations for optimizing a database?

   (a) Database Documenter

   (b) Database Splitter

   (c) Performance Analyzer

   (d) Table Analyzer

3. Which of the following is typically stored in a back-end database after it has been split?

   (a) Forms

   (b) Queries

   (c) Tables

   (d) Reports

4. Which of the following is *false* about encrypted databases?

   (a) Database encryption alters the contents of the database so that it cannot be opened without a password.

   (b) Encrypted databases can be broken into with ease.

   (c) Passwords can be removed from a database.

   (d) Passwords to an encrypted database can be changed by anyone who opens the database.

5. Which password is weakest?

   (a) 1_2fi&ty5

   (b) Butt3rCup!

   (c) mypassword

   (d) eXploring!2019

6. What is the benefit of creating an Access Database Executable?

   (a) The database will be protected against hackers.

   (b) Users cannot change forms and reports.

   (c) Table contents cannot be modified.

   (d) The navigation in the database will be greatly improved.

7. Which of the following statements about normalization is *false*?

   (a) A database in 3NF must also be in 2NF.

   (b) There are only three normal forms.

   (c) Normalization reduces repetition of data.

   (d) The Table Analyzer can help normalize tables.

8. What might be an outcome of running the Table Analyzer tool?

   (a) A report listing information about the tables (such as data types and field names)

   (b) Two files—a front-end and a back-end database

   (c) An optimized set of tables

   (d) A password-protected database

9. Which normal form will remove dependencies on a non-key field?

   (a) 3NF

   (b) 1NF

   (c) 2NF

   (d) None of these

10. Normalization can be defined as:

    (a) combining tables together to form a single table.

    (b) eliminating repetition of data.

    (c) adding a layer of security to a database.

    (d) a database with multiple tables.

Practice Exercises

Info Labs, a clinical studies company in Mississippi, employs 14 people; most employees fall in the categories of manager, account rep, or trainee. The employee database holds information about each employee, including salary, gender, title, and location. You have been asked to review the database to see if the employee table was designed properly. Refer to Figure 9.42 as you complete this exercise.

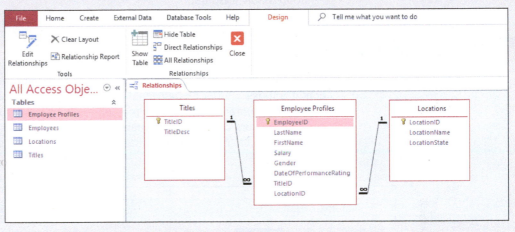

FIGURE 9.42 Clinic Database Relationships

a. Open *a09p1Clinic*. Save the database as **a09p1Clinic_LastFirst**.

b. Open the Employees table in Datasheet view and examine the data. Determine if the data meet the three normalization rules: 1NF, 2NF, and 3NF.

c. Close the Employees table. You decide to use the Table Analyzer for help with normalizing the Employees table.

d. Click **Analyze Table** in the Analyze group on the Database Tools tab. When the first wizard screen displays, click **Next** twice.

e. Accept the default **Employees table** when the *Which table contains fields with values that are repeated in many records?* screen displays. Click **Next** twice.

f. Verify the Employees table has been split into three tables on the next screen. Click **Table1**, click **Rename Table**, and then type **Employee Profiles** as the new name of this table. Click **OK**.

g. Click **Table2**, click **Rename Table**, and then type **Locations** as the new name of this table. Click **OK**.

h. Click **Table3**, click **Rename Table**, and then type **Titles** as the new name of this table. Click **OK**.

i. Click **Next**.

j. Click **LocationID** in the Locations table and click **Set Unique Identifier** to set LocationID as the primary key.

k. Click **EmployeeID** in the Employee Profiles table and click **Set Unique Identifier** to set EmployeeID as the primary key.

l. Click **Next**. Accept the default *No, don't create the query option* and click **Finish**. Click **OK** when the information message appears.

m. Review the new tables and confirm that the Analyzer moved fields from the Employees table into the two new lookup tables. Close all the tables.

n. Click **Relationships** on the Database Tools tab in the Relationships group. Click **All Relationships** to reveal the relationships created by the Table Analyzer. Your relationships should match Figure 9.42. Close the Relationships window, and click **No**.

o. Click the **File tab** and click **Encrypt with Password**. Access displays the message *You must have the database open for exclusive use*. Click **OK**. Close the database.

p. Use the Open command on the File tab to locate the *a09p1Clinic_LastFirst* database. Click the database, click the **Open arrow** at the bottom of the dialog box, and then select **Open Exclusive** from the list.

q. Click the **File tab** and click **Encrypt with Password**. Type **eXploring!2019** as the password. Click **OK**. Click **OK** in response to the *Row level locking will be ignored* message.

r. Close the database and reopen it. Type **eXploring!2019** in the Enter database password box.

s. Close the database and exit Access. Based on your instructor's directions, submit a09p1Clinic_LastFirst.

2 Metropolitan Art Museum

The Metropolitan Art Museum invites its patrons to become members of the museum. For a donation of $50 per year for an individual or $100 for a family membership, members are entitled to special discounts and member-only promotions. Your task is to review the database tables for normalization errors, check the performance, create a lookup field, and save the database as an Access Database Executable. Refer to Figure 9.43 as you complete this exercise.

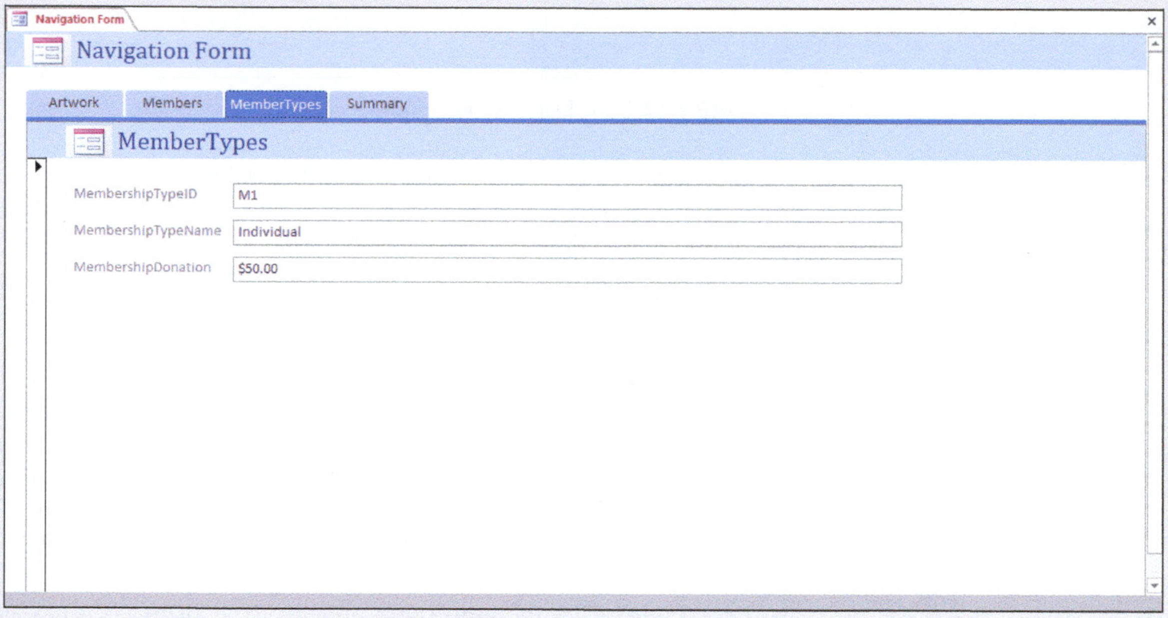

FIGURE 9.43 Museum Database Navigation Form

a. Open *a09p2Members*. Save the database as **a09p2Members_LastFirst**.

b. Open the Members table and examine the data. Determine if the data meet the three normalization rules: 1NF, 2NF, and 3NF.

c. Close the Members table. You decide to normalize the table manually.

d. Click **Query Design** in the Queries group on the Create tab. Double-click the **Members table** to add it to the query design grid and click **Close** in the Show Table dialog box.

e. Double-click the **MembershipTypeID**, **MembershipTypeName**, and **MembershipDonation** fields to add them to the query design grid. Click **Run** in the Results group to run the query. Take note of the repeating rows of data.

f. Switch to Design view. Click **Totals** in the Show/Hide group to eliminate the duplicate rows. Run the query.

g. Switch to Design view. Click **Make Table** in the Query Type group and type **MemberTypes** in the Table Name box. Click **OK**. Click **Run** in the Results group to create the MemberTypes table. Click **Yes** to the warning message.

h. Save the query as **Create Member Types** and close the query.

i. Open the **MemberTypes table** in Design view. Set the **MembershipTypeID field** as the primary key. Save and close the table.

j. Open the **Members table** in Design view and complete the following steps:
  • Change the MembershipTypeID data type to **Lookup Wizard**.
  • Click **Next** in the first Lookup Wizard step, select **Table: MemberTypes** in the next step, and then click **Next**.
  • Click >> to include all fields in the Lookup field. Click **Next** three times.
  • Click **Finish**, and click **Yes** to save the table. The two tables are now joined using the MembershipTypeID field.

k. Switch to Datasheet view. Click the **MembershipTypeID field** in the first row and verify that the Lookup field is working to see if the values are visible in the list.

   You can choose either of the two membership types from the menu. Next, you will delete the redundant fields in the Members table.

l. Switch to Design view. Select the **MembershipTypeName** and **MembershipDonation fields**. Click **Delete Rows** in the Tools group. Click **Yes** to confirm the deletion. Save and close the table.

m. Select the **Artwork table**. Click the **Create tab** and select **Form** to create a form based on the Artwork table. Save the form with the default name, and close the form.

n. Create forms for the Members and MemberTypes tables using the same method as Step m. Delete the subform that displays as part of the MemberTypes form. Save the forms with the default name and close the forms.

o. Click the **Create tab** and select **Report** to create a basic report based on the Members table using the Report tool. Save with the default name and close the report.

p. Click the **Navigation arrow** in the Forms group and select **Horizontal Tabs**. Drag the **Artwork form**, **Members form**, **MemberTypes form**, and **Members report**, in that order, to the Navigation form.

q. Double-click the **fourth tab**, and type **Summary**. Switch to Form view and click each **tab** to ensure the form works. Compare your results with Figure 9.43. Close the Navigation form, saving with the default name when prompted.

r. Click **Close** to close the dialog box.

s. Click the **File tab**, click **Options**, and in the Access Options dialog box, click **Current Database**.

t. Scroll to the Navigation section of the dialog box and deselect **Display Navigation Pane**.

u. Click the **arrow** next to Display Form in the Navigation Options and select **Navigation Form**. Click **OK** to close the dialog box. Click **OK**. Click **OK** to close the warning message that displays.

v. Click the **Database Tools tab** and click **Analyze Performance**. Click the **All Object Types tab**, click **Select All**, and then click **OK**. The first idea in the Results window suggests you save your application as an MDE file. When Access suggests you create MDE files, it should refer to ACCDE files. This is a known inconsistency in the program. Close the dialog.

w. Click the **File tab** and click **Save As**. Double-click **Make ACCDE**. Change the name to **a09p2MembersExecutable_LastFirst**. Click **Save**.

x. Close the database and exit Access. Based on your instructor's directions, submit the following:

   a09p2Members_LastFirst

   a09p2MembersExecutable_LastFirst

Mid-Level Exercises

1 The Computer Store

ANALYSIS CASE

Bytes and Bits, a computer store based in Florida, sells computer products to individuals and small businesses. You have been hired to assist with the daily computer operations, including management of the order processing database. Your plan is to analyze the database, create a front end for the users, and transfer the tables to a back-end database. After splitting the database, you will create a Navigation form to open the database objects.

a. Open *a09m1Computers*. Save the database as **a09m1Computers_LastFirst**.

b. Open the Database Documenter. Click **Options** and uncheck all options in the Include for Table section to deselect them. Select the **Names, Data Types, and Sizes option** in the Include for Fields section and select **Nothing** in the Include for Indexes section. Click **OK**. Click the **Customers table check box** to select it and click **OK**. In the generated report, note the Size (the third column) of each field. Notice that the values for the ZipCode and PhoneNumber field sizes in the Customers table are very large.

c. Click **Close Print Preview** in the Close Preview group. Open the **Customers table** in Design view, and adjust the field sizes to an appropriate size. The field size for the ZipCode and Phone-Number should be 10 and 14 characters respectively. Save and close the table.

d. Click the **Database Tools tab**, click **Access Database** in the Move Data group, and then click **Split Database** to split the database into a front-end and a back-end database. Save the split database in the same folder as your other solution files, accepting the default file name.

e. Open the **Customers table** and type your first and last names as the next customer, leaving the other fields blank. Close the table.

f. Open the a09m1Computers_LastFirst_be database, and open the Customers table. Verify your name is in the Customers table. Close the back-end database.

> **TROUBLESHOOTING:** If you open the front-end database at a later time on a different computer, you may get an error stating the file path is not valid. Use the techniques learned in a previous chapter to link the front-end database to the back-end database.

g. Create three objects in the a09m1Computers_LastFirst database: a form named **Customers** based on the Customers table using the Form tool, a form named **Products** based on the Products table using the Form tool, and a report named **Customer List** based on the Customers table using the Report tool. Close all objects.

h. Create a Navigation form using the **Vertical Tabs, Left template**. Add the **Products form**, followed by the **Customers form**, followed by the **Products List report**, followed by the **Customer List report**.

i. Test the Navigation form in Form view. Save the form with the default name and close the form.

j. Add the Navigation form to the Display Form option in the Current Database portion of the Access Options so the Navigation form opens when the database opens.

k. Locate and change the option in the Access Options so that the Navigation Pane does not display when the database is opened.

l. Close the database and exit Access. Based on your instructor's directions, submit the following:

a09m1Computers_LastFirst

a09m1Computers_LastFirst_be

2 Boats for All Seasons

The owners of Boats for All Seasons have asked you to assist in improving their database. They have plans for some additional forms and reports and also modifications to their main table. They are having a problem with the database when customers who bought boats from them years ago return to purchase again. The owners are unsure how to record a second transaction for the same customer. They have also asked for any other suggestions you may have for making the database more secure.

a. Open *a09m2Boats*. Enter the database password **exploring** to open the database.

b. Save the database as **a09m2Boats_LastFirst**. Enter the password **exploring** again.

c. Open the Customers table and review the contents of the table. Notice customer 2 (Frank Billingslea) is the same as customer 62, with identical addresses. James Windon (30 and 63) and Kathy Mcdowell (35 and 61) also have repeated information. In the following steps, you will split the customers table into two tables: a Customers table and a BoatPurchases table.

d. Open the Customer Purchases query and examine the results.

e. Modify the Customer Purchases query so it only shows values that are not null in the BoatType field. Run the query. Your query should list only customers who purchased a boat (56 records).

f. Switch to Design view. Click **Make Table** in the Query Type group and type **BoatPurchases** in the Table name box. Click **OK**. Run the query and click **Yes** at the warning. Save and close the query.

g. Open the BoatPurchases table in Design view and change the CustomerID Data Type to **Number**. Save the table and switch to Datasheet view. Sort the records by CustomerID in ascending order, locate the three customers who purchased more than one boat (Billingslea, Windon, and Mcdowell), and then update their CustomerIDs so that both purchases show the smaller ID. For example, change the second Billingslea CustomerID from 62 to **2**.

h. Switch to Design view and change the CustomerID field to a Lookup Wizard displaying CustomerID, LastName, and FirstName from the Customers table, sorted by LastName and then by FirstName, both in ascending order. Hide the key column. Accept the default field name. Save the table and click **Yes** at the prompt.

i. Switch to Datasheet view. The customer LastName and FirstName should display when you click the arrow at the right of any CustomerID field. Verify that the name in column 1 matches the names in columns 2 and 3. If it does, switch to Design view and delete the **LastName** and **FirstName fields**. These two fields were for reference only until you verified that the data matched. Save and close the BoatPurchases table.

j. Open the Customers table in Design view and delete the **BoatType**, **BoatPurchaseDate**, and **BoatPurchaseAmount fields**.

k. Save the table and switch to Datasheet view. Sort the table by LastName in ascending order. Locate the three customers who purchased more than one boat (Billingslea, Windon, and Mcdowell) and delete the three duplicate records with the larger CustomerID. For example, delete the second Billingslea record with a CustomerID of 62.

l. Close the database and reopen using the Open Exclusive option. Decrypt the database to remove the weak password. Encrypt the database with a stronger password of **eXploring!2019**. Click **OK** to close the warning message that appears.

m. Create a new form using the Form tool and a new report using the Report tool based on the BoatPurchases table. Save with the default name, and close each object.

n. Save the database as an Access database executable. Type **a09m2BoatsExecutable_LastFirst** for the file name.

o. Display the options for the database. In the Current Database tab, change the Application Title to **Boats for All Seasons**, and click the option for **Compact on Close** to select it. Notice the title bar now displays Boats for All Seasons.

p. Close the database and exit Access. Based on your instructor's directions, submit the following:

a09m2Boats_LastFirst

a09m2BoatsExecutable_LastFirst

Running Case

New Castle County Technical Services

New Castle County Technical Services (NCCTS) provides technical support for a number of local companies. A new hire will be working with you on the database, so to help prepare her, you will create a report to document the relationships for her, and you will split the database into two files so both of you can use the database on the NCCTS network. You will also create a Navigation form and set it to open automatically, while hiding the Navigation Pane. You will additionally create an Access Database Executable and add a password to help protect the database from accidental changes. Finally, you will apply your knowledge of normalization to analyze whether the database can be optimized.

a. Open *a09r1NCCTS* and save the database as **a09r1NCCTS_LastFirst**.

b. Use the Database Documenter tool to create a report displaying the relationships for all tables. Save the report as a PDF file named **a09r1NCCTSRelationships_LastFirst** and close Print Preview.

c. Create a new Navigation form using the **Horizontal Tabs, Two Levels layout**. Include the **Customer Information form** and **Calls by Customer report**, in that order from left to right. Save the form as **Navigation Form** and close the form.

d. Use the Table Analyzer tool to evaluate the **Customers table** and move through the steps using the default settings. Notice that the tool suggests you split the City and State fields into one table and the Zip in another. You will leave this window open for reference for the moment.

e. Open Microsoft Word. Write a short memo to your supervisor explaining what the Table Analyzer has suggested and whether you think it is a good suggestion. Make sure you discuss normalization as part of your explanation. Save the document as **a09r1NCCTSMemo_LastFirst** and close Word.

f. Cancel the Table Analyzer because you will not make any changes without discussing them with your supervisor.

g. Create an Access Database Executable from the database, using the name **a09r1NCCTSExecutable_LastFirst** as the file name.

h. Close the database. Reopen the **a09r1NCCTSExecutable_LastFirst** database in exclusive mode.

i. Set the **Navigation Form** to open automatically each time the database is opened.

j. Hide the Navigation Pane from the Options menu so that the Navigation Pane does not show when the database is opened.

k. Use the Database Splitter tool to split the database into a front-end and back-end database. Save the back-end database with the default name of **a09r1NCCTSExecutable_LastFirst_be**.

l. Close the database and exit Access. Based on your instructor's directions, submit the following:

a09r1NCCTS_LastFirst

a09r1NCCTSRelationships_LastFirst

a09r1NCCTSMemo_LastFirst

a09r1NCCTSExecutable_LastFirst

a09r1NCCTSExecutable_LastFirst_be

Disaster Recovery

Event Planning

You are the general manager of a large hotel chain. You recently moved all data for the company's event planning to an Access database. However, as the database size has increased, the database has become slower, so you have decided to use the built-in Access utilities to improve performance. You have also decided to add a password to improve security. Open *a09d1Hotel* and save it as **a09d1Hotel_LastFirst**. To improve the performance, you will run the Performance Analyzer tool, selecting all objects, and implement all four of the recommendations and ideas the program displays. When implementing the suggestion to create an MDE file, use the name **a09d1HotelExecutable_LastFirst**. You will also run the Table Analyzer tool on the Location table and accept the suggested change to the table name. After you have implemented these changes, add a password of **eXploring!2019** to the database. Close the database and exit Access. Based on your instructor's directions, submit the following:

a09d1Hotel_LastFirst

a09d1HotelExecutable_LastFirst

Capstone Exercise

Baseball Trading Cards

You and your partner Stann Dupp have a small business selling baseball cards online through eBay. As the more computer-savvy partner; you created an Access database with records of the cards you have in stock. As it turns out, Stann was attempting to manage the card inventory and ended up modifying crucial aspects of the database that impact the general operation of the database. You will reverse those changes and create other safeguards to protect this from happening in the future. The database tables may already be normalized; however, you will examine the tables to verify.

Restore Database Relationships

You have noticed the existing database has problems with relationships. You will open the database and create the relationships between the tables to make sure data are consistent in the database.

1. Open *a09c1Cards* and save the database as **a09c1Cards_LastFirst**.
2. Open each table in the database and look for normalization errors.
3. Open the Relationships window. Notice there are currently no relationships.
4. Add the Cards, Brands, and Rarity tables to the layout. Restore relationships between the Cards, Brands, and Rarity tables via the Brand ID and Rarity ID fields.
5. Set the options to **Enforce Referential Integrity** and **Cascade Update Related Fields** for each relationship you create.
6. Save the changes and close the Relationships window.

Analyze Database Performance

It is important to verify that the database performs properly when it is used in a production environment. You will run the Performance Analyzer tool and take note of the recommendations, suggestions, and ideas in the analysis results.

7. Open the Performance Analyzer dialog box, click the **All Object Types tab**, click **Select All**, and then click **OK**.
8. Verify that the first item on the list (an idea) suggests creating an MDE file (which is called ACCDE in Access 2019). You will create an ACCDE file later.
9. Verify the second item on the list (an idea) suggests you change the data type of Year field in the Cards table from Short Text to Long Integer. You decide not to make this change.
10. Close the Performance Analyzer.

Split the Database

You have decided to split the database to enable you and Stann to customize the individual front-end databases while the back end (the tables) remains safe and secure.

11. Split the database, accepting the default back-end name **a09c1Cards_LastFirst_be**. The front-end copy of the database remains open.
12. Look for the linked tables in the front-end copy of the database.

Create a Navigation Form and Hide the Navigation Pane

You will create a Navigation form that displays a new form and the five reports in the database. You will also set the database to hide the Navigation Pane and open the Navigation form whenever the database is opened.

13. Create a new form based on the Cards table using the Form tool.
14. Save the form as **Add or Edit Cards**.
15. Create a Navigation form based on the **Horizontal Tabs** template.
16. Drag the new **Add or Edit Cards form** to the first tab position.
17. Drag the reports to fill the next five tab positions.
18. Switch to Form view and test the Navigation form. Save the Navigation form with the default name and close it.
19. Set the database to open the Navigation form when the database opens and to hide the Navigation Pane.
20. Test the Navigation form by closing and reopening the database.

Encrypt the Database with a Password and Create an ACCDE File

You will encrypt the front-end database with a password. In addition, you will convert the front-end database to the ACCDE file format.

21. Close the database. Reopen the database in exclusive mode.
22. Display the Set Database Password dialog box.
23. Type the database password **eXploring!2019** in both dialog boxes and click **OK**.
24. Close and reopen the database to test the password.
25. Save the database as an Access Database Executable. Save the file with the name **a09c1CardsExecutable_LastFirst**.
26. Close the database and exit Access. Based on your instructor's directions, submit the following:

    a09c1Cards_LastFirst
    a09c1Cards_LastFirst_be
    a09c1CardsExecutable_LastFirst

Enhanced Database Techniques

LEARNING OUTCOME You will create and use macros and SQL to manage data within a database.

OBJECTIVES & SKILLS: After you read this chapter, you will be able to:

Macro Design

OBJECTIVE 1: UNDERSTAND THE PURPOSE OF A MACRO 554
Understand How a Macro Automates Tasks in a Database

OBJECTIVE 2: CREATE A STANDALONE MACRO 555
Create a Standalone Macro with the Macro Designer, Edit a Standalone Macro with the Macro Designer

OBJECTIVE 3: ATTACH AN EMBEDDED MACRO TO AN EVENT 557
Create an Embedded Macro with the Command Button Wizard, Format a Command Button, Create an Embedded Macro in an Event Property, Create a Message Box

HANDS-ON EXERCISE 1 561

Data Macros

OBJECTIVE 4: IDENTIFY WHEN TO USE A DATA MACRO 568
Use a Data Macro to Automate Data Entry

OBJECTIVE 5: CREATE AN EVENT-DRIVEN DATA MACRO 568
Create a Before Change Data Macro, Test a Data Macro, Modify a Data Macro

OBJECTIVE 6: CREATE A NAMED DATA MACRO 569
Create a Named Data Macro, Attach a Named Data Macro to a Form

HANDS-ON EXERCISE 2 572

Structured Query Language

OBJECTIVE 7: UNDERSTAND THE FUNDAMENTALS OF SQL 578
Create a Simple Query with SQL Statements

OBJECTIVE 8: INTERPRET AN SQL SELECT STATEMENT 579
Create a Query and View the Equivalent SQL Statement

OBJECTIVE 9: USE AN SQL SELECT STATEMENT AS A RECORD SOURCE 581
Create an SQL SELECT Statement as a Record Source

HANDS-ON EXERCISE 3 584

CASE STUDY | Retirement Plan Contributions

Terry Jackson, owner of Sunshine Therapy Services, offers a 401(k) retirement plan to all full-time employees. Employees can contribute a percentage of their salaries (generally not to exceed $18,000 per year) to their 401(k) accounts as a payroll deduction and receive a tax deduction on their federal tax returns for the amount they save. For employees who have been with the company for at least one year, the company will match the employees' contributions up to 5% of their salaries. For example, if an employee contributes 6% or more to the retirement plan, the company will match it with 5%. Employees who contribute 5% or less earn a dollar for dollar match.

You have been asked to verify the accuracy of the Sunshine employee data and the employee contributions, ensuring that they fall within the plan guidelines. For example, only employees who have worked for the company for at least one year are eligible for the company match. Terry also wants a monthly report that shows the detailed contributions per employee and the company's matching contributions.

CHAPTER 10

Using Macros and SQL in Access

Sfio Cracho/Shutterstock

FIGURE 10.1 Retirement Plan Contributions Database

CASE STUDY | Retirement Plan Contributions

Starting File	File to be Submitted
a10h1Sunshine	a10h3Sunshine_LastFirst

MyLab IT Grader An alternate version of this project is available as a MyLab IT Grader Assessment

Macro Design

Access provides database designers with a variety of tools and wizards to create tables, queries, forms, and reports, the four basic objects of an Access application. However, sometimes you want to have more control over how the objects in a database behave individually or in relation to other objects. For example, you may want to create a button on a form that when clicked, opens a related report. This type of functionality in the user interface can be accomplished using two different programming methods in Access—by creating macros and procedures using Microsoft Visual Basic for Applications (VBA). VBA is a programming language that works with Access and enables you to create procedures that run in the application. VBA requires knowledge of programming code and more expertise than creating a macro. A ***macro*** is a series of actions that can be organized to automate tasks or provide user interaction in Access without specific programming experience. It is easier to create a macro than a VBA procedure because Access includes a development tool for creating macros, the Macro Designer. VBA will not be covered in detail in this chapter; however, macros can be converted to VBA without having to write any complex programming code whatsoever. Because the Macro Designer provides an easy to use development tool, database professionals and end users alike can create helpful macros.

In this section, you will learn how to create two types of macros: standalone macros and embedded macros. You will also learn how Access can create macros automatically when you add command buttons to forms and reports.

STEP 1 Understanding the Purpose of a Macro

Macros can be used to automate repetitive tasks or perform specific actions. You can use a macro to organize a series of commands and instructions into a single database object to accomplish tasks when the macro executes. For example, if you import data from the same Excel workbook into a database each week, you can create a macro that displays in, and is executed from, the Navigation Pane to automate this task. Another useful example of a macro is that you can add a button to a form to run a specific report each time you click it. A button makes the user interface more intuitive and friendlier to work in. Access creates macros automatically when you add certain controls to forms or reports; for example, if you create a command button in a form to open a report or print a customer order, navigation in the database is simplified. The macro associated with the button executes when the button is clicked. Macros that work with "user interface" objects, such as forms, reports, and buttons, are known as UI macros. Data macros, which operate on tables when certain actions are performed, are discussed later in this chapter.

Access provides two categories of macros: standalone macros and embedded macros. A ***standalone macro*** is a database object that you create and use independent of other controls or objects. Standalone macros display as objects in the Navigation Pane. Figure 10.2 shows four standalone macros.

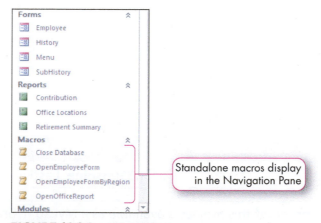

FIGURE 10.2 Standalone Macros

An *embedded macro* executes when an event attached to a control or object occurs. An *event* occurs when a user enters, edits, or deletes data; events also occur when users open, use, and close forms and reports. Embedded macros do not display in the Navigation Pane, but instead become an integrated part of an object, such as a form or report.

On Close is an example of an event attached to an object. Whenever you close a form or a report, the On Close event is triggered, and Access executes the steps stored in the macro if there is one attached to the On Close event.

STEP 2 ## Creating a Standalone Macro

A standalone macro displays as an object in the Navigation Pane and can be run independent of other objects. You use the Macro Designer to create a standalone macro. The *Macro Designer* was developed to make it easier to create or edit macros and to add or delete actions from macros.

Open the Macro Designer by clicking Macro on the Create tab. When you begin to design a macro, you add one or more actions that will list the tasks that you want the macro to perform. For example, you may want to add a MessageBox action to the macro to display a pop-up message to users when the macro runs. When there are multiple actions in a macro, Access executes the actions in the order in which they are listed in the Macro Designer window. After adding an action to the macro, specify the arguments you want for the action. An *argument* is a variable, constant, or expression that is used to produce the output for an action. For example, the MessageBox action contains four arguments: Message, Beep, Type, and Title, as shown in Figure 10.3. To see a short description of each argument, click in the argument box, move the pointer over the argument box, and Access displays a ScreenTip with a short description.

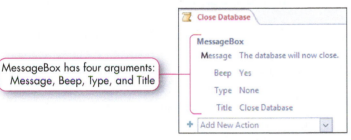

FIGURE 10.3 MessageBox Action with Arguments in Macro Designer

Actions are the individual steps that make up a macro. You can add actions to a macro with the Macro Designer in one of three ways:

- Click the Add New Action arrow and choose the action you want to add to the macro.

- Type the action name directly into the Add New Action box; Access autocompletes the action name as you type.

- Locate an action in the Action Catalog and click and drag (or double-click it) to add it to the macro. Actions are grouped by category in the Action Catalog pane. You can browse through the categories to find an action, or you can search for an action by typing in the Search box at the top of the pane.

You can also create an action by dragging a database object from the Navigation Pane to an empty row in the Macro Designer. If you drag a table, query, form, or report to the Macro Designer, Access automatically adds an action that opens the table, query, form, or report. If you drag a macro to the Macro Designer, Access adds an action that runs the macro. Figure 10.4 shows an OpenForm action that was created by dragging the Employee form from the Navigation Pane into a new macro.

It is always a good practice to test a macro to determine if it produces the expected results. Double-click the macro name in the Navigation Pane to run and test a standalone macro.

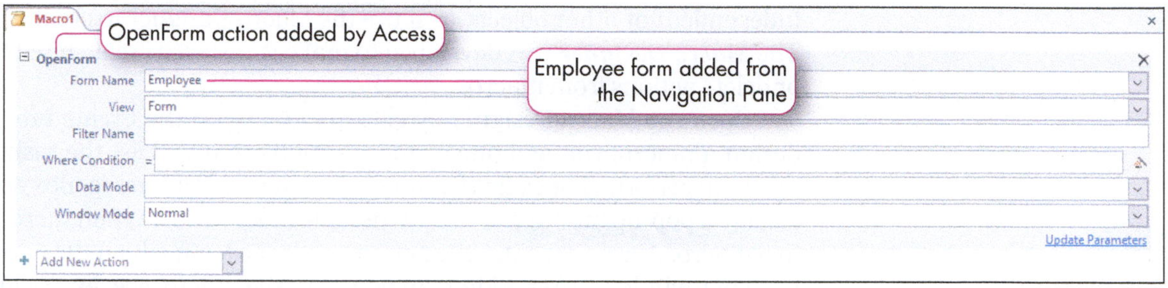

FIGURE 10.4 Drag the Employee Form into a Macro

To create a standalone macro using the Macro Designer, complete the following steps:

1. Click Macro in the Macros & Code group on the Create tab. The Macro Designer is displayed.
2. Ensure that the Action Catalog is open by selecting Action Catalog in the Show/Hide group on the Design tab.
3. Add an action to the Macro Designer using one of the methods mentioned above.
4. Specify the arguments you want for the action you added to the macro.
5. Add actions and arguments as needed to continue to build the macro.
6. Click Save when you finish building the macro.
7. Type a descriptive name for the macro. The macro name will display in the Navigation Pane.

STEP 3 **Edit a Standalone Macro in the Macro Designer**

After you have created a standalone macro and have determined that it works correctly, you might decide to modify, add, or delete actions. Right-click the macro name in the Navigation Pane and select Design View from the shortcut menu to open the Macro Designer. Modify the macro and then save and close it.

Attaching an Embedded Macro to an Event

Unlike a standalone macro that is an individual object in a database, an embedded macro is attached to an event of a control on a form or report (such as a button) or to an event of the form or report itself (such as Open or Close). After Update is an example of an event associated with a control. The After Update event is triggered each time you enter or update data in a field on a form. You can attach an embedded macro to the After Update event to evaluate the value entered in the field and verify that it falls within a set of parameters. In the Sunshine database, for example, if a user enters a 401(k) contribution in a form, a macro can verify whether the amount is less than or equal to a certain percentage of an employee's salary and determine the company match. There are two primary ways to create embedded macros. One way is to attach a macro to a specific event (such as After Update) in the Property Sheet of an object; the other method is to have Access create an embedded macro automatically using the Command Button Wizard.

STEP 4 Create an Embedded Macro with the Command Button Wizard

Command buttons are commonly used to start an action or a series of actions. Clicking a command button can open a form or report, close an object, or exit Access. You can use the Button control in the Controls group on the Design tab, as shown in Figure 10.5, to create an embedded macro automatically. The Command Button Wizard launches when you place a button on a form or report. After the wizard is finished, an embedded macro is inserted into the On Click event property of the button you have added. Using the wizard is an advantage because the step-through process prompts you through creating the button automatically as opposed to creating it manually, and then associating a macro with it in a separate step. The wizard creates both the button and its associated macro. The On Click event defines what will happen when an object, such as a command button on a form, is clicked. For example, clicking the command button could run a macro that will open a report related to a record on the form.

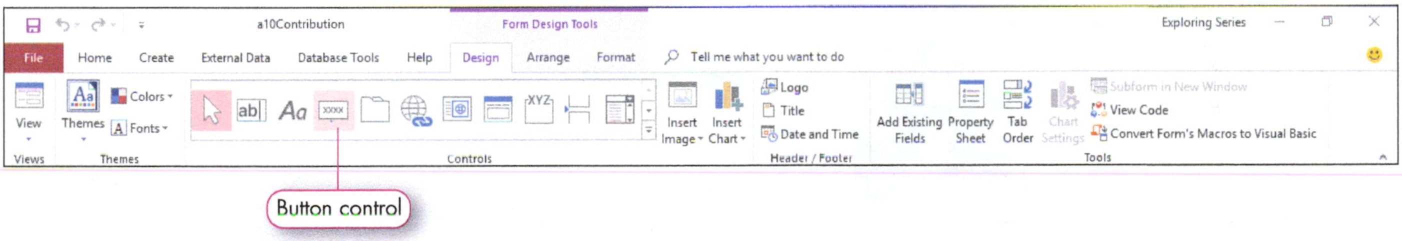

FIGURE 10.5 Button Control

To create an embedded macro with the Command Button Wizard, complete the following steps:

1. Open a form or report in Design view, click the Button control in the Controls group on the Design tab, and then click in the form (or report) to place the button. The Command Button Wizard will launch.

2. Select a category from the Categories list and select an action from the Actions list, as shown in Figure 10.6. Click Next.

3. Continue to step through the wizard and select the option to display text or an image on the command button, as shown in Figure 10.7. If the Text option is selected, type text to display on the button and click Next.

4. Type the name for the button as it will be referenced in Access, as shown in Figure 10.8, and click Finish.

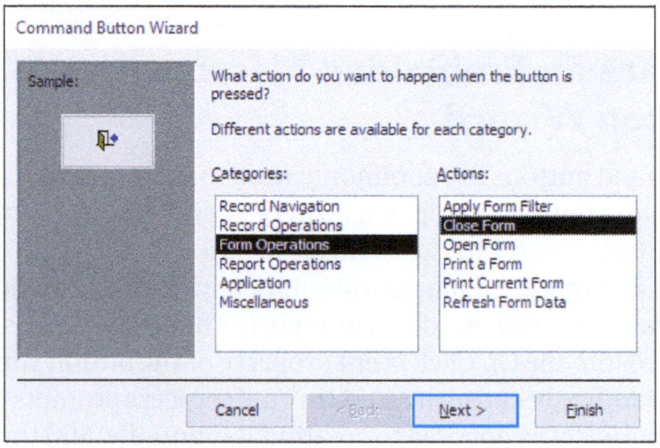

FIGURE 10.6 Select a Category and Action in the Command Button Wizard

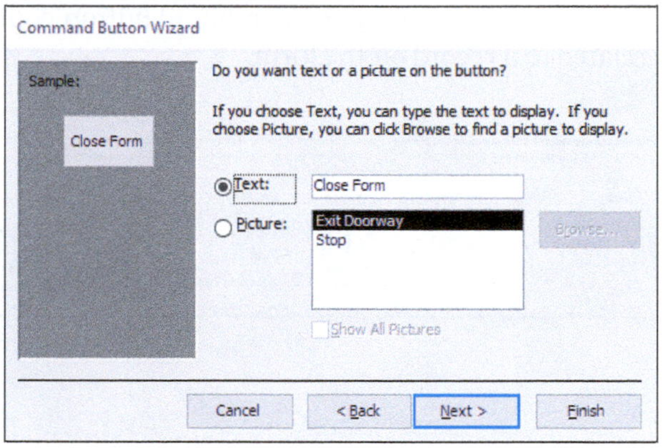

FIGURE 10.7 Select Text or a Picture to Display on Command Button

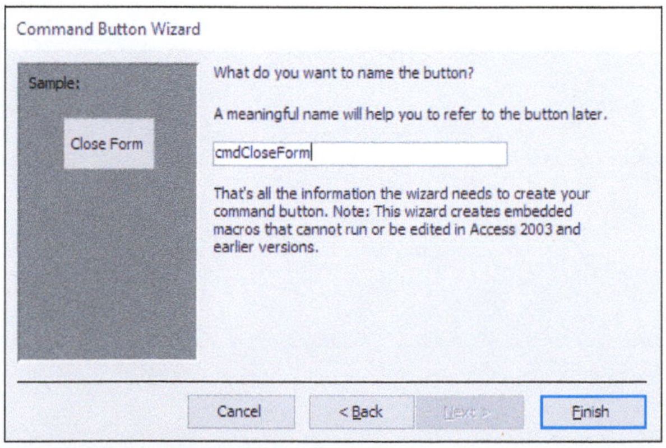

FIGURE 10.8 Type the Button Name and Finish the Wizard

Create an Embedded Macro in an Event Property

You can also add a macro to an existing control manually by clicking the ellipsis ··· in the event box of the control or object in the Property Sheet. When you add a macro to an event (such as the After Update event of a control or the On Click event of a button), Access embeds a macro in the object or control. The Event tab in the object's Property Sheet also enables you to open and edit the embedded macro. Figure 10.9 shows how an embedded macro displays in the Property Sheet for a control.

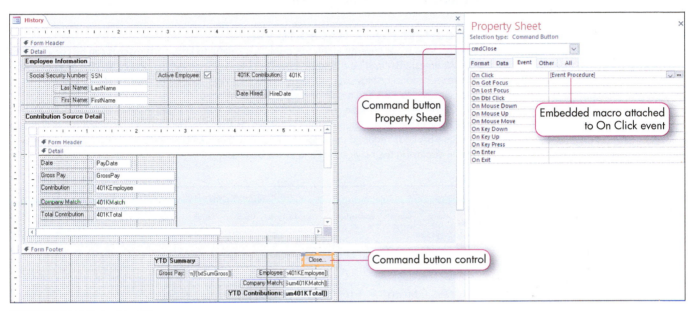

FIGURE 10.9 Embedded Macro

To attach an embedded macro to an event of a control, complete the following steps:

1. Open the object in Design or Layout view and open the Property Sheet.
2. Click the control you want to add the macro to and click in the event property box on the Event tab of the Property Sheet. When you click in an event property box, the ellipsis displays on the right side of the box, as shown in Figure 10.10.
3. Click the ellipsis, ensure that Macro Builder is selected, and then click OK.
4. Add actions to the macro.

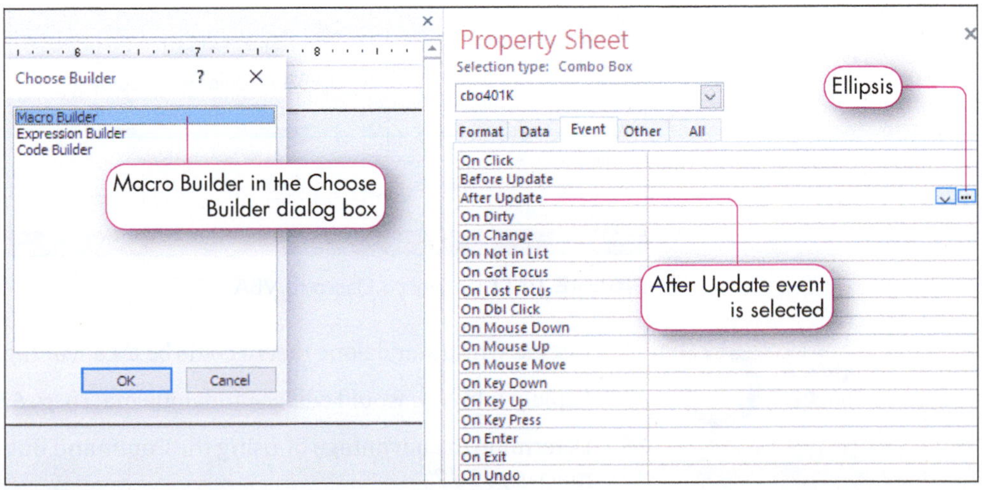

FIGURE 10.10 Create an Embedded Macro

The Macro Designer opens and you can add actions using the same methods you used for the standalone macro. For example, you can create a macro to compute employee 401(k) contributions. The macro can display a message after the 401(k) contribution is selected, informing the employee (or the user) the amount that will be deducted each paycheck (by displaying the 401K Contribution Percent multiplied by the weekly Salary).

To edit an embedded macro, open the form or report in Design view. In the Property Sheet, click in the event property box that contains the embedded macro. Click the ellipsis to open the Macro Designer and display the actions associated with the macro. Modify the embedded macro, save, and close it.

TIP: CONVERTING A MACRO TO VBA

Although VBA is not covered in this textbook, it is helpful to know that macros can be converted to VBA. At times, VBA may be a better choice for automating an Access object, as VBA enables more complex functionality. However, rather than creating VBA code from scratch, you can convert an existing macro to VBA and modify the VBA code as needed.

To convert a standalone macro to VBA, open the macro in Design view. Click Convert Macros to Visual Basic in the Tools group on the Design tab, as shown in Figure 10.11. A new module is created with the VBA code required to perform the same automated tasks as the original macro. The VBA module displays in the Navigation Pane of the database.

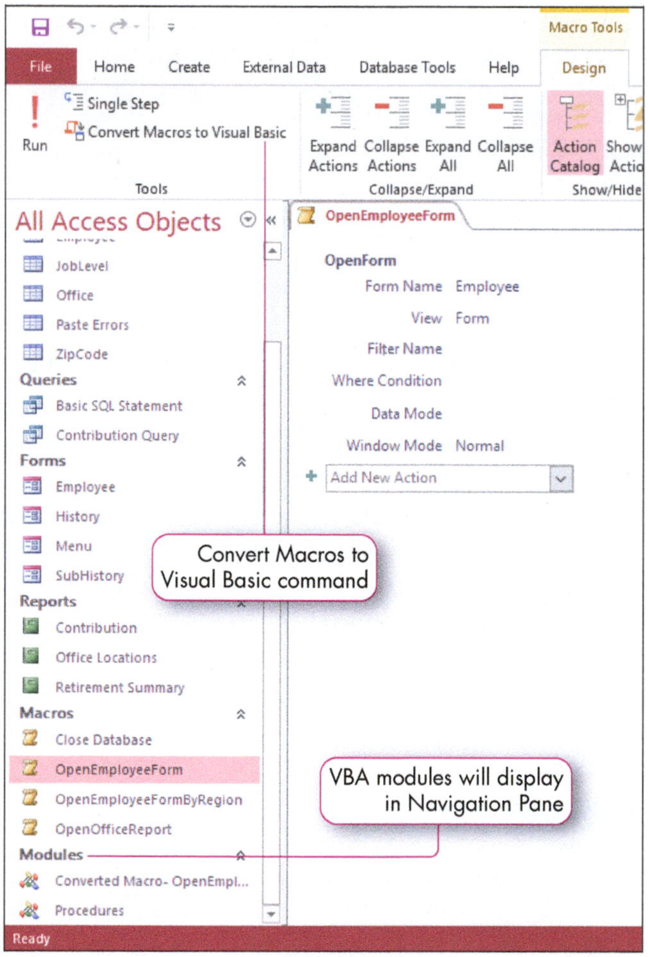

FIGURE 10.11 Convert a Macro to VBA

Quick Concepts

1. Discuss why a standalone macro could be an advantage over an embedded macro. *p. 554*

2. Explain why you would edit a standalone macro. *p. 556*

3. Determine the advantage of using the Command Button Wizard to create an embedded macro. *p. 557*

Hands-On Exercises

MyLab IT HOE1 Sim Training

Watch the Video for this Hands-On Exercise!

Skills covered: Understand How a Macro Automates Tasks in a Database • Create a Standalone Macro with the Macro Designer • Edit a Standalone Macro with the Macro Designer • Create an Embedded Macro with the Command Button Wizard • Format a Command Button • Create an Embedded Macro in an Event Property • Create a Message Box

1 Macro Design

You were hired to manage the 401(k) plan database at Sunshine Therapy Services. After you examine the design of the database, you decide to use standalone and embedded macros to display the forms and reports used to administer the plan.

STEP 1 UNDERSTAND THE PURPOSE OF A MACRO

Because this is your first time working with the Sunshine Therapy Services database, you examine the existing version by opening each table in Datasheet view. Next, you will open the Relationships window to see which tables are related. You will also open the forms and reports that are used frequently and determine that a macro can be created to open several objects automatically. Refer to Figure 10.12 as you complete Step 1.

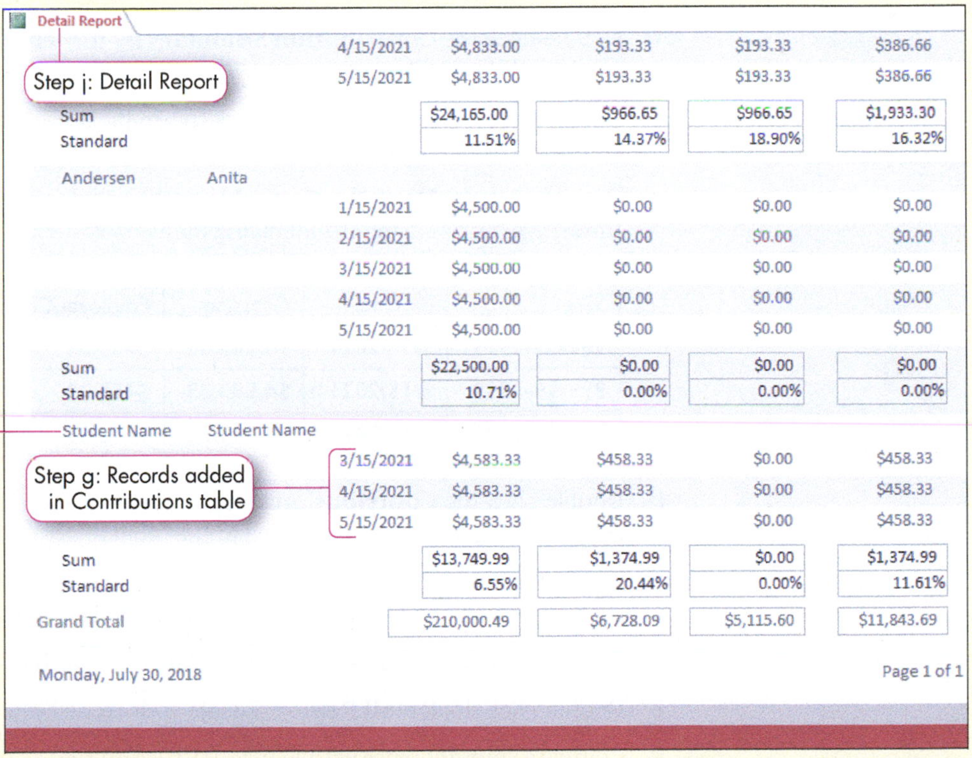

FIGURE 10.12 Sunshine Database Detail Report

a. Open *a10h1Sunshine* and save it as **a10h1Sunshine_LastFirst**.

TROUBLESHOOTING: If you make any major mistakes in this exercise, you can close the file, open *a10h1Sunshine* again and then start this exercise over.

b. Double-click the **Employee table** to open it in Datasheet view and examine the records. Open the **Contribution table** and examine the records. Open the remaining tables and examine the records.

You examine the data in each table to get acquainted with the database. The Contribution table contains the 401(k) contributions for each employee. The Employee table contains personal information for each employee.

c. Close all tables. Click **Relationships** in the Relationships group on the **Database Tools tab** to open the Relationships window.

You examine the table relationships to help you understand the data entry rules of the database. The Employee table contains a unique Social Security number (SSN) for each employee. The Contribution table contains an SSN field, but multiple contributions can be entered for each SSN.

d. Close the Relationships window. Double-click the **Employee table** and add your data as a new record to the table.

SSN	**999-99-9999** (do not type the dashes)
LastName	**Your last name**
FirstName	**Your first name**
Gender	**Your gender**
Other fields	**The same data as Anita Andersen's record**

e. Close the Employee table.

f. Double-click the **Contribution Summary by Job Title query** and review the contributions by job title.

You will use this information to track the employee and employer contributions summarized by job title.

g. Double-click the **Contribution table** and scroll down to the bottom of the records. Add three new entries using the following data:

SSN	PayDate	GrossPay	EmployeeContribution	CompanyMatch
999-99-9999	**3/15/2021**	**$4,583.33**	**$458.33**	**$0.00**
999-99-9999	**4/15/2021**	**$4,583.33**	**$458.33**	**$0.00**
999-99-9999	**5/15/2021**	**$4,583.33**	**$458.33**	**$0.00**

h. Double-click the **Contribution Details form** and scroll down to view the last three records in the form that you added in the table.

i. Double-click the **Employees form**. Advance to your record by clicking **Last record** in the Navigation bar. Change the **HireDate** to today's date. Close all open objects.

The HireDate will be used later to calculate the length of employment.

j. Double-click the **Detail Report**. Locate your record (the last record of the report).

k. Compare your database with Figure 10.12. You realize that several of the objects in the database are used regularly and determine that a macro that opens multiple objects automatically would be useful.

l. Close the report.

STEP 2 CREATE A STANDALONE MACRO

You begin to create and test a standalone macro to automatically open the Contribution Summary by Job Title query. Once you determine that your initial macro works, you will add to it in a later step. Refer to Figure 10.13 as you complete Step 2.

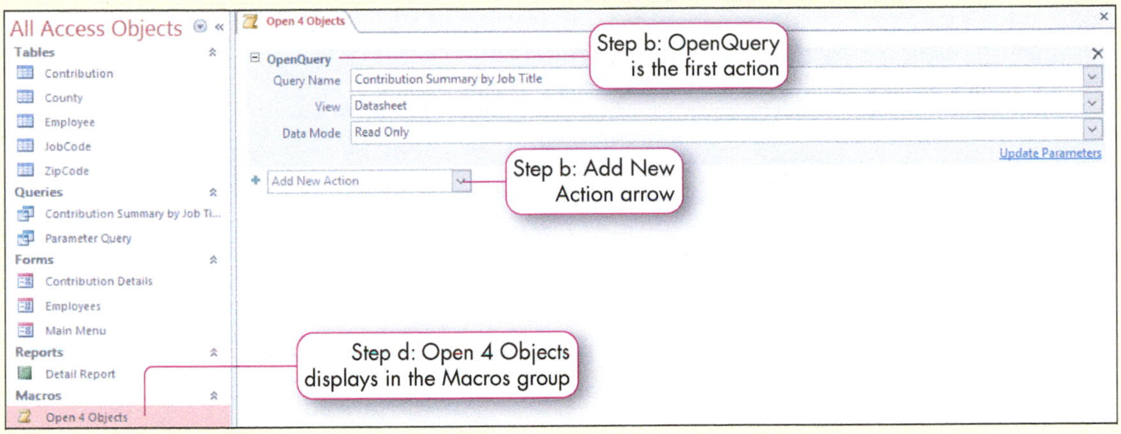

FIGURE 10.13 Use the Macro Designer to Create a Standalone Macro

a. Click **Macro** in the Macros & Code group on the **Create tab.**

The Macro Designer opens.

b. Click the **Add New Action arrow**, scroll down, and then select **OpenQuery** from the list of options.

The OpenQuery arguments are displayed. The OpenQuery action will open a query automatically.

c. Click the arrow at the end of each box and select the following arguments:

Query Name	**Contribution Summary by Job Title**
View	**Datasheet**
Data Mode	**Read Only**

d. Save the macro as **Open 4 Objects**. Close the macro.

The Open 4 Objects macro now displays in the Macros Group in the Navigation Pane.

e. Double-click the **Open 4 Objects macro** to run it.

Only one object, the Contribution Summary by Job Title query, opens.

f. Close the query.

EDIT A STANDALONE MACRO WITH THE MACRO DESIGNER

You created and tested a standalone macro in the previous step. Because the macro you created to open the query works correctly so far, you decide to edit the macro and add three more frequently used objects, two forms and a report. All four objects will open when you run the Open 4 Objects macro. Refer to Figure 10.14 as you complete Step 3.

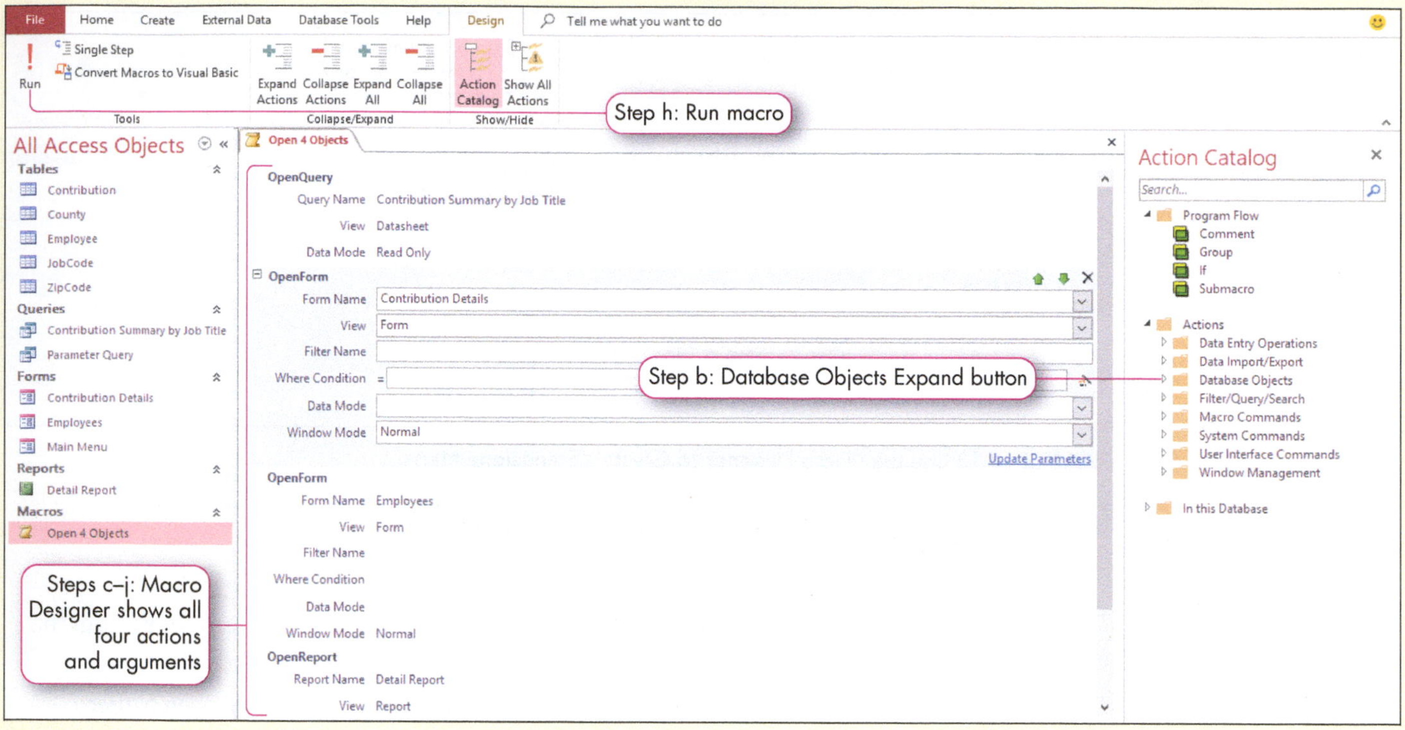

FIGURE 10.14 Use the Macro Designer to Edit a Standalone Macro

a. Right-click the **Open 4 Objects macro** in the Navigation Pane and select **Design View**.

The Macro Designer opens.

b. Click the **Database Objects Expand button** in the Action Catalog pane, below Actions. Click and drag the **OpenForm action** to the Add New Action box. The OpenForm arguments are displayed.

c. Click the **Form Name arrow** in the Action Arguments pane and select **Contribution Details**.

Select the following additional arguments:

View	Form
Window Mode	Normal

The remaining arguments are left blank.

d. Click in the **Add New Action box** and type **OpenForm**.

The OpenForm arguments are displayed for the second form.

e. Select the following arguments:

Form Name	Employees
View	Form
Window Mode	Normal

The remaining arguments are left blank.

f. Click the **Add New Action arrow** and select **OpenReport**.

The OpenReport arguments are displayed for the report.

g. Select the following arguments:

Report Name	**Detail Report**
View	**Report**
Window Mode	**Normal**

The remaining arguments are left blank. The macro now has an OpenQuery action, two OpenForm actions, and one OpenReport action added to it.

h. Save the macro. Click **Run** in the Tools group on the Design tab.

The Open 4 Objects macro runs and opens the four objects automatically, one after the other.

i. Close the four objects and close the macro.

CREATE AN EMBEDDED MACRO WITH THE COMMAND BUTTON WIZARD

You created a standalone macro. Next, you will create an embedded macro attached to a control on a form. You will add a command button to the main menu with an embedded macro; the macro will open the Parameter Query when the button is clicked. The Parameter Query will prompt the user to enter a minimum salary and then displays the employees who earn at least that amount. Refer to Figure 10.15 as you complete Step 4.

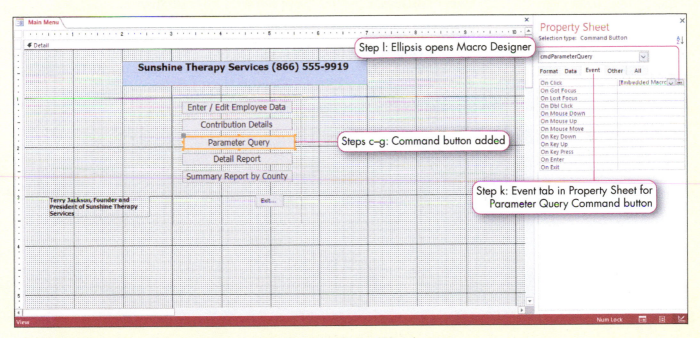

FIGURE 10.15 Create an Embedded Macro with the Command Button Wizard

a. Double-click **Parameter Query** in the Navigation Pane. When prompted, type **50000** and press **Enter**.

The query displays eight employees who earn at least $50,000.00.

b. Close the query. Right-click the **Main Menu form** in the Navigation Pane and select **Design View** from the shortcut menu.

The Main Menu opens in Design view.

c. Click the **Button control** in the Controls group on the Design tab and click in the space between the Contribution Details and Detail Report buttons.

The Command Button Wizard opens automatically, and you are ready to add an action to the button you created.

d. Select **Miscellaneous** from the Categories list and select **Run Query** from the Actions list. Click **Next**.

e. Select **Parameter Query** and click **Next**.

f. Select the **Text option** and type **Parameter Query** as the display text. Click **Next**.

g. Type **cmdParameterQuery** as the name for the button. Click **Finish**.

You created a command button on the form that will run the Parameter Query when you click it.

h. Ensure that the button is selected and the Property Sheet is open. Click the **Format tab** in the Property Sheet, set the button width to **2.25"** and the height to **.25"**. Click the **Font Size arrow** and select **12**. Leave the Property Sheet open. Click and drag the **Parameter Query button** so that its left edge is aligned with the left edge of the buttons above and below it.

i. Switch to Form view and click the **Parameter Query button**.

The query opens and prompts for the minimum salary amount.

j. Type **50000** and press **Enter**.

The query results display all the employees with a salary of at least $50,000.

k. Close the query and switch to Design view of the Main Menu form. Click the **Parameter Query button** and click the **Event tab** in the Property Sheet.

[Embedded Macro] displays in the On Click property box.

l. Click the **ellipsis** ⋯ on the right side of the On Click property box. The Macro Designer opens and enables you to make modifications to the embedded macro. There are no modifications needed at this time. Close the Macro Designer.

m. Save and close the Main Menu form.

CREATE AN EMBEDDED MACRO IN AN EVENT PROPERTY

Terry asks you to display a message when an employee runs the Detail Report. She wants to add a reminder to send the report to her every Friday. Refer to Figure 10.16 as you complete Step 5.

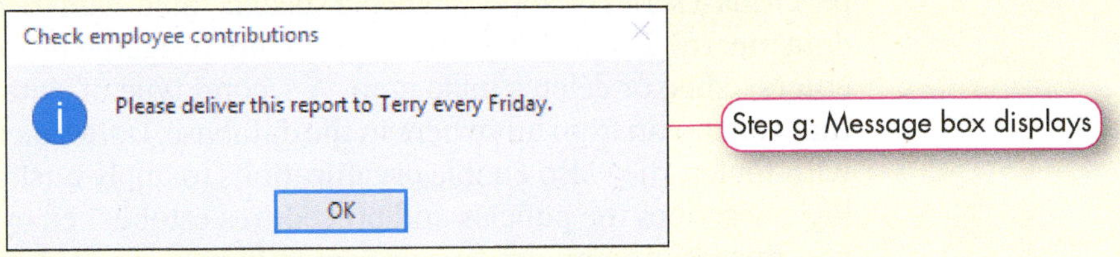

FIGURE 10.16 Message Displays When the Report Opens

a. Right-click **Detail Report** in the Navigation Pane and select **Design View** from the shortcut menu.

The Detail Report opens in Design view.

b. Ensure that the Property Sheet is displayed. Ensure that the Event tab is selected on the Property Sheet.

c. Click in the **On Open property box**. Click the **ellipsis** on the right side of the property box. Macro Builder is selected by default. Click **OK**.

The Macro Designer opens and enables you to create an embedded macro.

d. Click the **Add New Action arrow** in the Add New Action box, scroll down, and then select **MessageBox**.

The MessageBox arguments are displayed.

e. Type **Please deliver this report to Terry every Friday.** (include the period) in the Message box.

f. Verify that *Yes* is in the Beep box. Select **Information** in the Type box. Type **Check employee contributions** in the Title box.

g. Save and close the macro. With the report in Design view, click the **View arrow** and select **Print Preview** in the Views group to test the macro.

A message displays immediately, reminding users to send the report to Terry every Friday.

h. Click **OK**, close Print Preview, and then save and close the report.

i. Keep the database open if you plan to continue with the next Hands-On Exercise. If not, close the database and exit Access.

Data Macros

So far, you have worked with user interface (UI) macros that operate with controls, forms, and reports. To build automation into a table, a data macro is required. A *data macro* performs a series of actions when a specific table event occurs (known as an event-driven data macro). Event-driven data macros are triggered by table events, such as when a user enters, edits, or deletes table data. A second type of data macro is a named data macro that can be run from anywhere in the database. Data macros combine programming logic with tables; they also enable organizations to apply business logic to databases. Business logic describes the policies and procedures established by an organization. For example, you may want a macro to compare values, such as dates in two different fields, when data are entered and perform an action as a result. When a form is based on a table that contains a data macro, the form contains the same logic and the same results of the data macro as the table.

Data macros, like standalone macros and embedded macros, are created with the Macro Designer. The actions available in the Macro Designer are somewhat different for data macros than for standalone or embedded macros; however, the user interface of the Macro Designer is the same for each macro type.

In this section, you will learn data validation techniques using data macros. You will learn how to create event-driven data macros and named data macros.

STEP 1 Identifying When to Use a Data Macro

You can use data macros to validate and ensure the accuracy of data in a table. In a previous chapter, you learned how to use a validation rule to apply business logic to a single field in a table. However, when business logic requires the comparison of two or more fields, you need to use a data macro. For example, in the Sunshine database, you can compare an employee's hire date with the current date. If the employee has been with the firm for at least one year, then he or she is eligible for an employer match on the 401(k) contribution; otherwise, no employer match is available. To automate this type of business logic, so that the eligibility field is updated based on the employee's hire date, a data macro is required.

Data macros can only be associated with table events; however, as stated earlier, a form that is based on a table that contains a data macro inherits the logic of the table. After you practice adding a few data macros, you will begin to see the power they add to a database.

STEP 2 Creating an Event-Driven Data Macro

Table events occur naturally as users enter, edit, and delete table data. Event-driven data macros, such as Before Change or After Delete, can be programmed to run before or after a table event occurs.

To attach a data macro to a table event, complete the following steps:

1. Open the table that will contain the data macro in Design view.
2. Click Create Data Macros in the Field, Record & Table Events group on the Table Tools Design tab, as shown in Figure 10.17.
3. Select the event to which you want to attach the macro. For example, to create a data macro that runs before a record is saved, select Before Change.
4. Add macro actions using the Macro Designer. If a macro was previously created for this event, Access displays the existing macro actions.
5. Save and close the macro.

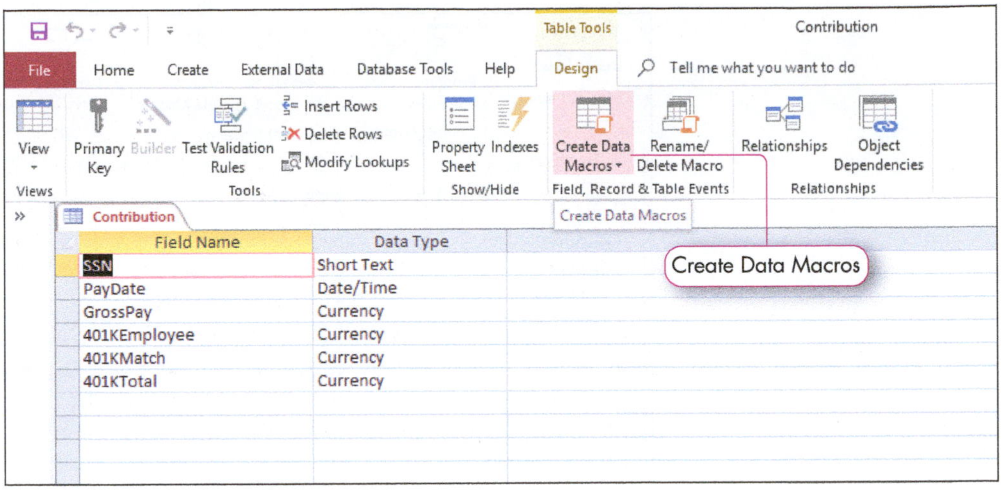

FIGURE 10.17 Create Data Macros

STEP 3 ▶ Test and Modify a Data Macro

To test the effect of a data macro, open the table to which the macro was added, and then add, delete, or update a record to trigger the macro. For example, if you attached a macro to the Before Change event, open the table, modify the data, and then advance to the next record to save the changes and trigger the Before Change event. The data macro will run and execute the actions you created. You can modify a data macro if you want to modify a condition or value, an outcome in an action, or to add or delete actions. To modify a data macro, select the Create Data Macros command and select the event to which the macro is attached to return to Design view.

STEP 4 ▶ Creating a Named Data Macro

In addition to creating data macros that are triggered by events, Access enables you to create named data macros. A named data macro also performs actions related to a table. You can access these macros from anywhere in the database, including running them from within another macro. In Design view of the table, click Create Data Macros in the Field, Record & Table Events group, and select Create Named Macro from the list (see Figure 10.18). Figure 10.19 portrays the Design view of a named data macro. You can run a named data macro from within another macro using the RunDataMacro action. Add the RunDataMacro action in the Macro Designer and select the named data macro using the Macro Name arrow. Figure 10.20 shows a named data macro attached to the After Update event of the Employee table. The macro sends an email to the database administrator each time a record in the Employee table is updated.

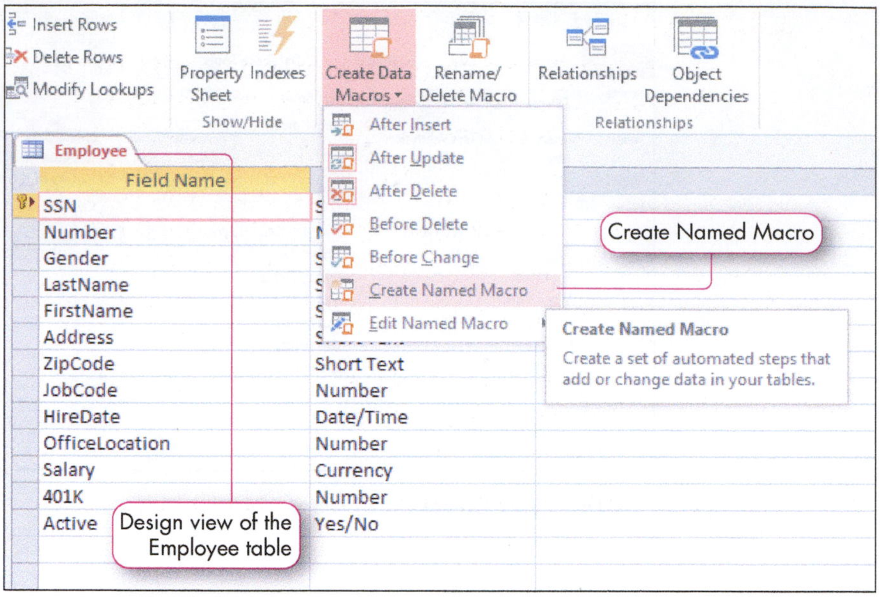

FIGURE 10.18 Create a Named Data Macro

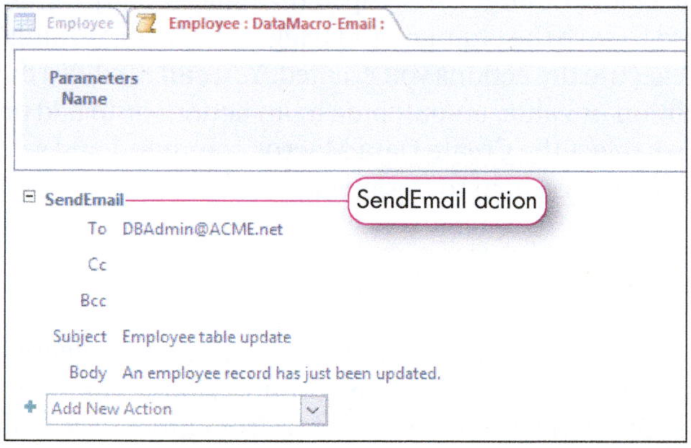

FIGURE 10.19 Named Data Macro Design

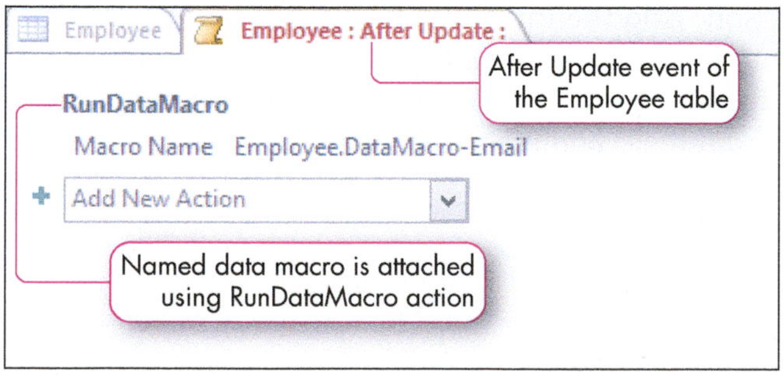

FIGURE 10.20 Attach a Named Data Macro to an Event

A named data macro can also be attached to an event in a form that is dependent on an underlying table. For example, you can associate a named data macro with an event property, such as After Update, in an employees form that is dependent on an employees table. Often users work with data in a form rather than the table itself. A data macro associated with a form event helps to automate tasks in a table, even when the edits are made through the associated form. The macro will operate the same way in the employees form as it would if were attached to the underlying table itself.

Quick Concepts

4. Compare how a data macro differs from other macros that you create using the Macro Designer. ***p. 568***

5. Discuss a specific reason as to why you would use an event-driven macro. ***p. 568***

6. Describe a situation where it would be beneficial to create a standalone macro. ***p. 554***

Hands-On Exercises

MyLab IT HOE2 Sim Training

Watch the Video for this Hands-On Exercise!

Skills covered: Use a Data Macro to Automate Data Entry • Create a Before Change Data Macro • Test a Data Macro • Modify a Data Macro • Create a Named Data Macro • Attach a Named Data Macro to a Form

2 Data Macros

You want to demonstrate the power of data macros to Terry. You will show her how data macros help reduce data entry errors by validating data values before they are added to a table. Although event-driven data macros are generally created from within tables, you will demonstrate that named data macros can be used with forms in the database to automate certain tasks. You will create a named data macro in a table to send an email and attach the same named data macro to a form.

STEP 1 IDENTIFY WHEN TO USE A DATA MACRO

You will identify an opportunity to create a data macro in the Employee table. Refer to Figure 10.21 as you complete Step 1.

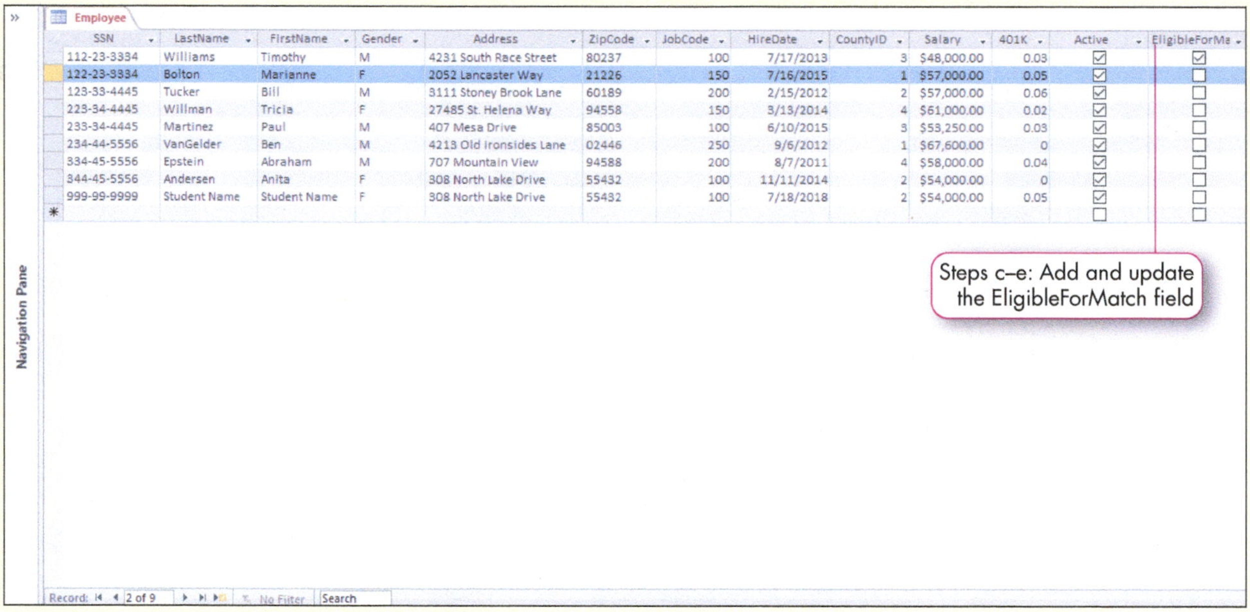

FIGURE 10.21 Identify When to Use a Data Macro

a. Open *a10h1Sunshine_LastFirst* if you closed it at the end of Hands-On Exercise 1, and save it as **a10h2Sunshine_LastFirst**, changing h1 to h2.

b. Right-click the **Employee table** and select **Design View**.

c. Add a new field, **EligibleForMatch**, with data type **Yes/No**, as the last field of the table. Save the table.

You will use the new field to indicate which employees are eligible for the company 401(k) matching contribution.

d. Switch to Datasheet view.

e. Click the **EligibleForMatch check box** in Record 1, for Timothy Williams.

Because Timonthy's HireDate was 7/17/2013, you indicate that he is eligible for the company match because he has been employed for a least one year.

> **TROUBLESHOOTING:** Ensure that your own record contains today's date as the date of hire. As you have only joined the organization today, you will not be eligible for the company match.

CREATE AN EVENT-DRIVEN DATA MACRO

The EligibleForMatch field can be updated automatically by a data macro based on the HireDate because the same eligibility rule applies to all employees. To eliminate the possibility of data entry errors, you will use the Before Change data macro to update the eligibility of an employee automatically. Refer to Figure 10.22 as you complete Step 2.

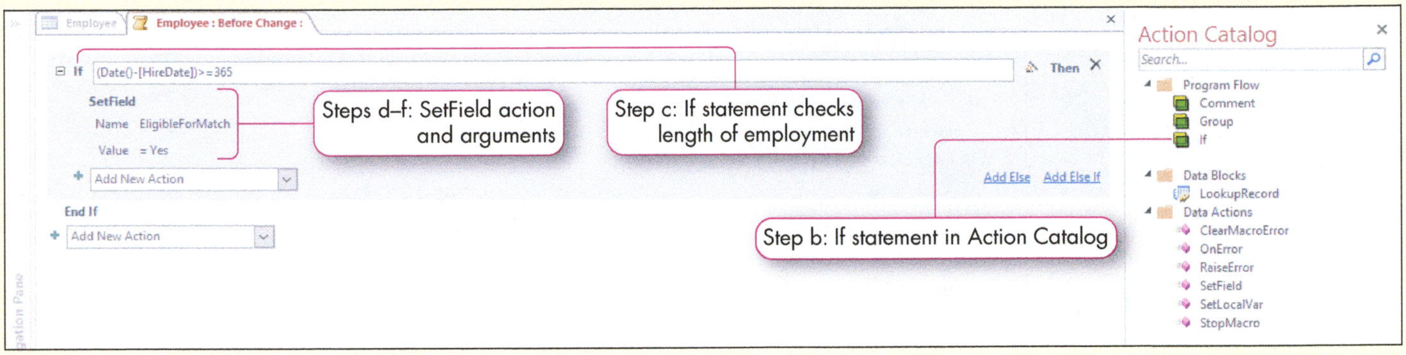

FIGURE 10.22 Before Change Data Macro

a. Switch to Design view. Click **Create Data Macros** in the Field, Record & Table Events group on the Design tab and select **Before Change**.

The Macro Designer displays.

b. Drag the **If statement** from the Program Flow folder in the Action Catalog to the Add New Action box in the macro.

The structure of the If statement is added to the macro.

c. Type **(Date()-[HireDate])>=365** in the Conditional expression box.

The expression determines if the employee has been employed at least one year (365 days) by subtracting the employee's hire date from today's date and evaluating that difference to determine if it is greater than or equal to 365. If true, the macro will set the value of the EligibleForMatch field to Yes.

d. Click the **Add New Action arrow** within the If action and select **SetField**.

The SetField arguments are added to the macro.

e. Type **el** in the Name box (and Access displays *EligibleForMatch*, the field name it predicts you are looking for). Double-click to accept the EligibleForMatch field.

f. Type **yes** in the Value box.

Access checks the EligibleForMatch check box if the length of employment expression evaluates to true.

g. Save and close the macro. Save the Employee table and keep it open for the next step.

You decide to test the Before Change macro using the employee records (1–9). You will change one field in each record in order to trigger the Before Change event and verify the macro correctly updates the EligibleForMatch check box. You will also add an extra condition to the If statement in the macro that will update the check box if the employee is not eligible for the match. Refer to Figure 10.23 as you complete Step 3.

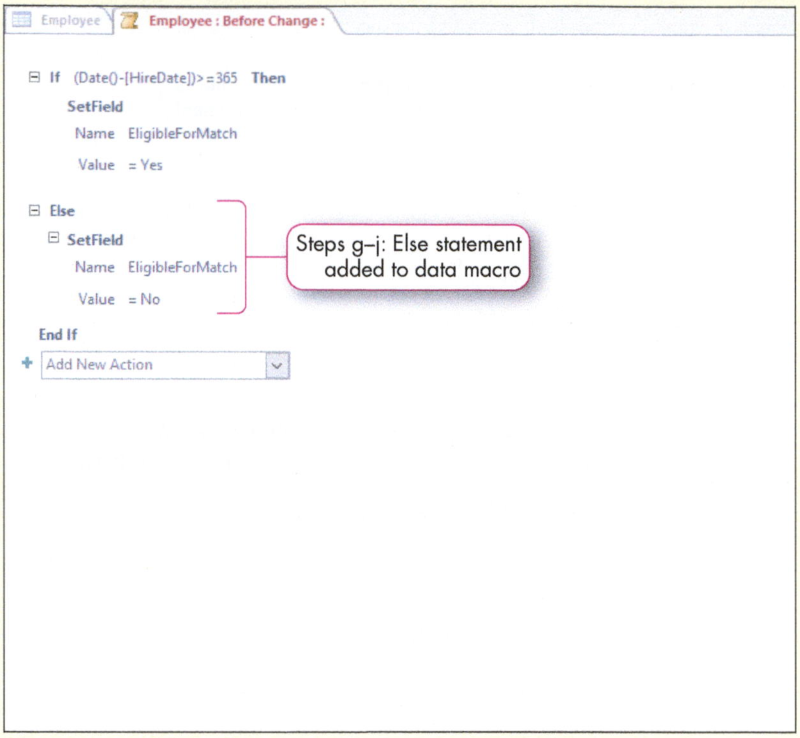

```
▦ Employee    ⚡ Employee : Before Change :

⊟ If  (Date()-[HireDate])>=365  Then
        SetField
          Name  EligibleForMatch
          Value  = Yes

⊟ Else
   ⊟ SetField
          Name  EligibleForMatch           ⟵  Steps g–j: Else statement
          Value  = No                            added to data macro

   End If
✚  [Add New Action              ▼]
```

FIGURE 10.23 Data Macro with Else Statement Added

a. Switch to Datasheet view.

To test the accuracy of the data macro, you will retype the 401(k) contributions for records 2 through 9 to trigger the Before Change event. The macro will automatically select the EligibleForMatch check box for the appropriate records. Later, when new records are added to the table, the macro will run each time a record is entered.

b. Type **0.05** in the **401K column** of record 2 (Marianne Bolton). Click in the **401K column** of record 3.

Because employee Marianne Bolton was hired on 7/16/2015, she is eligible for the 401(k) match. The data macro checks the check box.

c. Type **0.06** in the **401K column** of record 3 (Bill Tucker). Click in the **401K column** of row 4.

Because employee Bill Tucker was hired on 2/5/2012, he is eligible for the 401(k) match. The data macro checks the check box.

d. Repeat the process for the remaining records.

You wonder if the macro will deselect an incorrectly checked EligibleForMatch check box. You decide to test the data macro for this condition.

e. Click the **EligibleForMatch check box** for your record to select it, and press ↓ to trigger the macro.

You realize that the check box remains checked even though you are not yet eligible for the company match. You decide to modify the data macro to update the check box if the employee is not eligible for the match.

f. Switch to Design view. Click **Create Data Macros** in the Field, Record & Table Events group on the Table Tools Design tab and select **Before Change**.

The Macro Designer displays the If statement you set up earlier.

g. Click in the **If action** and click the **Add Else hyperlink** on the right side of the Macro Designer window to add the Else statement.

You will add another SetField statement to deselect the EligibleForMatch check box if employees are employed for less than one year.

h. Type **s** in the Add New Action box below the Else statement; Access displays the *SetField* action. Press **Tab** to accept the SetField action.

i. Type **el** in the Name box; Access displays the *EligibleForMatch* field name. Double-click to accept EligibleForMatch.

j. Type **no** in the Value box. Access attempts to add the Now function when you type *no*. Press **Tab** two times.

The data macro will now deselect the EligibleForMatch check box if the length of employment expression evaluates to false, that is, the length of employment is less than one year.

k. Save the macro. Close the macro. Save the Employee table.

l. Switch to Datasheet view, locate your record, and then change your proposed 401(k) contribution to **0.05**. Press ↓ to save your change.

The EligibleForMatch check box is unchecked by the data macro because you are not eligible for the match.

STEP 4 ## CREATE A NAMED DATA MACRO

Terry wants to be notified when any changes are made to the Employee table. You decide to create a named data macro that will send an email whenever a change is made to the Employee table. Refer to Figure 10.24 as you complete Step 4.

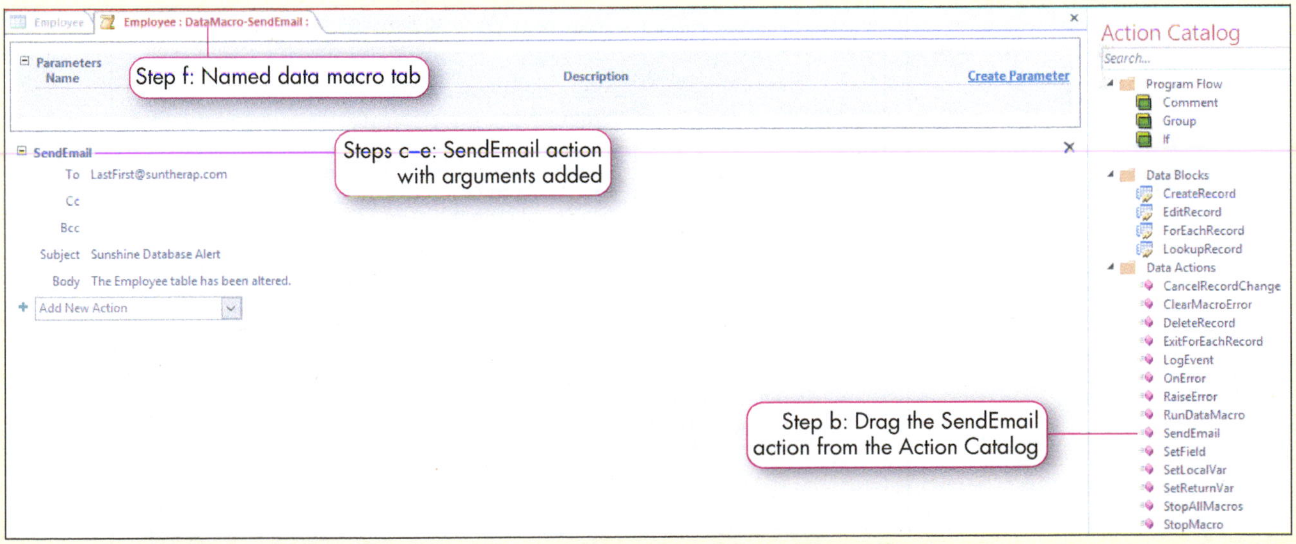

FIGURE 10.24 Create a Named Data Macro

a. Switch to Design view. Click **Create Data Macros** in the Field, Record & Table Events group on the Table Tools Design tab and select **Create Named Macro**.

The Macro Designer displays.

b. Drag the **SendEmail action** from the Data Actions folder in the Action Catalog to the Add New Action box.

The SendEmail action and its five arguments are added to the macro.

c. Type your email address in the To argument box. Skip the Cc and Bcc arguments.

> **TROUBLESHOOTING:** Your instructor may provide you with an alternate email address to complete this step.

d. Type **Sunshine Database Alert** in the Subject argument box.

e. Type **The Employee table has been altered.** (include the period) in the Body argument box.

f. Save the macro as **DataMacro-SendEmail**. Close the macro.

g. Save the Employee table. Close the table.

ATTACH A NAMED DATA MACRO TO A FORM

You will attach the named data macro to a form event because many updates to the Employee table will be done through the Employees form. You decide to use the After Update event as the trigger for the send email macro. Refer to Figure 10.25 as you complete Step 5.

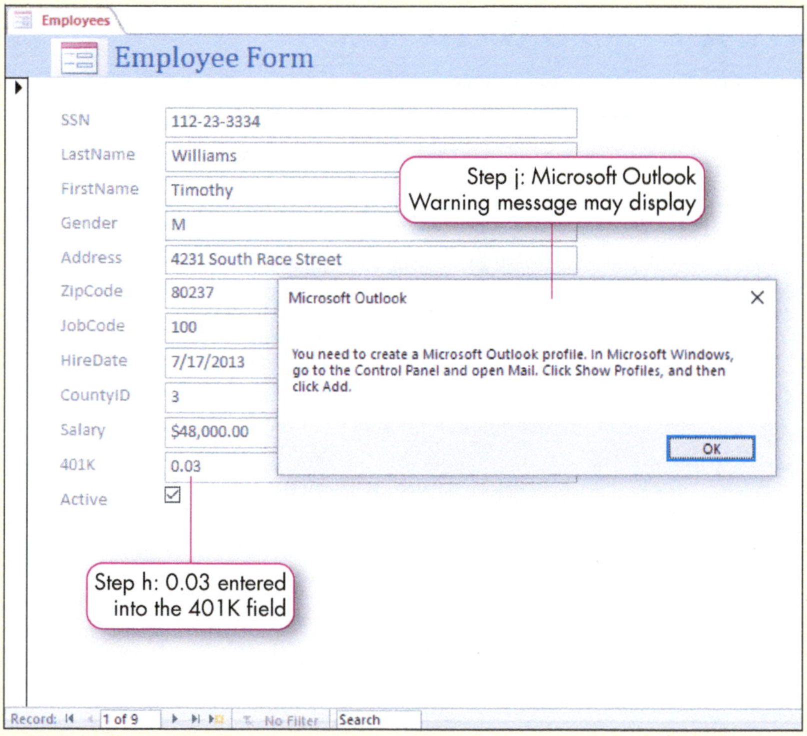

FIGURE 10.25 Test a SendEmail Named Data Macro

a. Open the Employees form in Design view.

b. Click in the **After Update property box** on the Event tab of the Property Sheet.

The ellipsis displays on the right side of the After Update property box.

c. Click the **ellipsis**, ensure that **Macro Builder** is selected, and then click **OK**.

The Macro Designer displays.

d. Click the **Add New Action arrow**, scroll down, and then select the **RunDataMacro action** from the list.

e. Click the **Macro Name arrow** and select **Employee.DataMacro-SendEmail**.

This macro is available because it was attached to the Employee table.

f. Save and close the macro.

g. Save the Employees form and switch to Form view.

h. Retype the existing 401(k) amount, **0.03**, in the 401K field of the first record (Timothy Williams).

i. Press **Tab** two times to advance to the second employee.

As soon as you move to the second employee, the After Update event is triggered and the SendEmail macro is activated. Access attempts to send an email using the parameters you typed in Step 4.

j. Click **Allow**. Check your email after a few minutes to see if you received the Sunshine Database Alert message.

TROUBLESHOOTING: If an email client is not set up on the computer you are using, you may have to cancel this step and stop the macro. Click OK if you receive the warning message shown in Figure 10.25. Click OK again and click Stop All Macros. If the warning message was not received as shown in Figure 10.25, and your computer is correctly configured to send the email, the macro will run as expected.

k. Save and close the form.

l. Keep the database open if you plan to continue with the next Hands-On Exercise. If not, close the database and exit Access.

Structured Query Language

Until now, whenever you wanted to ask a question about the data in a database, you created a query. The query's Design view enables you to select the tables you want to include and select the required fields from those tables. You can also add criteria and sorting in the query design grid. Whenever you create a query, you create a Structured Query Language (SQL) statement simultaneously. Access stores the SQL statement in the background.

In this section, you will learn the basics of SQL and the correlation between Design view and SQL view of a query. You will also learn how to use an SQL statement as the record source of a form or report.

STEP 1 | Understanding the Fundamentals of SQL

Structured Query Language (SQL) is the industry-standard language for defining, manipulating, and retrieving the data in a database. All of the queries you created so far in this textbook were created using the built-in query tools; however, they could have been created using SQL. You can use SQL to create a new query or to modify an existing query.

When you learn SQL, you are learning the data retrieval and data manipulation language of all the industry-leading databases—SQL Server, Oracle, and SAP Sybase, to name a few. If you learn SQL in connection with Access databases, your skills will be useful if you work in other database environments.

Figure 10.26 shows a basic query that was created in Design view. This query extracts all records from the Contribution table for the employee with SSN 456667778. Figure 10.27 shows the results in Datasheet view; the results contain 12 records. You can switch to SQL view to examine the statements generated by any query you create. To switch to SQL view, click the View arrow and select SQL View (see Figure 10.27).

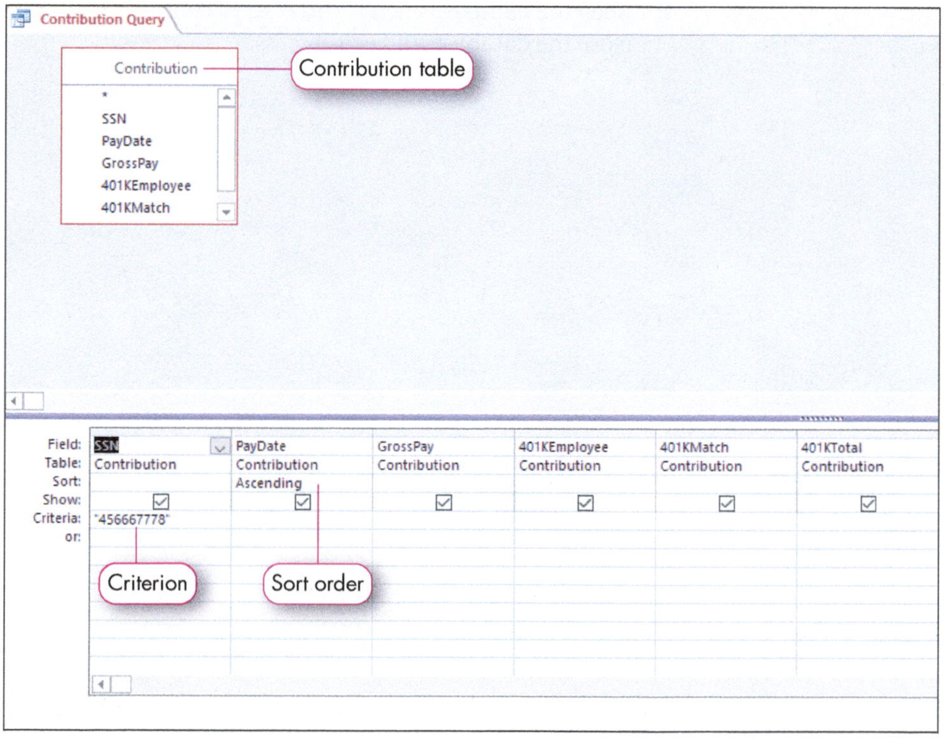

FIGURE 10.26 Contribution Query in Design View

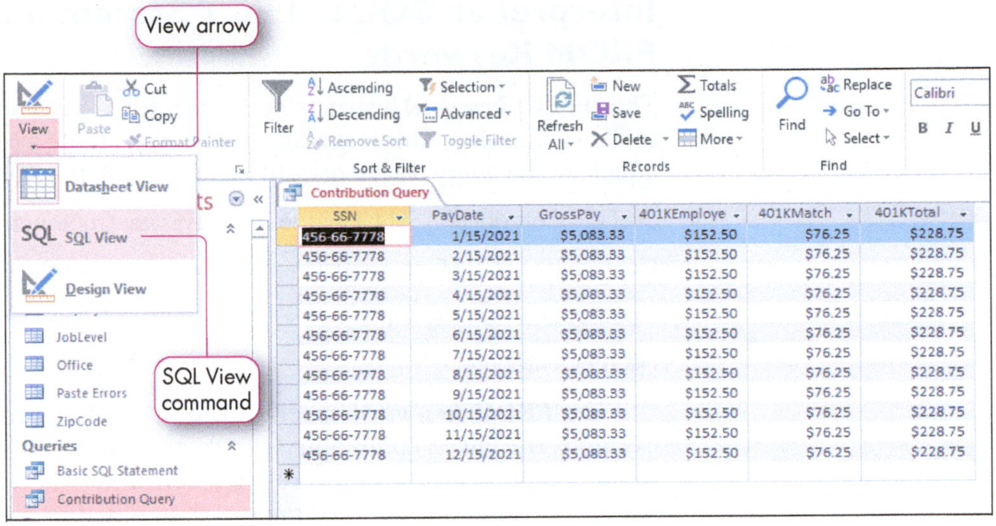

FIGURE 10.27 Contribution Query in Datasheet View

> **TIP: SWITCHING TO SQL VIEW**
> When you are working with queries in Access, you can switch to SQL view using three methods. In addition to clicking the View arrow to switch to SQL view, you can right-click the query tab and select SQL View from the shortcut menu, or from the open query, you can click the SQL icon at the bottom right of the Access window.

STEP 2 Interpreting an SQL SELECT Statement

Similar to a select query, an **SQL SELECT statement** is used to retrieve data from tables in a database. Figure 10.28 shows the equivalent SQL SELECT statement of the Contribution query created earlier in Design view (refer to Figure 10.26). The words shown in UPPERCASE are SQL keywords. An **SQL keyword** defines the purpose and the structure of an SQL statement. To use SQL, you will first learn the four basic keywords found in a typical SQL SELECT statement—SELECT, FROM, WHERE, and ORDER BY. Table 10.1 lists the four basic keywords of an SQL SELECT statement, along with their purposes. Notice the correlation between the SQL keywords and the parameters found in Design view.

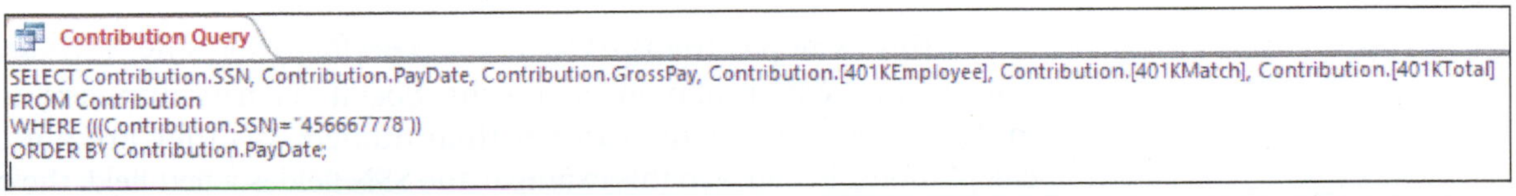

```
Contribution Query
SELECT Contribution.SSN, Contribution.PayDate, Contribution.GrossPay, Contribution.[401KEmployee], Contribution.[401KMatch], Contribution.[401KTotal]
FROM Contribution
WHERE (((Contribution.SSN)="456667778"))
ORDER BY Contribution.PayDate;
```

FIGURE 10.28 Contribution Query in SQL View

TABLE 10.1	Four Basic Keywords of an SQL SELECT Statement and Their Purposes
Keyword	**Purpose**
SELECT	Specifies the fields to include in the query
FROM	Specifies the table(s) or query (or queries) where the fields can be found
WHERE	Sets the criteria for the rows in the results
ORDER BY	Determines how the rows will be sorted

Interpret an SQL SELECT Statement: SELECT and FROM Keywords

The **SELECT keyword** instructs Access to return data from specific fields from one or more tables (or queries). This is similar to when you create a select query by adding fields from a table to the query design grid. In Figure 10.28, the SQL statement begins as follows:

SELECT Contribution.SSN, Contribution.PayDate, Contribution.GrossPay,

Contribution.[401KEmployee], Contribution.[401KMatch],

Contribution.[401KTotal]

FROM Contribution;

The **FROM keyword** specifies the table that contains the fields. In the above example, the FROM command is instructing Access to pull data from the Contribution table. When a query or expression containing a SELECT statement is executed, Access searches the specified table(s) designated in the FROM statement, extracts the designated data, and displays the results. In the statement above, field names are listed after the SELECT statement, separated by commas. If fields from different tables have the same name, the table name prefix followed by a dot is required. In the above example, *Contribution.* displays before each field name because the same field names are used in other tables in the database. When a field name has a leading numeric character, such as 401KEmployee, 401KMatch, and 401KTotal, the field name is enclosed by brackets [ ].

If all fields in a table are required for a query, you can use the asterisk character (*) to select all of the fields in a table. For example, the following SELECT statement returns all fields and records from the Contribution table:

SELECT *

FROM Contribution;

Interpret an SQL Statement: WHERE Keyword

After you select the table(s) and fields using SELECT and FROM, you can then filter the resulting records using the WHERE keyword. The **WHERE keyword** specifies the criteria that records must match to be included in the results. This is like specifying criteria in the design grid of a select query. If the query does not include the WHERE keyword, the query will return all records from the table(s). In Figure 10.28, the SQL statement contains the following clause:

WHERE ((((Contribution.SSN)="456667778"))

In this example, the WHERE clause specifies that only records with SSN equal to 456667778 will display in the results. Social Security numbers are generally stored in databases as text values rather than numeric, as they are not used in arithmetic calculations. Because in this example, the SSN field is a text field, the quotes are required around the SSN criterion.

Interpret an SQL Statement: ORDER BY Keyword

Typically, you want the query results to be arranged in a particular order. The **ORDER BY keyword** is used to sort the records by a certain field in either ascending or descending order. The ORDER BY clause must be added to the end of an SQL statement after the WHERE clause. In Figure 10.28, the SQL statement contains the following clause:

ORDER BY Contribution.PayDate;

In the statement above, the ORDER BY clause sorts the records in ascending order by PayDate. The ORDER BY sort order is ascending by default, so it is not necessary to specify when the records are to be sorted in ascending order. However, to sort in descending order, add DESC to the end of the ORDER BY clause. To sort the above records beginning with the most recent pay date, the statement would be as follows:

ORDER BY Contribution.PayDate DESC;

Explore More Advanced SQL Statements

The easiest way to learn more advanced SQL statements is to create Access queries in Design view and view the SQL statement in SQL view. Although some statements might seem complex at first, the more you work with SQL, the easier it will become to understand SQL statements. You will begin to recognize that each SQL statement contains a shared syntax. For example, most SQL statements begin with SELECT and end with a semicolon (;).

Action queries can also be translated into SQL statements. Update queries, append queries, make table queries, and delete queries each have their equivalent SQL keywords and syntax. For example, suppose you wanted to add all the records in Figure 10.27 to a new table named Archive. To do this, you would create a Make Table query. The equivalent SQL statement would be:

SELECT Contribution.SSN, Contribution.PayDate, Contribution.GrossPay,

Contribution.[401KEmployee], Contribution.[401KMatch],

Contribution.[401KTotal] INTO Archive

FROM Contribution

WHERE ((((Contribution.SSN)="456667778"))

ORDER BY Contribution.PayDate;

Using an SQL SELECT Statement as a Record Source

When you create a form or a report in Access, the first step is to select a record source, such as a table or a query, in the Navigation Pane. The next step is to click the Create tab and select the Form tool, Report tool, or another tool so that Access can create the new object. After the record source is selected and the form or report has been created, you can identify it in the Property Sheet of the database object. A sample report based on the Contribution table is shown in Figure 10.29.

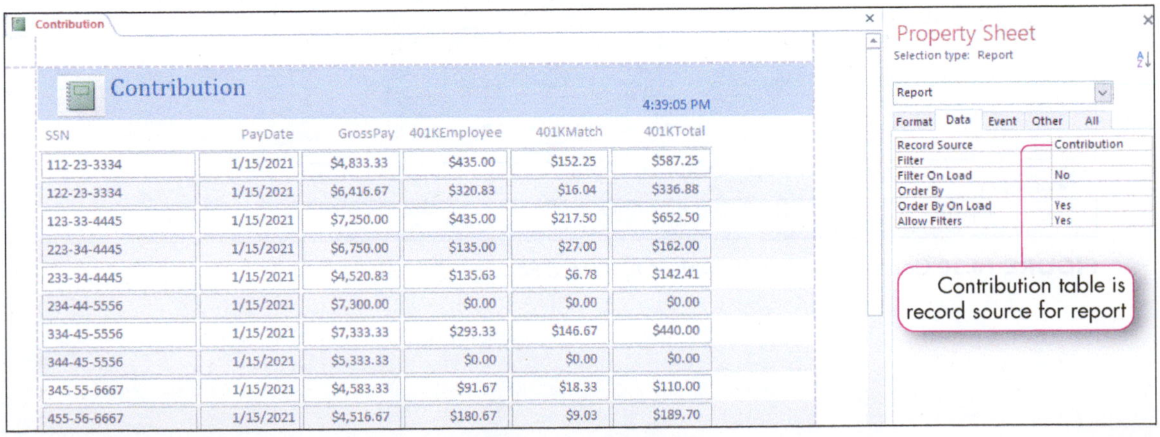

FIGURE 10.29 Contribution Report Created from the Contribution Table

Create an SQL Record Source for a Report

Based on the information you learned about SQL in this section, you should be able to create an SQL statement as the record source for a report. You know that the basic structure of an SQL statement is as follows:

SELECT *field names*

FROM *table name*

WHERE *specified criteria must be met*

ORDER BY *field name;*

The sample Contribution report, as shown in Figure 10.29, contains all of the records from the Contribution table; therefore, no WHERE clause is required. The records are not sorted in a different order than the SSN order found in the Contribution table, so no ORDER BY clause is needed. Based on this information, you can replace the existing record source (the Contribution table) with the SQL statement as follows:

SELECT *

FROM Contribution;

In addition, an SQL statement can be used instead of a query as the basis for a form or report. Instead of creating a separate query, the SQL statement would identify the table, fields, and criteria that a select query would use. A query that has been created as a separate database object can easily be deleted or modified and affect any form or report that depends on that query. Using an SQL statement as the record source in a form or report embeds the query requirements in the form or report itself with no dependency on a "named" query that exists apart from the report.

STEP 3 ▶ Copy an SQL Statement from SQL View

Refer back to the query discussed earlier, shown in Figure 10.26, which contains SSN criteria and is sorted by PayDate. When you switch the query to SQL view, as shown in Figure 10.28, the SQL statement is displayed. Because the SQL statement is in text format, you can copy the statement and paste it into the record source of a report. For example, in the sample Contribution report, you can copy the SQL statement from the Contribution query and paste it into the Record Source property box (similar to what was done in Figure 10.30). View the report in Print Preview, as shown in Figure 10.31.

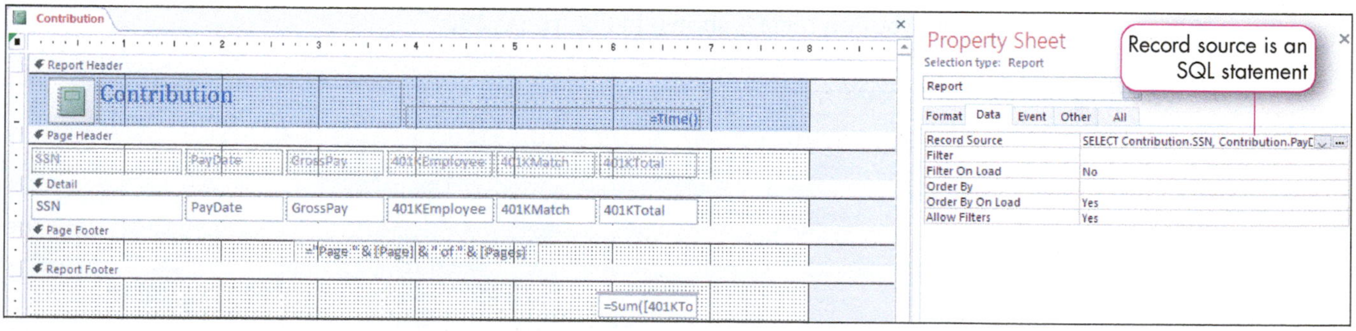

FIGURE 10.30 Contribution Report with SQL Record Source

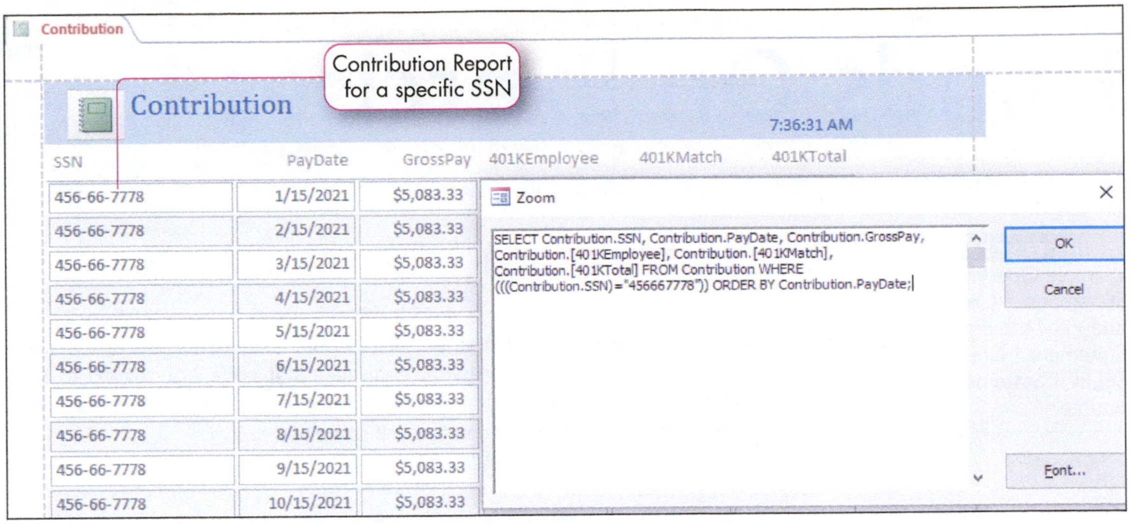

FIGURE 10.31 Contribution Report with Modified SQL Record Source

---

To use an SQL statement as a record source, complete the following steps:

1. Open the report (or form) in Design view and open the Property Sheet.
2. Ensure that Report (or Form) displays in the Selection type box at the top of the Property Sheet.
3. Click the Data tab and click in the Record Source property box.
4. Delete the existing value (for example, Contribution, the underlying table used in the report in Figure 10.30) from the Record Source, and type the SQL statement, such as SELECT Contribution.SSN; etc. in its place. Alternatively, you can copy and paste an SQL statement from the SQL view of a query into the Record Source, as shown in Figure 10.30.
5. Click View in the Views group on the Design tab to display the report in Print Preview (or a form in Form view) to test the change.

TIP: ZOOM TO WORK WITH A LENGTHY SQL STATEMENT
When you paste an SQL statement into a record source, it might appear that the statement will not fit into the record source's property box. However, the Record Source property can hold most SQL statements, including those statements that are very long. Use Shift+F2 to open the Zoom window to view or paste a lengthy SQL statement (as shown in Figure 10.31).

Quick Concepts

7. Discuss the purpose of Structured Query Language (SQL). **p. 578**
8. Review the purpose of the SQL WHERE statement. **p. 580**
9. Explain when you would use an SQL statement as a record source for a report. **p. 582**

Hands-On Exercises

MyLab IT HOE3 Sim Training

Watch the Video for this Hands-On Exercise!

Skills covered: Create a Simple Query with SQL Statements • Create a Query and View the Equivalent SQL Statement • Create an SQL SELECT Statement as a Record Source

3 Structured Query Language

SQL statements will be used in the Sunshine database in special circumstances. You will create two queries in the database. In the first case, you will use SQL statements to create a query; in the next you will create a query in Design view and view the equivalent SQL code. You suggest to Terry that you can use an SQL statement as the record source of a report. You explain that an SQL statement can be used in place of a query as a record source to create a self-contained report.

STEP 1 UNDERSTAND THE FUNDAMENTALS OF SQL

You want a query that will display only employees who are social workers, sorted by hire date, and you have decided to create it in SQL before making any changes to the Sunshine objects. You begin to create a new query and switch to SQL view, where you can practice writing an SQL statement. Refer to Figure 10.32 as you complete Step 1.

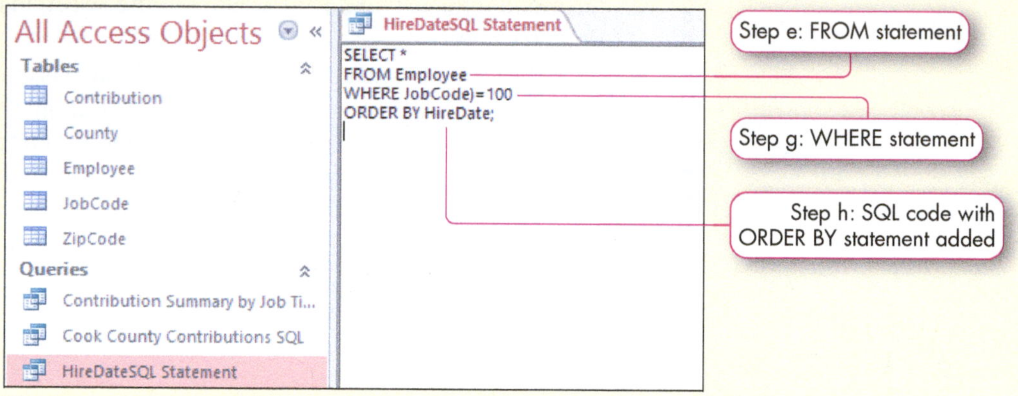

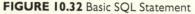

FIGURE 10.32 Basic SQL Statement

a. Open *a10h2Sunshine_LastFirst* if you closed it at the end of Hands-On Exercise 2, and save it as **a10h3Sunshine_LastFirst**, changing h2 to h3.

b. Click **Query Design** in the Queries group on the Create tab.

Query1 opens and the Show Table dialog box displays.

c. Close the Show Table dialog box without adding any tables.

You will create a query using SQL statements rather than the usual query design interface.

d. Click **SQL** in the Results group.

The SELECT statement displays in SQL view of the query window.

e. Move the insertion point after *SELECT* and before the semicolon (;), type * and then press **Enter**. Type **FROM Employee** to complete the SQL statement and click **Run** in the Results group.

The records for all nine employees are displayed in the results. All fields from the Employee table display.

f. Click the **View arrow** in the Views group and select **SQL View**.

The current SQL statement displays in SQL view of the query window.

g. Move the insertion point before the semicolon (;), press **Enter**, revise the SQL statement to add **WHERE JobCode = 100**, and then click **Run**.

You added a WHERE clause to extract only the employees who are social workers (JobCode = 100). Only four employees are displayed in the results.

h. Click the **View arrow** and select **SQL View**. Move the insertion point before the semicolon (;), press **Enter**, revise the SQL statement to add **ORDER BY HireDate**, and then click **Run**.

The same four employees are displayed in the results, except now they display in HireDate order.

i. Save the query with the name **HireDateSQL Statement**. Click the **View arrow** and select **Design View** to view the SQL statement in Design view. Close the query.

You saved an SQL statement as a named query in the database.

STEP 2 **CREATE A QUERY AND VIEW THE EQUIVALENT SQL STATEMENT**

You want to create a query that will show all the 401(k) contributions for Cook County employees. You want to see the equivalent SQL statement after you create the query in Design view. Refer to Figure 10.33 as you complete Step 2.

```
Cook County Contributions SQL
SELECT Contribution.SSN, Contribution.PayDate, Contribution.GrossPay, Contribution.EmployeeContribution, Contribution.CompanyMatch, Contribution.EmployeeTotal, Employee.CountyID
FROM Employee INNER JOIN Contribution ON Employee.SSN = Contribution.SSN
WHERE (((Employee.CountyID)=1))
ORDER BY Contribution.EmployeeTotal DESC;
```
Step f: Query displayed in SQL view

FIGURE 10.33 SQL Statement to Extract Cook County Contributions

a. Click **Query Design** in the Queries group on the Create tab.

b. Add the **Contribution** and **Employee tables** to the query design window and close the Show Table dialog box.

c. Add all six fields from the Contribution table to the query design grid. Add the **CountyID field** from the Employee table. Run the query.

All the fields of all 43 contributions are displayed in the results. You will add the criterion for Cook County.

d. Switch to Design view and type **1** in the CountyID criteria row. Run the query.

The numeral 1 is the Cook County ID and is used as the criterion for the search. Ten contributions now display in the results.

e. Switch to Design view and select **Descending** in the EmployeeTotal sort row. Run the query.

The same ten contributions are now displayed in descending EmployeeTotal order.

f. Switch to SQL view to see the equivalent SQL statement.

You created a query in Design view first and viewed the equivalent SQL statement in SQL view.

g. Save the query as **Cook County Contributions SQL**. Close the query.

Terry asks you to create an employee report in which the JobCode is greater than 150. You decide to create the report based on the Employee table using the Report tool. You will then replace the Employee table record source with an SQL statement to display the results you want. Refer to Figure 10.34 as you complete Step 3.

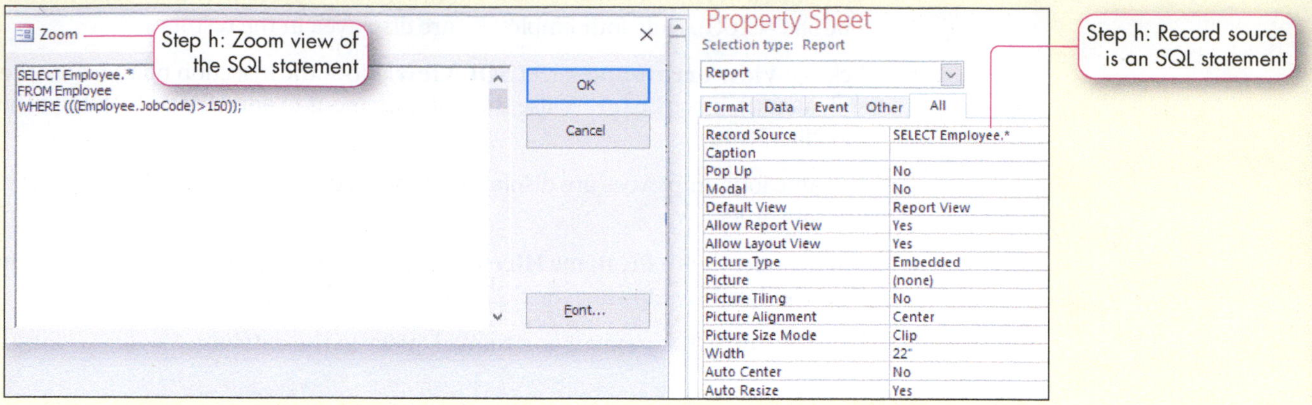

FIGURE 10.34 Report with an SQL Record Source

a. Click the **Employee table** and click **Report** in the Reports group on the Create tab.

   Access creates a new tabular layout report.

b. Switch to Design view, open the Property Sheet, select **Report** in the Selection type box, and then verify that the Record Source on the Data tab for the new report reads *Employee*.

c. Click the **Create tab** and click **Query Design** in the Queries group.

d. Add the **Employee table** to the query design window. Close the Show Table dialog box.

e. Double-click the * field from the Employee table to add it to the query design grid. Run the query.

   Nine employees are displayed in the results.

f. Switch to Design view and double-click to add the **JobCode field** to the second column of the query design grid. Click the **Show box** for JobCode to deselect it and type **>150** in the JobCode Criteria row. Run the query.

   Three employees who match the criterion are displayed in the results.

g. Switch to SQL view, ensure the code is selected, and then press **Ctrl+C** to copy the statement in the SQL window.

h. Click the **Employee report tab** and ensure that the Property Sheet is open. Delete the existing Record Source and press **Ctrl+V** to paste the SQL statement you copied into the box. Press **Shift+F2** and compare your statement with Figure 10.34.

i. Click **OK** to close the Zoom dialog box. Open the report in Print Preview to test the new record source.

   The report does not fit onto one page.

j. Change the orientation to **Landscape**. Close Print Preview, switch to Layout view, and delete the **Address** and **ZipCode** columns. Resize the columns and move the page number control so that all values are visible on the page. Save the report as **Employee Report** and close it.

k. Close the query without saving it.

   The report is self-contained and does not depend on a named query to display the records you want in the results; instead, it uses the SQL statement as the record source.

l. Close the database and exit Access. Based on your instructor's directions, submit a10h3Sunshine_LastFirst.

Chapter Objectives Review

After reading this chapter, you have accomplished the following objectives:

1. Understand the purpose of a macro.

- A macro is an Access object that enables you to execute an action or series of actions. You can use macros to group a series of commands and instructions into a single database object to accomplish repetitive or routine tasks. A macro can be set to run automatically based on the status of a button, a form, or a report.

2. Create a standalone macro.

- A standalone macro displays as an object in the Navigation Pane and can be run independent of other objects. You use the Macro Designer to create a standalone macro. The Macro Designer is a tool in Access that makes it easier to create and edit macros. To run a standalone macro, double-click the macro name in the Navigation Pane.
- Edit a standalone macro in the Macro Designer: After you have created a standalone macro and determined that it works correctly, you can modify, add, or delete actions. You can use the Macro Designer to edit macros in Design view. The user interface simplifies the tasks of adding actions and parameters to pre-existing macros.

3. Attach an embedded macro to an event.

- Embedded macros are attached to an event of a control on a form or report, or to an event of the form or report object itself. They can only be run from within the object.
- Create an embedded macro with the Command Button Wizard: You can add a control that automatically creates an embedded macro by using the Command Button tool to launch a wizard that prompts you through the steps. A command button can be placed on a report that will print the report or close it, for example.
- Create an embedded macro in an event property: You can attach an embedded macro to an event by clicking the ellipsis in the Property Sheet of a specific control and associating the macro name with it.

4. Identify when to use a data macro.

- Data macros are only used with table events. You might add a data macro to a table to verify that a customer has no outstanding invoices before placing a new order, to keep track of any changes made to a specific table, or to send a confirmation email when a contributor makes a donation. A form based on a table that contains a data macro inherits the logic of the table.

5. Create an event-driven data macro.

- Event-driven data macros are triggered when a table event, such as After Delete or Before Change, occurs.
- Test and modify a data macro: To attach a data macro to a table event, open the table you want to add the data macro to (in Design view) and click Create Data Macros in the Field, Record & Table Events group on the Design tab; to modify a data macro, reopen the macro and edit as needed.

6. Create a named data macro.

- You can access named data macros from anywhere in the database. You can run the named data macro from inside another macro using the RunDataMacro action.
- Attach a named data macro to a form: A named data macro can be run from within a form; for example, after a record is updated in a form, a macro that sends an email can be executed.

7. Understand the fundamentals of SQL.

- Structured Query Language (SQL) is the industry-standard language for defining, manipulating, and retrieving the data in a database. In fact, all Access queries use an SQL SELECT statement—behind the scenes—to extract data from tables.

8. Interpret an SQL SELECT statement.

- When you view an SQL SELECT statement in SQL view, the words shown in uppercase are SQL keywords. An SQL keyword defines the purpose and the structure of an SQL statement. The four basic keywords found in a typical SQL SELECT statement are SELECT, FROM, WHERE, and ORDER BY.
- Interpret an SQL SELECT statement—SELECT and FROM keywords: The SELECT keyword instructs Access to return the specific fields from one or more tables (or queries). The FROM keyword specifies the table(s) (or query or queries) that will be searched.
- Interpret an SQL statement—WHERE keyword: The WHERE keyword specifies the criteria that records must match to be included in the results.
- Interpret an SQL statement—ORDER BY keyword: The ORDER BY keyword is used to sort the records by a certain field in either ascending or descending order.
- Explore more advanced SQL statements: The easiest way to learn more advanced SQL statements is to create Access queries in Design view and view the SQL statement in SQL view.

9. Use an SQL SELECT statement as a record source.

- After a query is created using Design view, the SQL statements can be viewed by switching to SQL view. A correlation exists between each SQL statement and a query parameter.
- Create an SQL record source for a report: After you know the basic structure of an SQL statement, you can use the SQL statement to create a record source that can be used as the basis for a report (or a form) rather than a table or a query.
- You can create a form or report without relying on an underlying query because the record source defining the fields and criteria is contained in the object itself.
- Copy an SQL statement from SQL view: Locate the Record Source property of the form or report and either type an SQL statement into the property box or copy and paste a statement from the SQL view window of a query.

Key Terms Matching

Match the key terms with their definitions. Write the key term letter by the appropriate numbered definition.

a. Argument
b. Data macro
c. Embedded macro
d. Event
e. FROM keyword
f. Macro
g. Macro Designer

h. ORDER BY keyword
i. SELECT keyword
j. SQL keyword
k. SQL SELECT statement
l. Standalone macro
m. Structured Query Language (SQL)
n. WHERE keyword

1. _____ A series of actions that can be programmed to automate tasks. **p. 554**

2. _____ A database object that you create and use independently of other controls or objects. **p. 554**

3. _____ A term that describes what occurs when a user enters, edits, or deletes data; also occurs when a user opens, uses, or closes a form or report. **p. 555**

4. _____ A macro that executes when an event attached to a control or object occurs. **p. 555**

5. _____ A user interface that enables you to create and edit macros. **p. 555**

6. _____ A variable, constant, or expression that is needed to produce the output for an action. **p. 555**

7. _____ The industry-standard language for defining, manipulating, and retrieving the data in a database. **p. 578**

8. _____ A keyword that defines the purpose and the structure of an SQL statement. **p. 579**

9. _____ A block of text that is used to retrieve data from the tables in a database. **p. 579**

10. _____ The keyword that specifies the table (or tables) that will be searched. **p. 580**

11. _____ The keyword that instructs Access to return data from specific fields from one or more tables (or queries). **p. 580**

12. _____ The keyword that is used to sort the records by a certain field in either ascending or descending order. **p. 580**

13. _____ The keyword that specifies the criteria that records must match to be included in the results. **p. 580**

14. _____ A macro that executes a series of actions when a table event occurs. **p. 568**

Multiple Choice

1. Which statement about macros is *true*?

   (a) Embedded macros display in the Navigation Pane.

   (b) Macros cannot be used to examine table data.

   (c) The Macro Designer is the only way to automate tasks in Access.

   (d) Standalone macros can be run independent of other objects in the database.

2. Which feature automatically creates an embedded macro in a control?

   (a) Macro Designer

   (b) Command Button Wizard

   (c) Data Macro Wizard

   (d) Form Wizard

3. Which statement is *true* about standalone macros?

   (a) Standalone macros are created with the Macro Designer.

   (b) Standalone macros exist outside the database.

   (c) Standalone macros require knowledge of VBA code.

   (d) Standalone macros can only be used with table data.

4. Which of these terms describes when a user enters, edits, or deletes data in a table or a form?

   (a) Command

   (b) Statement

   (c) Argument

   (d) Event

5. Which statement is *false* for a named data macro?

   (a) It must be created in a table.

   (b) It cannot be attached to an event.

   (c) It can be modified using the Macro Designer.

   (d) It can be referenced using RunDataMacro.

6. Which of the following events can automatically trigger a macro to run?

   (a) Updating a record

   (b) Creating a report

   (c) Clicking a command on the ribbon

   (d) Sorting a table

7. Which statement is *true* about SQL?

   (a) It was originally invented to create formatted reports.

   (b) When you create a query, SQL is created automatically.

   (c) FROM statements sort data from tables.

   (d) SQL code can only be created using a special developer's interface.

8. Which SQL keyword sorts records based on a criterion?

   (a) SELECT

   (b) FROM

   (c) WHERE

   (d) ORDER BY

9. Which is a macro that performs actions related to a table and can be run from within another macro?

   (a) Data macro

   (b) Embedded macro

   (c) Named data macro

   (d) Standalone macro

10. Which of the following is *not* a valid record source for a report?

   (a) A form

   (b) An SQL SELECT statement

   (c) A table

   (d) A query

Practice Exercises

1 Advertising Specialists, Inc.

Advertising Specialists, Inc. is a leading advertising agency with offices in Atlanta, Chicago, Miami, and Boston. The company asked you to create a new form named Chicago Employees that only displays employees located in Chicago. You will use an SQL statement as the record source for the form and create a macro to close the form and display a message. You have also been asked to create a menu that users can use to open the three reports and one form. You decide to use the Form Design tool to create a menu from scratch. Creating a menu from scratch to navigate around the database offers an opportunity for total customization and control over your design. Refer to Figure 10.35 as you complete this exercise.

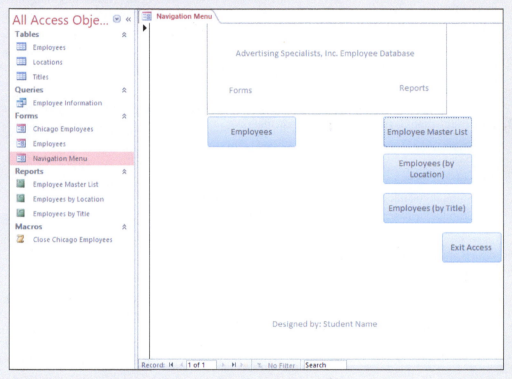

FIGURE 10.35 Menu Created with Command Buttons

a. Open *a10p1Advertise* and save it as **a10p1Advertise_LastFirst.**

b. Open the Employees table, and add yourself as a new record. Type **88888** as your EmployeeID. Type your last name, first name, and gender. Use the same values as the previous record (Marder) to complete the remaining fields. Close the table.

c. Open the Employees form in Design view. Click the **File tab**, click **Save As**, click **Save Object As**, and then click **Save As**. Type **Chicago Employees** in the Save As dialog box and click **OK**. You will create a form that displays only Chicago employees.

d. Ensure that the Property Sheet is open, click the **Data tab**, and then click in the **Record Source property box**. Press **Shift+F2** to see a zoom view of the record source property.

e. Type **Select * From Employees Where LocationID="L03";** in the Record Source property to replace the existing Employees table with an SQL statement as the record source. Include the ending semicolon (;). Click **OK**.

f. Save the form and switch to Form view. Advance through all the records to verify that only Chicago location (L03) employees are displayed.

g. Add a command button that will close the Chicago Employees form by creating a macro as follows:
  * Click **Macro** in the Macros & Code group on the Create tab.
  * Enter **RunMenuCommand** in the Add New Action box. Press **Enter**.

- Enter **Close** in the Command box.
- Save the macro as **Close Chicago Employees**.
- Close the Macro Designer.
- Right-click the macro in the Navigation Pane and select **Design View** from the shortcut menu.
- Select **MessageBox** in the Add New Action box.
- Type **Thank you for your attention to detail.** (include the period) in the Message box. Press **Enter**.
- Select **Information** in the Type box.
- Type **Thank you!** in the Title box. Press **Enter**.
- Enter **CloseWindow** in the Add New Action box.
- Enter **Form** in the Object Type box.
- Enter **Chicago Employees** in the Object Name box. Ensure that *Prompt* displays in the Save box.
- Save and close the macro.

h. Switch to Design view of the Chicago Employees form. Drag the **Close Chicago Employees macro** from the Navigation Pane into the Form Header and drop it so that its left edge aligns with the 5-inch mark on the horizontal ruler. Resize the command button to a width of 1.75 inches so that all of the text displays.

i. Save the form and switch to Form view. Click the **Close Chicago Employees button** and when the message box displays, click **OK**.

j. Open the **Employee Master List report** in Design view. Ensure that the Property Sheet is open, and note that the record source is the Employee Information query.

k. Open the **Employee Information query** and switch to SQL view.

l. Copy the entire SQL statement from the query window, including the ending semicolon (;). Paste the SQL statement into the Record Source property box of the Employee Master List report, replacing *Employee Information*.

m. Switch to Report view of the Employee Master List report. Save and close the report, and then close the query.

n. Click **Form Design** in the Forms group on the **Create tab**.

o. Add the following labels, using Figure 10.35 as a guide:
- A title label: **Advertising Specialists, Inc., Employee Database**
- A subtitle label: **Forms**
- A subtitle label: **Reports**

p. Click **Button** in the Controls group on the Design tab. Use the Command Button Wizard to add the following buttons, using Figure 10.35 as a guide:
- A button to open the Employees form. Set the text to display on the button as **Employees** and name the button **cmdEmployees**. Adjust the button position and size as shown.
- A button to open the Employee Master List report. Set the text to display on the button as **Employee Master List** and name the button **cmdMasterEmployee**. Adjust the button position and size as shown.
- A button to open the Employees by Location report. Set the text to display on the button as **Employees (by Location)** and name the button **cmdEmployeesLocation**. Adjust the button position and size as shown.
- A button to open the Employees by Title report. Set the text to display on the button as **Employees (by Title)** and name the button **cmdEmployeesTitle**. Adjust the button position and size as shown.

q. Add the following button, using Figure 10.35 as a guide:
- A button to quit the application. Set the text to display on the button as **Exit Access** and name the button **cmdExitAccess**.
- Adjust the button position and size as shown.

r. Add the following design elements, using Figure 10.35 as a guide:
- A rectangle surrounding the title and the subtitle labels
- A label at the bottom of the report: **Designed by: your name**

s. Save the form with the name **Navigation Menu**.

t. View the Menu form in Form view. Click each button to test the functionality. Click the **Exit Access button** to test it; if Access closes, then your testing is complete.

u. Ensure that the database and Access are closed. Based on your instructor's directions, submit a10p1Advertise_LastFirst.

2 Reliable Insurance, Inc.

Reliable Insurance, Inc. has decided to raise the salary of any employee with a good performance rating by 5% and that of an average employee by 2.5%. You will create a data macro to help implement this new policy. The company also creates a PDF file containing all employees from location L02 (Boston). The report is sent to the corporate office each month. The office manager wants to automate this process with a macro. Refer to Figure 10.36 as you complete this exercise.

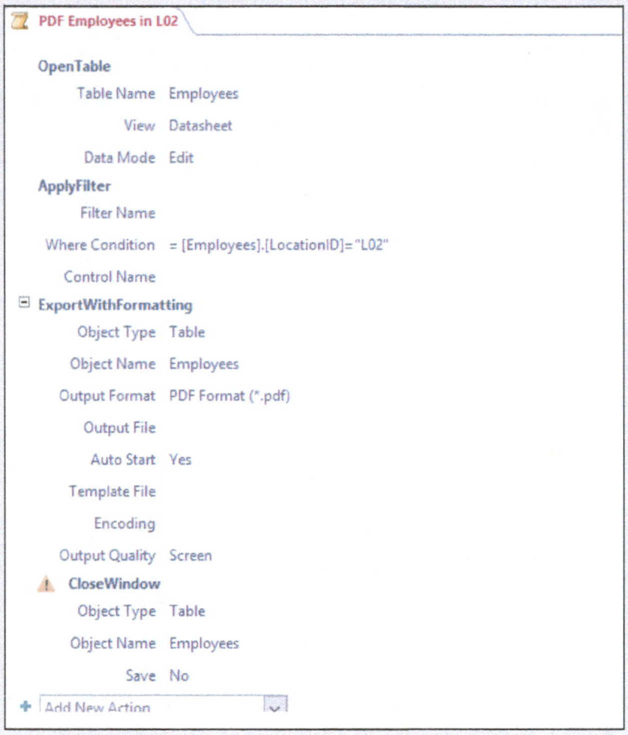

FIGURE 10.36 Macro to Export Data to Excel

a. Open *a10p2Reliable* and save it as **a10p2Reliable_LastFirst**.

b. Open the Employees table, and add yourself as a new record. Type **88888** as your EmployeeID. Type your last name, first name, and gender. Type **L01** for your location. Use the same values as the previous record (Marder) to complete the remaining fields.

c. Switch to Design view, and add a new field under the Salary field, named **SalaryAdjusted**, with data type **Currency**. Save the table.

d. Click **Create Data Macros** in the Field, Record & Table Events group on the Design tab and select **Before Change**. The Macro Designer opens. Complete the following steps:
- Drag the **If statement** from the Program Flow folder in the Action Catalog to the Add New Action box in the macro.
- Type **[Performance]="Good"** in the Conditional expression box.
- Select **SetField** from the Add New Action arrow within the If action.
- Type **SalaryAdjusted** in the Name box.
- Type **[Salary]*.05+[Salary]** in the Value box.

- Save and close the data macro.
- Click **Create Data Macros** in the Field, Record & Table Events group on the Design tab and select **Before Change**. The Macro Designer reopens so that you can modify the macro.
- Click in the **If action** and click the **Add Else hyperlink**.
- Drag the **If statement** from the Program Flow folder in the Action Catalog to the Add New Action box in the macro.
- Type **[Performance]="Average"** in the Conditional expression box.
- Select **SetField** using the Add New Action arrow.
- Type **SalaryAdjusted** in the Name box.
- Type **[Salary]*.025+[Salary]** in the Value box.
- Save and close the data macro. Save the table.

e. Switch to Datasheet view. Retype **Good** in the Performance field of the third employee (Johnson). Press ↓ to move to the next record and activate the data macro.

The new increased salary displays in the SalaryAdjusted field.

f. Repeat the process for all employees rated Good, upgrade your own performance value from Average to **Good**, and press ↓. Close the table.

g. Click **Macro** in the Macros & Code group on the **Create tab** to open the Macro Designer. You will create a macro to display employees in location L02.

h. Click in the **Add New Action box** and type **OpenTable**. Press **Enter**.

i. Add the following arguments:

Table Name	**Employees**
View	**Datasheet**
Data Mode	**Edit**

j. Click in the **Add New Action box** and type **ApplyFilter**. Press **Enter**.

k. Add the following arguments:

Filter Name	*(blank)*
Where Condition	**[Employees].[LocationID]="L02"**
Control Name	*(blank)*

l. Save the macro as **PDF Employees in L02**. Click **Run** in the Tools group to test the macro results so far. If the macro is working, the Employees table should open with only the L02 employees displayed. If not, open the macro in Design view to make necessary corrections and run the macro again. Close the filtered Employees table.

m. Click in the **Add New Action box** and type **ExportWithFormatting**. Press **Enter**.

n. Add the following arguments:

Object Type	**Table**
Object Name	**Employees**
Output Format	**PDF Format (*.pdf)**
Output File	*(blank)*
Auto Start	**Yes**
Template File	*(blank)*
Encoding	*(blank)*
Output Quality	Screen

o. Click in the **Add New Action box** and type **CloseWindow**. Press **Enter**.

p. Add the following arguments:

Object Type	Table
Object Name	Employees
Save	No

q. Save the macro. Close the macro. You will test the macro when all data entries are completed.

r. Open the **Employees table**. Navigate to Record 9 (Mark Brown), select **Poor** in the Performance field, type **Average**, and then press **Tab** until Record 10 is selected.

s. Navigate back to Record 9 and note that because Mark's performance rating is Average, his adjusted salary is increased when calculated by the data macro. For each employee where there is no adjusted salary, retype the Performance value and move to the next record. All employees with Average or Good ratings will receive salary increases. Close the Employees table.

t. Run the **PDF Employees in L02 macro** by double-clicking the macro name in the Navigation Pane. The results should export the L02 (Boston) employees to a PDF file. Save the file as **Boston Employees**. Close the reader window, and the macro closes the Employees table.

u. Close the database and exit Access. Based on your instructor's directions, submit a10p2Reliable_LastFirst.

Mid-Level Exercises

1   Northwind Exporters

Northwind Exporters provides specialty foods to businesses around the world. You have been asked to filter the Orders form so that each employee can see only his or her orders. You will also filter a report using an SQL statement.

a. Open *a10m1Exporters* and save it as **a10m1Exporters_LastFirst**.

b. Open the Employees table and note that nine employees are shown. Close the table.

c. Open the Orders form. Advance through the orders using the Next record button at the bottom of the form. Notice that the EmployeeID value changes as you move to each order. Switch to Design view.

d. Click the **1 button** on the form. Notice that the records in the form are filtered so that only orders for EmployeeID 1 are displayed.

e. Add a second button to the form in Design view, approximately three dots to the right and top-aligned with the first button. Click **Cancel** when the Command Button Wizard displays. Open the Property Sheet. Set the caption of the command button to **2**. Set the size of the button to **.25"** high and **.25"** wide.

You will create an embedded macro to filter the order records for EmployeeID 2 when the command button is clicked.

f. Ensure that the new 2 button is selected, and in the Property Sheet, click in the **On Click property box** on the Event tab. Click the **ellipsis**, and with Macro Builder selected, click **OK**.

g. Type **ApplyFilter** in the Add New Action box. Type **[EmployeeID]=2** in the Where Condition box. Save and close the macro.

h. Switch to Form view. Click **2** and notice the total orders (5) for EmployeeID 2 in the Current Record box. Advance through the orders and verify the EmployeeID is 2 for each order.

i. Switch to Design view, copy the **2 button**, paste it approximately three dots to the right and top-aligned with the second button, and then set **3** as the caption. In the Property Sheet, with button 3 selected, click in the **On Click property box**, and then click the **ellipsis**. Modify the Where Condition box so it reads **3** instead of *2*. Test the new button in Form view.

j. Add buttons 4 to 6 using the same method as in Step i.

k. Create a seventh button with the caption **Remove Filters** and a width of **1.25"** to remove the filters so that all the orders will display in the form. Locate the appropriate action in the Add New Action list.

l. Test each new button in Form view when finished and save the form.

m. Switch to Design view. Select the seven buttons. Click **Align** in the Sizing & Ordering group on the Arrange tab to align the tops of the seven buttons. Ensure that the horizontal spacing between the buttons is such that about three dots of space remain between each. Save and close the form.

n. Open the Customers report and take note of the range of countries represented.

o. Switch to Design view. Ensure that the Property Sheet is open, select the report, and then, on the Data tab, click the **Record Source property**. Type **SELECT * FROM Customers WHERE Country = [Enter a country];** in the record source in place of the Customers table.

p. Save the report. Switch to Print Preview and type **Switzerland** in the Enter Parameter Value dialog box. Click **OK** and close the report.

q. Close the database and exit Access. Based on your instructor's directions, submit a10m1Exporters_LastFirst.

2 Payroll Service, Inc.

ANALYSIS CASE

Payroll Service, Inc. provides payroll services to midsized businesses in Massachusetts, Illinois, Colorado, and California. You have been assigned to help the company set up business logic rules using macros and data macros. Your first task is to set the default number of exemptions an employee can claim (based on marital status). You begin by setting single employees to claim only one exemption. You will also create a macro that will email the current list of employees to the main office. The main office needs the list in HTML format. Finally, you will create an SQL record source for a report.

a. Open *a10m2Salaries* and save it as **a10m2Salaries_LastFirst**.

b. Open the Employee table in Design view. Click **Create Data Macros** in the Field, Record & Table Events group, and click **Before Change**.

c. Drag the **If statement** from the Program Flow folder in the Action Catalog to the Add New Action box in the macro.
   - Type [**MaritalStatus**]="**single**" in the If action box.
   - Select **SetField** from the Add New Action arrow.
   - Type **Exemptions** in the Name box.
   - Type **1** in the Value box.
   - Save and close the data macro.
   - Save the table.

d. Switch to Datasheet view. In the first record, type **2** in the Exemptions field. Press ↓ to move to the second row to trigger the Before Change event and the data macro. The number *2* changes to *1*. Repeat the test on the second record. Close the table.

e. Click the **Create tab** and click **Macro** in the Macros & Code group to open the Macro Designer.

f. Click in the **Add New Action box** and type **EMailDatabaseObject**. Press **Enter**.

g. Add the following arguments:

Object Type	Table
Object Name	Employee
Output Format	HTML (*.htm; *.html)
To	Your email address
Cc	(*blank*)
Bcc	(*blank*)
Subject	Email Employee Table
Message Text	The Employee table is attached in HTML format.
Edit Message	No
Template File	(*blank*)

h. Save the macro with the name **Email Table**. Close the macro.

i. Double-click the **Email Table macro**. The macro runs and attempts to send the Employee table as an attachment. Click **OK** if you receive the Microsoft Outlook warning message, as shown in Figure 10.25. Click **OK** again and click **Stop All Macros**. If the warning message was not received, click **Allow**. Check your email after a few minutes to see if you received the Email Employee Table message.

j. Open the Salaries by Gender report in Design view. Open the Property Sheet and verify the Record Source property contains Employee. Determine from the database which job code refers to which job title. Note the job code for Associate Consultant and the data type for this field, which you will use in the next step.

k. Type an SQL statement into the Record Source property. The report should include all records from the Employee table except Associate Consultants. Switch to Print Preview, and verify the report contains 10 records with the overall average salary of $79,650.00. Set the report to **Landscape orientation**. Save the report. Close the report.

l. Close the database and exit Access. Based on your instructor's directions, submit a10m2Salaries_LastFirst.

Running Case

New Castle County Technical Services

New Castle County Technical Services (NCCTS) provides technical support for a number of companies in the greater New Castle County, Delaware area. Now that you have completed Chapter 10, you are ready to work with macros and SQL.

a. Open the database *a10r1NCCTS* and save it as **a10r1NCCTS_LastFirst**.

b. Open the **Archived Calls table** in Datasheet view, observe the data, and then switch to Design view.

c. Add a new field named **Satisfied** to the last position in the table with a data type of **Yes/No**. Save the table.

d. Create a data macro attached to the Before Change event.

e. Use the SetField Action to populate the Satisfied field in the table. The Satisfied value will be set to **Yes** if the CustomerSatisfaction field contains a value of 3 or more. Otherwise, the Satisfied field will be set to **No**.

f. Save the macro. Close the macro. Save the table.

g. Switch to Datasheet view. For CallID 001, retype the Customer Satisfaction value as **5**, the next as **3**, the next as **2**, and the next as **1**. Modify the value for CallID 005 from 5 to **4** and click in the next record. Observe that the Satisfied field updates automatically as the values are entered. Close the table.

h. Open the **Customer Information form**, observe the data, and switch to Design view. Add an **Open Calls by Customer button** to the top-right corner of the form at the 0" mark on the vertical ruler and the 8.25" mark on the horizontal ruler, with a height of **0.5"** and a width of **1.7"**.

i. Set the button to open the Calls by Customer report and name the button **cmdOpenCalls**.

j. Save the form, switch to Form view, and then click the **Open Calls by Customer button** to ensure that the report opens. Close the report and the form.

k. Open the **Calls by Customer report** in Design view. Open the Property Sheet and click the **Record Source property box**. Right-click in the property box, and from the shortcut menu, select **Zoom**.

l. Add a WHERE clause to the end of the existing SQL statement that selects records from the Calls table with a customer satisfaction rating of less than 3.

m. Test the report in Print Preview, ensure that all Customer Satisfaction values are below 3, and save and close the report.

n. Close the database and exit Access. Based on your instructor's directions, submit a10r1NCCTS_LastFirst

Disaster Recovery

Troubleshoot: Fix a Macro

Open *a10d1Bonus* database and save it as **a10d1Bonus_LastFirst**. A macro named Macro—Open Objects was created to open the Employees table, the Employees Form, and the Employees Report. The macro is not working properly; the third object does not display at all, and the first two objects are read-only—you want them to open in Edit mode. Analyze the macro and fix it so that the first two objects open as required, and the report opens when the macro runs. Save and run the macro to ensure that it works properly. Based on your instructor's directions, submit a10d1Bonus_LastFirst.

Capstone Exercise

Specialty Foods

You are employed at Specialty Foods, Ltd., a small international gourmet foods distributor. The company asked you to modify the database and improve the reliability of the data entry process. You decide to create a few macros and add a menu for the common forms and reports. You will also modify the record source of one of the reports.

Create an Event-Driven Data Macro

1. Open *a10c1Specialty* and save it as **a10c1Specialty_LastFirst**.
2. Open the **Orders table** in Design view. Add a new field, **ExpectedShipDate** with the data type **Date/Time** below the OrderDate field. You will populate this new field when a new order is added using a data macro. Save the table.
3. Switch to Datasheet view, observe the data, and then switch back to Design view.
4. Create a data macro attached to the Before Change event.
5. Use the **SetField Action** to populate the ExpectedShipDate in the table. The ExpectedShipDate will always be five days after the OrderDate.
6. Save the macro. Close the macro. Save the table.

Test the Data Macro

You will change a value in the first record and then move to the second record to trigger the macro.

7. Switch to Datasheet view of the Orders table.
8. Retype the OrderDate in the first record (Order No 10248), and press ↓. The macro will be triggered and automatically fill in the ExpectedShipDate with a date five days after the OrderDate.
9. Repeat the test on the second and third records (10249 and 10250). Close the table.

Modify a Menu Form

You will modify a menu form using Form Design view; add three command buttons for the three forms in the database, and then add three command buttons for the three reports in the database.

10. Open the Main Menu form in Design view.
11. Add three buttons below the Forms label that will open the three forms in the database: **Enter Customers**, **Enter Orders**, and **Enter Suppliers** (in that order). Set the first one at the **2"** mark on the vertical ruler and the **1"** mark on the horizontal ruler. Set the height of the button to **0.5"** and the width to **1"**. The first button should have the caption **Enter Customers** with the button named as **cmdEnterCustomers**.

12. Repeat the same procedure for **Enter Orders** and **Enter Suppliers**, setting each button immediately below the one before it.
13. Add three buttons below the Reports label that will print preview the three reports in the database: **Employees**, **Orders**, and **Products** (in that order). Set the first one at the **2"** mark on the vertical ruler and the **4"** mark on the horizontal ruler. Set the height of the button to **0.5"** and the width to **1"**. The first button should have the caption **Employees** with the button named as **cmdEmployees**.
14. Repeat the same procedure for **Orders** and **Products**, setting each button immediately below the one before it.
15. Save the form, switch to Form view, and then test the buttons. Close all objects except the Main Menu form.
16. Switch to Design view, add a **Close Database button** that exits Access at the top-right corner of the form, at the **0"** mark on the vertical ruler and the **5"** mark on the horizontal ruler, with a height of **0.5"** and a width of **1"**. Name the button **cmdExit**.
17. Modify the embedded macro in the **On Click property** of the cmdExit button. Add a **MessageBox action** to the macro to display the message, **Please check all updates before exiting!** and set the Type to **Information**. Move the action up to before the QuitAccess action. Change the option under QuitAccess from *Prompt* to **Exit**. Save and close the macro.
18. Save the form, switch to Form view, and then set the **Main Menu** form to display when the database opens. Test the **Close Database button**. Reopen the database.

Add an SQL Statement as a Record Source

You want to modify the records displayed in the Employees report. You will modify the record source so that only employees who live in London display in the report.

19. Open the Employees report in Design view. Open the Property Sheet and click in the **Record Source property box**.
20. Type an SQL statement into the Record Source property of the report. The statement should select all fields (*) for employees in London. Save the report.
21. Test the report in Print Preview and close the report.
22. Close the database and exit Access. Based on your instructor's directions, submit a10c1Specialty_LastFirst.

Access Application Capstone Exercise (Chs. 1–4)

MyLab IT Grader

You were recently hired by your local college to help with registering all transfer students. The college's Transfer Advising Department is a one-stop location for transfer students to come with questions. They have been working with Excel spreadsheets generated by the Information Technology department, but they are hoping to do more with an Access database. They have had a number of problems, including employees putting information in the wrong fields, putting information in the wrong format, and creating incorrect formulas. They are also hoping for more consistent ways of finding information, as well as being able to generate reports. Your tasks include importing an existing Excel worksheet as a table into your Access database; modifying the table; creating a relationship between two tables; creating queries with calculated fields, functions, and totals; creating a form for input and one for navigation; creating a report; and backing up the database.

Open a Database and Import from External Sources

To start, you have been provided with a database the Information Technology department created. The database has one table and one form. You will be importing an Excel spreadsheet into a table and creating a primary key.

1. Open *aApp_Cap1_Advising* and save the database as **aApp_Cap1_Advising_LastFirst**.
2. Import the *aApp_Cap1_Transfer.xlsx* Excel workbook into a new table named **Transfer Schools**. While importing the data, ensure that *StudentID* has a data type of Short Text and select **StudentID** as the primary key.

Modify a Table in Design View

Now that you have imported the data from the workbook, you will modify the field properties in the Transfer Schools table and demonstrate sorting.

3. Open the Transfer Schools table in Design view.
4. Set the field size for the StudentID field to **10** and remove the @ symbol from the format property. Change the AdmittingSchool field size to **75** and change the RegistrationFee and TuitionDue fields to have **0** decimal places.
5. Switch to Datasheet view. Resize the AdmittingSchool column by double-clicking on the border between AdmittingSchool and AdmissionDate.
6. Sort the Transfer Schools table on the CreditsTransferred field in ascending order.
7. Save and close the table.

Create Relationships

Now that the table is imported and modified, you will create a relationship between the Transfer Schools and Transfer Students tables.

8. Add the Transfer Schools and Transfer Students tables to the Relationships window.
9. Create a one-to-one relationship between the StudentID field in the Transfer Students table and the StudentID field in the Transfer Schools table. Enforce referential integrity between the two tables and cascade updates.
10. Save the changes and close the Relationships window.

Modify Data in a Form

You will demonstrate changing information in a form.

11. Open the Transfer Students Data Entry form.
12. Locate the record for *Ellen Sullivan* and change her major to **History**. Close the form.

Create a Multitable Query

Adam McChesney, an adviser in the center, wants your assistance in helping him find certain information. You will create a query for him and demonstrate how he can change information.

13. Create a new query. From the Transfer Students table, add the FirstName, LastName, Major, Class, and GPA fields. From the Transfer Schools table, add the AdmissionDate, TuitionDue, CreditsEarned, and CreditsTransferred fields.

14. Set the criteria in the AdmissionDate field to **1/1/2021**. Save the query as **Transfer Credits**. Run the query (19 records will display).

15. Enter the TuitionDue for Bianca Bain as **$2200** and the GPA for Edgar Conway as **3.65**.

16. Save and close the query.

Create Calculated Fields

You will create a second query for Adam that will calculate the number of credits students lost upon transfer, the tuition payments for which they will be responsible (assuming three payments per semester), and the due date of the first payment.

17. Create a copy of the Transfer Credits query. Name the copy **Transfer Calculations**. Remove the criteria from the AdmissionDate field.

18. Create a calculated field named **LostCredits** that subtracts CreditsTransferred from CreditsEarned.

19. Create another calculated field named **TuitionPayments** that uses the payment function and determines tuition paid in four quarterly installments. The student's tuition payment and a 2.5% interest rate should be used in the function. Use **0** for the future_value and type arguments. Ensure that the payment appears as a positive number. Format the TuitionPayments calculated field as **Currency**.

20. Create another calculated field named **FirstPayment** that adds 30 to the admission date. Run the query and verify that the three calculated fields have valid data. Expand the fields to ensure the data is visible.

21. Add a Total row to the datasheet. Sum the TuitionDue column and average the TuitionPayment column. Save and close the query.

Create a Totals Query

Cala Hajjar, the director of the center, wants summarized information about the transfer students for the 2020–2021 academic year to present to the College's Board of Trustees. You will create a totals query for her to summarize the number of transfer students, average number of credits earned and transferred, and total tuition earned by transfer institution.

22. Create a query using the Transfer Schools table; add the AdmittingSchool, StudentID, CreditsEarned, CreditsTransferred, and TuitionDue fields.

23. Sort the query by AdmittingSchool in ascending order.

24. Show the Total row. Group by AdmittingSchool and show the count of StudentID, the average of CreditsEarned, the average of CreditsTransferred, and the sum of TuitionDue. Format both average fields as **Standard**.

25. Change the caption for the StudentID field to **NumStudents**, the caption for the CreditsEarned average to **AvgCreditsEarned**, the caption for the CreditsTransferred average to **AvgCredits Transferred**, and the caption for the sum of TuitionDue to **TotalTuition**.

26. Widen the columns in the query Datasheet view to ensure all column captions are fully visible. Save the query as **Transfer Summary**. Close the query.

Create a Form

Hideo Sasaki, the department's administrative assistant, will handle data entry. He asked you to simplify the way he inputs information into the new table. You will create a form based on the new Transfer Schools table.

27. Create a Split Form using the Transfer Schools table as the source.

28. Change the height of the AdmittingSchool field to be approximately half the current height. Remove the layout from all the labels and fields. Shrink each field so it is approximately as large as it needs to be.

29. Click record **123455** in the bottom half of the split form. Make sure all fields are still visible in the top half of the form. If not, adjust the controls so all values are visible.

30. Move the CreditsTransferred field so it is to the right of the CreditsEarned field on the same row. Move the RegistrationFee field so it is just below the CreditsEarned field. Move the TuitionDue field so it is just below the CreditsTransferred field.

31. Change the title of the form to **Transfer Schools Overview** and save the form as **Transfer Schools Form**. Close the form.

Create a Report

Cala is hoping you can create a more print-friendly version of the query you created earlier for her to distribute to the Board of Trustees. You will create a report based on the Transfer Calculations query.

32. Create a report using the Report Wizard. Add the **Major**, **FirstName**, **LastName**, **Class**, **GPA**, and **LostCredits** fields from the Transfer Calculations query. Do not add any grouping or sorting. Ensure that the report is in Landscape orientation.

33. Save the report as **Transfer Students Report** and view the report in Layout view.

Format a Report

Now that you have included the fields Cala asked for, you will work to format the report to make the information more obvious.

34. Apply the **Wisp theme**.

35. Group the report by the Major field. Sort the records within each group by LastName then by FirstName, both in ascending order.

36. Adjust the text boxes so the values for the Major field are completely visible.

37. Switch to Print Preview mode and verify that the report is only one page wide (Note: it may be a number of pages long).

38. Export the results as a PDF document saving the file as **aApp_Cap1_Transfer_LastFirst.pdf**.

39. Save and close the report.

Close and Submit the Database

40. Create a backup of the database. Accept the default name for the backup.

41. Close all database objects and exit Access.

42. Based on your instructor's directions, submit the following:

aApp_Cap1_Advising_LastFirst

aApp_Cap1_Advising_LastFirst_*CurrentDate*

aApp_Cap1_Transfer_LastFirst.pdf

Access Comprehensive Application Capstone Exercise (Chs. 5–10)

Insurance Brokers

You have been hired by ABC Insurance Brokers Co. to begin to develop a database to track drivers and their associated insurance data. A small database has been created, and you will continue to add data and features to it. In this project, you will add fields to a table and set data validation rules. You will also import a text file into a database, design advanced queries, and create a navigation form. Additionally, you will use SQL to modify a record source and create an embedded macro to automate opening a report You will add a chart to a report to compare license issue years.

Import a Text File into the Database

You have discovered that the insurance company data you want is stored in an external text file, so you will import the file as a table into the database, and not need to design the table from scratch.

1. Start Access. Open the file named *aApp_Cap2_Drivers* and save it as **aApp_Cap2_Drivers_LastFirst**.
2. Create a table in the database by importing the delimited text file named *aApp_Cap2_Insurance_Text.txt*. Use the first row of the file as field names, use **InsuranceID** as the primary key, and then name the table **InsuranceCos_Text**. Accept all other default options. Do not save the import steps.

Modify a Table

You will modify a table to add fields that store the websites and photos of agents, add a lookup field, and set data validation to ensure that valid values are entered in a field.

3. Create a new field in the **Agency Info table** after *InsPhone* named **Website** with the **Hyperlink data type**. In Datasheet view, add the website **http://William_Smith.com** to the William Smith record.
4. Create a new field in the Agency Info table after *Website* named **AgentPhoto** with the **Attachment data type**. In Datasheet view, in the William Smith record, add the picture file named *aApp_Cap2_WmSmith.jpg* to the **AgentPhoto field**.
5. Set the validation rule of the **InsuranceCo field** to accept the values **AS**, **NAT**, or **SF** only. Set the validation text to read **Please enter AS, NAT, or SF.** (include the period).
6. Make **InsuranceCo** a lookup field in the Agency Info table. Set the lookup to get values from the **InsuranceID field** in the InsuranceCos_Text table. Accept the default label and save the table. In Datasheet view, select the first **InsuranceCo value**, type **AT** and press **Enter**. When the message box displays, click **OK**. Click the **arrow** to view the options, select **AS** from the list, and then press the **down arrow** to save the record. Close the table.

Create Queries to Analyze, Update, and Delete Records

You will create queries to locate records that have missing values, update values in a table, and delete specific records from the database.

7. Create a new query using Design view. From the Insurance table, add the **DriverID**, **AutoType**, **TagID**, and **TagExpiration fields** (in that order). Save the query as **Missing Tag Dates**.
8. Set the criteria in the **TagExpiration field** to find null values. Run the query (two records will display). Save and close the query.

9. Create a new query using Design view. From the Drivers table, add the **Class field**. Change the query type to **Update** and set the criteria to update drivers whose class is *Minor* to **Junior**. Run the query (eight records will update). Save the query as **Driver Class_Update**. Run the query again and note that there are no records to update. Close the query. View the updates in the Drivers table and close the table.

10. Create a new query using Design view. From the Drivers table, add the **Class field**. Save the query as **Driver Class_Delete**.

11. Change the query type to **Delete** and set the criteria to delete drivers whose class is **Special**. Run the query (one record will be deleted). Save and close the query. View the changes in the Drivers table and close the table.

Create a Query to Prompt for Data

Creating a query to prompt for a value enables you to display results dynamically based on user input. You will create a query that outputs data based on the year entered at the prompt.

12. Create a new query using Design view. From the Insurance table, add the **InsuranceAgentID**, **AutoType**, **AutoYear**, and **TagID fields** (in that order). Save the query as **Agent_Parameter**.

13. Set the criteria in the **InsuranceAgentID field** to display the prompt as **Enter the Agent ID:** and run the query. In the parameter prompt, enter **AS8842**, and click **OK** to view the results (two records). Save and close the query.

Use the Performance Analyzer

The Performance Analyzer makes suggestions as to how a selected table can be made more efficient or to work better with other tables in the database.

14. Use the Analyze Performance tool to analyze the Drivers table. Note the idea to change the data type of the Weight field from Short Text to Long Integer. Close the Performance Analyzer dialog box. In the Drivers table, set the data type of the **Weight field** to **Number (Long Integer)**, then save and close the table.

Create a Navigation Form

A navigation form enables users to select key objects in the database in a user-friendly manner. The form will launch automatically to present the frequently used forms and report to end users.

15. Create a **Navigation Form** based on the **Vertical Tabs, Left template**. Drag and drop the **Drivers form** onto the first tab of the form. Drop the **Insurance form** onto the second tab.

16. Drag and drop the **Drivers report** onto the third tab of the Navigation form. View the form in Form view, click each of the tabs, and then save the form as **Navigator**. Close the form.

17. Set the option in the database so that the Navigator form launches automatically when the database opens. Close the database and reopen it to ensure that the Navigator form opens. Close the form.

Add an SQL Statement as a Record Source in a Report and Create an Embedded Macro in a Form

You will modify the record source of a report to display specific records. The report will not rely on an underlying query to select records; the criteria is handled by the SQL statement. You will add a command button to a form that will open a form with associated records.

18. Open the Drivers report in Design view. Modify the record source of the report using a SQL statement to select all **Drivers records** with a Class of **Adult**. Print Preview the report (eight records will display).

19. Modify the SQL record source to display **Junior** drivers. Print Preview the report (eight records will display). Save and close the report.

20. Open the Drivers form in Design view, click to add a **command button** at the intersection of the 6-inch mark on the horizontal ruler and the 3-inch mark on the vertical ruler.

21. Set the command button to open the Insurance form. Use the default picture as the button. Set the name and the caption of the button to **Open Insurance Form**. Set the width of the button to **1.5"**. Save the form. View the form in Form view and click the **command button**. Use the Find command in the Insurance form to locate the insurance record for the Driver ID **123456789**. Close the forms.

Add a Chart to a Report

You will create a chart in a report that compares the number of licenses that were issued by year. The chart will graphically depict the mix of drivers according to the years of driving experience.

22. Open the **Auto Year report** in Design view. Click the **Report Footer section bar**. Open the Property Sheet and set the height of the Report Footer section to **3"**. Close the Property Sheet. Click in the **blank space** below the Count function.

23. Insert a pie chart by clicking at the **0.5" mark** on the vertical ruler and the **2.5" mark** on the horizontal ruler. In the Chart Settings pane, set the **Auto Year_Parameter query** as the data source. In the parameter prompt, type **2012**. In the Axis (Category), select the **AutoType check box**, then in the parameter prompt, type **2012**. Close the Chart Settings pane.

24. Click in the **Chart Title box** in the Property Sheet, and type **Auto Type**. Close the Property sheet, then save and close the report. Reopen the report and type **2010** at the prompts. Note that the data in the report and chart displays according to the year input. Close the report.

25. Close all database objects, close the database, and exit Access. Based on your instructor's directions, submit aApp_Cap2_Drivers_LastFirst.

Microsoft Office 2019 Specialist Access

Online Appendix materials can be found in the Student Resources located at **www.pearsonhighered.com/exploring**.

MOS Obj #	MOS Objective	Exploring Chapter	Exploring Section Heading
1. Manage Databases			
1.1 Modify database structure			
1.1.1	Import objects or data from other sources	**Access Chapter 2**: Tables and Queries in Relational Databases	Multitable Queries
1.1.2	Delete database objects	Online Appendix	Online Appendix
1.1.3	Hide and display objects in the Navigation Pane	**Access Chapter 1**: Introduction to Access	Databases Are Everywhere!
1.2 Manage table relationships and keys			
1.2.1	Understand relationships	**Access Chapter 2**: Tables and Queries in Relational Databases	Multitable Queries
1.2.2	Display relationships	**Access Chapter 2**: Tables and Queries in Relational Databases	Multitable Queries
1.2.3	Set primary keys	**Access Chapter 2**: Tables and Queries in Relational Databases	Table Design, Creation, and Modification
1.2.4	Enforce referential integrity	**Access Chapter 2**: Tables and Queries in Relational Databases	Multitable Queries
1.2.5	Set foreign keys	**Access Chapter 2**: Tables and Queries in Relational Databases	Table Design, Creation, and Modification
1.3 Print and export data			
1.3.1	Configure print options for records, forms, and reports	**Access Chapter 4**: Basic Forms and Reports	Create Basic Reports to Present Information
1.3.2	Export objects to alternative formats	**Access Chapter 4**: Basic Forms and Reports	Create Basic Reports to Present Information
2. Create and Modify Tables			
2.1 Create tables			
2.1.1	Import data into tables	**Access Chapter 2**: Tables and Queries in Relational Databases	Multitable Queries
2.1.2	Create linked tables from external sources	**Access Chapter 2**: Tables and Queries in Relational Databases	Multitable Queries
2.1.3	Import tables from other databases	**Access Chapter 2**: Tables and Queries in Relational Databases	Multitable Queries
2.2 Manage tables			
2.2.1	Hide fields in tables	**Access Chapter 2**: Tables and Queries in Relational Databases	Table Design, Creation, and Modification
2.2.2	Add total rows	**Access Chapter 3**: Query Calculations and Expressions	Aggregate Functions
2.2.3	Add tables descriptions	**Access Chapter 1**: Introduction to Access	Databases Are Everywhere!

MOS Obj #	MOS Objective	Exploring Chapter	Exploring Section Heading
2.3	**Manage table records**		
2.3.1	Find and replace data	**Access Chapter 1**: Introduction to Access	Filters and Sorts
2.3.2	Sort records	**Access Chapter 1**: Introduction to Access	Filters and Sorts
2.3.3	Filter records	**Access Chapter 1**: Introduction to Access	Filters and Sorts
2.4	**Create and modify fields**		
2.4.1	Add and remove fields	**Access Chapter 2**: Tables and Queries in Relational Databases	Table Design, Creation, and Modification
2.4.2	Add validation rules to fields	**Access Chapter 2**: Tables and Queries in Relational Databases	Table Design, Creation, and Modification
2.4.3	Change field captions	**Access Chapter 2**: Tables and Queries in Relational Databases	Table Design, Creation, and Modification
2.4.4	Change field sizes	**Access Chapter 2**: Tables and Queries in Relational Databases	Table Design, Creation, and Modification
2.4.5	Change field data types	**Access Chapter 2**: Tables and Queries in Relational Databases	Table Design, Creation, and Modification
2.4.6	Configure fields to auto-increment	**Access Chapter 2**: Tables and Queries in Relational Databases	Table Design, Creation, and Modification
2.4.7	Set default values	**Access Chapter 2**: Tables and Queries in Relational Databases	Table Design, Creation, and Modification
2.4.8	Apply built-in input masks	**Access Chapter 2**: Tables and Queries in Relational Databases	Table Design, Creation, and Modification

3. Create and Modify Queries

MOS Obj #	MOS Objective	Exploring Chapter	Exploring Section Heading
3.1	**Create and run queries**		
3.1.1	Create simple queries	**Access Chapter 2**: Tables and Queries in Relational Databases	Single-Table Queries
3.1.2	Create basic crosstab queries	**Access Chapter 6**: Action and Specialized Queries	Summarizing Data with a Crosstab Query
3.1.3	Create basic parameter queries	**Access Chapter 5**: Data Validation and Data Analysis	Create a Parameter Query
3.1.4	Create basic action queries	**Access Chapter 6**: Action and Specialized Queries	Action Queries
3.1.5	Create basic multi-tab queries	**Access Chapter 2**: Tables and Queries in Relational Databases	Multitable Queries
3.1.6	Save queries	**Access Chapter 2**: Tables and Queries in Relational Databases	Single-Table Queries
3.1.7	Run queries	**Access Chapter 2**: Tables and Queries in Relational Databases	Single-Table Queries
3.2	**Modify queries**		
3.2.1	Add, hide, and remove fields in queries	**Access Chapter 2**: Tables and Queries in Relational Databases	Multitable Queries
3.2.2	Sort data within queries	**Access Chapter 2**: Tables and Queries in Relational Databases	Single-Table Queries
3.2.3	Filter data within queries	**Access Chapter 2**: Tables and Queries in Relational Databases	Single-Table Queries
3.2.4	Format fields within queries	**Access Chapter 3**: Query Calculations and Expressions	Calculated Fields and Expressions

MOS Obj #	MOS Objective	Exploring Chapter	Exploring Section Heading
4.	**Modify Forms in Layout View**		
4.1	**Configure form controls**		
4.1.1	Add, move, and remove form controls	**Access Chapter 4**: Basic Forms and Reports	Create Basic Forms to Simplify Data Management
4.1.2	Set form control properties	**Access Chapter 4**: Basic Forms and Reports	Create Basic Forms to Simplify Data Management
4.1.3	Add and modify form labels	**Access Chapter 4**: Basic Forms and Reports	Create Basic Forms to Simplify Data Management
4.2	**Format forms**		
4.2.1	Modify tab order on forms	**Access Chapter 7**: Advanced Forms and Reports	Set the Tab Order
4.2.2	Sort records by form field	**Access Chapter 4**: Basic Forms and Reports	Create Basic Forms to Simplify Data Management
4.2.3	Modify form positioning	**Access Chapter 4**: Basic Forms and Reports	Create Basic Forms to Simplify Data Management
4.2.4	Insert information in form headers and footers	Online Appendix	Online Appendix
4.2.5	Insert images on forms	**Access Chapter 4**: Basic Forms and Reports	Create Basic Forms to Simplify Data Management
5.	**Modify Reports in Layout View**		
5.1	**Configure report controls**		
5.1.1	Group and sort fields on reports	**Access Chapter 4**: Basic Forms and Reports	Create Basic Reports to Present Information
5.1.2	Add report controls	**Access Chapter 4**: Basic Forms and Reports	Create Basic Reports to Present Information
5.1.3	Add and modify labels on reports	**Access Chapter 4**: Basic Forms and Reports	Create Basic Reports to Present Information
5.2	**Format reports**		
5.2.1	Format a report into multiple columns	**Access Chapter 4**: Basic Forms and Reports	Create Basic Reports to Present Information
5.2.2	Modify report positioning	**Access Chapter 4**: Basic Forms and Reports	Create Basic Reports to Present Information
5.2.3	Format report elements	**Access Chapter 4**: Basic Forms and Reports	Create Basic Reports to Present Information
5.2.4	Change report orientation	**Access Chapter 4**: Basic Forms and Reports	Create Basic Reports to Present Information
5.2.5	Insert information in report headers and footers	**Access Chapter 4**: Basic Forms and Reports	Create Basic Reports to Present Information
5.3.6	Insert images on reports	**Access Chapter 4**: Basic Forms and Reports	Create Basic Reports to Present Information

Glossary

Access Database Executable (ACCDE) A type of database file that prohibits users from making design and name changes to forms or reports within the database, and prohibits users from creating new forms and reports.

Action query A query that adds, updates, or deletes data in a database.

Add-in A custom program or additional command that extends the functionality of a Microsoft Office program.

Aggregate function A calculation performed on an entire column of data that returns a single value. Includes functions such as Sum, Avg, and Count.

AND logical operator A condition in a query that returns only records that match all specified (at least two) criteria.

Anomaly An error or inconsistency within a database that occurs when you add, edit, or delete data.

Append query A query that selects records from one or more tables (the source) and adds them to an existing table (the destination).

Application part A feature that enables you to add a set of common Access components to an existing database, such as a table, a form, and a report for a related task.

Argument A variable, constant, or expression that is needed to produce the output for a function or action.

Ascending A sort that lists text data in alphabetical order or a numeric list in lowest to highest order.

Attachment control A control that enables you to manage attached files in forms and reports.

Attachment field A field used to store multiple files of various formats and then launch those files from within Access.

AutoNumber A number that automatically increments each time a record is added.

Back-end database Tables that can be used in a linked front-end database, but not manipulated by users.

Backstage view A component of Office that provides a concise collection of commands related to an open file.

Backup Database A utility that creates a duplicate copy of the entire database to protect from loss or damage.

Bound control A control whose source of data is a field in a table or query.

Calculated control A control containing an expression that generates a calculated result.

Calculated field A field that displays the result of an expression rather than data stored in a field.

Caption property A property that is used to create a more understandable label than a field name that displays in the top row in Datasheet view and in forms and reports.

Cascade Delete Related Records When the primary key value is deleted in a primary table, Access will automatically delete all records in related tables that contain values that match the primary key.

Cascade Update Related Fields An option that directs Access to automatically change all foreign key values in a related table when the primary key value is modified in a primary table.

Cloud storage A technology used to store files and to work with programs that are stored in a central location on the Internet.

Column heading The field name used to display values at the top of a crosstab query.

Combo Box control Displays a menu of options from which the user can select a single value.

Command A button or area within a group that you click to perform tasks.

Compact and Repair Database A utility that reduces the size of a database and fixes any errors that may exist in the file.

Comparison operator An operator such as greater than (>), less than (<), greater than or equal to (>=), and less than or equal to (<=) used to limit query results that meet the criteria.

Composite key A primary key that is made of two or more fields.

Constant A value that does not change.

Contextual tab A tab that contains a group of commands related to the selected object.

Control A text box, button, label, or other tool used to add, edit, and display the data in a form or report.

Copy A command used to duplicate a selection from the original location and place a copy in the Office Clipboard.

Criteria row A row in the query design grid that determines which records will be selected.

Crosstab query A query that summarizes a data source into a few key rows and columns.

CSV text file A file format that uses a comma to separate one column from the next column, enabling the receiving software to distinguish one set of field values from the next.

Cut A command used to remove a selection from the original location and place it in the Office Clipboard.

Data macro A macro that executes a series of actions when a table event occurs.

Data redundancy The unnecessary storing of duplicate data in two or more tables.

Data type Determines the type of data that can be entered and the operations that can be performed on that data.

Data validation A set of constraints or rules that help control how data are entered into a field.

Database A collection of data organized as meaningful information that can be accessed, managed, stored, queried, sorted, and reported.

Database Documenter A tool that creates a report containing detailed information for each selected object.

Database management system (DBMS) A software system that provides the tools needed to create, maintain, and use a database.

Database Splitter A tool that enables you to split a database into two files: a back-end database and a front-end database.

Datasheet view A grid containing fields (columns) and records (rows) used to view, add, edit, and delete records.

Date function A Date/Time function that returns the current date.

DatePart function A Date/Time function that examines a date and returns a portion of the date.

Default value A database setting that specifies a value that is automatically entered into a field when a new record is added to a table.

Delete query A query that selects records from a table and then removes them from the table.

Delimiter A special character that surrounds the criterion's value.

Descending A sort that lists text data in reverse alphabetical order or a numeric list in highest to lowest order.

Design view (form/report) A view that gives users advanced design settings not available in Layout view, (such as changing the tab order of a form) providing more control over the form and report design. Also used to create a new report or form from scratch by adding fields and controls manually to a blank object.

Design view (query) A detailed view of a query's structure and is used to create and/or modify a query's design by specifying the tables, fields, and criteria required for output.

Design view (table) A view that gives users a detailed view of the table's structure and is used to create and modify a table's design by specifying the fields it will contain, the fields' data types, and their associated properties.

Detail section The section of the form or report where records are displayed.

Dialog box A box that provides access to more precise, but less frequently used, commands.

Dialog Box Launcher A button that when clicked opens a corresponding dialog box.

Embedded macro A macro that executes when an event attached to a control or object occurs.

Encryption The process of altering digital information by using an algorithm to make it unreadable to anyone except those who possess the password.

Enforce referential integrity A relationship option that ensures that data cannot be entered into a related table unless it first exists in a primary table.

Enhanced ScreenTip A small message box that displays when you place the pointer over a command button. The purpose of the command, short descriptive text, or a keyboard shortcut if applicable will display in the box.

Event Occurs when a user enters, edits, or deletes data; events also occur when users open, use, or close forms and reports.

Expression A combination of elements that produces a value.

Expression Builder An Access tool that helps you create more complicated expressions.

Field The smallest data element in a table, such as first name, last name, address, or phone number.

Field property A characteristic of a field that determines how it will look and behave.

Field selector The column heading of a datasheet used to select a column.

Filter A feature that enables users to specify conditions to display only those records that meet those conditions.

Filter by Form A more versatile method of selecting data, enabling users to display records based on multiple criteria.

Find duplicates query A query that helps you identify repeated values in a table.

Find unmatched query A query that compares records in two related tables, and then displays the records found in one table, but not the other.

First normal form (1NF) A criterion satisfied when a table contains no repeating groups or repeating columns.

Fixed-length text file A file type that allocates a certain number of characters for each field.

Footer Information that displays at the bottom of a document page.

Foreign key A field in a related table that is the primary key of another table.

Form A database object that is used to view data, or add data to, or edit data in a table.

Form footer A section that displays one time at the bottom of a form.

Form header A section that displays once at the top of each form.

Form tool A tool used to create data entry forms for customers, employees, products, and other tables.

Form view A view that provides a simplified user interface primarily used for data entry; does not enable you to make changes to the layout.

Format Painter A feature that enables you to quickly and easily copy all formatting from one area to another in Word, PowerPoint, and Excel.

FROM keyword Specifies the table (or tables) that will be searched in an SQL Select Statement.

Front-end database A database that contains the queries, forms, and reports of the database.

Function A predefined computation that simplifies creating a complex calculation and produces a result based on inputs known as arguments.

Functional dependency A condition that occurs when the value of one field is determined by the value of another.

Gallery An Office feature that displays additional formatting and design choices.

Group A subset of a tab that organizes similar tasks together.

Group footer A section in a report that displays just below the Detail section in Design view. The group footer appears once each time the grouping field value changes.

Group header A section in a report that displays just above the Detail section in Design view, along with the name of the field by which you are grouping. The group header appears once each time the grouping field value changes.

Grouping A method of summarizing data by the values of a field.

Header An area with one or more lines of information at the top of each page.

Hyperlink A data type that enables you to quickly link to any file on your computer or to any webpage on the Internet.

IIf function Evaluates an expression and displays one value when the expression is true and another value when the expression is false.

Importing A process that enables you to copy external data into your database without linking it to its source file.

Index A setting for a field that reduces the time it takes to run queries and reports.

Indexed property A setting that enables quick sorting in primary key order and quick retrieval based on the primary key.

Input mask Enables you to restrict the data being input into a field by specifying the exact format of the data entry.

Input Mask Wizard A tool used to quickly assist with applying an input mask to a field.

IsNull function Checks whether a field has no value.

Join line A line used to create a relationship between two tables using a common field.

Keyboard shortcut A combination of two or more keys pressed together to initiate a software command.

Label Wizard A feature that enables you to easily create mailing labels, name tags, and other specialized tags.

Landscape orientation A document layout in which a page is wider than it is tall.

Layout control A tool that provides guides to help keep controls aligned horizontally and vertically and give your form a uniform appearance.

Layout view A view that enables users to make changes to a layout while viewing the data in the form or report.

Linking A process that enables you to connect to a table or spreadsheet without having to import the table data into your database.

Live Preview An Office feature that provides a preview of the results of a selection when you point to an option in a list or gallery. Using Live Preview, you can experiment with settings before making a final choice.

Lookup field Provides the user with a finite list of values to choose from in a menu.

Lookup Wizard Creates the menu of pre-defined values (lookup fields) by asking you questions and using your answers to create the options list.

Macro A series of actions that can be programmed to automate tasks.

Macro Designer The user interface that enables you to create and edit macros.

Make table query A query that selects records from one or more tables and uses them to create a new table.

Margin The area of blank space that displays to the left, right, top, and bottom of a document or worksheet.

Microsoft Access A relational database management system in which you can record and link data, query databases, and create forms and reports.

Microsoft Excel An application that makes it easy to organize records, financial transactions, and business information in the form of worksheets.

Microsoft Office A productivity software suite including a set of software applications, each one specializing in a particular type of output.

Microsoft PowerPoint An application that enables you to create dynamic presentations to inform groups and persuade audiences.

Microsoft Word A word processing software application used to produce all sorts of documents, including memos, newsletters, forms, tables, and brochures.

Mini Toolbar A toolbar that provides access to the most common formatting selections, such as adding bold or italic, or changing font type or color. Unlike the Quick Access Toolbar, the Mini Toolbar is not customizable.

Module An advanced object written using the VBA (Visual Basic for Applications) programming language.

Multiple Items form A form that displays multiple records in a tabular layout like a table's Datasheet view, with more customization options than a datasheet.

Navigation Form A tabbed menu system that ties the objects in the database together so that the database is easy to use.

Navigation Pane An Access interface element that organizes and lists the objects in an Access database.

Non-key field Any field that is not part of the primary key.

Normal form The rules to optimize and fix potential repetition issues (data redundancy) in a database.

Normalization The process of efficiently organizing data so that the same data are not stored in more than one table, and that related data are stored together.

Object A component created and used to make the database function (such as a table, query, form, or report).

Office Clipboard An area of memory reserved to temporarily hold selections that have been cut or copied and enables you to paste the selections.

OneDrive Microsoft's cloud storage system. Saving files to OneDrive enables them to sync across all Windows devices and to be accessible from any Internet-connected device.

One-to-many relationship When the primary key value in the primary table can match many of the foreign key values in the related table.

Open Exclusive A mode that guarantees that you are the only one currently using the database.

OR condition A query condition that returns records meeting any of the specified criteria.

ORDER BY keyword Used to sort the records by a certain field in either ascending or descending order in an SQL Select Statement.

Order of operations A set of rules that controls the sequence in which arithmetic operations are performed. Also called the *order of precedence*.

Page footer A footer that appears once at the bottom of each page in a form or report.

Page header A header that appears once at the top of each page in a form or report.

Parameter query A query that prompts the user for criterion (the parameter) at run time.

Paste A command used to place a cut or copied selection into another location.

Performance Analyzer A tool that evaluates a database and then makes recommendations for optimizing the database.

Picture A graphic file that is retrieved from storage media or the Internet and placed in an Office project.

Pmt function A financial function that calculates the periodic loan payment given a fixed rate, number of periods (also known as *term*), and the present value of the loan (the principal).

Portable Document Format (PDF) A file type that was created for exchanging documents independent of software applications and operating system environment.

Portrait orientation A document layout in which a page is taller than it is wide.

Primary key The field (or combination of fields) that uniquely identifies each record in a table.

Print Preview A view that enables you to see exactly what the report will look like when it is printed.

Property sheet The location where you change settings such as number format and number of decimal places.

Query A question about the data stored in a database, with answers provided in a datasheet.

Query Design view Enables you to create queries; the Design view is divided into two parts—the top portion displays the tables and the bottom portion (known as the query design grid) displays the fields and the criteria.

Quick Access Toolbar A component of Office 2013, located at the top-left corner of the Office window, that provides handy access to commonly executed tasks such as saving a file and undoing recent actions.

Read-only form A form that enables users to view, but not change, data.

Record A group of related fields representing one entity, such as data for one person, place, event, or concept.

Record selector A small box at the beginning of a row used to select a record.

Record source The table or query that supplies the records for a form or report.

Referential integrity Rules in a database that are used to preserve relationships between tables when records are added, deleted, or changed.

Related tables Tables that are joined in a relationship using a common field.

Relational database management system (RDBMS) A database management system that uses the relational model to manage groups of data (tables) and rules (relationships) between tables.

Relationship A connection between two tables using a common field.

Report A database document that outputs meaningful, professional-looking, formatted information from underlying tables or queries.

Report footer A section that displays one time at the bottom of a report.

Report header A section that displays once at the top of each report.

Report tool A tool used to instantly create a tabular report based on the table or query currently selected.

Report view A view that enables you to determine what a printed report will look like in a continuous onscreen page layout.

Report Wizard A feature that prompts you for input and then uses your answers to generate a customized report.

Ribbon The command center of Office applications. It is the long bar located just beneath the title bar, containing tabs, groups, and commands.

Rich Text Format (RTF) A format that enables text-based documents to be opened in a variety of word-processing applications.

Round function A math expression function that returns a number rounded to a specific number of decimal places.

Row heading The field name used to display values along the left side of a crosstab query.

Run command Used to produce query results (the red exclamation point).

Second normal form (2NF) A criterion satisfied when a table meets 1NF criteria and all non-key fields are functionally dependent on the entire primary key.

Section Part of a form or report that can be manipulated separately from other parts of the form or report.

Section bar Marks the top boundary of a section in a form or report.

SELECT keyword Determines which fields will be included in the results of an SQL Select Statement.

Select query A type of query that displays only the records that match criteria entered in Query Design view.

Selection filter A method of selecting that displays only the records that match a criterion you select.

Shortcut menu A menu that provides choices related to the selection or area at which you right-click.

Show row A row in the Query Design view that controls whether the field will be displayed in the query results.

Simply Query Wizard Provides a step-by-step guide to help you through the query design process.

Smart Lookup A feature that provides information about tasks or commands in Office and can also be used to search for general information on a topic, such as *President George Washington*.

Sort A feature that lists records in a specific sequence.

Sort row A row in the Query Design view that enables you to sort in ascending or descending order.

Split form A form that combines two views of the same record source—one section is displayed in a stacked layout and the other section is displayed in a tabular layout.

Splitter bar Divides a form into two halves.

SQL keyword Defines the purpose and the structure of an SQL statement.

SQL SELECT statement Used to retrieve data from the tables in a database.

Stacked layout Arrangement that displays fields in a vertical column.

Standalone macro A macro that can be used independently of other controls or objects.

Status bar A bar located at the bottom of the program window that contains information relative to the open file. It also includes tools for changing the view of the file and for changing the zoom size of onscreen file contents.

Structured Query Language (SQL) The industry-standard language for defining, manipulating, and retrieving the data in a database.

Subform A form inserted into another form that displays records that are related to the records in a main form.

Syntax A set of rules that governs the structure and components for properly entering a function.

Tab Located on the ribbon, each tab is designed to appear much like a tab on a file folder, with the active tab highlighted.

Tab order The sequential advancing in a form from one field or control to the next when you press Tab.

Tab stop The location to which the insertion point moves each time Tab is pressed.

Table The location where all data are stored in a database; organizes data into columns and rows.

Table Analyzer A tool that analyzes the tables in a database and normalizes them for you.

Table row A row in Query Design view that displays the data source.

Tabular layout An arrangement that displays fields horizontally across the screen or page.

Tag A data element or metadata that is added as a document property. Tags help in indexing and searching.

Tell me box A box located to the right of the last tab that enables you to search for help and information about a command or task you want to perform and also displays a shortcut directly to that command.

Template A predefined database that includes professionally designed tables, forms, reports, and other objects that you can use to jumpstart the creation of your database.

Text file A file that stores data without formatting and is commonly used for exchanging information between two computer systems.

Theme A collection of design choices that includes colors, fonts, and special effects used to give a consistent look to a document, workbook, presentation, or database form or report.

Third Normal Form (3NF) A criterion satisfied when a table meets 2NF criteria and no transitive dependencies exist.

Title bar The long bar at the top of each window that displays the name of the folder, file, or program displayed in the open window and the application in which you are working.

Toggle command A button that acts somewhat like a light switch that you can turn on and off. You select the command to turn it on, then select it again to turn it off.

Total row A method to display aggregate function results as the last row in Datasheet view of a table or query.

Totals query A way to display aggregate data when a query is run.

Transitive dependency A condition that occurs when the value of one non-key field is functionally dependent on the value of another non-key field.

Unbound control A control not tied to a specific field.

Uniform resource locator (URL) The location of a website or webpage on the Internet.

Update query A query that changes the data values in one or more fields for all records that meet specific criteria.

Validation rule A field property setting that limits the data values a user can enter into a field.

Validation text A field property setting that displays a custom error message to the user when incorrect data are entered into a field.

View The various ways a file can display on the screen.

WHERE keyword Specifies the criteria that records must match to be included in the results of an SQL Select Statement.

Wildcard A special character that can represent one or more characters in the criterion of a query.

XML Paper Specification (XPS) A file format developed by Microsoft and designed to display a printed page onscreen identically on any computer platform.

Zoom slider A feature that displays at the far right side of the status bar. It is used to increase or decrease the magnification of the file.

Index

A

Access Database Executable (ACCDE), 74, 534–535, 539
Action Catalog, 556
action queries
    append query, 346, 351–353, 360–361
    backing up database, 348, 357–358
    delete query, 346, 355–356, 362–363
    determining usage, 346–348
    introduction to, 346
    make table query, 346, 353–355, 361–362
    update query, 346, 348–350, 358–359
add-ins in Microsoft Office, 17–18
advanced forms
    Auto Order command, 394–395, 402
    combo boxes, 391–394
    introduction to, 390
    read-only form, 390, 399–400
    restricting edits, 390–391
    subforms, 396–398, 404
    tab order, 394–396, 402–403
    tab stop, 394, 395–396, 403
aggregate functions
    creating queries, 227–231
    to datasheet, 232
    totals query, 227–231, 233–235
All Commands function, 12
AND criteria, 171
anomaly, defined, 502
append query, 346, 351–353, 360–361
application part, 113–114
argument, defined, 555
argument, in functions, 218
attachment controls, 445–447
attachment field, 442–444, 450
Auto Order command, 394–395, 402
AutoCorrect, 34
AutoNumber, 141
AutoSave, 7

B

back-end database, 523
Back Up Database, 88–90
Backstage Navigation Pane, 25–26, 50
Backstage view, 6, 51–52
Blackwood Maintenance Service (BMS) case study, 438–439
blank database, 110
blank document, 6
blank fields, 305
Blank Form tools, 257
bound control, 405
built-in functions, 218–221

C

calculated control, 405, 406–408, 420–422
calculated field queries, 204–209, 231
calculated results, 214
caption, 143
cascade options, 154–155
chart control, 408–410, 422–423
Check Document, 32–34
cloud storage, 6
coffee shop case study, 248–249
column heading, 364
columns in Microsoft Access, 259, 280–281
Combo Box control, 391
combo boxes, 391–394, 400–401
Command Button Wizard, 557–558
common interface components, 9–15
common query errors, 210–211, 215–216
Commonwealth Federal Bank case study, 132–133
Compact and Repair Database utility, 90
comparison operators, 170
composite key, 506
Compress Pictures, 36
conditions in a totals query, 229–230
constant, defined, 207
contextual tabs, 10
controls
    attachment controls, 445–447
    bound control, 405
    calculated control, 405, 406–408, 420–422
    chart control, 408–410, 422–423
    introduction to, 405
    label control, 408
    line/rectangle controls, 410
    page break control, 410–411
    Text Box control, 406, 420–421
    unbound control, 405, 408
    understanding controls, 405–411
copy text, 30, 40–41
Crop tool, 36
crosstab query, 364–369, 376
Crosstab Query Wizard, 365–368, 375–376
CSV text files, 478
Current Database tab, 516
cut text, 30, 40–41

D

data analysis
    advanced functions, 319–326
    customizing output, 317–319
    Date function, 320–321, 329
    DatePart function, 324–326, 331
    IIf function, 321–324, 330–331
    IsNull function, 324, 330–331
    parameter query, 317–318, 327–328
    parameter report, 319, 327–328
    Round function, 321, 329
data in Microsoft Access
    adding, 152, 160–161
    controlling format, 307–309
    existing data and validation rule, 306
    importing from multiple sources, 149–152
    input mask, 307–309, 313–314
    lookup field, 309–310, 314–316
    from Microsoft Excel, 149–151, 157–158
    redundancy, 137
    in tables, 134–135, 136, 139
    Total row to summarize query data, 181
    types of, 139
data in Microsoft Excel, 149–151, 157–158
data macros
    defined, 568
    event-driven data macro, 568–569, 573
    named data macro, 569–571, 575–577
    test and modify, 569, 574–575
    when to use, 568, 572
data validation
    default field value, 305, 311–312
    defined, 304
    establishment of, 304–306
    require a field, 304–305
    validation rule with validation text, 305–306, 312–313
Database Documenter tool, 515, 516–518, 525–526
database in Microsoft Access
    Access Database Executable, 74, 534–535, 539
    back-end database, 523
    backing up, 348, 357–358
    blank database, 110
    built-in analysis and design tools, 515–524
    Database Documenter, 515, 516–518, 525–526
    Database Splitter, 515, 523–524, 528–529
    defined, 72
    encryption of, 532–533
    front-end database, 523–524
    navigation form, 530–532, 536–537
    normalization, 502–510
    object types, 74–78
    password protection, 532–534, 537–538

database in Microsoft Access (*continued*)
  Performance Analyzer, 515, 518–520, 526–527
  security of, 530–535
  Table Analyzer, 515, 520–523, 527–528
  using templates, 109, 111–113, 115–118
  utilities, 88–90, 97
database management system (DBMS), 72, 515
Database Splitter, 90, 515, 523–524, 528–529
Datasheet view
  action queries, 349
  adding/editing attachments in, 444, 451
  aggregate functions, 232
  overview of, 79–80
  removing attachments in, 442–444, 452
  tables and, 138–139, 144, 145–146, 148
Date function, 320–321, 329
DatePart function, 324–326, 331
default field value, 305, 311–312
delete query, 346, 355–356, 362–363
Design view
  calculated control, 407
  crosstab query, 368–369
  forms and, 254
  hyperlink field, 440–442
  overview of, 81–82
  Rectangle control, 410
  sections and, 412–414
  tables and, 144, 147–148
  verifying update query from, 350
Detail section, 412
Dialog Box Launcher, 10
dialog box in Microsoft Word, 10–11, 48
digital signatures, 535
document properties Microsoft Office, 50–51, 56
document properties Microsoft Word, 50–51
document views, 45, 46
duplicate records with queries, 369–371, 376–377

E

embedded macros, 555, 557–560, 565–567
encryption of database, 532–533
Enhanced ScreenTips, 17
enterprise-level DBMS database programs, 515
event, with embedded macros, 555, 557–560
event-driven data macro, 568–569, 573
existing data and validation rule, 305–306, 312–313

exporting data
  to Excel, 454–457, 464–466
  to PDF/XPS documents, 460–462, 467–468
  to Word, 457–459, 466–467
Expression Builder, 217–218, 222–223, 405, 407
expressions formula, 204–207, 212–213
external file connections
  attachment controls, 445–447
  attachment field, 442–444, 450
  exporting data to Excel, 454–457, 464–466
  exporting data to PDF/XPS documents, 460–462, 467–468
  exporting data to Word, 457–459, 466–467
  exporting objects, 462–463
  hyperlink field, 440–442, 448–449
  hyperlink value, 449–450
  introduction to, 440

F

fields
  adding/deleting in forms, 259–260
  adding/deleting queries in, 179, 182–183
  adding/removing in reports, 280
  attachment controls, 446
  default field value, 305, 311–312
  defined, 75
  lookup field, 309–310, 314–316
  non-key field, 505
  properties, 82, 142–144, 146–147
  require a field in data validation, 304–305
File Explorer in Microsoft OneDrive, 6
files/folders in Microsoft Office
  creating new file, 6
  open saved file, 7–8, 20–21
  previewing and printing, 51–52, 57
  saving file, 7, 19–20
  working with, 6–9
Filter by Form, 100–101, 106–107
filters in Microsoft Access, 98–101
find duplicate queries, 369–371, 376–377
find unmatched queries, 371–374, 377
first normal form (1NF), 503–505, 511
fixed-length text files, 478
Font Dialog Box Launcher, 10
Font group, 9
footers in Microsoft Office, 49–50, 55
foreign key, 142
form, defined, 76, 250
form controls, 260–261
Form Design tool, 257
form footer, 412
form header, 412
form layout control, 261–262, 269–270, 406
Form tools, 250–258, 264–266
Form view, 253, 258, 266–267

Form Wizard, 257, 396
Format Painter, 17
formatting
  Microsoft Access, 307–309
  Microsoft Excel, 474, 482–483
  Microsoft Office, 28–29, 39–40
forms. *see also* advanced forms
  add/delete fields, 259–260
  adjusting column widths, 259
  attachment controls, 445–446
  Blank Form tools, 257
  controls, 252
  Design view, 254
  exporting to another database, 469–470
  form controls, 260–261
  Form Design tool, 257
  form layout controls, 261–262, 269–270, 406
  Form tools, 250–258, 264–266
  Form view, 253, 258, 266–267
  Form Wizard, 257
  Layout view, 254, 258–259, 267–269
  modifying forms, 258–261
  multiple items form, 256
  named data macro and, 571, 575–577
  Navigation form, 256
  print selected records, 257–258
  record source, 251–252
  sorting records, 263
  split form, 255
  subform, 255
FROM keyword, 580
front-end database, 523–524
functional dependency, 505
functions, 218–221
  advanced functions, 319–326
  Date function, 320–321, 329
  DatePart function, 324–326, 331
  IIf function, 321–324, 330–331
  IsNull function, 324, 330–331
  Round function, 321, 329
future_value argument, 220

G

gallery, defined, 11
Get Add-ins, 17
grammar check in Microsoft Office, 32–34, 42
graphical user interface (GUI), 515
group, defined, 9
group footer, 417–419
group header, 416–417, 425–426
grouping, 229

H

headers in Microsoft Office, 49–50, 55
Help tab, 16
Home tab, 9
hyperlink field, 440–442, 448–449
hyperlink value, 449–450

I

IIf function, 321–324, 330–331
images, adding to sections, 415, 423–424
importing data to Microsoft Access
   Excel spreadsheet, 474, 476–477, 482–485
   introduction to, 471
   linking to a table, 471–473, 481–482
   text files, 477–479, 486–488
index, with Performance Analyzer tool, 519–520
Input Mask property, 143
Input Mask Wizard, 307–309, 313–314
insert pictures, 34–35
IsNull function, 324, 330–331

J

join lines, 136, 180

K

keyboard shortcuts, 14–15

L

label control, 408
Label Wizard, 276
landscape orientation, 47
layout control, 252
Layout view, 254, 258–259, 267–269
line control, 410
linking
   defined, 471
   to Excel spreadsheet, 474–476, 483–484
   hyperlink field, 440–442, 448–449
   hyperlink value, 449–450
   to a table, 471–473, 481–482
list boxes, 392
Live Preview, 11
loan payment with Pmt function, 220, 224–225
lookup field, 309–310, 314–316

M

Mac-based Office applications, 4
macro design
   defined, 554
   embedded macros, 555, 557–560, 565–567
   purpose of, 554–555, 561–562
   standalone macro, 554–557, 563–565
Macro Designer, 555, 560, 564–565, 569
macro object, 78
make table query, 346, 353–355, 361–362
margins, 47, 281
MessageBox action, 555–556
Metropolitan Zoo case study, 500–501

Microsoft Access
   data, 85–88, 93–96
   database creation, 109–114
   database object types, 74–78
   database utilities, 88–90, 97
   Datasheet view, 79–80, 139
   Design view, 81–82
   exporting data to Excel, 454–457, 464–466
   exporting data to Word, 457–459, 466–467
   Filter by Form, 100–101, 106–107
   filters in, 98–101
   interface examination, 78
   introduction to, 4, 72
   modifying, adding, saving data, 85–88, 93–96
   navigating and locating records, 80–81
   opening, saving, enabling content, 72–74, 91–92
   primary key in, 75, 136, 140–141, 146
   print information, 90
   records, 86, 93–96
   renaming and describing tables, 82–84
   sorts, 102–103, 107–108
   tables, 138–144
   templates, 109, 111–113, 115–118
Microsoft account, 5–6
Microsoft Excel
   add-ins, 17
   changing document views, 45
   data in, 149–151, 157–158
   importing data from Access, 454–457, 464–466
   importing data to Microsoft Access, 474, 476–477, 482–485
   introduction to, 4
   launching from Access, 440
   linking to spreadsheet, 474–476
   spelling/grammar check, 32
   summarizing query data, 181, 185
Microsoft Office
   add-ins, 17–18
   changing document views, 45–46
   common interface components, 9–15
   customizing ribbon, 12–13
   dialog box, 10–11, 21–22
   document properties, 50–51
   Enhanced ScreenTips, 17
   headers and footers, 49–50, 55
   Help tab, 16
   introduction to, 4–5
   keyboard shortcuts, 14–15
   Microsoft account, 5–6
   Mini Toolbar, 29
   modifying text, 27–29
   Office Clipboard, 31
   page layout, 46–48
   Quick Access Toolbar, 13–14, 22
   relocating text, 30–31
   reviewing a document, 32–34
   ribbon, 9–10
   shortcut menu, 14, 23

   spelling/grammar check, 32–34, 42
   starting an application, 5–6
   Tell me box, 15–16, 24
   templates, 25–26, 37–38
   themes, 26, 38
   working with files, 6–9
   working with pictures, 34–36, 43–44
Microsoft OneDrive, 4, 6–7
Microsoft PowerPoint, 4, 17, 32, 45
Microsoft SQL Server, 515
Microsoft Visual Basic for Applications (VBA), 554
Microsoft Word, 4, 440, 457–459, 466–467
Mini Toolbar, 29
module, defined, 78
multiple items form, 256
multitable query creation, 177–181, 183–185
My Add-ins, 17
MySQL, 515

N

named data macro, 569–571, 575–577
Navigation form, 256, 530–532, 536–537
Navigation Pane, 74–75, 92–93, 473, 531–532, 536–537, 554–557
non-key field, 505
normal forms, 502–510
normalization of database
   defined, 502
   finalizing design of, 509–510, 514
   first normal form, 503–505, 511
   second normal form, 505–506, 512
   third normal form, 507–508, 513
Northwind Traders case study, 70–71
NOT criteria, 171
null criteria expressions, 170–171
num_periods argument, 220

O

objects in Microsoft Access, 74–78, 462–463
Office Clipboard, 31
On Click event, 557
On Close event, 555
one-to-many relationship, 155–156
open saved file, 7–8
OR criteria, 171
Oracle, 515
ORDER BY keyword, 580
order of operations, 208
orientation in page layouts, 47, 281

P

page break control, 410–411
page footer, 412
page header, 412
pages/page layout in Microsoft Office, 46–48, 54–55
parameter query, 317–318, 327–328

parameter report, 319, 327–328
Passaic County Community College (PCCC) case study, 202–203
password protection of database, 532–534, 537–538
Paste arrow, 10
paste text, 30–31, 40–41
PDF (Portable Document Format), 277, 440, 460–462, 467–468, 517
Performance Analyzer, 515, 518–520, 526–527
Pickit image app, 17
pictures in Microsoft Office, 34–36, 43, 44
Pmt function, 220, 224–225
portrait orientation, 47
PowerPoint Themes gallery, 11
present_value argument, 220
previewing files, 51–52
primary key, 75, 136, 140–141, 146
Print Preview, 277, 284–285, 517
print/printing
    Microsoft Access, 90, 257–258, 277
    Microsoft Word, 51–52, 57
    Quick Access Toolbar, 13–14
Property Sheet, 209, 559

Q

Query Design view, 165–166
query/queries. *see also* specialized queries
    adding/deleting fields, 179, 182–183
    built-in functions, 218–221
    calculated field queries, 204–209, 231
    calculated results, 214
    copying and modifying, 172–173, 176
    defined, 75
    exporting to Excel, 455–456, 464–465
    Expression Builder, 217–218, 222–223
    expressions formula, 204–207, 212–213
    joinlines in multitable queries, 180
    loan payment with Pmt function, 220, 224–225
    multitable query creation, 177–181, 183–185
    order of operations, 208
    Query Design view, 165–166
    Query Wizard, 167–168, 174–175
    recovering from common errors, 210–211, 215–216
    single-table query, 164–166
    sort order, 172, 175
    Total row to summarize query data, 181
    totals query, 227–231, 233–235
    update query, 346, 348–350, 358–359
Query Wizard, 167–168, 174–175
Quick Access Toolbar (QAT)
    customizing ribbon, 12
    defined, 9
    file saving, 7
    use and customizing, 13–14, 22

R

rate argument, 220
read-only form, 390, 399–400
Recent Documents list, 8–9
record source and SQL SELECT statement, 581–583
records in Microsoft Access
    adding to a table, 86–87, 94–95
    defined, 75
    deleting from a table, 87–88, 96–97
    modifying in table, 86, 93–95
    navigating and locating, 80–81
    saving in a table, 88
    sorting in forms and reports, 263
    source, 251–252
rectangle control, 410
referential integrity, 153–154, 162–163
relationships
    database after normalization, 509–510, 514
    one-to-many relationship, 155–156
    tables in Microsoft Access, 84–85, 152–156, 161–162
relocating text, 30–31
renaming tables/worksheets, 82–84
report footer, 412
report header, 412, 415–416
report/reports
    adding/removing fields, 280
    attachment controls, 446–447, 452–453
    column widths, 280–281
    defined, 76, 271–272
    exporting to Excel, 456–457, 465–466
    Label Wizard, 276
    margins and orientation, 281
    modifying, 285–286
    Print Preview tab, 277, 284–285
    record source and, 581–582
    report tool, 272–273, 278–280, 283–284
    Report view, 277
    Report Wizard, 273–275
    sorting and grouping, 281–282, 287
report tool, 272–273, 278–281, 283–284
Report view, 277
Report Wizard, 273–275
retirement plan contribution case study, 552–553
ribbon
    changing document views, 45
    customizing ribbon, 12–13
    defined, 9
    modifying files, 20–21
    tabs on, 9–10
Round function, 321, 329
row heading, 364
RTF (Rich Text Format), 457–459

S

second normal form (2NF), 505–506, 512
section bar, 415

sections
    adding images, 423–424
    defined, 412
    show, hide, resize, 414–415
    understanding sections, 412–419
security of database, 530–535
select query, 348
select text in Microsoft Office, 27–28
selection filter, 98–100, 104–105
shortcut menu in Microsoft Word, 14, 23
Show Training, 16
Simple Query Wizard, 167–168
single-table query, 164–166
Smart Lookup, 16
sorts in Microsoft Access, 102–103, 107–108
specialized queries
    crosstab query, 364–369, 376–377
    duplicate records with, 369–371, 376–377
    introduction to, 364
    unmatched records with, 371–374, 377
spell check, 32–34, 42
split form, 255–256
Spotted Begonia Art Gallery case study, 2–3
SQL keyword, 579–581
SQL SELECT statement, 579–583, 585–586
stacked layout, 252
standalone macro, 554–557, 563–565
status bar, 46
Structured Query Language (SQL)
    defined, 578
    fundamentals of, 578–579, 584–585
    record source and, 581–583
    SQL SELECT statement, 581–583, 586
subforms, 255, 396–398, 404
syntax in functions, 218

T

tab order, 394–396, 402
tab stop, 394, 395–396, 403
Table Analyzer, 515, 520–523, 527–528
table/tables
    accommodating calculations, 137
    adding data, 152, 160–161
    adding records, 86–87, 94–95
    AND, OR, and NOT criteria, 171–172
    cascade options, 154–155
    common fields between, 136–137
    comparison operators, 170
    copying and modifying a query, 172–173, 176
    creating and modifying, 138–144
    current/future design needs, 135
    data in, 134–135
    data type, 139–140
    Datasheet view, 144, 145–146, 148
    defined, 75
    deleting records from, 87–88, 96–97

Design view, 81–82, 144, 147–148
designing, 134–137
examine in source database, 480
exporting to another database, 462–463, 468–469
field properties, 82, 142–144, 146–147
foreign key, 142
importing data from multiple sources, 149–152, 157–159
linking to, 471–473, 481–482
modifying imported design, 152, 159–160
modifying records in, 86, 93–97
multitable query creation, 177–181, 183–185
null criteria expressions, 170–171
one-to-many relationship, 155–156
primary key, 75, 136, 140–141, 146
query sort order, 172, 175
Query Wizard, 167–168, 174–175
referential integrity, 153–154, 162–163
relationship between, 84–85, 152–156, 161–162
renaming and describing, 82–84
saving records from, 88
single-table query, 164–166
specifying query criteria, 169–172, 175
storing data, 136
wildcards, 169–170

tabs on ribbon, 9–10
tabular layout, 252
Tell me box, 15–16, 24
templates
    Microsoft Access, 109, 111–113, 115–118
    Microsoft Office, 25–26, 37–38
Text Box control, 406, 420–421
text boxes, conversion to combo boxes, 392, 400–401
text files, importing to Microsoft Access, 477–479, 486–488
text in Microsoft Office, 27–29, 39–40
themes, 25, 26–27, 38, 281
third normal form (3NF), 507–508, 513
title bar, defined, 9
toggle commands, 29
Toggle Filter, 100
Tommy's Shelter case study, 302–303
total rows, 181, 185
totals query, 227–231, 233–235
type argument, 220

U

unbound control, 405, 408
uniform resource locator (URL), 440
unmatched queries, 371–374, 377
update query, 346, 348–350, 358–359

V

validation rule, 143, 305–306, 312–313
values in Microsoft Access, 100, 105
violations in first normal form, 504
Virtual Registry, Inc. case study, 344–345, 355
Visual Basic for Applications (VBA), 554

W

WHERE keyword, 580–581
wildcards in Microsoft Access, 169–170
Windows-based Office applications, 4

X

XPS (XML Paper Specification), 460–462, 467–468

Y

Yellowstone County Technical Services case study, 388–389

Z

zoom slider, 46